IMPERIAL GERMANY, 1871

NORTH SEA

BALTIC SEA

SWEDEN

DENMARK

MECKLEN-BURG

HAMBURG

BREMEN

OLDENBURG

PRUSSIA

TSARIST RUSSIAN EMPIRE

KINGDOM OF NETHERLANDS

KINGDOM OF BELGIUM

THÜRINGEN

SAXONY

HESSE

LUXEMBURG

PALATINATE (BAV.)

ALSACE-LORRAINE

BADEN

WÜRTTEM-BERG

BAVARIA

AUSTRO-HUNGARIAN EMPIRE

FRANCE

SWITZERLAND

KINGDOM OF ITALY

ADRIATIC SEA

OTTOMAN EMPIRE

Modern Germany

Garland Reference Library of the Humanities (Vol. 1520)

Advisory Board

Modern Germany

An Encyclopedia of History, People, and Culture, 1871–1990

Volume I
A–K

Editors
Dieter K. Buse
Juergen C. Doerr

Garland Publishing, Inc.
A member of the Taylor and Francis Group
New York & London, 1998

Library of Congress Cataloging-in-Publication Data

Modern Germany : an encyclopedia of history, people, and culture, 1871–1990 /
    edited by Dieter K. Buse and Juergen C. Doerr.
        p.   cm. — (Garland reference library of the humanities; vol. 1520)
        Includes bibliographical references and index.
        ISBN 0-8153-0503-6 (alk. paper)
        1. Germany—History—1871– —Encyclopedias.   2. Germany—
Intellectual life—Encyclopedias.   3. Germany—Civilization—Encyclopedias.
I. Buse, Dieter K. II. Doerr, Juergen C., 1939–   . III. Series.
DD14.M64   1998
943.08—dc21   97–13829
                                                                      CIP

Cover photograph: The Cologne Cathedral with the Hohenzollern bridge.
    Cologne, Germany. Copyright © Paul Stepan, Photo Researchers Inc., New York
Design Credit: Lawrence Wolfson Design, New York

Printed on acid-free, 250-year-life paper
Manufactured in the United States of America

Contents

Volume I

vii   Introduction

ix   Subject Guide

xxv   Chronology

xxxix   Contributors

li   Acronyms

3   The Encyclopedia A–K

Volume II

579   The Encyclopedia L–Z

1115   Index

Introduction

Since the political unification of the majority of German-speaking states in 1871, Germans have collectively experienced and reflected the best and the worst of modern civilization. However complex the issue of collective and individual guilt, Germans bear the main responsibility for the Holocaust and for many horrors and crimes associated with World War II and the Nazi era. Germans played a vital role as well in World War I, sharing the responsibility both for its outbreak and its severity.

Simultaneously, Germans contributed decisively to the aesthetic, scientific, and social achievements of the modern age, especially in philosophy, social welfare, and technology. The period of the Weimar Republic epitomizes the German reach for a modern, socially sensitive, politically progressive, and artistically innovative society. The subsequent Nazi era demonstrated the depth to which the same nation could plunge.

The two post–World War II German republics—the Federal Republic of Germany and the German Democratic Republic—sought to move toward the political and social norms on the different sides of the Iron Curtain. Since the 1960s, the era of extremes in German history—racist and radical politics, militarist and nationalist ideologies—seems to have passed. Despite much excitement and some violence, the German political reunification in 1990 appears to have confirmed the viewpoint that Germans have been integrated into Europe.

The richness of Germany's past, the country's contributions to many fields, and its complex path to the present need to be drawn together. Placing the major events, actors, and trends within an encyclopedic collection can help students to move away from simple stereotypes while providing a comprehensive information base. As a reference tool for scholars, this encyclopedia encourages an interdisciplinary approach to national history.

In general, *Modern Germany: An Encyclopedia of History, People, and Culture, 1871–1990* presents information commonly accepted by most scholars rather than interpretations espoused by a specific school of specialists. The editors have complemented the traditional emphasis on politics by including entries on personalities, events, institutions, and issues in such diverse fields as literature, music, art, religion, science, philosophy, economics, technology, the media, and society. This is the first English-language work of such comprehensiveness. However, limits of space have reinforced selectivity and demanded conciseness from contributors.

The diversity of modern German history is explored through individual biographies of writers, scientists, artists, entrepreneurs, social activists, academics, and politicians. Specific issues or topics, such as ABORTION, ARCHAEOLOGY, THE BASIC LAW, BERLIN WALL, CODETERMINATION, CUSTOMS, FEMINISM AND ANTI-FEMINISM, FOOD, *GERMANISTIK*, THE HANDICAPPED, HOUSING AND SLUMS, INVENTIONS, JOURNALISM, LEGAL PROFESSION, LIBRARIES, MILITARISM, MUSIC FESTIVALS, SCIENCE AND NATIONAL SOCIALISM, STAB-IN-THE-BACK LEGEND, and WANNSEE CONFERENCE (to name some) are presented at a detailed but terse level. More far-ranging examinations provide overviews of fields of knowledge, of professional activities in technology or culture, and of social problems. These include short essays ranging from AGRICULTURE, DIPLOMACY, FEDERALISM through to OLD AGE, PAINTING, VOCATIONAL EDUCATION, and WOMEN'S OCCUPATIONS. To provide an integrative overview of German political complexities, a set of longer essays covers the Imperial, Weimar, and National Socialist periods as well as the Federal Republic of Germany and the German Democratic Republic. Not every worthy topic could be included and some have been subsumed under others, but in all cases the bibliographies lead to further explorations.

Maps and charts accompany some entries. The maps demonstrate the difficulty of defining Germany politically. When considering culture, the difficulties of delineating "Germany" or "German" are multiplied; political boundaries become fences that defy and distort the layout of the land. Included among the entries are some on Swiss and Austrian individuals who have enriched "German" culture, though they may have lived, been born, or died outside the political borders of Germany. Some worked within a German-speaking environment, others lived in Germany for part of their careers, and some had seminal works published in the German language. How could we have excluded Franz Kafka, Max Frisch, the Vienna School, Arnold Schönberg, or Bruno Walter? To further illustrate the complexity of Germany's place on the European cultural and political map, we offer a series of entries outlining Germany's federal states and the country's relationships with nearly every one of its neighbors.

Since this is the first work of its kind in English—a German publisher is putting out an encyclopedic history series with over a hundred volumes on political themes—we have tried to attain a balanced coverage as we recruited authors known for their scholarly expertise. As we developed the list of topics, we also recognized the limits of any editors' expertise. Although we had decided to find the scholars who had written the main study on a given subject, we recognized that we needed help to create a balanced list of topics and contributors. Hence, we enlisted an advisory board to provide guidance, especially regarding literature, music, science, and technology. The editors found coordinating the efforts of about 400 contributors and 1300 entries a frustrating, but ultimately rewarding, experience. We remain particularly grateful to members of the advisory board and to contributors who followed instructions on bibliographies, length, and deadlines. The entries were requested on a staggered time line and thus were written between 1992 and 1995.

The project relied on the help of very dedicated individuals, including our wives and children, without whose hands-on cooperation the project would not have been completed. Dr. Tom Spira helped initiate the project and did a tremendous amount of high quality editing; Laurentian University, Sudbury, St. Thomas University, Fredericton, and the University of Prince Edward Island, Charlottetown provided significant financial and clerical help; Uta Doerr did most of the translations; Dale Dasset, Susan Delorme, Rose May Démore, Carole Desautel, Catherine Drover, Donna Mayer, Gaby Miller, Cindy O'Donnell, and Susan Parsons did retyping and reformatting; Robert Wittmer helped scan materials into WordPerfect format. The German Information Center, New York, the German Embassy in Ottawa and Inter Nationes in Bonn, Germany, generously provided illustrations. Robert Evans of Audio Visual Services at the University of New Brunswick, Fredericton, prepared the illustrations. Special thanks also to Marianne Lown, Helga McCue, and Jennifer Brosious of Garland Publishing for guiding us through the last stages of the publication process.

Dieter K. Buse
Laurentian University

Juergen C. Doerr
St. Thomas University

Subject Guide

Aeronautics
    Aeronautics
    Air Forces
    Braun, Wernher von
    Dornberger, Walter
    Dornier, Claude
    Göring, Hermann
    Heinkel, Ernst
    Junkers, Hugo
    Lilienthal, Otto
    Milch, Erhard
    Space
    Sperrle, Hugo von
    Vogt, Richard
    Zeppelin, Ferdinand

Agriculture and Rural Society
    Agrarian Leagues
    Agriculture
    Aristocracy
    Böckel, Otto
    Cooperatives
    Country Life
    Darré, R. Walther
    David, Eduard
    Depression, 1873–95
    Food
    Four Year Plan
    Heim, Georg
    Lübke, Heinrich
    Migration
    Peasantry
    Protectionism
    Urbanization

Alcohol and Anti-Alcoholism
    Alcohol
    Food
    Morality
    Temperance Movements
    Workers' Culture

Anarchism and Anarchists
    Anarchism
    Baader-Meinhof Group
    Extra-Parliamentary Opposition
    Landauer, Gustav
    Most, Johann
    Mühsam, Erich
    Reinsdorf, August
    Rocker, Rudolf
    Toller, Ernst

Anti-Semitism
    Anti-Semitism
    Auschwitz
    Böckel, Otto
    Chamberlain, Houston Stewart
    Crystal Night (*Kristallnacht*)
    Fritsch, Theodor
    Goebbels, Josef
    Heydrich, Reinhard
    Himmler, Heinrich
    Hitler, Adolf
    Holocaust
    Jews, 1869–1933
    Jews, 1933–90
    Lagarde, Paul de
    Langbehn, Julius
    National Socialism
    Nationalism
    Pan-German League
    Racism
    Stoecker, Adolf
    Streicher, Julius
    Treitschke, Heinrich von

Völkisch Ideology
Wannsee Conference

Archaeology
    Archaeology
    Schliemann, Heinrich

Architecture
    Architecture and Urban Design
    Bauhaus
    Behrens, Peter
    Gardens and Landscape
        Architecture
    Gropius, Walter
    Housing and Slums
    Jugendstil
    Mies van der Rohe, Ludwig
    Speer, Albert
    Urbanization
    Werkbund

Aristocracy
    Aristocracy
    Agrarian Leagues
    Country Life
    Diplomatic Corps and Diplomacy
    German Conservative Party
    German National People's Party
    Imperial and Free Conservative
        Party
    Imperial Germany: Military
    Prussia
    Resistance
    Social Mobility

Art, Art History, and Artists
    Artists
    Arts and Crafts

Baluschek, Hans
Barlach, Ernst
Baselitz, Georg
Baumeister, Willi
Beckmann, Max
Berlin Secession
Beuys, Joseph
Blaue Reiter, Der
Corinth, Lovis
Cremer, Fritz
Dada
Decadence
Decorative Arts
Dix, Otto
Ernst, Max
Exhibitions (Art)
Expressionism (Visual Arts)
Fritsch, Katharina
German Democratic Republic:
    Arts and Politics
Grosz, George
Heartfield, John
Heckel, Erich
Herzfelde, Wieland
Höch, Hannah
Hödicke, Karl
Hofer, Karl
Immendorff, Jörg
Impressionism
Jugendstil
Kandinsky, Wassily
Kiefer, Anselm
Kirchner, Ernst
Klee, Paul
Kokoschka, Oskar
Kollwitz, Käthe
Liebermann, Max
Lüpertz, Markus
Marc, Franz
Menzel, Adolph
Munich Secession
Münter, Gabriele
Museums
National Socialist Germany: Art
Naturalism, 1880s–1890s
Nay, Ernst
Nesch, Rolf
Nolde, Emil
Painting
Panofsky, Erwin
Pechstein, Max
Penck, A.R.
Photography
Polke, Sigmar
Prussian Art Academy
Richter, Gerhard
Schmidt-Rottluff, Karl

Schwitters, Kurt
Sculpture
Slevogt, Max
Stuck, Franz
Trockel, Rosemarie
Uhde, Fritz
Warburg, Aby
Werkbund
Werner, Anton
Wölfflin, Heinrich

Banking and Bankers
Abs, Hermann
Banking
Bleichröder, Gerson von
Bundesbank, Deutsche
Cooperatives
Currency
Deutsche Bank
Fürstenberg, Carl
Helfferich, Karl
Inflation and Hyperinflation
Raiffeisen, Friedrich
Schacht, Hjalmar
Schulze-Delitzsch, Hermann
Warburg, Max

Bourgeoisie
Bildung und Bildungsbürgertum
Bourgeoisie
Civil Service
Education
Leisure
Liberalism
Professions
Students
Universities
Zoological Gardens

Chancellery and Chancellors
Adenauer, Konrad
Bauer, Gustav
Bethmann Hollweg, Theobald von
Bismarck, Otto von
Brandt, Willy
Brüning, Heinrich
Bülow, Bernhard von
Caprivi, Leo von
Chancellor's, Office
Cuno, Wilhelm
Ebert, Friedrich
Erhard, Ludwig
Fehrenbach, Konstantin
Hertling, Georg von
Hitler, Adolf
Hohenlohe-Schillingsfürst,
    Chlodwig zu

Kiesinger, Kurt
Kohl, Helmut
Luther, Hans
Marx, Wilhelm
Max von Baden, Prince
Müller, Hermann
Papen, Franz von
Scheidemann, Philipp
Schleicher, Kurt
Schmidt, Helmut
Stresemann, Gustav
Wirth, Joseph

Chemistry (Biochemistry) and
    Chemists
Baeyer, Adolf
BASF
Bayer AG
Bergius, Friedrich
Boveri, Theodor
Butenandt, Adolf
Chemistry: Scientific and
    Industrial
Duisburg, Carl
Fischer, Emil
Haber, Fritz
Hahn, Otto
Henkel
Hofmann, August
I.G. Farbenindustrie AG
Kekulé, August
Kolbe, Hermann
Meitner, Lise
Merck
Nerst, Walther
Ostwald, Wilhelm
Pharmacy
Staudinger, Hermann
Warburg, Otto
Willstätter, Richard

Christian Democracy, Christian
    Democratic/Social Union
    and Figures
Adenauer, Konrad
Barzel, Rainer
Bertram, Adolf
Biedenkopf, Kurt
Blank, Theodor
Carstens, Karl
Catholic Women's Association
Catholicism, Political
Christian Democratic Union
Christian Social Union
Döpfner, Cardinal Julius
Ehard, Hans
Erhard, Ludwig

Frings, Joseph
German Democratic Republic:
    Churches
Heinemann, Gustav
Herzog, Roman
Imbusch, Heinrich
Kaiser, Jacob
Kiesinger, Kurt
Kohl, Helmut
Lieber, Ernst
Lübke, Heinrich
Maizière, Lothar de
People's Association for a
    Catholic Germany
Preysing, Konrad
Roman Catholic Church
Schröder, Gerhard
Schwarzhaupt, Elisabeth
Strecker, Gabriele
Strauss, Franz Josef
Süssmuth, Rita
Weber, Helene
Weizsäcker, Richard

Cinema, Film, and Filmmakers
    Cinema
    Fassbinder, Rainer Werner
    Goebbels, Joseph
    Herzog, Werner
    Hugenberg, Alfred
    Kluge, Alexander
    Kracauer, Siegfried
    Riefenstahl, Leni
    Schlöndorff, Volker
    Syberberg, Hans-Jürgen
    Third Reich: Film
    Third Reich: Propaganda and
        Culture
    Trotta, Margarethe von
    Ufa

Colonies and Empire
    Bismarck, Otto von
    Bülow, Bernhard von
    Colonies and Colonial Society
    Nationalism
    Peters, Carl
    Rohrbach, Paul
    Social Imperialism
    Weltpolitik

Communism, Communist Party, and
    Communists
    Brandler, Heinrich
    Fischer, Ruth
    German Communist Party
    German Democratic Republic

Honecker, Erich
Levi, Paul
Liebknecht, Karl
Luxemburg, Rosa
Münzenberg, Willi
Party of Democratic Socialism
Pieck, Wilhelm
Radek, Karl
Social Unity Party of Germany
Soviet–German Relations,
    1918–90
Spartacist League
Thälmann, Ernst
Ulbricht, Walter
Wehner, Herbert
Zetkin, Clara

Composers
    Berg, Alban
    Brahms, Johannes
    Bruckner, Anton
    Composers
    Dessau, Paul
    Eisler, Hanns
    Hindemith, Paul
    Liszt, Franz
    Mahler, Gustav
    Orff, Carl
    Pfitzner, Hans
    Reger, Max
    Schönberg, Arnold
    Stockhausen, Karlheinz
    Strauss, Richard
    Wagner, Richard
    Webern, Anton
    Weill, Kurt
    Wolf, Hugo

Conductors
    Conductors
    Furtwängler, Wilhelm
    Karajan, Herbert von
    Liszt, Franz
    Mahler, Gustav
    Walter, Bruno

Conferences
    Potsdam Conference
    Versailles, Treaty of
    Wannsee Conference
    Yalta Conference

Conservativism and Conservatives
    Adenauer, Konrad
    Bethmann Hollweg,
        Theobald von
    Bismarck, Otto von

Brüning, Heinrich
Bülow, Bernhard von
Caprivi, Leopold von
Center Party
Christian Democratic Union
Christian Social Union
Conservativism, 1871–1918
Conservativism, 1918–45
Erhard, Ludwig
Freyer, Hans
German Conservative Party
German National People's Party
Hertling, Georg von
Heydebrand und der Lasa,
    Ernst von
Hohenlohe-Schillingsfürst,
    Chlodwig zu
Hugenberg, Alfred
Imperial and Free Conservative
    Party
Imperial League against Social
    Democracy
Jung, Edgar
Kiesinger, Kurt
Kohl, Helmut
Kreuzzeitung
Langbehn, Julius
Lieber, Ernst
Moeller van den Bruck, Arthur
Papen, Franz von
Protestant Women's League
Puttkamer, Robert Viktor von
Radical Right
Spengler, Oswald
Strauss, Franz Josef
Treviranus, Gottfried
Zehrer, Hans

Cooperatives
    Cooperatives
    Schulze-Delitzsch, Hermann

Culture and Cultural Values
    Aesthetics
    Bildung und Bildungsbürgertum
    Counterculture, 1945–90
    Customs
    Decadence
    Folklore
    Human Sciences
    Inventions
    Kultur
    Morality
    Mythology, Classical and
        Germanic
    Understanding (Verstehen, Com-
        prehension, Hermeneutics)

Workers' Culture
Working-Class Literature
Youth Movements

Disarmament and Demilitarization
Disarmament
Pacifism and Peace Movement
Rearmament
Versailles, Treaty of
Yalta Conference

Drama and Dramatists
Borchert, Wolfgang
Braun, Volker
Brecht, Bertolt
Drama
Dürrenmatt, Friedrich
Expressionism (Literature)
Handke, Peter
Hasenclever, Hans
Hauptmann, Gerhart
Hochhuth, Rolf
Kaiser, Georg
Müller, Heiner
Naturalism
Piscator, Erwin
Radio Plays
Reinhardt, Max
Satire
Schnitzler, Arthur
Sternheim, Carl
Strauss, Botho
Theater
Toller, Ernst
Wedekind, Frank
Weiss, Peter
Zuckmayer, Carl
Zweig, Arnold

Ecology and Environmental
    Movement
Ecology
Engels, Friedrich
The Greens: Movement, Party,
    Ideology
Haeckel, Ernst
Kelly, Petra
Völkisch Ideology
Youth Movements

Economics, Economy, and Economists
Brentano, Lujo
Cartels
Coal Industry
Codetermination
Dawes Plan
Depression (1873–95)

(Great) Depression (1929–33)
Domestic Industry
Economic Miracle
Economics
Economics of German
    Reunification
Erhard, Ludwig
Exports and Foreign Trade
Federal Republic of Germany:
    Economy
Food
Founding Years
Four Year Plan (1936–42)
German Democratic Republic:
    Economy
Hilferding, Rudolf
Inflation and Hyperinflation
Marshall Plan
Mittag, Günter
Oldenburg, Karl
Political Economy
Postwar Reconstruction
Protectionism
Raiffeisen, Friedrich
Regional Economic
    Development
Reparations
Schacht, Hjalmar
Schiller, Karl
Schmoller, Gustav
Sombart, Werner
Wagner, Adolph
Weber, Alfred

Education
Althoff, Friedrich
Bildung und Bildungsbürgertum
Civil Service
Education
Education for Girls and Women
Falk, Adalbert
Geography
German Democratic Republic:
    Education
Honecker, Margot
Information Processing
Libraries
Literacy
National Socialist Germany:
    Education
Pedagogy since 1871
Rust, Bernhard
Schools
Schrader-Breymann, Henriette
Students
Teaching
Technological Training, Technical

Institutes and Universities
Vocational Education
Youth
Zahn-Harnack, Agnes von

Federal Republic of Germany
Adenauer, Konrad
Basic Law
Berlin Wall
Brandt, Willy
Christian Democratic Union
Christian Social Union
Erhard, Ludwig
Federal Republic of Germany
Federal Republic of Germany:
    Armed Forces
Federal Republic of Germany:
    Economy
Federal Republic of Germany:
    Foreign Policy
Federal Republic of Germany:
    Internal Security
Federal Republic of Germany:
    Judicial System
Federal Republic of Germany:
    Literature
Federal Republic of Germany:
    Political Radicalism and
    Neo-Nazism
Federal Republic of Germany:
    Political Terrorism
Federal Republic of Germany:
    Postwar Refugee and
    Expellee Organizations
Federal Republic of Germany:
    Women
Feminism in the Federal
    Republic
Free Democratic Party
Globke, Hans
Grand Coalition
The Greens: Movement, Party,
    Ideology
Heinemann, Gustav
Herzog, Roman
Heuss, Theodor
Kiesinger, Kurt Georg
Kohl, Helmut
Reunification
Schiller, Karl
Schmidt, Helmut
Social Democratic Party (SPD),
    1919–1990
Strauss, Franz Josef
Süssmuth, Rita
Trade Unions, 1945–90
Weizsäcker, Richard von

Feminism and Feminists
    Abortion
    Bäumer, Gertrud
    Cauer, Minna
    Feminism and Anti-Feminism
        (1871–1918)
    Feminism and Anti-Feminism
        (1918–45)
    Feminism in the Federal
        Republic of Germany
    Feminist Writing
    Heymann, Lida
    Lange, Helene
    Otto, Louise
    Salomon, Alice
    Schwarzer, Alice
    Selbert, Elisabeth
    Sex Reform and Birth Control
    Stöcker, Helene
    (Bourgeois) Women's Movement,
        1871–1933
    Zahn-Harnack, Agnes von
    Zetkin, Clara
    Zietz, Luise

Festivals
    Carnival
    Christmas
    Customs
    Festivals
    National Holidays
    Workers' Culture

Foreign Relations and Diplomats
    Adenauer, Konrad
    Allied High Commission to
        Germany
    Allied Occupation Statute
    American-German Relations
    American Occupation
    Anglo-German Relations
    Anschluss of Austria
    Austro-German Relations
    Bahr, Egon
    Basic Treaty
    Belgian-German Relations
    Berlin Blockade
    Bethmann Hollweg, Theobald
        von
    Bismarck, Otto von
    Bizone
    Blankenhorn, Herbert
    Brandt, Willy
    Brentano, Heinrich
    British Occupation Policy
    Brockdorff-Rantzau, Ulrich von
    Bülow, Bernhard von

Central Powers
Cold War and Germany
Danish-German Relations
Dawes Plan
Detente and Germany
Diplomatic Corps and
    Diplomacy
Dutch-German Relations
Eulenburg-Hertefeld, Philipp zu
Federal Republic of Germany:
    Foreign Policy
Fischer, Oskar
Franco-German Relations
Genscher, Hans-Dietrich
German Democratic Republic:
    Foreign Relations
German-German Relations
Germany Treaty
Gorbachev and the German
    Question
Hallstein, Walter
Hassell, Christian von
Imperial Germany: Foreign Policy
Israeli-German Relations
Italian-German Relations
Japanese-German Relations
Kiderlen-Wächter, Alfred von
Kohl, Helmut
Marschall von Bieberstein, Adolf
Marshall Plan
McCloy, John
Münzenberg, Willi
National Socialist Germany:
    Foreign Relations
Nato and Germany
Neurath, Constantin von
Oder-Neisse Line
Ostpolitik
Pfleiderer, Karl
Polish-German Relations, 1871–
    1918
Polish-German Relations, 1918–
    45
Polish-German Relations (after
    1945)
Postwar European Integration
    and Germany
Rapallo Treaty
Reparations
Reuter, Ernst
Ribbentrop, Joachim von
Robertson, Brian
Russian-German Relations
Scheel, Walter
Schröder, Gerhard
Schuman Plan
Schweinitz, Lothar von

Seyss-Inquart, Arthur
Soviet-German Relations
Soviet Occupation of Germany
Stalin Notes
Sudeten Problem
Swiss-German Relations
Weimar Republic: Foreign
    Relations
Weiszäcker, Ernst von
Weltpolitik

Foundations
    Althoff, Friedrich
    Foundations and Research
        Institutes
    Kaiser Wilhelm/Max Planck
        Societies
    Volkswagen
    Zeiss, Carl

German Democratic Republic
    Ackermann, Anton
    Anti-Fascism
    Axen, Hermann
    Berlin Wall
    Economics of German
        Reunification
    Fischer, Oskar
    Free German Trade Union
        Federation
    Free German Youth
    German Democratic Republic:
        Arts and Politics
    German Democratic Republic:
        Churches
    German Democratic Republic:
        Collapse
    German Democratic Republic:
        Constitutions
    German Democratic Republic:
        Economy
    German Democratic Republic:
        Education
    German Democratic Republic:
        Foreign Relations
    German Democratic Republic:
        Government System
    German Democratic Republic:
        Judicial System
    German Democratic Republic:
        Literature and Literary Life
    German Democratic Republic:
        Marxism-Leninism
    German Democratic Republic:
        Media
    German Democratic Republic:
        National People's Army

German Democratic Republic:
    Nationalism
German Democratic Republic:
    Opposition
German Democratic Republic:
    Political Culture
German Democratic Republic:
    Political Party System
German Democratic Republic:
    Sports
German Democratic Republic:
    State Security
German Democratic Republic:
    Technical Intelligentsia
German Democratic Republic:
    Women
Grotewohl, Otto
Hager, Kurt
Honecker, Erich
Honecker, Margot
Maizière, Lothar de
Mielke, Erich
Milch, Erich
Mittag, Günther
Modrow, Hans
Party of Democratic Socialism
Pieck, Wilhelm
Reunification
Sindermann, Horst
Socialist Unity Party
Stoph, Willy
Tisch, Harry
Ulbricht, Walter
Verner, Paul
Vogel, Wolfgang
Wolf, Markus

History and Historians
Archives
Bitburg
Burckhardt, Jacob
Delbrück, Hans
Dilthey, Wilhelm
Droysen, Johann Gustav
Fischer Controversy
Frank, Walter
Harnack, Adolf von
Hintze, Otto
Historikerstreit
History
Holocaust: Historiography
Huch, Ricarda
Human Sciences
Kehr, Eckart
Kempowski, Walter
Kracauer, Siegfried
Lamprecht, Karl

Löwith, Karl
Ludwig, Emil
Mehring, Franz
Meinecke, Friedrich
Mommsen, Theodor
Oncken, Hermann
Ranke, Leopold von
Sonderweg
Spengler, Oswald
Sybel, Heinrich
Third Reich: Historiography
Treitschke, Heinrich von
Troeltsch, Ernst
Weber, Alfred
Weber, Max

Holocaust
Anti-Semitism
Auschwitz
Baeck, Leo
Barbie, Klaus
Concentration Camps
Crystal Night (Kristallnacht)
Eichmann, Adolf
Einsatzgruppen
Euthanasia
Goebbels, Josef
Gypsies
Heydrich, Reinhardt
Himmler, Heinrich
Hitler, Adolf
Holocaust (World War II)
Holocaust: Historiography
Jews, 1933–90
Memory, Collective
Mitscherlich, Alexander
Mitscherlich, Margarete
Nazi War Crimes Trials and
    Investigations
Ravensbruck
Schindler, Oskar
Schutzstaffel (SS)
Stein, Edith
Stuttgart Declaration of Guilt
Wannsee Conference

Imperial Germany
Aristocracy
Bethmann Hollweg, Theobald von
Bismarck, Otto von
Bülow, Bernhard von
Caprivi, Leo von
Daily Telegraph Affair
Expressionism (Literature)
Expressionism (Visual Arts)
Hohenlohe-Schillingsfürst,
    Chlodwig zu

Imperial Germany
Imperial Germany: Army
Imperial Germany: Foreign
    Policy
Imperial Germany: Literature
Prussia
Weltpolitik
Wilhelm I
Wilhelm II
Zabern

Independent Social Democratic Party
Bernstein, Edward
Haase, Hugo
Independent Social Democratic
    Party, 1917–22
Kautsky, Karl
Zietz, Luise

Industrial Firms and Industrialists
Abbe, Ernst and Zeiss Werke
AEG AG
Audi
Automobile Industry
Balke, Siegfried
Ballin, Albert
BASF
Bayer AG
Beitz, Berthold
Benz, Karl
Berg, Fritz
BMW (Bavarian Motor Works)
Bosch, Carl
Bosch, Robert
Camphausen, Ludolf
Central Association of German
    Industrialists
Coal Industry
Daimler, Gottlieb
Daimler-Benz AG
Duisberg, Carl
Federation of German Industry
Flick Family
Friedrich, Otto A.
Fürstenberg, Carl
Heinkel, Ernst
Henkel
I.G. Farbenindustrie AG (1925–
    ·45)
Krupp: Family and Firm
Mannesmann: Family and Firm
Merck
Nordhoff, Heinrich
Nuclear Power and the Nuclear
    Industry
Pharmacy
Porsche, Ferdinand

Pressure and Special Interest
    Groups
Rathenau, Walther
Ruhrlade
RWE (Rheinisch-Westfälisches
    Elektrizitätswerk)
Schmitz, Hermann
Siemens AG
Siemens, Werner von
Silverberg, Paul
Sohl, Hans-Günther
Stinnes, Hugo
Steel Industry
Stumm-Halberg, Carl von
Third Reich and Industry
Thyssen, Fritz
Volkswagen
Zeiss, Carl

Industrialization and Economic
    Conditions
Cartels
Clothing
Coal Industry
Codetermination
Cooperatives
Domestic Industry
Electricity
Energy
Factory Laws and Reform
Federation of German Industry
Food
Housing and Slums
Industrialization and Its Social
    and Political Consequences
Inflation and Hyperinflation
Information Processing
Inventions
Labor Laws
Migration
Regional Economic
    Development
Steel Industry
Taxation
Trade Fairs
Urbanization
Wages
Women
Women's Occupations
Work
Working Conditions

Journalism and Journalists
Dietrich, Otto
Dirks, Walter
Dönhoff, Marion von
Freyer, Hans

Freytag, Gustav
Goebbels, Josef
Harden, Maximilian
Joos, Joseph
Journalism
Jung, Ernst
Kogan, Eugen
Magazines
Moeller van den Bruck, Arthur
Mosse, Rudolf
Mühsam, Erich
Niekisch, Ernst
Ossietzky, Carl von
Rohrbach, Paul
Satire
Schwarzer, Alice
Tucholsky, Kurt
Wallraff, Günter
Wolff, Theodor
Zehrer, Hans

Language
German as an International
    Language
Germanistik
Law and Lawyers
Federal Republic of Germany:
    Judicial System
Freisler, Roland
German Democratic Republic:
    Judicial System
Judicial System of Imperial and
    Weimar Germany
Law, German Conception of
Legal Profession (1871–1990)
Nazi War Crimes Trials and
    Investigations
Nuremberg Trials
People's Court
Schmitt, Carl
Third Reich: Legal Profession

Leisure
Bestsellers
Books
Carnival
Cinema
Customs
Festivals
German Democratic Republic:
    Sports
Libraries
Magazines
Media
National Holidays
Parks, Public
Radio

Sport
Television
Work
Workers' Culture
Zoological Gardens

Liberalism and Liberal Political
    Figures and Parties
Bamberger, Ludwig
Bassermann, Ernst
Bennigsen, Rudolf von
Camphausen, Ludolf
Dehler, Thomas
Erkelenz, Anton
Forckenbeck, Max von
Free Democratic Party
Genscher, Hans-Dietrich
German Democratic Party
German People's Party
Hamm-Brücher, Hildegard
Heuss, Theodor
Koch-Weser, Erich
Lambsdorff, Otto von
Lasker, Eduard
Liberalism, 1871–1933
Lüders, Marie-Elisabeth
Luther, Hans
Maier, Reinhold
Mende, Erich
Miquel, Johannes von
National Liberal Party
Naumann, Friedrich
Payer, Friedrich von
Pfleiderer, Karl
Richter, Eugen
Scheel, Walter
Schiffer, Eugen
Stresemann, Gustav
Weber, Max
Wolff, Theodor

Literature and Literary Figures
Andersch, Alfred
Andreas-Salomé, Lou
Autobiography
Bachmann, Ingeborg
Becher, Johannes R.
Becker, Jurek
Benn, Gottfried
Bergengruen, Werner
Bernstein, Elsa
Biermann, Wolf
Böll, Heinrich
Borchert, Wolfgang
Braun, Volker
Brecht, Bertolt
Broch, Hermann

Busch, Wilhelm
Canetti, Elias
Carossa, Hans
Celan, Paul
Children's Literature
Comedy
Döblin, Alfred
Drewitz, Ingeborg
Dürrenmatt, Friedrich
Eich, Günter
Enzensberger, Hans Magnus
Exile Literature
Expressionism (Literature)
Fairy Tale
Fallada, Hans
Federal Republic of Germany:
    Literature
Feminist Writing
Feuchtwanger, Lion
Fontane, Theodor
Freytag, Gustav
Fried, Erich
Frisch, Max
George, Stefan
German Democratic Republic:
    Literature and Literary Life
Germanistik
Grass, Günter
Grimm, Hans
Handke, Peter
Hasenclever, Walter
Hauptmann, Gerhart
Hein, Christoph
Henscheid, Eckhard
Hesse, Hermann
Heym, Stefan
Historical Novel
Hochhuth, Rolf
Hofmannsthal, Hugo
Holz, Arno
Huch, Ricarda
Imperial Germany: Literature
Johnson, Uwe
Johst, Hanns
Jünger, Ernst
Kafka, Franz
Kaiser, Georg
Kant, Hermann
Kaschnitz, Marie
Kästner, Erich
Kempowski, Walter
Kirsch, Sarah
Koeppen, Wolfgang
Kraus, Karl
Kunert, Günter
Langgässer, Elisabeth
Lasker-Schüler, Else

Lenz, Siegfried
Literary Criticism
Loest, Erich
Lowenthal, Leo
Mann, Heinrich
Mann, Thomas
May, Karl
Müller, Heiner
Musil, Robert
Mystery and Detective
    Fiction
Mythology, Classical and
    Germanic
National Socialist Germany:
    Literature
Naturalism, 1880s–1890s
Novel
Patriotic Literature
Raabe, Wilhelm
Radio Plays
Realism (Literary)
Remarque, Erich Marie
Rilke, Rainer Marie
Roth, Joseph
Salomon, Ernst
Satire
Schädlich, Hans
Schmidt, Arno
Schnitzler, Arthur
Seghers, Anna
Serial Literature
Sternheim, Carl
Storm, Theodor
Strauss, Botho
Symbolism
Trakl, Georg
Walser, Martin
Weimar Republic: Literature
Weiss, Peter
Wolf, Christa
Workers' Culture
Working-Class Literature
Zuckmayer, Carl
Zweig, Arnold
Zweig, Stefan

Mathematics and Mathematicians
Bieberbach, Ludwig
Cantor, Georg
Hilbert, David
Klein, Felix
Landau, Edmund
Mathematics
Weyl, Hermann

Media (Newspapers, Radio, Television)
Bild Zeitung

Der Spiegel
Die Welt
Die Weltbühne
Die Zeit
Electrical Information
    Transmission
Frankfurter Allgemeine Zeitung
German Democratic Republic:
    Media
Press and Newspapers
Radio
Süddeutsche Zeitung
Television
Third Reich: Propaganda and
    Culture
Völkischer Beobachter

Medicine and Medical Figures
Bacteriology
Biology
Boveri, Theodor
Butenandt, Adolf
Disease
Ehrlich, Paul
Eugenics
Handicapped
Health
Insanity
Koch, Robert
Medical Profession
Medicine
Pettenkofer, Max
Pharmacy
Physiology
Psychiatry
Psychoanalysis
Sauerbruch, Ferdinand
Virchow, Rudolf

Military and Military Figures
Air Forces
Armaments Policy
Baudissin, Wolf von
Bauer, Max
Beck, Ludwig
Blank, Theodor
Blomberg, Werner von
Brauchitsch, Walter von
Disarmament
Dönitz, Karl
Duesterberg, Theodor
Einem, Karl von
Falkenhayn, Erich von
Federal Republic of Germany:
    Armed Forces
Fritsch, Werner von
German Army League

German Democratic Republic:
    National People's Army
Gessler, Otto
Groener, Wilhelm
Guderian, Heinz
Halder, Franz
Hammerstein-Equord,
    Kurt von
Heusinger, Adolf
Hindenburg, Paul von
Hintze, Paul von
Hoffmann, Heinz
Imperial Germany: Military
Jodl, Alfred
Keitel, Wilhelm
Kluge, Günther von
Ludendorff, Erich
Maizière, Ulrich de
Manstein, Erich von
Milch, Erhard
Militarism
Moltke, Helmuth von (1800–91)
Moltke, Helmuth von (1848–
    1916)
Müller, Georg
National Socialist Germany:
    Military
Naval Mutinies of 1918
Navy and Naval Policy
Navy League
Noske, Gustav
Officer's Corps
Paramilitary Organizations
Paulus, Friedrich von
Raeder, Erich
Rearmament
Richthofen, Wolfram von
Rommel, Erwin
Rundstedt, Gerd von
Schlieffen, Alfred von
Seeckt, Hans von
Seldte, Franz
Sperrle, Hugo von
Schutzstaffel (SS)
Stab-in-the-Back Legend
Stahlhelm
Sturmabteilung (SA)
Tirpitz, Alfred von
Veterans' Organizations
Waldersee, Alfred von
Waffen-SS
Weimar Republic: Army

Minorities
    Citizenship and Foreigners
    German-Jewish Organizations
    Gypsies

Jews, 1869–1933
Jews, 1933–90
Minorities, Ethnocultural and
    Foreign

Monarchs
    Friedrich (Frederick) III
    Ludwig II
    Wilhelm I
    Wilhelm II

Music
    Ballet (Music)
    Chamber Music
    Choral Music
    Composers
    Conductors
    Keyboard Music
    Music Festivals
    National Socialist Germany:
        Music
    Opera
    Operetta
    Orchestral Music
    Orchestras
    Solo Lied

National Identification
    Bitburg
    Heimat (Homeland)
    Historikerstreit
    History
    Memory, Collective
    Mitscherlich, Margarete
    National Holidays
    National Identity
    National Symbols
    Nationalism

National Socialist Germany
    Concentration Camps
    Coordination (Gleichschaltung)
    Crystal Night (Kristallnacht)
    Exile Literature
    Hitler, Adolf
    National Socialism
    National Socialist Germany:
        Art
    National Socialist Germany:
        Education
    National Socialist Germany:
        Foreign Relations
    National Socialist Germany:
        Literature
    National Socialist Germany:
        Military
    National Socialist Germany:

Music
National Socialist Germany:
    Propaganda

National Socialist Organizations
    German Labor Front
    Gestapo
    Hitler Youth
    Kripo (Reich Kriminalpolizei)
    League of German Girls
    National Socialist Factory Cell
        Organization
    Reich Security Office
    Schutzstaffel (SS)
    Security Office of the SS
    Security Police (Sipo)
    "Strength Through Joy"
    Sturmabteilung (SA)
    Waffen-SS

National Socialists and Affiliated
    Supporters
    Barbie, Klaus
    Bormann, Martin
    Darré, R. Walther
    Eichmann, Adolf
    Frank, Hans
    Frank, Walter
    Freisler, Roland
    Frick, Wilhelm
    Funk, Walther
    Goebbels, Joseph
    Göring, Hermann
    Hess, Rudolf
    Heydrich, Reinhard
    Himmler, Heinrich
    Hitler, Adolf
    Höss, Rudolf
    Hugenberg, Alfred
    Johst, Hanns
    Kaltenbrunner, Ernst
    Keitel, Wilhelm
    Ley, Robert
    Papen, Franz von
    Ribbentrop, Joachim von
    Riefenstahl, Leni
    Röhm, Ernst
    Rosenberg, Alfred
    Rust, Bernhard
    Sauckel, Fritz
    Schacht, Hjalmar
    Scheubner-Richter, Max
    Schirach, Baldur von
    Scholtz-Klink, Gertrud
    Speer, Albert
    Stark, Johannes
    Strasser, Gregor

Strasser, Otto
Streicher, Julius

Nationalism
    Chamberlain, Houston Stewart
    Class, Heinrich
    Colonies and Colonial Society
    Eastern Marches Society
    Fatherland Party (1917–18)
    Geopolitics
    German Army League
    German Democratic Republic:
        Nationalism
    Grimm, Hans
    Hitler, Adolf
    Hugenberg, Alfred
    Imperial League Against Social
        Democracy
    Imperialism
    Jünger, Ernst
    Keim, August
    Ludendorff, Erich
    Moeller van den Bruck, Arthur
    Nationalism
    Nationalist Women's Associations
        (1871–1933)
    Navy League
    Pan-German League
    Patriotic Literature
    Peters, Carl
    Political Cartography
    Radical Nationalism
    Radical Right
    Ratzel, Friedrich
    Treitschke, Heinrich von
    Völkisch Ideology
    Weltpolitik
    World War I

Opposition in German Democratic
        Republic
    Becker, Jurek
    Biermann, Wolf
    German Democratic Republic:
        Opposition
    Harich, Wolfgang
    Havemann, Robert
    Reich, Jens

Optics
    Optics
    Zeiss, Carl

Pacifism
    Counterculture
    Heymann, Lida
    Pacifism and the Peace

Movement (1871–1990)
    Quidde, Ludwig

Peacemaking
    Brest-Litovsk
    Potsdam Conference
    Versailles, Treaty of
    Yalta Conference

Philosophy and Philosphers
    Adorno, Theodor
    Arendt, Hannah
    Benjamin, Walter
    Bloch, Ernst
    Cassirer, Ernst
    Dilthey, Wilhelm
    Frankfurt School
    Gadamer, Hans-Georg
    Gehlen, Arnold
    Habermas, Jürgen
    Heidegger, Martin
    Husserl, Edmund
    Jaspers, Karl
    Löwith, Karl
    Lukás, Georg
    Marburg School
    Marcuse, Herbert
    Marx, Karl
    Nietzsche, Friedrich
    Philosophy
    Popper, Karl
    Rickert, Heinrich
    Scheler, Max
    Schweitzer, Albert
    Strauss, Leo
    Understanding (Verstehen,
        Comprehension,
        Hermeneutics)
    Vienna Circle
    Wertheimer, Max
    Windelband, Wilhelm
    Wittgenstein, Ludwig

Photography
    Becher, Bernd and Hilla
    Photography
    Struth, Thomas

Physics and Physicists
    Bethe, Hans
    Boltmann, Ludwig
    Born, Max
    Einstein, Albert
    Franck, James
    Hahn, Otto
    Heisenberg, Werner
    Helmholtz, Hermann von

Laue, Max von
Lenard, Philipp
Mach, Ernst
Meitner, Lise
Pauli, Wolfgang
Physics
Planck, Max
Röntgen, Wilhelm
Schrödinger, Erwin
Sommerfeld, Arnold
Stark, Johannes
Weizsäcker, Carl-Friedrich von

Poetry and Poets
    Becher, Johannes R.
    Benn, Georg
    Biermann, Wolfgang
    Celan, Paul
    Expressionism (Literature)
    Fried, Erich
    George, Stefan
    Hermlin, Stephan
    Hofmannsthal, Hermann
    Kunze, Reiner
    Langgässer, Elisabeth
    Loerke, Oskar
    Poetry
    Rilke, Rainer Maria
    Symbolism
    Trakl, Georg

Political Parties and Politics
    Baader-Meinhof Group
    Basic Law
    Bavarian People's Party
    Center Party
    Christian Democratic Union
    Christian Social Union
    Constitutions
    Elections
    Extra-Parliamentary Opposition
    Fatherland Party
    Federal Republic of Germany:
        Political Radicalism and
        Neo-Nazism
    Federal Republic of Germany:
        Postwar Refugee and
        Expellee Organizations
    Federalism
    Free Democratic Party
    German Communist Party
    German Conservative Party
    German Democratic Party
    German Democratic Republic:
        Constitutions
    German Democratic Republic:
        Government System

German Democratic Republic:
    Political Culture
German Democratic Republic:
    Political Party System
German National People's
    Party
German People's Party
Grand Coalition
The Greens: Movement, Party,
    Ideology
Imperial and Free Conservative
    Party
Independent Social Democratic
    Party
Local Government
National Liberal Party
National Socialism
Parliamentary System
Parties and Politics
Party of Democratic Socialism
Social Democratic Party
Socialist Unity Party of Germany
    (SED)
Suffrage

Political Science, Political Scientists,
    and Theorists
Arendt, Hannah
Bernstein, Edward
Jung, Carl
Kautsky, Karl
Kogon, Eugen
Luxemburg, Rosa
Marx, Karl
Neumann, Franz
Political Science
Public-Opinion Surveying
Schmid, Carlo
Schmitt, Carl
Spengler, Oswald
Strauss, Leo
Weber, Max

Political Violence
Violence
Zabern

Presidency and Presidents
Carstens, Karl
Ebert, Friedrich
Heinemann, Gustav
Herzog, Roman
Heuss, Theodor
Hindenburg, Paul von
Hitler, Adolf
Lübke, Heinrich
Presidency

Scheel, Walter
Weizsäcker, Richard von

Professions
Anthropology
Archaeology
Artists
Astronomy
Banking
Biology
Chemistry: Scientific and
    Industrial
Civil Service
Clergy, Protestant
Composers
Conductors
Engineering
Geology
History
Journalism
Legal Profession
Mathematics
Medical Profession
Officers' Corps
Philosophy
Physics
Physiology
Policing
Political Science
Professions
Psychiatry
Psychology
Sociology
Teaching
Theology

Protestantism and Protestants
Barth, Karl
Bonhoeffer, Dietrich
Bultmann, Rudolf
Clergy, Protestant
Confessing Church
Dibelius, Otto
German Christians
German Democratic Republic:
    Churches
Harnach, Adolf
Moltmann, Jürgen
Ritschl, Albrecht
Schweitzer, Albert
Tillich, Paul
Troeltsch, Ernst
Weizsäcker, Richard von
Wurm, D. Theophil

Psychology and Psychologists
Adler, Alfred

Andreas-Salomé, Lou
Dilthey, Wilhelm
Freud, Sigmund
Fromm, Erich
Helmholtz, Hermann von
Husserl, Edmund
Insanity
Jung, Carl
Köhler, Wolfgang
Lewin, Kurt
Mitscherlich, Alexander
Mitscherlich, Margarete
Psychiatry
Psychoanalysis
Psychology
Wertheimer, Max
Wundt, Wilhelm

Publishing and Publishers
Amann, Max
Bestsellers, Contemporary
Books
Fischer, Samuel
Herzfelde, Wieland
Hugenberg, Alfred
Journalism
Magazines
Mosse, Rudolf
Piper, Reinhard
Press and Newspapers
Publishing and Book Trade
Rowohlt, Ernst
Sonnemann, Leopold
Springer, Alex
Ullstein Publishing
Unseld, Siegfried

Race and Racism
Anti-Semitism
Chamberlain, Houston Stewart
Eugenics
Günther, Hans
Haeckel, Ernst
Himmler, Heinrich
Hitler, Adolf
Racism
Radical Right
Science and National Socialism
Social Darwinism
Völkisch Ideology

Refugees and Exiles
Becher, Johannes R.
Benjamin, Walter
Biermann, Wolf
Brecht, Bertolt
Broch, Hermann

Einstein, Albert
Eisler, Hanns
Emigration
Exile Literature
Expulsion and Exile of Scientists
    and Scholars
Heym, Stefan
Honecker, Erich
Mann, Thomas
National Committee for a Free
    Germany
Refugees
Roth, Joseph
Salomon, Alice
Seghers, Anna
Tucholsky, Kurt
Ulbricht, Walter
Weill, Kurt
Zuckmayer, Carl
Zweig, Arnold
Zweig, Stefan

Regions and Political Territories
Alsace-Lorraine
Baden-Württemberg
Bavaria
Berlin
Berlin Wall
Bonn
Brandenburg
Bremen
Danzig, Free City of
Federalism
Hamburg
Hesse
Local Government
Lower Saxony
Mecklenburg-Vorpommern
North Rhine–Westphalia
Oder-Neisse Line
Prussia
Regional Economic
    Development
Rhineland-Palatinate
Ruhr Region
Saar
Saxony
Saxony-Anhalt
Schleswig-Holstein
Sudeten Problem
Thuringia
Upper Silesia
Versailles, Treaty of

Religion and Theologians
Baeck, Leo
Balthasar, Hans

Barth, Karl
Biblical Criticism
Bonhoeffer, Dietrich
Buber, Martin
Bultmann, Rudolf
Clergy, Protestant
Confessing Church
Döpfner, Cardinal Julius
German Christians
German Democratic Republic:
    Churches
Guardini, Romano
Haeckel, Ernst
Harnack, Adolf von
Jews, 1869–1933
Küng, Hans
Moltmann, Jürgen
Niemöller, Martin
Protestant Theology
Protestantism, Protestant Church
Rahner, Karl
Ritschl, Albrecht
Roman Catholic Church
Schweitzer, Albert
Stoecker, Adolf
Strauss, David Friedrich
Stuttgart Declaration of Guilt
Tillich, Paul
Troeltsch, Ernst

Reparations
Dawes Plan
Rapallo, Treaty of
Young Plan

Resistance to Nazism
Anti-Fascism
Canaris, Wilhelm
Delp, Alfred
Dohnanyi, Hans
Faulhaber, Michael von
Galen, Clemens August von
Gerstenmaier, Eugen
Gisevius, Hans Bernd
Goerdeler, Carl
Hammerstein-Equord, Kurt von
Hassell, Christian von
Hoegner, Wilhelm
Leber, Julius
Leuschner, Wilhelm
Lichtenberg, Bernard
Lubbe, Marinus van der
Mierendorff, Carlo
Moltke, Helmuth James von
National Committee for a Free
    Germany
Niemöller, Martin

Olbricht, Friedrich
Oster, Hans
Resistance
Schlabrendorff, Fabian von
Schulenburg, Fritz-Dietlof von
Schumacher, Kurt
Stauffenberg, Claus von
Stülpnagel, Carl-Heinrich von
Thälmann, Ernst
Tresckow, Henning von
Trott zu Solz, Adam
White Rose
Witzleben, Erwin von
Wundt, D. Theophil
Yorck von Wartenburg, Peter

Roman Catholicism and Catholic
    Political Figures (pre-1945)
Adenauer, Konrad
Bertram, Adolf
Brüning, Heinrich
Catholic Women's Association
Catholicism, Political
Center Party
Döpfner, Julius
Erzberger, Matthias
Faulhaber, Michael von
Fehrenbach, Konstantin
Frings, Joseph
Galen, Clemens August von
Heim, Georg
Hertling, Georg von
Imbusch, Heinrich
Joos, Joseph
Kaas, Ludwig
Kaiser, Jacob
Ketteler, Wilhelm von
Kulturkampf (1871–87)
Lieber, Ernst
Marx, Wilhelm
Papen, Franz von
People's Association for Catholic
    Germany
Preysing, Konrad von
Roman Catholic Church
Spahn, Martin
Stegerwald, Adam
Strecker, Gabriele
Weber, Helene
Windthorst, Ludwig
Wirth, Joseph

Satire and Satirists
Biermann, Wolfgang
Böll, Heinrich
Brecht, Bertolt
Busch, Wilhelm

Cabaret
Comedy
Dada
Feuchtwanger, Lion
Fried, Erich
Grass, Günter
Grosz, George
Harden, Maximillan
Hasenclever, Walter
Henscheid, Eckhard
Kästner, Erich
Kraus, Karl
Mann, Heinrich
Ossietzky, Karl
Satire
Schmidt, Arno
Schwitters, Kurt
Sternheim, Carl
Tucholsky, Kurt
Wedekind, Franz

Science
Anthropology
Astronomy
Atom Bomb
Bacteriology
Biochemistry
Biology
Chemistry, Scientific and
    Industrial
Expulsion and Exile of Scientists
    and Scholars
Folklore
Geography
Geology
Human Sciences
Kaiser Wilhelm/Max Planck
    Societies and Their
    Institutes
Linde, Carl von
Mathematics
Physics
Physiology
Science and National Socialism
Science in the Postwar
    Germanies
Space
Technology
Zoological Gardens

Sculpture
Barlach, Ernst
Beuys, Joseph
Cremer, Fritz
Expressionism (Visual Arts)
Fritsch, Katharina
Heckel, Erich

Kirchner, Ernst
Kolbe, Georg
Kollwitz, Käthe
Marcks, Gerhard
Schmidt-Rottluff, Karl
Sculpture

Social Conditions and Trends
Abortion
Alcohol
Artisans/Craftsmen
Childbirth and Motherhood
Clothing
Crime
Disease
Domestic Industry
Emigration
Euthanasia
Factory Laws and Reform
Family
Fertility
Food
Handicapped
Health (1871–1990)
Hirschfeld, Magnus
Homosexuality-Lesbianism
Housing and Slums
Infants, Children, and
    Adolescents
Insanity
Jews, 1869–1933
Labor Laws
Leisure
Literacy (1871–1990)
Marriage and Divorce
Minorities, Ethnocultural and
    Foreign
Morality
Old Age
Poverty
Pressure and Special Interest
    Groups
Prostitution
Rape
Sex Reform and Birth Control
Social Insurance
Social Mobility
Social Reform
Strikes
Suicide
Temperance Movements
Trade Unions
Unemployment
Wages
Welfare State
Women's Occupations
Work

Working Conditions

Social Democracy, Social Democratic
    Figures and Party
Baader, Ottilie
Bebel, August
Bernstein, Eduard
Brandt, Willy
Braun, Lily
Braun, Otto
David, Eduard
Ebert, Friedrich
Eisner, Kurt
Engels, Friedrich
Erler, Fritz
Fuchs, Anke
Heilmann, Ernst
Heinemann, Gustav
Hilferding, Rudolf
Hoegner, Wilhelm
Juchacz, Marie
Kautsky, Karl
Kopf, Hinrich
Kubel, Alfred
Liebknecht, Karl
Liebknecht, Wilhelm
Luxemburg, Rosa
Mehring, Franz
Mierendorff, Carlo
Müller, Hermann
Noske, Gustav
Ollenhauer, Erich
Rau, Johannes
Renger, Annemarie
Reuter, Ernst
Scheidemann, Philipp
Schiller, Karl
Schmid, Carlo
Schmidt, Helmut
Schmidt, Robert
Schumacher, Kurt
Selbert, Elisabeth
Social Democratic Party (SPD),
    1871–1918
Social Democratic Party (SPD),
    1919–90
Severing, Carl
Strobel, Käthe
Trade Unions, 1871–1945
Trade Unions, 1945–90
Vollmar, Georg
Wehner, Herbert
Wels, Otto
Wissell, Rudolf
Workers' Culture
Zetkin, Clara
Zietz, Luise

Social Welfare
    Association for Social Policy
    Berlepsch, Hans
    Gierke, Anna von
    Health
    Posadowsky-Wehner, Arthur von
    Salomon, Alice
    Social Insurance
    Strobel, Käthe
    Unemployment
    Virchow, Rudolf
    Weber, Helen
    Welfare State
    Youth
    Zahn-Harnack, Agnes von

Socialist Unity Party
    Ackermann, Anton
    Axen, Hermann
    Fischer, Oskar
    German Democratic Republic
    German Democratic Republic:
        Government System
    German Democratic Republic:
        Political Culture
    German Democratic Republic:
        Political Party System
    Grotewohl, Otto
    Hager, Kurt
    Hoffmann, Heinz
    Honecker, Erich
    Honecker, Margot
    Krenz, Egon
    Mielke, Erich
    Mittag, Günther
    Modrow, Hans
    Pieck, Wilhelm
    Sindermann, Horst
    Social Unity Party of Germany
        (SED)
    Stoph, Willi
    Ulbricht, Walter
    Verner, Paul

Sociology and Sociologists
    Adorno, Theodor
    Elias, Norbert
    Freyer, Hans
    Gehlen, Arnold
    Horkheimer, Max
    Lowenthal, Leo
    Lukács, Georg
    Mannheim, Karl
    Marcuse, Herbert
    Michels, Robert
    Simmel, Georg
    Sociology

    Tönnies, Ferdinand
    Troeltsch, Ernst
    Weber, Alfred
    Weber, Max

Sport
    German Democratic Republic:
        Sports
    The Olympic Games: 1936 and
        1972
    Sport

Spying and Spies
    Federal Republic of Germany:
        Internal Security
    German Democratic Republic:
        State Security
    Mielke, Erich
    Political Loyalty Decree
    Red Orchestra
    Vogel, Wolfgang
    Wolf, Markus

State and Its Roles
    Archives
    Armaments
    Basic Law
    Bundesbank, Deutsche
    Censorship
    Civil Service
    Constitutions
    Currency
    Delbrück, Rudolf von
    Diplomatic Corps and
        Diplomacy
    Economics
    Education
    Federal Republic of Germany:
        Internal Security
    German Democratic Republic:
        State Security
    Inflation and Hyperinflation
    Judiciary
    Kulturkampf
    Labor Laws
    Libraries
    Local Government (1871–
        1990)
    Minorities, Ethnocultural and
        Foreign
    Policing
    Political Economy
    Political Loyalty Decree (1972)
    Protectionism
    Sammlungspolitik
    Social Imperialism
    State and Economy

    Strikes
    Taxation
    Third Reich: Propaganda and
        Culture
    Universities
    Welfare State
    World War I
    World War II

Students
    Burschenschaft
    Counterculture
    Dutschke, Rudi
    Students
    Universities
    White Rose

Technology
    Abbe, Ernst and Zeiss Werke
    Aeronautics
    Automobile Industry
    Benz, Karl
    Chemistry, Scientific and
        Industrial
    Daimler, Gottlieb
    Diesel, Rudolf
    Electricity
    Energy
    Engineering
    German Democratic Republic:
        Technical Intelligentsia
    Inventions
    Linde, Carl von
    Nuclear Power and the Nuclear
        Industry
    Otto, Nikolaus
    Porsche, Ferdinand
    Railroads
    Siemens, Werner von
    Space
    Technological Training, Technical
        Institutes and Universities
    Technology
    Zeiss, Carl

Theater, Actors, and Playwrights
    Brecht, Bertolt
    Cabaret
    Drama
    Gründgens, Gustaf
    Hauptmann, Gerhart
    Henze, Hans
    Piscator, Erwin
    Reinhardt, Max
    Theater
    Third Reich: Propaganda and
        Culture

Wedekind, Frank
Zuckmayer, Carl

Trade Unions and Unionists
  Böckler, Hans
  Christian Trade Unions
  Codetermination
  Free German Trade Union
      Federation in the GDR
  Hanna, Gertrud
  Imbusch, Heinrich
  Kaiser, Jacob
  Ketteler, Wilhelm von
  Labor Laws
  Legien, Carl
  Leipart, Theodor
  Leuschner, Wilhelm
  Pressure and Special Interest
      Groups
  Stegerwald, Adam
  Tisch, Harry
  Trade Unions, 1871–1945
  Trade Unions, 1945–90
  Wissell, Rudolf

Transport
  Aeronautics
  Automobile Industry
  Railroads

Universities
  Althoff, Friedrich
  Bildung und Bildungsbürgertum
  Foundations and Research
      Institutes
  Kaiser Wilhelm/Max Planck
      Societies and Their Institutes
  Libraries
  Students
  Technological Training, Technical
      Institutes and Universities
  Universities

Urban Development
  Architecture and Urban Design
  Gardens and Landscape Architec-
      ture
  Housing and Slums
  Parks, Public
  Urbanization
  Zoological Gardens

Völkisch Ideas and Movement
  Chamberlain, Houston Stewart
  Darré, R. Walter
  Grimm, Hans
  Günther, Hans

Himmler, Heinrich
Hitler, Adolf
Lagarde, Paul de
Langbehn, Julius
Moeller van der Bruck, Arthur
National Socialism
Pan German League
Race
Radical Right
Rosenberg, Alfred
Social Darwinism
Völkisch Ideology
Wagner, Richard

Voting and Voting Systems
  Constitutions
  Elections
  Federalism
  Suffrage

War
  Air Forces
  Allied Bombing
  Burgfrieden
  Disarmament
  Einsatzgruppen
  Federal Republic of Germany:
      Armed Forces
  German Democratic Republic:
      National People's Army
  Imperial Germany: Armed Forces
  Inflation and Hyperinflation
  Militarism
  Naval Mutinies of 1918
  Nazi War Crimes Trials and
      Investigations
  Nuremberg Trials
  Officers' Corps
  Paramilitary Organizations
  Postwar Reconstruction
  Prisoners of War
  Rearmament
  Revolution of 1918–19
  Schlieffen, Alfred von
  Schmidt, Robert
  Soviet Occupation of Germany
  Stab-in-the-Back Legend
  Stahlhelm
  Stalingrad, Battle of
  Submarine Warfare
  Todt, Fritz
  Versailles, Treaty of
  Veterans' Organizations
  Waffen SS
  Weimar Republic: Army
  World War I
  World War II

Weimar Republic
  Constitutions
  (Great) Depression, 1929–1933
  Ebert, Friedrich
  Elections
  Great Depression
  Groener, Wilhelm
  Hindenburg, Paul von
  Inflation and Hyperinflation
  Papen, Franz von
  Paramilitary Organizations
  Parliamentary System
  Parties and Politics
  Presidency and Presidents
  Pressure Groups
  Prussia
  Putschism
  Reparations
  Revolution of 1918–19
  Ruhr Crisis
  Schleicher, Kurt von
  Seeckt, Hans von
  Stab-in-the-Back Legend
  Suffrage
  Versailles Treaty
  Weimar Republic: Army
  Weimar Republic: Foreign Policy
  Weimar Republic: Literature

Women and Women's Movements
  Abortion
  Andreas-Salomé, Lou
  Baader, Otalie
  Bäumer, Gertrud
  Braun, Lily
  Catholic Women's Association
  Cauer, Minna
  Childbirth and Motherhood
  Dönhoff, Marion von
  Education for Girls and Women
  Family
  Federal Republic of Germany:
      Women
  Feminism and Anti-Feminism,
      1871–1918
  Feminism and Anti-Feminism,
      1918–45
  Feminist Writing
  German Democratic Republic:
      Women
  Gierke, Anna von
  Hamm-Brücher, Hildegard
  Hanna, Gertrud
  Heymann, Lida
  Homosexuality and Lesbianism
  Jewish Women, League of
  Juchacz, Marie

Lange, Helene
League of German Girls
Lüders, Marie-Elisabeth
Marriage and Divorce
Morality
Nationalist Women's
    Associations
Otto, Louise
Prostitution
Protestant Women's League
Rape
Renger, Annemarie
Salomon, Alice
Scholtz-Klink, Gertrud
Schrader-Breymann, Henriette
Schwarzhaupt, Elisabeth
Selbert, Elisabeth
Sex Reform and Birth Control
Stöcker, Helene
Strecker, Gabriele
Strobel, Käthe
Süssmuth, Rita
Weber, Helene

Weber, Marianne
Women, 1871–1918
Women, 1918–45
(Bourgeois) Women's Movement,
    1871–1933
Women's Occupations
Zahn-Harnack, Agnes von
Zetkin, Clara
Zietz, Luise

Workers and Working Class
Artisans/Craftsmen
Christian Trade Unions
Codetermination
Factory Laws and Reform
Free German Trade Union
    Federation
Juchacz, Marie
Joos, Joseph
Labor Front
Labor Laws
Legien, Carl
Leipart, Theodor

Leisure
Ley, Robert
National Socialist Factory Cell
    Organization
Schmidt, Robert
Strikes
Temperance Movements
Trade Unions
Unemployment
Wages
Women's Occupations
Workers and National Socialism
Workers' Culture
Working-Class Literature
Working Conditions

Youth and Youth Movements
Free German Youth
Hitler Youth
League of German Girls
Schirach, Baldur von
Youth
Youth Movements

Chronology

1871

Founding of German Empire proclaimed in Hall of
Mirrors at Versailles (January 18)

Otto von Bismarck elected first chancellor of newly
founded German Empire

Kulturkampf against the Roman Catholic Church
initiated

Berliner Tageblatt launched by Rudolf Mosse

1872

Welfare facilities for workers set up by Krupp firm; a few
firms followed suit

Leopold von Ranke, who had been teaching at the
University of Berlin since 1825, retired

Verein für Sozialpolitik (Association for Social Policy)
founded

Resin-like material (precursor to synthetic material
production) created from phenol and formaldehyde by
Adolph von Baeyer

Die Ahnen (The ancestors) by Gustav Freytag published

1873

Three Emperors' League (Austria-Hungary, Germany,
Russia) established

Federal regulations standardizing weights, measures, and
coinage came into effect

1874

Reich Press Law to protect freedom of the press
promulgated

Liberal journal, *Deutsche Rundschau*, launched

1875

Civil marriage made obligatory

German Social Democratic Party formed at Gotha
Congress

Centralverband deutscher Industrieller (Central Association
of German Industrialists) established

1876

Bayeuth Festival inaugurated

Reichsbank (German Federal Bank) opened for business

Otto engine (first four-stroke combustion engine) constructed

First compression (ammonia) refrigerator constructed by
Carl von Linde

Grundlegung der politischen Ökonomie (Foundations of
political economy) by Adolph Wagner published

1877

Reich patent office established

Anton von Werner completed painting "Proclamation of
the Kaiser at Versailles"

With the purchase of the *Berliner Tageblatt* Leopold
Ullstein founded his publishing company

1878

Anti-socialist legislation passed by Reichstag

Adolf Stoecker and Adolph Wagner founded the Christian
Social Workers Party

Semper Opera House in Dresden completed

Germany's first soccer club founded in Hannover

Congress of Berlin concerning the allotment of colonial
territories held

1879

Bismarck's alliance with Liberals ended; new political allies
sought among conservative parties; protectionist
legislation passed, dismantling of the *Kulturkampf*
began

First volume of Heinrich von Treitschke's *Deutsche
Geschichte im neunzehnten Jahrhundert* (published as
German History in the Nineteenth Century) published

First electric locomotive constructed by Werner von
Siemens

Die Frau und der Sozialismus (published as *Woman Under
Socialism*) by August Bebel completed

Austro-German (Dual) Alliance established

1880

First electrically operated elevator built by Werner von
    Siemens

1881

Three Emperors' Alliance (Austria-Hungary, Germany, and
    Russia) established
Leopold von Ranke's *Weltgeschichte* (published as *World
    History*) published

1882

Triple Alliance created with addition of Italy to Dual
    Alliance (Austria, Germany)
Friedrich Althoff made head of university system in
    Prussian Ministry of Education
Rudolf Virchow, eminent scientist, first elected to the
    Reichstag
Tubercle bacillus discovered by Robert Koch

1883

With passage of Sickness Insurance Law (1884: Accident
    Insurance Law, 1889: Old Age and Disability),
    major welfare state program initiated by Bismarck's
    government
Also sprach Zarathustra (published as *Thus Spake
    Zarathustra*) by Friedrich Nietzsche published
Precursor to Allgemeine Elektrizitäts-Gesellschaft (AEG)
    launched by Emil Rathenau

1884

Active colonial policy initiated by Bismarck's government
Process for production of seemless pipes developed by
    Mannesmann brothers (Reinhard and Max)
Social Democratic Party newspaper *Berliner Volksblatt*,
    renamed *Vorwärts* in 1890, launched

1885

German Agricultural Society founded by Max Eyth

1886

King Ludwig II of Bavaria drowned in Lake Starnberg
S. Fischer Verlag founded by Samuel Fischer
Hamburg-America Line taken over by Albert Ballin
First "motor coach" introduced by Carl Benz

1887

Triple Alliance (Germany's alliance with Austria-Hungary
    and Italy) renewed
Russian-German Treaty (Reinsurance Treaty) signed
Britain insisted that all imported goods from Germany
    be labeled with "Made in Germany"
    inscription
German Writers' Association founded

1888

Emperor Wilhelm I died; succeeded by Frederick
    (Friedrich) III (March 9); within three months

Frederick III died and succeeded by Wilhelm II
    (June 15)
Association for the Reform of Women's Education founded
Association for Women's Welfare (Verein Frauenwohl)
    founded by group of feminist activists, led by Minna
    Cauer
Electromagnetic waves (Hertzian waves) discovered by
    Heinrich Hertz
Theodor Fontane's *Irrungen und Wirrungen* and Theodor
    Storm's *Der Schimmelreiter* (published as *The Rider on
    the White Horse*) published

1889

Three-volume *History of Dogma* completed by Adolf Harnack
Franz von Stuck appointed professor at the Munich
    Academy of Fine Art
Der Vogelflug als Grundlage der Fliegekunst (Bird flight as the
    basis of aviation) published by Otto Lilienthal
The novella *Papa Hamlet* by Arno Holz published

1890

Otto von Bismarck forced to resign as German chancellor;
    succeeded by Leo von Caprivi
Reinsurance Treaty with Russia not renewed by Germany
Johannes Miquel appointed Prussian Minister of Finance
Rembrandt als Erzieher (Rembrandt as educator) published
    by Julius Langbehn
Expiration of Imperial anti-Socialist legislation

1891

Establishment of the nationalistic Pan-German Association
SPD Erfurt Program proclaimed
Frühlings Erwachen (published as *Spring Awakening*)
    published by Franz Wedekind
Illustrated magazine *Die Woche* launched by August Scherl

1892

Lehrbuch der Geschichte der Gegenwart published by
    Wilhelm Windelband
Die Weber (published as *The Weavers*) published by Gerhart
    Hauptmann
First publication of Karl May's adventure stories
The Munich Secession established
Political weekly *Die Zukunft* launched by Maximilian Harden

1893

First German school for girls, which would enable them to
    matriculate (obtain *Abitur*), opened in Baden
A new "umbrella" feminist organization, Bund deutscher
    Frauenvereine, (BDF; Federation of German Women's
    Associations), formed
Agrarian League founded
High pressure oil combustion engine developed by Rudolf
    Diesel
Central Verein deutscher Staatsbürger jüdischen Glaubens
    (Central Association of German Citizens of the Jewish
    Faith) founded

1894

Resignation of Leo von Caprivi as chancellor; succeeded by Prince Chlodwig zu Hohenlohe-Schillingsfürst

Mechanism of chemical process of catalysis discovered by Wilhelm Ostwald

Caligula by Ludwig Quidde published

Reichstag building in Berlin completed

Advance publication of Theodor Fontane's *Effi Briest* by Deutsche Rundschau

First mass-produced vehicle, the Velo, manufactured by Benz Patent Motor Car Co.

1895

Motion that women be given the vote made by August Bebel in Reichstag

X-rays discovered by Wilhelm Röntgen

Etchings on "A Weavers' Rebellion" by Käthe Kollwitz published

Introduction by Max and Emil Skladanowsky of technology for recording and projecting moving images marked beginning of a German film industry

Kiel Canal opened

Studien über Hysterie (published as *Studies in Hysteria*) by Sigmund Freud published

1896

National Social Union founded by Friedrich Naumann after break with Adolf Stoecker

A hiking group, predecessor of the Wandervogel movement founded in 1901, formed by Karl Fischer

Publication of *Simplicissimus* begun by Albert Langen

Kruger Telegram, which strained Anglo-German relations, sent by William II

1897

Foreign Ministry taken over by Bernhard von Bülow; Alfred von Tirpitz appointed Secretary of State for the Navy. They initiated Germany's *Weltpolitik*

Commercial manufacture and distribution of diphtheria antitoxins pioneered by Paul Ehrlich

Politische Geographie (Political geography) by geographer Friedrich Ratzel published

Collection of poems, *Das Jahr der Seele,* by Stefan George published

1898

Navy League founded

First of a series of bills expanding the navy passed by Reichstag

Death of Otto von Bismarck

Death of Theodor Fontane

New daily *Berliner Morgenpost,* introduced by Ullstein

1899

Verband fortschrittlicher Frauenvereine (Federation of Progressive Women's Associations) formed

Foundations of the Nineteenth Century by Houston Stewart Chamberlain published

Journal, *Die Fackel,* founded by Karl Kraus

1900

Hohenlohe resigned as chancellor; succeeded by Bernhard von Bülow

Second Naval Bill passed

Accident insurance extended to new occupations

New civil code went into effect

Max Planck established quantum theory

Grundriss der allgemeinen Volkswirtschaftslehre by Gustav Schmoller published

First heavier-than-air airship flown by Ferdinand von Zeppelin

Die Traumdeutung (published as *Interpretation of Dreams*) by Sigmund Freud published

1901

Women allowed to study at universities in Baden

Buddenbrooks by Thomas Mann published

Culmination of *Jugendstil* movement with major exhibition at the artist colony Mathildenhöhe in Darmstadt

First private motor cars appeared on Berlin streets

Wilhelm Röntgen received Nobel Prize for Physics

Wandervogel youth movement founded

Pergamon Museum in Berlin opened

1902

Historian Theodor Mommsen received Nobel Prize for Literature

Emil Fischer awarded Nobel Prize for Chemistry

Deutscher Verein für Frauenstimmrecht (German Society for Women's Suffrage) founded by radicals Lida Gustava Heymann and Anita Augspurg

Aby Warburg founded Kulturwissenschaftliche Bibliothek Warburg (Warburg Library for Cultural Scholarship)

Robert Bosch's first engineer, Gottlob Honold, developed the high tension magneto and Bosch spark plug

1903

German Museum for Science and Technology established in Munich

Theodor Boveri recognized chromosomes as basis of heredity

1904

Jüdischer Frauenbund (League of Jewish Women) founded

In Berlin Max Reinhardt staged spectacular rendition of Shakespeare's *Midsummer Night's Dream*

1905

Founding of expressionist group *Die Brücke* in Dresden; it included Ernst L. Kirchner, Erich Heckel and Karl Schmidt-Rottluff

Albert Einstein developed "special theory of relativity"

Die Schaubühne (the theatrical stage), which in 1918

became *Die Weltbühne* (the world stage), established by theater critic Siegfried Jacobsohn

Nobel Prize won by Philipp Lenard (physics), Adolf von Baeyer and Eduard Buchner (chemistry) and Robert Koch (medicine)

Weltgeschichtliche Betrachtungen (published as *Force and Freedom: Reflections on History*) by Jacob Burckhardt published

Chief of the General Staff, Schlieffen, formulated military strategy plan bearing his name and partly followed in 1914

1906

Theodor Wolff became editor in chief of the *Berliner Tageblatt*

1907

Gustav Mahler became director of both the Vienna and New York Metropolitan orchestras

The Werkbund founded in Munich by a group of progressive artists, architects and industrialists. Peter Behrens, a Werkbund founder, appointed to AEG arts advisory board at suggestion of Emil Rathenau

Double-piston engine invented by Hugo Junkers

Reichstag elections centered on colonial and national questions

Weltbürgertum und Nationalstaat (published as *Cosmopolitanism and the Nation State*) by Friedrich Meinecke published

1908

Prussian Law of Association repealed; women and persons over 18 free to join parties and engage in political activities.

Ernst Rowohlt established first publishing house

Nobel Prize for Medicine awarded to Paul Ehrlich

Daily Telegraph Affair exacerbated Anglo-German relations

1909

Bernhard von Bülow resigned as chancellor; succeeded by Theobald von Bethmann Hollweg

First practical process for synthesizing ammonia produced by Fritz Haber

Nobel Prize for chemistry awarded to Wilhelm Ostwald

1910

Das Finanzkapital (published as *Finance Capital*) by Rudolf Hilferding published

1911

Kaiser Wilhelm Society for the Advancement of Science founded with Adolf von Harnack as president

Première of Richard Strauss' *Der Rosenkavalier* with libretto by Hugo von Hofmannsthal

Die Hose (published as *The Underpants*) by Carl Sternheim published

1912

Social Democratic Party received largest number of seats in Reichstag elections

Gerhart Hauptmann awarded Nobel Prize for Literature

The *Deutsche Bücherei* (German Library) established in Leipzig

Der blaue Reiter (The Blue Rider) Almanac assembled in 1911 by Wassily Kandinsky and Franz Marc and published by Piper Verlag

1913

Zabern Affair

Together with Carl Bosch, Friedrich Bergius developed process for the liquefaction of coal through high-pressure hydrogenation

The Stark Effect, the splitting of spectral lines, discovered by Johannes Stark, who was subsequently awarded Nobel Prize for physics in 1919.

Der Heizer by Franz Kafka published

Birth of biochemistry with addition of small chemistry section to Kaiser Wilhelm Institute of Biology

1914

World War I began contributing increasingly to inflation, food shortages, political and social upheaval

The three-volume *Der Dreissigjährige Krieg* (Thirty years' war) by Ricarda Huch published

The painter August Macke killed in military action

Max von Laue awarded Nobel Prize for physics

Battle of the Marne; the Schlieffen Plan failed

Through Battle of the Masurian Lakes, Paul von Hindenburg gained immense prestige

1915

Kunstgeschichtliche Grundbegriffe (published as *Principles of Art History*) by Heinrich Wölfflin published

Richard Willstätter awarded 1915 Nobel Prize in chemistry for studies of the constitution of chlorophyll and other plant pigments

The *Lusitania* was sunk off the coast of Ireland by German submarine

1916

Spartacus League formed by Rosa Luxemburg and Karl Liebknecht

Battle of Verdun resulted in approximately 1,000,000 deaths

Erich von Falkenhayn replaced as chief of the General Staff by Paul von Hindenburg; Erich Ludendorff appointed quarter-master-general

Battle of Jutland

Battle of the Somme opened

1917

Social Democratic Party split; Independent Social Democratic Party of Germany established

Germany introduced unrestricted submarine warfare

Chancellor Bethmann Hollweg forced out of power and replaced by Georg Michaelis who, in turn, was soon replaced by Georg von Hertling

Reichstag passed resolution calling for peace without
annexations

Ufa (Universum Film Aktiengesellschaft) founded at the
instigation of General Ludendorff

Hyper-nationalist German Fatherland Party founded

1918

Treaty of Brest-Litovsk signed with Soviet Union

Georg von Hertling replaced as chancellor by Prince Max
of Baden

The German High Command considered the war lost and
asked the German government to sue for peace on the
basis of president Woodrow Wilson's Fourteen Points

Erich von Ludendorff deposed as quarter-master general
and replaced by Wilhelm Groener

Mutinies broke out among crews of German navy at Kiel

Revolutions broke out in Munich; Bavarian king abdicated

Philipp Scheidemann announced the abdication of
Wilhelm II (who escaped to Holland) and proclaimed
the birth of the German (Weimar) Republic

SPD chairman Friedrich Ebert headed new republican
government

Armistice ending World War I signed

Women granted the franchise

Eight-hour working day proclaimed

Max Planck awarded Nobel Prize for physics; Fritz Haber
for chemistry

Der Untertan (published as *The Patrioteer*) by Heinrich
Mann published

1919

German Communist Party (KPD) founded

Communist Party leaders Karl Liebknecht and Rosa
Luxemburg murdered by Free Corps units

Constituent National Assembly elected with no party
gaining majority; coalition of SPD, Center Party, and
liberals formed

Germany signed the Treaty of Versailles

Friedrich Ebert elected Reich president by the Constituent
Weimar National Assembly

Weimar Constitution adopted

German Workers Party (later National Socialist German
Workers Party, NSDAP) founded; Adolf Hitler
became a member

Bauhaus established at Weimar

Arnold Sommerfeld published his *Atombau und Spektralinien*
(published as *Atom Structures and Spectral Lines*) which
became the bible of atomic physics

1920

Right-wing Kapp Putsch collapsed under pressure of of
general strike by workers

General elections for new Reichstag resulted in "Weimar
coalition" (coalition of SPD, Center Party, and
liberals) losing its majority

Towns of Eupen and Malmedy turned over to Belgium

Walther Nernst awarded the Nobel Prize for chemistry

Danzig proclaimed a free city under League of Nations
auspices

1921

Part of Ruhr occupied by Allies

Plebiscite held in Upper Silesia

Matthias Erzberger assassinated

Albert Einstein awarded the Nobel Prize for physics

Germany accepted Allied reparation terms

Max Born appointed head of physics department at
Göttingen University; his associates included Werner
Heisenberg, Robert Oppenheimer, Edward Teller, and
Enrico Fermi

1922

Germany signed Treaty of Rapallo with the Soviet Union

Walther Rathenau assassinated

German inflation became hyperinflation

Oswald Spengler completed his *Der Untergang des
Abendlandes* (published as *Decline of the West*)

Wilhelm Furtwängler became director of Leipzig
Gewandthaus Orchestra while remaining chief
conductor of the Berlin Philharmonic

1923

Belgian and French troops occupied the Ruhr

Separatist movement lauched in Rhineland with encouragement of Belgian and French authorities

Gustav Stresemann became chancellor and foreign minister

The German inflation reached its climax

German popular radio launched

Hjalmar Schacht directed efforts to establish new currency,
the Rentenmark

Adolf Hitler undertook abortive Munich Beerhall Putsch

Arnold Schönberg wrote his first 12-tone work, *Five Piano
Suites*

1924

Institute of Social Research established in Frankfurt am
Main

Der Zauberberg (published as *The Magic Mountain*) by
Thomas Mann published

Dawes Plan on reparation payments accepted by Germany

1925

Death of President Ebert; Paul von Hindenburg elected as
successor

Treaties of Locarno signed and ratified by Germany

Part I of Adolf Hitler's *Mein Kampf* (published as *My
Struggle*) published

I.G. Farbenindustrie AG formed by the merger of eight
companies

Franz Kafka's *Der Prozess* (published as *The Trial*) published

James Franck and Gustav Hertz awarded the Nobel Prize
for physics

Der fröhliche Weinberg (The merry vineyard) by Carl
Zuckmayer published

1926

Germany and the Soviet Union extended Treaty of Rapallo by signing treaty of friendship and neutrality

Germany joined the League of Nations

Volk ohne Raum by Hans Grimm published

Benz & Cie. and Daimler-Motoren-Gesellschaft amalgamated to form Daimler-Benz AG.

Gustav Stresemann awarded the Nobel Peace Prize

1927

Being and Time by Martin Heidegger published

Mies van der Rohe directed the Werkbund Exhibition, "The Dwelling" (Weissenhof settlement), a co-production of European avant garde architects at Stuttgart

Ludwig Quidde awarded the Nobel Peace Prize

Steppenwolf by Herman Hesse published

1928

Der Aufstand der Fischer von St. Barbara (published as *The Revolt of the Fishermen*) by Anna Seghers published

World première in Berlin of Bertolt Brecht's and Kurt Weill's *Drei Groschen Oper* (published as *Three Penny Opera*)

Publication of *Emil und die Detektive* (published as *Emil and the Detectives*) by Erich Kästner

1929

Germany accepted Kellog-Briand Pact

Gustav Stresemann dies

Germans accepted Young Plan in a referendum

Thomas Mann awarded the Nobel Prize for literature

Berlin Alexanderplatz by Alfred Döblin published

Im Westen nichts Neues (published as *All Quiet on the Western Front*) by Erich Maria Remarque published

Ideologie und Utopie (published as *Ideology and Utopia*) by Karl Mannheim published

1930

Intensification of Germany's economic crisis and unemployment

Herman Müller's cabinet, Weimar's last majority government, resigned and replaced by the first presidentially-appointed cabinet, led by Heinrich Brüning

Otto Warburg appointed director of the new Kaiser Wilhelm Institute of Cell Physiology in Berlin. A year later received Nobel Prize for medicine for his work on respiration

Der Mythos des 20. Jahrhunderts (The myth of the 20th century) by Alfred Rosenberg published

The first part of Robert Musil's *Der Mann ohne Eigenschaften* (published as *The Man Without Qualities*) published

Première of Josef von Sternberg's UFA film *Der blaue Engel* (published as *The Blue Angel*) based on Heinrich Mann's novel *Professor Unrat*

The Nazi Party achieved sizable gains (107 seats) in Reichstag elections

Mario und der Zauberer (published as *Mario and the Magician*) by Thomas Mann published

Hermann Hesse's *Narziss und Goldmund* (published as *Narziss and Goldmund*) published

1931

Deepening of economic and financial crises contributed to closure of German banks, savings banks, and stock exchanges

Announcement of Austro-German customs union; the union successfully challenged by France

Carl Bosch and Friedrich Bergius shared Nobel Prize for chemistry

Carl Zuckmayer's play *Der Hauptmann von Köpenick* (published as *The Captain of Köpenick*) published

1932

Germany's unemployment total topped 6 million

Paul von Hindenburg re-elected as president

Kleiner Mann-was nun ? (published as *Little Man, What Now?*) by Hans Fallada published

Werner Heisenberg awarded the Nobel Prize for physics

Heinrich Brüning resigned as chancellor and replaced by Franz von Papen

Government ban on SA (Storm Troopers) lifted

Coup d'état engineered in Prussia by Papen and the Nazis

July elections gave the Nazi party the largest number of seats (230) in the Reichstag

November Reichstag elections reduced Nazi seats to 180

Papen succeeded as chancellor by Kurt von Schleicher

1933

Adolf Hitler appointed chancellor (January)

Presidential decree significantly limited freedom of the press and assembly

Reichstag burned

Hindenburg granted Hitler emergency powers

New and controlled Reichstag elections gave Nazis 44% of popular vote; their coalition partners received 8%

Enabling Act gave Hitler government dictatorial powers

Coordination process quickly set in motion: federal structures replaced by exclusive central, national structures; civil service and judiciary brought in line; opposition political parties eliminated; worker organizations dissolved; persecution of Jews began

KPD and SPD political activities driven underground, some leaders exiled; KPD operated from Moscow, SPD from Prague, Paris, then London and Stockholm

Concentration camps set up for "enemies of the Reich"

Book-burnings took place in a number of German cities

Heinrich Himmler appointed political police commander in Bavaria

Joseph Goebbels appointed minister of public enlightenment and Propaganda

Hjalmar Schacht became Reichsbank president

Center Party disbanded voluntarily as Germany signed Concordat with Vatican

Growth of elitist SS; *Leibstandarte* SS Adolf Hitler, personal bodyguard units created

Erwin Schrödinger awarded the Nobel Prize for physics

1934

Bothersome SA leadership and other potential enemies of Hitler such as Kurt von Schleicher and Gregor Strasser eliminated (Night of the Long Knives)

Nazi putsch in Vienna led to assassination of Austrian Chancellor Dollfus

Death of President Hindenburg; Hitler combined offices of chancellor and president and became Führer

Paul Hindemith completed opera *Mathis der Maler* (Mathis the artist)

Walter Gropius left Germany for England

Leni Riefenstahl completed film *Triumph des Willens* (Triumph of the will)

Labor Front created under leadership of Robert Ley

1935

Majority of voters in Saar voted to rejoin Germany

Hitler rejected disarmament clauses of Treaty of Versailles; male conscription introduced

Anglo-German naval agreement signed

Nuremberg racial laws enacted

Carl von Ossietzky awarded Nobel Peace Prize

1936

Germany repudiated Treaty of Locarno and re-occupied the Rhineland

Four-Year Plan under direction of Hermann Göring for economic expansion and rearmament launched

Heinrich Himmler, in charge of the ever-expanding SS, became head of all German police. Police state firmly in his hands, subject only to Hitler's control

Olympic Games held in Berlin and Garmisch-Partenkirchen

Adolf Butenandt appointed director of the prestigious Kaiser Wilhelm Institute for Biochemistry in Berlin-Dahlem

Rome-Berlin Axis established

Anti-Comintern Pact signed by Japan and Germany

1937

Carl Orff completed opera *Carmina Burana*

Degenerate Art exhibition held in Munich

Encyclical *Mit brennender Sorge* (With burning sorrow) published by Pope Pius XI

Italian dictator Benito Mussolini visited Berlin

Hitler outlined his foreign policy plans at secret meeting of Germany's diplomatic and military leadership

1938

German Labor Front established Volkswagen company in Wolfsburg (Lower Saxony).

Minister of War Werner von Blomberg and commander in chief of the army Werner von Fritsch dismissed. Hitler took over Ministry of War. General von Brauchitsch became commander in chief of the army

Konstatin von Neurath replaced as Foreign Minister by Joachim von Ribbentrop

Chief of the army General Staff Lugwig Beck resigned and was replaced by Franz Halder

Austria annexed (Anschluss)

At Munich Conference Britain and France agreed to the dismemberment of the Czechoslovakian state; Germany occupied the Sudetenland

During Crystal Night (*Kristallnacht*) Jewish shops and synagogues plundered and set on fire. Individual Jews beaten up; Jews banned from the economy

1939

Hjalmar Schacht dismissed as Reichsbank president

German troops occupied the rest of Czechoslovakia

Auf den Marmorklippen (On the marble cliffs) by Ernst Jünger published

Nazi-Soviet Non-Aggression Pact signed

Germany invaded Poland; World War II began

Western Poland incorporated into the Reich

Adolf Butenandt awarded the Nobel Prize for chemistry

1940

German forces invaded and occupied Denmark, Norway, Belgium, Holland and France

Germany began aerial attacks on Britain (Battle of Britain); the British retaliated by bombing German cities

Germany invaded Romania

Hungary, Bulgaria and Romania joined the Berlin-Rome-Tokyo Pact

1941

Germany invaded Yugoslavia

German troops led by Erwin Rommel landed in Africa

Rudolf Hess fled to Scotland

Première performance in Zurich of Bertolt Brecht's *Mutter Courage und ihre Kinder* (published as *Mother Courage and Her Children*)

Germany invaded the Soviet Union

Bishop Clemens A. von Galen, in series of sermons, denounced Nazi program of euthanasia

Martin Bormann informed Gauleiter (regional Nazi Party leaders) that "National Socialism and Christianity are irreconcilable"

German siege of Leningrad began

All Jews in Nazi Germany required to wear identifying Star of David

Beginning of mass deportation of Jews from the Reich to ghettos of Eastern Europe

Germany declared war on the United States (December)

1942

At Wannsee Conference "Final Solution" measures deliberated

Start of mass gassing at Auschwitz

Albert Speer appointed minister of armaments

British intensified bombing of German cities

Anna Segher's novel *Das siebte Kreuz* (published as *The Seventh Cross*) published abroad (Mexico, Britain, and USA)

1943

Leaders of White Rose student resistance arrested and executed

Germany lost Battle of Stalingrad

The Allies announced "unconditional surrender" policy toward Germany; Goebbels called for "total war" effort

Siege of Leningrad ended in German withdrawal

Germans put down Warsaw ghetto uprising

Erwin Rommel's Africa Corps surrendered

Soviet counter-offensive against Germans gained momentum

1944

Successful Allied invasion of Normandy

July 20 resistance efforts to eliminate Hitler failed; a number of prominent civilian and military resistance participants executed

Otto Hahn awarded the Nobel Prize for chemistry

1945

City of Dresden laid to waste by concerted Allied bombing raid

Yalta meeting of Big Three to consider future of Germany

Hitler, Goebbels, and Himmler committed suicide

Unconditional German surrender effected

Germany came under Four-Power control

Potsdam meeting of Big Three (Stalin, Truman, and Churchill/Attlee) to consider future of Germany

International Military Tribunal met in Nuremberg to judge leadership of Third Reich

The victorious wartime Allies began large-scale dismantling of German industrial plants

1946

Local elections in western zones of occupation gave the Christian Democrats a majority

In Soviet zone of occupation Social Democrats and Communists merged into the Socialist Unity Party (SED)

Hamburg weekly, *Die Zeit*, appeared

The International Tribunal at Nuremberg reached decisions on the Nazi leadership

Hermann Goering escaped gallows by committing suicide

The German Library established in Frankfurt, taking on for the western zones the functions formerly carried out by German Library in Leipzig

Hermann Hesse awarded the Nobel Prize for literature

American and British foreign secretaries signed agreement to fuse their zones of occupation (Bizone)

Rebuilt Volkswagen Works started mass production

Carl Zuckmayer's three-act play *Des Teufels General* (published as *The Devil's Advocate*) published

1947

Landtag elections in the western zones gave the Social Democrats majorities in some *Länder* (states), in other *Länder* the Christian Democrats received a majority

Meetings of the the Big Four foreign ministers in Moscow and London failed to produce a common German

policy beyond the formal abolition of the state of Prussia

Doktor Faustus (published as *Dr. Faustus*) by Thomas Mann published

Bizonal Economic Council established

Premiere of W. Borchert's *Draussen vor der Tür* (published as *The Man Outside*)

The literary Group 47 founded by by A. Andersch and H. W. Richter

Die Welt, a daily founded by British military government, sold to Axel Springer

Rudolf Augstein launched weekly, *Der Spiegel*

1948

Bizonal structures extended

Soviet officials quit the Allied Control Council for Germany

The United States, the United Kingdom, France, and the Benlux countries (Belgium, Netherlands, Luxembourg) agreed on international control of the Ruhr, German participation in the Marshall Plan, and on process of uniting the three western zones of occupation into a new West German state

A new currency (the deutsche mark) for the western occupation zones and West Berlin announced. In response Soviet occupation officials introduced separate currency for their zone

The Free University of Berlin founded; historian Friedrich Meinecke chosen as its first president

Under the leadership of Otto Hahn, the Kaiser Wilhelm Society reconstituted as the Max Planck Society. Hahn remained president until 1960 when succeeded by Adolf Butenandt

Soviet officials began the blockade of Berlin; the Western Powers responded with airlift of supplies

A parliamentary council began discussion of the Basic Law, the new West German constitution

Separate governments established for East and West Berlin; Ernst Reuter elected chief mayor of West Berlin

1949

Basic Law for new Federal Republic of Germany accepted

Berlin Blockade officially ended

In Soviet zone, People's Congress elected which adopted draft constitution for German Democratic Republic

Bundestag elections held in Federal Republic of Germany; the Christian Democratic Union (CDU) won plurality of seats

Theodor Heuss chosen first president of the Federal Republic; Konrad Adenauer elected first chancellor

Establishment of Federal Republic of Germany (FRG) ended Allied military government and Allied Occupation Statute came into effect

New German Democratic Republic established with Wilhelm Pieck president and Otto Grotewohl minister-president

Bonn chosen as temporary site for the governmental structures of the FRG

The Petersberg Agreement improved Allied economic terms for West Germany

The FRG joined the International Ruhr Agency

Annual Frankfurt Book Fair reopened

Frankfurter Allgemeine Zeitung founded

1950

The FRG joined Council of Europe

Discussions on the remilitarization of the West German state begun

Special office for foreign affairs established within Adenauer's federal chancellery

The Suhrkamp Verlag founded

Poland and the German Democratic Republic agreed to recognize Oder-Neisse line as the boundary between the two respective states

The Rowohlt Verlag published first German paperbacks

1951

The Bundestag accepted the codetermination law

Foreign Office re-established; Konrad Adenauer took on the foreign affairs portfolio

Agreement on founding of European Coal and Steel Community signed

FRG federal constitutional court set up in Karlsruhe

Der Fragebogen (The questionnaire) by Ernst von Solomon published

Annual Bayreuth Wagner festival re-established

1952

Bundestag agreed, in principle, to West German participation in European Defense Community

Stalin "Note" proposed discussions for reunification of Germany

German Treaty granting FRG sovereignty signed

Second SED party conference agreed to extension of GDR socialist structures

FRG and Israel signed restitution agreement

Death of SPD party leader Kurt Schumacher; succeeded by Erich Ollenhauer

Agreement signed to effect FRG membership in International Bank for Reconstruction and Development

Regular German television service begun

1953

Bundestag ratified law setting minimal electoral support for political party representation in Bundestag at 5%

Worker uprising against SED-dominated GDR state

SED party leadership purged; Walter Ulbricht chosen first Secretary of SED

Hermann Staudinger awarded the Nobel Prize for chemistry

Federal election produced second Konrad Adenauer administration

1954

Soviet government recognized GDR sovereignty

Theodor Heuss elected to second term as FRG president

Following rejection by French National Assembly of European Defense Community agreement, London nine-power conference negotiated new terms for western integration, including military integration, of FRG (Paris Treaties)

Max Born shared Nobel Prize for physics with Walter Bothe

Herbert von Karajan appointed conductor of the Berlin Philharmonic Orchestra

FRG membership in NATO and the Western European ratified by French National Assembly

1955

Paris Treaties giving the FRG sovereignty went into effect upon ratification by West German and French parliaments

At Geneva conference of leaders of the US, the USSR, Britain, and France failed to resolve the German problem

Adenauer negotiated with Soviet leadership in Moscow; established diplomatic relations with USSR

In East Berlin, Soviet First Secretary Nikita Krushchev announced two (German)-nation doctrine

FRG postulated Hallstein Doctrine claiming sole representation of Germans of GDR as well as FRG

Warsaw Pact formed; GDR became a member

Eros and Civilization by Herbert Marcuse published

FRG and GDR Olympic Committees decided to send joint team to 1956 Olympic Games in Melbourne

First of the *documenta* exhibitions of contemporary art held at Kassel

Nuclear power program initiated by Germany

1956

Law for the creation of the National People's Army (NVA) and a Ministry of National Defense enacted by GDR Volkskammer

FRG Constitutional Court declared German Communist Party and its various organs to be illegal

1957

The Saar rejoined (West) Germany and became 11th Land (state) of the FRG

Treaty of Rome forming EEC signed by representatives of the FRG

First West Germans conscripted into Bundeswehr

Willy Brandt elected chief mayor of West Berlin

Third federal election gave the CDU/CSU coalition majority of seats in the Bundestag

GDR philosopher Wolfgang Harich received long-term jail sentence for criticizing government

Alfred Andersch's novel *Sansibar oder Der letzte Grund* (published as *Flight to Afar*) published

1958

Krushchev and the government of the GDR demanded that Berlin be demilitarized and made a free independent political entity

1959

Heinrich Lübke chosen president of the FRG

SPD decided on new party program (end of Marxism) at Bad Godesberg congress

Die Blechtrommel (published as *The Tin Drum*) by Günter Grass published

Mutmassungen über Jakob (published as *Speculations about Jacob*) by Uwe Johnson published

1960

Death of GDR President Wilhelm Pieck

Willy Brandt chosen SPD candidate for position of chancellor

Martin Walser's novel *Halbzeit* (Half-time) published

1961

Berlin Wall built

Heinrich von Brentano stepped down as FRG foreign minister; succeeded by Gerhard Schröder

Federal election victory enabled Adenauer to construct his fourth and last coalition government

1962

Spiegel Affair; publisher Rudolf Augstein and other members of *Spiegel* editorial staff arrested

Adolf Eichmann, central Holocaust figure, executed in Israel

Friedrich Dürrenmatt's *Die Physiker* (published as *The Physicists*) premiered in Zurich

1963

Franco-German treaty of cooperation signed by Adenauer and French President Charles de Gaulle

Second German Television channel began operations

In FRG, June 17 declared national day of commemoration of 1953 GDR uprising

Konrad Adenauer retired as chancellor; long-serving Economics Minister Ludwig Erhard chosen as successor

Death of Theodor Heuss

Governments of the GDR and West Berlin signed first pass agreement enabling West Berliners to visit relatives in East Berlin

Death of SPD leader Erich Ollenhauer

Rolf Hochhuth's *Der Stellvertreter* (published as *The Deputy*) premiered in Berlin

1964

Willy Brandt elected SPD party leader

Radical right National Democratic Party (NPD) founded

Peter Weiss' *Marat-Sade* premiered in West Berlin

German team, with members from both FRG and GDR, participated in Tokyo Olympic Games

1965

The FRG established diplomatic relations with the state of Israel

Fifth federal election led to renewed CDU/CSU/FDP coalition government. Ludwig Erhard re-elected chancellor

New Ruhr University opened in Bochum

Kursbuch, a critical magazine edited by Hans Magnus Enzensberger, began publication

1966

Disintegration of Erhard's coalition government; Baden-Württemberg Minister-President Kurt Georg Kiesinger chosen by CDU/CSU as its candidate for chancellor

Grand Coalition government of CDU/CSU/SPD formed; Kiesinger chosen chancellor, Willy Brandt chosen vice-chancellor and foreign minister

Professor Robert Havemann expelled from GDR Academy of Sciences

First GDR nuclear power station started operating

German Writers' Union of GDR held first annual conference

1967

Death of Konrad Adenauer

Student demonstrations in West Berlin led to shooting death of the student Benno Ohnesorge

Walter Hallstein resigned as president of the Commission of the European Community

Romania first Warsaw Pact member to establish diplomatic relations with the FRG

Alexander and Margarete Mitscherlich published *Die Unfähigkeit zu trauern* (published as *The Inability to Mourn*)

1968

The value-added tax introduced in the FRG

Walter Scheel succeeded Erich Mende as leader of the FDP

Warsaw Pact troops, including those from the GDR, entered Czechoslovakia to force an end to the reform movement

The Bundestag passed new emergency powers legislation

GDR adopted new constitution

For the first time FRG and GDR represented by separate teams for the Mexico Olympic Games

Christa Wolf's *Nachdenken über Christa T.* (published as *The Quest for Christa T.*) published

Siegfried Lenz's novel, *Die Deutschstunde* (published as *The German Lesson*) published

Under GDR government pressure, the eastern dioceses of the Protestant churches separated into the Federation of Evangelical Churches (BEK)

1969

Heinrich Lübke resigned as FRG president; succeeded by Gustav Heinemann

Sixth federal election led to formation of a SPD/FDP coalition government with Willy Brandt as chancellor and Walter Scheel as foreign minister and vice-chancellor

FRG government announced willingness to negotiate with

GDR on equal terms; adopted concept of two states in one German nation

1970

GDR Prime Minister Willi Stoph and FRG Chancellor Willy Brandt met, first in Erfurt, a few months later in Kassel

The Moscow treaty between the USSR and the FRG recognizing the status quo signed

Willy Brandt visited Warsaw to sign the Warsaw Treaty accepting the status quo between Poland and the FRG; Brandt kneeled at the memorial for the victims of the Warsaw ghetto liquidation by the Nazis

1971

Walter Ulbricht resigned as first secretary of the SED; succeeded by Erich Honecker

Terrorrist activities continue in the FRG

The Four-Power Treaty on Berlin signed

Rainer Barzel succeeded Kurt Georg Kiesinger as CDU party leader. Barzel also nominated as CDU/CSU candidate for the position of chancellor

Publication of Heinrich Böll's *Gruppenbild mit Dame* (published as *Group Portrait with Lady*)

Willy Brandt awarded the Nobel Peace Prize

1972

In the Bundestag, the CDU/CSU coalition initiated but lost a constructive vote of no-confidence in the Brandt/Scheel government

The Bundestag ratified the Moscow and Warsaw treaties

Terrorist activities intensified; a number of prominent terrorists, including Andreas Baader, Ulrike Meinhof, and Gudrun Ensslin, were arrested

Economics and Finance Minister Karl Schiller resigned from the federal cabinet; succeeded in portfolio by Defense Minister Helmut Schmidt

The XX Summer Olympic Games take place in Munich. The terrorist group, Black September, attacked the quarters of the Israeli Olympic team; 11 Israelis killed.

Seventh federal elections gave SPD its first plurality; the SPD/FDP coalition government renewed with Willy Brandt as chancellor and Walter Scheel as foreign minister and vice-chancellor

Heinrich Böll awarded Nobel Prize for literature

Annemarie Renger elected first woman president of the Bundestag

The Basic Treaty between the FRG and the GDR signed

1973

Rainer Barzel resigned as leader of CDU; succeeded by Helmut Kohl

The FRG and the GDR become members of the United Nations

Czechoslovakia and the FRG signed treaty and established full diplomatic relations

The FRG established diplomatic relations with Bulgaria and Hungary

In response to Arab oil embargo, FRG government introduced measures to limit use of oil products

Death of Walter Ulbricht

1974

The Bundestag ratified the nuclear non-proliferation treaty

The FRG and GDR exchanged their first permanent diplomatic representatives

Günter Guillaume, member of Willy Brandt's chancellery staff arrested for espionage on behalf of the GDR. Brandt resigned; Helmut Schmidt chosen by Bundestag as chancellor. Hans-Dietrich Genscher became foreign minister and vice-chancellor

Walter Scheel elected fourth president of the FRG

USA and GDR established diplomatic relations

New GDR consitution, which removed references to German nation, introduced

Hans-Dietrich Genscher chosen by the FDP as new party head

Hans-Jürgen Syberberg's film, *Karl May,* premiered

1975

Werner Herzog's *Jeder für sich und Gott gegen alle* (published as *Every Man for Himself and God Against All, or the Enigma of Kaspar Hauser*) awarded Prix Spécial at 1975 Cannes Film Festival

Otto Fischer replaced Otto Winzer as GDR foreign minister

Harry Tisch became chairman of FDGB (GDR Trade Union Federation)

1976

Ulrike Meinhof committed suicide

Death of Gustav Heinemann

Large-scale demonstrations against the building of nuclear power station at Brokdorf

Wolf Biermann exiled from the GDR

New GDR civil code went into effect

Eighth federal election gave CDU/CSU coalition a plurality but SPD/FDP coalition government continued. Helmut Schmidt continued as chancellor, Hans-Dietrich Genscher as foreign minister and vice-chancellor

Christa Wolf's novel *Kindheitsmuster* (published as *Patterns of Childhood*) published

1977

Terrorists murdered federal prosecutor Siegfried Buback along with his driver, banker Jürgen Ponto, industrialist Hanns Martin Schleyer and his driver, as well as three policemen

Death of Ludwig Erhard

GDR writer Reiner Kunze left GDR for FRG

Special federal anti-terrorist units freed a highjacked Lufthansa plane in Mogadishu, Somalia

Jailed terrorists Baader, Ensslin, and Raspe committed suicide

1978

Initial steps taken towards creation of the Greens political movement

Rainer Werner Fassbinder's *Die Ehe der Maria Braun* (The marriage of Maria Braun) premiered

SED member and critic Rudolf Bahro received eight-year jail sentence; in 1979 expelled to FRG

1979

Karl Carstens elected fifth FRG president

Bavarian Minister-President Franz Josef Strauss chosen as the CDU/CSU candidate for the office of chancellor

Bundestag decided that genocide and murder not subject to the statute of limitations

Völker Schlöndorff's film *Die Blechtrommel* (The tin drum) (based on Gunter Grass's novel of same title), won Golden Palm Prize at Cannes and an Oscar for the best foreign film

1980

Ninth federal election led to renewal of SPD/FDP coalition government with Helmut Schmidt chancellor and Hans-Dietrich Genscher as foreign minister and as vice-chancellor

The Green party officially founded

GDR became nonpermanent member of UN Security Council for two-year term

1981

Richard von Weizsäcker elected chief mayor of West Berlin

Elias Canetti awarded Nobel Prize for literature

Wolfgang Petersen's *Das Boot* (published as *The Boat*) premiered

Mass demonstrations against the NATO double-track decision on nuclear arms

FRG Chancellor Schmidt visited GDR

1982

The SPD/FDP coalition government disintegrated. The CDU/CSU and FDP agreed to topple minority government of Helmut Schmidt, to elect CDU leader Helmut Kohl as the new chancellor and to call new elections for March 1983

Filmmaker Rainer W. Fassbinder died at the age of 37

1983

The CDU/CSU/FDP government coalition re-elected. Helmut Kohl re-elected chancellor; FDP leader Hans-Dietrich Genscher serves as foreign minister and vice-chancellor

Greens elected to the Bundestag for the first time

Radical right Republikaner Party (REP) formed

GDR celebrated 500th anniversary of Martin Luther's birth

1984

Richard von Weizsäcker chosen sixth president of the FRG

Commercial television introduced in FRG

1985

For the first time, Greens participated in a government through a coalition with the SPD in the state of Hessen

FRG President Richard von Weizsäcker acknowledged German responsibility for war and Holocaust in speech on the fortieth anniversary of Germany's surrender in 1945

US President Ronald Reagan undertook controversial visit to Bitburg war veterans' cemetery

Volker Braun's novel *Hinze-Kunze-Roman* published

1986

Historians Ernst Nolte and Andreas Hillgruber and philosopher Jürgen Habermas initiated the *Historikerstreit* on the nature of the Holocaust

1987

Willy Brandt stepped down as leader of the SPD; succeeded by Hans-Jochen Vogel

SED First Secretary Erich Honecker officially visited FRG for four days

A number of prominent CDU and FDP politicians found guilty of illegally funnelling monies into party coffers in the so-called Flick Affair trial

Uwe Barschel, minister-president of the state of Schleswig-Holstein, apparently committed suicide after being accused of dirty-tricks politics

In the eleventh federal election the CDU/CSU/FDP government coalition re-elected. Helmut Kohl re-elected as chancellor, FDP leader Hans-Dietrich Genscher as foreign minister and vice-chancellor

Number of foreigners living in FRG topped 4 million (6.8% of total population)

1988

Death of Franz Josef Strauss

Former FRG Defense Minister, Manfred Wörner, chosen first German to hold the post of secretary general of NATO

1989

The FRG and GDR celebrated their fortieth anniversaries

Richard von Weizsäcker elected to a second term as president of the FRG

USSR General Secretary Mikhail Gorbachev greeted enthusiastically during his first visit to the FRG

Hungary opened its borders to the West, initiating a flood of emigration by East Germans to the FRG

Increasing numbers of demonstrators in GDR towns and cities, particularly Leipzig, demanded reform and dialogue with SED regime

Many East Germans left the GDR through Czechoslovakia and Poland

The Soviet Union made clear that it would not provide force to shore up the disintegrating SED regime

Erich Honecker succeeded by Egon Krenz as SED first secretary and head of the GDR government

Hans Modrow replaced Willi Stoph as GDR prime minister

Berlin Wall opened; its dismantling began

FRG Chancellor Helmut Kohl announced a "10-Point Plan for German Unity"

Gregor Gysi replaced Egon Krenz as chairman of the SED, the Socialist Unity Party of Germany—Party of Democratic Socialism

Brandenburg Gate opened by FRG Chancellor Helmut Kohl and GDR Minister-President Hans Modrow

1990

GDR elections gave majority to a coalition of conservative forces similar to that governing in Bonn. Lothar de Maizière, head of the GDR CDU chosen minister-president, heading a grand coalition of political forces including the GDR SPD but excluding the PDS

The FRG and GDR formed a currency union

At midnight on October 3 official unification of the FRG and GDR effected

First postwar all-German elections held; the CDU/CSU/FDP coalition returned to power

Difficult process of "growing together" of the two Germanies begun

Contributors

Donald Abenheim
Hoover Institution
Standford, CA

Lynn Abrams
Lancaster University
Lancaster
UK

Leslie A. Adelson
Ohio State University
Columbus, OH

Ann T. Allen
University of Louisville
Louisville, KY

Ulrich Ammon
Universität Duisburg
Duisburg
Germany

Margaret Lavinia Anderson
University of California
Berkeley, CA

Celia Applegate
University of Rochester
Rochester, NY

Leslie Armour
University of Ottawa
Ottawa, ON
Canada

Werner Arnold
Herzog August Bibliothek
Wolfenbüttel
Germany

Mitchell G. Ash
University of Iowa
Iowa City, IA

Dolores L. Augustine
St. John's University
Jamaica, NY

Shelley Baranowski
University of Akron
Akron, OH

David E. Barclay
Kalamazoo College
Kalamazoo, MI

Peter Barker
University of Reading
Reading
UK

Kenneth Barkin
University of California
Riverside, CA

Dagmar Barnouw
University of Southern California
Los Angeles, CA

Omer Bartov
Rutgers University
Rutgers, NJ

Mark Bassin
University College London
London
UK

Gerhard P. Bassler
Memorial University of Newfoundland
St. John's, NF
Canada

Thomas A. Baylis
University of Texas
San Antonio, TX

Richard J. Bazillion
Brandon University
Brandon, MN
Canada

Rolf Becker
R. Bosch GMBH
Stuttgart
Germany

Hugo Bekker
Ohio State University
Columbus, OH

Doris L. Bergen
University of Notre Dame
Notre Dame, IN

Volker R. Berghahn
Brown University
Providence, RI

Nina Berman
University of Texas
Austin, TX

Karen Bingel
McGill University
Montreal, QC
Canada

Richard Blanke
University of Maine
Orono, ME

Heinz Boberach
Bundesachiv
Koblenz
Germany

Rebecca Boehling
University of Maryland
 Baltimore County
Baltimore, MD

Claus Boerner
German Council of Trade Fairs
 and Exhibitions
Köln
Germany

Douglas Bokovoy
Universität der Bundeswehr
München
Germany

Heinrich Bortfeld
Herder Gymnasium
Berlin-Lichtenberg
Germany

Kathrin Bower
University of Wisconsin
Madison, WI

Gerard Braunthal
University of Massachusetts
Amherst, MA

Richard Breitman
The American University
Washington, DC

Steven J. Breyman
Rensselaer Polytechnic University
Troy, NY

George C. Browder
State University of New York
Fredonia, NY

Gisela Brude-Firnau
University of Waterloo
Waterloo, ON
Canada

Kathryn Brush
University of Western Ontario
London, ON
Canada

John H. Bryant
University of Michigan
Ann Arbor, MI

Phillip J. Bryson
Brigham Young University
Provo, UT

Arden Bucholz
State University of New York
Brockport, NY

Wolfgang Bügel
Henkel KGaA
Düsseldorf
Germany

Gordon J.A. Burgess
University of Aberdeen
Aberdeen
UK

Dieter K. Buse
Laurentian University
Sudbury, ON
Canada

John Lee Butler-Ludwig
University of Chicago
Chicago

David Cahan
University of Nebraska
Lincoln, NB

William M. Calder III
University of Illinois
Urbana, IL

Kenneth R. Calkins
Kent State University
Kent, OH

Gerd Callesen
The Labour Movement Library
 and Archive
Kopenhagen
Denmark

Joan Campbell
University of Toronto
Toronto, ON
Canada

Jane Caplan
Bryn Mawr College
Bryn Mawr, PA

Andrew R. Carlson
Western Michigan University
Kalamazoo, MI

Noel D. Cary
Holy Cross College
Worcester, MA

David C. Cassidy
Hofstra University
Hempstead, NY

Lamar Cecil
Washington and Lee University
Lexington, VA

Peter Chametzky
Adelphi University
Garden City, NY

Attila Chanady
University of Regina
Regina, SA
Canada

William M. Chandler
McMaster University
Hamilton, ON

Roger Chickering
Georgetown University
Washington, DC

Geoffrey Cocks
Albion College
Albion, MI

Irwin Collier
Freie Universität Berlin
Berlin
Germany

Alessandra Comini
Southern Methodist University
Dallas, TX

Alon Confino
University of Virginia
Charlottesville, VA

John S. Conway
University of British Columbia
Vancouver, BC
Canada

James S. Corum
USAF Air University
Maxwell AFB, Alabama

Roy C. Cowen
University of Michigan
Ann Arbor, MI

Gareth Cox
University of Limerick
Limerick
Ireland

Sabine Cramer
Vanderbilt University
Nashville, TN

Marielle Cremer
Universität Hamburg
Hamburg
Germany

Gabor Csepregi
Dominican College of Philosophy
   and Theology
Ottawa, ON
Canada

John Davidson
Cornell University
Ithaca, NY

Belinda Davis
Rutgers University
New Brunswick, NJ

Istvan Deak
Columbia University
New York, NY

James Deaville
McMaster University
Hamilton, ON
Canada

Mike Dennis
University of Wolverhampton
Dudley
UK

Marion Deshmukh
George Mason University
Fairfax, VA

James DiCenso
Trinity College
Toronto, ON
Canada

Jeffry M. Diefendorf
University of New Hampshire
Durham, NH

James M. Diehl
Indiana University
Bloomington, IN

Hans-Liudger Dienel
Deutsches Museum
München
Germany

Donald J. Dietrich
Boston College
Chestnut Hill, MA

Sabine von Dirke
University of Pittsburgh
Pittsburgh, PA

Juergen C. Doerr
St. Thomas University
Fredericton, NB
Canada

Uta Doerr
St. Thomas University
Fredericton, NB
Canada

David R. Dorondo
Western Carolina University
Cullowhee, NC

James R. Dow
Iowa State University
Ames, IO

Dieter Dowe
Friedrich-Ebert-Stiftung
Bonn
Germany

Jost Dülffer
Universität zu Köln
Köln
Germany

Heidrun Edelmann
Tübingen
Germany

Geoffrey H. Eley
University of Michigan
Ann Arbor, MI

Moritz Epple
Johannes Gutenberg Universität
Mainz
Germany

Michael H. Ermarth
Dartmouth College
Hanover, NH

Ellen L. Evans
Georgia State University
Atlanta, GA

Brett Fairbairn
University of Saskatchewan
Saskatoon, SK
Canada

Helen Fehervary
Ohio State University
Columbus, OH

Gerald D. Feldman
University of California
Berkeley, CA

Susan Felleman
School of Visual Art
New York, NY

Jürgen Fijalkowski
Freie Universität Berlin
Berlin
Germany

Susan M. Filler
Chicago, IL

Carole Fink
Ohio State University
Columbus, OH

Conan Fischer
University of Strathclyde
Glasgow
UK

Jens Flemming
Gesamthochschule Kassel
Kassel
Germany

Françoise Forster-Hahn
University of California
Riverside, CA

Ben Fowkes
Polytechnic of North London
London
UK

Ronald Francisco
University of Kansas
Lawrence, KS

Gabriele Franke
University of Waterloo
Waterloo, ON
Canada

Karl-Heinz Füssl
Paul-Löbe Institut
Berlin
Germany

Mary Fulbrook
University College of London
London
UK

Catherine Gelbin
Universität Potsdam
Potsdam
Germany

Andre Gerolymatos
McGill University
Montreal, QC
Canada

Katherina Gerstenberger
University of Cincinnati
Cincinnati, OH

Eva Geulen
University of Rochester
Rochester, NY

Sander L. Gilman
Cornell University
Ithaca, NY

Mark P. Gingerich
Ohio Wesleyan University
Delaware, OH

Kees Gispen
University of Mississippi
University, MS

Jerry Glenn
University of Cincinnati
Cincinnati, OH

Paul H. Gleye
Bauhaus Dessau
Dessau
Germany

Gerd Göckenjan
Universität Bremen
Bremen
Germany

Gert Gröning
Hochschule der Künste Berlin
Berlin
Germany

Atina Grossman
Columbia University
New York, NY

Mark M. Gruettner
Washington University
St. Louis, MO

Peter Guenther
University of Houston
Houston, TX

Arthur B. Gunlicks
University of Richmond
Richmond, VA

Amy Hackett
New York, NY

Sabine Hake
University of Pittsburgh
Pittsburgh, PA

James F. Harris
University of Maryland
College Park, MD

Steve Harris
Department of National Defence
Ottawa, ON
Canada

Dieter Haselbach
Aston University
Birmingham
UK

Peter Hayes
Northwestern University
Evanston, IL

Jürgen Heideking
Universität zu Köln
Köln
Germany

Elizabeth Heineman
Bowling Green State University
Bowling Green, OH

Winfried Heinemann
Militärgeschichtliches
    Forschungsamt
Potsdam
Germany

Guntram Herb
Middlebury College
Middlebury, VT

Sabine Hering
Universität Siegen
Siegen
Germany

Patricia Herminghouse
University of Rochester
Rochester, NY

Dagmar Herzog
Michigan State University
East Lansing, MI

Erika Hickel
Technische Universität
    Carolo-Wilhelmina
Braunschweig
Germany

Leonidas E. Hill
University of British Columbia
Vancouver, BC
Canada

John R. Hinde
Nanaimo, BC
Canada

Hansjoachim Hinkelmann
Optisches Museum
Oberkochen
Germany

Steven L. Hochstadt
Bates College
Lewiston, ME

Alfred Hoelzel
University of Massachusetts
Boston, MA

Dieter Hoffmann
Max Planck Institute—
   History of Science
Berlin
Germany

Peter Hoffmann
McGill University
Montreal, QC
Canada

Brian Holbeche
MacQuarie University
Sydney, NSW
Australia

Thomas Hollweck
University of Colorado
Boulder, CO

Martyn Housden
University of Bradford
Bradford
England

Michael G. Huelshoff
University of New Orleans
New Orleans, LA

John Jay Hughes
Archdiocese of St. Louis
St. Louis, MO

Julia Hughes
Smith Falls, ON
Canada

Georg Iggers
State University of New York
Buffalo, NY

Sigrid Jacobeit
Mahn- und Gedenkstätte
   Ravensbrück
Fürstenberg
Germany

Kyle Jantzen
McGill University
Montreal, QC
Canada

Konrad H. Jarausch
University of North Carolina
Chapel Hill, NC

Peter C. Jelavich
University of Texas
Austin, TX

Eric A. Johnson
Central Michigan University
Mt. Pleasant, MI

Jeffrey A. Johnson
Villanova University
Villanova, PA

Sheila Johnson
University of Texas
San Antonio, TX

Larry Eugene Jones
Canisius College
Buffalo, NY

Nancy Kaiser
University of Wisconsin
Madison, WI

Marion Kaplan
City University of New York
New York, NY

Alan Keele
Brigham Young University
Provo, UT

Paul Kelley
Atkinson College
York University
Toronto, ON
Canada

Katharine D. Kennedy
Agnes Scott College
Decatur, GA

Peter Kent
University of New Brunswick
Fredericton, NB
Canada

Lothar Kettenacker
German Historical Institute
London
UK

Peter Kirchberg
Auto Union GMBH
Ingolstadt
Germany

Martin Kitchen
Simon Fraser University
Burnaby, BC
Canada

Klemens von Klemperer
Smith College
Northampton, MA

Christoph Klessmann
Universität Bielefeld
Bielefeld
Germany

Dwight Klett
Rutgers University
New Brunswick, NJ

Henning Köhler
Freie Universität Berlin
Berlin
Germany

Eric D. Kohler
University of Wyoming
Laramie, WY

Wolfgang Kokott
Universität München
München
Germany

Patricia Kollander
Florida Atlantic University
Boca Raton, FL

Donald P. Kommers
Notre Dame Law School
Notre Dame, IN

Karlheinz Koppe
Bonn
Germany

Susanne Kord
George Washington University
Washington, DC

Harald Kötter
Ausstellungs- und Messe-Ausschuss
   der Deutschen Wirtschaft eV.
Köln
Germany

Frank Krause
Keele University
Keele
UK

Gerhard Krebs
Militärgeschichtliches
   Forschungsamt
Potsdam
Germany

Henry Krisch
University of Connecticut
Storrs, CT

Thomas Küster
Universität Münster
Münster
Germany

Manfred Kuxdorf
University of Waterloo
Waterloo, ON
Canada

Konrad Kwiet
MacQuarie University
Sydney, NSW
Australia

Brian Ladd
Rensselaer Polytechnic University
Troy, NY

Robert Lauterbach
Leipzig
Germany

Heide-Marie Lauterer
Universität Heidelberg
Heidelberg
Germany

Steven W. Lawrie
University of Aberdeen
Aberdeen
UK

Kenneth F. Ledford
Case Western Reserve University
Cleveland, OH

Andrew Lees
Rutgers University
Camden, NJ

Lyman H. Legters
William O. Douglas Institute
Langley, WA

Christiane Lemke
Freie Universität Berlin
Berlin
Germany

Russel Lemmons
Jacksonville State University
Jacksonville, AL

John A. Leopold
Western Connecticut State
   University
Danbury, CT

Katherine Anne Lerman
University of North London
London
UK

Herbert S. Levine
Schiller International University
Berlin,
Germany

Richard S. Levy
University of Illinois
Chicago, IL

Beth Irwin Lewis
The College of Wooster
Wooster, OH

Vernon Lidtke
John Hopkins University
Baltimore, MD

Georg Lilienthal
Johannes Gutenberg Universität
Mainz
Germany

Derek S. Linton
Hobart and William Smith Colleges
Geneva, NY

Colin T. Loader
University of Nevada
Las Vegas, NV

Rose-Carol W. Long
City University of New York
New York, NY

Clifford R. Lovin
Western Carolina University
Cullowhee, NC

Alfred D. Low
Marquette University
Milwaukee, WI

Kristie Macrakis
Michigan State University
East Lansing, MI

Maria Makela
Maryland Institute, College of Art
Baltimore, MD

Kristin Makholm
University of Minnesota
Minneapolis, MN

Patrick Malcolmson
St. Thomas University
Fredericton, NB
Canada

Michael R. Marrus
University of Toronto
Toronto, ON
Canada

Stefan Martens
Deutsches Historisches Institut
Paris
France

Dirk Martin
Centre de Recherches et d'Etudes
   Historiques
de la Seconde Guerre Mondiale
Brussels
Belgium

Benoit Massin
Freie Universität Berlin
Berlin
Germany

William Mathews
State University of New York
Potsdam, NY

Ellen Maurer
München
Germany

Frank A. Mayer
California State University
Los Angeles, CA

Claudia I. Mayer-Iswandy
Université de Montréal
Montréal, QC
Canada

Eva A. Mayring
Deutsches Museum
München
Germany

Lisa McLean
Laurentian University
Sudbury, ON
Canada

David McKibbin
University of Northern Iowa
Cedar Rapids, IA

David A. Meier
Dickinson State University
Dickinson, ND

Lothar Meinzer
BASF AG
Ludwigshafen
Germany

Volker Meja
Memorial University of
   Newfoundland
St. John's, NF
Canada

Inge Melber
BMW AG
München
Germany

Christina Melk-Haen
München
Germany

James A. Mellis
University of Aberdeen
Aberdeen
UK

Richard Merritt
University of Illinois
Urbana, IL

†Ben Meyer
Les Verrières
Switzerland

Michael Meyer
California State University
Northridge, CA

Susanne Miller
Bonn
Germany

Dieter Misgeld
Ontario Institute for Studies
   in Education
Toronto, ON
Canada

James Moran
Atkinson College, York University
North York, ON
Canada

Gordon Mork
Purdue University
West Lafayette, IN

John A. Moses
University of Queensland
St. Lucia
Australia

Walter Mühlhausen
Stiftung Reichspräsident-Friedrich-
   Ebert-Gedenkstätte
Heidelberg
Germany

Ingo Müller
Justizministerium
Bremen
Germany

Wolfgang Müller
Dickinson College
Carlisle, PA

Ferdinand Müller-Rommel
Universität Lüneburg
Lüneburg
Germany

Jerry Z. Muller
Catholic University of America
Washington, DC

Joyce Mushaben
University of Missouri
St. Louis, MO

Richard Myers
St. Thomas University
Fredericton, NB
Canada

Ronald Nabrotzky
Iowa State University
Ames, IA

Andres Nader
Cornell University
Ithaca, NY

J. Alden Nichols
University of Illinois
Urbana, IL

Donald L. Niewyk
Southern Methodist University
Dallas, TX

Bill Niven
University of Aberdeen
Aberdeen
UK

Helmut Norpoth
State University of New York
Stony Brook, NY

Otto Nübel
Daimler-Benz AG
Stuttgart
Germany

Colin O'Connell
St. Paul University
Ottawa, ON
Canada

Fred Oldenburg
Bundesinstitut für Ostwissenschaftliche
    und internationale Studien
Köln
Germany

Dietrich Orlow
Boston University
Boston, MA

Jonathan Osmond
University of Wales
Cardiff
Wales

P. Friedrich Ott
University of Massachusetts
Boston, MA

Richard J. Overy
University of London
London
England

Paul Paret
Princeton University
Princeton, NJ

James D. A. Parker
York University
North York, ON
Canada

Kim Ian Parker
Memorial University
    of Newfoundland
St. John's, NF
Canada

Maarten L. Pereboom
Salisbury State University
Salisbury, MD

Harmut Petzold
Deutsches Museum
München
Germany

Joachim Petzold
Berlin
Germany

Helmut F. Pfanner
Vanderbilt University
Nashville, TN

Peter C. Pfeiffer
Georgetown University
Washington, DC

Otto Pflanze
Bard College
Annandale-on-Hudson, NY

Ann L. Phillips
The American University
Washington, DC

Diane Pitts
Sir Wilfred Grenfell College
Corner Brook, NF
Canada

Ernest D. Plock
International Trade Administration–
    United States Department of
    Commerce
Washington, DC

Karl Heinrich Pohl
Universität Bielefeld
Bielefeld
Germany

Michael Pohlenz
Bayer Archiv
Leverkusen
Germany

Carol Poore
Brown University
Providence, RI

Ingunn Possehl
E. Merck OA/Firmenarchiv
Darmstadt
Germany

Elisabeth Prégardier
Bischöfliche Aktion Adveniat
Essen
Germany

Frank Priess
Konrad Adenauer Stiftung
Sankt Augustine
Germany

Joachim Radkau
Universität Bielefeld
Bielefeld
Germany

Joseph G. Ramisch
Carleton University
Ottawa, ON
Canada

Nancy Reagin
Pace University
New York, NY

Mark W. Rectanus
Iowa State University
Ames, IA

Klaus Reiff
Friedrich-Ebert-Stiftung
Bonn
Germany

Joachim Remak
University of California
Santa Barbara, CA

Wolfgang Renzsch
Friedrich Ebert Stiftung
Bonn
Germany

James Retallack
University of Toronto
Toronto, ON
Canada

Kenneth Reynolds
McGill University
Montreal, QC
Canada

Mary Beth Rhiel
University of New Hampshire
Durham, NH

Thomas Ringmayr
University of Washington
Seattle, WA

James S. Roberts
Duke University
Durham, NC

John Robertson
McMaster University
Hamilton, ON
Canada

Mark W. Roche
Ohio State University
Columbus, OH

Alan J. Rocke
Case Western Reserve University
Cleveland, OH

Silvia A. Rode
Vanderbilt University
Nashville, TN

Steven B. Rogers
United States Department of Justice
Washington, DC

Zoltan Roman
University of Calgary
Calgary, AB
Canada

Katherine Roper
Saint Mary's College
   of California
Moraga, CA

Ronald J. Ross
University of Wisconsin
Milwaukee, WI

Nancy Roth
University of Manchester
Manchester
UK

David E. Rowe
Johannes Gutenberg-Universität
Mainz
Germany

Marilyn Rueschemeyer
Rhode Island School of Design
Providence, RI

Linda H. Rugg
Ohio State University
Columbus, OH

Hermann J. Rupieper
Martin-Luther-Universität
Halle-Wittenberg
Germany

Jennifer M. Russ
Bootham School
York
UK

Kenneth C. Russell
St. Paul University
Ottawa, ON
Canada

Katharine Sams
McGill University
Montreal, QC
Canada

Amy E. Sanders
Columbia University
New York, NY

John Sandford
University of Reading
Reading
UK

Raffael Scheck
Colby College
Waterville, ME

Ulrich Scheck
Queen's University
Kingston, ON
Canada

Carol Scherer
University of Chicago
Chicago, IL

Donald Schilling
Denison University
Granville, OH

Hanna Schissler
University of Minnesota
Minneapolis, MN

Wolfgang Schlauch
Eastern Illinois University
Charleston, IL

Felix Schmeidler
Deutsches Museum
München
Germany

Gustav Schmidt
Ruhr-Universität
Bochum
Germany

David Schoenbaum
University of Iowa
Iowa City, IA

Klaus Schönherr
Militärgeschichtliches Forschungsamt
Potsdam
Germany

Helga Schreckenberger
University of Vermont
Burlington, VT

Gerd Schroeter
Lakehead University
Thunder Bay, ON
Canada

Georg Schütte
Alexander-von-Humboldt-Stiftung
Bonn
Germany

Frederic J. Schwartz
University College London
London
UK

Thomas A. Schwartz
Vanderbilt University
Nashville, TN

David Scrase
University of Vermont
Burlington, VT

Donald E. Shepardson
University of Northern Iowa
Cedar Falls, IA

Marilyn Shevin-Coetzee
George Washington University
Washington, DC

Wesley Shoemaker
Lynchburg College
Lynchburg, VA

Dennis E. Showalter
Colorado College
Colorado Springs, CO

Alan Sica
Pennsylvania State University
University Park, PA

Marc Silberman
University of Wisconsin
Madison, WI

Stephen J. Silvia
The American University
Washington, DC

Sara Gregg Skerker
University of Chicago
Chicago, IL

James Skidmore
Sir Wilfried Laurier University
Waterloo, ON
Canada

William Smaldone
Willamette University
Salem, OR

Ronald Smelser
University of Utah
Salt Lake City, UT

Woodruff D. Smith
University of Massachusetts
    at Boston
Boston, MA

Christian Søe
California State University
Long Beach, CA

Elaine G. Spencer
Northern Illinois University
DeKalb, IL

Peter D. Stachura
University of Stirling
Stirling
UK

Rod Stackelberg
Gonzaga University
Spokane, WA

James D. Steakley
University of Wisconsin
Madison, WI

Stewart Stehlin
New York University
New York, NY

Irmgard Steinisch
York University
North York, ON
Canada

Uwe Stender
Sewickley Academy
Sewickley, PA

William H. Stiebing Jr.
University of New Orleans
New Orleans, LA

Raymond Stokes
University of Glasgow
Glasgow
UK

Gunnar Stollberg
Universität Bielefeld
Bielefeld
Germany

Margaret Stone
University of Aberdeen
Aberdeen
UK

Bernd Stöver
Universität Potsdam
Potsdam
Germany

Carl Strikwerda
University of Kansas
Lawrence, KS

William Sweet
St. Francis Xavier University
Antigonish, NS
Canada

Charles Sydnor
Central Virginia Educational
    Telecommunications Corporation
Richmond, VA

Andrij Szanajda
McGill University
Montreal, QC
Canada

James F. Tent
University of Alabama
Birmingham, AL

Charles S. Thomas
Georgia Southern University
Statesboro, GA

Wayne C. Thompson
Virginia Military Institute
Lexington, VA

Wolfgang Thöner
Bauhaus Dessau
Dessau
Germany

Richard Tilly
Universität Münster
Münster
Germany

Frank B. Tipton
University of Sydney
Sydney, NSW
Australia

Edmund N. Todd III
University of New Haven
West Haven, CT

Mary Lee Townsend
University of Tulsa
Tulsa, OK

Ulrich Trumpener
University of Alberta
Edmonton, AB
Canada

R. Steven Turner
University of New Brunswick
Fredericton, NB
Canada

Gérard Vallée
McMaster University
Hamilton, ON
Canada

†Robert Vogel
McGill University
Montreal, QC
Canada

Heinz-Jürgen Vogels
Deutscher Akademischer
    Austauschdienst
Bonn
Germany

Elisabeth Waghäll
Davidson College
Davidson, NC

Mark Walker
Union College
Schenectady, NY

Lori Walsh
West Norriton, PA

Margaret E. Ward
Wellesley College
Wellesley, MA

Wolfhard Weber
Ruhr-Universität
Bochum
Germany

Ronald D. E. Webster
York University
North York, ON
Canada

Gregory Wegner
University of Wisconsin
La Crosse, WI

Paul Weindling
University of Oxford
Oxford
UK

Sheila Weiss
Clarkson University
Potsdam, NY

David Welch
University of Kent
Canterbury
UK

Edward B. Westermann
U.S. Airforce Academy
Colorado Springs, CO

Robert H. Whealy
Ohio University
Athens, OH

Dan S. White
State University
Albany, NY

Craig R. Whitney
The New York Times
New York

Sabine Wilke
University of Washington
Seattle, WA

David Williamson
Highgate School
London
UK

Josef Wittmann
MAN AG
Augsburg
Germany

Nancy Travis Wolfe
University of South Carolina
Columbia, SC

Stefan L. Wolff
Universität München
München
Germany

Manfred K. Wolfram
University of Cincinnati
Cincinnati, OH

Joachim Wolschke-Bulmahn
University of Hannover
Hannover
Germany

Reinhard K. Zachau
University of the South
Sewanee, TN

Bernhard Zimmermann
Universität Siegen
Siegen
Germany

E. R. Zimmermann
Lakehead University
Thunder Bay, ON
Canada

Acronyms

AEG	Allegemeine Elektrizitäts-Gesellschaft (General Electric Company)
APO	Ausserparlamentarische Opposition (Extraparliamentary Opposition)
BDF	Bund Deutscher Frauenvereine (Federation of German Women's Associations)
BdI	Bund der Industriellen (Federation of Industrialists)
BDM	Bund Deutscher Mädel (League of German Girls)
BHE	Bund der Heimatvertriebenen und Entrechteten (Federation of Expellees and Disenfranchised)
BMG	British Military Government
BMW	Bayerische Motoren Werke (Bavarian Motorworks)
BVP	Bayerische Volkspartei (Bavarian People's Party)
CDU	Christlich Demokratische Union (Christian Democratic Union)
CSU	Christlich Soziale Union (Christian Social Union)
DAF	Deutsche Arbeits Front (German Labor Front)
DGB	Deutscher Gewerkschaftsbund (German Trade Union Federation)
DDP	Deutsche Demokratische Partei (German Democratic Party)
DKP	Deutsch-Konservative Partei (German Conservative Party)
DNVP	Deutsch-Nationale Volkspartei (German National People's Party)
DVP	Deutsche Volkspartei (German People's Party)
ECSC	European Coal and Steel Community
EDC	European Defense Community
EEC	European Economic Community
FDGB	Freier Deutscher Gewerkschaftsbund (Free German Trade Union Federation)
FDJ	Freie Deutsche Jugend (Free German Youth)
FDP	Freie Demokratische Partei (Free Democratic Party)
FRG	Federal Republic of Germany
GDR	German Democratic Republic
Gestapo	Geheime Staatspolizei (Secret State Police)
KdF	Kraft durch Freude (Strength through Joy)
KPD	Kommunistische Partei Deutschlands (German Communist Party)
MfS	Ministerium für Staatssicherheit (Ministry for State Security)
NATO	North Atlantic Treaty Organization
NPD	Nationaldemokratische Partei Deutschlands (National Democratic Party of Germany)
NSDAP	Nationalsozialistische Deutsche Arbeiterpartei (National Socialist German Workers' Party)
NVA	Nationale Volksarmee (National People's Army)
OKW	Oberkommando der Wehrmacht (High Command of the Armed Forces)
OMGUS	Office of Military Government for Germany, United States
PDS	Partei des Demokratischen Sozialismus (Party of Democratic Socialism)
RAF	Rote Armee Fraktion (Red Army Faction)
RSHA	Reichssicherheitshauptamt (Reich Security Main Office)

SA	Sturmabteilung (Stormtroopers)
SBZ	Sowjetische Besatzungszone (Soviet Occupied Zone)
SD	Sicherheitsdienst (Security Service)
SED	Sozialistische Einheitspartei (Socialist Unity Party)
Sipo	Sicherheitspolizei (Security Police)
SMAD	Soviet Military Administration in Germany)
SPD	Sozialdemokratische Partei Deutschlands (Social Democratic Party of Germany)
SS	Schutzstaffel
Stasi	Staatssicherheit (State Security) (see MfS)
USPD	Unabhängige Sozialdemokratische Partei Deutschlands (Independent Social Democratic Party of Germany)

Modern Germany

Volume I
A–K

A

Abbe, Ernst (1840–1905) and the Zeiss Werke

Ernst Abbe was one of the foremost German optical theorists and industrialists of his day. He created a theory of image formation in microscopes and invented a series of microscopical instruments and measuring devices. The result was the first scientific understanding of microscopy to be embodied in practical microscopes and other optical systems. He thereby transformed the provincial workshop of Carl Zeiss in Jena into the world's leading optical concern, the Zeiss Werke.

Abbe was born in Eisenach on January 23, 1840, the son of Georg Adam Abbe, a spinning-mill worker of limited means, and Elisabeta Adam. After graduating from the Eisenach Gymnasium in 1857, he studied physical science first at Jena University, where he met Carl Zeiss, the owner of a small local optical workshop, and then for two more years at Göttingen, where he graduated in 1861. After teaching for two years (1861–63) at the Physikalischer Verein in Frankfurt am Main, Abbe qualified as a lecturer (1863) at Jena in mathematics, physics, and astronomy but soon limited his lecturing to aspects of optics, partly because in 1866 he also began working for Zeiss. In 1870, he was promoted to extraordinary professor. The following year he married Elise Snell, with whom he had two daughters. In 1876, Abbe became a full partner in the Zeiss Werke, and in 1889 became the sole owner of the firm and its associated business, the glassworks firm Otto Schott and Co. In 1889 he created the Carl-Zeiss Stiftung to promote scientific research (above all at Jena University) and enhance public welfare. He eventually endowed his entire estate to the Stiftung. He died by his own hand in Jena on January 14, 1905.

Between 1866 and 1872, Abbe created a new theory of the image-formation process in the microscope, thereby determining the limits of resolving power. Abbe realized that to develop a theory of the image-formation process required understanding the behavior of diffracted as well as of reflected and refracted light. He reasoned that to increase resolution required objectives with apertures sufficiently large to include at least some of the diffracted light rays. To capture diffracted rays, Abbe used oblique illumination and large-angle objectives. And to obtain a uniform image, he discovered that two conjugate points required a constant ratio between the sines of the two angles across the aperture.

The fulfillment of this condition, known since as Abbe's sine condition, allowed the imaging of both the axial and diffracted light rays. Abbe also applied this theoretical reasoning to a formula for microscope design and for determining the theoretical limits of resolving power.

Ernst Abbe. Courtesy of Inter Nationes, Bonn.

Along with and following the development of his imaging theory, Abbe and the Zeiss Werke also created a series of optical instruments, apparatuses, and measuring devices that enormously increased the resolving power of microscopes and that helped to place microscopy on a more precise basis: the focometer, the refractometer, the substage illuminator, the Abbe spectrometer, the apertometer, the spherometer, the comparator, immersion objectives, and apochromats. In addition, Abbe encouraged Schott to develop new types of glass with optical properties specifically designed to eliminate or minimize chromatic and spherical aberrations.

In addition to producing microscopes, the Zeiss Werke also manufactured eyeglasses and opera glasses, photographic lenses and objectives, butter and milk refractometers, field glasses, stereoscopic range finders, sighting telescopes, micro-photographic apparatuses, photometers, dilatometers, and telescopes. By the late 1880s, Zeiss optical products ranked among the high technology of the day, and the name Zeiss on a product was the sign of the finest quality. By 1902, the Zeiss Werke's annual sales reached about 3.6 million marks and it employed more than 1,300 people.

During the last third of the nineteenth century, Ernst Abbe became the major figure in establishing scientific foundations for microscopy. At the same time, he transformed a small workshop based on trial-and-error methods into a major, scientifically grounded technological firm that dominated the world market in optical products.

David Cahan

See also Inventions; Optics; Technology; Zeiss, Carl: Firm and Foundation

References

Abbe, Ernst. *Gesammelte Abhandlungen von Ernst Abbe.* 5 vols. Jena: Gustav Fischer, 1904–40.

Auerbach, Felix. *Ernst Abbe. Sein Leben, sein Wirken, seine Persönlichkeit nach den Quellen und aus eigener Erfahrung geschildert.* Leipzig: Akademische Verlagsgesellschaft, 1918.

Kühnert, Herbert, ed. *Der Briefwechsel zwischen Otto Schott und Ernst Abbe über das optische Glas, 1879–1881.* Jena: Gustav Fischer, 1946.

Rohr, M. von. "Zur Geschichte der Zeissischen Werkstätte bis zum Tode Ernst Abbes." *Forschungen zur Geschichte der Optik (Beilage zur Zeitschrift für Instrumentenkunde)* 2 (1936–38), 1–119.

Volkmann, H. "Ernst Abbe and His Work." *Applied Optics* 5 (1966), 1720–31.

Wittig, Joachim. *Ernst Abbe.* Leipzig: BSB B.G. Teubner, 1989.

Abortion

Prior to reunification, abortion rights in West Germany were highly restricted, requiring a doctor's certification that a woman's appeal to terminate a pregnancy fell under one of four "indicators" (medical, criminal, embryopathological, or social hardship). East German law, by contrast, guaranteed free and legal abortions upon demand during the first trimester of pregnancy. Deliberately excluded from the 1990 Unity Treaty because of its controversial nature, abortion has been declared "illegal but free from punishment" by the Federal Constitutional Court, effective June 16, 1993, for all women in unified Germany. The Bundestag had to approve a revised law no later than December 1994, ratifying restrictions specified in the court's May 28, 1993 verdict.

State interest in overcoming the decimating effects of recurrent wars in Europe led to Germany's first abortion ban in 1851. Chancellor Otto von Bismarck's consolidation of the Empire continued the trend, imposing a sentence of five years at hard labor under Paragraphs 218 and 219 of the 1871 Criminal Code. Efforts by the Independent Socialists, Social Democrats, and Communists to strike the prohibition from the code during the Weimar Republic resulted in a mitigation of punishment for violators by 1926. During the Great Depression of the 1930s, the Health Ministry estimated that there were 4,000 deaths among the one million abortions performed annually; doctors opposing Paragraph 218 set the fatality figure at 40,000. In 1930, the same year that Pope Pius XI condemned all forms of contraception and declared abortion a mortal sin, 356 Berlin physicians called for a "social hardship" indicator, as well as for dispensations to save the life of the mother and to end pregnancies involving rape, incest, or fetal deformity.

In 1931, more than 300 physicians were arrested simultaneously, giving rise to 800 local "action committees." Communists and socialists joined in a campaign to abolish Paragraphs 218 and 219, as did bourgeois and socialist women's movements, whose appeal rested on the belief that women's special responsibility for the protection of national well-being could be upheld only through their production of quality offspring.

Reform efforts ceased when the Nazis attained power in 1933 and the principle of "eugenic health" was displaced by the notion of "racial hygiene." The "Law for Protection against Congenitally Ill Offspring" eliminated the ban for "non-Aryans," leading to mass sterilizations and forced abortions among those women alleged to bear "life not worth living." But the number of legal abortions among "Aryans" fell to 2,275 by 1939. Individuals charged with "continuing efforts to harm the vitality of the German people" faced the death penalty after 1942.

Although a renewed debate commenced upon Germany's surrender in 1945, the 1871 Criminal Code remained in force until the promulgation of new constitutions in 1949. Enforcement of the old statutes was initially lax, as a result of the widespread rapes that occurred during the military occupation of major cities. Those by Soviet troops alone resulted in 6,000 abortion-related deaths; French troops in Stuttgart perpetrated 1,198 reported rapes; 971 American soldiers were criminally convicted. Campaigns waged from 1946 to 1948 produced no direct changes in Paragraph 218, although hard labor and the death sentence were formally stricken in 1953. Thus, the same paragraphs that had led to "procreation hygiene" abuse under the Nazis continued to restrict legal access to abortion, al-

though penal sentences were largely suspended for those performed on the basis of the specified "indicators" by 1969.
Convictions for violators decreased from 1,033 (30 percent
of all prosecutions) in 1955 to 802 in 1965, to 276 in 1969,
and to 154 in 1972. States governed by Social Democrats consistently defined the indicators more liberally than those under Christian Democratic control.

The birth of an autonomous women's movement coincided with the first Social Democratic/Free Democratic coalition under Chancellor Willy Brandt (1913–92) and led to
hopes for decriminalization of abortion. Feminists' stress on
a guaranteed right to abortion during the first three months
of pregnancy found majority support within the unions and
the Communist and liberal parties, as well as youth groups and
the national Social Democratic caucus. The ruling social-liberal majority adopted trimester legislation in April 1974 by a
vote of 247 to 233, which a conservative Bundesrat majority
immediately sought to block. Bolstered by strong church opposition to reform, five Christian Democratic Union/Chris-
tian Social Union (CDU/CSU) state governments joined 193
conservative parliamentarians (only ten women) in taking the
case to the constitutional court. On February 25, 1975, the
court upheld the state's obligation to see pregnancy carried to
full term. The judges obliged the Bundestag to pass a new law
in May 1975, legalizing the procedure only if a doctor certified that one of four "indicators" were met. The law, enacted
in June 1976, foresaw criminal penalties (up to five years of
imprisonment and/or a fine); it applied to resident foreigners as well as to citizens seeking abortions abroad. In June
1976, independent women's groups organized chartered buses
to the Netherlands, where provisions were more liberal.

By contrast to West Germany, beginning in 1972, the
GDR permitted abortion on demand for twelve weeks after
conception, provided the woman had not terminated a pregnancy during the previous six months. Article 31 of the formal Unity Treaty, signed on September 6, 1990, postponed
decisions regarding abortion rights until December 31, 1992,
yet obliged the all-German parliament to establish a regulation that would guarantee "the protection of unborn life
and . . . provide [pregnant women] necessary forms of aid
beyond the point of birth."

Both West and East German laws were applied through
December 1992 under an "operative site" principle, as opposed to the more restrictive "residency" principle that the
CDU/CSU originally sought to impose. The Bundestag commenced deliberations on the "Pregnancy and Family Assistance Act" in September 1991, approving the (tri-partisan)
Group Resolution by a vote of 357 to 283 on June 25, 1992.
The 1992 vote was followed by a repeat of 1974: 248 conservatives (215 men, 33 women) called on the judiciary to block
the new statute. Composed of seven males and one female justice, the second chamber of the constitutional court imposed
a temporary injunction on August 4, 1992, prohibiting full
implementation; provisions involving mandatory counseling
and a three-day waiting period took immediate effect.

On May 28, 1993, the court outlined an "Interim Law,"
which gave the Bundestag until December 1994 to generate

a new statute and declared abortion "illegal but free from
punishment." The judges decreed that lawmakers had no
power under the existing constitution to render abortion a
general "right" of women, although they recognized the trimester principle as well as the woman's ultimate right to
choose. The "stick" of criminal punishment during the first
twelve weeks of pregnancy has been replaced with the "carrot"
of obligatory counseling at an accredited center at least three
days prior to a termination. Officially approved advisors must
"encourage" all women to continue their pregnancies by outlining available forms of public assistance. The cost of abortions falling outside the medical, criminal, and embryopathic
"indicators" (ranging between 300 and 1400 deutsche marks)
will no longer be covered by the health-insurance system. The
ruling thus eliminates the "social hardship" indicator, which
formerly accounted for 80 percent of all certified abortions.
In the case of demonstrated financial need, costs may be covered by social-assistance payments.

Joyce Mushaben

See also Federal Republic of Germany: Women; Feminism and
Anti-Feminism; Feminism in the Federal Republic of Ger-
many; Fertility; German Democratic Republic: Women;
Health; Medicine; Morality; Sex Reform and Birth Control

References
Bridenthal, Renate, ed., with Atina Grossman and Marion
    Kaplan. *When Biology Became Destiny: Women in
    Weimar and Nazi Germany.* New York, NY: Monthly
    Review Press, 1984.
Däubler-Gmelin, Herta and Renate Faerber-Husemann.
    §218 — Der tägliche Kampf um die Reform. Bonn:
    Neue Gesellschaft, 1987.
Doormann, Lottemi, ed. *Keiner schiebt uns weg: Zwischen-
    bilanz der Frauenbewegung in der Bundesrepublik.*
    Weinheim: Beltz, 1979.
Hervé, Florence, Elly Steinmann, and Renate Wurms, eds.
    Kleines Weiberlexikon. Dortmund: Weltkreis Verlag,
    1985.
Merkl, Peter. "The Politics of Sex: West Germany." *Women
    in the World: A Comparative Study.* Ed. Lynn B. Iglitzin
    and Ruth Ross. Santa Barbara, CA: ABC-Clio, 1976.
Moeller, Robert G. *Protecting Motherhood: Women and the
    Family in the Politics of Postwar West Germany.* Berke-
    ley, CA: University of California Press, 1993.
Schwarzer, Alice. *Weg mit dem §218.* Cologne: EMMA
    Frauenverlag, 1986.

Abs, Hermann J. (1901–94)
Hermann J. Abs, the most prominent and influential banker
in the Federal Republic of Germany (FRG), played a critical
role in creating the financial conditions that shaped the FRG's
"economic miracle" in the 1950s and 1960s.

Born in 1901 to an upper-middle-class family in Bonn,
Abs graduated from a classical Gymnasium and studied at
the Friedrich Wilhelm University. He lost interest in higher
education within a year and in 1919 became a trainee in

Louis David's merchant banking house in Bonn. He spent most of the 1920s in various banking positions outside of Germany, then returned in 1929 as a foreign-investment expert employed by the Delbrück Schickler & Co. bank in Berlin. By 1937, his performance in this post led to an appointment to the managing board of the Deutsche Bank, where he became responsible primarily for international banking. In this capacity, he also served as a member of the supervisory board of a number of major corporations, including, from 1940, I.G. Farbenindustrie AG. Controversy clouds Abs's activities during the Nazi period. In 1970, the East German historian Eberhard Czichon accused Abs of participating in the "Aryanization" of German business during the Nazi period, but in 1972 a court found this accusation unfounded.

Abs had attained prominence within German financial circles by the end of the 1930s. In the post-1945 period his career flourished. Initially stripped of his positions at the Deutsche Bank and elsewhere, Abs nonetheless gained the confidence of influential members of the British military government. They enabled him to establish his business interests in Hamburg and invited him to serve as economic and financial advisor to the military governor, Sir Sholto Douglas. In 1948, Abs was named vice-chairman of the Kreditanstalt für Wiederaufbau, a credit facility formed to distribute counterpart funds made available through the Marshall Plan for investment in German industry and the economy. Abs became chairman of that organization in 1959.

Abs emerged as a prominent figure in West German domestic politics and became a close friend and confidant of Chancellor Konrad Adenauer. He used his influence with Adenauer and the federal cabinet to promote the reconstruction and expansion of heavy industry, particularly through helping to draft the investment aid law for basic industries of 1952. Abs's activities extended well beyond the domestic sphere, however—he headed the West German delegation to a London conference on war debts that resulted in the London War Debt Agreement of 1953. The West German government agreed to repay a certain proportion of Germany's foreign debts incurred prior to 1945. Since the sum was much smaller than the former Allies had initially demanded, and since the agreement finally settled a number of outstanding financial issues stemming from World War II, the Agreement helped to restore West Germany's solvency and political sovereignty and established the basis for future economic growth in the FRG. Another agreement negotiated by Abs provided restitution to Israel and to Jews who had suffered under National Socialism. This bill was passed by the Bundestag in March 1953.

While undertaking these activities as a representative of the federal government, Abs was also active in the private sphere. He sat on the managing board of the Süddeutsche Bank, one of the successors to the Deutsche Bank, beginning in 1952. Abs helped to organize the re-creation of the Deutsche Bank in 1957, and he chaired the managing board until his retirement in 1967. Both before and after his retirement, he served on the supervisory boards of a number of

major German corporations, including BASF, Daimler-Benz, Lufthansa, and RWE.
Raymond Stokes

See also Adenauer, Konrad; Banking; Deutsche Bank; I.G. Farbenindustrie AG; Israeli-German Relations; Marshall Plan

References
Abs, Hermann J. *Entscheidungen 1949–1953: Die Entstehung des Londoner Schuldenabkommens.* Mainz: Haase & Koehler, 1991.
———. *Lebensfragen der Wirtschaft.* Düsseldorf: Econ, 1976.
Czichon, Eberhard. *Der Bankier und die Macht: Hermann Josef Abs in der deutschen Politik.* Cologne: Pahl-Rugenstein, 1970.

Ackermann, Anton (Eugen Hanisch) (1905–73)

Anton Ackermann (legal name, Eugen Hanisch) was the leading theoretician of the German Communist Party (KPD) and then of the Socialist Unity Party (SED) in the immediate post–World War II period. Ackermann, from the more "liberal" wing of the KPD, formulated the "Separate German Roads to Socialism" theory that guided first KPD, then SED, policy from December 1945 until September 1948. His personal life represents a pattern of struggle and displacement common to Communists in the Europe of his generation. The highs and lows of his career mark the turbulent conditions within the SED and East Germany in the first postwar decade.

Ackermann, a worker with only a primary-school education, joined the Free Socialist Youth in 1919 and then the KPD in 1926. He advanced rapidly in the party apparatus. After graduating in 1928 from the Lenin School in Moscow, he worked in the Germany division of the Comintern. In 1935, he became a member of the Central Committee and candidate member of the *Politbüro* of the KPD. He fought in the Spanish Civil War and then emigrated to the Soviet Union. In late April 1945, he led a group of Communists home to Berlin.

The high point of Ackermann's career and influence was from 1945 to 1953. In those years he was a member of the Central Committee, candidate member of the *Politbüro*, member of parliament, and state secretary in the Foreign Ministry.

The "Separate German Roads to Socialism" thesis reflected not only Moscow's German policy but also the disillusionment with the Soviet system felt by a significant cohort of German Communists who had spent the war years in Moscow. It argued that the Soviet model was not applicable to Germany because of its advanced stage of industrialization. In addition, it offered the hope that German Communists might be able to distance themselves from Soviet occupation policies. "Separate Roads to Socialism" was standard policy throughout Eastern Europe until 1948, when consolidation of Soviet influence entered a new phase in response to international developments and the challenge of Marshal Josip Tito. Ackermann was forced to recant the policy in September 1948.

Ackermann was relieved of all party functions in July 1953 in retaliation for his support of the *Politbüro* group (Zaisser-Herrnstadt) that unsuccessfully tried to oust SED

General Secretary Walter Ulbricht (1893–1973). Despite his rehabilitation in 1956, he never regained political influence.
Ann L. Phillips

See also German Communist Party; German Democratic Republic; Socialist Unity Party of Germany; Ulbricht, Walter

References

Ackermann, Anton. "Über den einzig möglichen Weg zum Sozialismus." *Neues Deutschland,* September 24, 1948.
———. "Wohin soll der Weg gehen?" *Deutsche Volkszeitung,* June 14, 1945.
Gniffke, Erich W. *Jahre mit Ulbricht.* Cologne: Verlag Wissenschaft & Politik, 1966.
Krisch, Henry. *German Politics under Soviet Occupation.* New York, NY: Columbia University Press, 1974.
Leonhard, Wolfgang. *Child of the Revolution.* London: Collins, 1957.
Phillips, Ann L. *Soviet Policy toward East Germany Reconsidered: The Postwar Decade.* New York, NY: Greenwood, 1986.
Schenk, Fritz. *Im Vorzimmer der Diktatur.* Cologne: Kiepenheuer & Witsch, 1962.
Weber, Hermann. *Von der SBZ zur "DDR."* 2 vols. Hannover: Verlag für Literatur und Zeitgeschehen, 1966–67.

Adenauer, Konrad (1876–1967)

Konrad Adenauer was the first chancellor of West Germany. He had great influence on the formation of the state and convinced the West Germans of the advantages of integration into the Western alliance as well as of parliamentary democracy. Adenauer was successful in simultaneously maintaining the West German demand for reunification while pursuing other priorities in practical politics.

Adenauer grew up in modest conditions. His father was a mid-level civil servant in Cologne. After obtaining a law degree, Adenauer began his career in Cologne's city administration. Due to his enormous efficiency, and with the help of the Catholic Center Party, Adenauer was elected lord mayor of Cologne in 1917. His experiences in this position proved to be of great significance when he became chancellor.

After being dismissed from office by the Nazis in March 1933 he sought safety in a cloister. Beginning in 1935 Adenauer lived as a recluse in Rhöndorf (just south of Bonn), rejecting all offers of active involvement in resistance against the Nazis. After the failed assassination attempt on Hitler in July 1944, Adenauer was one of the suspects rounded up and placed in prison. Although the United States Army installed him as lord mayor of Cologne in March 1945, Adenauer would remain only shortly in office. Cologne became part of the British occupation zone, and the British removed him from office in October 1945, citing unauthorized political activity. Adenauer had made connections with French officers and begun talks about the establishment of a Rhineland state—involving the Ruhr industrial area, parts of Hesse, and the Palatinate—that would maintain close ties to France.

Portrait of Konrad Adenauer by Hans-Jürgen Kallmann. Courtesy of German Embassy, Ottawa.

As lord mayor of Cologne he had supported similar plans after World War I, from 1919 to 1923. These ideas did not involve separatist ambitions, however. His motivation lay in the healthy egoism of a Rhinelander during catastrophic situations. Although none of the plans for the creation of a Rhineland state had a chance, they are important in understanding Adenauer's political outlook. In times of relative political stability, the Adenauer record was one of a German patriot. During unstable times he developed his Rhineland plans. This ambivalence proved significant for his political career after 1945.

Adenauer's early acceptance of a separate West German state represented a concentration on the politically attainable. Simultaneously he presented himself to the Western allies as a valuable partner, one who would not consider separate dealings with the Soviet Union.

His dismissal as lord mayor in late 1945 allowed Adenauer to pursue other political goals. In January 1946, Adenauer, at age 70, began his career as a machine politician. The Christian Democratic Union (CDU) had been founded without his assistance. Within several weeks he became head of the CDU in the British zone, thereby influencing the party's political platform. Simultaneously Adenauer established contacts to the CDU organizations in the other Western occupation zones. He placed no importance on the Soviet zone. Its head, Jacob Kaiser (1888–1961), was a strong proponent of all-German solutions as well as of Berlin's role as capital.

With the fusion of the American and British zones into the Bizone in 1947 and the creation of the parliamentary body, Adenauer organized a coalition with the Free Democratic Party

(FDP) and the Deutsche Partei (DP) against the Social Democratic Party (SPD). He considered the SPD to be the chief
opponent, a party only slightly different than the Communists.
This coalition held the upper hand in the Wirtschaftsrat (Economic Council) and also in the Parlamentarischer Rat (Parliamentary Council), which under Adenauer's chairmanship
formulated the Basic Law in 1948–49.

The coalition won a majority in the first elections on
August 14, 1949. Adenauer surprised many by nominating
himself as chancellor despite his age. But he proved through
indefatigable effort and energetic command of his governmental duties that he was Bonn's leading political force.
Adenauer's political strategy had three goals: defense against
the Communist threat; ending of Allied occupation in West
Germany; and incorporation of West Germany into a united
Western Europe.

Initially there were difficulties. The Western powers remained reluctant. In August 1950, shortly after the outbreak
of the Korean War, Adenauer recommended the rearmament
of West Germany to the Allies, not so much as a bargaining
chip to gain sovereignty, but out of genuine fear of Communist aggression. He did not succeed. West German rearmament occurred in 1955, after the European Defense Community had been vetoed by France in 1954. The year 1955 saw
the establishment of West German sovereignty (with certain
limitations) and its acceptance into NATO.

Adenauer's policy of Western integration was unpopular
until 1952. In the elections of 1953 Adenauer nonetheless won
a great victory. This triumph was achieved because of growing
economic prosperity, the success of his first trip to the United
States in April 1953, and the suppression of a revolt in the
Soviet zone in June 1953. The success of Adenauer's visit to
the United States was in large part based on an agreement
ratified between West Germany and Israel involving high financial demands on the West German government.

Adenauer's anti-Communism was defensive. He regarded negotiations with the Soviets unacceptable, and thus
he rejected the Stalin Note of March 1952. How then should
the reunification of Germany be realized? He believed that the
Soviets, impressed only by power, would make concessions if
West Germany maintained its own military forces and the
Western alliance remained superior. Adenauer held this belief
his entire life, despite the Khrushchev Ultimatum of 1958
demanding the transformation of Berlin into a "free city" and
the building of the Berlin Wall in 1961. At the beginning of
1958 he offered the Soviets the "Austrian solution," which
meant abandoning German reunification if East Germany
were rendered neutral and given full democratic rights. Like
the planned Rhineland state in the West, East Germany was
to receive special status. The Soviets did not accept.

Adenauer's Moscow trip in September 1955 is widely
considered his greatest triumph. In reality he was the victim
of Soviet extortion. Moscow was willing to release German
prisoners of war only in exchange for the establishment of
diplomatic relations. The absolute majority that Adenauer
won in the elections of 1957, the first and only one in FRG
history, was possible thanks to the bloody suppression of the

Hungarian revolt by the Soviets and to Adenauer's generous
campaign promises.

Adenauer's most ambitious goal, the equipping of the
West German army with atomic warheads, proved unattainable. In 1957–58 he planned the production of atomic weapons together with France and Italy. He then demanded that
West Germany have a voice in NATO's nuclear strategy. The
Americans made halfhearted promises. Adenauer's excessive
anxiety concerning American protection of the Federal Republic in case of a Soviet nuclear attack annoyed Washington. Sour
relations with the Kennedy administration exacerbated matters dramatically. Kennedy had delayed plans for a NATO
multilateral nuclear force and then blocked West German
access to nuclear weapons with the 1963 nonproliferation
agreement. This reinforced Adenauer's fears that Washington
might reach an agreement with Moscow at the cost of West
Germany. He turned to Paris for help, signing the Elysée Treaty
in January 1963, a clear affront to Washington and London.
Under de Gaulle's influence he gave up earlier plans for a supranational Western Europe.

Adenauer's political decline began in 1959, when he decided to run for federal president and then quickly reversed
this decision, citing the unacceptability of Ludwig Erhard
(1897–1977), the father of the economic miracle, as his successor. His decline was further hastened by his slow reaction
to the Berlin Wall in August 1961 and the "*Spiegel* Affair" in
late 1962. His party forced him to retire in October 1963.

The secret of Adenauer's success was his political instinct,
his work ethic, and the extraordinary breadth of his political
program. He presented himself as a nationalist but pushed for
a Rhineland state; preached the "policy of strength" but hesitated with the unpopular build-up of German military forces.
He was considered a guarantor of close relations with Washington but became increasingly mistrustful. Big business had
his ear, but he pushed for social security reforms. He made
amends with Holocaust survivors and supported Israel, but he
secured the pardoning of German war criminals.

What were his achievements? He brought West Germany
into the Western family of nations. Through his long chancellorship he created stability, something not experienced since 1914.
He demonstrated that democracy and strong leadership were
not mutually exclusive. He held antidemocratic forces at bay.
Although an authoritarian, Adenauer trained an entire generation in democratic methods. He was himself confronted and defeated democratically. He became an unforgotten father figure.

Henning Köhler

See also Allied High Commission to Germany; Allied Occu-
pation Statute; American-German Relations; American Oc-
cupation; Anglo-German Relations; The Basic Law; Berlin
Wall; Blank, Theodor; Blankenhorn, Herbert; Brentano,
Heinrich von; Catholicism, Political; Center Party; Christian
Democratic Union; Erhard, Ludwig; Federal Republic of
Germany; Federal Republic of Germany: Foreign Policy;
Franco-German Relations; German Treaty; Globke, Hans;
Heuss, Theodor; Lübke, Heinrich; NATO and Germany;
Postwar European Integration and Germany; Postwar Recon-

struction; Rearmament; Soviet-German Relations; Stalin Notes; Strauss, Franz Josef

References

Adenauer, Konrad. *Briefe.* Bearbeitet von Hans Peter Mensing. 4 vols. Berlin: Siedler, 1983.

———. *Erinnerungen.* 4 vols. Stuttgart: Deutsche Verlags-Anstalt, 1965–68.

———. *Teegespräche.* Bearbeitet von Hanns Jürgen Küsters. 3 vols. Berlin: Siedler, 1985–88.

Blumenwitz, Dieter et al. *Konrad Adenauer und seine Zeit: Politik und Persönlichkeit des ersten Bundeskanzlers.* 2 vols. Stuttgart: Deutsche Verlags-Anstalt, 1976.

Dönhoff, Marion Gräfin. *Foe into Friend: The Makers of the New Germany from Konrad Adenauer to Helmut Schmidt.* Trans. Gabriele Annan. New York, NY: St. Martin's Press, 1982.

Köhler, Henning. *Konrad Adenauer.* Berlin: Propyläen Verlag, 1994.

Prittie, Terence. *Konrad Adenauer, 1876–1967.* London: Tom Stacey Ltd., 1972.

Schwarz, Hans-Peter. *Adenauer: Der Aufstieg 1876–1952.* Stuttgart: Deutsche Verlags-Anstalt, 1986. Translated by Louise Willmot, *Konrad Adenauer: From the German Empire to the Federal Republic, 1876–1952.* Providence: Berghahn Books, 1995.

———. *Adenauer: Der Staatsmann 1952–1967.* Stuttgart: Deutsche Verlags-Anstalt, 1991.

Adler, Alfred (1870–1937)

Alfred Adler, an Austrian physician, founded the school of individual psychology. Born in Vienna and graduated from the University of Vienna Medical School in 1895, Adler was in private practice when he was invited by Sigmund Freud (1856–1939) to join a small group of colleagues interested in studying and promoting psychoanalysis. This group evolved into the Vienna Psychoanalytic Society, with Adler serving as president from 1910 to 1911.

Although an early supporter of Freud, Adler quickly developed ideas that departed from Freudian psychoanalysis. With the publication of *Studie über die Minderwertigkeit von Organen* (Organ inferiority and its physical compensation), 1907, for example, Adler presented a theory that linked organ inferiorities (a sense of deficiency in one or another organ) to the feelings of inferiority that played an essential role in personality development. This essay challenged Freud's ideas about the importance of the sex instinct in the development of personality and psychopathology.

Unable to reconcile his theories with Freud's work, Adler resigned from the Vienna Psychoanalytic Society in 1911 and quickly established an independent association, the Society for Individual Psychology. The first systematic treatment of his challenges to Freudian psychoanalysis was presented in his first book, *Über den nervösen Charakter* (The neurotic character), 1912, in which he suggested that the lifelong struggle to overcome feelings of inferiority was the principal motive underlying human behavior.

After his break with Freud, Adler became interested in working with children and their families. In the 1920s he established a number of child-guidance clinics in Austria. With the publication of books such as *Menschenkenntnis* (Understanding human nature), 1927, and *The Education of Children,* 1930, Adler achieved international recognition in the areas of child psychology and education. By the late 1930s, individual-psychology organizations thrived in various European and North American cities, including Berlin and Frankfurt. Adler emigrated to the United States in 1934, and died during a lecture tour to Scotland in 1937.

James D.A. Parker

See also Freud, Sigmund; Psychoanalysis; Psychology

References

Ansbacher, H.L. and R.R. Ansbacher, eds. *Adler: A Systematic Presentation in Selections from His Writings.* New York, NY: Harper and Row, 1964.

Bottome, P. *Alfred Adler: A Portrait from Life.* New York, NY: Vanguard Press, 1957.

Orgler, H. *Alfred Adler: The Man and His Work.* London: Sidgwick and Jackson, 1963.

Rattner, J. *Alfred Adler.* New York, NY: Ungar, 1983.

Stepansky, P.E. *In Freud's Shadow: Adler in Context.* Hillsdale, NJ: Analytic Press, 1983.

Adorno, Theodor Ludwig Wiesengrund (1903–69)

Theodor Adorno was born on September 11, 1903 in Frankfurt, son of the wealthy wine merchant Oskar Wiesengrund and Maria Calvelli-Adorno, a professional singer of Corsican and Genovese origin (whose name he later adopted).

As a founding member of the "Frankfurt School" of critical sociology, he is best known for his theoretical contributions to social thought, to the sociology of culture (including music, literature, and "mass culture"), to studies of prejudice and anti-Semitism, and to psychopathologies of modern civilization. He created a distinctive prose style eventually known as "Adorno Deutsch" (Adorno German)—a Hegelianized refusal to write directly or simply in a rhetorical effort to reproduce stylistically the dialectical nature of life and thought. Adorno unintentionally played a pivotal role in providing the theoretical grounding of the "New Left" during the 1960s in Europe and the United States, where his works, along with those of Max Horkheimer (1895–1973), Herbert Marcuse (1898–1979), Walter Benjamin (1890–1940), and (to some extent) Erich Fromm (1900–80), were widely read and employed for political and cultural ends. However, a humiliating public confrontation in 1969 with members of the German New Left, who believed that his position was elitist and counterrevolutionary, preceded his death by only a few months.

Adorno's precocity would have seemed "elitist" to virtually any period of history. He was educated in that "Buddenbrooks" atmosphere of Central European upper-bourgeois comfort, position, and correlated ambition that produced some of the most learned and intellectually adventurous scholars in recent Western history (e.g., Georg Lukács [1885–

1971], Karl Mannheim [1893–1947], Ernst Bloch [1885–1977], and Marcuse). He was simultaneously at home in the most technically arcane aspects of modern music (helping Thomas Mann with *Doktor Faustus*), philosophy, social theory, certain aspects of psychology, cultural history, modern languages—all in a way that is unimaginable today. His peers and friends were among the most revered social analysts of the century, and he was more theoretically adept and broadly original than most of this august group. Perhaps only Walter Benjamin, his close friend and sometime theoretical opponent, matched his theoretical imagination.

The principal intellectual contribution Adorno made might be said to hinge on his notion of "negative dialectics." Anchored in a unique reading of Hegel and Marx, and surely abetted by atonal musical theory, this idea held that analytical concepts that claim to subsume or "speak for" both the subject and the object in some totalistic sense are inherently false, misrepresenting the social or cognitive world. Genuine dialectics, and the enlargement of knowing that went with it, had to be negative—to participate in "the great refusal," the popular term coined by his friend Marcuse.

Yet, from apparently the other pole, Adorno also argued against positivist/empiricist social science, which accepts at face value "objective" the responses of interviewees as to questions that, by their nature, cannot capture the reified quality of commodified life. As in all his most creative work, he refused to take sides clearly with one simple position against another, insisting instead that the philosophical or sociological investigator resist the temptation to make apodictic assertions and instead trust in some "fearlessly passive" orientation to empirical reality. Ironically, though, and in a way Adorno would have appreciated, such a position inflamed his readers, positively or negatively, and became, in good dialectical fashion, anything but "passive."

Adorno's works were widely read and influential, and remain indispensable to an understanding of twentieth-century social analysis.

Alan Sica

See also Benjamin, Walter; Bloch, Ernst; Frankfurt School; Fromm, Erich; Horkheimer, Max; Lukács, Georg; Mannheim, Karl; Marcuse, Herbert; Sociology

References

Adorno, Gretel and Rolf Tiedemann, eds. *Gesammelte Schriften*. 20 vols. to date, with 23 planned. Frankfurt am Main: Suhrkamp Verlag, 1970–present.

Adorno, Theodor, L.W. *Aesthetic Theory*. Ed. Gretel Adorno and Rolf Tiedemann. Newly translated, edited, and with a translator's introduction by Robert Hullot-Kentor. Minneapolis, MN: University of Minnesota Press, 1997.

———. *Against Epistemology*. Cambridge, MA: MIT Press, 1983.

———. *Alban Berg: Master of the Smallest Link*. Cambridge: Cambridge University Press, 1991.

———. *Aspects of Sociology*. Boston, MA: Beacon Press, 1972.

———. *The Authoritarian Personality* (co-author). New York, NY: Harper, 1950.

———. *The Culture Industry: Selected Essays on Mass Culture*. London: Routledge, 1991.

——— with Max Horkheimer. *Dialectic of Enlightenment*. New York, NY: Seabury, 1972.

———. *Hegel: Three Studies*. Cambridge, MA: MIT, 1993.

———. *Introduction to the Sociology of Music*. New York, NY: Seabury, 1976.

———. *The Jargon of Enlightenment*. Evanston, IL: Northwestern University Press, 1973.

———. *Kierkegaard: Construction of an Aesthetic*. Minneapolis, MN: University of Minnesota Press, 1989.

———. *Mahler: A Musical Physiognomy*. Chicago, IL: University of Chicago Press, 1992.

———. *Minima Moralia: Reflections from Damaged Life*. London: NLB, 1974.

———. *Negative Dialectics*. New York, NY: Seabury, 1973.

———. *Notes to Literature*. 2 vols. New York, NY: Columbia University Press, 1991.

———. *Philosophy of Modern Music*. New York, NY: Seabury, 1973.

———. *The Positivist Dispute in German Sociology*. (sections) London: Heinemann, 1976.

———. *Prisms: Cultural Criticism and Society*. London: Spearman, 1967.

———. *Quasi Una Fantasia: Essays on Modern Music*. London: Verso, 1992.

Jameson, Fredric. *Marxism and Form*. Princeton, NJ: Princeton University Press, 1971.

Martin, Jay. *Adorno*. Cambridge, MA: Harvard University Press, 1984.

Rose, Gillian. *The Melancholy Science*. New York, NY: Columbia University Press, 1978.

Zuidervaart, Lambert. *Adorno's Aesthetic Theory*. Cambridge, MA: MIT Press, 1991.

AEG (General Electric) AG

In 1881, Emil Rathenau (1838-1915) observed the Edison electric lighting system at the Paris Electrical Exhibition. He acquired licenses for the Edison patents and, in 1883, established the Deutsche Edison Gesellschaft für angewandte Elektrizität. After signing a municipal supply contract, Rathenau began operating his first electric station, serving a city block, in 1884. In 1887, Deutsche Edison was reorganized as the Allgemeine Elektrizitäts-Gesellschaft (AEG), which became Germany's second-most-important electrical manufacturer.

The AEG established a number of subsidiaries to serve as customers for its electrical equipment. The Berliner Elektrizitätswerke, which supplied Berlin, was taken over by the city in 1915. The Allgemeine Local- und Strassenbahn-Gesellschaft functioned as an operating and financing company for electric traction. The AEG demonstrated the benefits of using alternating current (AC) for long-distance transmission at the Frankfurt Electrical Exhibition in 1891. Although attempts during the 1880s to divide the lighting business with

Siemens & Halske failed, the two electrical manufacturers established several joint subsidiaries, most notably Telefunken in 1903 for radios, Osram in 1919 for light bulbs, and Kraftwerk Union in 1973 for nuclear energy.

Before World War I, an AEG engineer, Georg Klingenberg (1870–1925), promoted a Prussian state system to regain control from competitors, especially Siemens, of electric generation for the AEG. It failed mainly due to the opposition of communal electric companies, which feared a loss of power control. After World War II, the AEG faced a crisis because its facilities were situated in Berlin and central Germany. It thereupon moved its headquarters to Frankfurt. In later years, the AEG avoided high-risk developments by transferring General Electric's (GE) light-water nuclear technology elsewhere (AEG had bought GE patent use rights). The test reactor that emerged in 1961 was based on GE's experience with boiling-water reactors. It produced steam for turbines directly in the reactor core, as did the AEG's first commercial nuclear power station (Gundremmingen). Encountering difficulties with GE, the AEG constructed the 670-megawatt Würgassen nuclear facility on its own, having resolved the developmental problems of boiling-water reactors in 1983. After merging with Telefunken, the AEG changed its name in 1967 to AEG-Telefunken. Facing a financial crisis in the early 1980s, AEG-Telefunken reorganized and in 1985 adopted its present name, AEG AG. In 1985, Daimler-Benz acquired a 56 percent interest in AEG; by 1993 it held 80.2 percent. Germany's second-largest electrical manufacturer is controlled by a holding company that includes Mercedes-Benz AG and Deutsche Aerospace AG.

Edmund N. Todd III

See also Daimler-Benz AG; Electricity; Rathenau, Walther; Siemens AG

References

Braun, Hans-Joachim and Walter Kaiser. *Energiewirtschaft, Automatisierung, Information seit 1914.* Propyläen Technikgeschichte, vol. 5. Ed. Wolfgang König. Berlin: Propyläen, 1992.

Feldenkirchen, Wilfried. *Werner von Siemens: Erfinder und internationaler Unternehmer.* Berlin: Siemens AG, 1992.

Jacob-Wendler, Gerhart. *Deutsche Elektroindustrie in Lateinamerika: Siemens und AEG, 1890–1914.* Stuttgart: Klett-Cotta, 1982.

Pohl, Manfred. *Emil Rathenau und die AEG.* Mainz: Hase & Koehler, 1988.

Siemens, Georg. *History of the House of Siemens.* Trans. A.F. Rodger and Lawrence N. Hole. 2 vols. Freiburg: Karl Alber, 1957.

Aeronautics

German aeronautics may be traced roughly to 1871. The first steps made by aeronautics pioneers in the 1870s followed two wholly different lines: Count Zeppelin's (1838–1917) work on dirigible airships (derived from contemporary French balloon technology), and Otto Lilienthal's (1848–96) glider experiments. Later aircraft motor technology was based on Hugo Junkers's (1859–1985) early work on thermodynamics at the Dessau gas works in the late 1880s. Scientific and engineering work proceeded in tandem.

World War I ended the first phase of passenger flight (with Zeppelin airships) and, like in other countries, caused the beginning of military aviation. The 1920s were marked by a boom of international and intercontinental passenger and mail aviation. The Junkers all-metal planes proved to be the first of a long line of aircraft, whereas the Dornier flying boats, after being the backbone of transatlantic air traffic, became obsolete in the 1930s. The Zeppelin airship went out of business after the catastrophe at Lakehurst, New Jersey, where the *Hindenburg* was destroyed by an explosion of its hydrogen tanks (1937).

The 1920s saw international cooperation in aviation and the aircraft industry. Restrictions imposed on Germany in the aftermath of World War I turned out to be an additional incentive for international cooperation in the military and industrial fields. The heavy rearmament instigated by the Nazi government in the pre–World War II years emphasized mass production of aircraft with existing technology. New developments, such as Heinkel's pioneering work in rocket and jet propulsion, took low priority; prototypes of several types of rocket and jet fighter planes existed by the end of the war but few saw service because of fuel shortages and Allied bombing of aircraft factories.

The postwar hiatus on aviation imposed by the Allied forces lasted until 1955. Subsequently, industrial facilities situated in the West slowly went into business again (e.g., Junkers, Messerschmitt, Heinkel, Dornier, Hamburger Flugzeugbau, VFW-Fokker, Siebel-ATG, and Focke-Wulf). The only newcomer was the Bölkow Developments Company, founded by Ludwig Bölkow (1912–), a former chief designer with the company of Willy Messerschmitt (1898–1978). By a series of mergers, Bölkow succeeded in establishing the firm of Messerschmitt-Bölkow-Blohm, which (together with its competitors VFW-Fokker and Dornier) was one of only three companies to survive the 1970s. Political necessity but even more the competition of American industry led to international (European) cooperative ventures (Panavia on the military side, Airbus for civilian aircraft). During the 1980s, the German aircraft industry was fully integrated into Deutsche Aerospace (DASA), a subsidiary of Daimler-Benz.

As in other countries, early research and engineering activities were undertaken by private organizations. After the example set by the Aeronautical Society of Great Britain, the Deutsche Verein zur Förderung der Luftfahrt (German Association for Advancement of Aeronautics) was founded in 1881. In 1912, the Wissenschaftliche Gesellschaft für Luftfahrt (Scientific Society for Aeronautics) followed. By government order it merged during 1937 with two other organizations into the Lilienthal Society for Aeronautical Research, which was re-established after World War II. In 1967, in the face of a declining membership and ensuing financial difficulties, it merged with the Society for Rocket Technology and Space to become the Deutsche Gesellschaft für Luft- und Raumfahrt (German Aerospace Society).

Systematic research into aerodynamics was the objective of the Modellversuchsanstalt für Motorluftschiffahrt und Flugtechnik (Model Research Institute for Motor Aeronautics and Aviation Technology) at Göttingen, established in 1907 by a private foundation. Its first director was Ludwig Prandtl, professor at the University of Göttingen. In 1918, the Institute became the famed Aerodynamische Versuchsanstalt (AVA; Aerodynamic Research Institute), affiliated with the Kaiser Wilhelm Society (called the Max Planck Society since 1948). The institute was merged in 1969 with the Deutsche Versuchsanstalt für Luftfahrt (German Aeronautics Experimental Station, also a private foundation since 1912) and the Deutsche Forschungsanstalt für Luftfahrt (German Aeronautics Research Institute before 1936) into the Deutsche Forschungs- und Versuchsanstalt für Luft- und Raumfahrt (German Aerospace Research and Development Organization).

Many industrial and research facilities had been located on the territory of the Soviet zone before 1945. Such establishments as had not been destroyed during the final phase of the war were integrated into the military and economic framework of Warsaw Pact and Comecon structures and mostly dismantled after reunification.

Wolfgang Kokott

See also Daimler-Benz AG; Dornier, Claude; Heinkel, Ernst; Junkers, Hugo; Lilienthal, Otto; Space; Vogt, Richard; Zeppelin, Ferdinand von

References

Bölkow, Ludwig, ed. *Ein Jahrhundert Flugzeuge: Geschichte und Technik des Fliegens.* Düsseldorf: VDI, 1990.

Brütting, Georg. *Das Buch der deutschen Fluggeschichte.* Vol. 3: *Die grosse Zeit der deutschen Luftfahrt bis 1945.* Stuttgart: Drei Brunnen, 1979.

Fritzsche, Peter. *A Nation of Fliers: German Aviation and the Popular Imagination.* Cambridge, MA: Harvard University Press, 1992.

Mondey, David, ed. *The International Encyclopedia of Aviation.* London: Octopus, 1977.

Supf, Peter. *Das Buch der deutschen Fluggeschichte.* 2 vols. Stuttgart: Drei Brunnen, 1956–58.

Trischler, Helmuth. *Luft- und Raumfahrtforschung in Deutschland 1900–1970. Politische Geschichte einer Wissenschaft.* Frankfurt am Main: Campus, 1992.

Wohl, Robert. *A Passion for Wings: Aviation and Western Imagination 1908-1918.* New Haven, CT: Yale University Press, 1994.

Aesthetics

If the idealist tradition has been a powerful but problematic legacy for modern German thinkers, the central role it ascribed to aesthetics has remained unchallenged. Modern philosophers in Germany, whatever their orientation, have ener-getically explored issues of artistic creation and reception as primary aspects of human experience.

Friedrich Nietzsche (1844–1900), the first major philosophical voice to emerge in Imperial Germany, mobilized the aesthetic in his attack on traditional academic philosophy. In *The Birth of Tragedy,* 1872, he took art as a source of redemption in a meaningless world; in his later work, he presented a radical aestheticism as an alternative to transcendent moral norms. An early dictum sums up Nietzsche's consistent position: "Only as an aesthetic phenomenon," he writes in the book on tragedy, "are existence and the world eternally justified."

Another challenge to traditional aesthetics was posed by the natural sciences, which sought to define alternative, nonphilosophical approaches to the subject. Gustav Fechner advocated an "aesthetics from below" drawing its data from controlled experiments. A more speculative psychological aesthetics ultimately had a greater influence, leading to the theory of "empathy" (*Einfühlung*) as systematized in Theodor Lipps's *Ästhetik* (Aesthetics), 1903–06, in which he explored aesthetic response as the projection of human emotions onto the inanimate forms of music, the visual arts, and language.

With phenomenology, the natural sciences' concern with perception emerged within a philosophical framework, with important consequences for aesthetics. In *Das literarische Kunstwerk* (The literary work of art), 1930, Roman Ingarden, a disciple of Edmund Husserl (1859–1938), sharply distinguished between a work of art, which is indeterminate, and the various possible "concretions" of it through the cognitive activity of a reader. Ingarden later applied his theories to other media. For the existential phenomenologist Martin Heidegger (1889–1976), issues of aesthetics were as central as they had been for Nietzsche. Heidegger saw hermeneutics or interpretation as the basic mode of human existence, and in "The Origins of the Work of Art," 1936, he explored how art offered access to this process, bringing, in effect, worlds into being.

In his *Wahrheit und Methode* (Truth and method), 1960, Hans-Georg Gadamer (1900–), like Heidegger, posited a nonconceptual truth content inherent in the work of art, but historicized the act of interpretation, grounding it in the context of a common tradition and the possibility of the "fusion of horizons." The different phenomenological approaches were extended and synthesized in the reception aesthetics of the Constance School. Wolfgang Iser's *Der Akt des Lesens: Theorie ästhetischer Wirkung,* 1975 (published as *The Act of Reading,* 1976) described the interaction between a constructive reader and the clues provided by a literary text, and the studies of Hans Robert Jauss traced the historical nature of the reception of works of various media.

A second major strain in twentieth-century aesthetics has been sociological and primarily Marxist. An orthodox Marxist aesthetic was developed in the German discourse by Georg Lukács (1885–1971), who, drawing on the literature of the nineteenth century, articulated a normative notion of realism. In works from the 1930s and after, Lukács identified the truth content of literature as its ability to reflect political and economic realities, regardless of the author's own political position. The work of Theodor Adorno (1903–69), culminating in *Ästhetische Theorie* (published as *Aesthetic Theory*), 1970, represented a different sort of Marxist aesthetics, one that rejected the reduction of the artwork to its context and stressed instead immanent qualities of form. Taking as his model the hermetic works of twentieth-century artists, he identified a socially critical moment of modernism in the anti-mimetic rejection of identity with the social *status quo*, and a utopian moment in the privacy of aesthetic experience as resistance to an administered world. Through his notion of "anticipatory illumination" in the *Das Prinzip Hoffnung* (published as *Principle of Hope*), 1938-47, Ernst Bloch (1885–1977) highlighted the utopian potential inherent in art to wake a revolutionary consciousness by the articulation of alternative realities. In *Das Kunstwerk im Zeitalter seiner technischen Reproduzierbarkeit* (The work of art in the age of mechanical reproduction), 1936, one of the most widely read works of twentieth-century aesthetics, Walter Benjamin (1892–1940) sought to define the political potential of new, technologized modes of artistic production and reception, at the same time introducing the notion of "aura" to describe the traditional, and perhaps obsolete, relation to aesthetic objects. Common to all these positions was their development outside the official academy and their emergence from an intense involvement with contemporary political and artistic tendencies.

Frederic J. Schwartz

See also Adorno, Theodor; Benjamin, Walter; Bloch, Ernst; Gadamer, Hans-Georg; Heidegger, Martin; Husserl, Edmund; Literary Criticism; Lukács, Georg; Nietzsche, Friedrich; Painting; Sculpture

References

Beardsley, Monroe C. *Aesthetics from Classical Greece to the Present: A Short History*. New York, NY: Macmillan, 1966.
Holub, Robert C. *Reception Theory: A Critical Introduction*. London: Methuen, 1984.
Jameson, Fredric. *Marxism and Form: Twentieth-Century Dialectical Theories of Literature*. Princeton, NJ: Princeton University Press, 1971.
Kaufmann, Walter. *Niezsche: Philosopher, Psychologist, Antichrist*. 4th ed. Princeton, NJ: Princeton University Press, 1974.
Palmer, Richard D. *Hermeneutics: Interpretation Theory in Schleiermacher, Dilthey, Heidegger and Gadamer*. Evanston, IL: Northwestern University Press, 1969.

Agrarian Leagues

Agrarian leagues influence life and structures in modern societies in many important ways. Through them, farmers try to obtain a hearing for their interests, especially in the political arena. They develop programs and ideologies, seek to influence public opinion, mobilize members and sympathizers, and pressure governments, parliaments, and parties. Primarily, such organizations seek to redistribute financial burdens onto other groups and thereby keep as much in their own pocket as possible.

In Germany, the tradition of agrarian leagues dates to the late eighteenth and early nineteenth centuries. Aristocrats, bourgeois rentiers, and large landowners, plus some academics, pastors, and teachers, would form economic organizations and rural clubs. They sought to foster agricultural progress by discussions of scientific farming, rationalization, utilization of machinery, market strategies, and education. They organized competitions and exhibitions. Often the impetus came from state bureaucrats who wanted to foster their own agrarian and political views. At the end of the nineteenth century, rural chambers followed in this tradition: as involuntary organizations, they drew many farmers of a region, yet as publicly registered organizations they were under state regulation. They operated in a dual role: as representatives of particular interests and as an extended arm of the state.

Next to these quasi-official institutions, some independent occupationally based organizations emerged in the second half of the century. The first were the Christian peasants' leagues in the Catholic areas. They supported the Catholic Church during the *Kulturkampf* as well as against urban and industrial liberalism. Later they agitated against the Social Democrats, putting the raising of the material and ethical–religious standard of the peasantry on their agenda and propagating cooperatives and self-help. After 1893, the Bund der Landwirte (Agrarian League) appeared, partly competing and partly cooperating with the older leagues. The Bund had its main support in the Protestant regions. In a short time it became a dynamic, well-organized mass movement that helped to politicize rural society and became dominant among the agrarian leagues.

For historians, the Bund der Landwirte serves as the prototype of the qualitatively new, robust, and hands-on interest group. It combined modern methods of leadership and propaganda techniques with reactionary ideologies and anti-Semitic resentments (the latter being firmly established in the rural population). Though peasants and farmers predominated, the power brokers of the league were the large landowners, the *Junkers*. They wished to protect German agriculture by tariffs and subsidies against lower-cost competition from abroad. In addition, they tried to use political means to compensate for the loss of economic power that the agrarian sector suffered during the industrialization process. Partners for this enterprise were found in the various parts of the bureaucracy, the National Liberals, the middle-class leagues, and the other associations, especially the conservatives, who generally controlled the Agrarian League. Conservative politics thus became synonymous with agrarian interest politics.

Although the room to maneuver became restricted by debts and inflation after World War I for the organized agrarian economy, little changed in the pattern of lobbying established during the Imperial era. The forms but not the substance of interest representation changed. In 1921, the Reichslandbund replaced the Bund der Landwirte. At first it supported the German National People's Party (DNVP), the successor of the Conservatives; after 1930, it increasingly supported the Nazis. In 1933, this league was eliminated in the *Gleichschaltung* (coordination) and became part of the Reichsnährstand (Reich Food Estate). The latter served as an occupational representative and state-supporting organization that made the peasants into "handmaidens" for war preparations and the war economy.

In West Germany, the Deutscher Bauernbund (German Farmers Association) and the chambers of agriculture adroitly took up the earlier organizational and economic-political traditions to win subsidies. They successfully moved to the international level in the Common Market. In Brussels, as in Bonn, the leagues have influenced prices, set production quotas, and introduced market controls applied to individual states.

Jens Flemming

See also Agriculture; Anti-Semitism; Aristocracy; Darré, R. Walther; German Conservative Party; German National People's Party; Lübke, Heinrich; Peasantry

References

Ackermann, Paul. *Der Deutsche Bauernverband im politischen Kräftespiel der Bundesrepublik: Die Einflussnahme des DBV auf die Entscheidung über den europäischen Getreidepreis.* Tübingen: Mohr, 1970.

Farquharson, John E. *The Plough and the Swastika: The NSDAP and Agriculture in Germany 1928-1945.* London: Sage, 1976.

Flemming, Jens. *Landwirtschaftliche Interessen und Demokratie: Ländliche Gesellschaft, Agararverbände und Staat 1890–1925.* Bonn: Neue Gesellschaft, 1978.

Gessner, Dieter. *Agrarverbände in der Weimarer Republik: Wirtschaftliche und soziale Voraussetzungen agrarkonservativer Politik vor 1933.* Düsseldorf: Droste, 1976.

Moeller, Robert G. *German Peasants and Agrarian Politics, 1914–1924: The Rhineland and Westphalia.* Chapel Hill, NC: University of North Carolina Press, 1986.

———, ed. *Peasants and Lords in Modern Germany: Recent Studies in Agricultural History.* Boston, MA: Allen and Unwin, 1986.

Puhle, Hans-Jürgen. *Agrarische Interessenpolitik und preussischer Konservatismus im Wilhelminischen Reich (1893–1914): Ein Beitrag zur Analyse des Nationalismus in Deutschland am Beispiel des Bundes der Landwirte und der Deutsch-Konservativen Partei.* 2nd ed. Bonn: Neue Gesellschaft, 1975.

Schumacher, Martin. *Land und Politik: Eine Untersuchung über politische Parteien und agrarische Interessen 1914–1924.* Düsseldorf: Droste, 1978.

Agriculture

In modern Germany, the agricultural sector has played a significant role in economic development. The political influence of large landowners and small peasants has been of enormous consequence throughout the period. The long-term trend since the late nineteenth century has been the reduction of agriculture's proportion of gross national product (GNP) and of farmers as a proportion of the working population.

Prior to 1945, large landed estates predominated east of the River Elbe; some were subdivided into leased farms. In much of northern, central, and southern Germany, middle-size, owner-occupied farms were the norm. In parts of the Rhineland, parceled smallholdings prevailed in agriculture. There, small and large cultivators grew staples, such as grains, potatoes, and root crops. The eastern territories developed large-scale rye production. Farmers in Bavaria grew wheat. Schleswig-Holstein in the north and Alpine Swabia in the south raised livestock and engaged in dairy production. Specialty crops also flourished: viniculture in the Rhineland, Franconia, and the southwest, hops in Bavaria, and tobacco in Baden and the Rhine-Palatinate.

Chancellor Otto von Bismarck's Empire was allegedly built on iron and rye. The rye-producing *Junker* landlords of eastern Germany played a political role disproportionate to their small numbers. They defended their own economic interests by supporting Bismarck's protective agricultural tariffs. There has been much debate over the extent to which the *Junkers* were agrarian capitalist entrepreneurs. Undoubtedly, they derived much profit from grain exports and from the tariff constraints imposed on imports. When Bismarck's successor, Leo von Caprivi, embarked on a more liberal bilateral trade policy, the *Junkers* launched a vociferous protection campaign, backed by smaller peasant farmers elsewhere in Germany. The farmers' organization, the Agrarian League, influenced the course of rural politics in much of Protestant Germany, and in Catholic areas as well.

Prior to World War I, various nongovernmental agrarian organizations had sponsored technical improvements in German agriculture. The exigencies of World War I and the Allied blockade necessitated the establishment of nationwide and regional authorities with wide-ranging responsibilities for determining production, setting prices, and requisitioning produce. The War Food Office (Kriegsernährungsamt) came to be the principal regulating agency during World War I. The Weimar Republic established new agricultural ministries and other authorities at the national and regional level, commencing with the Reich Ministry for Food and Agriculture in 1920. Stringent controls caused widespread agrarian protests. This period coincided with the inflation of 1923. Farmers were angry and well-organized at a time when they were generally advantaged in comparison with most other sectors of society.

The postinflation period after 1924 witnessed a rapid return to the relative financial constraints that had begun before 1914. Many small German farmers became insolvent due to their inability to compete with small dairy producers in Denmark and the Netherlands and with larger-scale grain exporters overseas. A general decline in world agricultural prices after the mid-1920s further eroded their economic position. Large producers were also affected by these conditions, but they were able to reap maximum benefits from state farming assistance. The "eastern aid" (*Osthilfe*) to landowners east of the Elbe River proved controversial among Germany's urban population and smaller farmers in the south and west. Many of the latter were facing financial ruin by the early 1930s. They proved susceptible to the populist blandishments of the Nazis, who combined a concern for the economic plight of small producers with rhetoric extolling German peasant traditions and racial strength. Most Protestant peasants and many of their Catholic counterparts contributed to the electoral successes of the Nazis and the advent of Adolf Hitler.

The Nazi regime emphasized the need to liberate agriculture from debt and uncertain prices. Farmers' fortunes revived in the later 1930s. However, controls by the state in the form of the Reich Hereditary Farm Law (Reichserbhofgesetz) of 1933, the battle of production (Erzeugungsschlacht) of the Reich Food Estate (Reichsnährstand), and Göring's Four-Year Plan, starting in 1936, revived peasant complaints about coercion from above. Nazi rhetoric that hailed the peasantry as a "new nobility of blood and soil" was belied by the forced flight of labor from the land into burgeoning industrial production centers. The war in 1939 brought few problems to German agriculture at first. The country was better prepared than it had been in 1914. In subsequent years, government controls, manpower losses, and the deterioration of land and equipment took their toll as they had in World War I. The final phase of the war damaged agricultural land and property in the battle zones, particularly as the Soviet army advanced westward through Brandenburg.

The division of Germany into occupation zones in 1945 and the loss of all territory east of the Oder-Neisse line marked an important break in the history of German agriculture. In the territories now administered by the Russians and the Poles, and in the Soviet zone of Germany, the *Junker* estate-owners had their properties expropriated swiftly and completely. In 1945 and 1946 a land reform (*Bodenreform*) in the Soviet zone redistributed the property of all those owning land in excess of 100 hectares and of those deemed prominent Nazis and/or war criminals. The new landholding pattern included a core of established middle-size farmers, especially in Thuringia. Previously landless farm laborers, or those who had fled westward in the final stages of the war, received tiny five-hectare plots. Many farmers were unable to fulfill the delivery requirements imposed on them by the Soviet authorities.

The land reform had several purposes—not least to terminate *Junker* power once and for all, and to create a rural political base for the Communists. But this was only an interim measure. In the late 1940s, the Soviets introduced cooperative structures, which made the smallholders dependent on centralized dispensation of machinery. In the early 1950s, the East German government (GDR) renewed its attack on so-called "large peasants" (those with over 20 hectares) and promoted agricultural cooperatives (*Landwirtschaftliche Produktionsgenossenschaften;* LPGs). Collectivization proved a slow process, completed by compulsion in 1959 and 1960. The rural population in East Germany endured immense pressures. Signs of unrest appeared, including westward flight, which was stemmed in August 1961 by the building of the Berlin Wall.

In the early 1960s, the LPGs became enlarged and specialized. Neighboring LPGs were amalgamated. In the second half of the 1970s, grain and livestock production were separated—a calamitous measure for efficient production and for the rural environment. This policy was partly reversed in the 1980s. The rural population of East Germany remained dis-

Farm near Buxtehude in northern Germany. Courtesy of Inter Nationes, Bonn.

proportionately large, because LPGs encompassed not only peasants directly involved in farming but also those who were active in the rural infrastructure of education, administration, and political supervision. The pressure to leave the country-side was reduced by subsidized, stable produce prices and markets and by housing difficulties in the towns. The agricultural proportion of the population nevertheless declined from 17.0 percent in 1960 to 10.8 percent by the mid-1980s. East German agriculture had little scope for private enterprise, although private plots worked by cooperative farmers were a major source of eggs and fruit.

After 1945, Germany's western occupation zones faced desperate food shortages, but no radical change ensued in the structure of agricultural property or production. Early discussion of land reform was abandoned, but over subsequent decades, many parts of West Germany instituted *Flurbereinigung* (land reparceling) measures, not to challenge private property, but to rationalize the use of fragmented and widely dispersed holdings. These measures generally increased the size of holdings and reduced the agricultural proportion of West Germany's population, a trend encouraged by West Germany's industrial successes. By 1984, only 5.4 percent of the population was engaged in agriculture.

In West Germany, agriculture comprised less than two percent of GNP, but subsidies from the Common Agricultural Policy of the European Community improved its productivity dramatically. Wheat yields in tons per hectare in West and East Germany in 1950 were 2.58 and 2.43, respectively. By 1988, the gap had widened to 6.84 in West Germany and 4.83 in the east. The rising quality of West German produce, coupled with a fairly resilient domestic demand for German foods, brought prosperity to most rural areas. Some produce also came to have a significant export potential, German wines and beers in particular. Prosperity and the decline of the agricultural population wrought enormous changes in West German villages and small towns, not always to their aesthetic or social advantage.

German economic and currency union in July 1990, followed by the full political incorporation of the German Democratic Republic (GDR) into the Federal Republic of Germany in October, brought an immediate crisis to East German agriculture. Home demand plunged, to the advantage of West German suppliers. Suddenly, the LPGs were faced with market-determined prices and competition with Western packaging and distribution expertise. Rural unemployment soared. There was also the threat of the LPGs being dismantled by those who wished to withdraw their property from the collective and by those who sought restitution of their properties seized during the GDR years. Only the land reform of the occupation years remained firmly in place.

Jonathan Osmond

See also Agrarian Leagues; Anti-Semitism; Aristocracy; Darré, R. Walther; David, Eduard; Food; Four-Year Plan; German Conservative Party; German National People's Party; Heim, Georg; Industrialization; Lübke, Heinrich; Peasantry; Protectionism; Urbanization

References

Corni, Gustavo. *Hitler and the Peasants: Agrarian Policy of the Third Reich, 1930–1939.* New York, NY: Berg, 1990.

Evans, Richard J. and W.R. Lee, eds. *The German Peasantry: Conflict and Community in Rural Society from the Eighteenth to the Twentieth Centuries.* London: Croom Helm, 1986.

Farquharson, John E. *The Plough and the Swastika: The NSDAP and Agriculture in Germany 1928-45.* London: Sage, 1976.

———. *The Western Allies and the Politics of Food: Agrarian Management in Postwar Germany.* Leamington Spa: Berg, 1985.

Gerschenkron, Alexander. *Bread and Democracy in Germany.* Ithaca, NY: Cornell University Press, 1989.

Henning, Friedrich-Wilhelm. *Landwirtschaft und ländliche Gesellschaft in Deutschland.* Vol. 2: *1750 bis 1976.* Paderborn: Schöningh, 1978.

Hess, Klaus. *Junker und bürgerliche Grossgrundbesitzer im Kaiserreich: Landwirtschaftlicher Grossbetrieb, Grossgrundbesitz und Familienfideikommiss in Preussen (1867/71–1914).* Stuttgart: Steiner, 1990.

Klein, Ernst. *Geschichte der deutschen Landwirtschaft im Industriezeitalter.* Wiesbaden: Steiner, 1973.

Moeller, Robert G. *German Peasants and Agrarian Politics, 1914–1924: The Rhineland and Westphalia.* Chapel Hill, NC: University of North Carolina Press, 1986.

———, ed. *Peasants and Lords in Modern Germany: Recent Studies in Agricultural History.* Boston, MA: Allen & Unwin, 1986.

Osmond, Jonathan. *Rural Protest in the Weimar Republic: The Free Peasantry in the Rhineland and Bavaria.* New York, NY: St. Martin's Press, 1993.

Sandford, Gregory W. *From Hitler to Ulbricht: The Communist Reconstruction of East Germany, 1945–46.* Princeton, NJ: Princeton University Press, 1983.

Air Force (Luftwaffe)

German military air power began modestly before 1914, but during World War I it developed rapidly to become a major force engaged in reconnaissance, in air combat over the front lines, and in long-range bombing, which was directed at London from 1915 to 1918. At the end of the war the force was disbanded, and Germany was denied an air force under the terms of the Treaty of Versailles. In 1933, Adolf Hitler authorized the secret establishment of new air forces, and in 1935 the new service was officially established. By 1939 it was the most technically advanced and formidable air weapon in the world. The air force contributed decisively to the lightning victories of 1939–41. But by the middle of the war, problems of production, technical development, and strategic planning reduced its effectiveness. In 1944, it was overwhelmed by the great numerical superiority of the Allied powers, and by the bombing offensive in particular. The air force was defeated almost a year before Germany finally surrendered.

During the 1930s, the German air force prepared largely for a combined role with the German army as a tactical, battlefield force. Very little attention was given to air-sea cooperation, a weakness that persisted into the war. Air force leaders, particularly the first chief of staff, Colonel Walter Wever, who died in 1936, also hoped to develop a long-range bombing capability once the necessary technology was available. In 1938, a new generation of long-range heavy bombers was authorized by the commander in chief, Hermann Göring (1893–1946), but constant technical difficulties held up their introduction and no serious independent bombing campaign could be mounted between 1939 and 1945.

Under the direction of successive chiefs of staff, most notably Hans Jeschonnek (chief from 1939–43), air-army cooperation reached a high level of tactical sophistication. The air forces played a crucial part, together with mobile infantry and tanks, in the new battle strategy of the armored punch, which involved fast-moving concentrations of armor and aircraft with massive firepower. Behind the punch lay large numbers of medium bombers whose task it was to attack the rear of the enemy line, destroying airfields, supply lines, stores, and reinforcements. The strategy worked well in all the major land campaigns to 1942.

The concentration on air-army cooperation left the German air force less well equipped for other tasks. The air attack on Great Britain in 1940 failed to defeat the Royal Air Force or compel the British to seek terms. When the Allied bombing offensive against Germany began in earnest in 1942, Germany had only a rudimentary air defense system and far too few fighters, most of which were engaged on the eastern front. Under General Kammhuber, a line of air defenses—fighters, anti-aircraft guns, and radar—was set up defending northern Germany, but the defensive effort drew aircraft away from the eastern front and led to a fragmentation of German air forces. The result was failure on all fronts. Bombing overwhelmed the German fighter forces following the "Big Week" attack on the German aircraft industry in the spring of 1944, and the Allied long-range fighter broke the back of German air power in the summer. For D-Day, June 6, 1944, the German air forces could muster only 500 aircraft against the 12,000 of the Allies on the western front.

Aircraft production was the chief factor that affected the wartime air force. Under the control of Colonel Ernst Udet, production stagnated between 1939 and 1942, and the new generation of German fighters and bombers failed for the most part to materialize. In 1942, aircraft output was taken over by Field Marshal Erhard Milch (1892–1972), state secretary in the Air Ministry since 1933. Production was rationalized and expanded, but by that time there was too much ground to make up. In 1944, Germany produced 39,000 aircraft, but most were destroyed by the enemy at the factories, in transit, or after only a few hours of combat.

Hitler blamed the air force for losing the war. In the autumn of 1944, he tried to disband it in order to distribute its manpower to the army. Göring persuaded him to keep the air force, but its contribution to the final defense of Germany was slight, despite the development of the first jet aircraft, the Messerschmitt Me 262, and the use of the V-2 rockets.

In 1945, the Allies once again denied Germany a peacetime air force. Not until 1957, and the founding of the Bundeswehr, did West Germany regain an air force, which became integrated into the NATO defense system.

Richard J. Overy

See also Allied Bombing; Federal Republic of Germany: Armed Forces; Göring, Hermann; Hitler, Adolf; Milch, Erhard; National Socialist Germany: Military; NATO and Germany; Sperrle, Hugo; World War II

References

Boog, Horst. *Die deutsche Luftwaffenführung, 1935–1945*. Stuttgart: Deutsche Verlags-Anstalt, 1982.

British Air Ministry. *The Rise and Fall of the German Air Force, 1933–1945*. London: Air Ministry, 1948 (reissued, Arms and Armour Press, 1983).

Cooper, Matthew. *The German Air Force, 1933–1945: An Anatomy of Failure*. London: Jane's, 1981.

Homze, Edward L. *Arming the Luftwaffe: The Reich Air Ministry and the German Aircraft Industry 1919–1939*. Lincoln, NE: University of Nebraska Press, 1976.

Murray, Williamson. *Luftwaffe: Strategy for Defeat 1933–1945*. London: George Allen and Unwin, 1985.

Nielsen, Andreas. *The German Air Force General Staff*. United States Air Force Historical Studies, No. 173. New York, NY: Arno Press, 1959.

Overy, Richard J. *The Air War 1939–1945*. London: Europa, 1980.

Suchenwirth, Richard. *The Development of the German Air Force 1919–1939*. United States Air Force Historical Studies No. 160. New York, NY: Arno Press, 1968.

Alcohol

Beer, wine, and distilled beverages have been produced and consumed in German-speaking Central Europe for centuries. Each of these beverages has played important economic roles locally, regionally, and nationally. At the same time, alcohol consumption has long been part of the German social fabric. In the last decade, historians and other social scientists have focused increasingly on alcohol consumption and drinking patterns as important indicators of social differentiation and cultural identity within German society. The period of rapid social, economic, and political change that marked the second half of the nineteenth century was accompanied by significant shifts in drinking behavior and the larger context in which it occurred. This confluence of major historical forces temporarily elevated what contemporaries called *Die Alkoholfrage* (the drink question) to the status of a major public issue that reflected and shaped discussions of a broad range of major social issues central to the emergence of an industrial society.

The level of public concern with the "Drink Question" may be traced to the reemergence of German temperance organizations in the 1880s, but despite the explosion of published material on the subject and the attention of government officials, the realities and nuances of actual drinking behavior are harder to discern. Historians have generally relied on the interpretation of per capita consumption data, derived primarily from government statistics maintained to enforce the state's traditional interest in taxing alcoholic beverages. Although such data fail to capture illicit domestic production and other forms of evasion, the aggregate trend information they provide is generally regarded as indicative of underlying patterns of consumption. Aggregate consumption data can be supplemented by more fragmentary quantitative information, such as family budget studies, and by abundant contemporary observations about drinking behavior, particularly that of the working class.

The facts appear to be that alcohol consumption reached an all-time high in Germany in the early 1870s at approximately four gallons of absolute alcohol (*i.e.,* pure ethanol content) per capita aged 15 and above, with significant increases in spirits, beer, and wine consumption from the 1850s. Spirits was the predominant beverage as a source of alcohol throughout this period by a factor of about 2:1 compared to beer. On the national scale, wine was relatively insignificant.

From the late 1870s, total alcohol consumed gradually declined, with an important shift in the relative importance of beer and spirits as a source of alcohol intake, with beer steadily increasing in importance and spirits steadily decreasing. At the end of the first decade of the twentieth century, however, the per capita consumption of both beverages began to decline, creating a much more rapid reduction in overall levels of alcohol consumption that was reinforced by the social, economic, and political dislocations of the period of the two world wars. Consumption rose rapidly in the first three post–World War II decades, led by beer and wine. By the late 1970s, per capita consumption had slightly surpassed the pre–World War I levels and then began a gradual decline in the 1980s.

The nineteenth-century pattern of consumption has been interpreted in the context of industrial and urban development with an emphasis on the drinking behavior of the working classes. Alcohol played important dietary and social roles, especially for the working-class male. With increasing purchasing power and few alternatives, workers spent substantial portions of their income on drink. This was not primarily the drinking of despair portrayed in popular stereotypes of a downtrodden and demoralized working class, but rather the satisfaction of social and physiological needs on and off the job in conventional ways—through drink and the social interactions it afforded—in a rapidly changing environment that made drinking more public and potentially more disruptive.

Although they did not embrace total abstinence and prohibition, middle-class observers were increasingly critical of working-class drinking behavior and associated it with all the ills of the industrial era, from political disobedience to poverty. By the early years of the twentieth century, working-class drinkers were investing their resources increasingly in alternative forms of consumption, and working-class drink-

ing probably became less distinctive in its intensity, especially in meeting basic physiological needs. After the world wars, what had once been a prominent public issue on the social and political agenda of the nation was now treated much more as an individual medical problem. In the meantime, with the postwar economic recovery, the enjoyment of alcoholic beverages had become a common feature of an increasingly prosperous consumer economy.

James S. Roberts

See also Food; Morality; Temperance Movements; Workers' Culture

References

Heggen, Alfred. *Alkohol und bürgerliche Gesellschaft im 19. Jahrhundert.* Berlin: Colloquium Verlag, 1988.

Hoffmann, W.G. *Das Wachstum der deutschen Wirtschaft seit der Mitte des 19. Jahrhunderts.* Berlin: Springer, 1965.

Roberts, Jarmes S. "Der Alkoholkonsum deutscher Arbeiter im 19. Jahrhundert." *Geschichte und Gesellschaft* 6 (1980), 220–42.

———. *Drink. Temperance and the Working Class in Nineteenth Century Germany.* Boston, MA: George Allen and Unwin, 1984.

Spode, Hasso. *Die Macht der Trunkenheit: Kultur- und Sozialgeschichte des Alkohols in Deutschland.* Opladen: Leske and Budrich, 1993.

Wyrwa, Ulrich. *Branntwein und "echtes" Bier: Die Trinkkultur der Hamburger Arbeiter im 19. Jahrhundert.* Hamburg: Junius, 1990.

Allied Bombing (1939–45)

British plans for a strategic bombing offensive against Germany were well advanced when World War II began. The important sectors of the German war economy—steel, oil, electric power, armaments and aircraft factories, and transportation networks—had been identified, and the most important plants and other facilities noted. American planners would produce essentially similar lists between 1939 and 1941. Optimists hoped that the threat of strong blows delivered early in the war might act as a deterrent, but they also thought if deterrence failed and hostilities broke out, that the combination of severe damage to the enemy's war economy and accompanying civilian casualties could bring victory quickly and relatively cheaply.

These plans, however, were beyond the capabilities of Bomber Command in September 1939 (it mobilized only 349 front-line machines, all of them twin-engined). The plans also did not fit comfortably with the intentions of the British government. Fearing what the Luftwaffe could do to London, the Cabinet imposed severe constraints on the kinds of targets the Royal Air Force could attack, and not until the late summer of 1940, when France had fallen and Great Britain was under attack, did the gloves come off. Although Berlin was bombed several times from late August, Bomber Command and the Air Staff still believed that best results would come from attacking specific industrial installations—attacks which, by now, were

Römerberg, Frankfurt am Main, 1945. Courtesy of Inter Nationes, Bonn.

invariably carried out by night, experience having proved that it was much too risky to penetrate German air space by day.

Lacking electronic navigation aids, night bombing proved woefully inaccurate; and following a study conducted in the summer of 1941, which found that over the Ruhr industrial basin only one bomber in ten came within five miles of the objective, the thrust of the British bombing offensive changed. Everyone hoped that the development of radio and radar aids to navigation and blind-bombing devices would make precision night bombing possible sometime in the future. In the interim, Bomber Command undertook what came to be known as "area bombing." The target would be an entire German city, and the object of the attack would increasingly be the destruction of the morale of the German civilian population through "de-housing," injury, or death. If physical damage to industrial plants also occurred, so much the better. By 1942, when the area campaign began, four-engined heavy bombers—Halifaxes and Lancasters—were replacing the smaller twin-engined machines. These planes could carry bigger payloads, larger bombs, and more effective incendiary devices.

If the thousand-bomber operation against Cologne at the end of May 1942 was the symbolic starting point for large area raids, the five-month Battle of Berlin, conducted from November 1943 to March 1944—which cost Bomber Command just over 500 crews (about 3,500 men) killed or taken prisoner—best epitomized the struggle: a dangerous and exhausting aerial slugging match that produced hundreds of acres of devastation, yet had relatively little impact on German war production. Bomber Command's worst night came during the Battle of Berlin. On March 31, 1944,

the German defenses shot down ninety-five bombers.

In the spring and summer of 1944, Bomber Command prepared the way for, and then supported, the D-Day landings. Subsequently, exploiting several different navigation aids, it conducted a number of accurate raids against oil refineries and other precision targets between September 1944 and May 1945. But the area raids continued. The first great firestorm—the product of concentrated bombing and abnormal weather conditions—had been produced at Hamburg in July 1943. This raid killed some 40,000 civilians. In February 1945, similar destruction leveled Dresden, an old city with few important military or economic objectives. About half a million Germans died as a result of Allied bombings. Bomber Command suffered 47,000 fatal casualties in operations.

The first American bomber crews arrived in England in 1942. Unlike the RAF, the United States Army Air Forces were determined to attack precise military objectives by day, but until long-range fighter escorts were made available in large numbers in the winter of 1943–44, their efforts were largely ineffective and costly. Beginning in January 1944, the Americans launched crushing blows against the German aircraft industry, severely weakened the German day-fighter force in the process, and then took on the enemy's oil industry, ball bearing factories, transportation networks, and arms factories. These attacks produced much more disruption in the German war economy than the RAF's nighttime area raids, but at times, particularly in bad weather, the Americans also launched daylight area raids.

Steve Harris

See also Air Force; Postwar Reconstruction; World War II

References

Anders, Gebhard. *History of the German Night Fighter Force, 1917–1945*. London: Jane's, 1976.

Craven, W.F. and J.L. Cate. *The Army Air Forces in World War II*. 4 vols. Chicago, IL: University of Chicago Press, 1949.

Middlebrook, Martin and Chris Everitt. *The Bomber Command War Diaries: An Operational Reference Book, 1939–1945*. Harmondsworth: Penguin, 1985.

Murray, Williamson. *Luftwaffe*. Baltimore, MD: Nautical and Aviation Publishing Company, 1985.

Overy, R.J. *The Air War 1939–1945*. London: Europa, 1980.

Terraine, John. *A Time for Courage: The Royal Air Force in the European War, 1939–1945*. New York, NY: Macmillan, 1985.

Webster, Sir Charles and Noble Frankland. *The Strategic Air Offensive against Germany, 1939–1945*. 4 vols. London: Her Majesty's Stationery Office, 1961.

Allied High Commission to Germany (1949–55)

At the Washington Conference of Western foreign ministers in April 1949, the United States, Great Britain, and France agreed to create the Allied High Commission (AHC), a civilian body that would replace military government for the newly created Federal Republic of Germany (FRG). The American State Department had planned to end direct military rule of West Germany as early as 1947, but increased Cold War tensions, culminating in the Berlin Blockade (June 1948–May 1949), caused a delay.

The Allied High Commission was to coordinate the policies of the three Western occupying powers while supervising the German government of Chancellor Konrad Adenauer. Under the Allied Occupation Statute the AHC retained "supreme authority" in West Germany and veto power over most decisions. In the most literal sense, the AHC looked down upon the Bonn government from its headquarters in the Petersberg Hotel in the Siebengebirge, just south of Bonn.

The Allied High Commission formally came into existence on September 21, 1949, and its limits as a supervising organization became clear almost immediately. Adenauer used interviews with Western journalists to bypass the AHC and speak directly to Western publics, urging a more lenient policy toward his government in order to bring the Germans onto the Western side in the Cold War. His early meetings with the AHC were marked by sharp clashes, as Adenauer insisted on his government's final authority over such matters as the German exchange rate, civil service reform, and tax legislation.

Differences within the AHC also became clear, with the French arguing for strict control and the United States and Great Britain favoring a more trusting policy. As early as November 1949, Adenauer exploited these differences to force a foreign ministers' meeting and obtained the Petersberg Agreement, which effectively ended the dismantling of German industries. The intensification of the Cold War in 1950 with the outbreak of conflict in Korea further strengthened Adenauer's hand, especially after the United States decided to proceed with German rearmament. By September 1951, the

Western powers had agreed in principle to eliminate the AHC and turn over most of its powers to the Germans.

The AHC played a critical role in negotiating the contractual agreements that replaced the occupation in the Germany Treaty (Deutschlandvertrag) of May 1952. The AHC functioned until May 1955 and ceased operations with the formal restoration of German sovereignty.

Thomas Schwartz

See also Adenauer, Konrad; Allied Occupation Statute; American-German Relations; Anglo-German Relations; The Cold War and Germany; Federal Republic of Germany; Federal Republic of Germany: Foreign Policy; Franco-German Relations; McCloy, John J.; Robertson, Brian

References

Rupieper, Hermann-Josef. *Der besetzte Verbündete: Die amerikanische Deutschlandpolitik 1949–1955*. Opladen: Westdeutscher Verlag, 1991.

Schwartz, Thomas. *America's Germany: John J. McCloy and the Federal Republic of Germany*. Cambridge, MA: Harvard University Press, 1991.

Allied Occupation Statute (1949–55)

The Allied Occupation Statute originated in the 1948 agreement of the United States, Great Britain, and France to establish a separate West German state. Their intention was to produce a statute that would specify every power or function retained by the Allies and enumerate those that would be restored to the Germans. However, because of sharp disagreements among the Allies about how much authority to grant the Germans, with the French favoring strict control and the Americans and British willing to grant more authority, the Western powers decided at the Washington Conference of April 1949 to agree to a simplified occupation statute. This statute reserved "supreme authority" in Germany for the Allies and kept primary responsibility for these undefined areas: foreign affairs, refugees, demilitarization, control over the Ruhr, restitution, reparations, decartelization, deconcentration of industries, displaced persons, foreign trade and exchange, the security of Allied forces, respect for the German Basic Law, and war criminals. Such broad reservations papered over the Allied disagreements but left the new German government of Chancellor Konrad Adenauer in doubt over how much effective authority it would possess.

At the formal ceremony presenting the Occupation Statute in September 1949, Adenauer called for immediate revisions in the statute. The chancellor also symbolically asserted his equality with the High Commissioners by positioning himself on the same carpet on which the Allied representatives stood. Only as the ceremony ended did the High Commissioners remember to give the chancellor his copy of the Occupation Statute. A French diplomat rushed to Adenauer's personal assistant, Herbert Blankenhorn (1904–91), and gave him the document saying, "Let's not talk about it anymore."

But talk about it they did. Adenauer challenged the Occupation Statute from the beginning, arguing that the Allies should not interfere with his pro-Western government and undermine its authority with the German people. In the Cold War atmosphere of the period, this argument found support in Washington. By May 1950, the Western powers agreed to review the statute, and it was formally revised in March 1951. By September 1951, the Western powers agreed to replace the Occupation Statute with contractual agreements to end the occupation and bring Germany into the Western alliance. In May 1952, with the signing of the Germany Treaty (*Deutschlandvertrag)*, the Occupation Statute was abolished. However, the delay in ratifying the treaty meant that the Statute remained formally in effect until May 1955.

Thomas Schwartz

See also Adenauer, Konrad; Allied High Commission; American-German Relations; The Basic Law; The Cold War and Germany; Federal Republic of Germany; Federal Republic of Germany: Foreign Policy; Germany Treaty; McCloy, John J.; Postwar Reconstruction

References

Rupieper, Hermann-Josef. *Der besetzte Verbündete: Die amerikanische Deutschlandpolitik 1949–1955.* Opladen: Westdeutscher Verlag, 1991.

Schwartz, Thomas. *America's Germany: John J. McCloy and the Federal Republic of Germany.* Cambridge, MA: Harvard University Press, 1991.

Alsace-Lorraine

Located in eastern France, Alsace-Lorraine is divided into three regions: Lorraine, Lower Alsace, and Upper Alsace. The area was repeatedly fought over by France and Germany between 1870 and 1945, and was a source of contention for many of the years in between.

The contested areas, under German control from 1871 to 1919 and 1940 to 1945, included the cities of Diedenhofen, Metz, and Chateau-Salins in northern Lorraine; Wissembourg, Hagenau, Saverne, Strasbourg, Erstein, and Selestat in Lower Alsace; and Colmar, Guebwiller, Thann, Mulhouse, and Altkirch in Upper Alsace. Alsace-Lorraine's linguistic-cultural division runs between German-speaking Alsace and French-speaking Lorraine.

With the outbreak of war with France in 1870, German nationalists clamored for the annexation of Alsace-Lorraine to extend Germany to its "natural frontier," the Vosges, and deter future French aggression. In the Treaty of Frankfurt of May 1871, France ceded Alsace-Lorraine to Germany. Within unified Germany, Alsace-Lorraine became known as the Reichsland, an administrative territory under the control of a governor-general, nominally under civilian control. The Prussian military exercised almost complete authority over its domestic affairs. Economically, it added substantially to Germany's industrial and natural resources. Combined with new technologies, these resources allowed Germany to overtake Great Britain in steel production by the end of the century.

Before World War I, various attempts were made to integrate Alsace-Lorraine firmly into Germany. In 1911, the German legislature accepted a new constitution for Alsace-Lorraine designed to facilitate integration. The Zabern Affair of November 1913, however, inflamed popular resistance against government policies and the presence of the Prussian military.

During the world wars, some of the heaviest fighting took place in Alsace-Lorraine. In 1916, the Germans massed a major assault against the French stronghold at Verdun, in the part of Lorraine that had remained under French control. Between February and November, French and German forces suffered some half a million casualties each. With the signing of the Treaty of Versailles in 1919, Alsace-Lorraine reverted to France. With the fall of France in June 1940, it again became part of Germany until 1945, when it was returned to France. The fighting during the liberation of Alsace-Lorraine during the spring of 1945 devastated much of the region.

Since the end of World War II, Alsace and Lorraine have been separate provinces within France. Lorraine's natural resources have made it an important part of Europe's process of economic integration. With the establishment of the European Economic Community in 1957, Alsace has played an important role in Europe's integration. Strasbourg is the seat of both the Council of Europe and the European Parliament. Consequently, Alsace and Lorraine have become focal points for European unity and cooperation.

David A. Meier

See also Federalism; Franco-German Relations; Versailles, Treaty of; World War I; Zabern

References

Cole, H.M. *The European Theater of Operations: The Lorraine Campaign.* Washington, DC: Department of the Army, 1950.

Hochstuhl, Kurt. *Zwischen Frieden und Krieg: Das Elsass in den Jahren 1938-1940: Ein Beitrag zu den Problemen einer Grenzregion in Krisenzeiten.* New York, NY: Peter Lang, 1984.

Kettenacker, Lothar. *Nationalsozialistische Volkstumpolitik im Elsass.* Stuttgart: Deutsche Verlags-Anstalt, 1973.

Silverman, Dan P. *Reluctant Union: Alsace-Lorraine and Imperial Germany, 1871–1918.* University Park, PA: Pennsylvania State University Press, 1972.

Wehler, Hans-Ulrich. *Krisenherde des Kaiserreichs 1871–1918.* Göttingen: Vandenhoeck & Ruprecht, 1970.

Willis, Roy F. *France, Germany and the New Europe 1945–63.* London: Oxford University Press, 1968.

Althoff, Friedrich (1839–1908)

Friedrich Althoff's influence on higher education in Prussia can be compared with that of Wilhelm von Humboldt and Carl Becker. Friedrich Althoff was born February 19, 1839, at Dinslaken near Wesel, son of *Domänenrat* (government estate manager) Friedrich Theodor Althoff and Julie von Buggenhagen. In 1865 he married Marie Ingenohl. He died childless in Berlin on October 20, 1908.

An intelligent, undisciplined youth, he attended Bonn University in 1856–61, preferring fraternity life to law and never earning a doctorate. After serving in several minor judicial posts in the Rhineland and Berlin, on May 5, 1871 he was appointed *Justitiar* (legal advisor) and *Referent* (department head) for church and school affairs in the Civil Commissioner's Office for Alsace-Lorraine in Strassburg. Here he learned the fundamentals of academic administration that later culminated in the Althoff System. On October 10, 1882 he was appointed privy councilor, senior executive officer, and head of the personnel division of the Prussian Ministry of Ecclesiastical, Educational, and Medical Affairs. This post made him, until his resignation on October 1, 1907, czar of higher education in Prussia.

Arguably, the great legacy of Wilhelmine Prussia to the modern world is the research university, and that legacy was created by Althoff. He made Prussian universities preeminent in humanities, law, natural sciences, and theology. The University of Chicago and Johns Hopkins University were modeled on Althoff's creations. He first conceived the idea of pure research institutions financed in part by private capital. In 1910, he established the Kaiser Wilhelm Society (today the Max Planck Society), the model for Princeton's Institute for Advanced Studies among many others.

Althoff was the rare autocrat who devoted his entire career to the uncompromising pursuit of excellence. The breadth of his interests (medicine to classics, philosophy, and theology) and his fairness were part of his achievement. Crucial to his system was the concentration of talent in favored institutions (e.g., Berlin and Göttingen). Appointment of the best person available was his highest priority. Faculties could only advise the ministry. Althoff decided regularly on the advice of his trusted agents within the universities, men like Theodor Mommsen (1817–1903), Edmund Zeller, Rudolf Virchow (1821–1902), Gustav von Schmoller (1838–1917), Friedrich Paulsen, Adolf von Harnack (1851–1930), Felix Klein (1849–1925), Ulrich Wilamowitz, and Wilhelm Lexis. He never hesitated to impose the best person against the will of a timorous faculty. He supported Jews and Catholics against reactionary locals whenever he considered them best. He encouraged international cooperation and orchestrated German representation at the Chicago Exposition in 1893 and at St. Louis in 1904. The Kaiser Wilhelm–Theodore Roosevelt Exchange Professorships were Althoff's creation. By 1918, 18 of 58 Nobel Prize winners in natural sciences were German, and 16 were Prussian. The number of university students in Prussia increased some 250 percent during his term in office.

William M. Calder III

See also Bildung und Bildungsbürgertum; Education; Kaiser Wilhelm/Max Planck Societies and Institutes; Professions; Prussia; Schools; Universities

References

Brocke, Bernhard vom. "Friedrich Althoff: A Great Figure in Higher Education Policy in Germany." *Minerva* 29 (1991), 269–93.

———. "Hochschul- und Wissenschaftspolitik in Preussen und im Deutschen Kaiserreich 1882–1907: Das 'Sys-

tem Althoff.'" *Preussen in der Geschichte 1: Bildungspolitik in Preussen zur Zeit des Kaiserreiches.* Ed. Peter Baumgart. Stuttgart: Klett-Cotta, 1980.

———. *Wissenschaftsgeschichte und Wissenschaftspolitik im Industriealter: Das "System Althoff" in historischer Perspektive.* 2nd ed. Hildesheim: Edition Bildung und Wissenschaft, Verlag A. Lax, 1991.

Calder, William M. III and Alexander Kosenina. *Berufungspolitik innerhalb der Altertumswissenschaft im wilhelminischen Preussen: Die Briefe Ulrich von Wilamowitz-Moellendorff an Friedrich Althoff (1883–1908).* Frankfurt am Main: Klostermann, 1989.

Amann, Max (1891–1957)

Max Amann served as director of the Nazi Party's publishing house, the Eher Verlag, for many years and remained one of Adolf Hitler's loyal followers.

Born in Munich, on November 24, 1891, Amann attended business school and served an office apprenticeship in a Munich law firm. During World War I, he served in the Bavarian army and was, for a time, Hitler's company sergeant. After being demobilized in 1919, he married and worked in a Munich mortgage bank. He joined the Nazi Party in February 1920 and participated as a trusted lieutenant in the Hitler-Ludendorff Beer-Hall *Putsch* of 1923. He was arrested and jailed for nearly a month in November 1923 for "aiding and abetting high treason."

When the Nazi Party was refounded in February 1925, the Party's publishing house, the Eher Verlag, was granted financial independence and Amann was given a free hand by Hitler. After the Nazis came to power in 1933, Amann continued to enjoy Hitler's confidence and he was moved into the key position in the National Publishers' Association. Amann's power was further extended in 1934, when the Nazi regional press was placed his under control. In 1935, the Eher Verlag—under what became known as the "Amann ordinances"—acquired all the important publishing properties, establishing it in a position of complete dominance from which it could dictate Nazi propaganda.

This huge publishing empire was fiercely defended by Amann, who could generally rely on Hitler's support. However, Amann would frequently come into conflict with Joseph Goebbels (1897–1945) and Otto Dietrich (1897–1952), the Reich press chief. In disputes with Dietrich, Amann usually prevailed, but he was no match for Goebbels, who was intellectually his superior. Amann was not a political activist in that he was neither a speaker nor debater. Moreover, as he had little interest in journalism or writing, he did not use his position to disseminate his own views. Indeed, although he controlled the Nazi Party press and gained a detailed knowledge of publishing, he left corporate finance to others. From 1936 he acted not only as Hitler's business manager but also served as his personal banker. The substantial royalties from *Mein Kampf* remained in Amann's accounts and when Hitler required funds he simply called on his trusted agent. Max Amann remained unshakably loyal to Hitler and as a result acquired a large personal fortune. For his services to the Party he was appointed *Reichsleiter* (Reich leader) and awarded the highest Party honors. After the war, de-Nazification tribunals stripped him of his property and business holdings and he died in extreme poverty.

David Welch

See also Dietrich, Otto; Goebbels, Joseph; Hitler, Adolf; National Socialism; National Socialist Germany; Third Reich: Propaganda and Culture; *Völkischer Beobachter*

References

Abel, K.D. and N. Frei. *Die Presselenkung im NS-Staat.* Berlin: Vistas, 1988.

Frei, N. and J. Schmitz. *Journalismus im Dritten Reich.* Munich: C.H. Beck, 1989.

Hale, O.A. *The Captive Press in the Third Reich.* Princeton, NJ: Princeton University Press, 1964.

Koszyk, K. *Geschichte der deutschen Presse, 1914–45.* Berlin: Colloquium Verlag, 1966–72.

Max Amann: Ein Leben für Führer und Volk. Munich: Ehler, 1941.

American-German Relations

The ups and downs of American-German relations since the times of President Ulysses S. Grant and Chancellor Otto von Bismarck reflect the changing power structure in the Atlantic world. During the last quarter of the nineteenth century, Germany, united under the Prussian monarchy, was widely recognized as a rising "giant" destined to lead the way into a new era of scientific and cultural progress. The United States, despite its dynamic industrial expansion, found itself still on the periphery of the European power system. Before 1914, many Americans studied in Germany and trade—especially in such staples as cotton—flourished. Slowly the image of the United States as a "young country" in need of tutoring by culturally advanced Germans gave way to a sense of growing American-German rivalry. This economic, political, and ideological antagonism erupted into enmity during World War I, when—following the American declaration of war in April 1917—German scholars publicly defended "true German culture" against "false American democracy," and American intellectuals produced overheated propaganda that equated German rule with barbarism.

The atmosphere cleared quickly at the end of the war, which saw—from the American perspective—a defeated, weakened, and revolutionized Germany surrounded by irreconcilable neighbors and shackled by the punitive Treaty of Versailles. The balance of power had definitely turned in favor of the United States, which emerged as the world's most important creditor country, and which came to be seen as the quintessential "modern" state, combining prosperity with democracy and cultural innovation. During the 1920s, the United States promoted the economic stabilization of Europe, concentrating on Germany as the industrial heartland of the continent and trying to discourage any German-Soviet collusion. Americans remained aloof, however, from the political problems of the "Old World," and they flatly rejected a linkage between German reparation payments and Allied war debts.

The efforts made in the Weimar era to reestablish and improve American-German contacts were disrupted by the Great Depression and Adolf Hitler's rise to power. Although diplomatic and economic relations remained correct, the Nazis' anti-Semitism and aggressive nationalism began to darken the American image of Germany. Nazi propagandists, in turn, revived the old stereotypes of a purely materialistic and decadent American society. Cultural exchange was replaced by a "brain drain" of German emigrants and exiles to the United States, involving thousands of politically and racially persecuted intellectuals.

Even after the outbreak of war in Europe, the Roosevelt administration had great difficulty overcoming the strong isolationist tendencies in American society. However, when Hitler declared war on the United States in December 1941, Nazi aggression and war crimes brought a determined military response from the United States that sealed the fate of the Third Reich. During the war, Americans began to explore the reasons for the irrational behavior of the German people and their leaders. From this debate emerged the concept of "reeducation" that was put into practice by the occupation authorities after the initial, mainly punitive, stage of "de-Nazification" had ended.

The occupation period from 1945 to 1949 witnessed the greatest inequality in American-German relations: a totally defeated, economically ruined, and morally discredited Germany was confronted by a victorious, prosperous, and self-confident United States that had risen to superpower status. Contrary to the post–World War I period, the Americans successfully translated their power and prestige into political leadership. Strengthened by growing fear of Soviet expansionism, American determination to engage permanently in European affairs found expression in the Marshall Plan and NATO, in the establishment of the Federal Republic of Germany, and in the support for European integration. The new West German state, under Chancellor Konrad Adenauer, fol-

President Kennedy, Mayor Brandt, and Chancellor Adenauer in Berlin, 1963. Courtesy of German Embassy, Ottawa.

lowed the American lead and opted for participation in the Western alliance and European community even at the risk of indefinitely postponing German reunification.

Overcoming their national trauma in the face of the Cold War, the great majority of West Germans accepted not only American political and economic leadership but also the cultural hegemony of the "American way of life." This close association with the West proved to be the surest way to political emancipation and national self-determination. As it turned out after 1989, the so-called "Westernization" of Germany, instead of being an obstacle to the realization of national aspirations, had been a precondition of reunification.

At the end of the twentieth century, the trans-Atlantic interdependencies have grown to such an extent that it appears difficult to maintain any longer the notion of an "American hegemony" over Europe. The success of America's leadership in the material and spiritual reconstruction of Germany after World War II, therefore, can be measured by the speed with which it was supplanted by a more balanced, mutually beneficial cooperation and partnership.

Jürgen Heideking

See also Adenauer, Konrad; Allied High Commission to Germany; Allied Occupation Statute; American Occupation; Anglo-German Relations; The Basic Law; Berlin Blockade; Berlin Wall; Bitburg; Brandt, Willy; The Cold War and Germany; Dawes Plan; Expulsion and Exile of Scientists and Scholars; Federal Republic of Germany: Foreign Policy; Franco-German Relations; Frankfurt School; Kohl, Helmut; Marshall Plan; McCloy, John J.; NATO and Germany; Political Science; Postwar Reconstruction; Potsdam Conference; Reunification; Schmidt, Helmut; Soviet-German Relations; Versailles, Treaty of ; World War I ; World War II; Yalta; Young Plan

References

Cooney, James A. et al., eds. *The Federal Republic of Germany and the United States: Changing Political, Social and Economic Relations.* Boulder, CO: Westview Press, 1989.

Diefendorf, Jeffry M., Axel Frohn, and Herman-Josef Rupieper, eds. *American Policy and the Reconstruction of West Germany, 1945–1955.* Washington, DC: German Historical Institute and New York, NY: Cambridge University Press, 1993.

Eisenberg, Carolyn. *Drawing the Line: The American Decision to Divide Germany, 1944–1949.* Cambridge: Cambridge University Press, 1996.

Gimbel, John F. *The American Occupation of Germany: Politics and the Military, 1945–1949.* Palo Alto, CA: Stanford University Press, 1968.

Hanrieder, Wolfram F. *Germany, America, Europe: Forty Years of German Foreign Policy.* New Haven, CT: Yale University Press, 1989.

Jonas, Manfred. *The United States and Germany. A Diplomatic History.* Ithaca, NY: Cornell University Press, 1984.

Link, Werner. *Die amerikanische Stabilisierungspolitik in Deutschland 1921–1932.* Düsseldorf: Droste, 1970.

Mayer, Frank. *Adenauer and Kennedy: A Study in German-American Relations, 1961–1963.* New York, NY: St. Martin's Press, 1996.

Ninkovich, Frank A. *Germany and the United States: The Transformation of the German Question since 1945.* Boston, MA: Twayne Publishers, 1988.

Pommerin, Reiner, ed. *The American Impact on Postwar Germany.* Providence, RI: Berghahn Books, 1995.

———. *Der Kaiser und Amerika: Die USA in der Politik der Reichsleitung 1890–1917.* Cologne: Böhlau, 1986.

Rupieper, Herman-Josef. *Die Wurzeln der westdeutschen Nachkriegsdemokratie: Der amerikanische Beitrag 1945–1952.* Opladen: Westdeutscher Verlag, 1993.

Schröder, Hans-Jürgen. *Deutschland und die Vereinigten Staaten 1933–1939: Wirtschaft und Politik in der Entwicklung des deutsch-amerikanischen Gegensatzes.* Wiesbaden: F. Steiner, 1970.

———, ed. *Confrontation and Cooperation: Germany and the US in the Era of World War I, 1900–1924.* Providence, RI: Berg, 1993.

American Occupation (1945–49)

In 1945, for the second time in one generation, an American army of occupation entered Germany. But the American military government (1945–49), known officially as the Office of Military Government (U.S.) for Germany or OMGUS, was more ambitious than the localized military force that had occupied the Rhineland (1919–23). In concert with the British, French, and Soviets, the Americans stated their goals at the Potsdam Meeting (July 1945) as the so-called "four Ds," namely de-Nazification, demilitarization, decartelization, and democratization of German society. Harsh realities quickly forced revisions of some of those goals.

Aware that it faced great responsibilities for administering the affairs of liberated and conquered peoples after World War II, the War Department had created a new division of civil affairs–military government (CAMG) and had trained hundreds of civil affairs personnel for occupation duties by war's end. However, planning efforts were hindered by President Roosevelt's avoidance of detailed postwar planning in order to hold together the uneasy wartime coalition. Consequently, confusion reigned over occupation policy following his death in April 1945. Opposing concepts were mirrored in Treasury Secretary Henry Morgenthau's punitive "pastoralization" scheme, whereby Germany would be deindustrialized, and in the reconstructionist policy championed by War and State Department officials that would allow the German people to hope for national revival and normal living standards in a new, democratic world.

A compromise Joint Chiefs of Staff policy, JCS 1067, emerged. It combined both punitive and reconstructionist elements, but it emphasized the punitive course. The newly appointed military governor, General Lucius D. Clay, was charged with administering the U.S. zone containing 20 million Germans—mostly in the south and west of Germany in Greater Hesse, Bavaria, and what became Baden-Württemberg, but also small enclaves in Bremen and the U.S.

sector in Berlin. Inexperienced in civil-affairs undertakings, the emerging military government took some time to organize and was hampered by rapid military demobilization and a subsequent stream of inexperienced replacement personnel to fill the ranks of OMGUS.

General Clay faced one of the most daunting tasks ever assigned an American official. He was charged with administering a hostile territory despite the total demise of government, vast destruction of cities and industries, complete economic and financial breakdown, widespread malnutrition, and paralyzing disagreements among the occupiers, especially with the Soviets and to a lesser degree the French. He also had to convince an unsympathetic U.S. Congress and the president to invest huge sums just to prevent starvation. Clay quickly concluded that the punitive JCS 1067 policy was unworkable, and using its "disease and unrest" loophole, the American authorities provided some measure of relief, ostensibly to protect their own occupation troops from a diseased and desperate population.

Convinced by Nazi atrocities of the need for a thoroughgoing political purge, General Clay launched an ambitious program of de-Nazification for the U.S. zone, eventually pressuring the Germans to create special *Spruchkammer* (de-Nazification courts). All adult Germans submitted *Fragebogen* (questionnaires) containing 131 questions about their political activities and were assigned to several categories of guilt ranging from "major offenders" to "followers," or else declared exonerated. Hundreds of thousands, mostly "followers," received light sentences, ranging from fines or loss of official or professional positions for a time, although more notorious cases were tried as war criminals. Originally conceived as a program of permanent exclusion, de-Nazification took on a rehabilitative function by 1946. The entire program threatened to break down from sheer weight of numbers, and Clay, who had used it in part to convince Congress of the vigorous activities of the military government, rapidly terminated American involvement in it in the spring of 1948, once the Soviets signaled an end to their de-Nazification program.

An adroit administrator, General Clay in 1947 secured increasing support from Congress to develop positive programs of reconstruction and allowed in massive charitable aid programs by the Quakers and other major churches. Especially notable was an umbrella organization, the Cooperative of American Remittances to Europe or CARE, which allowed individual Americans to donate the famed CARE packages. While rigorously pursuing de-Nazification and demilitarization, Clay slowed and then stopped Soviet reparation plans that originally had involved the dismantling of some German industrial plants in the West. By 1946, he allowed the reemergence of German local and state (*Land*) political parties and governments in free elections. Clay resisted internationalization and socialization of the vast Ruhr industrial district, and with British help created an economic merger of their respective zones into the Bizone (1947). With considerable pressure, the French were convinced to add their zone to make the Trizone (1948).

Helped by the emergence of the Cold War, Clay pressed for a revision of American occupation policy, replacing the punitive JCS 1067 with the more positive JCS 1779, and in June 1948 he instituted an ambitious currency reform, introducing the new and valuable deutsch mark, indispensable for the economic miracle to come. Currency reform precipitated an open breach with the Soviet Union, in which Stalin blockaded West Berlin, a policy that backfired when the Americans, led by Clay, countered with the famed Berlin Airlift.

Increasingly viewing the German people—with whom they got along surprisingly well—as allies, the American occupation authorities instituted an ambitious but loosely defined policy of reeducation whereby they intended to influence German social and political institutions to create a more democratic, peaceable society. Their objective was to get Germans themselves to create or recreate political parties and constitutions that were democratic. They also sought to influence the press, mass media, educational systems, church, family, grass roots organizations, and other pressure points in society so that they reflected more democratic practices in the Germans' daily lives. Although some particulars of reeducation were ill-conceived or naïve, the basic goals were sound, and the involvement of Germans in them was vital to any long-term progress.

One clear-cut victory of Americans supporting a democratic German initiative occurred in Berlin in the spring of 1948, when Communist-persecuted students from the old Berlin University in the Soviet sector fled to the American sector and began creating the Free University of Berlin (FUB). General Clay gave the initiative crucial moral and financial backing, and the FUB became a model of a new, democratic university in which the older, maturer founding students, many of them veterans, helped to administer their own institution and were represented at all levels of administration, including admissions and the board of trustees. The Free University solidified and prospered in the 1950s.

Reeducation's greatest triumph may have been the ambitious cultural exchange programs in which the American military government organized the movement of thousands of young Germans with leadership and professional potential to the United States and other democratic European countries to observe democracies in action at first hand.

Although marked by confusion and cross-purposes, especially in the opening stages when memories of Nazism and the death camps were fresh, the American occupation of Germany after World War II ultimately proved to be an outstanding success that helped to create the Federal Republic of Germany with a democratic, peaceable, and prosperous society integrated into the affairs of Europe.

James F. Tent

See also Adenauer, Konrad; Allied High Commission to Germany; Allied Occupation Statute; American-German Relations; The Basic Law; Berlin Blockade; The Cold War and Germany; Marshall Plan; McCloy, John J.; Postwar Reconstruction; Potsdam Conference; World War II; Yalta Conference

References

Clay, Lucius D. *Decision in Germany*. Garden City, NY: Doubleday, 1950.

Diefendorf, Jeffry M., Axel Frohn, and Herman-Josef Rupieper, eds. *American Policy and the Reconstruction of West Germany, 1945–1955.* Washington, DC: German Historical Institute and New York, NY: Cambridge University Press, 1993.

Eisenberg, Carolyn. *Drawing the Line: The American Decision to Divide Germany, 1944–1949.* Cambridge: Cambridge University Press, 1996.

Gimbel, John. *The American Occupation of Germany.* Palo Alto, CA: Stanford University Press, 1968.

Peterson, Edward N. *The American Occupation of Germany: Retreat to Victory.* Detroit, MI: Wayne State University Press, 1977.

Pommerin, Reiner, ed. *The American Impact on Postwar Germany.* Providence, RI: Berghahn Books, 1995.

Tent, James F. *The Free University of Berlin: A Political History.* Bloomington, IN: Indiana University Press, 1988.

———. *Mission on the Rhine: Reeducation and Denazification in American-Occupied Germany.* Chicago, IL: University of Chicago Press, 1982.

Anarchism

Although individuals such as Max Stirner (1806–56) espoused anarchist ideas as early as the 1830s and 1840s, not until the 1870s did an anarchist movement emerge. The history of anarchism in Germany is one of many publications and some deeds.

The first German anarchist program was drawn up on October 2, 1875 and called for an organization of society based on a new economic foundation that involved the common possession of the soil, the mines, capital, the major lines of communication, and the tools of work. The first German anarchist newspaper, the *Arbeiter Zeitung* (Workers journal), 1876–77, was published in Bern. It called for the absolute emancipation of all workers, including the use of violent methods. August Reinsdorf (1849–85) smuggled the *Arbeiter Zeitung* into Germany and established a small anarchist group in Leipzig. One of his followers, Max Hödel (1857–78), attempted to assassinate Emperor Wilhelm I on May 11, 1878. Carl Nobling, who wounded Wilhelm I on June 2, 1878, may also have been in contact with Reinsdorf.

In the 1870s and 1880s, the German anarchist movement was controlled from outside Germany, first from Bern, where the *Arbeiter Zeitung* and *Der Rebell,* 1881, 1884–86, were published, and later from London, where *Der Rebell* was forced to move. *Die Autonomie,* 1886–93, which superseded *Der Rebell,* was also published in London by the Group Autonomie, a group of German exiles.

Johann Most (1846–1906) became a leading figure in the German anarchist organization in London after leaving Germany in December 1878. In London he established *Die Freiheit* (Freedom), 1879–1910, to be smuggled into Germany. At its peak, 4,500 copies went into Germany and Austria. He established an anarchist cell organization in Germany but it was infiltrated by police spies. Johann Most advocated the extreme forms of "propaganda by deed" via publications that contained instructions on how to make explosives and construct bombs.

Attempts at propaganda by deed fostered by Hermann Stellmacher and Anton Kammerer had the effect of turning most workers against anarchism. The liberals also spurned against the anarchist cause and reinforced the state's case against them. Reinsdorf's grandiose plans included murdering the Berlin Police President Madai, blowing up the Reichstag building, and killing all the leading members of the royal family at the dedication of the Niederwald Monument on September 28, 1883. The first two schemes were discovered and stopped. The last was attempted by two of his accomplices. For his part Reinsdorf was beheaded in 1885.

One of the leaders in the smuggling operation of anarchist newspapers was John Neve, who was called the soul of the German movement. His arrest in 1887 opened old wounds among the exile anarchists in London; it also cut off the key route by which newspapers and explosives were smuggled into Germany and distributed. The leadership of the movement fell victim to an exchange of allegations between the two groups. For all practical purposes the early German anarchist movement was dead by late 1887.

A new movement emerged after 1890, less committed to action. The majority of those in the movement continued to be workers, but the leadership included a number of intellectuals. Unsuccessful attempts were made to move into rural areas. The earlier movement had been composed primarily of artisans, whereas the new movement was made up of industrial workers.

Many anarchist newspapers appeared in Germany in the 1890s, such as *Kampf, Aktion,* and *Sturm. Der Sozialist,* 1891–99, edited by Gustav Landauer, which had a press run of 10,000 in 1891, led the field. The leaders in the new movement were a group of young men, known collectively as the *Jungen,* who had been expelled from the Social Democratic Party for anarchist leanings. Among them were Gustav Landauer (1870–1919), Rudolf Rocker (1873–1958), Bruno Wille, Bernard Kampfmeyer, and Max Reinhardt. A new aspect was the *Siedlung* idea, developed by Landauer, of self-contained cooperative settlements.

In 1909, in conjunction with the establishment of the Sozialistischer Bund (Socialist League), *Der Sozialist,* 1909–14, again started publication with a circulation of 500 to 1,500. It proved to be on too high a level for most workers. Simultaneously, in Munich, Erich Mühsam (1878–1934) published *Kain,* 1909–14, a monthly with a circulation of 3,000, aimed at revolutionary academic youth and Bohemian artists.

The late 1890s saw the development of groups interested in individualist anarchism. Max Stirner's *Der Einzige und sein Eigentum,* 1844, (published as *The Ego and His Own,* 1963), was the source of their philosophy. The movement expanded rapidly after World War I, with a number of groups and newspapers being founded, such as *Der Einzige,* Berlin, 1919–25, edited by Salomo Friedlaender; *Der individualistische Anarchist,* Berlin, 1919, edited by Benedict Lachmann; *Der Freiheitkünder* (Freedom herald), Hannover, 1924–25, edited by Carl Dopf with a circulation of 3,500; and *Der Ziegelbrenner* (The brickburner), Munich, 1917–21, edited by Ret Marut (1882–1969). Some authors see a parallel between Stirner's "Union of Egoists" and Rudi Dutschke's (1940–79)

Sozialistischer Deutscher Studentenbund (SDS; Socialist German Student League) of the 1960s.

The Weimar Republic witnessed much anarchist and anarcho-syndicalist activity. Rudolf Oestreich (1878–1963) started to republish *Der freie Arbeiter*, 1919–33, as the organ of the Föderation Kommunistischer Anarchisten Deutschlands (FKAD), which reached a high point in 1923 with a run of 7,200.

The syndicalist movement, of which Rudolf Rocker was the chief organizer and theoretician, was much larger than any other group. It achieved a membership of 150,000 by 1921, but fell to 50,000 by 1924, when its strikes and direct action failed. The main newspaper, *Der Syndikalist: Organ der Freien Arbeiter-Union Deutschlands* (The syndicalist: organ of the free German workers union), Berlin, 1919–33, had a circulation of 120,000 in 1921, falling to 25,000 subscriptions by 1924. It ceased publication in May 1933. A large anarcho-syndicalist youth organization had as its main newspaper *Junge Anarchisten* (Young anarchists), Leipzig/Offenbach/Bauten, 1923–31. Many of the anarcho-syndicalist youth groups continued to meet after the Nazis came to power. They met for discussion and reading of anarchist newspapers that were smuggled into Germany from Sweden, Spain, France, and the Netherlands up to 1939. Many were arrested and sent to concentration camps. They also worked in conjunction with the Edelweiss Pirates. Another anarchist organization active during the Nazi period was the *Schwarzen Scharen* (Black band).

After 1945, the number of anarchist and anarchist-influenced periodicals increased tremendously. Between 1945 and 1985, over 350 such periodicals were printed. Many prewar anarchists, such as Rocker, again participated.

The student movement of the 1960s, which was concerned with extra-parliamentary opposition, antiwar activities, the peace movement, and environmentalism, saw the number of anarchist periodicals increase dramatically. A few examples: *Die Freie Gesellschaft* (The free society), Hannover, 1981*ff.*; *Schwarzer Faden: Anarchistische Vierteljahresschrift* (Black thread: anarchist quarterly), 1979*ff.*, with a circulation of 2,000; *Trafik: Journal zur Kultur der Anarchie* (Tobacco shop: journal for the culture of anarchism), 1981 *ff.*; and *Aktion*, 1981 *ff.*, published in the Rhine-Main area.

Thousands of young people, such as Dutschke and the SDS, were involved in anarchist activities or stood on the perimeter of anarchism. Others, such as the Baader-Meinhof Group, while reminiscent of the propaganda-by-deed era of anarchism of the early 1880s, seem not to fall into the anarchist camp because they accepted some forms of government while rejecting others. Anarchism remains a belief that many still maintain.

Andrew R. Carlson

See also Baader-Meinhof Group; Dutschke, Rudi; Extra-Parliamentary Opposition; Landauer, Gustav; Most, Johann; Reinsdorf, August; Rocker, Rudolf; Toller, Ernst; Wilhelm I

References

Anarchismus in Deutschland. Vols. I–III. Hannover: Fackelträger Verlag, 1972–73.

Bock, Hans Manfred. "Bibliographischer Versuch zur Geschichte des Anarchismus und Anarcho-Syndikalismus in Deutschland." *Arbeiterbewegung Theorie und Praxis* 1 (1973), 299–335.
———. *Syndikalismus und Linkskommunismus von 1918–1923.* Meisenheim am Glan: A. Hein, 1969.
Carlson, Andrew R. *Anarchism in Germany.* Metuchen, NJ: The Scarecrow Press, Inc. 1972.
Klan, Ulrich and Dieter Nelles. *Es lebt noch eine Flamme: Rheinische Anarcho-Syndikalisten/-innen in der Weimar Republik und im Faschismus.* Grafenau-Döffingen: Trotzdem Verlag, 1990.
Linse, Ulrich. *Die anarchistische und anarcho-syndikalistische Jugendbewegung 1918–1933.* Frankfurt am Main: dipa-Verlag, 1976.
———. *Organisierter Anarchismus im Deutschen Kaiserreich von 1871.* Berlin: Duncker & Humblot, 1969.

Andersch, Alfred (1914–80)

Alfred Andersch authored novels, short stories, poems, and travelogues as well as radio plays and features, television dramas, and film adaptations of his own works. He made a name for himself as a publicist through avant-garde literary journals and experimental radio series, and as an essayist engaged in a lifelong fight to restore humanity after its total negation brought about by the nationalism and chauvinism of Nazi Germany. Due to his multitude of achievements, Andersch—who insisted on artistic freedom and simultaneously on realism in literature—has come to be considered one of the most influential voices in postwar German intellectual life.

In his controversial first book, *Deutsche Literatur in der Entscheidung* (German literature in crisis), 1948, the title of which hints at Andersch's reception of French existentialism, he defined artistic creation as an act of resistance of intellectual freedom against political power, an act that transcended the example of recent German history. All of his theoretical writings as well as his key novels, from the early *Die Kirschen der Freiheit* (The cherries of freedom), 1950, and *Sansibar oder der letzte Grund* (Zanzibar or the last reason), 1957, to *Winterspelt*, 1974, reiterate this rather conservative concept of an aesthetic resistance for the sake of the individual's freedom and the ideal of humanity. His heroes exemplify the author's existential decision to claim this freedom through political action. The common context of the Nazi period in these novels provides little more than the historical backdrop that forces such a decision.

Despite being the son of a German-nationalist officer, Andersch joined the Communist Party's youth organization. After the burning of the Reichstag on February 27, 1933, he was detained in the Dachau concentration camp and remained under continuous Gestapo surveillance thereafter. This experience initially led Andersch to refrain from politics and escape into literature and the aesthetic. In 1944, Andersch, who had been forced into a special battalion for former political prisoners, deserted on the Italian front and was taken to the United States as a prisoner of war (POW). He became a writer and an editor for *Der Ruf* (The call), the journal of the German POW camps. In 1945, he returned to Munich with his own model for a self-reliant reeducation of the German people. This became the aim of *Der Ruf*, the successor of the above journal, which he co-edited with Hans Werner Richter until it was banned by the American military government in 1947, following Andersch's public rejection of the "collective guilt postulate."

In 1947, Andersch and Richter became founding members of the literary association Gruppe 47. Its aim was to constitute a new German literature in the context of the European avant garde. In 1958, Andersch severed his associations with German literary circles and retreated to Berzona in Switzerland. In 1972 he accepted the offer of Swiss citizenship but continued to comment on political developments in Germany, often, as in his 1976 poem *Artikel 3 (3)* (referring to the Basic Law) against the *Radikalenerlass* (decree concerning radicals) and the related *Berufsverbote* (work ban). He warned of a resurgence of antidemocratic tendencies which might well result in the destruction of West German parliamentary democracy or, as Andersch provokingly put it, in new concentration camps for those who, like himself, voiced their dissent.

The idea of intellectual freedom and especially the concept of a reeducation of Germany's youth (who seemed to return from the war as a lost generation) through an exchange of ideas across national borders had run through Andersch's work since his *Das junge Europa formt sein Gesicht* (The young Europe forms its face), 1946, in which he envisioned European unity under the auspices of a socialist humanism and a European reawakening, which would end the slavery of nationalism forever. In "Die freie deutsche Republik als Brücke" (The free German republic as bridge), which also first appeared in *Der Ruf* of 1946, Andersch sharply criticized the Allies who accused all Germans who wished for German unity of nationalism and, by way of this spurious argument, denied a people its right to self-determination. He warned that this failure to seriously address the "German question" posed the real danger, because it prohibited making Germany into a bridge between west and east.

Decades after the separation of Germany into two states by the Cold War, Andersch still mourned the death of this historic opportunity in his essay, "Öffentlicher Brief an einen sowjetischen Schriftsteller" (Open letter to a Soviet writer), 1977. In an article of the same year entitled "Welche Aufgabe hat der Schriftsteller heute?" (What is the task of a contemporary writer?), he compared, in a provocative manner, the anti-Communism of the West to Hitler's fixed idea of a Jewish world conspiracy and, pointing to its historical result, pleaded for an end to the arms race for the sake of humanity's survival and the beginning of a reasoned dialogue about a new world order, in which the writer, the dissident per se, would have a part.

As in *Artikel 3 (3)* of 1976, Andersch took a radical stand in his essay, "Meine Himbeeren und Peter Paul Zahl" (My raspberries and Peter Paul Zahl), 1979, in which he defended the imprisoned West German "anarchist poet." He saw the evils brought about by nationalism *in extremis*, i.e., German National Socialism, resurface in the hysterical reaction to a perceived Communist threat. In the case of West Germany,

the hunt for so-called enemies of the state since the *Radikalenerlass* culminated in the *Deutscher Herbst* (German autumn) of the late 1970s. To Andersch, the implicit threat of the hasty antiterrorist legislation to civil liberties and democracy seemed a reminder of the German past.

During these years, Andersch—who once said that nobody who rightfully calls himself a writer can escape his time in his work— kept minding the garden in his Berzona retreat. His writings, whether as a poet or as a political essayist, resisted the signs of his times thanks to his aesthetic concept.

Gabriele Franke

See also The Cold War and Germany; Federal Republic of Germany: Literature; Gestapo; Richter, Hans Werner

References
Andersch, Alfred. *Werke in 18 Einzelausgaben.* Zürich: Diogenes, 1993.

Haffmanns, Gerd, ed., in collaboration with Rémy Charbon and Franz Cavigelli. *Über Alfred Andersch. Bibliographie der Werke und Auswahl-Bibliographie der Kritik.* 3rd expanded edition. Zurich: Diogenes, 1987.

Heidelberger-Leonard, Irene. *Alfred Andersch: Die ästhetische Position als politisches Gewissen.* Frankfurt am Main: Lang, 1986.

Reinhardt, Stephan. *Alfred Andersch: Eine Biographie.* Zurich: Diogenes, 1990.

Wagenbach, Klaus, Winfried Stephan und Michael Krüger, eds. *Vaterland, Muttersprache: Deutsche Schriftsteller und ihr Staat seit 1945. Ein Nachlesebuch für die Oberstufe* (a reference book for upper level [students]). Berlin: Wagenbach, 1979.

Wehdeking, Volker. *Alfred Andersch.* Stuttgart: Metzler, 1983.

Andreas-Salomé, Lou (1861–1937)

Lou Andreas-Salomé was born in 1861 into a German-speaking community in St. Petersburg, Russia. She moved to Zürich at age 19 and ultimately settled in Germany. Intellectually gifted with an inquiring and incisive mind, she studied philosophy, religion, history, and psychology, and wrote extensively on the psychology of religion, philosophy, art, femininity, and eroticism.

Although perhaps best known for her liaisons and friendships with Friedrich Nietzsche (1844–1900), Rainer Maria Rilke (1875–1926), and Sigmund Freud (1856–1939), Salomé was an original philosophical thinker, respected psychoanalyst, and acknowledged novelist in her own right. Her essays on philosophy, religion, and the psychology of woman were an inspiration to Nietzsche and Freud. Salomé studied with Freud in Vienna, but developed her own views on psychoanalysis, especially regarding the unconscious, where she differed from her teacher in her emphasis on its positive and creative capacities.

Her work on femininity and eroticism, most notably the essay "Der Mensch als Weib" (The human as woman), 1899, and the study *Die Erotik* (The erotic), 1910, was ground-breaking in its challenge to accepted views of woman and sexuality, and offered a revaluation of the feminine essence, focusing on woman's self-sufficiency, multiplicity, and utopian possibility. Salomé herself defied categorization and earned the criticism of many nineteenth-century German feminists because of her apparently contradictory views of woman, eroticism, and marriage, and for her own manipulation of social conventions.

Salomé focused on femininity and social conventions also in her fiction. Two representative works are *Fenitschka*, 1886, and *Eine Ausschweifung* (A debauchery), 1898. In these stories she explored the hybrid nature of woman, whom she later delineated in her analytical work on femininity. She constructed female characters who model her theoretical construction of woman as resistant to regulation and classification. Salomé offered a complex depiction of woman through these characters, intended to subvert and critique conventional turn-of-the-century attitudes toward women. She remained fascinated with issues of love, sexuality, and marriage until the end of her life. Her posthumously published memoirs, *Lebensrückblick* (Retrospective on life), 1951, testify to her continued resistance to social expectations that she found restrictive to her sexual and intellectual freedom.

Salomé was a brilliant and controversial figure whose prolific work provides insights not only into her own life as an intellectual, independent woman active in a community of the most noted minds in Europe, but also into the psychology and structure of modern German society as it was evolving and changing at the turn of the century.

Kathrin Bower

See also Feminism and Anti-Feminism, 1871–1918; Feminist Writing; Freud, Sigmund; Imperial Germany: Literature; Nietzsche, Friedrich; Psychoanalysis; Rilke, Rainer Maria

References

Andreas-Salomé, Lou. *Looking Back: Memoirs*. Trans. Breon Mitchell. New York, NY: Paragon House, 1991.

Gropp, Rose-Maria. *Lou Andreas-Salomé mit Sigmund Freud. Grenzgänge zwischen Literatur und Psychoanalysis*. Weinheim: Beltz, 1988.

Koepcke, Cordula. *Lou Andreas-Salomé. Leben, Persönlichkeit, Werk: Eine Biographie*. Frankfurt am Main: Insel, 1986.

Martin, Biddy. *Woman and Modernity: The (Life)Styles of Lou Andreas-Salomé*. Ithaca, NY: Cornell University Press, 1991.

Salber, Linda. *Lou Andreas-Salomé*. Reinbek bei Hamburg: Rowohlt, 1990.

Welsch, Ursula and Michaela Wiesner. *Lou Andreas-Salomé: Vom 'Lebensurgrund' zur Psychoanalyse*. Munich: Internationale Psychoanalyse, 1988.

Anglo-German Relations

Before unification in 1871, Germany was judged by an Englishman to be "a cluster of insignificant states under insignificant princelings." The fusion of these petty states under the leadership of Prussia produced a new dynamic power in the middle of Europe whose energy was unprecedented. The prevailing attitude in Great Britain to this new colossus was expressed by Prime Minister Disraeli as early as 1871: "The balance of power has been entirely destroyed and the country which suffers most and feels the effects most of this great change is England." This theme was to be taken up again by Prime Minister Thatcher when she tried in vain to slow down the process of German reunification in 1990. However, the two events could not be more different.

Anglo-German relations were compromised from the start by the fact that unification in 1871 was forged on the battlefield as a result of three successive wars. Chancellor Otto von Bismarck and Prime Minister Gladstone came to represent two contrasting political cultures: power politics versus liberal reform and "world opinion." Rapid industrialization and modernization in Germany were not matched by constitutional change as in Great Britain. German colonial aspirations after 1884, systematically fostered as a substitute for political change, were clearly directed against Great Britain. Imperial Germany strove for world-power status with all the brusqueness of an arriviste. Germany was already the strongest military power on the continent, and Admiral von Tirpitz's plans for a large battle fleet were a direct challenge to Great Britain's maritime supremacy.

The settlement of colonial disputes between Great Britain and France in 1904 led to the diplomatic isolation of Imperial Germany. German and British public opinion could not be reconciled: on the one side stood anxiety about encirclement, on the other fears of German hegemony in Europe. The rigid system of alliances and the determinative nature of military planning, such as the plans of General Alfred von Schlieffen (1833–1913), precipitated the outbreak of war in August 1914. Inevitably, Great Britain sided with France when Belgium was invaded. The duration of the war, new forms of popular propaganda, and the enormous casualty figures (nearly one million British soldiers died, twice as many as in World War II) brought Anglo-German antagonism to fever pitch.

German defeat in 1918 and the establishment of democracy could have been the beginning of a new era, had not the Treaty of Versailles been vehemently rejected by all German parties. Peaceful revision of the Treaty was the main objective of British endeavors vis-à-vis France and Germany until 1933 and beyond. Chancellor Gustav Stresemann's policy of gradually improving Germany's position was a cause for optimism. The menace posed by Adolf Hitler was not realized in time, and Germany's hectic rearmament program was not matched by equivalent efforts in Great Britain. Appeasement was seen as the only viable way of reaching a general settlement with the dictators. However, contrary to common belief, this was a policy of active involvement on the continent. This was certainly not what Hitler wanted, since he hoped to be able to trade German colonial claims for a free hand in Eastern Europe. Great Britain's guarantee to Poland in 1939 was the clearest sign that such a deal was unacceptable. The Second World War, which began as a gesture of British and French defiance against Hitler in September 1939, ended in Europe with the unconditional surrender of Germany in May 1945. The devastating effects of air raids meant that the civilian populations on both sides were directly affected by the war far more than ever before. Consequently, the psychological impact of the war was much more traumatic and enduring than any previous war.

To eradicate "Prussian militarism and Nazi tyranny," according to Churchill, were Great Britain's chief war aims. She was ahead of her allies in postwar planning for Germany: she devised the idea of joint Allied occupation, consisting of a Control Commission in Berlin and separate zones of occupation. The effect of the Cold War was that these provisional arrangements were to shape the future of Central Europe for nearly half a century. Military defeat and occupation were supposed to "re-educate" the Germans and bring about lasting peace in Europe. The decentralization of power and the restructuring of the federal system (the creation of new *Länder* [states] from the remainder of Prussia) were perhaps the most important British contributions to the new Germany after 1945.

Great Britain fully supported the integration of the Federal Republic into the Western Alliance, but remained outside the European Economic Community (1957). Germany became Great Britain's staunchest ally in her repeated attempts to join the European club. While popular reservations about Germany lingered on in Great Britain, the two governments established an ever-closer relationship, especially after the advent of Chancellor Willy Brandt's (1913–92) government in 1969. The new German *Ostpolitik* (eastern policy) was welcomed in London as a means of overcoming the division of Europe, even though the final outcome was not anticipated.

The consolidation of federal democracy and economic success in Germany led to a change of positions. West Germany, once the foster child of the British occupation authorities, increasingly came to be seen as a model for the regeneration of Great Britain. This was an extension of the Tariff Reformers' debate before 1914 about the lessons that could be learned from German efficiency. Both industrial societies realized that they had much in common and could learn from each other's experience. The reunification of Germany in 1990 was cast within the framework of four-power control, once invented and now reemployed by Great Britain. The united Germany was to remain firmly rooted in the Western security system.

Lothar Kettenacker

See also Adenauer, Konrad; Air Force; Allied Bombing; American-German Relations; Bethmann Hollweg, Theobold von; Bismarck, Otto von; The Cold War and Germany; Colonies and Colonial Society; Federal Republic of Germany: Foreign Policy; Franco-German Relations; Friedrich III; NATO and Germany; Naval Policy; North Rhine–Westphalia; Postwar European Integration and Germany; Potsdam Conference; Robertson, Brian; Ruhr Region; Soviet-German Relations; Stresemann, Gustav; Tirpitz, Alfred von; Versailles, Treaty of; Wilhelm II; World War I; World War II; Yalta Conference

References

Dockrill, Saki. *Britain's Policy for West German Rearmament.* Cambridge: Cambridge University Press, 1991.

Foschepoth, Josepf and Rolf Steininger, eds. *Die britische Deutschland- und Besatzungspolitik 1945–1949.* Paderborn: Schöningh, 1985.

Kennedy, Paul M. *The Rise of the Anglo-German Antagonism 1860–1914.* London: Allen Unwin, 1980.

Kettenacker, Lothar. *Krieg zur Friedenssicherung: Die Deutschlandplanung der britischen Regierung während des Zweiten Weltkrieges.* Göttingen: Vandenhoeck & Ruprecht, 1989.

Uhlig, Ralph. *Die Deutsch-Englische Gesellschaft 1949–1983: Der Beitrag ihrer 'Königswinter-Konferenzen' zur britisch-deutschen Verständigung.* Göttingen: Vandenhoeck & Ruprecht, 1986.

Watt, Donald C. *How War Came.* London: Heinemann, 1989.

Weidenfeld, Werner. *Die Englandpolitik Gustav Stresemanns.* Mainz: Von Hase und Köhler, 1972.

Wendt, Bernd Jürgen, ed. *Das britische Deutschlandbild im Wandel des 19. und 20. Jahrhundert.* Bochum: Studienverlag Dr. N. Brockmeyer, 1984.

Anschluss of Austria (1918–45)

Between 1918 and 1938, the movement for Austria to become a part of Germany (*Anschluss* = attachment) went through several phases. In 1918–19, when the Social Democrats ruled on both the German and Austrian sides of the Inn River, some looked back to the democratic, pre-Bismarckian Greater Germany program of the Revolution of 1848. However, Germany was unable to press the issue for fear of having to make territorial sacrifices elsewhere in exchange for a possible union. In 1931, the first phase of the *Anschluss* movement reached an unimpressive climax in a customs-union project, which was promptly rejected by the Allies, just as they had blocked any immediate postwar union through the Treaty of Versailles.

Adolf Hitler's power seizure initiated the last phase of the *Anschluss* movement. The Austrian government under chancellors Engelbert Dollfuss (1892–1934) and Kurt von Schuschnigg (1934–38), supported only by a small minority of the Austrian population, steered a semi-Fascist course, carrying on a two-front war against the Social Democrats on the one hand and the Nazi extremists and their nationalist allies on the other. 1934 was a troublesome year for Austria. In February, a civil war raged that involved the regular army and Fascist *Heimwehr* (home front) units against armed Socialist workers. A second civil war erupted with the German-inspired Nazi *Putsch* of July 25, 1934, during which Dollfuss was assassinated by native Nazis. Benito Mussolini, the Italian duce, dispatched troops to the Brenner Pass to protect Austria; Berlin was compelled to disavow the coup.

Thereafter, Hitler and Rudolf Hess tactically discarded violence; they wanted an *Anschluss* without causing resistance and bloodshed. Actually, the so-called "evolutionary" solution did not exclude sudden violent, revolutionary jolts, nor did it change the Nazi leaders' ultimate intentions. On the first page of *Mein Kampf*, Hitler had proclaimed that Germany and Austria ought to be one state: "Ein Volk—ein Reich." By the mid-1930s, most German Austrians had become adherents of such a pan-German ideology. Austrian patriotism, especially for the republic, was weak. In addition, the West's appeasement policy and Fascist Italy's illusions of becoming Germany's ally and a dominant power helped to bury Austria's independence.

In view of the common danger of a German expansion into Austria, France and Italy seemed for a time prepared to settle their differences and coordinate their policies. But the Stresa Front, which they established with Great Britain in 1935, turned out to be transitory. Great Britain never considered making any definite military commitment regarding Austria's independence and integrity. With the remilitarization of the Rhineland, France lost her access routes to Central Europe. Italy's military capacity to assist Austria gradually diminished in view of Mussolini's far-flung adventures in Ethiopia and Spain. The "pacific" July Agreement of 1936 between Austria and Germany, encouraged by Mussolini, was the wedge that Germany used to gain predominance in Austria and Central Europe.

In February 1938, Hitler invited Schuschnigg to Berchtesgaden. There, he forced him to make crucial concessions to Berlin. When, instead, the Austrian chancellor decreed an early Austrian plebiscite, Hitler opted for a military intervention. Schuschnigg was forced to accept the Nazi ultimatum, which demanded cancellation of the plebiscite, his resignation, and the formation of a new cabinet headed by Arthur Seyss-Inquart (1892–1946), an inveterate Austro-Nazi. On March 13, 1938 Hitler proclaimed the absorption of the "Ostmark" as a province in the Third Reich.

After World War II, the idea of another *Anschluss* did not reappear on the German and Austrian political agenda.

Alfred D. Low

See also Austro-German Relations; Hitler, Adolf; Italian-German Relations; National Socialist Germany: Foreign Policy; Seyss-Inquart, Arthur; Versailles, Treaty of

References

Eichstaedt, Ulrich. *Von Dollfuss zu Hitler: Geschichte des Anschlusses Österreichs, 1933–38.* Wiesbaden: F. Steiner, 1955.

Gehl, Jürgen. *Germany and the Anschluss 1931–1938.* New York: London: Oxford University Press, 1963.

Low, Alfred D. *The Anschluss Movement, 1918–1919 and the Paris Peace Conference.* Philadelphia, PA: American Philosophical Society, 1974.

———. *The Anschluss Movement 1918–1938, Background and Aftermath: An Annotated Bibliography of German and Austrian Nationalism.* New York, NY: Garland, 1984.

———. *The Anschluss Movement, 1931–38 and the Great Powers.* New York, NY: Garland, 1985.

Schuschnigg, K.v. *The Brutal Takeover: The Austrian Ex-Chancellor's Account of the Anschluss of Austria by Hitler.* London: Weidenfeld and Nicolson, 1971.

Stourzh, G. & B. Zaar, eds. *Österreich, Deutschland und die Mächte: Internationale und österreichische Aspekte des Anschlusses vom März 1938.* Vienna: Verlag der Österreichischen Akademie der Wissenschaften, 1990.

Anthropology, Physical

Anthropology in the German tradition until the 1970s refers essentially to physical, racial, or biological anthropology, or the study of human physical variation or "races"—a highly sensitive science in the successive political contexts from the Wilhelmine Empire to the Third Reich. Anthropology was nothing but "applied racial science," according to some Nazi luminaries. After the late 1890s, and particularly between 1920 and 1945, it was also named *Rassenkunde* (raciology).

The institutionalization of physical anthropology as a self-organized scientific discipline, with the founding of the first journals and scientific societies, started in Germany in the positivistic period of the 1860s and 1870s. As in most other countries, it generally combined during this first phase with ethnology (*Völkerkunde*) and prehistory-archaeology (*Urgeschichte*), as in the case of the Berlin Society (founded in 1869) and the first national society, the Deutsche Gesellschaft (society) für Anthropologie, Ethnologie und Urgeschichte (1870). Both were organized under the leadership of the famous medical pathologist and progressive politician Rudolf Virchow (1821–1902). In universities, only one chair—established in Munich in 1886—was available for the teaching of physical anthropology in all of Germany until 1906. Until World War I, most significant physical anthropologists were professors of anatomy or physicians.

Contrary to what is usually assumed, and compared to the French and American (pre-Boasian) schools, German physical anthropology was, from its foundation in the 1860s up to the mid-1890s, politically liberal or at least humanitarian, monogenist (i.e., asserting, in contrast to the polygenists, the unity of the human species respecting the "colored" races), and—in contemporary terms—anti-racist. Until 1918, the leaders of the discipline, scientists such as Virchow, Johannes Ranke (1836–1916, general secretary of the national society from 1878 to 1908), Julius Kollmann, and Felix von Luschan (first professor in Berlin in 1900), strongly reacted against the new political and "racial" anti-Semitism of the 1880s.

When the first "modern race theories" of Houston Stewart Chamberlain (1855–1924), Ludwig Schemann (Arthur Comte de Gobineau's apostle and translator in Germany who founded a "Gobineau Society" in 1894), Ludwig Wilser, Otto Ammon, and Ludwig Woltmann (founders of a Social Darwinist and Nordic racist "anthroposociology") surfaced in Germany at the turn of the century, the liberal founding generation rejected them as unscientific. Because of its ethical humanitarianism, the prevailing monogenism, and three decades' imperviousness to Darwinism (which anthropologists such as Virchow derogatorily named the "ape theory"), German anthropologists resisted attempts by Anglo-Saxon polygenists or German Darwinists (such as Ernst Haeckel) to expel "savages" from humanity by "animalizing" them or considering them as the "missing link" between the civilized human kind and its ape ancestors.

Despite this, many anthropologists supported German colonialism in one way or another after 1890, and most assumed the presence of a cultural hierarchy from the savagery of *Naturvölker* (primitive peoples) to the civilization of

Kulturvölker (civilized peoples), with their physiological and racial correlates. In the mid-1890s, when German physical anthropologists began converting to Darwinism, they replaced the peaceful humanitarian traditions derived from Herder and Humboldt by an inequalitarian racial and biological materialism.

The second generation of anthropologists, such as Felix von Luschan (1854–1924), Georg Buschan, Gustav Schwalbe (1844–1916), and Hermann Klaatsch (1863–1916), proved to be less democratic and more Darwinian. They increasingly succumbed to ideas of imperial and colonial expansion, Social Darwinist legitimation of war, and the system of eugenics. Besides the discovery of a number of prehistoric human remains at the turn of the century, the surrender of positivist liberal anthropology to Darwinism and eugenics was facilitated by the fact that since 1890, the "old craniology" faced an epistemological, methodological, and conceptual blind alley.

Just before the outbreak of World War I, a third generation of physical anthropologists, motivated by eugenics and fearing the "degeneration" of the German nation, abandoned pure craniometry and, with the help of Mendelian genetics and biometry, focused their scientific interest on questions of human heredity. They were led by Eugen Fischer (1874–1967), who became the main authority in the discipline in the mid-1920s. In 1927, he occupied the Berlin chair and the direction of the main German research center on human biology, the newly founded Kaiser Wilhelm Institute for Anthropology, Human Genetics, and Eugenics in Berlin. During the Weimar Republic, several new chairs were established in German universities. The political popularization of "raciology" by Nordic racists, such as H.F.K. Günther (1891–1968), benefited its institutionalization. While German-speaking anti-racist and progressive intellectuals, such as the sociologists F. Hertz, Ferdinand Tönnies (1855–1936) and F. Oppenheimer, had around 1900 embraced neo-Lamarckism, which was scientifically defeated in the 1920s, the neo-Darwinian camp, which happened to be politically pessimistic and frequently linked to a biological nationalism, won the upper hand. By 1930, most anthropologists had converted to eugenics (including Social Democrats, for instance Karl Brandt, professor at Cologne) when not, like Eugen Fischer (at Berlin) or Otto Reche (at Leipzig), to Nordic "race hygiene."

When Adolf Hitler came to power in 1933, very few physical anthropologists emigrated (Franz Weldenreich, Heinrich Münter, and Karl Brandt were exceptions), and still fewer resisted (Karl Saller) or were persecuted (Fritz Paudler). Most anthropologists (such as Fischer, Reche, Lothar Loeffler, Hans Weinert, Wilhelm Gieseler, Gerhardt Heberer, and Friedrich Keiter) joined the Nazi Party and other Nazi organizations, or at least praised the new regime for founding its politics on the "science of race" (Walther Scheidt and Egon von Eickstedt). The new regime created many new courses, chairs, and institutes for racial biology, and anthropologists served the racial policy of the Third Reich in many ways (counseling for the sterilization of "bastards," racial and genealogical certification for "half-Jews" and individuals of du-

bious descent, racial surveys and "resettlement" plans for the populations of the eastern occupied territories, surveys and "solutions" for German racial minorities, such as Gypsies and Jews), within several organizations or ministries. Besides serving as experts on racial matters, the anthropologists trained the SS physicians who made the racial "selections" in the eastern territories. As a whole, racial anthropology was as deeply involved and compromised with the regime's racial politics as were other biomedical disciplines with sterilizations, euthanasia, extermination, and human experiments (human genetics, psychiatry, criminal biology, and medicine).

Germany's defeat in 1945 did not induce major changes in university personnel. Although several institutes were closed (especially in the Soviet zone), most compromised anthropologists remained, retired, or found new positions in the 1950s, the 1960s, and even up to the 1970s. Scientists defended themselves individually and collectively against potential accusations by accusing "ignorant politicians" for enforcing a "pseudo-science" and by presenting the apologetic legend of their science having been a victim of totalitarianism. However, the development of population genetics and its criticism of the traditional thinking, combined with the international condemnation of Nazi racism, brought the concept of "race" into disrepute. In Germany itself, although anthropologists gained seven new chairs and institutes in the 1960s and 1970s, the discipline lost its scientific and academic significance and, except for prehistoric anthropology and paleoanthropology, trailed behind the scientifically more progressive and "politically correct" human genetics and cultural sciences, which showed little desire to cooperate scientifically with physical anthropologists.

Benoit Massin

See also Chamberlain, Houston Stewart; Eugenics; Euthanasia; Günther, Hans; Haeckel, Ernst; National Socialism; Racism; Social Darwinism; Tönnies, Ferdinand; Virchow, Rudolf

References

Lilienthal, G. "Anthropology and National Socialism." *Encyclopedia of the Holocaust*. Vol. 3. Ed. I. Gutman. New York, NY: Macmillan, 1990.

Massin, B. "Anthropologie raciale et national-socialisme; heurs et malheurs du paradigme de la 'race.'" *La science sous le Troisieme Reich*. Ed. J. Olff-Nathan. Paris: Editions du Seuil, 1993.

———. "Fin-de-Siecle Physical Anthropology and 'Modern Race Theories' in Imperial Germany (1890–1914)." *Volksgeist as Method and Ethic: Essays on Boasian Ethnography and the German Anthropological Tradition*. Ed. G.W. Stocking. Madison, WI: University of Wisconsin Press, 1996.

Proctor, Robert. "From Anthropologie to Rassenkunde in the German Anthropological Tradition." *Bones, Bodies, Behavior*. Ed. G.W. Stocking. Madison: University of Wisconsin Press, 1988.

Schwidetzky, I. *History of Biological Anthropology in Germany*. International Association of Human Biologists, Occasional Papers 3 (1992).

Weindling, Paul. *Health, Race and German Politics between National Unification and Nazism (1870–1945)*. Cambridge: Cambridge University Press, 1989.

Weingart, P., J. Kroll, and K. Bayertz. *Rasse, Blut und Gene: Geschichte der Eugenik und Rassenhygiene in Deutschland*. Frankfurt am Main: Suhrkamp, 1988.

Anti-Fascism

Anti-Fascism originally referred only to opposition to Mussolini's Fascist movement in Italy. After his assumption of power in October 1922, anti-Fascism became an international concept, since simultaneously in other countries similar alliances among radical right elements took place. In 1923, an international anti-Fascism congress convened in Frankfurt.

Communists saw themselves as the avant garde of the anti-Fascist struggle. Their ideologically and programmatically expanded definition of Fascism, formulated during the Fifth World Congress of the Comintern in 1924, viewed Fascism as "the classical form of counter-revolution in the decline of capitalist society." The definition was subsequently employed to include even Social Democracy as "social Fascism." In 1935, at the Seventh Congress of the Comintern, this notion was revised to exclude Social Democrats. The subsequent Popular Front strategy created a broader anti-Fascist resistance.

At the end of the war in Germany spontaneous groups termed "Antifa" (short for "anti-Fascist") organized liberation committees and tried to create a democratic mass movement. Most members were Communists, socialists, and Social Democrats, but this attempt at working-class liberation and self-organization was quickly repressed by the occupying powers.

The official anti-Fascism that first appeared in the Soviet occupation zone, later the German Democratic Republic (GDR), was based on the idea of a unified front (*Einheitsfront*) and Soviet Marshal Zhukov's Order #2 of June 10, 1945, according to which parties were admitted. The fusion of the Communist Party and the Social Democratic Party (SPD), which occurred under extensive Soviet pressure and which created the Socialist Unity Party (SED) on April 21, 1946, as well as the union of the "bourgeois" forces in the "bloc parties" of the GDR, made anti-Fascism the basis for national reconstruction. SED officials claimed that structural de-Nazification, founded on the concept of anti-Fascism, necessitated the land reform of 1945 and the expropriation of heavy industry in 1946.

The years 1945–48, described by GDR historiographers as the phase of the "anti-Fascist democratic revolution," were also considered the first phase of the socialist revolution. At the same time, East German officials hoped that anti-Fascism would gain a foothold in the Western occupation zones. These hopes were dashed by the prevailing anti-Communist attitude of the West, especially that of SPD party leader, Kurt Schumacher (1895–1952). The anti-Fascist committees, which had arisen spontaneously in the Western zones before war's end, and in which Communists and socialists were represented, were dissolved in the wake of the ban on political activity. It is also likely that the Western Allies viewed them as Communist sympathizers.

In the GDR, anti-Fascism became identified with official policy. This appeared in the constitutions of 1949 and 1968. In the latter, anti-Fascism was explicitly declared a fundamental constitutional premise. From this perspective, anti-Fascism was the political basis of all progressive forces, and was particularly directed against the Western capitalist states. The designation of the Berlin Wall as an "anti-Fascist bulwark" made this function evident.

This one-sided, politically motivated view of anti-Fascism is reflected in Marxist-Leninist GDR historiography. The activities of the Communist resistance (which were exaggerated as massive) were deemed to be a class struggle for the creation of the "people's democracy," which was consequently assigned a higher moral value than other political systems. It thus became difficult to consider bourgeois resistance as anti-Fascist.

Anti-Fascism is essentially defined by its opposition to Fascism; this vagueness, however, is problematic. From a Marxist-Leninist perspective, anti-Fascism, especially in the GDR, became central to defining and justifying the official ideology. This led the West to distance itself from the concept.

Bernd Stöver

See also Axen, Hermann; German Democratic Republic: Marxism-Leninism; Honecker, Erich; National Committee for a Free Germany; National Socialism; Resistance; Schumacher, Kurt; Seghers, Anna; Socialist Unity Party of Germany; World War II

References
Badstübner, Rolf. "Die antifaschistisch-demokratische Umwälzung im Spannungsfeld der Auseinandersetzungen in und um Deutschland." *Jahrbuch für Geschichte* 30 (1984), 7–70.

Borsdorf, Ulrich and Lutz Niethammer. *Zwischen Befreiung und Besatzung*. Wuppertal: Hammer Verlag, 1976.

Doerry, Thomas. *Antifaschismus in der Bundesrepublik: vom antifaschistischen Konsens in 1945 bis zur Gegenwart*. Frankurt am Main: Roderberg, 1980.

Grunenberg, Antonia. *Antifaschismus, ein deutscher Mythos*. Reinbek bei Hamburg: Rowohlt, 1993.

Plum, Werner. "Widerstand und Antifaschismus in der marxistisch-leninistischen Geschichtsauffassung." *Vierteljahreshefte für Zeitgeschichte* 9 (1961), 50–65.

Wippermann, Wolfgang. *Antifaschismus in der DDR: Wirklichkeit und Ideologie. Beiträge zum Thema Widerstand*. Vol. 16. Berlin: Informationszentrum Berlin, 1980.

Anti-Semitism (1871–1933)

Two crucial factors converged to produce the anti-Semitic movement of the 1870s in Germany. First, between 1848 and 1871, the Jews of Germany achieved emancipation, freeing them to move to urban centers, attend universities, enter the professions, and participate in public and cultural life. Their former lowly status gave way to a highly visible upward mobility. The second factor, the economic downturn following the Depression of 1873, further victimized a lower middle class and peasantry already having difficulty with the transition from an agricultural to a capitalist market economy. The resulting economic and social turmoil provided both the producers and consumers of anti-Semitic ideology, and introduced anti-Semitism as a tool of mobilization to German political life.

The anti-Semitic ideologues and leaders of the political organizations that began appearing around 1878–79 came from varying backgrounds. Christian conservatives, such as Hermann Wagener (1815–89) and Adolf Stoecker (1835–1909) depicted Jews as agents of social decomposition, sowing revolutionary discontent and undermining hierarchical authority. The doyen of nationalist historians, Heinrich von Treitschke (1834–96), wrote in his influential booklet, *Ein Wort über unser Judenthum* (A word about our Jewry), 1880, that "the Jews are our misfortune." He warned against the threat posed by assimilated Jews to a young, vulnerable German national unity and became the major inspiration for anti-Semitic students organized in the *Verein deutscher Studenten* (Association of German Students), 1880. By far the largest number of anti-Semitic politicians, however, came out of the ranks of the educated lower middle class. Failed academics, thwarted intellectuals, hand-to-mouth journalists—many of them erstwhile liberals or democrats—gave the movement its tone, saddling Jews with responsibility for most of the economic, cultural, and moral evils of the times.

Although these men built upon centuries of Jew-hatred, they saw themselves as innovators. Wilhelm Marr (1819–1904), a revolutionary democrat in 1848, coined the term anti-Semite in 1879 in order to distinguish between coarse Jew-baiting and religious bigotry and a new, up-to-date ideology based on race. Anti-Semites developed a theory of history, an analysis of the present, and a tool for predicting the future, all drawing upon the notion of a Jewish world conspiracy. Theirs was a full-time commitment to take action against the Jewish danger, and they succeeded in institutionalizing anti-Semitism with journals, newspapers, publishing houses, reform clubs, and political parties.

Those whose first priority was "solving the Jewish question" arranged themselves in small and fractious political parties appealing to Protestant peasant and urban lower-middle-class constituencies. Court Chaplain Stoecker's Christian Social Party (1878), closely allied to the Conservatives, lost its footing in Berlin by the mid-1880s and relied on supporters from rural districts in Westphalia. The Antisemitische Volkspartei (Anti-Semitic Peoples Party) established in Hesse in 1889 by Otto Böckel (1859–1923), the Saxon-based Deutsche Reformpartei (German Reform Party), 1880, of Oswald Zimmermann (1854–1910), and the Deutschsoziale Partei (German Social Party), 1889, led by Max Liebermann von Sonnenberg (1848–1911) united briefly as the Deutschsoziale Reformpartei (1894–1900). But personal rivalries, embarrassing scandals, and shifting fortunes at the polls led to frequent schisms.

Notwithstanding variations in rhetorical style and in the personal respectability of their leaders, the anti-Semitic parties had much in common. For campaign personnel and as a source of always uncertain finances, they relied at the grassroots level on approximately 140 reform clubs. Leaders earned

their living by writing for or editing numerous, usually short-lived and shabby, newspapers, 25 to 40 of which were associated with one of the parties. The programs of the parties sought to solve the Jewish question, while improving the lot of their constituents, through conventional legislative means. They all advocated exclusion of Jews from governmental offices and employment in public schools, limitations on Jewish immigration, and the taking of a special, racially based census.

None of these measures, which collectively would have amounted to a revocation of Jewish emancipation, came close to adoption in the national or state parliaments. Unable to penetrate the Catholic working-class masses, the anti-Semites of the Imperial era failed to build a strong mass movement. They achieved their high-water mark in the Reichstag elections of 1893 with 16 deputies (8 from Hessen; 6 from Saxony; 1 each from Brandenburg and Pomerania). Perhaps 350,000 votes (4.4 percent) were cast for identifiable anti-Semites from all parties. From this point, however, their percentage of the vote declined steadily. In the last Reichstag elections before World War I, they mustered only 131,000 votes, and during the course of the war, the anti-Semites disappeared into various right-wing parties.

The bankruptcy of conventional, parliamentary anti-Semitism cleared the way for those who had never accepted the feasibility of solving the Jewish question through party politics. For such deeply undemocratic persons, parliaments and parties were symptoms of the Judaic disease afflicting Germany. According to them, all levels of German society would have to be indoctrinated with anti-Semitism before sweeping measures to cleanse German life of false values could be undertaken. Normal politics were useless in this struggle for survival. The Russian Revolution of 1917 and the German collapse of 1918 corroborated their worst fears and readied German society for a more radical brand of anti-Semitism.

Anti-Semitic activism in the Weimar era continued to be the province of warring lower-middle-class organizations and parties. While many of the charges against Jews remained the same, powerful new images of the Jewish war profiteer, Bolshevik gangster, or oversexed plutocrat intruded into public discourse. The already sizable circulation of anti-Jewish literature—always a hallmark of the German anti-Semitic movement—rose to yet higher levels. Copies of *The Protocols of the Elders of Zion* (German editions from 1920) and Henry Ford's *The International Jew,* 1922, numbered in the hundreds of thousands.

A new breed of anti-Semite, more radically disaffected and willing to resort to violence, displaced the few survivors from the prewar era. In the Imperial period, anti-Semites had been hemmed in by generally respected institutions and norms of behavior. But Weimar democracy enjoyed no such legitimacy, making it far more difficult for organizations defending Weimar democracy and state agencies to fight anti-Semitism. Elements of the German elite of property and education, which had indulged in a manipulative and occasional anti-Semitism before the war, were now much more willing to finance anti-Semitic activities as a means of defending their interests. The respectable Pan-German League (1894), for example, "declared war against Jewry" and funded the distribution of 10 million anti-Semitic publications by the Deutschvölkischer Schutz- und Trutzbund (German People's Defense League) (1919–24), members of which carried out the murder of Walther Rathenau in 1922.

Particularly in Bavaria, following the abortive socialist and Soviet republics (1918–19), anti-Semitic groups of radical stamp flourished. Among them, the Nazi Party made extreme anti-Semitism central to its attempt to mobilize followers and after 1933 made solution of the Jewish question one of the chief tasks of the German state.

From 1871 to 1933, the anti-Semitism of the German right accustomed Germans to fanaticism and wildly improbable claims regarding Jewish plans of conquest. Just how actively appealing anti-Semitism was to ordinary Germans remains a moot issue. But there can be little doubt that anti-Semitism became entrenched in political culture, poisoned political life, and persuaded citizens to look upon the rights of Jews with indifference. Such apathy made the Final Solution possible.

Richard S. Levy

See also Böckel, Otto; Chamberlain, Houston Stewart; Fritsch, Theodor; Goebbels, Joseph; Hitler, Adolf; Holocaust; Jews, 1869–1933; Lagarde, Paul de; Langbehn, Julius; National Socialism; Nationalism; Pan-German League; Racism; Radical Right; Stoecker, Adolf; Treitschke, Heinrich von; *Völkisch* Ideology

References

Fricke, Dieter. *Die bürgerlichen Parteien in Deutschland: Handbuch der bürgerlichen Parteien und anderer bürgerlicher Interessenorganisationen vom Vormärz bis zum Jahre 1945.* 2 vols. Berlin: Das europäische Buch, 1968.
Jochmann, Werner. *Gesellschaftskrise und Judenfeindschaft in Deutschland, 1870–1945.* Hamburg: Christians, 1988.
Katz, Jacob. *From Prejudice to Destruction: Anti-Semitism 1700–1933.* Cambridge, MA: Harvard University Press, 1980.
Kauders, Anthony. *German Politics and the Jews: Düsseldorf and Nuremberg, 1910–1933.* New York, NY: Oxford University Press, 1996.
Levy, Richard S. *Antisemitism in the Modern World: An Anthology of Texts.* Lexington, MA: Heath, 1991.
———. *The Downfall of the Anti-Semitic Political Parties in Imperial Germany.* New Haven, CT: Yale University Press, 1975.
Lohalm, Uwe. *Völkischer Radikalismus: Die Geschichte des Deutschvölkischen Schutz- und Trutz-Bundes.* Hamburg: Leibniz Verlag, 1970.
Massing, Paul. *Rehearsal for Destruction: A Study of Political Anti-Semitism in Imperial Germany.* New York, NY: Harper, 1949.
Mosse, Werner E. and Arnold Paucker, eds. *Deutsches Judentum in Krieg und Revolution, 1916–1923.* Tübingen: J.C.B. Mohr, 1971.
Niewyk, Donald. *The Jews in Weimar Germany.* Baton Rouge, LA: Louisiana State University, 1980.
Paucker, Arnold. *Der jüdische Abwehrkampf gegen Anti-Semitismus und Nationalsozialismus in den letzten Jahren der Weimarer Republik.* Hamburg: Leibniz Verlag, 1966.
Pulzer, Peter G. J. *The Rise of Political Anti-Semitism in Germany and Austria.* New York, NY: John Wiley, 1964. Revised edition, 1988.
Rürup, Reinhard. *Emanzipation und Anti-Semitismus: Studien zur "Judenfrage" der bürgerlichen Gesellschaft.* Göttingen: Vandenhoeck & Ruprecht, 1975.

Archaeology

In the late nineteenth and early twentieth centuries, German archaeologists established national archaeological societies within Germany as well as German research institutes in Mediterranean lands. They improved archaeological methodology and became widely respected for their careful, "scientific" technique. Although non-German archaeologists, such as Giuseppe Fiorelli, Augustus Pitt Rivers, and W. M. Flinders Petrie, simultaneously developed improved excavation methods, German excavators introduced orderly excavation techniques, observed occupational strata, and kept meticulous records.

In 1829, the Prussians established the Istituto di Correspondenza Archaeologica to coordinate and systematize the study of Italian, and especially Etruscan, antiquity. After the unification of Germany, this institution became known as the German Archaeological Institute in Rome. The Deutsche Orient Gesellschaft (German [Near] Eastern Society) and the German Archaeological Institute in Athens were other important German institutions created to conduct research in ancient civilizations.

From 1875 to 1881, the German Archaeological Institute in Athens subsidized Ernst Curtius's influential excavations at Olympia in Greece. Though Greek law required that all of the thousands of objects excavated, including the expedition's most significant find, the *Hermes* of Praxiteles, remain in Greece, the institute spared no expense in the work. This was one of the first archaeological undertakings conducted purely for the sake of the knowledge to be gained. These excavations provided the training ground in systematic, stratigraphical digging for Wilhelm Dörpfeld, the person who introduced order and method into Heinrich Schliemann's (1822–90) excavations, and they served as a model for archaeologists of other nationalities working in mainland Greece and the Aegean, including the Greeks themselves.

The Deutsche Orient Gesellschaft sponsored several significant expeditions in the pre–World War I period. Under its aegis, Robert Koldewey uncovered the ruins of Babylon (1899–1917) and Walter Andrae unearthed Asshur, first capital of ancient Assyria (1902–14). Like the German work at Olympia, these expeditions in Mesopotamia demonstrated the value of precise, stratigraphical excavation methodology. This society was also responsible for Ludwig Borchardt's work at Tell el-Amarna in Egypt (1904–14), where the famous bust of Queen Nefertiti was discovered in 1912.

However, public interest in the recovery of ancient classical and Near Eastern civilizations had a negative effect on some German prehistorians and nationalists who felt their own past being slighted. Foremost among this discontented group was Gustav Kossinna, professor of German prehistory at the University of Berlin from 1902 until his death in 1931. Like Houston Chamberlain (1855–1927) in *The Foundations of the Nineteenth Century,* 1899, Kossinna promoted the greatness of German antiquity. He combined elements from linguistics, physical anthropology, and prehistoric archaeology to claim that European culture had begun in a "Germanic homeland" and then spread outward to the "inferior peoples" in other parts of Europe. He also asserted that the ancient Germanic territory had included places such as Poland, Czechoslovakia, and other areas where "Germanic" prehistoric artifacts had been found.

In the years following Germany's defeat in World War I, many people, including Adolf Hitler, were attracted to Kossinna's views. When the Nazis gained power in 1933, Kossinna's ideas formed the basis for state policy on archaeology. The new government created eight new university chairs in German prehistory, established several institutes and museums for prehistory, and funded prehistoric excavations in Germany on a scale unparalleled in the past. Prehistoric archaeology became an instrument for propagating Nazi ideology and promoting patriotism through popular journals such as *Germanen-Erbe* (Germanic heritage) and organizations such as the Reichsbund für Deutsche Vorgeschichte (National Federation for German Prehistory).

Many otherwise respectable professional archaeologists promoted these Nazi claims. Other archaeologists silently conformed to the requirements of Nazi-dominated funding sources. On the other hand, those archaeologists who openly opposed the Nazi misuse of prehistoric archaeology, for example, Gerhard Bersu, were dismissed from their positions and persecuted.

After World War II, most university posts in archaeology continued to be filled by the same people who had held them under the Nazis, or by scholars who had been trained during the 1930s and 1940s. While they quickly abandoned Nazi racial theories, many archaeologists, especially prehistorians, found it difficult to come to grips with the role of archaeology during the Nazi era. Furthermore, archaeologists in East Germany now had to conform to state-sponsored Communist ideology. These problems impeded German archaeological research throughout the Cold War period. However, by 1990, most of the Nazi-era archaeologists had died. The new generation of younger archaeologists and graduate students seemed more willing to confront the recent past of their discipline and to restore German archaeology to the eminence it had once possessed.

William H. Stiebing, Jr.

See also Racism; Schliemann, Heinrich; *Völkisch* Ideology

References

Arnold, Bettina. "The Past as Propaganda: How Hitler's Archaeologists Distorted European Prehistory to Justify Racist and Territorial Goals." *Archaeology* 45 (July-August 1992), 30–37.

———. "The Past as Propaganda: Totalitarian Archaeology in Nazi Germany." *Antiquity* 64 (1990), 464–78.
Daniel, Glyn and Colin Renfrew. *The Idea of Prehistory.* 2nd ed. Edinburgh: Edinburgh University Press, 1988.
Marchand, Suzanne L. *Down from Olympus.* Princeton, NJ: Princeton University Press, 1996.
McCann, William. "The National Socialist Perversion of Archaeology." *World Archaeology Bulletin* 2 (1988), 51–54.
———. "'Volk and Germanentum': The Presentation of the Past in Nazi Germany." *The Politics of the Past.* Eds. Peter Gathercole and David Lowenthal. London: Unwin Hyman, 1989.
Stiebing, William. *Uncovering the Past: A History of Archaeology.* Buffalo, NY: Prometheus Books, 1993.

Architecture and Urban Design

Immediately following the Franco-Prussian War in 1871, economic expansion, urbanization, and industrialization brought rapid development to cities and an extension of urbanized areas. Until then, many German cities had expanded only marginally beyond their medieval boundaries, though beginning in the eighteenth century fortified walls had been dismantled. While small-scale industries, railroad stations, and a few dwelling districts had been constructed beyond the medieval boundaries, many cities retained a strong historic character.

During the post-1871 "founding era" (*Gründerzeit*), districts of stately homes for the managerial class and *Mietskaserne* (literally, "rental barracks") for the working class replaced former agricultural land at city edges. The typical *Mietskaserne* in large cities comprised rows of five-story walk-up apartment buildings, with each stairwell serving two or four apartments per floor. Often the building formed an approximate rectangle covering an entire city block, with a small courtyard in the center where sanitary facilities could be installed. An applied architectural style often suggested the income level of residents. Facades of buildings for the lowest-income workers were simply articulated, while pretentions of primarily neoclassical adornment increased proportionally with the cost and size of apartments. In urban design, *Mietskaserne* districts usually comprised rows of unrelieved rectangular blocks.

The lack of sanitary facilities led to movements toward health reform, calling for water and sewer lines to serve expanding cities. This interest, along with the need to move the increasing vehicle and pedestrian traffic more efficiently through expanding cities, led to a more formal, geometric street design pattern that imposed fundamental changes on the traditional urban character rooted in the medieval city.

The increasingly engineering-oriented layout of urban districts encouraged a reconsideration of traditional forms in urban design, as represented by the influential book by the Austrian Camillo Sitte, *Der Städtebau nach seiner künstlerischen Grundsätzen* (City planning according to artistic principles), 1889. In 1890, Josef Stübben's *Der Städtebau* appeared, which defended the position of the "regularists," thus setting the stage for the competing visions of "traditional" versus "modern" that would dominate German architecture and urban design through much of the twentieth century.

As a result of these debates, aesthetic considerations strongly influenced German city planning at the turn of the century, as seen in the plans for Aachen, Danzig, Darmstadt, Dresden, Karlsruhe, Munich, and Stuttgart. In architectural style, *Jugendstil* (art nouveau) and influences of the Viennese Secession enjoyed prominence in the years shortly after 1900.

Expanding industrialization and prosperity also led to a desire by city dwellers to live in less dense surroundings. Theodor Fritsch's (1852–1933) book *Stadt der Zukunft* (City of the future), 1906, introduced the Garden City movement to Germany, and by the 1910s, *Siedlungen* (cooperative or factory-owned housing estates) would characterize German working-class dwelling construction. In style, many *Siedlung* dwellings hearkened to medieval German traditions, forming clusters of dwellings having small-paned windows and steeply pitched roofs (for example, the Krupp factory *Siedlung* Margarethenhöhe in Essen, designed by Georg Metzendorf), or began to explore proto-Modern reductionist ideas (Hellerau *Siedlung* near Dresden, by Heinrich Tessenow, 1908). Simultaneously, what would become the modern movement began to develop its own architectural aesthetic. In 1907, Hermann Muthesius formed the Werkbund (work association), an organization intended to bring designers into industry and improve German manufactured goods. The architect Peter Behrens (1868–1940), a Werkbund founder, assumed the role of head designer for the AEG industrial concern in 1907 and among other achievements bridged the gap between avant-garde aesthetics and architecture by designing the AEG Turbine Factory building in Berlin, which would become a standard monument of early modernist architecture.

The architect Walter Gropius (1883–1969) worked in Behrens's office from 1907 to 1910, when he formed his own office and received the commission to design what would be another standard monument of modernism: the Fagus shoe last factory in Alfeld an der Leine. Not only did Gropius substitute steel and glass curtain walls for the traditional masonry load-bearing walls, he celebrated the aesthetic of steel and glass, thereby proclaiming what would be a dominant characteristic of the "international style" in the 1920s. In 1926, Gropius designed another modernist building that would largely define the international style: the Bauhaus in Dessau, where stark masses of white stucco walls played against transparent glass curtains with black steel window frames. However, modernist architecture of the 1920s would more generally fall under the term *Neue Sachlichkeit* (New Objectivity) of practical and somewhat conventional large-scale buildings. The huge Schaltwerk-Hochhaus for Siemens in Berlin (1927; Hans Hertlein), which forms a huge gridded slab of piers and windows, is an excellent remaining example.

Economic hardship during the 1920s precluded most large-scale urban design programs but led to intense interest in the "housing problem." Some attempts to apply modernist architectural ideas to the provision of suitable housing were successful, at least on a small scale. The Weissenhofsiedlung in Stuttgart (1926) comprised experimental dwellings by a

Potsdamer Platz, Berlin, 1914 and after 1990 collapse of East Germany. Courtesy of German Embassy, Ottawa.

number of prominent modern architects, such as Le Corbusier and Mies van der Rohe. On the other hand, the residents of Walter Gropius's *Siedlung* Törten in Dessau (1926–28), comprising 314 concrete-frame row houses of "rationalized construction," began replacing the narrow steel-framed windows with traditional, wood-framed, shuttered windows shortly after the complex was completed.

Most innovative German architecture of the 1920s, however, remained traditional in its use of brick. Much of the expressionist movement in architecture of the 1920s celebrated the angular, intricate, hard-edged properties of dark, hard-fired clinker brick—in large-scale buildings it combined a sense of monumentality with a display of hand-craftsmanship—both of which properties directly contradicted the opposing international style model. The 11–story, brick-clad administration building for Borsig AG in Berlin (1922; Eugen Schmohl), for example, culminated in a zig-zag tower form.

Gigantism had characterized German architecture since the 1870s. In 1890–96 Bruno Schmitz designed the 81-meter-high Kyffhäuser Monument on a mountaintop in the Harz and in 1898–1913 created the 91-meter-high Völkerschlacht Monument in Leipzig. Both structures were masonry cenotaphs. Office buildings and factories of the expressionist and *Neue Sachlichkeit* movements of the 1920s began to dominate townscapes in a similar way, though the movements were truncated by the end of the Weimar Republic.

National Socialist architecture and urban design of the 1930s was not a unitary concept, but borrowed both from trends of large-scale monumentality and small-scale traditionalism, employing each in exaggerated form. Albert Speer's Zeppelin Field in Nuremberg represented the former, while in many cities dwelling blocks of a traditional style, with steeply pitched roofs and a central courtyard, equally represented National Socialist architecture. Despite the official suppression of international style modernism, industrial buildings continued to be constructed with functional character. Nazi urban design plans, remaining almost entirely unbuilt, tended toward grand axes flanked by monumental buildings inspired by classical architecture.

Postwar German architecture and urban design in the two German states represented the opposed societal visions governing them. In the 1950s, the ideological confrontation manifested itself in architecture, as West Germany fully embraced postwar modernism while East Germany rejected it. Frankfurt am Main became West Germany's financial center, its downtown increasingly characterized by free-standing high-rise structures in contrast to the contextual, low-rise traditional German city. The destroyed historic center of Kassel was redesigned in an orthogonal pattern with its *Treppenstrasse* (Stairway street) pedestrian zone from the mid-1950s. The influential book by R. Göderlitz, *Die Gegliederte und Aufgelockerte Stadt* (The structured and dispersed city), 1957, proposed the deconcentration of the traditional city center and opening the city to automobile access. Urban design solutions frequently incorporated long building slabs accompanying wide traffic-oriented streets, borrowing from the *Mietskaserne* tradition.

Early 1950s urban design in East Germany shared the aspiration for the automobile city, as represented in the plan for Stalinallee in Berlin (after 1950), though the architecture of the Stalinist period borrowed primarily from the "socialist realism" movement emanating from the Soviet Union in the 1930s. Called Nati Tradi (architecture of national tradition), early 1950s East German building hearkened specifically to German traditions: buildings along Lange Strasse in Rostock were rebuilt as a twentieth-century interpretation of German Brick Gothic architecture, while Nati Tradi architecture in Dessau evoked the region's eighteenth-century classicism.

The pace of its building being too slow and labor-intensive, East Germany abandoned the National Tradition movement in the mid-1950s and increasingly committed its centrally planned building industry to *Plattenbau*, large-scale, concrete, panel-prefabricated buildings that generally accommodated no significant urban design planning. In 1973, East Germany joined the "dispersed city" trend by accelerating its building program with large-scale prefabricated housing complexes on urban fringes.

As the negative effects of dispersed cities became clearer in the 1970s, both East and West Germany supported the transformation of central city districts into pedestrian zones, removing streetcar lines and automobile traffic from main shopping streets (Heidelberg) or enhancing "old city" cores as traffic-free shopping and leisure districts (Düsseldorf, Erfurt). However, until German unification, both West and East Germany had produced a tradition of postwar urban design dominated by the challenge of accommodating the increasing numbers of automobiles in the city.

Architecture of the 1980s in West Germany gravitated toward a modest "postmodernism" of playful forms in lively colors (Rob Krier's Stadtvillen in Berlin, 1983), while East Germany turned to a modest contextualism, fitting prefabricated buildings into remnants of historic centers (Kolonnadenstrasse in Leipzig, 1988). By reunification in 1990, however, buildings throughout East Germany had reached a condition of serious deterioration, and urban districts had not been planned to anticipate Western automobile ownership levels. These problems would pose major post-unification challenges in architecture and urban design.

Paul H. Gleye

See also Bauhaus; Behrens, Peter; Gardens and Landscape Architecture; Gropius, Walter; Housing; *Jugendstil*; Mies van der Rohe, Ludwig; Speer, Albert; Urbanization; Werkbund

References

Burchard, John. *The Voice of the Phoenix: Postwar Architecture in Germany*. Cambridge, MA: MIT Press, 1966.

Dal Co, Francesco. *Figures of Architecture and Thought: German Architecture Culture 1880–1920*. New York, NY: Rizzoli, 1990.

Kinser, Bill and Neil Kleinman. *The Dream That Was No More a Dream: A Search for Aesthetic Reality in Germany, 1890–1945*. New York, NY: Harper and Row, 1969.

Lane, Barbara Miller. *Architecture and Politics in Germany, 1918–1945*. Cambridge, MA: Harvard University Press, 1968. Rev. ed. 1985.

Posener, Julius. *From Schinkel to the Bauhaus*. London: Lund Humphries for the Architectural Association, 1972.

Taylor, Robert. *The Word in Stone*. Berkeley, CA: University of California Press, 1974.

Topfstedt, Thomas. *Städtebau in der DDR, 1985–1974*. Leipzig: Seemann, 1988.

Archives

Owing to the federalist structure of the German Reich and the Federal Republic, the archival sources of German history from 1871 to the present are located in a multitude of archives whose holdings complement each other. Subsequent to the destruction of archival material during World War II, many primary sources had to be replaced by secondary materials.

Only in 1919 was an archive, specifically the Reichsarchiv in Potsdam, founded to house the documents of the central government departments (*Reichsbehörden*). Most of the documents taken over from the civic authorities (*zivile Reichsbehörden*) and dating from before 1914 have remained intact and, after 1945, formed the nucleus of the holdings of the central German archives (Deutsches Zentralarchiv), subsequently the central state archives of the German Democratic Republic (GDR) and since 1990 of the Federal Archives (Bundesarchiv), Potsdam Division.

The records of the Prussian-German Army and of the Reichswehr, which were located in the army archives (Heeresarchiv) in Potsdam after 1937, were, in part, destroyed by an air raid in 1945. Most of the records of the major Reich departments and the Nazi Party offices, as well as the documents of the armed forces that had not been destroyed, were confiscated by the Allied troops in 1945 and taken to Great Britain (Whaddon Hall), to the United States (Alexandria, Va.), and to the Soviet Union; but most were repatriated in the 1950s.

In the Federal Republic these documents were placed in the Federal Archives, which has been in Koblenz since 1952, and its military division (Abteilung Militärarchiv) has been located in Freiburg since 1968. In the GDR they were combined with the holdings of the Reichsarchiv at Potsdam. There are some exceptions, however, namely: 1) most of the post-1871 documents of the Foreign Office (Auswärtiges Amt) and of the German diplomatic service, which are located in the political archives (Politisches Archiv) of the Foreign Office in Bonn; 2) the personnel material of the Nazi Party and its organizations, which were in the American-controlled Berlin Document Center and which became a branch of the Federal Archives in July 1994; and 3) concentration camp records, which are kept by the International Tracing Service (the Internationaler Suchdienst) in Arolsen, Hesse. Only in 1990 did it become known that the Soviet Union had retained sizable German files in special Moscow archives, now called the Center for the Preservation of Historical Documentary Collections (Zentrum für die Aufbewährung historisch-dokumentarischer Sammlungen).

The branches of the Federal Archives in Koblenz, Potsdam, and Freiburg will in the future combine most of the records of the central authorities of the German Empire, the Nazi Party, the occupation zones from 1945 to 1949, the GDR, the Federal Republic, the Wehrmacht (including the records of the navy [Kriegsmarine] since 1871 and the national people's army [Volksarmee], plus the holdings of the former GDR military archives) and the Bundeswehr.

Both the archives of Germany before 1945 and the Federal Archives have acquired the comprehensive personal papers of politicians, among them high-ranking officials and several chancellors of the Reich; party records and records of associations have also been secured; and their activities are documented by collections of posters and pamphlets. In the former West Germany, the archives of the political parties, financed through endowments, largely fulfilled this function, namely the Archives of Social Democracy of the Friedrich Ebert-Stiftung (foundation) in Bonn, the Archives for Christian-Democratic Politics of the Konrad Adenauer-Stiftung in St. Augustin near Bonn, and the Archives of German Liberalism of the Friedrich Naumann-Stiftung in Gummersbach (North Rhine–Westphalia). The archives of the parties and mass organizations of the former GDR, especially the central party archives of the SED (Zentrales Parteiarchiv der SED) were taken over through an endowed institute within the Federal Archives in Berlin.

Since their foundation, the Federal Archives have also established film archives for documentaries and feature films and have absorbed the holdings of the former GDR film archives containing some materials from the Reichsfilmarchiv.

Among the archives of the German states (Länder), for the period prior to 1933, the secret state archives (Geheimes Staatsarchiv) for the endowment for Prussian cultural heritage (Stiftung Preussischer Kulturbesitz) in Berlin-Dahlem are primary. It now contains the capacious files of the central Prussian authorities, which had been kept in Merseburg in the Historical Division II of the Central State Archives of the GDR (Historische Abt. II des Zentralen Staatsarchivs der DDR). Other nationally significant archives are the Bavarian State Archives (Bayrisches Hauptstaatsarchiv) in Munich, the Generallandesarchiv in Karlsruhe and the Hauptstaatsarchiv in Stuttgart for the Baden-Württemberg region, and the Staatsarchiv Dresden in Saxony.

Frequently, sources that are missing elsewhere can be found in the archives of the central offices (Zentralbehörden) of the smaller states, as for example the Archives of Lower Saxony in Oldenburg as well as in some 40 regional state archives, such as the archives of the former Prussian provinces, some of which continue to exist as Polish archives. For post–World War II history, the main archives (Hauptstaats- or Landeshauptarchive) of the newly created West German states deserve to be mentioned; they are located in Düsseldorf, Hannover, Schleswig, Wiesbaden, Koblenz, Saarbrücken and in the city-states of Hamburg, Bremen, and Berlin.

Some non–state-owned archives have important holdings: the Stiftung Bundeskanzler-Adenauer-Haus in Bad Honnef-Rhöndorf, which contains the papers of the first West German chancellor and which is remotely comparable to the American presidential libraries; the archives of Otto von Bismarck in Friedrichsruh, which preserve the papers of the first chancellor of the Reich; the Krupp Archives in Essen and the Siemens Archives in Munich with respect to the economy; and the Evangelisches Zentralarchiv (Protestant central archive) in Berlin for matters relating to the Protestant churches.

Heinz Boberach

See also Foundations and Research Institutes; Libraries; Socialist Unity Party of Germany

References
Aly, Götz and Susanne Heim. *Das Zentrale Staatsarchiv in Moskau ("Sonderarchiv")*. Düsseldorf: Hans-Böckler-Stiftung, 1992.
Boberach, Heinz, ed. *Inventar archivalischer Quellen des NS-Staates*. 3 vols. Munich: Saur, 1990.
Branig, Hans, Winfried Bliss, and Werner Petermann, eds. *Übersicht über die Bestände des Geheimen Staatsarchivs in Berlin-Dahlem*. Teil 11. Zentralbehörden, andere Institutionen, Sammlungen. Cologne: Grote, 1967.
"Das Archivwesen der Bundesrepublik Deutschland: Ein Überblick." *Der Archivar* 37 (1984), 313–479 (also published in English).
Granier, Gerhard et al., eds. *Das Bundesarchiv und seine Bestände*. Boppard: Boldt, 1977.
Guides to German Records Microfilmed at Alexandria, Va., by the American Historical Association. 62 vols. Washington: National Archives and Records Service, 1958 *ff.*

Kahlenberg, Friedrich. *Deutsche Archive in West und Ost: Zur Entwicklung des staatlichen Archivwesens seit 1945.* Düsseldorf: Droste, 1972.

Kent, George O., ed. *A Catalog of Files and Microfilms of the German Foreign Ministry Archives 1920–1945.* 4 vols. Palo Alto, CA: Hoover Institution Press, 1962–72.

Lötzke, Helmut and Hans-Stephan Brater, eds. *Übersicht über die Bestände des Deutschen Zentralarchivs Potsdam.* Berlin: Rütten & Loening, 1957.

Mommsen, Wolfgang. *Die Nachlässe in den deutschen Archiven.* 2 vols. Boppard: Boldt, 1983.

Wolfe, Robert, ed. *Captured German and Related Records: A National Archives Conference.* Athens, OH: Ohio University Press, 1974.

Arendt, Hannah (1906–75)

One of the important political philosophers of the twentieth century, Hannah Arendt was the most thought-provoking historian of the German-Jewish catastrophe. Her pathbreaking writings include *The Origins of Totalitarianism,* 1951, *The Human Condition,* 1958, *Eichmann in Jerusalem,* 1963, *On Revolution,* 1963, and *The Life of the Mind,* 1978.

Born in Königsberg, East Prussia, into an assimilated middle-class German-Jewish family, Arendt received a classical education and studied philosophy at the universities of Marburg, Freiburg, and Heidelberg with, among others, Martin Heidegger (1889–1976) and Karl Jaspers (1883–1969) (who directed her doctoral thesis, completed in 1928, on the concept of love in Saint Augustine). She was married twice: to Günther Stern (1929; divorce 1936) and to Heinrich Blücher (1940). Exile in Paris (1933–41) was followed by emigration to the United States (1941).

In the 1930s, Arendt was influenced by the critical Zionism of Kurt Blumenfeld. Her social-intellectual biography of Rahel Varnhagen, *Rahel Varnhagen: The Life of a Jewess,* completed 1938, first published 1958, sought to establish a historical model of the troubled social and political discourse of educated German Jews desiring assimilation. She enlarged this model in *Origins of Totalitarianism,* a political-historical analysis of the connection between the rise of political anti-Semitism and the decline of the nation-state, and of the meanings of Jewish participation in European history. In the 1940s, increasingly critical of the emphasis of political Zionism on a fated, irreversible anti-Semitism, Arendt wrote political commentary on the Arab-Jewish question (posthumously collected in *The Jew as Pariah: Jewish Identity and Politics in the Modern Age,* 1978, and in 1948 collaborated with Judah L. Magnes on the proposal for a binational Jewish-Arab state.

Her best-known work in political philosophy, *The Human Condition,* reconstructs, from the vantage point of an experienced collapse of modernity, a model of political intercourse that integrates important aspects of the political realm in classical antiquity. It provides the bridge between her previous work and two books published in 1963: on the trial of Adolf Eichmann, a study of the "bad citizen" responsible for the German *Zivilisationsbruch* (break with civilization), and on the American Revolution, a celebration of the "good citi-

Hannah Arendt. Courtesy of German Information Center, New York.

zen" responsible for the ideal of American democracy. Her shrewd and incisive essays on the difficulties faced by this democracy in the 1960s and 1970s were collected in *On Violence,* 1970, and *Crises of the Republic,* 1972. In her last years she returned to the philosophy of her youth with *The Life of the Mind,* posthumously published in 1978, edited by Mary McCarthy.

Arendt's political philosophy owes its enduring significance to her focus on the historicity of the human condition, which keeps in balance a realistic recognition of human limitations and an insistence on the realization of human potential.

Dagmar Barnouw

See also Anti-Semitism; Eichmann, Adolf; Heidegger, Martin; Holocaust; Jaspers, Karl; Jews; Philosophy

References

Barnouw, Dagmar. *Visible Spaces: Hannah Arendt and the German-Jewish Experience.* Baltimore, MD: Johns Hopkins University Press, 1990.

Beiner, Ronald, ed. *Hannah Arendt: 4 Lectures on Kant's Political Philosophy.* Chicago, IL: The University of Chicago Press, 1982.

Canovan, Margaret. *Hannah Arendt: A Reinterpretation of Her Political Thought.* Cambridge: Cambridge University Press, 1992.

Hill, Melvyn A., ed. *Hannah Arendt: The Recovery of the Public World.* New York, NY: St. Martin's Press, 1979.

Kateb, George. *Hannah Arendt: Politics, Conscience, Evil.*
Oxford: Martin Robertson, 1983.
Young-Bruehl, Elisabeth. *Hannah Arendt: For Love of the World.* New Haven, CT: Yale University Press, 1982.

Aristocracy

Like the other European nations, Germany possessed a status group whose principal, though by no means exclusive, mode of entry was birth, and whose main basis of support was land. Yet this aristocracy was unusually diverse; its internal divisions reflected not only the legal distinctions between upper and lower nobles dating back to the decentralization of the Holy Roman Empire but also the regionalism and particularism that persisted long after unification in 1871. As such, German aristocrats constituted an implicit challenge to national unity and identification, although most of them accommodated themselves, albeit grudgingly, to "Germany" as a single entity. Their relationship to the Prussian-dominated German state, even during the Imperial era, could at times be mutually supportive, but it could also involve serious conflict, even for the Prussian *Junkers,* a lower nobility whom the patronage of the Prussian state had benefited since the consolidation of Hohenzollern absolutism.

Aristocrats included not only the *Junkers,* whose origins lay in the German colonizations of the east during the late middle ages and who have been frequently assigned the primary responsibility for Germany's tragic recent history. They also included Catholic *Stiftsadel* (those with an ancient family lineage) in the west who lost their independence as an estate during the Napoleonic invasions of the early nineteenth century, and other regionally prominent nobles, such as those of Hesse, who retained their distinctive identities and political influence even after unification. Although many nobles were determined to preserve their exclusivity through endogamous marriages, their ranks had always been subject to periodic expansion by monarchical ennoblements, either of worthy officials or, under the Empire, of successful businessmen. Those nobles who owned land also confronted the intrusions of bourgeois proprietors, who throughout the nineteenth century acquired landed estates with increasing frequency.

Nevertheless, social distinctions survived and prospered after unification, not only among the aristocrats themselves (divided by region, religion, type of landownership, and wealth), but also between the aristocracies and the bourgeoisies of education and wealth. Recent evidence suggests that, in the latter case, both nobles and bourgeois chose to preserve the social distance between them. The once taken-for-granted "feudalization" of the *haute bourgeoisie*—the upper middle classes' adoption of aristocratic values and life style—was more apparent than real.

The German aristocracies faced numerous challenges to their social position, not only from the increasing visibility and prosperity of the middle classes and the shifting priorities of the state in response to industrial and urban growth, but also from the spread of mass politics with its implicit threat to the genteel notable politics (*Honoratiorenpolitik*) that the well-born would have preferred. Yet on the whole, aristocrats proved remarkably successful in adapting to the political and economic consequences of the rapid industrialization that followed unification. Those who owned land modernized their estates, while nobles occupied high positions in the national and regional bureaucracies as well as in the military. They acquired the technical skills and education that the modern instruments of state demanded. Others solidified their local authority through patronage of the major churches, Protestant and Catholic. Most importantly, however, nobles assumed the leadership of the major agrarian leagues and pressure groups, namely the Catholic peasant leagues (Bauernvereine) and the Agrarian League (Bund der Landwirte). They also played prominent roles in two major political parties, the Catholic Center and the eastern Prussian, and mainly Protestant, German Conservative Party (which after World War I merged with the German National People's Party). Such influence frequently bought them into conflict with the state, which had to juggle the competing claims of the major economic factions that sought its protection, and underscored the aristocratic penchant for resistance to central authority.

Although their ancient and legally recognized estatist privileges disintegrated throughout the nineteenth century, a process that the Empire accelerated and the Weimar Republic formally and finally confirmed, aristocrats remained a significant political and social force until the end of the Third Reich. For all of their rhetoric valorizing the peasantry, the Nazis did nothing directly to undermine estate agriculture, the principal foundation of aristocratic survival. A good many younger nobles, in fact, became fervent Nazis.

The Third Reich's volatile blend of meritocracy and populism ultimately offended many aristocrats, even if they at first welcomed the Nazi regime as an appropriately authoritarian antidote to republicanism. To name but two examples, the subordination of the army in 1938 to Hitler's direct command and the Third Reich's attempts to undermine organized Christianity, one of the most important determinants of aristocratic self-identification, drove many nobles into the anti-Hitler resistance that coalesced as war grew imminent. A number of them lost their lives after the unsuccessful coup attempt of July 20, 1944.

Not until the German defeat in 1945 were the German aristocracies collectively undermined as a distinctive caste. Soviet land reform, the loss of many of the eastern territories to Poland, and the determination of the German Democratic Republic to create a "workers' and peasants' state," brought dispossession, exile, and even death to the Prussian *Junkers.* And although West Germany preserved noble titles and provided on the whole a friendlier climate for the aristocratic families of both the east and west who survived the war, the social status of nobles depended on the degree to which they accommodated themselves to a thoroughly bourgeois and capitalist parliamentary democracy.

Shelley Baranowski

See also Agrarian Leagues; Bourgeoisie; Catholicism, Political; Center Party; Clergy, Protestant; Diplomatic Corps and Diplomacy; German Conservative Party; German National People's

Party; Imperial Germany; Peasantry; Protestantism and the Protestant Church; Prussia; Resistance; Social Mobility

References

Augustine, Dolores L. "Arriving in the Upper Class: The Wealthy Business Elite of Wilhelmine Germany." *The German Bourgeoisie: Essays on the Social History of the German Middle Class from the Late Eighteenth to the Early Twentieth Century.* Ed. David Blackbourn and Richard J. Evans. London: Routledge: 1991.

Brunner, Reinhold. "Landadliger Alltag und primäre Sozialisation in Ostelbien am Ende des 19. Jahrhunderts." *Zeitschrift für Geschichtswissenschaft* 39 (1991), 995–1011.

Carstens, Francis L. *Geschichte der Preussischen Junker.* Frankfurt am Main: Suhrkamp, 1988.

Hess, Klaus. *Junker und bürgerliche Grossgrundbesitzer im Kaiserreich: Landwirtschaftlicher Grossbetrieb, Grossgrundbesitz und Familienfideikommiss in Preußen (1867/71–1914).* Stuttgart: Franz Steiner Verlag, 1990.

Kaudelka-Hanisch, Karin. "The Titled Businessman: Prussian Commercial Councillors in the Rhineland and Westphalia during the Nineteenth Century." *The German Bourgeoisie: Essays on the Social History of the German Middle Class from the Late Eighteenth to the Early Twentieth Century.* Ed. David Blackbourn and Richard J. Evans. London: Routledge, 1991.

Machtan, Lothar and Milles, Dietrich. *Die Klassensymbiose von Junkertum und Bourgeoisie: Zum Verhältnis von gesellschaftlicher und politischer Herrschaft in Preußen-Deutschland 1850–1878/79.* Frankfurt am Main: Ullstein, 1980.

Moeller, Robert G. ed. *Peasants and Lords in Modern Germany: Recent Studies in Agricultural History.* Boston, MA: Allen and Unwin, 1986.

Muncy, Lysbeth. *The Junker in the Prussian Administration under William II, 1888–1914.* Providence, RI: Brown University Press, 1944.

Pedlow, Gregory W. *The Survival of the Hessian Nobility 1770–1870.* Princeton, NJ: Princeton University Press, 1988.

Reif, Heinz. "Der Adel in der modernen Sozialgeschichte." *Sozialgeschichte in Deutschland: Entwicklung und Perspectiven im internationalen Zusammenhang.* Ed. Wolfgang Schieder. Vol. 4. Göttingen: Vandenhoeck & Ruprecht, 1987.

———. "Mediator between Throne and People: The Split in Aristocratic Conservatism in 19th Century Germany." *Language and the Construction of Class Identities: The Struggle for Discursive Power in Social Organization: Scandinavia and Germany after 1800.* Ed. Bo Strath. Gothenburg: Kompendietryckeriet, 1990.

Rogalla von Bieberstein, Johannes. *Adelsherrschaft und Adelskultur in Deutschland.* Frankfurt am Main: Verlag Peter Lang, 1989.

Rosenberg, Hans. "Die Pseudodemokratisierung der Rittergutsbesitzerklasse." *Machteliten und Wirtschaftskonjunkturen: Studien zur neueren deutschen Sozial-und Wirtschaftsgeschichte.* Ed. Hans Rosenberg. Göttingen: Vandenhoeck & Ruprecht, 1978.

von Treskow, Rüdiger. "Adel in Preußen: Anpassung und Kontinuität einer Familie 1800–1918." *Geschichte und Gesellschaft* 17 (1991), 344–69.

Wehler, Hans-Ulrich. *The German Empire 1871–1918.* Trans. Kim Traynor. Leamington: Berg Publishers, 1985.

Armaments Policy

Armaments policy from 1871 on involves a set of tensions—between ends and means, and between state control and private enterprise. Prussia's cameralist traditions were nowhere stronger than in the arms industry dominated by state factories and a few small private firms under virtually permanent contracts. When, in the 1850s, the firm of Alfred Krupp (1812–87) offered the army cannon barrels made of cast steel, he found buyers only because bronze and iron, the traditional gun metals, were plainly unusable for the rifled cannon just entering service. The introduction of steel gave Prussia modern artillery light enough for field service and durable enough to be cost-effective. It began two decades of limited state involvement with bourgeois entrepreneurs.

Until the 1890s, Imperial Germany did little more than keep technical pace with its neighbors. The Reichstag refused to vote funds for constant, apparently minor, improvements in arms technology. Most weapons were still being produced in government arsenals. The War Ministry therefore regarded private firms primarily as sources of new designs whose undesirable features could be modified by the army. In the 1890s, industries sought to make the alliance of "rye and iron" economically as well as politically profitable. The demands of the new navy for big guns, armor plate, and high-powered engines opened a market that could not be supplied within traditional contexts. Like the army, the navy refused to become dependent on one or two suppliers. The relationships between high naval officers and industrialists nevertheless inevitably became more comprehensive and more symbiotic than those of the army with its suppliers.

In the Wilhelmine years the army revised its attitudes to technical innovation. If the War Ministry preferred to sustain an army of relatively limited size as a royal guard, it had to accept an emphasis on state-of-the-art weapons and up-to-date logistical support as force multipliers. If the General Staff favored a mass force, it had to recognize that the large numbers of men involved would require correspondingly increased amounts of hardware. Both factions paid correspondingly different levels of attention to developments in design and production.

One result was that previously diversified industrial firms increasingly specialized in weapons that could be sold in Germany and abroad. Krupp, Rheinmetall, and their counterparts sought to share markets through cartelization while competing fiercely for lucrative government contracts. The army and navy played the congenial role of final arbiters.

The integration of military and industrial institutions in Imperial Germany must not be exaggerated. Corporations nursed long lists of grievances against military procurement agencies, while economics formed no part of an officer's education. Even in the years immediately before World War I practical cooperation was minimal. Business continued to dominate key issues such as increasing shell production. Small wonder that in late 1914, when the short-war illusion faded, captains of industry such as Walter Rathenau were appalled at the absence of preparation for the war of attrition that Germany found itself compelled to wage.

Wartime conversion essentially involved taking up slack in a civilian economy already distorted by shortages of raw materials and by mobilization policies that heedlessly stripped factories of their skilled workers. German prewar weaponry proved little more than competitive. The infantry's rifle was a good cut below the British Enfield; the principal field gun of the artillery was inferior to the British 18-pounder and the French 75. Nor were German warships significantly superior to their British rivals, despite the myths that grew around the Battle of Jutland. The situation did not improve during the war. The few tanks that Germany produced were designed by a committee. Their appearance and performance reflected their genesis. Even the air force, the most modern of the services, was unwilling to standardize aircraft designs. Until the end of the war, front-line squadrons usually flew more than one type of plane, with predictable problems in tactics and maintenance.

Generals Hindenburg and Ludendorff delivered the final blow to German armaments procurement in World War I. Their grandiose "1916 program" exemplified military vitalism at its worst. It ignored human and material realities, and strained beyond the breaking point a system that was increasingly unable to respond even to the most forcefully delivered commands of the country's most powerful generals. If by 1918 the German army was a hollow shell, this was in good part the consequence of waste and confusion on a home front systematically mismanaged by men who had exceeded their professional training.

In the Weimar period, the Reichswehr (the army) drew the logical conclusion that future war required comprehensive integration of strategic and economic planning. This approach seemed even more necessary as Weimar Germany fell further and further behind in an arms race that was no less real for being less open than the one prior to 1914. Junior business executives and bright young colonels found point after point on which to agree. Even before Adolf Hitler's rise to power, the Reichswehr's plans for rapid, technical rearmament suitable for an offensive war were firmly in place.

The Third Reich is frequently credited with rearming "in breadth": planning for a constantly changing mix of forces to conduct short decisive campaigns against single enemies under varying conditions. In fact, Nazi Germany prepared from its inception for total war under conditions of total mobilization. The main impediment was the structural inefficiency of Hitler's state—in this context exacerbated by Hitler's initial decision to place Hermann Göring (1893–1946) in charge

of the war economy—and by bitter internal conflicts over resource allocation.

Years of deprivation, accompanied by dreams of what could be accomplished with sufficient funds and material, led the generals and admirals to behave like uniformed children let loose in a toy shop. The navy's Z-plan projected an ocean-going fleet to challenge those of Great Britain and the United States. The Luftwaffe committed itself to an independent role featuring strategic bombing. The army sought to expand its numbers and simultaneously create a high-tech armed force. No one was willing to compromise; no one was able to develop a coherent grand strategy. By 1939, the Reich needed everything from engine oil to small arms if its economy were not to overheat and self-destruct. Economics as well as ideology ultimately motivated Hitler's decision for war.

For all its early conquests, Nazi Germany proved unable in either Western or Eastern Europe to move beyond the crudest forms of direct economic exploitation. The increase in war production under Albert Speer (1905–81) after 1943 involved taking up slack in an economy that produced butter as well as guns as part of Hitler's plan to keep his people contented. Nor did Speer's achievements keep the army from fighting much of its war with captured rifles. Even more than during World War I, German weapons systems showed flaws of hasty design and shortcomings reflecting fractured communications between drawing boards and fighting fronts. Tanks and warships alike were plagued by engine problems. With the notable exceptions of the FW 190 and the Me 262, the Luftwaffe ended its war with the planes it had used in the Battle of Britain. Even sound airframes such as the BF 109 and the Ju 88 could bear only so much updating. By 1945, Germany was once again virtually disarmed in quantitative and qualitative terms.

The two Germanys that emerged from the Cold War followed different paths in armaments production. East Germany was controlled by the Soviet Union, which allowed it neither to design nor to produce any significant weapons systems. The Federal Republic's initial intentions of eschewing arms manufacturing gave way in the 1950s to a policy of developing an independent defense industry. This policy was regarded as necessary to avert dependence on West Germany's NATO allies and to ensure participation in spinoffs—the civilian proliferation of techniques and ideas allegedly generated by the Cold War arms race. As a result, the Federal Republic emerged as a producer and exporter of a solid range of such conventional arms as Leopard main battle tanks and diesel-powered attack submarines. To date, reunited Germany has not designed complex systems such as high-performance aircraft independently. It continues as well to eschew nuclear armaments.

Dennis E. Showalter

See also Adenauer, Konrad; Air Force; Blank, Theodor; Federal Republic of Germany: Armed Forces; Four Year Plan; German Democratic Republic: National People's Army; Groener, Wilhelm; Hindenburg, Paul von; Hitler, Adolf; Imperial Germany: Army; Krupp: Family and Firm;

44 ARMAMENTS POLICY

Ludendorff, Erich; Militarism; National Socialist Germany: Military; Navy and Naval Policy; Rearmament; Schleicher, Kurt von; Seeckt, Hans von; Speer, Albert; Tirpitz, Alfred von; Weimar Germany: Army; World War I; World War II

References

Deist, Wilhelm. *The Wehrmacht and German Rearmament.* Toronto: University of Toronto Press, 1981.

Feldman, Gerald D. *Army, Labor, and Industry in Germany, 1914–1918.* Princeton, NJ: Princeton University Press, 1966.

Geyer, Michael. *Deutsche Rüstungspolitik 1860–1980.* Frankfurt am Main: Suhrkamp, 1984.

Homze, Edward L. *Arming the Luftwaffe: The Reich Air Ministry and the German Aircraft Industry, 1919–39.* Lincoln, NE: University of Nebraska Press, 1976.

Milward, Alan S. *The German Economy at War.* London: The Athalane Press, 1965.

Overy, Richard. *Goering, The "Iron Man."* London: Routledge and Kegan Paul, 1984.

Showalter, Dennis. *Railroads and Rifles: Soldiers, Technology and the Unification of Germany.* Hamden, CT: Archon, 1975.

Artisans/Craftsmen (Guilds)

The category of artisans and craftsmen covers the "handicraft" (*Handwerk*) portion of the industrial sector and has always been distinguished from "domestic industry" (*Hausindustrie*). A master tailor might make the same sort of clothes as a seamstress, and a shoemaker might make the same sort of boots as a worker in a shoe factory, but in both cases he would be distinguished by his independence, his lifestyle, his selection of

a marriage partner, and the regard in which he would be held by the local community. Production in *Handwerk* has always been intimately bound up with the family. In the artisan household/firm, wives and daughters traditionally worked as unpaid auxiliaries, and sons were groomed for apprenticeships with other similar household/firms. As apprentices the boys received the training they would need to establish their own independent positions.

Because of its size, and also because of its links with traditional social structures, any perceived "decline" of this social group has been viewed with alarm. An impressive array of laws continues to support the position of the craft trades, and the Association of German Artisans (Zentralverband des Deutschen Handwerks) vigilantly protects the interests of its members.

Legislation undermined the monopoly powers of the guilds during the nineteenth century. The most famous laws were the Prussian law of 1807 and the Zollverein law of 1861. Nevertheless, although they were reduced to the status of voluntary organizations, guilds remained influential and master artisans remained powerful figures in many communities. Guilds controlled entry into trades by restricting access to apprenticeship, training apprentices only from respectable families, employing only journeymen with proper credentials, and most importantly, by limiting the number of master artisans in each town. Laws regulating opening hours, apprenticeship, and employment of family members reinforced the position of the artisan/craftsman despite the formal existence of occupational freedom.

The fate of individual artisans, of guilds, and of branches of *Handwerk* has varied from region to region and from industry to industry. Although often dismissed as outmoded, the

Professional small-business women's congress. Courtesy of Inter Nationes, Bonn.

household/firm and its attendant social structures have proved resilient. The rise of modern factory industry and the penetration of isolated districts by modern transportation threatened some artisans but provided opportunities for others. Globally, the census results show that the percentage of industrial workers in firms with five or fewer employees declined from 64 percent in 1875 to 31 percent in 1907 and 25 percent in 1925. However, artisanal craftsmen did not disappear. The absolute number of "independent" persons in the industrial sector declined only slightly before World War II, from 2.2 million in 1875 to 1.9 million in 1925. In some cases, such as shoemaking, artisanal craftsmen increasingly sold and repaired products that they received from factories, but in other trades the small independent manufacturers maintained themselves. This was particularly the case where specialized customer needs had to be met, and even in some technically advanced sectors, such as machine building, artisan firms have maintained themselves into the twentieth century.

In the Federal Republic, employees in firms with five or fewer workers made up 16 percent of the labor force in 1950. The line separating production and sales, which the official statistics had attempted to maintain, became blurred. In absolute terms, the number of "independent" persons in industry declined from 1 million in 1950 to 907,000 in 1959, but "independent" persons in trade rose from 991,000 to 1.1 million. By the mid-1960s, about one-third of all artisans/craftsmen reported to interviewers that they considered themselves to be equally "*Kaufmann*" (businessman) and "*Handwerker*" (artisan). Artisanal craftsmen had always sold the products they had made themselves, but many now regarded themselves as entrepreneurial figures as well. They continued to see themselves as a separate group, however, and in particular considered themselves distinct and different from industrial-commercial "managers" or owners of large firms. Their lifestyles, patterns of social interaction, and preferred marriage partners have continued to reflect their separate identity.

The number of craft firms continued to decline—to 500,000 in the 1980s—but the number of persons employed in these firms rose from some 3 million in the 1950s to some 4 million in the 1980s, about 8 employees per firm. Some of the "craft" occupations provided specialized business services and expanded, while others fell victim to factory competition. The number of building cleaners rose from 14,000 in 1956 to 331,000 in 1980, for instance, but the number of tailors declined from 188,000 to 28,000.

It was extremely difficult by the 1980s to achieve a position as an "independent" business owner without a higher education, above-average income, and substantial capital. This led to complaints of polarization within the craft sector. On the one hand, one-fifth of all craft apprentices sank to the level of unskilled workers, but on the other hand, one-fifth of all "independent" business owners ranked in the top two percent of income earners. In the 1990s, discussion of the craft sector is focusing on the prospects for independent small businesses in the former East Germany. As in most sectors, the legislation of the Federal Republic has been imposed on the east. This will probably make possible a substantial expansion of

the sector as the eastern economy is reconstructed, but in the longer run the artisans of the east will be subject to the same sorts of pressures as in the past.

Frank B. Tipton

See also Factory Laws and Reform; Family; Trade Unions (1871–1945); Women's Occupations

References
Kocka, Jürgen. *Arbeiterverhältnisse und Arbeiterexistenzen: Grundlagen der Klassenbildung im 19. Jahrhundert.* Bonn: J.H.V. Dietz, 1990.
Lenger, Friedrich. *Sozialgeschichte der deutschen Handwerker seit 1800.* Frankfurt am Main: Suhrkamp, 1988.
Volkov, Shulamit. *The Rise of Popular Antimodernism in Germany: The Urban Master Artisans, 1873–1896.* Princeton, NJ: Princeton University Press, 1978.

Artists
For much of the last century and a half, German artists have worked under the competing agendas of international modernism and the repeated, often virulent call for an exclusively nationalistic art. Moreover, the dramatic transformation of everyday life through industrialization and urbanization gave rise to a radical transformation of the institutions of art. The traditional and essentially democratic means of academic education and public exhibition were replaced by the demands of the art market, which encouraged innovation and promoted elitism in the construction of artistic identity.

In the years following the *Gründerzeit* (founding years), the art world fractured between the traditional academic system, represented by such artists as Berlin's Anton von Werner (1843–1915), and an art market that turned artists such as Munich's Franz von Lenbach (1836–1904) into veritable art princes. This distinction was reflected in the competing visions offered by Munich and Berlin artists over who and what would constitute a native German art. In Berlin, the Kaiser, with Werner as his agent, hoped to use art to further Imperial policy at home and abroad. Berlin's cultural hegemony was effectively opposed by Munich's artists and intellectuals until the very end of the century.

In the 1890s, the conflict over equal access to markets gave rise to the phenomenon of secessionism, whereby elite groups of artists sought to distinguish themselves from the mass of the state-sponsored international exhibitions. The Munich Secession of 1892, led by Fritz von Uhde (1848–1911), and the Berlin Secession of 1898, led by Max Liebermann (1848–1935), promoted both internationalism and elitism in the name of quality. They affiliated themselves with the international art market, thereby inadvertently helping to pave the way for both the commercial success of French modernism in Germany and for Berlin's emergence as the art capital of Central Europe.

The rise of German expressionism to national prominence after 1910 demonstrates both the influence of modernist French art and the by-then international art market. The expressionists can be divided roughly into two camps: those who affiliated with like-minded artists abroad, as was the case with the artists of the *Blaue Reiter* (Blue rider) under the leadership of the Russian emigré Wassily Kandinsky (1866–1944) and Franz Marc (1880–1916), and those who sought to create an indigenous German art, such as the artists of the *Brücke* (bridge). One of its members, Ernst Ludwig Kirchner (1880–1938), went so far as to deny the *Brücke's* obvious indebtedness to French art. Yet both groups owed their success to the commercial gallery system and their fame marks the final triumph of the art market over the institutions of the academy and the state exhibitions.

During the Weimar Republic, expressionism became institutionalized in the art academies and the museums, constituting an unofficial national style. The expressionists, however, came under attack by the dadaists such as George Grosz (1893–1959) for their continued elitism and perceived complicity with the political and moral bankruptcy of Weimar society. By the mid-1920s, a cool, anti-expressionist style interested in achieving art appealing to the proletariat and in reflecting the new industrial, urban environment, called the *Neue Sachlichkeit* (New Objectivity), prevailed in Germany and embraced not only the social criticism of artists like Grosz and Otto Dix (1891–1969), but also the machine-inspired aesthetic of the widely influential design school, the Bauhaus.

After 1933, Hitler and his agents attempted to roll back the institutional gains made by modernism and encouraged a return to a pre-secessionist Germanic art. The 1937 *Entartete Kunstausstellung* (degenerate art exhibition) ridiculed the modernist artist as both sick and fundamentally foreign, while the simultaneous *Grosse Deutsche Kunstausstellung* (great German art exhibition) proposed an alternative canon of healthy, authentically German artists. Both expressionists and dadaists faced international or internal exile; Max Beckmann (1844–1950), for example, fled Germany, while Emil Nolde (1867–1956), after seeking in vain to join the Nazi Party, was forbidden to paint.

In the wake of World War II and under a divided Germany, West German artists hoped to reenter the international community by repudiating their immediate past and by seeking a politically unpolluted artistic language in abstract painting, one opposed to the realism of the 1930s and the continued totalitarian aesthetics of contemporary social realism in the Soviet Bloc, including East Germany. This tendency culminated in the 1959 exhibition *documenta II* in Kassel, where nonobjective painting was celebrated as a manifestation of personal freedom within a democratic, capitalist society. In the 1960s and 1970s, German artists began to return to the forbidden legacy of the Nazi past while also engaging directly in the values and the images of contemporary life. German pop artists, such as Sigmar Polke (1941–), appropriated popular, consumer culture for their art, rendering its commercial, elitist character transparent. Such work has been read both as a capitulation to and an ironic critique of contemporary consumer society. Joseph Beuys's (1921–86) return to the problems of historical memory has also been widely influential, as was his call for an egalitarian art that would seek to create an egalitarian society.

During the 1980s and 1990s, German artists achieved heretofore unrivaled preeminence in international art markets and the world's museums. Characteristically, Anselm Kiefer's (1945–) difficult images dealing with the horror of the Holocaust and his many investigations of German identity have made him both celebrated abroad and controversial at home, where his work is read both as potentially neo-Fascist art and as a means of recognition and acceptance of Germany's history. What effect reunification and the increasing subordination of German identity to pan-European economic and political interests will have on the nature of art in German society remains to be seen.

John Lee Butler-Ludwig

See also Arts and Crafts; Baluschek, Hans; Barlach, Ernst; Baselitz, Georg; Bauhaus; Baumeister, Willi; Beckmann, Max; Berlin Secession; Beuys, Joseph; *Blaue Reiter*; Corinth, Lovis; Cremer, Fritz; Dada; Decadence; Decorative Arts; Dix, Otto; Ernst, Max; Exhibitions (Art); Expressionism; Founding Years; Fritsch, Katharina; German Democratic Republic: Arts and Politics; Gropius, Walter; Grosz, George; Heartfield, John; Heckel, Erich; Herzfelde, Wieland; Höch, Hannah; Hödicke, Karl Horst; Hofer, Carl; Immendorff, Jörg; Impressionism; Jugendstil; Kandinsky, Wassily; Kiefer, Anselm; Kirchner, Ernst; Klee, Paul; Kokoschka, Oskar; Kolbe, Georg; Kollwitz, Käthe; *Kultur*; Liebermann, Max; Lüpertz, Markus; Marc, Franz; Marcks, Gerhard; Menzel, Adolph; The Munich Secession; Münter, Gabriele; Museums; National Socialist Germany: Art; Nay, Ernst; Nesch, Rolf; Nolde, Emil; Pechstein, Max; Penck, A.R.; Photography; Polke, Sigmar; Schmidt-Rottluff, Karl; Schwitters, Kurt; Sculpture; Slevogt, Max; Struth, Thomas; Stuck, Franz von; Trockel, Rosemarie; Uhde, Fritz von; Werkbund; Werner, Anton von

References

Degenerate Art: The Fate of the Avant-garde in Nazi Germany. Los Angeles, CA: Los Angeles County Museum, 1991.

Documenta: Idee und Institution: Tendenzen, Konzepte, Materialien. Munich: Bruckmann, 1983.

German Art in the 20th Century: Painting and Sculpture 1905–1985. New York, NY: Prestel-Verlag, 1985.

Grosslein, Andrea. *Die internationalen Kunstausstellungen der Münchner Künstlergenossenschaft im Glaspalast in München von 1869 bis 1888.* Munich: Stadtarchiv München, 1987.

Harzenetter, Marcus. *Zur Münchner Secession.* Munich: Stadtarchiv, 1992.

Jensen, Robert. *Marketing Modernism in Fin de Siècle Europe.* Princeton, NJ: Princeton University Press, 1994.

Paret, Peter. *The Berlin Secession: Modernism and Its Enemies in Imperial Germany.* Cambridge, MA: Harvard University Press, 1980.

Tisdall, Caroline. *Joseph Beuys.* New York, NY: Thames and Hudson, 1979.

Weinstein, Joan. *The End of Expressionism: Art and the November Revolution in Germany.* Chicago, IL: University of Chicago Press, 1989.

Werckmeister, Otto Karl. *The Making of Paul Klee's Career.*
    Chicago, IL: University of Chicago Press, 1989.
Westkunst: Zeitgenössische Kunst seit 1939. Cologne:
    DuMont, 1981.

Arts and Crafts

The arts and crafts movement originally started in the second half of the nineteenth century in England, with William Morris as its leading figure. From the 1890s, it influenced German artists and architects. However, there did not exist an arts and crafts movement in the British sense in Germany. The most important transmitter of British ideas was the architect Hermann Muthesius (1861–1927), who worked for the German embassy in London from 1896 to 1903. He published several articles and books on British art and architecture and made it popular in Germany. Most recently, Stefan Muthesius dealt with the British influence within Germany. The first British artists known and admired in Germany were Charles R. Ashbee (1863–1942), Walter Crane (1845–1915), and M.H.B. Baillie Scott (1865–1945). After Ashbee and Baillie Scott decorated rooms in 1897 for the Duke of Hesse and his British wife in Darmstadt, they became known in Germany. Walter Crane, who exhibited in Germany from 1893, was better known in Germany than William Morris in the 1890s. In the formative years of *Jugendstil* (art nouveau), Crane exhibited also with the Secession in Munich. Several articles, for example by Hans E. von Berlepsch-Valendas (1849–1921), a promoter of arts and crafts ideas, were published on Crane in German papers. In 1896, Crane's book *Claims of Decorative Art*, 1892, appeared in German.

Although German artists and architects were intrigued by British ideas, their perception of how to reform the arts and crafts was quite different. The main points were to produce good design for everybody and sell it. Both saw establishing the equality of fine arts and decorative arts as the basis for a reform. Many of the German designers were originally painters, not architects or craftsmen, who turned to the crafts for economic reasons. Socialist ideas, which motivated British arts and crafts artists, never played any role in Germany. The designs usually were executed by craft firms and not by the artists themselves. This led to the need to protect the artists and supervise the quality of production. Hence several artists' companies were founded, such as the Vereinigte Werkstätten (united workshops) in Munich and the Munich Workshops for Domestic Furnishings (which merged in 1907 with the Deutsche Werkstätten [German workshops] in Hellerau), founded by Karl Schmidt in 1898.

In Dresden, the Workshops for German Furnishings were established by Theodor Müller, and smaller enterprises developed throughout Germany. In 1897, for the first time, modern crafts were exhibited together with fine arts in the Glaspalast (glass palace) in Munich. The exhibition was hailed by Berlepsch-Valendas in *Deutsche Kunst und Dekoration* (German art and decoration) as "finally a turning point." As a result, the Vereinigte Werkstätten in Munich were founded by Bruno Paul, Bernhard Pankok, Richard Riemerschmid, and other artists in June 1898. Their goal was not to create a uto-

pian community but a marketing system for the artist. All products showed the name of their designer to protect the copyright, and the artists could sell their products through the sales bureaus of this company.

The means to create good design was thought to be the reform of art schools and the education of the public through exhibitions. In the tradition of the teachings of Gottfried Semper, art historians promoted the new design with exhibitions, courses, and writings. Among them were Justus Brinckmann and Alfred Lichtwark in Hamburg and Friedrich Deneken in Krefeld. Artists such as Berlepsch-Valendas and Peter Behrens were hired to teach craftsmen in Krefeld and Nuremberg the basis of good design. Private art schools, such as the Debschitz School in Munich, founded by Wilhelm Debschitz and Hermann Obrist, tried to reform art school teaching. The Debschitz School introduced a obligatory preliminary course and thus became a kind of predecessor of Bauhaus teaching. Reform ideas were accompanied by an interest in folk art. According to Alois Riegl in *Volkskunst, Hausfleiss und Kunstindustrie* (Folk art, house work and industrial art), 1894, folk art was "good art" since it was not produced for a market but because of the producers' own needs, who thus had the maximum interest to make it as good and functional as possible. The reformers wanted to create a kind of new folk art, meaning good modern design accepted by a broad public. Nevertheless, Hermann Obrist already recognized the hopelessness of this goal, because common people did not want simple and plain design but preferred luxurious ornaments.

The reformers emphasized practical training in workshops, based on Gottfried Semper's writings. They were not promoting handicraft as an end in itself. In contrast to the teachings of Semper, the reformers wanted to educate the craftsman and the customer about the necessity of reasonable prices. This led to the main difference between the German and British reformers, which was their attitude toward machine production. Morris promoted handicrafts and saw machine work as evil. In Germany, the artists wanted to use the machine for good design, although the first enterprises still were largely based on craftsmanship and not on mass production. Soon, Richard Riemerschmid, Bruno Paul, and others had recognized the elite character of craft work and tried to produce cheaper goods for a broader public. They developed the so-called *Typenmöbel* (build-on furniture). The positive attitude toward the machine found its expression in the foundation of the Werkbund (work association) (1907) and eventually in the ideas promoted by the Bauhaus (1919).

Christina Melk-Haen

See also Artists; Bauhaus; Behrens, Peter; *Jugendstil*; The Munich Secession; Museums; Werkbund

References

Bott, Gerhard, ed. *Von Morris zum Bauhaus—eine Kunst gegründet auf Einfachheit.* Hanau: Peters, 1977.
Campbell, Joan. *The German Werkbund: The Politics of Reform in the Applied Arts.* Princeton, NJ: Princeton University Press, 1978.

Heskett, John. *Design in Germany 1870–1918.* New York, NY: Taplinger, 1986.

Muthesius, Hermann. *Das Englische Haus.* 3 vols. Berlin: E. Wasmuth, 1904–05.

Muthesius, Stefan. "Das englische Vorbild." *Studien zur Kunst des 19. Jahrhunderts.* Vol. 26. Munich: Prestel Verlag, 1974.

Pevsner, Nikolaus. *Pioneers of the Modern Movement from William Morris to Walter Gropius.* 2nd ed. Harmondsworth: Penguin Books, 1972.

———, ed. *The Anti-Rationalists.* London: Architectural Press, 1973.

Riemerschmied, Richard. *Vom Jugendstil zum Werkbund: Werke und Dokumente.* Munich: Prestel, 1982.

Ziegert, Beate. "The Debschitz School, Munich 1902–1914." *Design Issue* 3 (Spring 1986), 28-41.

Association for Social Policy (Kathedersozialisten)

The Kathedersozialisten (literally translated as Socialists of the Chair) were a group of German economists and university professors who emerged in the Bismarck era as advocates of some form of state socialism. The name was originally given to them by one of their liberal critics. It soon won general acceptance, for it aptly reflected the academic and bourgeois status of these men as well as their intellectual stance between Marxist socialism and laissez-faire liberalism. Like the Marxists, the Socialists of the Chair insisted that government had a key role to play in improving the lot of the lower classes, but unlike the Marxist socialists, they were convinced that the "social question" could be solved without resort to revolution. Thus, the historical economist Gustav von Schmoller (1838–1917), one of the group's most influential early members, maintained that the existing government could, through legislation, end the exploitation of the workers and make possible a gradual rise in the general standard of living. This would enable the working masses to bridge the gap that divided them from the possessing classes and eventually prepare them to participate fully in all aspects of the country's cultural life.

From the first, significant policy differences divided the group. For example, although both Schmoller and Adolph Wagner (1835–1917), a specialist in public finance, sought to overcome the growing rifts between social classes primarily in order to strengthen Germany abroad, they did not agree on how to achieve this end. Wagner, a true state socialist, in the 1870s advocated the nationalization of major service industries, notably the railways. After 1879, due to his conviction that only protectionist measures could check the advance of industry and preserve the traditional structures of the rural Germany that he valued, he broke ranks and allied himself with the conservatives' campaign for agricultural duties.

Schmoller, on the other hand, did not believe that either nationalization or protectionism could solve the social question in Germany. He argued that the state should direct its efforts to moderating the inevitable conflict between capital and labor through factory legislation and government-run social insurance schemes.

A third approach was that of Lujo Brentano (1844–1931), a somewhat younger and more liberal-minded economist. Abroad, his liberalism led Brentano to espouse the cause of free trade and to advocate international cooperation. At home, he favored legislation to enshrine the rights of the trade unions and urged implementation of the English model of industrial relations, including compulsory unionization, collective bargaining, and arbitration.

From 1872, the Socialists of the Chair had an organizational focus in the newly formed Verein für Sozialpolitik (Association for Social Policy) of which Schmoller, Wagner, and Brentano were co-founders. Although the Association soon abandoned its hope of seeing its initiatives translated directly into legislation, its high-caliber internal debates and its well-researched publications undoubtedly influenced policy formation. By 1890, many of the reforms first broached in Association circles had already been partly or fully implemented. After the collapse of Imperial Germany and the establishment of the Weimar Republic, the Association continued to prepare the ground for social reform legislation, especially through its case studies and statistical analyses publications. In 1934, however, it dissolved itself rather than become part of the Nazi new order.

Joan Campbell

See also Brentano, Lujo; Economics; Helfferich, Karl; Naumann, Friedrich; Oldenberg, Karl; Schmoller, Gustav von; Wagner, Adolph; Weber, Alfred; Weber, Max

References

Ascher, Abraham. "Professors as Propagandists: The Politics of the Kathedersozialisten." *Journal of Central European Affairs* 23 (1963), 282–302.

Boese, Franz. *Geschichte des Vereins für Sozialpolitik 1872–1932.* Schriften des Vereins für Sozialpolitik 188. Berlin: Duncker & Humblot, 1939.

Gorges, Irmela. *Sozialforschung in Deutschland, 1872–1914. Gesellschaftliche Einflüsse auf Themen- und Methodenwahl des Vereins für Sozialpolitik.* Königstein/Ts: Hain Verlag, 1980.

Plessen, Marie-Louise. *Die Wirksamkeit des Vereins für Sozialpolitik von 1872–1890: Studien zum Katheder- und Staatssozialismus.* Berlin: Duncker & Humblot, 1975.

Ringer, Fritz K. *The Decline of the German Mandarins: The German Academic Community 1890–1933.* Cambridge, MA: Harvard University Press, 1969.

Astronomy

The development of astronomy in Germany in the last 150 years was generally similar to that in other countries. Its main feature was the rise of astrophysics, beginning about 1850, which led to German astronomers concentrating on astrophysical research (positional astronomy) as the predominant domain of astronomical science. In the middle of the nineteenth century, most astronomers in Germany worked on the determination of the positions and movements of the stars, whereas today the physical state of the celestial bodies is the main object of astronomical research.

In the nineteenth century, German astronomers collaborated intensively with international colleagues. In the twentieth century, the two world wars inevitably caused some isolation. Only after 1950 were international contacts resumed. The Astronomische Gesellschaft (Astronomical Society) (1863), sought to accommodate astronomers from all countries. It organized the observation of the positions of the stars down to the eighth magnitude; in that work, observatories in many countries took active part. The result was a number of catalogues of star places. Since then, the whole study has been repeated twice (around 1930 and about 1960) in order to determine the precise motions of the stars. Several fundamental catalogues of reference stars have been compiled by the scientists of the Astronomisches Rechen-Institut (Astronomical Calculations Institute), the last of which was the *FK5*, published during the 1980s.

Leading scientists at the turn of the twentieth century were Hugo Seeliger (1849–1924), Robert Emden (1862–1940), and Karl Schwarzschild (1873–1916). Seeliger's main work was investigating the structure of the Milky Way; he developed methods of statistical astronomy in order to explore the distribution of stars in space. Emden applied the laws of thermodynamics to the problem of the internal structure of the stars. Schwarzschild made important contributions to stellar photometry and to the measurement of the effect of radiation in stellar atmospheres. Ejnar Hertzsprung published the Hertzsprung-Russell diagram for the first time in 1905. Important work, for example the *Potsdamer photometrische Durchmusterung* (photometric scanning) and investigations of the temperatures of the stars, was performed at the Potsdam Astrophysical Observatory, which had been founded in 1874 in order to promote astrophysical research in Germany.

Between the world wars, international isolation as well as economic and political circumstances obstructed scientific work. However, some star catalogues of international stature were constructed; for instance, the *Göttinger Spektralphotometrie* (spectral photometry) was a pioneer work. By collaboration among German observatories, the *Spektraldurchmusterung* (spectral scanning) of the northern and southern sky was accomplished. Ludwig Biermann (1905–86) and Albrecht Unsöld (1907–) accomplished theoretical work on the interior structure and the atmospheres of stars.

World War II caused many setbacks for German astronomy. Some observatories were heavily damaged by bombs; after 1945, the partition of Germany created problems. Nevertheless, scientific work in astronomy did not stop entirely. Extensive research on double stars by Wilhelm Rabe (1893–1958) proceeded at the Munich Observatory. The Unsöld school continued investigation on stellar atmospheres with great success. Observations of comets enabled Biermann to discover the important phenomenon of the solar wind. Cuno Hoffmeister (1892–1968) of the Sonneberg Observatory discovered about 10,000 variable stars.

International contacts, which had existed only occasionally since 1914, were renewed after 1945. German astronomers took an active part in founding the the European Southern Observatory in Chile during the 1960s. A similar observatory was established at Calar Alto in southern Spain.

German scholars contributed much to the writing of the history of astronomy after 1870. In 1873, Heinrich Mädler published his *Geschichte der Himmelskunde* (History of astronomy) in two volumes. Rudolf Wolf's *Geschichte der Astronomie* (History of astronomy) appeared in 1877. Between the world wars, Hans Ludendorff (1873–1970) published extensively on Mayan astronomy, and Ernst Zinner (1885–1970) published a number of studies, several of which are still standard works on the history of astronomy. Willy Hartner (1905–82) also engaged in important research on the history of astronomy.

Currently, astronomy in Germany is concentrated in three fields: the construction of new kinds of astronomical instruments, galactic astronomy, and the study of the structure and development of stars.

Felix Schmeidler

See also Kaiser Wilhelm/Max Planck Societies and Institutes; Physics

References

Bruggencate, P. ten. *Naturforschung und Medizin in Deutschland 1939–1946, Band 20, Astronomie, Astrophysik und Kosmogonie.* Wiesbaden: Dieterische Verlagsbuchhandlung, 1948.

Herrmann, D. *Geschichte der modernen Astronomie.* Berlin: Aulis Verlag Deubner & Co., 1984.

Litten, F. *Astronomie in Bayern 1914–1945.* Stuttgart: Franz Steiner Verlag, 1992.

Pyenson, Lewis. *Cultural Imperialism and the Exact Sciences: German Expansion Overseas, 1900–1930.* New York, NY: Peter Lang, 1985.

Schmeidler F. *Die Geschichte der Astronomischen Gesellschaft: Jubiläumsband 125 Jahre Astronomische Gesellschaft.* Hamburg: Astronomische Gesellschaft, 1988.

Atom Bomb (German Development of)

Germany never completed an atomic bomb. Instead, a research program involving 70 to 100 academic scientists, which began at the start of World War II, investigated all possible economic and military applications of nuclear fission. The administration of the project was under military or Nazi Party control for most of the war: from September 1939 to the fall of 1942, Army Ordnance scientist Kurt Diebner oversaw the research; from the fall of 1942 to the end of 1943, Abraham Esau, a respected technical physicist and influential Party member, managed the project as Hermann Göring's (1893–1946) plenipotentiary for nuclear physics. Walther Gerlach, an academic scientist, took over as head of the project only in 1944.

In practice, the project was divided into several sections, each of which was delegated to a leading scientist who directed this research at his own institute. The measurement of nuclear constants and other preliminary work was carried out under Walther Bothe in Heidelberg. Isotope separation and heavy-water production were pursued by two physical chemists,

Klaus Clusius in Munich and Paul Harteck in Hamburg. Harteck was by far the most dynamic and effective member of the project. Finally, nuclear reactor experiments were performed in three places: by Robert Döpel in Leipzig, by Karl Wirtz in Berlin, and under Diebner at Army Ordnance. Werner Heisenberg (1901–76) made an important contribution at the very beginning of the project by developing the theoretical foundation for applied nuclear fission and recognizing that the pure isotope uranium 235 would be a nuclear explosive. In 1940, Carl Friedrich von Weizsäcker (1912–) discovered that a nuclear reactor would produce transuranic elements (plutonium) with similarly explosive properties.

The status of the research project at the end of the war was comparable to what the Americans, British, and continental emigrés had achieved by the summer of 1942: a nuclear reactor that was close to maintaining a self-sustaining chain reaction and an isotope-separation process that had managed a slight enrichment of the ratio of isotope uranium 235 to uranium 238 (the Germans concentrated on ultracentrifuges, the Allies on electromagnetic and gaseous diffusion technologies). This performance was due in large part to the changing fortunes of the war. During the Blitzkrieg phase, from 1939 to the end of 1941, it appeared that Germany would win the war soon, so no "wonder weapons" were needed. When the war turned sour for Germany in the winter of 1941–42 and German Army Ordnance asked its researchers whether nuclear weapons could be produced in time to influence the outcome of the war, the answer was clearly no. These scientists therefore never had to confront the question, should we build nuclear weapons for Hitler?

Since 1945, a contentious and persistent debate has raged over the German atom bomb. The arguments used in this debate have generally fallen into one of two categories: (1) an "apologetic" thesis (created first by Weizsäcker and Heisenberg, popularized by the author Robert Jungk, and most recently argued by Thomas Powers) that if there had been a chance to make the bomb, then these scientists would have denied these weapons to Hitler; and (2) a "polemic" thesis (created first by the scientist Samuel Goudsmit, supported by Leslie Groves, the military head of the Manhattan Project, and most recently argued by Arnold Kramish) that if there had been a chance to make the bomb, then these scientists would have done their best so that Germany would not lose the war. Thus the "myth of the German atom bomb" is actually a controversy over what might have been, not what was.

The debate surrounding the German work on nuclear fission during World War II has played an important role in the postwar politics of the two German republics and in particular in the matter of German rearmament and nuclear weaponry. Depending on which thesis one favors, the "German atom bomb" can be either used as proof that German scientists and thus Germany can be trusted never to misuse nuclear research or as proof that the German scientific community and Germany surrendered themselves to the radical aims of a Fascist ideology and might do so again. The truth probably lies somewhere in between.

Mark Walker

See also Armaments Policy; Göring, Hermann; Hahn, Otto; Heisenberg, Werner; Hitler, Adolf; Kaiser Wilhelm/Max Planck Societies and Institutes; Meitner, Lise; Weizsäcker, Carl Friedrich von; World War II

References
Cassidy, David. *Uncertainty: The Life and Science of Werner Heisenberg*. New York, NY: Freeman, 1991.
Charles, Frank, ed. *Operation Epsilon: The Farm Hall Transcripts*. Berkeley, CA: University of California Press, 1993.
Jungk, Robert. *Brighter Than a Thousand Suns*. New York, NY: Harcourt, Brace, and Company, 1958.
Kramish, Arnold. *The Griffin*. Boston, MA: Houghton Mifflin, 1985.
Powers, Thomas. *Heisenberg's War: The Secret History of the German Bomb*. New York, NY: Knopf, 1993.
Walker, Mark. *German National Socialism and the Quest for Nuclear Power, 1939–1949*. Cambridge, MA: Cambridge University Press, 1989.

Audi (Auto-Union AG)
Audi was founded in 1909 in Zwickau by August Horch, one of the pioneer engineers of automotive technology. Audi cars were among the most successful sports cars produced in series (as opposed to hand-crafted) before World War I. In 1921, Audi was the first automobile manufacturer to equip its cars with left-hand drive on a large scale. Audi also pioneered the use of a filter for the intake of air, hydraulic brakes, and front-wheel drive for medium-size cars.

In 1932, Audi amalgamated with Horch, DKW, and Wanderer to form Auto-Union AG, headquartered in Chemnitz. Horch had produced eight-cylinder engines exclusively since 1926 and had become the most significant producer of eight-cylinder cars. In 1937, Horch's market share of the luxury car market amounted to approximately 50 percent. DKW was the largest German producer of small cars and the first to build vehicles with front-wheel drive (1930–31). It used the fuel-efficient two-stroke engines exclusively. DKW, with 35 percent of all new motorcycles produced in Germany, also became the largest manufacturer of these vehicles, whereas Wanderer cars set the standard for medium-size cars in the upper price range.

With 24.5 percent of all new vehicles produced, Auto-Union became Germany's second-largest automobile producer, after Opel. Auto-Union distinguished itself by research on the aerodynamics of car bodies and on safety features; its systematized crash tests, inaugurated in 1938, were the first in Germany. In 1938, Auto-Union had 20,000 employees, a turnover of 276.4 million reichsmarks, and 3,000 patents.

During the Nazi era, Auto-Union collaborated closely with Ferdinand Porsche (1875–1951) in the development of advanced technological products, one notable result of which was the 16-cylinder mid-engine racing car. This became the most successful German Grand Prix racing vehicle between 1934 and 1937. It won 32 of 50 races.

In 1945–46, Auto-Union was dismantled by the Soviet occupation forces. The company rebuilt in Ingolstadt (Bavaria)

in 1949, where it initially produced DKW cars with the traditional two-stroke engine but later also manufactured motor scooters, all-terrain vehicles, and mopeds. In 1957, Auto-Union became the first German company to produce cars with an automatic clutch. During 1964, Auto-Union merged with Volkswagen; since then, all cars under the brand name Audi have been powered by four-stroke engines.

Among the technologically significant innovations first introduced in mass production by Audi were the constantly engaged four-wheel-drive system in a passenger car (Quattro; 1980), the optimized aerodynamic car body (1982), the ten-point security system (Europe only; 1986), the V-8 aluminum engine (1988), and the highly fuel-efficient direct-injection turbo diesel engine (1990). With its 37,000 employees (1992), 16 billion deutsche mark turnover, and approximately 400,000 cars produced per annum, Audi is one of the leading German car manufacturers.

In the Chemnitz region of the German Democratic Republic (GDR), the Auto-Union cars continued production under the trademark IFA. There too, production began with the prewar DKW F8 and F9. In 1951, research on plastic materials for car bodies began with the aim of providing a substitute material for the unavailable high-grade steel. The first German car (type P70) with a mass-produced plastic body shell appeared in 1955. In 1958, the P50, with its air-cooled two-cylinder engine, followed under the name Trabant. Over 2.5 million cars of an improved but externally unchanged version—the P601—were built between 1964 and 1990.

The car manufacturing companies of the former GDR were not viable in a united Germany. However, in 1990, Volkswagen established a new car assembly plant in Zwickau, which has continued the manufacturing tradition of the Auto-Union.

Peter Kirchberg

See also Automobile Industry; Porsche, Ferdinand; Volkswagen

References

Etzold, Hans Rüdiger. *Ewald Rother and Thomas Erdmann: Im Zeichen der Ringe.* 1: 1873–1945. Ingolstadt: Edition quattro Gmbh, 1992.

Kirchberg, Peter. *Bildatlas Auto Union.* Berlin: Motorbuch Verlag, 1987.

———. *Horch, Audi, DKW and IFA—80 Jahre Geschichte des Autos aus Zwickau.* Berlin: VEB Verlag für Verkehrswesen, 1980.

Mirsching, Gerhard. *AUDI: Vier Jahrzehnte Ingolstädter Automobilbau—der Weg von DKW und Audi nach 1945.* Gerlingen: Bleicher, 1988.

Auschwitz

Located near the Polish village of Oswiecim in Upper Silesia, Auschwitz was the largest German concentration and extermination camp. It played a unique role in the Nazi policy of mass murder—principally mass gassing of Jews, but also of Poles, Russians, and Gypsies. After the war, the horrors of Auschwitz became legendary—the name became not only synonymous with the brutal excesses of Nazi terror but also a metaphor for the crisis and collapse of civilization, society, and culture. Diametrically opposed to this are the notorious international Holocaust denial campaigns, central to which are the catch cries of the "Auschwitz Lie" or the "Auschwitz Myth."

In the first period of its existence during 1939, Auschwitz functioned as a concentration camp in which predominantly Poles were incarcerated. In 1941, after a visit by Heinrich Himmler (1900–45), the Stammlager (central camp), known as Auschwitz I, was extended. The new camp, Birkenau or Auschwitz II, served as the killing center. Only a short railway track had to be laid connecting the *Rampa*—the place of arrival and "selection" of victims in Birkenau—with Auschwitz station, which had direct rail links with Berlin, Vienna, Warsaw, and Krakow.

After experimental gassings using a pesticide known as Zyklon B, the SS authorities had gas chambers, crematoria, and other installations built, permitting efficient, assembly-line extermination to take place. On October 29, 1942, under the heading of "Implementation of Special Treatment," the overall construction costs for the expansions were assessed at 8,225,300 reichsmarks. The number of European Jews murdered by gas is estimated to have been in excess of one million at Auschwitz, which was one of six major killing camps. The camp complex also incorporated Auschwitz III, or Monowitz, a vast forced-labor compound comprising numerous subsidiary or satellite camps, where German business firms, especially the I.G. Farben concern, established factories and workshops. I.G. Farben's Buna plant produced synthetic oil and rubber. 150,000 slave laborers perished there.

When Auschwitz was abandoned in January 1945, 58,000 inmates were driven westward to other camps in death marches. Only a few of them lived to be liberated. Several investigations and trials conducted against guards and officials in Germany and abroad spanned decades. Many, however, who had engaged in the design, administration, and commercial exploitation of Auschwitz went unpunished.

Konrad Kwiet

See also Anti-Semitism; Concentration Camps; Gypsies; Heydrich, Reinhard; Himmler, Heinrich; Hitler, Adolf; Holocaust; Holocaust: Historiography; Höss, Rudolf; Jews, 1933–90; Memory, Collective; Nazi War Crimes Trials and Investigations; Nuremberg Trials; Polish-German Relations; Racism; Ravensbrück; Schutzstaffel (SS); World War II

References

Auschwitz: Geschichte und Wirklichkeit des Vernichtungs-lagers. Reinbek bei Hamburg: Rowohlt, 1980.

Gutman, Yisrael, Michael Berenbaum, Yehuda Bauer, Raul Hilberg, and Franciszek Piper, eds. *Anatomy of the Auschwitz Death Camp.* Bloomington, IN: Indiana University Press, 1994.

Höss, R. *Commandant of Auschwitz: The Autobiography of Rudolf Höss.* Cleveland, OH: Popular Library, 1959.

Levi, Paul. *Survival in Auschwitz: The Nazi Assault on Humanity.* New York, NY: Collier, 1981.

Pressac, J.-C. *Auschwitz: Technique and Operation of the Gas Chambers.* New York, NY: Beate Klarsfeld Foundation, 1989.

Austro-German Relations

For more than a millennium, Austria has been part of the German *Kulturnation* (cultural nation). German literature has been enriched by the works of such Austrian authors as Walther von der Vogelweide, Franz Grillparzer, Adalbert Stifter, Hugo von Hofmannsthal (1874–1929), Arthur Schnitzler (1862–1931), Stefan Zweig (1871–1929), Robert Musil (1880–1942), and Peter Handke (1842–). The Burgtheater in Vienna is one of the leading stages in the German-speaking world, and the compositions of Joseph Haydn, Wolfgang Mozart, Franz Schubert, and Johann Strauss (father and son) have long been considered products of German culture. For hundreds of years, Vienna was one of the German world's preeminent centers of trade and learning; Europe's oldest remaining German-speaking university was founded in Vienna in 1365. Not until the mid–nineteenth century were German-speaking Austrians forced to consider whether a unified German nation-state should include them.

During the Revolution of 1848, Austria had sent representatives to the Frankfurt Assembly, which sought in vain to draft a liberal constitution for all German-speaking people. However, Austria failed to thwart Prussian, later German, Chancellor Otto von Bismarck's subsequent policy to achieve a "small German" unification centered on Prussia and excluding Austria. In 1866, Austria suffered a crushing defeat at the hands of the Prussian army at the battle of Königgrätz, and she dared not support the French in the Franco-Prussian War of 1870–71. Austria was politically excluded from the newly unified Germany in 1871. The two German-speaking states became economic, diplomatic, and military partners, with Austria as the junior partner except in the cultural sphere. Germany needed a trustworthy ally, and for the next half a century Austria played that role. But multinational Austria-Hungary became increasingly weakened in an age of rising nationalism and tried in vain to swim against the current of the times. Thus, Austria overreacted when Archduke Franz Ferdinand and his wife were murdered in June 1914 by a Serb nationalist in Sarajevo. Backed by Germany and the other Central Power allies, Austria made unacceptable demands upon Serbia, thereby helping to set off a chain reaction which led to World War I.

During the war, Austria-Hungary lost political and military cohesion as losses mounted and Germany's military power ebbed. In 1918, many of her non-German nationalities were in open rebellion, and an exhausted Austria simply stopped fighting. On November 11, Austrian Emperor Karl abdicated, and the next day, the German-Austrian Republic was proclaimed, comprising the small German remnant of the former empire. In the Treaties of Trianon (with Hungary) and St. Germain, Austria's other territory was distributed to Romania and Italy, or was used to construct the new states of Hungary, Poland, Czechoslovakia, and Yugoslavia. Such fragmentation destroyed the Austrian economy, producing the worst possible foundation for an untried democracy. For the next two decades, Austria was in turmoil.

In desperation, many Austrians demanded to join the newly formed German republic to the northwest. The provisional government declared the new country to be a constituent part of Germany, and early in 1919, the German and Austrian foreign ministers signed a protocol paving the way for unification. But the victorious powers vetoed such a combination and ordered Austria to eliminate the prefix "German" from its name. Nevertheless, *Anschluss* ("joining" with Germany) dominated Austrian debates, and plebiscites on it in 1921 won majorities of 90 and 78 percent in Tyrol and Salzburg, respectively.

Not until 1937 did Germany, ruled since 1933 by an Austrian, Adolf Hitler, decide to force an *Anschluss*; a previous (1934) German-instigated *Putsch* had failed. In February 1937, a currency union was proclaimed. Under orders from Berlin, the pro-Nazi Austrian interior minister, Arthur Seyss-Inquart (1892–1945), seized power in 1938 and called upon the German Reich to save Austria from alleged Communist chaos. On March 11, 1938, three days before a scheduled national referendum to determine whether Austria should become an integral part of Germany (which the unifiers were expected to lose), German troops entered Austria. Two days later it became a province (with its designation from a millennium earlier: the Carolingian "Ostmark") of the Third Reich. By March 14 when Hitler greeted the cheering crowds at the Heldenplatz in Vienna, 70,000 Austrians had already been put into jails or concentration camps.

During this seven-year *Anschluss*, Austrians were both victims of and participants in the Nazi terror. One-fourth of all adult Austrian males joined the Nazi Party, a higher percentage than in Germany. Also, about one-fourth of the convicted Nazi war criminals were Austrian. On the other hand, Austria had been occupied against its people's legally expressed will in 1938 and had had no alternative than to fight alongside Germany. Hoping to foment an Austrian revolt against Germany, the Allied powers declared in Moscow in October 1943 that Germany's annexation of Austria had made the latter state "the first free country to fall victim to Hitlerite aggression."

After the war, many Austrians gladly embraced this interpretation, along with the collective absolution and release from reparations it offered. At the same time, unpleasant memories of the war experience helped to convince most Austrians that their destiny was no longer linked directly to Germany. The Austrian government, media, and schools embarked upon a persistent and successful policy of instilling in their citizens' minds that Austria is a nation separate from Germany. In a 1956 poll, 46 percent of Austrians still indicated that they belonged to the German nation, but in 1991 three-fourths of those polled said that an Austrian nationality already existed, and only 5 percent rejected Austrian nationhood.

However, the comforting notion that Austria did not share Germany's history and that the experience between 1938 and 1945 had been an aberration to be disregarded was seriously jolted in 1986, when Kurt Waldheim was elected federal president. He was haunted by revelations that he had lied about being a member of the Nazi student union and the SA (brown shirts) and that he had served in a Wehrmacht unit involved in war crimes in the Balkans. This scandal not only placed a straightjacket on Austria's foreign relations until he stepped down in 1992, but it again brought to light Austria's complicity in Germany's war effort and crimes.

Since the Allies had declared that Austria had been illegally occupied by Germany in 1938 and had been "liberated" in 1945, its 1920 constitution, as amended in 1929, and all laws passed prior to March 5, 1933, went into effect on May 1, 1945; not until 1954 did West Germany declare the 1938 *Anschluss* Law to be void. Unlike Germany, Austria was permitted to have its own civilian government from the very beginning after World War II, so that Allied control was always indirect, rather than direct, as in Germany. The four Allies prevented official, bilateral contacts between Austria and West Germany until 1950, and not until November 1955 were ambassadors exchanged.

In 1955, Austria regained its unity and full sovereignty. The Soviet Union agreed to withdraw its troops and hand over the economic assets it had seized on the condition that Austria adhere to a policy of neutrality on the Swiss model. On May 15, the Austrian State Treaty was signed. Moscow's main motive was related to West Germany, which it wanted to prevent from entering NATO. Many Germans wanted to see their country reunified, and by dangling before their eyes an attractive example of what a low price might have to be paid for national unity and a withdrawal of foreign troops, Moscow hoped to persuade them to remain neutral and to work out a mutually acceptable form of German national unity. Chancellor Adenauer's government rejected this plan and joined NATO in May 1955.

The Austrian State Treaty and the 1961 Kreuznach Treaty, which settled outstanding bilateral disputes over compensation for Austrian victims of Nazi crimes, residual German assets in Austria, and the status of ethnic German refugees from Eastern Europe living in Austria, opened the way for much more extensive and intimate Austro-German relations. Bilateral trade boomed. In 1952, Austria's imports from and exports to West Germany were 20.1 and 21.6 percent, respectively, of the totals; by 1992, those figures had grown to 42.9 and 39.8 percent, making Germany Austria's most important trading partner and source of tourist income. The Austrian schilling is tied to the deutsche mark, and by 1991, 40 percent of Austria's industry and 70 percent of its daily newspapers (including the leading quality newspapers, *Der Standard* and *Kurier*) were owned or controlled by German investors.

Considering Germany's economic importance for Austria and the fact that two-thirds of Austria's trade is with the European Community (EC), it is not surprising that Austria applied for EC membership in 1989, with Germany as its main supporter. Austrians have little to fear that they will be dominated by their western neighbor, although in other EC countries there are unarticulated fears that Austria's entry might increase the weight of a "German bloc" within the EC.

Since the appeal of any form of *Anschluss* has disappeared, most Austrians reacted without anxiety to Germany's unification in 1990. But the prospect that Austria will meld with a unified Europe, in which all borders will became blurred, could weaken Austria's fragile identity, which has been carefully nurtured to enable Austria to escape from the German legacy.

Wayne C. Thompson

See also Anschluss; Bismarck, Otto von; Central Powers; Diplomatic Corps and Diplomacy; Hitler, Adolf; Holocaust; Imperial Germany: Foreign Policy; Italian-German Relations; National Socialist Germany: Foreign Policy; Prussia; Seyss-Inquart, Arthur; Versailles, Treaty of; Weimar Germany: Foreign Policy; World War I; World War II

References
Bader, William B. *Austria Between East and West, 1945–1955*. Palo Alto, CA: Stanford University Press, 1966.

Basset, Richard. *Waldheim and Austria*. New York, NY: Penguin, 1988.

Bluhm, William T. *Building an Austrian Nation: The Political Integration of a Western State*. New Haven, CT: Yale University Press, 1973.

Johnson, Lonnie. *Introducing Austria: A Short History*. Riverside, CA: Ariadne, 1992.

Katzenstein, Peter. *Disjoined Partners: Austria and Germany since 1815*. Berkeley, CA: University of California Press, 1976.

Kreisky, Bruno. *Im Strom der Politik: Der Memoiren Zweiter Teil*. Berlin: Seider, 1988.

Mitten, Richard. *The Politics of Antisemitic Prejudice: The Waldheim Phenomenon in Austria*. Boulder, CO: Westview Press, 1992.

Parkinson, F., ed. *Conquering the Past: Austrian Nazism Yesterday & Today*. Detroit, MI: Wayne State University Press, 1989.

Riedlsperger, Max E. "Austria and Germany: A Not-So-Foreign Relationship." *The Germans and Their Neighbors*. Ed. Dirk Verheyen and Christian Søe. Boulder, CO: Westview Press, 1993.

Ritter, Harry. "Austria and the Struggle for German Identity." *German Studies Review* (Winter 1992), 111–129. (Article prompted by the controversy surrounding an 1989 essay by Kiel historian Karl Dietrich Erdmann, "Die Spur Österreichs in der deutschen Geschichte: Drei Staaten, zwei Nationen, ein Volk?" [Zürich: Manesse Bücherei, 1989]. A response to Ritter's article and his reply are in *German Studies Review* [October 1993], 515–23.)

Segar, Kenneth and John Warren, eds. *Austria in the Thirties: Culture and Politics*. Riverside, CA: Ariadne, 1992.

Thompson, Wayne C. "Austria." *Western Europe*. Ed. W.C. Thompson. Harpers Ferry, WV: Stryker-Post Publications, 1982–annually updated.

Autobiography

Critical perceptions of autobiography have undergone even more substantial changes in the past twenty or thirty years than is the case with most other literary genres and forms. Until well into the second half of the twentieth century, the term was generally reserved for works that narrated a significant portion of an individual's life with the intention of offering a factually accurate account in a manner that reflected a unified perspective. Although the boundaries were vague in some cases, attempts were made to distinguish between autobiographies and related forms such as diaries, memoirs, reminiscences, and autobiographical novels. In Germany, Wolfgang Goethe remained the standard and the model. Among those who wrote autobiographies in the traditional sense are the literary figures Karl Gutzkow (1811–78), Gustav Freytag (1816–95), Theodor Fontane (1819–98), Gerhart Hauptmann (1862–1946), and Hans Carossa (1878–1956), and, in other cultural areas (a list that could be significantly lengthened), Sigmund Freud (1856–1939), Albert Schweitzer (1875–1965), Albert Einstein (1879–1955), and George Grosz (1893–1959). Important political figures who wrote autobiographies include Kaiser Wilhelm II (1859–1941), and chancellors Willy Brandt (1913–92) and Konrad Adenauer (1876–1967). Those by military leaders such as Paul von Hindenburg tend toward apologia.

The traditional literary autobiography is not dead, as Carl Zuckmayer (1896–1977) and Elias Canetti (1905–94), a winner of the Nobel Prize, demonstrate, but between 1955 and 1975 both the attitude of critics and the practice of belletristic writers changed radically. Reality came to be viewed as fragmentary and relative, so the very premises of traditional autobiography were called into question, and forms such as the diary were accorded validity. Similarly, "truth" was no longer recognized as an absolute, and the distinction between a supposedly accurate autobiography and an admittedly fictionalized autobiographical novel was largely lost. In the early 1960s, Peter Weiss (1916–82) wrote narratives that were characterized as fiction but that are now universally included in studies of autobiography. The tendency to write fiction with strong autobiographical tendencies accelerated as "new subjectivity" emerged toward the end of the decade, resulting in the production of dozens, even hundreds, of fictionalized autobiographies in the 1970s, a trend that continues until the present day in spite of the significant changes in literary taste that have taken place. Major novelists whose works reflect this development include Hermann Lenz (1913–), Thomas Bernhard (1931–89), and Peter Handke (1942–). As a result of the simultaneous emergence of the feminist movement, women writers are especially prominent in this group; Barbara Frischmuth (1941–) was one of the first, and others who deserve special mention are Gabrielle Wohmann (1932–), Elisabeth Plessen (1944–), and, most important, Christa Wolf (1929–), whose *Kindheitsmuster* (published as *Patterns of Childhood*, 1976) is perhaps the most frequently discussed autobiographical work in recent German literature.

Around 1980, a number of works appeared in which the authors examine their childhoods, with particular attention to their fathers, especially the fathers' actions and attitudes during the Nazi years; prominent in this group are Peter Henisch (1943–) and Christoph Meckel (1935–). The extent to which the older concept of factual accuracy has been discarded is reflected in that among the novels sometimes discussed in the framework of autobiography are Uwe Johnson's (1934–84) four-volume *Jahrestage* (Anniversaries), 1970–83, in which the protagonist is a woman, and Ingeborg Bachmann's (1926–73) extraordinarily complex and nonrealistic *Malina,* 1971.

Interestingly and paradoxically, more critical attention in studies of autobiography is now focused on works that are labeled as fiction than on those that are called autobiographical. The important authors Marie Luise Kaschnitz (1901–74) and Hilde Domin (1912–) come immediately to mind, as does Erich Fried (1921–88), who says in the afterword to one of his collections of stories that he "actually experienced" everything contained in them. Recent expressly autobiographical writing, including that by the authors just mentioned, displays a strong tendency toward the episodic and the fragmentary, as evident in the subtitle of one of the few recent books that superficially resembles the traditional autobiography, *Auf dem falschen Dampter,* 1988 (published as *On the Wrong Track: Fragments of an Autobiography,* 1993) by Milo Dor (1923–).

Jerry Glenn

See also Adenauer, Konrad; Bachmann, Ingeborg; Bismarck, Otto von; Brandt, Willy; Canetti, Elias; Einstein, Albert; Fontane, Theodor; Freud, Sigmund; Freytag, Gustav; Fried, Erich; Grosz, George; Handke, Peter; Hauptmann, Gerhart; Hindenburg, Paul von; Johnson, Uwe; Kaschnitz, Marie Luise; Schmidt, Helmut; Schweitzer, Albert; Weiss, Peter; Wolf, Christa; Zuckmayer, Carl

References

Frieden, Sandra. *Autobiography: Self into Form. German-language Autobiographical Writings of the 1970s.* Frankfurt am Main: Lang, 1983.

Goodman, Katherine. *Dis/Closures: Women's Autobiography in Germany between 1790 and 1914.* New York, NY: Lang, 1986.

Pascal, Roy. *Design and Truth in Autobiography.* Cambridge, MA: Harvard University Press, 1960.

Paulsen, Wolfgang. *Das Ich im Spiegel der Sprache: Autobiographisches Schreiben in der deutschen Literatur des 20. Jahrhunderts.* Tübingen: Niemeyer, 1991.

Automobile Industry

In 1886, the world's first automobile driven by an internal combustion engine was invented in Germany, but no major commercial benefit of this innovation ensued until the early twentieth century. In 1901, 12 firms in Germany produced 900 vehicles; by 1909, the number of firms had risen to 50, and the number of vehicles manufactured reached about 9,500. Most of the early workshops had originally produced bicycles, sewing machines, and baby carriages (e.g., Opel, Brennabor). Those who had been producing engines (e.g.,

Daimler, Benz) shifted to the manufacture of high-quality luxury cars. Luxury car production shaped the German automobile industry, especially as its products earned a worldwide reputation for superior standards. All vehicles were hand built individually.

During World War I, the production of cars ceased in favor of army vehicles. As demand soared during the war, a developing supply industry took over the production of parts and aggregates. After the war, the German car industry failed to modernize or to introduce technical improvements, even during the brief sham boom of the inflation years, and consequently German car makers could not keep up with world standards. Nevertheless, the number of producers, which had been reduced during the war, increased to 71 by 1924.

Import restrictions on automobiles, which were imposed by the German government at the beginning of World War I, were abolished in 1925. Thereafter, the importation of foreign automobiles rapidly increased. A graduated tariff scale could only temporarily deter this trend. Thanks to lower duties on car parts, foreign companies hurriedly built assembly plants on German soil (Citroën and Mathis, 1926; Peugeot, 1927; Ford, 1930). In 1927, their combined production of passenger cars represented more than one-sixth of domestic output, and in 1928, the market share of foreign brands rose by much more than one-third. In view of such competiton, numerous German car makers went bankrupt. Others amalgamated: Daimler and Benz merged with Mercedes in 1926; Audi, Horch, Wanderer, and DKW formed Auto-Union in 1932. The remaining firms adopted labor-saving production methods and reduced the number of their models.

In 1928, German makers built a total of some 100,000 cars and 21,000 trucks. The average labor productivity had risen by 260 percent compared with 1913, whereas prices had decreased on the average by one-third. The lack of funds and high taxation kept German car production low; German car makers could not compete with the much cheaper imports from the United States, France, and Great Britain. Conditions deteriorated in the late 1920s, and sales diminished drastically during the Great Depression, which caused the collapse of many firms. In 1929–30, General Motors of the United States took over Opel, which prided itself on being the most modern German car factory. With the infusion of American funds, Opel's lead within Germany increased.

Following the world economic crisis, the German car industry experienced an enormous boom, which was partly the result of economic recovery and partly brought about by tax concessions, which reduced maintenance costs, especially for commercial cars. Existing production capacity enabled the automobile industry to satisfy the increasing demand without noticeable new investments, and the industry began to recover from the losses of the 1920s. The production of passenger cars, which would have restored good health to the industry, was terminated by increased Nazi war preparations in the mid-1930s. Production lagged due to restrictions on the allocation of raw materials, high fuel costs, and army needs. In 1938, Germany produced only 277,000 cars and about 64,000 trucks.

Volkswagen Plant, Wolfsburg. Courtesy of Inter Nationes, Bonn.

During World War II, the production of civilian cars was forbidden, whereas the building of army trucks received a great impetus. After World War II the automobile industry in West Germany became a key sector. Today, it supports itself based on an expanded network of suppliers. Thanks to the gains in the export market and the promotion of private ownership within Germany, the automobile industry has outstripped all other industrial branches in growth. The number of car manufacturers (BMW, Daimler-Benz, Ford, Opel, Porsche, and Volkswagen, which included Audi) and the number of truck producers (Auwärter, Daimler-Benz, Faun, Kässbohrer, Magirus-Deutz, and MAN) eventually leveled off at six conglomerates each. In 1992, the sales revenue in the German automobile industry amounted to 235 billion deutsche marks (DM) (motor vehicles and engines: DM 163 billion; vehicle parts and accessories: DM 58 billion; trailers, bodies, and containers: DM 14 billion). In 1960, West German car makers produced 1,816,779 motor vehicles; in 1980, this figure rose to 3,520,934, and in 1992 production attained 4,863,721. Out of these, 2,084,254 units were exported in 1980 and 2,729,949 in 1992. The automobile industry had by then become Germany's most important exporter. In East Germany production runs remained low, though the Trabant, with its two-cycle engine, demonstrated high durability, and during the 1980s the Wartburg moved toward western technological norms. After reunification the eastern state-owned plants were taken over by the main West German firms.

Heidrun Edelmann

See also Audi; Benz, Carl; BMW; Bosch, Robert; Daimler, Gottlieb; Daimler-Benz AG; Diesel, Rudolf; Krupp: Family and Firm; Mannesmann: Family and Firm; Nordhoff, Heinrich; Otto, Nikolaus; Porsche, Ferdinand; Volkswagen

References

Bellon, Bernard P. *Mercedes in Peace and War: German Automobile Workers 1903–1945.* New York, NY: Columbia University Press, 1990.

Mommsen, Hans. *Das Volkswagenwerk und seine Arbeiter im Dritten Reich.* Düsseldorf: ECON Verlag, 1996.

Reich, Simon. *The Fruits of Fascism: Postwar Prosperity in Historical Perspective.* Ithaca, NY: Cornell University Press, 1990.

Seherr-Thoss, Hans C. Graf von. *Die deutsche Automobil-industrie: Eine Dokumentation von 1886 bis 1979.* 2nd ed. Stuttgart: Deutsche Verlagsanstalt, 1979.

Axen, Hermann (1916–91)

Hermann Axen was a member of the *Politbüro* of the Socialist Unity Party (SED) and secretary of the Central Committee for International Relations. Born in Leipzig into a Communist family (his father was a party functionary) of partial Jewish background, he joined the Communist youth organization in 1932.

Axen's fate during the Nazi era is contested. According to official East German sources, Axen was incarcerated in a succession of concentration camps. Western sources contend that he was released to the Soviets in the wake of the Nazi-Soviet Non-Aggression Pact of 1939 and spent the war years in the Soviet Union as a teacher in an "Antifa" (Anti-Fascism) school. He built a career in the SED apparatus, rising to the top echelons of the party.

Although Axen was a member of the *Politbüro* after 1970 and secretary of the Central Committee for International Relations after 1971, he was never part of the inner circle composed of Erich Honecker (1912–94), Günter Mittag (1926–94), Joachim Herrmann, and Erich Mielke (1907–). Generally regarded as a colorless, orthodox adherent of the old guard, Axen was at least linked to "new thinking" on security issues, which attempted to redefine relations between competing systems in the 1980s. He headed the SED team that—together with the opposition Social Democrats in West Germany—developed two model security initiatives: one to establish a chemical weapons–free zone and the second, a nuclear weapons–free corridor. He is not, however, generally credited with important substantive contributions to those discussions.

In 1988, he was the highest-ranking member of the SED ever to visit the United States; at the time it was seen as a prelude to a state visit by Erich Honecker, general secretary of the SED and chairman of the State Council.

Ann L. Phillips

See also Anti-Fascism; German Democratic Republic; Honecker, Erich; Mielke, Erich; Mittag, Günter; Socialist Unity Party of Germany; Ulbricht, Walter

References

Axen, Hermann. *Aktuelle Fragen der internationalen Beziehungen der Sozialistischen Einheitspartei Deutschlands und der Deutschen Demokratischen Republik.* Berlin: Dietz Verlag, 1965.

———. *Aus dem Referat des Genossen Hermann Axen zu Fragen der europäischen Sicherheit.* Berlin: Dietz Verlag, 1972.

———. "Fascism and Militarism Have Been and Remain Exterminated Forever in the GDR." *Panorama* 1989.

———. *Kampf um Frieden—Schlüsselfrage der Gegenwart: Ausgewählte Reden und Aufsätze.* Berlin: Dietz Verlag, 1986.

———. *Sozialismus und revolutionärer Weltprozess: Ausgewählte Reden und Aufsätze.* Berlin: Dietz Verlag, 1976.

———. *Starker Sozialismus, sicherer Frieden: ausgewählte Reden und Aufsätze.* Berlin: Dietz Verlag, 1981.

———. *Zur Entwicklung der sozialistischen Nation in der DDR.* Berlin: Dietz Verlag, 1973.

———. *Zur internationalen Lage und zur Entwicklung des Kräfteverhältnisses.* Berlin: Dietz Verlag, 1967.

Krenz, Egon. *Wenn Mauern fallen: die friedliche Revolution.* Vienna: Paul Neff, 1990.

Schabowski, Günter, with Frank Sieren and Ludwig Koehne. *Das Politbüro.* Reinbek: Rowohlt Taschenbuch Verlag, 1990.

Spittmann, Ilse, ed. *Die SED in Geschichte und Gegenwart.* Cologne: Verlag Wissenschaft und Politik, 1987.

B

Baader-Meinhof Group (BMG)

Ulrike Meinhof and Andreas Baader became the leading strategists in a left-wing extremist group, the Baader-Meinhof Gruppe (Group; BMG), during the late 1960s and early 1970s. It continued as the Red Army Faction (RAF), after their deaths in 1972. The BMG operated as a self-styled guerrilla movement, whose purpose it was to trigger ever-more-repressive responses from the state in hopes of destroying popular support for the capitalist system.

Although its campaigns of violence evinced internationalist features, the Baader-Meinhof Group left a legacy that is also one of the more ambiguous "national" ties binding the former East and West German states. The collapse of the Honecker regime in 1989 led to revelations that the German Democratic Republic (GDR) had granted new names and identities to many former RAF terrorists who then settled into normal family and work lives; many have been prosecuted since reunification.

The group's founding members acquired their political consciousness from the 1950s to the mid-1960s. From the vantage point of these radical cohorts, the 14-year reign of Chancellor Konrad Adenauer appeared to restore many anti-democratic tendencies that had led to the Third Reich. Many younger leftists also lost faith in the Social Democrats as a force for "real opposition," as a result of the Godesberg Program of 1959 and the party's participation in the Grand Coalition (1966–69).

During the 1960s, the proliferation of New Left organizations on university campuses began to eclipse the resurgence of radical right wing forces in West Germany. Rooted initially in demands for free speech and impelled by the processes of generational change, in 1967 the movement took a radical turn that sanctioned the use of physical force. The catalyst was the death of a Free University of Berlin (FUB) student, Benno Ohnesorge, shot by police on June 2 during a rowdy demonstration in front of the Berlin Opera against the Shah of Iran; later, numerous letters claiming responsibility for specific terrorist acts were signed "the June 2nd Movement." Most of the

BMG's original hardcore activists attended university prior to their conversion to militant activism. They initially enjoyed a measure of ideological sympathy from leftist intellectuals (for example, the author Heinrich Böll [1917–85] and Peter Brandt, son of Chancellor Willy Brandt [1913–92]) and even from some members of the legal community (Klaus Croissant, Otto Schily, and Horst Mahler), who identified with the group's ends, if not with its means.

The campaign of violence commenced with fires set in two Frankfurt department stores by Baader and his "revolutionary bride," Gudrun Ensslin, on April 2, 1968. Born in May 1943, Baader was a sulky, troublesome pupil who did not complete the *Abitur* (senior matriculation); he moved to Berlin to avoid conscription in 1963 and met Ensslin in 1967. Ensslin was born in August 1940 to a Lutheran pastor father and a Swabian-pietist mother; she attended high school for a year in Pennsylvania on a Christian youth exchange, then studied philosophy, English, and German literature at the University of Tübingen. She enrolled under a doctoral scholarship at the FUB in 1965, joined the Social Democrats, then the Students for a Democratic Society (Sozialistischer Deutscher Studentenbund; SDS). Baader and Ensslin took up with radicals at the University of Frankfurt in 1968.

Ulrike Meinhof, born in October 1934, was raised by a history professor qua peace activist in Hamburg after her father's death in 1939 and the loss of her mother to cancer in 1948. She studied philosophy, pedagogy, sociology, and German literature in Marburg, Münster, and Hamburg. As a journalist and mother of twin daughters, Meinhof was married for seven years to Klaus Röhl, publisher of *Konkret*—a radical-chic magazine financed by "Communist gold" funneled through East Berlin. She participated in the "Fight Atomic Death" campaign. After her divorce in 1968, she moved to Berlin, where she did freelance work for radio and television and lectured at the FUB. The fourth member of the inner circle was a Berlin sociologist associated with the Kommune II (semi-anarchist counter-culture group), the Austrian Jan-Carl Raspe, who was born in July 1944 and raised in East Berlin. Other names soon added to the "most wanted" posters were Holger Meins, lawyer Horst Mahler, Irmgard Moeller, Ingeborg Barz, Astrid Proll, and Rolf Pohle.

A major police sweep resulted in the arrest of core BMG members in June 1972, following a countrywide bombing campaign. They were incarcerated and tried in a specially built, top-security prison in Stammheim in 1974; members of the original "gang of four" were tried directly for 5 murders and 54 attempted murders, along with numerous robberies and explosions. Meins died of a hunger strike in 1974, and Meinhof hanged herself in her cell on May 8, 1976. Raspe, Baader, and Ensslin committed suicide while in solitary confinement at the prison.

Later actions by members of the RAF "successor generation" included bank robberies, more bombings, abductions, and the murders of prominent West German politicians and entrepreneurs. Among the more sensational cases were the murder of Berlin Superior Court President Günter von Drenkmann and the kidnapping of Berlin Interior Minister Peter Lorenz in 1974, along with the assassinations of Federal Prosecutor-General Siegfried Buback and Dresdener Bank chief Jürgen Ponto in 1977. The BMG-RAF accounted for 28 assassinations, 93 injured, and 15 hostage-takings during its first decade of operations. Between 1970 and 1978, 215 suspects were convicted of terrorist activity, 94 additional ones underwent criminal investigation, and 42 remained on the "wanted" list. The RAF has also claimed responsibility for the post-unification murders of Alfred Herrenhausen, head of the Deutsche Bank, and Detlef Rohwedder, director of the Trust Agency (Treuhandanstalt).

The BMG's legacy includes numerous measures restricting the civil liberties of younger leftists and lawyers. The Contact Ban Law of 1977 imposes solitary confinement for hardcore suspects and restricts the activities of defense lawyers. Witnesses willing to "tell all" have been guaranteed reduced sentences in hopes of tracking down the group's remaining members.

Joyce Mushaben

See also Anarchism; Böll, Heinrich; Brandt, Willy; Extra-Parliamentary Opposition; Federal Republic of Germany; Federal Republic of Germany: Political Radicalism and Neo-Nazism; Federal Republic of Germany: Political Terrorism; German Democratic Republic: State Security; Violence

References
Aust, Stefan. *The Baader-Meinhof Group: The Inside Story of a Phenomenon.* London: Bodley Head, 1989.

Baumann, Bommi (Michael). *Terror or Love? Bommi Baumann's Own Story of His Life as a West German Urban Guerrilla.* Trans. Helene Ellenbogen and Wayne Parker. New York, NY: Grove Press, 1979.

Becker, Jillian. *Hitler's Children: The Story of the Baader-Meinhof Terrorist Gang.* Philadelphia, PA: J.B. Lippincott Company, 1977.

Civil Liberties and the Defense of Democracy against Extremists and Terrorists: A Report on the West German Situa-
tion. Freiburg im Breisgau: Rombach, 1980. Issued by Atlantic Brücke.

Meinhof, Ulrike. *Die Würde des Menschen ist antastbar: Aufsätze und Polemiken.* (Posthumously published.) Berlin: Klaus Wagenbach Verlag, 1986.

"Sonderkommission Bonn" und Bundesamt für Verfassungsschutz, ed. *Der Baader-Meinhof Report: Dokumente–Analysen–Zusammenhänge.* Mainz: v. Haase & Koehler Verlag, 1972.

Baader, Ottilie (1847–1925)

Along with Clara Zetkin (1857–1933) and Luise Zietz (1865–1922), Ottilie Baader was one of the leading personalities of the socialist women's movement in Imperial Germany. She was an active fighter for women's suffrage, education, and protective labor laws for women and children, and presented her views at numerous national and international conferences.

Born into a worker's family near Frankfurt an der Oder, she had to take over the household after her mother's early death and supplement her family's income as a seamstress. She was compelled to gain her extensive education through self-study.

In the 1880s, she joined the socialist women's movement, became a member of the Berlin Women's Agitation Commission, and after 1895 served as Social Democratic Party (SPD) contact person for a Berlin electoral district and later for all of Berlin. In 1900, at the first national conference of Social Democratic women, which she co-chaired with Zetkin, she was elected as the first contact person (*Zentralvertrauensperson*) for women, especially women workers. Under great difficulties she expanded the system of contact persons created by the SPD in 1894 as a means of circumventing the law that made political activity of women illegal. By 1908, her network included more than 400 female regional contact persons.

On the difficult issue of cooperation between bourgeois and proletarian women's movements, Baader acted as the loyal partner of Zetkin against Lily Braun, who regarded cooperation as a necessity. Braun thereupon became isolated from the party's mainstream.

The Association Law (Reichsvereinsgesetz) of 1908 granted women the right to become regular members of political parties. Baader thought that a separate women's organization and contact persons were now superfluous, so the women's movement became integrated into the SPD. However, she demanded appropriate representation by women in the organizations and structures of the party.

Under the leadership of Zietz, who became the first woman elected to the national executive in 1908, Baader worked in the party's women's bureau. In 1917, Zietz moved to the more radical Independent Social Democratic Party. Baader lost her position when the party split and she was assigned to a menial position on the SPD journal *Parteikorrespondenz.* She had little influence thereafter.

Walter Mühlhausen

See also Braun, Lily; Social Democratic Party, 1871–1918; (Bourgeois) Women's Movement; Zetkin, Clara; Zietz, Luise

References

Baader, Ottilie. *Ein steiniger Weg: Lebenserinnerungen einer Sozialisten.* 3rd ed. Berlin: Dietz, 1979.

Dertinger, Antje. *Die bessere Hälfte kämpft um ihr Recht: Der Anspruch der Frauen auf Erwerb und andere Selbstverständlichkeiten.* Cologne: Bund-Verlag, 1980.

Evans, Richard J. *Comrades and Sisters: Feminism, Socialism and Pacifism in Europe, 1870–1945.* New York, NY: St. Martin's Press, 1987.

Quataert, Jean H. *Reluctant Feminists in German Social Democracy 1885–1917.* Princeton, NJ: Princeton University Press, 1979.

Bachmann, Ingeborg (1926–73)

Within the genres of poetry, radio play, short story, novel, and essay, Ingeborg Bachmann is recognized as one of the eminent writers of the twentieth century. She began by writing poetry and was "discovered" by the Gruppe (group) 47, Germany's postwar artistic avant garde, which awarded her its annual prize in 1953. That year she published her first of two volumes of poetry, *Die gestundete Zeit* (published as *Mortgaged Time*, available with other selected poems in *In the Storm of Roses*, 1986).

Bachmann's writing was greeted at every stage by prestigious German or Austrian prizes. Even before the publication of her final collection of poetry, *Aufrufung des Grossen Bären* (Invocation of the great bear), 1956, Literary Prize of Bremen, 1957, Bachmann had written the first two of her three now-classic radio plays, *Ein Geschäft mit Träumen* (A shop with dreams), 1952 and *Die Zikaden* (The crickets), 1954. For the third, *Der gute Gott von Manhattan* (The good God of Manhattan), 1957, she was honored with the coveted Radio Play Prize of Blind Veterans (1959).

After the late 1950s, Bachmann concentrated mainly on writing prose, although her work as lyricist for Hans Werner Henze (1955–65) and her translations of poetry by Giuseppe Ungaretti should be noted. She began as a prose writer with a series of four lectures, essays she delivered at Frankfurt University during the winter semester 1959–60, where she initiated the ongoing series of Frankfurt Lectures on Poetics. A year later, Bachmann's first collection of short stories, *Das dreissigste Jahr*, 1961 (published as *The Thirtieth Year*, 1964) garnered the literary prize of the Association of German Critics (commensurate with the Pulitzer Prize) and membership in the Berlin Academy of Arts. A 1964 collection of her poems, short stories, a radio play, and essays brought her the prestigious Georg Büchner Prize (1964).

Malina, 1971 (published in English, 1989), Bachmann's only completed novel, and her second collection of short stories, *Simultan* (1972), were published before she died in 1973. *Malina* won her a second Austrian literary prize in 1971. She had been given the Great Austrian State Prize in 1968. With *Simultan* (published as *Three Paths to the Lake*, 1989), she received full recognition as a prose-writing poet. The progression of her extraordinary literary career was linked closely to her personal history.

Bachmann was born on June 25, 1926, in Klagenfurt, Austria, close to Slovenia and Italy. Her youth was marked by

Ingeborg Bachmann. Courtesy of German Information Center, New York.

the Nazi *Anschluss* of her country. Her young womanhood was marred by the impressions of violence left by the war and its aftermath. Bachmann received a doctorate from the University of Vienna (1950), with a dissertation on the existential philosophy of Martin Heidegger. For two years, she worked as scriptwriter and then as editor for the Austrian radio station Red-White-Red, the only period in which she received a regular salary. By August 1954, she had gained wide recognition as an author, including appearing on the cover of *Der Spiegel.* She lived in Italy with the composer Henze, for whose music she wrote libretti for a decade, and between 1958 and 1962 with the Swiss writer, Max Frisch (1911–91). During that time, she involved herself publicly in political causes and was inducted into the Berlin Academy of Arts. In 1963, the Ford Foundation invited her to spend a year in Berlin, and, after travels to Prague, Egypt, and the Sudan, she returned in 1965 to Rome, where she became severely dependent on drugs. On September 25, 1973, she suffered burns in a fire resulting apparently from a cigarette in her bed. She died three weeks later.

The major themes of Bachmann's entire oeuvre were closely related to her personal experience. Philosophical questions concerning the responsibilities of thinking and language frame her texts. Like the Austrians Wittgenstein and Hofmannsthal before her, Bachmann experienced a crisis of language (*Sprachkrise*). She was a modernist in her treatment of alienation and dehumanization, problems she addressed through woman narrators who struggled to find their own voice. Bachmann proved to be at least a decade ahead of the war protests and feminist movements in Europe.

Since her death, various works from Bachmann's literary estate have been published, including *Der Fall Franza* (The Franza case) and *Requiem für Fanny Goldmann* (Requiem for Fanny Goldmann). These unfinished novels replaced *Malina* at the center of the feminist Bachmann canon during the 1980s. Feminist criticism has increasingly revealed the timelessness of her writings. From the image of woman as victim to that of subversion of norms in a society in which the powerless are silenced, Bachmann's writing as well as her individual existence were shaped by a tension resulting from her desire to overcome barriers (*Grenzüberschreitung*) yet at the same time to live within the bounds of an ordered existence (*Innerhalb der Grenzen*). By taking human interactions to their frightful consequences (*Todesarten*), Bachmann's writing points beyond these boundaries with a suggestion of utopian hope. Among the writers on whom she has had direct influence are Christa Wolf (1929–), Günter Grass (1927–), Max Frisch, Thomas Bernhard, Erich Fried (1921–88), and Peter Handke (1942–).

Sheila Johnson

See also Federal Republic of Germany: Literature; Feminist Writing; Fried, Erich; Frisch, Max; Grass, Günter; Handke, Peter; Henze, Hans Werner; Novel; Poetry; Radio Plays; Wolf, Christa

References

Achberger, Karen R. *Understanding Ingeborg Bachmann.* Columbia, SC: South Carolina University Press, 1993.

Albrecht, Monika. *"Die andere Seite": Zur Bedeutung von Werk und Person Max Frischs in Ingeborg Bachmanns "Todesarten."* Würzburg: Könighausen & Neumann, 1989.

Arnold, Heinz Ludwig, ed. *Ingeborg Bachmann.* Vol. 1. Munich: Text + Kritik, 1971.

Bachmann, Ingeborg. *Werke.* 4 vols. Munich: Piper, Sonderausgabe, 1978, reprinted, 1982.

Bieken, Peter. *IB.* Munich: Beck, 1988.

Hapkemeyer, Andreas, ed. *IB, Bilder aus ihrem Leben, Mit Texten aus ihrem Werk.* 4th ed. Munich: Piper, 1992, 1987.

———. *Ingeborg Bachmann: Entwicklungslinien in Werk und Leben.* Wien: Österreichische Akademie der Wissenschaften, 1990.

Lennox, Sara. "The Feminist Reception of Ingeborg Bachmann." *Women in German Yearbook.* Lincoln, NE: Nebraska University Press, 1993.

Remmler, Karen. "The Use and Abuse of Feminist Criticism: Ingeborg Bachmann." *Monatshefte* 85 (1993), 211–17.

Swiderska, Malgorzata. *Die Vereinbarkeit des Unvereinbaren: IB als Essayistin.* Tübingen: Niemeyer, 1989.

Bacteriology

During the "golden age of bacteriology" (c. 1880–1910), German scientists led the field. Robert Koch (1843–1910) and his coworkers identified bacteria that cause major communicable diseases and laid the foundations of immunology and chemotherapy. The German school of bacteriology was noted for developing rigorous research methods, applying new techniques, and founding major research institutes. Bacteriological research, which received substantial support from the Imperial government, the military sanitary corps, and state and local governments, promised cheap solutions to public-health problems, advanced tropical medicine (indispensable for German colonial ventures), and added to the international prestige of German science. By 1910, Emil Behring (1901), Koch (1905), and Paul Ehrlich (1908) had won Nobel Prizes in medicine, testimony to the preeminence of German bacteriology.

Although the botanist Ferdinand Cohn (1828–98) systematically classified bacteria in the 1870s, Robert Koch defined the field. At the Imperial Health Office (1880–85) Koch and his assistants invented the essential techniques of clinical bacteriology. By cultivating pure cultures of pathogenic bacteria and then infecting laboratory animals, they showed that specific bacteria cause diseases. Koch isolated the tubercle bacillus in 1882 and discovered the cholera vibrio in 1884. These discoveries established the primacy of German bacteriology over the French school of Louis Pasteur. Koch and his coworkers experimented extensively with photomicroscopy, bacterial stains, and disinfectants. Koch also trained doctors in diagnostic uses of bacteriology. The importance of diagnostic tests and disinfection for containing the spread of infectious disease was confirmed during the cholera epidemic of 1892 in Hamburg.

The contributions of bacteriologists to disease control were manifest, but rapid therapeutic benefits were few. Claims that Koch had found a cure for tuberculosis in 1891 proved embarrassingly premature. But Koch's assistant, Emil Behring (1854–1917), had already noticed that blood serum of laboratory animals previously infected with diphtheria bacteria contained antitoxins that countered the bacteria's toxic effects. Transferring this serum to uninfected animals conferred passive immunity. This work marked the beginnings of immunology and enabled Behring to produce a serum against diphtheria that reduced infant mortality in the late 1890s.

Paul Ehrlich (1854–1915), another Koch assistant, later formulated the first comprehensive theory of the immune system. Having detected the affinity of bacterial species for particular dyes, Ehrlich began searching for chemicals that could kill specific bacteria. His greatest success in chemotherapy came in 1910 with the demonstration that the arsenic compound Salvarsan cured syphilis. Behring and Ehrlich maintained close ties to German chemical firms. Chemotherapy became a specialty of the chemical industry, as evidenced by the work of Gerhard Domagk (1895–1964) at I.G. Farben, which resulted in the synthesis of sulfa drugs in the mid-1930s.

By the time of Koch's death in 1910, bacteriology was solidly institutionalized. Koch's Institute for Infectious Diseases and Ehrlich's Institute for Experimental Therapy were conducting innovative research. German universities had built research centers, and most large cities had established laboratories to test food, water, and pathological samples. The army sanitary corps had recognized the importance of bacteriology for military hygiene. Bacteriology proved effective during colonial campaigns and even more impressive during the World War I, when death rates from infectious diseases and tetanus in the field were remarkably low.

By 1918, the golden era of bacteriology was over. Bacteriology had become a routine science. The relatively easy victories had been achieved and the first generation of bacteriologists was dead. The Weimar Republic fostered social rather than bacteriologic hygiene. Nor did bacteriology occupy a prominent role in Nazi biological ideology. Racial hygienists had long criticized bacteriology for helping to preserve the supposedly biologically unfit. Nonetheless, pioneer bacteriologists, such as Emil Behring and Robert Koch, were still celebrated as German geniuses, the latter in the 1939 film, *Robert Koch: Kämpfer des Todes* (Robert Koch: fighter of death), starring Emil Jannings. By contrast, the public memory of Ehrlich, who was Jewish, was obliterated. The Nazis represented Jews and other racially persecuted minorities as deadly bacteria or disease carriers. In part because of such political perversions of science, Germany forfeited its lead in bacteriology and immunology during the Nazi era.

Derek S. Linton

See also Diseases; Ehrlich, Paul; Health; I.G. Farbenindustrie AG; Koch, Robert; Virchow, Rudolf

References

Bäumler, Ernst. *Paul Ehrlich: Forscher für das Leben.* Frankfurt am Main: Societäts-Verlag, 1979.

Brock, Thomas D. *Robert Koch: A Life in Medicine and Bacteriology.* Madison, WI: Science Tech Publishers, 1988.

Forster, W.D. *A History of Medical Bacteriology and Immunology.* London: William Heinemann Medical Books, 1970.

Silverstein, Arthur M. *A History of Immunology.* San Diego, CA: Academic Press, 1989.

Weindling, Paul. *Health, Race and German Politics between National Unification and Nazism 1870–1945.* Cambridge: Cambridge University Press, 1989.

Zeiss, H. and R. Bieling. *Behring: Gestalt und Werk.* Berlin: Bruno Schulz Verlag, 1941.

Baden-Württemberg

Baden-Württemberg is a relatively young state, the product of World War II and the resulting American and French occupation of this southwest part of Germany. After considerable debate and a number of plebiscites, the two prewar *Länder* (states) of Baden and Württemberg were united in 1952, with Reinhold Maier (1889–1971; Free Democratic Party) as its first minister-president. The capital is Stuttgart.

The German southwest has a rich, complex history. Here, in the nineteenth century, liberalism and democracy found fertile ground. Baden and Württemberg played an active role in the Revolutions of 1848, but both states also readily supported, after the defeat of Austria in 1866, the unification of Germany under Prussian leadership.

In the post–World War II years, Baden-Württemberg became a consistent stronghold of the Christian Democratic Union (CDU). With the demise of Reinhold Maier's coalition government in 1953, the CDU began its monopoly as the chief government party. Kurt Georg Kiesinger (1904–88),

Neues Schloss *in Stuttgart, capital of Baden-Württemberg. Courtesy of German Embassy, Ottawa.*

who became federal chancellor in 1966, Hans Filbinger, and Lothar Späth were three prominent CDU minister-presidents.

Baden-Württemberg, one of the wealthiest of the German *Länder*, has a richly varied economy reflecting the diverse geography of the state. Small-scale farming, often mixed and part-time, produces a wide range of products, including grapes. Agriculture is still a vital sector of the Baden-Württemberg economy, but industry, ranging from small firms to giants such as Bosch and Daimler-Benz, predominates. Forestry, and in this case its concomitant, tourism, also contribute to the diversity of the economy, especially in the Black Forest region.

Among the German *Länder*, Baden-Württemberg attracts the second-largest number of tourists (Bavaria attracts the most). Baden-Württemberg is one of the leading German export states, yet it has not been blessed with an abundance of natural resources. Furthermore, it has been handicapped by its deep inland location and distant export markets. Traditionally, Baden-Württemberg industry has been labor intensive, emphasizing quality finished products. Generally, it has been highly successful in responding to market demand and technological innovation. The three leading industrial sectors are the production of machines, motor vehicles, and electronics. Building on its handicrafts tradition, Baden-Württemberg also offers a diversity of precision tool and handicraft products (not just cuckoo clocks). IBM and Hewlett-Packard have their German headquarters in Baden-Württemberg.

The generally vibrant economy has made Baden-Württemberg the third most populous of the German *Länder* (9.6 million in 1992); it is also third in size (13,803 square miles). The capital city of Stuttgart has a population of 571,000. Other important urban centers are Karlsruhe (265,000), Mannheim (300,000), Heidelberg (131,000), Freiburg (183,000), and Ulm (106,000).

Baden-Württemberg also has a rich cultural tradition. Roman Catholicism has predominated in Baden, whereas Protestantism, especially of a pietistic strain, is prevalent in Württemberg. Romanticism, mysticism, and rationality, but also pragmatic, bourgeois realism, have deep roots in the German southwest. Friedrich Schiller (1759–1805), Friedrich Hölderlin (1770–1843), Georg W.F. Hegel (1770–1831), and Martin Heidegger (1889–1976) are but some of the prominent contributors to this rich heritage.

Baden-Württemberg has a number of prominent institutions, including the oldest university in Germany (Heidelberg was founded in 1386), and the oldest technical college in Germany (at Karlsruhe), as well as a number of research institutes, such as the German Cancer Research Center in Heidelberg, the Nuclear Research Center at Karlsruhe, and a number of Max Planck Institutes. The German Federal Court of Justice and the Federal Constitutional Court, Germany's highest tribunals, are both located in Karlsruhe.

Juergen C. Doerr

See also Bosch, Robert; Christian Democratic Union; Daimler-Benz; Federal Republic of Germany: Judicial System; Federalism; Kiesinger, Kurt Georg; Meier, Reinhold

References

Borst, Otto. *Wege in die Welt: Die Industrie im deutschen Südwesten seit Ausgang des 18. Jahrhunderts.* Stuttgart: Deutsche Verlag-Anstalt, 1989.

———. *Württemberg: Geschichte und Gestalt eines Landes.* Konstanz: Stadler, 1980.

Miller, Max and Gerhard Taddey, eds. *Baden-Württemberg.* Handbuch der Historischen Stätten Deutschlands, Vol. 6. Stuttgart: Kroner, 1965.

Rinker, Reiner and Wilfried Setzler, eds. *Die Geschichte Baden-Württembergs.* Stuttgart: K. Theiss, 1986.

Sauer, Paul. *Die Entstehung des Bundeslandes Baden-Württemberg.* Ulm: Süddeutsche Verlagsgesellschaft, 1977.

Schulz, Werner. *Landesbibliographie von Baden-Württemberg.* Stuttgart: W. Kohlhammer, 1978.

Baeck, Leo (1873–1956)

Leo Baeck was born in Lissa, Posen in 1873. His journey through life was characterized by the attempt to uphold and preserve his Jewish existence. An intensive public debate among theologians provided him with the opportunity to gain a reputation as an eminent scholar. In 1905 he presented his classic work, *Das Wesen des Judentums* (The essence of Judaism), as a response to the book by the Protestant theologian Adolf von Harnack, *Das Wesen des Christentums* (The essence of Christianity), 1902. His research and teaching were conducted at the renowned Berlin Hochschule für die Wissenschaft des Judentums (Center for Judaic Studies). Baeck held rabbinical appointments in Oppeln, in Silesia, in Düsseldorf, and—from 1912 until 1942—in Berlin. During World War I he served as an army chaplain. After 1918 he threw himself into a variety of activities, establishing himself as the leading representative of German Jewry. Other posts included that of chairman of the General Association of German Rabbis, grandmaster of the B'nai B'rith Lodge, and executive member of the Central Verein (Central Association of German Citizens of the Jewish Faith).

In 1933, when the Nazis seized power and the Jews experienced the cancellation of the implicit civil contract of Jewish-German fraternity, a new organization emerged, the Reichsvertretung der Juden (Reich Representation of German Jews). Under the leadership of Baeck, it tried to protect and maintain Jewish life and its continued existence in Germany. Baeck left no doubt that his strategies for the defense of the community would be restricted exclusively to measures within the bounds of prevailing law, an approach that later unleashed anger and criticism in some Jewish quarters. He protested repeatedly against the defamations, slander, and discrimination. Twice arrested by the Gestapo but each time released, he rejected offers to seek refuge abroad.

In early 1943 he was deported to the Theresienstadt ghetto. As a member of the Jewish Council of Elders he knew about the fate that awaited the Jews at Auschwitz. Baeck refused to convey his "terrible secret" to his fellow inmates, which also attracted criticism. After liberation in 1945 he settled in London, where he assumed the chairmanship of the

Council of Jews from Germany and of the World Union for Progressive Judaism. He died in London in 1956. A Seminary for Progressive Rabbis in London, a secondary school in Haifa, and the leading research centers and publication series on the history of German Jewry are dedicated to honor his memory.

Konrad Kwiet

See also Anti-Semitism; Auschwitz; German-Jewish Organizations; Holocaust; Israeli-German Relations; Jews, 1933–90

References

Baker, L. *Days of Sorrow and Pain: Leo Baeck and the Berlin Jews.* New York, NY: Macmillan, 1978.

Friedländer, A.H. *Leo Baeck: Teacher of Theresienstadt.* Woodstock, NY.: Overlook Press, 1991.

Baeyer, Adolf von (1835–1917)

Johann Friedrich Wilhelm Adolf von Baeyer, probably the most successful chemistry teacher of the last third of the nineteenth century, was a master of test-tube organic chemistry. His many syntheses included indigo, then the "king of dyes." For his achievements he was knighted and awarded the 1905 Nobel Prize in Chemistry.

Born in Berlin to a scholarly general who promoted geodetic surveying and to a mother descended from a distinguished Jewish family, Baeyer learned organic chemistry with August Kekulé (1829–96) at Heidelberg and Ghent, obtained his doctorate at the University of Berlin (1858), and for 12 years (1860–72) taught in the Berlin Gewerbeinstitut (Berlin Trades Institute) later merged into the Technische Hochschule (Technical University). Here he worked on uric acid and related compounds, then indigo; in his laboratory, Carl Graebe and Carl Liebermann developed a practical synthesis for alizarin dye (1868), the first major success of the German coal-tar dye industry. Baeyer co-founded the Deutsche Chemische Gesellschaft (German Chemical Society) in Berlin (1867). His marriage to Lydia Bendemann produced a daughter and two sons who followed academic careers until forced out in 1933.

After a brief tenure as full professor at Strassburg University (1872–75), Baeyer succeeded Justus von Liebig at the University in Munich. Baeyer's new laboratory building (the largest in Germany until 1900) became a world center for organic chemistry, producing some 1,600 publications and many distinguished academic and industrial chemists among its 395 doctorates awarded during his tenure to 1915. Baeyer set the standards but did not personally direct most of the research.

Considering himself a self-taught empiricist, Baeyer actually worked within the theoretical framework of classical organic chemistry formulated by Kekulé and others. Three main areas may be emphasized: acetylene chain compounds and the relationship of structural "strain" to explosive instability; the structure of valences in the six-membered ring of benzene and its derivatives (1885–93) (a question not clarified until the development of twentieth-century electron-bond theories); and of course the structure and synthesis of many dyestuffs, particularly indigo, and the relationship of molecular structure to color. Although many of Baeyer's early dye dis-

coveries were commercialized through collaboration with Heinrich Caro of the BASF corporation, his indigo syntheses (1878–83) proved uneconomical, and Baeyer abandoned the problem. The first commercial synthetic indigo came much later (1897).

Baeyer was the epitome of the German organic chemist, a model teacher and researcher who remained creative until old age and whose work enriched scientific knowledge and theory as well as industry.

Jeffrey A. Johnson

See also BASF; Chemistry, Scientific and Industrial; I.G. Farbenindustrie AG; Kekulé, August

References

Fruton, Joseph S. *Contrasts in Scientific Style: Research Groups in the Chemical and Biological Sciences.* Philadelphia, PA: American Philosophical Society, 1990.

Willstätter, Richard. *From My Life: The Memoirs of Richard Willstätter.* Lilli S. Hornig, trans. New York, NY: W.A. Benjamin, 1965.

Bahr, Egon (1922–)

Salesman, journalist, foreign and security policy advisor and strategist, and prime architect of the *Ostpolitik* of the social-liberal coalition of Willy Brandt (1913–92) and Walter Scheel (1919–), Egon Bahr was born in Treffurt, Thuringia. As the son of a civil servant he grew up in Torgau (where American and Soviet forces met in 1945). There he joined the choir of the castle church that Martin Luther had founded. As a member of the choir he developed his musical interests, which stayed with him. In 1938 the family moved to Berlin, where Bahr finished his gymnasium studies in 1940. Prevented by the Nazis from studies in music because his grandmother was not Aryan, he joined the sales department of the steel firm of Borsig. He was drafted into an anti-aircraft unit but was dismissed when his grandmother's non-Aryan status was discovered. He rejoined Borsig for the duration of the war.

At the close of the war, Bahr began his journalistic career writing for a number of Berlin newspapers; he also joined RIAS (Radio in the American Sector) and served as editor in chief in 1953–54. In these postwar years, he also became acquainted with Kurt Schumacher (1895–1952), leader of the Social Democratic Party (SPD) in West Germany, but following Schumacher's advice, he did not yet join the SPD. Schumacher was apparently concerned that SPD membership might hinder Bahr's journalistic career. Willy Brandt repeated this advice, but in 1956, influenced by the Soviet defeat of the Hungarian uprising, he became a party member. In 1959 Brandt, who had succeeded Otto Suhr as mayor of Berlin in October 1957, appointed Bahr as the press and information officer for the Berlin state government. The close cooperation and friendship of the two men had begun, a relationship which gained Bahr the epithet of Brandt's political "alter ego."

As a journalist, Bahr had developed a particular interest in foreign policy. By the late 1950s, the division of Germany and East-West tensions seemed far from resolution; the building of the Berlin Wall in 1961 marked the most intense phase of the Cold War. Bahr believed that the impasse could be overcome. In 1963 in a paper presented at the *Evangelische Akademie Tutzing* (Tutzing Protestant Academy), he outlined his prescription of "Wandel durch Annäherung" (change through closer relations). In cooperation with the Americans and other Western allies, the West Germans were to seek improved relations, both politically and economically, first with the Soviet Union, then with its European satellite states. Detente, a temporary acceptance of the political *status quo*, would ultimately create favorable conditions for overcoming the division of Germany.

When Brandt became foreign minister in 1966, Bahr became, first, special ambassador, then head of the Foreign Office Planning Staff. He was in a position to flesh out and to implement his unconventional, imaginative ideas. He was placed in charge of the initial negotiations (completed by Walter Scheel), which led to the Moscow and Warsaw treaties of 1970. He was also chief West German negotiator for the 1971 Quadripartite Agreement on Berlin and the 1972 Basic Treaty with East Germany, as well as the subsequent treaties with Czechoslovakia, Hungary, and Bulgaria. With the completion of the fundamental *Ostpolitik* structures, Bahr continued to serve as special foreign and security policy advisor to Brandt.

In 1972, Bahr became a member of the Bundestag, an office he held until 1990. He was a member of the Brandt (special tasks) and Schmidt (minister of economic cooperation and development) cabinets. With the demise of the Schmidt-Genscher coalition in October 1982, Bahr next year became head of the Institute for Peace and Security at the University of Hamburg, and in that position remained an influential and provocative commentator on foreign policy and security matters. He has received various awards, including the Theodor-Heuss-Prize, the Gustav-Heinemann-Bürger Prize and the title of Professor from the University of Hamburg.

Juergen C. Doerr

See also Basic Treaty; Berlin; Brandt, Willy; Detente and Germany; Disarmament; Federal Republic of Germany: Foreign Policy; German-German Relations; *Ostpolitik*; Schumacher, Kurt; Social Democratic Party, 1918–90; Soviet-German Relations; Wehner, Herbert

References

Bahr, Egon. *Sicherheit für und vor Deutschland: Vom Wandel durch Annäherung zur Europäischen Sicherheitsgemeinschaft.* Munich: Hanser, 1991.
———. *Was wird aus den Deutschen? Fragen und Antworten.* Reinbek: Rowohlt Verlag, 1982.
———. *Zum europäischen Frieden: Eine Antwort auf Gorbatschow.* Berlin: Corso bei Siedler, 1988.
Lutz, Dieter, ed. *Das Undenkbare denken: Festschrift für Egon Bahr zum siebzigsten Geburtstag.* Baden-Baden: Nomos Verlag, 1992.
Schröder, Karsten. *Egon Bahr.* Rastatt: Arthur Moewig Verlag, 1988.

Balke, Siegfried (1902–84)

Siegfried Balke, an engineer who was active in the chemical industry from the mid-1920s until the early 1950s, became a prominent politician in the Christian Social Union (CSU) during the 1950s and early 1960s. He served as head of a number of different ministries between 1953 and 1962, with his most important accomplishment being the steering of the Federal Republic of Germany toward establishing a large-scale nuclear power industry.

Balke was born in Bochum on June 1, 1902. He attended the Technische Hochschule (technical university) at Munich, from which he graduated as a Diplom-Ingenieur in 1924. He earned a doctorate one year later, after which he began a career as a chemical engineer and manager in a number of small chemical firms.

Only after 1945 did Balke rise to prominence, first as a member of upper management at Wacker Chemie GmbH, but also as a chemical industry lobbyist within the fledgling chemical industry trade association. In 1953, he assumed the post of federal minister of posts and telegraphs, moving on to head the Ministry for Atomic Questions in 1956, the Ministry for Atomic Energy and Water Supply and Distribution from 1957 to 1961, and the Ministry for Nuclear Energy in 1961 and 1962. The planning and construction of much of West Germany's nuclear power capacity occurred under his stewardship, a project that involved extensive cooperation between government and private industry.

Balke finished his career as he had begun it, in the private sector, although he now moved into a branch of industry that was more closely associated with nuclear power. He was a member of upper management at SIGRI Elektrographit in Meitlingen betwen 1964 and 1967. Between 1964 and 1969 he was also president of the Bundesvereinigung der Deutschen Arbeitgeberverbände (Federation of German Employers Associations).

Raymond Stokes

See also Christian Social Union; Nuclear Power and the Nuclear Industry

References

Balke, Siegfried. *Kernkraftwerke und Industrie: Das Kernkraftwerksprogramm der Bundesrepublik Deutschland und seine industriellen Probleme.* Bonn-Bad Godesberg: Deutsches Atomforum/Bundesministerium für Wissenschaftliche Forschung, 1966.
———. *Vernunft in dieser Zeit: Der Einfluss von Wirtschaft, Wissenschaft und Technik auf unser Leben.* Düsseldorf: Econ, 1962.
Müller, W.D. *Geschichte der Kernenergie in der Bundesrepublik Deutschland: Anfänge und Weichenstellungen.* Stuttgart: Schäffer, 1990.

Ballet (Music)

The musicologist Paul Nettl once wrote, "German romantics thought of ballet as un-German and un-romantic." This intolerant attitude toward ballet, a dance form that achieved its greatest success in France, Italy, and Russia, and later in England and the United States, was only occasionally overcome by the achievements of individual German choreographers. The composition of music especially for ballet fared somewhat better than the art of dance itself.

Most ballet in the German-speaking countries has been traditionally centered around the major opera houses rather than in independent companies. Visiting foreign dancers have also been traditionally more famous than native-born dancers. However, a major development in the notation of choreography was achieved by Rudolf von Laban (1879–1958), who published his system of "Labanotation" in *Kinetographie Laban* (first published in Germany, 1928). Many important choreographers studied with Laban, but almost all were foreigners; the only first-rank native German choreographer to have studied with Laban was Kurt Jooss (1901–79), who became famous outside Germany with such works as *Persephone* and *The Green Table*.

Both Laban and Jooss left Germany and accomplished their most prominent work in France and the United States as a result of the policies of the Nazis, who essentially abolished forms of dance that were not amenable to the masses. The most popular form of dance during that regime was folk dance. Male dancers were drafted into military service during the war; many were taken prisoner, wounded, killed, or sent to concentration camps.

The work of Erika Hanka at the Vienna Opera after World War II did much to make ballet respectable as an art form in its own right, and it has since been imitated by major opera houses in many cities in Germany and Austria.

German and Austrian composers traditionally shunned ballet as a second-class musical form and concentrated their work instead on the forms in which they were acknowledged experts: opera, symphony, concerto, and chamber music, among others. When a composer did write music for a ballet on commission, it was rarely regarded as a major work comparable to that in other genres (for example, Richard Strauss's [1864–1949] ballets *Schlagobers* and *Josephslegende* are barely known even today, compared with his operas, tone poems, or *Lieder*).

However, five major composers in the German-speaking countries have given serious attention to ballet music. Egon Wellesz composed the music for six ballets (*Das Wunder der Diana, Die Prinzessin Girnara, Persisches Ballett, Achilles auf Skyros, Die Nächlichen,* and *Die Opferung des Gefangenen*). Boris Blacher wrote seven such works, among them *Harlekinade, Lysistrata, Hamlet,* and *Der Mohr von Venedig.* Paul Hindemith (1895–1963) wrote three ballets: (*Herodiade, Der Dämon,* and *Nobilissima Visione,* the latter one of his most famous works) as well as the overture to a ballet, *Amor und Psyche.* The predominance of non-German themes in these works is not surprising, and all three composers were blacklisted under the Nazi regime as non-Aryans, cultural Bolsheviks, or both.

Two other composers who cooperated with the Nazi regime were nevertheless influential in the history of ballet composition in Germany after the Third Reich: Carl Orff (1895–

John Neumaier's ballet Peer Gynt *in Hamburg. Courtesy of German Embassy, Ottawa.*

1982) who composed *Carmina Burana*, and Werner Egk. The work of these composers has been important in the recent trend toward purposely written ballet scores as a countermove against the sometimes regrettable fashion of basing new ballets on pre-existing music composed for other venues and purposes.

Susan M. Filler

See also Composers; Conductors; Hindemith, Paul; National Socialist Germany: Music; Opera; Orchestral Music; Orff, Carl; Strauss, Richard

References

Coton, A.V. *The New Ballet: Kurt Jooss and His Work.* London: D. Dobson, 1946.

Koegler, Horst. *The Concise Oxford Dictonary of Ballet.* 2nd ed. Oxford: Oxford University Press, 1987.

Laban, Rudolf von. *Kinetographie Laban.* 2 vols. Vienna: Universal Edition, 1928–30.

———. *Principles of Dance and Movement Notation.* London: Macdonald and Evans, 1956.

Regitz, Hartmut, ed. *Tanz in Deutschland: Ballett seit 1945— eine Situationsbeschreibung.* Berlin: Quadriga, 1984.

Ballin, Albert (1857–1918)

Albert Ballin served from 1888 until his death as the chairman of the Hamburg-America Line, or HAPAG, which on the eve of World War I was the world's largest steamship company. As one of Imperial Germany's leading businessmen, he was in frequent contact with Kaiser Wilhelm II and other important political figures.

Ballin came from humble circumstances and lacked formal education, but he was a man of prodigious intellect, entrepreneurial flair, and engaging personality. He succeeded in capturing a major share of both the freight and passenger trade of the Atlantic by offering superior service and competitive prices and went on to send HAPAG ships around the world. The line's motto deservedly was "My Field Is the World" (*Mein Feld ist die Welt*). The principal casualties of the HAPAG's success were British steamship lines that had formerly held a commanding lead, and in some places a monopoly, in various world markets.

Ballin was proud of his line's success and he believed that Germany's national destiny was to become the superior economic force in the world, but he was convinced that the expansion of trade meant that there was a place for both Great Britain and Germany. He was therefore eager to diminish the problems in Anglo-German relations that arose from commercial and naval rivalry, and he worked hard with his business friends in London to inaugurate negotiations over naval armaments, notably in arranging the ultimately unsuccessful 1912 Berlin mission of the British Secretary of War, Lord Haldane.

Ballin knew Wilhelm II quite well, for the sovereign was an enthusiastic supporter of German merchant shipping. The Kaiser was frequently Ballin's guest in Hamburg and on his passenger ships, and Ballin used these occasions to stress that German national sentiments, such as fleet building and diplomatic aggressiveness, needed to be kept within reasonable limits to insure the continuation of European peace. War would destroy not only the Hamburg-America Line but Germany's entire economy. Unfortunately, the outbreak of hostilities, in part caused by Berlin's disregard of Ballin's sound advice, did exactly that. Ballin, broken by the disaster of Germany's approaching defeat, died on November 9, 1918, the day of the fall of the monarchy.

Lamar Cecil

See also Anglo-German Relations; Hamburg; Harden, Maximilian; Navy and Naval Policy; Tirpitz, Alfred von; Wilhelm II

References

Cecil, Lamar. *Albert Ballin: Business and Politics in Imperial Germany.* Princeton, NJ: Princeton University Press, 1967.

Huldermann, Bernhard. *Albert Ballin.* Oldenburg i.O.: Stalling, 1922.

Stubmann, Peter F. *Mein Feld ist die Welt: Albert Ballin, sein Leben.* Hamburg: Hans Christians Verlag, 1960.

Wile, Frederic W. *The Men around the Kaiser: The Makers of Modern Germany.* Indianapolis, IN: Bobbs-Merrill, 1914.

Balthasar, Hans Urs von (1905–88)

Hans Urs von Balthasar was a member of the Society of Jesus from 1929 to 1950. After leaving the order he lived in Basel, served as director of the Johannesgemeinschaft (a lay pastoral institute), and was involved in retreat work as well as conferences on spirituality. In 1972 he founded the periodical *Communio.* He is best known for his multivolume treatise on aesthetics and religion, titled *Herrlichkeit: Eine theologische Ästhetik* (The glory of the lord: A theological aesthetic), 1961–69. Nominated as cardinal by Pope John Paul II, he died two days before the honor was conferred.

Balthasar's fundamental theology emerged as part of an ongoing intellectual dialogue with Henri de Lubac and Karl Barth (1886–1968). Inspired by these theologians, Balthasar focused his reflections explicitly on the relationships between reason and faith, as well as between philosophy and theology. His *Theologik,* 1985, stressed that phi-

losophy was not only before but also in theology.

The theology of Balthasar consists of two interwoven threads. The first is the analogy that an interpersonal love relationship can provide the foundation for the encounter of the person with God. The second is the analogy that the act of aesthetic experience can provide for the perception of God's glory. The ontology behind this intersection of theology and aesthetics consists of a metaphysics of transcendentals. Thus, the encounter with every reality can be seen as an encounter with God in some fashion. In his system, the aesthetic experience is to be subsumed into a loving encounter with the God of love, who appears in all of creation.

In Balthasar's fundamental theology, aesthetics and interpersonal love encounter each other and fuse into one. A metaphysics of the transcendental reality and an anthropologically rooted vision of every meeting as ultimately an encounter with God seem to be held in a sophisticated mutual transparency. Balthasar is a master of synthesis and his thought flows lithely from one level of reflection to the other. For him, divine beauty becomes the manner in which God's goodness is expressed by God and understood by humans as the truth.

Donald J. Dietrich

See also Roman Catholic Church

References

Mooney, Hilary A. *The Liberation of Consciousness: Bernard Lonergan's Theological Foundations in Dialogue with the Theological Aesthetics of Hans Urs von Balthasar.* Frankfurt am Main: Verlag Josef Knecht, 1992.

O'Hanlon, Gerard. *The Immutability of God in the Theology of Hans Urs von Balthasar.* Cambridge: Cambridge University Press, 1990.

Riches, John. *The Analogy of Beauty: The Theology of Hans Urs von Balthasar.* London: T. and T. Clark, 1986.

Baluschek, Hans (1870–1935)

This realist painter's works highlighted the strains of rapid German industrialization during the Imperial period. Born in Breslau, Hans Baluschek studied in Stralsund and at the Royal Academy of Art in Berlin.

In the 1890s, Baluschek illustrated for the satiric periodical *Narrenschiff* (Ship of fools) and executed 39 graphics centering around the theme of industrialization's consequences for impoverished Berlin women. In the middle and late 1890s, he completed a thematic cycle of graphic prints, entitled *Between East and West,* which visually described Berlin's petty bourgeoisie, vagabonds, prostitutes, and drunks against a backdrop of city streets and factories. Among his most famous paintings— though during his career he painted few—was *Proletariat Women,* 1900, evoking women's estrangement from their traditional familial occupations and revealing the collective dilemma of monotonous factory labor.

Baluschek was a founding member of the Berlin Secession, and this affiliation afforded him greater visibility and recognition. He received commissions for railroad canvases during the first decade of the twentieth century. Critics labeled

Baluschek, along with the graphic artist Heinrich Zille, the "chronicler" of Berlin life. His countless graphics record workers during various times of the day—during lunch breaks, carting wagons of coal—from daybreak to evening evoking a Dickensian atmosphere of overwhelming difficulty in the face of daily life. The literary naturalism of Emile Zola, Arno Holz, and Gerhart Hauptmann influenced Baluschek's work, and the artist frequented the theatrical world.

After World War I, Baluschek taught at a Berlin high school and received various commissions for murals (e.g., the wine cellar of Lutter and Wegener). Stylistically, Baluschek's art represented social realism and had a didactic quality and message. Both style and technique remained remarkably consistent throughout his career. Politically he was on the left, but his art was firmly on the aesthetic right during his entire life.

Marion Deshmukh

See also Artists; Berlin Secession; Hauptmann, Gerhart; Holz, Arno; Painting; Workers' Culture

References

Bröhan, Margrit. *Hans Baluschek, 1870–1935: Maler, Zeichner, Illustrator.* Berlin: Nicolaische Verlagsbuchhandlung, 1985.

Esswein, Hermann. *Hans Baluschek.* Munich: R. Piper, 1905.

Gedächtnis-Ausstellung Hans Baluschek. Berlin: Magistrat von Gross-Berlin, 1948.

Hans Baluschek. Intr. Günter Meissner. Leipzig: VEB Seemann, 1966.

Hans Baluschek, Ausstellung. Berlin: Deutsche Akademie der Künste, 1955.

Wendel, Friedrich. *Hans Baluschek, eine Monographie.* Berlin: Dietz, 1924.

Widerra, Rosemarie. *Hans Baluschek: Leben und Werk.* Berlin: Mark Museum, 1974.

Zieseke, Christiane and Monika Hoffmann, eds. *Hans Baluschek.* Berlin: Staatliche Kunsthalle, 1991.

Bamberger, Ludwig (1823–99)

Ludwig Bamberger was born in Mainz on July 22, 1823. He was old enough to begin his public political career in the Revolution of 1848; he pursued his activities in politics during the entire second half of the nineteenth century.

After a university education in law between 1842 and 1845, Bamberger entered government service at the lowest level in the Bavarian Palatinate, where Jews enjoyed more freedom than elsewhere. Bamberger's future expanded nationally with the revolutions. In 1848, Bamberger regarded himself as a German and a democrat rather than as a Jew. Unlike most of his liberal colleagues, Bamberger participated in the 1848 revolution as a radical democrat rather than as a moderate liberal. During the revolution, Bamberger confined his activities to writing in the new left-wing political press and speaking before countless public audiences. But when the larger German states, led by Prussia and Bavaria, rejected the Frankfurt Constitution in the spring of 1849, Bamberger fought on the side of a relative handful of radical democrats in the Palatinate and, after being defeated, fled to Switzerland.

After travels in England, Belgium, and Holland, Bamberger settled in exile in Paris, where he married. Faced not only with the failure of the revolution but also with forced emigration, Bamberger began a career in banking, which is not surprising in view of his own and his wife's family connections in finance. By 1866, he was nonetheless able to devote himself far more to politics than to the boardroom. He gave up Parisian life in 1866 and returned to Mainz in order to participate in what appeared to be the construction of a new Germany.

Bamberger's parliamentary career began in 1868 with election to the Zollparlament, a legislative body not of a state but of a collection of independent states, the German Confederation sponsored by Prussia. In 1871, Bamberger won election to the Reichstag and served there until shortly before his death in 1899.

Politically, Bamberger defined his liberalism in national and economic terms, reflected by his patriotic support for a unified Germany. Despite reservations about Chancellor Otto von Bismarck and his methods, he continued his support by joining the National Liberal Party. Although involved in a wide variety of legislative activity, he made his name on issues involving free trade, currency, and banking. In his conflict with Bismarck over the introduction of a protective tariff and the outlawing of the fledgling Social Democratic Party, which the government regarded as responsible for assassination attempts on the Kaiser in 1878, Bamberger sided with the left wing of the National Liberal Party. When the left wing seceded in 1881 and formed a new party, the Sezessionisten (secessionists) Bamberger followed, and in 1884 helped to transform that party into the Freisinnigepartei (Progressive Party). Repeated attempts to reconstruct a new liberal party of the middle failed, leaving Bamberger and others in his position exposed to political life in a splintered party. Remarkably, probably testifying to his personal popularity and abilities, Bamberger continued to win election in the area around Mainz despite a considerable Catholic political presence in the area. His success was all the more remarkable because it came during a period of rising political anti-Semitism. Much of Bamberger's local success stemmed from his national opposition to Bismarck, especially to Bismarck's economic and colonial policies. Catholic voters appear to have been favorably disposed toward an opponent of the most important supporter of the *Kulturkampf*, the war against Catholicism.

James F. Harris

See also Bismarck, Otto von; *Kulturkampf*; Liberalism; National Liberal Party

References

White, Dan S. *The Splintered Party: National Liberalism in Hessen and the Reich, 1867–1918.* Cambridge, MA: Harvard University Press, 1976.

Zucker, Stanley. "Ludwig Bamberger and the Rise of Anti-Semitism in Germany, 1848–1893." *Central European History* 3 (1970), 332–52.

———. *Ludwig Bamberger: German Liberal Politician and Social Critic, 1832–99*. Pittsburgh, PA: University of Pittsburgh Press, 1975.

Banking

Banking has a prominent place in the modern economic history of Germany, because banks are known to have played a significant role in financing that country's economic development. In fact, in international and historical perspective, the role of banks in the German economy is one of the country's most striking features. Comparative economic and banking histories have long stressed the distinction between the specialized Anglo-American banking model and German "universal banking" (which combined short-term money market with long-term capital market transactions), and historical research on German banking has bestowed a disproportionately large amount of attention on the causes and consequences of this particular institutional evolution.

The causes of "universal banking" have been traced to two special features of Germany's nineteenth-century industrialization. First, German industrialization since around 1830 built significantly on new, capital-intensive technologies borrowed from abroad, mainly from Great Britain and France. Financing these technologies, e.g., ironmaking and railroads, was a major problem, because Germany had no tradition of gradual capital accumulation. The solution was the emergence of banks that not only supplied industry with short-term credits and means of payment but also provided long-term finance and entrepreneurial initiative in organizing (and reorganizing)

large-scale industrial enterprises. The development of such banks could thus be regarded as a demand-induced phenomenon; and this argument is a central part of Gerschenkron's celebrated typology of industrialization.

Second, in Germany government institutions early established a high degree of control over the currency and payments system—much more so than in Great Britain or the United States. Moreover, these institutions, such as the Bank of Prussia, founded in 1846, and later its nationwide successor, the Reichsbank, founded in 1876, proved willing to provide the commercial banks with liquidity and credits in times of need. Those commercial banks were therefore encouraged to concentrate fewer resources in the more conventional, highly liquid forms of banking activities, and more on entrepreneurial and investment banking. The development of universal banking in Germany became a function of government policy and hence, indirectly, of politics.

In the early stages of industrialization, until about 1870, commercial banking was dominated by private family firms, and many of these were, in effect, universal banks. After the 1870s, joint-stock banks became increasingly dominant, but they developed the universal banking form still further. By the eve of World War I, a handful of huge joint-stock banks with close ties to large industrial enterprises remained dominant. This was a unique development; so striking, indeed, that it served as the basis for a number of theories of capitalist development, namely those of Hilferding ("Finance Capital"), Schumpeter, and Lenin.

Germany's pre-1914 banking arrangements were not exclusively products of the large, universal banks. By concen-

Frankfurt City Hall with banks in background. Courtesy of German Embassy, Ottawa.

trating on large enterprises and wealthy capitalists, those banks were neglecting important branches of the economy: agricultural and rural credit needs, urban housing, small and especially new business enterprises, and lower-class savings. Special-purpose institutions, the most important of which were the public savings banks, the credit cooperatives, and the mortgage banks, emerged to serve these needs. In recent years, savings banks and credit cooperatives ("people's banks") have grown more than the large commercial banks.

The periodization of German banking history follows that of German history in general: pre-1914, World War I, the interwar years, World War II, and post-1945. World War I subordinated banks to government fiscal needs, while inflation (1919–23) gutted them. They had not yet recovered from this setback—their autonomy became limited by their dependence on foreign capital—when the Great Depression erupted in 1929 and led to their temporary collapse. Under the Nazi regime, banks once more became largely the servants of public finance. After World War II, the United States agitated for a remodeling of the German banking system along American lines. The proposed breakup of the "great banks" failed after a brief experiment with decentralization. By the 1950s, the banks were reconcentrating, and public discussion of the problem of bank power had resumed. However, the reintroduction of a central bank of issue independent of the government was effective, first in the form of the Bank deutscher Länder (bank of the German states), then in 1957 as the Bundesbank (federal bank). It proved an effective guarantor of price stability in the postwar period, although Germany's experience with two inflations created a favorable political environment for this policy.

How banking contributed to the overall growth and stability of the German economy is a difficult question. During the period of heavy industrialization (until 1914), commercial banks financed new and risky investments and large-scale enterprises. Due to cooperation between the central bank and commercial banks, growth proved relatively stable. During the interwar period, the situation was basically dismal, and the political environment was not propitious for progress. In the course of the postwar resurgence of the German economy, the commercial banks once again became prominently linked to successful industries and enterprises. Clearly, the correlation between bank growth and the rise of the economy in the 1850–1914 and post-1945 periods does not settle the matter of success or failure—nor do references to individual stories of success, in the financing of enterprises or industries. Despite some controversy on the role of banks in the pre-1914 period, research suggests that the banks made a basically positive contribution. German banks seem to have been better able to overcome informational problems, which were crucial for financial relationships, than those of most other countries. On the other periods the picture is not so clear.

Richard Tilly

See also Abs, Hermann J.; Bleichröder, Gerson von; Bundesbank, Deutsche; Currency; Depression, 1873–95; Deutsche Bank; Fürstenberg, Carl; (Great) Depression, 1929–33; Helfferich, Karl; Industrialization; Inflation and Hyperinfla-

tion; Schacht, Hjalmar; Schultze-Delitzsch, Hermann; Warburg, Max

References

Born, K.E. *International Banking in the 19th and 20th Centuries.* Leamington Spa: Berg, 1983.
Feldman, G.D. *The Great Disorder: Politics, Economics and Society in the German Inflation 1914–24.* Oxford: Oxford University Press, 1993.
Gerschenkron, A. *Economic Backwardness in Historical Perspective.* Cambridge, MA: Belknap Press, 1962.
Hilferding, Rudolf. *Finance Capital: A Study of the Latest Phase of Capitalist Development.* Boston, MA: Routledge & Kegan Paul, 1981.
Holtfrerich, C. "Zur Entwicklung der deutschen Bankstruktur." *Deutscher Sparkassen- und Giroverband.* Ed. Standort Bestimmung. Stuttgart: 1984.
Klein, Ernst. *Deutsche Bankengeschichte.* Vol. 3. Frankfurt am Main: Knapp, 1983.
Pohl, Manfred. *Einführung in die deutsche Bankengeschichte.* Frankfurt am Main: Knapp, 1976.
———. *Konzentration im deutschen Bankenwesen (1848–1980).* Frankfurt am Main: Knapp, 1982.
Tilly, R. "German Banking, 1850–1914: Development Assistance to the Strong." *Journal of European Economic History* 15 (1986), 113–52.
Wellhoner, V. *Grossbanken und Grossindustrie im Kaiserreich.* Göttingen: Vandenhoeck & Ruprecht, 1989.

Barbie, Klaus (aliases Altmann, Wilms, Müller) (1913–91)

The SS/SD *Hauptsturmführer* (captain) and war criminal Klaus Barbie was nicknamed "the Butcher of Lyons." Born in Bad Godesberg on October 25, 1913, he was part of a generation of Germans who matured with the bitter legacy of a lost war.

By his twenties, Barbie was ripe for the Nazi message of rage and hatred. Facing unemployment on graduation from secondary school in 1934, he joined the Hitler Youth. Party life agreed with the young man. On September 26, 1935, he joined the SS. Shortly thereafter he entered the SS Sicherheitsdienst, the party's security service. In 1937, when the Nazi Party reopened its membership rolls, Barbie gained immediate admission. In April 1940 he attained the rank of SS *Untersturmbahnführer* (second lieutenant).

Barbie's crimes began with his arrival in Lyons in early spring 1942. Lyons was a major textile manufacturing and banking center. Located 80 miles from unoccupied France's Swiss mountain frontier, the city was the capital of the French Resistance—battles with the German occupier became especially bitter.

Following the German occupation of southern France in autumn 1942, Barbie's job was to obtain intelligence on the French Resistance and make its existence as precarious and miserable as possible. Cold, ruthless, fanatical, and brutal, Barbie excelled at interrogation. In that role he became closely connected to the collaborationist French Militia. When it betrayed the whereabouts of the Gaullist resistance leader Jean

Moulin to Barbie, he presided over Moulin's interrogation, torture, and later, death.

The collapse of Fascist Italy before an Allied invasion during the summer of 1943 exposed German-occupied southern France to a new threat, and Barbie met it with murderous ruthlessness. Wherever he went in his pursuit of the Resistance and Jews, torture and massacres of innocent hostages became the order of the day. In February 1943, he commanded a raid on the headquarters of Lyons's Jewish Aid Society. The 85 persons arrested there were deported to Auschwitz. Similarly, Barbie exercised supervisory authority over the raid on a Jewish orphanage at Izieu, a village 40 miles to the east of Lyons. The 44 arrested children were deported to Auschwitz. In August 1944, as the Germans were preparing to abandon Lyons to the Allies, Barbie supervised the evacuation and murder of the inmates incarcerated in the city's Montluc Prison.

By war's end Barbie was hiding in Germany. With the onset of the Cold War, he obtained employment with American Intelligence, which aided his escape to Bolivia in 1951. He was discovered by the Nazi hunter Beate Klarsfeld in 1971. Not until 1983 was he expelled and extradited to France. Amidst much publicity and soul searching over French collaboration with the Germans, he stood trial for his crimes. In 1987 he was found guilty of various crimes and sentenced to life imprisonment.

Eric D. Kohler

See also Anti-Semitism; Auschwitz; Franco-German Relations; Hitler Youth; Holocaust; Nazi War Crimes Trials and Investigations; Schutzstaffel (SS)

References

Hoyos, Ladislas de. *Klaus Barbie.* New York, NY: McGraw-Hill, 1985.

Paris, Erna. *Unhealed Wounds: France and the Klaus Barbie Affair.* New York, NY: Grove Press, 1986.

Barlach, Ernst (1870–1938)

A sculptor, graphic artist, and dramatist whose work focused on themes of human spirituality, suffering and endurance, Ernst Barlach was a central figure in the development of modern and expressionist art in Germany during the first decades of the twentieth century.

The son of a physician, Barlach was born in Wedel, near Hamburg, and studied at the School of Applied Arts in Hamburg (1888–91), the Dresden Art Academy (1891–95), and the Académie Julian in Paris. Not until a 1906 journey to southern Russia to visit his brother Hans, an engineer working in Kharkov, did Barlach find his own themes and style. Sketches, diary entries, and Barlach's own later statements all attest to the profound impact of the vast landscape and people of the Ukraine. After returning to Germany, Barlach fashioned his first sculptures in wood and soon developed an innovative figurative style, which combined naturalism with a strong corporeality and an increasingly angular sense of form.

In 1908, Barlach joined the Berlin Secession and signed a contract for the exclusive sale of his noncommissioned works with the art dealer Paul Cassirer, who would also publish his

Ernst Barlach. Courtesy of Inter Nationes, Bonn.

plays—the first, *Der Tote Tag* (The dead day), 1912, accompanied by 27 Barlach lithographs—as well as other graphic cycles. In 1910 Barlach moved to Güstrow, a small town in Mecklenburg, where he worked with few interruptions and in increasing isolation for the rest of his life.

Barlach's deepest sympathies lay not with any political ideology but with human suffering and spiritual despair. After initial patriotic enthusiasm when World War I started in 1914, Barlach soon turned against the war and created a number of strong pacifist images, such as the lithograph *From a Modern Dance of Death,* 1916, published in Cassirer's wartime journal, *Der Bildermann* (The picture man). War memorials, unusual for their emphasis on sorrow and mourning rather than honor and sacrifice, were completed in Güstrow (1927), Kiel (1928), Magdeburg (1929), and Hamburg (1932). A larger-than-life-sized figure with arms folded and eyes closed, the Güstrow Memorial hangs suspended horizontally from an arch in the town's cathedral.

By 1930, seven of Barlach's dramas had been performed publicly (six years earlier he had been awarded the Kleist Prize for literature), and his 60th birthday that year was honored by a retrospective exhibition by the Prussian Academy of Arts, of which he had been a member since 1919.

Under the Third Reich, Barlach was denounced for his pessimistic imagery, the Slavic features of his figures, and his connections to international and Jewish modernism. Performances of his dramas were prohibited, and by mid-1937 381 of his works had been seized or removed from museums and churches. A bronze version of his sculpture *The Reunion (Christ and John),* 1926, was included in the well-known 1937 *Degenerate Art* exhibition.

Barlach's dramas are barely known outside of Germany, but his sculptures and graphics have gained international recognition. The visceral quality of his best work, especially his sculptures and woodcuts, and his efforts to convey the inwardness of men and women isolated in the world, place him among the early expressionists, although he rejected the label as meaningless. Barlach never relinquished the human figure for pure abstraction, and his work is linked to German impressionism as well as to expressionism; he combined elements and tendencies of both directions into images of unique individuality.

Paul Paret

See also Artists; Berlin Secession; Expressionism; National Socialist Germany: Art; Painting; Prussian Art Academy; Sculpture

References

Barlach, Ernst. *Das Dichterische Werk.* 3 vols. Ed. Friedrich Dross. Munich: R. Piper, 1956–59.
———. *Die Briefe 1888–1938.* 2 vols. Ed. Friedrich Dross. Munich: R. Piper, 1968–69.
———. *A Selftold Life.* Trans. Naomi Jackson Groves. Waterloo, Ont.: Penumbra, 1990.
Carls, Carl Dietrich. *Ernst Barlach.* New York, NY: Praeger, 1969.
Jansen, Elmar, ed. *Ernst Barlach: Werk und Wirkung.* Frankfurt am Main: Athenäum, 1972.
Schult, Friedrich. *Ernst Barlach, Werkverzeichnis.* 3 vols. Hamburg: Dr. Ernst Hauswedell & Co., 1959–71.

Barth, Karl (1886–1968)

This Swiss (Reformed) theologian taught in Germany from 1921 to 1935. Karl Barth is known for his literary output and for the important role he played in the opposition to the Nazi regime. His daunting theological production will be best remembered for the impressive volumes of his *Kirchliche Dogmatik* (Church dogmatics), 1932–68.

World War I convinced Barth that traditional theology, especially the so-called "liberal theology" of the time, was in need of a radical reorientation. It had failed in ethics. Unable to contribute anything positive to prevent the war, it was still, after the war, unsuited to speak a relevant word to contemporary society. Hence Barth was led to initiate a movement called "dialectical theology," which sought to terminate the dubious subservience of theology to the goals of the state, and to re-establish the proper theme of theology: the revelation of God, the "Wholly Other," who pronounces a critical judgment on all human affairs, claims, and pretensions, even on people's very religion.

The ground was thus prepared for a theology uncompromisingly centered on God's work and critical of all human endeavor. Barth's later works witnessed a further change of direction; the distant God he had come to know through his Calvinist tradition gradually gave way, thanks to a renewed attention to Luther's conception of God, to a more "human" concept of God, Who stooped to the human level in order to bring people to His level.

In his early years, Barth had joined the religious socialists. Teaching in Germany (1921 Göttingen, 1925 Münster, 1930 Bonn), he became actively involved in the movement of opposition to Adolf Hitler, especially within the Protestant Church and its branch known as the Confessing Church. He was among the principal authors of the Barmen Declaration, which became the charter of the Protestant Resistance. This activity earned his expulsion from the Reich. He spent the rest of his career and life in Basel, ceaselessly active on the theological as well as the political scenes.

Barth stands out among the giants on this century's theological scene. He propounded a theology that is able to stand on its own and, at the same time, is equipped to pronounce an independent judgment on the social and political questions of the time.

Gérard Vallée

See also Confessing Church; Protestant Theology; Protestantism and the Protestant Church; Resistance

References

Ahlers, R. *The Barmen Declaration of 1934: The Archeology of a Confessional Text.* Lewiston, ME: E. Mellen Press, 1986.
Balthasar, H. Urs von. *The Theology of Karl Barth.* New York, NY: Holt, Rinehart and Winston, 1971.
Bromiley, G.W. *An Introduction to the Theology of Karl Barth.* Grand Rapids, MI: Eerdmanns, 1979.
Busch, E. *Karl Barth: His Life From Letters and Autobiographical Texts.* Philadelphia, PA: Fortress Press, 1976.
Drewes, H.A. and H.M. Wildi. *Bibliographie Karl Barth.* Zürich: Theologischer Verlag, 1984.
Hunsinger, G. *How to Read Karl Barth: The Shape of His Theology.* New York, NY: Oxford University Press, 1991.
Jüngel, E. *Karl Barth: A Theological Legacy.* Philadelphia, PA: Westminster Press, 1986.
Kwiran, M. *Index to Literature on Barth, Bonhoeffer, and Bultmann.* Basel: F. Reinhardt, 1977.
Scholder, K. *The Churches and the Third Reich.* 2 vols. Philadelphia, PA: Fortress Press, 1988.
Stoevesand, H. *Karl Barth Gesamt-Ausgabe.* Zürich: Theologischer Verlag, 1971.
Sykes, S.W., ed. *Karl Barth: Centenary Essays.* New York, NY: Cambridge University Press, 1989.

Barzel, Rainer (1924–)

Parliamentary president from 1983 to 1984, Rainer Barzel was born on June 20, 1924, in Braunsberg (East Prussia). During the investigation into political payoffs by the Flick industrial concern, he resigned in October 1984.

Completing his Gymnasium studies in Berlin, Barzel served with the air forces from 1941 to 1945. After the war, Barzel studied law and economics at the University of Cologne and in 1949 completed his doctoral degree. Barzel's political career began in 1949. He served the state government of North Rhine–Westphalia and after 1955 as special counselor to Minister-President Karl Arnold. With the defeat of the Christian Democratic Union (CDU) in 1956, Barzel helped to reorganize the CDU at the state level. In 1957 he became a member of the Bundestag, and by 1960 he was a leading figure in the CDU. Barzel led the CDU/Christian Social Union (CSU) caucus in the Bundestag from 1964 to 1973. In 1971, he beat out his rival Helmut Kohl as head of the CDU.

In opposition to Chancellor Willy Brandt's (1913–92) *Ostpolitik* (eastern policy), Barzel attempted in April 1972 to remove the Brandt government through the use of a "constructive vote of no confidence," as permitted by the constitution. The popular backlash against the CDU came in November 1972 in the form of the worst postwar electoral results. Consequently, Barzel resigned as chair in 1973.

Barzel had held a number of positions in the federal government. In Chancellor Adenauer's last cabinet, from 1962 to 1963, Barzel served as the federal minister for German questions. From 1977 to 1979, he chaired the Economic Council of the Bundestag. From 1980 to 1983, he assumed Carlo Schmid's (1896–1979) role as coordinator for French-German Cooperation (until December) and as president of the German-French Institute. Barzel also chaired the Bundestag's Foreign Affairs Committee (1980–82). Within Helmut Kohl's cabinet, from October 1982 to March 1983, Barzel served as federal minister for Inner-German Relations, and then as president of the Bundestag.

A prolific commentator on German politics, Barzel has consistently criticized the political establishment for lacking a vision of Germany's identity and firm integration into the European community. Given the emphasis on political parties in Germany, he believes that they hold the key to Germany's long-term well-being.

David A. Meier

See also Adenauer, Konrad; Brandt, Willy; Christian Democratic Union; Kohl, Helmut; North Rhine–Westphalia; *Ostpolitik*; Parliamentary System; Parties and Politics

References

Barzel, Rainer. *Geschichten aus der Politik*. Frankfurt am Main: Ullstein, 1987.
———. *Im Streit und Umstritten*. Frankfurt am Main: Ullstein, 1986.
———. *Plädoyer für Deutschland*. Frankfurt am Main: Ullstein, 1988.
———. *Unterwegs: Woher und Wohin?* Munich: Droemer-Knaur, 1982.

Baselitz, Georg (Hans-Georg Kern) (1938–)

As one of the most important painters and sculptors to emerge in Germany since the 1960s, Georg Baselitz has reinvigorated painting and invested the human figure with new meaning. His signature style, the upside-down motif, emphasizes artistic values over specific objects and realigns his art with the expressive tradition of his predecessors.

Born Hans-Georg Kern in Grossbaselitz, Saxony, in 1938, Baselitz fought the restrictions of the dominant style of socialist realism in East Germany before registering at the Staatliche Hochschule für bildende Künste (state academy for the visual arts) in West Berlin in 1957, one year before his permanent emigration to the West. Initial studies of the abstract color theories of Ernst Wilhelm Nay (1902–68) heightened his interest in the human form and flesh, awakened by viewing the sensuous paintings of Chaim Soutine (1894–1943) while on a trip to Amsterdam in 1959.

The search for a new art based on personal expression led Baselitz to consider surrealism, symbolism, Artaud's "theater of cruelty," and the art of the mentally ill, all of which influenced his "Pandemonium Manifesto," written with the artist Eugen Schönebeck (1936–) in 1961, the same year he adopted the surname of Baselitz. The first solo exhibition of Baselitz's crude, naked figures and portrayals of diseased body parts, at the Galerie Werner & Katz in Berlin in 1963, was closed because of an outcry about his alleged violation of public decency. The incident helped to brand Baselitz as an *enfant terrible* of the art world. A scholarship to the Villa Romana in Florence in 1965 introduced Baselitz to Italian mannerism and a new romanticism, both of which influenced his series of *Heroes*, works that represent distorted and aggrandized archetypal rebel figures, a homage to painting and the idealism of the artistic enterprise.

Baselitz's attempts to "liberate representation from content" resulted in Fracture Paintings (1966–69), which divide the composition into disjunctive bands, and the upside-down paintings, beginning with *The Wood on Its Head*, 1969, which emphasize the color, paint, and composition of the inverted subject versus its recognizability. Since 1969, the inverted motif has been Baselitz's signature style and has further influenced the artist to blend figure and background in woodcuts, etchings, linocuts, and paintings. Baselitz's insistence on painterly gesture and color made reference to, yet kept at a distance, the eagles, figures, and nostalgic images from the artist's childhood.

Baselitz became a professor at the Hochschule der Künste (Academy for the Arts) in Berlin in 1983, after having taught for five years at the Academy in Karlsruhe. His paintings of the 1980s and 1990s engage in a dialogue with earlier artists, including Edvard Munch and the members of the Dresden *Brücke* (the bridge), as do his monumental sculptures first exhibited in the German Pavilion at the Venice *Biennale* in 1980. Like his paintings, these rough-hewn wooden figures and heads emphasize process, material, and expression over verisimilitude; the most recent ones have added vibrant colors to the mix. With the broad reappraisal of representation in painting since the early 1980s, Baselitz has enjoyed a heightened reputation and has had an increasing number of international solo exhibitions.

Kristin Makholm

See also Artists; Exhibitions (Art); German Democratic Republic: Arts and Politics; Nay, Ernst; Painting; Sculpture; Symbolism

References

Caldwell, John. "Baselitz in the Seventies: Representation and Abstraction/Baselitz in den siebziger Jahren: Gegenständlichkeit und Abstraktion." Trans. Elisabeth Brockmann. *Parkett* (Zürich) 11 (1986), 84–97.

Franzke, Andreas. *Georg Baselitz.* David Britt, trans. Munich: Prestel Verlag, 1989.

Gohr, Siegfried, ed. *Georg Baselitz: Retrospektive 1964–1991.* Exhibition catalogue. Munich: Hirmer Verlag, 1992.

Kuspit, Donald. "Pandemonium: The Root of Georg Baselitz's Imagery." *Arts Magazine* 60 (Summer 1986), 24–9.

Waldman, Diane. *Georg Baselitz.* Exhibition catalogue. New York, NY: Guggenheim Museum, 1995.

BASF Research Laboratory– Ludwigshafen. Courtesy of Inter Nationes, Bonn.

BASF (Badische Anilin- and Soda-Fabrik)

BASF, founded in 1865, is today one of the world's leading international chemical companies. Its operating divisions are oil and gas, products for agriculture, plastics and fibers, chemicals, dyestuffs and surface coatings, magnetic media, and pharmaceuticals. The headquarters of BASF is at Ludwigshafen on the Rhine. Its important inventions include dyestuffs (indigo), fertilizers (by the Haber-Bosch process), and plastics (Styropor).

BASF was founded as an *Aktiengesellschaft* (joint-stock corporation) on April 6, 1865 by Friedrich Engelhorn (1821–1902). Its object was the production of coal-tar dyes and the corresponding precursors and intermediates. It soon achieved great success in the synthesis and production of important dyestuffs such as alizarin (red madder, 1870) and indigo (1897). The same period saw developments in process technology, such as the contact process for sulfuric acid (1888) and the liquefaction of chlorine (1888).

Economic successes led to the company's rapid growth. In 1900, BASF employed nearly 7,000 people, making it one of the largest chemical companies in the world. More than two-thirds of its production was exported, and BASF built its own production facilities in important markets (France, Russia, and the United Kingdom).

After the turn of the century, BASF opened up a completely new field in chemistry with the synthesis of ammonia from nitrogen and hydrogen. On the basis of research carried out by Fritz Haber (1868–1934), Carl Bosch (1874–1940) developed the industrial-scale chemical production of ammonia and nitrogen fertilizers (1913). The new high-pressure technology paved the way for further applications, which resulted in the first industrial-scale syntheses of urea (1922), methanol (1923), and gasoline from coal (1927).

In 1925 BASF, whose payroll that year included some 22,000 people, merged with other German chemical companies to form I.G. Farbenindustrie AG. Until 1945, research and development at Ludwigshafen concentrated on the new acetylene chemistry of Walter Reppe (1892–1969), the first plastics (polystyrene, 1930), and synthetic rubbers. In 1934 the company developed the Magnetophon tape for recording.

As in World War I, the chemical industry proved to be a key factor, along with conventional armaments production, in World War II, especially since the German war economy was isolated from the world market. I.G. Farben, too, played an important part in the Nazi policy of self-sufficiency and re-armament after 1933, especially with products such as nitrogen, gasoline, rubber, plastics, and light metal. The company participated in the employment of forced labor and concentration-camp inmates.

In 1945, the production facilities at Ludwigshafen were largely destroyed, and until the completion of the decartelization of I.G. Farben the works were under foreign control—first American, then French. In 1952 BASF was refounded as an independent company. In addition to the laborious process of reconstruction, the focus during the 1950s was on the establishment and expansion of the plastics sector, the changeover from coal as the raw material for chemical products to petrochemistry based on oil and natural gas, and the new activity of producing crop-protection agents.

By 1990, BASF employed some 135,000 people worldwide and had sales of 46.6 billion deutsche marks. Further developments included the internationalization of the company's business and the building of production plants all over the world. Another step was to secure the raw materials base by becoming involved in the oil (1969) and natural gas (1990) businesses. The company also added divisions of higher value-added chemistry, such as surface coatings (1965), pharmaceuticals (1968), and vitamins (1970).

Lothar Meinzer

See also Bosch, Carl; Chemistry, Scientific and Industrial; Haber, Fritz; I.G. Farbenindustrie AG

References

BASF AG, ed. *Im Reiche der Chemie.* Düsseldorf: Econ-Verlag, 1965.

———. *Chemistry Looks to the Future—125 Years of BASF.* Ludwigshafen: BASF, 1990.

Haber, Lutz F. *The Chemical Industry 1900–1930.* Oxford: Clarendon Press, 1971.

———. *The Chemical Industry during the Nineteenth Century.* Oxford: Clarendon Press, 1958.

Holdermann, Karl. *Im Banne der Chemie: Carl Bosch, Leben und Werk.* Düsseldorf: Econ-Verlag, 1953.

Plumpe, Gottfried. *Die I.G. Farbenindustrie AG: Wirtschaft, Technik, Politik 1904–1945.* Berlin: Duncker & Humblot, 1990.

Schröter, Hans. *Friedrich Engelhorn: Ein Unternehmerporträt des 19. Jahrhunderts.* Landau: Pfälzische Verlagsanstalt, 1991.

Stokes, Raymond G. *Divide and Prosper: The Heirs of I.G. Farben under Allied Authority 1945–1951.* Berkeley, CA: University of California Press, 1988.

Travis, Anthony S. *The Rainbow Makers: The Origins of the Synthetic Dyestuffs Industry in Western Europe.* Bethlehem, PA: Lehigh University Press; London: Associated University Press, 1993.

The Basic Law

The Basic Law (Grundgesetz) is Germany's constitution. Adopted by the Parliamentary Council on May 8, 1949, it was called a basic law rather than a constitution (*Verfassung*) in order to underscore its provisional character. According to the document's original text, the Basic Law would "cease to be in force on the day on which a constitution adopted by a free decision of the German people comes into force." In 1990, however, East Germany agreed to unite with West Germany under the authority of the Basic Law. The Basic Law now serves as united Germany's constitution.

An imposing document composed of 146 articles, the Basic Law provides for a parliamentary democracy overlaid by a complicated system of separated powers and checks and balances. In addition, it divides power between federal and state governments, confers its blessing on political parties as important agents of political representation, creates an independent judiciary, establishes the conditions for the exercise of emergency powers, and includes a catalogue of fundamental rights anchored in the principle of human dignity that are absolutely binding on all units and branches of government.

In writing the Basic Law, the Parliamentary Council drew its inspiration from previous German constitutions in the democratic tradition, particularly the 1919 constitution of the Weimar Republic. The Basic Law recreates many of Weimar's democratic institutions but modifies them to eliminate the defects thought to have contributed to the Republic's collapse in 1933. One such reform was the creation of a strong chancellor. Under Article 67, parliament (Bundestag) may dismiss a chancellor only by electing his successor. The Basic Law also provides for a dual executive, dividing authority between the federal government (i.e., the chancellor and his cabinet) and the federal president. But unlike Weimar's powerful and popularly elected president, who was empowered to dissolve parliament, the indirectly elected chief of state created by the Basic Law has largely ceremonial functions. Finally, committed to an indirect democracy, the Basic Law bars the use of popular initiatives and referenda at the federal level.

The Basic Law is distinguished from previous German constitutions in other important respects. First, the Basic Law is more than exhortatory. Like the United States Constitution, it is a law of superior force and obligation and is directly enforceable as law by a judicial establishment crowned by the authority of the Federal Constitutional Court. Second, transient majorities cannot easily amend the Basic Law; rather, it takes a two-thirds vote in the Bundestag and the Bundesrat. Third, the Basic Law commits the Federal Republic to internationalism. It bans actions intended to disturb the peace among nations, makes the general rules of public international law an integral part of federal law, and authorizes the Federation to transfer its sovereign powers to international institutions. Fourth, it creates a "militant democracy." Mindful of Hitler's rise to power on the cusp of a popular movement, the Basic Law bans political parties and associations whose activity or purposes would threaten the liberal democracy it created. Article 28 requires all state governments to abide by the "principles of republican, democratic, and social government based on the rule of law."

The Basic Law is declared to be unamendable with respect to these basic principles of state order (i.e., federalism, rule of law, separation of powers, independent judiciary, and multiparty democracy) and the basic right to human dignity. Supreme among all the values of the Basic Law, human dignity, which the state is obligated to enforce and protect under Article 1, manifests itself in an extensive list of individual rights, including freedom of speech, press, assembly, and religion, the right to property and equality under law, and the right to the free development of one's personality. These rights, however, are limited by the state's responsibility under the Basic Law's social-welfare clause to provide for the fundamental needs of its citizens.

Donald P. Kommers

See also Adenauer, Konrad; Constitutions; Federal Republic of Germany; Federal Republic of Germany: Judicial System; Federalism; Heuss, Theodor; Parliamentary System; Parties and Politics; Schmid, Carlo; Schumacher, Kurt

References

Currie, David P. *The Constitution of the Federal Republic of Germany.* Chicago, IL: University of Chicago Press, 1994.

Hucko, Elmar M. *The Democratic Tradition: Four German Constitutions.* Leamington Spa: Berg Publishers Limited, 1987.

Karpen, Ulrich, ed. *The Constitution of the Federal Republic of Germany.* Baden-Baden: Nomos Verlagsgesellschaft, 1988.

Kirchhof, Paul and Donald P. Kommers, eds. *Germany and Its Basic Law: Past, Present and Future.* Baden-Baden: Nomos Verlagsgesellschaft, 1993.

Koch, H.W. *A Constitutional History of Germany in the Nineteenth and Twentieth Centuries.* London: Longman Gray, 1984.

Kommers, Donald P. *The Constitutional Jurisprudence of the Federal Republic of Germany.* Durham, NC: Duke University Press, 1989.

Starck, Christian, ed. *Main Principles of the Basic Law.* Baden-Baden: Nomos Verlagsgesellschaft, 1983.

Basic Treaty (1972)

The Basic Treaty (Grundvertrag), an agreement signed by the Federal Republic of Germany (FRG) and the German Democratic Republic (GDR) in December 1972, ended the two states' post–World War II mutual nonrecognition.

The document provided for an exchange of diplomatic missions, affirmed each government's autonomy in domestic and foreign affairs, permitted both leaderships to continue to define the question of German nationality according to separate doctrines, and laid the foundation for a substantial expansion of FRG and GDR popular contacts through the resulting increase in inner-German travel. In particular, the treaty halted the perceived national estrangement of Germans, who had been separated by the postwar division, and it ultimately weakened the efforts of the East German ruling Socialist Unity Party (SED) to establish a "GDR national consciousness" and to portray Bonn as the obstacle to closer mutual relations.

The treaty constituted the inner-German application of Chancellor Willy Brandt's (1913–92) program of cooperation with the FRG's eastern neighbors (*Ostpolitik*), which had been unveiled in the early 1970s. This policy recognized existing European geopolitical realities, in that Bonn pledged to respect Europe's postwar state frontiers and forswore attempts to forcibly alter them, even though Brandt's government did not unequivocally recognize the GDR. The treaty signified West Germany's acknowledgment that closer popular contacts between divided Germans to promote the unity of the German nation could only arise from practical cooperation with a GDR political elite that appeared to be a permanent feature. This decision represented a considerable gamble by West Germany's Social Democratic-Free Democratic governing coalition. The danger continually loomed that officially sanctioned dealings with the GDR regime and the treaty's acknowledgment of the GDR's legal autonomy could over time strengthen the SED's efforts to mold a separate, convincing GDR identity in the eyes of East Germany's inhabitants. In such an event, Bonn's program to nurture a common German identity and yearnings for reunification in East Germany might lose force.

This careful balancing act by West German governments began to pay dividends by the 1980s. The travel and communication contacts inaugurated by the Basic Treaty reinforced the attractiveness of West Germany as East Germans became exposed to western everyday life. This development was reflected in a sizable increase in emigration from the GDR to the West by 1984. The national feeling after the collapse of the Berlin Wall in 1989 and the westward flood of East Germans bore few similarities with traditional German nationalism that exalted German state power or supposed ethnic virtues. This new nationalism discredited East German socialism in preference to West German political and consumer life.

Bonn rarely employed the provisions of the Basic Treaty to force changes in, for example, SED human rights practices. However, the treaty formula allowed West German governments to continue to profile themselves as the "guardians" of Germans in the GDR, both through financial assistance and the maintenance of West German constitutional standards that retained reunification as a goal of state policy. The framework of the treaty, like overall *Ostpolitik*, helped to counteract the more extreme nationalist appeals voiced in the Federal Republic by permitting West Germany's governments to conduct a "German policy" that was notably more dynamic than the diplomatic approaches of the 1950s and 1960s, which merely emphasized the need for maintaining the *status quo* between the two German states.

Ernest D. Plock

See also American-German Relations; Bahr, Egon; Brandt, Willy; The Cold War and Germany; Detente and Germany; Federal Republic of Germany: Foreign Policy; German Democratic Republic; German-German Relations; Honecker, Erich; *Ostpolitik*; Soviet-German Relations

References

Birnbaum, Karl E. *East and West Germany: A Modus Vivendi.* Westmead, Farnborough and Hants: Saxon House, 1973.
Bundesministerium für innerdeutsche Beziehungen. *Materialien zum Bericht zur Lage der Nation.* Kassel: A.G. Wenderoth, annual publication.
———. *Zehn Jahre Deutschlandpolitik: Die Entwicklung der Beziehungen zwischen der Bundesrepublik Deutschland und der Deutschen Demokratischen Republik 1969–1979.* Melsungen: Verlagsbuchdruckerei A. Bernecker, 1980.
Cramer, Dettmar. *Deutschland nach dem Grundvertrag.* Stuttgart: Verlag Bonn Aktuell, 1973.
Frey, Erich G. *Division and Detente: The Germanies and Their Alliances.* New York, NY: Praeger, 1987.
Garton Ash, Timothy. *In Europe's Name: Germany and the Divided Continent.* New York, NY: Random House, 1993.
Mahnke, Hans Heinrich. "Der Vertrag über die Grundlagen der Beziehungen zwischen der Bundesrepublik und der DDR." *Deutschland Archiv* 6 (1973), 1163–80.
Niclauss, Karlheinz. *Kontroverse Deutschlandpolitik.* Frankfurt am Main: Alfred Metzner Verlag, 1977.
Plock, Ernest D. *The Basic Treaty and the Evolution of East-West German Relations.* Boulder, CO: Westview Press, 1986.
Ress, Georg. *Die Rechtslage Deutschland nach dem Grundlagenvertrag vom 21. Dezember 1972.* Berlin: Springer Verlag, 1978.
Seiffert, Wolfgang. *Das ganze Deutschland: Perspektiven der Wiedervereinigung.* Munich: Piper-Verlag, 1986.

Bassermann, Ernst (1854–1917)

Ernst Bassermann represented a second generation of leadership in the National Liberal Party of the Imperial era. As head of his party's Reichstag delegation from 1899 and then party chairman from 1905 until his death in 1917, Bassermann pursued an extended yet ultimately frustrated effort to place the National Liberals at the fulcrum of parliamentary politics in the Empire and to strengthen their standing among the middle strata of German society. His attempts culminated in the Bülow Bloc of 1907–09, in which the National Liberals anchored a liberal-conservative parliamentary partnership allied to the chancellor, after whom the coalition was named.

Following the collapse of the Bloc, however, over the final eight years of his career Bassermann was plunged into a prolonged struggle to maintain unity among the factionalized ranks of his party.

Bassermann was born on July 26, 1854 in Wolfach, Baden. He was descended from a family that had been prominent in the politics of southwestern Germany, but it was only when he was in his thirties and a successful lawyer that he became active in National Liberal affairs. His rise was rapid. In 1893, he was elected to the Reichstag from Mannheim. Two years later he became secretary of the National Liberal parliamentary delegation, and in 1899 he was chosen as its leader, following the retirement of Rudolf von Bennigsen (1824–1902). The most serious task Bassermann faced was to overcome the political and economic divisions that sapped the effectiveness of the party. The solution he sought was twofold: to associate National Liberalism with Germany's drive toward great-power status on the world stage, and to link it to internal reforms that would assure the middle strata greater political influence nationally.

National Liberal support of the Empire's foreign policy particularly aided Bassermann, as it attracted the party's representatives of heavy industry, who ordinarily disagreed with him on political and social questions. It was also a means of reiterating the great theme of National Liberalism's founding years, as well as of recapturing parliamentary leverage unwillingly ceded to the Center Party, which proved more supple on economic questions but less dependable to the government on international issues. All of the advantages and limitations of Bassermann's strategy were displayed in the Bülow Bloc. In the elections of January 1907, the pro-imperialist multiparty coalition orchestrated by the chancellor gave the National Liberals their largest electoral and parliamentary totals since the 1890s and made them the middle link in Bülow's "mating of the conservative and liberal spirit."

But if the national issue was the ladder on which the party climbed back into influence, the financial problems that confronted the Bloc became the test of Bassermann's ability to align the National Liberals with policies favorable to the middle classes. Industrial and agrarian elements were soon chafing at the terms of the relatively mild tax reform proposed by the government. Bassermann kept nearly all of the party's deputies loyal to the Bloc when the Conservatives defected and brought down the coalition in 1909. This failure initiated a period of recrimination and internal conflict among the National Liberals, which lasted to the outbreak of World War I.

The war brought the party a brief respite from its factional clashes. True to his German nationalism, Bassermann championed annexationist policies and found common ground with many National Liberals who had opposed him on domestic issues. But agreement on war aims could not heal the divisions within the party. When Bassermann died, on July 24, 1917 in Baden-Baden, the rifts were widening again. One year later, they were the fault lines along which the party collapsed.

Dan S. White

See also Bennigsen, Rudolf von; Bülow, Bernhard von; Liberalism; National Liberal Party; Parliamentary System; Parties and Politics

References

Bassermann, Karola. *Ernst Bassermann: Das Lebensbild eines Parlamentariers aus Deutschlands glücklicher Zeit*. Mannheim: Verlag Dr. Haas, 1919.

Eschenburg, Theodor. *Das Kaiserreich am Scheideweg: Bassermann, Bülow und der Block*. Berlin: Verlag für Kulturpolitik, 1929.

Heckart, Beverly. *From Bassermann to Bebel: The Grand Bloc's Quest for Reform in the Kaiserreich, 1900–1914*. New Haven, CT: Yale University Press, 1974.

Mittelmann, Fritz, ed. *Ernst Bassermann: Sein politisches Wirken; Reden und Aufsätze*. Berlin: K. Curtius, 1914.

Reiss, Klaus-Peter, ed. *Von Bassermann zu Stresemann: Die Sitzungen des nationalliberalen Zentralvorstandes 1912–1917*. Düsseldorf: Droste Verlag, 1967.

Roon-Bassermann, Elisabeth von. *Ernst Bassermann: Eine politische Skizze*. Berlin: Staatspolitischer Verlag, 1925.

Thieme, Hartwig. *Nationaler Liberalismus in der Krise: Die nationalliberale Fraktion des Preussischen Abgeordnetenhauses 1914–1918*. Boppard am Rhein: Harald Boldt Verlag, 1963.

White, Dan S. *The Splintered Party: National Liberalism in Hessen and the Reich, 1867–1918*. Cambridge, MA: Harvard University Press, 1976.

Baudissin, Wolf von (1907–93)

A German officer from 1926 to 1945, Wolf von Baudissin was a founding organizer of the German armed forces (1951–56), and as lieutenant general, he was deputy chief of staff for plans and operations, Supreme Headquarters Allied Powers, Europe (1965–67).

Wolf von Baudissin emerged in West Germany during 1950–55 among the organizers of a German contribution to Atlantic defense as an outspoken advocate of civil-military reform. He became linked in the public mind with the controversial reordering of command and obedience in army ranks that at the same time sought to assure civil rights to the soldiers of a second German democracy. From retirement in 1967 until his death shortly after German unification, Baudissin assumed the roles of defense intellectual, peace researcher, and commentator on international affairs.

Born in Trier on May 8, 1907 to a noble family in the Prussian bureaucracy, Baudissin spent his youth in West Prussia. In April 1926, he joined the Infantry Regiment No. 9 at Potsdam. In the years before the outbreak of war, Baudissin underwent infantry officer training and held company-grade assignments. Among his comrades and contemporaries were such leading figures of the anti-Hitler Resistance as Henning von Tresckow (1901–44) and Axell vom dem Bussche. During the war Baudissin served as an intelligence officer in divisional and corps staffs. Erwin Rommel (1891–1944) selected him to join his own staff in the North African campaign, in which Indian forces captured Baudissin at

Tobruk in April 1941. He served out the war behind Australian and British barbed wire, where he reflected on the failings of his profession and how the inability of German soldiers to understand democracy before 1933 had made them susceptible to their own professional failings and Nazi enticements thereafter.

After his release from a POW camp in July 1947, he sculpted garden ceramics, performed church social work in the Ruhr mines, and volunteered in the evangelical academics. These experiences, together with a devotion to the Pietist tradition and lay Protestantism, moved him to advocate a more prominent role for ethical principles in public institutions. In the fall of 1950, Baudissin was invited to attend a planning conference of a "Committee of Experts" to prepare the rearmament of West Germany. The group provided the Federal Chancellery with what became a blueprint for the Bundeswehr, the so-called Himmerod Memorandum. Baudissin co-authored a section on the "inner structure" of the new army that contained details of reformed and enlightened leadership, command, obedience, and morale.

On May 8, 1951, Baudissin joined the small defense office of the Federal Chancellery, together with such former Wehrmacht general staff officers as Adolf Heusinger (1897–1982), Johann-Adolf Kielmansegg, and Ulrich de Maizière (1912–). From 1951 until 1958, Baudissin and his colleagues in uniform as well as parliamentarians and interested members of the professions attempted to carry out the military reforms first drafted in the Himmerod Memorandum. This reform became best known for the terms "citizen in uniform" and "*Innere Führung*" (inner guidance). This latter term is an untranslatable expression for an enlightened style of command, leadership, obedience and morale suitable to the civil-military and human-rights clauses of the Basic Law of 1949.

In June 1958, he left the Ministry of Defense for the command of an infantry brigade in Göttingen. By November 1961, he had been promoted to major general. He served as chief of staff of intelligence and operations in the NATO Allied Force Central Europe Staff (Fontainebleau) during 1961–63, being promoted to lieutenant general (1964) and chief of the Rome NATO Defense College (1963–65) thereafter. In February 1965 he received the Freiherr vom Stein Prize of the city of Hamburg, together with de Maizière and Kielmansegg, in recognition of the West German military reforms.

By this time, however, Baudissin had become disillusioned with the course of the reforms and with certain conservative general officers in the Bundeswehr who appeared to undermine *Innere Führung*. Baudissin ended his military career as deputy chief of staff for intelligence, plans, policy, and operations in Supreme Headquarters Allied Powers, Europe and retired on December 31, 1967. That only led to a new phase of his public life.

In October 1968, he became a lecturer on modern strategy in the economics and social sciences faculty of the University of Hamburg. In 1971 he founded and became director of the Hamburg Institute of Peace Research and Security Policy associated with the same university and lectured on the social sciences at the nearby Bundeswehr University. His numerous publications, articles, and television appearances during the time of the social-liberal coalition and the Intermediate Nuclear Forces deployments (1969–85) gained him a wide publicity that continued into the period of German unification, when interest in *Innere Führung* and German civil-military relations grew with the need to expand NATO into Central and Eastern Europe.

Donald Abenheim

See also Armaments Policy; Federal Republic of Germany: Armed Forces; Heusinger, Adolf; Maizière, Ulrich de; NATO and Germany; Rearmament; Rommel, Erwin

References
Abenheim, Donald. *Reforging the Iron Cross: The Search for Tradition in the West German Armed Forces.* Princeton, NJ: Princeton University Press, 1988.

Baudissin, Wolf Graf von. *Abschaffung des Krieges: Beiträge zu einer Realistischen Friedenspolitik.* Gütersloh: G. Mohn, 1983.

———. *Konflikte, Krisen, Kriegsverhütung: Fragen, Analysen, Perspektiven.* Baden-Baden: Nomos, 1981.

Genschel, Dietrich. *Wehrreform und Reaktion: die Vorbereitung der Inneren Führung.* Hamburg: R.v. Decker, 1972.

Harder, Hans-Joachim and Norbert Wiggershaus. *Tradition und Reform in den Aufbaujahren der Bundeswehr.* Herford: E.S. Mittler, 1985.

Krüger, Dieter. *Das Amt Blank: Die schwierige Gründung des Bundesministeriums für Verteidigung.* Freiburg: Rombach, 1993.

Lutz, Dieter S., ed. *Im Dienst für Frieden und Sicherheit.* Baden-Baden: Nomos, 1985.

Militärgeschichtliches Forschungsamt, ed. *Anfänge westdeutscher Sicherheitspolitik.* 3 vols. Munich: Oldenbourg, 1982–93.

Bauer, Gustav (1870–1944)

Among the leaders of the second generation of unionists and the Social Democratic Party (SPD), Gustav Bauer became one of the first working-class people to hold ministerial office in Germany. He held many important posts but has been credited with few achievements, even though he helped to inaugurate the Works Council Law of 1920.

Bauer served as an assistant clerk who helped to organize the office-workers' union, which he then led by 1895. He became vice-chair of the trade union federation (Generalkommission der Gewerkschaften Deutschlands) during its expansionary period from 1908 to 1918. As Reichstag member for the SPD, he served on important committees, especially during World War I. Like most union leaders, he supported war credits and suggested that Germany had the right to expand territorially. He fostered the integration of labor into the national community.

Under Prince Max von Baden (1867–1929), Bauer served as state secretary for labor. He held a similar post during the Revolution of 1918, when he became minister of labor in the first Weimar Republic cabinet. He accepted the chancellorship during the crisis over the Treaty of Versailles, but had to resign because of his indecisive leadership during the Kapp *Putsch* in 1920.

Bauer represented the SPD in two additional coalition governments, under Hermann Müller (1876–1931) and Joseph Wirth (1879–1956). He held important posts, such as minister of finance and minister of transport as well as vice-chancellor, but is more known for having been involved in scandals than in innovative legislation. The SPD ousted him because he had made personal gains from his involvements in public office, but then rehabilitated him in 1925. From 1912 to 1928 Bauer sat almost uninterruptedly in the Reichstag, but then retired to private life and died during World War II.

Dieter K. Buse

See also Max von Baden; Müller, Hermann; Revolutions of 1918–19; Social Democratic Party; Trade Unions (1871–1945); Versailles, Treaty of; Wirth, Joseph

References

Golecki, Anton, ed. *Das Kabinett Bauer.* Boppard am Rhein: Boldt, 1980.

Potthoff, Heinrich. *Freie Gewerkschaften 1918–1933.* Düsseldorf: Droste, 1987.

Rintelen, Karlludwig. *Ein undemokratischer Demokrat: Gustav Bauer: Gewerkschaftsführer—Freund Friedrich Eberts—Reichskanzler. Eine politische Biographie.* Frankfurt am Main: Peter Lang, 1993.

Bauer, Max (1869–1929)

Colonel Max Bauer was born in Quedlinburg on January 31, 1869, to a family of lawyers, though his father was a gentleman farmer. Having briefly studied law and medicine in Berlin, he became an officer cadet in the Foot Artillery Regiment No. 2 in Swinemünde in 1888. He passed his exams with the compliments of Kaiser Wilhelm II and in 1892 was appointed adjutant to his regiment. In 1905 he was posted to the General Staff as an artillery expert without having attended the War Academy. In 1909, he became a staff officer under General Erich Ludendorff (1865–1937).

Bauer soon made his mark as an arrogant and self-willed officer, championing the huge Krupp 42–inch cannon (at a time when the German army's largest caliber was 30.5 cm) against the opposition of the Artillery Inspection Commission and the War Ministry. In 1912, he was posted to Colmar, but returned to the General Staff in 1913. In 1914 he was appointed head of the Heavy Artillery and Fortifications section of the Army High Command (OHL) and won the Pour le Mérite and an honorary doctorate from Berlin University for his part in the seizure of Antwerp. Under General Erich Falkenhayn (1861–1922) he was made responsible for the production of artillery shells, worked on the use of gas, and was largely responsible for the introduction of steel helmets.

Under generals Paul von Hindenburg (1847–1934) and Erich Ludendorff, Bauer became one of the most powerful men in Germany. He worked out the details of the auxiliary labor law in late 1916 and was largely responsible for labor policy, finance, wages, profits, coal delivery, transport, the allocation of raw materials, food, agriculture, population policies, and the care of war wounded. His ambition was to fully militarize the economy. An inveterate intriguer, he undermined Chancellor Bethmann Hollweg's position and attacked Chancellor Hertling and the Kaiser for their weakness. Prince Max von Baden tried to get rid of him. When Ludendorff resigned, Bauer reported sick. He suffered from a severe depression, heart disease, and concussion after a car crash in July 1918. Later he blamed himself for not staying and forcing the Crown Prince to lead the army against the Social Democrats. In 1919, Bauer co-founded, with Major Waldemar Papst, the National Association (Nationale Vereinigung), which called for an authoritarian regime encompassing soldiers and workers. During the Kapp *Putsch* of 1920 he was chief of staff to General Walther von Lüttwitz and was appointed secretary of state to Wolfgang Kapp. Following the failure of the *Putsch* he hid in Berlin, Bavaria, Hungary, and Vienna until granted an amnesty by the Reichstag in 1925.

In 1923 Bauer had been invited to the Soviet Union and later in the year he went to Spain as an advisor on civil aviation. In 1925 he went to Argentina to organize the use of spray planes to deal with a plague of locusts. In 1926 he returned to Germany and worked on Germany's illegal rearmament in Holland, Switzerland, and Sweden. During these years, Bauer elaborated the details of his theory of "Pangynismus," which held women responsible for materialism, egoism, and hedonism, in that men submitted to them and gave them their money, which the women frivolously wasted. In 1927, Bauer went to China as an advisor on building up the Chinese chemical industry, and then organized Mission B, a group of German experts to advise Chiang Kai-shek. Bauer died of smallpox in Shanghai on May 6, 1929.

Martin Kitchen

See also Bethmann Hollweg, Theobald von; Falkenhayn, Erich; Hertling, Georg von; Ludendorff, Erich; Max von Baden; Wilhelm II; World War I

References

Bauer, Max. *Der Grosse Krieg in Feld und Heimat: Erinnerungen und Betrachtungen.* Tübingen: Osiander, 1921.

Feldman, G.D. *Army, Industry, and Labor in Germany, 1914–1918.* Princeton, NJ: Princeton University Press, 1966.

Fischer, Fritz. *Griff nach der Weltmacht.* Düsseldorf: Droste, 1961.

Kitchen, Martin. *The Silent Dictatorship: The Policies of the German High Command under Hindenburg and Ludendorff, 1916–1918.* London: Croom Helm, 1976.

Bauhaus (1919–32)

The Bauhaus, originally a school of arts and crafts established in Weimar in 1919, exerted a worldwide influence in the field of design.

The founding director, Walter Gropius (1883–1969), rejected the traditional separation of "arts" and "crafts," as well as their association with the production of luxury items. He directed the school toward forging a unity of arts and crafts as a basis for the design of mass-produced goods. He organized the school into "workshops" in painting, sculpture, metal- and woodworking, textiles, pottery, stained glasswork, typography, graphics, and stagecraft. He borrowed from the master-apprentice tradition—Bauhaus "apprentices" learned by doing with the more experienced "masters." Prior to entering the workshops, apprentices had to complete a six-month preliminary course (*Vorkurs*) that explored general color and form theory.

The radical designs and teaching emanating from the Bauhaus were never popular in the provincial city of Weimar, and in 1925, political pressures forced Gropius to move the school to the industrial city of Dessau. Here he could design a new building for the Bauhaus. His structure, completed in 1926 and characterized by black-framed glass curtain walls juxtaposed against flat expanses of white stucco, became a standard monument of the international style.

Despite the frequent association of the name Bauhaus with architecture, architectural education itself played a relatively minor role there. Gropius appointed no architects as masters until after the school moved to Dessau, when he introduced a department of architecture under the direction of Hannes Meyer in 1927. Meyer replaced Gropius as Bauhaus director in 1928, and was succeeded in 1930 by the architect Ludwig Mies van der Rohe (1886–1969), who served until the school in Dessau was closed by the local authorities in 1932. In its later years, the Bauhaus moved away from its original design-oriented precepts into greater emphasis on building, advertising, and sociological perspectives that caused internal dissension and a rapid turnover of staff.

Although some Bauhaus students continued to influence design, the institution's long-term importance derived primarily from the uniquely creative group of artists and craftspeople serving as Bauhaus masters. Johannes Itten, Josef Albers, and László Moholy-Nagy developed the *Vorkurs* in Weimar, whereas Paul Klee (1879–1940), Wassily Kandinsky (1866–1944), Lyonel Feininger, Oskar Schlemmer, Marcel Breuer, Herbert Bayer, Gerhard Marcks (1880–1981) and Georg Muche served as workshop masters. In addition, first-year programs based on the *Vorkurs* became widely adopted in

design schools elsewhere and emerged as a standard part of design education.

The Bauhaus building in Dessau, damaged in World War II, was restored in 1976. It was used for various purposes until 1987, when the Bauhaus Dessau was reestablished as a research institute.

Paul H. Gleye

See also Architecture and Urban Design; Artists; Behrens, Peter; Gropius, Walter; Kandinsky; Wassily; Klee, Paul; Marcks, Gerhard; Mies van der Rohe, Ludwig

References

Dearstyne, Howard. *Inside the Bauhaus*. New York, NY: Rizzoli, 1986.

Droste, Magdalena. *Bauhaus*. Cologne: Taschen, 1991.

Naylor, Gillian. *The Bauhaus Reassessed*. London: Herbert, 1985.

Neumann, Eckard. *Bauhaus and Bauhaus People*. Rev. ed. New York, NY: Van Nostrand Reinhold, 1993.

Whitford, Frank. *Bauhaus*. London: Thames and Hudson, 1984.

———, ed. *The Bauhaus; Masters and Students by Themselves*. London: Conran Octopus, 1992.

Wingler, Hans M. *The Bauhaus: Weimar, Dessau, Berlin, Chicago*. Cambridge, MA: MIT Press, 1969.

Baumeister, Willi (1889–1955)

A prolific modernist artist, Willi Baumeister enjoyed a career as a painter, printmaker, collagist, and stage and graphic designer. He links the Weimar, and even pre–World War I, avant gardes to the post–World War II reestablishment of modernism in West Germany.

From 1905 to 1914, Baumeister studied off and on at the Stuttgart Academy of Art, under Adolf Hölzel (1853–1934) and alongside fellow Swabian Oskar Schlemmer (1888–1943), with whom he formed a friendship, artistic kinship, and local reputation. After service in World War I, Baumeister developed a geometric and constructivist style, paralleling Schlemmer's. His first breakthrough to national and international prominence came with his *Wall Paintings*, 1920–24, machine-aesthetic abstractions, sometimes with figurative associations and often in relief. These were shown and written about in Berlin and Paris as parallels to the contemporary works of the French artist Fernand Léger, with whom Baumeister shared an exhibition at Berlin's Der Sturm gallery in 1922. From 1925 to 1929, Baumeister painted in a more naturalistic style, often depicting sports themes.

Always involved in graphic design and advertising, Baumeister became a professor in this area at the Städel School of Art in Frankfurt, where Max Beckmann (1884–1950) taught painting. The Nazis dismissed Baumeister from his teaching post in March 1933, and showed four of his paintings in the notorious *Degenerate Art* exhibition in Munich in 1937. But Baumeister, who had a wife and two daughters, stayed in Germany, finding refuge in researching historical painting techniques at Kurt Herberts's Wuppertal paint and

Bauhaus in Dessau, Saxony, Anhalt. Courtesy of German Embassy, Ottawa.

lacquer factory. Since 1930, Baumeister's paintings had become ever more abstract, biomorphic, and surrealistic (*Eidos* series, 1938–41). During 1943–45 he produced cycles of drawings inspired by ancient texts, including the Sumerian Gilgamesh legend and the Old Testament stories of Saul and Esther, which have been interpreted as an inner resistance to Nazi ideology. Privately, he also produced and distributed collages lampooning Nazi-sponsored art.

After the war, Baumeister was quickly appointed professor at the Stuttgart Academy. He assumed a central role in Germany's cultural life, partly by virtue of his career prior to the Nazi period and his unblemished record during it. His historical and theoretical book (*Das Unbekannte in der Kunst*) was one of the first postwar German justifications of modern art. His public statements, and the flowering of his abstract paintings to greater size, with more vibrant and nuanced colors and in greater number than ever before, enhanced his fame.

Peter Chametzky

See also Artists; Beckmann, Max; National Socialist Germany: Art; Painting

References

Barron, Stephanie. *"Degenerate Art": The Fate of the Avant-Garde in Nazi Germany*. Los Angeles, CA: Los Angeles County Museum of Art, 1991.

Baumeister, Willi. *Das Unbekannte in der Kunst*. Stuttgart: Curt Schwab, 1947; Cologne: DuMont, 1960, 1974 and 1988.

Chametzky, Peter. *Autonomy and Authority in German Twentieth-Century Art: The Art and Career of Willi Baumeister (1889–1955)*. Ann Arbor, MI: University of Michigan Press, 1991.

Grohmann, Will. "Marginal Comments, Oppositional Work: Willi Baumeister's Confrontation with Nazi Art." Ed. Staatsgalerie Stuttgart. *Willi Baumeister: Zeichnungen, Gouachen, Collagen*. Stuttgart: Edition Cantz, 1989.

———. *Willi Baumeister: Life and Work*. New York, NY: Abrams, 1965.

Kermer, Wofgang. *Der schöpferische Winkel: Willi Baumeisters pädagogische Tätigkeit*. Stuttgart: Staatliche Akademie der Bildenden Künste, 1992.

Nationalgalerie Berlin. *Staatliche Museen Preussischer Kulturbesitz: Willi Baumeister*. Stuttgart: Edition Cantz, 1989.

Bäumer, Gertrud (1873–1954)

Gertrud Bäumer dominated the middle-class women's movement of Germany from the early twentieth century to 1933. An educator, writer, and politician, she was president of the Federation of German Women's Associations (Bund Deutscher Frauenvereine; BDF) from 1910 to 1919, remaining on the executive until 1933. Moderate in her tactics and nationalist in orientation, Bäumer sought to expand career opportunities for women, insisting that women's nature was particularly suited for work in education and social services. Her many publications include analyses of cultural and intel-

lectual figures such as Fichte and Goethe, pedagogical and historical studies, and commentaries on women's issues.

Bäumer's father was a Protestant pastor who later became a superintendent of schools. She too trained as a teacher and possessed a strong sense of Christian duty. Bäumer received a doctorate in 1904. Formative influences on her included the liberal nationalist Friedrich Naumann and the publicist and activist for women teachers' rights, Helene Lange (1858–1930). Together Bäumer and Lange produced a four-volume account of the women's movement in Europe, *Handbuch der Frauenbewegung* (Handbook of the women's movement), 1901–02. In collaboration with Lange from 1916 until 1930, and then alone, Bäumer edited the BDF's monthly, *Die Frau* (The woman).

In 1914, immediately after the announcement of German mobilization, Bäumer organized the National Women's Service (*Nationaler Frauendienst*) to coordinate women's contributions to the war effort. In writings such as *Der Krieg und die Frau* (The war and the woman), 1914, she rallied women to the cause, comparing mothers' experiences of sacrifice to death on the battlefield.

Bäumer's career during the Weimar Republic reflected key issues in Germany. When Alice Salomon (1872–1948), a convert from Judaism to Christianity, was chosen to become president of the BDF in 1919, Bäumer called it a tactical mistake to give a Jew that post. Accordingly, Marianne Weber (1870–1952) succeeded Bäumer instead. Bäumer favored retaining protective legislation for women workers and opposed decriminalizing abortion. She believed that the form of government mattered little for women's issues and considered democratic politics the epitome of self-interest. Nevertheless, she served in the National Assembly in 1919 and in the Reichstag from 1920 to 1932 for the German Democratic Party (Deutsche Demokratische Partei; DDP), with particular involvement in youth issues. She abhorred the Treaty of Versailles yet represented Germany on the League of Nations commission for social and humanitarian questions.

In 1933, after Hitler became chancellor, Bäumer presided over the dissolution of the BDF. That same year she lost her position as a specialist on youth welfare in the Interior Ministry. Bäumer requested but did not receive a post in the National Socialist bureaucracy, even though she informed Nazi authorities of her sympathy to their cause. Despite criticism from some Nazi women, she was allowed to continue issuing *Die Frau* until 1944.

After the defeat and collapse of the Nazi regime, Bäumer was denounced to the United States occupation authorities but declared fully rehabilitated. In *Der neue Weg der deutschen Frau* (The new path of the German woman), 1946, she described Hitler's Reich as a "demonic interlude" in German history and called on women to rebuild German society. A co-founder of the Christian Social Union (CSU), she was later active in the Christian Democratic Union (CDU).

Doris L. Bergen

See also Christian Democratic Union; Christian Social Union; German Democratic Party; Lange, Helene; Nationalism;

Naumann, Friedrich; Salomon, Alice; Social Reform; Versailles, Treaty of; Weber, Marianne; (Bourgeois) Women's Movement

References
Bach, Marie Luise. *Gertrud Bäumer: Biographische Daten und Texte zu einem Persönlichkeitsbild.* Weinheim: Deutscher Studien-Verlag, 1989.
Bäumer, Gertrud. *Im Licht der Erinnerung.* Tübingen: R. Wunderlich Verlag Hermann Leins, 1953.
Evans, Richard J. *The Feminist Movement in Germany, 1894–1933.* London: Sage, 1976.
Frevert, Ute. *Women in German History: From Bourgeois Emancipation to Sexual Liberation.* Oxford: Berg, 1989.
Greven-Aschoff, Barbara. *Die bürgerliche Frauenbewegung in Deutschland, 1894–1933.* Göttingen: Vandenhoeck & Ruprecht, 1981.
Hervé, Florence, ed. *Geschichte der deutschen Frauenbewegung.* Cologne: Papy Rossa, 1990.
Huber, Werner. *Gertrud Bäumer: Eine politische Biographie.* Augsburg: Dissertationsdruck W. Blasaditsch, 1970.
Koepcke, Cordula. *Frauenbewegung zwischen den Jahren 1800 und 2000.* Heroldsberg: Glock & Lutz, 1979.
Koonz, Claudia. *Mothers in the Fatherland: Women, the Family, and Nazi Politics.* New York, NY: St. Martin's, 1987.

Bavaria

Of all of the German states, Bavaria has traditionally claimed to have the oldest continuous political and cultural existence. Like the other German lands, Bavaria has experienced numerous changes of borders and populations. In the late nineteenth century, it assumed its current form, dominating the southeastern corner of Germany. Encompassing 27,238 square miles and possessing a population of some 11 million, Bavaria is the largest federal state in area and second largest in number of citizens.

Bavaria's geographic core before 1871 was, as it is today, the southern region bounded roughly by the Danube in the north, by the River Lech in the west, by the Bavarian Alps in the south, and by the River Inn in the east. This is the famous "parallelogram" within which the first Bavarian state, the duchy of the Agilolfinger dynasty, arose as a tributary to Charlemagne. This core eventually passed into the hands of the House of Wittelsbach in the twelfth century. Experiencing a fairly typical series of dynastic subdivisions in the medieval period, and severely tested during the Reformation and the Wars of Religion, the duchy nevertheless emerged after 1648 as a principal supporter of Roman Catholicism and what would later be called *grossdeutsch* (greater Germany) politics. Only in 1777, however, were the ancestral lands of southern Bavaria politically (though not geographically) united with the dynastically related Rhenish Palatinate under Duke Karl Theodor.

In the nineteenth century, Bavaria grew rapidly. Under the influence of the French Revolution and Napoleon, Bavaria found itself moving quickly into the age of the Enlightenment, though the Wittelsbachs remained firmly seated in Munich. Indeed, they and Bavaria profited materially from the Napoleonic upheavals. In 1806, under Napoleon's aegis, Bavaria was elevated to the status of a monarchy under King Max Josef I (1806–25). In addition, large and heavily Protestant territories in Franconia and Swabia were added to Catholic Bavaria. For a brief time Napoleon's ally in Bavaria even controlled the Tyrol, and Bavaria contributed significantly to the French emperor's campaign in Russia.

Bavaria's subsequent opposition to France during the Wars of Liberation guaranteed Munich's retention of most of its Napoleonic gains. By 1866 Bavaria had acquired the territorial extent and influence in German affairs that would shape most of its subsequent policies until World War II. That same year witnessed Bavaria's invasion and defeat by Prussia as Munich unsuccessfully attempted to support Austria in the Seven Weeks' War. Thereafter Bavaria was forced to pay reparations, surrender certain northern territories and sign an offensive and defensive alliance with Bismarck's Prussia. Though Bavaria was technically independent of all foreign powers, its independence was precarious and short-lived.

In 1870, Bavaria was swept into war against France by the same nationalist enthusiasm coursing through all of Germany. Thus followed Bavaria's inclusion in the German Empire on January 18, 1871. Only on certain conditions, however, did Bavaria accept membership. Berlin allowed Bavaria to retain a separate postal and rail system, an independent army and command structure, and separate diplomatic representation. Munich retained its taxes on beer and spirits, which contributed significantly to its financial independence. Citizenship, residency, colonization, and emigration remained independent of Reich control. In addition, Bavaria retained permanent seats on the Imperial committees of defense and foreign affairs, the latter of which Munich chaired.

Such reserved rights, it was hoped, would preserve Bavaria's identity in the new empire. This preservation was crucial in an age of wrenching social and economic change. As elsewhere in Germany, industrial development and urbanization proceeded in Munich, Augsburg, and Nuremberg, though the state as a whole remained predominantly agricultural. In addition, Bavaria's tradition of Roman Catholicism set it apart from most other regions of the empire. Though possessed of a vibrant and influential Protestant minority in Franconia, the state retained a majority of Roman Catholics. Consequently, Bavaria was at odds with Bismarck during the *Kulturkampf* which, despite Berlin's efforts, reinforced the Catholic self-image of the state. The Bavarian Patriots' Party (Patriotenpartei), founded in 1869, strongly represented these Catholic interests, as would later the Bavarian wing of the Catholic Center Party.

Taking great pride in the earlier revival of Bavaria's cultural traditions during the reign of King Ludwig I (1825–48), the state was essentially leaderless in the closing years of his grandson, the unfortunate Ludwig II (1864–86). The waning nineteenth century nevertheless saw a great artistic flowering in Munich in literature, the theater, the graphic arts, and architecture, even as the Empire slid toward the abyss of war in 1914. Still largely an agrarian state, Bavaria was to send fully 900,000 soldiers (200,000 of whom were killed) to all European fronts by 1918. In the process, however, Bavarians resentfully perceived themselves to be increasingly at the mercy of Berlin's drive toward economic and political centralization.

The Revolution of 1918 swept away the Wittelsbachs' ancient dynasty and ushered in a prolonged period of political disquiet in Bavaria. The troubled life of the Weimar Republic was characterized, in Bavaria, by continuous resentment over the removal of all of the reserved rights of the imperial period. Further, Bavaria's native conservatism, well represented by the ruling Bavarian People's Party (Bayerische Volkspartei), allowed for a disturbing toleration of proto-Nazi violence before 1923. After that year, the fledgling Hitler movement grew and was allowed to exist relatively undisturbed until the "seizure of power" in 1933. Like all the German states, Bavaria was reduced, after 1933, to the status of a party satrapy in the convoluted Nazi hierarchy. Divided into party districts (*Parteigaue*), Bavaria suffered all of the neo-pagan Nazi excesses, including the first concentration camp at the one-time artists' colony of Dachau. Though a stubborn streak of Catholic resistance would occasionally surface, Bavaria experienced the same catastrophic fate as all of Germany by 1945.

By the whim of American occupation authorities, Bavaria remained intact in 1945, save the loss of the Palatinate to the French zone. Political and economic reconstruction followed under Allied tutelage. As a postwar West German state took shape, Bavarian leaders pressed for a decentralized, federal arrangement in keeping with Bavarian tradition. Between 1946 and 1948, Bavaria's new ruling party, the Christian Social Union (CSU), adamantly maintained that only a federal republic could prevent a recurrence of dictatorship while safeguarding citizens' and Bavaria's rights. This advocacy influenced other western German leaders already inclined to support federalist plans, and in May 1949 the Federal Republic of Germany was inaugurated in Bonn.

Between 1949 and Germany's reunification in 1990, Bavaria remained federalism's and the states' (*Länder*) most vociferous, and most conservative, champion. The CSU controlled every Bavarian government after 1945 except one and oversaw Bavaria's transformation from an agrarian to an industrial state. Particular economic success was achieved in the aerospace, automotive, electronic, and machine-tool industries as well as in tourism. The presence of some two million Sudenten German refugees added significantly to handicrafts. Agriculture, though less important, remained a major economic factor in Bavaria and, not coincidentally, a base of conservative support for the CSU. Nationally, Bavaria's ruling party allied itself with the forces of Christian Democracy. This alliance permitted Bavarian, and more specifically CSU, concerns to be voiced at the highest level, especially by Franz Josef Strauss (1915–88). Bavaria is now one of 16 federal states, instead of West Germany's previous 11. Bavarians and their leaders confidently believe that their state will continue to play a prominent role in the life of the nation.

David R. Dorondo

See also Bavarian People's Party; Bismarck, Otto von; BMW; Christian Social Union; Ehard, Hans; Eisner, Kurt; Erhard, Ludwig; Federalism; Heim, Georg; Högner, Wilhelm; *Kulturkampf*; Ludwig II; National Socialism; *Putschism*; Röhm, Ernst; Strauss, Franz Josef

References

Dorondo, D.R. *Bavaria and German Federalism: Reich to Republic, 1918–33, 1945–49*. New York, NY: St. Martin's, 1992.

Golay, John Ford. *The Founding of the Federal Republic of Germany*. Chicago, IL: University of Chicago Press, 1958.

Kock, Peter Jakob. "Bayerns Weg in die Bundesrepublik." *Studien zur Zeit* 22 (1983).

Kraus, Andreas. *Geschichte Bayerns*. Munich: Verlag C.H. Beck, 1983.

Zorn, Wolfgang. *Bayerns Geschichte im 20. Jahrhundert 1900–1966*. Munich: Verlag C.H. Beck, 1986.

Bavarian People's Party (1918–33)

The Bavarian People's Party (Bayerische Volkspartei; BVP) was the largest and most influential of the regional and special-interest parties that appeared during the Weimar Republic. Founded on November 12, 1918, on the initiative of Bavarian peasant leader Georg Heim (1865–1938), the BVP received strong support from the leaders of the Bavarian organization of the German Center Party (Deutsche Zentrumspartei), who were disenchanted with the national party's drift to the left under Matthias Erzberger (1875–1921). Though ostensibly interconfessional, the BVP was closely allied to the Catholic aristocracy and Catholic clergy in Bavaria and depended heavily on the support of the Catholic peasant unions. Karl Friedrich Speck (1862–1942) served as national chairman from 1919 to 1929 and was succeeded by Fritz Schäffer (1888–1967), who served in this capacity until the party's dissolution on July 4, 1933.

The central feature of the BVP's political program was its call for the unification of the various German states, including Austria, on a federalist basis without the domination of any single state. Though committed to the parliamentary system of government, the BVP opposed the centralist features of the Weimar constitution and pursued an increasingly antirepublican course under Gustav von Kahr (1862–1934) from 1920 to 1923. Following Kahr's disgrace in connection with the abortive Hitler-Ludendorff *Putsch* of November 1923, the BVP came under the influence of more moderate forces represented by Heinrich Held (1868–1938), the Bavarian minister-president from 1924 to 1933. Under Held, the BVP repaired its relations with the Center Party, took part in various national cabinets from 1924 to 1928, and actively supported the policies of Chancellor Heinrich Brüning (1885–1970) from 1930 to 1932. The BVP's prominence in Bavarian politics exposed it to a steady barrage of attacks from the Nazis in the last years of the Weimar Republic. Following the Nazi seizure of power in Bavaria on March 9, 1933, party officials were summarily removed from positions of influence in the state government.

Larry Eugene Jones

See also Bavaria; Brüning, Heinrich; Catholicism, Political; Center Party; Erzberger, Matthias; Parties and Politics; Weimar Germany

References

Schönhoven, Klaus. *Die Bayerische Volkspartei 1924–1932.* Düsseldorf: Droste, 1972.
———. "Zwischen Anpassung und Ausschaltung: Die Bayerische Volkspartei in der Endphase der Weimarer Republik." *Historische Zeitschrift* 224 (1977), 340–78.
Schwend, Karl. *Bayern zwischen Monarchie und Diktatur: Beiträge zur bayerischen Frage in der Zeit von 1918 bis 1933.* Munich: R. Pflaum, 1954.
———. "Die Bayerische Volkspartei." *Das Ende der Parteien 1933.* Ed. Erich Matthias and Rudolf Morsey. Düsseldorf: Droste, 1960.

Bayer AG

Since its establishment in 1863, Bayer AG has developed from a manufacturer of synthetic dyes to a broadly diversified international chemicals and health care company with operations in about 150 countries. Its activities are divided into 21 business groups in the fields of polymers, organic chemicals, industrial products, health care, agrochemicals, and imaging technologies. Bayer is one of the largest employers in Germany.

On August 1, 1863, a merchant named Friedrich Bayer (1825–80) and a master dyer named Johann Friedrich Weskott (1821–80) founded the company Friedr. Bayer et comp. in Wuppertal-Barmen to manufacture and market synthetic dyes. The company expanded rapidly. Within two years, Bayer and Weskott acquired a stake in the first American factory for coal-tar dyes in Albany, New York. In 1876 they started their first foreign "factory" in a cellar in Moscow.

Many of the social and welfare benefits still enjoyed by the company's employees date back to its origins. For example, in 1873 the company set up a relief fund to assist employees in the event of illness. This was the forerunner of the company's present health-insurance fund.

New factories, a worldwide sales network, and above all laboratories and scientific research were expensive. To raise capital and to safeguard the company's future, on June 1, 1881 the company was transformed from a general partnership to a joint-stock company, Farbenfabriken vorm. Friedr. Bayer & Co. By then it had over 300 employees. Shortly afterward the company opened a central scientific laboratory that set new standards of industrial research. Bayer's discoveries included many organic and inorganic chemicals, dyes, and pharmaceuticals, including the "wonder drug" aspirin. A pharmaceutical department was established in 1888 and in 1904 Bayer entered the field of photographic chemistry with the manufacture of developing agents for photographic film. Starting in 1891, Carl Duisberg (1861–1935), who was the company's managing director from 1912 to 1925, built up a second production site in Leverkusen, near Cologne. In 1912 the company, which now had a workforce of 10,000, transferred its headquarters to this new, modern site.

World War I interrupted the company's rapid expansion. Bayer was increasingly integrated into the war economy, manufacturing essential war supplies including explosives and chemical weapons instead of dyes and pharmaceuticals. The war took a heavy toll on the company. Most of its foreign assets were confiscated and it was denied access to export markets, which were vital for further expansion. In 1919 sales were only two-thirds of their 1913 level and inflation was eating into financial reserves.

In an effort to restore competitiveness and strengthen the German dye industry on the world market, the German coal-tar dye manufacturers decided to merge in 1925. Bayer was among the companies that transferred their assets to the new I.G. Farbenindustrie AG and ceased to exist as a separate entity. However, the "Bayer tradition" continued in I.G. Farben's Lower Rhine consortium, which comprised factories in Leverkusen, Dormagen, Elberfeld, and Uerdingen. Moreover, the name Bayer was used for products marketed by the pharmaceuticals division of I.G. Farben. In the 1930s, research focused on the synthesis of rubber (Perbunan), modern polymer chemistry (polyurethanes), and pharmaceuticals. With the discovery of the therapeutic action of sulfonamides (Prontosil), Gerhard Domagk made an enormous contribution to chemical therapy of infectious diseases. In 1939 he was awarded the Nobel Prize for Medicine for his discovery.

During World War II, the Lower Rhine consortium's factories were regarded as "essential for the war effort." Production was maintained by employing, under horrendous conditions, forced laborers without pay from German-occupied countries in Europe.

At the end of the war, the Allies ordered the dissolution of I.G. Farbenindustrie AG. In 1951–52 12 successor companies were established in Germany, among them Farbenfabriken Bayer AG. The reconstruction of Bayer went hand in hand with the "Economic Miracle" in West Germany. The discovery of new plastics, fibers, agrochemicals, and pharmaceuticals and the company's successful return to the world market laid the foundations for rapid development. In 1963, a hundred years after its foundation, Bayer had 78,000 employees worldwide and marketed 8,500 products. In 1972 the company was renamed Bayer Aktiengesellschaft (Bayer AG). Focusing primarily on Western Europe and the United States, Bayer expanded its international activities. In 1974 it acquired Cutter Laboratories Inc. in the United States, followed by Miles Laboratories Inc. in 1978. Since 1981, Agfa-Gevaert AG has been a wholly owned subsidiary of Bayer AG.

Growing awareness of environmental issues in the 1970s has led to the development of modern environmental-protection technologies, such as Bayer Tower Biology for the treatment of waste water. By 1985 Bayer was spending a billion deutsche marks annually on environmental protection. Today the company's research concentrates on new pharmaceuticals and methods of treatment, diagnostic agents, new crop-protection products, and innovative imaging technologies. Bayer employs about 77,000 people in Germany and a total of over 153,000 people in 150 countries.

Michael Pohlenz

See also BASF; Chemistry, Scientific and Industrial; Duisberg, Carl; I.G. Farbenindustrie AG; Pharmacy

References

Beer, John J. *The Emergence of the German Dye Industry.* Urbana, IL: University of Illinois Press, 1959.

Hayes, Peter. *Industry and Ideology: IG Farben in the Nazi Era.* Cambridge: Cambridge University Press, 1987.

Mann, Charles C. and Mark L. Plummer. *The Aspirin Wars: Money, Medicine and 100 Years of Rampant Competition.* New York, NY: Knopf, 1991.

Bebel, (Ferdinand) August (1840–1913)

No other leader shaped the course of the socialist labor movement between the 1860s and the 1910s more than August Bebel. Although he had only a *Volksschule* (elementary school) education and artisanal training as a woodturner, Bebel had qualities that compensated for his modest beginnings: a clear and penetrating mind, the capacity to digest information quickly, an outstanding talent for public speaking, a flair for organizational and parliamentary politicking, a strong will, and an unwavering devotion to socialism and the emancipation of the working class. For his outspoken political radicalism he served many years in prison. It was assumed that Bebel would always be a member of the Executive Committee of the Social Democratic Party, and he served as a Reichstag deputy almost without interruption from the founding of the North German Confederation (1867) to his death in 1913.

August Bebel. Courtesy of German Embassy, Ottawa.

Although Bebel first learned about socialism through the work of Ferdinand Lassalle (1825–64), he did not join the Lassallean Allgemeiner Deutscher Arbeiterverein (General German Workers' Association) but began his involvement with the labor movement in the liberal-sponsored Arbeiterbildungsverein (Workers' Educational Association) in Leipzig. Under the influence of Wilhelm Liebknecht (1819–1900), Bebel turned more and more to Marxism, and the two of them were the chief founders of the Social Democratic Workers' Party (1869), which affiliated with the First International (1864–72), led from London by Karl Marx (1819–83). At the time of the Franco-Prussian War (1870–71), Bebel's public denunciation of German unification under Prussia and his open endorsement of the Paris Commune (1871) created a deep fissure between the young socialist movement and the new German Empire.

Political realism persuaded Bebel that the socialists needed to use the Reichstag for tactical reasons, but a lively utopian strain also characterized his worldview. He believed unceasingly that the collapse of capitalism was to occur at any moment. He mastered the art of leading a mass movement, but in doing so he also became the chief advocate of centrist policies on almost all issues that faced German Social Democracy. He fought vigorously against Eduard Bernstein's (1850–1932) revisionism, but in the end he helped to fashion a compromise that even Bernstein could embrace.

In addition to his heavy speaking schedule, Bebel published scores of pamphlets and articles, and numerous books, including a study of Charles Fourier. Although Bebel was not a theorist, his book, *Die Frau und der Sozialismus* (published as *Woman under Socialism*), 1879, was enormously popular and widely accepted as an authoritative statement on Social Democratic theory and goals. To rank-and-file members of the labor movement and to the German public at large, Bebel seemed to embody everything that typified German Social Democracy.

Vernon Lidtke

See also Bernstein, Eduard; Ebert, Friedrich; Kautsky, Karl; Liebknecht, Karl; Liebknecht, Wilhelm; Luxemburg, Rosa; Marx, Karl; Social Democratic Party, 1871–1918; Vollmar, Georg von

References

Bebel, August. *Ausgewählte Reden und Schriften.* 10 vols. Munich: K.G. Sauer, 1994–96.

———. *August Bebels Briefwechsel mit Friedrich Engels.* Ed. Werner Blumenberg. The Hague: Mouton, 1965.

———. *Aus meinem Leben.* 3 vols. Stuttgart: J.H.W. Dietz, 1910–14.

Hermann, Ursula and Volker Emmerich, eds. *August Bebel: Eine Biographie.* Berlin (East): Dietz Verlag, 1989.

Hirsch, Helmut. *August Bebel: Sein Leben in Dokumenten, Reden und Schriften.* Cologne: Kiepenheuer & Witsch, 1968.

Maehl, William Harvey. *August Bebel: Shadow Emperor of the German Workers.* Philadelphia, PA: American Philosophical Society, 1980.

Schraepler, Ernst. *August Bebel-Bibliographie*. Düsseldorf: Droste Verlag, 1962.

Seebacher-Brandt, Brigitte. *Bebel: Künder und Kärrner im Kaiserreich*. Bonn: J.H.W. Dietz, 1988.

Becher, Bernd (1931–) and Hilla (1934–)

The husband-and-wife team of Bernd and Hilla Becher have lived and worked together since the late 1950s, when they began systematically to photograph industrial structures such as water towers, gas tanks, blast furnaces, grain elevators, and factory façades. They traveled throughout Europe and the United States to do so. Adopting their exacting photographic craftsmanship, as well as the concept of a photographic archive, from certain photographers of the Weimar period, the Bechers ordinarily show their work in grid formation devoted to a particular architectural form, in order to provide not only formal but also functional comparisons across a range of time and geography. Their work may be viewed in the context of art, but it also functions as industrial archeology, and it documents technologies becoming obsolete.

Bernd Becher was born in Siegen, in the Ruhr district, in 1931; wife, Hilla, in Berlin in 1934. They were married in 1961. Their first book, provocatively entitled *Anonyme Skulpturen* (Anonymous sculptures), 1970, discussed minimalist and conceptual sculpture. Their work evolved notably through direct contact with the American sculptor Carl Andre. Since then they have published five more books, each devoted to a specific architectural form: *Framework Houses from the Siegen Industrial Area*, 1977; *Fördertürme, Chevalements, Mineheads*, 1985; *Watertowers*, 1988; *Blast Furnaces*, 1990; and *Pennsylvania Coal Mines Tipples*, 1991. The Bechers' photographs document a remarkable diversity and idiosyncracy—even personality—in buildings, each of which is wholly devoted to one highly specific industrial purpose. They trace an interaction between specific, human, and historical conditions and impersonal, abstract economic structures.

Thanks to their exhibitions and books, and the role of the faculty at the Staatliche Kunstakademie (state art academy) in Düsseldorf since 1976, the Bechers have strongly influenced a younger generation of artist-photographers, including several with substantial reputations in their own right, e.g., Thomas Struth and Thomas Ruff.

Nancy Roth

See also Artists; Painting; Photography; Sculpture

References

Andre, Carl. "A Note on Bernhard and Hilla Becher." *Artforum* 11 (December 1972), 59–61.

Aus der Distanz: Photographien von Bernd und Hilla Becher, Andreas Gursky, Candida Höfer, Axel Hütte, Thomas Ruff, Thomas Struth, Petra Wunderlich. Exhibition catalogue. Düsseldorf: Kunstsammlung Nordrhein-Westfalen, 1991.

Becher, Bernd und Hilla Becher. *Framework Houses from the Siegen Industrial Area*. Munich: Schirmer/Mosel Verlag, 1977.

———. *Anonyme Skulpturen: Eine Typologie technischer Bauten*. Düsseldorf: Art Press Verlag, 1970.

———. *Fördertürme, Chevalements, Mineheads*. Munich: Schirmer/Mosel Verlag, 1985.

———. *Industrial Facades*. Cambridge, MA: MIT Press, 1995.

———. *Water Towers*. Cambridge, MA: MIT Press, 1990.

———. *Pennsylvania Coal Mines Tipples*. New York, NY: Dia Center for the Arts, 1991; Munich: Schirmer/Mosel Verlag, 1991.

Becher, Johannes Robert (1891–1958)

The poet and politician Johannes R. Becher had an important role in socialist literary movements between the wars and was a Communist deputy to the Reichstag. During his exile in Moscow he co-founded the National Committee for Free Germany in 1943. In 1945, he returned to the Soviet zone and was the first minister of culture of the German Democratic Republic (GDR) from 1954 to 1958.

Becher was born in Munich in 1891 and studied philosophy and medicine in Munich, Jena, and Berlin. He was a leading figure in the expressionist movement, and under the influence of World War I, in which he refused to serve, became convinced of the political mission of literature. His autobiographical novel, *Abschied* (Farewell), 1940, traces his revolt against his affluent family background and his development of socialist sympathies. He joined the Independent Social Democratic Party (USPD) in 1917, and became the president of the Bund Proletarisch-Revolutionärer Schriftsteller (League of Proletarian-Revolutionary Authors) on its foundation in 1928.

Becher was charged with high treason in 1925 on the basis of his poems, "*Der Leichnam auf dem Thron*" (The corpse on the throne), 1925. The case was, however, dropped, then renewed in 1927 on the basis of his anti-war novel, *Levisite oder Der einzig gerechte Krieg* (Levisite or the only just war), 1926. After massive protests, the proceedings were again abandoned. In 1933, Becher had to leave Germany; from 1935 he lived in the Soviet Union as editor of the German edition of *International Literature* and in 1943 was a co-founder of the National Committee for Free Germany, which worked with German prisoners of war to prepare for postwar reconstruction. In 1945, he returned to Berlin, where he played a central role in organizing the cultural life of the Soviet zone; he was the first president of the League of Culture for the Democratic Renewal of Germany and helped to establich the Aufbau publishing house and the literary periodical *Sinn und Form* (Meaning and form). From 1954 to 1958, Becher was the first minister of culture of the GDR. He died in Berlin in 1958.

Becher's career divides into three parts: the early bohemian expressionist, the politically committed author and organizer, and the cultural functionary. His early lyrics, dealing with self-discovery, renewal, and religious motifs, are at the extreme limit of the expressionist dissolution of language. His earlier political works continue to experiment, not always successfully, with language and form. Later, his view of the artist's mission as communicator led him to adopt a more popular tone, as in the epic *Der grosse Plan* (The great plan), 1931.

After the division of Germany in 1949, Becher remained strongly committed to the ideal of Germany as a united socialist country. He wrote the words of the East German national anthem "Auferstanden aus Ruinen" (Arisen from ruins), 1949, set to music by Hanns Eisler (1898–1962). This contained the line, *"Deutschland, einig Vaterland"* (Germany, united fatherland), which later conflicted with the East German policy on unification and was deleted. In 1989, *"Deutschland, einig Vaterland"* was resurrected as the chant of demonstrators in Leipzig and elsewhere.

The demands of functioning as East Germany's "state poet," supplying occasional verse for Party festivities, together with having Stalinist dogma inflicted on his literary form, conflicted with Becher's own creativity. This resulted in conventional, stilted, and often sentimental poetry, as in the collection *Neue deutsche Volkslieder* (New German folksongs), 1950. His diaries, *Auf andere Art so grosse Hoffnung* (And yet such great hopes), 1951, make more rewarding reading. They give an insight into the searching conflicts and pressures he faced:. Becher's later importance lay not so much in the literary production of the state poet as in his attempts to mediate between German culture and Cold War politics.

James A. Mellis

See also Eisler, Hanns; Expressionism (Literature); German Democratic Republic; Independent Social Democratic Party; National Committee for a Free Germany; Poetry

References

Gansel, Carsten, ed. *Der gespaltene Dichter: Johannes R. Becher: Gedichte, Briefe, Dokumente 1945–1958.* Berlin: Aufbau, 1991.

Haase, Horst. *Johannes R. Becher, Leben und Werk.* Berlin: Volk & Wissen, 1981.

Richter, Hans. "Vollendung träumend. . . : Johannes R. Becher's Later Writing." *Socialism and the Literary Imagination: Essays on East German Writers.* Ed. Martin Kane. Oxford: Berg, 1991.

Rohrwasser, Michael. *Der Weg nach oben: Johannes R. Becher: Politiken des Schreibens.* Basel: Stroemfeld and Roter Stern, 1980.

Beck, Ludwig (1880–1944)

As chief of the General Staff from 1933 to 1938, Ludwig Beck rapidly built a strong German army. In retirement, he and Carl Goerdeler became the older generation's leading figures in the conservative Resistance. The son of a prosperous Rhineland industrialist, Beck left school at 18 for an army career. Transferred to the General Staff in 1913, he held staff positions until the 1918 defeat, which he attributed to a "stab in the back." He opposed the revolution, bolshevism, and the Weimar Republic; in 1923, he would have installed the Crown Prince as dictator. In the Reichswehr, he helped to demobilize the armies, was in Breslau during the struggle over Silesia, then held staff and command positions. He applauded the Nazi electoral success in September 1930, and he defended some officers devoted to Adolf Hitler, who testified at their treason trial in Leipzig. Beck was impressed with Hitler.

Beck's preparation in 1931 and 1932 of a handbook for tactical operations, late to be used in World War II, resulted in his promotion to lieutenant general and command of a cavalry division. Together with a number of officers, he welcomed Hitler's assumption of power. After October 1933, as Chief of the Truppenamt, the disguised General Staff, Beck pressed at all stages for rapid army expansion and modernization as well as withdrawal from the Disarmament Conference and League of Nations, conscription, and reoccupation of the Rhineland. He wanted the military and political establishments to share power equally, and the military to have a monopoly of force. Hence he approved the destruction of Röhm's SA on June 30, 1934 and resisted the challenge of Himmler's SS.

Beck was disturbed by Nazi attacks on Christianity, by the falsified charge of homosexuality against General Fritsch, and by Hitler's bellicose speech at the November 5, 1937 conference to which Foreign Minister Konstantin von Neurath and the military chiefs were invited. He feared that a general war might arise from military action against Austria or Czechoslovakia. Shocked by the *Anschluss*, and then by Hitler's order of May 1938 to prepare for an invasion of Czechoslovakia, he argued in memoranda during the summer of 1938 that an attack on Czechoslovakia would result in war and Germany's defeat by a coalition. He urged the generals to wage a strike early in August, but obtained little support because the reports of the military attachés and the results of war games contradicted his prognosis. Further, most generals refused to confront Hitler.

Beck resigned and was succeeded by General Halder. Only after the invasion of Poland did Beck actively promote the overthrow of the regime. In 1939–40 he hoped for British acceptance of much of the territory that Germany had acquired. Pessimistic about the invasions of Denmark, Norway, and Western Europe, he recognized that only defeat, as happened at Stalingrad, would stimulate a military coup d'état. Beck hoped to be the leader of the new Germany. When the July 20, 1944 attempt on Hitler's life failed, as a conspirator he was allowed to commit suicide, but having twice failed, he was executed.

Despite his sympathy for Nazism and the mainly military nature of his differences with the regime before 1939, Beck acquired a moral and political dimension thanks to his conservative opposition. Yet his territorial aims, and his effort to save Germany's military power for a successor regime that would be neither democratic nor parliamentary, have been viewed critically.

Leonidas E. Hill

See also Fritsch, Werner von; Goerdeler, Carl; Hitler, Adolf; National Socialist Germany: Foreign Policy; National Socialist Germany: Military; Resistance; Stauffenberg, Claus Schenk von

References

Beck, Ludwig. *Studien.* Stuttgart: D.F. Koehler, 1955.
Hoffmann, Peter. "Ludwig Beck: Loyalty and Resistance." *Central European History* 14 (December, 1981), 332–50.

Müller, Klaus-Jürgen. *The Army, Politics and Society in Germany 1933–45: Studies in the Army's Relation to Nazism.* Manchester: Manchester University Press, 1987.

———. *General Ludwig Beck: Studien und Dokumente zur politisch-militärischen Vorstellungswelt und Tätigkeit des Generalstabschefs des deutschen Heeres 1933–1938.* Boppard am Rhein: H. Boldt, 1980.

Reynolds, Nicholas. *Treason Was No Crime: Ludwig Beck, Chief of the German General Staff.* London: Kimber, 1976.

Schramm, Wilhelm Ritter von, ed. *Beck und Goerdeler: Gemeinschaftsdokumente für den Frieden 1941–1944.* Munich: Gotthold Müller, 1965.

Becker, Jurek (1937–97)

Jurek Becker asserts that he became a German writer merely by chance. Born in 1937 in the Polish city of Lodz, he and his Jewish parents were confined to the ghetto in 1939 until being sent to separate concentration camps in Germany. Having lost his mother, Becker was reunited at war's end with his father, who remained in the Soviet sector of Berlin, convinced that anti-Semitism would be less likely to surface in defeated Germany than in Poland. Becker ascribed his sensitivity to language to his experiences as a schoolboy, when he began to learn German at the age of eight. He later studied philosophy in East Berlin until being dismissed from the university for political reasons. He then wrote for cabaret, television, and film. His first novel, *Jakob der Lügner*, 1969 (published as *Jacob the Liar*, 1975), initially prepared as a screenplay, was not produced until 1974.

In the concentration camps Becker may have acquired the gift for storytelling that characterizes *Jacob the Liar*, with its affinities to the oral tradition and to writers such as Isaac B. Singer and Sholem Aleichem. Becker, who insists on maintaining his identity as a Jew without retaining any ties to religion, cites Franz Kafka (1893–1924) as a major influence. Jakob Heym, the "liar" of Becker's first novel, is a storyteller who becomes entrapped in the compulsion to invent reports of imminent liberation by the Red Army in order to help his fellow ghetto dwellers maintain hope in a hopeless situation.

Becker responded to an apparent relaxation of German Democratic Republic (GDR) censorship in the arts with the publication of *Irreführung der Behörden* (Misleading the bureaucrats), 1973, whose central figure is likewise a storyteller, for whom the study of law is only a cover for private preoccupations in the realm of imagination. The price of success, however, is political compromise and personal crisis.

Whatever artistic freedom seemed possible in the early 1970s ended with the drastic measures by East Germany against Wolf Biermann (1936–) in 1976 and the subsequent repressions against Becker and others who protested this action. After his expulsion from the Socialist Unity Party and his resignation from the Writers' Association, Becker was allowed to move to West Berlin, maintain his GDR citizenship, and continue to publish in East and West Germany. He remained outspoken in matters of German domestic and foreign politics.

Becker's writing revolves around the themes of his first works: the Holocaust and its aftermath on the one hand (*Der Boxer*, 1976; *Bronsteins Kinder*, 1986 [published as *Bronstein's Children*, 1988]) and critical depictions of opportunism, marital discord and deception under GDR socialism, on the other (*Schlaflose Tage*, 1978 [published as *Sleepless Days*, 1979]; *Aller Welt Freund* [Everyone's friend], 1982; *Amanda herzlos* [Heartless Amanda], 1992). His recent writing for film and television included a popular video series, *Liebling Kreuzberg* (Darling Kreuzberg), 1986–88.

In addition to numerous prizes and visiting professorships, Becker was elected to the Darmstadt Akademie für Sprache und Dichtung (Darmstadt Academy for Language and Poetry), 1983, and in 1989 to the guest professorship in poetics at the University of Frankfurt; his lectures there were published under the title of *Warnung vor dem Schriftsteller* (Warning about the author), 1990.

Patricia Herminghouse

See also Biermann, Wolf; Federal Republic of Germany: Literature; German Democratic Republic; Novel; German Democratic Republic: Literature and Literary Life

References
Heidelberger-Leonard, Irene, ed. *Jurek Becker.* Frankfurt am Main: Suhrkamp, 1992.

Johnson, Susan M. *The Works of Jurek Becker: A Thematic Analysis.* New York, NY: P. Lang, 1984.

Beckmann, Max (1884–1950)

A painter and graphic artist concerned more with the spiritual than the political, Max Beckmann grew out of German postimpressionism to become a major international figure in modern art.

Born in Leipzig, Beckmann studied art in Weimar (1900–03) and in 1904 settled in Berlin, where he met relatively quick success. In 1906 Beckmann received the Villa Romana prize for study in Florence and exhibited at, and joined, the Berlin Secession. In the following years he had one-man exhibitions in Magdeburg, Weimar, and Berlin, and by the outbreak of World War I was among the best-known young painters in Germany.

During the war Beckmann's experience as a medical orderly resulted in a nervous breakdown in 1915 that had a profound impact on his work. The fluid mixing of colors and painterly romanticism of his prewar years was replaced by a flatter application of bold color and a harsh angular distortion that make paintings such as *Deposition*, 1917 (The Museum of Modern Art, New York) and *The Night*, 1918–19 (Kunstsammlung Nordrhein-Westfalen, Düsseldorf) powerful evocations of horror and tragedy. In 1925 Beckmann signed a contract with his friend, the art dealer I. B. Neumann, and was appointed as a master teacher at the Stadelschule in Frankfurt; the following year he received his first museum retrospective, in Mannheim.

With the coming of the Third Reich, Beckmann was discharged from his teaching position and under mounting

Max Beckmann: Self-portrait. Courtesy of Inter Nationes, Bonn.

political pressure the newly opened Beckmann room in the National Gallery in Berlin was closed. In 1937 over 530 of his works were confiscated from German museums, and 21 paintings and prints were included in the *Degenerate Art* exhibition. The same year, Beckmann emigrated to Amsterdam, where he remained throughout the war. In 1947, he moved to the United States and never returned to Germany.

The strong contours and shallow spaces of many of Beckmann's paintings show the influence of northern medieval art. Exploring existential themes of spiritual and physical relations, Beckmann painted complex allegories containing a highly personal and autobiographical imagery. While much of his work shares the restless distortion of expressionism, Beckmann, who in the early 1920s was also considered a proponent of New Objectivity, opposed a purely abstract art and never identified himself with any artistic movement. In his large-scale triptychs, such as *Departure,* 1932–35, (The Museum of Modern Art, New York), Beckmann created mythic statements of the individual in the modern world that have had an international resonance.

Paul Paret

See also Artists; Expressionism (Visual Arts); National Socialist Germany: Art; Painting

References

Belting, Hans and Max Beckmann. *Tradition as a Problem in Modern Art.* Peter Wortsman, trans. New York, NY: Timken, 1989.

Buenger, Barbara C. "Max Beckmann's Ideologues: Some Forgotten Faces." *The Art Bulletin* 71 (1989), 453–78.

Fisher, James L., ed. *Max Beckmann Prints from the Museum of Modern Art.* New York, NY: Abrams, 1992.

Göpel, Erhard and Barbara Göpel. *Max Beckmann: Katalog der Gemälde.* 2 vols. Bern: Kornfeld und Cie, 1976.

Hoffmann, Carla and Judith C. Wiess, eds. *Max Beckmann, Retrospective.* Munich: The Saint Louis Art Museum and Preste-Verlag, 1984.

Behrens, Peter (1868–1940)

Peter Behrens trained as a painter, but made his reputation as a typographer, pioneer industrial designer, and architect. A founding member of the German Werkbund (work association), he was that association's most representative figure before World War I because of his association with the German General Electric Company (AEG). Under contract to the AEG from 1907 to 1914 as the firm's artistic advisor and architect, Behrens was able to realize the Werkbund ideal of an alliance between art and industry by helping to form everything that the AEG produced, from arc lamps to advertising, from factories and offices to workers' housing.

Behrens established a successful architectural practice in Berlin before World War I and became well-known at home and abroad. Among his most significant projects were a turbine factory for the AEG (Berlin, 1909) and the German Embassy in St. Petersburg (1911–12). Walter Gropius (1883–1969), Ludwig Mies van der Rohe (1886–1969), and Charles Edouard Jeanneret (Le Corbusier) were among the notables of the modern movement who served as his assistants at various times.

At the beginning of World War I, Behrens, a staunch patriot, was one of 93 prominent artists and intellectuals to sign a manifesto denying German responsibility for the outbreak of war. Subsequently, however, he helped to found the Bund deutscher Gelehrter (Federation of German Scholars), which advocated a negotiated peace without annexations.

In 1922, Behrens became a professor of architecture at the Akademie in Vienna, where he opened a second office. He continued to design major projects in Germany, including a headquarters building for the Hoechst Dyeworks (1920–24), a warehouse complex at Oberhausen for the Gutehoffnungshütte (1921–25), and an apartment building for the Werkbund's housing exhibition at the Weissenhof in Stuttgart (1927).

When Hitler came to power, Behrens, although he was never a member of the Nazi Party, sought to make his peace with the new regime and to continue his work. He was able to defend himself against charges of "philo-Semitism" and "cultural Bolshevism" laid by former employees and Nazi ideologues thanks to the favor of Albert Speer (1905–81) and the good will of Adolf Hitler, who admired his St. Petersburg Embassy building. In 1936, Behrens accepted an appointment as head of the Berlin Akademie der Künste's Master School of Architecture. His last major project, never executed, was a new AEG headquarters designed to occupy a key position on the north-south axis of Speer's master plan for Berlin. Behrens died in Berlin in 1940.

Joan Campbell

See also Architecture and Urban Design; Bauhaus; Gropius, Walter; Hitler, Adolf; *Jugendstil*; Mies van der Rohe, Ludwig; Speer, Albert; Werkbund

References

Buddensieg, Tilmann and Henning Rogge. *Industriekultur: Peter Behrens and the AEG, 1907–1914.* Trans. Iain Boyd Whyte, Cambridge, MA: MIT Press, 1981.

Kadatz, Hans-Joachim. *Peter Behrens: Architekt, Maler, Graphiker und Formgestalter, 1868–1940.* Leipzig: E.A. Seeman, 1977.

Windsor, Alan. *Peter Behrens: Architect and Designer.* London: The Architectural Press, 1981.

Beitz, Berthold (1913–)

Berthold Beitz, who was born on September 26, 1913, was raised in Pomerania, in the remote German northeast. He wanted to be an official of the Reichsbank.

Starting his career at Shell in 1939, he was soon occupied with collecting raw materials for war purposes. In 1941, he was made commercially responsible for the Karpathen Oel AG (Carpathian oil) in Boryslaw in occupied Poland. Here he became aware of the mass murder of Jews and the Polish resistance. He saved several hundred lives by requesting their services for his firm.

After World War II, Beitz began a career in the insurance industry, rising to the presidency of Iduna-Germania Insurance in 1949. During 1953–55 he became chief representa-

Berthold Beitz. Courtesy of Inter Nationes, Bonn.

tive for Alfried Krupp (1907–67) in Essen. Following the Allied divestment order of 1953, Alfried Krupp, as sole owner of the Krupp firm, had to sell the mining and steelmaking operations, with the heart of the concern (*Gusstahlfabrik*) being wrecked and dismantled. Beitz, who was a newcomer to heavy industry as well as to the Ruhrgebiet (Ruhr region), reorganized the remaining pieces of the former industrial empire.

Beitz pried open the markets of the eastern and Communist countries. By 1967, he urgently needed supplier credits. Then the company underwent reforms: Krupp's son Arndt gave up his inheritance and a foundation (Alfried Krupp von Bohlen und Halbach Stiftung) became owner of the company. After Alfried Krupp died in 1967, Beitz at once became president of the foundation's board of trustees and he presided over the supervisory board of the company from 1970 until 1989.

Beitz, who had outmaneuvered Hermann Abs of the Deutsche Bank and the interest holders of the neighboring steel community for control of Krupp, could not diversify the company beyond shipbuilding and steel rapidly enough, so that after the 1975 steel crisis Krupp was in need of cash. Beitz skillfully evaded participation by German banks and instead invited Iran, offering 25 percent of the assets of the Krupp holding company, Friedrich Krupp GmbH, as well as 40 percent in the Brazilian iron-ore firm, Campo Limpo, which together with some more Iranian investments in 1974 brought 1.3 billion deutsche marks (DM) in cash.

In 1954–1955, the Krupp company had 40,000 workers and an annual cash turnover of 1.6 billion DM. An additional 40,000 people worked in companies under Krupp trusteeship. In 1990, the turnover in the 230 Krupp companies was 15.3 billion DM (50 percent of which was located outside of Germany) employing some 59,000 workers. Among the earnings, mechanical engineering brought in 3.2, construction 2.2, electronics 0.7, steel 7.7, and services 2.5 billion DM. Krupp bought out two longtime steel rivals: the Bochumer Verein, in 1965, and the Hoesch concern in Dortmund, which exceeded Krupp in size, in 1992.

Beitz became a member of the International Olympic Committee and through his foundations emerged as a prominent figure in sponsoring scientific and cultural projects. He received special attention and honors from Poland and Israel because of his actions during the war.

Wolfhard Weber

See also Deutsche Bank; Krupp: Family and Firm; Schindler, Oskar and Helpers of the Jews; Third Reich: Industry; World War II

References

Friz, Diana Maria. *Alfried Krupp und Berthold Beitz: Der Erbe und sein Statthalter.* Zürich: Orell Fussli, 1988.

Koehne-Lindenlaub, Renate. "Friedrich Krupp GmbH." *International Directory of Company Histories.* Vol. 4. London: 1992,

Schmalhausen, Bernd. *Berthold Beitz im Dritten Reich: Mensch in unmenschlicher Zeit.* Essen: P. Pomp, 1991.

Belgian-German Relations

From a Belgian viewpoint, relations with their big eastern neighbor Germany were extremely important. Still, they must be considered within the larger context of interaction with other European powers, and, as of 1944, also with the United States. For Germany, relations with Belgium were only a matter of secondary importance, but, due to its geopolitical location, the smaller country never really escaped the attention of Berlin.

In 1830, Prussia had only grudgingly accepted the "revolutionary" establishment of the new Belgian kingdom and had, in consort with the other powers, imposed a neutral status on the country. After 1850, Belgium felt increasingly threatened, first by Imperial, and later by Republican France, which moreover was forging closer ties with Great Britain, traditionally Belgium's protector. By the late nineteenth century, the country became more inclined to turn to Germany, a tendency that was reinforced by extensive economic relations.

Disillusionment followed in 1914, and the "Boches" (Germans) subsequently became enemy number one. For four years, Belgian and German troops faced each other at the Ijzer, while the German military governor pursued a tough occupation policy. The Germans had hoped to use King Albert I as a mediator in the world conflict, but that hope was in vain. The king and the government in exile sided with France and its allies. In 1918, Belgium demanded harsh territorial and financial reprisals to be imposed on a disarmed Germany. The major powers—the United States, Great Britain, and France—took little account of these demands. Brussels concluded that only a complete alignment with Paris would yield some profit, and thus joined France in the 1923 occupation of the Ruhr. Neither the Weimar Republic nor the German public felt much sympathy for Belgium thereafter.

Belgium's tough stance eventually yielded little in the way of material rewards. When an international detente set in after 1924, Belgium joined a collective-security system that implied the restoration of Germany's great-power status. Within the framework of the Locarno treaties (1925) Belgium and Germany pledged to respect each other's borders (Rhine Pact, 1925). The normalization of German-Belgian relations was proceeding apace when Hitler became Germany's chancellor in 1933.

It soon became apparent that Hitler was aggressively committed to pursue Germany's supremacy. In the following few years the Nazi Reich sought to ease Belgium away from its wartime allies, but without success.

In German geopolitical calculations, Belgian territory had to be neutralized politically and militarily to prevent a French preventive attack through Belgium. Beginning in 1933, the Reich started offering conciliatory gestures to Belgium, which at first ignored them. Not until the international situation deteriorated, and especially when France (where a leftist Popular Front regime gained power in 1936) allied itself with the Soviet Union (1935), did Belgian foreign policymakers decide on a change in the country's orientation.

In October 1936, King Leopold III proclaimed a new policy of independent action. Belgium did not wish to be drawn into a war in order to preserve the Locarno treaties, and would therefore reduce its international commitments. In practice this gesture amounted to an overture to the Reich. Economic ties were strengthened and Berlin was thrilled. It only remained to render Belgium's aloofness from its former allies permanent.

Belgian policymakers had few options apart from a policy of appeasement. The strong moral position they attributed to their neutrality policy was dubious, considering the circumstances. Ideological factors may have played a part in Belgium's brief rapprochement with Nazi Germany. The relatively small political circle within the foreign office would consider pro-German Flemish public opinion only if it suited them. The prospect of good economic relations with the Reich must have been attractive.

In 1940, as in 1914, Belgium discovered that the value Germany attached to its small neighbor was relative indeed, and conditioned by the Reich's lust for power. Those in Berlin who believed that respecting Belgian neutrality would yield more than a military occupation lost the day. The German victory was overwhelming. While occupying Belgium, the Nazis led a large part of the establishment and the population to believe that the country would be able to remain more or less independent within a Fascist Europe. Insofar as the German war effort was not threatened, and within the framework of the law-and-order policy of the military regime, the Belgian administration was permitted to function, even if hampered by Fascist collaboration movements. Deteriorating material conditions, Great Britain's resistance, the first German defeats, and the increasingly harsh actions of the occupiers, however, gradually turned public opinion against the Germans.

This second German occupation triggered strong anti-German and anti-Nazi attitudes among most of the population and its policymakers. Despite these apprehensions, Belgium agreed, shortly after 1945, to the increasingly complete integration of West Germany into Western Europe. This decision was mainly due to the Cold War and Belgium's important position in it.

The American viewpoint was that peace and the growth of a capitalist world economy could be achieved only if Germany became a full partner. After some hesitation, Belgium adopted the American position. Now the USSR had become the main enemy. Europeans feared the military threat posed by the Soviet Union far less than they dreaded Communism itself, which would destroy European civilization as they knew it. Logic decreed that Belgian policymakers concede that the Federal Republic of Germany (FRG) had to be integrated into the West. Reconciliation with the German "hereditary enemy," the supranational enthusiasm, and the pro-American orientation were merely a continuation of policies pursued by earlier Belgian diplomacy: keep the peace and promote the economic prosperity of the country and that of its partners.

Belgium's approval of the FRG's entry into NATO through the Western European Union meant that after the economic and political integration of West Germany, its military integration in postwar Western Europe was now also a fact. Belgium had never questioned the matter seriously; it had even promoted the integration process through its minister for foreign affairs, Paul-Henri Spaak. Bilateral German-Belgian relations became completely normalized shortly afterward.

All of this does not mean that the two countries would always see eye to eye. In the early 1960s, it became clear that for Belgium, Atlantic defense orthodoxy carried more weight than it did for the FRG. Whereas West German Chancellor Konrad Adenauer was not ill-disposed toward a "gaullistic" Europe along a Bonn-Paris axis, Spaak did not share his views. For him, the United States remained the exclusive point of reference.

A few years later, however, and even after the crushing of the 1968 uprising in Prague, both countries promoted a policy of detente toward the East. In Brussels, Pierre Harmel had succeeded Spaak as foreign minister, and the Christian Democrat got on very well with the Social Democratic FRG Chancellor Willy Brandt (1913–92).

Dirk Martin

See also Federal Republic of Germany: Foreign Policy; Payer, Friedrich von; Postwar European Integration and Germany; Ruhr Crisis; Stresemann, Gustav; Weimar Germany: Foreign Policy; World War I; World War II

References

Coolsaet, R. *Buitenlande Zaken.* Leuven: Kritak, 1987.

Kieft, D.O. *Belgium's Return to Neutrality: An Essay in the Frustrations of Small Power Diplomacy.* Oxford: Clarendon Press, 1972.

Klefisch, P. *Das Dritte Reich und Belgien.* Frankfurt am Main: Lang, 1988.

Lademacher, H. *Die belgische Neutralität als Problem der europäischen Politik 1830–1914.* Bonn: Röhrscheid, 1971.

Miller, J.K. *Belgian Foreign Policy between Two Wars.* New York, NY: Bookman Associates, 1951.

Spaak, P.H. *Combats inachevé.* Paris: Fayard, 1969.

Vanlangenhove, F. *L'elaboration de la politique étrangere de la Belgique.* Brussels: Academies, 1980.

Warmbrunn, Werner. *The German Occupation of Belgium 1940–1944.* New York, NY: Peter Lang, 1993.

Benjamin, Walter (1892–1940)

Walter Benjamin was one of the most significant philosophers and intellectual critics in the period between the two world wars. But not until the 1960s did his writings gain widespread recognition. Though the Frankfurt School—Theodor W. Adorno (1903–69) in particular—was largely responsible for the initial "Benjamin renaissance," the relation of Benjamin to Frankfurt School critical theory was always problematic. In fact, Benjamin's rich and heterogeneous work defies any narrow categorizations. Even today, his writings continue to provide innovative impulses for disciplines ranging from film theory and materialist aesthetics to cultural studies, literary theory, and the philosophy of language.

Born in 1892 to affluent Jewish parents in Berlin, Benjamin spent most of his life as an impoverished intellectual

Walter Benjamin. Courtesy of Inter Nationes, Bonn.

without institutional support or ties. He concluded his studies at Berlin and Munich with a philosophical dissertation on *Der Begriff der Kunstkritik in der deutschen Romantik* (The concept of art-critique in German Romanticism), 1919, which is both an homage to and a distinguished critique of German Romanticism. Benjamin was among the first to discover the relevance of German Romantic philosophy to theories of modernity. The dissertation marked the beginning of Benjamin's continuing interest in an alternative to idealist aesthetics. By 1925 he had completed, in addition to numerous shorter articles and reviews on diverse subjects, his second book, *Ursprung des deutschen Trauerspiels* (The origin of the German mourning play). This dense and hermetic study on a seemingly arcane topic analyzes the emergence of the mourning play against the backdrop of modern aesthetic movements such as expressionism. The work was originally planned as an academic *Habilitation* project (qualification for university teaching), but under pressure from friends and professors who predicted the failure of his idiosyncratic analysis and foresaw anti-Semitic resentments, Benjamin eventually gave up his plans for a university career and withdrew his petition for the University of Frankfurt to accept his *Habilitation* project.

Among the many travels Benjamin undertook during the following years, his trip to Moscow to visit Asia Lacis was particularly significant. It resulted in an increasing attention to Communism and historical materialism and spawned a variety of works relating to these interests. Shortly after the Nazis came to power in 1933, Benjamin emigrated to Paris, where he continued to work, under unbearable living conditions and with almost no financial support, on the project that was to occupy him for the rest of his life.

The so-called *Arcades Project* is a gigantic collection of citations from numerous sources relating to Paris in the nineteenth century, sparingly interspersed with Benjamin's own comments and reflections. A fragment, it was conceived and organized as an innovative cultural historiography from a materialist point of view. Benjamin focused on the early, phantasmagoric phase of consumer capitalism and excavated those artifacts and dreams which have long since vanished—like the briefly fashionable shopping arcades themselves, which soon fell victim to George-Eugène Haussmann's architectural "beautification" of Paris. This archaeology of early capitalism was the culmination of Benjamin's persistent concern for theories of remembrance and memory, a theme evident from the early "Doctrine of the Similar" to his personal childhood memoirs in *Berliner Kindheit* (Berlin childhood), 1926, and essays on Marcel Proust (1939).

When Hitler's troops marched into Paris, Benjamin fled further south, anxiously awaiting a visa to enter the United States, which he finally obtained in August upon the intervention of Max Horkheimer. At the Spanish border near Port Bou, he and his companions were barred from leaving France for lack of French exit visas. Before being turned back and interned in a French camp, they were allowed to spend the night in a hotel. There, on September 25, 1940, Benjamin took his life with an overdose of morphine. On the next morning his companions were allowed to enter Spain.

Walter Benjamin's life and oeuvre are marked by, but not reducible to, a number of intellectual influences. A brief but intense involvement with the German Wyneken movement (he met Gustav Wyneken personally in 1912) came to an abrupt end in 1914–15. Other encounters with Kantian philosophy, Husserlian phenomenology, Freudian psychoanalysis, cabbalistic thought (often mediated through his friend Gershom Scholem), and Bertolt Brecht's (1898–1956) materialist theories of art have all left traces in his work. Not surprisingly, the critical reception of Benjamin's work has been characterized by the attempts of various groups to claim his legacy. The battles between those who identify Benjamin as either a messianic theologian or a Marxist theoretician have been particularly dominant. The key texts in this debate are the posthumously published theses *Über den Begriff der Geschichte* (On the concept of history), 1940, and the famous essay "Das Kunstwerk im Zeitalter seiner technischen Reproduzierbarkeit" (The artwork in the age of mechanical reproduction), 1936, in which Benjamin diagnoses the decay of the magic power of auratic artwork and expresses the necessity to supplant outmoded aesthetic concepts by a revolutionary aesthetics. His response to aestheticization of fascist politics was to politicize art and aesthetics.

Readers of Benjamin's oeuvre—which encompasses radio plays for children and literary criticism (essays on Goethe, Keller, Kafka, and others) as well as poetry and philosophy—have to conclude that it does not fall neatly along the lines of disciplines or positions. There exist, however, underlying concerns that lend the work a certain coherence, such as the re-

gard for a concept of experience that would avoid the shortcomings of both rationalism and positivism and the search for a nonidealist aesthetic. Handy categories fail to do justice to Benjamin's powerful intellectual endeavor, which continues to challenge disciplinary and ideological boundaries.

Eva Geulen

See also Adorno, Theodor; Aesthetics; Brecht, Bertolt; Frankfurt School; Jews, 1933–90

References

Benjamin, Walter. *Illuminations.* Ed. Hannah Arendt, trans. Harry Zohn. New York, NY: Harcourt, Brace & World, 1968.
———. *Reflections: Essays, Aphorisms, Autobiographical Writings.* Ed. Peter Demetz, trans. Edmund Jephcott. New York, NY: Harcourt Brace Jovanovich, 1978.
Buck-Morss, Susan. *The Dialectics of Seeing: Walter Benjamin and the Arcades Project.* Cambridge, MA: MIT Press, 1990.
Smith, Gary, ed. *On Walter Benjamin: Critical Essays and Recollections.* 2nd ed. Cambridge, MA: MIT Press, 1991.
Witte, Bernd. *Walter Benjamin: An Intellectual Biography.* Ed. Liliane Weissberg, trans. James Rolleston. Detroit, MI: Wayne State University Press, 1991.

Benn, Gottfried (1886–1956)

Gottfried Benn, one of twentieth-century Germany's outstanding poets, was a master craftsman who also wrote essays, prose works, and dramatic sketches. Benn's career began before World War I with his depictions of cancer wards and rotting flesh; it culminated in his refined poems of the post–World War II period. Throughout Benn employed language in innovative ways, creating often obscure montages with material ranging from mythology to contemporary science. He was briefly enamored of the Nazis but eventually wrote unusual poems of resistance, elevating the stasis of aesthetic form in response to the dizzying movement of history.

Benn studied philology and theology in Marburg (1903–04) before pursuing a degree in military medicine at the Kaiser Wilhelm Academy in Berlin (1905–10). A specialist in skin and venereal diseases, he integrated into his creative works not only a coldly cynical dissection of life but also a richly scientific vocabulary. His first collection of poems, *Morgue* (1912), shocked readers with its base images and hopelessness. In *Gehirne* (Brains), 1916, Ronne, a young physician, analyzes, even as he experiences, alienation and the disintegration of reality. In response to his sense of intellectual decay, the early Benn was drawn toward primitivism, the unconscious, and myth.

In his radio address of 1933, "Der neue Staat und die Intellektuellen" (The new state and the intellectuals), Benn declared his allegiance to Hitler. Benn mistakenly thought that the Nazis did not view art as subordinate to politics, as did the socialists, and he was attracted to the idea of a mythological collective. Benn was quickly disillusioned: he recognized his misreading of the Nazi view of art (even as Benn sometimes longed for an aestheticized politics, he was repulsed by the politicization of art), and he rejected the violence evident in the Röhm purge. His works were soon criticized in the *Völkischer Beobachter* (People's observer) as decadent, and in 1938 he was forbidden to publish.

Because of his initial support of the Nazis, Benn could not publish in Germany immediately after the war, but his works, initially released in Switzerland, were enthusiastically received (especially by younger poets, who admired his magisterial use of language). In a transformation of Nietzsche, the poems from the mid-1930s into the 1950s extol static form as beyond the inevitable changes of history. Artistic expression is the only absolute, the one salvation in a nihilistic world. In his influential poetological essay, "Probleme der Lyrik" (Problems concerning lyrics), 1951, Benn stresses the technical aspects of poetry and embraces the absolute poem, written for itself and addressed to no one.

Benn was a nihilist convinced of the meaninglessness and absurdity of history. He longed for salvation, shortly aligning himself with Nazism and later opposing this movement by elevating the absolute stillness of artistic form. Because Benn could recognize no valid content, his desire for the formal transcendence of chaos enabled his embrace of Nazism and his later rejection of it in favor of aestheticism.

Mark W. Roche

See also National Socialist Germany: Literature; Nietzsche, Friedrich; Poetry

References

Alter, Reinhard. *Gottfried Benn: The Artist and Politics (1910–34)*. Bern: Lang, 1976.

Benn, Ilse and Gerhard Schuster, eds. *Benn, Gottfried: Sämtliche Werke*. 7 vols. Stuttgarter Ausgabe. Stuttgart: Klett-Cotta, 1986– .

Dierick, Augustinus P. *Gottfried Benn and His Critics: Major Interpretations 1912–1992*. Columbia, SC: Camden House, 1992.

Roche, Mark William. *Gottfried Benn's Static Poetry: Aesthetic and Intellectual-Historical Interpretations*. Chapel Hill, NC: University of North Carolina Press, 1991.

Sander, Volkmar, ed. *Benn, Gottfried: Prose, Essays, Poems*. New York, NY: Continuum, 1987.

Schröder, Jürgen. *Gottfried Benn: Poesie und Sozialisation*. Stuttgart: Kohlhammer, 1978.

Wellershoff, Dieter. *Gottfried Benn: Phänotyp dieser Stunde: Eine Studie über den Problemgehalt seines Werkes*. Cologne: Kiepenheuer, 1958.

Wodtke, Friedrich Wilhelm. *Gottfried Benn*. 2nd ed. Stuttgart: Metzler, 1970.

Bennigsen, Rudolf von (1824–1902)

No political figure of later nineteenth-century Germany better exemplifies the marriage of moderate liberalism and nationalism than Rudolf von Bennigsen. Co-founder and then president of the Nationalverein (National Union) from 1859 to 1867, Bennigsen fulfilled that role for the National Liberal Party from its creation in 1867 through most of its first three decades of existence. Yet he never held office outside his native Hannover, and, as significant as were his accomplishments and as personally respected as he became, Bennigsen fell short of his own and his party's hopes of constructing a liberal constitutional state for the united Germany.

Born at Lüneburg on July 10, 1824, Bennigsen was descended from an aristocratic family that had sent its sons into state service for generations. His early career followed this model: after completing studies in law, he became a judge in Göttingen. But Bennigsen had also been influenced by the liberal and national currents of the Revolution of 1848, and in the early 1850s he moved increasingly into opposition to the reactionary Hannoverian regime. In 1856, he resigned his office when the government refused to allow him to become a candidate for the second chamber. Elected to the legislature, he quickly became the leader of the liberals there. Three years later he arrived on the national political scene through his involvement with the Nationalverein.

Bennigsen achieved leadership in the Nationalverein and later the National Liberal Party through the gift of a mediating temperament combined with a commitment to liberal nationalism. It accorded with his character and beliefs for him to accept compromise with Otto von Bismarck when the Prussian statesman unified North Germany in 1866, even though Hannover's military defeat and the deposition of its royal house fired anti-Prussian sentiments in Bennigsen's homeland (which separated him from many old friends). With the foundation of the National Liberal Party in 1867, Bennigsen began a decade of cooperation with Bismarck that produced an array of liberal institutions for the new North German Confederation and then, after the completion of unification in 1871, for the German Empire.

By the midpoint of the 1870s, the legislative agenda of National Liberalism was either completed or stalemated. The question of power thereupon became central in the relations between the party and Bismarck. In 1877, when the chancellor tried to finesse the issue and split the National Liberals by offering a ministry to Bennigsen alone, the Hannoverian refused out of regard for party unity. Over the following two years, Bismarck then sought out more compliant parliamentary allies among former antagonists—the Conservative and Catholic Center parties. Assured of their support on tariff issues, Bismarck broke with the National Liberals in 1879.

The result was a crisis of direction for the party. Whether it should stand in opposition or seek realliance with the government was a choice that Bennigsen could not mediate, and in 1880 the oppositional faction seceded. Bennigsen headed the depleted National Liberals for two years and then withdrew from parliamentary politics. He had taken the post of *Landesdirektor* (land director) in Hannover in 1867. He retreated to it, capping his administrative career in 1888 with elevation to the office of *Oberpräsident* (governor). By then, however, he had returned to the Reichstag in the *Kartell* elections of 1887, which temporarily restored the bond between the National Liberals and Bismarck. A decade of renewed parliamentary activity followed. Neither Bennigsen nor his party, however, could recapture their former influence. He retired in 1898, and died at his estate at Bennigsen on August 7, 1902, the embodiment of the achievement and the limitations of the moderate liberalism of his era.

Dan S. White

See also Bismarck, Otto von; Imperial Germany; *Kulturkampf*; Liberalism; National Liberal Party; Parliamentary System; Parties and Politics

References

Aschoff, Hans-Georg, et al. *Der Nationalliberalismus in seiner Epoche, Rudolf von Bennigsen: Gedenkschrift anlässlich der Gründung der Rudolf-von-Bennigsen Stiftung.* Baden-Baden: Nomos Verlagsgesellschaft, 1981.

Heyderhoff, Julius and Paul Wentzcke, eds. *Deutscher Liberalismus im Zeitalter Bismarcks: Eine politische Briefsammlung.* 2 vols. Bonn: Kurt Schroeder Verlag, 1925–26.

Kiepert, Adolf. *Rudolf von Bennigsen: Rückblick auf das Leben eines Parlamentariers.* 2nd ed. Hannover: C. Meyer, 1903.

Na'aman, Shlomo. *Der Deutsche Nationalverein: Die politische Konstituierung des deutschen Bürgertums 1859–1867.* Düsseldorf: Droste Verlag, 1987.

Oncken, Hermann. *Rudolf von Bennigsen: Ein deutscher liberaler Politiker.* 2 vols. Stuttgart: Deutsche Verlags-Anstalt, 1910.

White, Dan S. *The Splintered Party: National Liberalism in Hessen and the Reich, 1867–1918.* Cambridge, MA: Harvard University Press, 1976.

Benz, Karl (1844–1929)

This engineer was the creator of the modern automobile, together with Gottlieb Daimler (1834–1900), who was also working on a motor carriage only 90 miles away. Neither knew the other. The Benz Patent motor car made its first officially attested journey on July 3, 1886, in Mannheim.

Karl Benz, a train engineer's son, grew up in Karlsruhe. His mother made certain that her son received a school education that matched his interest in technology. Inspired by the efforts of riding a "bone-shaker," an early, primitive bicycle, Benz concentrated on experiments for the construction of vehicle propulsion systems, initially in a small technical workshop he had founded in Mannheim in 1871.

After five years and numerous experiments, Benz presented his first design: a three-wheel car with a two-stroke, one horsepower combustion engine that managed approximately 250 revolutions per minute (rpm). On New Year's Eve, 1879, the engine completed its first problem-free test run.

Although Benz founded a factory in Mannheim in 1883—Benz & Cie. Rheinische Gasmotoren-Fabrik—it took some time before he was able to build his first motorized vehicle. He lacked funds and his partner failed to understand the usability of such a means of transport.

Not until January 29, 1886 was Benz able to gain a patent, No. 37435, for his motor car, an extremely light vehicle. It still had three wheels because of problems with the steering; it had a horizontal, exposed single-cylinder engine, electric spark plug, surface carburetor, and water cooling. It achieved a top speed of nine miles per hour. Both rear wheels were driven by chains. This vehicle was the model of all modern cars, and may be found in the German Museum in Munich.

Economic success began for Benz & Cie. at the beginning of the 1890s with the first four-wheel model, the Benz Victoria (1893) and with the small Benz Velo (1894), the first car in the world to be mass-produced. Two Benz buses opened up the first bus route in Germany (1895). In the first car races, too, the rather slow but reliable Benz vehicles constantly won first place, for instance in the Paris-Rouen race (1894) or the Milwaukee-Chicago race (1895).

In 1900, with 400 workers and an annual production of 603 cars, Benz & Cie. was the biggest car factory in the world. An economic crisis in his company forced Benz to withdraw from management (1903). The company later flourished with the production of luxury cars, marine engines, and aircraft. Among other achievements it made a decisive contribution to the development of the diesel engine as a motor-vehicle propulsion system and with the Blitzen-Benz, the fastest vehicle on earth (1911). In 1926, Benz & Cie. merged with Daimler-Motoren-Gesellschaft to become Daimler-Benz AG.

Benz himself continued to produce a few cars in his own small factory in Ladenburg. Esteemed all over the world as the father of the motor car, he died in Ladenburg in 1929.

Otto Nübel

See also Automobile Industry; Daimler, Gottlieb; Daimler-Benz AG

References

Benz, Karl. *Lebensfahrt eines deutschen Erfinders: Die Erfindung des Automobils. Erinnerungen.* Leipzig: v. Hase & Koehler, 1943.

Nixon, St. John C. *The Invention of the Automobile (Karl Benz and Gottlieb Daimler).* London: Country Life Ltd., 1936.

Schildberger, Friedrich. *Gottlieb Daimler und Karl Benz: Pioniere der Automobilindustrie.* Göttingen: Musterschmidt, 1976.

Siebertz, Paul. *Karl Benz: Ein Pionier der Motorisierung.* Stuttgart: Reclam, 1950.

Williams, Brian. *Karl Benz.* New York, NY: Bookwright, 1991.

Berg, Alban (1885–1935)

Alban Berg, an Austrian composer, was one of the two chief disciples of Arnold Schönberg (1874–1951); together with Anton Webern (1883–1945), the three formed what is popularly known as the Second Viennese School of composition, one of the main movements of twentieth-century modern music.

Berg's musical education consisted of private lessons in composition with Schönberg from 1904 to 1908. As one of the landed but genteelly impecunious minor gentry, he managed a living from an odd combination of a small private income and often temporary professional work—teaching, editing, and administration. During World War I, he spent three years in noncombatant army service. His disorganized lifestyle limited his creative output to two operas, a few instrumental works, and some two dozen pieces for solo voice with accompaniment.

Despite his small output, Berg shines as the composer who united—at the highest, uniquely personal, creative level—the viable elements of musical tradition (such as lyricism transmitted through Gustav Mahler [1860–1911]) with the artistically most fruitful achievements of the Schönberg school. His Violin Concerto, 1935, has long been in the standard repertoire and his songs are rapidly gaining similar acceptance. However, it was with his transcendent operas, *Wozzeck,* 1922, and *Lulu,* 1935, the latter composition completed by Friedrich Cerha, that Berg assured himself of immortality; they belong to the best of the genre, regardless of style or historical period.

Zoltan Roman

See also Composers; Mahler, Gustav; Opera; Orchestral Music; Schönberg, Arnold; *Solo Lied;* Webern, Anton

References
Brand, Julian, Christopher Hailey, and Donald Harris, eds. *The Berg-Schönberg Correspondence: Selected Letters.* New York, NY: Norton, 1987.

Carner, Mosco. *Alban Berg: The Man and the Work.* 2nd ed. London: Duckworth, 1983.

Jarman, Douglas, ed. *The Berg Companion.* London: Macmillan, 1989.

Perle, George. *The Operas of Alban Berg.* 2 vols. Berkeley, CA: University of California Press, 1980 and 1985.

Reich, Willi. *Alban Berg.* Trans. Cornelius Cardew. London: Thames and Hudson, 1965.

Berg, Fritz (1901–79)
The longtime head of the Federation of German Industry was born on August 27, 1901 and died on February 3, 1979. His father owned a small plant processing iron wire in Altena. Berg turned to a study of political economy at the University of Cologne and from 1925 to 1928 stayed in the United States learning the theory and practice of the new methods of rationalizing millwork, Taylorism and Fordism.

His unpretentious but firm and religious character, and his direct way of addressing people and problems, were characteristic of relations in the small-scale industry of his home region. His rough but sincere character was appreciated by the Americans, who convinced him that the leaders of the German economy had much to learn from them. His personality and attitude created a certain kind of kinship with Konrad Adenauer, who backed his various international goodwill tours to demonstrate that the Germans had rejected

their previous hegemonial strivings and were now seeking cooperation. Berg favored economic cooperation within the European community.

His career as first president of the Federation of German Industry (Bundesverband der Deutschen Industrie; BDI), from 1949 to 1971, would hardly have been predicted in 1940, when he inherited the small firm from his father. Regionally important as head of the Hagen Chamber of Commerce (1946–1972) in the mountainous south of the Ruhr region, he was also president of the industrial association of manufacturers of iron, sheet, and metal (Wirtschaftsverband der Eisen, Blech and Metall verarbeitenden Industrie). Berg's presidency of the BDI can be well interpreted as an attempt by heavy industry (the traditional branch supplying the lobby groups with one of "their" men) to support a candidate from an industry whose leaders were scrutinized less by the victorious Allies than by the managers of the big steel concerns. Consequently, in 1972, he was followed as head of the BDI by Thyssen steel manager H.G. Sohl (1906–89). Berg, however, was a firm supporter of the *Mittelstand* (lower middle class)—and a strong anti-socialist.

When the Investment Aid Law (Investitionshilfegesetz) of 1952 supported heavy industry and electricity, it was the Industriebank that collected the capital—a foundation of the BDI, which thus continued the structures of the pre-1933 era.

Wolfhard Weber

See also Adenauer, Konrad; Central Association of German Industrialists; Codetermination

References
Berghahn, Volker R. *The Americanization of West German Industry 1945–1973.* Cambridge: Cambridge University Press, 1986.

Braunthal, Gerard. *The Federation of German Industry in Politics.* Ithaca, NY: Cornell University Press, 1965.

Bergengruen, Werner (1892–1964)
Werner Bergengruen was active from the 1920s through the 1950s as a short-story writer, poet, and novelist. Deeply committed to Christian ideals (he converted to Catholicism in 1936), Bergengruen gained renown as a conservative writer whose work retained the stylistic flavor of nineteenth-century German prose. Popular during most of his life, his works did not weather well the arrival of a new generation of postwar writers.

Born in Riga to a Baltic-German doctor, Bergengruen attended the Gymnasium Katharineum in Lübeck. He fought on the German side in World War I, yet was also a member of the Baltic National Guard in 1919, the year he married Charlotte Hensel. He was working as a journalist in Berlin and as a translator of Russian literature in the 1920s when his first works of fiction began to appear.

In the 1930s, Bergengruen met with genuine success as a writer with *Der Grosstyrann und das Gericht* (The tyrant and the court), 1935, and *Am Himmel wie auf Erden* (In heaven as it is on earth), 1940. The former work, planned originally as a *Novelle* (novella), has been understood as a condemnation of Nazi justice, although the Nazis found the novel acceptable as a reaffirmation of their leadership ideals. In the latter book, a historical novel about the Elector Joachim von Brandenburg, Bergengruen argues that humankind must place greater faith in the wisdom of God's plan for humanity and thus accept, without fear or loathing, the fate that God ordains. Considered unfit for participation in the task of national renewal, and removed from the Reichsschrifttumskammer (Reich's Writers Guild) in 1937, Bergengruen was still able to publish throughout the 1930s and 1940s, and his works were even issued as *Feldpostausgabe* (army military editions), although *Am Himmel wie auf Erden* was banned in 1941. He also delivered pamphlets for the White Rose resistance group.

After the war, Bergengruen settled in Zurich, where he wrote *Das Feuerzeichen* (The beacon), 1949, *Der letzte Rittmeister* (The last master of horses), 1952, and *Die Rittmeisterin: Wenn man so will, ein Roman* (The mistress of horses. If you wish: a novel), 1956, a *Novelle,* and two collections of prose that solidified his reputation as a writer who still believed in a world that made sense. His popularity reached its apogee in the 1950s, but the arrival on the literary scene of Günter Grass (1927–), Heinrich Böll (1917–85), and other modern writers highlighted the innocence of his message and the archaic style of his prose. Yet despite the apparent naïvete of his works, the popularity of his writing during the war years and their aftermath serves as a reminder of his eloquence in expressing the desire of many Germans for a culture dominated by more traditional values.

James Skidmore

See also Federal Republic of Germany: Literature; National Socialist Germany: Literature

References

Banziger, Hans. *Werner Bergengruen: Weg und Werk.* DALP Taschenbücher 353. Bern: A. Francke Verlag, 1961.

Kampmann, Theoderich. *Die Welt Werner Bergengruens.* Warendorf: Verlag J. Schnellsche Buchhandlung (C. Leopold), 1952.

Peters, Eric. "Werner Bergengruen—Realist and Mystic." *German Life and Letters* 2 (1949), 179–87.

Weiss, Gerhard. "Das Haus des Schicksals als Ausgangspunkt in den Prosawerken Werner Bergengruens." *Monatshefte* 53 (1961), 291–97.

———. "Die Prosawerke Werner Bergengruens." Unpublished doctoral disseration. University of Wisconsin, 1956.

Bergius, Friedrich (1884–1949)

Friedrich Bergius shared the 1931 Nobel Prize in Chemistry with Carl Bosch (1874–1940) for pioneering work on the liquefaction of coal through the process of high-pressure hydrogenation, which supplied Germany with liquid fuel during World War II.

Born in Goldschmieden, near Breslau, as son of the director of an aluminum works, Bergius began practical study in a metalworks, then completed a dissertation on physical chemistry at Breslau University (1907). After serving as postdoctoral assistant to Walther Nernst (1864–1941) and Fritz Haber (1868–1934) (who had just developed a process for producing synthetic ammonia through heat and pressure), Bergius joined Max Bodenstein at the *Technische Hochschule* (technical university) in Hannover, where he became a *Privatdozent* (private lecturer) in 1912, and studied high-pressure chemistry and the transformation of wood to coal. By 1913 he had patented several processes, including one for converting coal to liquid hydrocarbons that could be used as lubricants or fuel for internal combustion engines.

Unable to maintain his expensive private laboratory, Bergius joined the Th. Goldschmidt corporation in Essen as research director just before the outbreak of World War I. The technical and financial problems in developing Bergius's hydrogenation process proved too great, forcing the company after the war into an international consortium. This in turn sold out to the BASF corporation, which under Bosch had successfully developed Haber's hydrogenation process to produce ammonia and now, as part of the new I.G. Farbenindustrie monopoly, employed a modified Bergius process in the first successful coal-oil hydrogenation plant accompanying its ammonia works in Leuna (1927).

Bergius meanwhile sought to produce sugars for hog fodder from wood cellulose obtainable from scrap lumber, a technology Richard Willstätter (1872–1942) had begun developing in cooperation with the Th. Goldschmidt firm during World War I. The Third Reich subsidized Bergius as a part of its autarky policy, but his process produced only moderate tonnages of fodder. Praised by Nazi propaganda for inventing "German petroleum" to break the chains of foreign monopolies, Bergius himself had no direct role in Nazi policymaking, not surprisingly for an individualist whose Weimar-era friends had included Carl Zuckmayer (1896–1977) and Thomas Mann (1875–1955). Following the war he emigrated, offered his services as advisor to several foreign countries, and died in Buenos Aires, Argentina.

Bergius exemplifies the tragedy of a scientist whose grand technological conceptions dwarfed his own means and, when finally realized largely without his participation, served inhumane ends.

Jeffrey A. Johnson

See also Bosch, Carl; Chemistry, Scientific and Industrial; Four-Year Plan; I.G. Farbenindustrie AG; Willstätter, Richard

References

Farber, Eduard. *Nobel Prizewinners in Chemistry, 1901– 1961.* Rev. ed. London: Abelard-Schuman, 1963.

Hughes, Thomas P. "Technological Momentum in History: Hydrogenation in Germany 1898–1933." *Past and Present* 44 (1969), 106–32.

Stranges, Anthony N. "Friedrich Bergius and the Rise of the German Synthetic Fuel Industry." *Isis* 75 (1984), 643–67.

Berlepsch, Hans Hermann von (1843–1926)

Trained in the study of the law at the Universities of Göttingen and Berlin, Hans Berlepsch entered the Prussian civil service at an early age and distinguished himself as an advocate of social reform, first within government and later outside it.

In the 1870s and 1880s, he rose from the position of county councilor (*Landrat*) in Kattowitz, Upper Silesia, through the presidency of the Düsseldorf district, to a position as *Oberpräsident* (governor) of the Rhine province. He acquired extensive familiarity with social problems in industrial areas, which induced him to seek compromise with organized labor. In 1889 he played a key role in negotiations with miners that terminated a major strike in the Ruhr area.

Promoted in early 1890 to the position of Prussian minister for commerce and industry, he played a major role in implementing the February Decrees of Kaiser Wilhelm II, which pointed toward a "new course" in domestic politics. Under Berlepsch's leadership, the Reichstag passed a major revision of the Industrial Code for the Empire as a whole in 1891. It forbade or restricted labor on Sundays and holidays for all workers in factories, in mines, and in commercial establishments, and it limited work by women and children on all days. It also regulated working conditions within factories. He successfully opposed attempts to pass a "revolution bill" (*Umsturzvorlage*) that would have imposed new restraints on working-class organizations, but he failed in his efforts to loosen existing ones. Opposition to his programs by defenders of entrepreneurial interests led him to resign his post in 1896.

Berlepsch sought social reform for another quarter of a century. Having assumed the editorship of the weekly magazine *Soziale Praxis* (Social practice) in 1897, he helped in 1900 to establish the International Association for the Legal Protection of Labor. In 1901, he founded the Association for Social Reform, which he headed until 1920. In line with views that he set forth in a programmatic work, *Warum treiben wir die soziale Reform?* (Why are we undertaking social reform?), 1901, he sought to mobilize a broad spectrum of political, confessional and occupational groups for the purpose of reaching an accommodation between the demands of organized labor and the existing social order. The Association's successes under the Empire were modest, but the organization enjoyed considerable significance during the early years of the Weimar Republic.

Andrew Lees

See also Factory Laws and Reform; Imperial Germany; Prussia; Social Reform; Wilhelm II; Working Conditions

References

Berlepsch, Hans Hermann Freiherr von. *Sozialpolitische Erfahrungen und Erinnerungen.* Mönchen-Gladbach: Volksvereins-verlag, 1925.

Berlepsch, Hans-Jörg von. *"Neuer Kurs" im Kaiserreich? Die Arbeiterpolitik des Freiherrn von Berlepsch 1890 bis 1896.* Bonn: Verlag Neue Gesellschaft, 1987.

Berlin

The founders of the German Empire in 1871 made Berlin its capital. Dating back to 1237, Berlin by the 1870s had all the characteristics of an emerging capital. Its population was growing, from 563,900 urban and suburban residents a decade earlier to 932,000 in 1871. It already served as Germany's political, economic, and cultural center. The "founders' boom" (*Gründerjahre*) launched in 1871 merely enhanced Berliners' self-confidence.

The capital-city function, Berlin's inextricable tie to the Empire and its successor states, tends to underplay Berlin's role as an urban center in its own right. After 1871 it gained strength: the population increased to 1.95 million in 1890. Canalization and a municipal water system of the 1870s were later followed by elevated railways ringing the city and electric street lighting. It gained autonomy: in 1881 Berlin broke from provincial Brandenburg to become a city-state. While the Imperial government was banning socialists after 1878, Berlin gained its reputation as the home of the working class in the new architecture and urban design of huge rental barracks.

After 1888 the new emperor's aggressive stance enhanced Berlin's expansion. The population grew from 2.7 million in 1900 to 3.7 million a decade later; and urban improvements, such as the Teltow canal, continued apace. Expanding firms, such as the electrical giants Siemens and General Electric (AEG), fueled its economy. In 1920 the city incorporated 59 communes and 27 landed estates into Greater Berlin, which had over 4 million people living in twenty boroughs. Wilhelm II's three-decade regime was nevertheless disastrous. Reliance on Germany's feudal elite aroused class struggles that strengthened Berlin's Social Democrats and other leftists. World War I and its deprivations led to massive strikes. The war left Berlin a hotbed of unrest, political murders, and insurrection.

The Weimar Republic found Berlin moving from political and economic disorder to a golden age of wealth and high culture. Bursts of scientific and artistic creativity in Berlin gave the world new visions. Simultaneously, a new cancer, Nazism, crept into the city. After 1926, when Joseph Goebbels (1897–1945) became the party's *Gauleiter* (regional leader) in Berlin, conflict among Nazis, Social Democrats, and Communists rocked the city. Unemployment—with 600,000 out of work among a 1932 population of 4.2 million—and poverty exacerbated social pressure.

Adolf Hitler's regime promised to heal Germany's ills and to put Berlin at the center of the world. Rearmament spawned economic prosperity; national policies brought many, but by no means all, Berliners into the fold of Nazism; and sometimes grandiose schemes, such as the 1936 Olympics and Albert Speer's architectual designs, gave the city attention.

Such gains were short-lived after Hitler's war broke out. Once the tide of battle turned in the winter of 1942–43, Berlin became the Allies' prime target. Allied bombing (especially the "blockbusters," begun in March 1943), the ever-approaching Red Army's shelling, and intense street fighting to stave off the inevitable destroyed a quarter of the city's housing units and damaged two-thirds of the remainder. Berlin became a wasteland: mounds of rubble cluttering the streets, public services broken down, surviving factories and shops without needed supplies, a third of all Berliners gone, and Soviet soldiers everywhere dismantling whatever property was left.

Worst of all, from the perspectives of Berliners, their city was under foreign occupation. The Four-Power occupation of Germany tore away Berlin's role and status as capital city. Each occupier had its own zone of Germany, supervised by the Allied Control Council in Berlin. Greater Berlin itself, located deep inside the Soviet zone, was divided into four occupation sectors under a Four-Power Kommandatura.

The principle of joint occupation policy soon broke down because of antagonistic Cold War politics. The Western powers, particularly the United States, pushed toward economic stability and a more independent Germany, even if the USSR would not agree. In March 1948 the Soviets withdrew from the Kommandatura. Three months later, after the West announced a currency reform, the USSR imposed the Berlin blockade. The West responded with a counterblockade of the Soviet zone and, to protect the 2.2 million West Berliners, inaugurated an airlift of needed supplies.

In May 1949, the USSR ended its blockade, but its impact remained: eastern and western Germany remained divided. In September 1948 Soviet pressure forced West Berlin legislators to abandon the city hall located in the Soviet sector and regroup in the western borough of Schöneberg. East Germans seized the occasion to reform the government that remained. A scramble between East and West Berlin employees developed as each group sought access to files, documents, equipment, personnel, and other necessities of

modern government. By March 1949, with great bitterness on both sides, Greater Berlin was effectively split into two different cities.

The next dozen years found Berliners learning to live with their division. Government offices, municipal services, and private bodies such as the Social Democratic Party adapted to the new status quo. Residents of both cities could maintain interpersonal contacts—although ever fewer did so. Of concern to East German officials, however, was Berlin's more or less open border, which let East Germans flee the country. In August 1961 they persuaded Soviet Chairman Nikita Khrushchev to permit the building of a wall around West Berlin to stop this flow.

The wall, besides damaging the German Democratic Republic's (GDR) image, served for a time to stabilize the East German economy, and to separate East from West Berliners still more. The West bore another cost: realization that the United States would not go to war for German interests led some Germans to rethink their priorities. This awakening, along with West German domestic issues and America's role in Vietnam, contributed in the late 1960s to a student protest movement that, although nationwide, originated and took its most virulent form in West Berlin. Some "alternative opposition" supporters later organized new kinds of political protest or turned to terrorism.

By September 1971, Chancellor Willy Brandt's (1913–92) eastern policy led to a series of Four-Power and inter-German agreements that, among other arrangements, improved the access of West Berliners to the East. The division of Germany and Berlin became "normal." The GDR's popu-

Berlin. Courtesy of German Embassy, Ottawa.

lar legitimacy nevertheless began to lag—until it collapsed in November 1989. It soon became clear that Germans, east and west, wanted the GDR to end and German unification to begin.

Agreements in 1990 between the two governments envisioned East Berlin's incorporation into West Berlin's political, economic, and judicial system. In 1991 the reunited Greater Berlin, with 3.4 million inhabitants distributed over 23 boroughs, regained its capital-city status. Greater Berlin has every prospect to regain the worldwide status it enjoyed in earlier times.

Richard Merritt

See also Architecture and Urban Design; Basic Treaty; Berlin Blockade; Berlin Secession; Berlin Wall; Bonn; Brandenburg; Brandt, Willy; Goebbels, Joseph; Hitler, Adolf; Industrialization; *Ostpolitik*; Prussia; Reuter, Ernst; Speer, Albert; Urbanization; Weizsäcker, Richard von

References

Friedrich, Otto. *Before the Deluge: A Portrait of Berlin in the 1920's.* New York, NY: Harper and Row, 1972.

Hillenbrand, Martin J., ed. *The Future of Berlin.* Montclair, NJ: Allanheld, Osmun & Co., 1980.

Merritt, Richard L. and Anna J. Merritt, eds. *Living with the Wall: West Berlin, 1961–1985.* Durham, NC: Duke University Press, 1985.

Read, Anthony and David Fisher. *Berlin: The Biography of a City.* London: Hutchinson, 1994.

Berlin Blockade (1948–49)

The German capital, which during 1945–90 was under the joint administration of the four victorious powers—France, Great Britain, the USSR and the United States—after 1945 mirrored the tensions and divergent interests of the Allies. Only in 1948 did these escalate into an open conflict. The actions in and around Berlin threatened, three years after the end of World War II, to produce a military confrontation between East and West. The conflict was decisive not only in determining the fate of the divided city but in the formation of two German states and the development and consolidation of an eastern and a western military bloc.

The blockade of the land and water approaches to Berlin began immediately upon the introduction of the currency reforms of June 20, 1948, in the western zones. The corridors for aircraft remained the only open connections between the western zones and Berlin. The official Soviet justification was "technical disturbances." The Soviet commander in chief, Marshal Sokolowski, let it be openly understood that these difficulties would continue only until plans for the establishment of a West German state were buried. Here lay the essential political motive for the blockade. What appeared to be a Soviet step toward expelling the Western powers from Berlin and the incorporation of the city into the Soviet zone was in essence a calculated political ploy to halt, at the last moment, the emerging West German state. By such means, the Soviet Union hoped to maintain the Four-Power administration and

Berlin airlift. German Embassy Ottawa.

thus to prevent its loss of influence throughout the whole of Germany.

The Western powers responded with a determined airlift, after General Clay's proposal to break the blockade by means of an armed convoy was rejected in Washington as being too risky. Americans and Britons accumulated aircraft and put them into transport service to Berlin. The operation proved to be amazingly smooth. Through air corridors from Hamburg, Hannover, and Frankfurt, aircraft landed within minutes and within short distances of each other to service the enclosed city. The daily transport capacity increased from 1,000 tons on July 7, 1948 to 13,000 tons in April of 1949. The unexpected success of this risky undertaking could not disguise the decisive impact on the lives of the population. Even before the airlift, the electricity supply could be barely maintained. The coal allotments became so meager that a major catastrophe was prevented only because of the mild winter. Industrial production in Berlin was reduced by half; the number of unemployed rose drastically.

The blockade also intensified the political division of the city. When the city legislature could no longer meet in the eastern part because of organized riots, it was transferred by its president, Otto Suhr, into the western section. On December 5, 1948, elections took place in the western sectors. The Social Democratic Party (SPD) emerged as the big winner, by gaining 64.5 percent of the vote. At its inaugural sitting, the new city legislature reaffirmed Ernst Reuter (1889–1953) as chief mayor of Free Berlin.

The blockade and the airlift quickly developed their own political dynamic. The Western Allies, West Germans, and West Berliners became allies, and, if it was the declared goal of the Soviet Union to prevent the founding of a West German state, the very opposite was achieved. On September 1, 1948, the parliamentary council began to meet in Bonn to create a constitution. Once Soviet leader Josef Stalin recognized the futility of the blockade, Soviet negotiators agreed on May 4, 1949, to lift the blockade. Thus, for the time being, the life-threatening danger for Berlin was removed. Left was a divided city with separate currencies and separate administrations and a divided land in which during the same year two governments would be constituted.

Christoph Klessmann

See also American-German Relations; Berlin; The Cold War and Germany; Federal Republic of Germany; Reuter, Ernst; Soviet-German Relations

References

Arnold-Foster, Mark. *The Siege of Berlin.* London: Collins, 1979.

Bell, Michael. "Die Blockade Berlins—Konfrontation der Alliierten in Deutschland." *Kalter Krieg und Deutsche Frage: Deutschland im Widerstreit der Mächte 1945– 1952.* Ed. Joseph Foschepoth. Göttingen: Vandenhoek & Ruprecht, 1985, 217–39.

Davison, W. Phillips. *The Berlin Blockade: A Study in Cold War Politics.* Princeton, NJ: Princeton University Press, 1958.

Morris, Eric. *Blockade: Berlin and the Cold War.* London: Hamish Hamilton, 1973.

Shlaim, Avi. *The United States and the Berlin Blockade, 1948–1949: A Study in Crisis Decision-Making.* Berkeley, CA: University of California Press, 1983.

Tusa, Ann. *The Berlin Blockade.* Sevenoaks: Coronet Books, 1989.

Berlin Secession

Critics and proponents alike viewed this modernist artists' association, founded on May 2, 1898, as the foremost venue for the exhibition and promotion of German and foreign avant-garde painting and sculpture. Its prominence was reached during the first decade of its existence, when, under the leadership of its president, the impressionist painter Max Liebermann (1848–1935), together with artists including Walter Leistikow, Lovis Corinth (1858–1925), Max Slevogt (1868–1932), Franz Skarbina, Hans Baluschek (1870–1935), Käthe Kollwitz (1867–1945), and the sculptors August Gaul and Louis Tuaillon, the organization held annual exhibitions showcasing the latest art from Germany and France.

Its selective shows usually exhibited no more than several hundred objects, in contrast to the large traditional salon exhibitions, sponsored by the Verein Berliner Künstler (association of Berlin artists), where literally thousands of artworks were on display. The Secession gallery openings became society events for the German capital, frequented by the west end's *Bildungsbürgertum* (educated middle class) viewing works of German and French impressionism, postimpressionism, expressionism, and symbolist art, together with other international modernism. The group achieved notoriety when Kaiser Wilhelm II, gave a speech in 1901 at the opening of Berlin's Avenue of Victory (Siegesallee), and condemned Secessionist art as "gutter art."

After 1910, critics on the political and anti-Semitic right assailed the organization for its "Jewish" leadership, targeting Liebermann and Paul Cassirer, the art dealer who managed the exhibitions and promoted the artists' works. Painters on the aesthetic "left," primarily the expressionists, founded rival groups, such as Neue Secession, after the Berlin Secession rejected 89 works by 27 artists in 1910, including paintings by Emil Nolde (1867–1956). Following the exit of the expres-

sionists, other rival groups formed, diminishing the organization's reputation as a venue for the newest art styles.

By the 1920s, the Berlin Secession was an integral part of the German art establishment and its exhibiting artists held important teaching posts in the major art schools. Liebermann was appointed president of the Prussian Academy of Art, a position he held until the Nazis took over the government in 1933, when he resigned. The Berlin Secession disbanded in the same year when its last president, Eugen Spiro, emigrated to the United States.

Marion Deshmukh

See also Artists; Baluschek, Hans; *Bildung und Bildungsbürgertum*; Corinth, Lovis; Expressionism; Kollwitz, Käthe; Liebermann, Max; Nolde, Emil; Prussian Art Academy; Slevogt, Max

References

Berliner Secession. Exhibition catalog. Berlin: Neuer Berliner Kunstverein, EV, n.d. [1981].

Deshmukh, Marion F. "Art and Politics in Turn-of-the-Century Berlin: The Berlin Secession and Kaiser Wilhelm II." *The Turn of the Century, German Literature and Art 1890–1915.* Ed. Gerald Chapple and Hans H. Schulte. Bonn: Bouvier Verlag. Herbert Grundmann, 1981.

Doede, Werner. *Die Berliner Secession.* Berlin: Propyläen Verlag, 1977.

Paret, Peter. "Art and the National Image: The Conflict over Germany's Participation in the St. Louis Exposition." *Central European History* (June 1978), 173–83.

———. *The Berlin Secession, Modernism and its Enemies in Imperial Germany.* Cambridge, MA: Belknap Press of Harvard University Press, 1980.

Pfefferkorn, Rudolf. *Die Berliner Secession.* Berlin: Haude & Spener, 1972.

Teeuwisse, Nicolas. *Vom Salon zur Secession Berliner Kunstleben zwischen Tradition und Aufbruch zur Moderne: 1871–1900.* Berlin: Deutscher Verlag für Kunstwissenschaft, 1986.

Berlin Wall (1961–89)

The Berlin Wall came to symbolize not only the division of Germany but also the schism of Europe into two competing systems. The first stage of this multilayered construction began overnight on August 13, 1961. The many physical layers were emblematic of the multiple significances of the Wall itself.

The Berlin Wall was conceived to eliminate West Berlin as a flashpoint between the United States and the Soviet Union and to stop the hemorrhaging of the population of the German Democratic Republic (GDR), which by 1961 had lost two and a half million people to the West. The Wall had at least three distinct, yet related impacts. On the international level, it defused the Berlin crisis, in which the Soviet Union, for a second time, challenged the uneasy four-power occupation agreement. It marked a unilateral change

New watchtower, Potsdamer Platz, Berlin, 1981. Courtesy of German Embasssy, Ottawa.

of the status quo in Berlin in violation of the European Advisory Commission agreement approved at the Yalta and Potsdam conferences; nonetheless, the evidence suggests that the Kennedy administration was not only relieved but had given what could be read as tacit consent to as yet undefined Soviet actions to stabilize the situation in the Soviet sector of Berlin.

For both German states the Wall underscored a weakening confluence of interests with their respective superpower patrons in the early 1960s. Although unhappy that the Soviet Union had failed to exact Western recognition of GDR sovereignty and independence, the East German regime did allow the Wall to stop the exodus and consolidate its power for almost three decades. The West German government began rethinking its entire strategy for overcoming Germany's division. The result was Chancellor Willy Brandt's (1913–92) *Ostpolitik*, which was premised on the new assumption that any improvement in German-German relations would have to be negotiated through Moscow with the inclusion of East Berlin.

For the people of the two German states, and particularly of Berlin, the Wall abruptly and arbitrarily separated families and friends. Its tragedy in human terms extends far beyond the hundreds who died trying to escape.

The combination of circumstances that effectively opened the Berlin Wall on November 9, 1989 marked the beginning of the end of the GDR. The hope of reform Communists and many of the grass-roots movements to create a democratic, socialist GDR was swept away with the flood of East Germans who sought their future in West Germany.

Ann L. Phillips

See also Adenauer, Konrad; American-German Relations; Brandt, Willy; The Cold War and Germany; German-Ger-

man Relations; Reunification; Soviet-German Relations

References

Gelb, Norman. *The Berlin Wall*. London: M. Joseph, 1986.
Keller, John Wendell. *Germany, the Wall and Berlin: Internal Politics during an International Crisis*. New York, NY: Vantage Press, 1964.
McAdams, A. James. "An Obituary for the Berlin Wall." *World Policy Journal* (Spring 1990).
———. *Germany Divided: From the Wall to Reunification*. Princeton, NJ: Princeton University Press, 1993.
Merritt, Richard L. and Ronald A. Francisco. *Berlin between Two Worlds*. Boulder, CO: Westview Press, 1986.
Wyden, Peter. *Wall: The Inside Story of Divided Berlin*. New York, NY: Simon and Schuster, 1989.

Bernstein, Eduard (1850–1932)

Eduard Bernstein contributed to the theoretical debates of the German Social Democratic Party (SPD) regarding Marxism after the late 1890s. His ideas have frequently influenced party policy.

The son of a Jewish locomotive engineer, Bernstein did not finish high school or attend university despite his interests and capabilities. He served as a bank clerk until 1878. In 1872 he joined the SPD and became very active, participating in the preparation of the Gotha Congress of 1875, where followers of Ferdinand Lassalle combined with those of August Bebel (1840–1913). Since party political actions and publications were forbidden under Chancellor Otto von Bismarck's antisocialist laws after 1878, Bernstein moved to Zurich and then to London, where he served as an editor of the party's main paper, *Der Sozialdemokrat*. Bernstein was in close contact with Friedrich Engels and became knowledgeable about the British labor movement, especially the intellectuals in the Fabian Society. Intimate friendship bound Bernstein to Karl Kautsky (1854–1938), with whom he shared the desire to transform the ideals of Marx and Engels into reality.

Bernstein returned to Germany in 1901. During his last years in London, he authored the most important of his many writings. He revised Marx's theories of impoverishment and questioned the necessity of revolution. Instead, he offered a better future through social reform and evolution. Bernstein's criticisms focused upon Marxist social analysis and historical determinism, which predicted the imminent collapse of capitalism and a revolutionary takeover by the proletariat. He favored the reformist practices of Social Democratic leaders and advocated a revision of the party program to align theory with practice.

Various SPD congresses, in particular the Dresden Congress of 1903, rejected Bernstein's proposals. Only in 1921, when the SPD voted for a new program that ended the dominance of the Erfurt Marxian synthesis of 1891, did Bernstein's views gain a hearing. His ideas had further influence in 1959, when the SPD accepted a non-Marxist credo; however, as in 1921, this was done without specific reference to Bernstein.

From 1902 to 1928, Bernstein served with short interruptions as a member of the Reichstag. During World War I he opposed the politics of the SPD majority. In 1917 he joined the Independent Social Democratic Party, but in 1919 he returned to the SPD. His political influence during World War I was limited, and during the Weimar Republic disappeared almost completely. Yet his significance as a theoretician and historian of the labor movement, as well as his moral values, were recognized after the Second World War and acknowledged by historians.

Susanne Miller

See also Bebel, August; Engels, Friedrich; Independent Social Democratic Party; Kautsky, Karl; Luxemburg, Rosa; Marx, Karl; Social Democratic Party, 1871–1918

References
Bernstein, Eduard. *Die Geschichte der Berliner Arbeiter-Bewegung.* 3 vols. Berlin: Dietz, 1907–10. Reprint, 1972. Bonn-Bad Godesberg: Dietz Nachfolger.
———. *Die Voraussetzung des Sozialismus und die Aufgaben der Sozialdemokratie.* Stuttgart: Dietz, 1899.
Carsten, Francis Ludwig. *Eduard Bernstein 1850–1932: Eine politische Biographie.* Munich: C.H. Beck, 1993.
Gay, Peter. *The Dilemma of Democratic Socialism: Eduard Bernstein's Challenge to Marx.* New York: Collier, 1952.
Grebing, Helga. *Der Revisionismus: Von Bernstein bis zum Prager Frühling.* Munich: C.H. Beck, 1977.
Gustafsson, Bo. *Marxismus und Revisionismus: Eduard Bernsteins Kritik des Marxismus und ihre ideengeschichtlichen Voraussetzungen.* 2 vols. Frankfurt am Main: Europäische Verlagsanstalt, 1972.
Heimann, Horst and Thomas Meyer, eds. *Bernstein und der Demokratische Sozialismus.* Berlin: Dietz, 1978.
Meyer, Thomas. *Bernsteins konstruktiver Sozialismus: Eduard Bernsteins Beitrag zur Theorie des Sozialismus.* Berlin: Dietz, 1977.
Schelz-Brandenburg, Till. *Eduard Bernstein und Karl Kautsky: Entstehung und Wandlung des sozialdemokratischen Parteimarxismus im Spiegel ihrer Korrespondenz 1879–1932.* Cologne: Böhlau, 1992.

Bernstein, Elsa (1866–1949)

More than many authors, Elsa Bernstein may be regarded as a representative of her era, because she participated in most major contemporary literary movements. She wrote naturalistic dramas (*Wir Drei* [We three], 1891; *Dämmerung* [Dawn], 1893; *Maria Arndt*, 1908), impressionist novellas (*Caprice*, 1893), neoromantic fairy tales (*Königskinder* [Royal children], 1894), a symbolistic dramatic requiem (*Mutter Maria* [Mother Maria], 1900) and neoclassical tragedies (*Nausikaa*, 1906 and *Achill*, 1910). In addition to 20 dramas, of which 8 were performed and 12 were printed, she authored numerous novellas and poems.

Bernstein was born as Elsa Porges in Vienna in 1866, the daughter of Jewish parents. After a short but successful career as an actress (1883–87), which she had to abandon because of failing eyesight, she turned to writing. Her immediate success permitted her to conduct a literary salon of great renown, initially with the writer and lawyer Max Bernstein, whom she had married in 1890. In 1942, Bernstein and her sister Gabriele were deported to the concentration camp Theresienstadt; Bernstein survived the experience and died in Hamburg in 1949.

Bernstein's dramas are noteworthy for her thorough and unconventional characterization (especially of female figures), her uninhibited language and treatment of taboo subjects, and her great attention to realistic detail. For her Greek tragedy *Themistokles* (1896), Bernstein did extensive research, learned ancient Greek, and traveled to Greece to visit the sites she described in the play. A frequent subject of her plays is the culturally sanctioned oppression of women; her female figures are often torn between adherence to social norms and desires for personal autonomy. Bernstein's insistence on a realistic portrayal of contemporary society is partly expressed in the fact that most of her autonomous heroines are forced back into conventional roles or uphold them voluntarily. The ambivalence and compromising nature of her dramatic endings has disappointed traditional and feminist critics alike.

Bernstein's greatest success was *Königskinder*, largely due to the incidental music written for the play by Engelbert Humperdinck (1845–1921; Humperdinck also rewrote the play as an opera). Stylistically, Bernstein experimented with many forms; her use of style defies analysis in terms of chronological or linear development—she worked simultaneously on her naturalistic drama *Wir Drei* and on her neoromantic fairy tale *Königskinder*; *Maria Arndt*, a return to the naturalistic style, chronologically falls between her neoclassical tragedies *Nausikaa* and *Achill.*

Although Bernstein was initially considered one of the most promising dramatic authors of her time, her popularity began to wane around 1910. Today, her name has been deleted from literary history; she is remembered, if at all, under her pseudonym Ernst Rosmer instead of her name, or as Humperdinck's librettist instead of as an author in her own right.

Susanne Kord

See also Feminist Writing; Imperial Germany: Literature; Naturalism

References
Kord, Susanne. *Ein Blick hinter die Kulissen: Deutschsprachige Dramatikerinnen im 18. und 19. Jahrhundert.* Stuttgart: Metzler, 1992.
Kriwanek, Gerhard. "Das dramatische Werk von Elsa Bernstein." Unpublished doctoral dissertation. University of Vienna, 1952.
Pierce, Nancy Jean Franklin. "Woman's Place in Turn-of-the-Century Drama: The Function of Female Figures in Selected Plays by Gerhart Hauptmann, Frank Wedekind, Ricarda Huch and Elsa Bernstein." Unpublished doctoral dissertation. University of California, Irvine, 1988.

Scholtz, Novak and Sigrid Gerda. "Images of Womanhood in the Works of German Female Dramatists 1892–1918." Unpublished doctoral dissertation. Johns Hopkins University, 1971.

Wiener, Kurt. "Die Dramen Elsa Bernsteins (Ernst Rosmers)." Unpublished doctoral dissertation. University of Vienna, 1983.

Zophoniasson-Baierl, Ulrike. *Elsa Bernstein alias Ernst Rosmer: Eine deutsche Dramatikerin im Spannungsfeld der literarischen Strömungen des Wilhelminischen Zeitalters.* Bern: Lang, 1985.

Bertram, Adolf (1859–1945)

Adolf Bertram served as bishop of Hildesheim (1906–14) and archbishop of Breslau (1914–45). Bertram's preference, as president of the German Bishops' Conference, for private bureaucratic protests rather than public declarations weakened the resistance of German Roman Catholics to Hitler's tyranny.

Bertram, the son of a Hildesheim shopkeeper, was a brilliant student who was forced by the *Kulturkampf* (which closed Catholic theological faculties in Prussia) to study for the priesthood at the University of Würzburg. There he was ordained priest in 1881 and received a doctorate in theology in 1883. In 1884, he gained a doctorate in canon law at Rome. Bertram's stammer caused his superiors to exclude him from parish ministry. He worked tirelessly in diocesan administration, attaining the important offices of cathedral canon (1894) and vicar general (1905) before becoming bishop of Hildesheim in 1906. He proved a late bloomer, traveling throughout his large "diaspora" diocese (where Catholics were a minority), reinvigorating clergy and laity alike.

In October 1914, to his surprise, Bertram was named archbishop of Breslau, with three-and-a-half million Catholics (many of them Polish-speaking)—then the most populous diocese in the Catholic world. A cardinal's hat followed in 1919. Bitter postwar quarrels over the removal of large portions of his diocese to Polish jurisdiction brought charges, both in Breslau and Rome, that Bertram lacked zeal in defending church rights.

This characteristic proved fateful during the Nazi period. As president, after 1920, of the Fulda Bishops' Conference (enlarged in 1933 by the accession of the Bavarian bishops), Bertram was a skilled chairman. From 1933, however, he responded to Nazi persecution of the Church with an avalanche of meticulously formulated private protests, which the authorities either rejected or ignored. Though not lacking in courage, Bertram held tenaciously to the conviction (born of his *Kulturkampf* experience) that open opposition to rulers who were devoid of moral scruples would be counterproductive. Only rarely did Bertram heed the pleas of prelates, such as Konrad von Preysing (1880–1950) of Berlin, for public protests.

In 1942 Bertram, then 83, resigned the conference presidency. The bishops' inability to agree on a replacement forced him to soldier on. He died on July 6, 1945.

John Jay Hughes

See also Catholicism, Political; Holocaust; *Kulturkampf*; National Socialist Germany; Preysing, Konrad von; Roman Catholic Church

References

Albrecht, Dieter, ed. *Katholische Kirche im 3. Reich.* Mainz: Grünewald, 1976.

Böckenförde, Ernst-Wolfgang. "German Catholicism in 1933." *Cross Currents* XI (Summer 1961), 283–304.

Buscher, F.M. and M. Phayer. "German Catholic Bishops and the Holocaust, 1940–1952." *German Studies Review* 11 (October 1988), 463–85.

Conway, John C. *The Nazi Persecution of the Churches.* London: Weidenfeld and Nicolson, 1968.

Conzemius, V. "Pius XII and Nazi Germany." *Historical Studies.* Ed. J.C. Beckett. London: Routledge and Kegan Paul, 1969.

Helmreich, E.C. *The German Churches under Hitler.* Detroit, MI: Wayne State University Press, 1978.

Lewy, Guenter. *The Catholic Church and Nazi Germany.* New York, NY: McGraw-Hill, 1964.

Ruhm von Oppen, Beate. "Revisionism and Counter-Revisionism in the Historiography of the German Church Struggle." *The German Church Struggle and the Holocaust.* Ed. F.H. Littell and H.G. Locke. Detroit, MI: Wayne State University Press, 1974.

Bestsellers, Contemporary

In Germany, the existence of bestsellers can be traced to the middle of the nineteenth century, when widespread literacy, new technologies in the printing industry, and cheaper paper favored the growth of the literary market and the expansion of the reading public. However, the term "bestseller" was introduced in West Germany during the 1950s in order to characterize books that sold extremely well during their first months after publication. Nowadays, the word is reserved for books that have sold at least 100,000 first-edition copies. This number does not include the sale of a pocket-book edition of the same title or the copies sold by book clubs.

The typical sales pattern of the bestseller is characterized by the fact that high sales do not decline after the first few months but increase continuously in irregular intervals. In other words, the sale of the book is multiplied during the process of its reception. Indisputably, bestsellers are in economic terms more important than ever before for the leading publishing companies in Germany. These companies' advertising budget has increased during the last decade to 15 percent of total income, and this budget is more or less reserved for the promotion of very few books that are being "pushed" to become bestsellers on the German market. Since the 1970s, production of bestsellers has become a fundamental commercial necessity for all big publishing houses. In 1972, 25 percent of the total turnover of the Langen-Müller-Herbig publishing house resulted from the sale of only one book, by Ephraim Kishon, which succeeded as a bestseller.

As a market phenomenon, the bestseller tends to cross the boundaries of national cultures and markets. A large number of books that succeed as bestsellers on the German book market are written by authors from abroad, particularly by those who have already succeeded on the Anglo-American book market. Authors such as Frederick Forsythe, Harold Robbins, Erica Jong, or Umberto Eco are better known to the German reading public than the vast majority of German authors, though quite a few German authors' books have become bestsellers on the German book market during the last decades.

At present, Johannes Mario Simmel is Germany's most successful author. Simmel's books are said to have sold more than 15 million copies worldwide. Novelists such as Heinz Konsalik or Uta Danella, who are almost equally successful as Simmel on the German market, share the image problem of many bestseller authors in Germany: they are widely read, but they have gained no literary reputation. Nevertheless, several German authors with extraordinarily high literary reputations have succeeded with bestsellers on the German market and abroad: Günter Grass (1927–), Heinrich Böll (1917–1985), Peter Handke (1942–), and Patrick Süskind (1949–) are prominent examples.

In the nonfiction realm, bestsellers are significantly more dependent on topicality than in the literary genre. However, various nonfiction bestsellers of German origin have succeeded as "steadysellers" on the German market: Joachim Fest's *Hitler* biography (first published in 1976) or *Wallenstein,* the biography written by Golo Mann (first published in 1979).

Bernhard Zimmermann

See also Böll, Heinrich; Books; Grass, Günter; Handke, Peter; Ludwig, Emil; Publishing and the Book Trade; Remarque, Erich Maria

References
Arnold, Heinz Ludwig, ed. *Deutsche Bestseller—deutsche Ideologie.* Stuttgart: Klett Verlag, 1975.

Faulstich, Werner. *Bestandsaufnahme Bestseller-Forschung.* Wiesbaden: Harrassowitz Verlag, 1983.

Hohendahl, Peter Uwe. "Promoters, Consumers, and Critics: On the Reception of the Best-Seller." *The Institution of Criticism.* Ed. P.U. Hohendahl. Ithaca, NY: Cornell University Press, 1982.

Richards, Donald Ray. *The German Bestseller in the 20th Century.* Bern: Lang Verlag, 1968.

Zimmermann, Bernhard. "Das Bestseller-Phänomen im Literaturbetrieb der Gegenwart." *Neues Handbuch der Literaturwissenschaft.* Vol. 22. Ed. Jost Hermand. Wiesbaden: Athenaion Verlag, 1979.

Bethe, Hans (1906–)

Hans Bethe, who ranks as one of the most eminent and erudite theoretical physicists, received the Nobel Prize (1967) for "contributions in the theory of nuclear reaction, especially his discoveries concerning the energy production of stars."

Bethe was born in Strassburg as the son of the distinguished physiologist A.T. Bethe; he grew up in Kiel and later in Frankfurt am Main, where he passed his *Abitur* (senior matriculation) in 1924 and concentrated on physics at the University of Frankfurt. He subsequently (1926) studied with Arnold Sommerfeld (1868–1951) at the University of Munich, where he received his Ph.D. in 1928; two years later he earned the title *Privatdozent* (private lecturer). During the next years he taught at the universities of Munich, Frankfurt, Stuttgart, and Tübingen; with a grant from the Rockefeller Foundation he moved to Rome. In 1933 he emigrated to Manchester, England, and in 1934 he was engaged by Cornell University (Ithaca, New York) where he taught physics.

During World War II, Bethe joined the Manhattan Project as director of the Theoretical Physics Division in Los Alamos. After the war, he publicly warned about the danger of nuclear warfare. During the 1950s and 1960s he was a leading member of the President's Science Advisory Committee and was engaged in general aspects of the scientific and political problems of energy.

Bethe made important contributions to the quantum-mechanical explanation of the behavior of electrons and other particles in crystals, as well as to the theory of metals and solid state-physics in general. In the 1930s, he explained how stars like the sun produce energy by nuclear fusion (Bethe-Weizsäcker cycle). The Manhattan Project focused his interest on nuclear physics in a very general way.

Dieter Hoffmann

See also Physics; Sommerfeld, Arnold

References
Bernstein, J. *Hans Bethe: Prophet of Energy.* New York, NY: Basic Books, 1980.

Bethe, Hans. *Elementary Nuclear Theory.* New York, NY: Wiley, 1956.

Bethe, Hans Albrecht and Edwin E. Salpeter. *Quantum Mechanics of One- and Two-Electron Atoms.* Berlin: Academic Press, 1957.

Marshak, Robert Eugene, ed. *Perspectives in Modern Physics: Essays in Honor of Hans A. Bethe on the Occasion of his 60th Birthday, July, 1966.* New York, NY: Interscience Publishers, 1966.

Bethmann Hollweg, Theobald von (1856–1921)

Born in Hohenfinow, Brandenburg, to a successful commercial and agrarian family, Theobald von Bethmann Hollweg was trained as a lawyer. He rose to the top of Prussia's civil service, becoming Prussian interior minister in 1905 and imperial secretary of state for the interior in 1907. In 1909 he succeeded Bernhard von Bülow as chancellor, a post he held until 1917.

A relatively open-minded Free Conservative, he was confronted with a need for reform at home and a way out of Germany's growing isolation abroad. In 1911 he introduced a comprehensive social-insurance law and a more liberal constitution for Alsace-Lorraine. Much of the good will gained by the latter reform was destroyed by his mishandling of an incident in 1913 caused by military mistreatment of civilians in the town of Zabern. He was never able to achieve his goal of reforming Prussia's unequal three-class electoral system.

In foreign affairs, his main concern was that Germany's bellicose behavior and development of a blue-water navy that could challenge Great Britain's was isolating Germany. The willingness of Kaiser Wilhelm II and the military to use that navy to rattle the German sword was demonstrated in 1911, when the gunboat *Panther* was dispatched to Morocco's port of Agadir. This crisis persuaded Bethmann Hollweg that an accommodation with Great Britain was essential. However, naval negotiations with London collapsed in 1912 because of Admiral Tirpitz's insistence, supported by the Kaiser, that Great Britain promise to remain neutral in any war involving Germany. Bethmann Hollweg was exasperated with the impatient German nationalism propagated by such groups as the Pan-German League and Naval League. He declared: "Politics cannot be made with these idiots!"

Bethmann Hollweg enjoyed the company and advice of Kurt Riezler (1882–1955), an eminent scholar of classical Greek philosophy. At age 25, Riezler had attracted the attention of the Kaiser, for whom he wrote speeches. Bethmann Hollweg made him his closest political advisor and confidant. Riezler kept a diary, which became a key historical source in examining Germany's policy at the time of the outbreak of World War I and its aims during the war. Both men shared the shock and indignation of all of Europe when the Austro-Hungarian Archduke Franz Ferdinand was assassinated in June 1914. On July 5 and 6, 1914, Bethmann Hollweg approved of Germany's granting Austria-Hungary a "blank check" to deal with the matter. Only in the final days of the crisis did he desperately try to regain control of events, which had slipped out of everyone's control. With Russia, Germany, and France mobilizing, a European war had become unavoidable. When Germany violated Belgian territory prior to invading France, Great Britain also entered the war. In a serious public-relations blunder, Bethmann Hollweg told London's ambassador that Great Britain's longstanding guarantee of Belgian neutrality was a mere "scrap of paper."

Riezler's diary offers the closest and most immediate account of the German leaders' thinking. It reveals that from the beginning, not merely at the end of the July crisis, German leaders recognized the possibility that a local war in the Balkans could expand into a European or world war. Bethmann Hollweg was willing to risk that eventuality, although he hoped that the Austro-Serbian conflict could be localized and that the Entente could be weakened or split by a humiliation of Serbia. Bethmann Hollweg neither deliberately led Germany into war nor saw the assassination at Sarajevo as a cue to rush into a long-prepared war to establish German hegemony in Europe or clear a path for German territorial annexation, as some critics later charged. Nor was he guided by notions of a preventive war against Russia, even though he was convinced that Russia's westward expansion was imminent. There is no evidence in the diary that "monopoly capitalists," industrialists, or any economic motives played a significant role in decisions made in Berlin during July. Direct pressure from nationalist groups, newspaper edi-

Theobald von Bethmann Hollweg. Courtesy of German Information Center, New York.

tors, or parliamentary leaders had little or no influence on the chancellor's decisions.

With peace no longer possible, Bethmann Hollweg set about to achieve a German victory. On September 9, 1914, Riezler wrote the famous "September Program," which combined elements of all the various demands from military, governmental, journalistic, and business circles concerning war aims in France, Belgium, Luxembourg, the Netherlands, Central Africa, and, most importantly, *Mitteleuropa* (a middle European economic union under German hegemony). The document was discovered in the 1960s by Hamburg historian Fritz Fischer, who saw in it clear proof of his theory that Bethmann Hollweg, who initialed the draft, and other German leaders had war aims for which Germany had unleashed the war. The "Fischer controversy" raged for years in Germany, as his supporters staunchly defended his position that Germany had been chiefly responsible for the outbreak of the war. Other documents discovered subsequently, as well as Riezler's diaries (published in 1973), revealed weaknesses in Fischer's thesis. The September Program, which had been marked "provisional," had not been written in the expectation of a rapid victory and contained maximum demands in the event that Germany had suddenly to enter negotiations. Fischer made no effort to determine the government's "fallback position," what negotiators would have actually hoped or expected to achieve in talks.

In 1916, Bethmann Hollweg unsuccessfully sought American mediation to end the conflict. He opposed unrestricted German submarine warfare because of the risk of bringing the United States into the war. Civilian leaders never had full control over the military leadership in the German Empire, and he was overruled on this question in 1917, as he was whenever he tried to ameliorate Germany's exploitative occupation policies in conquered countries. An exasperated Riezler wrote at the time: "Never was a *Volk* more capable of conquering the world and more incapable of ruling it!" Confronted by opposition from both the Reichstag and from generals Hindenburg and Ludendorff, Bethmann Hollweg was forced to resign in 1917. He retired to his estate in Hohenfinow to write his memoirs.

Riezler returned to the Foreign Ministry to coordinate Germany's wartime revolutionary policy. He helped to put Lenin into power in Russia, where he guided the German mission in 1918. A member of the German Democratic Party, he supported the Weimar Coalition after the war, but he resigned from public life to protest the severity of the Treaty of Versailles. He became president of the University of Frankfurt, but his scorn toward the Nazis led to his dismissal. He was married to the daughter of the Jewish painter Max Liebermann (1848–1935), and accepted a chair at the New School for Social Research in New York, where he taught philosophy until his retirement in 1952.

Wayne C. Thompson

See also Alsace-Lorraine; American-German Relations; Anglo-German Relations; Austro-German Relations; Belgian-German Relations; Chancellor's Office; The Fischer Controversy; Hindenburg, Paul von; Imperial Germany; Ludendorff, Erich; Naval League; Navy and Naval Policy; Pan-German League; Parliamentary System; Parties and Politics; Rathenau, Walther; Social Democratic Party, 1871–1918; Tirpitz, Alfred von; Wilhelm II; World War I; Zabern

References

Bethmann Hollweg, Theobald von. *Betrachtungen zum Weltkrieg*. 2 vols. Berlin: Reimar Hobbing, 1919 and 1921. London: T. Butterworth, 1920–21. (The first volume was translated in 1920 as *Reflections on the World War*).

Erdmann, Karl Dietrich, ed. *Kurt Riezler, Tagebücher, Aufsätze, Dokumente*. Göttingen: Vandenhoeck & Ruprecht, 1972.

Fischer, Fritz. *Griff nach der Weltmacht: Die Kriegszielpolitik des kaiserlichen Deutschland 1914–1918*. 4th ed. Düsseldorf: Droste, 1971. New York, NY: W.W. Norton. (An earlier edition was translated in 1967 as *Germany's Aims in the First World War*).

Jarausch, Konrad H. *The Enigmatic Chancellor: Bethmann Hollweg and the Hubris of Imperial Germany*. New Haven, CT: Yale University Press, 1973.

Riezler, Kurt (under pseudonym J.J. Ruedorffer). *Grundzüge der Weltpolitik in der Gegenwart*. Stuttgart: Deutsche Verlags-Anstalt, 1914.

Thompson, Wayne C. *In the Eye of the Storm: Kurt Riezler and the Crises of Modern Germany*. Iowa City, IA: University of Iowa Press, 1980.

Beuys, Joseph (1921–86)

Sculptor, draftsperson, conceptualist, performance artist, environmentalist, political activist, and teacher, Joseph Beuys was among the most influential artists of post–World War II Germany. He was responsible for expanding the concept of art to include all creative activity and for cultivating the idea of the artist as a modern shaman. Beuys's diverse output is linked by the repeated use of the wound as a metaphor for the divisions in society between spirit and matter, intellect and intuition, man and nature, and east and west, as well as the implied references to the healing of that wound.

Born in Krefeld, Beuys grew up in the nearby town of Cleves, where the marshy, waterlogged terrain sparked his lifelong passion for nature and wildlife. After running away as an adolescent to join a traveling circus—an experience that Beuys later drew on in his performance art—he was drafted into the *Luftwaffe* (air force) at the age of 19 and trained as a combat pilot. According to his account of his life, the veracity of which has been questioned by some scholars, he was then shot down over the Crimea during the winter of 1943 and badly wounded in the crash. Tartar nomads found and rejuvenated him by covering his body in fat to regenerate warmth and by wrapping him in felt to insulate him. Being saved from a modern technological holocaust by the "primitive" methods of these tribal nomads gave Beuys his preoccupation with regeneration and healing as well as substance for some of his materials.

After studying with Josef Enseling and Ewald Matare at the Düsseldorf Academy of Art from 1947 to 1951, Beuys began to work with heavy gray felt, animal fat, sleds, and certain technological items that had the look of the war years, such as old batteries and transmitting devices. Other characteristic materials came to include honey and wax, which symbolize (through association with bees) communities in which individuals accommodate their own needs to the needs of the whole. Together with hares, stags, bees, and horses, these emblems of healing and of collectivism appear in installations such as *The Pack,* 1969, and *Honey Pump at the Workplace,* 1977; in performances such as *The Chief—Fluxus Chant,* 1964, and *How to Explain Pictures to a Dead Hare,* 1965; and in drawings. Highly critical of the dollar-backed Economic Miracle of the 1950s and 1960s, Beuys intended these materials at least in part as an antidote to what he believed was a rapacious, materialistic German society.

Beuys regarded his political activism as inseparable from art. As all creative activity, it was, in his view, "social sculpture." In 1967, he founded the German Students' Party (Deutsche Studentenpartei), the first of the organizations with which he sought to counter the domination of West German democracy by the political parties. This was followed in rapid succession by the Organization of Non-Voters and Free Plebiscite (Organisation der Nichtwähler, Freie Volksabstimmung) in 1970, the Organization for Direct Democracy by Plebiscite (Organisation für direkte Demokratie durch Volksabstimmung) in 1971, and the Free International University for Creativity and Interdisciplinary Research (Freie Internationale Hochschule für Kreativität und interdisziplinäre Forschung) in 1973. In 1976, Beuys ran for a seat in the West German Parliament as a nonparty candidate, and again in the elections for the European Parliament in 1979 as the candidate of the ecology party, the Greens. Although the Greens ultimately distanced themselves from him, Beuys supported an ecological platform throughout his career. *7,000 Oaks*, for example, was one of Beuys's "social sculptures" that began at the 1982 art exhibition *documenta 7* in Kassel. By its conclusion at *documenta 8* in 1987, 7,000 oak trees had been purchased by donors and planted throughout the urban area of Kassel.

The legacies of Beuys are many and diverse, but among the most important is his message that art *is* life, and that artists must therefore immerse themselves in all of life's social, political, environmental, and economic aspects.

Maria Makela

See also Artists; Painting; Sculpture

References

Adriani, Götz, Winfried Konnertz, and Karin Thomas. *Joseph Beuys: Life and Works.* Trans. Patricia Lech. Woodbury, NY: Barron's Educational Series, 1979.

Kunstsammlung Nordrhein-Westfalen, Düsseldorf. *Josef Beuys: Natur, Materie, Form: 30 November 1991–9 February 1992.* Munich: Schirmer and Mosel, 1991.

Philadelphia Museum of Art. *Thinking Is Form: The Drawings of Joseph Beuys: 10 October 1993–2 January 1994.* Philadelphia: Philadelphia Museum of Art; New York, NY: The Museum of Modern Art, 1993.

Schellmann, Jörg. *Joseph Beuys: Die Multiples: Werkverzeichnis der Auflagenobjekte und Druckgraphik.* Munich: Edition Schellmann, 1992.

Stachelhaus, Heiner. *Joseph Beuys.* New York, NY: Abbeville Press, 1991.

Tisdall, Caroline. *Joseph Beuys.* New York, NY: The Solomon R. Guggenheim Foundation, 1979.

Biblical Criticism

Since its inception in the early part of the nineteenth century, German biblical criticism has come to dominate biblical scholarship. German criticism has been largely influenced by historical and philological matters concerning the dating, integrity, and authenticity of the various biblical texts. A plurality of historical-critical methods, such as "source criticism" (*Literarkritik*), "form criticism" (*Formsgeschichte*), and "redaction criticism" (*Redaktionsgeschichte*), have developed and become an integral part of the larger biblical scene.

Historical criticism of the Bible in Germany came of age in the context of earlier nineteenth-century German historiography. Two scholars in particular, Julius Wellhausen (1844–1918) and H.J. Holtzmann (1832–1910), consolidated the insights of previous historiography and incorporated them into their own source-critical analyses. In the monumental *Prolegomena zur Geschichte Israels* (Prolegomena to the history of Israel), 1878, Wellhausen develops the history of Israel based on the identification and dating of four literary strands of the Pentateuch (J, E, D, P), incorporated earlier by W.M.L. de Wette (1740–1849), Eduard Reuss (1804–91), and K.H. Graf (1815–69). In the New Testament, Holtzmann's *Die synoptischen Evangelien* (The synoptic gospel), 1863, presupposed some of the earlier work of the Tübingen school of F.C. Baur (1792–60) and D.F Strauss (1808–74) and synthesized the insights of C.G. Wilke (1786–1854) and C.H. Weisse (1801–66) to establish a "two-source hypothesis," in which Matthew and Luke are said to have used Mark and an anonymous collection of Jesus's sayings (later called "Q") as the major sources of their gospels.

By the beginning of twentieth century, however, interest in Germany shifted from studying the sources of the tradition as factual historical information (however confused or disordered that information may be in the text) to a comparison of other religions in the ancient world, and to uncovering the oral history of the traditions. Archaeological discoveries and the deciphering of religious texts in the Orient, the Near East, and the Greco-Roman world prompted a group of scholars of the *religionsgeschichtliche Schule* (school of history of religion) such as J. Weiss (1863–1914), W. Bousset (1865–1920), W. Wrede (1859–1906), and H. Gunkel (1862–1932) to study the Bible as a product of its religio-historical environment. Further, the text came to be seen as more the product of a community through which it had been orally transmitted rather than as the literary product of a gifted individual. Gunkel uncovered various biblical "genres" (*Gattungen*) of oral transmission that reflected the religious needs of the people or their cultic interests (*Formsgeschichte*). The process by which this material came to be written down Gunkel viewed as the key to understanding the life situation of the community (*Sitz im Leben*).

The emphasis on the *Sitz im Leben* engendered further developments in the critical study of the Bible after World War I. The literary history of the historical traditions replaced specific events or institutions as a focus of study. In the Old Testament, Albrecht Alt (1883–1956) and two of his students, Gerhard von Rad (1901–71) and Martin Noth (1902–68), studied the history of the traditions (*Überlieferungsgeschichte*), with the intention of discerning how the Israelite community may have perceived its destiny as a result of a series of purposive saving acts of its God (*Heilsgeschichte*). In the New Testament, Rudolf Bultmann (1884–1976), drawing on the theologically preoccupied exegesis of Karl Barth (1886–1968), combined the form criticism of Gunkel with the modern existentialist philosophical movements of his friend Martin Heidegger (1889–1976). The result was an "existentialist theology," which viewed the gospel writers as collectors of small units of tradition that helped them to understand their own existence rather than to depict objective reality. They stressed "proclamation" (*kerygma*) of the gospel message rather than its purported historical accuracy, and the "mythological" language of the New Testament was to be translated into the discourse of human existence by "demythologizing" (*Entmythologisierung*).

Bultmann's synthesis of existentialist theology and the history of traditions school held sway in Germany until the end of the Second World War and elsewhere until the 1960s. In its stead a method known as "redaction criticism" (*Redaktionsgeschichte*), developed by three New Testament critics (W. Marxsen [1919–] on Mark, H. Conzelmann [1915–] on Luke, and G. Bornkamm [1905–] on Matthew) arose, and was applied to Genesis by Claus Westermann (1909–) and to the Pentateuch by Rolf Rendtorff (1925–). Based on the findings of source and form criticism, redaction criticism is concerned with the theological motivation of the author/community responsible for the editing of the final work. This historical-critical method still dominates the Biblical scene in Germany, whereas other approaches, such as sociological and "new-literary" ones, which the Anglo-American world has adopted, have not had any serious impact.

Kim Ian Parker

See also Barth, Karl; Bultmann, Rudolf; Heidegger, Martin; Protestant Theology; Roman Catholic Church; Strauss, David Friedrich

References

Clements, R.E. *A Century of Old Testament Study.* Guildford and London: Lutterworth Press, 1976.

Grant, R.M. and David Tracy. *A Short History of the Interpretation of the Bible.* 2nd revised ed. Philadelphia, PA: Fortress Press, 1984.

Kümmel, W.G. *The New Testament: The History of the Investigation of Its Problems.* Nashville, TN: Abingdon Press, 1972.

Morgan, Robert and John Barton. *Biblical Interpretation.* Oxford: Oxford University Press, 1989.

Neil, S. and T. Wright. *The Interpretation of the New Testament: 1861–1986.* 2nd ed. Oxford: Oxford University Press, 1988.

Rogerson, W. *Old Testament Criticism in the Nineteenth Century: England and Germany.* Philadelphia, PA: Fortress Press, 1984.

Soulen, R.N. *Handbook of Biblical Criticism.* Atlanta, GA: John Knox Press, 1981.

Bieberach, Ludwig (1886–1982)

The leading proponent of "Aryan mathematics," Bieberbach studied at the University of Heidelberg from 1905 to 1906, and thereafter in Göttingen, where in 1910 he took his doctorate under Felix Klein (1849–1925). After spending three years as a *Privatdozent* (private lecturer) at Zürich and Königsberg, Bieberbach was appointed to a full professorship in Basel in 1913. He then took a position in Frankfurt am Main, where he taught from 1915 to 1921 before assuming a chair in Berlin.

Because the University of Frankfurt had been founded with private donations from wealthy Frankfurt citizens, many of whom were Jewish, it was widely regarded as a haven for Jewish scholars. Although aware of this, during his years there Bieberbach apparently manifested no overt signs of anti-Semitism. In Berlin, he read and was deeply influenced by Pierre Boutroux's *L'ideal scientifique des mathématiciens dans l'antiquité et dans les temps modernes,* 1920, which proposed that mathematical thought reflects two diametrically opposed orientations. In preparation for the German translation (1927), Bieberbach delivered a lecture in 1926 in which he identified Boutroux's two *Wissenschaftsideale* (scientific ideals) with David Hilbert's (1862–1943) formalist ideas, on the one hand, and Klein's intuitive, *anschauliche* (graphic) approach, on the other. Like Boutroux, Bieberbach stressed the vitality of the latter approach, and argued further that the dominant formalist orientation posed a dire threat to the discipline.

This lecture served as the prelude to an open conflict between the Göttingen mathematician Hilbert and Bieberbach. Already in 1925, Italian mathematicians had begun making preparations for the International Congress of Mathematicians to be held in Bologna in 1928. As the first postwar congress to which German mathematicians were invited, the event promised to mark a breakthrough in international scientific relations. Bieberbach, however, supported the plans of L.E.J. Brouwer (1881–1966), who sought to organize a German boycott to undercut other schools of thought of the Bologna Congress. As secretary of the *Deutsche Mathematiker-Vereinigung* (DMV; Association of German Mathematicians), Bieberbach circulated a letter that discouraged attendance. Hilbert then responded by denouncing Bieberbach's position, which he described in private as a form of "political blackmail of the worst kind." The boycott effort failed, and when Hilbert led the German delegation into the Congress hall they were greeted by thunderous applause.

Although late to jump on the Nazi bandwagon, after 1933 Bieberbach swiftly moved to politicize the German mathematical community. By then, many of his powerful enemies in Göttingen had been forced to scatter following implementation of the new Aryan laws for "purifying" the civil service. Some of Göttingen's leading figures were placed on "vacation," whereas others simply left "voluntarily." One of the few who stayed, the Jewish mathematician Edmund Landau (1877–1938), found Sturmabteilung (SA) guards posted at the doorway of his lecture hall and one lone student inside. Landau drew the logical conclusion and applied for early retirement.

In the wake of these events, Bieberbach delivered a widely publicized speech that scandalized the international mathematical community. Drawing on the same kinds of stereotypes he had borrowed from Boutroux, he elaborated these ideas into a blatantly racist characterization of mathematical creativity. Landau served as his prime example of the "Jewish S-type," and Bieberbach praised the German students who boycotted his classes for their healthy aversion to this "degenerate" mathematical style.

In September 1934, Bieberbach sought to invoke the *Führerprinzip* (leadership principle) and thereby gain control of the DMV. At the annual meeting held in Bad Pyrmont, he nominated the second-rate Nazi mathematician Erhard Tornier for the post of führer of the DMV. After this coup attempt failed, Bieberbach tried to intimidate his rivals by exploiting his connections in the ministry. When they refused to back down, he resigned from the executive committee of the DMV. One year later, he founded the journal *Deutsche Mathematik* (1936–42) in an effort to publicize Aryan mathematics. It attracted little serious interest among leading German mathematicians.

Bieberbach served as dean of the faculty at Berlin during the war. Immediately afterward, he was forced to resign his position at the university. Although largely ostracized from the mathematical community, he continued to publish books and articles until his death.

David E. Rowe

See also Anti-Semitism; Hilbert, David; Klein, Felix; Landau, Edmund; Mathematics; Science and National Socialism

References

Biermann, Kurt-R. *Die Mathematik und ihre Dozenten an der Berliner Universität, 1810–1933.* Berlin: Akademie-Verlag, 1988.

Mehrtens, Herbert. "Ludwig Bieberbach and 'Deutsche Mathematik.'" *Studies in the History of Mathematics.* MAA Studies in Mathematics, vol. 26. Ed. Esther R. Phillips. Washington, DC: Mathematical Association of America, 1987.

———. *Moderne Sprache Mathematik: eine Geschichte des Streits um die Grundlagen der Disziplin und des Subjekts.* Frankfurt am Main: Suhrkamp, 1990.

Rowe, David E. "'Jewish Mathematics' at Göttingen in the Era of Felix Klein." *Isis* (1986) 422–49.

Schappacher, Norbert. "Das Mathematische Institut der Universität Göttingen 1929–1950." *Die Universität Göttingen unter dem Nationalsozialismus.* Ed. Heinrich Becker, Hans-Joachim Dahms, and Cornelia Wegeler. Munich: K.G. Saur, 1987.

———. "Fachverband—Institut—Staat." *Ein Jahrhundert Mathematik, 1890–1990: Festschrift zum Jubiläum der DMV.* Ed. Gerd Fischer et al. Braunschweig: Vieweg, 1990.

Biedenkopf, Kurt (1930–)

Minister-president of Saxony (Sachsen) since 1990, Kurt Biedenkopf has been on the left wing of the Christian Democratic Union (CDU). Biedenkopf sees democracy in Germany as dependent on political parties, which must continually renew and reinvigorate their credibility with the electorate. Biedenkopf has criticized the political establishment (as well as his own party) for failing to meet this challenge.

Born on January 28, 1930, in Ludwigshafen am Rhein, he attended the *Realgymnasium* in Merseburg and then in Gross-Umstadt after 1945. Biedenkopf's academic life began at Davidson College (Davidson, North Carolina), where he studied political science from 1949 to 1950. Afterward, he studied law and economics in Munich and Frankfurt am Main. In 1958 he received his doctorate in law.

Between 1958 and 1962, Biedenkopf attended Georgetown University (Washington, D.C.) and completed his master of law degree. He began his teaching career at Frankfurt am Main and Tübingen in 1963. After settling at Bochum in

1964, Biedenkopf became head of the law school (1966–67) and then rector of the university (1967–69). Concurrently, Biedenkopf made his first forays into politics through the federal government's Management Commission from 1968 to 1970. Leaving academic life in 1971, Biedenkopf became head manager of the Henkel firm in Düsseldorf.

Biedenkopf's political career originated in June 1973. A member of the CDU since 1965, Biedenkopf was chosen as the new general secretary (1973–77). A member of the Bundestag, (1976–80 and 1987–90), Biedenkopf also played a leading role on the CDU's executive council (1977–83), served as the CDU's chair in Westphalia-Lippe (1977–86) and in North Rhine–Westphalia (1986–87), and served as chair of the CDU's Economic Committee (1979–80).

With the fall of the Berlin Wall in 1989, Biedenkopf returned to academic life in Leipzig. The lure of politics, however, proved too strong. In 1990, he led the CDU through Saxony's first free elections since 1932. With the CDU taking 54 percent of the vote, Biedenkopf became Saxony's minister-president. Since 1990, Biedenkopf has given first priority to creating a market economy in Saxony and overcoming the east-west cultural division. In 1994, his government was reelected with an increased majority, receiving 58 percent of the popular vote.

David A. Meier

See also Christian Democratic Union; Kohl, Helmut; Reunification; Saxony

References

Biedenkopf, Kurt H. *Die neue Sicht der Dinge: Plädoyer für eine freiheitliche Wirtschafts- und Sozialordnung.* Munich: Piper, 1985.

———. *Fortschritt in Freiheit: Umrisse einer politischen Strategie.* Munich: Piper, 1974.

———. *Zeitsignale: Parteienlandschaft im Umbruch.* Munich: Bertelsmann, 1989.

Brandon, Henry, ed. *In Search of a New World Order.* Washington, DC: Brookings Institute, 1992.

Calleo, David P. and Claudia Morgenstern, eds. *Recasting Europe's Economies.* Lanham, MD: University Press of America, 1990.

Miegel, Meinhard, ed. *Sentenzen am Wege: Kurt Biedenkopf zum Sechzigsten.* Stuttgart: Bonn Aktuell, 1990.

Biermann, Wolf (1936–)

Wolf Biermann is important both in his own right as a lyric poet and songwriter/performer—and as a symbol for the way in which the German Democratic Republic (GDR) dealt with writers and artists who attracted its disapproval. The withdrawal of his GDR citizenship in 1976 marked the beginning of a wave of departures to the west.

Biermann was born in 1936 in Hamburg to a family that suffered from the Nazi persecution of Jews and Communists; his father died in Auschwitz in 1943. In 1956, at the age of 20, Biermann moved to the GDR, where as a student he began to write poems and songs. Although a committed Communist, he

*Wolf Biermann.
Courtesy of Inter
Nationes, Bonn.*

had repeated conflicts with the authorities because of his critical approach. After participation in the *Lyrikabend* (evening of lyrics) at the Akademie der Künste (academy of the arts) in December 1962, he was forbidden to perform publicly and his candidacy for the Socialist Unity Party (SED) was rejected. In 1963 he was again permitted to perform, and in 1964 and 1965 he was allowed to give concerts in West Germany. His first collection of songs and poems, *Die Drahtharfe* (The wire harp), was published in West Berlin in 1965.

As a consequence of the publicity in West Germany, Biermann was again banned from performing in the GDR, this time until 1976. During this period he extended his reputation within the GDR as a critical socialist, maintaining close contacts with the dissident Robert Havemann (1910–82). Further collections and recordings of his works were published in West Germany and smuggled into the GDR, among them the songs and poems of *Mit Marx- und Engelszungen* (With the tongues of Marx and of Engels), 1968, and the verse epic *Deutschland: Ein Wintermärchen* (Germany: a winter tale), 1972, a homage to Heinrich Heine's work with the same title. In 1976, he was unexpectedly allowed to leave the GDR to give a concert in West Germany, and his citizenship was withdrawn to prevent him from returning.

This maneuver by the GDR authorities provoked waves of protest by leading East German writers and artists, including Stefan Heym (1913–) and Christa Wolf (1929–). The protestors suffered repercussions of various kinds, and many of them left for West Germany in the following years. Biermann adapted with some difficulty to life and work in the west, where he attracted less general approval once his criticism was no longer directed at the GDR. The content of his West German collections such as *Preussischer Ikarus* (Prussian Icarus), 1978, reflected his changed circumstances by turning at the same time to more international and more personal concerns. In the 1980s, Biermann gave active support to the West German peace movement. After an enforced absence of 13 years, with the opening of the Berlin Wall he was invited back to the GDR to give a public concert in Leipzig in December 1989.

Biermann's songs, ballads, and poems are written in a very direct and immediate style. His influences include

François Villon, Heine, and Bertolt Brecht (1898–1956), and the subject matter ranges from political and social criticism to love poetry. Biermann's position as a political dissident within the GDR and as a symbol of literary censorship in the "Biermann affair" has tended to overshadow his real significance as a powerful and original lyric poet.

James A. Mellis

See also Brecht, Bertolt; German Democratic Republic; German Democratic Republic: Opposition; German Democratic Republic: Politics and Culture; German Democratic Republic: State Security; Havemann, Robert; Heym, Stefan; Reunification; Wolf, Christa

References

Arnold, Heinz Ludwig, ed. *Wolf Biermann.* 2nd ed. Munich: Edition Text und Kritik, 1980.
Biermann, Wolf. *The Wire Harp: Ballads, Poems, Songs.* Trans. Eric Bentley. New York, NY: Harcourt, Brace and World, 1968.
Graves, Peter J., ed. *Three Contemporary German Poets: Wolf Biermann, Sarah Kirsch, Reiner Kunze.* Leicester: Leicester University Press, 1985.
Keller, Dietmar and Matthias Kirchner, eds. *Biermann und kein Ende: eine Dokumentation zur DDR-Kulturpolitik.* Berlin: Dietz, 1991.
Rosellini, Jay. *Wolf Biermann.* Munich: Beck, 1992.
Stein, Hannes, ed. *Wolf Biermann: Klartexte im Getummel: 13 Jahre im Westen von der Ausbürgerung bis zur November-Revolution.* Cologne: Kiepenheuer & Witsch, 1990.

Bild Zeitung (1952–)

The daily "nonpartisan" *Bild* was the brainchild of its owner, Axel Cäsar Springer (1912–85). The tabloid appeared on West Germany's newsstands on July 24, 1952, with an initial edition of 250,000 copies. Its reception was phenomenal. Within two years, circulation rose to 1.3 million, and by 1983 the paper crossed the 5 million mark. Today, *Bild*, a supra-regional paper with local inserts for Hamburg, Frankfurt, Hannover, and Berlin, is read by more Germans than any other publication. Indeed, *Bild* is the largest paper of its kind in Europe.

Bild is easily attainable because it is cheap and sold at every conceivable public place. Its headlines are bold and simple. Red ink is used lavishly, emphasizing the headlines even further. The paper's vocabulary is not demanding, yet it is forceful and relies on linguistic stereotypes. Many photographs support the modest text.

To underestimate the paper and its influence would be a grave mistake. *Bild* "creates" public opinion. It provides dialogue for millions of people. It is the defender of national interests (so it claims). *Bild* will praise lavishly as well as condemn easily. It has not shied away from suppressing and even from falsifying news items. Indeed, the largest daily in Germany is also its most controversial.

Bild's editorial position was clearly determined by its owner, Axel Springer, who controlled Germany's largest newspaper publishing group. A staunch defender of the Western alliance and an outspoken anti-Communist, Springer used *Bild*, his pitbull, time and again to influence public opinion and to affect political life in West Germany. He never accepted the existence of a second, Communist German state, any East-West rapprochement, nor any German-German dialogue.

The years 1966 to 1972 were marked by bloody student unrest that found the Springer press in the midst of the controversy. The radical student movement singled out publisher Springer and *Bild* (and other Springer publications) as the most dangerous yellow press in West Germany. On June 2, 1967, a student was killed by police action during the unrest in Berlin. *Bild* reacted with bold headlines, condemning the student movement for having provoked the authorities in causing this tragedy. On June 5, 1967, *Bild* published inflammatory headlines, escalating its diatribe against the student movement: *"Studenten drohen: wir schiessen zurück"* (students threaten: we shoot back).

The writer, Günter Grass (1927–), found himself in *Bild's* crossfire as well. Grass publicly defended Arnold Zweig (1887–1968), an East German writer, against a false and damaging story in *Bild*. Immediately, *Bild* decried and viciously attacked Grass. On April 11, 1968, Rudi Dutschke (1940–79), leader of the Sozialistischer Deutscher Studentenbund (SDS; Socialist German Students' Association) was shot. Bloody confrontations spread across 27 German cities and 400,000 people rioted in the streets. *Bild's* editorial office in Munich was destroyed. Springer's publishing house and print shop in Hamburg and Berlin were under siege. Delivery trucks of the Springer press were stopped and set ablaze. Radical students tried to prevent the distribution of *Bild* and other Springer publications. By daybreak, 2 people were dead, 500 were injured and 600 arrested. On May 19, 1972, two bombs exploded at Springer's printing plant in Hamburg and injured 19 employees. Yet these sad statistics did not sway Springer, who stayed his course. *Bild* remained the most widely read tabloid in Germany.

On July 24, 1992, *Bild* celebrated its 40th anniversary. The tabloid will still find its critics as well as those who are full of praise. As Willy Brandt, (1913–92) former chancellor of West Germany (1969–74) and former chairman of the Social Democratic Party (SPD) said when asked about *Bild*: "It would be foolish not to know what is written in Germany's largest daily."

Manfred K. Wolfram

See also Extra-Parliamentary Opposition; Journalism; Press and Newspapers; Springer, Axel; Wallraff, Günter

References

Bild, Historische Verlags-Dokumentation. Hamburg: Axel Springer Verlag, October 11, 1993.
Brumm, Dieter. "Sprachrohr der Volksseele? Die Bild-Zeitung." *Porträts der deutschen Presse: Politik und Profit.* Ed. Michael Wolf Thomas. Berlin: Volker Spiess, 1980.
"40 Jahre: Ein Dokument für unsere Leser." *Bild, Sonderdruck.* July 24, 1992.
Wallraff, Günther. *Das BILD-Handbuch bis zum Bildausfall.* Hamburg: Konkret Literatur, 1981.

Bildung und Bildungsbürgertum (Cultivation and Cultivated Bourgeoisie)

The notion of "cultivation" was once the educational ideal of the German-speaking countries. Around 1800, philosophers, theologians and public officials elaborated the concept of a general humanistic cultivation (*allgemeine Menschenbildung*). For the Prussian reformer Wilhelm von Humboldt this anti-utilitarian vision was supposed to overcome the social divisions of estate society. Foremost, cultivation sought to perfect all individual faculties in order to achieve a well-rounded, self-governing personality. Studying Greek texts and artifacts would ennoble the mind through the best examples of human creativity. By revealing the fundamental unity of all knowledge as well as encouraging rational thinking and restrained feeling, scholarly study (*Wissenschaft*) would free humanity. In the classical tradition, even physical forces might be trained through gymnastics. For the educated in Central Europe this ideal of cultivation became a powerful secular ethic that governed their entire lives.

In implementation, *Bildung* fell somewhat short of its aspirations. Much of the cultural baggage was inculcated by bourgeois mothers through reading, drawing, or making music with their children. More formally, the state provided a three-tiered educational system that was open to everyone. In theory, all children went to a common primary school; some gifted ones advanced to the gymnasium to learn classical languages and sciences; and the most talented went on to the universities for professional training. In practice, workers' and farmers' offspring often failed in primary institutions, lower-middle-class children dropped out of secondary training, and only the sons of educated, propertied families persevered until higher learning. Moreover, rote learning and grammatical exercises hardly inspired nobler sentiments in pupils. Yet after graduation, cultivation continued informally through reading clubs, theater groups, concerts, and museums, thereby creating a shared cultural style.

At the beginning of the twentieth century, the ideal of cultivation faced increasing strains. Since the advancement of scholarship rested on specialization, the philosophical unity of knowledge became fractured. Moreover, middle-class parents demanded the inclusion of modern and useful subjects, such as English, in the official curriculum, triggering a veritable "school-war" between the defenders of the gymnasium and the advocates of more "realistic" training. At the same time, technical and commercial institutions, as well as pedagogical academies, clamored for equality with the classically-oriented universities. Due to the expanding secondary and tertiary enrollments and the influx of lower-middle-class children, the ethos of self-directed learning lost its motivating force, so that many critics warned against mediocrity due to mass education (*Vermassung*). As a result of these pressures, the cultivated felt beleaguered by social change and often yielded to a sense of cultural pessimism.

The social product of cultivation was the *Bildungs-*

bürgertum. Unique to Central Europe, this stratum was based on common educational patents that entitled their holders to certain positions (*Berechtigungswesen*). Because the free professions lagged due to the lateness of industrialization, secondary school graduates (*Abiturienten*) and university degree holders (*Akademiker*) looked to the state for employment. Claiming greater merit, they sought to replace the aristocracy by virtue of their better performance on competitive examinations. Though less wealthy, they tried to separate themselves from the propertied middle class through cultural sophistication. The privilege of reserve officer's standing, obtained by only one year of military training (*Einjährige*), made them superior to the more numerous white-collar employees and the lower middle class. In a bureaucratic system, this noneconomic middle class could play a larger role than in wealthier societies of the West.

The politics of the *Bildungsbürgertum* shifted dramatically. Although the educated were found in every ideological camp and lacked organization, their shared discourse displayed similar tendencies. Initially, the ideal of cultivation acted as a liberalizing impetus that promoted individual responsibility, constitutional government, and national unity. After unification, many of the educated grew defensive and became anti-Semitic or imperialist. Threatened by hyperinflation and depression after World War I, they remained skeptical of the Weimar Republic and hoped for a return to order and authority, even from the Nazis, whom they despised as plebeians. After the disaster of the Third Reich, the *Bildungsbürgertum* experienced an Indian summer that restored its institutions and values in the early Federal Republic. But in the East, the Socialist Unity Party abandoned the bourgeois specialists and trained a new Communist intelligentsia. In the West, the cultural revolution of the 1960s shattered the ideal of *Bildung* as well as the social stratum based on it and replaced it with a new group of democratic intellectuals.

Konrad H. Jarausch

See also Aristocracy; Bourgeoisie; Burschenschaft; Education; German Democratic Republic: Politics and Culture; *Kultur;* Professions; Students; Universities

References

Blackbourn, David and Richard J. Evans, eds. *The German Bourgeoisie: Essays on the Social History of the German Middle Class from the Late 18th to the Early 20th Century.* New York, NY: Routledge, 1991.

Bruford, Walter H. *The German Tradition of Self-Cultivation: Bildung from Humboldt to Thomas Mann.* Cambridge: Cambridge University Press, 1975.

Conze, Werner and Jürgen Kocka, eds. *Bildungsbürgertum im 19. Jahrhundert.* Stuttgart: Klett-Cotta, 1985.

Engelhardt, Ulrich. *Bildung: Begriffs- und Dogmengeschichte eines Etiketts.* Stuttgart: Klett-Cotta, 1986.

Jarausch, Konrad H. "Die Krise des deutschen Bildungsbürgertums im ersten Drittel des 20. Jahrhunderts." *Bildungsbürgertum im 19. Jahrhundert.* Vol. 4. Ed. Jürgen Kocka. Stuttgart: Klett-Cotta, 1989.

Kocka, Jürgen and Alan Mitchell, eds. *Bourgeois Society in Nineteenth Century Europe.* Oxford: Berg, 1993.

Ringer, Fritz K. *Education and Society in Modern Europe.* Bloomington, IN: Indiana University Press, 1979.

Biochemistry

The term *Biochemie* was first used by Felix Hoppe-Seyler (1825–95) in 1877, but the subject had developed out of "physiological chemistry" in the 1840s. In 1842, Justus Liebig's (1803–73) work *Animal Chemistry* stimulated a heated debate on whether life could be explained in terms of inorganic forces and substances. Although biochemistry linked organic chemistry with the chemical aspects of physiology, biology, and medicine, it remained divided as a discipline between institutes of chemistry and physiology. The founding of university chairs for physiological chemistry research remained sporadic in the nineteenth century.

After mid-century, much progress was made. Hoppe-Seyler analyzed active substances in the organism. Nineteenth-century biochemists discovered "enzymes" (the term dates from 1877) and "nuclein" (discovered by Friedrich Miescher [1844–95] in 1869). Biologists paid much attention to analyzing the constituents of the cell. Physicians concerned with physiology and hygiene, as well as pharmacologists, chemists, and agriculturalists, made numerous advances in the discipline. Exploration of the chemistry of basic physiological processes such as respiration and digestion, and of infection and immunity, resulted in an impressive array of discoveries.

Biochemistry remained a marginal discipline in interwar Germany, which lacked specialized university institutes. The Kaiser Wilhelm Society, however, maintained specialized laboratories, for which the Rockefeller Foundation provided substantial funds. Noted researchers in the Weimar period included Gustav Embden (1874–1933), who discovered the pathways of glucose metabolism, and Otto Warburg (1883–1970), noted for his studies in oxidation (the process responsible for the energy source of cell functions), particularly of carbohydrates. He was joined in this work by Otto Meyerhof (1884–1951), who then mapped out the chemical physiology of muscular contraction. Max Bergmann (1886–1944) was a noted protein chemist. The new concept of "biotechnology" wedded biochemistry to industry and agriculture. When the Nazis forced many Jewish biochemists to emigrate (including Meyerhof, Bergmann, and Hans Krebs [1900–81]), enzyme chemistry came to have an important impact on Anglo-American medicine. Warburg (classified as a half-Jew) remained and was able to continue research. Adolf Butenandt (awarded a Nobel Prize in 1931 for his work on enzymes) became director of the Kaiser Wilhelm Institute for biochemistry, which supported research in virology.

Since 1945, institutionalization and research priorities have conformed to the American model, which cultivated a separate discipline of biochemistry. The nucleic acids, which Miescher had discovered in 1869, became a major focus of attention after the Anglo-American breakthroughs in understanding the molecular basis of heredity. The period marked a shift from nutrition and applied research to metabolic studies and molecular biology. Concern to boost molecular biology resulted in major funding initiatives, for example, by the Volkswagen Foundation in the mid-1960s. This research led to industrial applications and the development of biotechnology.

Paul Weindling

See also Boveri, Theodor; Butenandt, Adolf; Kaiser Wilhelm/ Max Planck Societies and Institutes; Warburg, Otto

References
Bud, Robert. *The Uses of Life: A History of Biotechnology.* Cambridge: Cambridge University Press, 1993.
Buttner, J. *History of Clinical Chemistry.* Berlin: de Gruyter, 1983.
Kohler, Robert E. *From Medical Chemistry to Biochemistry: The Making of a Biomedical Discipline.* Cambridge: Cambridge University Press, 1982.
Nachmansohn, David. *German-Jewish Pioneers in Science, 1900–1933.* New York, NY: Springer Verlag, 1979.

Biology

Not only have German academics excelled in biological research, but much popular interest has centered in biology and natural history. In 1797, the Romantic philosopher Theodor Roose first used the term *Biologie*, which implied a synthetic and integrated approach to the study of organisms. Karl Friedrich Burdach and Gottfried Treviranus adopted the term in 1800 as a reference to all aspects of human life. Major discoveries in comparative morphology and taxonomy enriched Romantic *Naturphilosophie* (natural philosophy) until the 1840s. Natural history remained popular, as exemplified by Alfred Brehm's studies of animal life.

In the 1830s, cell theory postulated common formative elements for all life forms. During the 1840s, radical materialists sought to identify common physico-chemical laws. Controversies divided mechanists, vitalists, and organicists over whether organization was itself a vital characteristic. After the 1850s, Darwinian biologists attempted to reconstruct the historical sequence of their development. Formulations of Darwinism were diverse, because Germany's premier biologists favored organic and cooperative theories of development over mechanistic selectionism. They formulated diverse social theories on the basis of the newly discovered biological laws of development and descent that offered alternatives to the controversial theory of natural selection.

In the 1880s, interest focused on hereditary mechanisms. This culminated in 1900 in the rediscovery of the Mendelian laws of heredity. Field studies also flourished in the twentieth century, exemplified by ecology and ethology. Differing nationalist and socialist readings of Darwinism and eugenics continued. Biological popularizations disseminated knowledge regarding reproduction and birth control. At the time of the anti-socialist laws (1878), biology was banned from school curricula. By the 1920s, biology served to promote health and sex education. In the 1920s and 1930s, much interest centered on experimental studies of mutation, especially in radiation biology and population genetics.

The Association of Biologists (Biologen-Verband) was established in 1931, partly in response to an awareness that the biology profession was being threatened by the socioeconomic crisis. In 1934, the association became affiliated with the Nazi teachers' *Bund* (federation). The Nazis, who capitalized on a lively public interest in biology, attempted to project the image of biology as a specifically National Socialist science. Academic debate continued to rage even among SS-affiliated researchers over a diversity of theories, ranging from reductionism to holism and Darwinian selectionism to vitalism.

After World War II, German biology in the Federal Republic conformed to international norms. In the GDR, the authorities pressured biologists to support Lysenkoism. Genetics research continued in agriculture. German researchers maintained their leading role in genetics and embryology. Since the 1980s, considerable controversy has raged surrounding genetic engineering.

Paul Weindling

See also Boveri, Theodor; Haeckel, Ernst; Science and National Socialism

References
Jahn, I., R. Löther, and K. Senglaub, eds. *Geschichte der Biologie.* Jena: Gustav Fischer, 1982.
Kelly, Alfred. *The Descent of Darwin.* Chapel Hill, NC: University of North Carolina Press, 1981.
Weindling, P.J. *Health, Race and German Politics between National Unification and Nazism.* Cambridge: Cambridge University Press, 1989.

Bismarck, Otto von (1815–98)

Otto von Bismarck was born at Schönhausen on the Elbe on April 1, 1815. Through his father, Ferdinand, he belonged to a noble family with estates in the Altmark and Pomerania. His mother was Wilhelmine Mencken, daughter of a cabinet secretary to Frederick the Great and his successors. Hence his heritage was both aristocratic and bourgeois; that the former predominated was natural, given the social values of the time, but it was reinforced by a disturbed oedipal relationship with the mother ("She spoiled my character"). On her insistence the family leased its estates and moved to Berlin, where Otto was enrolled in a boarding school at age six and subsequently attended the gymnasium. Afterward he attended the universities of Göttingen and Berlin. The humanistic values of his formal education appear to have affected him little. And yet he read widely both then and later in literature and history. After passing the state examination, he was rejected for the Prussian foreign service but accepted into the judiciary. Two attempts at a civil service career, at Aachen and Potsdam, ended in failure, giving him a lifelong contempt for routine bureaucrats ("Pride bids me command rather than obey"). He retired in frustration to manage family estates at Kniephof and Schönhausen, where he spent the years 1838–47.

Bismarck sensed that his future lay in politics and regretted the absence in Prussia of a parliament, where he could make a name for himself as had Peel, O'Connell, and

Mirabeau. His opportunity came in 1847, when King Friedrich Wilhelm IV summoned a United Diet to consider new taxes. Here he appeared as a staunch supporter of the crown, one of the few capable speakers for the conservative cause in a chamber dominated by liberal critics of the regime. During the Revolution of 1848 he participated in the camarilla of reactionaries close to the King who plotted the overthrow of the revolution. His reward was appointment as Prussian envoy to the Diet of the German Confederation, at that time the most important post in the Prussian foreign service. Bismarck served in Frankfurt until 1859, when after a change of regime in Berlin he was posted as ambassador to St. Petersburg and then briefly to Paris before his appointment as Prussian minister-president on September 22, 1862.

Basic to Bismarck's character was, by his own admission, the need to dominate and control. But narcissism was tempered by a sense of responsibility grounded in his Lutheran religious faith. The skepticism of his early years was overcome in 1846 by a genuine religious conversion encouraged by local gentry of pietistic conviction. Among them was Johanna von Puttkamer, whom he married in 1847 and by whom he had three children—Marie, Herbert, and Wilhelm. Through these events he attained a stability and certainty of mission and purpose that lasted a lifetime. Bismarck was a monarchist with an intense personal loyalty to the Hohenzollern dynasty and Prussian state. In principle he opposed absolute government, that is, direct rule by the monarch in other than military and foreign affairs. He believed, however, that ministers should be chosen and appointed by the ruler and not by parliament. In his view parliament (in bicameral form) was an indispensable institution, valuable for its capacity to criticize and obstruct in some degree unwise policies pursued by the ruler and his ministers. But he never found his own policies "unwise."

Bismarck became Prussian minister-president in 1862 because of a developing struggle between the crown and the Prussian chamber of deputies over the government's plan to reorganize and enlarge the army. King Wilhelm I and his generals were convinced that the army was inadequate to fulfill its mission to defend the country on a continent that had experienced two dangerous wars in seven years. But they also wished to extend the years of compulsory service from two to three years in order to make military service a "school" for civil discipline and political obedience. As minister-president Bismarck fulfilled the king's expectation by ruling the country for four years in defiance of parliament (the Constitutional Conflict). In 1867 his administration was "indemnified" by the chamber of deputies owing to his successes in foreign policy.

During the 1850s Bismarck became convinced that Prussia must expand its frontiers and attain parity with Austria in the affairs of the German Confederation. But he was also convinced that the Habsburg empire would never willingly concede equality of status in Germany to the Hohenzollern monarchy. Coercion would be needed. The first strategy he advocated was to secure the friendship of Tsarist Russia and the cooperation of France, thereby isolating and threatening Austria. As the decade advanced, an expanding

Otto von Bismarck. Courtesy of German Information Center, New York.

Prussian-German economy and increasing agitation for German national unity created material and spiritual needs that only Prussia could satisfy. Accordingly Bismarck enlarged the range of his political strategy to include national unity under a reformed confederation, including a national parliament based on universal male suffrage. Although he kept all options open as long as possible, the last and most extreme option was the one that ended with the creation of the German Empire in 1871, and that gave to Bismarck the sobriquet of "white revolutionary."

Another sobriquet, "man of blood and iron," was less deserved. It stemmed from a chance remark Bismarck made to the budget committee of the Prussian chamber of deputies in 1863. "The great questions of the day," he said, "will not be settled by speeches and majority decisions—but by blood and iron." The final words have been interpreted to mean that Bismarck was an unprincipled man of violence. But Bismarck relied primarily not on war but on diplomatic finesse to attain his ends. At this he was one of the great masters of the balance-of-power system. He persuaded Austria to join Prussia in the war of 1864 against Denmark, which fought alone and was compelled to cede parts of Schleswig-Holstein to Austria and Prussia. In 1866, he isolated Austria, and Prussia's generals and troops defeated her and her German Catholic allied states. In 1870, the same fate befell France under Napoleon III. In the second of these wars most of Germany's small states sided with Austria. In the third and last war, all Germany (with the exclusion of Austria) fought under Prussian leadership against

France, which was compelled to cede Alsace and Lorraine to a unified German Empire dominated by Prussia.

After 1871, Bismarck, now chancellor of the Second German Reich, considered Germany a satiated nation-state. For its consolidation he sought to Germanize its Polish, Danish, and French minorities, but he advised the German-speaking peoples of Central and Eastern Europe not to look to the German Empire for assistance. The balance-of-power system, as reconstructed in 1866–71, now became the shield behind which Berlin could consolidate and fortify its control over the German Empire, a federal union under Prussian hegemony. In a system of five great powers (France, Great Britain, Russia, Austria, and Germany), he remarked, Germany must always strive to be one of a coalition of three. Since he believed France irreconcilable and because Great Britain stood aloof from the continent, Germany-Austria-Russia was the preferred combination. But frictions between Russia and Austria in Balkan affairs threatened to upset the "League of Three Emperors" in the late 1870s and 1880s. Bismarck managed to hold the combination together during these troublesome events. He acted in Germany's interest as he conceived it, rejecting the advice of generals who urged a preventive strike against France. But his diplomatic skill also helped Europe avoid a general war.

Bismarck's internal policies were less successful. In league with the National Liberals he did succeed in expediting the development of a national economy, which continued to expand despite the crash of 1873, a period of depression to 1879, and a wavering business cycle to 1894. But his effort, again with liberal support, to crush the German Center Party was ill advised. He considered the Center, which represented German Catholics, to be a "mobilization against the state," but his attack upon "ultramontanism" (called the *Kulturkampf*) became an assault on Catholicism itself and merely consolidated his foes. After 1878 Bismarck became more concerned about the progress of the German Social Democratic Party (SPD) at the polls and in the labor movement. To halt the alienation of labor, he sponsored the first general system of social insurance (health, old age, and unemployment benefits). But he also launched a series of "exceptional laws" against socialists. His "anti-socialist laws" were no more successful against socialism than were the *Kulturkampf* laws against Catholicism. After a series of strikes in 1889, beginning in the coalfields and spreading later to other industries, Bismarck desired a coup to abolish equal suffrage in national elections.

To his death in 1888, King of Prussia and Kaiser Wilhelm I continued to depend on Bismarck's leadership in internal and foreign affairs. His son and successor Friedrich III, who in earlier years might have dismissed Bismarck, was deathly ill of throat cancer and lasted only 99 days on the throne. His successor, Wilhelm II (Wilhelm I's grandson), soon became restless under Bismarck's tutelage and was eager to establish his "personal government." The inevitable clash of wills led to Bismarck's dismissal on March 18–20, 1890 and his "promotion" to the honorific title of Duke of Lauenberg. In retirement on his new estates at Varzin in Pomerania and Friedrichsruh (near Hamburg), Bismarck subjected the government of his

successors and Wilhelm II himself to withering attacks in the public press. A reconciliation came in 1894, but it was superficial. Bismarck's memoirs written in these years (*Gedanken und Erinnerungen*) were a repudiation of Wilhelm II and his government. He died on July 30, 1898 at Friedrichsruh, deeply concerned about Germany's future.

Otto Pflanze

See also Anglo-German Relations; Austro-German Relations; Bebel, August; Bleichröder, Gerson von; Catholicism, Political; Center Party; Colonies and Colonial Society; Conservatism; Constitutions; Delbrück, Rudolf von; Diplomatic Corps and Diplomacy; Federalism; Forckenbeck, Max von; Founding Years; Franco-German Relations; Friedrich III; German Conservative Party; Imperial and Free Conservative Party; Imperial Germany; Imperial Germany: Army; Imperialism; *Kreuzzeitung*; *Kulturkampf*; Ketteler, Wilhelm; Lasker, Eduard; Liberalism; Liebknecht, Wilhelm; Ludwig II; Militarism; Moltke, Helmuth von (the Elder); National Liberal Party; Parliamentary System; Parties and Politics; Polish-German Relations, 1871–1918; Protectionism; Prussia; Railroads; Roman Catholic Church; Russian-German Relations; Schweinitz, Lothar von; Social Democratic Party, 1871–1918; Social Insurance; Virchow, Rudolf; Welfare State; Wilhelm I; Wilhelm II; Windthorst, Ludwig

References

Bismarck, Otto von. *Die gesammelten Werke.* 15 vols. Ed. Hermann von Petersdorff et al. Nendeln: Kraus Reprint, 1972.

———. *Reflections and Reminiscences.* Ed. Theodor Hamerow. New York, NY: Harper & Row, 1968.

Crankshaw, Edward. *Bismarck.* London: Macmillan, 1981.

Engelberg, Ernst. *Bismarck: Das Reich in der Mitte Europas.* Berlin: Siedler, 1990.

———. *Bismarck: Urpreusse und Reichsgründer.* Berlin: Siedler, 1985.

Gall, Lothar. *Bismarck, the White Revolutionary.* 2 vols. Trans. J.A. Underwood. London: Allen & Unwin, 1986.

Kent, George, O. *Bismarck and His Times.* Carbondale, IL: Southern Illinois University Press, 1978.

Pflanze, Otto. *Bismarck and the Development of Germany.* 3 vols. Princeton, NJ: Princeton University Press, 1990.

Stern, Fritz. *Gold and Iron: Bismarck, Bleichröder, and the Building of the German Empire.* New York, NY: Alfred A. Knopf, 1977.

Taylor, A.J.P. *Bismarck: The Man and the Statesman.* London: Hamish Hamilton, 1955.

Bitburg

Situated in the western state of Rhineland-Palatinate, Bitburg is a small town (12,200 adult residents) once known largely for its beer (with its slogan "*Bitte, ein Bit . . .*") and its proximity to a United States air force base where Nike-Hercules missiles were formerly deployed. The significance of the area was politically redefined in 1985, owing to a controversial visit paid to a local cemetery by American President Ronald Reagan commemorating the 40th anniversary of Germany's unconditional surrender on May 8, 1945. The politics behind that visit have come to symbolize a conflict between those forces within the postwar state who seek to "close the book" on Germany's Nazi experience and those who believe that Germany has yet to process that past effectively.

The key events are outlined in a publication furnished by the German Press and Information Office, under the title *Remembrance—Sorrow and Reconciliation*. The controversy began with reports that Chancellor Kohl had been barred from participation in June 1984 activities memorializing the D-Day landings at Normandy during World War II, although Kohl later claimed to have communicated earlier that he was "not interested in being invited." The West German leader did participate, however, in a second anniversary ceremony in September 1984, holding hands with French President Mitterrand as a gesture of reconciliation on the World War I battlefield of Verdun. In November, the chancellor personally invited President Reagan to visit a German military cemetery during his next European trip, the aim of which would be "to achieve peace and reconciliation" with another of Germany's former adversaries "across the graves." Reagan labeled the idea a "very noble gesture" but was reluctant to accept a further suggestion that he visit the Dachau concentration camp. The president stressed his desire not to focus on the past but on the future.

American and West German advance teams nonetheless eventually agreed to schedule a presidential trip to the Kolmeshöhe cemetery at Bitburg. Reagan reiterated his refusal to visit a concentration camp on March 21, 1985, based on his personal conviction that "none of them [the German people] who were adults and participating in any way" in the war would still be alive, adding that "very few . . . even remember the war. . . . They have a guilt feeling that's been imposed upon them, and I just think it's unnecessary." On April 15 came the first media reports that the Bitburg cemetery held the remains of roughly 30 (later revised to 49) former members of the Waffen-SS which was characterized by a West German government spokesperson as a matter "of secondary importance." After a survey of the burial records, Kohl argued that 30 of those laid to rest "had not had a chance to evade conscription" and that the aim of the cemetery visit would be to provide "a sign for young people serving in the Bundeswehr, indicating that we have learned the lesson of history."

Over the next weeks, representatives of the United States Holocaust Memorial Council, as well as 53 members of the American Senate, petitioned Reagan to cancel the Kolmeshöhe excursion. Reagan justified his plans, observing "there is nothing wrong with visiting that cemetery where those young men are victims of Nazism also. . . . They were victims as surely as the victims in the concentration camps." His relativization of Waffen-SS roles triggered new cries of outrage, resulting in a White House announcement on April 19, 1985 that Reagan would also pay his respects at the Bergen-Belsen concentration camp. On April 20, the floor leader of the West German Christian Democratic Union

(CDU), Alfred Dregger, wrote to Senator Howard Metzenbaum (one of the initiators of the Congressional petition) that efforts to bring about a cancellation amounted to an "insult to my brother and his fallen comrades." (Dregger himself had served 1939 and 1945, rising to the level of battalion commander in the Wehrmacht.) On April 21, Kohl stressed his country's special historical responsibility "for the crimes of the Nazi tyranny . . . a responsibility reflected not least in neverending shame." The chancellor would repeat that line in his speech at Bergen-Belsen, ostensibly contradicting his other public ruminations on "the blessing of late birth." Four days later, 257 members of United States House of Representatives sent their own letter, urging the chancellor to release Reagan from his promise to visit Bitburg, paralleling a motion put to a Bundestag vote by the Greens (rejected 398 to 24). On April 26, the United States Senate affirmed a proposal exhorting Reagan reconsider his itinerary. Two days later, *The New York Times* revealed that the SS soldiers buried at Bitburg had been members of "*das Reich*" (the Second SS Tank Division), responsible for one of the worst civilian massacres of World War II, the killing of 642 French villagers in Oradour-sur-Glane in June 1942. By a vote of 390 to 26, the House of Representatives passed a second resolution calling upon Reagan to reconsider his planned cemetery visit.

On May 5, 1985, the 40th anniversary of the war's end, both the American and the West German leaders placed wreaths and offered a short address at Bergen-Belsen, followed by a stop at the Kolmeshöhe site; Reagan then moved on to speak at the nearby United States air force base. The President's remarks at Bergen-Belsen bore witness to his own selective remembrances of history: "Here lie the people—Jews—whose death was inflicted for no reason other than their very existence"; he did not mention the 50,000 Soviet prisoners of war who had been among the first to perish in the camp. The day was marked by protest demonstrations at the camp and graveyard sites.

That same day West German President Richard von Weizsäcker (1920–) addressed the Bundestag, delivering one of the most eloquent and candid speeches ever made by a government official regarding the Holocaust. Weizsäcker sought to name and embrace all of Hitler's victims (including women, Communists, and homosexuals, as well as Roma and Sinti "gypsies"). He appealed universally to postwar Germans: "All of us, whether guilty or not . . . must accept the past. We are all affected by its consequences and liable for it. . . . The more honest we are in observing this day, the freer we will be to face its consequences responsibly." On June 13, 1985, the West German parliament approved the "Law against Auschwitz Lies," rendering it a criminal offense for anyone to deny the authenticity of atrocities committed under the Nazi regime. One day later Helmut Kohl became the first German chancellor since Adenauer to attend a reunion of the Schlesienbund, made up of ethnic Germans expelled from Silesia by the Soviets after Germany's unconditional surrender, suggesting support for the Schlesienbund's forty-year-old demands for a return of the eastern territories.

Joyce Mushaben

See also American-German Relations; Federal Republic of Germany; Kohl, Helmut; Memory, Collective; National Socialist Germany; Waffen-SS; World War II

References
Hartman, Geoffrey H., ed. *Bitburg in Moral and Political Perspective.* Bloomington, IN: Indiana University Press, 1986.
Press and Information Office of the Government of the Federal Republic of Germany, ed. *Remembrance, Sorrow and Reconciliation. Speeches and Declarations in Connection with the 40th Anniversary of the End of the Second World War in Europe.* Bonn: Press and Information Office of the Government of the Federal Republic of Germany, 1985.
Sultanik, Kalman. "An Overview of 'Bitburg.'" *Midstream* (October, 1985).

Bizone (1947–49)

By January 1947, a joint economic administration had been established in the two occupation zones in Germany controlled by the American and British military governments after World War II. After the economic crisis and the hunger during the winter of 1946–47, this combined economic area formed an important fundament for economic reconstruction in Germany, the revival of industries and foreign trade. The Bizone comprised 60 percent of German territory and people.

As it seemed impossible to reach a four-power understanding on the question of German economic unity, and with the failure of the Council of Foreign Minsters at Paris in June 1946, the American secretary of state, James Byrnes, offered to his British colleague, Ernest Bevin, to merge their respective occupation zones. Already in September/October 1946, five agreements had been made to establish bizonal German administrations for food, transport, economy, finance, and post. By June 1946, the bizonal administrations were centralized at Frankfurt. The first Economic Council (*Wirtschaftsrat*) consisted of 52 deputies delegated from the parliaments of the states (*Länder)* of the American and British zones; the Executive Committee (*Verwaltungsrat*) formed a coordinating committee of the directors of the five bizonal administrations. However, these bizonal bodies did not have clearly defined functions. After the breakup of the London Foreign Ministers' meeting on the issue of German unity in December 1947, the Bizone was reorganized by the Frankfurt Charter of February 9, 1948, which delegated more executive functions. The second Economic Council comprised 104 deputies, and the new states committee (*Länderrat*) held the right to veto and to initiate laws. Although the bizonal administrations lacked any political powers, they became a board for important discussions and issued 171 laws (final authority lay with the occupation powers). In 1948, economic policy in the Bizone turned from economic control to a market economy advocated by Ludwig Erhard at the Economic Council. When the French agreed to cooperate in the currency reform of June 20, 1948, and with the subsequent discussions for the establishment of a constitution, the Bizone was transformed into a

political state on a trizonal level. Though concentrating on economic cooperation and consolidation, the combined economic area also developed a dynamic force on a political level. In September 1949, with the foundation of the Federal Republic of Germany, the bizonal administration was dissolved.

Eva A. Mayring

See also American-German Relations; American Occupation; Anglo-German Relations; British Occupation Policy; The Cold War and Germany; Federal Republic of Germany; Franco-German Relations; German Democratic Republic; Robertson, Brian; Ruhr Region; Soviet-German Relations; Soviet Occupation

References
Foschepoth, Josef and Rolf Steininger, eds. *Die britische Deutschland- und Besatzungspolitik 1945–1949.* Paderborn: Ferdinand Schöningh, 1985.
Marshall, Barbara. *The Origins of Postwar German Politics.* London: Croom Helm, 1988.
Pronay, Nicholas and Keith Wilson, eds. *The Political Re-Education of Germany and Her Allies After World War II.* London: Croom Helm, 1985.
Scharf, Claus and Hans-Jürgen Schröder, eds. *Die Deutschlandpolitik Grossbritanniens und die Britische Zone 1945–49.* Wiesbaden: Franz Steiner Verlag, 1979.
Turner, Ian D., ed. *Reconstruction in the Post-War Germany: British Occupation Policy and the Western Zone, 1945–55.* Oxford: Berg, 1989.

Blank, Theodor (1906–72)

From 1950 to 1955, Blank was security advisor to Chancellor Konrad Adenauer, and then minister of defense from 1955 to 1956. Blank's efforts enabled the rearmament of West Germany to be achieved within a multinational defense structure, NATO. The new German defense force, the Bundeswehr, was a democratic structure, one that promoted not the "state within a state" mentality of the Reichswehr, but a "citizen in uniform" with the duty to defend democratic values.

Born in 1906 at Elz on the Lahn in the upper Rhine Valley, Blank became, at the age of 25, general secretary of the Christian Factory and Transportation Workers' Union in Dortmund. He was ousted by the Nazis when he refused to cooperate with Adolf Hitler's policies. Drafted into the army during World War II, he was decorated for bravery. After the war he returned to the trade union movement, and in 1949 was elected to the Federal parliament. A convinced democrat, Blank was loyal to the policies of Konrad Adenauer, who enlisted Blank's political and managerial talents when Germany's allies raised the issue of rearmament.

Adenauer recognized that rearmament would facilitate his efforts to gain full sovereignty for the West German state. To demonstrate to the Allies that the newly created republic was committed to democratic principles and civilian control, Adenauer asked Blank on October 23, 1950, to head a security office, the Amt Blank, to develop and coordinate defense issues. On December 1, 1950, Blank's office consisted of 19 people, but within five years it grew to a staff of over 1,000. In June 1955, it became a full-fledged defense ministry.

Between 1951 and 1952, Blank and his staff, composed of soldiers—some of whom had served in Hitler's military—and civilians, created a new military organization. They consulted the tradition of the early-nineteenth-century Prussian military reformers, such as Gerhard von Scharnhorst and Carl von Clausewitz, to create a citizen in uniform who functioned in unison with his society. Screening boards would prevent officers with antidemocratic or neo-Nazi sympathies from entering the new military force. On May 9, 1955, West Germany formally became a NATO member, and on November 12, 1955, the bicentennial of Scharnhorst's birthday—a date Blank chose to symbolize a new chapter in German military history—the first 101 volunteers of the Federal Republic's defense force took their service oath.

The Federal Republic promised to provide its NATO allies with 96,000 troops by December 31, 1956, and with 270,000 men by December 31, 1957. Lack of equipment, training facilities, and volunteers prevented Blank from reaching these goals. Also, many West Germans questioned Germany's revised military tradition and refused to accept rearmament. To silence criticism, in October 1956 Adenauer dismissed Blank as defense minister. Theodor Blank nonetheless proved a major influence in the creation of a postwar democratic military structure in the Federal Republic of Germany.

Frank A. Mayer

See also Adenauer, Konrad; American-German Relations; Baudissin, Wolf; The Cold War and Germany; Federal Republic of Germany; Federal Republic of Germany: Armed Forces; German Democratic Republic: National People's Army; NATO and Germany; Rearmament

References

Abenheim, Donald. *Reforging the Iron Cross: The Search for Tradition in the West German Armed Forces.* Princeton, NJ: Princeton University Press, 1988.

Greiner, Christian. "Dienststelle Blank." *Militärgeschichtliche Mitteilungen* 17 (January 1975), 99–124.

Large, David Clay. *Germans to the Front: West German Rearmament in the Adenauer Era.* Chapel Hill, NC: The University of North Carolina Press, 1995.

Lowry, Montecue J. *The Forge of West German Rearmament, Theodor Blank and the Amt Blank.* New York, NY: Peter Lang, 1990.

McGeehan, Robert. *The German Rearmament Question.* Urbana, IL: University of Illinois Press, 1971.

Nelson, Walter Henry. *Germany Rearmed.* New York, NY: Simon and Schuster, 1972.

Blankenhorn, Herbert (1904–91)

Herbert Blankenhorn, a diplomat and Chancellor Konrad Adenauer's right-hand man, contributed significantly to fundamental political decisions during the early years of the Federal Republic and had considerable influence in shaping foreign policy.

Blankenhorn was an officer's son. His diplomatic career, which began in 1929, led Blankenhorn to Athens, Washington, Helsinki, and Bern prior to 1945. From 1946 to 1948, he worked in the German Office of the Occupation Zone Advisory Council in the British zone; in 1948, he became Secretary General of the Christian Democratic Union (CDU) Occupation Zone Committee in the British zone. In this capacity, he became known to Adenauer, who subsequently appointed him as his personal assistant.

Blankenhorn, who was pragmatic and flexible and had a quick mind, soon became an indispensable advisor to the chancellor. As director of the office providing the liaison with the Allied High Commission, he was the only one to accompany Adenauer in the negotiations with the Allied commissioners on the November 1949 Petersberg Agreement, which not only called for concessions in the industrial dismantling process but also assured Germany's entry into the International Ruhr Agency.

Blankenhorn was the right man for addressing complicated tasks. Adenauer named him head of the secret division, known under the code name of "Central Office for Home Service," which was installed in the Federal Chancellery in the spring of 1950 and which dealt with defense issues and German rearmament.

However, Blankenhorn's appointment as minister and director of the Office for Foreign Affairs in the Chancellery, which had been created in June 1950 and which was the nucleus of the future Foreign Office, came to naught because, like most diplomats before 1945, he had been a member of the Nazi Party. Nevertheless, in addition to Walter Hallstein (1901–82), he remained the chancellor's most important advisor in foreign affairs. After the creation of the West German Foreign Office in 1951, Blankenhorn took charge of its Political Division.

Blankenhorn asked Adenauer to appoint him as a permanent representative at the NATO offices in Paris, presumably for health reasons, but largely because of his dislike for Heinrich von Brentano (1904–64), who had become foreign minister in 1955. In the mid-1950s, Blankenhorn proposed a dialogue with Moscow. He cautioned against General Charles De Gaulle's reform plans, which would give the Western defense alliance enhanced autonomy in matters of defense planning. He rejected a too-close cooperation between France and Germany, lest it alienate other Allied countries. His diplomatic career reached its apogee when, between 1958 and 1970, he became ambassador first in Paris, then in Rome and London. Subsequently he worked for UNESCO.

Walter Mühlhausen

See also Adenauer, Konrad; Allied High Commission to Germany; American-German Relations; Brentano, Heinrich von; British Occupation Policy; Christian Democratic Union; Diplomatic Corps and Diplomacy; Federal Republic of Germany; Federal Republic of Germany: Foreign Policy; Franco-German Relations; NATO and Germany; Rearmament

References

Baring, Arnulf. *Aussenpolitik in Adenauers Kanzlerdemokratie: Bonns Beitrag zur Europäischen Verteidigungsgemeinschaft.* Munich: Oldenbourg, 1969.

Blankenhorn, Herbert. *Verständnis und Verständigung: Blätter eines politischen Tagebuchs 1949 bis 1979.* Frankfurt am Main: Propyläen Verlag, 1980.

Köhler, Henning. *Adenauer: Eine politische Biographie.* Frankfurt am Main: Propyläen Verlag, 1994.

Lademacher, Horst and Walter Mühlhausen, eds. *Sicherheit, Kontrolle, Souveränität: Das Petersberger Abkommen vom 22. November 1949: Eine Dokumentation.* Melsungen: Kasseler Forschungen zur Zeitgeschichte, 1985.

Schwarz, Hans-Peter. *Adenauer: Der Aufstieg: 1876–1952.* Stuttgart: Deutsche Verlags-Anstalt, 1986.

———. *Adenauer: Der Staatsmann: 1952–1967.* Stuttgart: Deutsche Verlags-Anstalt, 1991.

Blaue Reiter, Der (The Blue Rider)

The term *Der Blaue Reiter* (The Blue Rider) refers to the name of an almanac conceived by Wassily Kandinsky (1866–1944) and edited by Kandinsky and Franz Marc (1880–1916); to two exhibitions mounted by the editorial board of the almanac; and, more generally, to a group of Munich artists affiliated with Kandinsky and Marc in the years immediately preceding World War I.

The Blue Rider almanac was assembled in 1911 by Kandinsky and Marc and published by Piper Verlag in 1912. The two artists conceived the book as a chronicle of important artistic events around 1911, and, more broadly, as an agent of healing for a society they felt was diseased by materialism and scientific empiricism. The almanac thus featured abstract-tending contemporary art that, the editors believed, evoked the inner, subjective world of spirit and emotion through line, color, and form not tied to the appearances of the objective world. Besides work by Kandinsky and Marc, paintings by Henri Matisse, Robert Delaunay, Paul Cézanne, Vincent van Gogh, and other modern artists were reproduced. The almanac also illustrated work whose seemingly unsophisticated execution the editors much admired. Drawings by children were reproduced beside masks and sculpture from Africa and the South Seas, woodcut prints from the Middle Ages, and German and Russian folk art. In keeping with the purpose of the book, many of these artifacts illustrated stories of exorcism, healing, and regeneration. In addition, a number of literary essays addressed, among other topics, the question of form in art, music, and theater. These texts underscored the message of the book's visual images that spiritual rejuvenation is fostered best not by an art of objective reproduction but by one of subjective suggestion. Although Kandinsky and Marc initially intended to publish such an almanac annually, ultimately only one appeared.

Kandinsky later claimed that *The Blue Rider* almanac was so named simply because Marc loved horses, Kandinsky loved riders, and both loved the color blue, but the book's title no doubt derived in part from the facts that numerous pagan and Christian "riders" were important agents of salvation (including Saint George, who is featured on the book's cover) and that blue, the color of the heavens, is traditionally associated with spirituality.

The almanac lent its name to a group of artists loosely affiliated in Munich with Kandinsky and Marc, including Paul Klee (1879–1940), Alexei Jawlensky (1864–1941), Marianne von Werefkin (1870–1938), Gabriele Münter (1877–1962), and August Macke (1887–1914). All innovators whose work paved the way for the emergence of a truly modern art, these painters were essentially outsiders when they were living and working in Munich. Indeed, the first exhibition of *The Blue Rider* came about when Kandinsky's *Composition V* of 1911 was rejected by the jury of the New Artists' Society of Munich (Neue Künstlervereinigung Münchens), which had little sympathy for abstract-tending art. Kandinsky, Marc, Münter, and Alfred Kubin (1877–1959) resigned in protest, and Marc and Kandinsky quickly organized an exhibition of their own at Munich's Thannhäuser gallery. Under the auspices of *The Blue Rider* almanac, the show consisted of 43 works by 14 artists, among them Kandinsky, Marc, Münter, Arnold Schönberg (1862–1931), Robert Delaunay, Henri Rousseau, and Albert Bloch. A second exhibition of graphic works opened at the gallery of Hans Goltz in Munich in February 1912.

The name "The Blue Rider" is thus linked to the almanac edited by Kandinsky and Marc, to the two exhibitions at the Thannhäuser and Goltz galleries, and to the circle of artists surrounding Kandinsky and Marc in Munich in the years before World War I. With the outbreak of hostilities, the group disintegrated. Macke and Marc died in combat, whereas

1911 title page by Wassily Kandinsky of Blue Rider *program notes. Courtesy of Inter Nationes, Bonn.*

the Russians Werefkin, Jawlensky, and Kandinsky were forced to leave Germany. Only Münter and Klee remained in Munich, and ultimately even Klee departed to accept an appointment at the Bauhaus in Weimar. The Blue Rider was thus a short-lived, though tremendously important, force in the evolution of modern art.

Maria Makela

See also Artists; Exhibitions (Art); Kandinsky, Wassily; Klee, Paul; Marc, Franz; Münter, Gabriele; Painting

References

Lankheit, Klaus, ed. *The "Blaue Reiter" Almanac.* New York, NY: Viking, 1974.

The Solomon R. Guggenheim Museum. *Kandinsky in Munich 1896–1914.* New York, NY: The Solomon R. Guggenheim Foundation, 1982.

Weiss, Peg. *Kandinsky in Munich: The Formative Jugendstil Years.* Princeton, NJ: Princeton University Press, 1979.

Zweite, Armin. *The Blue Rider in the Lenbachhaus, Munich.* Munich: Prestel-Verlag, 1989.

Bleichröder, Gerson von (1822–93)

Gerson von Bleichröder was perhaps the most successful German banker of the Jewish faith in the second half of the nineteenth century. Specializing in international merchant banking and industrial financing, he greatly expanded his father's Berlin firm, S. Bleichröder, which he took over in 1855. He became banker and advisor to Chancellor Otto von Bismarck, as well as to many other prominent individuals.

His connection with the Paris Rothschilds brought Bleichröder to the attention of Bismarck, who made him his banker in 1859. Bleichröder's star rose with Bismarck's, as Bleichröder helped to finance Prussia's Wars of Unification. His assistance during the Austro-Prussian War of 1866 was crucial, because the Prussian parliament had suspended funding as part of a constitutional conflict (1859–66). In later decades as well, Bleichröder provided funds in support of numerous foreign and domestic policy initiatives. Conservative, but not a supporter of neofeudal reaction, Bleichröder became Bismarck's close and trusted personal advisor. Using his international financial connections, he supplied Bismarck with information vital to the formulation of policy, as well as to the optimal management of Bismarck's investment portfolio.

Bleichröder's relationship with Bismarck, along with his vast network of connections in high places, was a constant source of information on which Bleichröder could base sensitive investment decisions, particularly abroad. He conducted countless informal diplomatic missions, at times representing Bismarck, at times promoting his own interests. Bleichröder brought his financial power to bear in support of Bismarck's policies—anti-socialist legislation, protectionism, railway nationalization, imperialism, and the campaign against left-liberals (many of whom were major opponents of anti-Semitism). He financed news agencies friendly to himself and

to Bismarck, and distributed bribes to journalists. Bleichröder also assisted King Leopold II of Belgium in establishing his colony in the Congo. Conversely, Bleichröder was able to influence government policy in some instances, notably in the case of the improvement of German relations with Russia. He had a major interest in loans to Russia, which brought him large profits. His role as Tsarist banker became the subject of a bitter fight between Bismarck and Kaiser Wilhelm II after 1888.

Bleichröder spoke to Russian officials on behalf of Jews. He also headed efforts to protect Jews from persecution in Romania. However, Bismarck cynically used the international campaign on behalf of Romanian Jews to coerce the Romanian government into repaying railway loans made by German aristocrats. Bleichröder remained silent. Although he amassed an enormous fortune through his financial dealings, Bleichröder was ultimately Bismarck's tool. As a Jew, he was greatly resented by members of Bismarck's entourage and vilified by anti-Semitic propagandists. As Fritz Stern has shown in a magisterial biography, Bleichröder's life vividly illustrates the triumphs and limitations of Jewish assimilation in Germany.

Dolores L. Augustine

See also Anti-Semitism; Banking; Bismarck, Otto von; Jews, 1869–1933; Wilhelm I; Wilhelm II

References

Landes, David S. "Bleichröders and Rothschilds: The Problem of Continuity in the Family Firm." *The Family in History.* Ed. Charles E. Rosenburg. Philadelphia, PA: University of Philadelphia Press, 1975.

Pflanze, Otto. *Bismarck and the Development of Germany.* 3 vols. Princeton, NJ: Princeton University Press, 1990.

Stern, Fritz. *Gold and Iron: Bismarck, Bleichröder, and the Building of the German Empire.* New York, NY: Alfred A. Knopf, 1977.

Bloch, Ernst (1885–1977)

One of the twentieth century's leading interpreters of Marx, Ernst Bloch was born to Jewish parents in Ludwigshafen on July 8, 1885. He studied philosophy in Munich, Würzburg (where he obtained his doctorate in 1908), and Berlin, where he studied under Georg Simmel. While in Berlin, Bloch met and became a friend of the Marxist philosopher Georg Lukács (1885–1971).

After several years in Heidelberg and Garmisch, Bloch emigrated to Bern, Switzerland, in 1917. Here he was active in the opposition to the German war effort and, in 1918, completed his first book, *Geist der Utopie* (Spirit of utopia). The idea of utopia, and Bloch's claims that human nature was fundamentally undetermined and that there was in consciousness a "not yet" (*noch nicht*)—an anticipation of future possibilities that nevertheless has a present effect on the actual—were to remain dominant themes in his work.

In 1919, he returned to Germany and spent most of the 1920s in Berlin, where in 1921 he met Bertolt Brecht (1898–

Ernst Bloch. Courtesy of German Information Center, New York.

1956). Bloch's distinctive approach to Marxism is particularly evident in his 1921 study of the early sixteenth-century German reformer Thomas Münzer (*Thomas Münzer als Theologe der Revolution*). Nevertheless, one also finds influences of Romanticism and of Hasidism in his writings, especially his early quasi-autobiographical *Spuren* (Traces), published in 1930.

Bloch left Germany in March 1933, after Hitler's accession to power, staying successively in Zürich (where he had a falling-out with Lukács), Vienna, Paris, and Prague. In 1938 he went to the United States. It was during this period that he undertook his major work, *Das Prinzip Hoffnung* (published as *Principle of Hope*).

In 1949, Bloch returned to East Germany as professor of philosophy at the Karl-Marx Universität Leipzig. He also became editor of the *Deutsche Zeitschrift für Philosophie* and, in 1954 and 1955, published the first two volumes of *Das Prinzip Hoffnung*. Bloch's idealistic reading of Marx and Hegel and his public criticism of the ruling Socialist Unity Party did not suit the authorities and, in 1957, he was forced to retire from teaching and publishing, though a third volume of *Das Prinzip Hoffnung* appeared in East Berlin in 1959.

In 1961, at the time that the Berlin Wall was erected, Bloch found himself coincidentally in West Berlin. He had with him the manuscript of *Naturrecht und menschliche Würde* (Natural law and human dignity), 1961. Bloch decided to stay in the West, and was named professor at the University of Tübingen. His later work particularly influenced the theolo-

gian Jürgen Moltmann (1926–) and played an important role in the dialog between Christianity and Marxism. Bloch died in Tübingen on August 4, 1977.

William Sweet

See also Brecht, Bertolt; German Democratic Republic; German Democratic Republic: Political Culture; Moltmann, Jürgen; Philosophy; Protestant Theology; Simmel, Georg

References

Bloch, Ernst. *Briefe (1903–1975)*. Frankfurt am Main: Suhrkamp, 1985.
———. *Gesamtausgabe*. 17 vols. Frankfurt am Main: Suhrkamp, 1959–77.
———. *Principle of Hope*. Trans. Neville Plaice, Stephen Plaice, and Paul Knight. Cambridge, MA: MIT Press, 1986.
Hudson, Wayne. *The Marxist Philosophy of Ernst Bloch*. New York, NY: St. Martin's, 1982.
Kushner, David. *Ernst Bloch: A Guide to Research*. New York, NY: Garland, 1988.
Münster, Arno. *Ernst Bloch: Messianisme et utopie*. Paris: Presses universitaires de France, 1989.
———. *Figures de l'utopie dans la pensée d'Ernst Bloch*. Paris: Aubier, 1985.

Blomberg, Werner von (1878–1946)

At President Paul von Hindenburg's (1847–1934) request, Colonel-General (later Field Marshal) Werner von Blomberg was appointed secretary of war in the Hitler administration on January 30, 1933. As secretary of war and commander in chief of the Wehrmacht (1935–38), he advocated wholeheartedly Adolf Hitler's policy of rearmament and assisted this policy unconditionally.

Blomberg was born in Stargard, Pomerania, on September 2, 1878. He started his military career in 1897. During World War I, he served as an officer on the General Staff. In 1919, during his tour of duty in the Department of War he was taken into the new Reichswehr. After several high postings, he became commander of No. 1 Military District (Königsberg) in 1929. From 1932 until his appointment as secretary of war he headed the German delegation to the Geneva Conference on Disarmament.

As secretary of war, Blomberg supported unreservedly Hitler's policy of rearmament. During the Röhm purge, he supported Hitler's elimination of the Sturmabteilung (SA) in order to maintain the Reichswehr as the only powerful armed formation in the Reich. After Hindenburg's death, Blomberg proved himself a loyal vassal by ordaining that the Reichswehr swear a personal oath to the führer. Blomberg thereby helped consolidate Nazi power in Germany. On Hitler's orders, he planned the military occupation of the Rhineland in 1936. Acknowledging Blomberg's unconditional loyalty, Hitler made him the Wehrmacht's first field marshal on April 20, 1936. In spite of some slight protests against Hitler's aggressive policies, Blomberg must be seen as generally submissive and devoted to Hitler.

Blomberg was forced to retire as secretary of war and commander in chief of the Wehrmacht on February 4, 1938, after his marriage to a Berlin prostitute. The intrigue over the marriage devised by Heinrich Himmler (1900–45) and Hermann Göring (1893–1946) caused Hitler to discharge Blomberg. The field marshal himself advised Hitler on January 27, 1938, to assume direct command of the Wehrmacht. Blomberg's retirement offered Hitler the opportunity to keep the armed forces under his personal control and to eliminate any opposition within the Wehrmacht. Despite the scandalous circumstances of his retirement, Blomberg remained one of Hitler's admirers until the end of the Nazi regime. After the war, he was arrested by the United States authorities in order to appear as a witness at the Nuremberg Military Tribunal. On March 22, 1946, he died in prison from illness.

Klaus Schönherr

See also Beck, Ludwig; Fritsch, Werner von; Himmler, Heinrich; Hindenburg, Paul von; Hitler, Adolf; National Socialist Germany: Armed Forces

References

Brett-Smith, Richard. *Hitler's Generals*. San Rafael, CA: Presido Press, 1976.
Huebsch, Norbert Arthur. *Field-Marshal Werner von Blomberg and the Politicization of the Wehrmacht*. Ann Arbor, MI: University Microfilms International, 1985.
Janssen, Karl-Heinz and Fritz Tobias, eds. *Der Sturz der Generäle: Hitler und die Blomberg-Fritsch-Krise 1938*. Munich: C.H. Beck, 1995.
Moll, Otto Ernst Eugen. *Die deutschen Generalfeldmarschälle 1935–1945*. Rastatt: Pabel, 1961.
Stumpf, Reinhard. *Die Wehrmacht-Elite: Rang- und Herkunftsstruktur der deutschen Generale und Admirale 1933 bis 1945*. Boppard: Boldt, 1982.

BMW (Bavarian Motor Works; Bayerische Motoren Werke)

In 1916, Bavarian Motor Works (BMW) became established as a manufacturer of aircraft engines. An aircraft powered by a BMW IV engine set a world record by climbing to an altitude of 32,013 feet in 1919. But the production of aircraft engines—then the only products the company made—in Germany was forbidden by the Treaty of Versailles.

In the early 1920s, BMW made a comeback through the manufacture of motorcycles. The R32, the first one launched (1923), was the fastest machine in the world. In the 1930s, BMW began the production of high-performance automobiles, including the Dixi 3/15. In the same decade, the company resumed the production of aircraft engines. The BMW Hornet and BMW Xa were the first radial engines produced at the BMW's Munich plant. During World War II, BMW produced war equipment, such as jet engines, and conducted research into rocket technology. At war's end the company was closed down by the victorious powers and dismantled.

Following a three-year ban on any production activities, BMW restarted automobile production. It suffered a financial setback in 1959, and the company was on the verge of bankruptcy. Joining forces in this crucial situation, the workers, minority shareholders, and dealers succeeded in making a new start, whereupon BMW developed into the bearer of an outstanding world trademark. The BMW 700 became the first of its successful models manufactured in large numbers. The BMW 1500, introduced in 1962, marked the turning point in BMW's model range, heralding the advent of a new range of sporting and compact touring cars. In 1972, the first BMW 5 Series was launched, followed by the 3 Series in 1975, and the 7 Series in 1977—the predecessors of the major current model ranges.

The history of BMW is one of technical innovations, such as the flat-twin engine, drive shaft, and programmable digital motor electronics. They provided the groundwork for BMW's solid reputation and economic success.

Inge Melber

See also Audi; Automobile Industry; Daimler-Benz AG; Volkswagen

References

Dymock, Eric. *BMW: A Celebration*. London: Pavillion Books Ltd., 1990.
Frostick, Michael. *BMW: The Bavarian Motor Works*. London: Dalton Watson Ltd., 1976.
Monnich, Horst. *The BMW Story: A Company in Its Time*. London: Sidgwick and Jackson Ltd., 1991.

Böckel, Otto (1859–1923)

"The peasant-king of Hessen" and the first avowed anti-Semite to enter the Reichstag (1887), Otto Böckel represented the Marburg-Kirchain district until 1903. He introduced a new style of populist agitation featuring torchlight parades, open-air meetings, party badges, and nonstop campaigning, thereby forever changing the face of politics in the German countryside.

Born into a middle-class family in Frankfurt am Main, Böckel received his doctorate in modern languages from Marburg University (1882), where he stayed on as an assistant librarian. Romantic and nationalistic, a self-proclaimed "Bismarckian," he wandered from village to village collecting and preserving folklore. In the process he became acquainted with the mounting troubles of a rural population in the throes of transformation from manorial to capitalistic agriculture: falling prices for farm products, indebtedness, and foreclosure. Moving within the organizational network of anti-Semitic clubs and newspapers that had sprung up in the early 1880s, he placed himself at the head of a peasant protest movement. In his own newspaper, the *Reichsherold* (1887–94), he associated the evils besetting Hessian peasants with the coming of Prussian administration (1866) and its alleged beneficiaries, the Jews, who performed many agricultural middleman functions in the region.

Supported by anti-Semitic reform clubs in Giessen, Kassel, and Marburg, and by student volunteers from the Verein deutscher Studenten (Association of German Students; Marburg branch established 1886), he ran for the Reichstag on the slogan "Against *Junkers* and Jews," and won a stunning victory in the first balloting. Anti-Semitic competitors thwarted his ambition to form a unified national anti-Semitic party "to solve the Jewish question" and rescue the peasantry; he settled instead for the Hesse-based Antisemitische Volkspartei (1889; merged with the Saxon anti-Semites as the Deutsche Reformpartei in 1893) and remained a power in regional politics until 1919.

Böckel combined conventional anti-Semitic ideology, as represented in his inflammatory pamphlet *Die Juden—die Könige unserer Zeit* (The Jews—the kings of our age), 1886, with a fully-developed agrarian movement. His *Mitteldeutscher Bauernverein* (Central German Farmers' Association; 15,000 members, 400 chapters in 1892) supported a youth group, consumer and producer cooperatives, "Jew-free" markets, cheap insurance, and membership in savings and loans. None of these were an unqualified success, but they did achieve Böckel's main objective—the binding of the small farmer to his party.

Having alerted more powerful forces to the potential of anti-Semitic politics as a tool of mobilization among the Protestant peasantry, Böckel was first coopted by the Agrarian League (founded 1893) and then relegated to obscurity for the last 20 years of his life.

Richard S. Levy

See also Agrarian Leagues; Anti-Semitism

References

Böckel, Otto. *Die Juden—die Könige unserer Zeit.* 5th ed. Berlin: A. Rusch, 1886.

Levy, Richard S. *The Downfall of the Anti-Semitic Political Parties in Imperial Germany.* New Haven, CT: Yale University Press, 1975.

Mack, Rüdiger. "Otto Böckel und die antisemitische Bauernbewegung in Hessen, 1887–1894." *Wetterauer Geschichtsblätter* 16 (1967), 113–47.

Böckler, Hans (1875–1951)

Hans Böckler was the first chair of the German Trade Union Federation (Deutscher Gewerkschaftsbund, DGB), German labor's dominant confederation, from 1949 to 1951.

Böckler was born in the small Bavarian town of Trautskirchen in 1875. A year later, his family moved to nearby Furth. When Böckler was 13 his father died. Consequently, Böckler left school and became an unskilled metalworker.

At age 19, Böckler joined the Deutscher Metallarbeiterverband (DMV; German Metalworkers Association) and the Social Democratic Party (SPD). Charisma enabled Böckler to rise quickly in both organizations, and in 1903 he moved to Saarbrucken to become a full-time DMV official. In 1907, Böckler was transferred to Frankfurt am Main, and in 1910 he assumed the leadership of the DMV's Breslau district. This appointment placed him within the top ranks of the union. Between 1912 and 1914, Böckler worked for the DMV newspaper in Berlin.

During World War I, Böckler was drafted, soon to be wounded seriously and discharged. He spent the rest of the war working as a DMV official in Danzig, Kattowitz, and Siegen.

In 1920, Böckler was transferred to the DMV's Cologne office. While in Cologne, Böckler served on the city council and clashed occasionally with the mayor, Konrad Adenauer. In 1927 Böckler moved to Düsseldorf to take over the leadership of the DMV's largest district, Rhineland–Westphalia/Lippe, a job he kept until 1933. Böckler also served as a member of the Reichstag for the SPD after 1928. In 1933, the Nazis arrested Böckler, falsely charged him with embezzlement, then released him in 1934. Böckler spent the next decade working in Cologne and Berlin while maintaining loose contact with the Resistance. In 1944, Gestapo persecution prompted him to move to the countryside outside Cologne.

After the war, despite his advanced age, Böckler became involved in reorganizing the postwar German labor movement. With other labor moderates he strove to unite the formerly divided democratic elements of the German labor movement. They succeeded in October 1949 by founding the DGB, which embraced the principles of nonpartisan and industrial unionism. Böckler was elected DGB chairperson. In 1950, Böckler relied on his widespread popularity among workers and his close relationship with Chancellor Adenauer to broker a compromise ensuring that a sweeping version of codetermination for the coal, iron, and steel industries passed through the Bundestag. He died unexpectedly in February 1951.

Stephen J. Silvia

See also Adenauer, Konrad; Codetermination; Trade Unions

References

Borsdorf, Ulrich. *Hans Böckler: Arbeit und Leben eines Gewerkschafters von 1875 bis 1945.* Cologne: Bund-Verlag, 1982.

Mielke, Siegfried and Peter Rütters, eds. *Gewerkschaften in Politik, Wirtschaft und Gesellschaft 1945–1949.* With contributions by Michael Becker. Cologne: Bund-Verlag, 1991.

Schneider, Michael. *A Brief History of the German Trade Unions.* Trans. Barrie Selman, Bonn: J.H.W. Dietz, 1991.

Thelen, Kathleen Ann. *Union of Parts: Labor Politics in Postwar Germany.* Ithaca, NY: Cornell University Press, 1991.

Böll, Heinrich (1917–85)

In his novels and short stories, but also in his interviews and essays, Heinrich Böll was the outstanding commentator on and critic of, the development of West German society from its beginnings in the aftermath of the defeat of Nazi Germany through the Economic Miracle of the late 1950s and 1960s to the social tensions of the 1970s and early 1980s. He won respect and honors abroad, including the presidentship of PEN International (1971) and the Nobel

Prize for Literature (1972), but in his own country he remained controversial throughout his life and was the subject of often bitter attacks.

Böll was born in Cologne in 1917 and served in the Wehrmacht from 1939 to 1945. His early works, including the novel, *Und sagte kein einziges Wort* (And said not a single word), 1953, deal with the absurdity of war and the postwar situation of ordinary people.

Böll's early novels and short stories introduce the themes he would develop throughout his life: the importance of remembering the past and learning from it and the role of the individual conscience. The central characters of these early works are weak, suffering, and human and are contrasted with the figures of those in power, opportunists who prosper under any system. The ideological position is one of Christian socialism, contrasting earthly and transcendental values. The Church, especially the hierarchy, is reminded of its duty to care for its flock. The imagery of the sacraments, particularly the sharing of bread in the mass, constantly recurs, but the Christian content is distanced from the Church and restored to the people, the poor and the hungry. Böll's treatment of sexual relationships is positive, compassionate, and without hypocrisy.

Böll's criticism of the Church focused on its relationship to the state—from its collaboration with the Nazis to its close links with the ruling Christian Democratic Union (CDU) in the early years of the Federal Republic of Germany (FRG). His

novel *Ansichten eines Clowns* (published as *The Clown*), 1963, provoked a furious backlash from the Church, the CDU, and the West German establishment. Böll's criticism of society was now less transcendental, more critical of society itself. The increasingly materialist values of West Germany, money, and the misuse of power became central targets in his literary works, essays, and interviews. In the early 1970s, Böll attacked how the Springer press whipped up hysteria about emerging urban terrorism, and as a result was himself subjected to attack and harassment by the press. His story *Die verlorene Ehre der Katharina Blum* (published as *The Lost Honor of Katharina Blum*), 1974, was both an illustration of the escalation of violence in society and a warning that constitutional freedoms were being eroded. Two of his novels, *Billard um halbzehn* (published as *Billiards at Half Past Nine*), 1959, and *Gruppenbild mit Dame* (published as *Group Portrait with Lady*), 1971, draw parallels between contemporary West German developments and prewar German history, presenting a panorama of German experience in the twentieth century.

Böll became president of PEN International in 1971 and from this position was able to intervene on behalf of dissident Eastern Bloc authors such as Aleksander Solzhenitsyn; in 1972, at the height of the controversy over his contribution to the Baader-Meinhof debate, he was awarded the Nobel Prize for Literature.

Criticisms of Böll's works have tended to center on their political content rather than their literary merit, although some critics have complained of sentimentality and oversimplification of character and conflict and his female characters have been criticized as idealized versions of male stereotypes. His treatment of social developments in West Germany from the 1940s to the 1980s makes Böll the representative literary chronicler of West German society.

James A. Mellis

See also Bild Zeitung; Extra-Parliamentary Opposition; Federal Republic of Germany: Literature

References

Conard, Robert C. *Understanding Heinrich Böll*. Durham, SC: South Carolina University Press, 1992.

Hoffmann, Gabriele. *Heinrich Böll: Leben und Werk*. Munich: Heyne, 1991.

Rademacher, Gerhard. *Heinrich Böll: Auswahlbibliographie*. Bonn: Bouvier, 1989.

Reid, James H. *Heinrich Böll: A German for His Time*. Oxford: Berg, 1988.

Sowinski, Bernhard. *Heinrich Böll*. Stuttgart: Metzler, 1992.

Boltzmann, Ludwig (1844–1906)

Ludwig Boltzmann, an outstanding nineteenth-century physicist, worked in many fields, but his reputation is founded mainly on the integration of thermodynamics with classical mechanics.

After attending the gymnasium in Linz, Boltzmann began his studies of mathematics and physics in Vienna in 1863. He received his doctoral degree in 1866 and became *Assistent*

Heinrich Böll. Courtesy of Inter Nationes, Bonn.

(assistant lecturer) to Josef Stefan. In 1868 Boltzmann gained the status of a *Privatdozent* (private lecturer), and in 1869 he was appointed to the chair of mathematical physics in Graz. From 1873, he was professor of mathematics at the University in Vienna for three years. Subsequently, Boltzmann returned to Graz as professor of experimental physics. In 1890 he accepted a newly founded chair for theoretical physics in Munich. After the death of Stefan, he became his successor in Vienna in 1894. There Boltzmann remained, except for two years (1900–02) when he taught in Leipzig. He had problems with his physical and psychological health and committed suicide in 1906.

As early as in his second paper of 1866, he sought a connection between the second law of thermodynamics and the principles of mechanics. According to the second law, the entropy of an isolated system in a non-equilibrium state must always increase. However, there was an apparent contradiction. It seemed impossible to reduce irreversible phenomena to the behavior of the molecules that obeyed the reversible equations of mechanics. Developing J.C. Maxwell's statistical concepts, Boltzmann responded to this problem by applying probability arguments to it. Boltzmann modified the law itself: a decreasing entropy is not impossible but extremely improbable, because most of the states of a system are equilibrium states. Therefore, the entropy almost always increases. Boltzmann illustrated this discovery in his so-called H-theorem of 1872. In 1877, he found that the entropy is proportional to the logarithm of the number of possible molecular configurations corresponding to a macroscopic state. Boltzmann designated this number as a probability. The famous relationship has been written on his tombstone.

Boltzmann was a protagonist of atomism. At the end of the century, he defended it against a growing skepticism. His techniques and the formula for entropy played a role in the formation of early quantum theory.

Stefan L. Wolff

See also Physics

References
Boltzmann, Ludwig. *Gesamtausgabe*. Vol 1: *Vorlesungen über Gastheorie*. Vol. 8: *Ausgewählte Abhandlungen der internationalen Tagung in Wien 1981*. Braunschweig: Vieweg, 1981, 1982.
———. *Populäre Schriften*. Leipzig: J.A. Barth, 1905.
———. *Wissenschaftliche Abhandlungen*. 3 vols. Ed. F. Hasenöhrl. Leipzig: J.A. Barth, 1909.
Broda, Engelbert. *Ludwig Boltzmann: Mensch, Physiker, Philosoph*. Vienna: Franz Deuticke, 1955.
Brush, Stephen. *The Kind of Motion We Call Heat*. 2 vols. Amsterdam: North-Holland, 1976 and 1986.

Bonhoeffer, Dietrich (1906–45)

Dietrich Bonhoeffer was the most prominent theologian to be executed by the Nazis, a result of his close association with leading members of the Resistance movement.

Born into a large and influential family of intellectuals and professionals, he studied theology, largely under the influence of Karl Barth, and took up an academic career at the University of Berlin. His broad international sympathies were strengthened by a year's study in New York in 1930–31, where he became interested in the ideas of pacifism and the example of Gandhi. He was early on opposed to the totalitarian and racial beliefs of Nazism, and from 1933 onward became one of the leading younger supporters of the Confessing Church, which sought to prevent the introduction of Nazi ideas and practices into the German Evangelical Church.

From 1933 to 1935, he served as Lutheran chaplain in London, where he provided information to leaders of the Ecumenical Movement, such as Bishop George Bell of Chichester, in their efforts to mitigate the church struggle in Germany. In 1935 he was appointed director of an unofficial, later illegal, training seminary in Pomerania for Confessing Church students.

After the outbreak of war in 1939, he was recruited through his family connections to be a contact between the military resistance group and foreign churchmen. In 1942 he met with Bishop Bell in Sweden, seeking support for the anti-Nazi opposition, and made clear his view that Hitler's crimes of aggression and racial oppression were so great that Germany would have to accept a "penitential" peace settlement. As a result of such activities, he was arrested by the Gestapo in April 1943 and subsequently, after the abortive coup of July 1944, was put to death in Flossenburg concentration camp only days before its liberation. From his prison cell he was able to smuggle out letters, later published as *Widerstand und Ergebung: Briefe und Aufzeichnungen aus der Haft*, 1953 (published as *Letters and Papers from Prison*, 1972) which included a series of significant theological reflections relating to the role of the church in national and political affairs. Following the war, his status as an anti-Nazi martyr gave his ideas an added acceptance as a percipient response to the dilemmas of how Christians should face the challenge of unbridled nationalism and totalitarianism.

John Conway

See also Barth, Karl; Confessing Church; National Socialist Germany; Protestant Theology; Protestantism and the Protestant Church; Resistance

References
Barnett, Victoria. *For the Soul of the People: Protestant Protest against Hitler*. New York, NY: Oxford University Press, 1992.
Bethge, Eberhard. *Dietrich Bonhoeffer: Man of Vision, Man of Courage*. Trans. E. Mosbacher et al., New York, NY: Harper and Row, 1970.
Bonhoeffer, Dietrich. *Ethics*. Trans. Neville H. Smith. New York, NY: Macmillan, 1965.
———. *Gesammelte Schriften*. 4 vols. Ed. Eberhard Bethge. Munich: Christian Kaiser Verlag, 1958–61.
———. *Letters and Papers from Prison*. Trans. R. Fuller, F. Clark, and J. Bowden, New York, NY: Macmillan, 1972.

Bonn

Located on the Rhine, where that river flows out of the Siebengebirge—the last hills before entering the north German plain—Bonn was a small university city before becoming the provisional capital of the Federal Republic of Germany (FRG) in 1949. Nicknamed *Bundesdorf* (federal village), its name came to symbolize political normality and democracy in contrast to the extremes of the ill-fated Weimar Republic and the Nazi era.

Bonn was chosen as provisional capital because the American military had a regional headquarters nearby on the Petersberg (one of the legendary seven hills) and Chancellor Konrad Adenauer had his home in nearby Rhöndorf. Other centers were rejected as being too peripheral or too damaged by the war.

Roman ruins, Romanesque churches, and Baroque palaces compete with shopping centers and boutiques in the small city center. The birthplace of Ludwig van Beethoven and a rococo Rathaus (city hall) represent the old Bonn that served as residence city for the electors, who reigned from Cologne, the large trading city 18 miles to the north. Parts of the university founded in 1818 are still housed in a baroque residence and in the Poppelsdorfer Schloss (Poppelsdorfer palace); the residence and Schloss are joined by a broad avenue.

The new Bonn is represented by an ugly concrete highrise— the new city hall—outside the ring of stately nineteenth-century mini-villas that surround the old city, roughly coinciding with Roman camp walls. It is also represented by the numerous administrative and apartment buildings that dominate what were neighboring peasant villages after World War II.

The amalgamation of villages by the "capital" in 1969 resulted in a town of some 30,000 inhabitants in 1948 growing into a city of 300,000 by 1990. Bonn's transport and housing were only slowly revamped in the 1960s to accommodate the demands of a growing state administration. Many state officials lived in outlying villages, but lack of planning led to a chaotic development in regional roads and public services.

As the FRG and the German Democratic Republic (GDR) appeared to become permanent entities, Bonn seemed destined to lose its provisional character. The foreign embassies—most of which had been located in Cologne—built grandiose quarters, and by the mid-1970s 103 countries had residences in Bonn. Huge edifices replaced the temporary barracks of the political parties. The parliament, located in a rebuilt teachers' college, received an ultramodern home by the 1990s, as had the Chancellery in the 1970s. The government built ever more ministry blocks; two large museums emphasized the history of the Federal Republic and of German art; a tunnel was planned to bring a super-express rail connection and ties to the Autobahn network. These measures had made Bonn an accessible and, to all appearances, permanent capital, plus a minor cultural entrepot.

Unification in 1990 renewed discussions regarding Germany's capital. After rancorous debate, the government chose Berlin instead of Bonn in June 1991. As the economic costs of the move became apparent, the decision was modified and the move delayed until the year 2000 for most ministries; some administrative offices will remain and some new federal agencies will be established in Bonn.

Dieter K. Buse

See also Adenauer, Konrad; Berlin; Federal Republic of Germany; Federalism; Parliamentary System; Parties and Politics; Reunification

References

Berlin Bonn: Die Debatte. Cologne: Kiepenheuer und Witsch, 1991.

Beyme, Klaus von. *Hauptstadtsuche: Hauptstadtfunktionen im Interessenkonflikt zwischen Bonn und Berlin.* Frankfurt am Main: Suhrkamp, 1991.

Bundesminister für Raumordnung, Bauwesen und Städtebau, ed. *Vierzig Jahre Bundeshauptstadt Bonn, 1949–1989.* Karlsruhe: Müller, 1989.

Ennen, Edith. *Vom Römerkastell zur Bundeshauptstadt: Kleine Geschichte der Stadt Bonn.* 4th ed. Bonn: Stollfuss, 1985.

Germany. *Bundestag (12., 34. Sitzung: 1991–1995) Die Hauptstadt-Debatte: Der stenographische Bericht des Bundestages.* Bonn: Bouvier, 1991.

Kohrs, Ekkehard. *Kontroverse ohne Ende: Der Hauptstadt-Streit: Argumente, Emotionen, Perspektiven.* Weinheim: Beltz, 1991.

Pommerin, Reiner. *Von Berlin nach Bonn: die Alliierten, die Deutschen und die Hauptstadtfrage nach 1945.* Cologne: Böhlau, 1989.

Rey, Manfred van und Norbert Schlossmacher, eds. *Bonn und das Rheinland: Beiträge zur Geschichte und Kultur einer Region: Festschrift zum 65: Geburtstag von Dietrich Horoldt.* Bonn: Bouvier, 1992.

Rummel, Alois, ed. *Bonn, Sinnbild deutscher Demokratie: zur Debatte um Hauptstadt und Regierungssitz.* Bonn: Bouvier, 1990.

Books

Originally, the word "book" meant an indefinite number of beechwood plates, sewn together and used as material on which to write. After the invention of printing, "book" came to denote any number of printed or empty pages, which were sewn together and provided with a cover or dust jacket. Even today there is no internationally standardized definition of the term "book." In England, a book has to cost at least six-pence in order to be labeled as such. In the United States, any printed material distributed by the publishing trade is defined as a book. In Germany, most experts use the term in accordance with the UNESCO definition, which classi-fies a book as nonperiodical printed material that contains at least 49 pages.

Despite the increasing importance of electronic media, books still play an important role in the cultural life of Ger-many. This is also emphasized by UNESCO statistics on in-ternational book production: together with the (former) So-viet Union and the United States, Germany has continuously held a leading position since 1976. West Germany currently has approximately 4,000 book stores and more than 1,000 book shops, various book clubs, and numerous specialized firms that distribute books. The density and efficiency of the book trade network in Germany is generally regarded as unique. Every German book can be acquired, ordered, or delivered anywhere in Germany under identical conditions and within a short time. However, and despite fixed shop prices for books, Germany's book trade is characterized by a relatively small profit on capital, a situation that is caused by increasing competition and the compulsion of specialization.

According to target groups, contents, and modes of de-piction, book production in Germany may be subdivided into various branches and genres: fiction and poetry, nonfiction, reference, children's books, picture books, and calendars. Book-market research in Germany currently differentiates among 25 specialized areas of book production. With 26–27 percent of all new publications, fiction and poetry is the largest individual branch of book production. This statistic includes a large volume of cheap pulp novels.

Since 1961, the share devoted to the printing of pocket books has increased continuously. Between 1967 and 1980, the percentage of pocket books has doubled. Today, approxi-mately 15 percent of all new publications are pocket books. In relation to the number of copies published, the share of the pocket-book market exceeds the 15 percent figure. As in book production in general, pocket books tend to concentrate in-creasingly on nonfiction and avoid fiction and poetry.

Despite the enormous density of the book trade network in Germany, bookstores garner less than 50 percent of the total turnover, far behind book clubs and supermarkets. The book industry in Germany is currently characterized by intensive economic concentration processes. Almost 50 percent of all new publications are produced by 2.5 percent of the publish-ing houses in Germany. The publishing companies that pro-duce most of the books and the books with the highest num-ber of copies, such as the Bertelsmann group or the Axel Springer group, are closely linked or interconnected with in-ternational media corporations. The tendencies toward eco-nomic concentration and multinational integration seem to be irreversible.

Bernhard Zimmermann

See also Autobiography; Bestsellers, Contemporary; Comedy; Drama; Exile Literature; Expressionism; Fairy Tales; Federal Republic of Germany: Literature; Feminist Writing; Fischer, Samuel; Folklore; German Democratic Republic: Literature and Literary Life; Historical Novel; Imperial Germany: Lit-erature; Libraries; Literacy; Literary Criticism; Mosse, Rudolf; Mystery and Detective Fiction; Myth; Mythology; National Socialist Germany: Literature; Naturalism; Patriotic Litera-ture; Piper, Reinhard; Poetry; Publishing and the Book Trade; Radio Plays; Realism; Rowohlt, Ernst; Satire; Serial Literature; Symbolism; Theater; Ullstein Publishing; Weimar Germany: Literature; Working-Class Literature

References

Börsenverein des deutschen Buchhandels, eds. *Buch und Buchhandel in Zahlen.* 17 vols. Frankfurt am Main: Börsenverein des deutschen Buchhandels, 1977–93.

Hutter, Martin and Wolfgang Langenbucher. *Buchgemein-schaften und Lesekultur.* Berlin: Spiess-Verlag, 1980.

Kohler, Ursula. "Lesekultur in beiden deutschen Staaten: 40 Jahre—ein Vergleich." *Archiv für Soziologie und Wirtschaftsfragen des deutschen Buchhandels* 64 (1990), 367–402.

Ziermann, Klaus. *Vom Bildschirm bis zum Groschenheft.* Berlin: Dietz Verlag, 1983.

Borchert, Wolfgang (1921–47)

An important example of *Trümmerliteratur* (literature relating to life in the postwar ruins), Borchert's short stories and poems call attention to the suffering of the German population in the period immediately following World War II. His only drama, *Draussen vor der Tür* (published as *The Man Outside*), 1947, brought the author instant fame and remains one of the most performed plays on German stages.

Before he was drafted into the army in 1941, Borchert had worked as a bookseller and actor in his native Hamburg. The Nazis repeatedly imprisoned Borchert for his radical pacifism and forced him back into military service despite the emerging symptoms of the severe liver disease that ultimately caused the writer's early death.

Right after the war, Borchert not only renewed his contacts with the theater but also wrote the majority of his literary works. The poem collection *Laterne, Nacht und Sterne* (Lantern, night, and stars), 1946, and the short-story collection *Die Hundeblume* (The dandelion), 1947, express the longing for humanity in a dehumanized world. The anthology *An diesem Dienstag* (This Tuesday), 1947, includes "Nachts schlafen die Ratten doch" (At night the rats do sleep), a narrative from the perspective of a German child survivor of the war, and "Die drei dunklen Könige" (The three dark kings), the story of three German soldiers returning from war and captivity.

Borchert's humanist critique focuses on average people as victims of inhumane hierarchical social systems. His dramatic anti-hero Beckmann in *Draussen vor der Tür* (Outside before the door) immediately turned into an identification figure for a generation of young people who felt betrayed by the Nazi regime and the war. With its emphatic appeal to individual resistance against war, Borchert's last text, the manifesto "Dann gibt es nur eins!" (Then there is but one!), 1947, has become a key text for the West German peace movement.

With the "naked" language of *Heimkehrerliteratur* (homecoming literature), Borchert formulated the experience of Fascism for a generation that characterized itself as "lost." Borchert's exclusive focus on German suffering pinpoints his historical location; his call for individual responsibility in the face of inhumanity still echoes.

Katherina Gerstenberger

See also Federal Republic of Germany: Literature; World War II

References

Borchert, Wolfgang. *Das Gesamtwerk.* Hamburg: Rowohlt, 1949.

Burgess, Gordon J.A. *Wolfgang Borchert.* Hamburg: Christians, 1985.

Rühmkorf, Peter. *Wolfgang Borchert in Selbstzeugnissen und Bilddokumenten.* Hamburg: Rowohlt, 1961.

Schröder, Claus B. *Draussen vor der Tür: Eine Wolfgang-Borchert-Biographie.* Berlin: Henschel, 1988.

Wolff, Rudolf, ed. *Wolfgang Borchert: Werk und Wirkung.* Bonn: Bouvier, 1984.

Bormann, Martin (1900–?)

Martin Bormann, as director of the Party Chancellery (1941–45) and secretary to Adolf Hitler (1943–45), became known as the "Brown Eminence." In the later stages of World War II, Bormann emerged as one of the most influential people in Germany.

Born in Halberstadt, Bormann dropped out of school and, after working on a farm, served in an artillery regiment during World War I. He subsequently joined a Freikorps (free corps) unit and later was imprisoned for his involvement in a political murder (1924). He joined the Nazi Party in 1927. His early party offices included provincial press officer, SA officer, and director of a party insurance plan.

After the Nazi Party seized power (1933), Bormann became deputy to Rudolf Hess (1894–1987), who was himself deputy leader of the Nazi Party. Bormann's administrative skills made him invaluable to Hitler. For example, he managed the Adolf Hitler Fund of German Business and organized the development of the Führer's estate on the Obersalzberg. From 1938, as Hitler became less and less compromise-minded, Bormann began to eclipse Hess in significance. After war broke out in September 1939, Bormann was constantly with the Führer at his military headquarters.

Bormann replaced Hess when the latter flew to Great Britain (May 1941), and his post was retitled "director of the Party Chancellery." As such, Bormann had authority over the *Gauleiter* (regional party leaders) and *Reichsleiter* (senior party officials). Bormann's key functions involved the passing on of orders from Hitler to these party men and the arrangement of meetings with the führer. His resulting intimate knowledge of the führer's wishes and his capacity to regulate access to Hitler conferred tremendous power on Bormann.

A constant presence at Hitler's side gave Bormann even greater significance. His capacity for providing Hitler with whatever information he wanted and his ability to crystallize Hitler's rambling thoughts into specific orders made Bormann invaluable to the führer and an integral part of how decisions were made in the later years of the Third Reich. Bormann was even able to persuade Hitler to take particular policy decisions through the skilful management of dinner conversations.

A Nazi by conviction, Bormann constantly pressed for action against the churches and advocated extreme racial measures. He remained with Hitler until his suicide (April 30, 1945); only then did he flee the bunker. It is uncertain whether Bormann died trying to cross Russian lines or whether he eventually escaped to South America. Whatever Bormann's end, his reputation rightly lives on as the model of a manipulative and unscrupulous government functionary.

Martyn Housden

See also Hess, Rudolf; Hitler, Adolf, National Socialism; National Socialist Germany

References
Broszat, M. *The Hitler State*. London: Longman, 1981.
Farago, L. *Aftermath: Martin Bormann and the Fourth Reich*. New York, NY: Simon and Schuster, 1974.
Fest, J.C. *The Face of the Third Reich*. London: Harmondsworth, 1972.
Lang, J. von. *The Secretary: Martin Bormann: The Man Who Manipulated Hitler*. New York, NY: Random House, 1979.
Orlow, D. *The History of the Nazi Party*. 2 vols. Pittsburgh, PA: University of Pittsburgh Press, 1969–73.
Peterson, F.N. *The Limits of Hitler's Power*. Princeton, NJ: Princeton University Press, 1969.
Smelser, R. and R. Zitelmann, eds. *The Nazi Elite*. London: Macmillan, 1993.

Born, Max (1882–1970)

Max Born, an eminent theoretical physicist, participated substantially in the development of quantum physics in the 1920s. Born grew up in Breslau, where his father was professor of anatomy. He began his studies at the university in his native town in 1901. After five semesters, including one in Heidelberg and one in Zürich, Born studied at Göttingen. In 1905 he became the private *Assistent* (assistant lecturer) of David Hilbert (1862–1943). A Rudolf Minkowski seminar directed his interest to electron theory. Born's dissertation of 1906 dealt with an elasticity problem, written in the context of a prize competition suggested by Felix Klein. But electrodynamics and the theory of relativity were the main subjects of Born's research at that time. In 1909, he wrote his qualification thesis (*Habilitationsschrift*) on the self-energy of the relativistic electron. Thereafter, crystal physics became the major field of Born's activity. In 1912, he published, together with Theodor von Kármán, a paper on lattice vibrations, which contained a method to calculate the specific heats of solids better than Albert Einstein's (1879–1955) of 1907. Born finished a book on the dynamics of crystal lattices in 1915.

In the same year, he obtained the position of associate professor of theoretical physics in Berlin, which had been established to relieve Max Planck of his teaching duties. In 1919, Born advanced to a full professorship in Frankfurt, and two years later he accepted a call from Göttingen. Since 1922, when Niels Bohr had delivered a lecture series there, Born had been seeking a new quantum mechanics. In 1925, he developed, together with Pascual Jordan and Werner Heisenberg (1901–76), matrix mechanics (*Dreimännerarbeit*). Born used Schrödinger's wave equation for the treatment of scattering and collision processes. This led him in 1926 to a statistical interpretation of a particle's wave function. Born considered the square of the absolute value of the amplitude as a probability per unit volume of finding the particle at a given place and time.

Because of his Jewish descent, Born was suspended from his teaching at the University of Göttingen in 1933. He left

Germany and emigrated to Cambridge, England. In 1936, he obtained a professorship in Edinburgh, where he remained until retirement in 1953. The next year, he reemigrated to Germany, and became politically active with his warnings about nuclear weapons. In 1957, he signed the "Appeal of the Göttingen 18" against the nuclear arming of West Germany.

In Göttingen, as well as in Edinburgh, Born gathered numerous talented students around himself. He greatly influenced the development of quantum mechanics. In 1954, Born received the Nobel Prize for his fundamental contributions, and especially for the statistical interpretation of the wave function.

Stefan L. Wolff

See also Einstein, Albert; Heisenberg, Werner; Hilbert, David; Kaiser Wilhelm/Max Planck Societies and Institutes; Klein, Felix; Physics; Planck, Max; Schrödinger, Erwin

References
Born, Max. *Ausgewählte Abhandlungen*. Vol. 2. Göttingen: Vandenhoeck & Ruprecht, 1963.
———. *Physics in My Generation*. London: Pergamon, 1956.
The Born-Einstein Letters. Correspondence between Albert Einstein and Max and Hedwig Born. London: Walker, 1971.

Bosch, Carl (1874–1940)

One of the towering figures in German economic life during the Weimar and Nazi periods, Carl Bosch decisively shaped the German chemical industry and increased the capacity of his resource-poor country to wage prolonged war.

His development (1912) of industrial methods of extracting nitrogen from the air under high pressures and temperatures, for which he received a Nobel Prize (1931), not only freed Germany from dependence on imported nitrates for the manufacture of fertilizers and explosives, but also laid the basis for German production of fuel from domestic supplies of coal. During his tenure as chairman of the managing (1925–35) and supervisory (1935–40) boards of the giant I.G. Farben chemicals combine, that firm became deeply drawn into the Nazi program of arms, autarky, and aggression.

Born in Cologne as the eldest of six children of a factory owner and wholesaler, Bosch earned his doctorate summa cum laude at Leipzig in 1898, then joined the BASF corporation. He became a member of its managing board in 1916 and its chairman three years later. In 1924 he persuaded the leaders of the major German organic chemicals firms to merge their operations into I.G. Farben, largely on his terms and in order to apply their combined strength to the production of fuel from coal via the hydrogenation process. When this costly initiative proved economically uncompetitive, he clung to it nevertheless, seeking government assistance to stem the losses. This the Nazis granted in December 1933, and the agreement set a precedent for subsequent forms of state assistance to I.G. Farben's production of light metals, synthetic fibers, and rubber.

The tragic irony of Bosch's career was that his technical achievements came to serve political goals with which he did not sympathize. A devoted advocate of a trade-oriented, laissez-faire political economy, he acted as midwife to an aggressive, authoritarian one. Though he mistrusted the Nazis before and after 1933, refused to join the Party, actively opposed attacks on Jewish Germans, and considered Hitler's economic course irrational, his interest in producing substitutes for imported raw materials laid a basis of mutual interest between his firm and the Third Reich. The result was a degree of corporate complicity in facilitating German expansionism that drove the always somewhat melancholy Bosch to despondency by the time of his death.

Peter Hayes

See also BASF; Chemistry, Scientific and Industrial; Four-Year Plan; I.G. Farbenindustrie AG; National Socialist Germany

References

Hayes, Peter. *Industry and Ideology: IG Farben in the Nazi Era.* New York, NY: Cambridge University Press, 1987.

Holdermann, Karl. *Im Banne der Chemie: Carl Bosch, Leben und Werk.* Düsseldorf: Econ-Verlag, 1960.

Bosch, Robert (1861–1942)

On November 15, 1886, Robert Bosch opened his Workshop for Precision Mechanics and Electrical Engineering in Stuttgart with a staff of two—a journeyman mechanic and an apprentice. This company rapidly expanded to become a world leader in automotive technology and numerous other products. The number of employees grew from 4,500 in 1912 to 21,000 in 1936, and reached 181,000 in 1991.

Bosch, the youngest son of an innkeeper and farmer, was born on September 23, 1861, in Albeck, a village near Ulm. A mechanic's apprenticeship in Ulm and one semester as a visiting student at the Technical University of Stuttgart were followed by the traditional journeyman's travels, which took him as far as Great Britain and the United States. He married in 1887 and had three children. His second marriage in 1927 produced two more children.

In 1887, Bosch constructed a low-tension magneto for stationary gas engines. Ten years later, after further development, it made its debut in an automobile engine. In 1902, Gottlob Honold (1876–1923)—Bosch's first engineer—developed the high-tension magneto and Bosch spark plug. This innovation, followed by subsequent Bosch engineering and manufacturing breakthroughs, made a significant contribution to the success of the automobile.

Bosch began diversifying his company as early as 1927, with the introduction of a line of power tools. Other products and acquisitions followed: film cameras and projectors (1932), refrigerators (1933), radios (1933), television sets, electronic cameras, and broadcasting equipment (1936).

In addition to his immense success as an industrialist, Bosch had a strong philanthropic inclination. In 1906, his company became one of the first in Germany to introduce the eight–hour day for employees. Because of his abhorrence of profits gained by war, Bosch donated more than ten million marks to the German people (1916). Between the world wars, he made a major attempt to reconcile the French and German peoples. To commemorate the company's fiftieth anniversary, Bosch endowed the trust for the Robert Bosch Hospital in Stuttgart.

Bosch and Hans Walz (1883–1974), his managing director and successor, opposed the Nazi regime. Bosch helped many Jewish and other persecuted people. The Yad Vashem Foundation of Israel honored this benevolence in 1970. Bosch (until his death in 1942) and Walz supported the German anti-Nazi Resistance group that plotted the abortive coup of July 20, 1944.

Bosch regarded his company as an organism whose task it was to create assets for the benefit of society. For this reason, in his will dated 1937, he handed over his company to executors, who created the Robert Bosch Foundation in 1964. Today, the foundation owns more than 90 percent of the shares of Robert Bosch GmbH.

Rolf Becker

See also Automobile Industry; Resistance; Schindler, Oskar and Helpers of Jews

References

Heuss, Theodor. *Robert Bosch: His Life and Achievements.* Trans. Susan Gillespie and Jennifer Kapezuski. New York, NY: H. Holt, 1994.

Schildberger, Friedrich. *Bosch und der Dieselmotor.* Stuttgart: Robert Bosch GmbH, 1950.

———. *Bosch und die Zündung.* Stuttgart: Robert Bosch GmbH, 1952.

Bourgeoisie (*Bürgertum*)

The German term *Bürgertum* (bourgeoisie) derives from *Bürger* (citizen), originally the burgher of the medieval and early modern town. In the nineteenth century, the unity and privileged position of the urban citizenry was destroyed, and the lower middle class (*Kleinbürgertum* or *Mittelstand*) came to be largely excluded from the bourgeoisie. The bourgeoisie of the Imperial period, consisting of upper-middle-class and elite elements, became a dominant force in German society while seeking a modus vivendi with the nobility and the monarchy. The postwar period brought both the bourgeoisification of German society and the downfall of the bourgeoisie as a distinct social class.

Many of the cultural and political ideals central to the concept of *Bürgertum* originated in the eighteenth-century Enlightenment. The term *"Bürger"* took on the connotation of a "free" individual, endowed with the rights of citizenship, including *"Bürgerrechte"* or civil rights. Together, these citizens formed a *"Bürgerliche Gesellschaft,"* or civil society, which was conceived to be a classless society of *Bürger*. It worked to undermine the absolutist system.

"Civil society" remained (and still remains) an uncompleted project, not only in Germany but in the West as a whole. The bourgeoisie of the late eighteenth and early nineteenth centuries challenged the dominant position of the nobility on moral and philosophical grounds. In its own eyes, the bourgeoisie stood for achievement as opposed to birthright, the work ethic, honesty, decency, rationality in everyday life, and autonomy. Central to the bourgeois ethos is the concept of *Bildung*, which means education, not only in the formal sense, but also in the sense of the Enlightenment ideal of the perfection of the human spirit. "Solid" family life, involving patriarchal authority, sexual morality, and women's devotion to the needs of the family, provided an emotional haven in a harsh world and a sphere in which children could be socialized to bourgeois life. Economic security and prosperity, as well as an urban setting, were the prerequisites for this kind of life.

Industrialization and modernization led to the decline of the urban lower middle class (consisting of artisans, shopkeepers, and the like) and the rise of a wealthy, powerful, and socially exclusive bourgeoisie dominated by businessmen (industrialists, bankers, large-scale merchants, and other capitalists). The other major component of the bourgeoisie, the *Bildungsbürgertum*, or educated and professional bourgeoisie, lost its once-dominant position within the bourgeoisie by 1871. It consisted of university professors, teachers at the gymnasium level, civil servants, Lutheran clergy, members of the free professions, and other people with a university education. Intermarriage and the spread of university education in business circles promoted ties between the two factions of the bourgeoisie.

Nonetheless, a fusion of *Bildungsbürgertum* and economic bourgeoisie did not take place in Germany. There have been considerable disagreements among historians concerning the role of the bourgeoisie in Imperial Germany and in German history as a whole. In the decades after World War II, it was often said that the bourgeoisie had failed in its "mission" to liberalize and democratize German society. It was too weak to bring about a revolution in Germany, and was coopted or "feudalized" by the aristocracy. Against this background, the downfall of liberalism and the political alliance between "rye and iron" would appear to be the result of bourgeois self-abnegation. However, as David Blackbourn and Geoff Eley have pointed out, it was because of the hostility of the working class, *Mittelstand,* and peasantry that the bourgeoisie did not try to attain a position of overt political predominance.

This was unnecessary in any case, because the German state, far from being the defender of the old order, carried out a true "revolution from above" and promoted what the bourgeoisie saw as progress in many areas: German unification and state interventionism to promote economic growth, the rule of law, and imperialism. The monarchial system served as a bulwark against revolution in the country with the largest and best-organized labor movement in the world. Blackbourn and Eley do, however, overstate the extent of bourgeoisification in prewar German society, which was strongly resisted by the nobility. Unlike in Great Britain, there was no fusion of aristocracy and bourgeoisie. Moreover, social and political divisions within the bourgeoisie (between the business class and *Bildungsbürgertum*, as well as among Catholics, Protestants, and Jews) and within the broader middle classes (between the bourgeoisie proper and the *Mittelstand*) limited the social, political, and cultural influence of the bourgeoisie. It is also important to note that the German bourgeoisie's close relationship with the state (evidenced by acceptance of state interventionism, for example), stood in the way of the development of the Enlightenment ideal of the autonomous *Bürger*.

The bourgeois era (if one may be said to have existed in Germany) was essentially over by 1918. In the Weimar period, the nobility lost all real significance, but the economic crisis and the realities of mass politics conspired to prevent a triumph of the bourgeoisie. The Nazis opposed everything that the *Bürgertum* had traditionally represented, and most of their supporters were peasants or members of the *Mittelstand* or even the working class. Nonetheless, the *Bürgertum* played a key role in the Nazi accession to power, a fact which was not forgotten after 1945. The postwar period brought the destruction of the East German bourgeoisie and a general bourgeoisification of West German society, although forces such as the social state, female emancipation, and mass unemployment have partially destroyed the foundations of bourgeois habits and values in the West. Scholars are in agreement that the *Bürgertum* no longer exists as a concrete social formation, but the contradictory traditions and values associated with it live on in contemporary German society and political life.

Dolores L. Augustine

See also Aristocracy; *Bildung und Bildungsbürgertum;* Burschenschaft; Free Democratic Party; German Democratic Party; German National People's Party; German People's Party; Liberalism; National Liberal Party

References

Augustine, Dolores L. *Patricians and Parvenus: Wealthy Business Families in Wilhelmine Germany*. Oxford: Berg Publishers, 1994.

Blackbourn, David and Geoff Eley. *The Peculiarities of German History: Bourgeois Society and Politics in Nineteenth-Century Germany*. Oxford: Oxford University Press, 1984.

Blackbourn, David and Richard J. Evans, eds. *The German Bourgeoisie: Essays on the Social History of the German Middle Class from the Late Eighteenth to the Early Twentieth Century*. London: Routledge, 1991.

Cocks, Geoffrey and Konrad Jarausch, eds. *German Professions, 1800–1950*. New York, NY: Oxford University Press, 1990.

Kaplan, Marion. *The Making of the Jewish Middle Class: Women, Family, and Identity in Imperial Germany*. New York, NY: Oxford University Press, 1991.

Kocka, Jürgen and Allen Mitchell, eds. *Bourgeois Society in Nineteenth-Century Europe*. Oxford: Berg, 1993.

Mosse, Werner. *The German-Jewish Economic Elite, 1820–1935: A Socio-Cultural Profile*. New York, NY: Oxford University Press, 1989.

Niethammer, Lutz et al. *Bürgerliche Gesellschaft in Deutschland: Historische Einblicke, Fragen, Perspektiven*. Frankfurt am Main: Fischer Verlag, 1990.

Boveri, Theodor (1862–1915)

Boveri has a reputation as one of the first researchers to fuse Mendelian genetics with investigations of cell biology, which were particularly advanced in late-nineteenth-century Germany.

Boveri was the second of four sons of a Franconian physician, Theodor Boveri, and he pursued his entire academic career in Bavaria. He studied zoology at the University of Munich, gained a doctorate in natural sciences in 1885, and then joined the institute of the cell biologist and zoologist Richard Hertwig, where he gained his *Habilitation* (qualification for university teaching). From 1893, he was professor of zoology and comparative anatomy at the University of Würzburg. His experimental cell biology represented a departure from Darwinian morphology.

Emulating many German biologists, Boveri studied problems of heredity and development in marine organisms, at a time when intense philosophical and theoretical debates raged about mechanistic and vitalistic theories of organic development. He experimentally defined the role of the nucleus in the cytoplasm, and in 1903 he made pioneering observations on relations between genes and chromosomes. But he personally undertook no substantive genetics research. This was typical of the initially weak German response to Mendelian genetics.

When offered the directorship of the new Kaiser Wilhelm Institute for Biology, Boveri enlisted the help of his brother Walther, an engineer (and partner in the firm of Brown Boveri). He shaped the staffing of the institute by selecting Carl Correns, Richard Goldschmidt, and the future Nobel laureate Hans Spemann, thereby fundamentally deter-mining the agenda of interwar biological research. The reasons why Boveri ultimately declined the directorship have been the subject of much speculation. His illness and a reluctance to lose the status of a university professor were factors.

Boveri had wide-ranging cultural and philosophical interests and an earthy sense of humor. He married an American biologist; his daughter was the distinguished journalist Margret Boveri.

Paul Weindling

See also Biochemistry; Biology; Kaiser Wilhelm/Max Planck Societies and Institutes

References

Baltzer, F. *Theodor Boveri: Life and Work of a Great Biologist, 1862–1915*. Trans. D. Rudnick. Berkeley, CA: University of California Press, 1967.

Horder, T.J. and P.J. Weindling. "Hans Spemann and the Organiser." *A History of Embryology*. Ed. T. J. Horder. Cambridge: Cambridge University Press, 1986.

Brahms, Johannes (1833–97)

At a time when modern German music was ruled by Franz Liszt (1811–86) and Richard Wagner (1813–83), the German composer Johannes Brahms was regarded by many—including some of those who championed him—as an arch-conservative. Yet today he has come to occupy that rare place of honor that we reserve for an artist whose work is both intrinsically splendid and a fountainhead for subsequent developments in the given art. In an age when it was common to excel in but one or two areas, he created prodigiously in all genres except opera.

Following a thorough grounding in piano and composition at an early age, Brahms first earned his living chiefly as a touring pianist and occasional conductor. Success in composition came to him slowly; he won general acclaim only after he settled in Vienna permanently in 1868.

The peculiar character of much of Brahms's music derives from two contrasting affinities: a love for the folk song, and an attraction to the art music of the past. As was his general habit, he worked hard at both interests, absorbing into his vocal and instrumental music techniques and colors not generally appreciated in his day.

Brahms wrote piano and vocal music throughout his life. Perhaps because he was a fine performer himself, the former category includes many of his most exquisitely controlled yet fantasy-rich large-scale works (e.g., the Händel Variations, 1861), as well as some of his most forward-looking pieces (e.g., the Intermezzos of 1892 and 1893). The vocal music (including some 200 songs worthy of a successor to Franz Schubert) ranges from the soaring testament of the *German Requiem*, 1868, to the ravishing lilt of the *Zigeunerlieder* (Gypsy songs), 1888.

Brahms was acutely aware of the "shadow" of Beethoven's accomplishments in the weightiest of "absolute" genres, orchestral and chamber music. Even if he did take 20 years to write his First Symphony because of it, in the end his genius

Johannes Brahms. Courtesy of Inter Nationes, Bonn.

and determination earned him the mantle of Beethoven's heir precisely in these areas. His two dozen chamber works are distinguished not only by superb workmanship but also by an astonishing variety, ranging from the traditional string quartet (three between 1873 and 1876) to a trio for clarinet, 'cello, and piano (1891). Pride of place, however, must go to Brahms's symphonies (four between 1876 and 1885): in an age infatuated with musical drama (whether on stage or in the concert hall) and rapidly approaching a stylistic no-return because of it, the collective weight of just these four works (accrued from an inexhaustible melodic invention, a rich but meticulously controlled harmonic palette, an imaginatively flexible use of the inherited form, and the unremitting integrity of the communicative intent) was great enough to stave off disintegration for a score more years.

Zoltan Roman

See also Chamber Music; Choral Music; Composers; Conductors; Keyboard Music; Liszt, Franz; Orchestral Music; Wagner, Richard

References

Bozarth, George S., ed. *Brahms Studies: Analytical and Historical Perspectives.* Oxford: Clarendon, 1990.

Brahms, Johannes. *Sämtliche Werke.* Ed. Gesellschaft der Musikfreunde/Wien. Ann Arbor, MI: J.W. Edwards, 1949.

Geiringer, Karl. *Brahms: His Life and Work.* 3rd ed. New York, NY: Da Capo, 1982.

Musgrave, Michael. *The Music of Brahms.* London: Routledge and Kegan Paul, 1985.

Quigley, Thomas. *Johannes Brahms: An Annotated Bibliography of the Literature through 1982.* Metuchen, NJ: Scarecrow, 1990.

Brandenburg

Among the five new federal states, Brandenburg has the largest area combined with a relatively low population density of 275 inhabitants per square mile; in 1990 the total number of inhabitants was 2.65 million. The state comprises the central core of the former Prussian state surrounding Berlin, with which it is closely associated. Berlin was excluded in 1920 from the Prussian province of Brandenburg, which in turn was subdivided into the administrative districts (*Regierungsbezirke*) of Potsdam and Frankfurt an der Oder.

After World War II Brandenburg lost the region east of the Oder (30 percent of its territory), which became part of Poland, and emerged as an independent state (*Land*). It existed until the dissolution of the states (*Länder*) of the German Democratic Republic (GDR) in 1952, when it was divided into the districts of Potsdam, Frankfurt an der Oder, and Cottbus. After reunification Brandenburg was reconstituted in October 1990 with some territorial modifications. The capital is Potsdam, the largest city (141,000 inhabitants). Potsdam is, on one hand, a symbol of Prussian militarism; on the other hand, it also represents the cultural efflorescence of Prussia with its palace and park of Sans Souci, and the Cecilienhof palace, in which the victorious Allies concluded the Potsdam Agreement in 1945.

In the first free elections to the Brandenburg legislature on October 14, 1990, the Social Democratic Party (SPD) received the highest percentage of the votes cast (38.3 percent). It formed a coalition with the Free Democratic Party (FDP; 6.6 percent) and the Bündnis 90 (Alliance 90; 9.2 percent). The Christian Democratic Union (CDU; 29.4 percent) and the successor of the Socialist Unity Party (SED), the Party of Democratic Socialism (PDS; 13.4 percent), formed the opposition. As a result of the 1994 state elections, the SPD gained an absolute majority with 54.1 percent of the vote, and was able to govern on its own (CDU 18.7 percent; Bündnis 90/Greens and the FDP failed to overcome the 5-percent hurdle).

Brandenburg's industrialization commenced during the Imperial era, mainly in the Berlin vicinity. The number of inhabitants in the administrative district of Potsdam tripled from 1871 to 1914, rising from 1 to 3 million. During the same period the population of the administrative district of Frankfurt an der Oder increased only from 1 million to 1.3 million. Election results also reflected the differential degree of industrialization. In the Potsdam district (Berlin excluded), the SPD obtained 54 percent of the votes in 1912 whereas the conservative parties obtained 20 percent; in the Frankfurt an der Oder district, the SPD and the conservative parties were equally strong (35 percent each). During the Weimar Republic the workers' parties' representation in the Potsdam district remained above the average. Conversely, the Nazis obtained above-average results in the administrative district of Frankfurt an der Oder during the final phase of the Republic.

Under the Nazi dictatorship, Brandenburg became one of the centers of arms production. Steel and rolling-mills in Eisenhüttenstadt, open-pit mining of brown coal in Cottbus (the state's second largest city, with 129,000 inhabitants), machine and vehicle construction, and large chemical plants played a preeminent role in the GDR. Babelsberg, near Potsdam, was the center of the German film industry. Here the UFA (during the GDR era the DEFA) produced its feature films. With the dissolution of the GDR the entire industry of Brandenburg plunged into a deep crisis owing to the restructuring from planned economy to market economy; the unemployment rate was 14.89 percent in 1992.

One of the special characteristics of Brandenburg is the presence of ethnic Sorbs, a Slavic minority of approximately 100,000 people, who maintain their own culture and language in the Lausitz region. In the future, Brandenburg will benefit from the relocation of the seat of the German government from Bonn to Berlin.

Walter Mühlhausen

See also Berlin; Federalism; Prussia

References

Demps, Laurenz. "Brandenburg als Stammland Preussens." *Die neuen Bundesländer.* Ed. Martin Greiffenhagen. Stuttgart: Kohlhammer, 1994.

Holmsten, Georg. *Brandenburg: Geschichte des Landes, seiner Städte und Regenten.* 2nd ed. Berlin: Haude & Spener, 1991.

Jann, Werner and Bernhard Muszynski. "Brandenburg." *Handbuch der deutschen Bundesländer.* Ed. Jürgen Hartmann. 2nd ed. Frankfurt am Main: Campus, 1994.

Krockow, Christian Graf von. *Fahrten durch die Mark Brandenburg: Wege in unserer Geschichte.* Stuttgart: Deutsche Verlags-Anstalt, 1991.

Stiftung Mitteldeutscher Kulturrat Bonn. *Brandenburg.* Würzburg: Weidlich, 1991.

Wolffsohn, Seew. *Wirtschaftliche und soziale Entwicklungen in Brandenburg, Preussen, Schlesien und Oberschlesien.* Frankfurt am Main: P. Lang, 1985.

Brandler, Heinrich (1881–1967)

Heinrich Brandler was unusual among interwar leaders of the Communist Party of Germany (KPD) in being genuinely working class by both social origin and profession. His father was a bricklayer; he too entered the building trade. Self-educated, he was a trade unionist from 1896 and a Social Democrat from 1901. Brandler gradually gravitated toward the extreme left of the Social Democratic Party (SPD) around Rosa Luxemburg (1870–1919) and Karl Liebknecht (1871–1919). During World War I he joined the Spartacist group and helped Fritz Heckert to bring over his local party organizations in Chemnitz.

Brandler's early reputation was based on the prompt and vigorous response of the Chemnitz district to the Kapp *Putsch* of 1920, which contrasted with the abject failure of the KPD as a whole. This gave him the credentials to lead the Left in 1921, when he shared much of the responsibility for initiating the disastrous March Action, a *Putsch* attempt. After a short interval in jail and exile he returned to lead the party in 1922. But he had changed. Now he was devoted to the "united front" tactic, defending it against the KPD leftists. As party leader during the critical year 1923, Brandler faced awkward decisions. Despite the atmosphere of political and social crisis, he was dubious about the possibilities for revolution. He allowed Comintern pressure to force him into agreeing to an immediate seizure of power. When the decisive moment arrived, however, in October 1923, he called off the action, correctly surmising that the left Social Democrats would refuse to follow the KPD's lead.

Brandler was the obvious scapegoat for the debacle of 1923. He was removed from the leadership in January 1924, summoned to Moscow, and kept there. After his unauthorized return to Germany in 1928 he was expelled from the party for organizing a "rightist" faction. He then proceeded to found a new party, the KPO (Communist Party Opposition), which aimed to bring Social Democratic and Communist workers together in joint opposition to Nazism. He continued to be politically active to the end of his life, first in exile, then back in Germany. Brandler was essentially an able organizer, not a theoretician or revolutionary leader, and it was his misfortune that he took over the KPD at a time of revolutionary turmoil, when qualities of leadership and independence of judgment were indispensable.

Ben Fowkes

See also Fischer, Ruth; German Communist Party; Luxemburg, Rosa; Social Democratic Party; Thälmann, Ernst

References

Angress, Werner. *Stillborn Revolution: The Communist Bid for Power in Germany 1921–1923.* Princeton, NJ: Princeton University Press, 1963.

Fowkes, Ben. *Communism in Germany under the Weimar Republic.* London: Macmillan Press Ltd., 1984.

Tjaden, Karl-Hermann. *Struktur und Funktion der KPD Opposition (KPO).* Hannover: SOAK-Verlag, 1983.

Weber, Hermann. *Die Wandlung des deutschen Kommunismus.* 2 vols. Frankfurt am Main: Europäische Verlagsanstalt, 1969.

Brandt, Willy (1913–92)

The mayor of West Berlin from 1957 to 1966, leader of the Social Democratic Party (SPD) from 1964 to 1988, foreign minister and chancellor of Germany from 1966 to 1974, Willy Brandt received the Nobel Peace Prize in 1971 for his efforts in normalizing relations with the Eastern European countries that Nazi Germany had terrorized. In many ways, he represented the success of postwar Germany coming to terms with the Nazi past, taking up a role as a peaceful diplomatic player on the European stage, and moving toward a pluralistic society.

The name Brandt emerged in March 1933 during his resistance to Nazism in the socialist underground. Born illegitimately as Herbert Frahm in Lübeck in December 1913, he identified with his working-class grandfather's and mother's left-wing unionism and politics. By 16 he had become an active member of the Social Democrats. In 1931 he joined with the more activist Socialist Workers' Party and through it worked in the Resistance, mostly as a journalist in Scandinavia.

In 1946, Brandt returned to Berlin as a journalist and Norwegian press attaché. He became a protegé of the SPD mayor Ernst Reuter (1889–1953) and his radicalism declined. In Berlin, he remarried in 1948 and added three sons to the daughter by his first wife. At age 70 he would marry once more after many affairs. He remained by his own admission a reserved person, though he was ebullient in public.

Four phases and significant contributions mark his life. As a young radical socialist he opposed Nazism. During that phase he learned a more moderate and pragmatic approach to questions of social justice from the Scandinavians. After the war, while he fought for leadership roles in the Social Democratic Party, he engaged in what one biographer termed "double-speak"—radical rhetoric combined with pragmatism, for instance in accepting German rearmament. In this second phase he became mayor of Berlin and exploited the publicity of a city suffering at the center of Cold War confrontations and the building of the Berlin Wall in 1961. As the "German Kennedy," he sought the leadership of the Social Democrats, which he finally attained in 1964. However, as in 1961, and again in 1965, his bid for the German chancellorship failed.

Brandt himself saw 1965—which marked the beginning of the third phase—as a dividing point in his life and claimed that personal ambition gave way to a focus upon creative purpose. That purpose became the normalization of relations among all the European states.

Brandt's political opportunity came with the recession of 1966—which the conservatives failed to master—and through his party finally receiving sufficient votes to attain office in coalition with the liberals. After three years as foreign minister in an uncomfortable coalition with the conservatives, Brandt headed a ministry that consummated *Ostpolitik*, a policy of normalization with Eastern Europe.

His treaties with the Soviet Union, Poland, and East Germany and the agreement on Berlin stabilized the situation in Central Europe. The acknowledgment that Germany had lost the war and its eastern territories was enshrined by Brandt's symbolic act of falling to his knees at the memorial for the victims of the Nazi liquidation of the Warsaw ghetto. Though his diplomatic successes were not matched by promised internal reforms, the break had been made with the elitist, conservative Germany of Konrad Adenauer, which often had protected Nazi collaborators and war criminals.

After resigning from the chancellorship because of a spy scandal, Brandt headed the Socialist International and the North-South Commission in the last phase of his public life. Through these organizations he attempted to achieve the normalization of relations on a global scale and to make the industrial world aware of the Third World's plight. More cries of conscience than substantive changes emerged.

Brandt represented the maturing of the second German democracy and ensured that it did not go the way of the first. As the first Social Democratic chancellor since 1930, he helped to integrate that party as it abandoned its radical ideology. In his diplomatic actions Brandt represented the return of Germany to the international stage, but in a positive fashion, in contrast to the first half of the century. And in his personal life Brandt unconventionally illustrated that public figures can have foibles, these can be known, and they should not sway public judgments. As an individual Brandt remains an enigma. He was judged as too emotional and too lacking in charisma during 1965, then seen as a highly charismatic figure and as a stable, capable tactician in the 1970s. From a longer perspective, his *Ostpolitik* will perhaps be seen as more decisive than Helmut Kohl's efforts in the process of unifying Germany.

Dieter K. Buse

See also Adenauer, Konrad; American-German Relations; Anglo-German Relations; Bahr, Egon; Basic Treaty; Berlin; Berlin Wall; The Cold War and Germany; Detente and Germany; Federal Republic of Germany; Federal Republic of Germany: Foreign Policy; German Democratic Republic; German Democratic Republic: State Security; Grand Coalition; Franco-German Relations; German-German Relations; Honecker, Erich; National Identity; Nationalism; *Ostpolitik*; Parliamentary System; Parties and Politics; Postwar European Integration and Germany; Resistance; Reuter, Ernst; Schmidt, Helmut; Social Democratic Party; Soviet-German Relations; Stoph, Willi; Ulbricht, Walter; Wehner, Herbert; World War II

References

Brandt, Willy. *In Exile: Essays, Reflections and Letters 1933–1947*. Translated by R.W. Last. London: Oswald Wolff, 1973.
———. *My Life in Politics*. Trans. Anthea Bell. Middlesex: Penguin, 1992.
———. *People and Politics: The Years 1960–1975*. Trans. J. Maxwell Brownjohn. London: Collins, 1978.
Marshall, Barbara. *Willy Brandt*. London: Cardinal, 1990.
Prittie, Terence. *Willy Brandt: Portrait of a Statesman*. London: Weidenfeld and Nicolson, 1974.

Brauchitsch, Walter von (1881–1948)

Field Marshal Walter von Brauchitsch was commander in chief of the German army from 1938 through 1941. Personal circumstances made him dependent on Adolf Hitler and a complaisant instrument of the führer's conduct of the war.

Brauchitsch was born in Berlin on October 4, 1881. He joined the military in 1900. Twelve years later, he was transferred to the army's Grand General Staff. During World War I, Brauchitsch held various positions as an officer of the General Staff on the western front. During the Weimar Republic he entered the Reichswehr as a major.

Brauchitsch held numerous positions until 1932, most of them on the General Staff. From 1933 until his appointment as the army's commander in chief on February 4, 1938, he was commander of the First Division and of No. 1 Military District (Königsberg, 1933–37), later commander of the Fourth Army Group in Leipzig (1937–38). The precondition for his assuming high office was a financial donation from Hitler that made it possible for Brauchitsch to divorce his first wife and marry again. However, this made him dependent on Hitler, and his second wife (a fanatic Nazi) added her influence to make Brauchitsch a ready supporter of Hitler's war policies. Although an excellent military thinker, he did not have the force of character to prevail against Hitler, even in military matters.

During the 1938 Munich crisis, Brauchitsch shared the doubts voiced by his chief of staff, General Ludwig Beck (1880–1944). Nevertheless, he did not consent to organized insubordination of the army generals to terminate Hitler's course, which seemed to make war inevitable. Brauchitsch organized the military aspects of the *Anschluss* of Austria (March 1938) as well as the occupation of the Sudetenland (October 1938) and the invasion of Bohemia and Moravia in March 1939. Cooperating closely with his new chief of staff, General Franz Halder (1884–1972), he planned and commanded the operations against Poland, Denmark, Norway, Belgium, Luxembourg, the Netherlands, France, and the Balkans. The victorious outcomes heightened his prestige, both in army circles and in Hitler's eyes. The campaign against the USSR was planned by Brauchitsch, who also led the operations until December 1941. Hitler then held his army commander in chief responsible for the military failure in Russia during the winter of 1941–42. He discharged the field marshal on December 19, 1941.

After the war, Brauchitsch, who was suffering from cardiac disease, was arrested by the British. He died in a military hospital on October 18, 1948, before he could stand trial for war crimes.

Klaus Schönherr

See also Beck, Ludwig; Halder, Franz; Hitler, Adolf; National Socialist Germany: Military; Weimar Germany: Army

References
Bond, Brian. "Brauchitsch." *Hitler's Generals.* Ed. Correlli Barnett. London: Weidenfeld and Nicolson, 1990.
Brett-Smith, Richard. *Hitler's Generals.* San Rafael, CA: Presido Press, 1976.
Moll, Otto Ernst Eugen. *Die deutschen Generalfeldmarschälle 1935–1945.* Rastatt: Pabel, 1961.

Braun, Lily von Kretschman (1865–1916)

During the two decades immediately preceding World War I, Lily Braun was one of Germany's outstanding feminist socialists. A tireless political agitator, the author of widely read scholarly works such as *Die Frauenfrage* (The women's question), 1903, a journalist, and—toward the end of her career—a novelist, she aroused widespread interest and controversy with her views both in the women's movement as a whole and in the Social Democratic Party (SPD).

Born into the Prussian nobility, Braun's father, Hans, rose to the rank of general before ultimately being disgraced in a conflict with Kaiser Wilhelm II. Braun's mother, Jenny, trained her daughter in a manner befitting traditional nineteenth-century aristocratic females, but Braun chafed at the narrowness of her upbringing. By the 1890s she began to educate herself more broadly in philosophical and political matters. She became active in the Women's Welfare Association and in the German Society for Ethical Culture, in which she espoused left-leaning ideas critical of Christianity, patriarchy, and the exploitation of the working class. In 1893, she married Georg von Gizycki, an independent socialist and associate professor of moral philosophy at the University of Berlin. Gizycki died in 1895. One year later, shortly after declaring herself a socialist and joining the SPD, Lily married Heinrich Braun, a leading party intellectual.

Braun became a controversial SPD figure primarily because her ideas on social reform challenged the views of the orthodox Marxist leaders of the party, including the head of its women's organization, Clara Zetkin (1857–1933). In general, Braun urged the SPD to fight for a variety of radical reforms that would improve conditions for women workers and mothers under capitalism. She believed that the establishment of household operatives, maternity insurance, legislation to protect domestic servants, and other measures would broaden the SPD's base of support and help prepare the ground for the gradual development of socialism. She thought the socialist women's movement should cooperate with bourgeois women's organizations for the achievement of these aims; she counseled the SPD to establish new institutions to study the condition of women and coordinate the activities of women's organizations.

The party adopted some of Braun's ideas (e.g., the demand for a maternity furlough), but leaders such as Zetkin and Karl Kautsky (1854–1938) generally viewed them as "utopian" and "reformist" distractions from the proletariat's struggle for political power. Driven by personal as well as ideological motives, Zetkin successfully isolated Braun in the party. Braun lost her post at *Die Gleichheit* (Equality), the SPD women's organization newspaper, and at the party congress of 1903, co-chairman August Bebel (1840–1913) denounced Braun and her husband as revisionists. Though not expelled from the SPD, they had difficulty thereafter in gaining access to the socialist press or earning their living through party activity.

Although isolated, Braun remained in the SPD until shortly before her sudden death in 1916, and she continued to present controversial and sometimes contradictory views on marriage, children's rights, and other issues. World War I disoriented her ideologically. While she joined the SPD majority who backed the German war effort, she also grew disillusioned with the party, which she thought had been corrupted by capitalist materialism. Braun still hoped for the creation of a socialist society after the war and was convinced that by mobilizing for work in the war economy and by bearing children, women would be laying the foundation of a future socialist society.

William Smaldone

See also Feminism and Anti-Feminism; Social Democratic Party, 1871–1918; Zetkin, Clara

References
Boxer, Marilyn J. and Jean H. Quataert, eds. *Socialist Women.* New York, NY: Elsevier, 1978.
Braun, Lily. *Memoiren einer Sozialisten.* Vol. I: *Lehrjahre.* Vol. II. *Kampfjahre.* Munich: Albert Langen, 1908, 1911.
———. *Selected Writings on Feminism and Socialism.* Trans. and ed. Alfred G. Meyer. Bloomington, IN: Indiana University Press, 1987.
Meyer, Alfred C. *The Feminism and Socialism of Lily Braun.* Bloomington, IN: Indiana University Press, 1985.
Quataert, Jean H. *Reluctant Feminists in German Social Democracy. 1885–1917.* Princeton, NJ: Princeton University Press, 1979.

Braun, Otto (1875–1955)

As the Social Democratic Party (SPD) head of the Prussian state from 1920 to 1932 (with short interruptions), Otto Braun tried to transform the largest German state into a republican and democratic entity. However, in July 1932, when Chancellor Papen employed a constitutional technicality to remove him from office, Braun offered little resistance and went into exile.

Braun typified a generation of SPD leaders who came from craft families, joined the party young, and practiced journalism. The son of a shoemaker, Braun learned the printing trade after completing public schooling. In 1889, he joined the Social Democrats in Königsberg and quickly became the head of the organization. By 1893, he edited the local party paper and was, along with his friend Hugo Haase (1863–1919), among a group accused of treason against the state. Elected to the party central in 1911, he served as a capable organizer and administrator. From 1913 to 1918 he served in the Prussian parliament and from 1918 to 1920 in the Reichstag. Ideologically, Braun identified with the orthodox "Marxist" middle of the party until World War I.

In August 1914, Braun revealed highly emotional and patriotic concerns about his East Prussian homeland, then invaded by the Russians. Despite losing his only son at the front in 1915, he sided with those Social Democrats who continuously favored war credits. Depressions and illness sometimes hindered his work as party treasurer and his fight against the left-wing antiwar faction in the party. By early 1918, he wrote stridently anti-Bolshevik articles and approved compromises with the middle-class parties.

During the Revolution of 1918–19, Braun participated in the workers' council of Berlin, but favored an immediate constitutional assembly. As Prussian agricultural minister in 1919, he tried to remove the most reactionary Prussian bureaucrats and fostered rural settlement programs for demobilized soldiers. Later he opposed the use of emergency decrees

by President Ebert, especially if carried out by the military on social and economic issues. He favored a coalition of middle-of-the-road parties, which he achieved for Prussia in 1921 (SPD, Democrats, Center, and People's Party), after he had been minister of agriculture for three years. As Prussian prime minister from 1921 to 1932, with two short interruptions, he was respected for his energy, integrity, and what a biographer called his "virtuosity in the use of power."

He competed as the SPD presidential candidate in 1925, but lost to General Paul von Hindenburg (1847–1934). Despite the defeat, "the red czar's" Prussia remained the democratic bulwark of Germany in opposition to the Reich, where cabinets ruled by presidential decree after 1930. Before the April 1932 elections in Prussia, Braun's cabinet issued legislation that the head of the Prussian government had to be elected by a majority of the Landtag (legislature). Though in a minority, Braun remained in office until Papen had the Prussian ministries occupied while Braun took holidays during July 1932. Braun refused to support a call for a general strike, but tried to fight back through the courts. After Adolf Hitler's accession to power he went into exile at Ascona, Switzerland. In his memoirs he blamed the Treaty of Versailles and the influence of Moscow for the demise of the Weimar Republic.

Personal reasons accompanied his lack of action in 1932: he wanted to care for his dying wife and his own health was failing. He had tired of politics in the Weimar style: "Given the choice between a cabinet position and becoming a manager of a garbage disposal company," he said toward the end, "I'd understand if somebody chose the latter. For you'd have twice the salary and only half the garbage to deal with."

Though Braun attended some Social Democratic congresses in Germany after 1945, he continued to live in Switzerland until his death. He exercised little influence in exile or after the war.

Dieter K. Buse and Joachim Remak

See also Ebert, Friedrich; Prussia; Revolutions of 1918–19; Social Democratic Party; Weimar Germany; World War I

References
Braun, Otto. *Von Weimar zu Hitler.* New York, NY: Europa Verlag, 1940.
Matull, Wilhelm. *Otto Braun: Preussischer Ministerpräsident der Weimarer Zeit.* Dortmund: Veröffentlichungen der Ostdeutschen Forschungsstelle im Lande Nordrhein-Westfalen, 1973.
Schulze, Hagen. *Otto Braun oder Preussens demokratische Sendung: Eine Biographie.* Berlin: Propyläen, 1977.

Braun, Volker (1939–)

Volker Braun, one of the most important and versatile of the generation of writers who began to publish in East Germany in the 1960s, is a lyricist, dramatist, and narrative prose writer; from his first collection of poems, *Provokation für mich* (Provocation for me), 1965, to his postunification drama, *Böhmen am Meer* (Bohemia by the sea), 1992, his works focus on the processes of social and political change.

Braun was born in Dresden in 1939. On leaving school in 1957, he worked as a printer and as a laborer before studying philosophy in Leipzig from 1960 to 1964. In 1965–66 and again from 1977 he was attached to the Berliner Ensemble; between 1972 and 1977, he was with the Deutsches Theater in Berlin. In his earlier works, Braun identified fully with the official ideals of the German Democratic Republic (GDR), while at the same time he uncompromisingly pointed to the contradictions between intention and reality. His youthful enthusiasm and impatience were not always welcome; his poems were criticized as overintellectual and removed from reality.

From the late 1960s, Braun's work became less intense, more reflective, but also less optimistic that socialism could overcome its shortcomings. The collections of the 1970s and 1980s—*Gegen die symmetrische Welt* (Against the symmetrical world), 1974, *Training des aufrechten Gangs* (Practice in walking unbowed), 1979, *Langsamer knirschender Morgen* (Slow grinding morning), 1987—developed his theme of the individual's right to self-development within society. In his poems, Braun uses a combination of collage, reference to earlier poets, and the jargon and colloquialisms of late-twentieth-century German to reflect his vision of historical development.

Braun's dramatic writing was initially strongly influenced by the work of Bertolt Brecht (1898–1956); it dealt with the attempt to introduce socialist relations of production in the GDR and focused on the contradictions inherent in that process. The key work, *Die Kipper* (The dumpers), went through a number of revisions between 1962 and 1972. In it, and his other works of the time, Braun resisted pressures to minimize conflicts and to idealize his central characters in line with the current understanding of socialist realism. In *Die Kipper*, Paul Bauch is an idealist and loner whose enthusiasm for socialist transformation sets him at odds with his workmates. Braun's later dramas, such as *Guevara,* 1978, *Grosser Frieden* (The great peace), 1979, and *Lenins Tod* (Lenin's death), 1970, first performed in 1988, turned away from the GDR to set the developments there in the more general context of international revolutionary struggle and setbacks.

Braun's narrative writings include the semi-autobiographical *Das ungezwungne Leben Kasts* (Kast's unconstrained life), 1972, extended in 1979, and *Unvollendete Geschichte* (Unfinished story), which appeared in the periodical *Sinn und Form* (Intellect and form) in 1975 but because of its critical content and call for greater openness was not published in book form in the GDR until 1988. His novel, *Hinze-Kunze-Roman* (Hinze and Kunze, a novel), 1985, the most recent product of Braun's long involvement with the Faust material, encountered similar censorship problems.

Despite his disillusionment with the GDR, Braun still hoped in 1989 that it could be reformed. Since German unification his work has reflected withdrawal and pessimism. His play *Böhmen am Meer* considers the future of the former Cold War adversaries faced with the chaos and uncertainty of the approaching twenty-first century.

James A. Mellis

See also Brecht, Bertolt; German Democratic Republic: Literature; German Democratic Republic: Political Culture

References

Arnold, Heinz Ludwig, ed. *Volker Braun.* Munich: edition text + kritik, 1977.

Jacquemoth, Jos. *Politik und Poesie: Untersuchungen zur Lyrik Volker Brauns.* Berlin: Schmengler, 1990.

Profitlich, Ulrich. *Volker Braun: Studien zu seinem dramatischen und erzählerischen Werk.* Munich: Fink, 1985.

Wallace, Ian. *Volker Braun: Forschungsbericht.* Amsterdam: Rodopi, 1986.

———. "Volker Braun's Lyric Poetry: Problems of Reception." *Studies in GDR Culture and Society* 3 (1983), 179–93.

Braun, Wernher von (1912–77)

One of the leading scientists who worked on German and American rocket propulsion, Wernher von Braun was born on March 23, 1912 at Wirsitz (Posen), the son of the then County Administrator (later Minister of Agriculture) Magnus von Braun. Wernher von Braun was first introduced to the idea of space travel as a high-school student by Hermann Oberth's book *Rakete zu den Planetenräumen* (Rockets into outer space).

During his undergraduate studies of mechanical engineering at the Technical University of Berlin (1930–32), he joined the team of the Verein für Raumschiffahrt (Association for Space Travel), experimenting with rocket engines at the rocket testing site Reinickendorf (Raketenflugplatz Reinickendorf). After graduating in 1932, he became a civilian employee of the Army Ordnance Office, working with Captain (later Major General) Walter Dornberger (1895–1980) on small rockets. Completing his graduate studies at Humboldt University at Berlin, he obtained his doctorate in physics in 1934 with a thesis on liquid rocket engines.

After several years of experimental work at Kummersdorf (near Berlin), the Army Development Center was established at Peenemünde, with von Braun as technical director. There he was responsible for the successful development of the A4 (V-2) rocket (1942). His openly expressed intention to use the rocket as a means to reach the moon led to his imprisonment by the Gestapo (1944), but charges were postponed "until the end of the war effort."

In 1945, von Braun and several hundred of his key specialists moved to Bavaria and communicated with the United States army. Von Braun and part of his team were subsequently transferred to the United States within the framework of Operation Paperclip, a secret operation that spirited leading German scientists to America in defiance of American laws against the immigration of such individuals. After some years at El Paso, Texas, they were established at the American Army Redstone Arsenal at Huntsville, Alabama, which in 1960 became NASA's George C. Marshall Space Flight Center under the directorship of von Braun. Based upon their experience from Peenemünde, they developed a series of highly successful liquid rockets. The first successful American satellite, Explorer I, 1958, was the first visible success of the team; the

Saturn V rocket used in the Apollo lunar landing program the climax. In 1970, von Braun became deputy associate administrator (planning) at NASA. From 1972 until 1975 he worked with Fairchild Co. (vice president, engineering and development). He died on June 16, 1977 at Alexandria, Virginia.

Wolfgang Kokott

See also The Cold War and Germany; Dornberger, Walter Robert; Space

References

Bergaust, Erik. *Reaching for the Stars*. New York, NY: Doubleday, 1960.

Bergaust, Erik. *Wernher von Braun*. Washington, DC: National Space Institute, 1976.

David, Heather M. *Wernher von Braun*. New York, NY: Putnam, 1967.

DeVorkin, David H. *Science with a Vengeance*. New York, NY: Springer, 1992.

Ordway, Frederick I., III, and Mitchell R. Sharpe. *The Rocket Team*. New York, NY: Crowell, 1979.

Stuhlinger, Ernst, and F.I. Ordway. *Wernher von Braun: Aufbruch in den Weltraum*. Esslingen: Bechtle, 1992.

Walters, Helen B. *Wernher von Braun, Rocket Engineer*. New York, NY: Macmillan, 1964.

Brecht, Bertolt (1898–1956)

Widely acknowledged as the most influential German dramatist of the twentieth century, Eugen Berthold Brecht—who adopted the name "Bertolt" as a young man—was born on February 10, 1898, to a middle-class family in the Bavarian city of Augsburg. After dabbling in the study of medicine and serving briefly in a military hospital, Brecht abandoned the quest for conventional respectability and found his lifelong métier in poetry and drama, beginning with his drama *Baal* (1922; dates given are those of publication of the German version, not for earlier stages of writing and performance), in which the title figure, a writer, breaks with his bourgeois origins and ruins himself and others in an orgy of excess. In the interval between writing this first work and *Trommeln in der Nacht* (published as *Drums in the Night*), 1923, and *Im Dickicht der Städte* (published as *In the Jungle of Cities*), 1927, Brecht also produced some of his most famous poetry, most of which appeared in his *Hauspostille* (Manual of piety), 1927. Two other important collections resulted from his years of exile in Scandinavia: *Svendborger Gedichte*, 1939, and the *Buckower Elegien* (Buckower elegies), 1954. Although Brecht is less known for his prose, the witty Keuner anecdotes, *Geschichten vom Herrn Keuner* (Stories about Mr. Keuner), 1930, and his *Kalendargeschichten* (Tales from the calendar), 1949, enjoy enduring popularity.

Following his acquaintance with Helene Weigel, Brecht moved to Berlin in 1924. Although he married Weigel in 1929, Brecht maintained sexual and creative alliances with other women who contributed in various degrees to his artistic success. The extent to which Brecht did or did not acknowledge the indebtedness of his work to them and others remains a topic of controversy in discussions of his work, ranging as it did from open adaptations of plays by famous dramatists to unacknowledged borrowings and silent collaborations. The early years in Berlin were also marked by Brecht's study of Marxism, reflected most strikingly in *Die Massnahme* (The measures taken), 1931, one of several "learning plays" (*Lehrstücke*), which Brecht identified as "the theater of the future." The innovative style of this and other such pieces entailed the use of a chorus to break down the distinction between spectator and performer and to give the audience experience in dialectical thinking. The Marxist turn in his thinking is also evident in dramas such as *Die heilige Johanna der Schlachthöfe* (published as *St. Joan of the Stockyards*), 1932/38, and *Die Mutter* (published as *The Mother*), 1930s, based on Maxim Gorki's novel of the same title. Of greater fame are other plays he produced in collaboration with leading musicians of his time: Kurt Weill (the ever-popular *Dreigroschenoper* [published as *The Threepenny Opera*], 1931, and the opera *Aufstieg und Fall der Stadt Mahagonny* [published as *The Rise and Fall of the City of Mahagonny*], 1930), Hanns Eisler (*Leben des Galilei* [published as *Life of Galileo*], 1955); and Paul Dessau (*Mutter Courage und ihre Kinder* [published as *Mother Courage and Her Children*], 1949, *Der gute Mensch von Sezuan* [published as *The Good Person of Setzuan*], 1953, and *Der kaukasische Kreidekreis* [published as *The Caucasian Chalk Circle*], 1949.)

With Adolf Hitler's rise to power in 1933, Brecht left Germany, living in Denmark, Sweden, and Finland until the outbreak of war in Europe led him to exile in Santa Monica, California in 1941. Displays of capitalist sex, violence, and greed in his work initially gave way to emphasis on the evils

Bertolt Brecht. Courtesy of German Information Center, New York.

of Fascism in works such as *Die Rundköpfe und die Spitzköpfe* (Roundheads and peakheads), 1933/38; *Furcht und Elend des Dritten Reichs* (The private life of the master race), 1938/45; and *Der aufhaltsame Aufstieg des Arturo Ui* (published as *The Resistable Rise of Arturo Ui*), 1957. Some of Brecht's most enduring works were written and produced in exile: *Galileo, Mother Courage,* and *The Caucasian Chalk Circle.* His sojourn in the United States ended with a subpoena in 1947 to the House Committee on Un-American Activities in Washington, D.C. Offered the opportunity to stage his work in a theater headed by Weigel, the Berliner Ensemble, Brecht took up residence at the Theater am Schiffbauerdamm in East Berlin until his death on August 14, 1956, but he maintained Austrian rather than East German citizenship.

Brecht's effort to construct a Marxist theory of drama was rooted in his conviction that the audience should remain aware that what it views on stage is not "reality" but merely a demonstration of events that should be observed with critical detachment and an awareness of the possibilities for change. Firmly rejecting the tradition from Aristotle to Stanislavsky that called for a theater of illusion and identification, Brecht's "epic theater" is known for its employment of the *Verfremdungs-Effekt* ("alienation" or "distancing effect"), which entails techniques of acting and staging that promote a critical stance. It is debatable, however, whether Brecht's late plays owe their success to this theory. Among the volumes of theoretical writing, his *Kleines Organon für das Theater* (Short organon for the theater), 1953, and the much less well-known *Dialoge aus dem Messingkauf* (The Messingkauf dialogs), 1963, are the most important.

Patricia Herminghouse

See also Drama; Expressionism (Literature); German Democratic Republic: Literature and Literary Life; National Socialist Germany: Literature; Theater; Weimar Germany: Literature

References

Brooker, Peter. *Bertolt Brecht: Dialectics, Poetry, Politics.* London: Croom Helm, 1988.
Esslin, Martin. *Brecht: A Choice of Evils: A Critical Study of the Man, His Work and His Opinions.* 3rd ed. London: Eyre Methuen, 1980.
Hayman, Ronald. *Brecht: A Biography.* London: Weidenfeld and Nicholson, 1983.
Mews, Siegfried, comp. *Critical Essays on Bertolt Brecht.* Boston, MA: G.K. Hall, 1989.
Volker, Klaus. *Brecht: A Biography.* Trans. John Nowell. New York, NY: Seabury Press, 1978.
Willett, John. *The Theater of Bertolt Brecht: A Study from Eight Aspects.* London: Methuen, 1959.

Bremen

The city and the state of Bremen became part of the North German Confederation in 1866 under threat of military occupation by Prussia. In 1871, the state and Hanseatic Free City became part of Imperial Germany, though both remained outside the German customs union until 1888.

In 1871, the city's population stood at 83,000; by 1910, it had increased to 247,000, while the city-state had 310,000 inhabitants. Thereafter, population growth slowed, with slight declines during the world wars, but increased to 550,000 for the city and 680,000 for the city-state by the 1970s, a level at which it has stayed.

Located on the silt-laden Weser River and dependent on foreign trade (the region had hardly any industries until the 1890s), Bremen had the heaviest debt load among Imperial German cities as it financed its outrigger port of Bremerhaven, modernized its harbors and created extensive public works. The shipping trade, led by Germany's second-largest shipping firm, the Norddeutscher Lloyd, funneled emigrants from Central Europe to North America and brought back staple commodities, such as sugar, tobacco, cotton, coffee, wool, rice, and petroleum. For a hundred years, the Bremen port has been continental Europe's largest transshipper of cotton and coffee. Whereas this trade in staples initially fostered rapid growth in population and subsidiary trades, by the end of the century it made Bremen a dependent supplier to Germany's industrial areas.

In legal, political, social, and most cultural matters Bremen had been integrated into Germany by the twentieth century, even if it kept some local peculiarities such as large parks, fierce local pride, and the Low German dialect. The Bremen labor movement was among the largest in Imperial and Weimar Germany, but its artisan composition and ideological makeup reflected national patterns. The split between those supporting the First World War and those opposed to it led to bitter infighting and a radicalization that provided a strong base for the Independent Social Democratic Party (USPD) and later the Communists.

Politically, this little republic was governed—like its larger sister-city, Hamburg—by lifetime senators with little regard for the legislature (selected by an eight-class system of voting until 1918). Though calling themselves "liberal," the ruling lawyers and shipping-firm families dominated in a conservative fashion until the Revolution of 1918. Then a radical coalition held power for a short time until forced out by the national government in 1919. Liberals and Social Democrats provided coalitions until the "coordination" (*Gleichschaltung*) by the Nazis ended all pretense of independence. Under a Nazi governor, Bremen easily adapted to the racist policies of the Hitler regime, just as many of its citizens had become nationalistic in Imperial Germany and flocked to its populist leagues.

World War II and its aftermath transformed Bremen politically and economically. Heavy bombing had destroyed many fine Renaissance buildings. After the war, the British and then the Americans occupied the port city. It became the smallest German *Land* (state) under the Basic Law of 1949, which reconstituted Bremen as a self-governing commune, with the emphasis on federalism. The Social Democrats have had a near-monopoly on political power, but the city's economic base, especially shipping and ship and airplane building as well as electronics, has declined. In the 1960s, half of the population still made its living from commerce, shipbuilding, and related trades, plus reprocessing of imports, such as coffee and tobacco.

At present, Bremen illustrates many of the problems of contemporary Germany: a high number of unintegrated foreign workers, racist incidents, high youth unemployment, and a moderate Social Democratic government partly challenged by the ecological movement. The well-restored Renaissance buildings at the city's center testify to a glorious past, but the concrete and crumbling area beyond the core portends a difficult future. Worpswede, the artists' colony thirty miles to the north founded early in the century, represents the positive cultural life of Bremen's many parks, theaters, museums, and the manageable size of a city not cut off from its rural hinterland.

Dieter K. Buse

See also Federalism; Urbanization

References

Buse, Dieter K. "Urban and National Identity: Bremen, 1860–1920." *Journal of Social History* 26 (1993), 521–37.

Engelsing, Rolf. "England und die USA in der bremischen Sicht des 19. Jahrhundert." *Jahrbuch der Wittheit zu Bremen* 1 (1955), 23–58.

Mielsch, B. *Denkmäler, Freiplastiken, Brunnen in Bremen 1800–1945.* Bremen: J.H. Schmalfeldt & Co., 1980.

Moring, Karl-Ernst. *Die Sozialdemokratische Partei in Bremen 1890–1914.* Hannover: Verlag für Literatur und Zeitgeschehen, 1968.

Schwarzwälder, Herbert. *Geschichte der Freien Hansestadt Bremen.* 4 vols. Bremen: Christens, 1974 *ff.*

Brentano, Heinrich von (1904–64)

Heinrich von Brentano, a Christian Democrat and consistent advocate of Western European union, was among Germany's main political leaders after 1945. As a constitutional expert, long-time Christian Democratic Union/Christian Social Union (CDU/CSU) party whip in the Bundestag, and foreign minister from 1955 to 1961, he ranks among the leading politicians in the Adenauer era. But he did not gain much popular support and was soon forgotten after his death.

A lawyer from Offenbach, he entered politics after World War II as one of the founding members of the CDU and became one of the most powerful men within the Hessian branch of the party. In the deliberations on the Hessian state constitution, he fathered a key compromise with the Social Democratic Party (SPD), and as leader of the CDU in the Landtag (legislature) he was instrumental in the formation of the so-called Grand Coalition between the SPD and CDU.

Brentano played an important part in the construction of the West German constitution, the Basic Law. After the federal elections of 1949, he initially advocated a coalition of CDU/CSU and SPD, but then joined Adenauer, who eventually created a bourgeois coalition with the Free Democrats (FDP) and the Deutsche Partei (DP). As party whip of the CDU/CSU from 1949 to 1955, he was loyal to Adenauer, but this relationship was not always free of tension.

In June 1955, when Brentano attained the office of foreign minister, which he had long coveted, the most important foreign policy decisions, such as integration with the West, had already been made and had his active support. At times, Brentano favored a strong Europe as a third power between the two blocs. During his term of office, the European Community was founded and the Saar issue was settled.

As foreign minister, Brentano was dogmatically pro-Western; owing to his profound anti-Communism and his distrust of the ruling powers in the Kremlin, he opposed the establishment of diplomatic relations with the Soviet Union. He firmly adhered to the Hallstein Doctrine, which entrenched the right of the Federal Republic to be the sole international representative of a German state (*Alleinvertretungsanspruch*) and according to which Bonn automatically severed diplomatic relations with countries that recognized the German Democratic Republic. On the other hand, Brentano was more flexible in his politics vis-à-vis the Eastern European states, especially Poland, to which he accorded special status. In 1956, he signaled West Germany's willingness to renounce the former German territories east of the Oder-Neisse Line.

When the CDU/CSU lost its absolute majority in the 1961 elections, Brentano fell victim to the negotiations to form a coalition with the FDP, which rejected him. His resignation opened the way for a coalition between the CDU/CSU and the FDP, and he again became CDU/CSU party whip in the Bundestag until his death.

Walter Mühlhausen

See also Adenauer, Konrad; American-German Relations; Christian Democratic Union; The Cold War and Germany; Diplomatic Corps and Diplomacy; Federal Republic of Germany: Foreign Policy; Franco-German Relations; Postwar European Integration and Germany

References

Baring, Arnulf. *Sehr verehrter Herr Bundeskanzler! Heinrich von Brentano im Briefwechsel mit Konrad Adenauer 1949–1964.* Hamburg: Hoffmann und Campe, 1974.

Baring, Arnulf and Daniel Koerfer. "Heinrich von Brentano." *Persönlichkeit und Politik in der Bundesrepublik. Politische Porträts.* Vol. 1. Ed. W. L. Bernecker and V. Dotterweich. Göttingen: UTB Vandenhoeck, 1982.

Gotto, Klaus. "Heinrich von Brentano (1904–1964)." *Zeitgeschichte in Lebensbildern.* Vol 4. Ed. J. Aretz, R. Morsey, and A. Rauscher. Mainz: Grünewald, 1980.

Kosthorst, Daniel. *Brentano und die deutsche Einheit: Die Deutschland- und Ostpolitik des Aussenministers im Kabinett Adenauer 1955–1961.* Düsseldorf: Droste, 1993.

Wengst, Udo, ed. *Auftakt zur Ära Adenauer: Koalitionsverhandlungen und Regierungsbildung in der Bundesrepublik: Politische Porträts.* Düsseldorf: Droste Verlag, 1985.

Brentano, Lujo (1844–1931)

One of Imperial Germany's most distinguished economists, Lujo Brentano taught from 1891 at the University of Munich. A charismatic figure and dynamic lecturer, he captivated generations of students, many of whom led successful academic careers. Brentano was a prolific scholar who also engaged in spirited polemical debates with opponents on the right and left.

Together with Gustav von Schmoller (1838–1917) and Bruno Hildebrand, Brentano founded the Verein für Sozialpolitik (Association for Social Policy) in 1873. Termed "Kathedersozialisten" (academic socialists) by the journalist Heinrich Oppenheim, Brentano and his associates drew the scorn of liberals because they believed that the German working class could organize itself in trade unions on the British model. Brentano's circle of "academic socialists" addressed a congeries of problems associated with industrial society known collectively as the "social question." Although Brentano at first opposed Chancellor Otto von Bismarck's state socialism, by the end of the 1880s he had reconciled himself to the government's social welfare measures.

As the Prussian *Junkers* acquired greater political influence during the 1890s, Brentano's outlook became more liberal and his defense of free trade more vigorous. In the immediate prewar years, Brentano realized that the conservative alliance of big business and the *Junkers* had vanquished the free market on which he had pinned his hopes for social evolution. Modifying lingering reservations about Germany's repressive political system, he concluded that the state alone could accomplish the social goals he wished to achieve.

Though a committed Anglophile, Brentano rallied to Germany's cause in 1914. He resolutely opposed imperialistic war aims, but confined his criticism of the government to its domestic policy. Germany's defeat left his own strong patriotic convictions intact. He nevertheless withdrew from public life in the 1920s and devoted himself to scholarly research until his death shortly before the Weimar Republic met its own end.

Despite a flirtation with the Progressive movement around the turn of the century, Brentano was in many ways a typical nineteenth-century "political professor." He enjoyed matching wits with his adversaries in the great debates of the day on issues of national concern, but he remained apolitical in outlook. Party politics, in Brentano's estimation, corrupted scholarship. Along with many of his fellow academics, he held politics and the political process in contempt. Brentano thereby helped to perpetuate attitudes that, in the end, deprived the country's best minds of a role in shaping public policy.

Richard J. Bazillion

See also Association for Social Policy; Industrialization; Liberalism; Social Reform

References

Barich, Werner. *Lujo Brentano als Sozialpolitiker.* Berlin: Triltsch & Huther, 1936.
Brentano, Lujo. *Mein Leben im Kampfe um die soziale Entwicklung Deutschlands.* Jena: E. Diederichs, 1931.
Sheehan, James J. *The Career of Lujo Brentano: A Study of Liberalism and Social Reform in Imperial Germany.* Chicago, IL: University of Chicago Press, 1966.

Brest-Litovsk (1918)

Brest-Litovsk connotes the three months of wrangling between the Central Powers, headed by Imperial Germany, and revolutionary Russia during World War I over peace terms. The German government wanted to end the exhausting two-front war. It had assisted Lenin's return to Russia at a crucial moment. The final settlement at Brest-Litovsk removed Russia from the Allied alliance against Germany and from the war altogether, thereby fulfilling one of Lenin's central promises to the Russian people when the Bolsheviks seized power in the October Revolution of 1917. But the price of peace was high.

Germany dictated the terms: Russia surrendered all of Poland, the Baltic states, Finland, large parts of Belorussia, Ukraine, and part of Transcaucasia. Losses totaled 1,300,000 square miles and 62 million people. The proposed peace caused a major crisis in the revolutionary government and within the Bolshevik party itself. Lenin won approval by the narrowest margin only by threatening to resign. The Left Social Revolutionaries left the government and returned to their strategy of political assassination—including an assault on Lenin—to arouse the masses.

Peace proved to be fleeting. The Allies intervened in the ensuing civil war on the side of the Whites—partly because of their antipathy toward the Bolsheviks, partly because they regarded Russia's withdrawal from the war as a betrayal, and most importantly to protect their investments. The Treaty of Brest-Litovsk became invalidated when Germany surrendered to the Western Allies, although many of Russia's territorial losses remained in place through the interwar period. The harshness of the treaty's terms did not prevent a realignment of European politics in the 1920s that for a time found Soviet Russia and Weimar Germany in tacit alliance as the two outcasts of Europe.

Ann L. Phillips

See also Soviet-German Relations; World War I

References

Baumgart, Winfried, ed. *Brest-Litovsk: Ausgewählt und eingeleitet von Winfried Baumgart und Konrad Repgen.* Göttingen: Vandenhoeck & Ruprecht, 1969.
Carr, Edward Hallett. *German-Soviet Relations between the Two World Wars, 1919–1939.* Reprint edition. New York, NY: Ayer, 1979.
Die Friedensverhandlungen in Brest-Litowsk und der Friede mit Russland: Authentische Berichte. Leipzig: Felix Meiner, 1918.
Magnes, Judah Leon. *Russia and Germany at Brest-Litovsk: A Documentary History of the Peace Negotiations.* New York, NY: Rand School of Social Science, 1919.

Wheeler-Bennett, John. *The Forgotten Peace: Brest-Litovsk, March 1918.* New York, NY: Morrow, 1939.

British Occupation Policy (1945–55)

British occupation policy in Germany resulted from the Allied victory over Nazi Germany in World War II. It comprised two aspects: the impact that the British had on overall Allied policy in Germany, and the policy that the British implemented in their occupation zone. Both orientations originated in various wartime arrangements and the agreement concluded at the Potsdam Conference in July-August 1945. The aim of British policy was to de-Nazify, demilitarize, and decentralize Germany, to restore democracy, and to take measures to prevent Germany from ever starting a war again.

Starting late in 1945, Allied unity in Germany was plagued by constant disagreements regarding, for example, policies to be pursued on reparations, central administration, economic unity, and the "German question." Occupation policy was difficult to implement because of complications arising from the emerging Cold War. Conflicts arose over implementations of policy, over the Council of Foreign Ministers, over the Allied Control Authority and Allied Control Council, and over the Allied command structure in Berlin. By 1948, the Allied powers were unable to reach unanimous decisions on most questions. The occupation powers concentrated on reorganizing the individual zones politically and economically.

Beginning in 1947, the British and American occupation zones became subject to a joint administration forming the Bizone, and in 1949 the Federal Republic of Germany (FRG) commenced operations on the combined territories of the Western zones, including the French sector. The Western Allies, through the Allied High Commission at Bonn-Petersberg, retained certain reserved rights, defined by the Occupation Statute. Allied-German relations were revised by general conventions in 1952 and 1954. The occupation period terminated in 1955 with the transfer of full sovereignty to the FRG.

The British pursued their own occupation policies in Germany. The British zone was the largest of the four zones in terms of population, and it was also the most highly industrialized area, with an abundance of primary and secondary industries situated along the Rhine and Ruhr rivers. Occupation policy was implemented by the British military government, by the Control Commission for Germany (British Element) at Berlin headquarters and at British zonal offices, and by regional military government establishments in each state (North Rhine–Westphalia, Lower Saxony, Berlin, Hamburg, and Schleswig-Holstein).

Policy on Germany and occupation was formulated and supervised in London by the Foreign Office, the War Office, and the Control Office for Germany and Austria. The British administered Germany by utilizing the principle of indirect rule. Politically, they particularly stressed the introduction of measures that would ensure the success of democracy. They established German administrative divisions, licensed political parties, authorized the functioning of the press and media, reorganized local government, and held local and regional elections. After the establishment of the *Länder* (states), starting late in 1946, the British military government gradually transferred legal responsibilities to the Germans.

Economically, the British concentrated on reconstructing the means of production, a goal that the British reached ahead of the Americans. British plans for nationalizing German industries failed, however, because the Americans vetoed the idea. On their own, the British could not ensure the national unity of Germany after World War II, but they did succeed in reorganizing a large portion of Germany politically and economically. They introduced a stable democracy in the devastated land and helped to integrate the FRG into the Western community.

Eva A. Mayring

See also Allied High Commission to Germany; Allied Occupation Statute; Anglo-German Relations; Bizone; Federal Republic of Germany; Federalism; Lower Saxony; North Rhine-Westphalia; Rearmament; Robertson, Brian; Ruhr Region; Schleswig-Holstein

References
Birke, Adolf M., Hans Booms, and Otto Herker, eds. *Akten der Britischen Militärregierung in Deutschland/Control Commission for Germany, British Element: Sachinventar 1945–1955/Inventory 1945–1955.* 11 vols. Munich: K.G. Saur, 1993.

Deighton, Anne. *The Impossible Peace: Britain, the Division of Germany and the Origins of the Cold War.* Oxford: Clarendon Press, 1990.

Roseman, Mark. *Recasting the Ruhr, 1945–1958: Manpower, Economic Recovery and Labour Relations.* Oxford: Berg, 1992.

Turner, Ian D., ed. *Reconstruction in Post-War Germany: British Occupation Policy and the Western Zones 1945–1955.* Oxford: Berg, 1989.

Broch, Hermann (1886–1951)

Hermann Broch's novels and essays explore the philosophic thoughts and social conditions that enabled the triumph of Nazism in Austria. He also offers insightful glimpses on human rights and on the resolution of international conflicts.

The scion of an upper-class, largely assimilated Viennese Jewish family, Broch was groomed to take over management of the family's textile mill by being trained as a textile engineer. In 1909 he converted to Roman Catholicism. In 1927, he sold the business and devoted himself to the study of mathematics, philosophy, and psychology. Following the occupation of Austria by Germany in 1938, he was incarcerated for two weeks. He fled to England, then emigrated to the United States. In 1950, Broch became honorary lecturer of German literature at Yale University (New Haven, Connecticut).

The intellectual and artistically creative atmosphere of interwar Vienna stimulated the essence of Broch's early critical essays. In the trilogy *Die Schlafwandler* (published as *The Sleepwalkers*), 1931–32, Broch documents the decay of values and shows a search for new ones through protagonists that illustrate the Wilhelmine era. The transition from the quasi-realistic style of his first volume to the multiplicity of forms of the third volume signals Broch's break with traditional narrative unity. In *Der Tod des Vergil* (The death of Vergil), 1945, he has the dying poet mirror the dichotomy of art and human suffering. He thereby demonstrates that ethical distinction is more meaningful than poetry. The mystical vision of the dying person evokes a visionary re-creation and ends in a dimension "beyond language."

Broch's novels, which retain inner monologue almost throughout, are among the most impressive linguistic and stylistic experiments in recent times. The historical guilt of indifferent, innocuous contemporaries is illustrated in the novella-novel, *Die Schuldlosen* (The innocents), 1950. *Die Verzauberung* (The enchantment; fragment, 3 versions, posthumously published in 1969), set in a mountain village, illustrates the mass hysteria aroused by a wandering preacher—a Hitlerian figure—who leads a group to xenophobic persecution and collective crime.

Broch's dramas and poems have not attained the standing or influence of his novels. In contrast, his theoretical writings are of timeless relevance; his tracts on human rights and his call for an international humanitarian party anticipated the stance of Amnesty International. His warnings about nuclear armament and studies on conflict management correspond to the discourse of later peace research. Broch's mass hysteria theory (*Massenwahntheorie*) analyzed European Fascism and showed how democracies can protect their constitutionality from being destroyed by dictators who legally come to power. Broch's expansive correspondence is like an autobiography of letters that effectively preserves his personality as well as his humane understanding. Together with Kafka, Robert Musil (1880–1942), and Elias Canetti (1905–94), Broch belongs to the literary avant-garde of the first half of the twentieth century and remains one of the most influential authors and thinkers of Austria.

Gisela Brude-Firnau

See also Canetti, Elias; Kafka, Franz; Musil, Robert; Novel; Weimar Germany: Literature

References

Broch, Hermann. *Kommentierte Werkausgabe.* 17 vols. Ed. Paul Michael Lützeler. Frankfurt am Main: Suhrkamp, 1974–81.

———. *Literature, Philosophy, Politics.* Ed. Stephen D. Dowden. Columbia, SC: Camden House, 1988.

Dowden, Stephen D. *Sympathy for the Abyss: A Study in the Novel of German Modernism: Kafka, Broch, Musil, and Thomas Mann.* Tübingen: Niemeyer, 1986.

Jonas, Klaus W. "Bibliographie der Sekundärliteratur zu Hermann Broch 1971–1984." *Hermann Broch.* Ed. Paul Michael Lützeler. Frankfurt am Main: Suhrkamp, 1986.

———. "Bibliographie Hermann Broch." *Hermann Broch/ Daniel Brody: Briefwechsel 1930–1951.* Frankfurt am Main: Buchhändler-Vereinigung, 1971.

Lützeler, Paul Michael. *Hermann Broch: Eine Biographie.* Frankfurt am Main: Suhrkamp, 1985.

Ritzer, Monika. *Hermann Broch und die Kulturkrise des frühen 20. Jahrhunderts.* Stuttgart: Metzler, 1988.

Ziolkowski, Theodore. *Hermann Broch.* New York, NY: Columbia University Press, 1964.

Brockdorff-Rantzau, Ulrich von (1869–1928)

Ulrich von Brockdorff-Rantzau, born on May 29, 1869, served as Germany's first ambassador to the Soviet Union from 1922 to 1928. He helped to bridge the gulf between Social Democrats and the old elite from which he had sprung—an important Holstein family and another distinguished aristocratic branch, the Brockdorffs. In 1894, he entered the foreign service as attaché, then served briefly in Brussels, St. Petersburg, and Vienna before being posted to Budapest as consul general from 1909 to 1912. At the age of 42, he became ambassador to Denmark, a favorable placement for one who, through his proximity to Schleswig, understood the country, which in 1914 gained strategic importance.

After the outbreak of the World War I, Rantzau feared that the German military would mistrust Copenhagen's neutrality and occupy the country. Bent on making a separate peace with Russia, Rantzau developed the thought that Germany must concentrate on "vanquishing the most dangerous opponent, England, which strove to annihilate Germany." In December 1917, he fantasized that Germany had the chance to reach Paris, "to annihilate the French army for good," to undercut Russia, and "to create a great [German] army dominating all of Europe."

During the Revolution of 1918–19, Rantzau assumed the post of foreign minister (January 2, 1919). His program stressed the importance of eliminating the old political and social system of Imperial Germany and the significance of a peace based on justice and Wilsonian principles of self-determination and the preservation of national dignity. In February 1919, Rantzau tried to assure the German and foreign public that a count can be a dedicated democrat, although his definition of democracy was a bizarre elitist-aristocratic conception.

Rantzau prepared for the Versailles peace conference, resolved to resist any challenge from friend or foe to his eminent role. According to legend, at the end of the conference he deliberately left his gloves on the negotiating table (as an insult). He had responded to the presiding officer of the conference, Georges Clemenceau, while remaining seated. As foreign minister, he repeatedly warned the Allies of the Bolshevik threat to Germany, hoping thereby to obtain more favorable peace terms. He also tried to maneuver the *Anschluss* of rump Austria to Germany. He championed the retention of Imperial Germany's boundaries, denied Germany's war guilt, and demanded a peace based on President Wilson's Fourteen Points and the prompt entry of Germany into the League of Nations. When the peace conference rejected Germany's terms, the German cabinet split, whereupon Scheidemann and Rantzau resigned.

To Rantzau, German policy toward Russia was always linked with his desire to avenge the personal and national humiliation of Versailles. Through a close relationship with Soviet Russia, he wanted to create a counterweight against the West. Surprised by the 1922 German-Russian Rapallo Treaty, he soon perceived the possibilities of terminating of both countries' isolation.

In 1922, after an internal struggle over the appointment to the Moscow ambassadorship, Rantzau prevailed. He developed excellent personal relations with Georgi Chicherin, Soviet commissar for foreign relations. Both men were "outsiders." However, Rantzau probably never developed a thorough understanding of Marxism-Leninism and of the various political forces operating in the Soviet Union, and he never learned Russian. The Soviets, in turn, distrusted the twists and turns of German diplomacy, the Locarno policy of Gustav Stresemann (1878–1929) with his pro-Western leanings.

Stresemann and Rantzau disagreed on the Locarno Treaty and differed on Germany's entry into the League of Nations. Russia seemed to be isolated with the abandonment of the Rapallo policy, yet no major change in Germany's *Ostpolitik* (eastern policy) followed. Prior to Germany's entry into the League (September, 1926), Berlin had concluded the April treaty with the Soviet Union, which calmed some Soviet fears and partly appeased Rantzau. He never abandoned the belief that intrigues spun by personal enemies and conspirators in Berlin had simply set aside his policy.

In August 1928, Rantzau returned for a vacation to Berlin. He was sick, dispirited, and disappointed, and died shortly thereafter. *Pravda* produced an unusual, highly laudatory obituary. The Soviet leaders believed that Rantzau had represented that German elite which wanted to cultivate friendship with Moscow. He had stood for the Rapallo policy despite initially rejecting it.

Alfred D. Low

See also Diplomatic Corps and Diplomacy; Rapallo Treaty; Soviet-German Relations; Versailles, Treaty of; Weimar Republic; Weimar Germany: Foreign Policy; World War I

References

Brockdorff-Rantzau, Ulrich Karl Christian, Graf von. *Dokumente.* Berlin: Deutsche Verlagsgesellschaft für Politik und Geschichte, 1920.

Haupts, Leo. *Ulrich Graf von Brockdorff-Rantzau, Diplomat und Minister in Kaiserreich und Republik.* Göttingen: Musterschmidt Verlag, 1984.

Holborn, Hajo. "Diplomats and Diplomacy in the Early Weimar Republic." *The Diplomats, 1919–1938.* Ed. G.A. Craig and F. Gilbert. Princeton, NJ: Princeton University Press, 1953.

Rosenbaum, Kurt. *Community of Fate.* Syracuse, NY: Syracuse University Press, 1965.

Wengst, Udo. *Graf Brockdorff-Rantzau und die aussenpolitische Anfänge der Weimarer Republik.* Frankfurt am Main: Peter Lang, 1973.

Bruckner, Anton (1824–96)

Born in Ansfelden, Upper Austria, the Austrian composer Anton Bruckner was best known as an organist during his lifetime; after his death, he was virtually forgotten. Despite growing recognition of the true significance of this deceptively simple genius over the past couple of decades, it is still virtually impossible to create a wholly reliable and objective portrait of the man and his music.

Throughout his life, Bruckner was saddled with the traits and effects of his humble origins. Showing unmistakable musical talent early on, he received training from his father (a village teacher and organist) and as a choirboy at the monastery of St. Florian, where he became organist in 1851; he was in his thirties before he could afford composition lessons in Vienna. Aside from a certain renown as a virtuoso organist, Bruckner spent much of his career in relative obscurity, teaching theory at the Conservatory (1868–91) and University of Vienna (1875–94); he was unpaid at first—only in his sixties was he recognized with an honorary doctorate and the Knight's Cross of the Order of Franz Joseph.

The effect of his lifelong diffidence had a most deleterious effect on Bruckner's work as a composer. Not abundantly prolific in any case (writing chiefly sacred and secular choral music and symphonies, with some organ and chamber works besides), he revised again and again much of what he wrote, all too often on the misguided advice of others. For this reason, five of his nine numbered symphonies (1866–96; the ninth is unfinished) exist in at least two versions.

Despite their troubled history, Bruckner's symphonies are increasingly valued as imposing and magisterial works in a unique style: they succeed in blending the absolute symphonic heritage of the past with the deeply dramatic intensity and immediacy of Wagner's musical language. The interior movements include some of the most splendid adagios and scherzos written since Beethoven, while the grandeur of the corner movements is much enhanced by the organist's penchant for a "registrated" use of the orchestral families of instruments.

Zoltan Roman

See also Composers; Orchestral Music; Wagner, Richard

References

Grasberger, Renate. *Bruckner-Bibliographie (bis 1974).* Graz: Akademische Druck und Verlagsanstalt, 1985.

———. *Werkverzeichnis Anton Bruckner.* Tutzing: Hans Schneider, 1977.

Simpson, Robert. *The Essence of Bruckner.* 2nd ed. London: Gollancz, 1977.

Wagner, Manfred. *Bruckner.* Mainz: Goldmann/Schott, 1983.

Watson, Derek. *Anton Bruckner.* London: Dent, 1975.

Brüning, Heinrich (1885–1970)

The politician Heinrich Brüning was born in Münster on November 26, 1885, and died at Norwich, Vermont, on March 30, 1970. In 1919, he became active in the Catholic Christian Trade Union movement. From 1920 to 1930 he was its general secretary, from 1924 to 1933 he was a Center Party deputy in the Reichstag, and in 1929 he became chairman of the party's Reichstag caucus. He served as chancellor during the crucial period of March 1930 to May 1932.

Known as an expert on financial matters, he was chosen by President Paul von Hindenburg (1874–1934) to become chancellor at the time of worsening global economic conditions. His program to overhaul and consolidate the budget by tax increases and budget cuts did not win Reichstag approval. Brüning therefore governed by presidential decree under Article 48 of the Constitution.

Brüning's program of lowering prices and wages only intensified the deflation and the fall in productivity. Unemployment exceeded six million in 1932, with a corresponding increase in popularity for the radical parties of the left and right. His critics urged him to increase the means of credit, strengthen buying power, and create new jobs. But Brüning's strategy was to enforce stringent saving measures in order to obtain a balanced budget. This in turn would improve foreign credibility and help efforts to get the Western powers to reduce the reparations, and grant Germany equality in weapons. This was all part of a general plan that would revise the Treaty of Versailles, which in turn would help to end the world economic crisis and lessen the growing appeal of the Nazis. Disagreements with Hindenburg over such issues as his agrarian policies caused the president to withdraw his support from Brüning, who thereupon resigned. In May 1933 Brüning took over leadership of the Center Party. While opposing the Enabling Act, he found it necessary, under pressure, to dissolve the party. In 1934 he emigrated to the United States, where he became professor at Harvard University (1939–50). He later returned and taught at Cologne (1951–54).

Brüning was known for his integrity and expertise in economic matters. He won the respect of many foreign observers for his efforts to guide his country through the Great Depression. A monarchist at heart, he was not an energetic supporter of the parliamentary system. Possessing a retiring personality, he lacked oratorical skills, tactical ability, and mass appeal. His position within the Center Party was conservative, and he was instrumental in bringing the Party back to a more rightist position than that of Matthias Erzberger and Josef Wirth earlier in the Weimar period. His policies helped Weimar to function for two years under Article 48, but his methods of governing by presidential decree helped to ease the way for Adolf Hitler to install his dictatorship.

Stewart Stehlin

See also Catholicism, Political; Center Party; Great Depression; Hindenburg, Paul von; Hitler, Adolf; Papen, Franz von; Schleicher, Kurt von; Versailles, Treaty of; Weimar Germany

References

Bracher, Karl Dietrich. "Brünings unpolitische Politik und die Auflösung der Weimarer Republik." *Vierteljahrshefte für Zeitgeschichte* 19 (1971), 113–23.
Brüning, Heinrich. *Briefe und Gespräche, 1934–1945*. Ed. Claire Nix. Stuttgart: Deutsche Verlags-Anstalt, 1974.
———. *Memoiren, 1918–1934*. Stuttgart: Deutsche Verlags-Anstalt, 1970.
Büttner, Ursula. "Politische Alternative zum Brüningschen Deflationskurs." *Vierteljahrshefte für Zeitgeschichte* 37 (1989), 209–51.
Conze, Werner. "Brüning als Reichskanzler. Eine Zwischenbilanz." *Historische Zeitschrift* 214 (1972), 310–34.
———. "Brünings Politik unter dem Druck der grossen Krise." *Historische Zeitschrift* 199 (1964), 529–50.
Helbich, W.J. *Die Reparationen in der Ära Brünings*. Berlin: Colloquium Verlag, 1967.
James, Harold. "Gab es eine Alternative zur Wirtschaftspolitik Brünings?" *Vierteljahrschrift für Sozial- und Wirtschaftsgeschichte* 70 (1983), 523–41.
Jones, Larry E. and James Retallack, eds. *Between Reform, Reaction, and Resistance. Studies in the History of German Conservatism from 1789 to 1945*. Oxford: Berg, 1993.

Buber, Martin (1878–1965)

One of the most influential German-Jewish religious thinkers of the twentieth century, Buber was born on February 8, 1878, in Vienna. His mother abandoned the family, for reasons unexplained, when Buber was three, and he was raised by his grandparents until he was fourteen. It has been argued that this episode lies at the root of Buber's interest in the importance of human relations.

Buber studied philosophy and art history at Leipzig, Berlin, and Zurich, and obtained his doctorate from Vienna in 1904. While in Leipzig, he became influenced by the ideas of Theodor Herzl, the founder of modern Zionism, but Buber's thought was also marked by the work of Georg Simmel (1858–1918) and Wilhelm Dilthey (1833–1911), his professors in Berlin. Beginning in 1904, Buber spent five years in an intensive study of Hasidic thought. The influence of the mysticism of the Hasidim, as well the Christian existentialism of such thinkers as Sören A. Kierkegaard, may be found throughout Buber's writings.

During the years 1901–24, Buber was involved in publishing and journalism, and he edited the Zionist newspaper *Der Jude* from 1916 until 1924. By 1916 he had written the first draft of his most important work, *Ich und Du* (I and thou), published in Berlin in 1923. Here he argued that association between persons in modern society often exhibits an impersonal and instrumental "I-it" form, whereas it is only in the more intimate "I-thou" relation that individuals are able to overcome their estrangement from both others and themselves and become truly human. This focus on interhuman relationships is also particularly evident in *Die Frage an den Einzelnen* (1936; published as *Between Man and Man*). Buber's view of religion reflects the same concern, though he maintained that the relation between humanity and God is rarely direct, but most often mediated through contact with other persons.

From 1924 until 1933, Buber held the Chair of Jewish Ethics and the Study of the Jewish Religion at the University of Frankfurt am Main. He also lectured at the Freies Jüdisches Lehrhaus (Free Jewish Institute of Learning) in Frankfurt, and

Martin Buber. Courtesy of German Information Center, New York.

was an important figure in the Jewish community in prewar Germany. In 1938, he emigrated to Palestine and he became professor of the sociology of religion at the Hebrew University of Jerusalem, where he taught until his retirement in 1951.

Buber's emphasis on the fundamental role of community and on the Jewish people as a witness to it was reflected in his staunch defense of the Israeli *kibbutz*. Still, he was an important advocate of Arab-Jewish cooperation (see his essay in *Towards Union in Palestine: Essays on Zionism and Jewish-Arab Cooperation*, 1945) and had a strong influence on Dag Hammarskjöld, secretary general of the United Nations from 1953 to 1961. Paradoxically, Buber's work came to have greater importance outside of Israel and the Jewish tradition than within. His influence on modern Christian thought, such as that of Paul Tillich (1886–1965) and H. Richard Niebuhr, is particularly profound. Buber died in Jerusalem on June 13, 1965.

William Sweet

See also Dilthey, Wilhelm; Jews; Philosophy; Protestant Theology; Simmel, Georg; Tillich, Paul

References

Buber, Martin. *Werke*. 3 vols. Munich: Kösel Verlag, 1964.
———. *The Writings of Martin Buber*. Ed. Will Herberg. New York, NY: World Publishing, 1956.
Cohn, Margot and Rafael Buber. *Martin Buber: A Bibliography of his Writings 1897–1978*. Munich: K.G. Saur, 1980.
Friedman, Maurice S. *Martin Buber: The Life of Dialogue*. 3rd ed. Chicago, IL: University of Chicago Press, 1976.
———. *Martin Buber's Life and Work*. 3 vols. New York, NY: Dutton, 1981–83.
Moonan, Willard. *Martin Buber and His Critics: An Annotated Bibliography of Writings in English through 1978*. New York, NY: Garland Publishing, 1981.
Schilpp, Paul A. and Maurice S. Friedman. *The Philosophy of Martin Buber*. La Salle, IL: Open Court, 1967.

Bülow, Bernhard von (1849–1929)

Prince Bernhard Martin Heinrich Carl von Bülow was the fourth chancellor of Imperial Germany (1900–09) and the longest-serving chancellor under Kaiser Wilhelm II. Widely regarded as a skillful political operator and gifted public speaker, he was adept at ingratiating himself with the monarch, on whom his position depended. But his political survival was achieved at the cost of a marked deterioration in Germany's domestic and international position during his chancellorship.

Bülow was the eldest son of Bernhard Ernst von Bülow, state secretary of the German Foreign Office (1873–79). After interrupting his education (1870) to fight in the Franco-Prussian War, he embarked on a diplomatic career (1873) and held responsible positions in Athens (1877), Paris (1879), and St. Petersburg (1884) before being appointed as minister in Bucharest (1888) and ambassador to Rome (1893). His appointment as state secretary of the Foreign Office (1897) owed as much to his close friendship with the Kaiser's best friend, Philipp zu Eulenburg-Hertefeld (1847–1921), as to his diplomatic talent, but he soon eclipsed the aging chancellor, Chlodwig zu Hohenlohe-Schillingsfürst (1819–1901), and replaced him in October 1900. His unrivaled position with the kaiser before 1906 was reflected in his rapid elevation to the status of count (1899) and prince (1905). These benefices underpinned his undisputed authority within the Imperial and Prussian executives.

After 1897, Bülow became closely associated with Germany's ambitious new *Weltpolitik* (world policy) and naval program. In his first speech to the Reichstag (December 1897), he articulated the aspirations of a postunification Wilhelmine generation by demanding that Germany, too, should have a "place in the sun." But, despite the acquisition of Kiaochow (1897) and the Caroline islands (1899), the more aggressively nationalist thrust of German diplomacy under Bülow mainly served to increase Germany's isolation. Until the last months of his chancellorship, he fully supported Alfred von Tirpitz's (1849–1930) plan to create a big battlefleet, and he subordinated German foreign policy to the requirements of the naval program. His disposition of the crises over Morocco (1905–06) and Bosnia (1908–09) alienated the other European powers, cemented the Triple Entente (1907), and nourished German fears of "encirclement."

In domestic policy, Bülow aimed at rallying all nonsocialist forces behind the monarchy and avoiding a confrontation with the Reichstag. After securing parliamentary approval of a more protectionist tariff (1902), he faced growing criticism of his avoidance of contentious issues, his conciliation of the Catholic Center Party, and his inability to halt the growth of the Social Democratic Party. Domestic and international difficulties precipitated a crisis of confidence in his chancellorship by 1906, not least at the kaiser's court. Bülow bolstered his position by dissolving the Reichstag, exploiting nationalist passions in the "Hottentot" elections (1907), and forging a new liberal-conservative coalition, the Bülow Bloc (1907–09). But he continued to shun fundamental reform, and the artificiality of his strategy (which was not extended to Prussia) was apparent even before the coalition disintegrated over financial reform (1909). Having lost the kaiser's confidence as a result of the *Daily Telegraph* Affair (1908), Bülow was forced to resign (June 1909).

Despite Wilhelm II's bitter hostility towards his former favorite, Bülow entertained hopes of being recalled to the chancellorship until the collapse of the monarchy in 1918. Having married a Catholic divorcée, Countess Marie von Dönhoff, née Princess Camporeale (1886), he lived for most of his retirement in Italy and undertook an unsuccessful mission to Rome in 1915 to keep Italy neutral in World War I. His book *Deutsche Politik* (German policy), 1916, and the four volumes of his highly controversial and unreliable memoirs (published posthumously in 1930–31), attempted to vindicate his conduct of German policy and emphasize his peaceful aims. His efforts confirmed his vanity and superficiality, demonstrated the bankruptcy of his diplomacy, and further damaged his historical reputation.

Katharine Anne Lerman

See also Anglo-German Relations; Bethmann Hollweg, Theobald von; Center Party; Colonies and Colonial Society; *Daily Telegraph* Affair; Diplomatic Corps and Diplomacy; Hohenlohe-Schillingsfürst, Chlodwig zu; Imperial Germany: Foreign Policy; Imperialism; Nationalism; Navy and Naval Policy; Parties and Politics; Russian-German Relations; *Sammlungspolitik*; Social Imperialism; Tirpitz, Alfred von; *Weltpolitik*; Wilhelm II

References
Bülow, Bernhard von. *Denkwürdigkeiten.* 4 vols. Berlin: Ullstein, 1930–31.
———. *Deutsche Politik.* Berlin: Reimar Hobbing, 1916.
———. *Reden.* 3 vols. Ed. J. Penzler and O. Hötzsch. Berlin: Georg Reimer 1907–10.
Fesser, Gerd. *Reichskanzler Bernhard Fürst von Bülow.* Berlin: Deutscher Verlag der Wissenschaften, 1991.
Hiller von Gaertringen, Friedrich. *Fürst Bülows Denkwürdigkeiten: Untersuchungen zu ihrer Entstehungsgeschichte und Kritik.* Tübingen: J.C.B. Mohr (Paul Siebeck), 1956.
Lerman, Katharine Anne. *The Chancellor as Courtier: Bernhard von Bülow and the Governance of Germany, 1900–1909.* Cambridge: Cambridge University Press, 1990.
Thimme, Friedrich, ed. *Front wider Bülow: Staatsmänner, Diplomaten und Forscher zu seinen Denkwürdigkeiten.* Munich: F. Bruckmann AG, 1931.
Winzen, Peter. *Bülows Weltmachtkonzept: Untersuchungen zur Frühphase seiner Aussenpolitik 1897–1901.* Boppard am Rhein: Harald Boldt Verlag, 1977.

Bultmann, Rudolf (1884–1976)

This Lutheran theologian and New Testament scholar attracted the attention of the scholarly world by his seminal contributions in the field of method and interpretation in biblical studies. His stirring proposals, though passionately criticized and in need of further refinements, still spur the field of biblical research.

Owing much to the extant schools of exegesis (historical and literary criticism; comparative study of religions), Bultmann may be regarded as summarizing more than a century of scholarship and advancing it one step further. He first became known with his epoch-making *Geschichte der Synoptischen Tradition,* 1922 (published as *History of the Synoptic Tradition,* 1963). Then, his career (1912 Marburg; 1916 Breslau; 1920 Giessen; 1921–51 Marburg) assumed an innovative turn under the influence of a Marburg colleague (1923–27), the philosopher Martin Heidegger (1889–1976), and Heidegger's existential categories. Inspired by this influence, Bultmann came to regard Christian faith as bestowing on the believer a new self-understanding and providing him with the means to achieve an authentic existence.

With Bultmann, the hermeneutics of the faith became linked with biblical studies. In 1941, Bultmann outlined his program for demythologizing the Christian message in "New Testament and Mythology," popularized in *Jesus Christ and Mythology,* 1951 (published in English in 1958, in German in 1964). He regarded the task of demythologizing as one of "seeing through" mythological representations, grasping the understanding of existence they embody, and re-expressing it in existential categories that contemporary people can relate to. Bultmann's commentary of *Das Evangelium des Johannes,* 1941 (published as *The Gospel of John,* 1971) and his *Theologie des Neuen Testaments,* 1948–53 (published as *Theology of the New Testament,* 1952, 1955) illustrate this program.

Bultmann's first dedication was to scholarly work, although he consistently appeared concerned with the social and political consequences of his teaching and writing. He never modified his lectures in order to mollify Nazi ideology during the "troubled years," and he disagreed with Heidegger that National Socialism could contribute to a spiritual and intellectual renewal in Germany. He joined the anti-Nazi Confessing Church at its inauguration in 1934.

Gérard Vallée

See also Biblical Criticism; Confessing Church; Heidegger, Martin; Protestant Theology

References
Boutin, M. *Relationalität als Verstehensprinzip bei Rudolf Bultmann.* Munich: Kaiser, 1974.
Hobbs, E.C., ed. *Bultmann: Retrospect and Prospect. The Centenary Symposium at Wellesley.* Philadelphia, PA: Fortress, 1985.

Jaspert, B. and G. Bromiley, eds. *Karl Barth and Rudolf Bultmann: Letters 1922–1966.* Grand Rapids, MI: Eerdmans, 1981.

Johnson, R.A. *Rudolf Bultmann: Interpreting Faith for the Modern Era.* London: Collins, 1987.

Jones, G. *Bultmann: Towards a Critical Theology.* Cambridge: Polity Press, 1991.

Kwiran, M. *Index to Literature on Barth, Bonhoeffer, and Bultmann.* Basel: F. Reinhardt, 1977.

Roberts, R.C. *Rudolf Bultmann's Theology: A Critical Interpretation.* Grand Rapids, MI: Eerdmans, 1976.

Robinson, J.M. *A New Quest of the Historical Jesus and Other Essays.* Phildadelphia, PA: Fortress, 1983.

Schmithals, W. *An Introduction to the Theology of Rudolf Bultmann.* London: SCM Press, 1968.

Thiselton, A.C. *The Two Horizons.* Grand Rapids, MI: Eerdmans, 1980.

Bundesbank, Deutsche (German Federal Bank)

The Deutsche Bundesbank, the central bank of the Federal Republic of Germany (FRG), is headquartered in Frankfurt am Main. Although legally owned by the federal government, the Bundesbank has independent authority to manage the German money supply and to regulate and support the banking system.

Shortly before the postwar currency reform, which introduced the deutsche mark in 1948, a new two-level central banking system reminiscent of the United States' Federal Reserve System came into being in the western occupation zones. At that time, the central banks in the individual German states, though legally independent, still lacked authority to issue banknotes. The new system created a Central Bank of the German States (Bank deutscher Länder) in Frankfurt am Main in March 1948. Each of the state central banks retained responsibility for its own region. The Bank of the German States was given responsibility for currency issue and foreign exchange management. A Central Bank Council set discount policy, introduced reserve requirements, and offered guidelines for credit and open market policy. The Bank of the German States, which functioned independently of German political authority in the conduct of monetary policy, gained autonomy from Allied control in 1951.

With the establishment of the Deutsche Bundesbank in July 1957, the two-level system of the Bank of the German States and the independent state central banks became consolidated into the unitary Bundesbank. Although retaining the title of state central bank, these state banks are no longer legally independent institutions but constitute the main administrative divisions of the Bundesbank. Branch offices of the state central banks (190 at the end of 1992) are responsible for meeting the currency needs of banks and for clearing bank transfers.

German monetary policy is determined by the Central Bank Council, the highest organ of the Bundesbank. The normally biweekly meetings of the Central Bank Council are chaired by the president of the Bundesbank. Resolutions are passed by a simple majority of the votes cast and are imple-

mented by the executive organ of the Bundesbank, the Directorate. The president of the Bundesbank also serves as chairperson of the directorate, which includes the vice-president of the Bundesbank and six additional members, who are selected especially for their technical competence in economic and banking affairs. The Central Bank Council includes all members of the directorate, together with the presidents of the state central banks.

The president, vice-president, and all other members of the directorate are appointed by the federal president upon the recommendation of the federal government to serve eight-year terms. The government may not discharge members of the directorate before the end of their terms, although under special circumstances they may be appointed for a shorter term. The presidents of the state central banks are likewise named by the federal president upon the recommendation of the Bundesrat and in consultation with the Central Bank Council. Presidents of the state central banks are usually nominated by the respective state governments. Other members of the board of directors of a state central bank (the vice president and up to two additional members) are nominated by the Central Bank Council and appointed by the Bundesbank president.

The Bundesbank is legally charged with safeguarding the German currency and with providing for the proper conduct of banking business in the FRG involving domestic and international payments. Safeguarding the currency has been understood at the Bundesbank to mean preventing and fighting inflation. In addition, the Bundesbank is legally charged with supporting the general economic policy of the federal government, which is committed to maintain the macroeconomic goals of high employment, a high sustainable economic growth rate, and a favorable international balance of payments, as well as a low inflation rate. To this end, mutual consultation between the Bundesbank and the federal government occurs on a regular basis. Members of the federal government can participate as nonvoting members in the deliberation of the Central Bank Council, and they can delay implementation of council resolutions for up to two weeks. The federal government is legally obliged to invite the president of the Bundesbank to hold discussions involving monetary policy. The Bundesbank is obliged to provide information on monetary matters upon a request by the federal government. The

German Federal Bank in Frankfurt am Main. Courtesy of Inter Nationes, Bonn.

Bundesbank is a nonvoting participant in the federal government's Fiscal Planning Council and the Business Conditions Council.

Whenever a low-inflation strategy has conflicted with other macroeconomic goals, the Bundesbank has demonstrated a desire for the single-minded pursuit of the goal of low inflation. There is no binding procedure to resolve fundamental policy conflict that may occur between the Bundesbank and the federal government, short of a change in the law governing the Bundesbank. In terms of the average annual inflation rate of consumer prices over the three decades between 1960 and 1990, the Deutsche Bundesbank has been the world's most successful central bank among the major industrial countries. Annual consumer price inflation over this period has averaged only 3.5 percent, compared to 4.9 percent in the United States and 7.7 percent in the United Kingdom.

Irwin Collier

See also Banking; Currency; Deutsche Bank; Economic Miracle

References
Bundesbank. *Wahrung und Wirtschaft in Deutschland 1876–1975.* Frankfurt am Main: Verlag Fritz Knapp, GmbH, 1975.
"Die Bankenaufsicht in der Bundesrepublik Deutschland." *Deutsche Bundesbank: Gesetz über das Kreditwesen.* Frankfurt am Main: Bundesbank, June 1994.
Die Deutsche Bundesbank. *Geldpolitische Aufgaben und Instrumente.* 6th ed. Sonderdrücke der Deutschen Bundesbank Nr. 7. Frankfurt am Main: Bundesbank, 1993. Also available in English.
Issing, Otmar. *Einführung in die Geldpolitik.* 5th ed. Munich: Verlag Franz Vahlen, 1993.
Kennedy, Ellen. *The Bundesbank.* London: Pinter, 1991.
Marsh, David. *The Bundesbank.* London: Mandarin, 1992.
Sturm, Roland. "The Role of the Bundesbank in German Politics." *West European Politics* 12 (1989), 1–11.

Burckhardt, Jacob (1818–98)
The Swiss historian and historian of art Jacob Burckhardt is perhaps best remembered for his history of the Renaissance, *The Civilization of the Renaissance in Italy,* 1860. His reputation as a scholar, however, was established by his earlier works of cultural history, *The Age of Constantine the Great,* 1852, and, not least, the popular guide to Italy's artistic and architectural treasures, *Die Cicerone,* 1855. Burckhardt's lecture notes were published posthumously as *Griechische Kulturgeschichte* (Greek cultural history), 1898–1902, and *Weltgeschichtliche Betrachtungen* (World historical observations), 1905, his most comprehensive theoretical statement on the nature of history.

Burckhardt was born into an old patrician family in Basel in 1818. With the exception of frequent trips to Italy, his student years in Berlin and Bonn (1839–43), and the years 1855–58 (when he taught in Zürich), Basel remained the center of his existence. In Berlin he studied history under two

of the most prominent historians of the nineteenth century—Leopold von Ranke (1795–1886) and Johann Gustav Droysen (1808–)—and art history under Franz Kugler (1808–58).

Despite the early influence of his mentor, Ranke, Burckhardt distanced himself from the main texts of Rankean historiography. He never considered history to be scientific, but rather described history as "sheer poetry." As a result of the emphasis on aesthetics, his works offer a unique mode of historical representation and visual imagery, rather than mere explanation. In addition, during a time of great political change and growing nationalism, Burckhardt, unlike his contemporaries, refused to write strict political and diplomatic history, choosing instead cultural history and developing it as a legitimate mode of historical discourse.

The rejection of the dominant nineteenth-century historical paradigm also reflected Burckhardt's criticism of contemporary society. His interest in the problems of modernity can be seen in his work on the Renaissance, in which he described the Renaissance Italians as the "firstborn among the sons of modern Europe." The sustained tension between the power of the state and the creative forces of culture, first evident in the Renaissance, remained a central theme in Burckhardt's work. Especially critical of the central state and those who wield power, a force he considered by nature evil, Burckhardt feared that the nationalism and popular democracy unleashed by the French Revolution of 1789 would lead to tyranny and disrupt the cultural unity of Europe.

Despite his cultural pessimism, Burckhardt believed that through historical study and the aesthetic re-creation of the past, the destructive potential of the forces of modernity could be overcome and the cultural continuum maintained. In an age of uncertainty and rejection of traditional approaches to the study of the past, Burckhardt's aesthetic understanding of the historical process is becoming increasingly attractive. As such, he remains one of the most widely studied historians today.

John R. Hinde

See also Droysen, Johann Gustav; History; Ranke, Leopold von

References
Burckhardt, Jacob. *Briefe.* 11 vols. Ed. M. Burckhardt. Basel: Benno Schwabe, 1949–1986.
———. *Gesamtausgabe.* 12 vols. Stuttgart: Deutsche Verlagsanstalt, 1930.
Gilbert, Felix. *History: Politics or Culture? Reflexions on Ranke and Burckhardt.* Princeton, NJ: Princeton University Press, 1990.
Kaegi, Werner. *Jacob Burckhardt: Eine Biographie.* 7 vols. Basel: Benno Schwabe, 1947–82.
White, Hayden. *Metahistory.* Baltimore, MD: Johns Hopkins Press, 1973.

Burgfrieden (1914–16)
Burgfrieden means literally "peace in the fortress" or "civic truce." It constitutes an agreement between traditionally hostile factions within a country to cease disputes for the duration of a national emergency. Such an arrangement was

achieved for a limited time between organized labor (both the political and industrial wings) on the one hand and the Imperial government and industrial leaders on the other in August 1914. The situation demanded a concentration of all elements of the population for the war effort. Accordingly, they agreed that all strikes, lockouts, and party-political opposition to the government would be discontinued.

The desired national unity seemed to have been achieved when the Social Democrats voted for war credits in the Reichstag on August 4, and the kaiser responded in his famous speech stating that he recognized no more party divisions but only Germans. However, this unity was more apparent than real. The attitude of the Social Democrats was crucial, but their unanimous vote for the war credits was really only an expression of party discipline, which concealed the deep-seated dissent originating from the anti-imperialist elements within the party. By the following year these had begun to protest against the war and openly to rebel against party discipline. Their activities led ultimately to the formation of the Independent Social Democratic Party and later to the Communist Party of Germany.

The *Burgfrieden*, however, was rigorously supported by the powerful trade union leadership under its chairman, Carl Legien (1861–1920), also a Social Democratic Reichstag deputy. He, above all, insisted on the maintenance of "the policy of 4 August" because he was convinced that solidarity with the government and industry in time of war was essential if the trade unions were to achieve full legal recognition as the representatives of the working class in the country through legislation. Also, the unions perceived themselves as the natural advocates of a modern social policy to improve the welfare of the working class within the state.

Legien's objective was in part achieved through the passing in 1916 of the national war auxiliary service bill (*Kriegshilfsdienstgesetz*), the aim of which was to mobilize all able-bodied workers between 16 and 60 for the war effort. Labor made some temporary gains, but the price was the virtual militarization of the entire country. The working class in particular was subjected to massive deprivations. The resultant unrest was expressed in a series of wild strikes in addition to the splitting of the Social Democratic Party.

In the end, the *Burgfrieden* was impossible to sustain despite the best efforts of its labor advocates, such as Legien, not least because the initial objects of the participants were irreconcilable. Labor wanted to defend the fatherland, maintain German prosperity, and extract more democratic concessions from the government as a recognition for loyal collaboration. Management and government wanted to strengthen the monarchical, antidemocratic system and expand Germany's borders in an imperialistic war. When this latter objective became more and more clear to labor circles, the rigorous maintenance of the *Burgfrieden* became illusory.

John A. Moses

See also Independent Social Democratic Party; Legien, Karl; Nationalism; Social Democratic Party; Wilhelm II; World War I

References

Feldman, Gerald D. *Army, Industry and Labor in Germany 1914–1918*. Princeton, NJ: Princeton University Press, 1966.

Fletcher, Roger. *Revisionism and Empire: Socialist Imperialism in Germany 1897–1914*. London: Allen and Unwin, 1984.

Kocka, Jürgen. *Facing Total War: German Society 1914–1918*. Leamington Spa: Berg Publishers, 1984.

Moses, John A. *Trade Unionism in Germany from Bismarck to Hitler, 1869–1933*. 2 vols. London: George Prior, 1982.

Burschenschaft

The Burschenschaft was the first modern student movement that sought to reform campus life as well as transform national politics. In 1815, returning volunteers from the Wars of Liberation tried to found a comprehensive organization at Jena University in order to improve student conduct by supplanting the older regional groups, called *Landsmannschaften*. For the 1817 tricentennial of the Lutheran Reformation, 500 students from all over Germany met in a festival at the Wartburg Castle to demand national unification and burn the symbols of political reaction. One year later, reformers created the Allgemeine Deutsche Burschenschaft (general German student's society), the first national student union to represent various German-speaking universities. When one radicalized member, Karl Sand, assassinated the minor poet and Russian informer August Kotzebue in 1819, Austrian Foreign Minister Klemens Metternich outlawed the movement through the "Carlsbad Decrees," passed by the German Confederation. The restored monarchies considered student ideas subversive because they contained curious blends of nationalism and constitutionalism as well as romanticism and Protestantism.

During the repression in the 1820s, the Burschenschaft went underground and continued its agitation in secret. Denounced as demagogical and hounded by the police, the movement split into a quietist (*Arminen*) and activist (*Germanen*) wing, with the latter trying to seize the police barracks in Frankfurt am Main, capital of the German Confederation, in 1833. After another wave of persecution by the Central Investigative Agency, the Burschenschaft reemerged in the 1840s as a "progressive movement" and propagated democracy as well as social reform. During the Revolution of 1848, many former members ran for parliament as liberals in order to put their aspirations of national unity and constitutional government into practice at the sessions of the first all-German Parliament meeting in St. Paul's Church in Frankfurt am Main. At the same time, radical students met in another Wartburg celebration to demand university reform as well as further political changes. The first cohorts of the German student movement therefore played a central role in the rise of national liberalism in Central Europe.

With the defeat of the Revolution, the Burschenschaft turned into a traditional fraternity. Seeking to rival the socially exclusive but apolitical Corps, it also adopted the drinking and dueling rites typical of German student associations. Since it retained some lingering political interest, the Burschenschaft applauded Chancellor Otto von Bismarck's unification of Germany, but under pressure of the anti-Semitic agitation of the 1880s forsook its liberal ideals and began to exclude Jews from membership. Championing German nationalism and imperialism, the monarchist fraternity enthusiastically embraced World War I, but it never quite accepted the legitimacy of the Weimar Republic. For these reasons the Burschenschaft played a leading role in antidemocratic student organizations of the 1920s and entered into electoral alliances with the rising National Socialist Student League. In spite of its nationalist credentials, the Nazis transformed it, like its other rivals, into local *Kameradschaften* (comradeships), which tenuously claimed to uphold their patriotic heritage. Initially banned by the World War II victors, the Burschenschaft reemerged during the 1950s to become a mainstay among conservative students of the Federal Republic. Its later development, therefore, shows a curious reversal from a progressive impulse into a reactionary force, only somewhat redeemed by more recent moderation.

Konrad H. Jarausch

See also Bildung und Bildungsbürgertum; Bourgeoisie; Nationalism; Students; Universities; Youth; Youth Movements

References
Heer, Georg and Paul Wentzke. *Geschichte der deutschen Burschenschaft.* 4 vols. Heidelberg and Frankfurt am Main: C. Winter 1919–1931. Reprinted 1965.
Jarausch, Konrad H. *Deutsche Studenten.* Frankfurt am Main: Suhrkamp, 1983.
———. *Students, Society, and Politics in Imperial Germany.* Princeton, NJ: Princeton University Press. 1982.
———. "The Sources of German Student Unrest, 1815–1848." *The University in Society.* Vol. 2. Ed. Lawrence Stone. Princeton, NJ: Princeton University Press, 1974.
Quellen und Darstellungen zur Geschichte der Deutschen Einheitsbewegung. Heidelberg: C. Winter, 1911 *ff.*
Weber, R. G. S. *The German Student Corps in the Third Reich.* New York, NY: Macmillan, 1986.

Busch, Wilhelm (1832–1908)

The artist, poet, and humorist Wilhelm Busch is best known for his hilarious and often gruesome picture stories, the most famous of which is *Max und Moritz,* 1865. His pithy verses are still quoted almost as frequently as those of Goethe and Schiller. Busch's tales of village life delight in the gratuitous violence of small children, the chaos caused by animals run amok, and the mayhem created by pranksters when they disrupt bourgeois complacency. Influenced by Charles Darwin (1809–82) and Arthur Schopenhauer (1788–1860), Busch offers exuberant entertainment in his satires, which also reflect his deep concern with aggression and his profound pessimism.

Born in rural north Germany, Busch trained as an engineer before studying art at the academies in Düsseldorf (1851), Antwerp (1852), and Munich (1854). He joined the rebellious Young Munich art circle and contributed regularly to the humorous weeklies the *Fliegende Blätter* (Flying pages) and the *Münchener Bilderbogen* (Munich picture pages) from 1859 to 1871. In all, Busch produced some 60 picture stories and nine hundred paintings, as well as poetry and prose.

Busch's humor ranged widely. In addition to bad boys and animal antics, the lifelong bachelor satirized sexuality, marriage, and family life. *Die Fromme Helene* (The pious Helen), 1872, runs the gamut from childish rebellion, religious hypocrisy, sexual precociousness, and symbolic castration to impotence, adultery, alcoholism, and death. Busch's final two picture stories, *Balduin Bahlamm,* 1883, and *Maler Klecksel* (The painter Klecksel), 1884, pillory the pompous self-deception of would-be poets and artists. At the time of German unification, Busch published the anti-Catholic satires, *Der heilige Antonius von Padua* (The holy Antonius from Padua), 1870, and *Pater Filucius* (Father Filucius), 1872, and a cruel anti-French skit in the 1870 *Münchener Bilderbogen.* These overtly political publications were the exceptions to an oeuvre that combined ironic insight into the absurdity of daily life and a persistent fascination with the dark side of the human condition.

Mary Lee Townsend

See also Artists; Imperial Germany: Literature; Painting; Poetry; Satire

References
Arndt, Walter, ed. and trans. *The Genius of Wilhelm Busch.* Berkeley, CA: University of California Press, 1982.
Bohne, Friedrich. *Wilhelm Busch: Leben, Werk, Schicksal.* Zürich: Fretz & Wasmuth, 1958.
Busch, Wilhelm. *Sämmtliche Briefe: Kommentierte Ausgabe.* 2 vols. Ed. Friedrich Bohne. Hannover: Wilhelm-Busch-Gesellschaft, 1968–69.
———. *Werke: Historisch-kritische Gesamtausgabe.* 4 vols. Ed. Friedrich Bohne. Hamburg: Standard-Verlag, 1959.
Kunzle, David. *The History of the Comic Strip: The Nineteenth Century.* Berkeley, CA: University of California Press, 1990.
Lotze, Dieter P. *Wilhelm Busch.* Boston, MA: Twayne, 1979.

Butenandt, Adolf (1903–95)

Adolf Friedrich Johann Butenandt was awarded the Nobel Prize in chemistry in 1939 for his work on sex hormones; he shared the prize with Leopold Ruzicka, who received it for his work on polymethylenes and higher terpenes. The German government forced Butenandt to decline the prize. Not until after the war, in 1949, did he receive the gold medal and the diploma.

The son of a businessman, he was born in Bremerhaven-Lehe on March 24, 1903, and attended school in Bremerhaven. Then he studied chemistry, biology, and physics at the universities of Marburg and Göttingen. He received his doctorate in 1927 under the direction of Adolf Windaus (Nobel Prize winner in chemistry, 1928) with a dissertation on the chemical constitution of rotenone at the University of Göttingen. In 1929, Butenandt isolated estrone, the hormone that determines sexual development in females, in pure crystalline form. This work led to the isolation of related hormones, and within a few years, he had isolated androsterone (1931), a male sexual hormone, and progesterone (1934), a hormone important for the biochemical processes involved in pregnancy.

After completing his *Habilitation* (thesis to qualify for university teaching) in 1931 on the follicular sex hormone, Butenandt became head of the organic and biochemical department of the chemistry laboratory at the University of Göttingen. In 1933, at the relatively young age of 30, he received an appointment as professor of organic chemistry and director of the organic chemical institute at the *Technische Hochschule* (technical university) in Danzig. After declining an offer to become a professor of biological chemistry at Harvard University in 1935, Butenandt received a joint appointment as director of the prestigious Kaiser Wilhelm Institute for Biochemistry in Berlin-Dahlem in 1936 and honorary professor at the University of Berlin, where he remained until the end of the war.

After the war, the Kaiser Wilhelm Society was dissolved and the Max Planck Society, its successor organization, was founded. Butenandt, who had moved to Tübingen in 1944, became director of the Tübingen Max Planck Institute for Biochemistry, and was professor of physiological chemistry at the University from 1945 to 1956. In 1952 he was appointed professor of physiological chemistry at the University of Munich. He became director of the physiological-chemical institute there from 1956 until 1960, when he became president of the Max Planck Society, a position he held until 1972, a period of intense expansion and institute building. Butenandt contributed much to the rebuilding of German science in the postwar period and became an influential science organizer.

Butenandt's most outstanding contribution to science was his work on sex hormones. Within five years (1929–34) he had isolated two female sex hormones, estrone and progesterone, and one male sex hormone, androsterone. He found that they all belonged to the same class of substances, the steroids, and that they had similar chemical structures, although they all had different physiological functions. Butenandt was unique in that his work on sex hormones focused on their chemical constitution. He always searched for new knowledge about life's processes and functions. This guided him to other branches of research—he also performed important work on the biochemistry of heredity, viruses, the relationship between cancer and hormones, and the active substances of insects.

Butenandt's isolation and elucidation of the structure of sex hormones assisted in the synthesis of other steroids; it also

Adolf Butenandt. Courtesy of German Information Center, New York.

had far-reaching importance for medicine. It hastened the production of cortisone on a large scale and fostered preparations that could be used therapeutically, such as estradiol for disturbances in the menstrual cycle, progesterone to prevent miscarriages, and estrogen as the basis for oral contraceptives.

   Kristie Macrakis

See also Biochemistry; Chemistry, Scientific and Industrial; Kaiser Wilhelm/Max Planck Societies and Institutes; Physiology

References

Butenandt, Adolf. *Das Werk eines Lebens.* Munich: Max-Planck-Gesellschaft; Göttingen: Vandenhoeck & Ruprecht, 1981.

Karlson, P. *Adolf Butenandt: Biochemiker, Hormonforscher, Wissenschaftspolitiker.* Stuttgart: Wissenschaftliche Verlagsgesellschaft, 1990.

Maisel, A.Q. *The Hormone Quest.* New York, NY: Random House, 1965.

C

Cabaret

Cabaret—in German *Kabarett*, also *Cabaret* in its early years—designates a genre of performance as well as the venue where it is performed. Cabaret is usually presented in a small theater, and consists of a variety of short songs, monologues, and skits that satirize contemporary politics, social attitudes, and consumer fashions.

Cabarets appeared in Paris in the 1880s. The first German cabaret was Ernst von Wolzogen's "Buntes Theater" (motley theater), founded in Berlin in 1901. In the wake of that venture's success, other cabarets were established, most notably Max Reinhardt's (1873–1943) "Schall und Rauch" (sound and smoke) and, in Munich, the "Elf Scharfrichter" (eleven executioners), where Frank Wedekind (1864–1918) sang morbid ballads. Since censorship limited the audacity of these stages, most cabarets of the Imperial era tended to present an innocuous mixture of jokes, skits, and semi-risqué songs.

The Weimar Republic marked a high point in the history of German cabaret. The lifting of censorship in 1918 opened the doors to political criticism, but writers such as Kurt Tucholsky (1890–1935) and Walter Mehring discovered that most spectators came to cabaret to be entertained, and were offended by overly biting lyrics. Consequently, politics played a secondary role in cabaret performances, which concentrated instead on the social mores, consumer fads, and sexual foibles of the day. Lively tunes were provided by highly prolific composers such as Friedrich Hollaender, Rudolf Nelson, and Mischa Spoliansky. The two most successful cabarets of the early 1920s were founded by women, namely Rosa Valetti's "Grössenwahn" (megalomania) and Trude Hesterberg's "Wilde Bühne" (wild stage). Kurt Robitschek's "Kabarett der Komiker" (cabaret of comedians) was Berlin's major venue later in the decade.

Cabaret's success spilled over into other areas. Berlin's immense revue stages likewise presented a variety of numbers, albeit in much more spectacular form. Cabaret songs were incorporated into dramas as well as films (such as *Der blaue Engel* [produced as *The Blue Angel*], 1930, with Hollaender's

numbers). Even the Communist Party was not immune: its agitprop troupes entertained proletarian audiences with cabaret-style shows that spread leftist ideals.

When the Nazis came to power, cabaret's most prominent performers, writers, and composers went into exile because of their Jewish ancestry or leftist leanings. Many who were captured after 1939 by Germany's advancing armies perished in the concentration camps. In the Reich itself, the "Tingel-Tangel" and Werner Finck's "Katokombe" (catacombs), the only Berlin cabarets that dared to make wisecracks about the Nazis after 1933, were forcibly closed in 1935. Thereafter, the regime tried to promote a type of "positive cabaret" that would support Nazi ideals, but the attempt failed owing to its total lack of wit. In the end, the so-called cabarets of the Nazi era presented mindless variety acts, featuring song-and-dance numbers in which "showgirls" played a prominent role.

The postwar years saw a reappearance of cabaret in the Western and Soviet zones. Unlike their forebears, the new stages focused mainly on political issues. The cabarets of the Federal Republic tended to be extremely leftist, and they addressed issues such as rearmament, the persistence of Nazis in public office and private industry, and the Vietnam War. In East Germany, cabarets were one of the very few officially sanctioned outlets for criticism. They routinely made light of problems such as consumer-goods shortages, inability to travel abroad, and bureaucratic red tape, but they refrained from attacking the leadership, the Soviet Union, or basic Communist precepts.

In the Federal Republic, there was much talk of a "cabaret crisis" in the 1970s and 1980s: the end of the Vietnam War and Germany's continued economic success dwindled the ranks of critical spectators. However, the social and economic dislocations brought about by the unification of Germany have given renewed impetus to cabarets in both the "old" and the "new" federal states. For the foreseeable future, it is unlikely that this lively art will lack targets for its satirical and parodistic barbs.

Peter C. Jelavich

See also Censorship; National Socialist Germany; Satire; Theater; Weimar Germany

References

Appignanesi, Lisa. *The Cabaret.* New York, NY: Universe Books, 1976.

Budzinski, Klaus. *Pfeffer ins Getriebe: So ist und wurde das Kabarett.* Munich: Universitas, 1982.

Jelavich, Peter. *Berlin Cabaret.* Cambridge, MA: Harvard University Press, 1993.

Otto, Rainer and Walter Rösler. *Kabarettgeschichte: Abriss des deutschsprachigen Kabaretts.* Berlin: Henschelverlag, 1977.

Rösler, Walter. *Das Chanson im deutschen Kabarett 1901–1933.* Berlin: Henschelverlag, 1980.

Camphausen, Ludolf (1803–90)

From headquarters located in Cologne, Ludolf Camphausen operated banking, railroad, and steamship enterprises that made him one of Rhenish Prussia's most successful entrepreneurs by 1830. An early advocate of steam transportation, he enlisted the support of the future Friedrich Wilhelm IV for his railroad-building projects. Camphausen's business and political acumen led to involvement in public affairs and to election as a Prussian legislature (Landtag) deputy in 1842.

An interest in economic modernization attracted Camphausen to the political reform movement. As a member of the provincial Landtag in 1843, he failed to persuade the government to institute press freedom and other liberal measures. His efforts to mitigate arbitrary rule established his credentials as a liberal during the 1840s. When Friedrich Wilhelm IV's "February Patent" of 1847 brought the liberal movement to life in Rhenish Prussia, Camphausen emerged as a leading figure. All liberals strove to achieve a constitutional state, a goal to be reached by convincing the king to convene the Landtag at regular intervals. Camphausen himself, while a deputy in the United Landtag of 1847, assumed a moderate attitude toward the government in Berlin.

Camphausen's willingness to compromise with the regime won him the office of prime minister of Prussia on March 29, 1848. Too interested, perhaps, in retaining the Crown's goodwill, he hesitated to appoint liberal-minded officials to vacant positions. He resigned in June when the government's constitutional initiatives failed to win legislative approval. Following the collapse of the Prussian Union scheme in 1850, he lost all hope for a liberal alliance with the Hohenzollern monarchy. Later, Camphausen, like many liberals of 1848–49, was beguiled by Chancellor Otto von Bismarck's successes. He once confessed that the events of 1871 meant the realization of "the impulse toward unity of the German nation, newly awakened in 1840." Yet Bismarck's constitutional innovations, notably universal manhood suffrage, struck him as dangerously radical.

Consistent in his moderate-liberal political principles, Camphausen remained ambivalent toward the modernization process. Though an early proponent of steam power, he disliked mechanized factories and believed that Germany would be better off as an agricultural rather than an industrial country. He therefore opposed the protectionist ideas of Friedrich List (1789–1846) and championed free trade. Essentially conservative in his response to the "social question," he did realize the need to do something to aid Germany's impoverished workers. His only practical suggestion, however, was to create savings banks intended to encourage thrift among the working class.

Richard J. Bazillion

See also Bismarck, Otto von; Liberalism

References

Angermann, Erich. "Ludolf Camphausen (1803–1890)." *Rheinische Lebensbilder.* 2 vols. Ed. Bernhard Poll. Düsseldorf: Rheinland-Verlag, 1966.

Brandenburg, Erich. *König Friedrich Wilhelm IV: Briefwechsel mit Ludolf Camphausen.* Berlin: Gebrüder Paetel, 1906.

Caspary, Anna. *Ludolf Camphausens Leben: Nach seinem schriftlichen Nachlass dargestellt.* Stuttgart: Cotta'sche Buchhandlung Nachfolger, 1902.

Hofmann, Jürgen. "Ludolf Camphausen: Erster bürgerlicher Ministerpräsident in Preussen." *Männer der Revolution von 1848.* Ed. Helmut Bleiber et al. Berlin: Akademie-Verlag, 1987.

Obermann, Karl. "Ludolf Camphausen und die bourgeoise Konterrevolution. Zur Rolle der liberalen Bourgeoisie in der Revolution 1848/49." *Zeitschrift für Geschichtswissenschaft* 18 (1970), 1448 *ff.*

Schwann, Mathieu. *Ludolf Camphausen.* 3 vols. Essen: G.D. Baedeker, 1915.

Canaris, Wilhelm (1887–1945)

Canaris was a naval officer (1905–35) who became head of the military intelligence organization, the Abwehr (1935–44). His role in the resistance to Adolf Hitler, although limited, resulted in his execution by the Nazis.

Canaris entered the navy in 1905 and was on the small cruiser *Dresden* when it was scuttled in battle at the Falklands. After fleeing internment in Chile, he returned to Germany and spied in Spain. After World War I, he helped organize volunteer troops (*Freikorps*) against the council movement during the Revolution of 1918 and was involved in the murders of Rosa Luxemburg (1870–1919) and Karl Liebknecht (1871–1919). While naval adjutant (1919–20) to Reichswehr Minister Gustav Noske (1868–1946), he joined the Kapp *Putsch*. Retained in the navy, he engaged in sale of arms abroad—especially torpedoes and submarine prototypes in Spain and Japan—illegal rearmament, and financing the Organization Consul, which murdered Walther Rathenau (1867–1922) and Matthias Erzberger (1875–1921). Press criticism of his testimony before a Reichstag committee in 1926 and his role in the Phoebus scandal in 1928 caused his transfer to the battleship *Schlesien*, which he commanded after September 1932.

Canaris remained a monarchist, opposed the Weimar Republic, welcomed Adolf Hitler's appointment, praised

National Socialism, including anti-Semitism, and supported rearmament, reoccupation of the Rhineland, and the acquisition of Austria, the Sudetenland, and the Polish Corridor. With the rank of captain, he was appointed in 1935 to chief of the Abwehr, which also undertook sabotage and diversionary operations. During 1935–36 Canaris talked frequently with Hitler and apparently urged intervention in the Spanish Civil War, cooperation with Italy there, and alliance with Rome. Hardly disturbed by the Sturmabteilung (SA) murders of June 30, 1934, Canaris criticized the Schutzstaffel (SS), Sicherheitsdienst (SD), and Gestapo because of their framing of General Fritsch in 1937. In contact with Ernst von Weizsäcker to prevent Germany's destruction by war in August-September 1938, and ready to unseat but not assassinate Hitler, Canaris warned Italy of impending war in 1938, as he did again in 1939, but did not commit treason or want fundamental changes in the Third Reich. A famous report on Hitler's August 22, 1939 speech reflects the tenor of Canaris's diary. Canaris had apparently recognized that Hitler was a murderous megalomaniac and warmonger.

Incensed—as a passionate anti-Communist—by the Nazi-Soviet Pact, especially resenting the expulsion of Germans from the Baltic states, Canaris did not plot against Hitler but protected Colonel Oster and others who did. Always pessimistic about the outcome of the war, and an opponent of the invasion of the USSR, he later dabbled in contacts with the Soviets in Stockholm for a separate peace. The Abwehr failed to detect the Soviet military buildup at Stalingrad, to predict the Allied landing in North Africa, and to prevent the acceptance of British disinformation. Its bureaucratic struggles with the Security Service of the SS (SD) and Reich Security Main Office (RSHA) brought about its demise and fusion with the RSHA early in 1944. Although Canaris had not had any part in the July 20, 1944 attempt on Hitler's life, he was close to a number of leading figures. He was executed in the last weeks of the Nazi regime.

Canaris was an elusive character who after 1945 acquired an inflated reputation as opponent of Hitler and intelligence chief. Earlier a Nazi, but disenchanted with the regime by 1938, he did little against it, and politically remained a Fascist and an advocate of "Great" Germany.

Leonidas E. Hill

See also Hitler, Adolf; Liebknecht, Karl; Luxemburg, Rosa; National Socialist Germany; Navy and Naval Policy; Paramilitary Organizations; Resistance; Soviet-German Relations

References

Brissaud, André. *Canaris*. London: Weidenfeld and Nicolson, 1973.

Colvin, Ian. *Canaris*. London: Victor Gollancz, 1951.

Fleischhauer, Ingeborg. *Die Chance des Sonderfriedens: Deutsch-sowjetische Geheimgespräche 1941–1945*. Berlin: Siedler, 1986.

Fraenkel, Heinrich and Roger Manvell. *The Canaris Conspiracy*. London: William Heinemann, 1969.

Hoehne, Heinz. *Canaris*. London: Secker and Warburg, 1979.

Kahn, David. *Hitler's Spies: German Military Intelligence in World War II*. New York, NY: Macmillan, 1978.

Whiting, Charles. *Canaris*. New York, NY: Ballantine, 1973.

Canetti, Elias (1905–94)

Elias Canetti was a writer, autobiographer and philosopher. His extensive work, *Masse und Macht* (Crowds and power), 1960, was an investigation in history, psychology, anthropology, philosophy, religion, and literature of the modern phenomenon: the mass. Canetti pursued this topic with particular dedication since World War II as a response to Nazi atrocities, but his novel *Die Blendung,* 1935, written in 1933, already explored the problematic relation between the individual and mass society.

Born in Russe, Bulgaria, to Ladino- and German-speaking Sephardic Jews, Canetti grew up in Bulgaria, England, Austria, Switzerland, and Germany. Canetti's childhood experiences, as well as the process by which German became his "acquired mother tongue" (and, consequently, the language in which he wrote) was described in his autobiography, *Die gerettete Zunge* (The tongue set free), 1977. In 1924, Canetti attended the University of Vienna, where he earned a doctorate in chemistry. *Die Fackel im Ohr* (Torch in my ear), 1980, the second part of his autobiography, describes Canetti's years in Vienna and contact with Karl Kraus (1874–1935). Kraus's influence on Canetti is most evident in his plays *Hochzeit* (Marriage), 1932, and *Komödie der Eitelkeit* (Comedy of ar-

Elias Canetti. Courtesy of Inter Nationes, Bonn.

rogance) written in 1934; first printing, 1964. *Das Augenspiel* (Play of the eyes), 1985, is the last part of his autobiography, which ends with his mother's death in 1937. In 1938 Canetti went into exile in London.

Canetti's critical studies include *Der andere Prozess* (Kafka's other trial), 1968, an analysis of Franz Kafka's (1883–1924) relationship with Felice Bauer. He has also published his copious notebooks under the titles *Aufzeichnungen 1942–1948* (Notes 1942–1948), 1965; *Alle vergeudete Verehrung. Aufzeichnungen 1949–1960* (All squandered adoration. Notes 1949–1960), 1970; *Die Provinz des Menschen. Aufzeichnungen 1942–1972* (The province of the human. Notes 1942–1972), 1976; and *Das Geheimherz der Uhr. Aufzeichnungen 1973–1985* (The secret heart of the clock. Notes 1973–1985), 1987.

Canetti's recognition has steadily increased in the English-speaking world since the translation of *Die Blendung* in 1946. In 1980, he was awarded the Kafka Prize and the Nobel Prize for literature. Canetti died in 1994.

Andres Nader

See also Federal Republic of Germany: Literature; Kafka, Franz; Kraus, Karl

References

Bensel, Walter, ed. *Elias Canetti: Eine Personalbibliographie.* Bremerhaven: DUX-Verlag, 1989.
Lawson, Richard H. *Understanding Elias Canetti.* Columbia, SC: University of South Carolina Press, 1991.
Piel, Edgar. *Elias Canetti.* Munich: Beck, 1984.
Stevens, Adrian and Wagner Fred, eds. *Elias Canetti: Londoner Symposium.* Stuttgart: Verlag Hans-Dieter Heinz, 1991.

Cantor, Georg (1845–1918)

Georg Cantor may be considered the founder of mathematical set theory. He also contributed to the professionalization of mathematics in Germany by founding the German Mathematical Society in 1890 and serving as its first president.

Cantor was born on March 3, 1845, in St. Petersburg into a wealthy Protestant merchant family. After studying mathematics in Zürich and Göttingen, he took his doctorate at Berlin, where his main teacher was the influential mathematician, Kurt Weierstrass (1815–97). In 1872, Cantor obtained a professorship at the University of Halle/Saale, and he remained there throughout his career. Beginning in 1884, he suffered from severe periodic attacks of depression. He died on January 6, 1918.

In his early work on real analysis, Cantor came to consider different types of point sets in the line of real numbers. In the course of these studies, he developed the concepts of general set theory. In particular, Cantor was led to introduce a hierarchy of "transfinite numbers," characterizing different kinds of infinite sets. Though he originally was motivated by rather concrete problems of real analysis, Cantor made strong philosophical claims about the nature of transfinite numbers. He considered his extension of the concept of number a decisive step in the evolution of mathematics. Trying to reject

criticisms of Aristotle and of the scholastic tradition with regard to the use of "actual infinities," Cantor separated the mathematical notion of the "transfinite" from the concept of an "absolute infinity," which he reserved for the theological domain. These considerations found some support among Catholic theologians.

On the other hand, important members of the mathematical community, notably the Berlin mathematician Leopold Kronecker (1823–91), had strong reservations about Cantor's new concepts. In spite of a famous defense of Cantor's transfinite methods by David Hilbert (1862–1943), the discussions about transfinite set theory went on during the first decades of the twentieth century, and were reinforced by the general recognition of the so-called "set theoretical paradoxes." In the Nazi era, Cantorian set theory was even criticized as a form of decadent "Jewish mathematics," as opposed to the healthy "Aryan" variety.

Cantor's general outlook on mathematics is perhaps best expressed in his famous sentence, "The essence of mathematics lies in its freedom" (*Gesammelte Abhandlungen* [Collected works], 1932) For him, mathematics was to be seen as a creation of the human mind, and not as a (part of) natural science. This conviction also motivated Cantor in his institutional activities. In 1890, he succeeded in his efforts to found an independent professional organization of German mathematicians, the Deutsche Mathematiker-Vereinigung (DMV). He also played a central role in the preparation of the first International Congress of Mathematicians (Zürich, 1897).

Thanks to his contributions to mathematical knowledge and to his organization of mathematics as a modern scientific discipline, Cantor may be considered one of the foremost figures of what has been called "mathematical modernism."

Moritz Epple

See also Hilbert, David; Mathematics; Science and National Socialism

References

Cantor, Georg. *Gesammelte Abhandlungen mathematischen und philosophischen Inhalts.* Ed. E. Zermelo. Berlin: Springer, 1932. Reprint: Berlin: Springer, 1980.
Dauben, Joseph Warren. *Georg Cantor: His Mathematics and Philosophy of the Infinite.* Cambridge, MA: Harvard University Press, 1979.
Mehrtens, Herbert. *Moderne Sprache Mathematik.* Frankfurt am Main: Suhrkamp, 1990.
Purkert, Walter. *Georg Cantor.* Basel: Birkhauser, 1987.

Caprivi, Leo von (1831–99)

Caprivi had won considerable distinction as a soldier and military administrator before his appointment in March 1890 as Imperial chancellor and minister-president of Prussia as successor to Prince Otto von Bismarck. He served as chancellor until October 1894, but resigned as minister-president in 1892.

Caprivi had the good fortune to be a young officer during the wars of the 1860s and 1870s, through which Bismarck achieved the unification of Germany under the King of Prussia. He fought with distinction, and after hostilities had been brought to an end in 1871 Caprivi was advanced through a number of administrative positions in the peacetime army, achieving a reputation as an able although hardheaded officer. A quiet, reclusive bachelor, Caprivi was without ambition for political office, but in 1890, Kaiser Wilhelm II, having dismissed Bismarck, believed that it would be prudent to replace him with a seasoned military figure. Caprivi, who was almost 60 and who bore a resemblance to the former chancellor, seemed the obvious choice.

Caprivi was under no illusions about the difficulties of his position, and the principal problem he identified as the kaiser. The two men never succeeded in working well together, not only because of personality clashes but also because Caprivi opposed what he considered Wilhelm's inordinate ambitions for the army and his reactionary domestic policies. Although himself a general, Caprivi as chancellor insisted that the ultimate force in the government be the civil administration, and he deprived the kaiser's beloved military attachés of much of their independence and succeeded in whittling down the large increases in the strength of the army that Wilhelm II desired. As a diplomat, Caprivi believed that Germany was entitled to a position in Europe commensurate with her political and economic power, but he was opposed to any kind of adventurism or bellicosity. Caution was Caprivi's watchword, and straightfoward loyalty to Germany's longtime ally, Austria-Hungary, was a fixed principle of his policy. Russia constituted a potential threat against whom Germany had to be vigilant, but at the same time Caprivi was prepared to bargain with St. Petersburg. In 1892, he succeeded in forging a trade treaty with Russia, for which Wilhelm rewarded his chancellor by promoting him to the rank of count.

By 1894, Wilhelm had grown tired of Caprivi's preceptorial manner and he was profoundly annoyed that the chancellor would not support an aggressive campaign against socialist elements in the working class who in 1894 had precipitated a number of strikes. Since the chancellor, notorious for his refusal to compromise, held firm in his resistance, Wilhelm allowed Caprivi to resign. The former chancellor lived quietly in retirement until his death five years later.

Lamar Cecil

See also Austro-German Relations; Bismarck, Otto von; Hohenlohe-Schillingfürst, Chlodwig zu; Imperial Germany; Russian-German Relations; Wilhelm II

References

Cecil, Lamar. *Wilhelm II, Prince and Kaiser, 1859–1900.* Chapel Hill, NC: University of North Carolina Press, 1989.

Nichols, J. Alden. *Germany after Bismarck: The Caprivi Era 1890–1894.* Cambridge, MA: Harvard University Press, 1958.

Röhl, John C.G. *Germany without Bismarck: The Crisis of Government in the Second Reich, 1890–1900.* Berkeley, CA: University of California Press, 1967.

Carnival in Rottweil in Black Forest Region. Courtesy of Inter Nationes, Bonn.

Carnival

Carnival is chiefly celebrated in Roman Catholic areas in the period preceding Lent. Celebrations vary, the festival itself being variously known as *Karneval* (Rhineland), *Fassenacht* (Mainz), *Fasching* (Bavaria), and *Fastnacht* or *Fasnet* (southwest Germany). Dressing up, mocking the establishment, street activity, and taking on the role of "fool" always play dominant parts. Major Carnival celebrations take place in Aachen, Cologne, Düsseldorf, Mainz, Munich, and Münster.

Particularly in the Rhineland, Carnival is a time of organized merry-making. The Carnival Committee organizes "sessions" (*Sitzungen*), balls, and visits to hospitals. The festivities in Cologne start after Epiphany (January 6) with the proclamation of the Carnival Triumvirate: the Prince, the Peasant Farmer, and the Maid (the last also played by a man). "Sessions" are held on many evenings during the season, climaxing in the "grand session" (*Prunksitzung*) on Rose Monday. This session starts with the entry of the guard of fools and features an appearance by the Triumvirate, specially written carnival songs, dancing groups, and comic acts, often in the local dialect. Many of the audience wear fancy dress and join in the communal singing, linking arms and swaying to the music.

The most colorful and frenzied days of the Cologne Carnival are those from the last Thursday before Lent through to the very last moments of Shrove Tuesday. Three of those days were commonly known as the "three mad days," starting with the women's Carnival. Women dress up and assume complete power for the day. At 11:11 A.M. they symbolically storm the Town Hall and any man foolish enough to wear a tie on this day risks having it cut off just below the knot. Children form a fancy dress procession through the streets on the Sunday afternoon, a foretaste of the splendor of the main Carnival procession on Rose Monday. This consists of countless decorated floats, carts, and coaches, several in the form of ships on wheels, and giant walking figures—often depicting well-known political or international figures—groups of carnival fools, and musical bands. The floats are filled with tons of packaged sweets, chocolates, and cellophane-wrapped bunches of flowers, which are thrown into the crowds. Celebrations continue at dances, parties, and sessions.

The rural *Fastnacht* celebrations have a much older history with a more obvious link with pre-Christian spring festivals. They vary from place to place, but very often involve fools' costumes, wooden masks, foxes' tails, bells, whips, water, soot, and noise, generally regarded as a protection against the demons considered to be a threat during the transitional period between winter and spring. Carnival normally ends with a sweeping out (*Kehraus*) of the carnival season or a burying of *Fasnet* in preparation for Lent.

Jennifer M. Russ

See also Customs

References

Beitl, Richard. *Wörterbuch der deutschen Volkskunde.* 3rd ed. Stuttgart: Kröner, 1974.

Russ, Jennifer M. *German Festivals and Customs.* London: Oswald Wolff, 1982.

Schönfeldt, Sybil Gräfin. *Das Ravensburger Buch der Feste und Bräuche.* Ravensburg: Otto Maier, 1980.

Carossa, Hans (1878–1956)

Hans Carossa was a medical doctor who made a literary career out of diaries, partially autobiographical fiction, and poetry. The recognition of Carossa as a modern-day disciple of Goethe made the writer an object of the Nazi cultural propaganda machine.

Carossa was born in Bavaria, where he lived most of his life, and practiced medicine with his father. His interest in Goethe started at an early age, and imbued him with a sense that art existed for reasons other than for its own sake. His first novel, *Doktor Bürgers Ende: Letzte Blätter eines Tagebuchs* (Doctor Bürger's death: last pages of a diary), 1913, is a fictional journal that has been called Carossa's "Werther." In it, a young doctor vacillates between a life devoted to art and one devoted to living, between a desire for death and for life. Carossa participated in the First World War as a medical officer, and recorded his experiences at the eastern front in *Rumänisches Tagebuch* (Romanian diary), 1924; it was republished in 1934 under the title *Tagebuch im Kriege*, famous for its admonition "Raube das Licht aus dem Rachen der Schlange!" (steal the light from the dragon's teeth) and notable for the absence of any bitterness toward the political ends of the war.

In the 1920s Carossa met Hedwig Kerber, with whom he was to have a child in 1930 and later marry, after the death of his wife Valerie Endlicher, in 1943. The success of *Der Arzt Gion* (Doctor Gion), 1931, ended a "dry" creative period. In this novel, the doctor is able to maintain a balance that eluded Doctor Bürger, and instead of committing suicide finds a place in society; he has been compared to the person of Pollux in Goethe's *Wilhelm Meister*.

Carossa remained in Germany during the Nazi regime. In a semi-autobiographical novel, *Geheimnisse des reifen Lebens* (Secrets of mature life), 1936, and in a description of the year 1900 in *Das Jahr der schönen Täuschungen* (The year of beautiful deceptions), 1941, Carossa gave voice, albeit unobtrusively, to his misgivings about the path Germany was following. As recipient of the Goethe Prize in 1938, Carossa found himself becoming an increasingly public figure, and was thus compelled by the government to accept the presidency of the Nazi-sponsored European Writers' Association in 1941, a post he never physically assumed. After the war, Carossa defended his political accommodations by claiming his actions had helped save others from worse fates.

Although not a very prolific writer, Carossa is recognized as an elegant twentieth-century apologist of Goethe's theory of *Bildung* (cultivation). His mildly religious poetry appears in many anthologies, and his friendships with Hofmannsthal, Rilke, Hesse, Mombert, and others attest to the high regard in which he was often held.

James Skidmore

See also Bildung und Bildungsbürgertum; Hesse, Hermann; Hofmannsthal, Hugo von; National Socialist Germany: Literature; Weimar Germany: Literature

References

Carossa, Hans. *Sämtliche Werke.* 2nd ed. Frankfurt am Main: Insel Verlag, 1978.

Falkenstein, Henning. *Hans Carossa: Köpfe des XX. Jahrhunderts.* Vol. 93. Berlin: Colloquium Verlag, 1983.

Henkel, Arthur. "Beim Wiederlesen von Gedichten Hans Carossas." *Zeit der Moderne: Zur deutschen Literatur von der Jahrhundertwende bis zur Gegenwart.* Ed. Hans-Henrik Krummacher, Fritz Martini, and Walter Müller-Seidel. Stuttgart: Alfred Kroner Verlag, 1984.

Langen, August. *Hans Carossa: Weltbild und Stil.* Berlin: Erich Schmidt Verlag, 1955.

Michels, Volker, ed. *Über Hans Carossa.* Frankfurt am Main: Suhrkamp, 1979.

Carstens, Karl (1914–92)

Karl Carstens, a member of the Christian Democratic Union (CDU) who became president of the Federal Republic of Germany (FRG) in 1979, was known for his conservative and Christian leanings. Among Germans he encouraged a sense of responsibility and a willingness to act tempered by objectivity and sensibility. He won popular affection for undertaking a series of hikes (walking tours) in order to spend time with Germany's youth.

Born in Bremen on December 14, 1914, Carstens studied law and political science at several German and French universities. He received his doctorate in law from the University of Hamburg in 1937. During the war, Carstens served in the artillery (1939–40) and later with anti-aircraft units near Bremen and Berlin.

Carstens returned to the legal profession in May 1945 and completed a master's in law from Yale University (1948–

49) in New Haven, Connecticut. After being legal advisor for Bremen's Senate (1949–54), Carstens taught at the University of Cologne and headed the Institute for the Law of the European Community (1960). In addition, Carstens represented the FRG on the Council of Europe in Strasbourg (1954–55). Working in the Foreign Office (1955–66), Carstens came to hold its second highest office. During Chancellor Kiesinger's Grand Coalition, Carstens moved into the Defense Ministry and then (1968) into Kiesinger's office as state secretary.

Active with the CDU in Schleswig-Holstein, Carstens entered the Bundestag in November 1972. With the resignation of Rainer Barzel (1924–) as head of the CDU/CSU (Christian Social Union) caucus in 1973, Carstens assumed that post after outmaneuvering Gerhard Schröder (1910–89) and Richard von Weizsäcker (1920–). The narrow victory of Helmut Schmidt's social-liberal coalition in 1976 and Helmut Kohl's drive to head the CDU/CSU in the Bundestag gave Carstens the support necessary for his election as president of the Bundestag (December 1976).

In 1979, Carstens sought to succeed President Walter Scheel (1919–). Despite an intensive press campaign focusing on his membership in the Nazi Party, Carstens became West Germany's fifth president by a vote of 520 to 431. After the social-liberal coalition was brought down (October 1982) through the use of the constructive vote of no confidence by the Christian Democrats, Carstens dissolved the Bundestag in January and called for new elections in March. Carstens was succeeded by Richard von Weizsäcker in 1984.

David A. Meier

See also Christian Democratic Union; Federal Republic of Germany; Federal Republic of Germany: Foreign Policy; Kiesinger, Kurt Georg; Kohl, Helmut; Presidency; Scheel, Walter; Schleswig-Holstein; Schmidt, Helmut; Schröder, Gerhard; Weizsäcker, Richard von

References
Carstens, Karl. *Vom Geist der Freiheit*. Stuttgart: Deutsche Verlags-Anstalt, 1989.
Wiedemeyer, Wolfgang. *Karl Carstens—Im Dienst unseres Staates*. Stuttgart: Verlag Bonn Aktuell, 1980.

Cartels

Cartels are horizontal or vertical agreements between independent firms to regulate their market behavior. Such agreements may include, for example, the limiting of production or the stipulating of quotas for cartel members. They may also involve price fixing. Some cartels arrange for the coordination of their sales organizations in so-called syndicates, which are responsible for the marketing of members' products. Because cartels consciously promote anti-competitive behavior, they have been deemed dysfunctional to a capital economy. But it should be remembered that individual companies may be just as keen to stabilize the market. The quest for security and predictability tends to be particularly strong in times of recession or depression.

Cartels first proliferated in Germany during the depression of the 1870s and 1880s, when they were formed as "children of an emergency situation" (*Kinder der Not*). Contrary to liberal economic theory, they were not dissolved again when the country moved into a boom period after 1895. At a time when the United States adopted its antitrust laws (Sherman Act of 1890), which banned the formation of cartels as anti-competitive and monopolistic, the Reich Court, in a decision of 1897, actually sanctioned them. Cartels were recognized as binding agreements between private parties and violations could thenceforth be pursued in the courts. Unlike American industry, where capitalism, despite various exceptions to the principle of competition, was pushed in the direction of oligopoly, German industry expanded its cartel system. By 1914, dozens of these agreements thrived in various branches of industry. The Weimar Republic saw further increases, and the Third Reich finally implemented total cartelization at the prompting of the top industrial associations. It was a peculiar capitalism in which the market had lost its traditional function.

Meanwhile, in the United States, the German cartel system was deemed to be contributing to the victory of Nazism, the regimentation of economic life, and ultimately to the unleashing of World War II. Washington was therefore determined to destroy the German cartel system (which would also serve as a means of undermining the cartel traditions of France, Italy, and Belgium, some of whose industries had joined the German-dominated international cartels of the interwar period). Decartelization thus became one of the American peace aims, and horizontal agreements were banned in 1945.

The question was whether this ban would be effective in the long run, or whether German businessmen would lapse into their anti-competitive behavior once the newly established Federal Republic of Germany (FRG) had gained full sovereignty. In 1950, Economics Minister Ludwig Erhard (1897–1977), no less eager than the Americans to avoid an economic relapse, drafted a bill to secure competition. The law also banned cartels, but it permitted some exceptions from the basic principle. Most of West German industry, by contrast, favored a return to a 1923 decree, which had allowed for the formation of cartels and threatened to ban them only when they could be proven to have abused their market power. After much acrimonious debate, Erhard's bill finally passed in 1957. Since then, German industry has developed market structures and behaviors that more resemble those of the United States, the hegemonic industrial power of the postwar period that was bent on building a multilateral, antiprotectionist world trading system to forestall the disasters of the 1930s and 1940s.

Volker R. Berghahn

See also Central Association of German Industrialists; Depression (1873–95); Economic Miracle; Erhard, Ludwig; I.G. Farbenindustrie AG; Ruhrlade; State and Economy

References
Berghahn, V.R. *The Americanisation of West German Industry, 1945–1973*. Leamington Spa: Berg, 1986.

Chamberlin, E.H., ed. *Monopoly and Competition and Their Regulation.* London: Macmillan, 1954.

Hentschel, V. *Wirtschaft and Wirtschaftspolitik im Wilhelminischem Deutschland.* Stuttgart: Klett-Cotta, 1978.

Levy, Hermann. *Industrial Germany.* New York, NY: A.M. Kelley, 1966.

Schachter, O. and R. Hellawell. *Competition in International Business.* New York, NY: Columbia University Press, 1981.

Cassirer, Ernst (1874–1945)

Philosopher and historian of philosophy, Ernst Cassirer was born in Breslau (now Wroclaw, Poland) on July 28, 1874. He studied at Berlin under Georg Simmel (1858–1918) and at Leipzig, Heidelberg, and Marburg, where he obtained his doctorate under Hermann Cohen (1842–1918) in 1899. His dissertation, "Descarte's Kritik der mathematischen und naturwissenschaftlichen Erkenntnis" (The critique of mathematical and physical knowledge in Descartes) was published in 1902 as the introduction to his magisterial *Leibniz' System in seinen wissenschaftlichen Grundlagen* (Leibniz' system: its fundamentals).

Cassirer's thought reflects the influence of the neo-Kantian Marburg School, and he is considered by many to be one of its most famous representatives. His early work focused on the problem of knowledge, such as *Das Erkenntnisproblem in der Philosophie und Wissenschaft der neueren Zeit* (The problem of knowledge in recent philosophy and science), 4 vols.: 1906, 1907, 1920, 1950, but he soon turned to research in the history of philosophy and published important articles and studies on the philosophy of law (*Freiheit und Form*, [Freedom and form], 1916) and on Hölderlin, 1917, Kant, 1918, Goethe, 1918, and Kleist, 1919. With Cohen he published an edition of Kant's collected works (1912–18). Cassirer taught as *Privatdozent* (private lecturer) at Berlin beginning in 1906 and, on its foundation in 1919, was named professor and later rector (1929–30) at the University of Hamburg.

In 1922 Cassirer turned to the question of form, and 1923 saw the publication of the first of three volumes of his major work, *Philosophie der symbolischen Formen* (The philosophy of symbolic form), 1923–29. Here he extended Kant's critique of reason to human culture. As Kant had argued concerning aesthetic judgement, Cassirer saw human reason as fundamentally dynamic. Unlike Kant, however, Cassirer believed that one can find a principle of invariability (which he identified with objectivity) not only in science, but in all "cultural forms": art, history, philosophy, and religion. Specifically, he located the "invariable" behind all diversity in the symbolic forms of myth, language, and technology. Cassirer's definition of human nature reflected this focus on symbol. He saw the human person primarily as a being that uses symbols (*animal symbolicum*) and understood cultural achievements to be the results of human symbolic activity.

By the late 1920s, Cassirer turned to the conflict between the rationalism of the Enlightenment tradition and the irra-

tionalist tendencies in recent German thought, such as the philosophy of Martin Heidegger (1889–1976). This concern is particularly evident in *Die Philosophie der Aufklärung* (The philosophy of the enlightenment), 1932, the last work Cassirer published in Germany. He resigned from his professorship at Hamburg upon Hitler's nomination as chancellor of the Reich in January 1933, and left Germany soon thereafter. From 1933 until 1935 he taught at Oxford and from 1935 until 1941 in Sweden at Göteborg, where he acquired Swedish citizenship. During this time he wrote an important critique of the principle of causality, *Determinismus und Indeterminismus in der modernen Physik* (Determinism and indeterminism in modern physics), 1936. In 1941 Cassirer moved to the United States to teach, first at Yale (1941–44) and later at Columbia (1944–45). In this latter period, Cassirer returned to the humanist themes of his work of the late 1920s and early 1930s (see his *An Essay on Man,* 1944, and *The Myth of the State,* 1946). He died in New York City on April 13, 1945.

Cassirer's work, like that of the Marburg School in general, is currently experiencing a renewed popularity in scholarly circles in France and Germany.

William Sweet

See also Heidegger, Martin; The Marburg School; Philosophy; Simmel, Georg

References

Eggers, Walter. *Ernst Cassirer: An Annotated Bibliography.* New York, NY: Garland, 1988.

Itzkoff, Seymour. *Ernst Cassirer: Philosopher of Culture.* Boston, MA: Twayne, 1977.

Klibansky, Raymond and W. Solmitz. "Bibliography of Ernst Cassirer's Writings." *Philosophy and History: Essays Presented to Ernst Cassirer.* Ed. H.J. Paton and Raymond Klibansky. Oxford: Clarendon Press, 1936; new edition, New York, NY: Harper and Row, 1964.

Krois, John Michael. *Cassirer: Symbolic Forms and History.* New Haven, CT: Yale University Press, 1987.

Schilpp, P.A. *The Philosophy of Ernst Cassirer.* 2nd ed. LaSalle, IL: Open Court, 1973.

Catholic Women's Association

The industrialization of German society, with its inevitable social challenges, initially drew women into the various religious chapters (*Ordensgemeinschaften*) that dealt with the burning social and educational issues of the nineteenth century. Fifty new orders were formed within the Franciscan tradition alone. In 1885, Pauline Herber founded the Association of German Catholic Teachers, the first denominational, occupational association for women who thus far had not had access to universities and professional associations. In 1899, Agnes Neuhaus founded the Association of Social Workers (today, the Sozialdienst katholischer Frauen [Catholic Women's Social Service]), which helped needy women and children. Elisabeth Gnauck-Kuhne, the first German female social scientist, launched the program of the Catholic Women's Association, which was created in 1903. A multitude of associations for women factory workers, women cottage workers, and domestics in western and southern Germany aimed at enhancing personal and professional development. The associations of mothers and young women first developed at the parish level, which then joined ranks regionally in 1915.

In 1918, German women obtained the franchise. The six women delegates of the Center Party who were elected to the constituent National Assembly (Hedwig Dransfeld, Agnes Neuhaus, Maria Schmitz, Christine Teusch, Helene Weber, and Marie Zettler) represented the women organized in the Catholic women's associations of the time. During the 14 years of the Weimar Republic, Catholic women delegates left their mark in the political arena by their participation in civic education and the elaboration of a constructive political culture. Hedwig Dransfeld inspired the establishment of the Women's Peace Church (*Frauensfriedenskirche*) in Frankfurt, which was inaugurated in 1929 and considered the work of all Catholic women's organizations. National Socialism excluded women from the political sphere, permitted only religious education by the associations, and prohibited all association publications.

After World War II, Catholic women's associations and Catholic women's groups united and formed a steering committee (*Arbeitsgemeinschaft*) of the Catholic Women's Associations, which now comprises some 20 associations representing approximately two million organized women. The *Arbeitsgemeinschaft* is a member of the German Women's Council.

The Catholic women's movement has been actively engaged in discussions concerning a number of significant but controversial sociopolitical issues in the Federal Republic of Germany, such as the realization of men's and women's equality pursuant to Article 3(2) of the Basic Law, as well as the constitutionally guaranteed protection of the family and marriage. In discussions of Paragraph 218 of the Criminal Law, the associations unequivocally endorsed the protection of the unborn child and a multitude of "pro-life" initiatives to support women and families in distress. The movement for renewal after the Second Vatican Council (1962–65) also spurred greater participation by the Catholic women's movement in Church committee work.

At a time of shifting religious commitment, the Catholic Women's movement regards its task as promoting the values of the Gospel, as participating actively in the societal processes, and as fostering international solidarity, especially by espousing the cause of underprivileged women in the Third World.

Elisabeth Prégardier

See also Catholicism, Political; Center Party; Christian Democratic Union; People's Association for a Catholic Germany; (German) Protestant Women's League; Weber, Helene

References

Kall, Alfred. *Katholische Frauenbewegung in Deutschland: Eine Untersuchung zur Grundung katholischer Frauen-vereine im 19. Jahrhundert.* Paderborn: F.S. Schöningh, 1983.

Prégardier, Elisabeth and Anne Mohr. *Politik als Aufgabe: Engagement christlicher Frauen in der Weimarer Republik.* Annweiler: Plöger Verlag, 1990.

Catholicism, Political

In Germany, the homeland of Martin Luther and the largest European polity with substantial numbers of both Catholics and Protestants, religious tension and politics have long been intertwined. Modern German politics has been marked by the rise of several subcultural groupings, each with its own outlook (*Weltanschauung*), institutions, and partisan tradition. Political Catholicism takes its place in this framework alongside socialism, Communism, liberalism, Fascism, and (Prusso-Protestant) conservatism. Although the other "-isms" are not as explicit as political Catholicism about their connection to the politics of religion, each of them, at least in Germany, has involved an anticlerical dimension.

Ideologically, modern political Catholicism developed in the nineteenth century as a unique blend of conservative and liberal precepts. Although Catholic theorists cherished the ideal of individual human dignity, they criticized what they termed the mechanistic misinterpretation of this ideal by the secular thinkers of the French Enlightenment. Society, these Catholic critics argued, was not simply the sum of its individual human parts, but an organic, interdependent corpus. Institutionalized religion was its lifeblood, because human dignity was inseparable from natural law, family values, social obligation, and the Golden Rule. From these principles, German Catholic theorists attempted to draw political conclusions that would apply to a world buffeted by the legacy of the French Revolution and by the dislocations caused by industrial capitalism.

Political Catholicism was further shaped by the distinctive circumstances of German national unification. Under the Holy Roman Empire, with its major religious wars and its numerous semi-autonomous component states, some of which were also religious enclaves, religion had often been an instrument of the power politics of the petty princes. After the Empire's demise during the Napoleonic period, Protestant Prussia acquired the Catholic Rhineland and Westphalia (1815). This annexation caused sporadic confessional incidents amid a generally prejudicial climate of perceived Catholic sociopolitical inferiority. Religious tensions flared more widely during the later 1860s, when Prussian Minister-President Otto von Bismarck succeeded in unifying most of Germany under Prussian leadership and without Catholic Austria. In the new, Protestant-dominated Germany, Catholics were labeled "anti-national" and made up only one-third of the population.

Under these circumstances, German political Catholicism advocated religious and civil parity for Catholics, socioeconomic protections for the disproportionately Catholic lower classes, and the defense of churchly prerogatives against infringement by the state (for example, in the realms of education and marriage). Beyond these points, Catholics sought to balance various aspects of sociopolitical thought: social corporatism versus individual rights, national patriotism versus regional cultural autonomy and religious internationalism, and respect for hierarchical authority versus constitutional protections against tyranny (a critical point for a minority). Although most Catholic politicians and theorists depicted these dichotomies not as "either/or" but as "both/and" propositions, differences invariably arose among Catholics who placed the point of balance further to one side or the other. Also at issue was whether the Catholic agenda ought to be pursued primarily through partisan parliamentary action or through diplomatic negotiations and concordats between governments and the Vatican.

The partisan development of political Catholicism dates from the revolutionary year of 1848, when Catholics formed their own caucuses in the Frankfurt Diet and the Prussian Diet. With German unification in 1870–71, Catholics formed a loose national party, the Center. In the subsequent period of organized anti-Catholic persecution (the *Kulturkampf*), the Center, as the key political agent of Catholic resistance, grew to be for a time the largest German party and acquired significant parliamentary power. Under the parliamentary Weimar Republic, Bavarian Catholics formed their own regional party (the Bavarian People's Party), but the Center Party remained strong in Prussia and Germany as a whole and participated regularly in governmental coalitions, often providing the chancellor.

Alongside the Church, the Catholic schools, the party, and the annual Catholic convocations or *Katholikentage* (still held today), Catholics maintained an extensive and well-organized press and a network of vocational and social organizations.

Heinrich Brüning, Center Party chancellor, 1930–32. Courtesy of German Information Center, New York.

The Catholic press association, the Augustinusverein, was the de facto press arm of the Center Party. Particularly noteworthy among the social organizations were those devoted to workers. Encouraged by Pope Leo XIII's social encyclical *Rerum novarum* (1891), clerical and lay activists built up the People's Association for a Catholic Germany (Volksverein), the Catholic Labor Leagues (Katholische Arbeitervereine), and the interdenominational but largely Catholic Christian trade unions.

With the coming of Nazism, much of the institutional edifice of political and social Catholicism came tumbling down. Ironically, the movement's eclectic adaptability, which had helped it to outlast Bismarck and later to switch with alacrity from monarchical to republican constitutionalism, now served it ill. Ensconced in their own political party, far fewer Catholics than Protestants supported the Nazi party before it came to power; but afterward, Catholics, fearing a new *Kulturkampf*, tried to make their peace with the Nazi state. In return for Nazi promises (later broken) to respect the Church's prerogatives, the Center Party put aside its scruples and voted for the Enabling Act, which gave Hitler dictatorial powers. Shortly thereafter, during negotiations for a concordat between Berlin and the Vatican, the Center disbanded.

Apart from sporadic protests and despite some persecution, the Church failed to muster a glorious record in resisting Nazi atrocities. But the old Catholic subcultural bonds, although loosened, did survive. After the war, with Prusso-Protestant conservatism thoroughly discredited, many Protestants accepted the leadership of Catholic ex-Centrists such as Konrad Adenauer in building an interdenominational political party. That party, the Christian Democratic Union (CDU), has proved central to Germany's democratic rebirth. Political Catholicism thus confirmed its position as one of the chief founts of partisan politics in Germany—the source of the Center Party, and the leading historical tradition behind Christian Democracy.

Noel D. Cary

See also Adenauer, Konrad; Bertram, Adolf; Brüning, Heinrich; Catholic Women's Association; Center Party; Christian Democratic Union; Christian Social Union; Christian Trade Unions; Erzberger, Matthias; Faulhaber, Michael von; Galen, Clemens August von; Heim, Georg; Hertling, Georg von; Kaas, Ludwig; Ketterler, Wilhelm von; Kohl, Helmut; *Kulturkampf*; Lieber, Ernst; Marx, Wilhelm; People's Association for a Catholic Germany; Preysing, Konrad von; Strauss, Franz Josef; Vatican-German Relations; Weber, Helene; Windthorst, Ludwig

References
Anderson, Margaret L. *Windthorst: A Political Biography.* New York, NY: Clarendon Press of Oxford University Press, 1981.
Cary, Noel D. *The Path to Christian Democracy: German Catholics and the Party System from Windthorst to Adenauer.* Cambridge, MA: Harvard University Press, 1996.

Conway, John. *The Nazi Persecution of the Churches, 1933–1945.* New York, NY: Basic Books, 1968.

Evans, Ellen L. *The German Center Party 1870–1933: A Study in Political Catholicism.* Carbondale, IL: Southern Illinois University Press, 1981.

Fogarty, Michael. *Christian Democracy in Western Europe, 1820–1953.* London: Routledge and Kegan Paul, 1957.

Loth, Wilfried. *Katholiken im Kaiserreich.* Düsseldorf: Droste Verlag, 1984.

Ross, R.J. *Beleaguered Tower: The Dilemma of Political Catholicism in Wilhelmine Germany.* South Bend, IN: Notre Dame University Press, 1976.

Smith, Helmut Walser. *German Nationalism and Religious Conflict: Culture Ideology, Politics, 1870–1914.* Princeton, NJ: Princeton University Press, 1995.

Sperber, Jonathan. *Popular Catholicism in Nineteenth Century Germany: Society, Religion, and Politics in Rhineland-Westphalia, 1830–1880.* Princeton, NJ: Princeton University Press, 1984.

Stehlin, Stewart A. *Weimar and the Vatican 1919–1933: German-Vatican Diplomatic Relations in the Interwar Years.* Princeton, NJ: Princeton University Press, 1983.

Windell, George. *The Catholics and German Unity 1866–1871.* Minneapolis, MN: University of Minnesota Press, 1954.

Cauer, Minna (1841–1922)

Minna Cauer is best known as leader of the radical wing of the bourgeois women's movement; her own successes and disappointments mirror that of the radical movement. Perhaps still more than her political allies, from Hedwig Dohm to Lily Braun (1865–1916), Anita Augspurg, and Lida Heymann (1868–1943), Cauer represents the movement's attempt to transcend class and party politics and to bridge the gap between the bourgeois and proletarian women's movements. Likewise, her own political and social isolation reflects the failure of the radicals to achieve their goals.

Cauer trenchantly criticized Wilhelmine party politics, espousing political democratization across both gender and class divides. She attacked both the more moderate bourgeois and the proletarian women's movements for what she perceived to be a subservience to male-defined political visions. An intense and uncompromising fighter for women's rights broadly conceived, Cauer also played a central role in representing specifically the interests of female white-collar workers (commercial workers, office employees, and teachers), and sought to expand the range of these women's educational and employment opportunities.

Twice widowed and in possession of a teaching degree, Cauer entered the women's movement in the early 1880s. In 1888, she founded the *Frauenwohl* (women's welfare) organization (initially as the women's counterpart to the *Deutsche Academische Vereinigung* [German Academic Association]), which emerged immediately as the hub of the left wing of the bourgeois women's movement. Cauer initiated the 1894 Berlin meeting of bourgeois women's groups, which led to the proclamation of support for women's voting rights. In 1895, she represented the minority position in the bourgeois women's movement regarding women's equal rights to political assembly. In the same year, she founded and assumed editorship of *Die Frauenbewegung* (Women's movement), the first organ of the radical wing, over which she held tight control until its dissolution in 1918. *Die Frauenbewegung* reflected Cauer's interest, not simply in welfare and "social reform," but in political rights broadly conceived; it also disclosed Cauer's influence in its aggressively political tone.

In 1898, frustrated by her continued marginality and lack of influence on the mainstream women's movement, Cauer called a general meeting of the Bund Deutscher Frauenvereine (Federation of German Women's Associations) in Hamburg. This meeting resulted in the split of the radical wing from the League, and Cauer's and Augspurg's founding of the alternative Verband Fortschrittlicher Frauenvereine (Federation of Progressive Women's Associations). In the first decade of the new century, Cauer led the Hamburg Deutsche Frauenstimmrechtsbund (Hamburg-German Federation of Suffragettes), and between 1912 and 1918 she acted as editor for the *Zeitschrift für Frauenstimmrecht* (Journal for Women's Suffrage).

Cauer saw herself as a strong patriot, but was committed to an international women's movement. Initially a supporter of World War I, from 1915 she took a courageous pacifist stance. Cauer continued to work for women's rights until her death in 1922.

Belinda Davis

See also Braun, Lily; Feminism and Anti-Feminism, 1871–1918; Heymann, Lida; Nationalist Women's Associations; Pacifism and the Peace Movement; Women, 1871–1918; (Bourgeois) Women's Movement

References

Canning, Kathleen. *Gender and the Changing Meanings of Work: Structures and Rhetorics in the Making of the Textile Factory Workplace in Germany, 1850–1914.* Ithaca, NY: Cornell University Press, 1995.

Cauer, Minna. *Die Frau im 19. Jahrhundert.* Berlin: S. Cronback, 1898.

Greven-Aschoff, B. *Die Bürgerliche Frauenbewegung in Deutschland, 1894–1933.* Göttingen: Vandenhoeck & Ruprecht, 1981.

Kalckstein, Karl von, Minna Cauer, and Albert Eulenberg. *Nationale und Humanistische Erziehung.* Kiel: Lipsius & Tischer, 1891.

Lüders, E. *Der "Linke Flügel": Ein Blatt aus der Geschichte der deutschen Frauenbewegung.* Berlin: W. & S. Loewenthal, 1904.

———. *Minna Cauer: Leben und Werk.* Gotha: Friedrich Andreas Perthes, 1925.

Naumann, Gerlinde. *Minna Cauer: Eine Kämpferin für Frieden, Demokratie und Emanzipation.* Berlin: Buchverlag der Morgen, 1988.

Celan, Paul (Paul Antschel) (1920–70)

Paul Celan, prolific lyricist, writer of short prose pieces, and translator of poetry from many literatures, wrote in an idiom all his own. Though done in German, his mature work during and in the wake of the Holocaust reveals an ambivalent attitude vis-à-vis the language—his mother tongue, but also the tongue of the destroyers of the Jews, his people. The uniquely colored language crisis resulted in a struggle with words that are recalcitrant to obey, in an ever-increasing preoccupation with language that wants to fall silent before the unsayable, in a house of poetry that is haunted by the ghosts of the past. Death looms large, even in the love poems.

Celan was born as Paul Antschel in the then Romanian, now Moldovan, town of Czernowitz. After graduating from a local gymnasium in 1938, he spent a year in Tours to prepare for a medical career. Upon his return to his hometown he studied Romance languages. His parents were deported in June 1942 to the German-occupied Ukraine, where they were murdered, and the young poet himself spent time in a Romanian forced-labor camp until early 1944. Upon his return to Czernowitz he studied English literature, then, in December, left for Bucharest, where he translated materials from Russian into Romanian for a publishing house. Early in 1948 the poet wended his way to Vienna. In July he went to Paris, where he taught German literature at a lyceum. His life came to an end when he slipped into the Seine.

Some 140 poems of the Czernowitz period have survived, among them his most famous, "Todesfuge" (Death fugue). In their aggregate these compositions reveal an astoundingly quick development and bear the signs of the many literary influences on this early work (medieval materials, Goethe, Hölderlin, Novalis, Trakl, Kafka, and above all Rilke). A heavy whiff of the tomb wafts through this collection. Judaic concepts are everywhere, as are borrowings of motifs derived from Greek mythology.

In Bucharest the poet moved in surrealist circles and, adopting the name Celan, wrote poetry in their vein, in German as well as Romanian. In the latter language he also produced short prose pieces.

In Vienna Celan wrote the commentary that accompanied the publication of etchings by the artist Edgar Jené (*Edgar Jené und der Traum vom Träume* [Edgar Jené and the dream of the dreams]). His own *Der Sand aus den Urnen* (The sand from the urns) came off the press in August 1948; Celan, already in Paris, took it off the market, allegedly because of its printing errors.

In Paris Celan married the artist Gisèle Lestrange, and it was Paris that saw him acquire an aura: *Mohn und Gedächtnis* (Poppy and memory) was published in 1952; it was followed by *Von Schwelle zu Schwelle* (From threshold to threshold), 1955, *Sprachgitter* (Speech grill), 1959, *Die Niemandsrose* (No-one's rose), 1963; dedicated to the Russian poet Ossip Mandelstamm, *Atemwende*, 1967, and *Fadensonnen* (Threadsuns), 1968. *Lichtzwang* (Light-compulsion), *Schneepart* (Snow-part), and *Zeitgehöft* (Homestead of time) were published posthumously. The stirring prose *Gespräch im Gebirg* (Conversation in the mountains) is from 1960. Celan's literary activities included many translations, of Russian, Italian, Romanian, Portuguese, Hebrew, and English pieces (Shakespeare's sonnets among them).

Celan was the recipient of prestigious prizes, including the City of Bremen Prize in 1958 and the Georg Büchner Prize in 1960. On the latter occasion he delivered "Der Meridian," a speech of literary importance.

The literature on Celan's oeuvre, begun well before 1970, is already vast, and is destined to increase, in part because of the hermeneutically colored and difficult-to-penetrate poetic idiom in which he speaks in the poetry of his maturity. Though full of ambiguities, oxymorons, and double entendres, this language nevertheless seeks to communicate, even if only to a selective audience. Celan's coining of words, his increasingly terser delivery, and his tortured syntax create the impression that he seeks to destroy the German language in order to replace it with a new one, his very own. It is a language that, however secular and however turned in upon itself it may become, strains for metaphysical reach, time and time again.

Hugo Bekker

See also Federal Republic of Germany: Literature; Holocaust; Jews, 1933–90; Kafka, Franz, Poetry; Rilke, Rainer Maria

References

Brierly, David. *"Der Meridian": Ein Versuch zur Poetik und Dichtung Paul Celans.* Frankfurt am Main: Peter Lang, 1984.

Celan, Paul. *Das Frühwerk.* Ed. Barbara Wiedemann. Frankfurt am Main: Suhrkamp, 1989.

———. *Gesammelte Werke.* 5 vols. Ed. Beda Allemann and Stefan Reichert. Frankfurt am Main: Suhrkamp, 1983.

Chalfen, Israel. *Paul Celan. Eine Biographie seiner Jugend.* Frankfurt am Main: Insel Verlag, 1979.

Felstiner, John. *Paul Celan: Poet, Survivor, Jew.* New Haven, CT: Yale University Press, 1996.

Glenn, Jerry. *Paul Celan.* New York, NY: Twayne Publishers, 1973.

Janz, Marlies. *Vom Engagement absoluter Poesie: Zur Lyrik und Ästhetik Paul Celans.* Königstein/Ts: Athenäum, 1984.

Meinecke, Dietlind. *Wort und Name bei Paul Celan: Zur Widerruflichkeit des Gedichts.* Bad Bomberg: Gehln Verlag, 1970.

Olschner, Leonard Moore. *Der feste Buchstab: Erläuterungen zu Paul Celans Gedichtübertragungen.* Göttingen: Vandenhoeck & Ruprecht, 1985.

Pöggeler, Otto. *Spur des Worts: Zur Lyrik Paul Celans.* Freiburg: Verlag Karl Alber, 1986.

Voswinckel, Klaus. *Paul Celan: Verweigerte Poetisierung der Welt: Versuch einer Deutung.* Heidelberg: Lothar Stiehm, 1974.

Wiedemann-Wolf, Barbara. *Antschel Paul-Paul Celan: Studien zum Frühwerk.* Tübingen: Max Niemeyer Verlag, 1985.

Censorship

Censorship of the arts has taken different forms in modern Germany, varying with the changing political regimes. If it is defined narrowly as preliminary censorship, then it was abolished permanently in 1918. But most writers and artists producing under subsequent governments would argue that state influence over the arts continued in various guises.

In Imperial Germany, preliminary censorship—whereby a work had to be submitted to the police for approval prior to public presentation—existed only for theater and, after the turn of the century, for film. Nevertheless, other arts could be kept under control by the paragraphs of the criminal code that prohibited the display or sale of works promoting "blasphemy," "obscenity," or "lese majesty." Some writers and artists were indeed brought to trial for these offenses, but prosecution often backfired: convictions were difficult to obtain, and every case inflamed the cultural community and generated publicity for the author or artist in question. Much heated discussion was generated by the proposed Lex Heinze, an attempt by conservative forces to pass a stronger law against "obscenity" in the arts; it was defeated in the Reichstag in 1900.

After the fall of the monarchy, preliminary censorship was abolished, along with the law against lese majesty. The Weimar constitution proclaimed: "There will be no censorship" (*Eine Zensur findet nicht statt*). Nevertheless, oppositional writers and artists, mainly of leftist persuasion, were occasionally brought to trial for obscenity, blasphemy, or even defamation of the Reichswehr (army) and treason. Generally, though, the arts were free to flourish in the 1920s, and many state and municipal governments under Social Democratic control even encouraged artistic experimentation.

That situation was radically reversed in the spring of 1933, when many of Germany's best-known artists fled the country. For those who remained, the Nazis did not have a formal system of censorship, but created a new, highly effective tool in the form of the Reich Chamber of Culture (Reichskulturkammer). Every writer and artist who wanted to produce works for public consumption had to join. Leftists and Jews were automatically excluded, as was any person who offended Nazi officialdom. In addition, the Nazis mounted "exhibitions of shame," culminating in the *Degenerate Art* exhibition held in Munich in 1937, where many of the artistic products of the Weimar era were held up to ridicule.

The two postwar German states developed highly different modes of controlling the arts. In the Federal Republic, occasional confiscations of "obscene" or "blasphemous" works still occurred, but the practice generally ceased in the 1960s with the relaxing of public sexual and moral standards. Debates about censorship came to be focused instead on the state-subsidized arts: theaters and museums, but especially mass media such as radio and television. These are not directly under state control, but since their governing boards consist of representatives from the various political parties as well as social and religious groups, some of the more truculent writers and artists claim that they tend to support a cultural *juste milieu* that avoids overly experimental or critical works.

In the German Democratic Republic (GDR), the government was able to exert direct control over cultural activity because almost all theaters, cinemas, publishing houses, and radio and television stations were state-owned. Furthermore,

all writers and artists had to belong to appropriate "unions," which gave them monthly stipends but also monitored their ideological conformity. The fact that so many East Germans could receive Western radio and television transmissions meant, however, that "capitalist" cultural influences could not be blocked out. Moreover, many artists and writers genuinely believed in the humanistic promises of socialism, and therefore were critical of the state's excessive control of society and the arts. The GDR saw constant swings between relative cultural openness and artistic repression, as the state tried—unsuccessfully—to find a tolerable middle ground between the conformity demanded by party ideologues and the desire of writers and artists for freedom of expression.

Peter C. Jelavich

See also German Democratic Republic: Political Culture; Imperial Germany; National Socialist Germany: Art

References
Barron, Stephanie, ed. *"Degenerate Art": The Fate of the Avant-Garde in Nazi Germany.* Los Angeles, CA: Los Angeles County Museum of Art, 1991.
Hochhuth, Rolf. "Zensur in der Bundesrepublik Deutschland." *Rolf Hochhuth: Dokumente zur politischen Wirkung.* Ed. Reinhardt Hoffmeister. Munich: Kindler, 1980.
Hütt, Wolfgang, ed. *Hintergrund: Mit den Unzüchtigkeits und Gotteslästerungsparagraphen des Strafgesetzbuches gegen Kunst und Künstler 1900–1933.* Berlin: Henschelverlag, 1990.
Leiss, Ludwig. *Kunst im Konflikt: Kunst und Künstler im Widerstreit mit der "Obrigkeit."* Berlin: Walter de Gruyter, 1971.
Lenman, Robin. "Art, Society, and the Law in Wilhelmine Germany: The Lex Heinze." *Oxford German Studies* 8 (1973–74), 86–113.
Stark, Gary. "Pornography, Society, and the Law in Imperial Germany." *Central European History* 14 (1981), 200–29.
"Symposium: The Censorship of Literary Naturalism." (Essays by Gary Stark, Peter Jelavich and Peter Paret.) *Central European History* 18 (1985), 326–64.
Willson, A. Leslie. "The Many Faces of Censorship in the Federal Republic of Germany." *The Germanic Review* 65 (1990), 98–110.
Zipser, Richard A.J. "The Many Faces of Censorship in the German Democratic Republic 1949–1989." *The Germanic Review* 65 (1990), 111–29.

Center Party (1871–1933)

From its origins in the age of Chancellor Otto von Bismarck to its dissolution under Adolf Hitler, the Center Party was the partisan vehicle of the loosely bundled set of outlooks known as political Catholicism and the major political representative of united Germany's large Catholic minority.

Faced with persecution or lingering bias throughout Imperial Germany, Catholics swarmed to the Center as the agent of confessional defense. Holding roughly one-quarter of the seats in the Reichstag during much of this period, the Center was intermittently the largest party. Despite a slow electoral decline and the breakaway of Bavarian Catholics as the Bavarian People's Party after World War I, the Center, though down to 12 percent of the vote by 1930, retained its influence. Due to its socially diverse constituency and its position in the middle of the party spectrum, it was an indispensable partner in every parliamentary government under the Weimar Republic.

The precursors of the German Center Party were the Catholic caucuses in the short-lived Frankfurt Parliament of 1848 and in the legislature of the predominantly Protestant state of Prussia. When the Prussian constitutional conflict overshadowed religious issues in the early 1860s, the Prussian Catholic caucus (known since 1858 as the Center) briefly disappeared. But in southern Germany, Prussia's victory over Catholic Austria in the war of 1866 gave rise to populist, clerically supported parties that were suspicious of German unification led by Prussia and defensive of the prerogatives of the existing smaller states. Fearing not just Prusso-Protestant conservatism but also the anticlerical tendencies in German national liberalism, Prussian Catholics revived the Center in the autumn of 1870. The following spring, south Germans joined the northerners to form a Center caucus in the first Reichstag of the newly unified German state.

The new Center Party insisted that it was opposed not to national unification but to Prussian chauvinism. Although it denied that it was a purely confessional grouping, its platform emphasized religious protection and civil parity for Catholics, states' rights for the Catholic south, churchly prerogatives in the schools, and diplomatic support for the Pope in his struggle to recover Rome from unified Italy. These positions made the Center anathema both to Bismarck and to the National Liberals, who cooperated to enact draconian anticlerical legislation. In the subsequent period of religious persecution (the *Kulturkampf*), Catholic political resistance was spearheaded by the Center. Under its parliamentary leader Ludwig Windthorst, the Center by 1878 was in a position to block governmental legislation, or to pass it in return for concessions in religious and federal affairs.

As a permanent minority party, the Center did not originally advocate parliamentary government. Yet parliaments were now the most significant loci of German Catholic power. By the end of the century, the Center, thanks to its broad constituency (including workers in the Christian Trade Unions), had become the chief political broker in the Reichstag, even when religious issues were not pressing.

When the Centrist politician Matthias Erzberger (1875–1921) persuaded his party during World War I to back the Peace Resolution together with the Social Democratic Party (SPD) and the democratic liberals, he was ushering in a sea change in German politics. This new grouping, which eventually became the Weimar coalition, wrote Germany's democratic, republican constitution in 1919.

The Weimar Republic is usually associated with the SPD and the German Democratic Party (DDP); yet, until the controversial cabinets of 1930–32, the most consistent facilitator of parliamentary governability was the Center. From 1919 until May of 1932, Germany had 19 different national governments; 9 of these were led by a Centrist such as K. Fehrenbach, J. Wirth, W. Marx, or H. Brüning. The Center never went into parliamentary opposition in Prussia or in the Reichstag. Yet it never committed itself irrevocably to republicanism in principle, which it carefully distinguished from its commitment to constitutional procedure. Based on its experience with the SPD, the Center held that governmental participation under its auspices would chasten and moderate extremists. Trying under this premise to make the parliamentary system function, the Center eventually entered national-level coalitions with all the major parties on the Left and Right except the Communists and Nazis (and even tried to negotiate a coalition with the latter in 1932). This dubious even-handedness led the party to be seen as opportunistic, even as it saw itself as conscientiously refusing to shirk responsibility.

Three times in its history, the Center demonstrated extraordinary moral and political strength: in its opposition to Bismarck and the *Kulturkampf*, in its pragmatic refusal to wallow in the nihilistic nationalism that afflicted Protestant conservatives after World War I, and in maintaining its electorate (alone among the non-Marxist parties) during the Nazi wave of the early 1930s. Yet, the same subcultural protectiveness from which the Center drew strength also rendered it vulnerable to bouts of defensiveness, sycophancy, and political expediency. By voting under pressure for the Enabling Act in March of 1933 (in effect amending the constitution to give Hitler dictatorial powers), the Center upheld the appearance of legality while dispensing with its substance. Anxious to head off new attacks on their religion and their patriotism, Catholics subsequently placed their hopes on negotiations for a concordat between Berlin and the Vatican. In the course of those negotiations (concluded in July 1933), the Center—the last legal non-Nazi party—voluntarily dissolved. Weakened by its own perception that it had compromised itself by associating with the godless, anti-nationalist Left (the SPD), the agent of political Catholicism proved an inadequate final obstacle to the dictatorship of the racial-nationalist Right.

Noel D. Cary

See also Adenauer, Konrad; Bavarian People's Party; Bertram, Adolf; Brüning, Heinrich; Catholicism, Political; Christian Democratic Union; Erzberger, Matthias; Galen, Clemens von; Hertling, Georg von; Joos, Joseph; Kaas, Ludwig; Ketteler, Wilhelm von; *Kulturkampf*; Lieber, Ernst Maria; Marx, Wilhelm; People's Association for Catholic Germany; Preysing, Konrad von; Spahn, Martin; Vatican-German Relations; Weber, Helene; Windthorst, Ludwig; Wirth, Joseph

References

Anderson, Margaret L. *Windthorst: A Political Biography*. New York, NY: Clarendon Press of Oxford University Press, 1981.

Bachem, Karl. *Vorgeschichte, Geschichte und Politik der Deutschen Zentrumspartei*. 9 vols. Cologne: J.P. Bachem, 1926–32.

Blackbourn, David. *Class, Religion and Local Politics in Wilhelmine Germany.* New Haven, CT: Yale University Press, 1980.

Cary, Noel D. *The Path to Christian Democracy: German Catholics and the Party System from Windthorst to Adenauer.* Cambridge, MA: Harvard University Press, 1996.

Epstein, Klaus. *Matthias Erzberger and the Dilemma of German Democracy.* Princeton, NJ: Princeton University Press, 1959.

Evans, Ellen L. *The German Center Party 1870–1933: A Study in Political Catholicism.* Carbondale, IL: Southern Illinois University Press, 1981.

Junker, Detlef. *Die Deutsche Zentrumspartei und Hitler 1932/1933.* Stuttgart: Ernst Klett Verlag, 1969.

Morsey, Rudolf. "The Center Party between the Fronts." Trans. John Conway. *The Path to Dictatorship: Ten Essays by German Scholars.* Garden City, NY: Doubleday, 1966.

———. *Der Untergang des politischen Katholizismus: Die Zentrumspartei zwischen christlichem Selbstverständnis und "Nationaler Erhebung" 1932/33.* Stuttgart: Belser Verlag, 1977.

———. *Die Deutsche Zentrumspartei, 1917–23.* Düsseldorf: Droste, 1966.

Ruppert, Karsten. *Im Dienst am Staat von Weimar: Das Zentrum als regierende Partei in der Weimarer Demokratie 1923–1930.* Düsseldorf: Droste, 1992.

Windell, George. *The Catholics and German Unity 1866–71.* Minneapolis, MN: University of Minnesota Press, 1954.

Zeender, John. *The German Center Party, 1890–1906.* New Series, vol. 66, part 1. Philadelphia, PA: Transactions of the American Philosophical Society, 1976.

Central Association of German Industrialists (Centralverband deutscher Industrieller)

Of the industrial interest groups that proliferated in Germany during the latter decades of the nineteenth century, the most well-known and influential was the Centralverband deutscher Industrieller. Formed in 1876 to spearhead an ultimately successful campaign for higher tariffs on manufactured goods, the Centralverband subsequently expanded its mission and began addressing a broad range of issues of concern to industrialists in their relations with the rest of German society. As justification for the policies it advocated, the organization appropriated the rhetoric of nationalism and claimed to speak for a stronger, wealthier, and more secure Germany.

In an era of increasing state intervention in economic and social issues, the Centralverband lobbied government officials and tried, although with less success, to influence legislative bodies and public opinion. The Centralverband launched numerous fiercely-fought crusades to block liberal and democratic reforms, acquiring a reputation as one of the foremost bastions of German authoritarianism. Characteristic of its initiatives were frustrated efforts in the 1890s to secure pas-

sage of repressive legislation designed to substitute for the recently lapsed anti-socialist laws as well as later attempts to secure the outlawing of picketing.

The Centralverband was a federation, its membership consisting largely of organizations representing various branches of German industry, among them metalworking, paper, leather, glass, and processed food products. The initiative in forming the Centralverband came primarily from the Northwest Group of the Verein deutscher Eisen- und Stahlindustrieller, a powerful association of Rhenish-Westphalian iron and steel industrialists, and the Verein süddeutscher Baumwollindustrieller, representing South German manufacturers of cotton textiles. These two groups remained influential in the Centralverband throughout its existence. This was especially true of the first—the Verein deutscher Eisen- und Stahlindustrieller was the largest and wealthiest member association. Its links to the Centralverband were so close that it even shared a common administration with that organization from 1893 to 1912 under the direction of their mutual business manager, the intransigent Henry Axel Bueck.

In the campaign for higher tariffs undertaken by the Centralverband in the late 1870s, protectionists in its ranks cast aside some of their earlier social and political prejudices to make common cause with estate owners in the east. The resulting *Junker*-industrialist alliance was a carefully calculated and often contentious relationship that underwent alternating periods of strain and rapprochement during the remaining decades of the imperial era. Whatever disagreements emerged over economic issues, a common commitment to an authoritarian order insured continued efforts on the part of influential leaders within the Centralverband to reestablish cooperation in national affairs with the agrarian camp. At the same time, however, advocates of collaboration had to contend with those Centralverband members who suspected such a policy. Symptomatic of its internal differences over relations with organized agriculture was the organization's balancing between the liberal, anti-agrarian Hansabund, formed in 1909, and the Kartell der schaffenden Stände (Cartel of Creative Estates), a loose coalition of antiparliamentary forces, including the agrarians' Bund der Landwirte, formed in 1913.

Although the Centralverband aspired to speak for all of German industry, its right to do so did not go uncontested. In 1895, a rival organization, the Bund deutscher Industriellen (Federation of German Industrialists), came into existence. The Bund claimed to provide a voice for export-oriented finished-goods manufacturers and challenged the increasingly cartelized basic industries concentrated in the Centralverband. Whereas the Centralverband consisted of industries characterized by large and middle-sized production units, many of the enterprises represented by the Bund were small. The creation of the Bund meant the Centralverband had to be more attentive to the divergent interests of its own members, not all of whom were willing or able to follow the unyielding policies advocated by the giants of heavy industry.

Just before World War I, the Centralverband and Bund moved toward closer cooperation. In 1913 the separate employers' federations associated with each other to form the

Vereinigung deutscher Arbeitgeberverbände (Federation of German Employers' Association). With the outbreak of war, the Centralverband and Bund cooperated in a common industrial war committee and jointly supported annexationist policies. And at war's end, confronted by the increased uncertainties brought by the collapse of Imperial Germany, the two industrial federations merged in the Reichsverband der deutschen Industrie (Federation of German Industry), achieving in defeat the organizational unity of German industry long sought by the leaders of the Centralverband.

Elaine Glovka Spencer

See also Coal Industry; Exports and Foreign Trade; Protectionism; State and Economy; Steel Industry

References

Böhme, Helmut. *Deutschlands Weg zur Grossmacht: Studien zum Verhältnis von Wirtschaft und Staat während der Reichsgründungszeit 1848–1881.* Cologne: Kiepenheuer & Witsch, 1966.
Bueck, Henry Axel. *Der Centralverband Deutscher Industrieller 1876–1901.* 3 vols. Berlin: Deutscher Verlag, 1902–05.
Kaelble, Hartmut. *Industrielle Interessenpolitik in der wilhelminischen Gesellschaft: Centralverband Deutscher Industrieller 1895–1914.* Berlin: de Gruyter, 1967.
Saul, Klaus. *Staat, Industrie, Arbeiterbewegung im Kaiserreich: Zur Innen- und Aussenpolitik des Wilhelminischen Deutschland 1903–1914.* Düsseldorf: Bertelsmann Universitätsverlag, 1974.
Spencer, Elaine Glovka. *Management and Labor in Imperial Germany: Ruhr Industrialists as Employers, 1896–1914.* New Brunswick, NJ: Rutgers University Press, 1984.
Stegmann, Dirk. *Die Erben Bismarcks: Parteien und Verbände in der Spätphase des Wilhelminischen Deutschlands: Sammlungspolitik 1897–1918.* Cologne: Kiepenheuer & Witsch, 1970.
Ullmann, Hans-Peter, ed. *Interessenverbände in Deutschland.* Frankfurt am Main: Suhrkamp Verlag, 1988.
Varain, Heinz Josef, ed. *Interessenverbände in Deutschland.* Cologne: Kiepenheuer & Witsch, 1973.

Central Powers

This term was originally applied to the Triple Alliance linking Germany, Austria-Hungary, and Italy, an alliance first concluded in 1882 and regularly renewed at five-year intervals until 1915. Actually, Italy had ceased to be a member a year earlier, when war broke out in Europe, because the alliance was to be invoked only in case of attack by another power, a condition that Italy did not consider to have been met.

After Italy had quit the alliance, the term was used more loosely (although also more frequently) to describe the wartime coalition of Germany, Austria-Hungary, Bulgaria, and Turkey. During World War I, the Central Powers were opposed by the Triple Entente, namely Great Britain, France, and Russia, plus all the countries that entered the war against the Central Powers, including the United States in 1917. Relations among the Central Powers were often tense as Germany came to dominate its partners because of Austrian military failures, especially on the eastern and southern fronts. The question of who ruled in Berlin, German politicians or military leaders, helped to undercut the war effort and led to the Central Powers' defeat, with Austria-Hungary suing for peace in October 1918.

Joachim Remak

See also Austro-German Relations; Diplomatic Corps and Diplomacy; Russian-German Relations; World War I

References

Craig, Gordon. "The World War I Alliance of the Central Powers in Retrospect: The Military Cohesion of the Alliance." *Journal of Modern History* 27 (1965), 336–44.
Langer, William L. *European Alliances and Alignments: 1871–1890.* 2nd ed. New York, NY: Alfred A. Knopf, 1960.
Schmitt, Bernadotte E. and Harold C. Vedeler. *The World in the Crucible, 1914–1919.* New York, NY: Harper and Row, 1984.

Chamber Music

In contrast to orchestral music, chamber music is defined according to the size of the instrumental complement. Usually it is written for one performer, rather than a whole section of instruments, playing each part. In effect, the conception of chamber music is based on writing for a group of soloists varying in numbers. With the passage of time, increasingly by the nineteenth century, this style required virtuoso performance standards of the individuals in a chamber group.

The paradox of chamber music in the nineteenth and twentieth centuries was its semi-public, semi-private nature; the demands placed on the individual performers exceeded much of what they were required to do in orchestral groups, but such standards may well have influenced writing for the orchestral sections which had not been individualistic in nature, especially among stringed instruments.

The piano trio and string quartet, which had been the mainstays of classical and early romantic chamber music, were seriously undermined in the late nineteenth century as composers searched for unusual combinations and sizes. A single chamber work by Richard Wagner (1818–83), the *Siegfried Idyll* (which was not meant for performance in public), stretched the definition of chamber music in both scope (thirteen instruments) and style (one movement instead of the usual three or four). It nevertheless provided an example of the possibilities for expansion of nonorchestral instrumental composition, since it fell within the definition of chamber music by virtue of the fact that one player performed each part. However, it touched the border of the definition of "chamber orchestra" because of the number of executants, at least as defined by Egon Wellesz in *Die neue Instrumentation* (The new orchestration), 1929–30.

The *Siegfried Idyll* may have been known to Arnold Schönberg (1874–1951) when he wrote *Verklärte Nacht* (Transfigured night) in 1899. Based on a poem by Richard Dehmel, this work was scored for string sextet (two violins, two violas, and two cellos). While not challenging the traditional conception of chamber music in term of size, since it is simply an expansion of the basic string quartet, this work— like the *Siegfried Idyll*—dispensed with the multimovement concept: it is essentially a one-movement work, although as varied in mood and instrumental technique as any multimovement work. Both works also broke new ground in another important way: they were based on extramusical conceptions (*Verklärte Nacht* on a poem of Dehmel, *Siegfried Idyll* on a distillation of concrete leitmotifs from the *Ring* cycle). Programmatic factors had affected many other forms of music in the nineteenth century before they influenced chamber music in such works as these, and the programmatic idea was never as widespread in this type of music as in others even after such experiments. Later works of chamber music by Schönberg and his followers increasingly returned to the original absolute conception, although experimentation with unusual instrumental combinations even resulted in the use of the human voice in works that still qualified as chamber music. Schönberg broke ground in this respect in such works as *Pierrot Lunaire*, using the voice as a co-participant with other instruments. In this he and his followers may have been influenced by techniques used by Gustav Mahler (1860–1911)—Mahler is not known as a composer of chamber music (only a single piano quartet from his student period survives), but his use of the human voice in several of his symphonies and in *Das Lied von der Erde* is often couched in almost chamberlike dimensions, and the voice is often more important for color than for text in such passages.

A parallel development, which appears to have been a separate phenomenon, was the appearance of the so-called "salon orchestra," comparable to the chamber group in size but performed with a different purpose entirely. The salon orchestra was commonly found in social venues, such as cafés, not in concert halls; it was wildly variable in makeup (being composed of whatever small combinations of instruments might be thrown together, including instruments, such as guitar and harmonium, unlikely to be used in formal chamber works). The music played by salon orchestras was usually arranged from familiar melodies in operas and popular concert works, primarily for entertainment, and is thus comparable to the anthologies of popular transcriptions for piano (see the entry on keyboard music).

The place of chamber music in the twentieth century, apart from the works of the Second Viennese School, was largely sustained by neoclassical composers. Paul Hindemith (1895–1963), who was a practicing violinist and violist, returned to the classical ideals of the string quartet, frequently playing his own works with his friends. However, in the series of works entitled *Kammermusik*, he stretched the definition of the term "chamber music"—these works varied from chamber-orchestra dimensions to small groups of soloists performing among themselves. He also wrote many works for

Chamber music concert in Nuremberg. Courtesy of Inter Nationes, Bonn.

unusual chamber combinations, particularly favoring instruments like the viola for which there had been little repertoire.

Organized chamber groups performing such music in the German-speaking countries have been rather unusual, the most well known in the early twentieth century being the Rosé Quartet and the Kolisch Quartet. Recently, groups like the Hagen Quartet have attempted to recoup the reputation of chamber music, which has been relatively neglected in the latter part of the twentieth century.

Susan M. Filler

See also Brahms, Johannes; Hindemith, Paul; Keyboard Music; Mahler, Gustav; Orchestral Music; Schönberg, Arnold; Wagner, Richard

References

Baron, John H. *Chamber Music: A Research and Information Guide.* New York, NY: Garland Publishing, 1987.

Cobbett, Walter Willson. *Cyclopedic Survey of Chamber Music.* 3 vols. 2nd ed. with supplementary material. Ed. Colin Mason. London: Oxford University Press, 1963.

Lemacher, Heinrich. *Handbuch der Hausmusik.* Graz: A. Pustet, 1948.

Salmen, Walter. *Haus- und Kammermusik: Privates Musizieren im gesellschaftlichen Wandel zwischen 1600 und 1900.* Leipzig: Deutscher Verlag für Musik, 1969.

Chamberlain, Houston Stewart (1855–1927)

Houston Chamberlain, an "elective German," wrote *Die Grundlagen des Neunzehnten Jahrhunderts,* 1899 (published as *Foundations of the Nineteenth Century,* 1911), among the most influential works of racial nationalism. A champion of Wagnerism and an admirer of Adolf Hitler, he devoted his life to preaching the superiority and inevitable triumph of Germans.

Chamberlain came from an upper-class English family—his father was an admiral—but spent most of his life on the continent. Educated in France and Germany, and suffering bouts of ill health, he fell under the spell of Richard Wagner (1818–83), overwhelmed first by his music, then by his thought. Although he never met the "god of Germanism," Chamberlain became his apostle, eventually settled in Bayreuth, and married one of Wagner's daughters (1908). From 1882, he tended the Wagner cult along with members of the family and a circle of devotees. A prolific writer, Chamberlain remains best known for his *Grundlagen*. A work of synthesis, equipped with full scholarly apparatus, but nonetheless a highly political polemic, the book advanced the "simple and clear revelation that the whole of modern culture and civilization is the work of one race: the Germanic." Chamberlain differed from other *völkisch* (racist) writers in his basic optimism about the future, a stance that survived the loss of World War I and the "degradation" of the Weimar Republic.

Chamberlain's anti-Semitism was also more refined, eschewing coarse vilification but still making it clear that Jews embodied only negative and dangerous traits. Among these was a programmatic mongrelizing of the Indo-Europeans in order to leave only one pure and therefore dominant race, the Jewish. Incapable of true religiosity, Jews could not have produced a Christ, who, according to Chamberlain, was a Nordic, blue-eyed blond from the "Aryan Galilee."

The doctrines of the *Grundlagen* made their way into the common intellectual property of nationalist and racist writers, including Hitler and the Nazi Party ideologue Alfred Rosenberg (1893–1946). Hitler acknowledged (and exploited) this debt by visiting the paralyzed Chamberlain, a dying man, and kissing his hands.

Chamberlain's pseudo-scholarly tone and lack of overt vulgarity, as well as the 28 editions of his major work (a quarter of a million copies printed by 1942), made racial thought available to those offended by the typical outpourings of *völkisch* lowbrows. Many respectable intellectuals took the *Grundlagen* a good deal more seriously than it deserved.

Richard S. Levy

See also Anti-Semitism; Hitler, Adolf; Racism; Rosenberg, Alfred; *Völkisch* Ideology; Wagner, Richard

References

Chamberlain, H.S. *Die Grundlagen des Neunzehnten Jahrhunderts.* Munich: Bruckmann, 1899.

———. *Richard Wagner.* Munich: Bruckmann, 1896.

Field, Geoffrey G. *Evangelist of Race: The Germanic Vision of Houston Stewart Chamberlain.* New York, NY: Columbia University Press, 1981.

Glaser, Hermann. *The Cultural Roots of National Socialism.* Trans. Ernest A. Menze. Austin, TX: University of Texas Press, 1978.

Mosse, George L. *The Crisis of German Ideology: Intellectual Origins of the Third Reich.* New York, NY: Grosset and Dunlap, 1964.

Schüler, Winfried. *Der Bayreuther Kreis von seiner Entstehung bis zum Ausgang der wilhelminischen Ära: Wagnerkult und Kulturreform im Geiste völkischer Weltanschauung.* Münster: Aschendorff, 1971.

Stackelberg, Roderick. *Idealism Debased: From Völkisch Ideology to National Socialism.* Kent, OH: Kent State University Press, 1981.

Chancellor's Office

The term "chancellor's office" (*Kanzleramt*) first appeared in the constitution of the North German Confederation of 1866. The office was established to support the federal chancellor, who had to supervise the implementation of administrative acts assigned to the federal level of government. With the founding of the empire in 1871, the chancellor (*Reichskanzler*) was the only government minister. He was appointed by and could be dismissed by the kaiser. He reported and answered to the Reichstag but was not responsible to it. In 1871, the office of Imperial chancellor (*Reichskanzleramt*) was established as the successor of the federal chancellery. It served as the central administrative office to support the chancellor. In the course of the expansion of governmental responsibilities, brought about by the constitution of the new state, it grew into a huge ministry. Its ever-widening tasks eventually included social, economic, and public-health affairs, and the office was renamed Reichsamt des Inneren (Ministry of the Interior). In May 1879, after an application from Chancellor Otto von Bismarck, a central bureau was established under the name of Reichskanzlei (Imperial chancellery) to assist him as chancellor.

During World War I, the small office of a few advisers and secretaries expanded as the chancellor displaced the kaiser at the center of decisionmaking. In 1917, Friedrich von Payer (1847–1931) became vice-chancellor and his office handled relations with the political parties. By November 1918, when Friedrich Ebert momentarily took over the chancellery, it had nearly twelve secretaries and aides, plus clerical staff, who served as a support system to the provisional six-member cabinet. The personnel comprised a mix of roles and duties: political advisers, private secretaries, and administrative assistants. They handled correspondence, agendas, and recordkeeping.

Under the Weimar Republic's constitution, the expansion of activities and personnel continued. The chancellery retained its role as the central office for the chancellor and as the main administrative support for the cabinet. It concentrated on supplying information to the chancellor, coordinating between ministries, and preparing agendas for the cabinet as well as implementing its decisions.

In January 1933, Adolf Hitler was appointed Reichskanzler by President Paul von Hindenburg (1847–1934). When Hindenburg died in August 1934, Hitler merged the offices of chancellor and president, though most of the presidential staff were retained. As head of state, Hitler used the chancellery but its legal status became ambiguous.

After World War II, the Frankfurt Direktorialkanzlei (Frankfurt directorate chancellery) emerged in April 1948. It sought to coordinate the Western zones' administrative departments, to accommodate press and information, and to sup-

Chancellery, Bonn. Courtesy of Inter Nationes, Bonn.

ply information to the chair of the administrative council. From autumn 1949 to its dissolution in May 1950, this office was based in Bonn. Chancellor Konrad Adenauer refused to take it over and instead founded a new federal chancellor's office (*Bundeskanzleramt*) for West Germany.

The Bundeskanzleramt became a key institution for all postwar chancellors in the Federal Republic. In the early 1950s, the office was solely responsible for the political agenda of Adenauer. In the 1960s, it developed into a "letter box" for passing proposals to cabinet. Under Chancellor Willy Brandt (1913–92), the office became an institutional watchdog over the ministries and a clearing house for bills submitted by ministries to cabinet. Today, the office supplies the chancellor with advice and information on the consideration of policy issues and links these with ministers and their departments. In general, the chancellor's office plays a major part in structuring cabinet decisions in accordance with the chancellor's views.

The office currently has a staff of 450, only a minority of whom are political appointees. They direct between 50 and 60 higher civil servants and their supporting and technical staff, spread over 41 policy units. Each unit mirrors a policy field in one of the departments of the government. The staff of the chancellor's office has come to play a large part in German politics. The functions of the staff are administrative and political. The staff members act administratively, in that they organize meetings of the cabinet and in particular the flow of business between the chancellor and the ministers. They are concerned with gathering, circulating, and, to an extent, controlling ministerial proposals. They also deal with the cabinet agenda, record and monitor cabinet decisions, and supervise the implementation of these decisions. They often play a part in the development of the long-term ideas about cabinet activities. The chancellor's staff exists in order to improve the efficiency of the cabinet.

Yet the chancellor's staff does not function solely at an administrative level. It also has political functions: its members make suggestions to the chancellor on policy questions and may develop their own policy proposals. For instance, on the instructions of Chancellor Helmut Kohl, the treaty of union between the FRG and the former German Democratic Republic (GDR) was developed by the bureaucrats in the chancellor's office. Similarly, the promotion of the eastern trea-

ties under Chancellor Willy Brandt and the preparation of the draft for the European monetary system under Chancellor Helmut Schmidt took place in the chancellor's office. The Bundeskanzleramt has remained instrumental in supporting the chancellors in organizing governmental policies.

Ferdinand Müller-Rommel

See also Adenauer, Konrad; Bauer, Gustav; Bismarck Otto von; Bethmann Hollweg, Theobald von; Brandt, Willy; Brüning, Heinrich; Bülow, Bernhard von; Caprivi, Leopold von; Cuno, Wilhelm; Ebert, Friedrich; Erhard, Ludwig; Fehrenbach, Konstantin; Hertling, Georg von; Hitler, Adolf; Hohenlohe-Schillingsfürst, Chlodwig zu; Kiesinger, Kurt Georg; Kohl, Helmut; Luther, Hans; Max von Baden; Marx, Wilhelm; Müller, Hermann; Papen, Franz von; Scheidemann, Philip; Schleicher, Kurt von; Schmidt, Helmut; Stresemann, Gustav; Wirth, Joseph

References

Berry, Phillis. "The Organization and the Influence of the Chancellery during the Schmidt and Kohl Chancellorships." *Governance* 2 (1989), 343–53.

Dyson, Ken. "The German Federal Chancellor's Office." *Political Quarterly* 45 (1974), 367–75.

Erdmann, Karl Dietrich, ed. *Die Akten der Reichskanzlei: Weimarer Republik*. Boppard am Rhein: Harald Boldt Verlag, 1969 *ff*.

Mayntz, Renate. "Executive Leadership in Germany." *Presidents and Prime Ministers*. Ed. Richard Rose and Ezra Suleiman. Washington, DC: AEI, 1980.

Miller, Susanne and Heinrich Potthoff, eds. *Die Regierung der Volksbeauftragten 1918/19*. Düsseldorf: Droste, 1969.

Müller-Rommel, Ferdinand. "The Chancellor and His Staff." *From Adenauer to Kohl*. Ed. Stephen Padgett. London: Hurst Publisher, 1993.

Müller-Rommel, Ferdinand and Gabriele Pieper. "Das Bundeskanzleramt als Regierungszentrale." *Das Parlament* 21–22 (1991), 3–13.

Chemistry, Scientific and Industrial
Chemistry in the Empire to 1914

Nineteenth-century German organic chemists were the first to engender a close interaction between academic and industrial scientists in order to perform large-scale, systematic research and development. German firms achieved world leadership in synthetic organic chemistry and acquired a nearly total world monopoly in the dye industry.

The intellectual and institutional elaboration of academic organic chemistry during the 1860s and 1870s provided the basis for German success. Anticipating economic benefits, state governments appointed leading organic chemists, including August Wilhelm Hofmann (1818–92; Berlin), August Kekulé (1829–96; Bonn), Adolf von Baeyer (1835–1917; Strassburg and Munich) and Hermann Kolbe (1818–84; Leipzig), to research chairs whose large new institutes shaped the next generation. Except for Kolbe, these leaders embraced the new structural organic chemistry as a powerful tool for science and industry. Under Hofmann's presidency, the German Chemical Society (founded in 1867) and its *Berichte* (reports) disseminated information regarding the latest organic research; by 1880, probably most of the world's research chemists were members.

Academic expansion went hand in hand with the emergence of a research-intensive industry in need of discovering coal-tar chemicals, beginning with dyes. Early on, synthetic alizarin displaced a major vegetable dyestuff (1868–73) and provided the first major source of profits for the nascent German coal-tar dye industry. Initially unencumbered by a national patent system and benefiting from easily available capital and trained chemists, German firms quickly outproduced their foreign rivals. The mid-1870s economic recession and Imperial patent laws (1876–77) combined to encourage small industries to consolidate into a relatively small number of research-intensive firms, predecessors of the later BASF, Hoechst, and Bayer corporations. These companies produced hundreds of new aniline dyes, culminating in BASF's discovery of synthetic indigo (1897). By 1914, the Germans controlled most of the world's dye production and were diversifying into related fields such as pharmaceuticals, which were promoted by a competitive branch of the industry led by a half-dozen smaller firms, such as Merck in Darmstadt.

By the 1890s, organic chemistry took up 90 percent of the space in German academic chemical publications. This imbalance led even organic chemists, such as Hofmann's successor Emil Fischer (1852–1919), to advocate founding new academic facilities for other branches of the discipline, an effort that helped to found the Kaiser Wilhelm Society. By 1914, pioneering physical chemists such as Wilhelm Ostwald (1853–1932), Walther Nernst (1864–1941), and Fritz Haber (1868–1934) had helped to restore parity between organic and nonorganic research in Germany and to promote the development of industrial electrochemistry as well as new technologies for the production of inorganic chemicals such as synthetic ammonia. Although German organic chemists such as Fischer and Richard Willstätter (1872–1942) still dominated the discipline, increasingly complex problems revealed the limits of their structural methods.

Chemistry in Crisis, 1914–49

In 1914, chemistry in Germany entered 35 years of almost perpetual crisis, punctuated by two world wars and by political and economic upheavals in which the chemical industry played a critical and highly controversial role. Simultaneously, its general economic significance in Germany grew to rival that of heavy industry.

World War I deprived the export-oriented German dye firms of their overseas markets and stripped them at least temporarily of many foreign affiliates and patents. The war also thrust them into a strategic role—they had to produce domestic substitutes for previously imported vital materials, such as nitrates. Tactically, they produced the explosives and poison gas that nearly achieved German victory on land. The war accelerated the process of industrial consolidation in the dye corporations. In 1925 this led to an amalgamation of major

firms known as the I.G. Farbenindustrie AG. This German synthetic chemicals monopoly recovered most of the international markets it had lost during the war. Building on wartime experience, the German chemical industry also sought to promote its technologies for the mass production of synthetic nitrates, oil, and rubber. This and the collapse of world trade during the early 1930s brought the chemical industry into accommodation with National Socialism.

Despite mutual distrust and some animosity between Nazi leaders and some older academic chemists in 1933, as well as the skepticism of I.G. Farben leaders such as Carl Duisberg (1861–1935) and Carl Bosch (1874–1940), the industry subsequently accommodated itself gradually to the Third Reich's emerging autarky policy, particularly after Carl Krauch, an I.G. Farben director, took a leading role in shaping the Four-Year Plan of 1936. As expected, synthetic nitrates, fuel, and rubber played a crucial role in supporting the German war effort after 1939. Although profiting greatly from early German victories, I.G. Farben became implicated in the atrocities of Auschwitz by using slave labor for plant construction and producing (through a subsidiary) Zyklon B cyanide pesticide, used in mass murder. The few I.G. Farben executives later convicted of these crimes by the Americans received relatively light sentences. The victorious Allies ordered I.G. Farben to be dissolved, but its successor firms remained highly concentrated.

Until the 1930s, systematic industrial subsidies helped German academic chemists to weather successive financial crises and to remain competitive in organic chemistry as well as in the "border areas" skirting chemistry, physics, and biology. Nazi-dictated dismissals affected substantial numbers of academic chemists, particularly on the border with physics, which caused weaknesses to emerge in theoretical chemistry. The Nazi regime offered chemistry substantial support in the quest for research that would promise industrial and military benefits. The support also aided the Kaiser Wilhelm Institutes (e.g., Otto Hahn's [1879–1968] nuclear chemistry and Adolf Butenandt's [1903–95] biochemistry). The perennial crises severely limited government funding for the expansion of university facilities, however, and many were destroyed in World War II.

Chemistry in a Divided Germany, 1949–90

After 1949, the chemical industry in West Germany rapidly recovered to enjoy successful growth, particularly in synthetic polymers (rubber, plastics, and fibers) as well as in pharmaceuticals, even as it fundamentally converted its coal-based production to petroleum. The Adenauer years brought favorable government policies (including tax incentives for industry), which helped chemistry share in the "economic miracle" years. By 1974, BASF, Bayer, and Hoechst, I.G. Farben's main successors, had become the world's largest chemical corporations (total sales: 58.8 billion deutsche marks (DM) vs. 4 billion in 1955). They maintained their favorable position despite rising oil costs, expensive pollution-control equipment installed during the 1970s, and government restrictions on the development of DNA biotechnology during the 1980s. The "big three" achieved a record 137 billion DM in sales and spent 7.3 billion DM on research in 1989. Nonetheless, in sales, the German chemical industry as a whole ranked behind its American and Japanese counterparts.

The smaller industries in the east recovered more slowly from the burden of Soviet reparations that involved dismantling and removing entire plants to the USSR. The German Democratic Republic (GDR) adopted petroleum-based technologies with the help of Soviet oil imports, but its industry remained far more dependent on obsolescent, uncompetitive lignite-based technologies. Lacking the West's prosperity and excluded from the influence of the environmental movement, the GDR also suffered extensive damage from pollution and ecological devastation in its industrial districts.

Postwar scientific chemistry is more complex, costly, team-oriented, and influenced by physical theory than the science that the Germans had once dominated. Industrial and academic success no longer necessarily go hand in hand. Between Hermann Staudinger's 1953 Nobel Prize and 1988, when three German chemists shared the prize, only four out of a total of fifty-three chemistry laureates were German (the GDR had none).

Academic and industrial chemistry developed within nineteenth-century German society in a pattern of mutual interaction that was typically modern both in the great scientific and technological successes it produced, as well as in the occasional destructive misuse that resulted from them.

Jeffrey A. Johnson

See also Auschwitz; Baeyer, Adolf von; BASF; Bayer AG; Bosch, Carl; Butenandt, Adolf; Duisberg, Carl; Fischer, Emil; Four-Year Plan; Haber, Fritz; Hahn, Otto; Henkel AG; Hofmann, August Wilhelm von; I.G. Farbenindustrie AG; Kaiser Wilhelm/Max Planck Societies and Institutes; Kekulé, August; Kolbe, Hermann; Meitner, Lise; Merck; Nernst, Walther; Ostwald, Wilhelm; Pharmacy; Staudinger, Hermann; Willstätter, Richard

References

Brock, William H. *The Norton History of Chemistry.* New York, NY: W.W. Norton, 1993.

Haber, L.F. *The Chemical Industry, 1900–1930: International Growth and Technological Change.* Oxford: Clarendon Press, 1971.

Hayes, Peter. *Industry and Ideology: IG Farben in the Nazi Era.* Cambridge: Cambridge University Press, 1987.

Homburg, Ernst. "The Emergence of Research Laboratories in the Dyestuffs Industry, 1870–1900." *British Journal for the History of Science* 25 (1992), 91–111.

James, Laylin K., ed. *Nobel Laureates in Chemistry, 1901–1992.* Washington, DC: American Chemical Society, Chemical Heritage Foundation, 1993.

Johnson, Jeffrey A. "Academic Chemistry in Imperial Germany." *Isis* 76 (1985), 500–24.

———. *The Kaiser's Chemists: Science and Modernization in Imperial Germany.* Chapel Hill, NC: University of North Carolina Press, 1990.

Morris, Peter J.T. "The Development of Acetylene Chemistry and Synthetic Rubber by I.G. Farbenindustrie

Aktiengesellschaft, 1926–1945." Unpublished doctoral dissertation. Oxford University, 1982.

Stokes, Raymond G. *Divide and Prosper: The Heirs of I.G. Farben under Allied Authority, 1945–1951.* Berkeley, CA: University of California Press, 1988.

———. *Opting for Oil: The Political Economy of Technological Change in the West German Chemical Industry, 1945–1961.* Cambridge: Cambridge University Press, 1994.

Travis, Anthony S. *The Rainbow Makers: The Origins of the Synthetic Dyestuffs Industry in Western Europe.* Bethlehem, PA: Lehigh University Press, 1993.

Childbirth and Motherhood

Childbirth and motherhood have been part of the experience of the large majority of German women. The number of children born per woman, however, has steadily declined from slightly under five per marriage entered before 1905 to one or two today; unmarried mothers have most typically had only one child. In addition, the proportion of women who cease their childbearing activity by the age of 30 has grown. The simultaneous increase in life expectancy has meant that a much lower proportion of German women's adult lives is dominated by childbearing and childrearing than was the case a century ago.

At the time of nineteenth-century unification, childbirth was dangerous for mothers and children alike. Over 20 percent of children died in their first year of life, and maternal mortality remained high. Over the following decades, improved cleanliness and better nutrition improved infants' chances of survival, and medicine's increasing ability to intervene effectively in risky births meant women were decreasingly likely to die in childbirth. On the eve of World War I, fewer than five births per thousand occurred in hospitals; hospital births are now nearly universal. The move to hospitals has affected not only women's chances of survival but also their experience of childbirth. A procedure once associated with female networks and a home environment is now associated with medical professionals and high-technology surroundings, even in cases of very low risk.

Motherhood has been highly politicized in modern Germany. During the Wilhelmine period, social scientists, medical professionals, and legislators expressed deep alarm that Germany's declining birth rate and fertility would put the country at a disadvantage against its European competitors. Bourgeois feminists often based their claim for improved status for women on women's role as mothers, and socialists glorified working-class mothers' role in raising revolutionaries. During World War I and again under the Nazis, governments portrayed motherhood as women's patriotic duty. The Federal Republic (FRG) after 1949 promoted the nuclear family—with the housewife-mother at its center—as a bulwark against Communism, while the German Democratic Republic (GDR) emphasized mothers' role in the education of socialist citizens.

The political uses of motherhood were reflected in a long history of legislation designed to ease the situation of mothers, but which usually also aimed to satisfy larger demographic, political, or economic goals of the state. Concerns about infant mortality motivated the passage of the Law to Protect Mothers (*Mutterschutzgesetz*) during the Weimar years. The law, whose provisions have been periodically expanded, prohibits pregnant women from performing certain tasks at the workplace, protects them from being fired, and provides paid leave at the end of the pregnancy and during the first weeks of nursing. Many of the provisions of the law were initially limited, however: women on leave received only a portion of their pay, and some types of female workers, such as domestic workers, were excluded. Thus the law was neither able to coax the most needy women from the workplace nor prevent them from returning to work immediately after delivery.

Governments worried about declining birth rates have attempted to encourage women to have more children, although the rewards offered have often been mainly symbolic. During the Weimar years, small family allowances were introduced for civil servants with children. The Nazi government presented racially and socially approved mothers of several children with the Mothers' Cross. More meaningful to mothers of fewer children were the marriage loans introduced under National Socialism: one-quarter of the loan was forgiven for each child a couple produced. Measures to prevent socially or racially unacceptable populations from reproducing, such as sterilization and restrictions on marriage, were more palpable.

Both postwar Germanys extended family allowances to the general population, both lent ideological support to large families, and both introduced programs in the 1980s to make it easier for working women to take a leave of absence during a child's first year. (The West German program, still in effect, is open to fathers upon application; the East German program allowed fathers to take time off only under unusual circumstances.) With the exception of the German Democratic Republic (GDR), all German governments have closely restricted access to abortion. No public policy, however, has shaken the tendency of women to have fewer children.

Perhaps the most notable change in mothers' experience has been the increasing trend towards combining care of young children with work outside the home. Through most of modern German history, mothers of small children who worked usually did so at home in some form of domestic industry. The requirements of wartime economies, however, brought large numbers of mothers into new places of work, as did the needs of both postwar German states. By the mid-1970s, 40 percent of West German mothers of children under age 15 were employed outside the home, and work outside the home became nearly universal for women in the GDR, regardless of motherhood status. West German mothers were more likely than their East German counterparts to take on part-time work; they were also more likely to experience difficulties in finding day care for their children. Reunification has brought the closing of nurseries and high female unemployment to the former GDR; considerable financial hardship has resulted for this new group of "just-housewives." The low birthrate is now an accepted feature of German society, but the need to combine motherhood with gainful employment remains an issue for mothers and policy-makers alike.

Elizabeth Heineman

See also Federal Republic of Germany: Women; German Democratic Republic: Women; Gierke, Anna von; Infants, Children, and Adolescents; Marriage and Divorce; Women; Women's Occupations; Working Conditions; Youth

References

Allen, Ann Taylor. *Feminism and Motherhood in Germany, 1800–1914.* New Brunswick, NJ: Rutgers University Press, 1991.

Beck-Gernsheim, Elisabeth. *Vom Geburtenrückgang zur neuen Mütterlichkeit: Über private und politische Interessen am Kind.* Frankfurt am Main: Fischer, 1984.

Bock, Gisela. "Antinatalism, Maternity and Paternity in National Socialist Racism." *Maternity and Gender Policies: Women and the Rise of the European Welfare States, 1880s-1950s.* Ed. Gisela Bock and Path Thane. London: Routledge, 1991.

Evans, Richard J. and W.R. Lee, eds. *The German Family: Essays on the Social History of the Family in Nineteenth- and Twentieth-Century Germany.* London: Croom Helm, 1981.

Helwig, Gisela. *Frau und Familie in beiden deutschen Staaten.* Cologne: Verlag Wissenschaft & Politik, 1982.

Koonz, Claudia. *Mothers in the Fatherland: Women, the Family and Nazi Politics.* New York, NY: St. Martin's, 1987.

Mason, Timothy. "Women in Germany, 1925–1940: Family, Welfare and Work." *History Workshop* 1 (1976), 73–113; 2 (1976), 5–32.

Moeller, Robert. *Protecting Motherhood: Women and the Family in the Politics of Postwar West Germany.* Berkeley, CA: University of California Press, 1993.

Usborn, Cornelie. *The Politics of the Body in Weimar Germany: Women's Reproductive Rights and Duties.* Ann Arbor, MI: University of Michigan Press, 1992.

Children's Literature

Four distinct yet continuous phases may be discerned in German children's literature between 1871 and 1990: 1871–1918, 1919–33, 1933–45, and 1945–90. In each, the influence of literary tradition remained paramount; nevertheless, new and original themes have slowly gained the interest and acceptance of authors, readers, and critics.

1871–1918

The German victory in the Franco-Prussian War of 1870–71 gave rise to a wave of nationalism that deeply influenced children's books during the period. Authors took to representing and promoting a patriotic image of Germany's past and the glories of its military achievements, with minimal regard for historical accuracy. This nationalistic urge was also motivated in overseas colonization and expansion, which found literary expression in the adventure novel, above all in Karl May's (1842–1912) tales of American Indians and of the Orient.

The stories of war and foreign adventure were clearly intended for boys. The development of girls' books was slower, as the first attempts were targeted at the upper classes. However, the *Backfisch* (silly teenage girl) genre (see Emmy von

Rhoden, *Backfischchens Leiden und Freuden* [Teen girls' misfortunes and joys], 1863) lost its class emphasis and rapidly won widespread popularity.

With the creation of mass literature in the second half of the nineteenth century, a new literary climate emerged in which literary quality was often of secondary importance. A response to this trend was the Jugendschriftenbewegung, a group of literary critics, among them many social democrats, who strove to combat the declining quality of children's books. One of the group's founders, Heinrich Wolgast (1860–1920) played a key role, and his 1898 work, *Das Elend unserer Jungendliteratur* (The poverty of our youth literature), stands as a model of the movement's criticisms.

However, there were books that did find both popular and critical acclaim. Such individual works as Johanna Spyri's (1829–1901) *Heidi*, 1882, and Agnes Sapper's (1852–1929) *Die Familie Pfäffling* (The Pfäffling family), 1907, met with instant approval and have appeared in innumerable editions. The other case is that of the picture book, which, especially as exemplified by Waldemar Bonsels's (1881–1955) *Biene Maja* (Maja the bee), 1912, and the works by Ernst Kreidolf (1863–1956) and Gertrud Caspari (1872–1948), is one of the rare genres of consistently high quality.

1919–33

The 1920s were marked by an increasing attention to the didactic potential of children's books. Following the model of Wolgast, many socialist and social democratic authors eschewed traditional conservative themes and wrote books that would show and teach the public the values of the progressive, humane society (e.g., Carl Dantz, *Peter Stoll, ein Kinderleben*, 1925 [Peter Stoll, a child's life]; Alex Wedding [Grete Weiskopf], *Edu und Unku*, 1932). The interwar period also witnessed the beginning of the careers of two of Germany's best-known writers: Erich Kästner (1899–1979) published *Emil und die Detektive* (Emil and the detectives), 1929, and Lisa Tetzner (1894–1963) published *Hans Urian oder die Geschichte einer Weltreise* (Hans Urian or the story of a world trip), 1919. Both authors are known for their pleas for world peace and tolerance, rare topics in Germany in the upcoming period between 1933 and 1946.

1933–45

Nationalistic literature endured despite the emergence of progressive writing, and it provided the foundation for Nazi literature. Hitler used children's books only as propaganda material to encourage strength, courage, and obedience (e.g., Karl Schenzinger, *Der Hitlerjunge Quex* [The Hitler youth quiz], 1932). Books that did not meet the ideological criteria were censored or banned. Authors such as Wedding, Kästner, Tetzner, and her husband Kurt Kläber (a.k.a. Kurt Held, 1897–1957, author of *Die rote Zora und Ihre Bande* [The red Zora and her gang], 1941), wrote while in exile, yet many more stayed, trying to publish their books in Germany. By the end of the war, the humanist and pacifist themes of the 1920s reemerged in works such as Jella Lepman's *Die Konferenz der Tiere* (The conference of the animals), 1949, Kästner's *Als ich ein Junge war* (published as *When I Was a Little Boy*), 1959, and Heinrich Maria Danneborg's, *Jan und das Wildpferd* (Jan and the wild horse), 1957.

1945–90

The division of Germany in 1949 set the development of children's literature on two separate paths. In the Federal Republic of Germany (FRG) three phases are evident: conservatism (1949–67), progressive experimentation (1968–77), and fantasy and cautious experimentation (1978–90). The need for authors—especially those who published in the Nazi state—to repress the recent past led them to treat traditional, "distant" themes in their work; only in the late 1960s did authors of children's books start to write about Fascism and the Holocaust.

Authors of children's literature responded to the changed atmosphere following the student revolts of the late 1960s, turning away from the conservatism of their elders and toward a discussion of contemporary society. This trend is particularly evident in the "problem literature," which drew attention to such problems as racism, poverty, the environment, and crime (e.g., Ursula Wölfel, *Die grauen und die grünen Felder* [The grey and the green fields], 1970s; Christine Nöstlinger, *Die feuerrote Friedricke* [The flaming red Friedricke], 1970). The 1960s also marked the beginning of one of Germany's most popular literary careers, that of Janosch, also known as Horst Eckert. As the influence of the student movement faded, authors frustrated with its outcome sought other sources of inspiration in fantasy and linguistic and symbolic experimentation (Michael Ende, *Unendliche Geschichte* [Neverending story], 1979).

In the German Democratic Republic (GDR), the state always gave children's literature high priority. Four phases can be distinguished between 1949 and 1990. From 1949 to circa 1955 writers invoked the anti-Fascist and solidarity themes popular among German and Soviet authors of the 1920s and 1930s. Important works from time period are Stephan Hermlin's *Die erste Reihe* (The first row), 1951, Ludwig Reno's *Trini*, 1954, and Erwin Strittmatter's *Tinko*, 1954.

During the 1950s, attention turned to the building of the GDR and, above all, the collectivization of farms (Benno Pludra, *Ein Mädchen, fünf Jungen und sechs Traktoren* [One girl, five boys, and six tractors], 1951). However, by the 1960s, industrial and urban growth and their problems attracted the attention of children's authors. But the need to view these topics from a socialist perspective often led to one-sided positivism, since an open critique of the political or economical system was prohibited. Yet as economic and social hardship dimmed the likelihood of a bright socialist future, subjectivity and guarded criticism made its way into GDR children's literature by the end of the 1960s. Finally, in the 1980s, after long having been banned from utopian themes, authors turned to fantasy and symbolism in order to respond to society's complexities without directly attacking the socialist system, as in the case of Christa Kozik's *Der Engel mit dem goldenen Schnurrbart* (The angel with the golden mustache), 1983, and Peter Abraham's *Affenstern* (Monkey star), 1988.

Elisabeth Waghäll

See also Hermlin, Stephan; Infants, Children, and Adolescents; Kästner, Erich; May, Karl

References

Aley, Peter. *Jugendliteratur im Dritten Reich: Dokumente und Kommentäre zur Jugendschriftumspolitik und Jugendschriftentheorie in der Zeit von 1933 bis 1945.* Gütersloh: Bertelsmann, 1968.

Altner, Manfred. *Die deutsche Kinder- und Jugendliteratur zwischen Gründerzeit und Novemberrevolution.* Berlin: Der Kinderbuchverlag, 1981.

Baumgärtner, Alfred Clemens, ed. *Deutsches Jugendbuch heute.* Velber: Friedrich Verlag, 1974.

Doderer, Klaus, ed. *Lexikon der Kinder- und Jugendliteratur: Personen-, Länder- und Sachartikel zu Geschichte und Gegenwart der Kinder- und Jugendliteratur.* 3 vols. Weinheim: Belz Verlag, 1973.

———. *Zwischen Trümmern und Wohlstand: Literatur der Jugend 1945–1960.* Weinheim: Beltz Verlag, 1988.

Dyrenfurth, Irene. *Geschichte des deutschen Jugendbuches.* Zürich: Atlantis Verlag, 1967.

Emmerich, Christian, ed. *Literatur für Kinder und Jugendliche in der DDR.* Berlin: Kinderbuchverlag, 1981.

Hürlimann, Bettina. *Three Centuries of Children's Books in Europe.* Cleveland, OH: World Publishing Co., 1954.

Kamenetsky, Christa. *Children's Literature in Hitler's Germany: The Cultural Policy of National Socialism.* Athens, OH: University of Ohio Press, 1984.

Mattenklott, Gundel. *Zauberkreide: Kinderliteratur seit 1945.* Stuttgart: J.B. Metzler, 1989.

Mayr-Kleffl, Verena. *Mädchenbücher: Leitbilder für Wirklichkeit.* Opladen: Leske Verlag, 1986.

Wild, Reiner, ed. *Geschichte der deutschen Kinder- und Jugendliteratur.* Stuttgart: J.B. Metzler, 1990.

Choral Music

The function of choral music in the eighteenth and early nineteenth centuries was governed by certain conditions. First was predominance of religious works based on the nature of the texts that formed the basis of the music, particularly masses, requiems, and quasi-religious stories in oratorios or cantatas, with use of the chorus as a separate character from those of the soloists. Second was similarity of musical style to the purely instrumental works written by the same composers (e.g. the symphonies and chamber music of Joseph Haydn and Wolfgang A. Mozart).

Ludwig van Beethoven first used a chorus in a form that had been purely instrumental until then: the symphony, which was changed forever in the last (choral) movement of his Ninth Symphony, 1824. At the same time, Beethoven expanded the scope of the chorus beyond all of his previous choral works in the *Missa Solemnis,* 1823. Such innovations set an example for the composers who followed Beethoven and challenged them to expand the use of choral forces in sacred and secular works.

Sacred choral works continued primarily in the forms of masses and requiems, which had been set to music since the Middle Ages, although the musical styles of such settings had naturally changed over the centuries. The influence of the Catholic Church was increasingly challenged in the nineteenth century, when works of a liturgical nature fell under the musical influence of opera, much to the chagrin of the Church hierarchy. The development of the oratorio, an unstaged equivalent of opera with a quasi-religious text, had helped to undermine the tenets of the religious musical style and to blur the stylistic line between secular opera and religious works.

Secular choral works are difficult to define beyond being non-sacred in form or extramusical meaning. They include chorus-sized, or at least chamber-sized, vocal ensembles, with instrumental accompaniment varying from nothing to a full-sized orchestra. The religiosity of a vocal text was sometimes quixotically contravened by its use in a purely secular form like the symphony; such unorthodox uses occurred increasingly in the nineteenth and twentieth centuries, largely because of societal interest in historical and folkloric events expressive of nationalism. In contrast to the Latin texts used for centuries in the religious works, the texts of secular works were based on drama (Goethe's *Faust,* for example, was a frequent subject), prose literature, or poetry. In many cases, the composer doubled as librettist, especially among the followers of Wagner, who had written his own texts.

Religious works lost favor compared with secular works starting with the late nineteenth century, but there were some such works that stand as models of their kind. Anton Bruckner (1824–96), best known as a symphonist, also composed settings of the Mass and late in his life wrote a *Te Deum,* 1881, perhaps influenced by his exposure to the liturgy during his work as organist of St. Florian. Paul Hindemith (1895–1963) composed an unusual Mass for voices alone, rare in his oeuvre, which was most often devoted to orchestral, chamber, operatic, and solo vocal works; it stands as an anomaly in the Germany of the 1920s and 1930s, in which few composers set any kind of religious texts to music because of the essentially secular trends after World War I, as well as the stand of the Nazi regime, in the German-speaking countries. In 1922, Arnold Schönberg wrote his oratorio *Jakobsleiter* (Jacob's ladder), which is a rare Jewish religious work among composers in the German-speaking countries.

Thomaner Choir, Leipzig. Courtesy of Inter Nationes, Bonn.

There had been certain quasi-religious usages in the symphonies of Gustav Mahler (1860–1911), which were neither mass nor requiem nor oratorio. In 1894 in the Second Symphony he had included a choral setting of the *Auferstehungsode* of Klopstock, in the Third Symphony of 1896 a setting of a religious poem from *Des Knaben Wunderhorn* (which may be considered a manifestation of religious faith in the folk traditions of the German people). Likewise, in 1906 in the Eighth Symphony, Mahler set the Catholic liturgical hymn *Veni, Creator Spiritus*, which may be comparable to Bruckner's *Te Deum* in its contrapuntal dramatic setting of a text that had by then escaped the control of the Church.

Many of the same composers who wrote such religious settings also set secular texts, thus proving that their choices of texts were governed by musico-dramatic considerations rather than principles of *Gebrauchsmusik* (everyday music). Bruckner's *Helgoland*, 1893, falls into the nationalist category. Mahler had written his own text for the cantata *Das klagende Lied*, 1880, based on stories by Ludwig Bechstein and the Brothers Grimm (which could quite easily have served as the basis of an opera). Schönberg, in his *Gurrelieder*, published 1911, used the chorus as a dramatic character equivalent to the soloists and even the orchestra. Hindemith, among other works, wrote a *Liederbuch für mehrere Singstimmen*, which resembles his Mass in 1963 in the intimacy of its vocal requirements. A total contrast appeared in the scenic cantatas of Carl Orff (1895–1982), especially *Carmina Burana*, 1937, which—while based on medieval texts from the same period as many liturgical sources—is quite pagan and sometimes even risqué in orientation.

A comparison of these diverse examples shows that the size of choral works in the late nineteenth and the early twentieth centuries bears no relation to the nature of the text; depending on the orientation of the composer and the circumstances of composition, choral works varied from the most intimate capella works (equivalent to instrumental chamber music) to gigantic choral-orchestral blockbusters. The single stylistic facet that most such works—sacred and secular—share is the use of dramatic word painting, which lent itself to romantic and expressionist influences. This trend has continued to the present, although the employment of choral forces in musical works has diminished somewhat in popularity in the latter part of this century.

Susan M. Filler

See also Bruckner, Anton; Composers; Hindemith, Paul; Keyboard Music; Mahler, Gustav; Orchestral Music; Orff, Carl; Schönberg, Arnold

References

Schünemann, Georg. *Führer durch die deutsche Chorliteratur.* 2 vols. Wolfenbüttel: Verlag für musikalische Kultur und Wissenschaft, 1935–36.

Ulrich, Homer. *A Survey of Choral Music.* New York, NY: Harcourt Brace Jovanovich, 1973.

Young, Percy M. *The Choral Tradition: An Historical Survey from the Sixteenth Century to the Present Day.* Rev. ed. New York, NY: W.W. Norton, 1981.

Christian Democratic Union (CDU)

Founded in 1945, the CDU emerged as an explicitly interconfessional Christian party with the aim of building a broad electoral alliance (in contrast to its Catholic ancestor, the pre-1933 Center Party). The choice of the term "union" (instead of "party") reflected this encompassing goal and set the stage for the CDU's electoral success.

With Konrad Adenauer's accession to the chancellorship following the first Bundestag election of 1949, the CDU became the primary party in the majority coalition. From that point, its function would be that of a chancellor-party with the task of reinforcing and building popular support for Adenauer. The overwhelming victory in the 1953 election demonstrated the CDU's ability to effectively integrate diverse social and economic interests. With this election the CDU convincingly established itself as Germany's prototypical catch-all formation.

Programmatically, the CDU quickly shifted away from its early postwar reformist and left-of-center Ahlen program to endorse the social market economy espoused by the father of the Economic Miracle, Ludwig Erhard (1897–1977). Throughout its history the pragmatic CDU has exhibited a strong centrist orientation manifested in a politics of the middle way.

Organizationally, the CDU was originally a loose association of regional parties sharing little more than a common label. Only after the first Bundestag election, at its party congress in Goslar in 1950, did the CDU unify itself within a single federal organization.

German Christian democracy retains a distinctly federalized structure. This is most evident in the special relationship between CDU and CSU (Christian Social Union). The CSU exists only in Bavaria, where it competes at all levels. Correspondingly, the CDU has no presence in this *Land* (state) but constitutes the Christian democratic party in the 15 other *Länder* (states). Hence the two parties never compete electorally against each other. In the Bundestag they form a single parliamentary caucus (*Fraktion*).

Because the CDU immediately became a party of government led by a popular chancellor, it found little need for organizational innovation and remained a party of regional notables. During its long period in power, membership did not expand significantly and organizational modernization remained neglected. After 1969, once the CDU was forced into the unaccustomed role of opposition party, it began an arduous phase of renewal that involved leadership change, membership expansion, and programmatic rethinking. By the beginning of the 1980s, the CDU had been transformed into a modern mass-membership party.

In 1982, as a result of the first successful use of the "constructive vote of no confidence" procedure (Article 67 of the Basic Law) Helmut Kohl became chancellor and the Christian Democrats returned to power in coalition with the Free Democrats (FDP). Following successive election victories in 1983 and 1987, Kohl and his party found themselves in control when the GDR collapsed. At that historic moment, Kohl took the lead in initiating a strategy for political and economic unification. This leadership earned the CDU crucial victories in the critical East German Volkskammer (parliament) election of March 1990, which was, in effect, a referendum on the question of rapid unification. The victory for the CDU-led Alliance for Germany also set in motion the negotiations leading to the unification treaties and the 1990 Bundestag elections. These ratified unity and confirmed the preeminence of the CDU in the immediate post-unity era.

William M. Chandler

See also Adenauer, Konrad; Barzel, Rainer; Bertram, Adolf; Biedenkopf, Kurt; Blank, Theodor; Carstens, Karl; Catholic Women's Association; Catholicism, Political; Center Party; Christian Social Union; De Mazière, Lothar; Ehard, Hans; Erhard, Ludwig; Frings, Joseph; Heinemann, Gustav; Herzog, Roman; Imbusch, Heinrich; Kaiser, Jacob; Kiesinger, Kurt Georg; Kohl, Helmut; Lieber, Ernst; Lübke, Heinrich; Schröder, Gerhard; Schwarzhaupt, Elisabeth; Spahn, Martin; Strecker, Gabriele; Stegerwald, Adam; Strauss, Franz Josef; Süssmuth, Rita; Weber, Helene; Weizsäcker, Richard von

References

Beyme, Klaus von. *Political Parties in Western Democracies.* Aldershot: Gower, 1985.

Cary, Noel D. *The Path to Christian Democracy: German Catholics and the Party System from Windthorst to Adenauer.* Cambridge, MA: Harvard University Press, 1996.

Chandler, William M. "The Christian Democrats and the Challenge of Unity." Ed. Stephen Padgett. *Parties and Party Systems in the New Germany.* Aldershot: Dartmouth, 1993.

Clemens, Clay. *Reluctant Realists: The Christian Democrats and West German Ostpolitik.* Durham, NC: Duke University Press, 1989.

Haungs, Peter. "Die CDU: Prototyp einer Volkspartei." *Parteien in der Bundesrepublik Deutschland.* Ed. Alf Mintzel and Heinrich Oberreuter. 2nd ed. Opladen: Leske and Budrich, 1992.

Mitchell, Maria. "Materialism and Secularism: CDU Politicians and National Socialism, 1945–1949." *Journal of Modern History* 65 (June, 1995), 278–308.

Smith, Gordon. *Democracy in Western Germany: Parties and Politics in the Federal Republic.* 3rd ed. New York, NY: Holmes and Meier, 1986.

Christian Social Union

After Germany's total defeat and occupation in 1945, the Christian Social Union (Christlich Soziale Union; CSU) represented a new hope for a resurrected party-political establishment. It was founded in Bavaria by, among others, the former trade-union leader from Franconia and cabinet minister Adam Stegerwald (1874–1945) and the Munich lawyer and Resistance member Josef "Ochsensepp" Müller.

In two critical respects, the CSU was intended to transcend the pre-1933 Bavarian party-political boundaries. First, the CSU appealed to both of the major Christian denominations in postwar Bavaria. Second, it aspired to become a genuine *Volkspartei* (people's party) by incorporating not only tra-

ditional middle-class elements of the Bavarian population but also workers, farmers, and professionals. Its founders thus hoped to create a party bridging the differences that had effectively aided the Nazis during the Weimar Republic by paralyzing the parliamentary system. Nevertheless, the CSU also hoped to remain the party representing the traditions of Bavaria, a state that had been badly tarnished as the "birthplace" of National Socialism. The CSU's founders could then lay claim to the mantle of Bavarian political uniqueness which had been trumpeted by the CSU's Bavarian predecessor, the Bavarian People's Party.

Between 1945 and 1949, two principal currents of thought dominated the CSU's internal workings. The first was represented by Stegerwald and Müller, two liberally inclined notables who hoped to give the new party a decidedly anticonservative orientation. Their influence enabled the CSU to win early support among north Bavarian Protestants and workers in several of Bavaria's major industrial cities. The second current found expression in the likes of former members of the Bavarian People's Party such as Anton Pfeiffer and Fritz Schäffer. These men and their supporters represented a much more conservative, Roman Catholic, south Bavarian orientation. Though the disagreements between these two currents often caused the CSU considerable organizational—and sometimes electoral—grief before 1949, the party nevertheless established an early dominance in postwar Bavarian politics. Although the conservative elements eventually managed to oust Müller from the chairmanship in 1949 and reduce the left-of-center influence of Müller's supporters, the CSU remained a party capable of appealing at least marginally to members and voters outside of its conservative redoubt.

Both segments of the party shared one of the CSU's most important political ideals—the desire to reform postwar Germany in a federalist fashion. All members of the party's leadership maintained that only a federated Germany could prevent either Communism or a return to Nazism while also preserving Bavaria's historical and cultural uniqueness. In this respect, the CSU and the Bavarian governments controlled by the party during the Federal Republic of Germany's early years contributed significantly to the creation of the first successful German democracy. In the process, the CSU also established a firm grip on the politics of its home state. Through an unwaveringly conservative position on almost every issue and unceasing self-identification of the party with Bavaria, the CSU succeeded in maintaining control of every Bavarian government, save one, between 1945 and 1993.

David R. Dorondo

See also Bavarian People's Party; Christian Democratic Union; Ehard, Hans; Federalism; Political Parties and Politics; Strauss, Franz Josef

References

Dorondo, D.R. *Bavaria and German Federalism: Reich to Republic, 1918–33, 1945–49.* New York, NY: St. Martin's, 1992.

Gurland, Arcadius R.L. *Die CDU/CSU: Ursprünge und Entwicklung bis 1953.* Ed. Dieter Emig. Frankfurt am

Main: Europäische Verlagsanstalt, 1980.

Gutjahr-Loser, Peter. *CSU: Portrait einer Partei.* Munich: Gunter Olzog Verlag, 1979.

Mintzel, Alf. *Die Geschichte der CSU: Ein Überblick.* Opladen: Westdeutscher Verlag, 1977.

Wolf, Konstanze. *CSU und Bayernpartei: Ein besonderes Konkurrenzverhältnis 1948–1960.* Cologne: Verlag Wissenschaft & Kultur, 1982.

Christian Trade Unions (1899–1933)

The League of Christian Trade Unions was founded in 1899 as a patriotic and religious alternative to the so-called "free trade unions" that had been organized earlier in the century by the Marxist and officially nonreligious Social Democratic Party (SPD). Opposing Marxist internationalism and the notion of an unremitting class struggle, the Christian unions nonetheless insisted that their own ideal—German national solidarity with a social conscience—required genuine collective bargaining. These unions thus had nothing in common with the so-called "yellow" or company-sponsored unions with which they sometimes have been lumped mistakenly.

Though the Christian trade unions were interdenominational (among their Protestant sponsors were Adolf Stoecker [1835–1909] and his Christian Social party), much of the impetus for their emergence came from political Catholicism and the social Catholic self-help movement of the late nineteenth century, led by such men as Wilhelm von Ketteler. In an era of rapid industrialization, prominent urban Catholics feared they might lose their mass base to the SPD unless the clergy and the Catholic Center Party took steps to satisfy the workers. Drawing upon the tradition of Adolf Kolping's mid-century network of journeymen's leagues, hostels, and adult education classes, two new organizations appeared in the early 1890s: the regionally autonomous Catholic Labor Leagues (Katholische Arbeitervereine) and the Rhenish-based People's Association of Catholic Germany (Volksverein). Yet it was a long step from these clerically tutored and exclusively Catholic organizations to real, interdenominational trade unions with the will and the numerical strength to stage viable strikes. For 15 years after their founding, the unions had to fight for their lives, as some Catholic notables tried to get the Vatican to forbid Catholics from joining. Like the free unions, however, the Christian unions emerged from World War I in a significantly strengthened position. From 330,000 members on the eve of the war (roughly 80 percent Catholic), the blue-collar Christian unions grew to about one million members by 1919. An additional 400,000 mostly Protestant white-collar workers were affiliated with the blue-collar Christian unions via the German National Union of Commercial Employees (DHV). Altogether, the Christian unions' umbrella organization, the Deutscher Gewerkschaftsbund (DGB; German Trade Union Federation), now represented one out of every five organized workers.

With the postwar change to republican and parliamentary government, Catholics and Protestants in the DGB found themselves on opposite sides of the partisan dividing line between government and opposition. In a bid to give Protestant workers a moderate and democratic alternative to the antire-publican German National People's Party (DNVP), the Catholic head of the DGB, Adam Stegerwald (1874–1945), proposed in 1920 the "Essen program." He urged the Christian and affiliated unions to launch a broad new interdenominational and socially diverse party (not a labor party). According to Stegerwald, the proposed new "Christian people's party" would split the DNVP, supplant the Center, outdraw the SPD, and become the prime party of government. Such a massive overhaul of the existing party system, however, proved impossible to achieve. This failure led in part to the ill-starred efforts during the 1930–32 tenure of Chancellor Heinrich Brüning (1885–1970), the DGB's former executive secretary, to compel greater cooperation among the parties through authoritarian measures.

During the Great Depression, many Protestant workers proved vulnerable to the self-styled "social" appeal of Nazism. Under the circumstances, some union leaders showed interest in Chancellor Kurt von Schleicher's (1882–1934) stillborn scheme late in 1932 to split the Nazi movement by forming a nonparliamentary emergency government backed by the army, the "social wing" of the Nazi party, and the socialist and Christian unions. After Adolf Hitler assumed power in January 1933, fearful Christian and socialist union leaders held merger talks. In May, however, the Nazis summarily shut down the free unions and selectively "coordinated" or liquidated Christian union organizations. Over the next twelve years, many Christian union leaders were harassed, periodically arrested, or (like the DHV's Max Habermann) killed. Several, including Habermann and Jakob Kaiser (1888–1961), became important figures in the Resistance.

Convinced that labor disunity had helped to pave the way for the Nazis, socialist and Christian labor leaders unified the trade union movement (and adopted the name DGB) after the war. Harkening back in part to the Essen program, trade unionists such as Kaiser, Karl Arnold, and Stegerwald himself (who died in 1945) were also key figures in the postwar founding of the interdenominational and socially pluralistic Christian democratic parties, the Christian Democratic Union and Christian Social Union. In defiance of Kaiser and Arnold, Christian secessionist trade unions were later reestablished. Most churchgoing workers, however, remained in the unified DGB.

Poised between the pre-industrial and industrial worlds, the early Christian trade unionists were socially progressive but culturally conservative. Although critical of capitalism, they rejected what they deemed to be the intolerance and utopian arrogance of the Marxists. Working-class dignity, they believed, could not be based on disdain for the dignity of others, but had to be grounded in mutual social (and religious) respect. Insisting that social anomie was a cultural as well as an economic and political problem, they sought to adapt social and democratic reforms to traditional values and mores. Unfortunately, their exalted ambitions were overrun by their own social and economic anxieties, as well as those of the other social classes whose partnership they sought. When their early hopes of constructing a tolerant "Christian, social, and national democracy" (Stegerwald) were dashed, some of these workers joined the mindless flight into the regimented solidarity of Nazism. Only after the firestorm that followed did they find the path to a new democratic synthesis.

Noel D. Cary

See also Catholicism, Political; Kaiser, Jakob; Kettler, Wilhelm von; National Socialist Germany; People's Association for a Catholic Germany; Stegerwald, Adam; Trade Unions, 1871–1945

References

Brose, Eric Dorn. *Christian Labor and the Politics of Frustration in Imperial Germany.* Washington, DC: Catholic University of America Press, 1985.

Cary, Noel D. *The Path to Christian Democracy: German Catholics and the Party System from Windthorst to Adenauer.* Cambridge, MA: Harvard University Press, 1996.

Conze, Werner, Erich Kosthorst and Elfriede Nebgen. *Jakob Kaiser.* 4 vols. Stuttgart: Kohlhammer, 1967–72.

Patch, William, Jr. *Christian Trade Unions in the Weimar Republic, 1918–1933: The Failure of "Corporate Pluralism."* New Haven, CT: Yale University Press, 1985.

Ross, R.J. *Beleaguered Tower: The Dilemma of Political Catholicism in Wilhelmine Germany.* South Bend, IN: Notre Dame University Press, 1976.

Schneider, Michael. *Die christlichen Gewerkschaften 1894–1933.* Bonn: Verlag Neue Gesellschaft, 1982.

Schorr, Helmut J. *Adam Stegerwald.* Recklinghausen: Kommunal-Verlag, 1966.

Christmas

Christmas celebrations, customs, and festivities actually start a month before December 25, with Advent. For children the highlight is St. Nicholas's Day on December 6, when they hope to find a shoe or boot full of sweets, biscuits, nuts, and fruit outside their bedroom door. A figure dressed as St. Nicholas, or Father Christmas (*Weihnachtsmann*), is seen regularly with his sack and his rod, with which to punish naughty children.

Each of the Sundays in Advent is celebrated with an Advent wreath, mostly made of greenery, with four red candles on it. On the first Sunday one of these is lit over afternoon coffee; on the second, two; on the third, three; and on the Sunday immediately prior to Christmas, all four candles burn. A splendid selection of *Weihnachtsgebäck* (Christmas biscuits), is eaten together with *Stollen*, a rich yeast fruit bread. Some children are still lucky enough to bake and decorate a gingerbread house at home, depicting the witch's house in the fairy tale about Hänsel and Gretel. Children also count the days to Christmas with an Advent calendar.

Christmas markets are held in most towns during Advent, the most famous being the Christkindelsmarkt in Nuremberg, which features a glittering array of Christmas goodies, most notably the traditional decorations and nutcrackers in the form of wooden soldiers from the Erzgebirge in the former East Germany. Other well-known wooden decorations are pyramids of varying sizes, with several layers of

Nuremberg "Christkindlesmarkt." Courtesy of German Embassy, Ottawa.

carved figures which are rotated by the heat of candles. Even more curious are the *Räuchermännchen*, wooden figures that emit smoke either through the mouth or pipe when a small cone of charcoal is ignited inside.

On December 24, the shops and offices close around noon and most people spend the afternoon at home. The Christmas tree is still central to the celebrations and is not decorated until the afternoon of Christmas Eve (the holy evening), often behind closed doors so that the children can believe that angels have done the decoration, the tinsel being their hair that became caught as they flew away. Often around 4 p.m. a bell is rung to announce that the tree is decorated and lit (still, in some cases, with real candles). Everyone wishes each other "Happy Christmas" (*Fröhliche Weihnachten*). The crib with figures is often to be found near the tree and the presents either under the tree or on a nearby table. The family sits around and hears the Christmas story, sings traditional carols such as "O, du Fröhliche" (Oh, how joyfully) or "Stille Nacht" ("Silent Night") before exchanging gifts. The "colorful" plate is still popular, made of cardboard decorated with Christmas motifs, and containing a selection of sweets to be nibbled through the festivities. There are no fixed Christmas foods, although a few families eat carp on Christmas Eve and goose the next day. Churchgoing families attend Christmas services either in the early evening or at midnight.

December 25 and 26 are very quiet days, normally devoted to family visits. Although the twelve days of Christmas contain the much noisier New Year celebrations, they end with the Three Kings' Day on January 6. In many, mostly Roman Catholic, areas boys still dress up as Kaspar, Melchior, and Balthazar and carry a big star from house to house, begging for money, sweets, or alcohol. As a sign of their visit, a chalked formula, thought to offer the house protection, is to be seen on many a lintel throughout the year, for example, 19K + M + B96 (i.e., 19 K[aspar] + M[elchior] + B[althazar] 96).

Jennifer M. Russ

See also Customs

References

Auerbach, Konrad. *Seiffener Weihnacht: Brauchtum im Erzgebirge.* Leipzig: GRAFA, 1991.

Beitl, Richard. *Wörterbuch der deutschen Volkskunde.* 3rd ed. Stuttgart: Kröner, 1974.

Bernhard, Marianne. *Gnadebringende Weihnachtszeit.* 4th ed. Munich: Südwest Verlag, 1972.

Buhl, Wolfgang. ed. *Der Nürnberger Christkindlesmarkt.* Würzburg: Echter, 1976.

Russ, Jennifer M. *German Festivals and Customs.* London: Oswald Wolff, 1982.

Schönfeldt, Sybil Gräfin. *Das Ravensburger Buch der Feste und Bräuche.* Ravensburg: Otto Maier, 1980.

Cinema

The technology for recording and projecting moving images was invented in Germany by Max and Emil Skladanowsky. They introduced their Bioscop in Berlin on November 1, 1895, but the system proved so cumbersome that they adapted the standard of 35mm film pioneered around the same time by more influential French and American inventors.

Owing to a strong cultural bias against the cinema as popular entertainment, traditionalists attempted to censure it. Hence, the development of the early cinema in Germany proceeded in the shadow of more powerful foreign producers. The only notable exception was Oskar Messter (1866–1943), who experimented with the entire spectrum of international genres and technologies. Not until 1913 did a domestic industry evolve as the cultural boycott was broken through a series of films with scripts by recognized authors and actors from famous theaters (e.g., Max Mack [1884–1973], *Der Andere* [The other], 1913; Stellan Rye [1880–1914], *Der Student von Prag* [The student of Prague], 1913). Although such films brought respectability to the cinema, they were not commercially successful, and with the onset of war in 1914, the promising development was interrupted.

After an official ban on film imports was imposed in 1916, domestic production companies proliferated. Even the state became involved when the military formed production units that—through a process of mergers—would become the Universal Film Company (*Universum Film Aktiengesellschaft*, Ufa). Despite the devastated economy, political unrest, and harsh anti-German measures by the victorious Allies after the war, the film industry blossomed. Paradoxically, the German film industry emerged from World War I in a strong position because of its isolation, and during the 1920s, it became the major competitor for Hollywood. The rampant inflation meant that German films were easy to export, which offered production companies an international economic advantage.

Familiar dramatic and comedy genres continued to dominate cinema fare, but other trends also appeared that would mark the "classic German cinema" of the 1920s. Ernst Lubitsch (1892–1947) adapted the popular genre of Italian historical epics with lavish costume dramas such as *Madame Dubarry* (produced as *Passion*, 1919) and *Anna Boleyn*, 1920, spectacles that opened the international market for the country's productions. Lubitsch not only translated the innovations of stage director Max Reinhardt's (alias Maximilian Goldmann, 1873–1943) innovations to the screen (e.g., crowd dynamics and gestic acting) but also devised new ways of editing for narrative continuity, achievements that made him the first of many German directors to be lured to Hollywood.

Another development was the expressionist cinema. Robert Wiene's (1881–1938) *Das Kabinett des Dr. Caligari* (produced as *The Cabinet of Dr. Caligari*), 1919, captured the public imagination with its stylized sets, distorted image composition, exaggerated acting, and distinctive editing. Directors such as Fritz Lang (1890–1976), Paul Leni (1885–1929), Friedrich Wilhelm Murnau (1888–1931), and Paul Wegener (1874–1948) pioneered a series of art films characterized by their expressive visualization of dreams, trauma, disorientation, horror, and angst. Their antirealistic style corresponded to thematic preoccupations with fantastic or magical events and threatening figures (phantoms, vampires, and criminals). Other directors focused on disastrous psychological situations in the *Kammerspielfilm* or "chamber drama," adapted from the theater.

Political and economic stabilization after 1925 and technological advances in the cinema (better lighting, camera mobility, sound recording) led to increasing centralization of the entire film sector in response to foreign (mainly American) competition. This phase terminated the contorted emotionalism of the expressionist cinema. The German film industry adapted to a more standardized international quality with a distinctive turn toward realism and social criticism (best exemplified in films by Georg Wilhelm Pabst [1885–1967]). The giant Ufa with its vertical monopoly structure grew out of this trend and eventually became the backbone of the Nazi-controlled film industry.

After the collapse of the Third Reich both victors and losers sought a new start. Since the four Allies rejected a centralized film industry in Germany, each one fostered its own policies based on self-interest and Cold War ideologies. The Soviets reconstructed production facilities quickly, and by 1946 the *Deutsche Film-Aktiengesellschaft* (Defa) was producing films committed to anti-Fascist and "democratic" re-education (e.g., those by Wolfgang Staudte [1906–84] and Kurt Maetzig [1911–]) in Postdam. The state-owned company was part of a larger cultural policy known as socialist realism, and because the cinema was considered to have a mass impact, it was particularly susceptible to state intervention. Nonetheless, directors like Konrad Wolf (1925–82), Frank Beyer (1932–), and Heiner Carow (1929–) produced a remarkable body of films for Defa, which became the largest studio facility in Europe during the 40-year history of the German Democratic Republic.

In the West, where the cinema was considered a form of commercial entertainment, the industry expanded only after the currency reform in 1948, when economic stabilization made it an attractive investment. Numerous small, undercapitalized production companies arose that were unable to compete in the international market, a situation that still characterizes the film sector in the Federal Republic of Germany (FRG). During the 1950s, this constraint led to conformist and profit-oriented cinema entertainment aimed exclusively at the domestic audience.

As in the rest of Europe, competition from television and expanded leisure-time activities eroded the traditional cinema audience and made room for a "new wave" in the 1960s. The Oberhausen Manifesto of 1962 announced the renewal of the directors' art cinema with small budgets and topical films committed to quality and experimentation. By the end of the decade a new generation of filmmakers had established the "young German film" (e.g., Alexander Kluge [1932–], Volker Schlöndorff [1939–], and Jean-Marie Straub [1933–]). Innovative government funding largely channeled through public television created a fresh burst of energy in the 1970s. Less a movement than a shared notion of independent film culture, the "new German cinema" gained international prestige, while ironically the unprecedented number of young, talented directors struggled in a home market dominated by American fare.

While directors like Werner Herzog (1942–), Rainer Werner Fassbinder (1945–82), and Wim Wenders (1945–) established international visibility with their large-scale productions, others—women, gay/lesbian, and experimental filmmakers—probed the limits of formal conventions and political narrative. At the threshold of the new century a unified Germany faces a surplus of talented filmmakers and increasingly large multinational media conglomerates. New forms of international funding under the auspices of the European Community and new electronic technologies in the audiovisual industries will write the future of the German cinema.

Marc Silberman

See also Fassbinder, Rainer Werner; Goebbels, Joseph; Herzog, Werner; Kluge, Alexander; Reinhardt, Max; Riefenstahl, Leni; Schlöndorff, Volker; Third Reich: Propaganda and Culture; Trotta, Margarethe von; Ufa

References

Bandmann, Christa and Joe Hembus. *Klassiker des deutschen Tonfilms 1930–1960.* Munich: Goldmann, 1980.

Barlow, John D. *German Expressionist Film.* Boston, MA: Twayne, 1982.

Bock, Hans-Michael, ed. *Cinegraph: Lexikon zum deutschsprachigen Film.* Munich: Edition Text + Kritik, 1984 *ff.*

Eisner, Lotte. *The Haunted Screen: Expressionism in the German Cinema and the Influence of Max Reinhardt.* Berkeley, CA: University of California Press, 1969.

Elsaesser, Thomas. *New German Cinema: A History.* New Brunswick: Rutgers University Press, 1989.

Jacobsen, Wolfgang, Anton Kaes, and Hans Helmut Prinzler. *Geschichte des deutschen Films.* Stuttgart: Metzler, 1993.

Kracauer, Siegfried. *From Caligari to Hitler: A Psychological History of the German Film.* Princeton, NJ: Princeton University Press, 1947.

Kreimeier, Klaus. *Die Ufa-Story: Geschichte eines Filmkonzerns.* Munich: Hanser, 1992.

Pflaum, Hans Günther. *Germany on Film: Theme and Content in the Cinema of the Federal Republic of Germany.* Ed. Robert Picht. Trans. Richard C. Helt and Roland Richter. Detroit, MI: Wayne State University Press, 1990.

Schenk, Ralf, ed. *Das zweite Leben der Filmstadt Babelsberg; DEFA-Spielfilme 1946–1992.* Berlin: Henschel Verlag, 1994.

Silberman, Marc. *German Cinema: Texts in Context.* Detroit, MI: Wayne State University Press, 1995.

Citizenship and Foreigners

In 1990, approximately 5.7 million foreigners—or 7.2 percent of the total population—lived in the Federal Republic of Germany (FRG). The largest group consists of labor migrants and their dependents; the other groups are asylum seekers (some 200,000 in 1990) and, lately, war refugees, particularly from the former Yugoslavia. In some metropolitan areas, such as Frankfurt, foreigners constitute more than 20 percent of the population; in Berlin, the capital of Germany, they constitute about 12 percent. The Turks, with 1.7 million, are the largest non-German ethnic group.

Some 60 percent of foreigners have been residing in Germany for ten or more years and more than two-thirds of foreign children were born in Germany. Despite their long residency, even the labor migrants who came to the FRG in the 1960s and in the early 1970s generally did not enjoy citizenship rights. For example, they could not vote or be candidates in local and national elections. Political marginalization and social isolation are only some of the problems that foreigners are facing in Germany today. The sharp increase in racially motivated violent attacks on foreigners and the rise of xenophobia after German unification in 1990 has been a cause for renewed concern about the civil, social, and political rights of minorities. At the core of the debate are the conceptions of nationhood and citizenship in unified Germany.

Citizenship is not simply a legal formula; it has become an increasingly salient political, social, and cultural fact and as such an instrument to include or exclude individuals in a society. Thus the issue of citizenship has legal, political, and cultural dimensions. The perception and definition of who is a "foreigner" and how to frame the issue of citizenship is shaped by each country's history in the building of the nation-state.

CITIZENSHIP AND FOREIGNERS

German notions of nationhood and citizenship emerged before the founding of the modern German state in 1871 and were tied to the idea of a "cultural nation," in which Germans are defined by their ethnicity. This ethnocultural notion of citizenship can be traced at least as far back as the founding of the German Empire in 1871. The strongly federal nature of the early modern German state delayed the passing of a national law on citizenship until 1913. The issue of Germans abroad (*Auslandsdeutsche*), large-scale immigration into the rapidly industrializing German Empire, and the rise of patriotic nationalism provided for a political climate in which the law granted citizenship on the basis of descent, rather than on membership in the political community, as in France. It established the still-extant model of *jus sanguinis* (law of blood). The Citizenship Law of 1913 offered citizenship rights based on common descent, language, and culture (*Volkszugehörigkeit*). It included ethnic Germans outside the home territory but excluded immigrants, which made naturalization extremely difficult.

The devastating experience with racial laws in Nazi Germany led the founders of the FRG in 1948–49 to craft a concept of citizenship based on universal civil and political rights, democratic citizenship, and generous provisions concerning political asylum. The Basic Law (Grundgesetz), or constitution, of 1949 contained liberal provisions for asylum (Article 16: "Persons persecuted on political grounds shall enjoy the right of asylum"). But the FRG also reestablished the citizenship law of 1913 according to the ethnocultural conception in which citizenship is based on descent. Much of postwar German political discourse on citizenship derives from a struggle between these two concepts, the liberal model based on universal civil rights and the traditional ethnocultural model rooted in membership in the ethnic community.

The latter concept enjoyed considerable support because it seemed to provide a legal and political framework for solving two decisive issues in postwar Germany: the large-scale refugee problem and the country's division during the Cold War. The preamble of the Basic Law included Germans in the former German Democratic Republic (GDR), granting citizenship automatically to the East Germans. Some two million citizens of East Germany moved to West Germany before the Berlin Wall was built; about half a million fled or moved during the dramatic 1989–90 events. In addition, Article 116.1 of the Basic Law, which defined membership in the political community on the basis of *Volkszugehörigkeit*, or descent, provided a legal ground to integrate expellees (*Vertriebene*) and "outsettlers" (*Aussiedler*). Of the 12.5 million Germans who fled or were expelled from Eastern Europe after the war, two-thirds settled in the FRG. Based on a broad postwar consensus, the FRG granted citizenship easily to East Germans as well as to ethnic Germans from Eastern Europe, even after the refugee problem was no longer pertinent.

In contrast to the inclusive notion of citizenship toward ethnic Germans living outside of FRG territory, the German citizenship law was, and still is, exclusive toward non-ethnic Germans living within the FRG. Naturalization rates, for example, are four to five times higher in France than in Germany

150,000 Germans in Frankfurt am Main demonstrating against hostility towards foreigners (1993). Courtesy of Inter Nationes, Bonn.

for the main group of migrant workers and their dependents; the gap is even higher for second- and third-generation immigrants. Whereas France expects assimilation and naturalization, the German government views naturalization as the exception. Labor migrants still find it difficult to integrate into the social fabric of German society.

The issue of foreigners, or *Ausländerpolitik*, has become a contentious, partisan issue in the 1990s. The term *Ausländer* (alien) is a highly charged phrase in German politics, often misused in the symbolic politics of post-unification Germany. Revisions in the asylum law are a case in point. Bowing to the pressure of a resurgent nationalistic right, the federal government under Chancellor Helmut Kohl has restricted the right to seek political asylum because of an alleged danger to the state by the influx of "foreigners." In May of 1993, the Basic Law was amended in parliament with the support of the Social Democrats and the Free Democrats, to severely restrict the right to seek political asylum in Germany.

There are some signs of a backlash in the new FRG. In the metropolitan areas as well as in small communities citizens have formed civic initiatives to fight the rise of xenophobia and racism. The revised aliens' law (Ausländergesetz) of 1990 provides for easier naturalization of second- and third-generation foreigners, and the administration now more often grants dual citizenship. Naturalization rates have increased in cities such as Berlin, which have large ethnic minorities. Procedural changes have at the same time made it more difficult for ethnic Germans in Eastern Europe to enter the FRG. With German unification in 1990, the territorial "openness" of the German question was once and for all settled and the borders fixed. Policies toward ethnic German minorities in post-Communist Europe have shifted to encouraging these groups to stay and to demand minority rights.

With European integration well under way, the issue of citizenship and the treatment of foreigners is no longer a national-jurisdiction issue alone. The ethnocultural German citizenship and nationhood conception in its premodern, predemocratic fashion are progressively more outmoded in a Europe with open borders. Once again the treatment of foreigners and the attitudes toward them is becoming a litmus test for the strength of civil society and civil liberties in Germany.
Christiane Lemke

See also The Basic Law; Minorities, Ethnocultural and Foreign; Nationalism; Racism; Refugees

References

Brubaker, Roger. *Citizenship and Nationhood in France and Germany.* Cambridge: Cambridge University Press, 1992.

Kanstroom, Daniel. "Wer sind wir wieder? Laws of Asylum, Immigration, and Citizenship in the Struggle for the Soul of the New Germany." *The Yale Journal of International Law* 18 (1993), 152–211.

Civil Service

The modern German civil service (*Beamtenschaft, Beamtentum*; civil servant: *Beamte*) dates from the eighteenth century, when the absolutist rulers of states such as Prussia, Bavaria, and Baden developed centrally controlled systems of public administration to replace the decentralized structures of aristocratic feudal rule. The new system integrated nobles rather than simply supplanting them. It continued the patronage and privileges characteristic of early modern states, but combined personal loyalty to the dynastic ruler with conformity to legally formalized standards and procedures. From the late eighteenth century, under the influence of the Enlightenment, the French Revolution, and the Napoleonic regime, state administrations were further professionalized and subjected to legal norms that governed administrative acts and the internal structure of the bureaucracy. In the reform era of the early nineteenth century, bureaucrats of Prussia and the Rhineland states were closely associated with the economic and political liberalization of civil society. The classical German professional civil service, or *Berufsbeamtentum*, emerged in this period.

The history of the civil service has been marked by these twin legacies of politicization and professionalism, their ambiguities described most famously by Max Weber (1864–1920). In their late-nineteenth-century heyday, Germany's civil services, especially in Prussia, were known for their political, social, and gender exclusivity; they were characterized by a rigidly hierarchical structure, subordination to a special body of substantive and procedural law, a strong corporate identity and ethos, and a narrow conception of public welfare. In the absence of a viable parliamentary system, the elite of the civil service also acted as the political leadership in Imperial Germany. Though official and conservative opinion glorified the efficiency, incorruptibility, and impartiality of German civil servants, critics distrusted their politicization, caste-like elitism, combination of authoritarian and subaltern mentality, and legalistic formalism.

The image of the civil service as an elite caste was in any case at odds with the fact that by the early twentieth century the civil administration was one of the largest employers in Germany (and the German administrative apparatus was larger than that of comparable countries). By 1907 it accounted for 10 percent of the German work force, with some 1.2 million Reich, *Land* (state), and local government personnel in a wide range of positions from ministerial officials to professors and postal workers. Alongside tenured *Beamte* proper, the public administration by now included a growing number of untenured public employees and workers (*Angestellte* and *Arbeiter*). Many of these were employed in quasi-commercial spheres such as transport and municipal services, and increasing numbers were women.

Although employees were excluded from the social honor and the legal and material privileges enjoyed by *Beamte* (tenure, pensions, and other allowances), the expense of the public administration imposed increasing strain on the public finances, and state governments began to look for ways to reduce costs. Civil servants responded by organizing collectively for the protection of their privileges, while other public employees strove to improve their own conditions of employment. By the beginning of the twentieth century, political and socioeconomic tensions had emerged between the concept of the elite, authoritarian *Beamtenstaat* (civil service state) and the modern realities of the mass bureaucratic state.

The Weimar Republic, with its substitution of political democracy for bureaucratic leadership, forced these tensions to center stage. However, its divided governments were unable either to meet civil servants' demand for economic security or to provide them with a new image, whether of bureaucratic corporatism or democratic professionalism. The political strategy adopted in 1919—buying civil servants' loyalty with a constitutional guarantee of their special legal status and traditional privileges—brought a costly, inflexible, and politically burdensome inheritance for the republic. Civil servants established themselves as a powerful interest group and exploited their new political freedom to campaign vigorously as members of political parties and professional lobbies. They resisted the halting efforts to create a somewhat more open civil service (e.g., by easing the regulations on training or seniority), obscuring the fact that it was not politicization or patronage they rejected but democratization.

Elite civil servants remained at best reserved and at worst openly hostile toward the republic, and most officials were deeply alienated after 1929, when retrenchment hit their salaries and threatened their protected status. The Nazis capitalized on these discontents, attracting civil service voters by assurances of concern for their material needs as well as more grandiose promises of antidemocratic, authoritarian renewal. After 1933, however, the Nazis gave no priority to programmatic administrative reform, except insofar as the wholesale destruction of democracy and the federal system vastly enlarged the authority of the Reich administration. But the regime's dynamic and polycratic style of government, far from strengthening the civil service, eroded its structure and practices. New, expanded, or hybrid bureaucratic systems—among them the police/SS, the Labor Front (DAF), and the Nazi Party's own numerous organizations—developed haphazardly. These were partly parasitic on traditional civil service departments, but often displaced them and provided new avenues to status and advancement for the ambitious. Although the sheer number of officials grew enormously after 1933, the traditional civil service was no longer readily recognizable in the institutional structures of Nazi Germany. Both institutionally and individually, civil servants were subjected to a combination of political pressure, neglect, and degradation that made a bitter reward for the support they had initially optimistically offered the Nazis.

Given the successive crises of civil service status and prestige between 1918 and 1945, it was a remarkable testimony to the political significance of the institution that its backers were able to reinstate it in postwar West Germany. In the Soviet zone, alongside de-Nazification and administrative reconstruction, the traditional civil service was simply abolished: ordinary labor law was extended to state employees, thus ending the special legal status of the *Beamte*. In the western zones, however, Allied efforts to extend de-Nazification into law reform and democratization were successfully resisted by the parties as well as by civil servants. The institution incorporated into the new Federal Republic by legislation of 1953 and 1965 was thus the recognizable descendant of the traditional *Berufsbeamtentum*, complete with its traditional monopolies and privileges, the predominance of trained jurists in its senior ranks, and the politicization of its ministerial elite.

At the same time, although the postwar administrative apparatus expanded from 2.1 million in 1950 to 3.7 million in 1981, its size was now comparable with the administrations of other European states. Of this expanding number, a declining proportion were *Beamte* proper; this testified to the largely service nature of the expanding sectors, in which too the growing numbers of women were disproportionately employed. These developments may suggest that the administrative balance had tipped toward bureaucratization, but at the same time senior civil servants remained closely identified with the government, and officials were disproportionately represented in the membership of the Bundestag. The decade after 1972 also saw a new phase of direct political control, the so-called *Berufsverbot* (job ban), which was intended to exclude opponents of the constitutional order from public employment.

In the German Democratic Republic (GDR), meanwhile, the socialization of the economy had created a vastly expanded state administration; whereas federalism was restored in West Germany, the GDR became a centralized state in 1952. A Soviet-style cadre policy was applied to the administration, with the aim of ensuring a versatile and loyal elite

schooled in political as well as administrative leadership. Together with changes in disciplinary law and pay structures in the 1960s, the cadre system tended to distinguish the politico-administrative leadership from the mass of functionaries almost as clearly as in the West, if for different reasons. Official commitment to sexual equality increased the number of women dramatically, yet they remained concentrated in the lower and middle ranks, with very few breaking into leadership positions.

The unification of the two German states since 1990 has itself been largely a bureaucratic process, enacted under a treaty of accession that provided for the assimilation of East Germany to West German law and practice. Major elements of administrative restructuring in the east include the restoration of federalism and the abolition of the many state and quasi-state apparatuses, from secret police to health clinics. Officialdom on both sides forestalled a centrally directed purge of the GDR state bureaucracy, providing instead that ministries would take charge of personnel reduction and reeducation in their respective areas.

Jane Caplan

See also Professions

References
Caplan, Jane. *Government without Administration: State and Civil Service in Weimar and Nazi Germany.* Oxford: Oxford University Press, 1988.
Gillis, John. *The Prussian Bureaucracy in Crisis 1840–1860: Origins of an Administrative Ethos.* Palo Alto, CA: Stanford University Press, 1971.
Kunz, Andreas. *Civil Servants and the Politics of Inflation in Germany 1914–1924.* Berlin: de Gruyter, 1986.
Rosenberg, Hans. *Bureaucracy, Aristocracy, and Autocracy: The Prussian Experience.* Boston, MA: Harvard University Press, 1966.
Wunder, Bernd. *Geschichte der Bürokratie in Deutschland.* Frankfurt am Main: Suhrkamp Verlag, 1986.

Class, Heinrich (1860–1954)

Heinrich Class was trained as a lawyer. During his undergraduate studies he came under the strong influence of Heinrich von Treitschke (1834–96) at Berlin University, and of the extremist newspaper publisher, Friedrich Lange, who founded and headed the anti-Semitic and radical nationalist Deutschbund (German League).

In 1908, upon the death of Ernst Hasse, Class became head of the Pan-German League. Unlike his predecessor, Class did not believe in a hands-off relationship with the government. During the chancellorship of Bethmann Hollweg, Class established a close partnership with official circles, especially with Foreign Secretary Alfred von Kiderlen-Wächter (1852–1912). Class and the League accepted government bribe funds for various nationalistic causes. In spite of this, Class strongly attacked the government, both directly and anonymously, whenever he believed it was not upholding Germany's worldwide national interests. Direct attacks were usually made on official policy in the pages of the League's journal *Alldeutsche Blätter*, and Class also wrote a number of anonymous pamphlets and books before 1914, in which he revealed an extremely outspoken attitude to issues of the day (e.g., *Wenn ich der Kaiser wär* [If I were the kaiser], using the pseudonym "Daniel Frymann," and *Deutsche Geschichte* [German history], using the pseudonym "Einhart").

By 1918, frustrated with the German government's inability to win the war, Class proceeded to lead the Pan-Germans into a much more radical direction. In 1920, seeking like-minded allies, he interviewed the fledgling politician Adolf Hitler, whom he rejected as a "savage." Indeed, B. Chamberlain has alleged that in 1921 Class was instrumental in urging Hitler to adopt an anti-Semitic political course.

Otherwise the League generally struggled after World War I, while Class soldiered on as its head. In 1933, he accepted an honorific seat in the Nazi-controlled Reichstag, only to have Hitler summarily dissolve the Pan-German League in 1939.

His 1930 memoirs, *Wider den Strom* (Against the stream), though replete with apologetics, have useful vignettes on some of the leading personages in German politics and the radical nationalist camp, especially during the League's heyday before 1914. Perhaps because his organization was dissolved by Hitler in 1939, Class managed to escape the humiliation of postwar de-Nazification. He died peacefully in 1954.

Class is emblematic of a whole generation of middle-class mandarins who spent their lives upholding an uncompromising radical-nationalist and racist ideology, only to see their dreams utterly shattered in the carnage of World War II.

Ronald D.E. Webster

See also Fatherland Party; Navy League; Pan-German League; Radical Nationalism; Radical Right

References

Chamberlin, B. "The Enemy on the Right: The Alldeutscher Verband in the Weimar Republic, 1918–26." Unpublished doctoral dissertation. University of Maryland, 1972.

Chickering, Roger. *We Men Who Feel Most German: A Cultural Study of the Pan-German League 1886–1914.* Boston, MA: Allen and Unwin, 1984.

Class, Heinrich. *Wider den Strom.* Leipzig: K.F. Koehler, 1932.

Eley, Geoff. *Reshaping the German Right: Radical Nationalism and Political Change after Bismarck.* New Haven, CT: Yale University Press, 1980.

Kruck, A. *Geschichte des Alldeutschen Verbandes 1890–1914.* Wiesbaden: Franz Steiner, 1954.

Schödl, G. *Alldeutscher Verband und deutsche Minderheitenpolitik in Ungarn 1890–1914.* Frankfurt am Main: Lang, 1978.

Webster, R.D.E. "Radical Nationalists of the Reich and the German Problem in Austria-Hungary, 1896–1914." Unpublished doctoral dissertation. University of Toronto, 1974.

Wertheimer, Mildred S. *The Pan-German League 1890–1914.* New York, NY: Columbia University Press, 1924.

Clergy, Protestant

The Protestant clergy has been an important component of the educated middle classes in Germany. Historically, it has assumed the responsibility for transmitting German culture, especially the heritage of the Reformation, to successive generations. The parsonage was widely seen as the appropriate model for society as a whole, both because of the patriarchal structure of the pastor's family and because of the harmony that was presumed to exist in the pastor's home. Thus, the model was both conservative and fundamentally antipluralist.

Until the end of the Second World War, the predominant outlook of Protestant pastors was indeed conservative and intensely nationalistic despite their division into a Lutheran majority and Reformed minority, and despite the theological and political controversies that frequently erupted among them. That conservatism was consistent with the state-supported status of the German Protestant churches, as well as with the status of clergymen as virtual state officials, both of which rendered criticism of government policy difficult. More importantly, the university training of Protestant pastors, their preponderantly middle- and lower middle-class social backgrounds, and the conservatism of the most committed Protestant laypersons (whose favor was crucial if the pastor expected to work effectively in his parish), all contributed to the clergy's lack of sympathy toward democracy, pluralism, socialism, and "cosmopolitanism."

Although most pastors resigned themselves to the collapse of Imperial Germany and the creation of the Weimar Republic, the Nazi movement's apparent respect for the Christian churches, its commitment to eliminating "moral decadence" and rolling back secularization, as well as its passion for restoring Germany as a great power, played well to clerical prejudices. A significant number joined the oppositional Confessing Church once the Nazi regime flouted the theological and institutional integrity of the Protestant churches, but the clergy as a whole, including Confessing ones, dissented minimally from the Third Reich's imperialism, anti-Semitism, and anti-leftism.

The same conservative tendencies resurfaced in the early postwar period, especially as leading Protestant (and Catholic) clerics intervened to protect many individuals with dubious pasts from Allied de-Nazification. Much occurred subsequently to diversify the Protestant pastorate: its openness to candidates with working-class backgrounds, the admission of women, the division of Germany into two states with two different social, economic, and political systems, and the apparent rootedness of parliamentary democracy in the West. In the late 1980s, the clergy in the German Democratic Republic played a critical role in bringing about the demise of the Socialist Unity Party in the name of democratization. Although the Protestant clergy must articulate the message of the Reformation—the central demand of their vocation—it can no longer be presumed to provide a single model for society as a whole.

Shelley Baranowski

See also Confessing Church; Protestant Theology; Protestantism and the Protestant Church; Roman Catholic Church

References

Besier, Gerhard, Jörg Thierfelder, and Ralf Tyra. *Kirche nach der Kapitulation: Das Jahr 1945—eine Dokumentation.* 3 vols. Stuttgart: Kohlhammer, 1989.

Diephouse, David. *Pastors and Pluralism in Württemberg 1918–1933.* Princeton, NJ: Princeton University Press, 1987.

Greiffenhagen, Martin, ed. *Das evangelische Pfarrhaus: Eine Kultur- und Sozialgeschichte.* Stuttgart: Kreuz Verlag, 1984.

Scholder, Klaus. *The Churches and the Third Reich.* Vol. 1. Philadelphia, PA: Fortress Press,1988.

Wright, J.R.C. *"Above Parties": The Political Attitudes of the German Protestant Church Leadership, 1918–1933.* Oxford: Oxford University Press, 1974. Expanded German version: *"Über den Parteien." Die politische Haltung der evangelischen Kirchenführer, 1918–1933.* Göttingen: Vandenhoeck & Ruprecht, 1977.

Clothing

In 1992, the German garment industry employed 167,000 workers, 0.5 percent of all wage and salary earners; apparel production contributed 0.4 percent to the German gross domestic product and 1.4 percent to total industrial production. The clothing industry has always been an important source of female employment. Women have held the most of the jobs in the garment sector for over half a century. Apparel manufacturing has declined as a share of German production and employment for almost 30 years. Clothing as a share of the German gross domestic product peaked in 1965 at 2.7 percent. Employment in the garment sector peaked a year later at 406,000, or 1.9 percent of the total dependent labor force. Advances in productivity, changing consumption patterns, and rising imports account for the declines since then.

Most clothiers that have survived over the past two decades have done so by relying on skilled labor to produce small batches of top-quality, high-priced clothing made out of expensive and sophisticated fabrics, and by adopting "mixed production," that is, using overseas facilities for labor-intensive operations and for providing lower-priced items in fashion lines but doing everything else domestically. The "up-market" and mixed-production strategies have enabled firms to remain profitable despite high German wages and intense competition from abroad. Other German firms have endured by specializing in traditional items, including the North Sea fisherman's cap, the alpine hat, *Lederhosen*, the oak-leaf sports jacket, and other regional attire. These creative business strategies have not, however, halted the relative or even the absolute decline of German apparel manufacturing. The increased economic difficulties resulting from German reunification have served only to exacerbate the sector's downward trend.

Before the twentieth century, most Germans made their own clothing at home. The most affluent ordered specially made articles from tailors. Advances in sewing machines and industrial organization at the turn of the century greatly lowered manufacturing costs and enabled mass-produced "ready to wear" garments virtually to displace home and specialty production within the space of two decades. Although a small amount of home and specialty apparel production has continued to this day, the overwhelming volume of clothing sold in the German market is mass produced. From 1900 to 1930, four regions dominated garment production: Bavaria, Berlin, Saxony, and Westphalia. Three factors, present to varying degrees in each region, explain their success: cheap labor, proximity to textile plants, and closeness to wholesalers. Nazi persecution of Jews all but wiped out the Berlin garment trade, but the other three regions remained important centers of apparel manufacturing.

When Communist authorities tightened control over eastern Germany after World War II, thousands of clothiers fled Saxony for the Franconian region of Bavaria, depleting Saxony of its small producers and precipitating a "start-up boom" of garment companies across the border. Nonetheless, Saxony remained the seat of clothing and textile production in the German Democratic Republic. Communist authorities eventually replaced small producers with mass manufacturing. East Germany concentrated on the mass production of standardized clothing and exported a large portion of its wares to the Soviet Union. In 1989, 102,900 employees, or 1.2 percent of the entire East German labor force, worked in the apparel industry. The collapse of Soviet markets and the arrival of new competition, particularly from Asia, injured the eastern German clothing industry. By 1992, only 19,900 eastern German garment workers still had jobs.

Today, Germany's clothing industry is concentrated in Bavaria and Westphalia. Germany's premier apparel trade fairs take place in Munich and Düsseldorf. Since the war, Düsseldorf has replaced Berlin as Germany's fashion capital. Expensive apparel boutiques populate the Königsallee, or the "Ko" as native Düsseldorfers call it, which is the premier fashion street in Germany. Since the late 1970s, Germans have become increasingly prominent in the fashion world. Karl Lagerfeld, chief designer for Chanel, ranks among the most influential forces in the international fashion scene, and Jil Sander has also become a prominent designer. German fashion houses, such as Hugo Boss, Joop, and Escada, have raised the profile of German fashion to unprecedented heights worldwide.

Stephen J. Silvia

See also Women's Occupations

References

Engel, Jürgen. *Internationale Wirtschaftsbeziehungen und Strukturwandel: Am Beispiel der bundesdeutschen Textil- und Bekleidungsindustrie.* Bremen: Skarabaus, 1985.

Friman, Richard H. *Patchwork Protectionism: Textile Trade Policy in the United States, Japan, and West Germany.* Ithaca, NY: Cornell University Press, 1990.

Wassermann, Wolfram. *Arbeitsgestaltung als Gegenstand gewerkschaftlicher Politik: Zur Soziologie der Arbeitsgestaltung am Beispiel der Textil- und Bekleidungsindustrie.* Bonn: Neue Gesellschaft, 1985.

Coal Industry

Coal has played a vital role in Germany's industrial success. The German coal mining industry has been unique in a number of ways. Mining companies organized themselves in the late nineteenth century into associations, usually called cartels or syndicates. Coal mining has also had extremely close connections to the all-important steel industry and has often had political importance because of its crucial economic role, its large and diverse work force, and the generally conservative mentality of its owners.

The most important coalfield has been in the Ruhr valley in Westphalia, which has been producing between 60 and 80 percent of the country's coal since the mid-nineteenth century. Smaller fields lie in the Saarland and, until it was lost to Poland after World War II, Silesia. Germany has also been exceptional in Europe in that about half of the coal mined has been brown coal, also known as soft coal or lignite, most of which comes from Saxony. Less useful for iron smelting than the more common hard coal, brown coal is suitable for burning for residential heating or power generation.

The Ruhr-Westphalian coal syndicate, founded in 1893 and lasting until World War I, was not a cartel in the classic sense of a monopoly that could control prices. Coal from the Saar and Silesia, and especially British coal imports, always provided competition. The syndicate acted most effectively as a sales organization to promote exports. The syndicate in coke (processed or hardened coal for use in smelting iron) acted similarly. Before World War II, Germany exported more coal than it imported, and it was usually the dominant exporter to Belgium, the Netherlands, France, and Italy. British exports of coal to Germany, however, were often large, especially to Berlin, Hamburg, and other areas on or near the coast.

By 1900, Ruhr coal mines had begun consolidating and merging with iron and steel companies, which were their major customers and whose production was rapidly expanding. The result was integrated firms (*Hüttenwerke*) which produced coal, iron, and steel and which were among the largest corporations in the world outside the United States. Gelsenkirchener, managed by Emil Kirdorf, mined 10 million tons of coal annually, almost half of Belgium's entire production. At the same time, Kirdorf's firm produced 275,000 tons of steel each year. Although advanced in their size and integration of production, these firms did not alter the traditional pick-and-shovel methods used to mine coal. Ruhr coal competed well because the coal veins were larger and more accessible than most of those located elsewhere in Western Europe. German annual coal production between 1870 and 1913 grew from 34 to 277 million tons, while Great Britain's grew from 112 to 292 million.

Before 1914, the coal mining industry experienced extremely high employee turnover rates. Many miners would quit and get a job at other mines. Over a quarter of the Ruhr miners were Polish, most of them German citizens from eastern Prussia. Ruhr employers tried to attract workers by providing housing and welfare benefits, but miners, organized in socialist, Christian, and Polish unions, launched massive strikes in 1889, 1905, and 1912 to obtain higher wages. Mine owners vigorously opposed unions and the socialists, and often allied themselves with conservative political forces in Imperial Germany.

During the interwar period, mine owners adopted electrical drills to mine coal and introduced modern mechanized means to haul coal out of mines. Germany became Europe's leading producer, a position it would hold until passed by the Soviet Union in the 1950s. Brown coal especially became increasingly important for electric power generation. As a political factor, coal mining lost influence to the steel industry and particularly to the newer chemical and electrical sectors. The chemical trust I.G. Farben was in charge of the Nazi program of producing oil from coal. In the late 1930s, coal exports nonetheless paid for vital raw materials for Nazi rearmament. During both world wars, coal was a crucial element in Germany's war effort. By failing to attract workers to mining and to provide adequate food for miners, however, the government failed to raise coal production and thereby eventually weakened its mobilization of the economy.

After World War II, joining German coal to French iron ore served as a prime argument for creating the European Coal and Steel Community, founded in 1950. Germany began the postwar era heavily dependent on coal, but industry and government allowed oil and gas to take much of its place. Between 1957 and 1967, oil went from supplying 11 percent to 48 percent of energy needs. Thanks to government intervention and a booming economy, the number of coal miners dropped by half without causing a major political crisis. Generating electricity became the primary function of coal. In 1975, 58 percent of West Germany's coal went to electricity, and only 16 percent to the iron and steel industry. Residential heating, transportation, and gas production absorbed the rest.

Unlike many other countries, West Germany did not expand coal production to offset the high price of oil during the late 1970s and 1980s. Because of environmental concerns, the high costs of mining the older veins of the Ruhr, and the cheapness of imported coal, Germany instead emphasized nuclear power and conservation. The government subsidized one-third of the mines, and it gradually shut down unprofitable operations. Between its postwar zenith in 1964 and 1986, coal production diminished from 255 to 201 million tons annually. Yet West Germany, as late as the early 1990s, relied on coal for over 30 percent of its energy needs, more than any other major industrial country. East Germany, by contrast, raised production enormously, first to promote industrialization, then to avoid importing expensive oil and gas. Production went from 104 million tons in 1947 to 315 million in 1986, virtually all of it brown coal. Repairing the ecological damage caused by burning excessive amounts of brown coal in the East and finding a more acceptable mix of energy sources were two of the major tasks united Germany faced in the 1990s.

Carl Strikwerda

See also I.G. Farbenindustrie AG; Postwar European Integration and Germany; Ruhr Region; Ruhrlade; The Saar; Saxony; Steel Industry; Trade Unions

References

Clark, John G. *The Political Economy of World Energy.* Chapel Hill, NC: University of North Carolina Press, 1991.

Feldman, Gerald and Klaus Tenfelde, eds. *Workers, Owners and Politics in Coal Mining: An International Comparison of Industrial Relations.* Oxford: Berg, 1990.

Gillingham, John. *Industry and Politics in the Third Reich: Ruhr Coal, Hitler and Europe.* London: Methuen, 1985.

Hardach, Karl. *The Political Economy of Germany in the Twentieth Century.* Berkeley, CA: University of California Press, 1976.

Henderson, W.O. *The Rise of German Industrial Power, 1834–1914.* Berkeley, CA: University of California Press, 1975.

Hickey, Stephen. *Workers in Imperial Germany: The Miners in the Ruhr.* Oxford: Oxford University Press, 1985.

Parker, William and Norman Pounds. *Coal and Steel in Western Europe.* Bloomington, IN: Indiana University Press, 1957.

Spencer, Elaine Glovka. *Management and Labor in Imperial Germany: Ruhr Industrialists as Employers, 1896–1914.* New Brunswick, NJ: Rutgers University Press, 1984.

Stockder, A.H. *History of the German Trade Associations of the German Coal Industry.* New York, NY: Henry Holt, 1924.

Codetermination (*Mitbestimmung*)

Codetermination is a system of relations between employers and employees (and their trade unions) that, instead of assuming a state of irreconcilable conflict between the two sides of industry (an "us" and "them" mentality), tries to establish modes of cooperation by creating special collaborative institutions.

Two different models of codetermination evolved. Employers, insofar as they were not wedded to the idea of conflict between capital and labor, were eager to preserve their position of dominance. Codetermination under this model was therefore unequal. Employees and unions had the right to participate in company affairs, but employers (management and shareholders) had the final voice in decisionmaking. By contrast, the unions during the Weimar Republic promoted a model that advocated parity between capital and labor (*paritätische Mitbestimmung*). Some trade unionists regarded parity as a step to transforming capitalism into socialism. Employer resistance to this parity model was fierce in the 1920s and again in 1947, when *paritätische Mitbestimmung* was to be introduced into a number of Ruhr steel trusts. At this point, capital and labor were to have had equal representation on the companies' supervisory boards under a "neutral" chairman; a "worker director" representing the workforce was to have been added, with equal rights, to the management board.

Because the British occupation authorities favored this first practical experiment in parity, employer resistance this time proved futile. The latter tried to reverse the fait accom-pli of 1947 in 1950–51 after the founding of the Federal Republic of Germany (FRG). The trade unions, on the other hand, wanted to extend the steel parity model to other large enterprises. After a fierce political battle, parity survived and was indeed extended to all large coal and steel companies. All other branches came to be governed not by the *Montanmitbestimmungsgesetz* (industrial codetermination law), but by the *Betriebsverfassungsgesetz* (industrial relations law) of 1952, which granted the work force limited rights of information and consultation but no parity. Although no longer regarded as a means of transforming capitalism into socialism, parity as a question reemerged in the 1960s. The reformist mood of that period and the balance of political forces in West Germany resulted in an extension of codetermination, though not quite to the level of parity. After long debates, the 1976 *Mitbestimmungsgesetz* (codetermination law) stopped short of a balanced representation on the supervisory board. The representatives of shareholders and management retained the majority.

Over some 45 years of *Mitbestimmung* practice, the balance sheet looks favorable. Although employers always saw the 1951 parity law as the thin end of the wedge, codetermination has in fact contributed to promoting peace between capital and labor and has facilitated the comparatively conflict-free experience of industrial relations in the FRG during the past four decades.

Volker R. Berghahn

See also Adenauer, Konrad; Berg, Fritz; Central Association of German Industrialists; Trade Unions, 1945–90

References

Blumenthal, W.M. *Codetermination in the German Steel Industry.* Princeton, NJ: Princeton University Press, 1956.

Muszynski, B. *Wirtschaftliche Mitbestimmung zwischen Konflikt- und Harmoniekonzeptionen.* Meisenheim: A. Hain, 1975.

Spiro, H.J. *The Politics of German Codetermination.* Cambridge, MA: Harvard University Press, 1958.

Thum, H. *Mitbestimmung in der Montanindustrie.* Stuttgart: Deutsche Verlags-Anstalt, 1982.

The Cold War and Germany

The Cold War evolved from World War II; the partition of Germany into two states was one of the main features of the Cold War and remained a central conflict until its end in 1989.

The wartime coalition of the United Kingdom, the Soviet Union, and the United States contained within it political tensions, such as Soviet expectations for a second front in Western Europe in 1942–43 and Western fears of a Soviet separate peace with the National Committee for a Free Germany. The Cold War also grew out of differences in political systems. Nevertheless, joint discussions of the German question from Tehran in 1943 to Yalta and Potsdam in 1945 brought some understandings. The matter of (temporary) zonal boundaries for immediate military occupation was re-

solved quickly in 1944. These temporary delineations, however, became the boundaries between the two German states for the whole Cold War era. Differences among the victorious powers increased at the end of war. At first Poland, then Iran, China, the Turkish straits, and the social revolution in Eastern and Central Europe were the sources of dispute; finally came the German question.

Although originally the Allies had planned to dismember Germany, at Potsdam they agreed to maintain German unity. Yet the Potsdam reparations agreement brought dissent: economic unity, which was an agreed aim, quickly proved unattainable because each victor was entitled to take its reparations with priority out of its own zone. This the Soviets did extensively. After the founding of the Bizone (January 1, 1947), Americans and Britons, and later also the French, tended to consolidate their respective zones economically and politically, ultimately (1949) forming a separate western state based on their own values. The Soviet Union forced a social revolution (land reform and socialization) in its zone, but continued to claim German unity according to its interpretation of the Potsdam agreement. The two German states created in 1949 grew out of the respective zones of influence established in Germany at war's end, but the division of Germany was also the product of the Cold War, which increasingly centered on Germany, as the Berlin Blockade (1948–49) confirmed.

The outbreak of the Korean War in 1950 heightened fears that the Cold War could escalate into a third world war should the German situation deteriorate any further. Many Germans became convinced that Communist subversion and possible aggression in Central Europe could force the Western powers to answer with an outright war. Certainly, the Cold War was crucial to the consolidation of the Federal Republic of Germany (FRG) and to Chancellor Adenauer's policy of anchoring the FRG in the West. At the same time, both strategies hindered reunification. Similarly, the Western powers tended to prioritize detente, especially by disarming or disen-

gaging over a solution of the German question. From the late 1950s, reunification became a rhetorical gesture whose primary purpose was to prevent the rise of new nationalist sentiments in the FRG, which in turn might lead to a separate arrangement between the FRG and the Soviet Union.

For the USSR, the German Democratic Republic (GDR) increasingly became the western keystone of its European zone of influence. The economic and political consolidation of this territory thus gained priority, but without much success. This was the framework for the second Berlin crisis (1958–61). Superficially viewed, Secretary General Krushchev wanted to debate the status of West Berlin, but his principal aim was to have the GDR recognized internationally through separate peace treaties with both of the German states. The Soviet leaders finally retreated from wishing to conclude separate peace treaties, which left the erection of the Berlin Wall (August 13, 1961) as a minimal solution. Both before and after the erection of the Wall, Berlin remained in danger of direct military confrontation—with which Krushchev tried to threaten American President John F. Kennedy at the Vienna summit in May 1961.

After 1963, the Western allies and the USSR took small steps toward achieving a modus vivendi in the German and Berlin questions. Tensions increased in East Asia, where the Vietnam war became a kind of war by proxy. In concordance with its Western partners, especially the United States, the FRG succeeded at introducing a series of eastern treaties, known as *Ostpolitik* (1969–74), in order to normalize relations with the Soviet Union, the GDR, Poland, and Czechoslovakia. These treaties did not bring formal acceptance of the GDR as a sovereign nation-state by the FRG, but they facilitated connections between the two German states. The partition of Germany (defenses at the frontier, the Berlin Wall) could not be overcome.

When Chancellor Helmut Schmidt pressed for NATO decisions to station new medium-range missiles if the Warsaw Pact countries would not draw back theirs, the question of deployment in Germany again formed a central point of conflict during this phase of the Cold War. The firmness of the West and especially the FRG, where deployment had already begun, led to a deep-rooted rethinking of the matter of confrontation through armaments. In this renewed Cold War between the United States and the Soviet Union during the 1980s, the two German states strove to uphold their relatively good bilateral relations ("Community of Responsibility"; "No more war from German territory!").

After 1985, when Mikhail Gorbachev took office in the Soviet Union, the idea gained support that confrontation through armaments could not be won either economically or politically. The new Soviet leadership wanted disarmament also as a prerequisite to liberalize the regimes in Eastern Europe according to national models. It may be that since 1986–87 Gorbachev also took unification of Germany into account, but he did not give up the claim of a reformed socialist society and a new consolidation of Russian influence. His policy was one of the prerequisites for the accelerating reunification process since 1989, which ended the Cold War, at least for the time being.

Jost Dülffer

See also Adenauer, Konrad; American-German Relations; Berlin; Berlin Blockade; Berlin Wall; Federal Republic of Germany: Foreign Policy; German Democratic Republic: Foreign Relations; *Ostpolitik*; Soviet-German Relations

References

Doerr, Juergen C. *The Big Powers and the German Question, 1941–1990: A Selected Bibliographical Guide.* New York, NY: Garland, 1992.

Foschepoth, Josef, ed. *Kalter Krieg und Deutsche Frage: Deutschland im Widerstreit der Machte, 1945–1952.* Göttingen: Vandenhoeck & Ruprecht, 1985.

Hillgruber, Andreas. *Europa in der Weltpolitik der Nachkriegszeit 1945–1963.* Ed. Jost Dulffer. 4th ed. Munich: R. Oldenbourg Verlag, 1993.

Loth, Wilfried. *The Division of the World 1941–1955.* New York, NY: St. Martin's Press, 1988.

———. *Ost-West-Konflikt und deutsche Frage.* Munich: DTV, 1989.

Poiger, Uta. "Rock 'n' roll, Female Sexuality, and the Cold War Battle over German Identities." *Journal of Modern History* 68 (September, 1996), 577–616.

Colonies and Colonial Society

Germany's brief career as a colonial power began in 1884–85 with the seizure of the coastal areas of Cameroon and Togo in West Africa, Southwest Africa (now Namibia), German East Africa (now mostly Tanzania), northeastern New Guinea, and a number of Pacific islands. Later, the boundaries of the colonies were defined through diplomatic interaction with other powers, and a few other possessions were added: part of Samoa, island groups in Micronesia, and the naval colony of Kiaochow in China. Germany completely lost her colonies in World War I.

The diplomacy and politics surrounding Germany's appearance as a colonial power were more important than any economic benefit Germany acquired from having overseas possessions. The idea of colonies as settlement areas for German emigrants and as trading bases harkened to pre-1848 liberalism, but an effective colonial movement was a product of national unification, economic expansion, and depression in the 1870s. The colonial movement, especially as manifested in organizations such as the German Colonial Society (1887), created some of the structural and ideological framework within which German radical nationalism developed its characteristic forms. Chancellor Otto von Bismarck, who had earlier opposed colonialism, decided to make Germany a colonial power in the early 1880s partly to attract the support of the mostly middle-class nationalists who joined the colonial movement and to draw them away from the liberal parties. Bismarck was not willing, however, to take large diplomatic risks in the race for colonies, and he wanted to limit the size of the overseas empire for financial reasons. The colonial movement therefore turned against him in the late 1880s.

After 1890, successive German governments attempted to rationalize the colonial empire and to develop the colonies as adjuncts to the German economy. These policies were increasingly attacked by the radical right (especially by the Pan-German League) as insufficiently expansionary, unsupportive of German settlers, and inadequately assertive of Germany's position as a great power. Much of German colonial politics centered around these attacks, to which issues of administration, economic development, and policy toward indigenous peoples were subordinated. The Colonial Society, with an establishment-based leadership, tended to support government development policy, but it had a radical wing that also sometimes attacked the government.

The impact of German rule on the colonies varied largely with the nature of economic exploitation. In Southwest Africa, development policies in support of European settlers engendered an indigenous revolt between 1904 and 1907 and a military campaign that came close to exterminating the Herero people. East Africa, the largest and potentially wealthiest colony, was the scene of efforts to develop both an African peasant economy and a settler society. It had its own revolt: the Maji Maji rebellion of 1905.

The Colonial Society remained active during the Weimar years, lobbying for the return of the colonies. Adolf Hitler paid lip service to colonial aspirations but refused to make overseas colonies a priority of the Third Reich.

Woodruff D. Smith

See also Bülow, Bernhard von; Imperialism; Rohrbach, Paul; *Weltpolitik*; Wilhelm II

References

Bley, Helmut. *South-West Africa under German Rule 1894–1914.* Trans. Hugh Ridley. Evanston, IL: Northwestern University Press, 1971.

Hausen, Karin. *Deutsche Kolonialherrschaft in Afrika: Wirtschaftsinterresse und Kolonialverwaltung in Kamerun vor 1914.* Zürich: Atlantis-Verlag, 1970.

Iliffe, John. *Tanganyika under German Rule 1905–1912*.
Cambridge: Cambridge University Press, 1969.

Smith, Woodruff D. *The German Colonial Empire*. Chapel
Hill, NC: University of North Carolina Press, 1978.

———. *The Ideological Origins of Nazi Imperialism*. New
York, NY: Oxford University Press, 1986.

Wehler, Hans-Ulrich. *Bismarck und der Imperialismus*.
Cologne: Kiepenheuer & Witsch, 1969.

Comedy

To examine German-language comedy from 1871 is to begin
in medias res. By the mid-nineteenth century, an established
body of comic dramatists had taken the works of Shakespeare
and Molière as models, although, unlike the latter, no prominent German playwright is known primarily for comedies.
Best known among the early comedies are G.E. Lessing's
Minna von Barnhelm, 1767, and H.W. Kleist's *Amphitrion*,
1807, and *Der zerbrochene Krug* (The broken jug), 1808.

Before the twentieth century, comedies characteristically
had happy endings, very often symbolized with a marriage,
and most were utopian. According to the eminent dramatist
and aesthetician Friedrich Schiller (1759–1805), comedy has
an even more important goal than tragedy, "and it would, if
it achieved [this goal], make all tragedy superfluous and impossible" (*Über Naive und Sentimentalische Dichtung* [*About
Naïve and Sentimental Writing*, 1795–96]). For nineteenth-
century theorists (e.g., A.W. Schlegel, G.F. Hegel, and F.Th.
Vischer), comedy also implied hope, a concept on which Ernst
Bloch expanded in the twentieth century.

The conservatively censurious edicts of the Congress of
Vienna (1815) brought a hiatus in the creation or performance of socially relevant comedies in the German-speaking
world for almost a century. Although comedies since recognized for their quality were written—for example, C.D.
Grabbe's *Scherz, Satire, Ironie und tiefere Bedeutung* (published
as *Joke, Satire, Irony, and Deeper Meaning*), 1827 and G.
Büchner's *Leonce und Lena*, 1836—they were not publicly
performed until much later (1907 and 1911, respectively, for
the examples above). Rural and regional comedies (*Volksstücke*)
(e.g., the Austrians Johann Nestroy's *Lumpazivagabündis*,
1833, and Ferdinand Raimund's *Der Verschwender* [The wast-
rel], 1834), continued to be written and presented in Germany and Austria. Indeed, the development of comedy in the
two countries cannot be separated. However, the more individual, less dialogic, forms of prose and lyric took precedence
over drama during most of the nineteenth century.

In the century's final two decades, however, a socially
critical approach to comedy developed, the style of which has
since characterized the best German-language comedy. It
evolved from the affirmative concept of a basically harmless
Humor. Unlike the American definition, the German term
implies conciliation with the darker side of life (*Wahrig*) and
the resigned or restrained irony of earlier dramas. The twentieth-century comedies are grounded in satire—didactic and/
or socially critical—which at times turns into the grotesque
or absurd. The happy ending either suggests its own obverse
or is abandoned entirely in favor of the open form. Comedy

often becomes tragicomedy. The audience is kept distanced
from the action and expected not only to think beyond the
final scene but also to undergo a change as a result of this critical thinking process. When, around 1880, naturalism became
the dominant aesthetic, the way for a more aggressive form of
comedy was opened.

Naturalism, a short-lived style concerned primarily with
the plight of the lower classes, produced one lasting comedy,
written by the Silesian Gerhart Hauptmann (1862–1946), *Der
Biberpelz* (published as *The Beaver Coat*), 1893, an analytical
comedy about a washerwoman, Mother Wolffen, who steals the
coat and gets away with it. Hauptmann satirizes the authoritarian bureaucratic strata, represented by the arrogant Berlin
official Wehrhahn. His 1911 Berlin tragicomedy, *Die Ratten*
(published as *The Rats*), relies on irony to comment negatively
on a morally bankrupt society. Between the 1870s and the early
twentieth century, the Viennese Ludwig Anzengruber (1839–
89) and the Bavarian Ludwig Thoma (1867–1921) were the
best known of those who wrote comedies set in a rural/pro-
vincial milieu. Whereas Anzengruber's comedies remain fixed
in nineteenth-century conciliatory humor, Thoma's (e.g., *Moral*,
1908) are grounded in a darker social satire.

Representative of the turn-of-the-century aesthetic, then
later of neoromanticism, was the Viennese Hugo von Hofmannsthal (1874–1929) who, in addition to his comic opera
lyrics (e.g., *Der Rosenkavalier* [Cavalier of the rose], *Adriadne auf
Naxos* [Adriadne on Naxos]), created two hopefully positive
comedies, *Der Schwierige* (published as *The Difficult Man*),
1920, a love story about Count Hans Karl Bühl, and *Der
Unbstechliche* (published as *The Incorruptible Man*), 1923, the
hero of which is the servant Theodor. Hofmannthal's contemporary Carl Sternheim (1878–1942) is the only successful dramatist of comedies among the expressionists (1910–25) and is
remembered primarily for *Die Hose* (published as *The Underpants*), first of the "Maske" tetralogy of 1911, 1914, 1915, and
1923. It offers ironic criticism of the Berlin bourgeoisie. Carl
Zuckmayer's (1896–1977) first, lusty, life-confirming *Volksstück*
comedy, *Der fröhliche Weinberg* (published as *The Happy Vineyard*), 1925, was followed by his tragicomedy, *Der Hauptmann
von Köpenick* (published as *The Captain from Köpenick*), 1931,
called a "German fairytale," which parodied Prussian militarism by using a uniform to symbolize the emptiness of its
authoritarianism. Further representatives of the "new" *Volksstück*
were Marieluise Fleisser (1901–73) with *Pioniere in Ingolstadt*
(published as *The Civil Engineering Corps in Ingolstadt*), 1928,
rev. 1968, and the Austrian Ödön von Horvath (1901–38) with
Geschichten aus dem Wiener Wald (published as *Stories from the
Vienna Woods*), 1931; both works are colored by the black humor of social criticism.

Determinative for modern comedy, not only in Germany,
but internationally as well, are the works and theories of
Bertolt Brecht (1898–1956). Whereas comic elements pervade
most of his dramas in the form of parody, satire, and exaggeration, two of his exile works, *Der aufhaltsame Aufstieg des Arturo
Ui* (published as *The Avoidable Rise of Arturo Ui*), 1941, and
Herr Puntila und sein Knecht Matti (Mr. Puntila and his servant Matti), 1948, embody the principles of comedy most

clearly. Mr. Puntila, in a plot reminiscent of Charlie Chaplin's *City Lights*, actually parodies Zuckmayer's *Der fröhliche Weinberg*.

With Karl Marx, Brecht believed that the last stage of a historical period is its comedy, because a cornerstone of the mature Brecht's dramatic theory is that art should entertain, which fits with the Marxian premise that people should "cheerfully leave their past behind." Formulator of the concept of the "alienation effect" (*Verfremdungseffekt*), Brecht used it didactically in conjunction with his comedies as with his oeuvre generally. Of the other playwrights in exile, Franz Werfel's (1890–1945) works stand out. His *Jacobowsky und der Oberst* (published as *Jacobowsky and the Colonel*) 1943, is "the comedy of [the] tragedy" of the eponynous Jew fleeing the Nazis.

In the former German Democratic Republic (GDR), Peter Hacks (e.g., *Moritz Tassow*, 1962) is the only author known primarily for his comedies. He worked within the framework of socialist realism, a style predicated on conciliatory humor not unlike that of the nineteenth century. The comedies of the Swiss Max Frisch (1911–91) (e.g., *Biedermann und die Brandstifter* [published as *Biedermann and the Arsonists*], 1958), and Friedrich Dürrenmatt [1921–90] reflect Brecht and encompass the grotesque and the absurd. In relation to *Der Besuch der alten Dame* (published as *The Visit*), 1956, Dürrenmatt, who theorized reactively on the basis of his own works (cf. *Theaterschriften und -reden* [Theater articles and speeches], 1966) declared that no longer tragedy, but only comedy was possible. Both his and Frisch's plays imply the tragedy behind the comedy.

In the 1960s Günter Grass (1927–) (*Die bösen Köche* [The nasty cooks], 1961) and Tankred Dorst (1925–) (*Die Kurve* [The curve], 1960) created socially critical farces with grotesque exaggeration and absurd situations. The following decade, the Austrians Thomas Bernhard (1931–89) (e.g., *Die Macht der Gewohnheit* [published as *The Power of Habit*, 1974]) and Wolfgang Bauer (1941–) (e.g., *Silvester oder Das Massaker im Hotel Sacher* [published as *Silvester or The Massacre in the Hotel Sacher*, 1971]) produced dark comedies, reflecting German society a century after its genesis in 1871 with bitter, uncompromising satire. And the comedy of Botho Strauss (1944–) in *Der Park* (published as *The Park*), 1983, is uncomfortably painful to watch in its sharp observation of the banalities of the alienated contemporary city-dweller. But the author, actor, director, and filmmaker Herbert Achternbusch (1938–), portrays the absurdities of rural and urban Bavaria as paradigms for the Western world in his comedies for stage (e.g., *Der Stiefel und sein Socken* [The boot and its sock], 1994) and film (e.g., *Punch Drunk*, 1987).

Beyond the stage, the dramatic media of the radio play and film have offered significant forums of comedy for women. In the 1950s and 1960s, the Austrians Ilse Aichinger (1921–) and Ingeborg Bachmann (1926–73) excelled in dramas for the radio reflecting aspects of the grotesque and absurd, colored by subtle humor and irony. In film, the range is from Helke Sander's (1937–) strong feminist satire and irony (e.g., *Der Anfang aller Liebe ist das Schrecken* [published as *The Beginning of All Love is Horror*], 1983) through Doris Dörrie's (1955–)

farcical movies in the screwball tradition (e.g., *Männer* [Men], 1985, and *Geld* [Money], 1989), to Ulrike Ottinger's (1942–) ironically grotesque, elaborately exotic persiflages, tinged with black humor (e.g., *Freak Orlando*, 1981). Ottinger has also staged two plays by Elfriede Jelinek (1946–) (*Clara S.*, 1983 and *Begierde und Fahrerlaubnis* . . . [published as *Greed and Permission to Drive* (a pornography), 1986]), with her even bitterer comedy, represents women's contribution to Germany's stage at the end of the century. The 1993 hit of the spring theater season was a travesty by Rolf Hochhuth (1931–) whose 1960s documentary plays and 1970s comedy, *Die Hebamme* (published as *The Midwife*), 1971, made him an author to be reckoned with. In 1993, his *Wessies in Weimar* ("Wessies" is the derogatory term with which East Germans refer to those from West Germany) was "the play to see," despite mixed reviews. In myriad ways creators of German comedy are leaving the century laughing, more openly but less hopefully than they began it.

Sheila Johnson

See also Bachmann, Ingeborg; Brecht, Bertolt; Dürrenmatt, Friedrich; Federal Republic of Germany: Literature; Frisch, Max; German Democratic Republic: Literature and Literary Life; Grass, Günter; Hauptmann, Gerhart; Hochhuth, Rolf; Hofmannsthal, Hugo von; Imperial Germany: Literature; National Socialist Germany: Literature; Satire; Sternheim, Carl; Strauss, Botho; Weimar Germany: Literature; Zuckmayer, Carl

References

Arntzen, Helmut. "Vorwort." *Komödiensprache*. Ed. H. Arntzen. Münster: Aschendorff, 1988.

Brauerhoch, Annette et al., ed. "Komödien." *Frauen und Film* 53 (1992).

Durzak, Manfred. *Dürrenmatt, Frisch, Weiss. Deutsches Drama der Gegenwart zwischen Kritik und Utopie*. Stuttgart: Philipp Reclam Jr., 1972.

Freund, Winfried, ed. *Deutsche Komödien*. Munich: W. Fink, 1988.

Grimm, Reinhold and Walter Hinck. *Zwischen Satire und Utopie*. Frankfurt am Main: Suhrkamp, 1982.

Guthke, Karl S. *Modern Tragicomedy: An Investigation into the Nature of the Genre*. New York, NY: Random House, 1968.

Heidsieck, Arnold. *Das Groteske und das Absurde im modernen Drama*. Stuttgart: Kohlhammer, 1969.

Hein, Jürgen. "Die Komödie." *Formen der Literatur*. Ed. Otto Knörrich. Stuttgart: Alfred Kroner, 1981.

Hinck, Walter. *Die deutsche Komödie*. Düsseldorf: A. Bagel, 1977.

Kiermeier-Debre, Joseph. *Eine Komödie und auch keine*. Stuttgart: Steiner, 1989.

Lorenz, Dagmar. "Humor bei zeitgenossischen Autorinnen." *The Germanic Review* 62 (Winter 1987), 28–36.

Martini, Fritz. *Lustspiele—und das Lustspiel*. Stuttgart: Klett, 1974.

Paulsen, Wolfgang, ed. *Die deutsche Komödie im zwanzigsten Jahrhundert*. Heidelberg: L. Stiehm, 1972.

Composers

The major composers in the German-speaking countries have been important influences in the dissemination of music in the last centuries. They are often classifiable according to the styles and forms most prevalent in the various movements listed below, which are not always exclusive.

Romanticism, which had been influenced by the innovations of Ludwig van Beethoven, Franz Schubert, Robert Schumann, and Carl Maria von Weber in the early nineteenth century, had developed two opposing factions in the latter part of the century. The idea of *program music* influenced by extramusical (often literary) ideas had been exemplified in opera and the solo song since the Baroque period, at least; exploitation of the concept in instrumental works, including the concert overture, symphonic poem, and symphony, was pioneered by Franz Liszt (1811–86), who bore a strong influence on the post-Romantic composers Hugo Wolf, Richard Strauss (1864–1949), Hans Pfitzner (1869–1949), and Erich Wolfgang Korngold (1897–1957).

The antithesis of the programmatic idea, found in *absolute music,* is best illustrated by the works of Johannes Brahms (1833–97), who widely influenced composers outside the German orbit in such forms as symphony, concerto, and chamber music. These forms had been used in their absolute state since the time of Mozart and Beethoven, but Brahms stood as champion of the absolute in the classical formal tradition. In many ways, the same may be said of Anton Bruckner (1824–96), who—while influenced by Richard Wagner (1813–83) in his orchestral and harmonic language—wrote ten symphonies as conservative in form and free from outside influence as any of Brahms's music.

Gustav Mahler (1860–1911) stood apart as a bridge between the two antithetical factions. Blatantly programmatic in his early symphonies, he never entirely abandoned the traditional forms; increasingly after the turn of the century, he became subtle in his application of programmatic influences and quite open in the use of absolute symphonic forms and almost Baroque contrapuntal techniques. By the end of his life, the programmatic element was almost entirely confined to his songs, the other major form in his oeuvre.

The immediate beneficiaries of Mahler's influence were Arnold Schönberg (1874–1951) and his students, including Alban Berg (1885–1935), Anton von Webern (1883–1945), and Egon Wellesz, who have become known as the Second Viennese School. These composers reworked long-established genres: opera, *Lieder,* chamber music, and orchestral works (although the symphony, which had been the backbone of Mahler's work, was transformed so much as to be unrecognizable and was often given a deceptive title). The innovations of Schönberg and his followers were harmonic rather than formal: they abandoned the traditional major/minor tonalities and went beyond chromaticism, ultimately arriving at dodecaphony or serialism (the use of the twelve tones in the octave in non-traditional progressions without reference to a tonal center).

Composers later in the twentieth century were profoundly influenced by these ideas (allowing for a period of disfavor during the Nazi regime). Among those who continued to exploit the twelve-tone system based on the innovations introduced by the Second Viennese School were Wolfgang Fortner, Rolf Liebermann, and Boris Blacher.

The influence of expressionism among composers was rather widespread beginning with the Second Viennese School (it may have been foreshadowed in Mahler's late works), but it cannot be considered a musical style in its own right. It was rather an extramusical influence in which content was illustrated by musical techniques that were often deliberately shocking and realistic, as in Berg's opera *Lulu.*

The use of jazz as an influence in concert music and opera seems to have developed from the ragtime style in the United States in the early decades of the twentieth century; it was exploited by George Gershwin and Darius Milhaud before German composers gave it serious attention. It was probably entirely independent of the twelve-tone style being concurrently used among the Austrian composers, being absolutely tonal and far less dissonant than the other style; there is no reason to consider it as a reaction to the extremes of the serial technique. German-speaking composers began to use the jazz style in the 1920s and 1930s; its eminent exponents were Paul Dessau (1894–1979), Hanns Eisler (1898–1962), and Kurt Weill (1900–50). The style was condemned by the Nazis as decadent, and the works of these composers (who survived by going into exile) were banned from performance in the Third Reich. Jazz was never again exploited in the German-speaking countries to a similar extent.

The dodecaphonists were taught by Schönberg to respect the long-established forms, but many younger composers abandoned the forms more or less completely, resulting in a backlash from composers considered *neoclassical.* The most prominent representative of this movement in the first half of the twentieth century was Paul Hindemith (1895–1963), who believed that the wildest dissonances should be controlled by order in forms that had existed since the baroque and classical periods. Hindemith's embrace of clarity in musical style should have sufficed to make him acceptable to the Nazi regime; but for other reasons his music was proscribed, and it was Carl Orff (1895–1982) and Werner Egk who carried the neoclassical torch in the Nazi countries and continued to do so internationally after World War II. A more recent example of neoclassicism is the Austrian Gottfried von Einem.

Other movements, including electronic and aleatoric music, have affected composers to a variable degree. The long-term effects of these styles among modern composers in Germany and Austria is questionable; Karlheinz Stockhausen (1928–) has experimented with many of these styles, but cannot be categorized by any one of them more than another.

The only movement among composers in the nineteenth and twentieth centuries that does not appear to have achieved widespread currency among the best German and Austrian composers is nationalism. The concept of nationalism in music was certainly influential in the case of Wagner, and it was therefore exploited by the Nazis who attempted to purge non-German influences from music in the Third Reich; but the movement was not successful in attracting the best composers of the era. Ironically, the German composers were generally too cosmopolitan to be influenced by a style based on political xenophobia and oppression.

Susan M. Filler

See also Ballet; Berg, Alban; Brahms, Johannes; Bruckner, Anton; Chamber Music; Choral Music; Dessau, Paul; Eisler, Hanns; Henze, Hans Werner; Hindemith, Paul; Keyboard Music; Liszt, Franz; Mahler, Gustav; Music Festivals; National Socialist Germany: Music; Operetta; Orchestral Music; Orff, Carl; Pfitzner, Hans; Reger, Max; Schönberg, Arnold; Stockhausen, Karlheinz; Strauss, Richard; Wagner, Richard; Webern, Anton; Weill, Kurt; Wolf, Hugo

References

Leibowitz, Rene. *Schoenberg and His School.* New York, NY: Philosophical Library, 1949.

Nebehay, Christian Michael. *Wien speziell—Musik um 1900: wo finde ich Berg, Brahms, Mahler, Schönberg, Hauer, Wolf, Bruckner, Strauss, Zemlinsky, Webern: Leben und Werk/Gedenk- und Wirkungsstätten/Museen und Sammlungen in Wien.* Vienna: Christian Brandstatter, 1984.

Neighbour, Oliver Wray. *The New Grove Second Viennese School: Schoenberg, Webern, Berg.* With Paul Griffiths and George Perle. New York, NY: Norton, 1983.

Rickett, Richard. *Music and Musicians in Vienna.* Vienna: Prachner, 1973.

Stuckenschmidt, Hans Heinz. *Germany and Central Europe.* Twentieth Century Composers, vol. 2. London: Weidenfeld and Nicolson, 1970.

Concentration Camps

Having abdicated all moral and judicial responsibilities, the Nazi regime established an extensive network of concentration camps. Controlled and administered by the SS, they were places of experimentation where specially selected and trained personnel introduced new techniques of oppression, terror, and mass murder. The goal was to create a society that had no place for persons who on political, social, or racial grounds were declared to be "enemies of the German people and nation." The brutalities unleashed went beyond all historical experience and the powers of the human imagination. Inmates lived a life on borrowed time, exposed to isolation and demoralization, forced labor and starvation, torture and "medical experiments," killings and other despotic acts. Incarcerated often under the pretext of "protective custody," they were divided into groups and subgroups, categorized and marked as political or religious opponents, resisters or hostages, "asocial" or criminals, homosexuals or mentally retarded, Jews or Gypsies.

In the initial years of Nazi rule the camps served primarily as special centers of detention designed to punish and "re-educate" political opponents, especially Communists. Dachau concentration camp, near Munich, was established in early 1933 and became the model for the structure and daily routine of all subsequent camps. From 1936—in the course of war preparations and expansion—economic considerations played an important part. Camps such as Buchenwald and

Dachau Concentration Camp Memorial. Courtesy of German Embassy, Ottawa.

Sachsenhausen, Flossenbürg and Mauthausen, Ravensbrück and Neuengamme were erected, providing not only the growing SS industry but also state and private enterprises with a vast reservoir of cheap slave labor.

A third function was allocated to camps constructed after 1941 in occupied Poland. Designed as extermination camps or "death camps," they were centers for the implementation of the program of the Final Solution. More than three million European Jews, but also Gypsies, Poles, Russians, and other "undesirable" elements, were put to death by poison gas. The number of Jews gassed in Chelmno is estimated at 320,000, in Belzec at 600,000, in Sobibor at 250,000, in Treblinka at 900,000, and in Auschwitz at far beyond one million.

In January 1945, some 700,000 prisoners of various nationalities were still held in camps (511,537 males and 202,674 females) guarded by 40,000 SS personnel. With the advance of the Allied troops the camps were gradually abandoned. Inmates were driven on death marches; some 250,000 perished. After the liberation of the camps numerous investigations and trials were conducted against guards and camp officials. Many perpetrators and accomplices went unpunished. Moreover, they also remained free of the "camp-syndromes" that tortured the surviving victims. The campaigns launched by anti-Semites and neo-Nazis after the war to deny the horrific crimes committed in concentration and extermination camps continue to be waged, and with increased vehemence at an international level. Of little impact, sadly, has been the historical evidence, let alone plaques, monuments, museums, and archives to be found at almost all the sites of former terror and murder.

Konrad Kwiet

See also Anti-Semitism; Auschwitz; Baeck, Leo; German-Jewish Organizations; Gestapo; Gypsies; Heydrich, Reinhard; Himmler, Heinrich; Holocaust; Höss, Rudolf; National Socialist Germany; Nazi War Crimes Trials and Investigations;

Racism; Ravensbrück; Resistance; Schutzstaffel (SS); *Völkisch* Ideology; Wannsee Conference

References

Arad, Y. *Belzec, Sobibor and Treblinka: The Operation Reinhard Death Camps.* Bloomington, IN: Indiana University Press, 1987.

Dachauer Hefte. Studien und Dokumente zur Geschichte der nationalsozialitischen Konzentrationslager (1985 *ff.*).

Gutman, Y. and A. Saf, eds. *The Nazi Concentration Camps.* Proceedings of the Fourth International Historical Conference. Jerusalem: n.p., 1984.

Kogon, E. *The Theory and Practice of Hell.* Trans. Heinz Norden. New York, NY: Farrar, Strauss & Co, 1953.

Krausnick, Helmut and Martin Broszat. *Anatomy of the SS State.* Trans. Dorthy Long and Marion Jackson. London: William Collins Sons, 1968.

Pingel, F. *Häftlinge unter SS-Herrschaft: Widerstand, Selbstbehauptung und Vernichtung in Konzentrationslägern.* Hamburg: Hoffmann und Campe, 1978.

Rückerl, A., ed. *Nationalsozialistische Vernichtungslager im Spiegel deutscher Strafprozesse: Belzec, Sobibor, Treblinka, Chelmno.* Munich: DTV, 1977.

Sofsky, Wolfgang. *The Order of Terror: The Concentration Camp.* Trans. William Templar. Princeton, NJ: Princeton University Press, 1997.

Conductors

Although conducting in the modern sense dates to about the year 1800, it took the activity of such figures as Carl Maria von Weber (1786–1826), Ludwig Spohr (1784–1859), and Felix Mendelssohn (1809–47) to establish conducting as a legitimate profession. The baton was only gradually accepted during the first half of the nineteenth century.

Two phenomena of the early nineteenth century proved essential for the emergence of the modern conductor: the image of the conductor as virtuoso and the creation of professional orchestras. At mid-century, both Richard Wagner (1813–83) and Franz Liszt (1811–86) championed music written by themselves as well as earlier masters and colleagues and pioneered modern concepts of baton technique and interpretation (see, for example, Wagner's *Über das Dirigieren* [On conducting], 1869). Partially in response to Wagner's music, a generation of conductors arose that would definitively establish a German hegemony: Hans von Bülow (1830–94), Hermann Levi (1839–1900), Hans Richter (1843–1916), Anton Seidl (1850–98), Felix Mottl (1856–1911) and Carl Muck (1859–1940).

It is not coincidental that the most prominent conductors in the New World initially came from German-speaking lands, for example Leopold Damrosch (1832–85), a Liszt pupil who founded the New York Symphony Society, and Theodore Thomas (1835–1905), who led the New York Philharmonic from 1877 to 1891 and then conducted the Chicago Symphony Orchestra. Despite the simultaneous development of the conducting profession in other European countries, none of those lands could match the German-speaking areas in terms of the quantity and diversity of conducting talent.

The turn of the century brought the juxtaposition of the composer-conductors with an ever-increasing number of professional conductors. In the former category belong the uncompromising perfectionists Gustav Mahler (1860–1911) and Richard Strauss (1864–1949) and the elegant practitioner Felix von Weingartner (1863–1942). The ranks of conducting specialists included such imposing figures as Arthur Nikisch (1855–1922) in Leipzig and Franz Schalk (1863–1911) and Ferdinand Löwe (1865–1925) in Vienna, all of whom championed the music of Anton Bruckner and other late-nineteenth-century and turn-of-the-century masters. Another generation of conductors came to maturity during the years between the wars, and some of them became leading figures in the musical world: Bruno Walter (1876–1962), Otto Klemperer (1885–1973), Wilhelm Furtwängler (1886–1954), and Hans Knappertsbusch (1888–1965). What united these rather disparate talents was their seriousness and their commitment to the German romantic traditions in repertory and interpretation. At the same time, a group of conductors emerged that specialized in newer compositions. The activity of Erich Kleiber (1890–1956), Hermann Scherchen (1891–1966), Hans Rosbaud (1895–1962), and Klemperer benefited not only the Second Viennese School of Schönberg, Berg, and Webern, but also such rising stars as Paul Hindemith (1895–1963) and Kurt Weill (1900–50).

The Nazi rise to power cut short their efforts, because most contemporary music was banned from performance and many of the conductors had to leave Germany (Fritz Busch and Bruno Walter [1876–1962], for example, emigrated to the United States). In general, the Nazis often replaced the leading conductors with less talented but racially pure or politically reliable musicians. Those who survived in Germany throughout the war years (for example, Furtwängler or Clemens Krauss [1893–1954]) had to be cleared of collaboration charges by the Allies after the war. As an alleged Nazi sympathizer, Herbert von Karajan (1908–89) had to be de-Nazified before he could resume conducting in 1947.

The resulting drain of talent from Germany during World War II meant that there was a certain dearth of conductors in the immediate postwar years, a hiatus that would be filled by such new faces as Hans Schmidt-Isserstedt (1900–73), Rudolf Kempe (1910–76), and Sergiu Celibidache (1912–). Among these postwar conductors, Karajan emerged as the dominant figure, creating an "empire" that would last well into the 1980s. Nevertheless, a number of German conductors born during the 1920s came to prominence during the 1960s, including such figures as Wolfgang Sawallisch (1923–), Klaus Tennstedt (1926–), Michael Gielen (1927–), and Christoph von Dohnanyi (1929–). East Germany also produced several conductors of prominence, above all the long-term music director of the Leipzig Gewandhaus Orchestra, Kurt Masur (1928–). In more recent years, several peripatetic younger talents such as Hans Zender (1936–) and, above all, Christoph Eschenbach (1940–) have risen to prominence, yet it is still too early to determine who, if anyone, will fill the gap left by Karajan's death in 1989.

James Deaville

See also Furtwängler, Wilhelm; Karajan, Herbert von; Mahler, Gustav; Opera; Operetta; Orchestral Music; Orchestras; Strauss, Richard; Wagner, Richard; Walter, Bruno

References

Galkin, Elliott W. *A History of Orchestral Conducting: In Theory and Practice.* New York, NY: Pendragon Press, 1988.

Laux, Karl and Georg Feder. "Dirigenten." *Die Musik in Geschichte und Gegenwart.* Vol. 3. Kassel: Bärenreiter, 1954, cols. 509–35.

Schonberg, Harold C. *The Great Conductors.* New York, NY: Simon and Schuster, 1967.

Schünemann, Georg. *Geschichte des Dirigierens.* Leipzig: Breitkopf und Härtel, 1913.

Weissmann, Adolf. *Der Dirigent im 20. Jahrhundert.* Berlin: Propyläen-Verlag, 1925.

Westrup, Jack. "Conducting." *The New Grove Dictionary of Music and Musicians.* Vol. 4. London: Macmillan, 1980.

Wooldridge, David. *Conductor's World.* New York, NY: Praeger Publishers, 1970.

Confessing Church

The name Confessing Church (*Bekennende Kirche*) was first adopted in 1934 by the section of the German Evangelical Protestant churches that opposed the attempts by the rival "German Christians" (*Deutsche Christen*) to impose pro-Nazi ideas and practices on church life. The subsequent conflict between these two groups became known as the German church struggle (*Kirchenkampf*). In 1933, the German Christians greeted the Nazi rise to power with enthusiasm as an opportunity for renewal and reorganization of the Protestant church. With the help of various Nazi agencies, they gained control of the church's structures and leading positions and promoted the establishment of a unified Reich church under a Reich Bishop, Ludwig Müller, Hitler's personal appointee. They called for the removal of all anti-Nazi elements from the church, including the eradication of all Jewish influences on Christianity.

In September 1933, Pastor Martin Niemöller (1892–1984) founded the Pastors' Emergency League to campaign for the defense of the church's autonomy along traditional and orthodox lines. During the following months, Karl Barth (1886–1968), Dietrich Bonhoeffer (1906–45), and others prepared a statement of their beliefs, which the Synod of Barmen, Rhineland, adopted in May 1934. This declaration became the basis of the Confessing Church's theological stance against the heretical innovations of the German Christians.

The Confessing Church explicitly limited its resistance to Nazism to the internal church sphere and never claimed to be opposed to the regime's political goals. Many of its members openly supported Hitler's nationalistic and social aims (including the subordination of the Jewish minority, due to the survival of traditional anti-Judaic prejudices). They failed to realize that the totalitarian ambitions of Nazism were all-encompassing, and were consequently increasingly caught between their patriotic and their ecclesiastical loyalties. Their successful protest against the Nazis' plans for "coordination" (*Gleichschaltung*) did, however, prevent a complete capitulation to Nazi wishes by a significant minority of the parishes. At the same time, because they claimed to be the true inheritors of Germany's Lutheran traditions, they refused to form a breakaway church.

From 1934 to 1937 the Confessing Church waged a valiant battle in the theological area, but was increasingly subject to harassment and intimidation. In 1937, Pastor Niemöller was arrested and was subsequently sent to a concentration camp. At the same time, the Confessing Church's training seminaries were prohibited, though they were later reconstituted illegally for a handful of ordinands, many of whom were to play leading roles in the post-1945 church. In 1938, the approaching threat of war over Czechoslovakia led to proposals for church services of repentance and confession, instead of the enthusiastic endorsement expected by the Nazis. The subsequent Nazi campaign of defamation led to confusion and uncertainty, so that only individual protests were voiced against the infamous Crystal Night (*Kristallnacht*) pogrom against the Jews in November 1938.

The conflict of personal loyalties led to divisions within the Confessing Church ranks. One group, led by bishops Marahrens of Hannover and Meiser of Munich, was prepared to reach accommodation with the Nazi state. The more militant followers of Niemöller, however, refused to make any concessions in their theological stance regardless of the consequences, for which many were to suffer surveillance, interrogation, and imprisonment. Their most notable theologian, Bonhoeffer, was executed in 1945.

With the outbreak of war in 1939, many Confessing Church pastors were called up for military service, and faced increasing unpopularity as a result of their alleged political disloyalty. As a small minority, their anti-Nazi political stance was ambivalent and hesitant. But the steadfast refusal of the few to worship the false gods of racism and expedience, and their readiness to suffer for their faith, saved the German Protestant church from total apostasy.

John Conway

See also Barth, Karl; Bonhoeffer, Dietrich; Clergy, Protestant; Dibelius, Otto; National Socialist Germany; Niemöller, Martin; Protestantism and the Protestant Church; Resistance

References

Barnett, Victoria. *For the Soul of the People: Protestant Protest against Hitler.* New York, NY: Oxford University Press, 1992.

Conway, John S. *The Nazi Persecution of the Churches 1933–1945.* New York, NY: Basic Books, 1968

Helmreich, Ernest. *The German Churches under Hitler: Background, Struggle and Epilogue.* Detroit, MI: Wayne State University Press, 1979.

Scholder, Klaus. *The Churches and the Third Reich.* 2 vols. London: SCM Press, 1987–88.

Conservatism, 1871–1918

For "conservatives of disposition"—people who had a natural inclination to favor the status quo over rapid change—life in Imperial Germany changed at a dizzying pace. The capitalist economy was expanding rapidly, changing structurally, and displacing many of the productive groups (for example, artisans) that conservatives believed to be bulwarks of the old order. In society, class relations were becoming more brittle, further undermining conservatives' (idealized) notion of a harmonious, corporate society. In politics, Germans quickly embraced universal manhood suffrage: the congenial "politics of notables" characteristic of the 1870s and 1880s slowly gave way to a new style, where the urgent need for grass-roots agitation and mass propaganda led to the rise of rabble-rousers within even the parties of the right. And in the world of avantgarde culture, previously accepted conventions and attitudes yielded to new uncertainties that further offended conservative sensibilities.

It was argued until recently that, despite these developments, the two principal conservative elites in Germany, the land-owning *Junkers* and the heavy industrialists, managed successfully to deflect the forces of modernity. According to this view, Chancellor Otto von Bismarck's dalliance with liberalism in the 1860s and 1870s came to an abrupt end with his turn to anti-socialist and protectionist measures in 1878–79. Thereafter, conservative groups rallied together to preserve "premodern" structures in state and society.

Many features of this interpretation remain valid. The corporate ethos of the Prussian bureaucracy, the Prussian parliament, the royal court, and the army—not to mention certain aspects of the justice and schooling systems—was clearly authoritarian, conservative, perhaps even reactionary. The continuing importance of these institutions prevented liberal reformers and socialist revolutionaries from redressing the galling unfairness that characterized much of German society and politics. Nevertheless, historians now tend to stress how the bastions of conservatism were crumbling after 1871, as their defenders retreated into enclaves that were bypassed by the mainstream of change. To take one example, the unwillingness of the German bourgeoisie to embrace revolutionary doctrines, though conservative in one sense, is no longer considered proof that upwardly mobile middle-class Germans were "feudalized" by older conservative elites. On the contrary: the rising importance of the educated and propertied bourgeoisie profoundly altered public opinion on such issues as constitutional reform, civil liberties, and municipal administration. It also began to dictate rules of conduct in public deportment and family life.

In politics, conservatives became more divided over time. Already by 1894, Kaiser Wilhelm II's appeal to the conservatives to defend "religion, morality, and order" (one might substitute "anti-socialism, protectionism, and imperialism") no longer sufficed to hold together anything resembling a single conservative interest. Why, then, did Germany escape a revolutionary fate before 1918? Two important aspects of any answer lie in the nature of the conservative parties themselves and in the structure of decisionmaking in the state.

Conservatives were divided principally among two nominal and two de facto conservative parties in the empire. On the far right stood the German Conservative Party, dominated by estate-owning *Junkers* in the Prussian east and determined to block every attempt to diminish this class's economic and political strength. Less reactionary and more pliable was the Free Conservative Party (also known nationally as the Imperial Party), which by 1914 had sunk to near insignificance. The National Liberal Party was more national than liberal, especially after 1890, and among its backers were iron and steel magnates in the Ruhr district. But like the Center Party, which represented German Catholics, National Liberalism was always characterized by an uneasy (and sometimes inconsistent) mix of liberal and conservative tendencies.

That a showdown never occurred between conservatives and their enemies is also due to the ambiguities of Germany's constitution and the inconsistent policies of its chancellors. Under Bismarck, anti-socialist laws were considered necessary to contain the growth of Social Democracy. By 1890, however, these laws had patently failed and were allowed to lapse. A conservative consensus was never available to endorse the kind of brutal anti-socialist repression adopted by the Nazis—perhaps there were too few "go-for-broke" reactionaries in Imperial Germany and too many "conservatives of disposition." Subsequently, the government pursued an unheralded but not inconsequential program of social reform and tentative political reform. By 1914, liberals and socialists had begun the difficult task of reconciling their differences, leaving conservatives increasingly on the sidelines.

The government of Chancellor Bethmann Hollweg (1909–17) reacted to these developments in contradictory ways. According to its own lights, its policy was staunchly conservative. Yet Bethmann Hollweg's impatience with the Conservative Party was clear even before 1914. The bankruptcy of conservatism in 1918 is largely explained by its failure either to embrace minimal reform in peacetime or to achieve victory on the battlefield. Nonetheless, its strength was demonstrated again only 15 years later when conservatives contributed to the collapse of the Weimar Republic.

James Retallack

See also Aristocracy; Bethmann Hollweg, Theobald von; Bismarck, Otto von; Bourgeoisie; Center Party; Conservatism, 1918–45; German Conservative Party; *Kreuzzeitung*; Parties and Politics; Wilhelm I; Wilhelm II

References

Eley, Geoff. *Reshaping the German Right: Radical Nationalism and Political Change after Bismarck.* New Haven, CT: Yale University Press, 1980.

Jones, Larry Eugene and James Retallack, eds. *Between Reform, Reaction, and Resistance: Studies in the History of German Conservatism from 1789 to 1945.* Oxford: Berg, 1993.

Peck, Abraham J. *Radicals and Reactionaries: The Crisis of Conservatism in Wilhelmine Germany.* Washington, DC: University Press of America, 1978.

Puhle, Hans-Jürgen. *Agrarische Interessenpolitik und preussischer Konservatismus im Wilhelminischen Reich 1893–1914: Ein Beitrag zur Analyse des Nationalismus in Deutschland am Beispiel des Bundes der Landwirte und der Deutsch-Konservativen Partei.* 2nd ed. Bonn: Verlag Neue Gesellschaft, 1975.

Retallack, James. *Notables of the Right: The Conservative Party and Political Mobilization in Germany, 1876–1918.* London: Unwin Hyman, 1988.

Stegmann, Dirk, Peter-Christian Witt, and Bernd-Jürgen Wendt, eds. *Deutscher Konservatismus im 19. und 20. Jahrhundert: Festschrift für Fritz Fischer.* Bonn: Neue Gesellschaft, 1983.

Conservatism, 1918–45

Conservatism from 1918 to 1945 was a diverse movement that assumed many ideological and organizational forms. As an ideology, conservatism opposed the dramatic changes that had taken place in the structure of German political life with the collapse of the monarchy and the establishment of the Weimar Republic. For the most part, conservatives rejected the Weimar state as the source and symbol of Germany's national fragmentation and supported the creation of a more authoritarian state free from the corrupting influence of mass party politics. In social and economic policy, conservatives generally supported the free-enterprise system, despite frequent calls for a more organic economy in which agriculture and the independent middle class would be accorded a privileged status.

In the Weimar Republic, political conservatism found its principal representative in the German National People's Party (Deutschnationale Volkspartei; DNVP), a monarchist party founded in November 1918 in the hope of fusing the various strains of prewar German conservatism into a coherent political force. By the end of the 1920s, however, it became apparent with the formation of conservative splinter parties, such as the Business Party of the German Middle Class (Wirtschaftspartei/Reichspartei des deutschen Mittelstandes), the Christian National Farmers and Peasants' Party (Christlichnationale Bauern- und Landvolkpartei), the Christian Social People's Service (Christlich-sozialer Volksdienst), and the Conservative People's Party (Konservative Volkspartei), that this effort had failed.

The bankruptcy of political conservatism in the Weimar Republic could also be seen in the shift of power from traditional conservatives such as Count Kuno von Westarp (1864–1945), DNVP party chairman from 1926 to 1928, to radical nationalists such as Alfred Hugenberg (1865–1961), DNVP party chairman from 1928 to 1933. At no point was the crisis of Weimar conservatism more apparent than in the period from 1930 to 1932, when the efforts of Chancellor Heinrich Brüning (1885–1970) to reform the Weimar constitution along essentially conservative lines encountered unrelenting opposition from Hugenberg and the leaders of the DNVP.

A further manifestation of this crisis was the emergence of new variants of conservative ideology, such as "young conservatism" or "revolutionary conservatism." Advocates of a "conservative revolution," such as Arthur Moeller van den Bruck (1876–1925), Oswald Spengler (1880–1936), and Edgar Jung (1894–1934), rejected the DNVP as the instrument of vested economic interests and called for a more radical transformation of German political life than traditional conservative spokesmen were prepared to accept. By the beginning of the 1930s, the German conservative establishment had become so fragmented along political as well as structural lines that it was no longer capable of formulating a coherent response to the collapse of the Weimar state and the rise of Nazism. Although many conservatives remained profoundly distrustful of Nazi demagogy, others sympathized with the movement's militant opposition to Weimar democracy and openly preferred it to a return to parliamentary rule following the era of government by presidential decree from 1930 to the end of 1932. As a result, individual conservatives, such as Hugenberg and Franz von Papen (1879–1969), proceeded to reach an accommodation with the Nazi leadership that cleared the way for Adolf Hitler's installation as chancellor on January 30, 1933.

In the Third Reich, conservatism ceased to exist as a coherent political or ideological force. Conservative organizations, such as the National Rural League (Reichslandbund), German National Union of Commercial Employees (Deutschnationaler Handlungsgehilfen-Verband), and the Stahlhelm (Steel Helmets), were either dissolved or coopted into the organizational structure of the Nazi state. Conservative intellectuals, including the exponents of a "conservative revolution," were either ostracized, ignored, or—in the case of Jung—murdered. Individual conservatives, such as Carl Goerdeler (1884–1945) and Hjalmar Schacht (1877–1970), on the other hand, continued to collaborate with the Nazi state in the hope of mitigating its evils. The Fritzsch-Blomberg crisis at the beginning of 1938 exposed the futility of such a strategy and lent new impetus to the emergence of a conservative resistance to Hitler. The Kreisau Circle (Kreisauer Kreis) under Count Helmuth James von Moltke (1907–45) served as a major forum for the discussion of conservative plans for the reconstruction of the German Reich after the Nazis had been removed from power. Goerdeler and other conservative opponents of the Nazi regime played a major role in the abortive attempt on Hitler's life on July 20, 1944, and were subsequently killed in the repression that followed.

Larry Eugene Jones

See also Aristocracy; Brüning, Heinrich; German National People's Party; Goerdeler, Carl; Hugenberg, Alfred; Jung, Edgar; Moeller van den Bruck, Arthur; Moltke, Helmuth James von; Papen, Franz von; Parties and Politics; Resistance; Schacht, Hjalmar; Spengler, Oswald; Stahlhelm

References

Jones, Larry Eugene and James Retallack, eds. *Between Reform, Reaction and Resistance: Studies in the History of German Conservatism from 1789 to 1945.* Oxford and Providence, RI: Berg, 1993.

Klemperer, Klemens von. *Germany's New Conservatism: Its History and Dilemma in the Twentieth Century.* Princeton, NJ: Princeton University Press, 1957.

Lebovics, Hermann. *Social Conservatism and the Middle Classes in Germany 1914–1933.* Princeton, NJ: Princeton University Press, 1969.

Mohler, Armin. *Die konservative Revolution in Deutschland 1918–1932: Ein Handbuch.* 2nd ed. Darmstadt: Wissenschaftliche Buchgesellschaft, 1972.

Petzold, Joachim. *Wegbereiter des deutschen Faschismus: Die Jungkonservativen in der Weimarer Republik.* Cologne: Pahl-Rugenstein, 1978.

Ritter, Gerhard. *Carl Goerdeler und die deutsche Widerstandsbewegung.* Munich: DTV, 1964.

Stegmann, Dirk, Bernd-Jürgen Wendt, and Peter-Christian Witt, eds. *Deutscher Konservatismus im 19. und 20. Jahrhundert: Festschrift für Fritz Fischer.* Bonn: Verlag Neue Gesellschaft, 1983.

Constitutions (1871–1933)

Between the proclamation of the German Empire in 1871 and the establishment of the Nazi dictatorship in 1933, Germany had two constitutions, each reflecting the substantially different historical circumstances under which it was completed. The first was a modified version of the constitution of the North German Confederation of 1867, originally conceived by Prus-

Page from the Basic Law, which has served as West Germany's constitution since 1949 and reunited Germany's constitution since 1990. Courtesy of Inter Nationes, Bonn.

Der Parlamentarische Rat hat das vorstehende Grundgesetz für die Bundesrepublik Deutschland in öffentlicher Sitzung am 8. Mai des Jahres Eintausendneunhundertneunundvierzig mit dreiundfünfzig gegen zwölf Stimmen beschlossen. Zu Urkunde dessen haben sämtliche Mitglieder des Parlamentarischen Rates die vorliegende Urschrift des Grundgesetzes eigenhändig unterzeichnet.

BONN AM RHEIN, den 23. Mai des Jahres Eintausendneunhundertneunundvierzig.

PRÄSIDENT DES PARLAMENTARISCHEN RATES

I. VIZEPRÄSIDENT DES PARLAMENTARISCHEN RATES

II. VIZEPRÄSIDENT DES PARLAMENTARISCHEN RATES

sian Minister-President Otto von Bismarck. It was approved by the governments and parliaments of the Confederation and the four south German states that, by way of formal treaties, had joined to create united Germany after the successful war against France in 1871. Subsequently, the new Federal Council (Bundesrat) and Parliament (Reichstag) also accepted it, and it was officially promulgated by the Prussian king in his new capacity as emperor. The second was the constitution of the Weimar Republic, born in defeat and revolution at the end of the First World War. It was the work of a freely elected National Assembly in 1919 and was based on the principle that all state authority emanated from the sovereign people.

In 1871, sovereignty derived from 22 monarchs and the senates of three city-states. Thus the Federal Council, consisting of 58 representatives of the 25 states, was the embodiment of national sovereignty and the guardian of the rights and interests of all member states. It had extensive legislative, administrative, and controlling powers. Its president was the Reich chancellor, who was personally responsible to the emperor and was also in charge of federal government business. The constitution made no provisions for a federal cabinet or ministries. But it provided the new emperor with prerogatives that, together with the personal union of the Prussian and imperial crowns, made him much more than a mere figurehead. He represented the Empire internationally, he was the commander in chief of the armed forces, and he had the right to appoint and dismiss the chancellor and all Reich officials and to convene and dissolve parliament.

The Reichstag was a popular assembly elected on the basis of universal manhood suffrage and an equal, direct, and secret ballot. It had to approve the annual budget and had the right to initiate federal legislation. Although these provisions gave it significant political clout, its members were not permitted to hold government office, nor were they paid a salary.

By contrast, the Reichstag of the Weimar Republic embodied popular sovereignty and was the supreme national legislative authority. The chancellor and all government ministers were directly responsible to it and required its confidence. The Reichsrat or Federal Council, on the other hand, lost its former position of preeminence, though it still represented the various states and enjoyed limited veto rights in the legislative process. But a proposed thorough reorganization of Germany's traditional dynastic, territorial structure, possibly involving the division of Prussia into federal administrative districts, did not take place.

Perhaps the most controversial aspect of the Weimar constitution was its attempt to combine representative and parliamentary with plebiscitary and presidential elements in the new political system. The president was to be elected for a period of seven years and was given significant powers, such as the right to appoint and dismiss the chancellor, Reich officials, and military officers. Article 48 also enabled him to rule by emergency decree, abrogate fundamental rights temporarily, and restore public law and order and enforce Reich laws using military force if necessary. These important functions resulted in a dual system, in which both parliament and president enjoyed popular legitimacy, and in a bipolar executive, with one pole, the chancellor, dependent on the confidence of parliament and the president.

A further plebiscitary feature of this system was the provision for popular initiative and referendum. In theory, this provision enabled one-tenth of the country's eligible voters to force what amounted to a popular intervention in the political process between presidential and parliamentary elections. Finally, a substantial second part of the Weimar constitution consisted of a long list of fundamental rights and duties of German citizens. But the various civil, social, economic, and cultural rights could be amended by a two-thirds parliamentary majority, or suspended by the president. They did not guarantee an immutable democratic order. The constitution of 1871 had not listed fundamental rights at all, though subsequent federal legislation did codify many rights, such as freedom of movement, association, and religion, and the protection of property.

The constitutions of 1871 and 1919 were both flexible enough to allow evolutionary change or adaption to changing circumstances. Both were results of political compromises and balancing acts, and as such, left a great deal open or inadequately defined. In the first, the combination of monarchical and democratic institutions, federal and unitary principles, and conservative political leadership and a liberal economic order was at best a temporary expedient, perhaps necessary under the circumstances of 1871, but less and less viable as years went by.

When, in October 1918, reforms finally established the primacy of parliament and abolished the three-class voting system in Prussia, they were too late to prevent the fall of the monarchy and the ensuing revolutionary upheaval. In 1919, the combination of presidential and parliamentary systems was equally problematic, and was certainly not conducive to political stability. Furthermore, neither constitution defined the role of parties. In the Empire, this omission reflected the anomalous situation in which the representatives of the politically mobilized masses played hardly any direct role in the political decisionmaking process, and had no influence on the emperor, bureaucracy, military, or federal council. In the Weimar Republic, the omission was a historical irony as much as an expression of distrust of parties in general. Many contemporaries referred to the republic disparagingly as the "party state," and the ultimate breakdown of the parliamentary system certainly had much to do with the nature and attitude of the parties. In the end, the Nazis had little difficulty in establishing a system without these parties, a system in which the Weimar constitution, though never formally abrogated, ceased to be meaningful.

Attila Chanady

See also Basic Law; Bismarck, Otto von; Federalism; German Democratic Republic: Constitutions; Imperial Germany; Judicial System of Imperial and Weimar Germany; Law, German Conception of; Legal Profession; Third Reich: Legal Profession; Weimar Germany

References

Bracher, K.D., M. Funke and H.A. Jacobsen, eds. *Die Weimarer Republik 1918–1933*. Düsseldorf: Droste, 1987.

Huber, E.R. *Deutsche Verfassungsgeschichte seit 1789*. Vols. 3 and 5. Stuttgart: W. Kohlhammer, 1963, 1978.

Hucko, E.M., ed. *The Democratic Tradition: Four German Constitutions*. Leamington Spa: Berg, 1978.

Koch, H.W. *A Constitutional History of Germany in the Nineteenth and Twentieth Centuries*. London: Longman, 1984.

Mommsen, Hans. *The Rise and Fall of Weimar Democracy*. Trans. Elborg Forster and Larry E. Jones. Chapel Hill, NC: University of North Carolina Press, 1996.

Mommsen, Wolfgang. *Imperial Germany 1867–1918: Politics, Culture, and Society in an Authoritarian State*. Trans. Richard Deveson. London and New York, NY: Arnold, 1995.

Stürmer, Michael. *Das kaiserliche Deutschland*. Düsseldorf: Droste, 1970.

Cooperatives

The German cooperative movement emerged in the last half of the nineteenth century to serve farmers, rural and urban borrowers, artisans, small businesses, and consumers. Agricultural and credit cooperatives remain strong and have served as models for development in other countries.

German writers sometimes stress the roots of the cooperative idea in preindustrial community (the word for cooperative, *Genossenschaft*, suggests this), but cooperatives in their modern form emerged only after 1850. Hermann Schulze-Delitzsch (1808–83), then F.W. Raiffeisen (for rural cooperatives), and others promoted similar ideas: autonomous organizations with voluntary membership, running businesses to serve their members, and controlled by the principle of one member, one vote. Today, the movement identifies its principles as "self-help, self-responsibility, and self-administration." Schulze-Delitzsch and Raiffeisen founded mainly credit cooperatives, though specialized agricultural cooperatives spread widely after the 1880s and consumer cooperatives started in the 1890s. Other forms of cooperation did not take root: worker cooperatives, advocated by Ferdinand Lassalle (1825–64), were not attempted on a large scale and did not last when they were tried.

Until 1920, the movement grew at an explosive rate, and also split on functional, regional, and political lines. Parallel to the Raiffeisen Generalverband (general association) among the rural cooperatives—and larger—was the more secular and pragmatic Reichsverband (national association) founded by National Liberal deputy Wilhelm Haas (1839–1913). Various agrarian organizations also had their own cooperatives and federations. The state became involved in 1895 through the Prussian Central Cooperative Bank, which provided subsidized credit and promoted the multiplication of cooperatives. The Prussian bank also sponsored the Hauptverband (primary association; 1901) for trade and artisanal cooperatives, which represented conservative ideas of *Mittelstandspolitik* (lower middle-class politics) as an alternative to the liberal Schulze-Delitzsch Allgemeiner Verband (general association).

In 1903, the Social Democratic, working-class consumer cooperatives also broke away from the Schulze-Delitzsch federation to form their own, the Central Association of German

Cooperatives (Zentralverband deutscher Konsumvereine); and in following years the Catholic consumer cooperatives organized to keep themselves separate from the socialists. From all of these divergent social, political, and regional forces emerged some fifteen to twenty thousand cooperatives by 1900, over 30,000 by 1914, and well over 50,000 at the peak in the 1930s.

A period of consolidation followed. The middle-class urban cooperatives were united when the Hauptverband joined the Schulze-Delitzsch federation in 1920. A similar unification of agricultural cooperatives was achieved with state help in 1930; rationalization of rural cooperatives continued under the National Socialist regime. The German Raiffeisen Union was reestablished in 1948 for rural cooperatives, and in 1972 it united with the Schulze-Delitzsch organization to create (for the first time) one common apex organization for all German cooperatives, the German Cooperative and Raiffeisen Federation. Consumer cooperatives were suppressed and broken up by the Nazis, and had difficulty reestablishing themselves after the war; except for one or two highly successful cooperatives, most were amalgamated into Co-op AG, a centralized joint-stock company that fell apart amidst scandal in the late 1980s. Independent cooperatives were not reestablished in the German Democratic Republic.

In the mid-1980s there were still over 10,000 cooperatives in the Federal Republic, including 3,700 cooperative banks, 4,300 agricultural and rural services cooperatives, nearly 1,200 housing-construction cooperatives, and some 800 cooperatives for trades and small business. Together, these cooperatives had about thirty billion deutsche marks in assets. Over fourteen million Germans were members, ten million of these in the credit cooperatives, and the number was rising.

Brett Fairbairn

See also Raiffeisen, Friedrich Wilhelm; Schulze-Delitzsch, Hermann; Social Democratic Party

References
Faust, Helmut. *Geschichte der Genossenschaftsbewegung.* 3rd ed. Frankfurt am Main: Fritz Knapp, 1977.
Hasselmann, Erwin. *Geschichte der deutschen Konsumgenossenschaften.* Frankfurt am Main: Fritz Knapp, 1971.
Novy, Klaus et al., eds. *Anders Leben: Geschichte und Zukunft der Genossenschaftskultur: Beispiele aus Nordrhein-Westfalen.* Berlin: Verlag J.H.W. Dietz Nachf, 1985.
Peal, David. "Self-Help and the State: Rural Cooperatives in Imperial Germany." *Central European History* 21 (1988), 244–66.

Coordination (*Gleichschaltung*) (1933–34)
The term *Gleichschaltung* (coordination) is used to describe the monopolization of authority in public and private institutions in 1933–34 during the Nazis' power seizure. The term, borrowed from the vocabulary of electrotechnology, had its first application in the Law for the Coordination of the *Länder* (states) with the Reich of April 7, 1933, which reconstituted the state legislatures to conform with the results of the March 1933 Reichstag elections. Special Reich commissioners were assigned to the states to control their administrations. With the dissolution of the federal upper house (the Reichsrat) in February 1934, Nazi centralization replaced state federalism.

The coordination process encompassed the formal and informal (sometimes violent) Nazification of other public bodies (for instance, town councils), the so-called "re-constitution" of the civil service, the banning of political parties, trade unions, and similar independent organizations, and their substitution by Nazi monopoly organizations (such as the German Labor Front or the National Socialist Women's Union); it also entailed the quasi-compulsory self-Nazification of the vast array of professional, cultural, and sports associations that studded German social life. These organizations expelled Jewish and other politically "undesirable" members and submitted to supervision or eventual takeover by Nazi structures. Though never total (for instance, the churches retained considerable independence), *Gleichschaltung* imposed wide membership in Nazi organizations, rendered voluntary social activity illegal, and contributed to the degradation of German social relations.

Jane Caplan

See also Constitutions; Federalism; Hindenburg, Paul von; Hitler, Adolf; National Socialist Germany; Parliamentary System; Political Parties and Politics; Sturmabteilung

References
Allen, Sheridan. *The Nazi Seizure of Power.* Rev. ed. New York, NY: Franklin Watts, 1984.
Peukert, Detlev. *Inside Nazi Germany: Conformity and Racism in Everyday Life.* New Haven, CT: Yale University Press, 1987.
Stachura, Peter D. *The Nazi Machtergreifung.* London: Allen and Unwin, 1983.

Corinth, Lovis (1858–1925)
Painter, draftsperson, and printmaker, Lovis Corinth was a key figure in the history of modern German art. Not only did he anticipate expressionism by nearly a decade in his early work of the 1890s, in the 1920s he pushed expressionism to its extreme in works on canvas and paper. A self-avowed monarchist and committed German patriot, Corinth often used this expressive style to make veiled sociopolitical statements.

Corinth's unusually long training period of nearly eleven years began in Königsberg, where he studied from 1876 to 1880, primarily with the genre painter Otto Günther (1838–84). He then worked from 1880 to 1884 in Munich, first at the private atelier of Franz von Defregger (1835–1921), subsequently at the Academy of Fine Arts (Akademie der bildenden Künste) with Ludwig Löfftz (1845–1910), and finally from 1884 to 1887 at the Academie Julian in Paris with William Adolphe Bouguereau and Tony Robert-Fleury. Corinth returned to Munich in 1891, settling there after brief stays in Berlin and Königsberg. Here he began not only to experiment with printmaking, but also to leave behind the sober realism of early works such as *Portrait of Franz Heinrich*

Corinth with a Wine Glass, 1883, for a more expressive idiom. In this regard, his figure compositions are particularly noteworthy. Characterized by the packed compositional spaces, rough figural energies, exaggeration, and overstatement that ultimately became the hallmarks of expressionism a decade later, works like *Temptation of St. Anthony,* 1897, are also typified by their burlesqued tone. Not only do they empty usually dignified scenes of all ethical import, these raucous paintings satirize time-honored artistic traditions of religious, mythological, and historical painting.

Although one of these compositions, *Deposition,* 1895, won a gold medal at the Munich salon in 1895, Corinth moved to Berlin in 1901. Here he gradually lightened his palette and rendered his brushwork more vehement, while blunting the satirical edge of his work, retaining only the exaggerated expressions and gestures of his early style in pictures such as *Capture and Blinding of Samson,* 1907. The earnestness that now came to characterize his figure compositions was further fostered both by the serious stroke Corinth suffered in 1911 and by the events of 1914–18 and of the early Weimar Republic. Not only was the artist deeply depressed about his own waning strength, the staunch monarchist and patriot was also distraught over the sociopolitical conditions of wartime and postwar Germany.

Rather than spoof literary subject matter, Corinth now often interpreted it metaphorically, using the passion of Christ, for example, as a poignant symbol of his own life and that of his country in *The Red Christ,* 1922. With their characteristic

Lovis Corinth. Courtesy of Inter Nationes, Bonn.

high-keyed color, their expressive distortions, and their hurriedly brushed, seemingly windswept forms, these pictures—as well as the many incisive portraits and landscapes he painted while at his vacation home in the mountains just south of Munich— elevated the emotional urgency of prewar expressionism to new heights. Corinth also used the graphic medium to express his postwar disillusionment, executing a number of lithographic and etched print cycles that delineate his antidemocratic stance.

Corinth was awarded the title of professor by the Prussian Ministry of Culture in 1917, and was the subject of numerous important exhibitions during his lifetime. A member of the Munich and Berlin secessions, he served as president of the latter from 1913 to 1925. Before his death in 1925, Corinth also authored several book-length autobiographies, a handbook on painting, and numerous art-historical essays.

Maria Makela

See also Artists; Berlin Secession; Expressionism; Munich Secession; Painting

References
Berend-Corinth, Charlotte. *Die Gemälde von Lovis Corinth.* Munich: Bruckmann, 1958.

Makela, Maria. "A Late Self-Portrait by Lovis Corinth." *Aspects of Modern Art at the Art Institute* 16 (1990), 56–69, 93–95.

———. "Aspects of Lovis Corinth's Graphic Work." *Lovis Corinth.* Exhibition Catalogue. New York: National Academy of Design. (May 14–June 28, 1992).

Müller, Heinrich. *Die späte Graphik von Lovis Corinth.* Hamburg: Lichtwarkstiftung, 1960.

Schwarz, Karl. *Das graphische Werk von Lovis Corinth.* 3rd enlarged ed. San Francisco, CA: Alan Wofsy Fine Arts, 1985.

Uhr, Horst. *Lovis Corinth.* Berkeley, CA: University of California Press, 1990.

Counterculture (1945–90)

Since World War II, both Germanys have had to cope with segments of their societies that opposed mainstream culture and tried to develop alternative models to it. Throughout the history of postwar Germany, these countercultural groups developed into a broad, politically motivated protest movement.

The rearmament of West Germany in the 1950s ignited the first prominent political protest movements (Ohnemich-Bewegung [count me out movement], Paulskirchen-Bewegung [St. Paul's church movement], Kampf-dem-Atomtod-Bewegung [death to the atomic bomb movement]), followed by the Easter March Movement in the 1960s. The developments in mainstream politics, particularly the Grand Coalition of the two major parties, radicalized West German society and the already existing political protest movements, which saw themselves as a necessary extra-parliamentary opposition (*Ausserparlamentarische Opposition,* APO). This protest was not yet a counterculture, because it focused on a single political issue, but it paved the way for the student-led protest of the late 1960s.

The student movement (approximately 1967–72) became the most significant extra-parliamentary opposition and countercultural development in postwar West Germany. In comparison to earlier cultural and political protest, the student movement combined political demands with the idea of a cultural revolution extending to all spheres of social life. Marxism and the "critical theory" of the Frankfurt School (Max Horkheimer [1895–1973], Theodor Adorno [1903–69], Herbert Marcuse [1898–1979], and Jürgen Habermas [1929–]) became the most significant foundations for the students' social and political theory. Their protest crystallized around the following issues: the emergency decree laws, the collective amnesia about the Nazi past, the Vietnam War as the most visible confrontation between the First and the Third Worlds, and authoritarian structures in family, school/university, and society at large. The student movement also introduced new modes of political activism developed by the United States student movement (teach-ins, sit-ins).

Though the student movement became politically paralyzed by factionalization, it left behind a strong legacy of political awareness and willingness to protest as well as new lifestyles and ideas such as *Wohngemeinschaften* (cooperative housing), communes, sexual liberation, and anti-authoritarian education. By the mid-1970s, criticism arose of the student movement's exclusive emphasis on the collective and the concept of class, which led to newly defined political paradigms: that of the politics of the self, first expressed in the women's movement's slogan "the personal is the political," and that of grass-roots democracy characterized by the citizens' initiatives. The counterculture of the 1970s and 1980s articulated itself in a variety of new social movements: the women's movement, the ecology movement, the squatters' movement (which was closely connected with the so-called Youth Revolt, 1981), the alternative movement, and the peace movement.

During the 1970s, citizens' initiatives concerned with environmental issues in their regions emerged across the country. The federal government's energy policy, which was based solely on the further expansion of nuclear power, became the focal point for a powerful mass movement. The *Anti-Atomkraft-Bewegung* (anti-nuclear movement) and the protest movement against the Startbahn West, a new runway at the Frankfurt airport for which a whole forest had to be cut down, managed to mobilize thousands of people and succeeded in establishing supra-regional organizational structures culminating in a legislative arm, the Green Party. Similar tendencies could also be observed in the GDR during the early 1980s, but on a much smaller scale because of the oppressive nature of the political system.

The peace movement achieved a high level of mobilization during the early 1980s (peace marches in Bonn in 1981 and 1982 drew 300,000 to 400,000 protesters). A strong peace movement also emerged in the GDR in the 1980s within the context of the church under the slogans "make peace without arms" and "swords into plowshares." The peace movement in the West lost momentum and mass support as soon as its main issue—prevention of the deployment of United States cruise missiles and Pershing IIs on West German territory—vanished from the political agenda when the government ratified the Missiles Treaty in November 1983.

Apart from their political demands, the new social movements of the 1970s and 1980s constituted the so-called *Alternativbewegung* (alternative movement) or *Alternativkultur* (alternative culture), because most of the activists in these movements also tried to realize their political agenda in their own lives. During the 1970s, the term "alternative" became a political signifier for an anti-institutional, leftist-ecological position with which the majority of the people involved in projects such as eco-stores, alternative bookstores, and dentists', lawyers', or any kind of craftsmen's collective identified. The alternative movement was not theoretically inclined, but a shift toward anti-rationalist, poststructuralist paradigms (Michel Foucault, Gilles Deleuze, and Felix Guattari) is apparent. Though the alternative movement peaked in the mid-1980s and has since lost momentum, the significance of countercultural movements may be seen in the enhanced gender and ecological awareness of mainstream Germany and in the importance of the peace movement for the formation of a strong opposition to the GDR regime, without which its "velvet revolution" and unification would not have been possible.

Sabine von Dirke

See also Adorno, Theodor; Armaments Policy; Detente and Germany; Disarmament; Dutschke, Rudi; Extra-Parliamentary Opposition; Federal Republic of Germany; Frankfurt School; Greens; Habermas, Jürgen; Horkheimer, Max; Marcuse, Herbert; Students; Universities

References

Bauss, Gerhard. *Die Studentenbewegung der 60er Jahre in der Bundesrepublik und West Berlin.* Cologne: Pahl-Rugenstein, 1976.

Brand, Karl-Werner, Detlef Busser, and Dieter Rucht. *Aufbruch in eine andere Gesellschaft: Neue soziale Bewegungen in der Bundesrepublik Deutschland.* Frankfurt am Main: Campus, 1983.

Cohn-Bendit, Daniel and Reinhard Mohr. *1968—Die letzte Revolution, die noch nichts vom Ozonloch wusste.* Berlin: Wagenbach, 1989.

Ehring, Klaus. "The Peace Movement in East Germany—Its Origin and Future." *Telos* 56 (Summer 1983), 183–192.

Hermand, Jost. *Die Kultur der Bundesrepublik. 1965–1985.* Munich: Nymphenburger, 1988.

Kolinsky, Eva, ed. *The Greens in West Germany: Organisation and Policy Making.* Oxford: Berg, 1989.

Offe, Claus. "New Social Movements: Challenging the Boundries of Institutional Politics." *Social Research* 52, 4 (1985), 817–68.

Otto, Karl A. *Die ausserparlamentarische Opposition in Quellen und Dokumenten.* Cologne: Pahl-Rugenstein, 1989.

Wasmuht, Ulrike, ed. *Alternativen zur alten Politik? Neue soziale Bewegungen in der Diskussion.* Darmstadt: Wissenschaftliche Buchgesellschaft, 1989.

Country Life

Useful generalization about country life in modern Germany is complicated by the vast variety of agricultural practices, growing conditions, village structures, social relationships, and historical traditions that have shaped rural cultures. This regional variety transcends the well-known distinctions between farming practices in western and central Germany, on the one hand, and the large landed estates of the *Junkers* east of the Elbe, on the other. Effective generalization is also complicated by persistent gaps in our knowledge of German rural history.

Since the late nineteenth century, Germany's rural population and agricultural work force have been steadily declining relative to the country's total population. In 1878–79, 49.1 percent of working Germans were employed in agriculture; in 1933, the figure was 33.9 percent, and by the 1950s, less than 20 percent. The number of agricultural enterprises has also dropped sharply, from 5.6 million in 1895 to about 630,000 in the Federal Republic in 1990. In the early 1960s, one-third of all West Germans still lived in communities with fewer than five thousand inhabitants, and only about one-third of those were still employed in agriculture.

Country life in Germany has been profoundly affected by processes of economic change, technological innovation, and cultural transformation. In modern times, the peasant village has, in fact, been neither a backwater nor an oasis; despite the nostalgia of some Germans for the alleged virtues of rural life, the self-contained world of the "traditional" peasant village disappeared long ago. By the late eighteenth century, many German peasants had begun to respond to new market forces, and the nineteenth century brought innumerable changes that forever altered "traditional" village structures and patterns of peasant behavior: e.g., peasant emancipation, the crisis of proto-industry, the rise of capitalist agriculture, crop specialization, the development of railways, rural-urban migration and emigration overseas, and an increasingly important role for national and international market forces. After 1871, rural Germany was constantly and sometimes traumatically influenced by a "zigzag" pattern (Robert G. Moeller) of political and economic conditions. The agrarian crisis of the early 1890s was followed by recovery at the end of that decade, whereas the unprecedented challenges of war and inflation between 1914 and 1924 yielded to an equally unprecedented agricultural crisis after the late 1920s.

Although recent research has shown that the countryside was not necessarily an unqualified reservoir of support for the Nazis, it is a well-known fact that rural voters turned in large numbers to the party and that Nazi leaders devoted a great deal of attention to rural issues. Many prominent Nazis—including Minister of Agriculture R. Walther Darré (1895–1953), Heinrich Himmler (1900–45) and of course Adolf Hitler—were convinced that the peasantry represented the "lifesource of the Nordic race," in contrast to the alleged degeneracy of urban dwellers. While Nazi propagandists constantly extolled the purity of peasant customs and village life, government efforts to stabilize and protect the peasantry through the Hereditary Farm Entailment Law (*Erbhofgesetz*) of 1933 or the policies of the Reich Food Estate (*Reichsnährstand*) were nei-

ther wholly successful nor especially popular. Indeed, recent studies have shown that peasants and agricultural workers were rarely passive instruments of powerful elites, whether *Junker* agrarians or Nazi ideologues.

After 1945, dramatic changes in the character and conditions of country life occurred in both German states. In the Federal Republic, agricultural producers continued to remain an important lobbying force through agrarian leagues, despite the ongoing decline in their numbers. Small farms still dominate the western German landscape; 90 percent are less than 20 acres in size. The transformation of country life in East Germany was far more thoroughgoing. In the Soviet occupation zone, land reforms eliminated the economic and social power base of the old landowning aristocracy east of the Elbe; these reforms were followed by the collectivization efforts of the German Democratic Republic. By the late 1980s, some 5,100 collective farms (*Landwirtschaftliche Produktionsgenossenschaften*; LPG) had replaced 600,000 individual agricultural enterprises. These collective units radically altered both the physical shape of the eastern German countryside and the nature of village life. After the unification of the two German states in 1990, the LPGs were privatized; by the end of 1991, about 75 percent of the original LPGs had been transformed into private enterprises of one sort or another.

David E. Barclay

See also Agrarian Leagues; Agriculture; Aristocracy; Customs; Darré, R. Walther; Leisure; Peasantry

References
Abel, Wilhelm. *Die drei Epochen der deutschen Agrargeschichte.* 2nd ed. Hannover: Verlag M. & H. Schaper, 1964.
Evans, Richard J. and W.R. Lee, eds. *The German Peasantry: Conflict and Community in Rural Society from the Eighteenth to the Twentieth Centuries.* New York, NY: St. Martin's Press, 1986.
Farquharson, John E. *The Plough and the Swastika: The NSDAP and Agriculture in Germany 1928–45.* London: Sage Publications, 1976.
Haushofer, Heinz. *Die deutsche Landwirtschaft im technischen Zeitalter.* Stuttgart: Verlag Eugen Ulmer, 1963.
Jacobeit, Wolfgang, Josef Mooser, and Bo Strath, eds. *Idylle oder Aufbruch? Das Dorf im bürgerlichen 19. Jahrhundert: Ein europäischer Vergleich.* Berlin: Akademie-Verlag, 1990.
Moeller, Robert G., ed. *Peasants and Lords in Modern Germany: Recent Studies in Agricultural History.* Boston, MA: Allen and Unwin, 1986.

Cremer, Fritz (1906–93)

This sculptor and graphic artist created the Buchenwald concentration camp monument and won numerous prizes in the German Democratic Republic (GDR). At the height of his career in the 1950s he asserted that his talents were employed to propagate the greatest good: socialism.

Born to a poor family in the Ruhr on October 22, 1906,

Cremer attended school in Essen, where he also apprenticed as a stone mason. He served as a mason's helper and participated in the Communist youth movement. When he moved to Berlin in 1929, he joined the Communist Party as well as studying with Wilhelm Gerstel at the Berlin Academy for Free and Applied Arts. Although he protested Käthe Kollwitz's exclusion from the Prussian Academy of Art in 1933, he was able to travel extensively. Study trips to Paris in 1934 and London in 1936 preceded a stay at the German Academy in Rome, 1937–38. Until conscripted in 1940, Cremer held a master's position with Gerstel and then the Prussian Academy. Although he later claimed to have participated in the anti-Fascist resistance, his artistic career hardly suffered.

After war service and prisoner-of-war status, Cremer became a professor in Vienna's Academy of Applied Arts in 1946. In 1950, he accepted a professorship in East Berlin, where he flourished with state support. In 1976, however, he joined a dozen leading GDR intellectuals, including Christa Wolf (1929–), in signing a protest declaration to the GDR leadership against the exiling of Wolf Biermann (1936–).

Cremer's early reliefs, as well as clay and stone works, evoke the peasant-like, despondent figures of Ernst Barlach's wood sculptures in their focus on suffering and the consequences of drudgery in work and war. A few emulate Georg Kolbe's (1877–1947) more refined nudes, but Cremer did not follow that sculptor's accommodation with Nazi muscularity. After the war, Cremer's work became more abstract, while continually evoking the downtrodden, especially in the faceless forms of suffering mothers. Some bathers, lovers, and plump nudes began to appear by the late 1940s, celebrating life and youth. Nonetheless, Cremer's main work focused on commissioned monuments to honor left-wing resistance fighters, opposition to war, and the concentration-camp dead (Mauthausen, Ebensee, and Berlin). The Buchenwald monument, with eight symbolic two-meter figures, took from 1952 to 1956 to complete. Cremer's numerous lithographs and woodcuts illustrated classic German themes, such as Faust. These dark-line drawings often served as book illustrations.

Cremer survived many regime changes. Throughout, his oeuvre remained a thought-provoking commentary on the difficulties of the human condition, even if he accommodated himself enough in each period—shifting themes and forms—to survive by producing works that fit with what was expected of a state-supported artist.

Dieter K. Buse

See also Artists; Barlach, Ernst; Biermann, Wolf; German Democratic Republic: Political Culture; Kollwitz, Käthe; Prussian Art Academy; Wolf, Christa

References

Deutsche Akademie der Künste. *Fritz Cremer.* Berlin: Akademie Verlag, 1956.
Fritz Cremer: Der Weg eines deutschen Bildhauers. Dresden: Verlag der Kunst, 1956.
Schmidt, Diether. *Fritz Cremer: Leben, Werke, Schriften, Meinungen.* Dresden: Verlag der Kunst, 1972.

Crime

German crime rates have never been considered exceptional by international standards, but crime has always been an issue closely tied to the German nationalist debate. From Germany's unification in 1871 to its reunification in 1990 and beyond, the quest for law and order has continually animated nationalistic discourse, and extreme nationalists have frequently branded their political, ideological, and socioeconomic opponents with the charge of either being lax on crime and criminals or of being criminals themselves. Accordingly, those perceived as being outside the German "national community"—from Jews, Poles, and Communist workers of Imperial Germany, the Weimar Republic, and the Third Reich to foreign "guest workers" and asylum-seekers in the Federal Republic—have often suffered under prejudicial public opinion and not infrequently under prejudicial laws and criminal-justice practices as well.

To be fair, however, popular and nationalist biases have affected every country's concerns over crime, and, except for the period of the Third Reich, German criminal-justice officials, institutions, and practices have had many admirers. Whereas German police have frequently been characterized as overbearing and militaristic, they also have often enjoyed the reputation of being highly trained and honest. German judges, lawyers, and prosecutors have always been the products of a rigorous educational and examination system. German criminal law, except in the Nazi period, has frequently been credited for its scientific and rational nature.

If Germany's criminal-justice institutions and personnel have helped to keep Germany's crime rates respectable in comparison with those of other countries (here it must be noted that comparing crime rates across national boundaries and often even within them is a questionable business, but highly respected scholars as early as Emile Durkheim in the late nineteenth century have often remarked upon Germany's low rates), many other factors have played a role as well. Since the passage of Otto von Bismarck's social insurance laws in the 1880s, Germany has always had one of the most comprehensive social welfare systems in the world. Since the late nineteenth century as well, German workers have nearly always received comparatively high wages and the gap between rich and poor in German society has usually been narrower than in many industrialized countries. Crime-retarding values, such as orderliness, honesty, and obedience to authority have long been stereotypical German traits.

Since the work of internationally respected criminal-justice scholars such as Georg von Mayr and Gustav Aschaffenburg in the late nineteenth and early twentieth centuries, crime and justice in Germany have received much scholarly attention. Though, as in all contentious issues, scholarly debate often overshadows scholarly consensus, the following observations about the history of German crime trends find much support:

1) Germany's rapid urbanization and industrialization of the late nineteenth and early twentieth centuries were not met by great upsurges in either violent crime (murder, manslaughter, assault and battery) or

property crime (theft, embezzlement), although urban-based populations were frequently charged with criminal culpability by conservative elites and official statistics demonstrate an upsurge in prosecutions for political offenses allegedly committed by these urban populations (e.g., workers, socialists, Jews) in the decades before World War I. Furthermore, rates of criminal prosecution for political offenses remained high in the Weimar Republic and reached extreme levels during the Nazi years.

2) From the Empire to the Federal Republic, official crime statistics have demonstrated repeatedly that large German cities have not had particularly high crime rates, especially in the category of violent crime (official statistics from the 1957 statistical yearbook of the Federal Republic show, for example, that Hamburg's crime rates were well below the national average and Berlin's and Bremen's were just barely above it).

3) Over the last 120 years, the greatest upsurges in crime rates have accompanied the economic hardship and political chaos following the two world wars of the twentieth century, but these upsurges have proved to be only temporary.

4) As in many other countries, young males in their late teens and early twenties have consistently had the highest rates of recorded crime, and women of all ages have consistently had the lowest rates of recorded crime (usually about one-fourth to one-fifth that of males).

5) Various non-ethnic German populations living in Germany have often had exceptionally high rates of recorded crime and continue to have higher than average rates today, but these rates must always be understood in relation to prevailing biases against them in the population and criminal-justice system.

The history of crime in Germany, like the history of German nationalism, has been scarred by an authoritarian, antipluralistic, and antiforeign bias. Many observers have regarded Bismarck's use of the legal system to crack down on Catholic and socialist political enemies as a prelude to Hitler's complete perversion of the police, laws, and justice system in his attempt to annihilate the Jews, socialists, and Communists whom he and other extreme nationalists denounced as "November criminals" after World War I. Although xenophobia and extreme nationalism continue to influence the debate concerning crime as Germany once again emerges as a unified nation, democratic and pluralistic forces today have the best chances of succeeding that they have had in Germany's troubled history.

Eric A. Johnson

See also Federal Republic of Germany: Political Terrorism; Judicial System of Imperial and Weimar Germany; Law, German Conception of; Minorities; National Socialism; Policing; Violence; Working Conditions

References

Blasius, Dirk. *Bürgerliche Gesellschaft und Kriminalität.* Göttingen: Vandenhoeck & Ruprecht, 1976.

———. *Kriminalität und Alltag: Zur Konfliktgeschichte des Alltagslebens.* Göttingen: Vandenhoeck & Ruprecht, 1978.

Dastner, Christian, et al. *Kriminalität in der Bundesrepublik: Ausmass und Reaktion.* Göttingen: Verlag Otto Schwartz, 1972.

Evans, Richard J. *Rituals of Retribution: Capital Punishment in Germany 1600–1987.* Oxford: Oxford University Press. 1996.

———, ed. *The German Underworld: Deviants and Outcasts in German History.* London: Routledge, 1988.

Funken, Christiane. *Frau—Frauen—Kriminelle: Zur aktuellen Diskussion über Frauenkriminalität.* Opladen: Westdeutscher Verlag, 1989.

Gellately, Robert. *The Gestapo and German Society: Enforcing Racial Policy 1933–1945.* Oxford: Oxford University Press, 1990.

Johnson, Eric A. *Urbanization and Crime: Germany 1871–1914.* New York, NY: Cambridge University Press, 1994.

Koch, H.W. *In the Name of the Volk: Political Justice in Hitler's Germany.* New York, NY: St. Martin's Press, 1989.

Zehr, Howard. *Modernization and Crime: Patterns of Criminality in Nineteenth Century Germany and France.* London: Croom Helm, 1976.

Crystal Night (*Kristallnacht*) (November 9, 1938)

The most violent expression of anti-Jewish sentiment prior to the war was named after the glass from the shattered windows of Jewish premises that littered the streets on the morning of November 10, 1938.

On November 9, 1938, Ernst vom Rath, third secretary of the German Embassy in Paris, was shot and killed by a 17-year-old Polish Jew, Herschel Grynszpan. The boy was acting out of revenge for the forcible deportation from Germany of his parents. With thousands of others, they had been dumped across the Polish border during the previous month.

Although Jews had been experiencing increased forms of discrimination and sporadic violence for some time, the *Kristallnacht* did not occur as a result of long-term planning. The events of November 9 were seized on by Propaganda Minister Joseph Goebbels (1897–1945), who was anxious to win back Hitler's favor after falling from grace because of an affair with the Czech actress Lida Baarova. Goebbels used the opportunity of an "old fighters" reunion in commemoration of the Munich *Putsch* of November 9, 1923, attended by Hitler, to proposed a coordinated campaign of terror against Jews. Groups of party activists and storm troopers were told to collect incendiary material to burn down their local synagogues and the police were ordered not to intervene. According to Nazi figures over 800 shops were destroyed, 191 synagogues set on fire, and 76 synagogues demolished; 91 Jews were killed, 20,000 arrested and taken to concentration

Nazi-sponsored boy-cotting of Jewish shops, November 9, 1939. Courtesy of Inter Nationes, Bonn.

camps. The total damage to property was estimated at 25 million reichsmarks.

The program was not in fact popular with the mass of the German people, who objected to the lawlessness, vandalism, and destruction of property involved. Nevertheless, *Kristallnacht* marked a radicalization of Jewish policy with the aim of driving Jews out of German economic life altogether. To add insult to injury, they were required to meet the cost of the damage to their property themselves, and on November 12, 1938 the Jewish community was ordered to pay a fine of one billion reichsmarks and was excluded from German economic life, thus formalizing the "Aryanization" of Jewish-owned property that had begun in the autumn of 1937.

The long-term significance of *Kristallnacht* was to convince the Nazi leadership of the limitations of an uncoordinated Jewish policy. In future, the "solution" to the so-called "Jewish problem" would be a more "rational" course of action, carried out by the SS and with the public largely excluded. Thus, *Kristallnacht* represents a crucial junction on the road to Auschwitz.

David Welch

See also Anti-Semitism; Goebbels, Joseph; Hitler, Adolf; Holocaust; Jews, 1933–90; National Socialist Germany

References

Bankier, D. *The Germans and the Final Solution: Public Opinion under Nazism.* Oxford: Blackwell, 1992.
Burleigh, M. and W. Wippermann. *The Racial State: Germany 1933–1945.* New York, NY: Cambridge University Press, 1991.
Gordon, Sarah. *Hitler, Germans, and the "Jewish Question."* Princeton NJ: Princeton University Press, 1984.
Schleunes, K. *The Twisted Road to Auschwitz: Nazi Policy towards German Jews 1933–39.* Urbana, IL: University of Illinois Press, 1990.
Welch, David. *The Third Reich: Politics and Propaganda.* London: Routledge, 1993.

Cuno, Wilhelm (1876–1933)

Born into a Catholic civil servant family, Wilhelm Cuno studied law at Heidelberg, Breslau, and Berlin universities. He entered the Imperial civil service in 1907 and served during World War I as head of the War Food Office (Kriegsernährungsamt). In 1918, he became director of the Hamburg-America Shipping Line (HAPAG). He was assigned as official government adviser in the German delegation to the Versailles peace conference and later became a leading spokesman for shipping interests.

When Social Democratic President Friedrich Ebert (1871–1925) asked Cuno to become chancellor in November 1922, Germany was faced with two major problems: reparations and the control of monetary inflation. His predecessor Joseph Wirth (1879–1956) had resigned because he had been unable to solve them. Furthermore, the political parties in the Reichstag were unable to agree on a new coalition government. Cuno did not belong to any party when he became chancellor, although he was close to the conservative German Peoples' Party (DVP). Cuno managed to form a government of so-called experts as chancellor from November 22, 1922 to August 12, 1923.

His cabinet was unique in many ways. Cuno had the trust of President Ebert, who believed in his personal integrity, expected him to succeed in negotiations with the major reparation powers (United States, Great Britain, and France), and hoped that the director of the HAPAG would gain the support of German business necessary to solve the reparation crisis. However, Cuno did not get the support of the parties in the Reichstag. He formed a cabinet above parties, which allowed individual party members to accept cabinet posts. Without a parliamentary basis, this weak cabinet did not request a vote of confidence in the Reichstag, but was accepted by the major parties as an easy way out of a parliamentary crisis.

Under normal conditions, the Cuno government would not have lasted long. Cuno's ideas about reparations and domestic reform did not differ much from his predecessor's, who had demanded a moratorium on reparations and negotiations with the Allied powers about a reduction of German payments. Cuno was not able to gain the support of German industry, nor was he able to open negotiations with the Allies. Instead, on January 11, 1923, French troops, accompanied by a small Belgian detachment, occupied the Ruhr district in order to enforce French reparation claims.

The Ruhr occupation united the German population and Cuno answered with a policy of passive resistance, ordering German civil servants, businessmen, and workers to reject any cooperation with the occupation forces. This policy was eased by British abstention from occupation and by American objections to it. However, after several months of fruitless resistance, the German economy had further deteriorated, the currency was destroyed in a hyperinflation, and Cuno was losing support for this policy. He resigned and returned to his work for the HAPAG.

Hermann J. Rupieper

See also Ebert, Friedrich; German People's Party; Inflation and Hyperinflation; Ruhr; Stresemann, Gustav; Weimar Germany

References

Harbeck, Harl Heinz, ed. *Das Kabinett Cuno: Akten der Reichskanzlei*. Boppard: Harold Boldt Verlag, 1968.

Jones, Kenneth Paul, ed. *U.S. Diplomats in Europe, 1919–1941*. Santa Barbara, CA: ABC-CLIO, 1983.

Nelson, Keith L. *Victors Divided: America and the Allies in Germany, 1918–1923*. Berkeley, CA: University of California Press, 1975.

Rupieper, Hermann J. *The Cuno Government and Reparations 1922/1923: Politics and Economics*. The Hague: Martinus Nijhoff Publishers, 1979.

Sternburg, Wilhelm von, ed. *Die Deutschen Kanzler von Bismarck bis Schmidt*. Königstein: Athenäum, 1986.

Currency

The history of German currency between 1871 and 1990 is less a history of dynastic succession of one currency by another than an evolution of monetary species. The deutsche mark of today is a fundamentally different creature from its evolutionary forebears.

Until 1871, the German states had six different systems of coinage and thirty-three note-issuing banks. In 1871 and 1873, the Empire officially introduced the mark as a monetary unit of account, equal to one-tenth of the value of a new gold coin, the *Reichsgoldmünze,* which had a parity of 1/279 kg of fine gold. The name of the new monetary unit reflected a political compromise struck between the competing thaler and gulden currency areas of northern and southern Germany, respectively. The new Reich chose the gold standard partly motivated by the example of England and partly by the possession of over five billion gold francs in French reparations payments. Silver coins circulated in Germany as legal tender until 1909.

In 1875, when the Bank of Prussia became the Reichsbank, Germany's first central bank, the other thirty-two banks continued to issue their bank notes privately, four of them until 1935. The notes issued by the Reichsbank became legal tender in 1909, which ratified what had long become a customary practice. Technically, the Reichsbank could redeem its notes in either gold or silver until 1909, but in practice its notes were being redeemed in gold alone long before that time. Neither the obligation nor the practice continued for long. Two days prior to World War I, the government suspended gold convertibility.

The unanticipated financial burdens of modern warfare vastly exceeded the planning capacities of military and civilian leaders. The Reichsbank covered the national debt by purchasing government war bonds with newly created fiat currency, trusting that most of it would be repaid upon victory. Instead, the Reichsbank launched hyperinflation.

The enormous debt generated by the lost war, veteran entitlements, and reparations payments exceeded the Weimar Republic's capacity to tax and borrow. The French and Belgian occupation of the Ruhr in 1923 further aggravated the fiscal situation. The Republic supported widespread strikes in the Ruhr by using proceeds from loans granted by the Reichsbank. Prices ultimately rose by one trillion percent during the fifteen months leading up to November 1923. The inflation peaked at 32,400 percent per month in October 1923. During that month, tax revenues accounted for only 1 percent of the Republic's expenditures. Freshly printed currency financed the remaining 99 percent.

The rentenmark, backed by a mortgage on land, stabilized the German monetary system. The Dawes Plan of 1924 changed the name of the currency to the reichsmark (RM), set at 4.2 RM to the gold-based American dollar. The old hyperinflated paper mark could be converted at a rate of one trillion to one. In order to ensure continued reparations payments, the Dawes Plan decreed that half the members of the Reichsbank be appointed by foreign representatives. Germany regained full monetary sovereignty in 1930, as part of the

Young Plan of 1929. Soon thereafter, the global banking crisis of July 1931 forced the Reichsbank to suspend the convertibility of the reichsmark into gold or American dollars.

The Third Reich gradually undermined the independence of the Reichsbank. In January 1939, Hitler dismissed its entire board of directors in response to a confidential memorandum that the central bank could not protect a currency against the onslaught of an outright inflationary fiscal policy. By then, the second major inflation of the German currency was well under way. Between 1935 and 1945, government debt increased twenty-six-fold, the currency in circulation ten-fold, and bank deposits about five-fold. The imposition of strict wage and price controls beginning in November 1936 made this inflation qualitatively different from that of 1922–23. Force of law temporarily suspended the link between the inflation of purchasing power and a spiral of wages and prices.

Equally strict foreign exchange controls prevented German wealth-holders from buying assets elsewhere, so that they accumulated government bonds and fiat currency relatively silently, i.e., without initiating a price inflation. This "suppressed inflation" became the monetary legacy of the Third Reich.

The Allied occupation powers continued the policy of suppressed inflation during the immediate postwar years. The coexistence of a currency explosion, shortages of goods, and price controls generated black markets, a barter economy, and increased use of commodity money, such as cigarettes.

The Western and Soviet representatives could not agree on a common economic policy for postwar Germany, whereupon the Western occupation zones independently implemented a currency reform. On June 21, 1948, they converted the reichsmark into the new currency, the deutsche mark (DM), at the rate of ten to one. Simultaneously, they decontrolled prices. The West German economic revival began with the birth of the deutsche mark, even though it could not yet be freely converted into other currencies. Only in 1958 did the deutsche mark become a currency that could be freely and completely exchanged, at the rate of 4.20 DM per American dollar.

The Soviet zone implemented a currency reform, also at the rate of ten reichsmarks to one mark. Suppressed inflation evolved into a centrally planned economy along Soviet lines. On July 1, 1990 a treaty on German monetary, economic, and social union converted the East German mark into the deutsche mark at an average rate of roughly 1.8 East German marks per DM.

According to the December 1991 Maastricht Treaty of the European Union, the final phase of a three-stage process to achieve economic and monetary union in Europe is to commence no later than 1999. For qualifying countries, the monetary sovereignty of their individual national central banks will be transferred to a European system of central banks. This plan will enable the deutsche mark to evolve into a fiscal token representing a common European currency.

Irwin Collier

See also Banking; Deutsche Bank; Economics; The Economics of German Reunification; Inflation and Hyperinflation

References

Deutsche Bundesbank. *Währung und Wirtschaft in Deutschland 1876–1975*. Frankfurt am Main: Verlag Fritz Knapp GmbH, 1985 *ff.*

Feldman, Gerald D. *The Great Disorder: Economics, Politics and Society in the German Inflation, 1914–24*. New York, NY: Oxford University Press, 1993.

Müller, Hans, ed. *Zur Vorgeschichte der Deutschen Mark: Die Währungsreformpläne 1945–1948: Eine Dokumentation*. Basel: Kyklos-Verlag, 1961.

Schinasi, G.J., L. Lipschitz, and D. McDonald. "Monetary and Financial Issues in German Unification." *German Unification: Economic Issues*. Ed. Leslie Lipschitz and Donogh McDonald. Washington, DC: International Monetary Fund, 1990.

Siedenberg, Axel and Helmut Kaiser. "German Monetary Unification (GMU)." *The New Palgrave Dictionary of Money & Finance*. Vol 2. Ed. P. Newman, M. Milgate, and J. Eatwell. London: Macmillan, 1992.

Welcker, Johannes. "Germany: Monetary and Financial System." *The New Palgrave Dictionary of Money & Finance*. Vol. 2. Ed. P. Newman, M. Milgate, and J. Eatwell. London: Macmillan, 1992.

Customs

Germany is still rich in customs marking various stages through life. On the first school day a child carries a big decorated cardboard cone filled with all kinds of small novelties that are unpacked during the course of the morning. Throughout the summer, *Kinderfeste*—special open-air parties for children—are held in most towns, with the simple aim of giving pleasure to the children.

Birthdays are celebrated with great enthusiasm not only by children but also by adults. The breakfast and afternoon coffee tables are often decorated with a special birthday wreath (*Geburtstagskranz*) with a white candle, the "life candle" (*Lebenskerze*) in the center. An alternative birthday candle holder is a wooden, heart-shaped base containing a wooden numeral and a small candle. Adults are expected to take special food or drink to work to offer to their colleagues, birthdays ending in a zero requiring special fare. Adult friends are invited in midafternoon for splendid cakes and coffee. All guests bring bouquets of flowers or presents. Special regional customs accompany particular birthdays—for example, an unmarried 30-year-old must sweep the steps of Bremen Cathedral.

Various celebrations are connected with houses and homes. The completion of a new house is preceded by the topping-out celebrations (*Richtfest*). Salt and bread are still symbolically given to people who have moved, and a surprise party (*Stühlerücken*) is often held for those who have just moved.

The rites of passage connected with the Church are similar to those in other countries. Births are usually announced with a simple printed card. Children will have their first communion or be confirmed between the ages of 8 and 16. At confirmation the young person receives many confirmation

Vine-dresser dance, Winnigen/Mosel. Courtesy of German Embassy, Ottawa.

presents or large sums of money. The day is marked by a family get-together with godparents at a special celebration meal.

Engagement celebrations, if they take place at all, follow no one prescribed pattern. The prospective children-in-law are usually invited by their respective parents-in-law to address them with the familiar *du* instead of the formal *Sie*, thus symbolizing their acceptance into the family circle. Friends and distant relatives are informed by printed announcements of the engagement and plain identical engagement rings are exchanged by the couple, to be worn on the third finger of the left hand by both partners until the marriage ceremony, when they are transferred to the corresponding finger of the right hand.

The wedding is made public by means of a printed announcement card sent out a few days before the event, and sometimes a press announcement is made, though the invited guests will have been informed much earlier.

The eve-of-the-wedding party is known as the *Polterabend*, because of the old belief that noise frightens away evil spirits. Some people still throw items of chipped crockery against a "wedding house" at the *Polterabend*, resulting in a pile of broken china by the door. This custom comes from the superstitious belief that broken fragments are lucky. The church wedding alone is insufficient under German law and has to be preceded by a civil ceremony at the Registry Office. The bridal couple then travels to church together, sometimes in a horse-drawn wedding coach, and they are preceded up the aisle by small children who strew flowers across their path. The reception can simply take the form of afternoon coffee or can include an evening meal followed by a dance. Friends of the couple often produce a newsletter containing humorous reminiscences and even songs to be sung by the whole wedding party. Sometimes the bride is "stolen" during the reception, but she is always found in a local hostelry where she can be freed when the bridegroom pays the ransom in the form of the bill for the robbers' drinks.

Nowadays most deaths are marked by a death announcement in the newspaper or sent through the post on black-edged stationery, followed by a simple funeral service and burial or cremation. Then the mourners often go to a nearby restaurant or house to drink coffee together and eat the special funeral cake, *Butterkuchen* or *Streuselkuchen*. This event, as do all meetings in Germany, ends with the shaking of hands and the sending of greetings to other members of the family not present.

Jennifer M. Russ

See also Carnival; Christmas

References

Beitl, Richard. *Wörterbuch der deutschen Volkskunde.* 3rd ed. Stuttgart: Kröner, 1974.

Rippley, LaVern. *Of German Ways.* New York, NY: Barnes and Noble, 1980.

Russ, Jennifer M. *German Festivals and Customs.* London: Oswald Wolff, 1982.

Schönfeldt, Sybil Gräfin. *Das Ravensburger Buch der Feste und Bräuche.* Ravensburg: Otto Maier, 1980.

Weber-Kellermann, Ingeborg. *Saure Wochen Frohe Feste: Fest und Alltag in der Sprache der Bräuche.* Munich: C.J. Bucher, 1985.

Dada

This provocative international art movement proclaimed an anti-aesthetic and anti-art (bourgeois/conventional) philosophy embracing all the arts. It was founded in 1916 in Zürich by Hugo Ball (1886–1927) and Emmy Hennings (1885–1948) as "Cabaret Voltaire." Its performances were outstanding examples of nonconformity and public provocations. Other participants in the early period were Richard Hülsenbeck (1892–1974), the French/Swiss Hans (Jean) Arp (1887–1966), and the Romanians Marcel Janco (1895–1984), Tristan Tzara (1896–1963), and Hans Richter (1888–1976).

The next Dada center, this one with strong political tendencies, sprang up in Berlin in 1918 with Hülsenbeck, Johannes Baader (1875–1956), Hannah Höch (1889–1978), Raoul Hausmann (1886–1971), and George Grosz (1893–1959). Max Ernst (1891–1976), Arp, and Johannes Theodor Baargeld (1892–1927) formed a Dada group in Cologne in 1919. Kurt Schwitters (1887–1948) formed a one-man offspring in Hannover. The most significant contributions consisted of collages and assemblages, experimentation with language (simultaneous and sound-poetry), abstract paintings and reliefs, "performances," and abstract films. The movement spread to Paris (1919), with Tristan Tzara, Francis Picabia, and André Breton, and had forerunners in New York (Alfred Stieglitz, Marcel Duchamp, and Man Ray).

The groups published a number of short-lived journals that contained their manifestos and examples of literary and visual works. Most participants wrote autobiographies and left collages and other works; a Dada Archives and Research Center is located at the University of Iowa. Some trends in surrealism were rooted in Dada.

Peter Guenther

See also Artists; Ernst, Max; Grosz, Georg; Höch, Hannah; Painting; Schwitters, Kurt

References
Ades, Dawn. *In the Mind's Eye: Dada and Surrealism.* Chicago, IL: Museum of Contemporary Art; New York, NY: Abbeville Publishers, 1985.
Freeman, Judi. *The Dada and Surrealist Word-Image.* Cambridge, MA: MIT Press, 1989.
Hülsenbeck, Richard. *Dada Almanach.* 2nd ed. Hamburg: Edition Nautilus, 1987.
Motherwell, Robert, ed. *The Dada Painters and Poets: An Anthology.* 2nd ed. Cambridge, MA: Bellknap Press, 1989.
Short, Robert. *Dada and Surrealism.* London: Lawrence King Publishers, 1994.

Daily Telegraph Affair (1908)

The *Daily Telegraph* affair in November 1908 was the most serious domestic crisis in the reign of Kaiser Wilhelm II before the outbreak of World War I. Although it did not engender constitutional reform, it focused public attention on the deficiencies of Wilhelmine government, provoked severe criticism of the kaiser's "personal rule," and caused acute national humiliation. It also shattered the monarch's confidence in his chancellor, Bernhard von Bülow (1849–1929), which forced Bülow to resign after the parliamentary defeat of the Reich financial reform (1909).

The affair resulted from the publication of Wilhelm II's remarks to friends in England (1907) in the form of an interview with Colonel Stuart-Wortley in the British newspaper *Daily Telegraph* on October 28, 1908. Intended to improve Anglo-German relations, the remarks "You English are mad, mad as March hares! What has come over you that you are so completely given over to suspicions quite unworthy of a great nation? What more can I do than I have done? . . . The prevailing sentiment amongst my own people is not friendly to England. I am in a minority in my own land. . . . That is another reason why I resent your refusal to accept my pledged word that I am the friend of England," were seen as politically inept and damaging, the latest in a long line of royal indiscretions that further compromised Germany's unenviable international position.

Since the kaiser had acted constitutionally in submitting the text of the interview to the chancellor for vetting prior to publication, public attacks were, in the first instance, directed against the incompetence of Bülow and the Foreign Office, but soon shifted to the irresponsibility of the kaiser's remarks. Even the German Conservative Party joined the public outcry and urged the monarch to be more restrained in the future. Bülow failed to defend the kaiser unequivocally in the crucial Reichstag debate of November 10–11 and thus incurred Wilhelm's lasting hostility. Despite the broad consensus within the executive, legislature, and press that constitutional safeguards ought to be erected against a repetition of the affair, Bülow was content to secure personal rather than political guarantees from the kaiser, thereby avoiding potential constraints on his own position. The Reichstag also proved unable subsequently to exploit the affair to increase its own powers. Although the affair prompted a deeply depressed Wilhelm II to consider abdication in November 1908, it ultimately had no political consequences save Bülow's eventual fall.

Katherine Anne Lerman

See also Anglo-German Relations; Bülow, Bernhard von; Imperial Germany; Wilhelm II

References

Lerman, Katherine A. *The Chancellor as Courtier: Bernhard von Bülow and the Governance of Germany 1900–1909*. Cambridge: Cambridge University Press, 1990.

Schüssler, Wilhelm. *Die Daily-Telegraph-Affaire: Fürst Bülow, Kaiser Wilhelm und die Krise des zweiten Reiches 1908*. Göttingen: Musterschmidt Wissenschaftlicher Verlag, 1952.

Daimler, Gottlieb (1834–1900)

Daimler was an engineer and businessman who, with Karl Benz (1844–1929), created the modern automobile. Benz, who lived only 100 miles away, worked simultaneously to patent a motor car. Neither knew of the other. Daimler's aim in life was not principally the construction of a car, but the motorization of transport on water, on land, and in the air. With the design of a small, high-speed internal combustion engine he achieved the crucial prerequisite for the development of modern transport.

Daimler came from Schorndorf, where his ancestors operated a small bakery and a wine bar. He trained in mechanical engineering to satisfy his own personal interests, toiled as a simple factory worker, and attained further education at a polytechnical institute in Stuttgart. His apprentice years frequently took him abroad, to Paris, London, Manchester, and Leeds. There he acquired considerable knowledge regarding the layout of factories and the organization of production processes.

In 1867, he took his first executive position at the Reutlingon Bruderhau machine factory, a charitable organization for orphaned children. He met the young, gifted Wilhelm Maybach, who was a superb designer. A lifelong, con-

Gottlieb Daimler. Courtesy of German Information Center, New York.

genial work relationship developed between them, without which Daimler's life work would have been less meaningful.

From 1872, both men were employed at the Deutz gas engine factory for ten years, Maybach as chief engineer and Daimler the technical director. In this position he managed the production of the four-stroke engine developed by Nikolaus August Otto at Deutz (1876). Sales of the four-stroke engine brought in high profits. In 1882, however, Daimler and Maybach withdrew following a difference of opinion with management. In a small experimental workshop in Stuttgart they attempted to develop a high-speed internal combustion engine of limited weight. This engine was designed to drive various means of transport.

In 1885, the first operational car engine ran: an upright, one-cylinder, four-stroke engine with an open hot-tube ignition system, curved groove control, and floating carburetor. It achieved an output of 1 hp at 600 rpm and was first built into a motorbike (1885), then a four-wheel coach and a boat (1886). Later applications included railway inspection cars, locomotives, fire pumps, streetcars, and exhibition trains (1887–88). It was even built into an airship that lifted off in 1888 from Daimler's factory grounds, thus marking the beginning of dirigible airship history in Germany.

Since performance and cooling of the engine were inefficient, Maybach quickly created, in sequence, the first two-cylinder V-engine (1889) for Daimler, the first four-cylinder in-line engine (the model of all modern in-line engines; 1890), the first gearbox in the history of the car

(1889), a water cooling system (1890), the air mist carbu-retor (1893), and the first individually designed cars, such as the wire-wheel car (1889) and the first truck (1896). These and the first Benz cars were the origins of Daimler-Benz AG production.

Daimler devoted himself to financial and business tasks, to founding the Daimler-Motoren-Gesellschaft in 1890, and to establishing international business relations. The beginnings of the French (Panhard, Levassor, Peugeot, 1890) and the British (Daimler Coventry, 1886) car industries were based on licenses for Daimler engines. In the United States, the first engines based on the Daimler license were built in Hartford, Connecticut (1891). At the same time, Steinway of New York made Daimler products available throughout the North American continent through a catalogue and an exhibition.

While his engine design quickly spread throughout the world, illnesses and disagreements with business partners about his financial holdings, the use of his patent, and the management of the company overshadowed the last years of Daimler's life. He died in 1900 in Stuttgart, highly honored among the founders of the automobile.

Otto Nübel

See also Automobile Industry; Benz, Karl; Daimler-Benz AG; Inventions; Otto, Nikolaus; Technology

References

Bird, Anthony. *Gottlieb Daimler, Inventor of the Motor En-gine.* London: Weidenfeld and Nicolson, 1962.
Schildberger, Friedrich. *Gottlieb Daimler und Karl Benz: Pioniere der Automobilindustrie.* Göttingen: Musterschmidt, 1976.
Siebertz, Paul. *Gottlieb Daimler—Ein Revolutionär der Technik.* 4th ed. Stuttgart: Reclam, 1950.

Daimler-Benz AG

The oldest auto manufacturer in the world, Daimler-Benz has developed into a high-technology group with four corporate units: Mercedes-Benz, AEG, Deutsche Aerospace, and Daimler-Benz InterServices (known as debis). The two original firms, Benz & Cie., founded by Karl Benz (1844–1929) in 1882–83, and Daimler-Motoren-Gesellschaft, founded by Gottlieb Daimler (1834–1900) in 1890, amalgamated in 1926 to form Daimler-Benz AG.

Its main field of activity remains the manufacture of motor vehicles under the trade name of Mercedes-Benz; production in 1991 was 578,000 cars and 296,000 commercial vehicles. Since 1985 the company has diversified into electrical engineering and electronics (AEG), aviation and space systems (Deutsche Aerospace), and the services sector (debis).

The history of the firm—and hence of the modern car—began with the construction of the first vehicles to be driven by high-speed internal combustion engines: the Benz Patent Motor Car and the Daimler motor carriage (1886). From Daimler's patents emerged the French car industry (Levassor,

Panhard, Peugeot), followed by the British (Daimler Coventry). America's first functional automotive engines were manufactured under Daimler license in Hartford, Connecticut. Daimler also built the first truck (1896). Benz manufactured the first mass-produced vehicle, the Velo (1894), as well as the first modern omnibuses (1895), and became into the world's biggest motor vehicle factory (1900).

Whereas Benz focused on the motorcar, Daimler concentrated on the engine, which he built into vehicles already available such as carriages, locomotives, and streetcars (1886–88), as well as fire-fighting pumps (1888), boats (1886), and the first airship to be driven by a gas engine (1888). He thereby anticipated the firm's later venues on land, on water, and in the air. When the first airplanes appeared, Benz and Daimler, both leading competitors in car manufacture, began to produce aircraft engines and airplanes. Both subsequently became involved in the arms industry during World War I. The difficult postwar economic situation led to the amalgamation of both firms into Daimler-Benz AG (1926).

Together they owned five factories; in Mannheim and Gaggenau (previously Benz's), and in Untertürkheim, Sindelfingen, and Berlin (previously Daimler's), in which initially only cars and commercial vehicles were manufactured (10,829 units) in 1927. They rapidly moved on to large engines for ships, airships, and airplanes, which led once again to arms deliveries during World War II, mainly aircraft engines and military vehicles. The company was as much part of the National Socialist armaments machine as was German industry in general. In the years 1933–45 it continued to play its traditional leading role in the German economy. As early as the 1920s, the diesel engine, designed as a vehicle propulsion unit by Benz in 1922–23, was introduced in commercial vehicles, and after 1936 was fitted into cars. The supercharged sports cars became world famous, as did the Daimler-Benz racing cars (Silver Arrows).

After the war, the plants were almost totally dismantled and had to be reconstructed over a number of years. Not until the 1950s did Daimler-Benz venture into the world market, with the export of trucks to India (1950), as well as to Brazil, Argentina, and the United States (1952), where the 300 SL sports car with gull-wing doors came to symbolize this era.

Daimler-Benz is now represented in almost 200 countries and regards itself, along with its production plant, as a global player. Today, Daimler-Benz is the largest industrial enterprise in Germany, with 1991 sales of approximately 95 billion deutsche marks and a workforce of 379,000.

Otto Nübel

See also Automobile Industry; Benz, Karl; Daimler, Gottlieb; Otto, Nikolaus

References

Bellon, Bernard. *Mercedes in Peace and War: German Auto-mobile Workers 1903–1945.* New York, NY: Columbia University Press, 1990.
100 Jahre Daimler-Benz: Das Unternehmen, Die Technik. Mainz: Von Hase & Koehler, 1986.

Oswald, Werner. *Mercedes-Benz Personenwagen 1886–1984.* 2nd ed. Stuttgart: Motorbuch, 1985.

Roth, Karl Heinz. "Der Weg zum Guten Stern des Dritten Reichs: Schlaglichter auf die Geschichte der Daimler-Benz AG und ihre Vorläufer (1890–1945)." *Das Daimler-Benz Buch: Ein Rüstungskonzern im "Tausenjährigen Reich."* Ed. Hamburger Stiftung für Sozialgeschichte. Nördlingen: Greno, 1987.

Danish-German Relations

After the war of 1864, Denmark lost her German-speaking territories in Schleswig-Holstein. However, in northern Schleswig the majority of the population was Danish, and since 1864, this ethnic group's existence has had a continuing influence on German-Danish relations.

German cultural influence in Denmark was considerable into the twentieth century. However, the Schleswig conflict created a tension that was mainly perceptible in Denmark, leading to a cooling off in the Danish-German interchange. German interest in "things Nordic," dating to the eighteenth century, however, meant that Danish literature found its way into the international mainstream via German translations.

After World War I, a referendum was held in Schleswig; the northern zone had a Danish majority and the southern a German. Although a new border was established, by 1921, it was not possible to reach a bilateral agreement concerning the rights of both minorities. Such an agreement was rejected by all Danish governments, as they wished to avoid interference by the great power Germany in internal Danish affairs. During the interwar years, Danish-German relations were strained because of the minority conditions, as neither side accepted the new border and many demanded that it be moved. However, the Social Democratic Parties (SPDs) in both countries, which had been cooperating for a long time, recognized the border in an accord (1923). Since the two parties exerted considerable influence, this was important for stability.

The Nazi ascension to power led to renewed tension and had as one consequence the Nazification of the German minority north of the border. Another consequence was that the SPD in Denmark chose a more "national" line, expressed, for instance, in its attitude to the defense question.

In 1940, Denmark was occupied by German troops. The Danish government continued in office until August 1943—albeit in a restricted manner. During 1943, a free general election to the parliament took place. But after the banning of the Communist Party in 1941, resistance to the Nazi occupation grew, and after Stalingrad the resistance movement gained broad support in the working classes. Extensive industrial strikes during 1943 forced the government to resign. The SPD, which since 1929 had wielded the dominating political power in Denmark, collaborated with the Germans, which made possible the special occupation policy that saw Denmark through the war without tremendous losses in human lives. It also made possible the rescue transfer of nearly all Danish Jews to Sweden.

The post-1945 period saw considerable change in the situation of the two minorities. In 1955, the governments of both countries made solemn declarations that regulated the conditions for the minorities. This policy of "detente" has meant that today, all national conflicts between Denmark and Germany are settled. However, the relationship is by no means identical to the situation prior to the beginning of the national struggle. German is no longer the world language it once was, nevertheless it is taught in Danish schools as the second foreign language; nor is Germany perceived as a threatening world power. Germany's importance to Denmark as a trading partner has varied over the period, but has at all times been considerable. German cultural influence in Denmark, however, has been largely replaced by Anglo-American impulses since 1945.

Gerd Callesen

See also Federal Republic of Germany: Foreign Policy; Holocaust; Minorities; National Socialist Germany; Resistance; Schleswig-Holstein; World War II

References

Brandt, Otto. *Geschichte Schleswig-Holsteins: Ein Grundriss.* 8th ed. Ed. Wilhelm Klüver. Kiel: Walter G. Mühlau, 1981.

Callesen, Gerd. *Die Schleswig-Frage in den Beziehungen zwischen dänischer und deutscher Sozialdemokratie von 1912 bis 1924: Ein Beitrag zum sozialdemokratischen Internationalismus.* Schriften der Heimatkundlichen Arbeitsgemeinschaft für Nordschleswig 21. Apenrade: Heimatkundliche Arbeitsgemeinschaft, 1970.

Fink, Troels. *Deutschland als Problem Dänemarks: Die geschichtlichen Voraussetzungen der dänischen Aussenpolitik,* Flensburg: Christian Wolff Verlag, 1968.

Jensen, Jens Christian, ed. *Vor hundert Jahren: Dänemark und Deutschland 1864–1900. Gegnern und Nachbarn.* Kiel: Kunsthalle, 1981.

Nissen, Henrik S., ed. *Scandinavia during the Second World War.* Oslo: Universitetsforlaget, 1983.

Søe, Christian. "Denmark and Germany: From Ambivalence to Affirmation?" *The Germans and Their Neighbors.* Ed. D. Verheyen and Christian Søe. Boulder, CO: Westwood Press, 1993.

Yahil, Leni. *The Rescue of Danish Jewry: Test of a Democracy.* Philadelphia, PA: Jewish Publication Society of America, 1969.

Danzig, Free City of (1920–39)

The Free City of Danzig was created by the Treaty of Versailles (Articles 100–108) as a compromise between the principle of national self-determination and Woodrow Wilson's 13th point, which assured Poland "a free and secure access to the sea." The German-speaking city and its environs (with a Polish minority of about 5 percent) were separated from Germany involuntarily but were permitted an autonomous government under the protection and constitutional supervision of the League of Nations, with certain prerogatives reserved for Poland. Danzig became important as a symbol of German resentment of the Treaty of Versailles and as an issue in German-Polish relations.

Danzig also provided a unique window into political life under National Socialism. The Nazi Party took power in the Free City after elections on May 28, 1933, gave the party 50.03 percent of the vote. However, it was not possible for *Gauleiter* (regional party leader) Albert Forster to establish a true copy of Hitler's dictatorship. The Nazi Party was forced to govern under the eyes of Poland and the League of Nations. The first Nazi president of Danzig, Hermann Rauschning, was a conservative who believed in following legal norms and who tried to use his post to reconcile Poland and Germany. Rauschning contributed to the improvement in relations that led to the German-Polish non-aggression pact of January 1934, and his cooperation with the League of Nations improved British-German relations. He served Hitler's purposes well in 1933 and 1934, but Forster was able to force him out of office in November 1934 and replace him with a more dedicated party man, Arthur Greiser.

Elections on April 7, 1935 produced not quite 59 percent for the Nazis, despite widespread election fraud and the intimidation of opponents. This countered the impression left by the Saar plebiscite of January 1935 that the entire German people supported Hitler. Most impressive was the ability of the opposition groups (Catholic Center, nationalist conservatives, and Social Democrats), to survive under difficult conditions and to work together against the Nazis. A serious economic downturn and a currency devaluation increased the popularity of the opposition. Petitions to force a supervised new election in late 1935 were rejected by the League Council. Had an election been held, the Nazis would likely have been resoundingly defeated.

The increasing weakness of the League and the essential indifference of Poland (provided Polish rights were respected) led to the destruction of the organized opposition by the end of 1937. Nor could the League prevent the introduction of anti-Semitic legislation late in 1938 and the increasing persecution of Danzig's remaining Jews. After March 1939, Danzig's Nazis contributed to the increasing pressure Germany placed on Poland. Danzig was readied as a staging area for the German invasion of Poland. The Free City was annexed to Germany on September 1, 1939, at the start of World War II.

Herbert S. Levine

See also National Socialist Germany: Foreign Policy; Polish-German Relations, 1918–45; Stresemann, Gustav; Versailles, Treaty of; Weimar Germany: Foreign Policy; World War I

References

Kimmich, Christoph M. *The Free City: Danzig and German Foreign Policy, 1919–1934.* New Haven, CT: Yale University Press, 1968.

Levine, Herbert S. *Hitler's Free City: A History of the Nazi Party in Danzig, 1925–39.* Chicago, IL: University of Chicago Press, 1973.

Darré, R. Walther (1895–1953)

R. Walther Darré was the author of two controversial books that argued that the Nordic peasant was the basis, both racial and cultural, for all that was great in German civilization. He was appointed by Adolf Hitler to organize the German peasants politically for National Socialism in 1930 and became minister of agriculture in 1933, a post he retained until May 1942.

Darré, born to a German merchant family in Belgrano, Argentina on July 14, 1895, came to Germany in 1905 for his education and was preparing to become a colonial farmer when World War I broke out. After serving as an officer, he spent time as a student, as a civil servant, and as a writer. In his most important work, *Das Bauerntum* (The peasantry), published in 1929, he argued that the peasant class was the life-source of the Nordic race, and, if its decline were not halted, German civilization was doomed. His ideas brought him to the attention of Hitler, and in 1930 Darré was appointed to organize the peasants for the Nazis.

The rural classes had paid little attention to Hitler before this time, but Darré was very successful in building a political machine, the *Agrarpolitischer Apparat*, which infiltrated existing agricultural organizations, and he developed appeals to farmers all over Germany based on his concepts of *Blut und Boden* (blood and soil). The result was apparent in the large electoral gains of the Nazis in 1932, which included many additional rural votes.

On June 29, 1933 Hitler appointed Darré to be minister of agriculture. He moved quickly to restructure German agriculture by developing the two laws, passed in September 1933, that created the *Reichsnährstand* (Reich Food Corporation) and the *Reicherbhöfe* (Reich Hereditary Farms). The first assured farmers of economic security by creating a market structure whereby all farm production and prices could be controlled, and the second guaranteed them honor by giving them a special place in the Nazi state. Darré believed that only if farmers were prosperous and happy could they serve as the source of racial and cultural purity. By 1936 Darré seemed to have succeeded. Agriculture was in better shape than it had been since World War I. Hitler, however, had other plans. He wanted the organization Darré had created to be harnessed to efficient war production. The Second Four-Year Plan effectively stripped Darré of his power, though he remained in Hitler's cabinet until 1942. After the war, in 1948, he was tried by the Nuremberg court as part of the Ministries Case, was found to be guilty of two of eight counts, and was sentenced to seven years in prison. He was released in 1950 and died in Munich of a liver ailment on September 5, 1953.

Darré was a curious figure in the Nazi hierarchy. He wanted to turn the clock backward in order to recreate an ideal agricultural past, while his colleagues sought to increase production through modernization. He wanted a self-sufficient, isolated Germany, while Hitler sought world domination. One can argue that Darré was not a real Nazi, and it is true that he was different from most of the others, but he played a crucial role in both Hitler's rise to power and the preparation for war.

Clifford R. Lovin

See also Agrarian Leagues; Agriculture; National Socialist Germany; Peasantry; Racism; *Völkisch* Ideology

References

Bramwell, Anne. *Blood and Soil: Richard Walther Darré and Hitler's Green Party.* Abbotsbrook: Kensal House, 1985.

Corni, Gustavo. *Hitler and the Peasants: Agrarian Policy of the Third Reich, 1930-1939.* New York, NY: Berg Publishers, 1990.

Darré, R. Walther. *Das Bauerntum als Lebensquelle der Nordischen Rasse and Neuadel aus Blut und Boden.* Munich: J.F. Lehmanns Verlag, 1929 and 1930.

Farquharson, J. E. *The Plough and the Swastika: The NSDAP and Agriculture in Germany, 1928-1945.* London: Sage Publications, 1976.

Reischle, Hermann. *Reichsbauernführer Darré, Der Kämpfer um Blut und Boden.* Berlin: Verlag und Vertriebsgesellschaft, 1933.

David, Eduard (1863–1930)

This influential Social Democratic politician (born June 11, 1863 in Ediger an der Mosel; died December 24, 1930) was the son of a state official. Eduard David achieved a doctorate in 1891 and became a secondary school teacher, but had to leave his post because of his activities for the Social Democratic Party (SPD). As editor of SPD newspapers, he attained a seat in the Hesse Landtag (legislature) in 1896 and won a by-election to the Reichstag in 1903.

In the SPD debates on agrarian policies (1894–95), David played an important role: he favored a policy of improving the situation of the small holding farmers and acted as the opponent of Karl Kautsky (1854–1938) at the party congress of 1895. Without letting himself be drawn into fine points of theoretical Marxism, he took the side of Eduard Bernstein (1850–1932) in the so-called revisionism debates.

In the Reichstag—his most important area of work—David concentrated upon economic, tax, and agrarian policies; after 1910, also foreign policy. He condemned any provocation of Great Britain by the German government and opted for understanding between Great Britain and Germany.

David achieved his optimum influence during World War I in pushing the leadership group around Friedrich Ebert (1871–1925) to collaborate with the German state. He was among the most important representatives of the right wing of the SPD Reichstag caucus, which sought a German victory, dropped all opposition to the government, and cooperated with the bourgeois parties. He had close contacts with the trade union leaders who supported these policies. David strongly favored Social Democratic participation in the government of Prince Max von Baden (1867–1929) in October 1918.

Although David was a member of the SPD-led government in 1919–20 and remained a Reichstag representative until his death, he had only limited influence during the Weimar Republic. Despite being a strong exponent of a na-

tional policy for the SPD during the world war and fostering collaboration with the middle-class parties, he has been nearly overlooked by his own party and in historical studies. Yet his views on reforms in agriculture and in internal policies have in effect become reality within the SPD.

Susanne Miller

See also Agriculture; Bernstein, Eduard; Ebert, Friedrich; Kautsky, Karl; Max von Baden; Peasantry; Social Democratic Party; World War I

References

Matthias, Erich, ed., with Susanne Miller. *Das Kriegstagebuch des Reichstagsabgeordneten Eduard David 1914 bis 1918.* Düsseldorf: Droste, 1966.

Schorske, Carl. *The Origins of the Great Schism: German Social Democracy 1905–1917.* Cambridge, MA: Harvard University Press, 1955.

Schwieger, Gerd. "Zwischen Obstruktion und Kooperation. Eduard David und die SPD im Kriege." Unpublished doctoral dissertation. Universität Kiel, 1970.

Dawes Plan

The Dawes Plan was named after Charles G. Dawes (1865–1951), American lawyer, financier, and general, who was appointed by the Allied Reparation Commission in 1923 as a semi-official American member of the Committee of Experts to report on means of balancing Germany's budget and stabilizing its currency. Dawes was selected chairman of the committee, which developed a plan to make the actual transfer of reparation payments conditional on the stability of the German exchange. It was an attempt to withdraw this highly complicated question from international controversy among the principal European powers, especially France and Germany.

When the report was finally published on April 9, 1924, after sharp disagreements concerning the amount of the German annuity, the nature of guarantees, and numerous other issues, it represented the maximum concessions of the various powers and paved the way for the later Locarno agreements. The Dawes Plan called for German reparation payments beginning with 1 billion reichsmarks (RM) in 1924–25 and rising gradually to a standard of 2.5 billion RM, a rate to be reached in 1928–29. Thereafter, Germany's obligations might be adjusted upward, according to an index of prosperity. The total amount for which Germany would be held liable would cover all costs arising from World War I and include the expenses for occupation armies, the control commissions, and interest on foreign loans to Germany, in addition to reparations. Only half of the standard annual payments would come from the German budget. The rest would be derived from interest on first mortgage bonds issued on the assets of German industry and the German railway system.

The plan also solved the transfer issue by creating an agent for reparation payments and a Bank of Issue in Berlin. Together with five financial specialists, the agent would determine how much Germany could safely transfer to the Allied powers without creating foreign exchange difficulties.

The Dawes Plan did not immediately end the Ruhr occupation, but it provided a substantial breathing space and an institutional framework suitable for working out a viable long-term reparation scheme. The German government did not achieve a balanced budget nor an export surplus by the time the question of a final settlement arose in 1928. By then, the situation was further complicated by the increasing pressure from the conservative American administration for the repayment of war loans, the growth of French financial power relative to that of Great Britain, and the German pressure for a definite solution. In fact, the policies of the major creditor countries remained unconducive to a rational reparation settlement. Even less could be expected from Germany, given that the coming negotiations were to be the preserve of bankers rather than of politicians.

Hermann J. Rupieper

See also American-German Relations; Anglo-German Relations; Currency; Franco-German Relations; German National People's Party; Inflation and Hyperinflation; Reparations; Ruhr Crisis; Versailles, Treaty of; Weimar Germany; World War I

References

Holz, Kurt A. *Die Diskussion um den Dawes- und Young-Plan in der deutschen Presse.* 2 vols. Frankfurt am Main: Haar und Herchen, 1977.

Kent, Bruce. *The Spoils of War: The Politics, Economics, and Diplomacy of Reparations 1918–1932.* New York, NY: Oxford University Press, 1985.

Link, Werner. *Die amerikanische Stabilisierungspolitik in Deutschland 1921–1932.* Düsseldorf: Droste Verlag, 1970.

Pohl, Karl Heinrich. *Weimars Wirtschaft und die Aussenpolitik der Republik 1924–1926: Vom Dawes-Plan zum internationalen Eisenpakt.* Düsseldorf: Droste Verlag, 1979.

Schuker, Stephen A. *American "Reparations" to Germany, 1919–1933: Implication for the Third World Debt Crisis.* Princeton, NJ: Princeton University Press, 1988.

———. *The End of French Predominance in Europe. The Financial Collapse of 1924 and the Adoption of the Dawes Plan.* Chapel Hill, NC: The University of North Carolina Press, 1986.

Decadence

Decadence (German equivalent *Entartung*) is a concept used in the German-speaking countries less as an objective assessment of quality than as a political catchword. A judgment of "decadence" is more likely to denote public misunderstanding of radical creative ideas than recognition of mediocre standards of creation. The forms in which the term is most likely to be applied—visual art, drama or film, literature or music—are notable in their use as the voices of individuals who comment on society, which are potentially useful in political ways and may ultimately escape beyond control. Therefore, the definition of decadence in a work of art is subject to variant interpretations and thus to abuse and misstatement, depending on the political beliefs of the observer.

In the German-speaking countries, preoccupation with the definition of decadence in individual cases centered around two main periods. The first was during the fin-de-siècle period in Vienna. It was born of a society without moral basis, pointed out by intellectuals in their work, therefore misunderstood by the general public. Among the creative geniuses who challenged the morality of the society in which they lived were artists Gustav Klimt and Oskar Kokoschka (1886–1980), writers Hugo von Hofmannsthal (1874–1929), Arthur Schnitzler (1862–1931), Franz Werfel, Hermann Bahr, and Theodor Herzl, and composers Gustav Mahler (1860–1911), Arnold Schönberg (1874–1951), Alban Berg (1885–1935), and Anton von Webern (1883–1945). A voice apart from these, who observed the effect of societal mores on the individual in the course of his work, was Sigmund Freud (1856–1939).

The connecting link between this period and the Third Reich, which was established on the principle of redeeming society from its decadence, was the person of Adolf Hitler, who developed his ideas as a young man while living in Vienna. As influenced by the anti-Semitic politicians Karl Lueger and Georg von Schönerer, Hitler transmuted his standards of "morality" into legal practice during the Third Reich. Almost all of the intellectuals listed above, many of them Jews, were condemned by the Nazis as un-German, and their works were banned from public access. One additional form of art was closely controlled by the political censors of the Third Reich. Film, in which the Germans were the acknowledged experts during the silent and early sound eras, had not achieved widespread circulation until after World War I. A comparison of the films created during the Weimar Republic with those made during the Third Reich suggests that one genre—the horror film—vanished so suddenly (within weeks of the seizure of power in 1933) as to be obviously banned. Among the eminent filmmakers who had specialized in this particular genre in the 1920s and were proscribed by the Nazis were Robert Wiene (*Das Cabinett des Doktor Caligari* [produced as *The Cabinet of Dr. Caligari*]), F.W. Murnau (*Nosferatu*), Fritz Lang (*Das Testament des Dr. Mabuse* [produced as *Dr. Mabuse*]), and Henrik Galeen (*Der Golem* [produced as *The Golem*]). It is therefore reasonable to assume that this kind of film was considered decadent.

In 1937 there was an *Exhibition of Degenerate Art*, officially supported by the Nazi Party; a year later, there was a similar *Exhibition of Degenerate Music*. The purpose of these exhibitions was the reeducation of the German public to the tastes acceptable to the political establishment. It is questionable if these exhibitions succeeded in their purposes, because the large number of viewers may have been drawn by curiosity about the forbidden artistic forms, especially when examples were labeled obscene. Even in guidelines relating to music (which is not generally judged in terms of moral standards), excessive dissonance (which the Nazis called "cultural Bolshevism") and jazz were condemned. Forbidden fruit tempted the average viewer or listener more than exhibitions of politically correct but often dull art and music.

Therefore, "decadence" may be, in the German political context, applied to creative styles that transcended the bounds established by a totalitarian government for the inculcation of values for the German masses. Any work of art created by a non-German (particularly a Jew) fell into the category, allowing xenophobia to become a factor in the judgment of creative quality.

Susan M. Filler

See also Aesthetics; Anti-Semitism; Cinema; Freud, Sigmund; Hitler, Adolf; Hofmannsthal, Hugo von; Kokoschka, Oskar; *Kultur;* Mahler, Gustav; Morality; National Socialist Germany: Art; National Socialist Germany: Music; Schnitzler, Arthur

References

Douglas, Drake. *Horror!* New York, NY: Collier Books, 1969.
Dümling, Albrecht and Peter Girth, eds. *Entartete Musik: zur Düsseldorfer Ausstellung 1938—eine kommentierte Rekunstruktion.* Düsseldorf: Kleinherne, 1988.
Eickhorst, William. *Decadence in German Fiction.* Denver, CO: A. Swallow, 1953.
Grunberger, Richard. *The Twelve-Year Reich: A Social History of Nazi Germany, 1933–1945.* New York, NY: Holt, Rinehart and Winston, 1971.
Kater, Michael. *Different Drummers: Jazz in the Culture of Nazi Germany.* New York, NY: Oxford University Press, 1992.
Reed, John Robert. *Decadent Style.* Athens: Ohio University Press, 1985.
Schorske, Carl. *Fin-de-Siècle Vienna: Politics and Culture.* New York, NY: Alfred A. Knopf, 1980; New York, NY: Vintage Books, 1981.

Decorative Arts

"Decorative arts" in German is *Kunstgewerbe*, a word that came into use in the second half of the nineteenth century. Together with the new term, a new type of museum—the so-called *Kunstgewerbemuseum*—came into being. This "museum of decorative arts" emulated the South Kensington Museum (1852) in London. According to Gottfried Semper's *Wissenschaft, Kunst und Industrie* (Knowledge, art, and industry), 1852, the museum was to teach the craftsman and the public. Among the first of such museums in German-speaking countries was the one in Vienna, founded in 1864. Its first curators were Rudolf von Eitelberger and Jakob Falke.

The general interest in decorative arts stimulated the foundation of the so-called *Kunstgewerbe-Vereine*, societies organized by craftsmen and businessmen. The Bayerische Kunstgewerbeverein (Bavarian Applied Art Association) in Munich (1851) was the most important and oldest one in Germany. It published its own journal and organized exhibitions for the public.

After 1850, fashions in decorative arts became influenced by exhibitions organized in Munich, the major contemporary art center. In 1876, the Bavarian Applied Art Association celebrated its 25th anniversary by organizing the first *National Art and Art Industry* exhibition. This show popularized the neo-Renaissance style, a vogue reinforced by Georg Hirth's publication, *Das deutsche Zimmer der Renaissance* (The German room during the Renaissance), 1880. The proponents of this style copied elements of the late Gothic and Northern Renaissance and identified it with the times of Martin Luther (1483–1546) and Albrecht Dürer (1471–1528), a glorious period in German history. Therefore it was regarded as the "true German" style.

After the war with France and the foundation of the German Empire in 1871, Germans sought a formal expression of the new state's political and economic power, which was to be independent of French predominance, including in the decorative arts. In 1888, a second *National Applied Art Exhibition* in Munich popularized neobaroque, which had already become fashionable through the fairytale castles of the Bavarian king Ludwig II. Anton Pössenbacher, who was employed by Ludwig II, also worked for the wealthy bourgoisie, many of whose members wanted to have little castles of their own. A third exhibition took place in Dresden in 1906, at a time when Munich was beginning to lose its leading role in the decorative arts.

By 1910, new stylistic tendencies and new production methods emerged. The old conservative applied art associations had become discredited. After the short interlude of the elaborate art nouveau (*Jugendstil*) the stricter, more classical neo-Biedermeier forms came into vogue. A *Neue Sachlichkeit* (new objectivity) and functionalism also emerged. These new objectives became apparent in the foundation of the German Werkbund in 1907 by Henry van de Velde, Karl Ernst Osthaus, and Hermann Muthesius, among others. Handicraft became increasingly supplemented by industrial design. The development toward the pure form in the decorative arts culminated in the Bauhaus style, founded in Weimar in 1919. The Bauhaus taught design for mass production. The rise of National Socialism in Germany interrupted this development and led to the closure of the Bauhaus in 1933. Neoclassical forms, such as those used by Paul Ludwig Troost and the so-called *Heimatstil* (provincial or regional style) architects became predominant in the Third Reich.

After World War II, the Bauhaus ideas and forms experienced a renaissance in Germany. They were promoted by the so-called Ulmer Schule (Ulmer school) and by designers such as Adolf Schneck in Stuttgart.

Christina Melk-Haen

See also Arts and Crafts; Bauhaus; *Jugendstil;* Ludwig II; Museums; Werkbund

References

Campbell, Joan. *The German Werkbund: The Politics of Reform in the Applied Arts.* Princeton, NJ: Princeton University Press, 1978.
Heskett, John. *German Design 1870–1918.* New York, NY: Taplinger, 1986.
Himmelheber, Georg and H. Kreisel. *Die Kunst des*

deutschen Möbels. Vol. 3: *Klassizismus, Historismus, Jugendstil.* Munich: Beck, 1973.

Makela, Maria. "Munich's Design for Living." *Art in America* (February 1989), 144–50.

Mundt, Barbara. *Historismus, Kunstgewerbe zwischen Biedermeier und Jugendstil.* Munich: Verlag Keyser, 1981.

Schack von Wittenau, Clementine, ed. *125 Jahre Bayerischer Kunstgewerbeverein.* Munich: Catalogue Münchner Stadtmuseum, 1976.

Schneck, Adolf. *Neue Möbel vom Jugendstil bis heute.* Munich: Bruckmann, 1962.

Selle, Gert. *Die Geschichte des Designs in Deutschland von 1870 bis heute.* Cologne: DuMont, 1978.

Semper, Gottfried. *Wissenschaft, Industrie und Kunst, Vorschläge zur Anregung eines nationalen Kunstgefühls.* Braunschweig, 1852. New edition: H.M. Wingler, ed. *Wissenschaft, Industrie und Kunst und andere Schriften.* Mainz: Neue Bauhausbücher, 1966.

Wichmann, Hans. *Aufbruch zum neuen Wohnen: Deutscher Werkbund, Werkstätten und WK-Verband-ihr Beitrag zur Kultur unseres Jahrhunderts.* Basel: Birkhauser, 1978.

Dehler, Thomas (1897–1967)

A leading member of the Free Democratic Party (FDP), Thomas Dehler was a trenchant public figure in the founding period of the Federal Republic of Germany (FRG). He attracted both admiration and controversy with his fervent commitment to traditional liberal ideals and German reunification. While federal minister of justice (1949–53), he helped to shape the new state's post-totalitarian judicial system. As FDP leader (1954–57), Dehler advocated greater efforts for national reunification, which he found neglected in Chancellor Konrad Adenauer's policy of Western integration.

Born near Bamberg in Bavaria, Dehler always identified with the liberal tradition of his native Franconia. After military service in World War I, he entered the legal profession and became an active member of the German Democratic Party (DDP). In the Third Reich, he was able to continue as defense lawyer in Bamberg, although he was an opponent of Nazism and his wife was partly Jewish. He had links to the resistance group around Carl Goerdeler (1884–1945), and was twice jailed briefly for political reasons.

After World War II, the Americans appointed Dehler to public offices in Bamberg. He resumed his liberal political activities and in 1946 became the first leader of the Bavarian FDP. Two years later, he was a member of the parliamentary council that drafted the Basic Law.

An outspoken member of Adenauer's first government, Dehler plunged into several controversies. He took a firm stand against a return to capital punishment. Politically more costly were his abrasive criticisms of organized labor in the debate on codetermination and of the Constitutional Court's decision on the Paris Treaties. The latter intervention seemed inappropriate for a justice minister, and he was not retained after the Bundestag election of 1953.

The FDP thereupon chose Dehler as its Bundestag leader and, in 1954, as its federal party leader. Outside the cabinet, Dehler became a strong critic of Adenauer's *Deutschlandpolitik*, although the FDP was still a government partner. One of the sharpest disagreements concerned the Saar, where Dehler rejected plans for the region's Europeanization. In early 1956, he led a majority of his party's parliamentary contingent out of the coalition.

These political conflicts took a heavy toll, even if they freed the FDP from the danger of being reduced to a satellite of the Christian Democrats. Dehler resigned as leader in 1957, a few months before his party's setback in the third Bundestag election. Although he would later be seen as a forerunner of the new *Ostpolitik*, his primary concern had been reunification. After becoming Bundestag vice-president in 1960, Dehler would on occasion reenter public debates. In a last major speech, in 1967, he advocated a "radical liberal" alternative to the Grand Coalition's proposed emergency legislation.

Christian Søe

See also Adenauer, Konrad; Federal Republic of Germany: Foreign Policy; Free Democratic Party; German Democratic Party; Goerdeler, Carl; Grand Coalition; *Ostpolitik*; Saar

References

Bald, Richard Hans. *The Free Democratic Party (FDP) and West German Foreign Policy, 1949–1959.* Unpublished doctoral dissertation. University of Michigan, 1963.

Bark, Dennis L. and David R. Gress. *A History of West Germany, From Shadow to Substance.* 2nd ed. Oxford: Basil Blackwell, 1993.

Cromwell, R.S. *The Free Democratic Party in German Politics: A Historical Study of a Contemporary Liberal Party.* Unpublished doctoral dissertation. Stanford University, 1960–61.

Glatzeder, Sebastian J. *Die Deutschlandpolitik der FDP in der Ära Adenauer: Konzeptionen in Entstehung und Praxis.* Baden-Baden: Nomos, 1980.

Klingl, Friedrich. *"Das ganze Deutschland soll es sein!" Thomas Dehler und die aussenpolitischen Weichenstellungen der fünfziger Jahre.* Munich: Olzog Verlag, 1987.

Delbrück, Hans (1848–1929)

The first modern military historian, Hans Delbrück wrote the four-volume *Geschichte der Kriegskunst im Rahmen der Politischen Geschichte* (published as *History of the Art of War*), 1900–18, a pathbreaking study because it joined politics, economics, and society with armies, battles, and leaders. From 1882 to 1922, Delbrück also edited the *Preussische Jahrbücher* (Prussian annals), the leading German political-commentary monthly. As professor of history at the University of Berlin (1882–1921) he was close to the family of Kaiser Friedrich III, became an opponent of a victory of annihilation during World War I, was a member of the German delegation to the Versailles

Peace Conference in 1919, and, at the end of his life, wrote a five-volume *Weltgeschichte* (published as *World History*), 1925–29, defended his country against war guilt claims, and championed the German liberals against charges of treason for their part in opposing a war of annihilation in 1917–18.

Delbrück was born in 1848 on the Baltic Sea island of Rügen, in the kingdom of Prussia, to a local court judge and his wife, the daughter of a Berlin professor. His studies at Heidelberg, Greifswald, and Bonn were interrupted by the Franco-Prussian War, in which he led troops in combat at St. Privat and Saarbrücken. He received his doctorate at the University of Bonn in 1873 under Heinrich von Sybel (1817–95). From 1874 to 1879, he served as a tutor in the household of the Crown Prince of Prussia, later Kaiser Friedrich III, and established a relationship with the Crown Princess, Queen Victoria's eldest daughter, that lasted until her death.

Joining Berlin University in 1881, he published the *Das Leben des Feldmarschalls Grafen Neidhardt von Gneisenau* (published as *Life of Field Marshall Gneisenau*), 1908, and began a lifelong battle to legitimize military history within the university and to establish the humanistic study of armies within the military. His major books, *Die Perserkriege und die Burgunderkriege: Zwei Kombinierte Kriegsgeschichtliche Studien* (published as *The Persian Wars and the Burgundian Wars*), 1882, *Strategie des Perikles erläutert durch die Strategie Friedrichs des Grossen* (published as *The Strategy of Pericles Described Through the Strategy of Frederick the Great*), 1900, *Geschichte der Kriegskunst,* and *Numbers in History,* 1913, were opposed by historians and General Staff officers. Historians believed that military history had no place in the university, whereas General Staff officers did not regard a civilian as qualified to write military history. Delbrück was elected to the Prussian parliament and to the Reichstag, which did not endear him to either professors or officers.

During World War I, Delbrück tried to combine contemporary military description with political criticism. But in the atmosphere of censorship and propaganda of the first catastrophe of global proportions, he failed to influence Germany's war policies. After 1918, he testified before the Reichstag committee that investigated the German collapse during World War I, and he engaged in celebrated legal battles against the "stab in the back" legend. In 1928 he was decorated by President Paul von Hindenburg (1847–1934) with the highest civilian award of the Weimar Republic. Delbrück wrote the inscription for his own gravestone: "I sought the truth and loved my country."

Arden Bucholz

See also Friedrich III; Hindenburg, Paul von; History; Sybel, Heinrich von; Versailles, Treaty of; World War I

References

Bucholz, Arden. "Hans Delbrück." *Research Guide to European Historical Biography*, Series 2. Vol. 2. Washington, DC: Beacham Publishing, 1992.
———. *Hans Delbrück and the German Military Establishment.* Iowa City, IA: University of Iowa Press, 1985.
Craig, Gordon. "Delbrück the Military Historian." *Makers of Modern Strategy from Machiavelli to the Nuclear Age.* Ed. Peter Paret. Princeton, NJ: Princeton University Press, 1986.
Delbrück, Hans. *The History of the Art of War.* 4 vols. Lincoln, NE: University of Nebraska Press, 1990.
———. *Numbers in History.* London: University of London, 1913.

Delbrück, Rudolf von (1817–1903)

Educated at the universities of Bonn, Göttingen, and Berlin, Rudolf von Delbrück joined the Prussian civil service in 1837. He spent most of his career in the Ministry of Commerce, whose foreign trade section he directed after 1848. For the next quarter-century, he fashioned economic policy, uncovered the latent political significance of the Prussian-German Customs Union (Zollverein), and proved himself adept in managing economic relations among Prussia and its Zollverein partners.

Austro-Prussian rivalry during the 1850s and 1860s enabled Delbrück to employ the Zollverein as an instrument of Prussian statecraft. He negotiated membership in the Customs Union for Hannover and Oldenburg in 1851 and kept a reluctant Saxony within the fold. Thereafter, in the political contest with Vienna, Berlin made skillful use of free trade to ensure the economic subordination of its adversary. Delbrück pursued his *Zollvereinpolitik* in a series of diplomatic missions, through which he persuaded the smaller members of the Customs Union to ratify the free-trade agreement concluded in 1862 between Prussia and France. None of the other German states dared to defy their senior partner by striking a political deal with Austria. Economic self-interest, as Delbrück anticipated, outweighed whatever enticements Vienna could offer.

Following the unification of Germany, Delbrück's career reached its apogee. Chancellor Otto von Bismarck appointed him head of the Reich Chancellery in 1871, and he served at the same time as Prussian minister without portfolio. In this dual role, Delbrück created a centralized federal bureaucracy responsive to the chancellor's will. He represented Bismarck in the Bundesrat and Reichstag, thereby gaining a reputation as the chancellor's "right hand." In all but name, Delbrück was Germany's vice-chancellor for several years. His authority waned in the mid-1870s, when economic prosperity faltered, free-trade ideas suffered an eclipse, and Bismarck abandoned his indifferent courtship of the Liberals. As the forces of protectionism gathered political strength, Delbrück's position deteriorated. Bismarck, for his part, blamed his deputy's "overbearing and obstinate character" for straining their professional relationship.

Delbrück left office with a patent of nobility in 1876, having conceded that he no longer enjoyed Bismarck's confidence. He won election to the Reichstag in 1878 and, as a deputy, vigorously opposed the imposition of tariffs on food and manufactured goods. Germany, however, had entered an age of protectionism, in which the laissez-faire economic doctrines espoused by Delbrück had no place.

Richard J. Bazillion

See also Austro-German Relations; Bismarck, Otto von; Chancellor's Office; Civil Service; Exports and Foreign Trade; Liberalism; Protectionism; State and Economy

References

Delbrück, Rudolf von. *Lebenserinnerungen 1817–1867: Mit einem Nachtrag aus dem Jahre 1870.* 2 vols. Leipzig: Duncker & Humblot, 1905.

Helfferich, K. *Biographisches Jahrbuch und deutscher Nekrolog.* Vol. 17. 1906 [1912].

Morsey, Rudolf. *Die oberste Reichsverwaltung unter Bismarck 1867–1890.* Münster: Aschendorff, 1957.

Pflanze, Otto. *Bismarck and the Development of Germany.* Vol. 2. *The Period of Consolidation, 1871–1880.* Princeton, NJ: Princeton University Press, 1990.

Delp, Alfred (1907–45)

A German Jesuit, Alfred Delp was arrested on July 28, 1944, as a member of the Resistance via the Kreisau Circle organized by Count Helmuth James von Moltke (1907–45). He refused a Gestapo offer to escape death by leaving the Society of Jesus and was hanged on February 2, 1945. His prison meditations, translated into several languages, have achieved international circulation.

Born in Mannheim on September 15, 1907 to middle-class parents, Delp was baptized into his mother's Catholic faith but raised a Protestant by his father. In his 14th year he chose Catholicism. Following a brilliant *Abitur* (senior matriculation) in 1926 he entered the Society of Jesus and was ordained a priest on July 24, 1936. His prewar scholarly publications show an interest in philosophy and social justice and a desire to develop a notion of patriotism free of Nazi perversions. Delp was a gifted preacher. His sermons in a Munich parish were recorded in shorthand and widely circulated in typescript. During the war he ministered to the victims of bombing and encouraged people to help the Jews.

Delp was an active member of the Kreisau Circle from its second meeting in October 1942. Following the attempt on Hitler's life on July 20, 1944, Delp was urged to go into hiding. He refused and was arrested in Munich eight days later. On January 11, 1945, after a 20-day trial with Moltke and others (during which the Nazi judge Roland Freisler [1893–1945] told the accused: "Christianity and National Socialism have only one thing in common: we both demand the whole man"), Delp was condemned to death.

John Jay Hughes

See also National Socialist Germany; Resistance; Roman Catholic Church; Schutzstaffel (SS); World War II

References

Conway, John C. *The Nazi Persecution of the Churches.* London: Weidenfeld and Nicolson, 1968.

Delp, Alfred. *The Prison Meditations of Father Alfred Delp.* New York, NY: Macmillan, 1963.

Helmreich, E.C. *The German Churches under Hitler.* Detroit, MI: Wayne State University Press, 1979.

Depression, 1873–95

Between 1873 and 1895, Germany passed through what Hans-Ulrich Wehler has called the "first phase of advanced industrialization." Uneven industrial expansion and crisis in agriculture characterized this period, yet by its end, Germany had emerged as the leading industrial power of Europe, overtaking Britain in steel production in 1895 and dominating the new chemical and electrical industries. The emergence of new industries and the relative or absolute decline of agriculture and older industries such as railways brought unemployment, overinvestment, overproduction, and a host of related problems. To label the entire period as one long depression is deceptive, but in fact periods of recovery lasted only relatively briefly, from 1879 to 1882 and from 1886 to 1890.

The depression affected the agricultural sector most sharply and permanently. By the turn of the century, Germany could no longer be called an agricultural state. In 1873, agriculture's share of Germany's gross domestic product was still about 20 percent larger than industry's. In 1889 they were equal, and by 1895 industry's share was 14 percent larger than agriculture's.

Investment in agriculture declined dramatically during the 1870s, and agricultural imports grew. Germany had been

Table 1. Population Growth of Major German Cities, 1860–1900

	Berlin	Cologne	Dresden	Frankfurt am Main	Hamburg	Königsberg	Leipzig	Munich	Ruhr area*	Stuttgart	Germany
1860–1861	548,000	121,000	128,000	76,000	134,000	95,000	78,000	148,000	191,000	56,000	35,567,000
1870–1871	826,000	129,000	177,000	91,000	240,000	112,000	107,000	169,000	311,000	92,000	41,059,000
1880–1881	1,122,000	145,000	221,000	137,000	290,000	141,000	149,000	230,000	408,000	117,000	45,234,000
1890–1891	1,579,000	282,000	277,000	180,000	324,000	162,000	295,000	349,000	556,000	140,000	49,428,000
1900–1901	1,889,000	373,000	396,000	289,000	706,000	188,000	456,000	500,000	774,000	177,000	56,367,000

Source: B.R. Mitchell, *European Historical Statistics, 1750–1975.* New York, NY: Facts on File, 1981, 30, 86–88.
*includes only Dortmund, Düsseldorf, Essen, and Wuppertal.

importing rye since 1852, but after the mid-1870s, it also became a net importer of oats, barley, and wheat.

Growing competition from the United States, Canada, Argentina, Australia, and Russia forced German agricultural prices down. When the price of Prussian wheat fell almost 30 percent between 1880 and 1886, the old elite of Prussian estate owners turned against free trade and supported stiff tariffs. The growth of grain imports also stirred nationalist fears. In 1891, Chancellor Leo von Caprivi (1831–99) declared to the Reichstag that "the existence of the state is at stake, when it is not in a position to live on its own sources of supply."

Such fears could not stop the forces of urbanization and industrialization. Germany's industrial revolution, focused on iron, mining, and railroads, had fostered unprecedented prosperity and growth from 1850 to 1873. Victory over France and the formation of the German Empire in 1871 helped to produce a speculative boom known as the *Gründerzeit* (founding years). In 1873, however, the stock market crashed; over the next year, more than 60 banks failed and 120 companies went bankrupt, including 4 railroads. The crisis turned into a severe depression that lasted until 1879. The brief recovery from 1879 to 1882 gathered little momentum and failed to restore confidence before the economy again turned downward. In the later 1880s growth was more vigorous; but recession returned in the 1890s. Despite the vicissitudes of capitalism and the fluctuations of the business cycle, the population of Germany's cities continued to grow at a rate much faster than that of the nation as a whole. Between 1860 and 1900, Germany's population increased 58 percent, but the population of most major cities more than tripled (see Table 1, p. 225).

Perceptions about the causes of the depression had profound consequences for German society. Economic hardship exposed economic liberalism to attack from socialists and conservatives alike. Urban industrial laborers, hard hit by reduced wages, fewer work hours, and layoffs, turned to the Social Democrats. Catholics and conservatives blamed liberals and Jews for the country's plight. Chancellor Otto von Bismarck, meanwhile, forged an antiliberal coalition united in its contempt for new money and "foreign" concepts of capitalism and free trade. Calls for protectionist tariffs used the term "national" in a sense that was xenophobic and anti-Semitic. These conflicts lingered as prosperity returned in the mid-1890s.

Maarten L. Pereboom

See also Agrarian Leagues; Agriculture; Anti-Semitism; Bismarck, Otto von; Caprivi, Leo von; Founding Years; Industrialization; Liberalism; Protectionism; Radical Nationalism; Radical Right; State and Economy; Unemployment; Urbanization

References

Hamerow, Theodore S. *The Birth of a New Europe: State and Society in the Nineteenth Century.* Chapel Hill, NC: University of North Carolina Press, 1983.

Hardach, G. *Deutschland in der Weltwirtschaft 1870–1970: Eine Einführung in die Sozial- und Wirtschaftsgeschichte.* Frankfurt am Main: Campus, 1977.

Henning, F.-W. *Die Industrialisierung Deutschlands 1800–1914.* Paderborn: Schöningh, 1976.

Hentschel, V. *Deutsche Wirtschafts- und Sozialpolitik 1815–1914.* Königstein: Athenäum, 1980.

Hoffman, W.G. *Das Wachstum der deutschen Wirtschaft seit der Mitte des 19. Jahrhunderts.* Berlin: Springer-Verlag, 1965.

Landes, David S. *The Unbound Prometheus: Technological Change and Industrial Development in Western Europe from 1750 to the Present.* London: Cambridge University Press, 1969.

Lee, W.R., ed. *German Industry and German Industrialisation: Essays in German Economic and Business History in the Nineteenth and Twentieth Centuries.* London: Routledge, 1991.

Stern, Fritz. *Gold and Iron: Bismarck, Bleichröder and the Building of the German Empire.* New York, NY: Vintage, 1979.

Wehler, Hans-Ulrich. *Bismarck und der Imperialismus.* 2nd ed. Frankfurt am Main: Suhrkamp, 1985.

———. *The German Empire, 1871–1918.* Trans. Kim Traynor. Leamington Spa: Berg, 1985.

(Great) Depression (1929–33)

By the time of the New York stock market crash in October 1929, Germany's economy was already in a state of depression. Industrial production fell and unemployment grew as foreign sources of credit, channelled through German banks, dried up. A banking crisis in central Europe during the summer of 1931 shattered all hopes for early recovery, and in the following year, unemployment reached almost six million, or almost one-third of the work force. A global trend toward protectionism devastated trade. The fragile constitution of the Weimar Republic, buffeted by these disasters, gave way to National Socialism.

The German economy had never really recovered from World War I; like its former adversaries, Germany had liqui-

---

Table 2. German Industrial Production, 1871–1900 (1913 = 100)

1871	21	1881	27	1891	41
1872	24	1882	27	1892	42
1873	26	1883	29	1893	43
1874	27	1884	30	1894	45
1875	27	1885	31	1895	49
1876	28	1886	31	1896	50
1877	27	1887	33	1897	53
1878	28	1888	35	1898	56
1879	27	1889	39	1899	58
1880	26	1890	40	1900	61

Sources: B.R. Mitchell. *European Historical Statistics, 1750–1975.* New York, NY: Facts on File, 1981, 375–76.
Germany. *Statistik des Deutschen Reichs.* 1873–1939.

Table 1. German Industrial Production, 1925–36 (1937=100)

1925	68	1929	79	1933	54
1926	61	1930	69	1934	67
1927	78	1931	56	1935	79
1928	78	1932	48	1936	90

Source: B.R. Mitchell, *European Historical Statistics, 1750–1975*. New York, NY: Facts on File, 1981, 376.

Table 2. Annual Average Unemployment, 1929–33

Year	Unemployed	Percentage of work force
1929	1,899,000	....
1930	3,076,000	15.3
1931	4,520,000	23.3
1932	5,575,000	30.1
1933	4,804,000	26.3

Source: B.R. Mitchell, *European Historical Statistics, 1750–1975*. New York, NY: Facts on File, 1981, 175–78.

dated most of its assets fighting the war. In the decade that followed, consumer demand did not increase and agriculture remained in a state of depression. To a large degree, capital for investment in Germany came from abroad, especially the United States. In keeping with longstanding tradition, German banks borrowed from private lenders on a short-term basis and in turn provided long-term loans to businesses. As the United States stock market rocketed upward in 1928, such short-term loans became increasingly difficult to obtain; net exports of American capital, which grew from $200 million in 1926 to over $1 billion in 1928, plunged back to $200 million in 1929. Suddenly, German banks had little money to lend.

The credit squeeze, combined with collapsing stock and commodities markets, produced economic disaster in Germany. Consumer industries had suffered a mild recession in 1928, and unemployment that year stood at over one million. From mid-1929 onward, heavy industry began an even steeper decline. The stock market, which had fallen 14 percent between June 1928 and September 1929, fell another 15 percent between September and December. Strife between the Social Democrats and the German Peoples' Party (DVP) in 1930 over contributions to the strained German Unemployment Insurance Fund made it impossible for any government to rule with a majority. Invoking emergency measures of the constitution, Chancellor Heinrich Brüning (1885–1970) began to rule by decree. The Reichstag's opposition led to elections in September 1930, which produced a major victory for the Nazis.

Hopes for recovery in 1931 faded as a banking crisis developed in Central Europe during the spring. Up to that point, banks had cooperated to keep the system of international finance working, but the length of the crisis eroded confidence and strained the capacity of the banks themselves

to assist one another in the interest of preventing collapse. In Germany, the bankruptcy of Nordwolle, a large textile company, caused the failure of the Danatbank (Darmstädter und Nationalbank) in July. A severe run on Germany's banks ensued. Public-private cooperation saved Germany's other major banks from failure and restored a measure of domestic confidence. A standstill agreement ended the ruinous withdrawal of foreign funds. Yet production fell to its lowest point and unemployment reached its highest level in 1932 (see Table 2). The economy, therefore, was improving as 1933 began; but the Weimar Republic did not survive the depression. Prosperity returned during the Nazi era to an autarkic Germany gearing up for war.

Maarten L. Pereboom

See also Brüning, Heinrich von; Hitler, Adolf; Müller, Hermann; National Socialism; Radical Nationalism; Radical Right; Sturmabteilung (SA); Unemployment; Weimar Republic; Young Plan

References

Bennett, E.W. *Germany and the Diplomacy of the Financial Crisis, 1931.* Cambridge, MA: Harvard University Press, 1962.

Born, K.E. *Die deutsche Bankenkrise 1931: Finanzen und Politik.* Munich: R. Piper, 1967.

Grotkopp, W. *Die grosse Krise: Lehren aus der Überwindung der Wirtschaftskrise 1929–1932.* Düsseldorf: Econ-Verlag, 1954.

Hoffman, W.G. *Das Wachstum der deutschen Wirtschaft seit der Mitte des 19. Jahrhunderts.* Berlin: Springer-Verlag, 1965.

Holl, Karl ed. *Wirtschaftskrise und liberale Demokratie.* Göttingen: Vandenhoeck & Ruprecht, 1978.

James, Harold. *The Reichsbank and Public Finance in Germany 1924–1933: A Study of the Politics of Economics during the Great Depression.* Frankfurt am Main: Fritz Knapp, 1985.

Kindleberger, Charles P. *The World in Depression, 1929–1939.* Rev ed. Berkeley, CA: University of California Press, 1986.

Stachura, Peter, ed. *Unemployment and the Great Depression in Weimar Germany.* London: Macmillan, 1986.

Stiefel, D. *Finanzdiplomatie und Weltwirtschaftskrise.* Frankfurt am Main: F. Knapp, 1989.

Turner, Henry A. *German Big Business and the Rise of Hitler.* New York, NY: Oxford University Press, 1985.

Der Blaue Reiter

See Blaue Reiter, Der

Der Spiegel

True to its name, *Der Spiegel* (The mirror) has virtually mirrored West Germany's postwar history since its creation in 1947. Conceived in Hannover by three young British occupation officers as a news magazine called *Diese Woche* (This week), it was quickly acquired by the 23-year-old Rudolf Augstein, who renamed it and moved it to Hamburg.

Regarded as a "*Sturmgeschütz der Demokratie*" (self-propelled cannon of democracy) by Augstein, who still personified *Der Spiegel* in 1996, it was regarded as a "*Schmierblatt*" (a rag) by Konrad Adenauer, the Federal Republic's first chancellor. Years later, even a former editor in chief, Claus Jacobi, was to recall it as "200 pages of no." Yet *The International Herald-Tribune* has hailed it as "a national institution."

Within *Der Spiegel's* first decade, its reporting had already led to indictments, resignations, and parliamentary investigations, while the steady growth of circulation and advertising revenues suggested readers who could not get enough. Despite the elegance and gusto of Augstein's urgings to the contrary, growing majorities continued to favor Adenauer, German NATO membership, and (West) German integration in the embryonic (West) European Community over a neutralized, reunified Germany.

In 1962, *Der Spiegel*, which was founded to report the news, inadvertently became the news when a challenge to Adenauer's defense minister, Franz Josef Strauss (1915–88), tested the magazine itself and the new West German democracy. Concerned with the numerical superiority of Warsaw Pact forces, Strauss had commissioned his staff to study whether nuclear preemption might limit damage from a Soviet strike. An agitated colonel then talked to Conrad Ahlers, one of Augstein's reporters.

On October 8, 1962, *Der Spiegel* published Ahlers's protracted critique of current strategy and defense planning—though without mention of the study that inspired it. The night of October 26, a swarm of magistrates and police officers raided editorial offices in Hamburg, Bonn, and Düsseldorf,

arresting six senior editors and executives, including Augstein. The next day, Ahlers returned mysteriously—transported by security agents—from a vacation in Spain. The defendants were charged with violation of official secrets.

The "*Spiegel* Affair" that followed caused Strauss to resign after denying his role in Ahlers's arrest. Under pressure from his Free Democratic coalition partners, Adenauer also agreed to resign before the 1965 election. In the end, no one ever came to trial.

In 1984, Sir James Goldsmith, a British publisher and Conservative politician, claimed that *Der Spiegel's* campaign against Strauss was based on Soviet misinformation. Augstein first charged libel, then settled out of court. Yet there could be no doubt that the sources of "the affair" were strictly German.

Never infallible, the magazine has also been embarrassed on occasion. For example, its quest for Austrian President Kurt Waldheim's Nazi past confirmed that even as perfect a news machine as *Der Spiegel* can fall for doctored documents. Despite claims that *Der Spiegel* might be losing its zest and aggressiveness, not to mention the trail of indictments, resignations, official investigations, and even an occasional suicide, the magazine has nonetheless persisted into the 1990s. An estimated six million readers continue to await its appearance every Monday.

David Schoenbaum

See also Adenauer, Konrad; Journalism; Magazines; Press and Newspapers; Strauss, Franz Josef

References

Bergner, Gert. *Rudolf Augstein und die Spiegel-Affäre*. Berlin: Stoetner, 1964.
Bunn, Robert F. *German Politics and the Spiegel Affair*. Baton Rouge, LA: Louisiana State University Press, 1968.
Schoenbaum, David. *The Spiegel Affair*. Garden City, NY: Doubleday, 1968.

Dessau, Paul (1894–1979)

Paul Dessau, one of the leading East German composers, was born to Jewish parents in Hamburg, where he studied composition and began a conducting career that led him to Cologne, Mainz, and Berlin. In 1933, he moved to Paris, where he met René Leibowitz. He then went to the United States in 1939, where he met Bertolt Brecht (1942). In 1948, after having taught and composed film music in Hollywood, he returned with Brecht to East Berlin, where he was appointed to the Academy of Arts. He taught music in Zeuthen near Berlin, and, after initially clashing with the socialist administration, became officially recognized as a state artist.

Dessau enjoyed early success with his chamber piece *Concertino*, 1924, which was performed at the prestigious Donaueschingen festival in 1925, and for which he was awarded the Schott Prize. His compositional development displays early Wagnerian influences and can be traced through expressionism and neoclassicism to employment of the twelve-tone method, Jewish folk songs, and musical quotations. His

Der Spiegel. *Courtesy of Robert Evans.*

opera *Einstein,* 1971–73, uses various compositional languages. Most of Dessau's vocal music after 1942 was set to texts written by Brecht, including the oratorio *Deutsches Miserere,* 1944–47, and the two operas, *Die Verurteilung des Lukullus* (The sentencing of Lucullus), 1949, and *Puntila,* 1966. A committed socialist, he believed that music had a major role to play in social and political thought.

Gareth Cox

See also Brecht, Bertolt; Composers; German Democratic Republic: Political Culture

References

Hennenberg, Fritz. *Paul Dessau: Eine Biographie.* Leipzig: Deutscher Verlag für Musik, 1965.

Detente and Germany

Detente commonly refers to that period from the mid-1960s through the mid-1970s when the United States and the Soviet Union expanded their relations in an effort to move beyond coexistence to a sturdier rapprochement. A web of connections was created that included not only arms-control negotiations, but economic ties and cultural, academic, and personal exchanges. The Helsinki Final Act, signed in 1975, represented the centerpiece of this phase of detente for both the Soviet Union and Europe.

Despite an apparent confluence of interests, each superpower pursued conflicting agendas through detente which, in turn, differed from the shared interests of Eastern and Western Europeans. The Soviet Union, Eastern Europe, and Western Europe viewed detente as a divisible agreement and applied its provisions primarily to Europe. The United States, in contrast, regarded detente as a global agreement. For the latter, the value of detente was measured in its ability to modify Soviet behavior, whereas the Soviet Union sought Western economic assistance to rejuvenate its sluggish economy without having to introduce fundamental reform. Eastern and Western Europeans became the strongest supporters of detente. They measured its success in personal terms of having more access to information over open borders, and in terms of a general internal relaxation in the USSR and East Europe. Europeans diverged increasingly from their two superpower patrons, who slipped back into confrontation patterns in the late 1970s through the mid-1980s.

West Germany's *Ostpolitik* flourished in the international environment of detente. Begun during the Grand Coalition (1966–69), *Ostpolitik* is closely associated with the chancellorship of Willy Brandt (1913–92) from 1969 to 1972. It marked a dramatic departure from Konrad Adenauer's strategy of overcoming the division of Germany by isolating and thereby undermining East Germany. The new approach sought to make the division of Europe and Germany more porous by accepting the post–World War II order. The Eastern Treaties signed in the early 1970s with Moscow, Warsaw, and Prague, and the Basic Treaty with East Berlin enshrined the principles of *Ostpolitik.*

Initially, the East German leadership felt particularly threatened by the relaxation of tensions. Walter Ulbricht (1893–1973) was deposed as first secretary of the SED in 1971, in part because of his opposition to improving relations with West Germany. His successor, Erich Honecker (1912–94), accepted rapprochement but coupled it with a policy of strict demarcation, or *Abgrenzung,* that emphasized the separate and distinctive characters of the two German states. He sought to restrict all unofficial contacts. By the 1980s, when relations between the United States and the Soviet Union had soured, the leaders of both German states were committed to pursuing a policy of detente.

Ann L. Phillips

See also Adenauer, Konrad; American-German Relations; Basic Treaty; Brandt, Willy; Federal Republic of Germany: Foreign Policy; German-German Relations; Honecker, Erich; *Ostpolitik*; Soviet-German Relations; Ulbricht, Walter

References

Davy, Richard. *European Detente: A Reappraisal.* London: Royal Institute of International Affairs, 1992.

Frey, Eric G. *Division and Detente: The Germanies and their Alliances.* New York, NY: Praeger, 1986.

Garthoff, Raymond L. *Detente and Confrontation: American-Soviet Relations from Nixon to Reagan.* Washington, DC: Brookings Institution, 1985.

Garton Ash, Timothy. *In Europe's Name.* London: Jonathan Cape, 1993.

Gati, Charles. *The Debate over Detente.* New York, NY: Foreign Policy Association, 1977.

Goldmann, Kjell. *Change and Stability in Foreign Policy: The Problems and Possibilities of Detente.* Princeton, NJ: Princeton University Press, 1988.

McAdams, A. James. *East Germany and Detente: Building Authority After the Wall.* Cambridge: Cambridge University Press, 1985.

Moreton, Edwina. *East Germany and the Warsaw Alliance: The Politics of Detente.* Boulder, CO: Westview, 1978.

Deutsche Bank

The Deutsche Bank received its charter from the Prussian government on March 10, 1870, and opened its doors for business on April 9, 1870. It was founded as a joint-stock bank, with an initial capital of five million thalers, by the liberal politician Ludwig Bamberger (1823–99) and the Berlin banker Adelbert Delbrück for the purpose of financing German foreign trade and thereby breaking what had been a virtual British monopoly in this sphere. Delbrück acted as chairman of the supervisory board. The management of the bank until 1900 reposed in the hands of Georg von Siemens, the first spokesman of the board of managing directors, and Hermann Wallich, who guided international operations. In 1876, the Deutsche Bank took over the Deutsche Union-Bank and the Berliner Bank-Verein, thereby becoming Germany's largest bill of exchange and investment bank.

Prior to World War I, the Deutsche Bank expanded its international activities through its branches and subsidiaries.

It opened its London Agency in 1873, founded the Deutsche Übersee-Bank (German Overseas Bank) in 1886 (renamed Deutsche Überseeische Bank in 1893), and, in collaboration with a consortium of other banks, founded the Deutsch-Asiatische Bank (German Asiatic Bank). The South American business of the bank was especially important, and the Banco Alemán Transatlantico, established as a branch office of the Deutsche Überseeische Bank in Buenos Aires, became the center of a network of branches in South America.

Prior to World War I, the Deutsche Bank also played a major role in German investment in Russia and in the Balkans, especially in the Romanian oil fields, and was the leading financier of the Berlin-Baghdad railway. Some of the bank's most famous personalities, who were or became major political figures—Arthur von Gwinner (spokesman from 1910 to 1918), Karl Helfferich (1872–1924), and Emil Georg Strauss—were involved in this venture. Gwinner also promoted investments in North America, especially in the Northern Pacific Railroad.

After 1880, the bank also functioned as the classic German universal bank in the financing of German industrial enterprise, most notably with respect to the Mannesmann concern, the electrical firms of AEG and Siemens, and the construction company of Philipp Holzmann. A good measure of the growing importance of domestic business was the bank's mergers with the major regional banks with which it previously had pooling arrangements. This process, which began before World War I, accelerated during the war and the postwar inflationary period. The bank also became engaged in the financing of heavy industry, and during the Weimar era it was especially active in financing the new industries of the Weimar period: automobiles (Daimler-Benz and BMW), motion pictures (Ufa), and air travel and transport (Lufthansa).

Much of the bank's expansion after 1918 compensated investors for heavy losses incurred through war and inflation. The opening gold mark balance of the Deutsche Bank in 1924 was 25 percent of what it had been in 1914. Industrial self-financing also weakened the bank's domestic business. The bank was an important intermediary in securing loans from the United States and in providing trade credits for the Soviet Union. In order to reduce competition and maintain its dominant position, the Deutsche Bank in 1929 merged with its chief competitor, the Disconto-Gesellschaft, to form the Deutsche Bank und Disconto-Gesellschaft. The merger undoubtedly helped the bank to weather the depression and banking crisis of 1931. The new company was renamed the Deutsche Bank in 1937.

During the National Socialist period, the bank was "Aryanized," and subsequently served as an instrument of the regime's racist and imperialist policies. The Nazi regime was hostile to big banks, so its influence was kept to a minimum.

After the war, under Allied pressure, the Deutsche Bank split into three regional banks in 1952: the Norddeutsche Bank (North German Bank) in Hamburg, the Rheinisch-Westfälische Bank (Rhenish-Westphalian Bank) in Düsseldorf, and the Süddeutsche Bank in Munich (South German Bank). Due to the brilliant tactical skills of Hermann J. Abs

(who had already joined the managing board of the bank in 1938), strong domestic pressures favoring big banks, and growing willingness by the Allies to reconsider their position, the three banks were reunited into a reconstituted Deutsche Bank in 1957. Thereafter, the bank moved into the mass personal account market, a process already begun in 1928, and in recent years (especially under Alfred Herrhausen, spokesman between 1985 and 1989, and his successor, Hilmar Kopper), has vastly expanded its international alliances and acquisitions.

Gerald D. Feldman

See also Abs, Hermann; AEG AG; Banking; BMW; Currency; Daimler-Benz AG; Helfferich, Karl; Inflation and Hyperinflation; Mannesmann: Firm and Family; Siemens AG; Ufa

References

Gall, Lothar, Gerald D. Feldman, Harold James, Carl-Ludwig Holtfrerich, and Hans E. Büschgen. *The Deutsche Bank, 1870–1995*. Munich: Beck Verlag; London: Weidenfeld and Nicolson, 1995.
Seidenzahl, Fritz. *100 Jahre Deutsche Bank*. Frankfurt am Main: Deutsche Bank, 1970.

Dibelius, Otto (1880–1967)

Dibelius's lengthy career as one of the most prominent leaders of the German Evangelical Church extended over 50 years until his retirement as Bishop of Berlin-Brandenburg in 1966. During World War I, he became a notable church spokesman urging loyalty to the Imperial dynasty and its authoritarian structures and espousing a highly nationalistic and antiforeign stance. Following Germany's defeat and the overthrow of the monarchy, however, he recognized the futility of nostalgia and instead propagated the role of the church as the true upholder of the nation's moral values. His book *Das Jahrhundert der Kirche* (The century of the church), 1927, called for a reassertion of the Protestant cause and a repudiation of the pluralistic, democratic values of the Weimar Republic.

His leadership talents and flair for publicity were recognized in 1925 when he became general superintendent of the region around Berlin (the Kurmark), one of the Prussian church's most prestigious positions. As a result he was chosen to preach before Hindenburg and Hitler at the opening of the Reichstag in Potsdam in March 1933. His staunchly conservative defense of the church's establishment, however, aroused the opposition of radical Nazis, which led to his suspension from office in June 1933. After spending a year as a resort chaplain in Italy, he returned to Berlin in 1934 to organize the Confessing Church's struggle for the defense of the church's autonomy against Nazi encroachments. Though repeatedly arrested, he was spared the fate of his colleague Martin Niemöller.

In 1945, he quickly took over control of the Berlin-Brandenburg church, assumed the title of bishop, and played a leading role in the proclamation of the Stuttgart Declaration of Guilt and in the reestablishment of the Evangelical Church in Germany. From 1949 to 1961 he was chairman of the

Otto Dibelius. Courtesy of German Information Center, New York.

church's executive council, and from 1954 to 1961 one of the presidents of the World Council of Churches. After 1949, he persuaded leading West German Protestants to support Adenauer's government, including its policies of rearmament and inclusion in NATO. As bishop of Berlin-Brandenburg, he led the church's opposition to the Communist-controlled East German regime. He caused considerable discussion when he repudiated its authority even in non-spiritual matters, which led in 1960 to his being barred from exercising his functions in the territory of East Germany. But his national and international prestige as a pragmatic upholder of conservative nationalist values, his resolute defense of traditional Protestant orthodoxy against the secularizing dangers of both Nazism and Communism, and his wide ecumenical vision in the post-1945 years established his reputation as a farsighted and shrewd ecclesiastical statesman.

    John Conway

See also Barth, Karl; Confessing Church; German Democratic Republic; Niemöller, Martin; Protestantism and the Protestant Church; Stuttgart Declaration of Guilt

References

Barnett, Victoria. *For the Soul of the People: Protestant Protest Against Hitler.* New York, NY: Oxford University Press, 1992.

Dibelius, Otto. *Ein Christ ist immer im Dienst.* Stuttgart: Kreuz-Verlag, 1961. English translation: *In the Service of the Lord.* New York, NY: Holt, Rinehart and Winston, 1964.

Scholder, Klaus. *The Churches and the Third Reich.* 2 vols. London: SCM Press, 1987–88.

Wright, Jonathan R. C. *"Above Parties": The Political Attitudes of the Protestant Church Leadership, 1918–1933.* Oxford: Oxford University Press, 1974.

Die Welt

One of Germany's quality papers, the daily *Die Welt* (The world) celebrated its 45th anniversary in 1991. With a circulation of 220,765 copies, it holds a firm position as a leading national paper and includes several local editions. *Die Welt* is known for its conservative stance, which was formulated by its owner and publisher, Axel Cäsar Springer (1912–85).

    Since autumn of 1992, the editorial staff of *Die Welt* has joined the company's corporate headquarters in Berlin, relocating from the former capital, Bonn. June 1, 1993, saw a local edition of *Die Welt* published in and for Berlin. The relocation effort and the Berlin edition of *Die Welt* are symbolic events, bringing to closure one phase of the often tumultuous history and embattled position of the paper and its publisher.

    Die Welt was conceived by the British government in October 1945. A need existed for a nonpartisan newspaper covering the entire British zone of occupation. Colonel Henry P. Garland, press chief for Hamburg and Schleswig-Holstein, was ordered to assemble an editorial staff, organize the distribution of the paper-to-be, and provide a print shop for this supra-regional edition. As senior editor, he hired an experienced journalist, the German Hans Zehrer (1899–1966), in December 1945. The publishing house was inaugurated in January 1946 and its owner was the British military government. The paper was launched on April 2, 1946. 160,000 copiesof the first six-page edition were printed in Hamburg . It appeared twice weekly, at first, then three times per week, and beginning with July 1, 1949, *Die Welt* was available daily with a circulation of 1,005,000 copies.

    Zehrer, who assembled the German editorial staff and who suggested the paper's definitive name, *Die Welt* (the original plan was to call it *Der Tag* [The day]), was released from his duties in March 1946 when his political past was questioned by the Social Democrats of Hamburg. The editorial position of the paper was firmly established by the British Information Services Control (ISC). Politics, business, and culture were the three main topics of coverage for the paper. Any typeset page had to pass a British controller, and preliminary censorship was the norm.

    Until September 1948, *Die Welt* was distributed throughout all of occupied Germany, including the Soviet zone. When the licensing requirements were dropped in 1949, the "British" *Die Welt* started to experience serious competition from German publications, resulting in an immediate decline in its circulation. Senior editors began to occupy revolving chairs. The year 1950, for example, witnessed the hiring and firing of six senior editors. By 1953, the circulation rate had dropped to 172,098. Something drastic had to done to save the paper. Management decided to privatize *Die Welt*. Among the 16 offers that were considered, Axel Springer's prevailed. On September 17, 1953, he became the new owner of *Die Welt* and ended the paper's British era. Springer reappointed as ninth senior editor Hans Zehrer, who guided the paper until May 1966. Springer began to identify with his paper personally. On his directive, *Die Welt*, which since May 1950 had carried the tagline *unabhängige Tageszeitung* (independent daily) changed the line to *unabhängige Tageszeitung für Deutschland* (independent daily for Germany) in February 1956. This was a defiant public statement, because "Germany," as a legal entity, did not exist.

Springer's political agenda became apparent in the formulation of his four guiding editorial principles, which became binding for all of the Springer publications. They were: (1), to strive toward a peaceful German unity; (2), to promote reconciliation of Jews and Germans and support the vital rights of the state of Israel; (3), to reject all forms of political extremism; and (4), to uphold the principles of a free social market economy. These guiding principles and Springer's consistent denial of the legitimacy of the East German state changed the editorial position of *Die Welt* from nonpartisan to pro-Western and anti-Communist.

Die Welt was published against the prevailing *Zeitgeist*, which favored steps toward detente. The Springer press opposed any attempt toward an East-West rapprochement or peaceful dialogue between the two Germanys. Slowly, anti–Springer/ *Die Welt* sentiments began to circulate. The slogan of the "ugly publisher" emerged and Springer was targeted by student radicals. In the fall of 1967, the Sozialistische Deutsche Studentenbund (SDS; Socialistic German Students' Association) announced its campaign to expose and smash the Springer publishing group. More than 100 writers, among them Günter Grass (1927–) and literary Nobel laureate Heinrich Böll (1917–85), signed their proclamation. Ironically, 1967 was the same year that the University of Missouri honored *Die Welt* as the Daily of the Year, in recognition of its "outstanding accomplishments in the area of journalism." In West Germany, however, the attacks on Springer publications escalated. The *Neue Linke* (New Left) called for action. The Easter holidays of 1968 were marked by bloody riots with tragic consequences. Springer publishing houses became the main targets. The circulation of *Die Welt* began to decline. Springer was not spared public ridicule, denunciation, and threats on his life. On May 19, 1972, two bombs at his printing plant in Hamburg injured 19 employees. Yet Springer, certain of his political conviction, remained opposed to any German-German dialogue. He stayed his course and so did *Die Welt*. After May 20, 1975, Springer personally headed the masthead of *Die Welt* as its publisher. He died on September 22, 1985, in Berlin, but the paper displayed his name on the masthead until October 2, 1990, the *Tag der Deutschen Einheit* (day of German unification). Through its cooperation with *The Washington Post*, *The Los Angeles Times*, and the *Yomiuri Shimbun* in Tokyo, *Die Welt* achieved world-class status. It is available in over 130 countries and it is recognized worldwide as one of Germany's leading dailies.

Manfred K. Wolfram

See also Bild Zeitung; Die Zeit; Federal Republic of Germany; Frankfurter Allgemeine Zeitung; Journalism; Magazines; Press and Newspapers; Springer, Axel; Süddeutsche Zeitung

References

Adler, Ernst-Dietrich. "Die Welt." *Zeitungsland Nordrhein-Westfalen: Geschichte—Profile—Struktur*. Ed. Bernhard Böll, Volker Schulze, and Hans Süssmuth. Bonn: ZV Zeitungs-Verlag Service GmbH, 1993.

Die Welt, Historische Verlags-Dokumentation. Hamburg: Axel Springer Verlag, 1993.

Harenberg, Karl-Heinz. "Aus Bonn für 'Deutschland': Die Welt." *Porträts der deutschen Presse: Politik und Profit*. Ed. Michael Wolf Thomas. Berlin: Volker Spiess, 1980.

Die Weltbühne (1918–33)

A famous and controversial cultural-political weekly, *Die Weltbühne* served as a main forum for Germany's left-wing intellectuals from the end of World War I to Adolf Hitler's assumption of power in 1933. It opposed the monarchist groups and institutions that the Weimar Republic had inherited from the German empire with the same acerbic wit that it used to castigate the leaders of the republic for not eliminating the monarchists.

Established in 1905 in Berlin as *Die Schaubühne* (The theatrical stage) by the outstanding theater critic Siegfried Jacobsohn, the journal first concerned itself almost exclusively with literary and theatrical affairs. It became increasingly political during World War I, however, and in 1918 it changed its name to *Die Weltbühne* (The world stage), heralding a profound involvement in all the concerns of humanity. While never abandoning the area of culture—in fact producing some of the best theater, film, psychology, and art writing in Europe—*Die Weltbühne* fought for revolutionary change in Germany. Disappointed in the pedestrian outcome of the republic, the journal's writers called Weimar alternately "a republic without republicans" or "a place with republicans but no republic."

After Jacobsohn's death in 1926, the journal's editorship passed to Kurt Tucholsky (1890–1935), Weimar Germany's most celebrated and most abominated political satirist and social critic. Tucholsky's tenure lasted only one year, but he lastingly defined the style and character of the journal with his enormous journalistic and literary output. His successor, Carl von Ossietzky (1889–1938), who edited the journal from 1927 to 1932, gave it an even more markedly left-wing and pacifist character. Under his leadership, the journal addressed such major issues as the need for judicial reform, homosexual rights, decriminalization of abortion, women's rights, European reconciliation, the unity of the German working class, and above all, universal disarmament.

Concentrating on their old enemies, the military and the conservatives, the writers of *Die Weltbühne* tended to overlook the threat of Hitler, whom they erroneously saw as a tool in the hands of reactionary forces. The Nazis abominated the journal, and once in power, they arrested Ossietzky. They also publicly burned issues of *Die Weltbühne*, as well as the writings of such of its contributors as Tucholsky, Heinrich Mann (1871–1950), Lion Feuchtwanger (1884–1958), and Ernst Toller (1893–1939). Other writers for the journal, most of whom were Jews, fell victim to racial persecution. The journal itself continued, first in Vienna, then in Prague, even later in Paris, and finally in post–World War II East Berlin, but it had become a crypto-Communist publication, meaning that it had lost its wit, its charm, its vitality, and worst of all, its political independence. *Die Weltbühne* still is seen as one of the foremost advocates of modernity in Weimar Germany.

Istvan Deak

See also Abortion; Censorship; Cinema; Drama; Feminism and Anti-Feminism; Feuchtwanger, Lion; Homosexuality/Lesbianism; Journalism; Literary Criticism; Mann, Heinrich; Morality; National Socialism; Ossietzky, Carl von; Pacifism and the Peace Movement; Satire; Sex Reform and Birth Control; Theater; Toller, Ernst; Tucholsky, Kurt; Weimar Germany; Weimar Germany: Literature

References

Deak, Istvan. *Weimar Germany's Left-wing Intellectuals: A Political History of the "Weltbühne" and Its Circle.* Berkeley, CA: University of California Press, 1968.

Enseling, Alf. *Die Weltbühne: Organ der Intellektuellen Linken.* Münster am Westfalen: C.J. Fahle, 1962.

Holly, Elmar E. *Die Weltbühne 1918–1933: Ein Register sämtlicher Autoren und Beiträge.* Berlin: Colloquium Verlag, 1989.

Madrasch-Groschopp, Ursula. *Die Weltbühne: Porträt einer Zeitschrift.* Königstein, Ts: Athenäum, 1983.

Die Zeit

In its fifth decade of publication, the "liberal voice of reason" *Die Zeit* (The time) has a readership of 1.49 million, making it one of the most widely distributed and read "quality" newspapers in the world and by far the largest of its kind in Germany. Since the first issue appeared on February 21, 1946 in Hamburg under "License No. 6" issued by the British military authorities, *Die Zeit*, a weekly newspaper, has maintained its skeptical yet serious attitude toward every facet of life in postwar Germany. Not affiliated with any political party, *Die Zeit* has earned a reputation as Germany's true opposition paper regardless of which party is in power. Theo Sommer (1930–), one of the paper's senior editors, characterizes *Die Zeit* as independently liberal, often in a position between both sides. It persistently stresses reason and quiet reflection.

Countess Marion Dönhoff (1909–), co-senior editor, expands Sommer's editorial position by including tolerance and political morality based on common sense, candor, evaluation of all available facts, and a willingness to admit when one is wrong. This editorial stance can create tension among its editors and publishers and alienate its readership. In 1955, for example, the subscription rate had dropped to 44,000 and the paper was near bankruptcy. Moreover, the original *Lizenzträger* (licensed partners) parted rather unceremoniously, further eroding the public's confidence in the paper.

Gerd Bucerius (1906–95) remained as publisher and sole owner of *Die Zeit*. A leading figure of the Christian Democratic Union (CDU) and three-term member of the Bundestag, he succeeded in guiding his paper through very difficult years. Only his controlling financial interests in the popular illustrated weekly *Stern* kept *Die Zeit* from certain financial ruin. Staying his course, he rebuilt a quality editorial staff and invited authors and guest contributors of national and international renown. Besides a slate of Nobel laureates, British prime ministers, U.S. senators, French cabinet members, and presidents of West Germany, the paper also published such well-known German writers as Heinrich Böll (1917–85), Günter Grass (1927–), and Hans Magnus Enzensberger (1929–). Yet it was the addition of Helmut Schmidt, former chancellor and the leader of the Social Democratic Party (SPD), as senior editor that seemed to be the crowning achievement of Gerd Bucerius. Schmidt Helmut, Marion Dönhoff, and Theo Sommer succeeded Bucerius as publisher.

Today, 490,000 copies of *Die Zeit* are sold weekly and read (in German) worldwide. The original eight pages of *Die Zeit* (1946) have grown to over a hundred pages for some weekly editions. Since October 1970, every issue of *Die Zeit* has contained the colorful *ZEITmagazin* supplement. The paper maintains its headquarters in Hamburg and has additional offices in Berlin, Bonn, Essen, Frankfurt, Brussels, Paris, and Moscow. Its foreign correspondents are located in London, Madrid, Rome, Vienna, Milan, Rio de Janeiro, New York, Warsaw, and Tokyo. *Die Zeit* is also published as an overseas edition in Toronto, Canada, just one day after the appearance of the original version in Hamburg. This 24-page compendium contains a selection of the most important articles from *ZEIT*.

Die Zeit is known for its lack of venerability which it complements by its prestige, influence, objectivity, morality, clarity of language, and sheer readability. With the addition of the overseas edition, *Die Zeit* has become a weekly forum for open discussion among its 104 journalists, its many guest contributors, and all of its readers worldwide.

Manfred K. Wolfram

See also Bild Zeitung; Die Welt; Dönhoff, Marion von; Federal Republic of Germany; *Frankfurter Allgemeine Zeitung;* Journalism; Magazines; Press and Newspapers; *Süddeutsche Zeitung*

References

Bucerius, Gerd. "Vierzig Jahre *Die Zeit.*" *Die Zeit.* February 21, 1986.

Dönhoff, Gräfin Marion. "Aus der Werkstatt der *Zeit*: Ein Blick in das Innenleben einer liberalen Zeitung." *Die Zeit.* December 16, 1988.

Dornberg, John. "*Die Zeit*: A liberal voice of reason." *Lufthansa's Germany* 1986, 36–41.

Meyn, Hermann. "Liberaler Kaufmanngeist, *Die Zeit.*" *Porträts der deutschen Presse: Politik und Profit.* Ed. Michael Wolf Thomas. Berlin: Volker Spiess, 1980.

Diesel, Rudolf Christian Karl (1858–1913)

In close cooperation with the firms of Maschinenfabrik Augsburg (MAN) and Friedrich Krupp, Rudolf Diesel developed the high-pressure oil combustion engine, which was later named after him. The first operational diesel engine was completed in Augsburg in 1897 and clearly surpassed all other thermal engines in efficiency. After overcoming the technical problems that occurred in the early engines—which were exclusively stationary installations—the diesel engine was introduced all over the world at the beginning of the twentieth century—even for ship propulsion. It would later be used as a prime mover for rail and road vehicles.

Diesel was born on March 18, 1858, to German parents in Paris. He was educated in Paris, Augsburg, and Munich. In 1883, he married Martha Flasche (1860–1944). He had three children: Rudolf (1884–1944), Hedwig (1885–1968), and Eugen (1889–1970). The last compiled a biography of his father: *Diesel–Der Mann, das Werk, das Schicksal* (published as *Diesel, the Man, His Work, His Fate*), 1937.

Diesel worked in the field of refrigeration engineering (Linde system) in France (1880–90) and Germany. In 1893 he went into business for himself. His patent number 67,207, "Working process and design for internal-combustion engines," as well as the contracts with MAN and Friedrich Krupp, formed the basis for the realization of his invention. Under the direction of Heinrich von Buz, MAN built a test engine, which proved to be effective after some modifications. The first operational diesel engine in the world achieved the then-extraordinary efficiency rate of 26.2

Rudolf Diesel. Courtesy of German Information Center, New York.

percent during tests in Augsburg under the supervision of Professor Moritz Schröter in 1897. Diesel and Schröter announced this new principle for an engine—high mechanical compression of the ambient air aspirated into the cylinder, auto-ignition of the fuel injected under high pressure, and combustion using a high temperature gradient—at the 1897 general meeting of the Association of German Engineers (VDI) in Kassel.

Diesel issued licenses globally for the construction of his engines. Later he experienced difficult disputes about his patents. In 1907 he was granted an honorary doctorate in engineering from his university, the Technische Hochschule München (Technical University, Munich).

Diesel anticipated that his engine would also be used to drive cars and rail vehicles, but he did not see his dream realized in practice. During a crossing from Belgium to England he passed away under mysterious circumstances during the night of September 29–30, 1913.

Diesel's invention changed the complexion of the world. The diesel engine currently has an efficiency rate in excess of 50 percent, and is still the most economical thermal engine in existence.

Josef Wittmann

See also Automobile Industry; Engineering; Krupp: Family and Firm; Mannesmann: Firm and Family

References

Cummins, C. Lyle Jr. *Diesel's Engine.* Lake Oswego, OR: Carnot Press, 1993.

———. *Diesel's Engine: Internal Fire.* Lake Oswego, OR: Carnot Press, 1976.

Grosser, Morton. *Diesel: The Man and the Engine.* New York, NY: Atheneum, 1978.

Niske, Robert W. and Charles M. Wilson. *Rudolf Diesel: Pioneer of the Age of Power.* Norman, OK: University of Oklahoma Press, 1965.

Thomas, Donald E. Jr. *Diesel: Technology and Society in Industrial Germany.* Tuscaloosa, AL: The University of Alabama Press, 1987.

Dietrich, Otto (1897–1952)

Otto Dietrich was the Nazi press chief who became chairman of the Reich Association of the German Press and vice-president of the Reich Press Chamber.

As head of the Nazi Party's press, Dietrich played an important role in securing the Party's electoral victory in 1933. Once in power, Dietrich attacked the Weimar press, accusing it of collaborating with the Marxists and of corrupting political life. He warned that the Nazi Party intended to eliminate what he referred to as "selfish publisher interest groups" and to replace them with a press that would more closely reflect nationalist values. Accordingly, the German press experienced the process of *Gleichschaltung* (coordination) that was a common feature of Nazi rule.

On April 30, 1933, the Reich Association of the German Press (RVDP) elected Dietrich as its chairman. He announced that membership in the association would be compulsory for all journalists and that all members would have to prove their "racial and political reliability."

Having regulated entry into the profession and the flow of news, Dietrich, together with Propaganda Minister Joseph Goebbels (1897–1945), tackled the problem of editorial policy and content. Nazi domination of the press was exerted through the Reich Press Chamber, one of seven chambers comprising the Reich Chamber of Culture established by the law of September 22, 1933. Grouped in the Reich Press Chamber were the two most important organisations, the RVDP and the Association of German Newspaper Publishers, with Max Amann (1891–1957), the head of the Nazi publisher Eher Verlag, as chairman.

From 1933, the Press Department of the Propaganda Ministry took over the daily press conferences that had been a regular feature of journalistic life during the Weimar Republic. The content of the newspapers was rigidly controlled through detailed directives issued by the Ministry. Such restrictions were soon to be reinforced by the "Editors Law" (*Schriftleitergesetz)* of October 4, 1933. Dietrich had been the driving force behind this law, which made editors of newspapers and political periodicals responsible for any infringement of government directives. In effect, the law reversed the roles of publisher and editor, reducing the publisher to the position of business manager. The obligatory character of all directives and decrees was stressed repeatedly, which ruled out editorial independence.

On November 15, 1933, Amann was appointed president of the Reich Press Chamber and Dietrich became vice-president. This marked the beginning of one of the longest-standing feuds within the Nazi party over control of the press. Dietrich, in his position as Reich press chief and later secretary of state within the Propaganda Ministry, controlled the editors and journalists, while Amann reigned supreme in the publishing field. As a result the press of the Third Reich became increasingly regimented and dull, with little opportunity for independent thought and action.

David Welch

See also Amann, Max; Coordination; Goebbels, Josef; National Socialist Germany; Press and Newspapers; Third Reich: Propaganda and Culture

References
Abel, K. D. *Die Presselenkung im NS-Staat.* Berlin: Colloquium, 1968.
Dietrich, Otto. *The Hitler I Knew.* London: Methuen, 1957.
Frei, Norbert and J. Schmitz. *Journalismus im Dritten Reich.* Munich: C.H. Beck, 1989.
Hale, Orion A. *The Captive Press in the Third Reich.* Princeton, NJ: Princeton University Press, 1964.
Koszyk, Kurt K. *Geschichte der deutschen Presse, 1914–45.* Berlin: Colloquium Verlag, 1966–72.

Dilthey, Wilhelm (1833–1911)

Wilhelm Dilthey was a wide-ranging German philosopher-historian best known for his efforts to base history and the other human sciences (*Geisteswissenschaften*) on an expanded theory of knowledge. He is also widely regarded as the "father" of modern intellectual history.

Born in Biebrich in the Rhineland, he began higher studies in theology at Heidelberg and Berlin but gravitated toward philosophy and history. After positions at Basel, Kiel, and Breslau, he assumed Friedrich Hegel's chair at Berlin in 1882; the following year saw the first volume of his *Introduction to the Human Sciences* (1883), his *Gesammelte Schriften* (Collected works) run to over 20 volumes.

Influenced by the non-speculative "realistic idealism" of Friedrich E. Schleiermacher, Johann G. Droysen (1808–84), and Friedrich A. Trendelenburg, he joined the intellectual reaction against positivism and metaphysics. As an extension of Immanuel Kant's critical effort, he sought to provide a "critique of historical reason," which would establish the cognitive validity of empathetic understanding (*Verstehen*) as the main method of history and other humane disciplines. He carried further Droysen's distinction between causal explanation and interpretive understanding, but never regarded them as entirely exclusive.

In his efforts he came to elaborate a new, radically reflective "life empiricism," or "life philosophy," which took its departure from ordinary experience within the matrix of culture. In this view, the world of actual, lived experience is always and already permeated with tacit meanings and coherent structures, which we reexperience (*nacherleben*) in our understanding and bring to reflective awareness. These coherences may constitute a more or less explicit worldview, compounded of factual beliefs, value judgments, and ultimate ends.

Along with his theory of understanding, Dilthey proposed a special discipline devoted to the explication of worldviews (*Weltanschauungslehre*). The attempt to define and to ground the human sciences—in which "being" and "knowing" (or object and subject) are not categorically distinct—brought Dilthey to theoretical quandaries and logical deadends. He came to enunciate the "circle of understanding," whereby parts and wholes are reciprocally illuminating and wherein the mind partakes of what it is trying to grasp.

Dilthey's exposition of human understanding issued in a critical theory of history is vastly different from the substantive philosophies of history in the manner of Hegel, August Comte, and Karl Marx (1819–83). Dilthey's evolving position also stood at odds with concurrent neo-Kantian efforts to base the human sciences on eternal values or transcendental norms. In hopes of achieving an ultimate foundational science, he pursued a descriptive psychology ("Ideen über eine beschreibende und zergliedernde Psychologie" [ideas toward a descriptive and analytical psychology], 1894), which treated mental contents as meaning-laden and embedded in coherences. Dissatisfied, he turned after 1900 toward hermeneutics (the theory of textual exegesis), based upon the triadic whole of experience/expression/understanding. This endeavor brought him into proximity to Edmund Husserl's (1859–1938) nascent phenomenology and Max Weber's (1864–1920) interpretive sociology.

Dilthey is often linked to kindred trends in German

Lebensphilosophie (Friedrich Nietzsche [1844–1900] and Georg Simmel [1858–1918]) and later existentialism (Karl Jaspers [1883–1959] and Martin Heidegger [1889–1976]), as well as the crisis of historicism (Ernst Troeltsch [1863–1923]). His thought has been criticized for alleged "mentalism," subjectivism, and relativism. His constant aim, however, remained a theory of human understanding as valid cognition—not an intuitive vision of either the self-reflecting ego or the sweep of history.

As a practicing historian, Dilthey produced broadly synthetic but meticulous studies of Schleiermacher (1870; enlarged 1922), the young Hegel (1904), Western natural law tradition (1887*ff*), the Enlightenment, romanticism, and many specific German literary figures and movements. True to his Rhenish liberal roots, Dilthey remained stalwartly cosmopolitan in the heyday of Wilhelmine chauvinism.

Dilthey has been aptly called "the German William James." His thought was continued by a "Dilthey school" of Georg Misch, Hermann Nohl, Eduard Spranger, Erich Rothacker, Bernard Groethuysen, and Theodor Litt. He also exerted a profound influence upon Jaspers, Heidegger, and José Ortega y Gasset. A major thinker who focused upon crucial issues of interpretive knowledge, Dilthey continues to exert a marked influence on the theory and practice of the humane disciplines.

Michael H. Ermarth

See also Droysen, Johann; *Germanistik*; Heidegger, Martin; History; Human Sciences; Husserl, Edmund; Jaspers, Karl; Nietzsche, Friedrich; Philosophy; Psychology; Simmel, Georg; Troeltsch, Ernst; Understanding; Weber, Max

References

Dilthey, Wilhelm. *The Essence of Philosophy.* Chapel Hill, NC: University of North Carolina Press, 1954.
———. *Gesammelte Schriften.* 20 vols. Stuttgart: Teubner, 1957*ff.*
———. *Introduction to the Human Sciences.* Princeton, NJ: Princeton University Press, 1988.
———. *Poetry and Experience.* Princeton, NJ: Princeton University Press, 1985.
———. *Selected Works.* Princeton, NJ: Princeton University Press, 1985.
———. *Selected Writings.* Cambridge: Cambridge University Press, 1976.
Dilthey-Jahrbuch für Philosophie und Geschichte der Geisteswissenschaften. Göttingen: Vandenhoeck & Ruprecht, 1983 *ff.* (Text in German and English).
Ermarth, Michael. *Wilhelm Dilthey: The Critique of Historical Reason.* Chicago, IL: University of Chicago Press, 1978.
Makkreel, Rudolf. *Dilthey: Philosopher of the Human Studies.* Princeton, NJ: Princeton University Press, 1975.
Plantinga, Theodore. *Historical Understanding in the Thought of Wilhelm Dilthey.* Toronto: University of Toronto Press, 1978.
Rickman, H-P. *Dilthey Today: A Critical Appraisal of the Contemporary Relevance of His Work.* New York, NY: Greenwood, 1988.
———. *Wilhelm Dilthey: Pioneer of the Human Studies.* Berkeley, CA: University of California Press, 1979.

Diplomatic Corps and Diplomacy

In 1867 the Foreign Office (FO) of Prussia was transferred to the North German Confederation and, in 1871, to the newly founded German Empire. Until 1918, the federated states kept their right to have diplomatic representatives in foreign countries, although political relations were solely conducted by the Imperial diplomatic service.

German diplomats in foreign countries formed a single corps, together with the officials of the FO in Berlin. The pre-unification social hierarchy was maintained, with preference given to members of the oldest aristocracy. Those of bourgeois origins served mainly in the lower ranks of the FO and were confined to the economic or justice departments. Prussian diplomats had their ranks supplemented by new members from the other German states. This enlarged the corps, but retained the aristocratic dominance. Protestants remained overrepresented. The financial and social requirements of diplomatic service enhanced its social exclusiveness. The priority given to social origins over academic degrees and specialized knowledge sometimes contributed to mistakes in policy.

The social factor became especially important after Chancellor Otto von Bismarck's dismissal in 1890, when Kaiser Wilhelm II claimed personal loyalty and social standing as essential requirements for the diplomatic corps. That Germany had become a highly industrialized country was not reflected in the structure of its diplomatic service.

A major reform was begun in 1917 and finally carried out in 1920. It unified the diplomatic and consular services, which welcomed personnel from the economic and scientific professions. A study of law became the usual qualification for foreign office service. During the Empire, most diplomats had favored the conservative parties (without regarding themselves as members of political parties); during the Weimar Republic, some members of liberal or Social Democratic parties entered the service, without basically altering its character.

Germany's foreign missions numbered 59 in 1876, rose to 173 in 1914, but declined to 112 in 1923 before rising to 171 in 1937. The number of the higher-service diplomats (consular level and above) inside and outside Germany rose from 142 (1874) to 351 (1914) to 433 (1923). After the first phase of the Weimar Republic, aristocratic or upper bourgeois diplomats continued to be overrepresented; they usually served the republic with loyalty but without commitment.

The conservative preferences of the Foreign Office were felt during the presidential governments (1930–33), but only eight diplomats were members of the Nazi Party before Hitler's takeover in 1933. During the Third Reich, large numbers of diplomats shifted their loyalty again and joined the Nazi Party; some of them accepted Schutzstaffel (SS) honorary ranks and became SS members. In later years many were recruited from the SS. Only one ambassador left the foreign service voluntarily in 1933. The Nazis established competing foreign policy

1878 Berlin Congress. Courtesy of Inter Nationes, Bonn.

agencies, some of which later were formally incorporated into the FO. When Ribbentrop, a Nazi outsider, became foreign minister in 1938, many of his followers entered the diplomatic service.

In 1951, the FO was revived in the Federal Republic of Germany (FRG), initially with many of its former personnel. Its forerunners were the *Deutsche Büro* (German Bureau) and the *Dienststelle für Auswärtige Angelegenheiten* (Service Office for Foreign Affairs) in the federal chancellor's office. The increasing number of decolonized states and the growing need for representation with international organizations was mirrored in the increased number of foreign missions, from 70 in 1952 to 175 in 1961 to 214 in 1990. Simultaneously, the higher-service personnel grew from 896 in 1953 to 1,279 in 1961 to 1,501 in 1990. In 1992, the higher service comprised some 1,632 officials.

Since the beginning of the century, diplomacy has undergone a functional change that has been accelerated since the 1950s: in transnational relations many state agencies and ministries define the course of foreign policy, and international institutions develop new kinds of diplomatic interchange. Innovations in communication techniques as well as frequent travel by leading politicians reduce the immediate political importance of individual diplomatic actions, but they multiply the need for an international diplomatic presence. The FO now seeks to recruit diplomats with general qualifications. Jurists still dominate the ranks, but those with abilities in the economic, cultural, and social-science branches are more deliberately integrated.

In contrast to the FRG, the German Democratic Republic (GDR), at its inception, started to build a completely new diplomatic service, mostly recruited from Communist Party functionaries with little experience in foreign countries. Until 1969, the GDR had diplomatic relations almost exclusively with the states of the "socialist world system." Only commercial missions were sent to most of the other countries, preferably to neutral ones. In the wave of recognition after 1972, the GDR was able to institute diplomatic posts worldwide, for which, in the meantime, a new generation of diplomats had

been educated. The Ministerium für Auswärtige Angelegenheiten (Ministry of Foreign Affairs) of the GDR was terminated upon German reunification on October 3, 1990; 235 members of the GDR higher service applied to the FO of the newly united FRG, but only 9 of them were accepted.

Jost Dülffer

See also Adenauer, Konrad; American-German Relations; Anglo-German Relations; Aristocracy; Austro-German Relations; Belgian-German Relations; Bethmann Hollweg, Theobald von; Bismarck, Otto von; Brandt, Willy; Brentano, Heinrich von; Bülow, Bernhard von; Civil Service; Eulenburg-Hertefeld, Philipp zu; Federal Republic of Germany: Foreign Policy; Fischer, Oskar; Franco-German Relations; Genscher, Hans-Dietrich; German Democratic Republic: Foreign Relations; Hallstein, Walter; Hohenlohe-Schillingsfürst, Chlodwig zu; Honecker, Erich; Imperial Germany: Foreign Policy; Italian-German Relations; Kiderlen-Wächter, Alfred; Marschall von Bieberstein, Adolf von; National Socialist Germany: Foreign Policy; *Ostpolitik*; Russian-German Relations; Schröder, Gerhard; Schweinitz, Lothar von; Soviet-German Relations; Stresemann, Gustav; Versailles, Treaty of; Weimar Germany: Foreign Policy; Wilhelm II; World War I; World War II

References

Cecil, Lamar. *The German Diplomatic Service.* Princeton, NJ: Princeton University Press, 1976.

Craig, Gordon A. and Felix Gilbert, eds. *The Diplomats, 1919–1939.* New York, NY: Atheneum, 1965.

Heinemann, John. *Hitler's First Foreign Minister: Constantin Freiherr von Neurath, Diplomat and Statesman.* Berkeley, CA: University of California Press, 1979.

Schwabe, Klaus, ed. *Das Diplomatische Korps 1871–1945.* Boppard: Boldt, 1985.

Dirks, Walter (1901–91)

The political journalist and writer Walter Dirks was a leading critic of German politics in his countless essays and commentaries, beginning in the Weimar Republic. After World War II, he was among the most important advocates of a Christian socialism.

Born to a Catholic family in Dortmund-Hörde, Dirks had special insight into the difficulties of workers through observing his mother's welfare work during his youth. A member of the Catholic youth movement, he studied philosophy, theology, and music before obtaining a post in 1924 with the newspaper the *Rhein-Mainische Volkszeitung* (Rhine-Main people's paper). Though only founded in 1923, this newspaper became a respected voice of the left wing of the Center Party.

Until the newspaper's ban in 1934, Dirks published opinion articles on social, cultural, and church policies as well as making a reputation as a music critic. He also wrote under the pseudonym Georg Risse for the unaffiliated republican journal *Deutsche Republik*. In 1935 he found a hiding place in the apolitical feature section of the *Frankfurter Zeitung,* until the Nazis forbade its publication in 1943. The latter paper had served as a fig leaf for the Nazis' attempt to prove to the world that they practiced freedom of the press.

After the war, Dirks thought the time for European socialism had arrived and demanded a completely new beginning. As one of the founders of the Christian Democratic Union (CDU), he wanted the new party to have the impress of the "Frankfurter" guidelines—which he had decisively influenced—from September 1945, with its program of a "socialism from Christian responsibility." Due to the dominance of the free market–conservative wing of the CDU, he withdrew from the party, where he had been more of an intellectual guide than a pragmatic politician.

Together with Eugen Kogon (1903–87), who had spent many years in concentration camps and who had illustrated the total inhumanity of the Nazi system of terror in his study *Der SS-Staat* (published as *The Theory and Practice of Hell*), 1950, Dirks began in 1946 to publish the journal *Frankfurter Hefte*. It was the most successful journal of politics and culture in the postwar era. Here this socially-oriented left-wing Catholic, engaging intellectuals and pacifists out of religious conviction, had a forum for his conception of the spiritual and moral renewal of the "second republic." Here too he had a chance to present his ideas on combining Christian thought with socialism. Dirks was a vehement proponent of European unity, especially French-German rapprochement, which he had advocated in his early years.

From 1956 to 1966, Dirks directed the main cultural department of West German Radio (Westdeutscher Rundfunk), and thereafter lived as a freelance journalist and author.

Walter Mühlhausen

See also Catholicism, Political; Center Party; Christian Democratic Union; Kogon, Eugen

References

Blankenberg, Heinz. *Politischer Katholizismus in Frankfurt am Main 1918–1933*. Mainz: Matthias Grünewald Verlag, 1981.

Dirks, Walter. *Der singende Stotterer: Autobiographische Texte*. Munich: Kosel-Verlag, 1983.

———. *Gesammelte Schriften*. Ed. Fritz Boll, Ulrich Bröckling, and Karl Prümm. 8 vols. Zürich: Ammann, 1987–91.

———. *War ich ein linker Spinner? Republikanische Texte— von Weimar bis Bonn*. Munich: Kosel-Verlag, 1983.

Focke, Franz. *Sozialismus aus christlicher Verantwortung: Die Idee eines christlichen Sozialismus in der katholisch-sozialen Bewegung und in der CDU*. Wuppertal: Hammer, 1978.

Gurland, A.R.L. *Die CDU/CSU. Ursprünge und Entwicklung bis 1953*. Ed. Dieter Emig. Frankfurt am Main: Europäische Verlagsanstalt, 1980.

Prumm, Karl. *Walter Dirks und Eugen Kogen als katholische Publizisten der Weimarer Republik*. Heidelberg: C. Winter, 1984.

Disarmament

Disarmament as a process may be imposed unilaterally in order to enforce arms-limitations measures on a defeated enemy or may be a result of multilateral negotiations whose aim is weapons reduction. Between 1870 and 1990, Germany twice experienced unilateral attempts to limit or destroy its ability to wage war. Since 1979, Germany has participated in numerous multilateral attempts to reduce various weapons systems. These attempts culminated in the July 16, 1990 agreement between the Soviet Union and the Federal Republic of Germany to limit the size of the German armed forces and to remove Soviet troops from a unified Germany.

On May 8, 1899, at the first Hague Peace Conference, Germany and its European neighbors spoke of limiting armaments but could not agree on mutual controls. Germany's defeat in 1918 led to the British, Americans, French, and Italians imposing extensive reductions in armaments in the Treaty of Versailles. Under General Seeckt and his followers, Germany secretly as well as openly avoided fulfilling the disarmament clauses. Nevertheless, the unilateral disarmament terms facilitated the rise of extremist political parties in Germany that demanded an end to arms limitation. Adolf Hitler's Nazi Party was the most successful of these groups.

After Germany's surrender on May 8, 1945, the victorious powers—the United States, the Soviet Union, and Great Britain—signed an official protocol on August 2, 1945 at the Potsdam Conference. This document instituted a policy of total disarmament of Germany. An Allied Military Security Board (MSB) outlawed the manufacture of all weapon systems; abolished, once again, the German General Staff; and even forbade the wearing of military decorations. The teaching of military history in the occupied and divided country was also prohibited.

The Cold War allowed West Germany to emerge as a respected sovereign state with a large military. By the late 1970s, its arms policy sought a multilateral approach to limiting those weapons systems capable of delivering nuclear weapons to European targets. West Germany had endorsed the 1967 Nuclear Non-Proliferation Treaty, and in September 1987, Chancellor Helmut Kohl agreed to scrap the intermediate-range Pershing missiles held in West Germany if the United States and Soviet Union would also phase out similar weapons. By December 1987, a treaty was signed in Washington, that called for the elimination of such weapon systems.

In the process of reunification after 1989, the leaders of Germany and the Soviet Union achieved a bilateral disarmament agreement, whereby Germany would reduce its armed forces from 500,000 to 375,000 men. In return, the 360,000 Soviet troops stationed in the former East Germany were to leave that area by 1994.

Frank A. Mayer

See also Bahr, Egon; The Cold War and Germany; Detente; Greens; Kohl, Helmut; Pacifism and the Peace Movement; Rearmament; Reunification; Seeckt, Hans von; Versailles, Treaty of

References

Brodie, Barnard. *War and Politics.* New York, NY: Macmillan, 1973.

Craig, Gordon A. *Politics of the Prussian Army.* 2nd ed. New York, NY: Clarendon, 1964.

Howard, Michael. *Studies in War and Peace.* New York, NY: Viking Press, 1971.

Neumann, William L. *After Victory: Churchill, Roosevelt, Stalin, and the Making of the Peace.* New York, NY: Harper and Row, 1967.

Disease

Although the German medical profession established its extraordinary international reputation in the last half of the nineteenth century with painstaking scientific research on the etiology, diagnosis, and treatment of diseases, public responses to disease and disease control generally ranged far beyond narrowly technical matters. Such responses, which affected health and social policies, were often shaped by ideological commitments, literary representations, and moral panics. As a result of professional interests and public fears, enormous gaps often opened between the perceived virulence of various diseases and their actual frequency and lethality, discrepancies that reveal much about national and social anxieties.

In broad terms, three major phases of response to disease and disease control may be identified after the nineteenth-century national unification. The first fell between 1871 and 1900, when public-health authorities emphasized the conquest of infectious diseases, especially those that afflicted Germany's burgeoning cities. During the second phase, which extended until 1945, attention shifted to the social consequences of infant mortality, tuberculosis, venereal diseases, nervous disorders, and alcoholism, which were portrayed as indicators of national degeneration, sapping Germany's vitality and imperiling its future. After the defeat of Nazi Germany in 1945, disease control largely reverted to the medical profession and became normalized. As in other advanced industrial countries, cancer and heart disease emerged as the leading killers and the foci of medical research. In recent decades, growing awareness of the environmental sources of some diseases, challenges to technocratic medicine, apprehensions over health care costs, and the AIDS epidemic have reawakened widespread public concern and discussion about disease.

Despite attempts by the Imperial Health Office (established in 1876) to collect comprehensive statistics on infectious diseases and causes of death in the German Empire, limitations in reporting in the various German states meant that accurate statistics were available only for the larger cities until after 1900. Average mortality rates for nineteenth-century Germany peaked at over 28 deaths per thousand in the early 1870s, when over one-third of all deaths were ascribed to tuberculosis, respiratory infections, and intestinal disorders. A host of infectious diseases, such as measles, diphtheria, typhus, and childbed fever accounted for another 10 percent of deaths. Such infectious diseases took a heavy toll among infants. At least one-fifth of all babies in German cities died before their first birthdays. Among infants of the poorest classes, mortality rates commonly reached 30 percent.

Such regular patterns of disease and death were often overshadowed, however, by murderous epidemics, to which Germany was still vulnerable. A smallpox epidemic spread by returning German troops at the end of the Franco-Prussian War killed over 120,000 in the state of Prussia alone. The Hamburg cholera epidemic of 1892 infected 17,000 persons and caused 8,600 deaths. By the turn of the century, however, large-scale epidemics had become rare and mortality rates from most infectious diseases were declining rapidly. Medical historians differ over the weight that should be assigned to various factors in bringing about these falling rates. Clearly contributing to this ameliorization were improved sewers and water supply systems, better diets, popularized hygiene, the social diffusion of professional medical care following the enactment of national health insurance in 1883, and the diagnostic and prophylactic advances made possible by bacteriology. Whatever the relative importance, during this era of scientific positivism the combination of higher living standards and sanitation stemming from public health campaigns clearly combined to diminish risk from infectious disease. Doctors and sanitary engineers legitimated their professions on the basis of their achievements in reducing the significance of epidemics.

Despite the decreased mortality from infectious diseases, strategies for disease control increasingly became issues of mass politics around the turn of the century. Middle-class alarm at the rapid fall in birth rates that marked the demographic transition, fears about national efficiency, and urban social reform impulses prompted the formation of numerous associations to combat various "diseases of the people." Medical reformers focused on tuberculosis, venereal diseases, childhood ailments, nervous disorders, and alcoholism, all of which were thought to weaken the population and diminish fertility. This politicization was accompanied by the emergence of ideologies of racial hygiene and pro-natalism and by demands for greater state intervention. Literary and artistic representations of disease also underwent profound mutations, with disease frequently being associated with decadence, as in Thomas Mann's best-selling novel of family decline, *Buddenbrooks,* 1901.

These changes may be illustrated by examining reactions to pulmonary tuberculosis (TB) between the turn of the century and 1945. During the 1890s medical opinion was sharply divided over treatment for TB. Bacteriologists such as Robert Koch (1843–1910) searched for a vaccine, whereas many physicians supported various natural therapies. Opponents of the bacteriologists were soon debating whether susceptibility to TB was largely environmental or hereditary. The socialists, who accepted the environmental explanation, favored free TB clinics, industrial hygiene, and housing reform. Given the failure of Koch's tuberculin cure and the mounting socialist agitation, middle-class welfare societies took the initiative in organizing a sanatorium movement, which they viewed as an instrument for improving national health, encouraging good hygienic habits among the lower classes, and undercutting the socialists. The movement enjoyed the patronage of the empress as well as the chancellor and other leading officials, and galvanized the energies of the Patriotic Women's League. By 1910, Germany's 97 public sanatoria and urban TB clinics had become a source of national pride, although only a small percentage of the estimated 600,000 German tubercular patients received treatment.

During and after World War I, much of this work was nullified as levels of TB incidence returned to 1890s levels. But public-health officials in the Weimar Republic could build on the foundation of clinics and sanatoria established in Imperial Germany. The 1925 TB law provided a framework for coordinating the campaign against TB. Moreover, with economic stabilization, the downward secular trend in TB, apparent since the late nineteenth century, reasserted itself. But attitudes toward TB were rapidly polarizing. Whereas Thomas Mann (1875–1955) could still ironically play on romantic affinities between TB, creativity, and spirituality in *Der Zauberberg* (The magic mountain), 1924, ideologues of the right increasingly represented TB as a disease of the weak-willed, dissolute, and criminally inclined. And whereas the democratic left proposed countering TB with neighborhood clinics, public health education, and improved living standards, racial hygienists called for restrictions on the marriages of, or even the sterilization of, tuberculars as part of a nationwide eugenics policy.

Although the Nazis were committed to eradicating TB, which in *Mein Kampf* Hitler had coupled with syphilis as a poison of the national body, even they refrained from such draconian policies. The Nazis instituted a program for early detection of TB, required registration of all cases, and passed legislation enabling health officials to confine tuberculars forcibly. TB was allowed as one of the few grounds for abortion. Those suffering from TB certainly were stigmatized under the Nazi regime. But because of divisions among Nazi medical officials, tuberculars were not among those slated for forced sterilization under the law of 1933. Nonetheless, in occupied Poland in 1942, SS leaders seriously discussed exterminating 35,000 tuberculosis patients. As was so often the case with Nazi biopolitics, campaigns to eradicate disease readily translated into plans to murder those labeled as disease carriers.

After World War II, the occupation administrations were intent on containing the spread of infectious disease, especially TB and venereal diseases, both of which grew to near-epidemic proportions as they had after World War I. Their public-health measures were largely successful. Soon after the founding of East and West Germany in 1949, the synthesis of numerous antibiotics rendered mortality negligible from those infectious diseases that had so long preoccupied public disease discourse. As the importance of these killers waned, Germans increasingly succumbed to diseases of affluent industrial civilizations, especially heart attacks, circulatory disorders, and cancer. Whereas in 1955 16.7 percent of all deaths in West Germany resulted from cancer and 16.6 percent from heart disease, by 1986 the corresponding figures had climbed to 24.5 percent and 21.5 percent.

With slight variation, East German trends paralleled those in the West. Doctors in both German states developed complex strategies to reduce risks of heart attacks and high blood pressure that included prescribing medication and persuading patients to adopt healthier lifestyles. Some German epidemiologists have recently suggested that similar preventive strategies should be directed against cancer. Intensified campaigns against smoking or efforts aimed at identifying environmental carcinogens might be more effective than the present emphasis on cancer treatment, which has shown remarkably few positive results in West Germany during the last 30 years.

Although debates over cancer and heart disease have been largely confined to the medical journals, the emergence of HIV and AIDS generated public policy debates in the 1980s. In morally charged rhetoric reminiscent of that of the radical right of the 1920s, conservative Bavarian politicians and some of the press demanded such punitive measures as mandatory registering of HIV-positive persons and even quarantining of HIV-positive prostitutes, homosexuals, and drug addicts in concentration camps. Cooler heads prevailed, however. Both Rita Süssmuth, the federal minister of health, and the parliamentary committee on AIDS have instead relied on massive informational and educational campaigns to curb the spread of the virus, with special efforts to reach high-risk groups. AIDS registration has remained voluntary. To date, this policy appears to have succeeded. Instead of the 100,000 cases of AIDS originally forecast, about 40,000 persons have been infected with HIV and around 5,400 have contracted AIDS. Cases are overwhelmingly concentrated in the larger cities. Physicians treating AIDS have lobbied to assure continued health insurance financing for prolonged care of AIDS patients and researchers have pressed for long-term funding. But public-health measures seem to have averted an epidemic of potentially catastrophic proportions.

Derek S. Linton

See also Alcohol; Bacteriology; Fertility; Food; Hamburg; Health; Koch, Robert; Mann, Thomas; Medical Profession; Medicine; Morality; National Women's Associations; Schutzstaffel; Temperance Movements; Virchow, Rudolf

References

Becker, Nikolaus, Elaine M. Smith, and Juergen Warhrendorf. "Time Trends in Cancer Mortality in the Federal Republic of Germany." *International Journal of Cancer* 43 (1989), 245–49.

Davis, Devra Lee and Hoel David, eds. *Trends in Cancer Mortality in Industrial Countries.* New York, NY: New York Academy of Sciences, 1990.

Die Gesundheitspolitik der DDR im Wandel. Bonn-Bad Godesberg: Friedrich Ebert Stiftung, 1989.

Kaeser, Rudolf and Vera Pohland, eds. *Disease and Medicine in Modern German Cultures.* Western Societies Occasional Paper no. 28. Ithaca, NY: Cornell University Press, 1990.

Light, Donald W. and Alexander Schuller, eds. *Political Values and Health Care: The German Experience.* Cambridge, MA: MIT Press, 1986.

McKeown, Thomas. *The Origins of Human Disease*. Oxford: Basil Blackwell, 1988.

Proctor, Robert N. *Racial Hygiene: Medicine under the Nazis*. Cambridge, MA: Harvard University Press, 1988.

Spree, Reinhard. *Health and Social Class in Imperial Germany: A Social History of Mortality, Morbidity, and Inequality*. Oxford: Berg, 1988.

Tuffs, Annette. "Germany: AIDS Policy, AIDS Research." *The Lancet* 337 (January 19, 1991), 165–66.

Usborne, Cornelia. *The Politics of the Body in Weimar Germany*. Ann Arbor, MI: University of Michigan Press, 1992.

Weindling, Paul. *Health, Race and German Politics between National Unification and Nazism 1870–1945*. Cambridge: Cambridge University Press, 1989.

Dix, Otto (1891–1969)

This graphic artist was born December 2, 1891, in Untermhaus near Gera. After six years of grammar school and a four-year apprenticeship as decoration (house) painter, Otto Dix received a stipend to study at the Kunstgewerbeschule (art and design school) in Dresden until 1914, when he was drafted into the army.

After the war he returned to Dresden and from 1919 to 1922 studied at the Kunstakademie (Academy of Art). He was a co-founder of the Dresden Secession Group of 1919. His early works showed expressionist and futurist tendencies, and he participated in the 1920 *First Dada Messe* (first Dada exhibition) at the Galerie Burkhard in Berlin. Many of his drawings and paintings memorialized the horrors of the war, especially the portfolio of 50 etchings and aquatints of 1924 and paintings of the trenches and of war cripples. From 1922 to 1925 he studied at the Kunstakademie at Düsseldorf. He became bitterly critical of the decadent 1920s and their erotic nightlife, which he depicted with a grotesque and cruel immediacy. After being appointed professor at the Academy of Art in Dresden, Dix became well known, with exhibitions at the *Biennale*, at the Brooklyn Museum, and in many cities in Germany.

In 1931 he was elected member of the Prussian Academy of Art, but in 1933 the Nazis forced his withdrawal from the prestigious institution, dismissed him from his teaching position, and prohibited the exhibition of his works. His veristic depictions (*Neue Sachlichkeit*) were the opposite of the heroic-cult images the Nazis desired.

Dix moved to Hemmenhofen and painted primarily landscapes, portraits, and religious subjects in the style and form of the fifteenth- and sixteenth-century masters. In 1937 the Nazis confiscated nearly 260 of his works in German museums and prominently displayed 26 of them in the "shameful" *Degenerate Art* exhibition in Munich. Although 54 years of age, he was drafted into the army in 1945 and returned in 1946 from a French prisoner-of-war camp. Afterward, the number of his exhibitions increased constantly. Yearly he visited Dresden, where he was appointed honorary senator of the Academy. He was elected member of the Academy of Art in East as well as in West Berlin, received numerous prizes (including the Cornelius and the Rembrandt prizes) and the Order of Merit of the Federal Republic of Germany. He died July 25, 1969, at Singen hospital and was buried at Hemmenhofen.

Peter Guenther

See also Artists; Dada; Decadence; National Socialist Germany: Art; Painting; Prussian Art Academy

References

Karsch, Florian, ed. et al. *Otto Dix, 1891–1969: Das graphische Werk*. Hannover: Fackelträger Verlag, 1970.

Löffler, Fritz. *Otto Dix, 1891–1969: Oeuvre der Gemälde*. Recklinghausen: Aurel Bongers, 1981.

———. *Otto Dix, Life and Work*. New York, NY: Holmes & Meier, 1982.

McGreevy, Linda F. *The Life and Works of Otto Dix, German Critical Realist*. Ann Arbor, MI: University of Michigan Research Press, 1981.

Döblin, Alfred (1878–1957)

Alfred Döblin's best-known work, the novel *Berlin Alexanderplatz,* 1929, describes Franz Biberkopf's struggle to make a life for himself in a Berlin that epitomizes modern mass society at its most disorienting for an individual. In a style reminiscent of James Joyce's, *Berlin Alexanderplatz* represents a radical departure from realism and narrative omniscience, and was

Otto Dix. Courtesy of Inter Nationes, Bonn.

among the first works in the German language to experiment freely with shifts in narrative perspective, with collage (children's rhymes and news announcements next to dictionary entries), and with stream-of-consciousness writing.

Born in Stettin to a Jewish family, Döblin grew up in Berlin and was a medical officer in the army from 1914 to 1918. While practicing as a neurologist and psychiatrist in Berlin, he was also involved in literary circles and in 1910 became a co-founder of the expressionist journal *Der Sturm* (The storm), where he began his writing career with the publication of short stories such as "Die Ermordung einer Butterblume" (The murder of a dandelion), 1913. Döblin experimented with narrative perspective in his early novels, of which *Die drei Sprünge des Wang-lun* (The three leaps of Wang-lun), 1915, brought him his first success.

At risk because of his Jewish background as well as his socialist activism, Döblin fled from Germany to France in 1933. There, he was involved in the Zionist movement—the beginnings of his interest in Jewish affairs is recorded in his *Reise in Polen* (Travels in Poland), 1925. In 1940 he escaped the Nazi troops marching into France and moved to the United States, an experience he described in *Schicksalreise: Bericht und Bekenntnis* (Fateful journey: report and confession), 1949.

In Hollywood, Döblin converted to Roman Catholicism during a personal crisis. He returned to Germany after the war as an education officer with the French army, but moved back to France in 1953. After falling ill in 1956, he returned to Emmendingen, near Freiburg, where he spent his last days.

Döblin remained a writer throughout his years of exile and published *Babylonische Wanderung, oder Hochmut kommt vor dem Fall* (The Babylonian migration, or arrogance precedes the fall), 1934, a fictional critique of the cult of heroes; *Pardon wird nicht gegeben* (Men without mercy), 1935; and a trilogy (*Die Fahrt ins Land ohne Tod*, [Journey to the land without death], 1937; *Der blaue Tiger*, [The blue tiger], 1938; and *Der neue Urwald*, [The new jungle], 1948) about the brutality of colonialism in South America as a foreshadow of the ills of the modern world. *Hamlet oder die lange Nacht nimmt ein Ende* (Hamlet or the long night ends), finished in 1946 but unpublished until 1956, is a novel of postwar trauma that in its second version ends in the decision to make a new beginning—rather than the retreat into a convent of the first version (which did not find a publisher).

Andres Nader

See also Expressionism; Expulsion and Exile of Scientists and Scholars; Novel; Weimar Germany: Literature

References

Kobel, Erwin. *Alfred Döblin: Erzählkunst im Umbruch.* Berlin: de Gruyter, 1985.

Neumann, Harold. *Leben: Wissenschaftliche Studien, Krankheiten und Tod Alfred Döblins.* St. Michael: Bläschke, 1982.

Prangel, Matthias. *Alfred Döblin.* 2nd rev. ed. Stuttgart: Metzler, 1987.

Dohnanyi, Hans von (1902–45)

This Resistance activist was born in Vienna on January 1, 1902, and died on April 8, 1945. Hans von Dohnanyi married Christine Bonhoeffer in 1925.

In 1929, the young lawyer joined the Reich Justice Ministry, where he was noted for his critical intelligence and reserved nature. In 1933 he became the personal assistant to Reich Minister of Justice Dr. Franz Gürtner. After the Reichstag fire, Dohnanyi attempted in vain to organize a judges' public inquiry into political terror. He worked with Gürtner on reform of the penal code and began to gather evidence of Nazi criminal activities from secret Justice Ministry files, hoping that his "Chronicle of Scandals" might later be used to convict party leaders of treason. In 1937, Dohnanyi was placed in charge of gathering evidence of homosexuality against Reichswehr (army) Commander Werner von Fritsch. This brought him into contact with Admiral Wilhelm Canaris (1887–1945) and Colonel Hans Oster (1888–1945), key anti-Nazis within the Abwehr (military intelligence).

Dohnanyi was posted in 1938 as a judge in the Leipzig Reichsgericht (supreme court), but in August 1939, at the outbreak of war, Dohnanyi was called up for military service and was appointed to the administrative branch of the Abwehr, where under Canaris and Oster, he headed the Office of Political Affairs. From there he linked Resistance circles among the military, labor, Confessing Church, and Kreisau intellectuals. In 1938 and 1939, Dohnanyi participated in military plots to arrest Hitler. His role was to conduct legal action to have Hitler declared insane by a panel of doctors under Dohnanyi's father-in-law, psychiatrist Dr. Karl Bonhoeffer. Brought into the Abwehr to handle paperwork for future military insurrections, Dohnanyi prepared propaganda to legitimize a coup. Through him conservative anti-Nazis were united with socialist and trade union leaders opposed to the regime. Following the failed plot of 1939, Dohnanyi helped to initiate Operation X, the mission of Catholic lawyer Dr. Josef Müller to the Pope, and rewrote Müller's report with a view to convincing the German generals to remove Hitler.

Dohnanyi used his position during the war to help the Confessing Church resistance, provided an Abwehr cover for Dietrich Bonhoeffer (1906–45), and frustrated Reich Sicherheit Haupt Amt (RSHA; Reich Security Main Office) investigations into the U7 plan to smuggle out Jews. Finally, in 1943, Dohnanyi participated in a planning meeting for Operation Flash in Smolensk, delivered the plastic explosives to be used by Major General Tresckow to blow up Hitler's plane, and would have relayed the code for the operation in Berlin had the explosives discharged.

On April 5, 1943, Dohnanyi and his wife Christine were arrested. His health failing under interrogation, Dohnanyi was paralyzed after an Allied bomb hit his cell. The discovery of Canaris's full diary sealed Dohnanyi's fate, and he was executed in Sachsenhausen on April 9, 1945.

Kyle Jantzen

See also Bonhoeffer, Dietrich; Canaris, Wilhelm; Confessing

Church; National Socialist Germany; Oster, Hans; Resistance; Tresckow, Henning von

References

Bethge, E. *Dietrich Bonhoeffer*. London: Collins, 1970.

Chowaniec, Elizabeth. *Der "Fall Dohnanyi" 1943–1945.* Munich: R. Oldenbourg, 1991.

Manwell, R. and H. Fraenkel. *The Canaris Conspiracy*. New York, NY: McKay, 1969.

Dönhoff, Marion (1909–)

Countess Marion Hedda Ilse Dönhoff, was born in 1909 on the East Prussian estate of Friedrichstein (in Pregaltal bei Königsberg). Her mother was a former lady-in-waiting to Empress Auguste Viktoria; her father was a member of the Prussian Herrenhaus (upper house) and of the Reichstag. Marion Dönhoff was not, in her words, "raised as the prince's child in the city but amidst the entire motley assemblage [of village life], albeit with special responsibilities."

Completing her *Abitur* (senior matriculation) in Potsdam, Dönhoff studied national economics in Frankfurt am Main, where her outspoken liberalism earned her the nickname "the red countess." When the Nazis seized power in 1933, she moved to Basel, Switzerland, where she obtained her doctorate in political science in 1935. Over the next three years she traveled extensively throughout Europe, Africa, and the United States before taking over as director of one of the family's agricultural complexes in 1938. While managing affairs at Quittainen, Dönhoff became actively involved in the Resistance and "lost all of [her] friends" as a result of the failed assassination attempt against Hitler of July 20, 1944. In January 1945, she fled the family estate shortly before the arrival of the Soviet army. Her best-selling book *Namen, die keiner mehr nennt* (Names that are no longer mentioned), 1962, recounts her six-day journey on horseback and also offers a moving historical treatment of her family's role in national political affairs over four centuries.

In 1946, the newly created weekly *Die Zeit* added Dönhoff to its staff as a writer. She left in protest when the publication allocated print-space to jurist Carl Schmidt, who had helped to "legitimize" the Nazi regime. Returning in 1955, she quickly advanced to head the political section, then emerged as deputy editor-in-chief the same year (1956) that she became a founding member of the German Society for Foreign Affairs (for which she served as vice president until 1981). Dönhoff attracted many readers with her political commentaries and her essay collection, *Die Bundesrepublik in der Ära Adenauer—Kritik und Perspektiven* (The federal republic in the Adenauer era—critique and perspectives), 1963, as well as with her reportage in collaboration with Rudolf Walter Leonhardt and Theo Sommer after a shared *Reise in ein fernes Land: Wirtschaft und Politik in der DDR* (Journey into a distant land: economy and politics in the GDR), published in 1964.

In July 1968, "the countess" became editor in chief of *Die Zeit*, then assumed the role of publisher in December 1972. She was the only German woman ever to hold a post of this distinction to date. After 1959, she abandoned her exclusively *Westpolitik* (Western-oriented) posture. Her personal appeal for reconciliation and improved relations between the Federal Republic of Germany (FRG) and the socialist states of Eastern Europe emerges as a consistent theme in her 1970 book, *Deutsche Aussenpolitik von Adenauer bis Brandt: 25 Jahre miterlebt und kommentiert* (German foreign policy from Adenauer to Brandt: 25 years of experience and commentary). The next year, she received the Peace Prize of the Börsenverein des Deutschen Buchhandels (association of the German Book trade). Further publications centering on developments in pre- and postwar Germany include a collage of 17 personal-historical profiles under the title *"Menschen, die wissen, worum es geht"—Politische Schicksale 1916–1976* (People who know what it's about—political fates), assembled in 1976; *Von Gestern nach Übermorgen: Zur politischen Geschichte der Bundesrepublik Deutschland* (published as *Foe into Friend: The Makers of the New Germany from Konrad Adenauer to Helmut Schmidt,* 1982), printed in 1981, and *Preussen—Mass und Masslosigkeit* (Prussia—measure and lack of moderation), 1987. Her involvement in international affairs, particularly her concerns regarding the heightening tensions during the years of United States President Ronald Reagan, is reflected in her *Amerikanische Wechselbäder* (American inconsistencies), 1983, and *Weit ist der Weg nach Osten* (The road to the east is long), 1985. Her interest in Africa, reflected in *Der südafrikanische Teufelskreis* (The South African devil's circle), 1987, has contributed to the FRG's growing awareness of the North-South nexus.

Marion Dönhoff. Courtesy of Inter Nationes, Bonn.

Among the countless honors Dönhoff has received, she admits to having been moved most deeply by the award of an honorary doctorate from a Polish university. She was the first woman ever to receive the Theodor Heuss Prize (1966). In 1982, the Academic Senate of the University of Hamburg accorded Dönhoff its highest award, the title of Honorary Senator. In celebration of her eightieth birthday, former Chancellor Helmut Schmidt (1913–) convened a symposium of "world-class" personalities under the rubric *Ende des Kommunismus—was nun?* (The end of communism—what now?).

For Dönhoff, November 9, 1989 (the opening of the Berlin Wall) is the most significant turning point in postwar history. She is engaged in an effort to bridge the political-cultural gap between East and West Germans. Her recently compiled manifestoes— *Weil das Land sich ändern muss* (Because the country must change), 1992, and *Weil das Land Versöhnung braucht* (Because the country needs reconciliation), 1993—call for a process of mutual understanding and accommodation. Dönhoff remains an active contributor to *Die Zeit* and a frequent panelist at international conferences.

Joyce Mushaben

See also American-German Relations; Aristocracy; Cold War; *Die Zeit*; Federal Republic of Germany; Federal Republic of Germany: Foreign Policy; Federal Republic of Germany: Postwar Refugee and Expellee Organizations; Journalism; Polish-German Relations; Press and Newspapers; Prussia; Soviet-German Relations

References

Dönhoff, Marion. *Amerikanische Wechselbäder*. Munich: Deutscher Taschenbuch Verlag, 1983.

———. *Kindheit in Ostpreussen*. Berlin: Siedler and Goldmann, 1991.

———. *Weit ist der Weg nach Osten*. Munich: Deutscher Taschenbuch Verlag, 1985.

"Marion Dönhoff wird 75 Jahre: Widersprüche aushalten, Spannungen leben." *Die Zeit*. November 30, 1984.

Dönitz, Karl (1891–1980)

The naval leader Karl Dönitz was born into a middle-class family at Grünau-bei-Berlin on September 16, 1891. Imbued by his father with a strong sense of service to the state, Dönitz entered the Imperial German Navy in 1910.

The outbreak of World War I found Dönitz in the Mediterranean aboard the light cruiser *Breslau*, and he remained with that vessel until the fall of 1916. Reassigned to submarine duty, Dönitz served initially aboard *Kapitänleutnant* Walter Forstmann's submarine, the *U-39*, before assuming command of his own vessel, the *UC-25*, in January 1918. On October 4, 1918, Dönitz was forced to scuttle his second command, the *UB-68*, and he spent the remainder of the war in British captivity.

Dönitz was repatriated to Germany in July 1919 and entered the Weimar Republic's Reichsmarine. As commander of the torpedo boat *T-157*, Dönitz sought to remain neutral during the Kapp *Putsch* of 1920, but fell under suspicion of being a *Putschist* and was relieved of command. With the col-

lapse of the *Putsch*, Dönitz was reinstated and held a number of significant ship- and shore-based commands throughout the 1920s. His service to the republic culminated with his assignment as First Admiralty Staff Officer at the Reichsmarine's North Sea Station at Wilhelmshaven.

Dönitz spent most of the first two years of the Nazi dictatorship on foreign assignment, initially as the recipient of a Hindenburg travel grant (1933), later as commander of the training cruiser *Emden* (1934–35). In September 1935, however, he was appointed commander of Germany's reconstituted submarine force. Between 1935 and 1939 he oversaw the expansion of that force and schooled his subordinates in the use of wolfpack tactics.

The wartime success of the U-boat force, particularly the campaigns of late 1940 and 1942 and individual exploits such as Günther Prien's torpedoing of the battleship *Royal Oak* on October 13, 1939, drew Adolf Hitler's favorable attention to Dönitz. Not surprisingly, Hitler named Dönitz as Grand Admiral Erich Raeder's (1876–1960) successor when the latter retired as naval commander in chief on January 30, 1943. Dönitz's appointment came at a time when the German surface fleet's fortunes were already in decline; by May 1943, Allied countermeasures were turning the tide against the submarine as well. Dönitz nevertheless sought to counter Allied material and technological superiority with more and improved submarines and renewed offensive spirit on the part of U-boat crews. This dogged determination, and the nearly complete absence of naval officers from the conspiracy of July 20, 1944, doubtless convinced Hitler to name Dönitz as his successor upon his suicide of April 30, 1945.

Dönitz surrendered what remained of German forces on May 7–8, 1945 and was arrested by the Allies on May 23. In 1946, the International Military Tribunal at Nuremberg sentenced him to ten years' imprisonment for war crimes. Released from Spandau Prison in 1956, Dönitz spent the remaining years of his life in retirement and died at Aumühle, West Germany, on December 24, 1980.

Charles S. Thomas

See also National Socialist Germany; Navy and Naval Policy; Nuremberg Trials; Raeder, Erich; Submarine Warfare; World War II

References

Dönitz, Karl. *Zehn Jahre und zwanzig Tage*. 4th ed. Frankfurt am Main: Bernard und Graefe, 1967.

Görlitz, Walter. *Karl Dönitz: Der Grossadmiral*. Göttingen: Musterschmidt, 1972.

Hoyt, Edwin Palmer. *The Death of the U-boats*. New York, NY: McGraw-Hill, 1987.

Padfield, Peter. *Dönitz: The Last Führer*. London: Gollancz, 1984.

Salewski, Michael. *Die deutsche Seekriegsleitung 1935–1945*. 3 vols. Frankfurt am Main: Bernard und Graefe, 1970–1975.

Steinert, Marlis G. *Capitulation 1945: The Story of the Dönitz Regime*. London: Constable, 1969.

Domestic Industry

The image of artisans practicing their trades in villages and small towns set in pastoral landscapes forms a recurrent theme in German literature and nationalist rhetoric from the mid-eighteenth century. Artisans were seen as a crucial component of the "old middle class" (*alter Mittelstand*), which was being threatened by modernization and industrialization. Despite the fact that the number of persons in artisan trades increased, the perceived "decline" of artisan trades was a key element in the antimodernism of the late nineteenth century. Many artisans supported anti-Semitic parties before World War I, and many later voted for the Nazi Party. But artisans also played an important role in the rise of the labor movement. Some trades, for instance the printers, moved directly from guild structures to modern forms of labor organization, and until World War I, the leaders of most unions and of the Social Democratic Party (SPD) were former artisan journeymen.

The analysis of domestic industry is compounded by definitional problems, which in turn can explain some of the inconsistency in the claims made about artisan trades and the responses of artisans to changing conditions. The occupational and industrial censuses undertaken by the German government did not distinguish between artisan and factory production, and also seriously underreported part-time workers and family members employed by artisans. In addition, the category "domestic industry" refers to two distinct forms of organization, artisan/handicraft production (*Handwerk*), e.g., shoemakers, and employment in the home (*Hausindustrie*), e.g., seamstresses. *Handwerk* referred to the trades controlled by guilds, male-dominated and with exclusively male membership since the seventeenth century. Guilds controlled entry into trades by restricting access to apprenticeship, employing only journeymen with proper credentials, and most importantly, by limiting the number of master artisans in each town. The legal authority of the guilds was progressively undermined by government legislation, and they had been reduced to voluntary associations by Prussian legislation in the 1850s and the Zollverein law proclaiming occupational freedom (*Gewerbefreiheit*) in 1861. Nevertheless, guilds remained influential and master artisans remained powerful in many communities until after World War I. In the artisan household/firm, wives and daughters worked as unpaid auxiliaries, and as such were reported by the censuses only as "assisting members of the family."

Hausindustrie went largely unreported in the censuses because the largely female labor force was perceived as not having a true occupation and therefore as not employed. In this sort of domestic industry, workers were employed on a piecework basis, working materials provided by their employers into finished products—seamstresses made up nearly half the total, but many thousands of women and their children, for example, wrapped cigars or soap or counted matches into matchboxes, for example. Whatever their family status, such workers were employed as individuals, without the protection of either the traditional guilds or the modern unions. In fact, guilds and unions perceived them as a threat; in the clothing industry, for instance, male master tailors and male workers in mechanized clothing factories feared the competition of non-guild, non-union seamstresses and saw unemployed women functioning as a "reserve army." The government's legislation to protect women might in fact have created the conditions for the expansion of *Hausindustrie* by increasing the cost of employing women in factories.

In 1850, virtually all metalworkers were members of artisan trades; by 1914, nearly all were industrial employees. This meant that many individuals in what had been a traditional artisan industry were condemned to spend their entire working lives as dependent workers and would never become independent masters. In other trades, such as shoemaking, artisan family firms shifted to retail sales and to the repair of products they had previously made but now received from factories. In still others, particularly in the clothing industry and particularly in Berlin, trades were transformed from male artisan *Handwerk* to female capitalist *Hausindustrie*, notably in the boom period from the 1890s to 1914. Such transitions were painful, and often led to discontent and protest, which could take either reactionary, antimodern forms or lead to support of the new labor movement.

Following World War II, many traditional handicraft products came to be produced in factories for the souvenir and tourist trade. Those which required manufacture or finishing by hand came to be produced on the piecework basis of *Hausindustrie*, with the labor now increasingly provided by the families of migrant workers. In addition, rising unemployment has recently contributed to a continuation of other forms of domestic manufacture, particularly clothing, as part of black or gray markets to avoid taxes and minimum-wage legislation.

Frank B. Tipton

See also Artisans/Craftsmen; Factory Laws and Reform; Industrialization; Social Democratic Party; Social Reform; Women's Occupations; Working Conditions

References

Franzoi, Barbara. *At the Very Least She Pays the Rent: Women and German Industrialization, 1871–1914.* Westport, CT: Greenwood, 1985.

Herzog, Marianne. *From Hand to Mouth: Women and Piecework.* Harmondsworth: Penguin, 1980.

Lenger, Friedrich. *Sozialgeschichte der deutschen Handwerker seit 1800.* Frankfurt am Main: Suhrkamp, 1988.

Volkov, Shulamit. *The Rise of Popular Antimodernism in Germany: The Urban Master Artisans, 1873-1896.* Princeton, NJ: Princeton University Press, 1978.

Döpfner, Julius (1913–76)

Bishop of Würzburg at 35, later bishop of Berlin and Archbishop of Munich, Julius Döpfner was one of the leading figures at the Second Vatican Council. His premature death deprived the Catholic Church of a voice for moderation and for dialogue with non-Catholics and the modern world that was heard beyond the borders of his own country.

Born on August 26, 1913, the fourth of five children of a hotel waiter in Bad Kissingen, Döpfner spent the prewar

Nazi years in Rome, where he was ordained a priest on October 29, 1939. He received a doctorate in theology with a dissertation on John Henry Newman in 1941. Following wartime service in Würzburg parishes, he became vice-rector of the seminary in 1946. He organized the restoration of 48 bombed churches; the building of 43 new ones and of church-subsidized housing; and promoted new initiatives in adult education, in the lay apostolate, and in friendly relations with Protestants. Döpfner's departure for Berlin in 1957 was widely regretted in Würzburg.

Though forbidden entry from 1958 into the eastern part of his diocese by the East German authorities, Döpfner was an energetic and popular bishop, rising to national prominence at the August 1958 Catholic Congress in West Berlin, by his appointment as cardinal in November, and by his pioneering 1960 appeal for German-Polish reconciliation through mutual forgiveness. In July 1961, Pope John XXIII appointed him archbishop of Munich, despite Döpfner's repeated plea that he was needed in Berlin, where the erection of the Berlin Wall on August 13 confronted the Church with new problems.

Döpfner's Munich years were closely connected with the Second Vatican Council (1962–65), in which he played a leading role: from 1963 he was one of the four council presidents. As vice-president of the papal Birth Control Commission Döpfner joined the majority in recommending a change in church teaching. When Paul VI rejected this advice in the encyclical *Humanae vitae* (July 1968), Döpfner, since 1965 president of the West German Bishops' Conference, shaped the Königstein Declaration, which respected both papal teaching and individual conscience.

In this question, as in the many other controversies which troubled the church after Vatican II, Döpfner tried to mediate between the partisans of tradition and renewal, criticizing rigidity on one side and irresponsibility on the other. Personally modest, open to dialogue, but firm in essentials, he suffered acutely from the post-conciliar polarization. The resulting stress may have been a factor in the heart attack which killed him in his 63rd year.

John Jay Hughes

See also Polish-German Relations after 1945; Roman Catholic Church

References

Morsey, Rudolf, ed. *Zeitgeschichte in Lebensbildern: Aus dem deutschen Katholizismus des 20. Jahrhunderts.* Vol. 3. Mainz: Grünewald.
New Catholic Encyclopedia. Vol. 17. New York. McGraw-Hill, 1967–79.

Dornberger, Walter Robert (1895–1980)

Artillery officer and engineer, Walter Dornberger pioneered the German rocket program; he was military chief of the Army Development Center at Peenemünde (1937–45), where the world's first liquid-propelled rocket (A4, known under its propaganda name V-2) was developed.

Born September 6, 1895 in Giessen, Walter Dornberger finished his high-school education just before World War I. He became an artillery lieutenant, and his wartime experiences became crucial for his subsequent professional career. After his release from a prisoner-of-war camp in 1920, he joined an artillery regiment in Minden under Major (later Field Marshal) Brauchitsch and studied engineering at the Technical University of Berlin, where he graduated in 1930 and received his doctorate in 1935. In 1928, then a captain, Dornberger joined the Army Ordnance Office (Heereswaffenamt) under Colonel (later General) Kurt Becker (1879–1940) and was given responsibility for the development of small, solid-fuel artillery rockets. Beginning in 1932, he initiated (with his civilian employee Wernher von Braun [1912–77]) the development of liquid-fueled rockets. After transferring the test facilities from Kummersdorf (near Berlin), he moved to the island of Usedom (1937). There, he became military commander of the Army Development Center (Heeresversuchsanstalt; HVA) in Peenemünde. After the first successful flight of the Aggregat 4 experimental rocket (1942), Colonel Dornberger became a major general (1943). His army rank and connections enabled him to successfully thwart the attempts by the Schutzstaffel (SS) to take control of the HVA, thus ensuring the continuity of development work during the final phase of World War II. Already in 1942, he had recognized the vast peacetime potential of the so-called "V-2" missile.

After some time as a prisoner of war in Great Britain (1945–47), Dornberger became an advisor to the United States Air Force at Dayton, Ohio. In 1950, he joined the Bell Aerosystems Company in Buffalo, New York, and participated in the development of large rocket planes; later (1959) he became vice-president (research), in particular pioneering defense systems against space-to-Earth rocket attacks. After his retirement (1965) he moved to Boston, Massachusetts and later to Mexico; in 1979 he returned to Germany. He died on June 26, 1980 at Ottersweier, Baden.

Dornberger received numerous honors recognizing his outstanding merits as rocket engineer and organizer. For his autobiographical book *V-2*, first published in 1951, he received the Edward G. Pendray Award of the American Rocket Society (1955). The Astronautics Award of the same organization (1959) recognized his activities in developing the technology of supersonic gliding planes.

Wolfgang Kokott

See also Aeronautics; Brauchitsch, Walter von; Braun, Wernher von; The Cold War and Germany; Inventions; National Socialist Germany; Science and National Socialism; Space; World War II

References

Dornberger, Walter. *V-2.* New York, NY: Viking, 1954.
Ley, Willy. *Rockets, Missiles, and Men in Space.* New York, NY: Viking, 1968.
Neufeld, Michael J. *The Rocket and the Reich: Peenemünde and the Coming of the Ballistic Missile Age.* New York, NY: The Free Press, 1995.

Speer, Albert. *Inside the Third Reich: Memoirs.* New York, NY: Macmillan, 1970.

Stoelzel, Heinz. "Walter Dornberger: General und Raketen-ingenieur." *Soldat und Technik* 7 (1965), 575–77.

Dornier, Claude Honoré Desiré (1884–1969)

Gifted engineer and successful entrepreneur, Claude Dornier brought to maturity the aeronautical industry established by Count Zeppelin on Lake Constance. He pioneered all-metal airplanes and was one of the first industrial managers to notice the future economic importance of new technologies such as space and electronics.

Born May 14, 1884 at Kempten, the son of a French-language teacher, Claude Dornier studied mechanical engineering at Munich. Following his diploma (1907), he went to work for several companies in southwestern Germany and eventually (1910) joined the Luftschiffbau Zeppelin (airship construction) at Friedrichshafen. Working at first in the experimental department, he became scientific advisor to Count Zeppelin in 1913 and, from 1914, head of development for all-metal seaplanes. From 1922, his *Zeppelin-werk Lindau* (zeppelin works) bore the name Dornier, and he later took full possession. Expanding his industrial activities into neighboring Switzerland as well as into Italy, his product line of heavy-duty sea and land planes was

Claude Dornier. Courtesy of German Information Center, New York.

during the 1920s and 1930s the backbone of German commercial aviation.

After 1933, additional business came from the military. Aircraft production ceased in 1944, following a devastating Allied air raid on Friedrichshafen. After World War II, Dornier took residence in Switzerland but supervised the gradual rebuilding of his enterprises, which were managed by several of his seven sons from two marriages. The most successful postwar plane was the Dornier Skyservant. Dornier's most far-sighted entrepreneurial decision was (1962) to establish the Dornier System company in Immenstaad (close to the former Friedrichshafen facility)—a subsidiary specializing in space and electronics.

Dornier died on December 5, 1969, in Zug, Switzerland. Besides his industrial empire (which later became part of the Daimler-Benz conglomerate), he left to his credit about two hundred engineering patents.

Wolfgang Kokott

See also Aeronautics; Air Force; Daimler-Benz AG; Zeppelin, Ferdinand

References

Meyer, Henry Cord. *Airshipmen, Businessmen and Politics, 1890–1940.* Washington, DC: Smithsonian Institution Press, 1991.

Wachtel, Joachim. *Claude Dornier: Ein Leben für die Luftfahrt.* Planegg: Aviatic, 1989.

Drama

The history of German drama since the late nineteenth century is one of discontinuity and disruption, of radical changes of direction that in turn reflect the social, economic, and political dislocations of the modern era.

Imperial Germany gave rise to two major revolutions in drama, the second of them extending well into the Weimar Republic. Naturalism (1880–1900) transformed drama into a vehicle of social analysis by means of an uncompromisingly realistic portrayal of middle- and working-class life, as in *Die Weber* (published as *The Weavers),* 1892, by Gerhart Hauptmann (1862–1946). Expressionism (1910–25) intensified the anti-bourgeois satire of two important forerunners, Frank Wedekind (1864–1918) and Carl Sternheim (1878–1942) and widened its critique to include the alienation generated by modern industrial capitalism, as, for example, in the *Gas* trilogy (1917–20) of Georg Kaiser (1878–1945). It rejected realism in favor of nonrepresentational imagery and a declamatory style that gave expression to its characteristic desire for the spiritual regeneration of society. World War I and the ensuing revolutionary upheavals gave the movement a sharper political focus, especially in the plays of Ernst Toller (1893–1939), such as *Masse Mensch* (Masses of mankind), 1921.

In the Weimar Republic, expressionism gradually gave way to a more restrained, realistic depiction of social behavior reflecting the "new objectivity" of the mid-1920s, and to the hard-edged treatment of specific contemporary issues. Drama participated in the general trend away from elitist culture, and popular genres were introduced or revived; for example the folk plays of Marieluise Fleisser (1901–74) and Ödön von Horvath (1901–38). However, the polarization and radicalization of national politics from 1930 on profoundly affected drama, which increasingly became an instrument of conflicting ideologies: right-wing plays, typically glorifying nationalist heroes, contrasted with a variety of left-wing forms, ranging from agitprop to the controversial didactic plays of Bertolt Brecht (1898–1956), such as *Die Massnahme* (Measures taken), 1930.

These tensions were a prelude to the complete division of drama after the Nazis assumed power in 1933, when theater was brought under the control of the Reichskulturkammer (Reich Chamber of Culture). Undesirable plays were banned and burned and their authors forced into exile. While within Germany approved dramatists produced work of negligible artistic value promoting Nazi ideology, the exiles, often working under extremely difficult conditions, created a significant body of drama, much of it overtly anti-Nazi, containing some of the century's most important plays—those written by Brecht in Scandinavia, including *Leben des Galilei* (The life of Galileo) and *Mutter Courage und ihre Kinder* (Mother Courage and her children). First versions of both were completed in 1939.

From 1949 to 1990 German drama again became divided along political lines. Despite the authoritative presence of Brecht in the early years, the development of drama in the GDR was stifled by Communist cultural policy, and only Heiner Müller (1929–95) emerged as a major talent. In the Federal Republic a substantial drama did not develop until the mid-1960s, which saw a wave of documentary plays, the most important of which was *Die Ermittlung* (The investigation), 1965, by Peter Weiss (1916–82)—a dramatization of the Frankfurt Auschwitz trial—and a successful revival of the folk play. However, the political and intellectual ferment of the 1960s found its fullest expression in Weiss's *Die Verfolgung und Ermordung Jean Paul Marats dargestellt durch die Schauspielgruppe des Hospizes zu Charenton unter der Anleitung des Herrn de Sade* (The persecution and assassination of Jean-Paul Marat: as performed by the inmates of Charenton under the direction of the Marquis de Sade), 1964, which combined a provocative debate of ideological issues with a spectacular "total theater." The 1970s brought another change of direction. As the conservative reaction to the 1960s set in, West German dramatists increasingly turned to a drama of "inwardness," associated especially with Botho Strauss (1944–).

Although the history of German drama since the 1880s has been turbulent, this has not always been a disadvantage, as it has fostered responsiveness to historical change and a willingness to innovate. These qualities have placed Germany in the vanguard of developments in modern European drama.

Brian Holbeche

See also Borchert, Wolfgang; Braun, Volker; Brecht, Bertolt; Dürrenmatt, Friedrich; Expressionism (Literature); Federal Republic of Germany: Literature; German Democratic Republic: Literature and Literary Life; Handke, Peter; Hasenclever, Hans; Hauptmann, Gerhart; Hochhuth, Rolf; Imperial Germany: Literature; Kaiser, Georg; Müller, Heiner; Naturalism; Piscator, Erwin; Radio Plays; Reinhardt, Max; Satire; Schnitzler, Arthur; Sternheim, Carl; Strauss, Botho; Theater; Toller, Ernst; Wedekind, Frank; Weimar Germany; Weimar Germany: Literature; Weiss, Peter

References

Grimm, Reinhold. *Nach dem Naturalismus: Essays zur modernen Dramatik.* Kronberg: Athenäum Verlag, 1978.
Hinck, Walter. *Das moderne Drama in Deutschland: Vom expressionistischen zum dokumentärischen Theater.* Göttingen: Vandenhoeck & Ruprecht, 1973.
———, ed. *Handbuch des deutschen Dramas.* Düsseldorf: August Bagel Verlag, 1980.
Innes, C.D. *Modern German Drama: A Study in Form.* London: Cambridge University Press, 1979.
Mennemeier, Franz Norbert. *Modernes deutsches Drama: Kritiken und Charakteristiken.* 2 vols. Munich: Wilhelm Fink Verlag, 1973-75.
Osborne, John. *The Naturalist Drama in Germany.* Totowa, NJ: Rowan and Littlefield, 1971.
Ritchie, James M. *German Expressionist Drama.* Boston, MA: Twayne, 1976.
———. *German Literature under National Socialism.* Totowa, NJ: Barnes and Noble, 1983.

Drewitz, Ingeborg (1923–86)

An engaged post-1945 writer of fiction and nonfiction, Ingeborg Drewitz characterized herself as the creator of Berlin realism. She made contributions in a wide variety of genres: essays, reviews, speeches, portraits, biography, autobiographical vignettes, radio plays, dramas, novels, short stories, and travel literature.

Of her eight novels published between 1958 and 1986, *Gestern war heute, hundert Jahre Gegenwart* (Yesterday was today, a century in the present), 1978, received the widest acclaim. It paints a broad historical canvas from 1923 to the late 1970s, with the experience of five generations of German women in the foreground.

Ingeborg Neubert was born into a lower-middle-class household in Berlin-Moabit. She managed to complete a doctorate in philosophy at Berlin's Humboldt University during World War II, despite her father's opposition and conscription into both compulsory labor service and war service. But she felt compelled to launch a writing career after 1945 because of the profound personal shock she had experienced when she learned of the genocide committed by the Germans. One of Drewitz's first works was a Holocaust drama, *Alle Tore waren bewacht* (All the gates were guarded), 1951–52, which daringly used a women's barracks in a concentration camp as a setting.

Drewitz depicts the years from 1923 to 1945 repeatedly in her fiction, as well as in a number of autobiographical sketches, collected in *Hinterm Fenster die Stadt* (The city behind the window), 1988, and *Lebenslehrzeit* (Formative years), 1985, in which she argues that one can begin to understand

Ingeborg Drewitz. Courtesy of German Embassy, Ottawa.

References

Haussermann, Titus, ed. *Ingeborg Drewitz: Materialien zum Werk und Wirken.* Stuttgart: Radius, 1983. 2nd rev. ed. 1988.

"Ingeborg Drewitz: Nachlass und Vermächtnis: Erinnertes und Hinterlassenes: Ingeborg Drewitz zu Ehren." *Die Horen* 32 (1987), 126–213.

Rogers, Gerhild Bruggemann. *Das Romanwerk von Ingeborg Drewitz.* Studies in Modern German Literature 26. New York, NY: Peter Lang, 1989.

Schweikert, Uwe, ed. *Ingeborg Drewitz: "Die ganze Welt umwenden": Ein engagiertes Leben.* Düsseldorf: Claassen, 1987. Reprint: Munich: Goldmann Taschenbuch, 1989.

Ward, Margaret E. "Ingeborg Drewitz." *Women Writers in German-Speaking Countries: A Bio-Bibliographical Source Book.* Ed. Elke Frederiksen. New York, NY: Greenwood Press, 1994.

Droysen, Johann Gustav (1808–84)

Johann Gustav Droysen was trained as a classical scholar and became famous with his groundbreaking studies of Hellenism, *Geschichte Alexanders des Grossens* (History of Alexander the Great), 1833, and *Geschichte des Hellenismus* (History of Hellenism), 1836 and 1843. Later works, *Geschichte der preussischen Politik* (History of Prussian policy), 1855–68, and his theoretical work *Historik* (History), 1868, however, reflected his concern for contemporary politics and the state of the historical discipline. His reputation primarily rests on his later works.

After studying classical philology at the University of Berlin (1826–33), where he came under the influence of August Boeckh (1785–1867) and G.W.F. Hegel (1770–1831), Droysen concentrated on the study of Greek antiquity, developing his concept of Hellenism. Through the turbulent 1840s, Droysen taught at the University of Kiel (1840–51). There he became politically involved in the German cause against Danish policy in the highly charged Schleswig-Holstein issue and subsequently became a leading figure in the Frankfurt Assembly of 1848, where he advocated German unification under Prussian auspices.

Fearing reprisals for his political activity during the Revolution of 1848, he left Kiel for Jena in 1851, where he remained until he was called to Berlin in 1859. His disappointment with the results of 1848 and 1866 did not lessen his political commitment, his belief in the need for a strong state, or his faith in the inevitability of Prussia's leading role in Germany. Indeed, these aspects of his thought were reflected in his *Geschichte der preussischen Politik*, which argued that since the fifteenth century Prussian rulers had actively sought a leading role in Germany and were destined to form the core of a new, strong, and unified German state.

Droysen was also one of the few nineteenth-century historians to examine historical theory in depth. His *Historik*, initially a series of lectures and courses, was perhaps the most comprehensive theoretical statement on the nature of history to emerge from the period. Droysen attempted to defend the

the Nazi period only by examining daily life. Drewitz's political activism may be traced to the student revolt of the 1960s, when she had to respond directly to the demands of the younger generation (to which her three daughters belonged). She gave speeches, edited and/or provided introductions for books, accepted teaching posts, participated in political demonstrations, wrote letters, and organized hundreds of exhibits and conferences, by means of which she drew attention to exile writers, Turkish writers, other women writers, and prisoners. She assumed leadership roles in the new German writers' union, founded in 1969, and in the New Society for Literature after 1973. She also reached out to writers in the German Democratic Republic. Her experiences as a young woman in the 1950s, struggling to gain access to a male-dominated culture industry, had convinced her that women writers needed to support each other. From 1961 to 1964 she therefore served as the head of GEDOK, an organization of German and Austrian women writers. She later came to identify personally with Bettine von Arnim (1785–1859), whose biography, *Bettine von Arnim: Romantik—Revolution—Utopie,* 1969, Drewitz wrote before the feminist rediscovery of Romantic women.

Although Drewitz received numerous literary prizes over three decades, she was never accepted by either mainstream or feminist critics as a major writer. Her other accomplishments were often the target of right-wing attacks in the press. Only belatedly did her work on behalf of minorities bring her acclaim. In 1980 she received the Carl von Ossietzky Medal from the German Section of the International League for Human Rights. A few weeks before her death in November 1986 she was awarded the Premio Minerva of the Club delle donne of Italy for her social and political activism, especially that on behalf of women.

Margaret E. Ward

See also Federal Republic of Germany: Literature; Feminist Writing; Historical Novel autonomy of historical thought against the onslaught of positivism and the belief that the methods of the natural sciences could be applied to the study of history. While he shared his contemporaries' faith in the meaningfulness of the historical process, he distanced himself from Leopold von Ranke's (1785–1886) "scientific history" by advocating a hermeneutic approach that emphasized intuitive understanding (*Verstehen*) rather than causal explanation.

Droysen's theoretical and practical work was unified by his underlying commitment to reason and objectivity and to the belief that history, as a rational inquiry, could lead to personal self-awareness and emancipation. This clearly reflected his belief in the autonomy of the historical discipline and the nineteenth century's elevation of history to the foremost authority and guide to understanding and representing the past.

John R. Hinde

See also History; Prussia; Ranke, Leopold von; Schleswig-Holstein; Understanding

References

Iggers, Georg G. *The German Conception of History.* 2nd ed. Middletown, CT: Wesleyan University Press, 1983.

Rüsen, Jorn. *Begriffene Geschichte: Genesis und Begründung der Geschichtstheorie J.G. Droysens.* Paderborn: Schöningh, 1969.

White, Hayden. "Droysen's *Historik*: Historical Writing as a Bourgeois Science." *The Content of the Form.* Ed. Hayden White. Baltimore, MD: Johns Hopkins University Press, 1987.

Duesterberg, Theodor (1875–1950)

The military career that Duesterberg, born October 19, 1875 in Darmstadt, originally chose was a distinguished one. It included service in China during the Boxer Rebellion, a tour of duty in the Prussian War Ministry in charge of officer training, and a battalion command in World War I. Under the impact of Germany's defeat, Duesterberg resigned from the army. He devoted his energies to a newly formed league of combat veterans called Der Stahlhelm, Bund der Frontsoldaten (Steel Helmets). At first, the Stahlhelm was nothing more than what its name indicated—a politically neutral veterans' group. Gradually, it became politicized, associating itself with the political right, a development in which Duesterberg played a major part. In 1924, thanks both to his organizational talents and to his generally well-received rhetorical attacks on the Treaty of Versailles and the Weimar Republic, he became the Stahlhelm's *Zweiter Bundesführer*, or Second National Leader, a somewhat misleading title, because rather than the Second Leader being deputy to the First Leader, Franz Seldte (1882–1947), the two were co-equal.

In the presidential election of 1932, Duesterberg ran as the candidate of both the Stahlhelm and the German National People's Party (DNVP) against Paul von Hindenburg and Adolf Hitler, but received less than 7 percent of the vote. During this election campaign the Nazis discovered that Duesterberg's paternal grandfather, a veteran of the Wars of

Liberation, had been born Jewish and baptized only in 1817. In the ensuing debate ("an indescribable hate campaign," Duesterberg wrote later, "in which there seemed to be no end to the anonymous abusive letters that I daily received"), most of the Stahlhelm leaders, Seldte included, stood by him and refused his offer to resign. That such a matter could become an issue at all says much about the poisoned atmosphere of Weimar's later years. The Nazi assumption of power thus put him at considerable personal risk. He was sent to the concentration camp at Dachau in 1934, and according to his testimony was saved from execution only through Hindenburg's personal intervention. Following his release later that year, he established contacts with a number of the regime's opponents, without, however, taking part in any of the active resistance.

After the war, Duesterberg tried to exculpate the Stahlhelm, playing down its anti-Weimar activities and playing up its conflicts with the Nazis. But while even opponents of his attested to his personal integrity, and both his dislike and distrust of Hitler were beyond doubt—he rejected the offer of a cabinet post in the proposed Hitler government—the effort to project a new image for the old Stahlhelm remained unconvincing. Nor were the attempts to revive the Stahlhelm organization in the years following 1945 accompanied by any greater success by the time of Duesterberg's death on November 4, 1950 in Hameln.

Joachim Remak

See also German National People's Party; Hindenburg, Paul von; National Socialist Germany; Paramilitary Organizations; Seldte, Franz; Stahlhelm; Veterans' Organizations; Weimar Germany

References

Berghahn, Volker R. *Der Stahlhelm, Bund der Frontsoldaten.* Düsseldorf: Droste, 1966.

Der Stahlhelm, Erinnerungen und Bilder. 2 vols. Berlin: Stahlhelm Verlag, 1932–33.

Duesterberg, Theodor. *Der Stahlhelm und Hitler.* Wolfenbüttel: Wolfenbüttler Verlagsanstalt, 1949.

Duisberg, (Friedrich) Carl (1861–1935)

Already famous in the Imperial era as an accomplished scientist and industrial organizer, Carl Duisberg provided the initial impetus behind the gradual merger of the German organic chemical industry into the I.G. Farben corporation (1925–45) and ended his career during the Weimar Republic as one of Germany's preeminent big businessmen. In that capacity, he failed in his efforts to stem the rise of Nazism and the economic ideology it represented.

Born in Barmen into the family of a ribbon weaver and educated at the universities of Göttingen and Jena, Duisberg owed his prominence to volubility, self-confidence, and boundless energy. He made his reputation early in the laboratories of Bayer, then married the niece of one of the firm's owners and went on to plan its massive Leverkusen works and write two persuasive memos (1904 and 1915) that pulled the major German chemical manufacturers toward consolidation.

contemporaries failed to heed his moderation. He labored unsuccessfully to keep I.G. Farben a loose federation of firms, to persuade it to abandon the production of fuel from coal that gave the firm and the Nazi regime a common interest, to defeat Hitler's bid for power, and to discredit the ideas that Germany could prosper by pursuing autarky, dominance in Eastern Europe, or a government-directed economy.

Peter Hayes

See also Bayer AG; Chemistry, Scientific and Industrial; Dawes Plan; Hindenburg, Paul von; I.G. Farbenindustrie AG; National Liberal Party; Third Reich: Industry; Young Plan

References

Flechtner, Hans-Joachim. *Carl Duisberg—vom Chemiker zum Wirtschaftsführer.* Düsseldorf: Econ-Verlag, 1960.
Hayes, Peter. *Industry and Ideology: IG Farben in the Nazi Era.* New York, NY: Cambridge University Press, 1987.

Dürrenmatt, Friedrich (1921–90)

Born on January 5, 1921, the son of a pastor in the German Swiss town of Konolfingen, Friedrich Dürrenmatt provoked more controversy through his ways of expressing his "Swissness" than his rather conventional origins might have suggested.

After university study in literature, philosophy, and science, Dürrenmatt combined his interests in painting and writing in a career that included work as a graphic artist, theater critic, director, dramatist, and prose writer. Together with his countryman Max Frisch (1911–91), Dürrenmatt became one of the dominant figures of postwar German literature, filling the void that existed particularly in West German dramatic writing in the early postwar years. An acknowledged moralist with an interest in the didactic function of the stage, Dürrenmatt maintained a critical attitude toward bourgeois society and its values without sharing Bertolt Brecht's faith in the potential of the proletariat to change the world. He did, however, share his concern for finding forms that could provoke contemporary audiences, seeing particularly in comedy (often satirical, tending toward the parable, and sometimes with traces of the absurd) probably the best opportunity to break free from the traditional "theater of illusion." Throughout his career, Dürrenmatt wrote critically about theater, commenting on its institutional aspects, developing his dramaturgical theories, explicating his own works and making suggestions for their performance. He repeatedly revised many of his plays.

As a dramatist, Dürrenmatt first gained notice with a controversial performance of *Es steht geschrieben* (It is written), 1946, which he later rewrote as a more brusque comedy, *Die Wiedertaufer* (The Anabaptists), 1967. His early stage successes—*Romulus der Grosse* (Romulus the great), 1949, *Die Ehe des Herrn Mississippi* (The marriage of Mr. Mississippi), 1952, *Ein Engel kommt nach Babylon* (An angel comes to Babylon), 1954—marked the beginning of a prolific period

Carl Duisberg. Courtesy of German Information Center, New York.

Prominent in the Hansa-Bund, in the chemical industry's trade associations, and in the National Liberal Party before 1914, as the first chairman of I.G. Farben's supervisory board (1925–35) and as president of the National Association of German Industry (1925–31), he stood out as the corporate world's leading paternalist toward labor and pragmatist in politics. He pioneered in the development of company-subsidized benefit programs and social activities to keep his workers content, even as he criticized the cost to business of the Weimar Republic's social welfare legislation. A vigorous advocate of the Dawes and Young reparations plans and the principle of free trade, he urged German executives to reach an accommodation with democracy, as well as with the victors of 1918, and to stand by moderately conservative parties and governments in the crisis of 1930–33. In 1932, he served as one of the national chairmen of President Hindenburg's re-election campaign against Hitler. Already retired by the time the Nazis obtained power, Duisberg in his few public comments or appearances thereafter ventured the hope that "the renewal of 1933" would succeed. His activities and views may be traced in his two-volume *Abhandlungen, Vorträge und Reden* (Papers and speeches), 1923 and 1933, and his memoir, *Meine Lebenserinnerungen,* 1933.

Though Duisberg, like many German executives of his era, was often imperious, heavy-handed, and nationalistic, what stands out in his final years are the instances in which that continued well into the 1970s. After the genuinely international fame that Dürrenmatt achieved with plays such as *Der Besuch der alten Dame* (The visit of the old lady), 1956, and *Die Physiker* (The physicists), 1961, however, his popularity on the stage faded. *Der Besuch*, perhaps his most famous play, was also made into a film starring Ingrid Bergman (1964) and an opera by Gottfried von Einem (1971). After a period of more intense work in the theater itself, where he staged his own adaptations of plays by Shakespeare, Lessing, Goethe, and Büchner, he increasingly devoted his efforts to political speeches and essays.

Dürrenmatt's early success as a dramatist has tended to eclipse his achievement as a writer of novels, short stories, and essays. The popularity of his grotesque comedies has its counterpart in detective and mystery stories, such as *Der Richter und sein Henker* (The judge and his hangman), 1952, *Der Verdacht* (The quarry), 1953, and *Das Versprechen* (The pledge), 1958, all of which were made into films. Two other stories, the comic *Grieche sucht Griechin* (Once a Greek . . .), 1955, and the much darker *Die Panne* (Traps), 1956, have also enjoyed enduring success. Although Dürrenmatt was not recognized as a poet during his lifetime, a collection of his poetry, *Das Mögliche ist ungeheuer* (The possible is immense), 1994, appeared after his death on December 14, 1990.

Patricia Herminghouse

See also Brecht, Bertolt; Drama; Frisch, Max

References

Dürrenmatt, Friedrich. *Writings on Theatre and Drama.* London: J. Cape, 1976.

Peppard, Murray B. *Friedrich Dürrenmatt.* New York, NY: Twayne Publishers, 1969.

Whitton, Kenneth S. *Dürrenmatt: Reinterpretation in Retrospect.* Oxford: Oswald Wolff Books, 1990.

Dutch-German Relations (1933–45)

Adolf Hitler's accession to power in January 1933 did not change the Dutch policy of neutrality. Not since Napoleon had war destroyed the peace of the Netherlands, and successive cabinets from 1933 to 1940 sought to preserve the peace they had enjoyed even in World War I.

As in World War I, the country's geographic position and its extensive trade with Germany underlined the practical need for neutrality, just as reliance on international law emphasized the theoretical basis for this policy. The same neutral principles that allowed the exiled Kaiser Wilhelm II to find asylum at Doorn in 1918 permitted over 30,000 Jews fleeing Nazi persecution to live in Holland after 1933.

The Germans repeatedly assured the Dutch that the Third Reich would respect their country's neutrality. The Great Depression and the importance of German trade encouraged the government to accept these verbal assurances. Unlike Belgium, the Dutch kingdom had had no guarantors pledged to defend its neutrality. As German policy became more aggressive and ultimately led to war after the invasion of Poland in 1939, various Dutch cabinets found no resolution to the dilemma of either arming and incurring the charge of collaborating with Germany's enemies or remaining passive and confronting a potential invasion with minimal forces.

On May 10, 1940, Case Yellow launched the invasion of the Netherlands, Belgium, and France. The Dutch fought valiantly, but the tactics of blitzkrieg overwhelmed the country within four days. Queen Wilhelmina and her cabinet fled to Great Britain and established a government in exile. Hitler chose the Austrian Arthur Seyss-Inquart (1892–1946) as *Reichskommissar* (Reich Commissioner) for the conquered country. The Nazis aimed at reversing the 1648 exclusion of the Netherlands from the Reich; more concretely, they wanted the support of the Dutch people and resources for Hitler's New Order. In contrast to the vicious occupational policy introduced in the Slavic east, German strategy in Holland sought to conciliate a "blood-related" people. A small minority organized in the Dutch National Socialist Movement under Anton Mussert actively collaborated with the Germans, but a majority of the country's nine million people refused to support the Nazis. Loyalty to the House of Orange and religious, liberal, and social traditions in the Netherlands evoked a deep resentment of the German occupation and ultimately facilitated an active resistance that prevented Seyss-Inquart from manipulating any Dutch *Anschluss.*

In February 1941, opposition to the Nazi policy of segregating Dutch Jews ignited economic discontent and precipitated a strike in Amsterdam—the first such action against the Germans in any conquered territory. Seyss-Inquart resorted to stronger measures, which he amplified after the invasion of Russia later that year. German determination ultimately meant that 70 percent of Dutch Jewry (the highest rate in any Western country) perished in killing camps such as Auschwitz-Birkenau and Sobibor. In May 1943, after the Nazis demanded that all Dutch veterans report for labor service in Germany, another strike broke out. From then, a strong and persistent resistance plagued the Nazi occupation forces.

The Allied invasion of Normandy and the rush to the Rhine and Ruhr rivers led to the liberation of the southern Dutch provinces in the summer of 1944. Seyss-Inquart continued to control the northern regions. Nazi intransigence led the railway workers to strike in support of the Allies, and cities such as Amsterdam and Rotterdam endured a "hunger winter," which caused the death of many civilians. In May 1945, with the collapse of the Third Reich imminent , Canadian forces liberated the remainder of the country. About a quarter of a million Dutch died as a result of the war and occupation.

To collect material, to provide assistance in legal procedures such as the trials of war criminals, and to analyze the history of this era, the Dutch government established in Amsterdam the State Institute for War Documentation. This organization continues to exist as a research center and has produced the authoritative history of this era.

John A. Leopold

See also Holocaust; Jews, 1933–90; National Socialist Germany; Seyss-Inquart, Arthur; World War II

References

de Jong, Louis. *Het Koninkrijk der Nederlanden in de tweede wereldoorloq.* Scholarly edition. 14 vols. The Hague: Martinus Nijhof, 1969–1991.

Verheyen, Dirk. "The Dutch and the Germans: Beyond Traumas and Trade." *The Germans and Their Neighbors.* Ed. C. Søe and D. Verheyen. Boulder, CO: Westview Press, 1993.

Warmbrunn, Werner. *The Dutch under German Occupation.* Palo Alto, CA: Stanford University Press, 1963.

Dutschke, Rudi (1940–79)

One of the leading personalities of the West German student movement of the mid-1960s, Rudi Dutschke grew up in the German Democratic Republic. He moved to the Federal Republic just two days before the closing of the border with the building of the Berlin Wall in 1961 and emerged as a leading student militant while studying sociology at the Free University in West Berlin.

Dutschke's initial political context was the Berlin section of a Situationist splinter group called Subversive Action, which as a result of its vigorous public interventions (the first was the so-called "poster action" that accompanied the first big Vietnam demonstration in February 1966) became the main element in the increasingly radicalized Berlin Socialist German Students League (SDS). The Berlin student left became identified with a politics of direct action and mass demonstrations, directed simultaneously against Western imperialism in the Third World (e.g., the demonstration against Moise Tshombe in December 1964, that against the Shah of Iran in June 1967, and the two Vietnam demonstrations of 1966) and right-wing politics inside West Germany itself (most famously against the power of the Springer press empire). During 1967–68, the confrontationism of the Berlin student movement escalated in response to the murder of a student protestor, Benno Ohnesorg, at the demonstration against the Shah, and this atmosphere of violent polarization culminated in an assassination attempt on Dutschke himself on April 11, 1968.

Dutschke survived the shooting, but suffered permanent injury. After unsuccessful attempts to settle in Great Britain and a brief stay in Ireland, he accepted an appointment at the Danish University of Aarhus in 1971. He reemerged as a public figure of the West German New Left during 1973, when he addressed another Vietnam demonstration in Bonn, and he played an important part in the negotiations between 1977 and 1980 that eventually produced the Greens. Dutschke himself could not participate in the Green breakthrough to regional and national importance—he died from complications from his 1968 injuries on December 24, 1979.

Politically and intellectually, Dutschke stood for an anti-Stalinist and noneconomistic form of socialism that eschewed the temptations of Maoist and Trotskyist sectarianism or the ethical desperation of strategies of armed struggle. He espoused a cautious utopianism, aimed at the long-term shifting of the terms of political debate. His Marxism was broadly Hegelian in inspiration, stressing the philosophical critique of capitalism via themes of alienation and domination, rather than political economy. The main influences on his ideas were George Lukács (1885–1971), Herbert Marcuse (1898–1979), and especially Ernst Bloch (1885–1977), and the foundation of his thinking was strongly Central European in this sense. It was also anti-Leninist, not in the sense of being hostile to Lenin and the Bolshevik revolution as such but because he rejected the bureaucratic Soviet socialism as a viable model for the Western European left and argued for the societal and historical specificity of the Russian Revolution, which therefore could not serve as a guide to events in the West. His major theoretical statement in these respects was published in 1974 as *Versuch, Lenin auf die Füsse zu stellen* (Attempt to stand Lenin on his feet).

   Geoff Eley

See also Bloch, Ernst; Extra-Parliamentary Opposition; The Greens: Movement, Party, Ideology; Lukács, Georg; Marcuse, Herbert; Students; Universities

References

Dutschke, Rudi. *Aufrecht gehen: Eine fragmentarische Autobiographie.* Berlin Kreuzberg: Olle & Wotter, 1981.
———. *Mein langer Marsch: Reden, Schriften und Tagebücher aus zwanzig Jahren.* Ed. Gretchen Dutschke-Klotz, Helmut Gollwitzer, and Jürgen Miermeister. Reinbek bei Hamburg: Rowohlt, 1980.

Rudi Dutschke. Courtesy of German Information Center, New York.

———. *Versuch, Lenin auf die Füsse zu stellen: Über den halbasiatischen und den westeuropäischen Weg zum Sozialismus.* Berlin: K. Wagenbach, 1974.

Eley, Geoff. "Germany Since '68: From the APO to the Greens." *Socialist Review* 18 (October–December, 1988), 130–42.

E

Eastern Marches Society (Ostmarkenverein)

The Deutscher Ostmarkenverein (Society for the Eastern Marches), otherwise known as the H-K-T Society or the Hakatisten after its three founders, Ferdinand von Hansemann (1861–1900), Hermann Kennemann (1815–1910), and Heinrich von Tiedemann-Seeheim (1843–1922), was formed in 1894 as a campaigning organization to strengthen German domination of the Polish-speaking areas of eastern Prussia. It aspired to rally the German population within a structure of aggressive patriotic solidarity, explicitly directed against the Poles and their claim to self-determination. The society used a combination of cultural promotion, economic support, and political mobilization. Its launch was part of the general opposition against the "new course" politics of the post-Bismarckian government of Leo von Caprivi (1831–99) and his successors between 1890 and 1904, which had involved minor concessions to Polish language in the schools, a somewhat reduced harassment of Polish agrarian organizations, and a relaxing of anti-Polish discrimination in public employment. The social context was provided by demographic pressures on the German population, particularly in Posen and parts of West Prussia, the most Polish of Prussia's eastern provinces, and by the flight of population to Berlin and Germany's industrialized west. The Ostmarkenverein's creation was consequently fueled by anxieties about the long-term erosion of German culture in the eastern borderlands.

The society's membership collapsed from an initial 20,000 to 9,400 after only three years but then grew steadily, reaching a total of 54,000 by 1914. In practice, its activities depended on close cooperation with the Prussian government and its provincial administration, which from the turn of the century adopted increasingly combative policies in relation to the Polish cultural presence. This was reflected in the society's membership, which was drawn mainly from civil servants, teachers, independent tradesmen, and the German farming population. Although the Ostmarkenverein originated in the founding moment of the so-called "national opposition," namely, the self-consciously "Bismarckian" backlash against

Caprivi's moderately liberalizing policies (which had also produced the Pan-German League in 1891), this symbiosis with the government's own anti-Polish apparatus held it back from any full-scale radical-nationalist critique of the Wilhelmine establishment. Moreover, the development of a populist language of politics, which was striking in the radical nationalism of the Navy League, was inhibited by the controlling and autocratic leadership style of Tiedemann, who kept the society's policy firmly in his own hands.

Geoff Eley

See also Agrarian Leagues; Caprivi, Leo von; Citizenship and Foreigners; Minorities, Ethnocultural and Foreign; Nationalism; Pan-German League; Polish-German Relations, 1871–1918; Radical Nationalism; Radical Right

References

Eley, Geoff. "German Politics and Polish Nationality: The Dialectic of Nation-Forming in the East of Prussia." *From Unification to Nazism: Reinterpreting the German Past.* Ed. Geoff Eley. London: Allen and Unwin, 1986.

———. *Reshaping the German Right: Radical Nationalism and Political Change after Bismarck.* Ann Arbor, MI: University of Michigan Press, 1991.

Galos, A., F.-H. Gentzen, and W. Jacobzyk. *Die Hakatisten.* East Berlin: Deutscher Verlag der Wissenschaften VEB, 1966.

Tims, R.W. *Germanizing Prussian Poland.* New York, NY: Columbia University Press, 1941.

Ebert, Friedrich (1871–1925)

The first president of the Weimar Republic (1919–25), Ebert co-headed the Social Democratic Party (SPD) after 1913 and led the transitional government during the Revolution of 1918–19. Historians differ on whether his involvements helped to create or destroy democracy, whether he aided or hindered social reform.

Friedrich Ebert.
Courtesy Dieter K. Buse.

Like many of his colleagues in the executive of the pre–World War I SPD, Ebert came from an artisan family, joined the socialist cause early, and practiced journalism for a time. Born in February 1871 as the son of a Heidelberg tailor of modest means, Ebert learned leatherworking after his public schooling. By 1889, he trekked as a journeyman through central Germany and joined the saddlers' union and SPD before they became legal in 1890. In Bremen, where he worked from May 1891 to December 1905, he became a nearly full-time party agitator and organizer while managing a pub, where he gave advice on social legislation. His speaking and organizational talents were recognized by election to many leading union and party positions. From 1900 to 1905 he served in the local parliament and as labor secretary, offering advice to the Bremen poor. Then he became a member of the Social Democratic executive in Berlin, where he served successfully as administrator and mediator between factions. Ideologically, Ebert took a middle position within the SPD.

World War I altered his political and personal life. In August 1914 he approved of war credits. By 1915 he had special authority in the party and tried to use its institutions to maintain unity, but by 1916 he had turned against the left-wing antiwar faction. Through Reichstag committees and war-supporting efforts Ebert came to know state officials and leaders of the bourgeois parties. All acknowledged the patriotism that cost him two sons, and all recognized that by 1917 he was the decisive leader of the Social Democrats.

Ebert favored compromises and alliances with the bourgeois parties to attain peace and a nonannexationist settlement to the war. He persuaded his party caucus to send representatives into Max von Baden's (1867–1929) cabinet, even though the war was lost and few reforms had been gained, in September 1918. By then Ebert, who during the war had kept to a dual policy of public opposition demanding reforms combined with secret cooperation aiding the state to support the war effort, opposed revolution.

During the Revolution of 1918–19, Ebert placed himself at the head of the revolutionary movement in order to contain it. He made a secret agreement with the old military leaders, in particular General Wilhelm Groener (1867–1939), to bring back troops in keeping with the armistice terms but also to restore order. Some historians think that he thereby doomed the new republic from the start by legitimizing and restoring an undemocratic officers' corps. Others think that he had few alternatives and that his actions to quickly obtain a constitutional assembly plus his efforts to overcome the postwar economic difficulties helped to establish a parliamentary democracy with significant social achievements.

In February 1919, the constituent assembly elected Ebert as temporary president, and in 1922 parliament reelected him. He organized a powerful new office and employed the decree powers of Article 48 of the constitution to oppose *Putsch*es from the left and from the right, as well as to implement social and economic legislation during the chaos of 1923. Again historians differ widely on the importance of his acts. Some claim that he acted in accordance with the constitution, while others accuse him of playing with dictatorship and setting precedents that would allow his successors to misuse the same powers. By repeatedly having to recreate cabinets—at least ten in six years—when coalitions fell apart over foreign affairs, especially reparations payments, Ebert influenced the governing of the country. He approved "Deutschland, Deutschland über alles" as the national anthem and compromised on which national flag to choose.

Though accused of having been the bureaucratic Stalin of the SPD, and acclaimed as having been the German Abraham Lincoln, Ebert was neither. He was a well-meaning and dedicated person who represented the German populace well as head of state but failed them as political leader. He could not control the military men with whom he had allied and his compromises with the liberals were not upheld from their side.

The political left, especially the Communists, accused Ebert of betraying the working class. The political right watched as Ebert was slandered and attacked in libel trials for alleged treason during the war; only after his death were the conservatives with whom he had worked willing to attest to his efforts to save the German state. Ebert died in office after an appendix operation, delayed partly because of the libel trials.

Dieter K. Buse

See also Bebel, August; Groener, Wilhelm; Haase, Hugo; Independent Social Democratic Party; Liebknecht, Karl; Luxemburg, Rosa; Max von Baden; Müller, Hermann; Presidency; Revolution of 1918–19; Scheidemann, Philipp; Seeckt, Hans von; Social Democratic Party; Trade Unions, 1871–1945; Versailles, Treaty of; Weimar Germany; Wels, Otto; World War I

References

Buse, Dieter K. "Ebert and the German Crisis, 1917–1920." *Central European History* 5 (1972), 234–55.

———. *Friedrich Ebert—Sein Weg zum Politiker von nationaler Bedeutung (1915–1918)*. Heidelberg: Stiftung Reichspräsident-Friedrich-Ebert-Gedenkstätte, 1994.

———. "Nationalism and Socialism, with Special Reference to Friedrich Ebert, 1913–1923." *History of European Ideas* 15 (1992), 187–92.

———, ed. *Parteiagitation und Walhkreisvertretung: Eine Dokumentation über Friedrich Ebert und seinen Reichstagswahlkreis Elberfeld-Barmen, 1910–1918*. Bonn: Neue Gesellschaft, 1975.

———. "Party Leadership and Mechanisms of Unity: The Crisis of German Social Democracy Reconsidered, 1910–1914." *Journal of Modern History* 62 (1990), 477–502.

König, R., H. Soell, and H. Weber, eds. *Friedrich Ebert und seine Zeit. Bilanz und Perspektiven der Forschung*. Munich: Oldenbourg, 1990. [Essays by P-C. Witt, D.K. Buse, S. Miller, R. Rürup, E. Jesse, H. Potthoff, K. Megerle, and G. Jasper on historiography, rise in the party, role during war, alternatives during the revolution, cabinet building, and constitutional practices.]

Mühlhausen, Walter and B. Braun, eds. *Friedrich Ebert und seine Familie: Private Briefe 1909–1924*. Munich: Oldenbourg, 1992.

Münch, Ronald A. *Von Heidelberg nach Berlin: Friedrich Ebert 1871–1905*. Munich: Oldenbourg, 1991.

Ecology

Ecology in Germany emerged as an independent field of study in the 1860s out of the convolutions in the natural sciences that had been stirred by Charles Darwin's *Origin of Species*, 1859, which had a particularly strong effect in Germany. Darwin offered a persuasive scheme of organic evolution that demonstrated that all life forms literally grew or evolved out of other forms, and that stressed the tight biological interconnectedness and interdependence of all organic life. Darwin's theory of natural selection also focused new attention on the problematic relationship of organic life to its immediate natural environment. In particular, it underscored that the environment influenced evolution and that organisms in turn responded to this influence through adaptation.

Insights such as these strongly influenced many young German "converts" to Darwinism, notably Moritz Wagner, Karl Semper, Anton Kerner, Fritz Müller, and Ernst Haeckel (1834–1919). Haeckel proposed the term *Oekologie* to identify broadly the study of the relationship of natural organisms to their surrounding environment. Researchers in various fields, including the biologists Karl Semper and Karl Möbius, the marine scientists Ernst Hensen and Karl Brandt, and the botanists Oscar Drude and Andreas Schimper, expanded and deepened the scope of ecology considerably in subsequent decades.

Through Haeckel and others, *Oekologie* emerged as a *Weltanschauung*, according to which the earth could be viewed as a single, unified organism, in which all elements tightly intertwined to form one interconnected and well-balanced system, all parts deriving from the same essential material and all obeying common laws. These ecological insights had anthropological implications. Darwin had demonstrated the "rightful" place of *Homo sapiens* in the chain of organic evolution. This was taken to mean that human beings belonged to the identical natural-ecological nexus of interdependencies and laws that conditioned and controlled all organic life.

The intellectual and cultural resonances of *Oekologie* in Wilhelmine Germany transcended the strict boundaries of natural science. Indeed, the singular historical significance of *Oekologie* lies precisely in its broader connection to contemporary politics. The socialists and Marxists had a substantial interest in it. As Friedrich Engels asserted in his *Dialektik der Natur* (The dialectic of nature), the left was as eager as anyone in fin-de-siècle Germany to incorporate the principles of natural science and Darwinism into its social theories and programs.

Even more significant, however, was the sympathetic response to Haeckelian ecology from the opposite end of the political spectrum. The conservative-nationalist *völkisch* (racist) movement shared with *Oekologie* its organicism, its strongly holistic view of humankind as an integral part of the natural world, and its critical stance against the technology and social organization of the modern world that tended to shatter this holism. An incipient "ecologism," to borrow Anna Bramwell's term (1989), clearly appeared by mid-century in the work of W.H. Riehl, who wrote a "natural history" of the German people, stressing the importance of *Einwurzelung*, or organic rootedness, in their native soil.

By the century's end, the *völkisch* movement had become a dominant force in the country, and the influence of the ecological *Weltanschauung* was manifest. In particular, the *Wandervogel*, or German youth movement, which inspired generations of young people with the urge to return to nature in order to reestablish an organic harmony with the natural world, mirrored the spirit of Haeckel's ecological teachings. One of the *Wandervogel's* ideological mentors, Willibald Hentschel, had taken a degree in zoology under Haeckel. In his writings, holism, organicism, and anti-modernism all blended with an intense longing for the national rejuvenation of the German *Volk*, to be achieved by reestablishing a vital connection with the natural environment. The doctrine of *Blut und Boden* (blood and soil), which emerged from the youth movement after 1918, was obviously inspired by this type of thinking. Through *Wandervogel* enthusiasts such as Heinrich Himmler (1900–45) and R. Walther Darré (1895–1953), a direct line linked the men of the late nineteenth century to the emerging National Socialist ideology. Indeed, a fairly well-defined "green wing" in the Nazi party operated chiefly under Darré's tutelage. During his tenure as minister of agriculture, Darré advanced programs to "re-peasantize" the

German population and reform German agriculture along bio-organic lines.

Even earlier, *Oekologie* had exerted an appreciable influence on the fledgling *Natur-* and *Heimatschutz* movements that emerged in the late nineteenth century, although it was by no means synonymous with these movements. Here as elsewhere, it frequently combined ·with a *völkisch*-nationalist orientation, as the writings and activities of the outstanding environmentalist Hugo Conwentz, among others, made clear. After 1945, ecology became even more strongly and explicitly identified with conservation and environmental protection, but it was no longer an exclusively patriotic project associated with an outspoken interest in protecting and rejuvenating the German *Volk* and nation. Instead, works such as Anton Böhm's *Epoche des Teufels* (The devil's epoch), 1955, or Werner Heisenberg's (1901–76) *Naturwissenschaft und Technik im politischen Geschehen unserer Zeit* (Natural science and technology in contemporary politics), 1960, presented the familiar dangers of uncontrolled technological advance and the resulting divorce of humankind from the rest of the natural world. These emerged as problems of global dimensions that threatened all human society, not only Germany.

After World War II, the environmental conservation movement in West Germany grew notably in mainstream political influence and number of adherents. During the early years of postwar reconstruction, for example, widespread opposition mobilized with some success against a variety of hydroelectric projects. The idea of "nature preserves" gained in appeal, with the result that by 1965 some 28 nature parks had been established across the country. Federal legislation advocated the protection of the environment, with laws on water management adopted in 1957, on clean air in 1959, and on pesticide control in 1968, among many others. A general nature conservation act legislated in 1976 capped all of these efforts. The emergence of the Green party as a powerful and enduring political force in national politics has been the most profound demonstration of the proliferation of ecological-environmental awareness and concern. Echoes of *Oekologie*'s earlier political associations resounded, and were quite apparent, in the political ambiguities and tensions that characterized the early years of the Greens in the late 1970s and 1980s.

Mark Bassin

See also Darré, R. Walther; Engels, Friedrich; The Greens: Movement, Party, Ideology; Haeckel, Ernst; Heisenberg, Werner; Himmler, Heinrich; Nuclear Power and the Nuclear Industry; Peasantry; Postwar Reconstruction; *Völkisch* Ideology; Youth Movements

References

Bramwell, Anna. *Blood and Soil: Walther Darré and Hitler's "Green Party."* Bourne End: Kensal, 1985.

———. *Ecology in the 20th Century: A History.* New Haven, CT: Yale University Press, 1989.

Cittadino, Eugene. *Nature as the Laboratory: Darwinian Plant Ecology in the German Empire 1880–1900.* Cambridge: Cambridge University Press, 1990.

Dominick, Raymond H. *The Environmental Movement in Germany: Prophets and Pioneers, 1871–1971.* Bloomington, IN: Indiana University Press, 1992.

Gasman, Daniel. *The Scientific Origins of National Socialism: Social Darwinism in Ernst Haeckel and the German Monist League.* London: Macdonald, 1971.

Hermand, Jost. *Grüne Utopien in Deutschland: Zur Geschichte des ökologischen Bewusstseins.* Frankfurt am Main: Fischer, 1991.

Mosse, George. *The Crisis of German Ideology: Intellectual Origins of the Third Reich.* New York, NY: Grosset and Dunlap, 1964.

Economic Miracle (*Wirtschaftswunder*)

In 1948, the Western occupation forces saw their mission in Germany coming to an end. Ludwig Erhard (1897–1977), minister of economics in the new German government, sparked the long-awaited economic recovery by completing a currency reform the Allies had favored and inaugurating policies of decentralization, privatization, and dismantling of the planning organization that the Allies had not been bold enough to sponsor. Complementary policies favored by Erhard included investment promotion, anti-cartel activities, foreign trade promotion, and extensive social policies to share the fruits of growth.

Encouraged by the improved business climate, West Germans had begun the process of economic reconstruction in earnest, filling empty stores with goods almost overnight. The Germans opened production bottlenecks and continued to modernize, retool, and expand their stock of capital equipment incessantly. The "social market economy" was so successful that it became known as the Economic Miracle (*Wirtschaftswunder*), capturing the attention of the world as total industrial production doubled from 1950 to 1957 and the gross national product (GNP) grew at a rate of nine to ten percent per year.

Fortunately, the brief central planning experience of the war had not deadened the skills of German management and entrepreneurship. The work force was highly trained and was disinclined to be politically engaged. Germans were prepared to sacrifice and work hard to achieve an orderly and comfortable existence. For years, the unions were prepared to forgo rapid wage increases and the people were willing to wait patiently for government and industrial investments to bear fruit. Nor had German social policy traditions, going back to Chancellor Otto von Bismarck, been forgotten in the war experience. Extensive transfer programs compensated for war losses and protected against the uncertainties that had called the welfare state into existence.

Labor was encouraged early in the postwar period by the adoption of the famous policy of codetermination (*Mitbestimmung*). The law required representation of workers on the boards of directors of corporations with two thousand or more employees, providing workers with a voice even in major policy decisions.

Maintaining an undervalued deutsche mark made it possible for West Germany to develop its economy on the basis of an export drive. The rapid growth of production of increasingly attractive quality, together with longstanding trading traditions, made it possible for Germany to achieve dramatic balance-of-trade surpluses. The concatenation of these circumstances and of Erhard's astute policies proved a boon to West Germany.

Phillip J. Bryson

See also Adenauer, Konrad; Christian Democratic Union; Codetermination; Currency; Erhard, Ludwig; Exports and Foreign Trade; Federal Republic of Germany; Marshall Plan; Trade Unions 1945–90; Unemployment

References

Hamel, Hannelore. *Soziale Marktwirtschaft—Sozialistische Planwirtschaft.* 5th ed. Munich: Verlag Vahlen, 1989.

Peacock, Alan and Hans Willgerodt, eds. *German Neo-Liberals and the Social Market Economy.* London: Macmillan, 1989.

Stolper, Gustav, Karl Hauser, and Knut Borchardt. *The German Economy: 1870 to the Present.* New York, NY: Harcourt, Brace and World, 1967.

Thieme, H. Jörg. *Soziale Marktwirtschaft: Ordnungskonzeption und wirtschaftspolitische Gestaltung.* Munich: Verlag C.H. Beck, 1991.

Wallich, Eli. *Mainsprings of the German Revival.* New Haven, CT: Yale University Press, 1955.

Economics

This social science analyzes the allocation of scarce resources and addresses aggregate and individual decision processes determining what is produced for whom. The branch of the discipline that investigates the decision processes of individual agents (for instance, consumers, managers, workers, and policymakers) is microeconomics; the aggregates of national economic activity are the substance of macroeconomic analysis.

Economists attempt to comprehend economic phenomena through theoretical methodologies. Deductive methods are used to understand the relationships between key economic variables: hypothetical conclusions are derived from logical processes proceeding from the formation of simplifying assumptions. The use of mathematical techniques is a standard part of the analysis of such relationships. Although the realism of specific assumptions occasionally strikes outsiders as less than desirable, those deductive processes leading to generally accepted conclusions are on sound footing. Milton Friedman argues that science need not be concerned about the perceived realism of such assumptions as long as they are associated with empirically testable hypotheses that predict economic outcomes accurately.

A separate branch of the discipline, econometrics, arose from the effort to empirically test and apply the logical, mathematical propositions of economic theory. It was developed when economists, curious especially about some new hypotheses from John Maynard Keynes's *The General Theory of Employment, Interest and Money,* 1936, began to utilize methods from mathematics and statistics to test those hypotheses. The statistical procedures employed in econometric studies can, of course, provide no sounder results than the data on which they are based.

Information on decisionmaking is also generated by the relatively new discipline of experimental economics. Modeling economic situations or environments, this technique uses properly motivated participants to simulate agents making choices. Other branches of economics deal with less general phenomena, and include money and banking, labor, public finance, comparative systems, public choice, and economic history.

The study of economics in contemporary Germany does not differ substantially from the approach in other Western countries. Before reunification, however, economics in East Germany bore only modest resemblance to its counterpart in the democratic market countries. Economists in East Germany focused on the organization and institutions of central economic planning, largely rejecting the "bourgeois" theories of the West. A central function of economists in the German Democratic Republic, as in other socialist countries, was to propagate Marxian doctrines and defend the ideological positions of the party. Generally, independent scientific work was difficult or impossible for economists·to achieve there.

In the Federal Republic, all the branches of the discipline, the major methodologies, and the important schools of economic thought are currently represented. Although there are numerous highly qualified theoreticians in Germany, German economists tend to deal with more practical, policy-oriented issues than, say, their American counterparts.

Germany has a strong economic tradition including, for example, the Austrian School. Worthy of note are Friedrich List (1789–1846), a contemporary of David Ricardo, who taught that free trade was sound policy only after the development process had made sufficient progress. J.H. von Thuenen (1783–1850), the father of German location studies, pioneered in optimization and mathematical techniques. His influence reached, for example, to Alfred Weber (1868–1958) and August Loesch (1906–45).

The Historical Schools of the British Isles and Germany had a tradition that challenged classical economics and its laissez-faire liberalism of the nineteenth century, especially as Germany progressed toward nationhood. Adherents generally disdained economic theory; they hoped from the uniqueness of history in its endless divergent possibilities to infer laws of economic development. An older school included Wilhelm Roscher (1817–94), Bruno Hildebrand (1812–78), and Karl Knies (1821–98); the younger historicists included Gustav von Schmoller (1838–1917), Arthur Spiethoff (1873–1957), Werner Sombart (1863–1941), and Max Weber (1864–1920). Karl Marx (1818–83) presented a more widely known alternative to classical economics in his acrid analysis of capitalism and prediction of its failure.

Examples of contemporary German influence include Carl Föhl (1901–73), who published a treatise (before the *General Theory*) containing many "Keynesian" concepts. Heinrich von Stackelberg (1905–46) contributed important ideas to the theory of oligopoly. Germany's "Ordo-liberals" are an important contemporary school. Building on foundations laid in the postwar period by Walter Eucken (1891–1950) and Paul Hensel (1907–75), a number of economists carry on their strong pro-market tradition, retaining an important influence in contemporary German economic policy, especially as it pertains to the economics of reunification. Generally, as they analyze the characteristics of the economic "order" or system pertaining in a given place or time, they search for principles that assure favorable economic outcomes. They see in their studies of central-planning systems elements of irrationality preventing optimal or even effective economic performance.

Phillip J. Bryson

See also Association for Social Policy; Brentano, Lujo; Erhard, Ludwig; Hilferding, Rudolf; Marx, Karl; Oldenburg, Karl; Professions; Schiller, Karl; Schmidt, Helmut; Schmoller, Gustav von; Sombart, Werner; Weber, Alfred; Weber, Max

References

Barkin, Kenneth D. *The Controversy over German Industrialization, 1890–1902.* Chicago, IL: University of Chicago Press, 1970.

Eatwell, John, Murray Milgate, and Peter Newman, eds. *The New Palgrave: A Dictionary of Economics.* 4 vols. London: Macmillan, 1987.

Friedman, Milton. "The Methodology of Positive Economics." *Essays in Positive Economics.* Ed. Milton Friedman. Chicago, IL: University of Chicago Press, 1953.

Lebovics, Herman. *Social Conservatism and the Middle Classes in Germany, 1914–1933.* Princeton, NJ: Princeton University Press, 1969.

Schumpeter, Joseph A. *History of Economic Analysis.* New York, NY: Oxford University Press, 1954.

Spiegel, Henry William. *The Growth of Economic Thought.* Englewood Cliffs, NJ: Prentice-Hall, 1971.

The Economics of German Reunification

The precipitous decline of the Honecker regime in 1989 and the inability of the successor regimes of Egon Krenz and Hans Modrow (1928–) to win the confidence of the East German

New Wharf, Wismar, Mecklenburg-Vorpommern. Courtesy of German Embassy, Ottawa.

people opened a window in global affairs for the reunification of Germany. Helmut Kohl, the "chancellor of unification," seized the opportunity to formalize economic, currency, and social unification on July 2, 1990. The process was consummated with breathtaking speed on October 3, the "day of German unity," of the same year, when the Federal Republic of Germany (FRG) incorporated five new eastern states. In turn, the east adopted the political/legal institutions of West Germany.

In spite of the early hopes of most participants, it was inevitable that the economic transformation of the east would produce widespread malaise and social pain. The jettisoning of the Marxist-Leninist social system, embedded in national life for 40 years, necessitated the elimination of the planning bureaucracy, the seemingly unjust redeployment of the not hopelessly tainted former elites, and the east's learning to understand the legal and social institutions associated with markets.

Most difficult, however, was the high unemployment. A slow work pace and extensive labor hoarding under socialism had resulted in the retention of excessive personnel at the enterprise level. These workers could not be retained once state subsidization of inefficiency ceased.

Not only did the East German political system disappear; the entire network of domestic East German and Eastern European socialist markets collapsed. In the fiercely competitive environment that followed the opening of the Berlin Wall, it was apparent that East German enterprises were inadequately equipped and technologically obsolete. Economic reality forced many East Germans to give up their old jobs and wait for better ones to be produced in the reemergence of East German industry.

Despite these difficulties, the reunification process brought East Germans numerous substantial benefits not available to other formerly socialist countries in the region. These were material benefits derived from their adoption by Western Europe's premier economic performer. While the threat of transformation failure remains real for other Eastern European countries, the East German future has been guaranteed by the unification treaties.

Reunification with West Germany also obviated the need of the new federal states to develop entirely new financial and other market institutions in support of the transformation effort, to achieve price stability and currency convertibility independently, to establish a comprehensive set of reliable market prices, and to learn how to avoid unsound state financial practices. Moreover, the FRG provided a very dependable social net for the adopted East Germans.

It was anticipated that reunification would bring the eastern states a large flow of investments from the FRG's private sector. The German government would also invest heavily in infrastructure improvements. Actual investment flows in the first years after reunification were not in the volumes anticipated. In part, this was because privatization uncertainties persuaded westerners to postpone investment plans. Rightful owners had to be sorted out and compensation or restitution made for verified ownership claims. The Trust Agency (Treuhandanstalt) sold off state-owned properties where buyers could be found. After the relatively facile sale of small properties, there remained the formidable task of selling off the larger, inefficient, technologically obsolete, and underequipped enterprises whose markets had collapsed.

In spite of the advantages of the association with West Germany, therefore, the transformation process was a trying one. It required not only privatization and marketization, but also the adaptation of economic agents to new conditions, new thinking, new challenges, and new possibilities. Maintaining patience, hope, and self-respect through the transition was difficult for the East Germans who experienced constant levels of unemployment around 20 percent. At the same time, providing assistance rather than mere criticism proved to be a challenge for the west. The levels of assistance provided would cause Westerners to forgo income growth for a number of years.

Phillip J. Bryson

See also Currency; German Democratic Republic: Collapse; Federal Republic of Germany: Economics; German Democratic Republic: Economics; Kohl, Helmut; Mittag, Günter; Modrow, Hans; Reunification; Unemployment

References

Bryson, Phillip J. "The Economics of German Reunification: A Review of the Literature." *Journal of Comparative Economics* 16 (1992), 118–49.

Deutsches Institut für Wirtschaftsforschung, Berlin, and Institut für Weltwirtschaft an der Universität Kiel. "Gesamtwirtschaftliche und unternehmerische Anpassungsprozesse in Ostdeutschland." *Wochenbericht* 58 (1991), 323–46.

Die Verträge zur Einheit Deutschlands. Munich: C.H. Beck Verlag, 1990.

Hartwig, Karl-Hans and H. Jörg Thieme, eds. *Transformationsprozesse in sozialistischen Wirtschaftssystemen: Ursachen. Konzepte, Instrumente.* Heidelberg: Springer-Verlag, 1991.

Schiller, Hans and Dietmar Schadow, eds. *Ordnungspolitik beim Übergang der DDR-Wirtschaft zur Marktwirtschaft.* Wirtschafts Report Special. Berlin (East): Institut für Wirtschaftswissenschaften, 1990.

Education

The German educational system of the late nineteenth century was internationally admired and even imitated, both for its rigorous and varied secondary schools and for its ubiquitous and effective elementary schools. Imperial Germany divided pupils according to class, gender, region, and religion and provided instruction deemed appropriate for students' presumed destinies. Educational reform, which expanded educational access for some pupils and modernized curricula, accompanied the political and economic changes of the twentieth century. By the second half of the twentieth century, schools were much more likely than before to be coeducational, urban, and secular, but different types of schools continued to recruit students from different social backgrounds.

The elementary school (*Volksschule*) educated over 90 percent of all children in Imperial Germany, including virtu-

ally all those of small farmers, industrial workers, and other wage laborers. No more than 8 percent of pupils attended secondary schools, which encompassed classical and modern schools for boys and higher girls' schools. Secondary-school pupils included not only a disproportionately large number of children from well-educated and prosperous families but also many children of shopkeepers and lower civil servants. The goals of compulsory elementary schooling, which lasted seven or eight years in the late nineteenth century, were "religious-moral" education and instruction in the knowledge and skills "necessary for practical life."

The most prominent subjects were reading, arithmetic, and religion, which alone occupied 15 to 20 percent of school hours. Religion lessons and stories in the reading books typically emphasized such values as obedience, thrift, and order. History and geography lessons received less class time and focused on regional topics, which in southern Germany, for example, meant minimal treatment of the Hohenzollern dynasty. In addition, girls had several hours of needlework classes, designed to teach domestic virtues and other basic skills. By the turn of the century, gymnastics classes, which included marching in formation with iron rods, were part of the curriculum for boys.

Most of these public elementary schools were either Protestant or Catholic schools, and in most regions local clergy served as school inspectors. The number of one-class schools declined in the late nineteenth century, with only about 10 percent of Prussian pupils attending such schools in 1911. Most elementary classes were coeducational, except in cities with enough pupils to permit separation by sex as well as grade level. Upon finishing school, pupils usually found employment, began apprenticeships, or entered private training programs. Few ever became full-time students again, but many attended continuation schools once or twice weekly to review their lessons and in some instances pursue vocational training. Girls had far fewer opportunities for vocational training than boys. Although elementary schooling in the Imperial era served to reinforce class differences, it was less effective in instilling piety, docility, and opposition to socialism. The schools had considerable success in teaching literacy, numeracy, and some basic knowledge.

The most prestigious boys' secondary school was the Gymnasium, a nine-year school that taught Greek and Latin and awarded the minority of students who actually graduated the *Abitur*, a certificate required for university admission. The Gymnasium continued to enroll the largest number of male secondary students, but its share of enrollment declined in the early twentieth century with the expansion of newer schools, most notably the *Realgymnasium*, which omitted Greek from its curriculum, and the *Oberrealschule*, which eliminated classical languages entirely and emphasized modern languages and science instead. Supporters of equal privileges for these modern schools argued that they provided better preparation for scientific and medical study, more German education, and less overburdening of pupils. After several decades of discussion, and intervention by Kaiser Wilhelm II, Prussia extended university admission to graduates of the modern schools in 1901.

Although successfully modernizing and expanding, the boys' secondary-school system remained exclusive.

Girls' secondary schooling took place in higher girls' schools, which taught no classical languages. As women gained access to universities in the early twentieth century, some girls' schools introduced courses to prepare pupils for the *Abitur*.

The German school system continued to evolve after World War I, with at least partial resolution of several longstanding disputes. In Imperial Germany it was common for boys' secondary schools to offer grades one through three in *Vorschulen* (preparatory schools) designed to prepare pupils for secondary-school admission at age nine. The constitution of the Weimar Republic, in response to advocates of common schooling, mandated that all children attend an elementary school (*Grundschule*) for the first four grades, thereby eliminating preparatory classes. This reform created for the first time a formal link between the two parts of the school system and reflected a republican effort at democratization.

Reform of religious education was more ambiguous, as the Center Party squelched liberal and socialist proposals to secularize schooling. School inspection by clerics was abolished, but religious schooling remained the norm in most regions. The percentage of girls' schools awarding the *Abitur* rose sharply to 60 percent by 1930, but coeducation at the secondary level remained rare in most states. Under the influence of reform pedagogy, individual elementary schools gained some control over some aspects of their curricula, but classes remained large, with 57 percent of pupils attending classes of 40. The majority of rural schools still had only one or two classrooms.

The Weimar constitution required civics instruction in all schools. The number and variety of secondary schools continued to expand in the 1920s, but working-class youth had minimal access. They comprised only 5 percent of secondary pupils in 1931, despite a constitutional provision that subsidized needy but able pupils. The percentage of the 11- to 19-year-olds attending secondary school rose from 6 percent in 1921 to 8.8 percent in 1931. Situated between secondary and elementary schools were an assortment of often private middle schools. Educational administrators in the Weimar Republic recognized middle schools by creating an intermediate certificate for their graduates, but this option became popular only in the Federal Republic of Germany (FRG). The Weimar Republic saw the continuation of many Wilhelmine educational reforms but no radical transformation.

While National Socialism eventually shaped the content, purpose, and structure of education in accordance with its ideology, the Nazi leadership was forced to compromise on some educational matters. Pressure from the Catholic Church prevented the elimination of religious schooling. Local power and resources limited the centralization of school administration. The Nazis reduced students' access to secondary education and attempted to unify the system of secondary education, diminishing the role of the Gymnasium. At the same time, Nazi policy expanded and systematized the middle schools to formalize a three-part school system. In all school types the Nazis lowered educational standards and emphasized physical and military training and racial and national in-

doctrination. War disrupted education at all levels.

After World War II, the United States, France, and Great Britain attempted to transform education in West Germany but had little success. The Americans favored a comprehensive school system that would have abolished the Gymnasium, the pride of educated Germans. Schooling resumed at the end of the war using textbooks and curricula from the Weimar Republic and often relying on makeshift classrooms. The FRG returned most responsibility for education to the states but promoted coordination among them.

In the Düsseldorf Agreement of 1955, the states' ministers of culture agreed to perpetuate the tripartite school system. The agreement gave the name Gymnasium to all secondary schools that required nine years of study (on top of the four years of elementary schooling) and prepared students for the *Abitur*. Typically, each Gymnasium had a disciplinary focus, on modern languages or mathematics and science, for example. English replaced Latin as the first foreign language in most schools. The second track, originally called the middle school and later the *Realschule*, offered ten years of study and prepared students to enter various technical schools for career training. The third track was the general school (*Hauptschule*), the successor to the *Volksschule*, with a nine-year course followed by at least three years of mandatory vocational training. As in the Weimar Republic, a four-year *Grundschule* prepared young children for all school types.

In a departure from the past, the school system of the FRG provided various opportunities for pupils to move from one track to another. Nonetheless, in 1960, only 12.4 percent of West Germans aged 11 to 19 attended a Gymnasium and only 5.4 percent earned the *Abitur*. Over half of the students who entered universities in the early 1960s came from the upper and upper-middle classes, with families of university-educated professionals, white-collar executives, and technical specialists especially well represented. Statistical analysis shows that representation of the lower and lower-middle classes at universities declined sharply from 1931 to 1963. By the 1960s there was growing concern about glaring inequities that continued to disadvantage students according to class, region, religion, and gender. Criticism of the three-track system produced some experimental comprehensive schools and alternative paths to higher education. By 1980, 27 percent of thirteen-year-olds attended Gymnasium and 25 percent attended *Realschule*, up from only 6 percent in 1955. From 1955 to 1980, the percentage of pupils in *Hauptschule* fell from 79 percent to 39 percent. West German education has demonstrated flexibility, but many features of the system inherited from the Imperial era have persisted.

Katharine D. Kennedy

See also Education for Girls and Women; Free German Youth; German Democratic Republic: Education; Hitler Youth; Literacy; National Socialist Germany: Education; Pedagogy; Roman Catholic Church; Schools; Schrader-Breymann, Henriette; Teaching; Technical Training, Technical Institutes, and Universities; Vocational Education; Universities; Wilhelm II; Youth; Youth Movements; Zahn-Harnack, Agnes von

References

Albisetti, James C. *Schooling German Girls and Women: Secondary and Higher Education in the Nineteenth Century.* Princeton, NJ: Princeton University Press, 1988.

———. *Secondary School Reform in Imperial Germany.* Princeton, NJ: Princeton University Press, 1983.

Berg, Christa, ed. *Handbuch der deutschen Bildungsgeschichte,* Vol. 4: *1870–1918: Von der Reichsgründung bis zum Ende des Ersten Weltkriegs.* Munich: C.H. Beck, 1991.

Kennedy, Katharine D. "Regionalism and Nationalism in South German History Lessons, 1871–1914." *German Studies Review* 11 (1989), 11–33.

Lamberti, Marjorie. *State, Society, and the Elementary School in Imperial Germany.* New York, NY: Oxford University Press, 1989.

Langewiesche, Dieter and Heinz-Elmar Tenorth, eds. *Handbuch der deutschen Bildungsgeschichte.* Vol. 5: *1918–1945: Die Weimarer Republik und die nationalsozialistische Diktatur.* Munich: C.H. Beck, 1989.

Müller, Detlef K. *Sozialstruktur und Schulsystem: Aspekte zum Strukturwandel des Schulwesens im 19. Jahrhundert.* Göttingen: Vandenhoeck & Ruprecht, 1977.

Müller, Detlef K. and Bernd Zymek. *Sozialgeschichte und Statistik des Schulsystems in den Staaten des Deutschen Reiches, 1800–1945. Datenhandbuch zur deutschen Bildungsgeschichte.* Vol. 2, part 1. Göttingen: Vandenhoeck & Ruprecht, 1987.

Müller, Detlef K., Fritz K. Ringer, and Brian Simon, eds. *The Rise of the Modern Educational System: Structural Change and Social Reproduction, 1870–1920.* Cambridge, MA: Cambridge University Press, 1987.

Ringer, Fritz K. *Education and Society in Modern Europe.* Bloomington, IN: Indiana University Press, 1979.

Shirley, Dennis. *The Politics of Progressive Education: The Odenwaldschule in Nazi Germany.* Cambridge, MA: Harvard University Press, 1992.

Tent, James F. *Mission on the Rhine: Reeducation and Denazification in American-Occupied Germany.* Chicago, IL: University of Chicago Press, 1982.

Education for Girls and Women

A gradual expansion of educational opportunities for women characterized the period from 1871 to 1990. Accompanying and shaping reforms in women's education were ongoing debates about the relative similarity and difference of women and men and about the relation between the public and private roles of women.

The institutions that exemplified gender-specific education for German girls were the higher girls' schools, nineteenth-century institutions that persisted through the first half of the twentieth century as *Lyzeen* and then as *Oberschulen.* Only around 5 percent of all German girls, virtually all of them from the middle and upper classes, attended higher girls' schools in the late nineteenth century. After nine or ten years of schooling, graduates could attend seminars for training women teachers—the only option for further study. In contrast with contemporaneous boys' secondary schools, girls' institutes offered several hours a week of instruction in needlework, fewer lessons in mathematics and science, no training in Greek and Latin, and more exposure to German and religion.

Although state educational officials apparently considered these mostly private girls' schools peripheral to the educational system, their students and teachers often became advocates of improved education for women. Teacher Helene Lange (1848–1930), in her "Yellow Brochure" (formally titled *Die höhere Mädchenschule und ihre Bestimmung*), published in 1887, argued for an enhanced role for women teachers in educating girls and for higher education for women. Especially controversial was Lange's view that the primary purpose of women's education was to serve women, not their future husbands. She also insisted that women's nature dictated an education equal to but different from men's. Lange was instrumental in establishing, in 1893, one of the first special courses to grant girls the *Abitur,* the certificate required for university admission. For some years, women had audited university lectures. In 1900, Baden became the first German state to permit women to matriculate, followed by Bavaria in 1903, Württemberg in 1904, and Saxony in 1906. In 1908, Prussia reformed its higher girls' schools to include an academic track culminating in the *Abitur,* as well as tracks for training teachers and for teaching housekeeping and childrearing skills. With this reform the girls' schools became recognized secondary schools.

A gradual movement toward coeducation has also characterized girls' secondary schooling in the twentieth century. Girls in Baden and Württemberg began attending boys' schools in the early years of the twentieth century, but most German girls attended girls' schools throughout the 1920s and 1930s. Bavaria introduced coeducation at the secondary level only after World War II.

The twentieth century witnessed a significant improvement in the quality of girls' secondary education and in women's access to higher education. In the early 1920s, slightly more than 10 percent of Prussian girls' schools granted the *Abitur,* but this increased to 60 percent by 1930, and by the end of the 1930s, most girls' secondary schools offered the credential required for university admission. By 1931, girls received 23 percent of *Abitur* certificates. Women's share of German university enrollment increased from 7 percent in 1914 to 16 percent in 1931, but fell to 11 percent in 1937–38 as the Nazis limited women's enrollment. The Nazis also introduced a women's *Abitur,* which emphasized home economics while restricting the academic curriculum.

Despite the Nazis' commitment to educating women only for domesticity, the percentage of women students increased during World War II, reaching 61 percent of the total in the winter of 1943–44. After the war, the percentages of girls among West German *Abitur* recipients were 33 percent in 1950, 36 percent in 1960, and 39 percent in 1975. Women's representation among West German university students rose from 16 percent in 1951 to 22 percent in 1960 and, with the expansion of West German higher education, to 41 percent in the late 1980s. Although the numbers and percentages of girls enrolled in advanced secondary and tertiary institutions rose dramatically, until the later part of the twentieth century most girls had little or no formal education beyond that of the *Volksschule* (elementary school).

Despite educators' preference for separating the sexes, most elementary schools in Imperial Germany were coeducational simply because separate classes in small schools would have been expensive and impractical. Most of the teachers in the elementary schools, 85 percent at the turn of the century, were men. The stories in the reading books used in these schools contained few female characters, suggesting that girls were little more than an afterthought in schools designed for boys. Required needlework classes for girls, intended both to teach skills and instill domestic virtues, were the exception to this. Larger schools introduced courses in cooking and home economics in the early twentieth century. Into the final decades of the twentieth century, girls were underrepresented among apprentices and more likely than boys to qualify only for unskilled or semi-skilled positions.

Growing numbers of German women benefited from expanding educational opportunities during the second half of the twentieth century, but women continued to lag behind men in earning credentials to pursue many academic and nonacademic careers. Tensions between educating girls for domesticity and preparing them for work outside the home persisted.

Katharine D. Kennedy

See also Education; Feminism and Anti-Feminism; Lange, Helene; Schools; Universities; Women, 1871–1918, 1918–45; (Bourgeoisie) Women's Movement; Women's Occupations

References

Albisetti, James C. *Schooling German Girls and Women: Secondary and Higher Education in the Nineteenth Century.* Princeton, NJ: Princeton University Press, 1988.

Allen, Ann Taylor. *Feminism and Motherhood in Germany, 1800–1914.* New Brunswick, NJ: Rutgers University Press, 1991.

Kennedy, Katharine D. "Domesticity (Hauswirtschaft) in the Volksschule: Textbooks and Lessons for Girls, 1890–1914." *Internationale Schulbuchforschung* 13 (1991), 5–21.

Mertens, Lothar. *Vernachlässigte Töchter der Alma Mater: Ein sozialhistorischer und bildungssoziologischer Beitrag zur strukturellen Entwicklung des Frauenstudiums seit der Jahrhundertwende.* Berlin: Duncker & Humblot, 1991.

Müller, Detlef K. and Bernd Zymek. *Sozialgeschichte und Statistik des Schulsystems in den Staaten des Deutschen Reiches, 1800–1945. Datenhandbuch zur deutschen Bildungsgeschichte.* Vol. 2, part 1. Göttingen: Vandenhoeck & Ruprecht, 1987.

Schluter, Anne, ed. *Pionierinnen, Feministinnen, Karrierefrauen? Zur Geschichte des Frauenstudiums in Deutschland.* Pfaffenweiler: Centaurus, 1992.

Simmel, Monika. *Erziehung zum Weibe: Mädchenbildung im 19. Jahrhundert.* Frankfurt am Main: Campus Verlag, 1980.

Ehard, Hans (1887–1980)

Born in the Upper Franconian town of Bamberg in northern Bavaria, Hans Ehard became one of the most important regional political figures in early post–World War II Germany.

Ehard first attained prominence in 1923–24 when he served as a prosecuting attorney in Adolf Hitler's treason trial following the Beer Hall *Putsch.* Only after Germany's collapse in 1945, however, did Ehard's real gifts as a seeker of consensus emerge. Bavaria's postwar reconstruction saw a new party, the Christian Social Union (Christlich Soziale Union; CSU), competing for power with the Bavarian Liberals and Social Democrats. Ehard was chosen by the CSU to head the first postwar elected Bavarian government. This choice was, in large measure, due to Erhard's skills as a political bridge builder, both within his own party and between it and the others. Following two-and-a-half stormy years in which he oversaw the initial implementation of Bavaria's new democratic constitution and refereed severe intraparty squabbling, Ehard also consented to serve as the CSU's chairman. He held this post and the minister-presidency until 1954. During his tenure as Bavaria's chief executive, Ehard held the additional post (in 1950–51) of president of the upper house (Bundesrat) of the parliament of the Federal Republic of Germany (FRG).

Ehard viewed this latter service as an important adjunct to his work as Bavarian minister-president. It is in the Bundesrat that Bavaria's and the other states' interests are immediately represented at the national level. Such a post Ehard considered crucial to preserving Bavaria's historic identity in the new republic, even if each *Bundesratspräsident* served for only one year. His duties as Bavarian minister-president and president of the Bundesrat also reflected Ehard's great personal faith in federalism's value as an organizational principle not only for Germany but for all Europe. This idea, about which Ehard wrote and spoke tirelessly, was for him and the CSU the most effective means to maintain Germany's democratic unity while simultaneously preserving the separate identities of Bavaria and the other federal states.

Following his service as minister-president, Ehard served (1954–60) as speaker of the Bavarian state assembly (Landtag). These years coincided with the single period to date in which Ehard's CSU did not control Bavaria's government. Ehard eventually became president of the Bavarian Red Cross and died in retirement in 1980.

David R. Dorondo

See also American Occupation; Bavaria; Christian Social Union; Federal Republic of Germany; Federalism

References

Dorondo, D.R. *Bavaria and German Federalism: Reich to Republic, 1918–33, 1945–49.* New York, NY: St. Martin's, 1992.

Ehard, Hans. *Bayerische Politik: Ansprachen und Reden des bayerischen Ministerpräsidenten.* Comp. Karl Schwend. Munich: Richard Pflaum Verlag, 1952.

Eschenburg, Theodor. *Geschichte der Bundesrepublik Deutschland. Band I: Jahre der Besatzung.* Ed. Karl

Dietrich Bracher, Theodor Eschenburg, et al. Stuttgart: Deutsche Verlags-Anstalt, 1983.

Morsey, Rudolf. "Zwischen Bayern und der Bundsrepublik: Die politische Rolle des bayerischen Ministerpräsidenten Hans Ehard 1946–1949." *Juristenzeitung* 10–11 (1981), 361–70.

Ehrlich, Paul (1854–1915)

Paul Ehrlich made significant contributions in the field of bacteriology, particularly in the areas of immunochemistry and anti-infective chemotherapy. His medical training began at the University of Breslau and he received his medical degree from the University of Leipzig in 1878. In 1896, Ehrlich was named director of the State Institute for Serum Research and Serum Testing in Steglitz. In 1899, he became the director of the Institute of Experimental Therapy in Frankfurt am Main.

Ehrlich's work may be classified into three areas. The first is the application of stains to the differentiation of cells and tissues for the purpose of revealing function (1877–90). This led to the development of the acid-fast stain to identify tubercle bacteria. In 1881, Ehrlich introduced methylene blue, a dye used extensively in microbiology. He described its ability to differentiate various blood cells by their staining characteristics, a method that laid the foundations for the fields of hematology and the study of anemia and leukemia.

Ehrlich's second major contribution involved the study of immunity (1890–1900). His chemical side-chain theory accounted for the specific interactions of antibodies with antigens. The theory explained the effect of bacterial toxins and led to the development of antitoxins.

Ehrlich pioneered the commercial manufacture and distribution of diphtheria antitoxins in 1897 by improving and standardizing the technique for producing highly potent diphtheria antitoxin from goats and horses. In 1908, Ehrlich won the Nobel Prize for medicine in recognition of his work, which had led to a diphtheria antitoxin serum dosage that could be safely used in clinical practice. The use of antitoxins became the first practical treatment for many infectious diseases.

In the last period of his life, Ehrlich concentrated on the study of chemotherapeutic agents (1907–15). He described the use of chemicals, which he called "magic bullets," and the modification of chemical dyes to attack disease. He tested in excess of six hundred dyes before discovering, in 1909, the arsenic compound salvarsan, also known as compound 606, which cured syphilis. During this period, 6 percent of all deaths were due to syphilis. Salvarsan was the first synthetic drug to be employed on a wide scale and was used extensively to protect German troops against syphilis in World War I.

Another result of Ehrlich's scientific work was the drug Prontosil, manufactured by the German dye industry in Domagk in 1935. Prontosil dramatically cured streptococcal infections and led to the development of the sulfonamide class of drugs, one of the twentieth century's most important discoveries in anti-infective therapy.

Paul Ehrlich is probably most revered for his work in the description of the agents that cause disease and the discovery

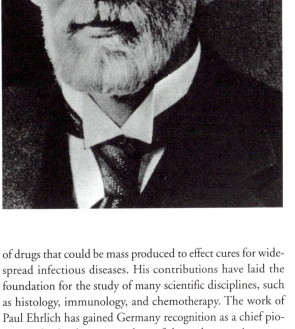

of drugs that could be mass produced to effect cures for widespread infectious diseases. His contributions have laid the foundation for the study of many scientific disciplines, such as histology, immunology, and chemotherapy. The work of Paul Ehrlich has gained Germany recognition as a chief pioneer in the development and use of chemotherapeutic agents.

Lori Walsh

See also Bacteriology; Biology; Chemistry, Scientific and Industrial; Disease; Health; Koch, Robert; Medicine; Pharmacy

References

Baumler, E. *Paul Ehrlich.* New York, NY: Holmes and Meier, 1984.

Bibel, Debra Jan. *Milestones in Immunology: A Historical Exploration.* Madison, WI: Science Tech Publishers, 1988.

Bullock, William. *History of Bacteriology.* New York, NY: Dover Publications, 1938.

David, Bernard D. *Microbiology: Including Immunology and Molecular Genetics.* Philadelphia, PA: Harper and Row, Publishers, 1980.

Ehrlich, Paul. "Die Wertbemessung des Diphtherieheilserums und deren theoretische Grundlagen." *Klinisches Jahrbuch* (1897), 299–326.

———. "Proceedings of the Royal Society, London." *Biology* 66 (1900), 424–48.

Himmelwert, F. *The Collected Papers of Paul Ehrlich.* New York, NY: Pergamon Press, 1956–58.

Long, Esmond R. *A History of Pathology.* New York, NY: Dover Press, Inc., 1965.

Marquandt, Martha. *Paul Ehrlich.* New York, NY: Henry Schuman, 1951.

Reid, Robert. *Microbes and Men.* New York, NY: Saturday Review Press, 1975.

Eich, Günter (1907–72)

This poet and radio play writer was born in Lebus on the Oder. Günter Eich studied Chinese and law at the universities of Berlin and Leipzig and at the Sorbonne. He had some poems published while still a student and in 1929 he wrote his first radio play, *Caruso,* for the newly established Berlin Radio. His first volume of poems, *Gedichte* (Poems), appeared in 1930. From 1933 to 1939 he worked for Berlin Radio and became one of the pioneers of the new radio plays. For the rest of his literary career Eich restricted himself almost exclusively to writing poetry and radio plays.

He served in the army for the whole of the Second World War and was taken prisoner by the Americans. After his release in 1946 he started to write again, at first mainly poems about his experiences in the war and in the prisoner-of-war camp and about the problems of coming to terms with Germany's Nazi past. But soon he also dealt with a wide range of fundamental issues, often in a highly critical and satirical voice. His poems tend to be short and often contain striking, highly original surrealistic and absurdist dream images and verbal abstractions. Many express a profound melancholy and pessimism. He published a number of anthologies: *Abgelegne Gehöfte* (Discarded farms), 1948, *Untergrundbahn* (Subway), 1969, *Botschaften des Regens* (Messages of the rain), 1961, *Zu den Akten* (To the files), 1964, *Anlässe und Steingärten* (Occasions and rockgardens), 1966, *Maulwürfe I* (Mules I), 1968, and *Maulwürfe II* (Mules II), 1970.

In 1947 Eich became one of the founding members of Group 47, an association of young authors and critics who wanted to revive German literature after the Nazi suppression. Eich also wrote successful and widely acclaimed radio plays. In 1952 he was awarded the prestigious Radio Play Prize of Blind Veterans for *Die Andere und ich* (The other and I). Among his best-known radio plays are: *Träume* (Dreams), 1950, *Die Mädchen aus Viterbo* (The girls from Viterbo), 1952, *Das Jahr Lazertis* (Lazertis's year), 1953, *Zinngeschrei* (Tin screams), 1955, *Die Brandung vor Setúbal* (The surf of Setúbal), 1956, *Allah hat hundert Namen* (Allah has a hundred names), 1957, and *Festianus Märtyrer* (Festianus martyr), 1958. He married the Austrian author Ilse Aichinger in 1953 and was awarded the Büchner Prize in 1959. Eich died in Salzburg.

Margaret Stone

See also Federal Republic of Germany: Literature; Poetry; Radio Plays

References

Arnold, Heinz Ludwig, ed. "Günter Eich: Text und Kritik." *Zeitschrift für Literatur* 5 (1979).

Eich, Günter. *Ein Lesebuch.* Frankfurt am Main: Suhrkamp, 1972.

———. *Gesammelte Werke.* 4 vols. Frankfurt am Main: Suhrkamp, 1973.

Goss, Marlies. *Günter Eich und das Hörspiel der 50er Jahre: Untersuchungen am Beispiel "Träume."* Frankfurt am Main: Peter Lang, 1988.

Krispyn, Egbert. *Günter Eich.* New York, NY: Twayne Publishers Inc., 1971.

Märki, Peter. *Günter Eichs Hörspielkunst.* Frankfurt am Main: Athenaion, 1974.

Müller-Hanpft, Susanne. *Über Günter Eich.* Frankfurt am Main: Suhrkamp, 1979.

Neumann, Peter Hort. *Die Rettung der Poesie im Unsinn: Der Anarchist Günter Eich.* Stuttgart: Klett, 1981.

Post, Klaus-Dieter. *Günter Eich. Zwischen Angst und Einverständnis.* Bonn: Bouvier, 1977.

Schafroth, Heinz Friedrich. *Günter Eich:* Munich: Beck, 1976.

Unseld, Siegfried, ed. *Günter Eich zum Gedächtnis.* Frankfurt am Main: Suhrkamp, 1973.

Eichmann, Adolf (1906–62)

Adolf Eichmann was a colonel in the Schutzstaffel (SS) and the Jewish affairs expert for the German Security Police and the Security Service (SD). A participant in the Wannsee Conference in 1942, Eichmann played an integral role in the "final solution of the Jewish question" in Europe.

Born in the Rhineland, Eichmann grew up in Linz, Austria, where he came under the influence of Ernst Kaltenbrunner (1903–46) and the Austrian Nazi movement. He joined the party and the SS in early 1932, but fled to Germany the following year after the Austrian Nazis were outlawed and he was dismissed from his job. Eichmann continued to train with the Austrian SS legion near Passau and was transferred to the Dachau concentration camp outside Munich in 1934 for additional military training.

In September 1934, Eichmann was sent to Berlin and assigned to the headquarters of the SD under Reinhard Heydrich (1904–42). He joined the newly-established Jewish Affairs Department in 1935. His duties included negotiations with Zionist leaders concerning the emigration of German Jews to Palestine, which Eichmann visited in late 1937. He opposed the mass deportation of Jews to Palestine because he viewed the creation of a Jewish state there to be contrary to Germany's national interests. The outbreak of the war in September 1939 eventually made it impossible for Germany to send Jews to British-controlled Palestine.

After the incorporation of Austria into the Reich in March 1938, Eichmann was sent to Vienna to supervise the local Jewish affairs department. He arranged for the forced emigration of the Austrian Jews through the creation of the Central Office for Jewish Emigration. Following the establishment of the Reich Protectorate of Bohemia and Moravia in March 1939, Eichmann was sent to Prague to effect the forced emigration of the Czech Jews. Eichmann's offices in Vienna and Prague served as a model for a central office for Jewish emigration established in the Reich Ministry of the Interior in January 1940.

Himmler created the Reich Security Main Office in September 1939 and Eichmann was assigned to the Jewish affairs section of the Gestapo. At this time, Eichmann switched his support from the policy of forced emigration to that seeking the mass deportation of Jews from areas incorporated into the Reich to concentration camps and ghettos in the German-occupied territories in the East. Eichmann also participated in the January 1942 Wannsee Conference, where the mass extermination of the European Jews was planned. Over the next two years, he arranged and scheduled the transport of the Jews to killing centers in the East. Eichmann went to Budapest in early 1944 in order to personally expedite the deportation of nearly half a million Hungarian Jews following the German occupation of its former ally.

After the war, Eichmann assumed various aliases and went into hiding in Germany until 1950, when he escaped to Argentina. He was apprehended by Israeli agents in Buenos Aires in May 1960 and tried the following year for war crimes and crimes against humanity. The Israeli court convicted him, and Eichmann was hanged in June 1962, the only Nazi war criminal to be brought to justice by the Jewish state.

Steven B. Rogers

See also Arendt, Hannah; Auschwitz; Austro-German Relations; Concentration Camps; Heydrich, Reinhard; Himmler, Heinrich; Hitler, Adolf; Holocaust; Israeli-German Relations; Jews, 1933–90; National Socialist Germany; Nazi War Crimes Trials and Investigations; Schutzstaffel; Wannsee Conference

References
Arendt, Hannah. *Eichmann in Jerusalem.* New York, NY: Penguin, 1984.
Gilbert, Martin. *The Holocaust.* New York, NY: Holt, Rinehart and Winston, 1985.
Hilberg, Raul. *Sonderzüge nach Auschwitz.* Mainz: Dumjahn Verlag, 1981.
Lang, Jochen von, ed. *Eichmann Interrogated.* New York, NY: Farrar, Strauss and Giroux, 1983.
Reitlinger, Gerald. *The Final Solution.* London: Vallentine, Mitchell and Co. Ltd., 1953.

Einem, Karl von (1853–1934)

Karl Wilhelm George August von Einem was born of an old patrician and military family on January 1, 1853, at Herberg in the Harz. A Prussian cadet in 1866, he became a commissioned officer during the Franco-Prussian War. He was appointed to the General Staff in 1880 without having attended the War Academy. In 1898, he was transferred to the War Ministry and in 1900 became head of the General War Department.

Appointed war minister in 1903, he opposed the efforts of General Alfred von Schlieffen (1833–1913) and Chancellor Bernhard von Bülow (1849–1929) to increase the size of the army, arguing that with the naval building program the financial resources of the empire were insufficient for both.

His real reason was that he believed in a small, politically reliable, and high-quality army and not in modern mass forces. He argued in favor of improved technology, particularly heavy artillery, machine guns, and improved defensive positions. On a different military issue, he gave his full support to the introduction of field-gray uniforms.

Though promoted to the rank of cavalry general in 1907, Einem was dismissed along with Bülow in 1909. He was then posted to command the Seventh Army Corps in Münster. On September 12, 1914, he became commander of the Third Army and withstood a number of fierce French assaults in the Champagne region. His army took part in the initially successful spring offensive in 1918, but was eventually driven back over the Maas. After the war, Einem retired completely from public life and wrote two volumes of memoirs. He died in Mühlheim on the Ruhr on April 7, 1934.

Martin Kitchen

See also Bülow, Bernhard von; Imperial Germany: Army; Officer Corps; Schlieffen, Alfred

References
Einem, Generaloberst von. *Ein Armeeführer erlebt den Weltkrieg.* Leipzig: K.F. Koehler, 1933.
Kitchen, Martin. *The German Officer Corps, 1890–1914.* Oxford: Oxford University Press, 1968.

Einsatzgruppen (Execution Squads)

The *Einzatzgruppen* (full name, *Einsatzgruppen der Sicherheitspolizei und des Sicherheitsdienstes*) were mobile and militarized police units of battalion size in Nazi Germany assigned to carry out the mass murder of designated Nazi racial and ideological enemies. They operated under the personal direction of Reinhard Heydrich (1904–42), head of the Reich Security Main Office, but were responsible to Heydrich's superior, Heinrich Himmler (1900–45).

During the Polish campaign the *Einsatzgruppen* suppressed uprisings behind the army lines and neutralized potential future resistance by eliminating groups regarded as hostile. Some army officers, however, interfered with the mass executions and plundering carried out by the *Einsatzgruppen* in Poland. The result was that the wave of terror in Poland, though claiming tens of thousands of victims, did not go quite as far as it might have. By the time of the German invasion of the USSR, however, Himmler and Heydrich, with Adolf Hitler's backing, had succeeded in freeing the *Einsatzgruppen* from military control. Mass executions began within days of the German attack, as these police, usually operating in company-sized units (*Einsatzkommandos*), followed the German armies eastward.

The standard technique for mass executions was to use ravines where they were available, or to dig ditches and trenches. The victims were lined up at the edge of ditches or placed in the ditches themselves; then the policemen shot them. The next victims were placed on top of the previous ones. The procedure was very methodical and quite standardized. Since late 1941, some *Einsatzkommandos* also received and used gas vans, which had sealed freight compartments. The victims were loaded into the rear, and then carbon monoxide exhaust was channeled back inside to kill them. Everywhere the *Einsatzkommandos* left masses of dead Jews, Soviet officials, prisoners of war, Gypsies, and "Asiatics" behind.

One historian's estimate has the four *Einsatzgruppen* operating in the Soviet Union killing a minimum of just over 700,000 people during the period June 1941–December 1942. Much of this data comes from the reports of the *Einsatzgruppen* themselves, which were sent to Berlin and edited in the Reich Security Main Office. All but one of these reports survive. That perhaps 3,000 men with little preparation and varied attitudes managed to execute some 700,000 victims within an 18-month period is evidence of the Nazi regime's ability to gain and hold followers who pursued its genocidal goals.

Richard D. Breitman

See also Gypsies; Heydrich, Reinhard; Himmler, Heinrich; Holocaust; Jews, 1933–90; National Socialist Germany: Military; Polish-German Relations; Prisoners of War; Reich Security Main Office; Soviet-German Relations; World War II

References

Breitman, Richard. *The Architect of Genocide: Himmler and the Final Solution.* Hanover, NH: University Press of New England, 1992.

Headland, Ronald. *Messages of Murder: A Study of the Reports of the Einsatzgruppen of the Security Police and the Security Service, 1941–1943.* Rutherford, NJ: Fairleigh Dickinson University Press, 1992.

Hilberg, Raul. *The Destruction of the European Jews.* 3 vols. Revised and definitive edition. New York, NY: Holmes and Meier, 1985.

Höhne, Heinz. *The Order of Death's Head: The Story of Hitler's SS.* New York, NY: Ballantine Books, 1969.

Krausnick, Helmut and Hans-Heinrich Wilhelm. *Die Truppe des Weltanschauungskrieges: Die Einsatzgruppen der Sicherheitspolizei und des SD, 1938–1942.* Stuttgart: Deutsche Verlags-Anstalt, 1981.

Krausnick, Helmut et al. *Anatomy of the SS-State.* New York, NY: Walker, 1968.

Reitlinger, Gerald. *The SS, Alibi of a Nation, 1922–1945.* New York, NY: Viking Press, 1957.

Einstein, Albert (1879–1955)

Albert Einstein grew up in Munich, but he dropped out of the Gymnasium there and eventually finished school in Aarau, Switzerland. He then studied mathematics and physics at the Zürich Polytechnic Institute, where he met and married a fellow student, Mileva Maric, with whom he had two sons. Unable to obtain a teaching position after graduation, he secured a post in the Swiss Patent Office at Bern. But his research soon brought him scientific recognition, appointments at various universities, and finally in 1914 a prestigious call to the University of Berlin. At the end of the war he divorced Mileva Maric and married his cousin Elsa, a widow with two daughters.

Einstein achieved international fame after 1919; he became the gentle magus of popular lore and a figure of undying fascination to adoring crowds. He used his fame to support the causes in which he believed, notably pacifism and Zionism. This activity made him the target of the anti-Semitic right in Germany, and in 1933 he left Germany to accept a position at the Institute for Advanced Study at Princeton, New Jersey. In 1939, at the urging of Léo Szilárd and others, Einstein abandoned his pacifism and wrote to President Roosevelt, warning him of the dangers of German research in nuclear fission.

In one of the famous 1905 papers, Einstein developed the revolutionary idea that radiation consists of independent particles of energy, or light quanta, rather than of waves. He used this bizarre assumption to explain several puzzling phenomena, including the photoelectric effect. Over the next two decades Einstein boldly developed the consequences of the so-called wave-particle duality while at the same time searching for a new theoretical foundation for physics that would resolve the paradox about the nature of radiation. But Einstein refused to accept the probabilistic interpretation of quantum mechanics urged by Niels Bohr and Werner Heisenberg (1901–76). His continuing insistence that "God does not play dice with the world" eventually led to his scientific isolation.

Einstein's second revolutionary paper of 1905 set out the Special Theory of Relativity. It treated several problems inherent in the classical physics of the later nineteenth century, including consistent experimental failures to detect the Earth's absolute motion through the ether. He traced these problems to the inability of observers in relative motion to establish unambiguously the simultaneity of two spatially separated events, the consequences of this for all measurement, and the resulting need for new transformation equations to replace the traditional Galilean ones. The new transformations eliminated effects due to absolute motion, but also predicted paradoxical changes in the dimensions, mass, and even the "local time" resulting from states of relative motion between observers. From these effects Einstein deduced the equivalence of mass and energy in his famous $E=mc^2$.

Einstein immediately began the struggle to extend his theory of relativity to apply to bodies in accelerated motion as well as to states of inertia. Adopting the views of mathematician Hermann Minkowski, he gave the theory a geometrical interpretation in terms of a four-dimensional space-time continuum. The completed General Theory of Relativity, announced in 1915, treated gravitational effects as local alterations in the metric of space-time induced by the presence of matter and electromagnetic fields. Until his death Einstein searched in vain for a "unified field theory" that would extend the geometrical interpretation to the electrodynamical field.

R. Steven Turner

See also Atom Bomb (German Development of); Expulsion and Exile of Scientists and Scholars; Heisenberg, Werner; Jews, 1869–1933; Kaiser Wilhelm/Max Planck Societies and Their Institutes; Pacifism and the Peace Movement; Physics; Planck, Max; Science and National Socialism

References

Clark, Ronald W. *Einstein. The Life and Times.* New York, NY: World Publishing Company, 1971.

Hoffmann, Banesh. *Einstein, Creator and Rebel.* New York, NY: New American Library, 1972.

Pais, Abraham. *The Science and the Life of Albert Einstein.* Oxford: Oxford University Press, 1982.

Pyenson, Lewis. *The Young Einstein: The Advent of Relativity.* Bristol: Adam Hilger Ltd., 1985.

Eisler, Hanns (1898–1962)

As one of the foremost composers of the German Democratic Republic (GDR), Hans Eisler mainly wrote vocal and dramatic music that espoused socialist ideology.

Eisler was born in Leipzig. From 1901 to 1925 he lived in Vienna, where he studied harmony and counterpoint with Karl Weigl at the New Vienna Conservatory and composition privately with Arnold Schönberg (1874–1951) and Anton Webern (1883–1945). In 1925 he began teaching in Berlin, where he became politically active, joining the German Communist party in 1926 and working within the political group Das rote Sprachrohr (the red mouthpiece). His enforced exile began in 1933 and, after living in Vienna, Paris, and Denmark, he moved to North America in 1938. He taught in New York and Mexico and in 1942 settled in Los Angeles, where he became musical assistant to Charlie Chaplin. The anti-Communist excesses of the McCarthy era forced him to return to Europe, and from 1949 until his death, Eisler lived in East Berlin, where he taught at the Academy of Arts and the Musikhochschule (conservatory).

Influenced by Schönberg, Eisler composed twelve-tone music, but following disagreements with Schönberg in 1926 over composers' responsibilities to new music, and because of his newly developed Marxist leanings, he turned to writing functional music that opposed capitalism and Fascism; *"Einheitsfrontlied"* (Song of the united front), is perhaps the best-known of these tonal left-wing marching songs. The year 1930 saw his important meeting with Bertolt Brecht (1898–1956), which resulted in two diatonic *Lehrstücke* (Didactic pieces), *Die Massnahme* (The measure), 1930, and *Die Mutter* (The mother), 1931. The anti-Fascist *Deutsche Sinfonie,* 1935–39, uses texts by Brecht, is basically tonal, and employs twelve-tone techniques. In Hollywood he wrote film scores and a book with Theodor Adorno (1903–69) on the techniques involved, *Composing for the Films,* 1947.

In the last decade of his life in the GDR, Eisler devoted himself primarily to writing so-called *angewandte Musik* (comprehensible music that is readily applicable to theater, cinema, or ballet and that is of societal and aesthetic value) producing vast amounts of songs (including the East German national anthem) and music for films and the theater.

Gareth Cox

See also Adorno, Theodor; Brecht, Bertolt; Composers; Expulsion and Exile of Scientists and Scholars; German Democratic Republic; Schönberg, Arnold; Webern, Anton

References

Betz, Albrecht. *Hanns Eisler: Political Musician.* Trans. Bill Hopkins. Cambridge: Cambridge University Press, 1982.

Grabs, Manfred. *Hanns Eisler: Kompositionen-Schriften-Literatur: Ein Handbuch.* Leipzig: VEB Deutscher Verlag für Musik, 1984.

Eisner, Kurt (1867–1919)

Socialist journalist, writer, and politician, Kurt Eisner proclaimed the Bavarian Republic on November 7, 1918, and served for one hundred days as its prime minister and foreign minister. Count Anton von Arco Valley assassinated him on February 12, 1919, an event that unleashed the bloody phase of the Bavarian revolution.

Son of a Jewish Berlin shopkeeper, Eisner quit university in 1889 to pursue journalism, first at the *Frankfurter Zeitung* and from 1893 as political editor of Marburg's *Hessische Landeszeitung,* where he was influenced by the neo-Kantian philosophy professor Herman Cohen. In 1897–98, he served nine months in jail on a charge of lese-majeste for a pseudonymous article ridiculing Kaiser Wilhelm II. This earned him the respect of Wilhelm Liebknecht (1826–1900), the patriarch of the Social Democratic Party (SPD), and appointment to the editorial board of Berlin's leading socialist newspaper, *Vorwärts* (Forward). In 1905, Eisner differed ideologically with his co-editors and was forced to resign.

Moving to Nuremberg, he became a political columnist and editor for the Social Democratic newspaper, *Fränkische Tagespost,* and published a critical history of Germany during the Napoleonic period, *Das Ende des Reiches* (The end of the Reich), 1907, which has been termed Eisner's "farewell to Prussia." In 1910, he arrived in Munich (after ending his 17-year marriage to Elisabeth Hendrich), where he and his second wife, Elise Belli, lived outside the city.

The long-haired, bearded Eisner became political editor of the newspaper *Münchner Post* and a member of Munich's Schwabing Bohemia, the artist, bohemian sector of Munich. From 1916 the discussion group at the Golden Anchor tavern was his political pulpit. In 1917 he attended the Gotha Conference and emerged as the Munich leader of the antiwar Independent Social Democratic Party (USPD). For being critical of the emperor and the war, his political newspaper column was banned, which limited him to a meager income from drama criticism. Jailed for organizing a munitions strike in January 1918, Eisner was released in October to run for parliament as a USPD candidate. His SPD opponent, Erhard Auer, miscalculated Eisner's charisma, the disaffection of antiwar soldiers, peasants, and workers, and the weariness of the general populace. Rallying on the Theresienwiese, Eisner and his followers seized the army barracks and the government in a bloodless coup that created the Bavarian Republic two days before the proclamation of the Weimar Republic in Berlin.

As prime minister, Eisner hoped to exploit the populist energies and antiwar sentiments that had created the Bavarian Republic. He found the parliament he headed insufficiently democratic and advocated the continual governmental use of councils of soldiers, peasants, and workers. This earned him little support, just as his foreign policy initiatives, advocating an immediate and full confession of German war guilt to achieve reconciliation with France, aroused the mistrust of the interim leaders of the Berlin government, Friedrich Ebert (1871–1925) and Philipp Scheidemann (1865–1939). With his government on the verge of collapse, Eisner was on his way to the session at which he would resign his position when Arco Valley shot him down in the street.

There is general doubt about Eisner's aptitude for practical politics. The intellectual depth of his book-length studies of Nietzsche (1892) and Liebknecht (1900) are unquestionable. Some disagreement exists over his creative achievement as a writer of didactic socialist parables (*Sozialmärchen* [Sociopolitical fairy tales], collected in *Feste der Festlosen: Hausbuch weltlicher Predigtschwänke* [Feasts of the feastless: handbook of secular sermon anecdotes], 1906). But generally, he is considered one of Imperial Germany's most important left-wing journalists.

Peter Chametzky

See also Bavaria; Ebert, Friedrich; Independent Social Democratic Party; Journalism; Liebknecht, Karl; Nietzsche, Friedrich; Revolution of 1918–19; Scheidemann, Philipp; Social Democratic Party

References

Eisner, Kurt. *Die Neue Zeit*. Munich: Georg Müller, 1919.
———. *Gesammelte Schriften*. 2 vols. Berlin: Paul Cassirer, 1919.
———. *Sozialismus als Aktion: Ausgewählte Aufsätze und Reden*. Ed. Freya Eisner. Frankfurt am Main: Suhrkamp, 1975.
Fechenbach, Felix. *Der Revolutionär Kurt Eisner: Aus persönlichen Erlebnissen*. Berlin: J.H.W. Dietz, 1929.
Grassmann, Josef von. "Kurt Eisner." *Deutsches Biographisches Jahrbuch* 2 (1917–20), 368–78. Stuttgart: Deutsche Verlags-Anstalt, 1928.
Grunberger, Richard. *Red Rising in Bavaria*. New York, NY: St. Martin's Press, 1973.
Gurganus, Albert. *The Art of Revolution: Kurt Eisner's Agitprop*. Columbia, SC: Camden House, 1986.
Hausenstein, Wilhelm. "Erinnerung an Eisner." *Der Neue Merkur* 3 (1919), 56–68.
Mitchell, Allan. *Revolution in Bavaria, 1918–1919: The Eisner Regime and the Soviet Republic*. Princeton, NJ: Princeton University Press, 1965.
Pierson, Stanley. *Marxist Intellectuals and the Working-Class Mentality in Germany, 1887–1912*. Cambridge, MA: Harvard University Press, 1993.
Schade, Fritz. *Kurt Eisner und die bayerische Sozialdemokratie*. Hannover: Verlag für Literatur und Zeitgeschehen, 1961.

Elections

Elections articulated the political culture of the German nation from 1871 to 1990, reflecting and influencing the political climate. Only from 1919–30 and in the post-1949 Federal Republic, however, did they directly shape government. The voting system changed markedly from one regime to the next; it is often thought that a stable democracy has emerged only since the 1950s.

The electoral law of Imperial Germany (law of May 31, 1869 of the North German Confederation, carried over through the constitution of April 16, 1871), gave the vote to all men 25 years of age or older, except members of the armed forces (excluded for fear of politicizing the army) and those who had lost their civil rights for various reasons. The percentage of the population entitled to vote edged up to 22 percent in 1912. This broad suffrage, broader than Great Britain's was before 1884, was instituted by Chancellor Otto von Bismarck in a bid to undermine the liberal parties—he hoped the masses would be susceptible to conservative influence. Instead, after 1890, the Reichstag suffrage facilitated the mobilization of new social groups and the emergence of mass politics. In contrast to state suffrages, which could be unequal like Prussia's three-class system or restricted to narrow groups like Saxony's pre-1896 suffrage, the Reichstag ballot was "universal, equal, secret, and direct" and became a symbol of democracy.

Voting occurred within 382 (after 1873, when Alsace-Lorraine was added, 397) constituencies, each having a population of roughly 100,000; each of the 26 federal states had a minimum of one constituency. Since these constituencies were not redrawn, urban areas became increasingly underrepresented: in 1912, the largest constituency had 338,900 voters, while the smallest had 10,700. Each constituency elected one deputy. If no candidate achieved an absolute majority on the first ballot, the two with the largest totals met in a runoff.

Reichstag campaigns sometimes revolved around nationalistic or patriotic issues, as in the *Kulturkampf* elections of 1874, the anti-socialist campaign of 1879, the campaigns of 1887 and 1893 based on the failure of military legislation desired by the government, and the campaign of 1907 occasioned by colonial policy. Other elections, notably those of 1881, 1898, 1903, and 1912, focused more on social-economic and taxation-related issues. Party programs were long-term and ideological; voter participation was high and reached 85 percent in 1912. Members of particular socioeconomic groups cast strong, "affirming" votes for the parties representing their beliefs. Catholics supported the Center Party, agrarian Protestants in the east voted for the Conservatives, and the working class voted increasingly for the Social Democrats (SPD), giving the SPD the largest vote total in 1890 and the largest seat total in 1912. The liberal parties lacked any such roots in solid, broad social-economic groupings.

Following the collapse of Imperial Germany and the declaration of the Weimar Republic, the SPD, the Center, and the left-liberal German Democratic Party (DDP)—the Weimar Coalition—took power in the elections of January 1919. The Weimar electoral law (April 27, 1920) confirmed the universal and equal suffrage introduced during the Revolution of 1918–19: all men and women 20 years of age and older could vote (still with exceptions for the armed forces and others) and proportional representation made ballots equal in effect. Under proportional representation, deputies were elected off party lists, one for every 60,000 votes received by a party within 35 large multi-deputy constituencies. Remainders of unused votes were pooled at regional and national levels to elect deputies off party lists at those levels. The number of deputies in the Reichstag varied with the number of votes cast. Proportional representation made it easy for small parties to enter the Reichstag, may have exaggerated the fragmentation of parties, and increased the power of the party bureaucracies, which drew up the candidate lists.

Electoral politics were more unstable than before, partly due to difficult economic and nationalistic issues (inflation, reparations, and as of 1929, unemployment and agricultural crisis) and partly due to structural factors. The Weimar Coalition parties permanently lost their majority in 1920. The SPD still won the highest vote totals of any party in all Reichstag elections until 1932, but right-wing parties often refused to cooperate with it, making coalitions difficult. In addition, the Communists now competed for SPD voters. Liberal and conservative voter support was very fragmented and volatile, often going to parties critical of the republic. This left room for the Nazis to mobilize increasing numbers of voters after 1928, especially rural Protestants and members of the lower middle class; but to a greater extent than most Weimar parties the Nazis drew some supporters from all classes. Meanwhile, the president elected in 1925 and 1932, General Paul von Hindenburg (1847–1934), had little enthusiasm for democracy; as of 1930 he permitted governments lacking parliamentary majorities to rule using "emergency" powers.

While the Nazi Party never won a majority in free Reichstag elections, its performance in July and November 1932 allowed it to become and remain the largest party in the Reichstag—assisted by grassroots terror and intimidation—and led to Hitler being invited to become chancellor in January 1933, a position he used to take over the German state and end all but the vestiges of democracy. Even in the manipulated elections of March 1933 the Nazis could not secure an absolute majority; but by then elections hardly mattered. Despite some yes-no referenda, officially achieving huge victories, there was no meaningful voting in Nazi Germany.

Frameworks for democracy were reestablished under the guidance of Allied occupation authorities in 1948–49. After the creation of the Federal Republic through the Basic Law (May 23, 1949), a new electoral law followed (June 15, 1949; significant amendments on July 8, 1953). All men and women 21 years of age or older (since 1969–70: 18 or older) had the vote in a complex system of "personalized proportional representation"—a combination of proportional representation with direct election from local constituencies. The first elections to the new Bundestag in August 1949 saw the Christian Democrats (CDU/CSU), heirs to the former Catholic and conservative parties, receive 139 seats and the SPD 131.

In the Soviet zone the German Democratic Republic was declared in October 1949. The Socialist Unity Party (SED), patronized by the Soviet authorities, dominated the new state. The Popular Assembly, "highest organ of the state," had 434 members, 110 from the SED, 180 from the East German CDU and other parties, and 144 from the "mass organizations" (trade unions and youth groups). While elections to the Popular Assembly were superficially conducted under a democratic system with all citizens 18 and older eligible to vote, the elections were exclusively controlled by SED functionaries through the nomination of a slate of candidates, the "Unity List of the National Front." Party pluralism and voting existed in a formal sense only. The last elections in the GDR were admitted to be fraudulent.

The electoral system in the west (carried over to united Germany) provides for a meaningful, if complicated, representative democracy. Half of the Bundestag is elected from party lists, the other half from local constituencies—roughly one constituency for every 110,000 voters. (Until 1990 there were 247 or 248 directly elected deputies, and usually about 496 deputies total.) Each voter casts two ballots, the first for a local candidate, to be elected by a plurality in the constituency; the second for a party. The party votes are pooled within each federal state, and each party is entitled to a share of the seats equal to its share of the votes. Its directly elected candidates count toward this entitlement, and the difference is then filled by candidates off party lists. However, to qualify for any representation, a party must win either three direct seats or 5 percent of the total vote in the whole Federal Republic (the "5 percent rule").

An interesting feature of this voting system is that it allows voters to split their two votes between a particular candidate and a different party. Another important aspect of the electoral system is the interlocking of state and federal politics: state elections affect the profile of leaders who go on to the federal level, can create a sense of momentum that affects federal campaigns, and can indirectly affect federal institutions such as the Bundesrat and the presidency.

Broad electoral trends in the Federal Republic include the elimination of most small parties by the "5 percent rule" after 1953—in effect, a multiparty system evolved into a two-and-a-half-party system. Since 1957, the two large parties (CDU/CSU and SPD) have won 80–90 percent of the vote, while the FDP dipped at times close to the 5 percent cutoff. Only once did any party win an absolute majority (the CDU/CSU in 1957 with 50.2 percent). The parties and their campaigns became less class- or ideology-based than before, more broadly integrative, though at times a regional division existed (SPD in the north, CDU/CSU in the south). Party support has been consistent: from 1961 to 1990 the CDU/CSU's support varied only between 44 and 49 percent, the SPD's only from 36 to 46. Until the 1960s, the CDU/CSU dominated, largely based on economic issues and relations with the west. But in the four elections of 1969–80, the SPD under Willy Brandt (1913–92) was finally able to gain more than 40 percent of the vote, and together with a change in the allegiance of the FDP, this produced SPD-led coalition governments. Another turning point came in 1982, when the social-liberal coalition disintegrated and the FDP again changed partners. The elections of 1983, 1987, and 1990 were victories for the center-right coalition, again based largely on promises of economic prosperity. Also in the 1980s, the Green Party emerged with an alternative politics that drew enough support to clear the 5-percent hurdle and obtain parliamentary representation.

Brett Fairbairn

See also The Basic Law; Center Party; Christian Democratic Union; Christian Social Union; Constitutions; Free Democratic Party; German Communist Party; German Conservative Party; German Democratic Party; German Democratic Republic: Political Culture; German National People's Party; German People's Party; Grand Coalition; The Greens: Movement, Party, Ideology; Imperial Germany; Independent Social Democratic Party; National Liberal Party; Parliamentary System; Parties and Politics; Political Science; Social Democratic Party; Socialist Unity Party; Suffrage; Weimar Germany

References
Büsch, Otto, Monika Wölk, and Wolfgang Wölk, eds. *Wählerbewegung in der deutschen Geschichte: Analysen und Berichte zu den Reichstagswahlen 1871–1933.* Berlin: Historische Kommission zu Berlin, 1978.

Cerny, Karl H., ed. *Germany at the Polls: The Bundestag Elections of the 1980s.* Durham, NC: Duke University Press, 1990.

Childers, Thomas. *The Nazi Voter: The Social Foundations of Fascism in Germany, 1919–1933.* Chapel Hill, NC: University of North Carolina Press, 1983.

Jones, Larry Eugene and James Retallack, eds. *Elections, Mass Politics, and Social Change in Modern Germany: New Perspectives.* Cambridge: Cambridge University Press, 1992.

Koch, H.W. *A Constitutional History of Germany in the Nineteenth and Twentieth Centuries.* London: Longman, 1984.

Padgett, Stephen, and Tony Burkett. *Political Parties and Elections in West Germany: The Search for a New Stability.* Rev. ed. New York, NY: St. Martin's, 1986.

Ritter, Gerhard A., with M. Niehuss. *Wahlgeschichtliches Arbeitsbuch: Materialien zur Statistik des Kaiserreichs 1871–1918.* Munich: C.H. Beck, 1980.

Suval, Stanley. *Electoral Politics in Wilhelmine Germany.* Chapel Hill, NC: University of North Carolina Press, 1985.

Vogel, Bernhard, Dieter Nohlen, and Rainer-Olaf Schultze. *Wählen in Deutschland: Theorie—Geschichte— Dokumente 1848–1970.* Berlin: de Gruyter, 1971.

Electrical Information Transmission

"Electrical information transmission" is a generic term including all technological systems that transmit information electrically, often over long distances. In each of these systems, signals that are perceptible to human senses are transformed into electrically transmissible ones. At their destination they are retransformed into perceptible signals.

Innovations began during the 1830s with the electrical telegraph, followed in 1876 by the telephone, at the turn of the century by various audio broadcasting systems (radio), and since the 1930s by video broadcasting systems (television). In the 1950s, computer networks came into being. In West Germany this development culminated in the installation of an Integrated Services Digital Network (ISDN) in the 1980s.

German developments were, in most cases, part of the international pattern, and governments in Germany have always been conscious of the importance of international systems affecting industry, commerce, culture, politics, and the military. Throughout the nineteenth and twentieth centuries, the state fostered pride in specifically German contributions (especially in radio and television) and emphasized the necessity of maintaining competitiveness.

After several experiments, the first electrical telegraph lines in the German states became operational in 1849. After 1871, the Reichstelegraphenverwaltung (Imperial Telegraph Administration) managed and developed the telegraph system. In the 1880s the Ministry of Posts assumed responsibility for telegraphic transmissions and later for telephones.

The German telephone network became established in large towns starting in 1877. By the mid-1980s most homes in West Germany had a telephone, unlike East Germany, which lagged far behind.

The German telex system (*Fernschreib-apparatus*) developed slowly. After experiments during the 1920s, the system rapidly improved after 1933. Until 1945, the National Socialist public authorities controlled numerous exclusive telex networks including that for Volksaufklärung und Propaganda (people's enlightenment and propaganda), though other state and party agencies such as the Wehrmacht, Luftwaffe, Marine, Labor Front, Reichsbahn, Sturmabteilung (SA), and Schutzstaffel (SS) had their own systems. In the late 1980s, telefaxes superseded telex.

Starting in 1923, a network of radio transmitters intended to cover the whole country as well as to contact ethnic Germans living abroad emerged. Beginning with the urban area of Berlin, the first steps toward a television transmitter network followed in the late 1930s. The National Socialists' ambitions to create comprehensive networks for occupied Europe and later the whole world were foiled by defeat in war. The completion of radio and television networks took place separately in the two German states. Since the 1960s radio transmission in stereo mode and television transmission in color has kept German broadcasting in line with international norms.

Hartmut Petzold

See also Electricity; Information Processing; Radio; Siemens AG; Television

References
Bausch, Hans, ed. *Rundfunk in Deutschland.* 5 vols. Munich: DTV, 1980.

Bruch, Walter und Heide Riedel. *PAL Das Farbfernsehen.* Berlin (West): Deutsches Rundfunk-Museum, 1987.

Goebel, Gerhart. "Der Deutsche Rundfunk bis zum Inkrafttreten des Kopenhagener Wellenplans." *Archiv für das Post- und Fernmeldewesen* (1950), 353–454.

Reiss, Erwin. *"Wir senden Frohsinn": Fernsehen unterm Faschismus.* Berlin: Elefanten-Press-Verlag, 1979.

Siemens, Georg. *History of the House of Siemens.* 2 vols. Freiburg: K. Alber, 1957.

"100 Jahre Fernsprecher in Deutschland." *Archiv für Postgeschichte* (special edition, 1977).

Electricity

The close relationship between electricity and magnetism became known during the nineteenth century. A wire moved through a magnetic field induces an electric current, which in turn produces a magnetic field. Turning a current on in one wire or alternating the current's direction induces a current in a nearby wire. This new understanding provided the basis for electromagnets and electric generators, motors, and transformers. Telegraph systems were the first practical use of electricity. In 1849, Germany's first telegraph line connected Berlin and Frankfurt am Main. Werner von Siemens (1816–92), who founded Siemens & Halske in 1847, developed a viable dynamo in 1866 and in 1879 displayed the first electric locomotive. Heinrich Hertz (1857–94) demonstrated in 1888 connections between electromagnetism and light that James Clerk Maxwell (1831–79) had predicted and that later were adapted to produce radio and television.

Electrical systems expanded rapidly. In 1881, Emil Rathenau (1838–1915) licensed Edison's lighting patents, based on direct current (DC), for Germany. He established the Allgemeine Elektrizitätsgesellschaft (AEG) in 1887. AEG and Siemens & Halske dominated the market for electrical products by 1902. Their initial systems used DC, supplying small areas but using batteries to balance the load on equipment. Generators operated steadily, charging batteries in periods of low consumption and working together with batteries during peak periods of consumption.

The first DC central stations were built in large cities, which, in the 1890s, added alternating current (AC) components to existing DC systems or built pure AC systems. Some cities built mixed AC-DC systems to gain the benefits of both. AC systems could not use batteries but could employ transformers to increase voltage and reduce power losses in long-distance transmission. Supplying larger areas might include customers with varied consumption patterns that could help to balance the load on equipment. In 1910, the installed capacity of AC stations surpassed that of DC stations, and in 1913 they surpassed that of mixed AC-DC stations. The amount of electricity delivered from public nets doubled every four years between 1900 and 1914 and every nine years after World War I. As the size of turbines increased from 5,800 kilowatts (kW) in 1905 to 50,000 kW in 1921, transmission systems increased from 10 to 110 kilovolts (kV).

Expanding power systems involved institutional innovation. In 1879, Werner von Siemens helped to organize the Elektrotechnischer Verein (Electrotechnical Association) in Berlin, which in 1880 began publishing the periodical *Elektrotechnische Zeitschrift* (Electrotechnical journal). In 1882 and 1883, the Technische Hochschulen (technical universities) in Darmstadt and Berlin established the first chairs for electrical engineering. Representatives of power companies founded their own association, the Vereinigung der Elektrizitätswerke (Federation of Electrical Power Plants), in 1892. Local professional societies merged in 1893 to form the national Verband Deutscher Elektrotechniker (Association of German electrotechnicians). Another innovation involved local government. Building central stations required cooperation from increasingly professionalized municipal administrators. Expanding into surrounding county regions affected other levels of administration. Combining public influence and private capital in mixed public-private corporations resolved the political and financial difficulties of building regional systems. Mixed corporations, like the RWE in Essen, expanded by taking over town or county systems in exchange for stock and influence.

After 1914, power companies expanded. During World War I, Reich financing expanded generating capacity to produce war materials such as nitrogen and aluminum. Although some 4,100 power companies supplied Germany, most electricity was generated by a few large corporations, which successfully opposed the Socialization Law of 1919. In 1926, 24 companies generated 62.5 percent of electricity in public nets. Large mixed corporations and municipal companies competed with growing state companies, such as Bavaria's Bayernwerk AG, Prussia's Preussische Elektrizitätswerk AG, and the Reich's Elektrowerke AG. These companies resolved their boundary problems and began interconnecting. By 1929, the RWE's new 220 kV line joined north German coal stations with hydroelectric stations in the Alps and connected the RWE, Preussische Elektrizitätswerk, and Bayernwerk. The Reich Electrical Law of 1935 simply confirmed relationships developed during the 1920s. Electrical generation doubled between 1934 and 1939, since the war proved to be only a brief interruption—by 1947 the capacity of 1942 had been regained.

In 1948, the larger companies formed the Deutsche Verbundgesellschaft e.V. to increase technical integration. Its eight members provided 80 percent of the electricity generated in 1992. Turbines steadily increased in size to 150 megawatt (mW) in 1955 and 300 mW in 1965. The first 380 kV high-voltage line began operating in 1957. In cooperation with the federal government, power companies and electrical manufacturers introduced nuclear power stations modeled on American reactors promoted by the American Atoms for Peace program. In 1961, the first German nuclear reactor, at Kahl on the Rhine, began delivering electricity into the net, although difficulties with nuclear power remain. After 1990, the major problem became weaning the five new states away from the eastern electrical grid by making their electrical system compatible with the western grid.

Electricity allowed significant changes in production and consumption. Steam engines required shafts and belts for transmitting power, and shop floors had to be arranged accordingly. During the 1880s, DC motors served a variety of functions. Their speed could be easily regulated, and they, together with batteries, provided advantages to DC systems over AC systems. Michael von Dolivo-Dobrowolsky (1862–1919), working for AEG, designed AC motors that were displayed at the Frankfurt Electrical Exhibition in 1891 and placed in wide use by 1900. DC and AC motors could be located to suit production and designed to match working characteristics of each piece of equipment. Electrical manufacturers and industries collaborated in developing such equipment. Only three German cities had electric streetcars in 1891; in 1900, 104 cities did. Eventually, regional systems combined streetcars and light railroads. Large-scale electrification of the Bundesbahn (federal railroad) began only in the 1950s. By the early 1930s, 85 percent of the farms in Germany had electrical connections, compared to 12 percent in the United States and 65 percent in France.

Some industries generated electricity for self-consumption. Coal and steel companies in the Ruhr used cheap fuels, such as unmarketable waste coal or blast-furnace gas. Some chemical companies produced steam at high pressure to drive turbines and generate electricity before using it in chemical processes. After World War II, industrial power systems became increasingly integrated into public utility systems. Although larger power companies had begun promoting household consumption during the 1920s, not until the 1950s did significant numbers of households move beyond lighting to a wide use of electrical products.

Edmund N. Todd III

See also AEG AG; Coal Industry; Ecology; Energy; The Greens: Movement, Party, Ideology; Hertz, Heinrich; Nuclear Power and the Nuclear Industry; RWE; Siemens AG

References

Braun, Hans-Joachim and Walter Kaiser. *Energiewirtschaft, Automatisierung, Information seit 1914.* Propyläen Technikgeschichte, Vol. 5. Ed. Wolfgang König. Berlin: Propyläen, 1992.

Hughes, Thomas P. *Networks of Power: Electrification in Western Society, 1880–1930.* Baltimore, MD: The Johns Hopkins University Press, 1983.

König, Wolfgang and Wolfhard Weber. *Netzwerke, Stahl und Strom: 1840–1914.* Propyläen Technikgeschichte, Vol. 4. Ed. Wolfgang König. Berlin: Propyläen, 1990.

Elias, Norbert (1897–1990)

In his best-known work, *Über den Prozess der Zivilisation* (published as *The Civilizing Process*), 2 vols., 1939, Elias analyzed the effects of state formation in Europe on changes of individual personality structure. Throughout his writings, Elias applied sociological, historical, and social psychological approaches to the empirical and theoretical study of long-term social processes. Elias initially called his distinctive approach "figurational sociology" (*Was ist Soziologie?* [What is sociology?], 1970), but later came to prefer "process sociology." His books include *Involvement and Detachment*, 1987, *Über die Einsamkeit der Sterbenden in unseren Tagen* (published as *The Loneliness of the Dying*), 1985, *Time*, 1984, *Studien über die Deutschen* (The Germans), 1989, and *The Society of Individuals,* 1987.

Elias studied medicine, philosophy, and psychology in Breslau and Heidelberg, where he did postgraduate work in sociology with Alfred Weber (1868–1958). From 1929 he was Karl Mannheim's assistant (1893–1947) in Frankfurt. After his forced emigration in 1933, he moved first to Paris, then to London, before being appointed as a lecturer at the University of Leicester (1954–62). He also held posts at the Universities of Ghana, Amsterdam, Frankfurt (where he was professor emeritus), Konstanz, and elsewhere. In 1977 he received the Adorno Prize of the city of Frankfurt. In the late 1970s he returned to Germany to work at the Zentrum für Interdisziplinäre Forschung (center for interdisciplinary research) in Bielefeld. From 1984 until his death he lived in Amsterdam.

Elias achieved fame late in life, in his seventies. Only in 1969 was *The Civilizing Process,* which had been released just before the war by a small Swiss publishing house, republished in Germany, It soon became something of a cult book among German and Dutch students. *The Court Society* was published in the same year. Elias worked out the theory that he had first formulated in *The Civilizing Process* in his many essays, especially in the sociology of knowledge and science. For Elias, contemporary sociology is too preoccupied with theory construction. The primary weakness of theories that are formulated at a high level of abstraction is that they fail to reflect on their initial partisan commitments and their dependence on a relatively narrow, contemporary point of departure. Theory as such is an insufficient remedy against the sociologist's involvement in the short-lived struggles of the moment. However, comparative historical research alone cannot provide the explanations sought by the sociologist, who aims at explanations of the long-term development of human societies. Both need to be integrated into a frame of reference without ideological encrustations. The high-level syntheses pursued by sociologists require the employment of theoretical models not merely for the sake of empirical testability but in order to safeguard the very object of sociological inquiry, which is to make the human past intelligible and to raise questions about the future of present-day societies.

Volker Meja

See also Kultur; Mannheim, Karl; Sociology; Weber, Alfred

References

Elias, Norbert. *The Germans: Power Struggles and the Development of Habitus in the Nineteenth and Twentieth Centuries.* Ed. Michael Schroter. New York, NY. Columbia University Press, 1996.

———. *Reflections on a Life.* Cambridge: Polity Press, 1994.

Gleichmann, P.R. et al., eds. *Human Figurations: Essays for Norbert Elias.* Amsterdam: Amsterdams Sociologisch Tijdschrift, 1977.

Korte, Hermann. *Über Norbert Elias. Das Werden eines Menschenwissenschaftlers.* Frankfurt am Main: Suhrkamp, 1988.

Mennell, Stephen. *Norbert Elias. Civilization and the Human Self-Image.* Oxford: Basil Blackwell, 1989.

Emigration

Any line graph depicting emigration from Germany between 1871 and 1990 would be characterized by steep ups and downs that resemble four large waves peaking in 1873, 1882, 1923, and 1950. Each of these waves represents a phase exhibiting unique push and pull factors, shifting source areas, and changing structural features. Between 1871 and 1990, gross emigration from Germany amounted to an estimated 4.7 million people.

The first two waves—1864–73, with more than one million emigrants, and 1880–93, with 1.8 million emigrants—formed the tail end of an exodus between 1820 and 1914 of almost 6 million Germans. Ten percent of them, however, are estimated to have returned. This mass exodus was mostly overseas migration, destined for the United States (89 percent), Canada (1.3 percent), Brazil (2 percent), Argentina (1871–1914: 0.9 percent) and Australia (1.3 percent). Major overland emigration to the Habsburg and Russian empires decreased drastically during the first half of the nineteenth century and ceased after 1871.

Traditionally, the bulk of Germany's emigrants had hailed from the southwestern regions of Alsace, Baden, Württemberg, Hesse, and the Palatinate. Not until the 1860s did central Germany become a major source area of emigration. By the 1880s, most of Germany's emigrants originated in the northeastern provinces of Prussia, which had hitherto contributed only minimally to emigration. The shifting of the geographical emigration center from southwest to northeast Germany accompanied a change in the structure of emigration. The southwest German emigration included largely families headed by small, independent farmers, tradesmen, and artisans. By the 1880s and early 1890s, Germany's northeast generated an increasing proportion of day laborers and farmhands gathered from the big estates east of the Elbe River; they tended to emigrate as individuals and exhibited a higher rate of return migration.

The chief underlying motivation for the nineteenth-century mass exodus was Germany's transition from an agrarian to an industrial state and the concomitant urbanization, internal migration, and revolution of rising (and at first unsatisfied) expectations. In the southwest, rapid population growth, traditional division of peasant inheritances, and occupational restructuring produced acute overpopulation and pauperism until, in the 1870s, industry became able to absorb the labor surplus. Improved communications and enterprising shipping promoters facilitated the exodus. The growth of the American economy held out the hope of rapid upward mobility for migrants in the New World. Networks of trans-Atlantic contacts, chain migrations, and prepaid tickets lowered the threshold of the individual's decision to emigrate. Not affected by any exit or entry restrictions, the nineteenth-century mass exodus developed a suction of its own until Germany's burgeoning industrial expansion and the end to the Depression of 1873–95 raised living standards and caused a labor shortage again.

Various restrictive factors, such as the postwar exclusion of German immigration (until 1921 in the United States,

1923 in Canada, 1925 in Australia, and 1928 in New Zealand), the American restrictive quota legislation, and Canada's preference for agriculturists, altered Germany's post–World War I immigration pattern. After 1930, Canada restricted access to wealthy farmers and American consuls drastically reduced the number of visas issued so that fewer than half of the German quota spaces were filled. Major push factors were the backlog of demand for emigration since 1914 and the uprooting experience of war, revolutionary upheaval, political instability, and economic insecurity. Also, influx of 1.4 million German refugees from the territories ceded by the Treaty of Versailles increased population density.

Structurally, post–World War I Germany's emigration pattern was even more typically than before the war a labor-migration system consisting of skilled and unskilled workers, farmhands, domestic servants, and office clerks. Of these, 60 percent migrated as single individuals without families. Germany contributed 604,700 emigrants for the period 1919–33. Of these, 71 percent went to the United States, 10.2 percent to Brazil, 8.6 percent to Argentina, and 5 percent to Canada. During the same period, the seaports of Hamburg and Bremen recorded 223,000 return migrants. The interwar emigration from Germany peaked in 1923 with 115,400 emigrants and reached its nadir in 1939 with 80,000.

Third Reich policies caused a German-Jewish exodus and a return migration of Germans from North America. From 1933 to 1939, European ports counted 117,000 overseas emigrants from Germany, but the actual German-Jewish exodus by 1941 has been estimated at 300,000 from Germany (1937 borders) and at 450,000-600,000 from the enlarged Germany of 1939. Many German Jews sought temporary asylum in neighboring European countries and in Shanghai. Between 1933 and 1941, about 100,000 of them emigrated to the United States, 80,000 to Latin America, and 55,000 to Palestine. In October 1941, Germany officially prohibited emigration. The recorded return of Germans from North America, between 1934 and 1937, was 190,000.

Unique post–World War II conditions shaped the fourth and last German emigration wave. Population pressure was enormous, as occupied and war-ravaged West Germany had to accommodate 11.6 million German expellees and refugees by 1950, plus 1.6 million non-German displaced persons (DPs) in 1946. Despite strong push factors for several years after 1945, German nationals were prohibited from leaving occupied Germany as well as from entering their traditional countries of immigration. Germany's only emigrants from 1945 to 1950 were 655,000 DPs resettled by the International Refugee Organization.

Not surprisingly, after the removal of exit and entry barriers in 1950, emigration from Germany soared to 128,600 arrivals recorded in the United States in 1950 and 125,000 departures recorded in Germany in 1951 (one-quarter of them identified as German expellees from the east). By 1958, the exodus leveled off at below 20,000, and Germany began recruiting a rapidly growing number of foreign "guest workers." From 1950 to 1961, German statistics registered 780,000 emigrants. Of the close to 1.2 million Germans who emigrated to North America and Australia between 1950 and 1969, the United States had admitted 775,000 and Canada 300,000.

Gerhard P. Bassler

See also Agriculture; Artisans/Craftsmen; Depression (1873–95); Expulsion and Exile of Scientists and Scholars; Migration; Minorities, Ethnocultural and Foreign; Poverty; Refugees; Regional Economic Development; Unemployment

References

Bade, Klaus J., ed. *Auswanderer, Wanderarbeiter, Gastarbeiter: Bevölkerung Arbeitsmarkt und Wanderung in Deutschland seit der Mitte des 19. Jahrhunderts.* Vol. 1. Ostfildern: Scripta Mercaturae Verlag, 1984.

———. *Deutsche im Ausland—Fremde in Deutschland: Migration in Geschichte und Gegenwart.* Munich: C.H. Beck, 1992.

Bickelmann, Hartmut. *Deutsche Überseewanderung in der Weimarer Zeit.* Wiesbaden: Steiner, 1980.

Grossmann, Kurt R. *Emigration: Geschichte der Hitler Flüchtlinge, 1933–1945.* Frankfurt am Main: Europäische Verlagsanstalt, 1969.

Köllmann, Wolfgang and Peter Marschalck. "German Emigration to the United States." *Perspectives in American History.* 7 vols. Ed. D. Fleming and B. Bailyn. Cambridge, MA: Harvard University Press, 1974, 499–554.

Marschalck, Peter. *Deutsche Überseewanderung im 19. Jahrhundert.* Stuttgart: E. Klett, 1973.

Moltmann, Günter. "American-German Return Migration in the Nineteenth and Early Twentieth Centuries." *Central European History* 8 (1980), 378–92.

Wetzel, Juliane. "Auswanderung aus Deutschland." *Die Juden in Deutschland 1933–1945.* Ed. Wolfgang Benz. Munich: C.H. Beck, 1989, 413–98.

Energy

Between 1870 and 1990, Germans obtained energy from a changing mixture of sources, including animals, wood, water, coal, petroleum, natural gas, and nuclear power. The particular mix of energy sources at a given time influenced and reflected dominant technological systems, domestic power relations, and Germany's foreign relations.

By far the most important source of energy from the mid-nineteenth century through the early 1960s was coal, of which Germany possessed two major types. Hard coal from the Ruhr district was particularly high in energy content and was also well suited to use in the steel industry that emerged in the last third of the nineteenth century. Lower in energy content than hard coal, brown coal was less economical to transport. Industries depending on it for power or raw materials had to be located near the mines. Main brown coal reserves lay near Cologne, with even greater holdings in central Germany.

Use of domestic coal stocks was closely connected to technological change in Germany. Coal fueled Germany's first industrial revolution, which featured widespread use of steam engines and large-scale production of iron and steel. It also played a vital role in the development of the key industries of the second industrial revolution, electrical goods and chemicals. Both phases used coal for power. Moreover, electrical goods themselves stimulated demand for coal; chemical products used it in the manufacturing of dyes and, later, of pharmaceuticals. By World War I, the chemical industry also used coal to produce synthetic nitrogen, synthetic rubber, and rudimentary plastics.

The centrality of coal to Germany's economic and technological development through World War I translated into political power for those who controlled the resource; coal, iron, and steel producers constituted one of the most powerful interest groups in Imperial Germany. They developed the country's transportation system, supplied the needs of German armies, shaped the tariff law of 1879, and influenced Germany's battleship-building program beginning in the late 1890s. The growing output of heavy industry was accomplished in part through an expansion of the labor force, which meant that it also became a locus for problems in labor relations.

Coal and the industries based on it also provided a basis for Germany's growing prominence and power in international affairs before 1914. Germany used the secure domestic resource to produce military hardware and also to enhance her foreign trade position. By 1913, for example, the German chemical industry controlled nearly 90 percent of the lucrative international trade in dyestuffs.

By the 1920s, petroleum challenged the status of coal and its associated industries around the world. Cleaner, higher in energy content, and more easily transportable than coal, petroleum was especially suitable for servicing the burgeoning automobile industry. Despite extensive exploration, Germans found little petroleum within their borders. However, German chemists developed processes to produce synthetic petroleum from domestic coal; large-scale production began in 1927. Gasoline produced from coal was relatively expensive, but provided a vital and secure input for the German military through 1945.

Synthetic fuel and other processes transformed domestic coal into materials that could substitute for imports; their significance thus extended beyond the economic sphere. From the 1920s through 1945, the ability of chemistry to overcome Germany's natural resource limitations in many vital areas enabled Nazis and others to dream of self-sufficiency, which for the Nazis was a step toward an aggressive war of expansion. Rapidly declining synthetic fuel production following intensive Allied bombing played an important role in the collapse of the Nazi regime in early 1945.

Two key trends characterize the history of German energy after 1945. First, beginning in the 1950s the German successor states developed nuclear power, which today supplies significant amounts of electricity. Second, both states began to rely far more heavily on petroleum as a primary energy source. This development was far more pronounced in the Federal Republic of Germany (FRG) than in the German Democratic Republic (GDR): by 1973, oil provided 55 percent of the FRG's energy needs. After the first oil crisis (1973–74), interest in petroleum declined slightly in favor of coal, natural gas, and alternative sources. In contrast, the GDR in 1970 used (primarily brown) coal to meet 87 percent of its energy needs, a figure that declined to 75 percent in 1984. Oil covered 11 percent of the GDR's demand in 1984.

As before 1945, energy choices had political consequences. Control of German coal was a primary motivation for moves toward European integration in the 1950s. The FRG's growing reliance on petroleum was also part of a trend toward increasing dependence on overseas trade and resources and was connected closely to the FRG's continued competitiveness internationally and to its integration into the Western world economy. The GDR's continued reliance on domestic coal resources resulted largely from its integration into the Soviet Bloc and its relative isolation from Western markets. The inefficiency of this energy source and resultant pollution helped to cause the decline of the GDR.

German unification in 1990 involved further changes in energy use and allocation. Decommissioning unsafe nuclear reactors, deemphasizing brown coal, and increasing reliance on petroleum and gas are the present policies in the former GDR. Increased emphasis on conservation and growing awareness of the environmental consequences of energy usage constitute major trends.

Raymond Stokes

See also Coal Industry; Electricity; Industrialization; Nuclear Power and the Nuclear Industry; Ruhr Region

References

Friedrich Ebert Stiftung, ed. *Die Energiepolitik der DDR: Mangelverwaltung zwischen Kernkraft und Braunkohle.* Bonn: Verlag Neue Gesellschaft, 1988.

Gillingham, John. *Coal, Steel, and the Rebirth of Europe: The Germans and French from Ruhr Conflict to Economic Community.* New York, NY: Cambridge University Press, 1991.

———. *Industry and Politics in the Third Reich: Ruhr Coal, Hitler and Europe.* New York, NY: Columbia University Press, 1985.

Horn, Manfred. *Die Energiepolitik der Bundesregierung von 1958 bis 1972.* Berlin: Duncker & Humblot, 1977.

Hughes, Thomas P. *Networks of Power: Electrification in Western Society, 1880–1930.* Baltimore, MD: Johns Hopkins University Press, 1983.

Landes, David. *The Unbound Prometheus: Technological Change and Industrial Development in Western Europe from 1750 to the Present.* New York, NY: Cambridge University Press, 1969.

Pounds, Norman. *An Historic Geography of Western Europe, 1800–1914.* New York, NY: Cambridge University Press, 1985.

Roseman, Mark. *Recasting the Ruhr, 1945–1958: Manpower, Economic Recovery and Labour Relations.* New York, NY: Berg, 1992.

Stokes, Raymond G. *Opting for Oil: The Political Economy of Technological Change in the West German Chemical Industry, 1945–1961.* New York, NY: Cambridge, 1994.

Walker, Mark. *German National Socialism and the Quest for Nuclear Power, 1939–1949.* New York, NY: Cambridge, 1989.

Weisbrod, Bernd. *Schwerindustrie in der Weimarer Republik.* Wuppertal: P. Hammer Verlag, 1978.

Winnacker, Karl and Karl Wirtz. *Nuclear Energy in Germany.* La Grange Park: American Nuclear Society, 1979.

Engels, Friedrich (1820–95)

The names of Friedrich Engels and Karl Marx (1818–83) are linked inextricably and for good reason. As the chief founders of modern Communism, they collaborated closely from 1844 until Marx's death, (1883), co-authored *The Communist Manifesto,* 1848, as well as other works, and, although some scholars have emphasized certain differences in their outlooks, they themselves believed themselves to be in essential agreement on all theoretical and political matters. As an author, Engels did much to popularize Marx's theories, but he also enjoyed considerable recognition as a socialist thinker through his own writings. Always a dependable and untiring correspondent, Engels also distinguished himself as an advisor to socialists in numerous countries, a contribution equaled by no other leading nineteenth-century socialist.

Engels's first-hand experience with English industrial workers commenced in 1842 when he arrived in Manchester to work in the family manufacturing firm. He published the results of his investigations in *Die Lage der arbeitenden Klasse in England* (published as *The Condition of the Working Class in England in 1844*), 1845, a book that soon became a socialist classic. Engels was a master polemicist, evident in his attack on Eugen Dühring, *Herr Eugen Dührings Umwalzung der Wissenschaft* (published as *Herr Eugen Dühring's Revolution in Science*), serialized in the newspaper, *Vorwärts,* 1877–78. Three chapters from this work were assembled in a small booklet, *Entwicklung des Sozialismus von der Utopie zur Wissenschaft* (published as *Socialism: Utopian and Scientific*), 1880, which quickly became one of the most popular and widely read introductions to Marxist socialism. In *Ursprünge der Familie, des Privateigentums und des Staates* (published as *The Origins of the Family, Private Property and the State*), 1884, Engels sought to develop a materialist anthropology, a task that Marx had intended to undertake. Engels was also deeply interested in military affairs and may be recognized as international socialism's first expert in that area.

At the apex of his reputation in the 1880s and 1890s, Engels devoted the final years of his life to editing volumes 2 and 3 of *Das Kapital* (published as *Capital*), 1885 and 1895, working closely with the leaders of the Second Socialist International after its founding (1889), and attempting, though unsuccessfully, to complete a major theoretical work on dialectics, science, and nature. *The Dialectics of Nature* (*Dialetik der Natur*) was published posthumously in English translation in 1940. Until the very end, socialists in many countries turned to Friedrich Engels for counsel and guidance.

Vernon Lidtke

See also Bebel, August; Bernstein, Eduard; Ecology; Kautsky, Karl; Liebknecht, Wilhelm; Luxemburg, Rosa; Marx, Karl; Social Democratic Party, 1871–1918

References
Cornu, Auguste. *Karl Marx et Friedrich Engels: Leur vie et leur oeuvre.* 4 vols. Paris: Presses universitaire de France, 1955.
Engels, Friedrich. *Engels as Military Critic.* Ed. W.H. Chaloner and W.O. Henderson. Manchester: Manchester University Press, 1959.
Eubanks, Cecil L. *Karl Marx and Friedrich Engels: An Analytical Bibliography.* 2nd ed. New York, NY: Garland Publishers, 1984.
Hunley, J.D. *The Life and Thought of Friedrich Engels: A Reinterpretation.* New Haven, CT: Yale University Press, 1991.
Levine, Norman. *The Tragic Deception: Marx contra Engels.* Santa Barbara, CA: Clio Books, 1975.
Mayer, Gustav. *Friedrich Engels: Eine Biographie.* 2 vols. 2nd ed. The Hague: Martinus Nijhoff, 1934.
Rigby, S.H. *Engels and the Formation of Marxism: History, Dialectics, and Revolution.* Manchester: Manchester University Press, 1992.

Engineering

Engineering, like most disciplines, possesses certain uniquely national features. In Germany, engineering in the late 1870s began a rapid ascent to global leadership in the design and manufacture of high-quality industrial machinery. It came to excel in complex, labor-intensive mechanical and electromechanical equipment for the domestic as well as the export market. Except for a brief interruption after World War II, Germany has been able to maintain this enviable position.

German engineering also has long had weaknesses. Standardization, capital intensity, mass production, distribution, and, since the 1960s, new fields such as computers and biotechnology have lagged behind the United States or Japan. Costs have been high since the 1920s. On balance, however, the strengths have outweighed the weaknesses, and the overall picture is one of a proud and thriving engineering tradition that dates back well over a century. Engineering therefore is rightly perceived as an island of steadfastness and success amid the trauma and discontinuity that have engulfed Germany's national experience since the 1870s. This and the rise of technological society in general have made engineering an increasingly important factor in post–World War II German society.

The national characteristics of Germany's engineering tradition are largely a product of nineteenth-century social circumstances. Two critical agencies in this regard were the long-standing social marginalization of engineering and the primacy of school culture over apprenticeship and experience in the training of engineers. Social barriers segregated work in industry and engineering from respectable pursuits such as government service and the academic professions. In a society dominated by neohumanist values and bureaucratic and military institutions, professional status rested on classical secondary schools, university education, and an elaborate system of educational certifications and career entitlements. Engineering had a separate, socially inferior educational system without classical preparation or the right to transfer to nontechnical schools and professions.

Other European countries knew similarly bifurcated systems of technical and nontechnical education before World War II, but none made the boundaries between them quite as rigid, invidious, and impenetrable as did nineteenth-century Germany. The caste-like German system effectively prevented the assimilation between engineers and the older elites that was possible elsewhere.

The other side of this, however, was that it gave Germany the self-sustaining, permanently energized, and successful engineering culture that set it apart from other European countries. German engineers were driven to build up their own—competing and alternative—systems of ideology and education, culminating in formidable institutes of higher technical education (*Technische Hochschulen*), their own professional and doctoral degrees (from 1899), and technocratic critiques of the empire's and the Weimar Republic's institutions. The history of the Verein Deutscher Ingenieure, Germany's largest and best-known professional engineering association (founded 1856), is exemplary in this regard.

The contrast with Great Britain is especially striking. Owing to opportunities of social assimilation and the absence of good engineering schools, Great Britain saw its technical lead slip away and its proud engineering tradition lose steam in the late nineteenth century. Germany averted a similar loss of momentum, even though its engineers after 1945 shed most of the countercultural aspects of their historic identity. Their separate, outsider culture moved into the void left by the destruction of the inherited sociopolitical hierarchy in the Third Reich. Engineering and technology thereby became a central part of the core values that have governed East and West German society after World War II.

Germany historically put much greater emphasis on schools to produce its engineering profession than did countries such as Great Britain and the United States. While the latter began moving toward school-based engineering education in the 1880s and 1920s, respectively, Germany had used technical schools as a way to promote industrialization and technological progress since the early nineteenth century. Largely because of socially inspired emulation of the universities and natural sciences, German engineering schools early on developed a penchant for theory, abstraction, and mathematics. They tended to neglect practical training and shop experience. This stimulated the emergence of a technological culture oriented toward individuality and perfectionism in design rather than ease of production and assembly. Production-related development took a back seat to innovation in the form of new designs on paper. Customization, labor intensiveness, high costs, and short production runs were the consequence.

School culture also encouraged the early academization and professionalization of engineers. This trend, however, was interrupted by the emergence of a new, second tier of nonacademic and more practical engineering schools after 1880. While the new schools strengthened the flexibility and breadth of German engineering, they also contributed to oversupply and career crowding after the early 1900s. These problems did not disappear until the mid-1930s and were a major factor in the discontent and unemployment of engineers during the Weimar period. The dualism between older, university-level engineering schools and newer, nonacademic ones also meant that engineering remained a heterogeneous and factionalized profession until the 1960s. By then academization of the second wave of engineering schools had evolved sufficiently far to initiate a phase of reconciliation and renewed homogenization.

Kees Gispen

See also Education; Inventions; Professions; Technical Training, Technical Institutes, and Universities; Technology; Universities

References

Gispen, Kees. *New Profession, Old Order: Engineers and German Society, 1815–1914.* Cambridge: Cambridge University Press, 1989.

Jarausch, Konrad. *The Unfree Professions: German Lawyers, Teachers, and Engineers, 1900–1950.* New York, NY: Oxford University Press, 1990.

König, Wolfgang, ed. *Netzwerke Stahl und Strom 1840 bis 1914. Propyläen Technikgeschichte,* vol. 4. Ed. Wolfgang König and Wolfhard Weber. Berlin: Propyläen Verlag, 1990.

Ludwig, Karl-Heinz. *Technik und Ingenieure im Dritten Reich.* Düsseldorf: Droste Verlag, 1974.

Ludwig, Karl-Heinz and Wolfgang König, eds. *Technik, Ingenieure und Gesellschaft: Geschichte des Vereins Deutscher Ingenieure 1856–1981.* Düsseldorf: VDI-Verlag GmbH, 1981.

Lundgreen, Peter, ed. *Ingenieure in Deutschland, 1770–1990.* Frankfurt am Main: Campus Verlag, 1994.

Enzensberger, Hans Magnus (1929–)

Hans Magnus Enzensberger is one of the most prolific contemporary West German intellectuals and authors. His work encompasses essays, theoretical treatises, radio features, translations, travel accounts, documentary literature, and plays. He lived for extended periods of time in Norway, Rome (scholarship at the Villa Massimo 1959–60), and the United States, where he left a visiting professorship (1968) in order to live in Cuba.

Poetry is Enzensberger's forte as a literary writer. His first anthology of politically committed poetry (*verteidigung der wölfe* [Defense of the wolves], 1957) represented a break with the hermetic style that dominated West German poetry after World War II. From 1964 to 1975, he took a break from poetry and devoted these years of political upheaval to documentary literature such as *Das Verhör von Habana* (published as *The Interrogation of Havana*), 1970 and *Der kurze Sommer der Anarchie* (The short summer of anarchy), 1972. He has

spoken out on many political issues. Much of his work focuses on the dialectic of politics and aesthetics and the role of the intellectual in a society of mass media, such as "Bewusstseins-Industrie" (Consciousness-industry), 1962.

Together with K.M. Michel, he founded and edited (until 1975) the monthly journal, *Kursbuch* (Timetable), which quickly became a mouthpiece of the New Left and the student movement (1967–72). When he turned away from the documentary genres in the mid-1970s with a new anthology of poetry (*Mausoleum*, 1975) and a new journal, *TransAtlantik*, the left denounced him as betraying its political project. This is, however, a misperception of an intellectual who has always been an independent thinker and a poet who knows about the value and the limitations of a committed literature in contemporary society.

Sabine von Dirke

See also Aesthetics; Drama; Extra-Parliamentary Opposition; Federal Republic of Germany: Literature; Literary Criticism; Poetry

References

Deitschreit, Frank. *Hans Magnus Enzensberger.* Stuttgart: Metzler, 1986.

Enzensberger, Hans Magnus. "Bewusstseins-Industrie." *Einzelheiten I.* Frankfurt am Main: Suhrkamp, 1962.

———. *Die Gedichte.* Frankfurt am Main: Suhrkamp, 1983.

———. *Politische Brotsamen: Essays.* Frankfurt am Main: Suhrkamp, 1982.

Grimm, Reinhold. *Texturen: Essays und anderes zu Hans Magnus Enzensberger.* New York: Peter Lang, 1984.

Grimm, Reinhold, ed. *Hans Magnus Enzensberger: Materialien.* Frankfurt am Main: Suhrkamp, 1984.

Erhard, Ludwig (1897–1977)

Ludwig Erhard, the person most identified with Germany's post–World War II Economic Miracle, was born on April 2, 1897, in Fürth, Bavaria. He studied business in Munich in 1913. After World War I, he studied economics, business, and sociology at the Trade College (*Handelshochschule*) of Nuremberg. He received his doctorate from the University of Frankfurt am Main in 1924 with a dissertation on money and international currencies. After a few years in business, Erhard joined the Institut für Wirtschaftsbeobachtung (Institute for Economic Observation) of the Nuremberg Trade College in 1928, and soon became its department head. In 1942, he became the director of Nuremberg's Institute for Industrial Research, focusing on consumer-goods industries.

During the war years, Erhard and others of the "Freiburg School," such as Alfred Müller-Armack, Wilhelm Röpke, Alexander Rüstow, Leonhard Miksch, and Walter Eucken, carefully considered overcoming the problems of the Fascist central-planning system. After the war, Erhard came to the attention of the American authorities in Nuremberg, and in September 1945 they made him minister for commerce and trade in Bavaria. In 1947 he became honorary professor of

Ludwig Erhard. Photo by Günter Rittner. Courtesy of German Information Center, New York.

Harvard, Columbia, and other universities. He contributed several publications to the literature on the social market economy.

Phillip J. Bryson

See also Adenauer, Konrad; Bizone; Chancellor's Office; Christian Democratic Union; Economic Miracle; Federal Republic of Germany; Postwar European Integration and Germany

References

Erhard, Ludwig. *Prosperity through Competition.* London: Thames and Hudson, 1958.

Hoell, Günter. "Ludwig Erhard." *Ökonomen Lexikon.* Ed. Werner Krause, Karl-Heinz Graupner, and Rolf Sieber. Berlin: Dietz Verlag, 1989, 137–38.

Loewenstern, Enno von. "The Man Who Pulled West Germany Out of Poverty." *The Wall Street Journal.* November 21, 1989, A18.

Pounds, Norman J.G. *The Economic Pattern of Modern Germany.* London: John Murray, 1963.

Thieme, H. Jörg. *Soziale Marktwirtschaft: Ordnungskonzeption und wirtschaftspolitische Gestaltung.* Munich: C.H. Beck, 1991.

Wünsche, Horst Friedrich. *Ludwig Erhards Gesellschafts- und Wirtschaftskonzeption: Soziale Marktwirtschaft als Politische Ökonomie.* Bonn: Verlag Bonn Aktuell, 1986.

economic policy at the University of Munich, where his preferences for a neo-liberal economic order became well known. In October 1947 he became chairman of the bizonal (American-British) Commission for Money and Credit in Frankfurt am Main. Here, foundations were laid for the currency reform of the following year and for the elimination of price and other controls that had been considered essential and retained under the occupation authorities.

In the elections of 1949, Erhard became minister of economics in the first coalition government under Chancellor Konrad Adenauer. He retained this position until 1963, during which time he presided over the establishment of the "social market economy." His convictions, which were liberal in the European sense, predisposed him to oppose economic planning, cartels, and trade protectionism. Once in a position of authority, he pursued the privatization of state-owned enterprises, the deregulation of the economy, and the achievement of a convertible currency. So strong was the resulting recovery that the effort came to be known as the Economic Miracle.

For Erhard, economic growth was not the end of policy but merely the means of promoting individual well-being; nothing could achieve this more effectively than the functioning of the free but "social" market. Such a market is directed by policies assuring that all citizens share in material improvements.

In 1963, he replaced Adenauer as chancellor of the Federal Republic, but served only until 1966. Later, Erhard was a visiting professor in Munich and Bonn, as well as at

Erkelenz, Anton (1878–1945)

A mechanic, liberal union functionary, and politician, Anton Erkelenz was a member of the German Democratic Party (DDP) in the Weimar Republic until 1930, when he joined the Social Democratic Party (SPD). He was also a prolific writer and, with Gertrud Bäumer (1873–1954), co-editor of Friedrich Naumann's (1860–1919) periodical *Die Hilfe* (Help), 1923–30, and the editor of the machinists' weekly *Der Regulator* (The regulator), 1919–33. His political career began in the liberal Hirsch-Duncker union movement in 1902. In 1919 he was elected to the National Assembly, and from 1920 to 1930 he was a DDP member of the Reichstag.

As a self-made man without formal education, Erkelenz was somewhat of an outsider in the DDP. Yet he was not only a prominent spokesman of its left-wing and social-liberal traditions, but also the chairman of its managing committee (*Vorstand*) from 1921 to 1929. The position was well-deserved. The party's Vorstand was concerned essentially with organizational matters and needed a man like Erkelenz who believed that politics had to be a full-time profession. He took Naumann's teachings seriously and tried to turn the DDP into a modern mass organization in a state of permanent mobilization. Furthermore, he was determined to infuse democratic principles, such as dispersal of authority and ultimate control of policymaking by the rank and file, into that organization. He hoped that a party based on such principles would accommodate not only educated middle-class liberals but also workers and commercial employees (whom he himself represented).

In matters of policy on national and international issues, Erkelenz was a forceful fighter for democratic liberalism and republicanism. He pleaded eloquently for close cooperation with the Social Democrats, opposed compromises with the nationalist, antirepublican right, and assiduously propagated ideas of international reconciliation. Ill health after 1927 forced him to give up the fight and his leadership positions, but it was the founding of the State Party in 1930 by other Democrats and the Young German Order that prompted him to quit and join the SPD.

In addition to the innumerable articles and pamphlets that Erkelenz published, he wrote, among other books, *Moderne Sozialpolitik* (Modern social policy), 1926, and edited *Zehn Jahre Deutsche Republik: ein Handbuch für republikanische Politik* (Ten years of the German republic: a handbook for republican politics), 1928.

Attila Chanady

See also Bäumer, Gertrud; German Democratic Party; Liberalism; Naumann, Friedrich; Social Democratic Party; Weimar Germany

References
Brantz, Rennie W. "Anton Erkelenz, the Hirsch-Duncker Trade Unions, and the German Democratic Party." Unpublished doctoral dissertation. Ohio State University, 1973.

Frye, Bruce B. *Liberal Democrats in the Weimar Republic: The History of the German Democratic Party and the German State Party.* Carbondale, IL: Southern Illinois University Press, 1985.

Hess, Jürgen C. *"Das ganze Deutschland soll es sein." Demokratischer Nationalismus in der Weimar Republik am Beispiel der Deutschen Demokratischen Partei.* Stuttgart: Klett-Cotta, 1977.

Jones, Larry E. *German Liberalism and the Dissolution of the Weimar Party System 1918–1933.* Chapel Hill, NC: University of North Carolina Press, 1988.

Schneider, Werner. *Die Deutsche Demokratische Partei in der Weimarer Republik 1924–1930.* Munich: Fink, 1978.

Stephan, Werner. *Aufstieg und Verfall des Linksliberalismus 1918–1933: Geschichte der Deutschen Demokratischen Partei.* Göttingen: Vandenhoeck & Ruprecht, 1973.

Erler, Fritz Karl Gustav (1913–67)

One of the sharpest minds among the younger generation of post-1945 Social Democratic Party (SPD) politicians, a leading proponent of party reform, as well as the party's foreign- and defense-policy spokesman, Fritz Erler was born in the Prenzlauer Berg working-class section of Berlin. His parents came from a petit-bourgeois and proletarian milieu. His father, a barber, staunchly supported Friedrich Ebert (1871–1925) and reform Social Democracy. Both parents were actively interested in working-class politics.

Fritz, the youngest of the Erler children, was the only one for whom sufficient resources were found to attend secondary school. He proved to be a brilliant student and gained his *Abitur* (senior matriculation) in 1932. Through a student exchange he went to France, where he became not only familiar with the native language but developed a lifelong sympathy for France. As a student he became politically active by joining the Sozialistische Arbeiterjugend (SAJ; Socialist Workers' Youth), in 1928. The leftist SAJ tended to be critical of the established SPD leadership, yet rejected the Communist Party and sought to overcome the division within the German working-class movement.

When the Nazis came to power, Erler joined the SAJ-affiliated underground opposition group Neu Beginnen (New Beginnings). In November 1938, he was arrested by the Gestapo and spent the rest of the Nazi years in prison and concentration camps. His experience with the totalitarian state strengthened his determination that Social Democrats must not only espouse humanitarian values but must gain power to put such values into effect.

At the end of the war, Erler joined the civil service of Württemberg-Hohenzollern and became an associate of Carlo Schmid, that state's provisional head of government. In 1947, he became a member of the Württemberg-Hohenzollern legislature as well as district administrator (*Landrat*) of Tuttlingen. He was also elected to the first FRG Bundestag in 1949. Over the next 15 years, he gained election to various party, Bundestag, and international institution offices, among them SPD central committee deputy party whip, SPD deputy chairman, Bundestag party caucus chairman, deputy chairman of the Bundestag standing committee on European security and defense, and vice president of the Institute for Strategic Studies in London.

Along with Carlo Schmid (1896–1979), Herbert Wehner (1906–90), and Willy Brandt (1913–92), Erler was one of the "young Turks" determined to reform the SPD and lead it to power. A brilliant parliamentary debater and an unsentimental political analyst, Erler prepared the SPD for the responsibilities of office in Bonn.

Juergen C. Doerr

See also Brandt, Willy; Federal Republic of Germany; Resistance; Schmid, Carlo; Social Democratic Party, 1918–90; Wehner, Herbert; Youth Movements

References
Soell, Hartmut. *Fritz Erler—Eine politische Biographie.* 2 vols. Berlin: Verlag J.H. Dietz Nachf., 1976.

Ernst, Max (1891–1976)

Surrealist artist Max Ernst, a prolific innovator in various media, was briefly associated with the German avant garde, but spent most of his career in France. In works such as *Oedipus Rex,* 1921, the collage-novel *Une Semaine de bonté,* 1934, and *Europe after the Rain,* 1940–42, Ernst explored the mysteries of human psychology and the natural world with protean imagination and unprecedented freedom.

Born in Brühl, near Cologne, Ernst attended university at Bonn, then served in the German army during World War I. Back in Cologne, he married Luise Strauss, and by 1919 was an active member of Dada, an international anti-art movement begun during the war. Less anarchic or political than Dada, Ernst's early work is characterized by visionary transformations of material. Collages such as *The Song of the Flesh*, 1920, employ images culled from obsolescent science texts and from commercial catalogues in irrational mixed-media compositions, often with obscure, poetic titles handwritten on the margins.

Ernst moved to Paris in 1921, and by 1924 was a central figure among the poets and artists who founded the surrealist movement. In his prodigious work of the next decade, the surrealist fascination with chance events, the unconscious, dreams, and sexual desire is evident. In 1925 he discovered *frottage*, pencil rubbings from textured surfaces, and produced his *Histoire Naturelle* series. In 1929 he published *La Femme 100 têtes*, the first of his major collage-novels, which recombined outmoded popular illustrations into haunting, psychosexual pictorial narratives.

In the 1930s, Ernst concentrated increasingly on painting, employing surrealist techniques in dense, vertiginous, hallucinatory pictures, such as *The Entire City*, 1935–36. He left his second wife, Marie-Berth Aurenche, moved in 1938 to southern France with English artist Leonora Carrington, and, in 1941, after repeated problems with French and German authorities, emigrated to the United States, sponsored by the American heiress and art collector Peggy Guggenheim (1898–1979), who soon became his third wife.

In New York, Ernst worked with André Breton (1896–1966) and other exiled surrealists on the journal *VVV* (1942–44). In 1946, he moved with his fourth wife, American painter Dorothea Tanning (1912–), to Sedona, Arizona, where they lived and worked for most of seven years, returning in 1953 to Paris. Ernst spent his last 23 years working to ever greater recognition and acclaim, his innovations having contributed to artistic developments as diverse as Jackson Pollock's (1912–56) drip paintings and the British television comedy, *Monty Python's Flying Circus*.

Susan Felleman

See also Artists; Dada; Painting

References

Camfield, William A. *Max Ernst: Dada and the Dawn of Surrealism*. Munich: Prestel, 1993.

Motherwell, Robert, ed. *Max Ernst: Beyond Painting and Other Writings by the Artist and His Friends*. New York, NY: Wittenborn, Schultz, 1948.

Russell, John. *Max Ernst: Life and Work*. New York, NY: Abrams, 1967.

Schneede, Uwe M. *Max Ernst*. New York, NY: Praeger, 1973.

Spies, Werner. *Max Ernst, Collages: The Invention of the Surrealist Universe*. New York, NY: Abrams, 1991.

———, ed. *Max Ernst Oeuvre-Katalog*. 5 vols. Houston and Cologne: Menil Foundation and DuMont, 1975–87.

———, ed. *Max Ernst: Retrospective 1979*. Munich: Prestel, 1979.

Erzberger, Matthias (1875–1921)

The politician Matthias Erzberger was born September 20, 1875 in Buttenhausen, Württemberg, and died near Bad Griesbach, Baden, on August 26, 1921. A primary school teacher, journalist, Center Party member of the Reichstag after 1903, strong critic of submarine warfare, member of the German Armistice Commission in 1918, and Reich minister of finance in 1919–20, he was assassinated in 1921 by right-wing extremists.

In 1905–06, as member of the Reichstag, he attacked the government's colonial policy, which contributed to improvements in colonial administration and aided his advancement within his own party. He specialized in financial and military questions. Because of his international connections, especially with the Vatican, Erzberger served Berlin for special missions before and during the war. Energetic, ambitious, endowed with oratorical skills, and willing to take responsibility, he could also be controversial in his choice of means toward reaching his objectives and was thus capable of making enemies. During and after the war he was active in steering the Center Party in a more liberal direction and advocating cooperation with the socialists and democrats.

Originally a strong nationalist and pro-annexationist, he changed his beliefs during the war and espoused constitutional reform and a peace of understanding. Dissatisfied with the government's wartime management, he was instrumental in Chancellor Theobald von Bethmann Hollweg's (1856–1921) fall and in initiating the peace resolution of 1917. In October 1918 he became state secretary without portfolio in the cabinet of Max von Baden and next month as one of the peace negotiators signed the armistice for Germany, for which he was branded a traitor, one of the "November criminals," by rightist groups.

In the National Assembly he worked for acceptance of the Treaty of Versailles and warned that rejection would result in Germany's total destruction. On July 21, 1919 he became Reich finance minister and carried through needed financial and tax reforms. A financial scandal overshadowed the rest of his political career. The rightist deputy Karl Helfferich (1872–1924) openly attacked him, accusing him of dissimulation and venality, and the compromising results of the investigation caused Erzberger to resign. In June 1920 he was once more elected to the Reichstag and wanted to resume his political activities, but in August 1921, while vacationing in the Black Forest, he was murdered by two rightist former military officers. Although at times impetuous and lacking in judgment, he was one of the most important democratic politicians during the Weimar period, devoted to his country and the Roman Catholic religion and an advocate of social justice.

Stewart Stehlin

See also Bethmann Hollweg, Theobald von; Center Party; Helfferich, Karl; Inflation and Hyperinflation; Max von Baden; Parliamentary System; Parties and Politics; Versailles, Treaty of; Weimar Germany; Wirth, Joseph; World War I

References

Epstein, Klaus. *Matthias Erzberger and the Dilemma of German Democracy.* Princeton, NJ: Princeton University Press, 1959.

Eschenburg, Theodor. *Matthias Erzberger: der grosse Mann des Parliamentarismus und der Finanzreform.* Munich: Piper Verlag, 1973.

Morsey, Rudolf. *Die deutsche Zentrumspartei, 1917–1923.* Düsseldorf: Droste Verlag, 1966.

Eugenics

In 1883 the British scientist Francis Galton coined the term "eugenics" to denote the social uses to which an understanding of heredity could be employed to "improve" the genetic substratum of a given population. By the second decade of the twentieth century, eugenics movements had achieved an intellectual vogue in many Western countries.

In Germany, an incipient eugenics movement was launched largely through the writings of two physicians, Wilhelm Schallmayer (1857–1919) and Alfred Ploetz (1860–1940). Ploetz's treatise, *Die Tüchtigkeit unserer Rasse und der Schutz der Schwachen* (The capability of our race and protection of the weak), 1895, is important for having popularized the term *Rassenhygiene* (race hygiene). Although used far more frequently than other German synonyms for eugenics, the plural ending "n" in the word *Rassen* suggested races, hence denoting that *Rassenhygiene* was about the improvement of the various anthropological races as well as the human race. Partisans of the term, many of whom would later become influential during the Third Reich, for instance Fritz Lenz (1887–1976), Eugen Fischer (1874–1967), and Ernst Rudin (1874–1953), felt all too comfortable with the word's double meaning.

Although eugenics had an early institutional start in Germany—indeed, the Gesellschaft für Rassenhygiene (Association for Racial Hygiene), founded in 1905, was the world's first such professional organization—the movement remained small during the Imperial era. In the early years, German eugenics was hardly distinguishable from its sister movements in Great Britain and the United States, with the possible exception that the Germans placed more emphasis on "positive eugenics" (the reproduction of the "fitter" elements in society) than on "negative eugenics" (policies designed to reduce the fecundity of the "less fit" or "*Minderwertigen*") than did the Anglo-Saxon countries.

The troubled Weimar Republic witnessed the popularization of eugenics to a far wider audience than had existed previously. The *Deutsche Gesellschaft* (German society), reflecting the increased political polarization of Germany following the Revolution of 1918, experienced serious internal divisions between those members (largely in Berlin) who wanted nothing to do with overly racist (*völkisch*) ideas, and those individuals (located primarily in Munich) who welcomed the inclusion of a "Nordic eugenics." Attempts to popularize eugenics were also accompanied by substantial institutional expansion. During the Republic two foundations for research in eugenics were established: The Kaiser Wilhelm Institute for Psychiatry (Munich) in 1924 and the Kaiser Wilhelm Institute for Anthropology, Human Heredity, and Eugenics (Berlin) in 1927.

Although German eugenics gradually caught the attention of government officials, social workers, and church-related charitable organizations during the Republic, race hygienists remained unsuccessful in passing any major eugenics legislation prior to 1933. Conservative race hygienists such as Lenz viewed Adolf Hitler as the only politician interested in and capable of promoting a eugenics worldview, and indeed the Nazi seizure of power enabled those German race hygienists willing to work for the New Order to help shape the racial population policy of the Third Reich while simultaneously furthering their own careers.

The Nazi leadership imposed significant changes on the race hygiene movement, the most important of which was the explicit emphasis on *Rassenpflege* (racial care) and *Aufnordung* (Nordification) as goals and the elimination of all Jewish, politically unreliable, and non-racist German eugenicists. Certainly, the 1935 Nuremberg Laws were viewed by Nazi officials as eugenic, although there is no evidence that any German race hygienist had a hand in their construction.

Despite the important changes that the movement underwent during the Third Reich, there was at least as much continuity as discontinuity. The new preoccupation with "race" after 1933 in no way lessened the attention devoted to the more traditional concerns of the older, meritocratic eugenics (e.g., increasing the birthrate of the "fitter" classes of society, reducing the number of "nonproductive" elements). The July 1933 law *Gesetz zur Verhütung erbkranken Nachwuchses* (law for the prevention of hereditarily diseased progeny), a draconian measure that resulted in the mandatory sterilization of approximately 400,000 individuals, was not only written and supported by race hygienists but was based on a failed Prussian proposal of 1932.

Eugenics research activities continued along similar pre-1933 lines in Berlin and Munich, although the occupation of large portions of Eastern Europe and the construction of the death and slave-labor camps during the war provided race hygienists with new opportunities and hitherto unavailable "human material" to continue their work. German eugenicists also taught race hygiene courses to SS doctors, provided expert testimony in cases coming before genetic health courts, and composed racial testimonials and genealogies.

Although most German race hygienists active during the Third Reich did not bear direct responsibility for initiating the "euthanasia action" and the Final Solution, they were significant historical actors in a project that ultimately ended in Auschwitz. Several important race hygienists, such as Lenz and Josef Mengele's advisor, Otmar Freiherr von Verschuer (1896–1969), were able to continue their careers as professors of human genetics in the postwar period.

Sheila Weiss

See also Anthropology; Biology; Concentration Camps; Euthanasia; Hitler, Adolf; National Socialism; Racism; *Völkisch* Ideology

References

Bock, Gisela. *Zwangssterilisation und Nationalsozialismus: Studien zur Rassenpolitik und Frauenpolitik.* Schriften des Zentralinstituts für sozialwissenschaftliche Forschung der Freien Universität Berlin 48. Opladen: Westdeutseher Verlag, 1986.

Kaupen-Haas, Heidrun, ed. *Der Griff nach der Bevölkerung: Aktualität und Kontinuität nazistischer Bevölkerungspolitik.* Schriften der Hamburger Stiftung für die Sozialgeschichte des 20. Jahrhunderts. Nördlingen: Franz Greno, 1986.

Lifton, Robert Jay. *The Nazi Doctors: A Study in the Psychology of Evil.* New York, NY: Basic Books, 1986.

Müller-Hill, Benno. *Murderous Science: The Elimination of Jews, Gypsies, and Others, Germany 1933–45.* Oxford: Oxford University Press, 1988.

Proctor, Robert. *Racial Hygiene: Medicine under the Nazis.* Cambridge, MA: Harvard University Press, 1988.

Schmuhl, Hans Walter. *Rassenhygiene, Nationalsozialismus, Euthanasie.* Göttingen: Vandenhoeck & Ruprecht, 1987.

Weindling, Paul. *Health, Race and German Politics Between National Unification and Nazism 1870–1945.* Cambridge, MA: Cambridge University Press, 1989.

Weingart, Paul, Jürgen Kroll and Kurt Bayertz. *Rasse, Blut und Gene: Geschichte der Eugenik und Rassenhygiene in Deutschland.* Frankfurt am Main: Suhrkamp, 1988.

Weiss, Sheila Faith. *Race Hygiene and National Efficiency: The Eugenics of Wilhelm Schallmayer.* Berkeley, CA: University of California Press, 1987.

Eulenburg-Hertefeld, Philipp zu (1847–1921)

Prince Eulenburg, promoted in 1900 by Kaiser Wilhelm II to that title from count, was a leading German diplomat from 1890 until 1902, and because of his unusually close friendship with the sovereign he enjoyed uncommon influence in German politics and diplomacy at the turn of the century.

Trained as a soldier, Eulenburg transferred to diplomacy while still a young man. A protegé of the powerful German chancellor, Otto von Bismarck, he was given choice assignments. During his service in the Prussian legation in Munich, he and young Prince Wilhelm of Prussia met and formed an instant friendship based on their common interest in spiritualism and the arts. Once Wilhelm ascended to the Prusso-German throne, Eulenburg became his leading advisor. The kaiser advanced Eulenburg in the diplomatic service, in 1894 giving him the ambassadorial post in Vienna, which he held until his retirement eight years later. Wilhelm saw to it that Eulenburg was frequently in attendance at court in Berlin. In time, Eulenburg came to possess a dominant influence on the always impressionable ruler, until in 1906 an accusation of homosexuality, followed by a highly publicized but indecisive trial, led to his disgrace and utter repudiation by Wilhelm II.

Eulenburg's influence on the kaiser was unfortunate. Eulenburg consistently urged Wilhelm to assert his prerogatives to the maximum, to hold other branches of government in Germany, such as the legislature, in contempt, and to entrench Prussian aristocrats in the leading positions they had historically enjoyed in the Empire. Eulenburg believed that the German nation possessed a unique moral and spiritual essence, one reflected in its medieval mythology, about which Eulenburg wrote musical dramas and songs much admired by the kaiser. Eulenburg was contemptuous of other European peoples, especially the British, and his influence had the effect of inflating Wilhelm II's already pronounced nationalist ardor and infusing it with a strong xenophobic character.

Lamar Cecil

See also Aristocracy; Diplomatic Corps and Diplomacy; Harden, Maximilian; Imperial Germany; Wilhelm II

References

Eulenburg-Hertefeld, Prince Philipp zu. *Aus 50 Jahren: Erinnerungen, Tagebücher und Briefe aus dem Nachlass.* Berlin: Paetel, 1923.

———. *Mit dem Kaiser als Staatsmann und Freund auf Nordlandsreisen.* 2 vols. Dresden: Carl Reissner, 1931.

Haller, Johannes. *Aus dem Leben des Fürsten Philipp zu Eulenburg-Hertefeld.* Berlin: Paetel, 1924.

Röhl, John C.G. *Kaiser, Hof und Staat: Wilhelm II und die deutsche Politik.* Munich: C.H. Beck, 1987.

———. *Philipp Eulenburgs politische Korrespondenz.* 3 vols. Boppard: Harald Boldt, 1976–83.

Euthanasia

The term "euthanasia" normally denotes the act of assisting in painlessly terminating the life of someone whose death is imminent, usually a victim of an incurable terminal illness. During the Third Reich, the term was mostly inappropriately used to describe the bureaucratically licensed extermination of 100,000 to 200,000 mentally and physically handicapped individuals in Germany, occupied Poland, and the Soviet Union between 1939 and 1945. Most of the victims were patients in state hospitals or mental institutions. "Euthanasia" was also meted out to concentration-camp prisoners deemed mentally ill or incapable of work ("Operation 14f13"), as well as to so-called "half-Jewish" children housed in correctional facilities.

Ideologically, "euthanasia" may be viewed as a logical consequence of the Social Darwinist philosophy and the cost-benefit analysis underlying the turn-of-the-century German eugenics movement. The 1920 publication of *Die Freigabe der Vernichtung lebensunwerten Lebens* (Allowing the destruction of unworthy life) by the lawyer Karl Binding and the psychiatrist Alfred Hoche launched a public discussion over the ethics and economics of keeping so-called "defective human beings" and "valueless" individuals alive. The two authors stressed, above all, the high cost, both in terms of money and personnel, of keeping "incurable imbeciles" and the untreatable sick in public institutions. A few other voices were raised in favor of "euthanasia" during the financially troubled Weimar Republic, yet unlike the case of the mandatory sterilization of the "unfit," there was never any consensus among German race hygienists that "euthanasia" was a viable eugenic measure, even during the early years of the Third Reich.

"Euthanasia" was an integral part of Adolf Hitler's program for "racial purification." By 1935, the führer had discussed plans for the elimination of the institutionalized mentally and physically handicapped in the event of war. With their grossly distorted and unflattering picture of the mentally ill and retarded, propaganda films such as *Das Erbe* (Heredity), 1935, and *Opfer der Vergangenheit* (Victim of the past), 1937, not only sought to popularize the mandatory sterilization law but also to pave the way for a general acceptance of "euthanasia." The widely viewed *Ich klage an* (I accuse), 1941, attempted to render the "mercy death" of the incurably sick acceptable.

A "euthanasia" law served to preserve the good conscience of those who would be participating in the killing. When the war began, however, a decision was made to keep the "euthanasia action" secret, and the law was never put into effect. In order not to implicate Hitler and the führer's chancellery, the latter, in conjunction with the Reich Ministry of the Interior, established, in 1940, the organizational headquarters of the "euthanasia" program in an inconspicuous building located in Tiergartenstrasse 4 in Berlin. For this reason the "euthanasia action" was code-named "Aktion T4."

The government employed fake state and quasi-state institutions to make contact with the outside world, especially with the numerous state and denominational hospitals that would be required to deliver thousands of their charges to transit centers (for camouflage purposes) and then to one of six killing institutions in Germany to be gassed. The selection of those patients to be killed was based on a questionnaire filled out by hospital personnel (for which they were paid) and evaluated by physicians working for T4. The family of the victims later received a standardized letter with false information regarding the cause of death.

In addition to the adult "euthanasia action," the government initiated a special "euthanasia" program for children in late 1938. At that time, the parents of a seriously deformed child wrote to Hitler begging to have their son released from his suffering. Hitler delegated his personal physician, Karl Brandt, to take care of the matter. At the same time, Hitler gave Brandt and Reichsleiter (Reich leader) Phillip Bouhler in the chancellery oral approval to proceed in the same manner with other such cases. Hospitalized children selected for "euthanasia" were placed in special pediatric wards, where they were later gassed. Many of these victims were used for "scientific observation" (medical experiments) before they were killed.

Protests, especially from the Catholic Church, forced an end to the gassing operations in August 1941. After this, the killing continued more discreetly through starvation and medication. Many of the T4 personnel wound up in Poland, where they aided in the extermination of Jews and others in the death and slave-labor camps. In the last years of the war, with the round-the-clock bombing of major German cities, patients were evacuated from mental institutions and sent to "euthanasia centers" so that the beds could be used for the wounded. "Euthanasia" was finally terminated with the arrival of the Allies.

A different euthanasia debate, begun in the 1980s in many countries about the right to help the aged and the terminally ill by assisted suicide, has been burdened in Germany by the history of "euthanasia" practice during the Third Reich.

Sheila Weiss

See also Eugenics; Galen, Clemens von; The Handicapped; Hitler, Adolf; Holocaust; Insanity; National Socialism; Racism

References

Dörner, Klaus et al., eds. *Der Krieg gegen die Psychisch Kranken*. Rehburg-Loccum: Psychiatrie Verlag, 1980.

Götz, Aly, ed. *Aktion T4, 1939–45: Die "Euthanasie"-Zentrale in der Tiergartenstrasse 4*. Berlin: Hentrich, 1987.

Klee, Ernst. *"Euthanasie" im NS-Staat: Die "Vernichtung Lebensunwerten Lebens."* Frankfurt am Main: Fischer, 1983.

Lifton, Robert Jay. *The Nazi Doctors: A Study in the Psychology of Evil*. New York, NY: Basic Books, 1986.

Müller-Hill, Benno. *Murderous Science: Elimination of Jews, Gypsies, and Others, Germany 1933–45*. New York, NY: Oxford University Press, 1988.

Nowak, Kurt. *Euthanasie und Sterilizierung im Dritten Reich: Die Konfrontation der evangelischen und katholischen Kirche mit dem "Gesetz zur Verhütung erbkranken Nachwuchses" und der "Euthanasie"-Aktion.* Göttingen: Vandenhoeck & Ruprecht, 1978.

Proctor, Robert. *Racial Hygiene: Medicine under the Nazis*. Cambridge, MA: Harvard University Press, 1988.

Rost, Karl Ludwig. *Sterilisation und Euthanasie im Film des "Dritten Reiches."* Abhandlungen zur Geschichte der Medizin und der Naturwissenschaften. Husum: Matthiesen Verlag, 1987.

Schmuhl, Hans Walter. *Rassenhygiene, Nationalsozialismus, Euthanasie*. Göttingen: Vandenhoeck & Ruprecht, 1987.

Weindling, Paul J. *Health, Race and German Politics between National Unification and Nazism*. Cambridge: Cambridge University Press, 1989.

Exhibitions (Art)

Since 1871, art exhibitions in Germany have been mounted by a variety of institutions. In Imperial Germany, public art academies organized annual or biennial exhibitions that were typically juried by members of the academy, together with official representatives of the state governments. These "salons," which often displayed hundreds upon thousands of artworks, were often international in scope and fairly conservative in composition.

Private artists' organizations, such as the Munich Artists' Association (Münchener Künstlergenossenschaft), mounted exhibitions as well. Although such shows were usually also very large in size and international in scope, they tended to be more cosmopolitan in composition than the academic exhibitions because they were typically organized by juries democratically elected by the membership at large. The many *Kunstvereine* (art associations), whose membership included both artists and collectors, likewise mounted exhibitions. These, however, were small in size and generally limited to the work of local painters, sculptors, and printmakers.

With the secessionist movement at the turn of the century and the subsequent splintering of the various art communities, private art associations proliferated, as did, therefore, the number of exhibitions. Although these were often international in scope, they, too, were small in comparison to the academic exhibitions and often more uniformly vanguard in character. Notable among them were the exhibitions of the Blue Rider (*Blaue Reiter*) and the Bridge (*Brücke*). Some of these shows were mounted in local galleries, whose owners also organized small exhibitions of art. In Berlin, for example, Herwarth Walden was an important disseminator of avantgarde ideas through the exhibitions he mounted in his Storm (Sturm) gallery. In all of the abovementioned shows, artworks were typically for sale.

During the Weimar period, the exhibitions of the public academies and of the large private art associations generally declined in number and importance, while those of the small artists' societies and of the private galleries increased in frequency and stature. Among the most notorious was the *First International Dada Fair (Erste Internationale Dada-Messe)*, held at the Otto Burchard Gallery in 1920. Here the artists Rudolph Schlichter and John Heartfield exhibited a uniformed dummy with a pig's head. Museums now began to play a more important role in the organization of exhibitions, with, for example, the director of the Kunsthalle (Art Gallery) in Mannheim, Gustav Hartlaub, mounting an important survey in 1925 on a recent trend in painting, New Objectivity (*Neue Sachlichkeit*). Alternative teaching institutions, such as the Bauhaus, likewise opened their doors to the public with shows that displayed the products of teachers and students.

The most notable exhibitions mounted during the Nazi period were the annual shows of officially sanctioned art that were held in Munich's Haus der Kunst (House of Art), and the *Degenerate Art (Entartete Kunst)* exhibition of 1937. In this notorious traveling show organized by the Ministry of Pro-

paganda, around six hundred works of modern art were disrespectfully installed in museums as examples of "degenerate" national culture. The exhibition opened in Munich and then moved to Berlin, Leipzig, Düsseldorf, Hamburg, Frankfurt am Main, Vienna, Salzburg, Stettin, and Halle. At its first venue alone it was seen by over two million visitors.

Although professional artists' associations, such as the Munich Secession (Münchener Sezession), continued to mount exhibitions in the postwar period, museum and gallery shows now dominated. An important exception is the *documenta* exhibition in Kassel, which is curated by independent art professionals. First mounted in 1955 and thereafter every four or five years, this exhibition is among the most important surveys of contemporary international art.

Maria Makela

See also Artists; Berlin Secession; *Bildung und Bildungsbürgertum; Blaue Reiter;* Bourgeoisie; Dada; Munich Secession; Museums; National Socialist Germany: Art; Painting; Sculpture

References
Berlin, Berlinische Galerie. *Stationen der Moderne: Die bedeutenden Kunstausstellungen des 20. Jahrhunderts in Deutschland.* Berlin: Berlinische Galerie, 1988.

Langenstein, York. *Der Münchner Kunstverein im 19. Jahrhundert:Ein Beitrag zur Entwicklung des Kunstmarkts und des Ausstellungswesens. Miscellanea Bavarica Monacensia.* vol. 122. Ed. Karl Bosl and Richard Bauer. Munich: Neue Schriftenreihe des Stadtarchivs, 1983.

Makela, Maria. *The Munich Secession: Art and Artists in Turn-of-the-Century Munich.* Princeton, NJ: Princeton University Press, 1990.

Paret, Peter. *The Berlin Secession: Modernism and Its Enemies in Imperial Germany.* Cambridge, MA: The Belknap Press of Harvard University Press, 1980.

Teeuwisse, Nicolaas. *Vom Salon zur Secession.* Berlin: Deutscher Verlag für Kunstwissenschaft, 1986.

Westecker, Dieter, Carl Eberth, Werner Lengemann, and Erich Müller. *documenta-Dokumente 1955–1968.* Kassel: Georg Wenderoth Verlag, 1972.

Exile Literature

Exile literature dates to Ovid, and isolated examples may be cited from various epochs throughout the centuries. Germany produced a number of such authors in the nineteenth century (notably Heinrich Heine and leftists such as Eduard Bernstein [1850–1932]), and a few German pacifists during the 1920s, most notably the dada group in Zürich, may be considered exile writers. Only with the emergence of twentieth century dictatorships in the Soviet Union, Italy, Spain, and especially Germany, however, did numerous authors go into exile. So many writers fled Adolf Hitler's Germany, including most of those with outstanding reputations, that scholars of German literature have used the term "exile literature" to refer almost exclusively to this group.

The first to flee Germany upon Hitler's assumption of power in January 1933 were leftists such as Bertolt Brecht

Art exhibition hall, Bonn. Courtesy of Inter Nationes, Bonn.

(1898–1956) who had actively opposed the Nazis, for whom the choice was immediate flight or prison. Most of the others left Germany in 1933 on the basis of moral principles. The Nazis, for example, actively courted Stefan George (1868–1933), who refused to remain in a country governed by them. Politically inactive Jews departed gradually over the next seven years, as their situation deteriorated. Many thoroughly assimilated Jewish writers hesitated to abandon a country whose culture and traditions they loved and respected; dozens in fact remained and ultimately became trapped in concentration camps, from which few emerged with their lives. Another group fled throughout Europe as Hitler annexed Austria, which had been a haven to numerous Jewish writers. Germany subsequently conquered many of the Western democracies, including France and Denmark, where some of the exiles had originally sought refuge.

Exiles eventually spread throughout the world, with large numbers in the United States (including Thomas Mann [1875–1955], Franz Werfel, and Carl Zuckmayer [1896–1977]), Latin America (Anna Seghers [1900–83]), the United Kingdom (Erich Fried [1921–88]), Sweden (Nelly Sachs), Switzerland (Robert Musil [1880–1942]), Palestine (Else Lasker-Schüler [1869–1945]), and the Soviet Union (Johannes R. Becher [1891–1958]); isolated individuals ended up elsewhere; Karl Wolfskehl in New Zealand, for example. Many of these authors (e.g., Mann, Seghers, and Becher) adapted to their new environment and continued being successful and productive, whereas others did not adjust (e.g., Musil, Lasker-Schüler); suicides were common (e.g., Walter Benjamin [1892–1940] and Stefan Zweig [1871–1942]). Aesthetically, the exiles were a heterogeneous group. They favored traditional lyric poetry and historical novels, but they also wrote important dramas (Brecht and Zuckmayer), topical novels (Seghers and Friedrich Torberg [1908–79]), and worked at the cutting edge of the avant garde (Hermann Broch [1886–1951]).

Only in the late 1960s did exile literature become a focus of literary scholarship. It has since come to be recognized as an important field of study. The definition of the term, however, remains problematical. At first, analysts tended to restrict "exile literature" to works produced between 1933 and 1945 (or 1948), for the practical reason of limiting the body of material available for investigation and on the theoretical grounds that by 1948 no valid reason existed to call those who did not return "exiles": they remained abroad by choice and had hence become emigrants.

In recent years, most scholars have adopted a broader definition. Not only are those who fled in the 1930s and chose to remain beyond 1948 called exiles, the term is now also applied to Jews who survived the war in Europe, in a camp or underground, and then chose not to remain in Germany or Austria; included in this group are Paul Celan (1920–70) and Jakov Lind (1927–). The latter represents a special problem, because he began to write in English around 1970. Less successful, on the other hand, have been attempts by a few scholars to extend the definition of exile literature to include writers such as Günter Grass (1927–), who were unable to

return to their homes in what had become Poland or the Soviet Union, or the many writers who were forced to leave the German Democratic Republic.

Jerry Glenn

See also Becher, Johannes Robert; Benjamin, Walter; Brecht, Bertolt; Broch, Hermann; Celan, Paul; Expulsion and Exile of Scientists and Scholars; Fried, Erich; Grass, Günter; Lasker-Schüler, Else; Mann, Heinrich; Mann, Thomas; Musil, Robert; Seghers, Anna; Tucholsky, Kurt; Zuckmayer, Carl; Zweig, Stefan

References

Broerman, Bruce M. *The German Historical Novel in Exile after 1933: Calliope contra Clio.* University Park, PA: Pennsylvania State University Press, 1986.

Heilbut, Anthony. *Exiled in Paradise: German Refugee Artists and Intellectuals in America, from the 1930s to the Present.* New York, NY: Viking Press, 1983.

Krispyn, Egbert. *Anti-Nazi Writers in Exile.* Athens, GA: University of Georgia Press, 1978.

Pfanner, Helmut F. *Exile in New York: German and Austrian Writers after 1933.* Detroit, MI: Wayne State University Press, 1983.

Spalek, John M. and Robert F. Bell, eds. *Exile: The Writer's Experience.* Chapel Hill, NC: University of North Carolina Press, 1982.

Strelka, Joseph P. *Exilliteratur: Grundprobleme der Theorie, Aspekte der Geschichte und Kritik.* Bern: Lang, 1983.

Strelka, Joseph et al., eds. *Protest-Form-Tradition: Essays on German Exile Literature.* University, AL: University of Alabama Press, 1979.

Exports and Foreign Trade

Foreign trade has long been a key part of German industrialization and growth. The basic pattern of trade changed little between 1871 and 1990. Germany has been a net importer of food and raw materials and a net exporter of manufactured goods. This relationship placed significant pressure on German foreign and domestic policy and led successive governments to embrace a variety of policies to manage this essential dependence.

Before German unification in 1871, the Prussian government had followed the lead of the Cobden Treaty in placing German trade with France on a most-favored-nation basis. That is, Germany offered the French access to its markets at the lowest possible level of tariff, in exchange for similar treatment from France. The Frankfurt Treaty ending the Franco-Prussian War extended this treatment to all commercial treaties signed by either France or Germany with other states. Almost immediately thereafter, however, German support for free trade came under a number of pressures.

First, the agricultural sector, which had supported the move to free trade, found that its exports were no longer competitive, especially as grain from Eastern Europe and the United States entered world markets. Additionally, the British iron industry remained competitive vis-à-vis German producers, especially after the recession of the early 1870s resulted in excess capacity in Great Britain, which increased incentives to export. Finally, the extension of most-favored-nation status to France opened German markets to French textiles. Combined, these changes in world markets upset the coalition of domestic political forces that favored free trade. Chancellor Otto von Bismarck, who had favored free trade, saw in the changing conditions an opportunity to further strengthen his political position, and began to shift German trade policy toward protection in 1878–79. Much of the protectionist pressure, however, was directed against Russian grain exports, which was inconsistent with Bismarck's efforts to strengthen German-Russian relations after the Russo-Turkish War.

After 1890, German protectionism grew slowly, partly because of opposition by Chancellor Caprivi and partly due to a series of strains in the "coalition of iron and rye." For example, the recession of 1890–91 encouraged industry to demand lower tariffs to encourage exports.

Pressures within the coalition of industry and agriculture resulted in a series of bilateral trade treaties that lowered German tariffs on agricultural products in exchange for lower tariffs on German industrial products. These tariffs rose again after the turn of the century, but on the average, German tariffs remained lower than those elsewhere in the international system. Successive German governments attempted to balance the increasingly divergent trade policy preferences of the agricultural and industrial sectors.

During the pre–World War I period, the ratio of German manufactured exports to total exports nearly doubled to 63 percent in 1913. Exports also grew, from 2.5 billion marks in 1872 to 10.1 billion in 1913. Imports grew at a similar pace, and during much of the period Germany ran a trade deficit. Almost three-quarters of all German exports in 1913 were in semi-manufactured and finished products (down about 10 percent from 1890). Foodstuffs and raw materials accounted for over two-thirds of all imports. Combined, these data emphasize the nature and significance of German dependence on the world market. This reliance was further demonstrated during World War I, as the Allied embargo on Germany greatly weakened the country and led the state to intervene in the domestic economy, the so-called "war socialism."

German trade during the Weimar period was heavily influenced by the crises in the German and world economies. First, the great inflation in the immediate postwar years limited the capacity of some German firms to export, as the war reparations limited their capacity to import. The post-1923 stabilization, in contrast, saw a significant increase in German trade, and a resumption of the prominent role of industrial goods in the structure of German exports. By the end of the 1920s, one in three German industrial workers was dependent on export markets. Hence, the collapse of the German, and world, economy after 1929 fell disproportionately upon German industry. German exports dropped from 13.5 billion reichsmarks in 1929 to 5.7 billion in 1932, and imports declined from 13.4 to 4.7 billion. These losses coincided with similar collapses among most advanced industrial states.

After 1933, foreign trade became the express means of political influence. Via clearing agreements, barter arrangements, import licensing, and export subsidies, the Nazi government pursued autarkic economic policies by dominating those trade relations that continued to exist. German trade policy emphasized neomercantilistic goals and encouraged similar behavior by Germany's traditional trading partners. As a result, German foreign exchange holdings remained low, and German trade shifted from traditional markets to Southeastern Europe, Latin America, and the Middle East.

After 1945, trade again became a central element in German economic policy. The "export-led growth" policies of all the postwar German governments played a key role in achieving the Economic Miracle. One motivation for German participation in the European Economic Community in 1958 was access to export markets, particularly France. German exports continued to be dominated by manufactured goods, which accounted for over 90 percent of all exports by the early 1950s. By the mid-1960s, imports were more evenly balanced between raw materials, foodstuffs, and manufactured goods, but the volume of foodstuffs, and raw materials imports, particularly as a proportion of domestic consumption, remained high. Postwar German governments have emphasized the value of free trade, but unlike the Anglo-Saxon countries, the German government supports free trade based less on ideology and more on German industrial interests.

Michael G. Huelshoff

See also Agriculture; Anglo-German Relations; Economic Miracle; Caprivi, Leo von; Depression; (Great) Depression; Franco-German Relations; Inflation; Protectionism; Russian-German Relations; State and Economy

References

Hardach, Karl. *The Political Economy of Germany in the Twentieth Century.* Berkeley, CA: University of California Press, 1980.
Henderson, William O. *The Rise of German Industrial Power 1834–1914.* Berkeley, CA: University of California Press, 1975.
Kitchen, Martin. *The Political Economy of Germany 1815–1914.* London: Croom Helm, 1978.
Lambi, Ivo. *Free Trade and Protection in Germany 1868–1879.* Wiesbaden: Franz Steiner Verlag, 1963.
Stolper, Gustav, Karl Häuser, and Knut Borchardt. *The German Economy 1870 to the Present.* 2nd ed. New York, NY: Harcourt, Brace, and World, 1967.

Expressionism (Literature)

"Expressionism" is the name of a revolutionary movement in German culture from about 1905 to 1925 that embraced art, literature, theater, film, and to a lesser extent music. The term had its origins in French art criticism and was first used in 1913 to describe the new German literature. Literary expressionism was mainly confined to the years 1910–20, sometimes called the "expressionist decade."

By 1910, a new generation of young writers rebelled against the values of the Imperial era and the alienating and depersonalizing effects of modern industrial civilization generally. Their revolt was one of youth against age, of sons against fathers, and this gave a special vehemence to their grotesque caricatures of the stolid burgher and their apocalyptic visions of mass destruction. In many cases there was an impassioned plea for more desirable alternatives, such as the unleashing of vital energies or the spiritual regeneration of mankind.

The expressionists also revolutionized the language of literature. In order to convey a subjective, emotionally charged vision of reality, the most important poets—Johannes R. Becher (1891–1958), Gottfried Benn (1886–1956), Georg Heym (1887–1912), Else Lasker-Schüler (1869–1945), Alfred Lichtenstein (1889–1914), Ernst Stadler (1883–1914), August Stramm (1874–1915), Georg Trakl (1887–1914), Jakob van Hoddis (1882–1942), and Franz Werfel (1890–1945)—often abandoned poetic and linguistic conventions and created powerful nonrepresentational images reminiscent of the distorted shapes and bold primary colors of expressionist painting.

These features are also characteristic of expressionist prose fiction, which is of lesser significance, and of drama. The dramatists utilized the visual language of expressionism to create a new theatrical style in which sets, costumes, and lighting often functioned as metaphors of emotional states. Their preferred form was the pseudo-religious station drama, which traced the stages of the central character's moral or spiritual transformation. Although few plays avoided verbal and visual hyperbole, the most important of them, such as *Mörder, Hoffnung der Frauen* (Murder, hope of the women), 1910, by Oskar Kokoschka (1886–1980), *Der Bettler* (The beggar), 1912, by Reinhard Johannes Sorge (1892–1916), *Der Sohn* (The son), 1914, by Walter Hasenclever (1890–1940), *Die Bürger von Calais* (The citizens of Calais), 1914, and the *Gas* trilogy, 1917–20, by Georg Kaiser (1878–1945), and *Masse Mensch* (Mass man), 1921, by Ernst Toller (1893–1939), achieved considerable emotional and theatrical power.

The immediate prewar years, which saw the publication of a large number of seminal plays and collections of poetry, were the high point of literary expressionism. World War I brought profound changes. Many expressionist writers died in the first year of fighting, and the energies of the movement were then largely devoted to opposing the war, resulting for example in antiwar plays such as *Seeschlacht* (Battle at sea), 1917, by Reinhard Göring (1887–1936) and *Ein Geschlecht* (One sex), 1917, by Fritz von Unruh (1885–1970). From 1917 on, a number of expressionists, including the poets Becher, Karl Otten (1889–1963), and Ludwig Rubiner (1881–1920) and the dramatist Toller, turned to revolutionary and socialist goals. However, with the failure of the Revolution of 1918–19 the movement lost its utopian élan, even though the style continued into the early 1920s, especially in the theater.

Expressionism remained a controversial literary phenomenon long after its demise. It was attacked as "degenerate art"

by the Nazis, and was the subject of a series of polemics, the so-called "expressionism debate," among exiled Marxist critics in the 1930s. While the initial tendency in the West after the renewal of interest in the movement in the 1950s was to stress its modernist innovations, subsequent more balanced assessments have acknowledged the value of the emancipatory and utopian elements of expressionism as well.

Brian Holbeche

See also Becher, Johannes Robert; Benn, Gottfried; Drama; Hasenclever, Walter; Heym, Stefan; Kaiser, Georg; Kokoschka, Oskar; Lasker-Schüler, Else; Poetry; Revolution of 1918–19; Toller, Ernst; Trakl, Georg; Werfel, Franz

References
Anz, Thomas and Michael Stark, ed. *Expressionismus: Manifeste und Dokumente zur deutschen Literatur 1910–1920.* Stuttgart: J.B. Metzler, 1982.
Brinkmann, Richard. *Expressionismus: Internationale Forschung zu einem internationalen Phänomen.* Stuttgart: J.B. Metzler, 1980.
Bronner, Stephen Eric and Douglas Kellner. *Passion and Rebellion: The Expressionist Heritage.* New York, NY: Columbia University Press, 1988.
Lloyd, Jill. *German Expressionism: Primitivism and Modernity.* New Haven, CT: Yale University Press, 1991.
Paulsen, Wolfgang. *Deutsche Literatur des Expressionismus.* Bern: Herbert Lang, 1983.
Raabe, Paul with Ingrid Hannich-Bode. *Die Autoren und Bücher des literarischen Expressionismus: Ein biliographisches Handbuch.* 2nd ed. Stuttgart: J.B. Metzler, 1992.
———. *The Era of German Expressionism.* Trans. J.M. Ritchie. Woodstock, NY: The Overlook Press, 1974.
Ritchie, James M. *German Expressionist Drama.* Totowa, NJ: Rowan and Littlefield, 1971.
Rötzer, Hans G., ed. *Begriffsbestimmung des literarischen Expressionismus.* Darmstadt: Wissenschaftliche Buchgesellschaft, 1976.
Sokel, Walter H. *The Writer in Extremis: Expressionism in Twentieth-Century German Literature.* Palo Alto, CA: Stanford University Press, 1959.

Expressionism (Visual Arts)

The term "expressionism" has come to refer to an aspect of international modernism that dominated the visual arts in Germany from approximately 1909 to 1921. Artists associated with the term used a multiplicity of antinaturalist, tension-producing devices to attack not only the conventions of nineteenth-century art but also the conventions of a society they found dehumanizing, commercial, and corrupt. Drawing upon an array of international political and social ideologies such as anarchism, socialism, and theosophy, the artists experimented with the use of emotive color, form, and composition to communicate their utopian visions.

Although the term expressionism was initially used to identify the turning away from impressionism by French art-

1911 Painting
Das gelbe Haus
(The yellow house)
by Gabriele Münter.
Courtesy of German
Embassy, Ottawa.

ists such as Henri Matisse and others in his fauve circle, by the time of the 1912 Cologne *Sonderbund* (Special group) exhibition, characterized as a survey of "the most recent movement in painting . . . expressionism," German painters such as Max Pechstein (1881–1955) and Ernst Kirchner (1880–1938) of the Dresden/Berlin *Brücke* (Bridge) group and Franz Marc (1880–1916) and the Russian-born Wassily Kandinsky (1866–1944) of the Munich *Blaue Reiter* (Blue Rider) group were viewed as part of the new style. But provincial artists and the general public reacted negatively to the bright colors, flattened shapes, and distorted forms of expressionism, continuing a long-standing aspect of German thought in which internationalist influences were seen as the direct cause of the decline of German art and culture.

As a result, supporters of expressionism such as the critics Wilhelm Worringer, Herwarth Walden, and Paul Fechter tended to justify the new developments by emphasizing the transcendental, metaphysical, and universal power of the new forms and, in Fechter's case especially, by pointing to the indigenous sources of expressionism in northern artists and the Nordic past. Artists, aware that most of the public was bewildered by their work, felt compelled to explain their approach in essays, tracts, and manifestos. Intellectuals from other fields—architecture, literature, and drama—soon became involved in expressionist issues.

Among the most highly debated topic was the question of communalism versus individualism. Because of the dominance of the state in artistic affairs during the Empire, artists and architects struggled to free themselves from national or state regulations that might determine the direction and content of their works. Social anarchism, with its promise of mutual help and a state that would wither away, set the frame for the expressionists' utopian and optimistic estimate of the possibilities of individual creativity. At the same time, artists associated with expressionism were consumed by questions about their public responsibility.

World War I became a catalyst for an even more activist stance among many of these artists. With the collapse of imperial rule in 1918 and the formation of the Weimar Republic, many artists who had been associated with expressionist groups before the war established new organizations, such as the *Arbeitsrat für Kunst* (Work Council for Art) and the

Novembergruppe (November group), which initially supported free art education, public museums, and mass participation in public projects. Expressionism, now infused with French cubism and Italian futurism, evoked innovation, internationalism, and opposition to the Imperial past and became a visual signifier of the new republic.

But the antinaturalism that most expressionists believed would stimulate change met with resistance from the workers they wished to inspire. Moreover, as the strikes and street battles of 1919 weakened the new republic, many artists and critics became disillusioned with the governing Social Democrats and turned dramatically against the cubo-expressionist style that had become associated with the posters and other visual images of the republic commissioned by the majority party. Communists such as George Grosz (1893–1959) and John Heartfield (1891–1968) began to view expressionism in formalist terms and turned away from their expressionist past. By 1920, even as the urban middle class began to embrace the stylistic manifestations of expressionism in theater design and film, many of the original supporters of expressionism, such as Worringer, began to write of its demise. Nonetheless, references to expressionism survived in the visual developments of Dada and *Neue Sachlichkeit* (New Objectivity), as well as in the art criticism of the 1920s and the 1930s. The Nazis made little distinction between any of these manifestations, referring to all aspects of modernism as "degenerate."

Rose-Carol W. Long

See also Artists; Beckmann, Max; *Blaue Reiter*; Dada; Dix, Otto; Grosz, George; Heartfield, John; Kandinsky, Wassily; Kirchner, Ernst; Marc, Franz; Pechstein, Max; Nolde, Emil; Painting; Schmidt-Rottluff, Karl

References

Barron, Stephanie. *German Expressionism, 1915–1925: The Second Generation.* Exhibition catalog. Los Angeles County Museum of Art, 1988.

———, ed. *"Degenerate Art": The Fate of the Avant-Garde in Nazi Germany.* Exhibition catalog. Los Angeles County Museum of Art, 1991.

Berlinische Galerie, Museum für moderne Kunst, Photographie und Architektur. *Stationen der Moderne. Die bedeutenden Kunstausstellungen des 20. Jahrhunderts in Deutschland.* 2 vols. Berlin: Museum für moderne Kunst, 1988.

Gordon, Donald E. *Expressionism: Art and Idea.* New Haven, CT: Yale University Press, 1987.

Heller, Reinhold et al. *Art in Germany: 1909–1936 From Expressionism to Resistance: The Marvin and Janet Fishman Collection.* Munich: Prestel Verlag, 1990.

Lloyd, Jill. *German Expressionism: Primitivism and Modernity.* New Haven, CT: Yale University Press, 1991.

Long, Rose-Carol Washton, ed. *German Expressionism: Documents from the End of the Wilhelmine Empire to the Rise of National Socialism.* New York, NY: G.K. Hall, 1993. Paperback edition: Berkeley, CA: University of California Press, 1995.

Los Angeles County Museum of Art. *German Expressionist Prints and Drawings, The Robert Gore Rifkind Center for German Expressionist Studies.* 2 vols. Los Angeles: Los Angeles County Museum of Art. 1989.

Rigby, Ida K. *An alle Künstler! War—Revolution—Weimar.* Exhibition catalog. San Diego, CA: San Diego State University Press, 1983.

Staatliche Museen zu Berlin. *Expressionisten: Die Avantgarde in Deutschland 1905–1920.* Exhibition catalog. Berlin: Henschelverlag Kunst und Gesellschaft, 1986.

Trauger, Susan. *The Catalogue of the Library of the Robert Gore Rifkind Center for German Expressionist Studies.* Boston, MA: G.K. Hall, 1989.

Weinstein, Joan. *The End of Expressionism: Art and the November Revolution in Germany, 1918–19.* Chicago, IL: University of Chicago Press, 1990.

Expulsion and Exile of Scientists and Scholars (1933–45)

With the assumption of power by the Nazi Party on January 30, 1933, anti-Semitism became a constituent of official German policy. However, at the beginning not all parts of society were concerned in the same way. In particular, universities and public research institutes suffered rather early under a series of measures whereby a considerable number of scholars lost their positions. On April 7, 1933 the process started with the "law for the restitution of the civil service." Besides the dismissals for political reasons, this law provided the exclusion of people who belonged to the "Jewish race." This affected not only those of Jewish religion. If only one of the grandparents had been a member of a Jewish community, the person in question was a "non-Aryan" and had to be removed from office. A few weeks later, these rules were extended to all university teachers, even if they did not belong to the civil service. Two exceptions were made but not always observed. Veterans and those who had been in office before World War I could remain in their positions. After the race laws of Nuremberg in 1935, which used a more narrow definition of "being Jewish," these exceptions were abandoned. In 1937, a further regulation led to the dismissal of all civil servants with a Jewish spouse. For such people it had been impossible since 1933 to get any new position.

There was almost no resistance from the universities to this policy. Max Planck, the president of the Kaiser Wilhelm Society (1858–1947), paid Hitler a visit on May 16, 1933. He failed in his attempt to convince the chancellor that for the sake of German science some of the Jewish scientists should be kept. Until 1938, about 1,400 of the university staff of approximately 11,000 persons were dismissed. The number increases if employees of nonuniversity institutes and recent graduates are added. Very few were able to get positions in private companies. The overwhelming majority had to leave Germany. After 1938 a new wave of emigration emerged from other countries because of the *Anschluss* of Austria, racist laws in Italy, and occupation of foreign territories by Germany.

A few emigrants built up an organization called Notgemeinschaft deutscher Wissenschaftler im Ausland (emergency association of German scientists in foreign lands). They tried to help their fellow sufferers to find positions outside Germany. Within a very short time, special organizations were founded in several countries to support the German scholars who could not continue their professional lives at home. The most important were the Academic Assistance Council (AAC, SPSL after 1936) in Great Britain and the Emergency Committee in Aid of Displaced German Scholars in the United States. They raised funds to enable employment of immigrants at universities in addition to the normal staff. The personal data, testimonials, and documentation of the displaced scholars were compiled by the committees. Universities could get this information and then decide if they wanted a dismissed scholar. The committees paid the salary or a part of it for a transitional period. This was intended to allow the immigrant to reestablish himself in his new surroundings. It was expected that afterward he would be capable of getting a permanent position. If this seemed unlikely, no grant was offered. In this way, financial aid was mostly restricted to first-class scholars. According to SPSL statistics, more than 2,000 persons looking for positions had been registered in November 1938; 524 of them were then placed permanently, 306 temporarily.

Until 1933, Germany still kept a leading role in many fields of research. Emigrants carried German knowledge and culture to the admitting countries. The preferred destinations were Great Britain and the United States. There, similar facilities existed, which led to interesting opportunities of intellectual interaction but sometimes also to problems of integration. In undeveloped Turkey, however, about 200 refugees had to rebuild education and research.

Great Britain could not absorb all immigrant scholars because of the comparative paucity of permanent academic positions. Therefore a considerable number of them had to emigrate once more and mainly went to the United States. Most of the remaining male refugees who did not hold British passports were imprisoned in internment camps as "enemy aliens" in the spring of 1940; some were deported to Canada and Australia. By March 1941 nearly all of the interned scholars had been released, not least due to the intercession of the SPSL. In the United States, the remarkable contributions of immigrants included advances in physics. Their participation in the development of nuclear weapons was spectacular. In philosophy, with the Vienna Circle as a prominent example, and in the social sciences, immigrant scholars also excelled.

Stefan L. Wolff

See also Anti-Semitism; Civil Service; Coordination; Emigration; Einstein, Albert; Jews, 1933–90; National Socialist Germany; Planck, Max; The Vienna Circle

References

Beyerchen, Alan D. *Scientists under Hitler.* New Haven, CT: Yale University Press, 1977.

Fermi, Laura. *Illustrious Immigrants: The Intellectual Migration from Europe 1930–1941.* Chicago, IL: University of Chicago Press, 1968.

Fleming, D. and B. Bailyn. *Intellectual Migration: Europe and America, 1930–1960*. Cambridge, MA: Belknap Press of Harvard University, 1969.

Lehmann, Harmut and James Sheehan, eds. *An Interrupted Past: German-speaking Refugee Historians in the United States after 1933*. Cambridge: Cambridge University Press, 1991.

Röder, Strauss, ed. *International Biographical Dictionary of Central European Emigres 1933–1945*. Munich: K.G. Saur, 1983.

Extra-Parliamentary Opposition (*Ausserparlamentarische Opposition*, APO)

This term functions as a collective name for the loose network of various left-liberal groups opposing the federal parliament's politics during the 1960s. The extra-parliamentary opposition (APO) represented a public response to the dysfunctionality of parliamentary democracy, in West Germany symbolized by the coalition government of the two major parties, the Christian Democratic Union/Christian Social Union (CDU/CSU) and Social Democratic Party (SPD) from 1966 to 1969. This so-called Grand Coalition eroded the system of checks and balances, because it left only the small Free Democratic Party (FDP) in the parliamentary opposition. It was not a homogeneous movement—the Campaign for Democracy and Disarmament, the Socialist German Student Association (SDS), and the unions became the organizational pillars of the APO.

The APO managed to temporarily transgress generational and ideological boundaries because of its central concern—the emergency laws introduced by the CDU in 1960. The emergency laws were designed to strengthen the executive power of the government in cases of national emergency. Left-liberal critics saw them, however, as a serious infringement of democratic rights and freedoms by an increasingly authoritarian state and compared them to the emergency laws of the Weimar Republic, which had paved the way for Hitler's smooth and semi-legal transformation of Germany into a dictatorship. The Grand Coalition government made it possible to pass these constitutional amendments, which require a two-thirds majority.

The failure to prevent the passage of these laws in the Bundestag, along with the continuous rearmament of the Federal Republic of Germany (FRG) and growing ideological differences within the extra-parliamentary opposition (particularly between its bourgeois-liberal wing and the student movement) led to its dissolution. Still, the APO had a lasting impact on the political culture. It represented the first mass movement against the elected representatives of the still-young FRG. Secondly, it helped to develop a protest culture and to articulate alternative political concepts (self-organization of those affected, erection of a counter-public sphere, democratization of society through mobilization of the grassroots), that became the foundation of the new social movements of the 1970s and 1980s.

Sabine von Dirke

See also Baader-Meinhof Group; Dutschke, Rudi; Federal Republic of Germany; Federal Republic of Germany: Political Radicalism and Neo-Nazism; Federal Republic of Germany: Political Terrorism; Grand Coalition; Students; Universities

References

Burns, Rob and W. van der Will. *Protest and Democracy in West Germany: Extra-Parliamentary Opposition and the Democratic Agenda*. New York, NY: St. Martin's Press, 1988.

Markovits, Andrei and Philip S. Gorski. *The German Left. Red, Green and Beyond*. New York, NY: Oxford University Press, 1993.

Otto, Karl A. *APO: Die ausserparlamentarische Opposition in Quellen und Dokumenten (1960–70)*. Cologne: Pahl-Rugenstein, 1989.

———. *Vom Ostermarsch zur APO: Geschichte der ausserparlamentarischen Opposition in der Bundesrepublik (1960–70)*. Frankfurt am Main: Campus, 1977.

Rupp, Hans Karl. *Ausserparlamentarische Opposition in der Ära Adenauer*. Cologne: Pahl-Rugenstein, 1980.

F

Factory Laws and Reform

Factory production came relatively late to Germany, but by the 1880s Germany had some of the largest and most modern plants in the world. This remains true today. Nonetheless, small factories have always been an important source of innovation and employment, engaging most of Germany's industrial workers. Factory reform in Germany has focused on two issues: working conditions and employee participation. Before World War II, conservatives introduced factory reforms to preserve traditional social patterns and to reduce the attractiveness of unions. Since 1945, however, organized labor and the Social Democrats have taken the lead in promoting reform.

The 1869 Commercial Ordinance (*Gewerbeordnung*) was the first factory-regulating act. It included a ban on Sunday work and on child labor under age nine and set a maximum ten-hour workday for children ages nine to twelve. An 1878 amendment of the *Gewerbeordnung* instituted periodic factory safety inspections and forbade women to work until three weeks after giving birth. The 1891 revision of the *Gewerbeordnung* banned nighttime work for minors and women, set a maximum eleven-hour workday for the latter, and recommended the creation of advisory "worker committees." Despite widespread employer resistance, by 1905 approximately 10 percent of all workplaces with 20 or more employees had worker committees.

The 1903 Child Labor Act forbade work for children under 12. Five years later, another revision of the *Gewerbeordnung* raised the child-labor age limit by one year for larger workplaces, set a maximum six-hour workday for 13- and 14-year-olds, banned night and holiday work for minors, and permitted children to work only after they had completed their required schooling.

During World War I, the Auxiliary Patriotic Service Act in 1916 required all civilian males between 17 and 60 to work and restricted people from changing jobs without their employers' permission. The act also obliged the creation of advisory worker and white-collar committees and established labor courts to hear industrial disputes. Employers' associa-

tions and unions signed a 12-point program on November 15, 1918 that recognized collective bargaining, agreed to the eight-hour day, banned company unions, and required works councils, which meant representation by workers in each plant to advise on working conditions.

The 1920 Works Council law provided a legal foundation for the new works councils but restricted their jurisdiction to a limited set of personnel issues. In 1923, the government used its emergency powers to suspend the eight-hour day until 1927 and introduced compulsory arbitration for labor disputes. During the early 1930s, the government, in a series of emergency measures, reduced wages and cut social benefits. These devices, however, did not revive the economy.

Once in power, the National Socialists quickly dismantled factory institutions. In 1933, the Nazis suspended unions and eliminated works councils, replacing them with the compulsory German Labor Front to serve as the party's arm in the workplace. Until 1937, the state pressured women to leave the work force and forbade using machinery on public works projects when humans could accomplish the task. "Labor trustees" (usually bosses) replaced collective agreements for setting wages and working conditions. The 1938 Working Time Ordinance, which is still in force today, lengthened the workday to ten hours, set limits on store hours, and banned night work for women. The last provision was found unconstitutional in 1993. The Nazis also issued employment registration books and took full authority over allocating labor.

After the war, the Allied Control Council issued several directives regarding factories. Directive No. 22 restored works councils, No. 26 reinstituted the eight-hour day, and No. 35 permitted collective bargaining. In 1947, "parity codetermination," which distributes seats on corporate boards of directors (*Aufsichtsräte*) equally between labor and management in the iron and steel industry, was introduced. The 1951 *Montanmitbestimmungsgesetz* (coal and steel codetermination law) extended parity codetermination to all coal, iron, and steel companies. A year later, the Works Constitution Act extended a much weaker version of codetermination to the rest of the economy. Employees would receive one-third of the seats on each board.

The postwar Social Democratic governments enhanced the power of works councils in 1972 by giving them the right to negotiate severance pay and expanded codetermination rights in 1976. The Social Democrats, with union backing, also initiated the "humanization of work" program, which reduced the physical and psychological strains of working in mass-production industries.

In 1982, Helmut Kohl's administration liberalized workplace regulations, and in 1985 it expanded opportunities to use part-time employees. Still, the liberalization measures have been moderate. The Kohl government also created a special, separate works council to represent middle management. Since the early 1980s, German employers have increasingly adopted Japanese models when reorganizing factories. This "leaner" and more team-oriented approach has devolved more responsibilities on employees but has also raised the physical and mental demands placed on them. During the 1980s, environmental restrictions on factories increased. This forced some firms to undertake research and production elsewhere.

In the German Democratic Republic, the factory served as the nexus of the economic and social lives of most East Germans, providing educational opportunities, vacation homes, cultural events, sports clubs, and child care. German unification ended this program, as factories were restructured according to the Western model in order to make them more economically viable and attractive to buyers. Little has been done since unification to restructure eastern German society to compensate for this loss.

Stephen J. Silvia

See also Codetermination; Federal Republic of Germany: Economy; German Democratic Republic: Economy; German Labor Front; Industrialization; National Socialist Factory Cell Organization; Social Democratic Party; Social Insurance; Social Reform; State and Economy; Trade Unions; Women's Occupations; Working Conditions

References

Barkai, Avraham. *Nazi Economics.* New Haven, CT: Yale University Press, 1990.

Herbig, Rudolf. *Notizen aus der Sozial-, Wirtschafts- und Gewerkschaftsgeschichte vom 14. Jahrhundert bis zur Gegenwart.* Frankfurt am Main: Union-Druckerei, 1980.

Kittner, Michael. *Arbeits- und Sozialordnung: Ausgewählte und eingeleitete Gesetzestexte.* 19th ed. Cologne: Bund, 1994.

Fairy Tales

The fairy tale is a story of wonder, often including elements of the fantastic or supernatural. The genre is generally divided into two subcategories: folk tales (*Volksmärchen*) and art fairy tales (*Kunstmärchen*). The folk tale has its origins in the oral tradition, whereas the art fairy tale is the work of an individual and does not necessarily conform to the folk-tale pattern. Some typical features of the European folk tale include 1) the main character belongs to the real world, while the protagonist's opponent is often supernatural; 2) the hero encounters a difficulty that he must surmount; 3) the plot resolves in a happy end. Generally the characters are unidimensional, and the style, while quick-paced, has little description.

In the early nineteenth century, Jakob Grimm (1785–1863) and his brother Wilhelm (1786–1859), whose interest in collecting tales had been stimulated by Clemens Brentano (1778–1842) and Achim von Arnim (1781–1831), popularized the folk tale in Germany with *Kinder- und Hausmärchen* (Children's stories and fairy tales), two volumes, 1812 and 1815. Their collection had a decisive impact on the development of the genre and remains popular today not only in German-speaking regions but also in numerous translations worldwide.

The art fairy tale flourished during the period of German Romanticism and was fostered by authors such as Brentano, Johann Wolfgang von Goethe (1749–1832), E.T.A. Hoffmann (1776–1822), Novalis (1772–1801), and Johann Ludwig Tieck (1773–1853). Representative authors of the genre in the period between Romanticism and Realism include Wilhelm Hauff (1802–27) and Eduard Mörike (1804–75). The realistic mid- to late-nineteenth-century literary trends were not conducive to the art fairy tale. Only a few writers successfully combined elements of the fairy tale with realistic tendencies. Theodor Storm's (1817–88) "Hinzelmeier," 1851, and Gottfried Keller's (1819–90) "Spiegel, das Kätzchen" (Mirror, the kitty), 1856, are examples from this period.

Study of the twentieth-century art fairy tale is fraught with debate over the application and definition of the term. At the turn of the century, Hermann Hesse (1877–1962), Hugo von Hofmannsthal (1874–1929), and Franz Kafka (1883–1924) experimented with the genre. Hesse employed fairy-tale elements in "Merkwürdige Nachricht von einem Stern" (Peculiar news from a star), 1915, which deals with the horrors of war, and "Iris," 1918.

The anthologies *Die goldene Bombe: Expressionistische Märchendichtungen und Grotesken* (The golden bomb: expressionist fairy tale and grotesque literature), 1970, *Märchen, Sagen und Abenteuergeschichten auf alten Bilderbogen, neu erzählt von Autoren unserer Zeit* (Stories, legends, and adventure stories with traditional illustrations, newly told by contemporary authors), 1974, and *Deutsche Märchen* (German stories), 1985, contain a cross-section of twentieth-century tales. Many of the stories in *Die goldene Bombe*, for example, Albert Ehrenstein's (1886–1950) "Die Schuld" (*Guilt*), 1916, are imbued with a strong element of social criticism. Satire is also common in many of the tales. The stories collected in *Märchen, Sagen und Abenteuergeschichten* share a common focus—literary reworkings of folk tales. Peter Hacks (1928–), better known for his dramatic works, is represented in this anthology with "Der Schuhu und die fliegende Prinzessin" (The schuhu and the flying princess), 1967, another tale with a satirical slant. *Deutsche Märchen* offers selections by diverse authors, including Alfred Döblin (1878–1957), Oskar Maria Graf (1894–1967), Kurt Schwitters (1887–1948), and Robert Walser (1878–1956).

The diverse fairy tales in the various anthologies illustrate that the concept of the genre has indeed broadened. The twentieth century has also witnessed the development of science fiction and fantasy, new literary forms that incorporate elements of the fairy tale.

Diane Pitts

See also Children's Literature; Döblin, Alfred; Hesse, Hermann; Hofmannsthal, Hugo von; Kafka, Franz; Schwitters, Kurt; Storm, Theodor; Walser, Martin

References

Borchers, Elisabeth, ed. *Deutsche Märchen.* 5th ed. Frankfurt am Main: Insel, 1985.

Geerken, Hartmut, ed. *Die goldene Bombe: Expressionistische Märchendichtungen und Grotesken.* Darmstadt: Agora, 1970.

Jung, Jochen, ed. *Märchen, Sagen und Abenteuergeschichten auf alten Bilderbogen, neu erzählt von Autoren unserer Zeit.* Munich: Moos, 1974.

Karlinger, Felix. *Grundzüge einer Geschichte des Märchens im deutschen Sprachraum.* Darmstadt: Wissenschaftliche Buchgesellschaft, 1983.

Lüthi, Max. *The Fairytale as Art Form and Portrait of Man.* Trans. Jon Erickson. Bloomington, IN: Indiana University Press, 1984.

———. *Märchen.* 8th ed. Stuttgart: Metzler, 1990.

Tismar, Jens. *Das deutsche Kunstmärchen des zwanzigsten Jahrhunderts.* Stuttgart: Metzler, 1981.

———. *Kunstmärchen.* 2nd ed. Stuttgart: Metzler, 1983.

Yount, Christel. *Expressionistische deutsche Märchen.* Munich: Profil, 1980.

Zipes, Jack David. *The Brothers Grimm: From Enchanted Forests to the Modern World.* New York, NY: Routledge, 1988.

Falk, Adalbert (1827–1900)

Although the son and grandson of Protestant pastors in Silesia, Adalbert Falk chose instead to pursue a legal career. Following the completion of his studies in 1847 at the University of Breslau, Falk entered the Prussian civil service where he held a variety of posts ranging from state attorney and judge in Lyck, Glogau, and Berlin to privy councilor in the justice ministry itself. His experience also included terms in the Landtag and the constituent Reichstag and service as Prussian delegate to the Bundesrat. Ultimately Falk's early career is only of passing interest because his prominence is associated with his role as minister of ecclesiastical affairs and education (*Kultusminister*) and as Otto von Bismarck's liberal associate during the *Kulturkampf.*

Appointed *Kultusminister* in 1872, Falk introduced important educational reforms. He revised the curriculum, improved teachers' training, upgraded both the salaries and status of teachers, and built new schools throughout Prussia. These achievements, however, were overshadowed by his role as the official most responsible for implementing Bismarck's *Kulturkampf* regulations against the Roman Catholic Church.

These laws limited church influence in educational matters, regulated the state-church relationship, introduced compulsory civil marriage, coerced recalcitrant clergy, suppressed religious orders and congregations, and reorganized the church at the community level.

Although enforcement of the *Kulturkampf* crippled the operation of the Roman Catholic Church, disrupted its organization, and brought real disturbance to the faithful at large, Falk in the end failed to reduce the Church and its followers to submission. Angered by this failure, Bismarck disparaged his associate and his methods. Falk was energetic enough in the drafting of legislation, Bismarck observed in 1875, but "when it comes to a question of implementation, the sensitive Silesian manifests itself" in the minister's character. The *Kultusminister* "thinks it possible to fight the ultramontanes with velvet gloves," Bismarck groused on another occasion, when in fact "iron claws are required."

While no one would suggest that Falk displayed special solicitude for civil liberties and human rights, it nonetheless remains true that the legal and administrative methods he employed during the *Kulturkampf* conformed in every respect to correct judicial forms and procedure. Falk believed in the rule of law, and he rejected suggestions that it might be possible to step outside its framework. Not only did Falk's methods ultimately antagonize Bismarck, but in the end his policies also estranged the royal court and orthodox Protestant elements. In 1879 Falk was obliged to resign, and he returned to the relative obscurity from which he had been plucked.

Ronald J. Ross

See also Bismarck, Otto von; Catholicism, Political; Center Party; Education; Imperial Germany; *Kulturkampf*; Liberalism; National Liberal Party; Roman Catholic Church; Schools

References

Foerster, Erich. *Adalbert Falk: Sein Leben und Wirken als Preussischer Kultusminister dargestellt auf Grund des Nachlasses unter Beihilfe des Generals d. I. Adalbert von Falk.* Gotha: Leopold Klotz Verlag, 1927.

Lamberti, Marjori. "State, Church, and the Politics of School Reform during the *Kulturkampf.*" *Central European History* 29 (1986), 63–81.

———. *State, Society, and the Elementary School in Imperial Germany.* New York, NY: Oxford University Press, 1989.

Ruhenstroth-Bauer, Renate. *Bismarck und Falk im Kulturkampf.* Heidelberg: Carl Winter Universitätsverlag, 1944.

Skalweit, Stephan. "Falk, Paul Ludwig Adalbert." *Neue Deutsche Biographie.* Vol. 5. Ed. Historischen Kommission bei der bayerischen Akademie der Wissenschaften. Berlin: Duncker & Humblot, 1961.

Falkenhayn, Erich von (1861–1922)

The war minister and one of the main strategists in the first part of World War I, Erich Georg Anton Sebastian von Falkenhayn was born on September 11, 1861 at Burg Belchau near Thorn. Having served as an officer cadet, he was commissioned as an officer in 1880. After three years at the War Academy, he was appointed to the topographical department of the General Staff in 1893. In 1896, he went to China, where he remained for six years. On his return to Germany he served as staff officer to his regiment.

After he was appointed war minister on July 8, 1913, he energetically defended the army against its critics over such issues as dueling, the mistreatment of soldiers, and the Zabern Affair of 1913. When Helmuth von Moltke the Younger (1848–1916) failed to implement to the letter the Schlieffen Plan, Falkenhayn was appointed to the High Command (OHL) on September 14, 1914, an assignment that was kept secret until November 3, 1914. He developed a strategy of *Ermattung* ("slowly wearing down"), which came to mean relentless bloodletting. He resigned as minister of war in January 1915 but remained at the head of the OHL, having resolutely deflected the mounting criticisms of generals Hindenburg and Ludendorff, who wanted a major campaign in the east to knock Russia out of the war.

In an attempt to break through the Entente lines in the West, Falkenhayn launched an ambitious and ingenious assault on Verdun in 1916, but owing to errors in planning and execution the strategy degenerated into a costly bloodbath and had to be terminated. In August 1916, Falkenhayn was replaced by Hindenburg at the OHL.

For the rest of the war, Falkenhayn served on the eastern and southeastern fronts. In September 1916, he was given command of the Ninth Army, having turned down the offer of an ambassadorship to Turkey. In a brilliantly executed campaign, he defeated the Romanian army. On July 9, 1917, he was given command of Army Group F in the east, where he soon found himself at loggerheads with his Turkish allies. In February 1918, he was posted to command the Tenth Army in Belorussia. On June 5, 1919 he retired to his family castle, where he lived in isolation. He died in Schloss Lindstedt, near Potsdam, on April 8, 1922.

Martin Kitchen

See also Bethmann Hollweg, Theobald von; Hindenburg, Paul von; Imperial Germany: Army; Ludendorff, Erich; Militarism; Moltke, Helmuth von (Younger); Officer Corps; Wilhelm II; World War I

References

Falkenhayn, Erich von. *Die Oberste Heeresleitung 1914– 1916 in ihren wichtigsten Entscheidungen.* Berlin: E.S. Mittler, 1920.

Janssen, K.-H. *Der Kanzler und der General: Die Führungskrise um Bethmann Hollweg und Falkenhayn.* Göttingen: Musterschmidt, 1967.

Fallada, Hans (Rudolf Ditzen) (1893–1947)

A popular novelist, Hans Fallada is best known for his depictions of the plight of the "little man" during the turbulent last years of the Weimar Republic. The most noteworthy of his many novels are *Bauern, Bonzen und Bomben* (published as *Farmers, Bigwigs, and Bombs*), 1931, *Kleiner Mann—was nun?* (published as *Little Man—What Now?*), 1932, *Wer einmal aus dem Blechnapf frisst* (published as *Who Once Eats of the Tin Bowl*), 1934, *Wolf unter Wölfen* (published as *Wolf among Wolves*), 1937, *Der eiserne Gustav* (published as *Iron Gustav*), 1938, *Jeder stirbt für sich allein* (published as *Each Dies for Himself Alone*), 1947, and *Der Trinker* (published as *The Drinker*), 1950. He also published short stories and two volumes of memoirs, *Damals bei uns daheim* (published as *At Home with Us Then*), 1942, and *Heute bei uns zu Haus* (published as *At Home with Us Today*), 1943. He adopted his pseudonym, derived from a Grimm fairy tale, for the publication of his first novel, *Der junge Goedeschal* (published as *The Young Goedeschal*), 1920.

Fallada led a troubled life, blighted by drug and alcohol addiction and complicated after 1933 by political pressures. Although sympathetic to neither movement, he was courted first by the Nazis, and then, after the war, by the Communists. He cooperated half-heartedly with both. Fallada's literary output is uneven in quality, much of it marred by sentimentality. However, his best work, a group of four novels set in the Weimar Republic, is characterized by an acute observation of the impact of social and political tensions on ordinary lives. The trial of members of the *Landvolk* (farmers') movement in Neumünster provided the material for *Bauern, Bonzen und Bomben*, his most political novel, which vividly captures the machinations of small-town politicians, businessmen, and journalists. Its successor, *Kleiner Mann—was nun?*, is the classic novel of the Great Depression in Germany, encapsulating the struggle of the white-collar worker to stay employed and preserve his class identity. While the Great Depression is also the setting of *Wer einmal aus dem Blechnapf frisst*, which depicts the difficulties faced by ex-prisoners attempting to reintegrate into society, the last of these novels, *Wolf unter Wölfen*, examines a favorite theme of Fallada's, the individual's search for guiding moral principles, against the backdrop of the inflation of 1923.

Although he does not belong to the first rank of modern novelists, Fallada occupies a special place in literary history as the chronicler of the petty bourgeoisie and as a social novelist able to depict the dislocations of the Weimar Republic from the perspective of the disorientated victims. A fluent, if conventional, narrative style has made him one of the most widely-read German novelists of the century.

Brian Holbeche

See also Great Depression; National Socialist Germany: Literature; Novel; Weimar Germany; Weimar Germany: Literature

References

Caspar, Günter. *Fallada-Studien.* Berlin: Aufbau Verlag, 1988.

Dünnebier, Enno. *Personalbibliographie Hans Fallada.* Neubrandenburg: Federchen Verlag, 1993.

Liersch, Werner. *Hans Fallada: Sein grosses kleines Leben: Eine Biographie.* 2nd ed. Hildesheim: Claassen Verlag, 1993.

Tinsley, R.L. *Hans Fallada's Concept of the Nature of the "Little Man": the Focal Point of His Narrative Work.* New Orleans, LA: Tulane University Press, 1965.

Family

With the rise of the bourgeoisie in Europe, a new family form emerged that supplanted the earlier *ganzes Haus* ("whole household"; a household including not only a couple and their offspring, but also its servants, journeymen, and other outsiders, all subject to the authority of the father). The *ganzes Haus* had been a working unit that tended to define relationships in terms of division of labor. Once production was moved out of the bourgeois family, the family came to be seen as the "private sphere," a haven in a harsh world, untouched by the struggle of economic endeavor. However, there was a considerable lag in the adoption of bourgeois family forms in nonbourgeois segments of society, notably the peasantry, where the *ganzes Haus* structure survived well into the twentieth century.

The modern family is the product of a series of social revolutions, one of which has been dubbed the "discovery of childhood." In traditional (pre-bourgeois) society, children were not valued for themselves, but rather for the work they performed. Small children were neglected, and older children sent off to work as soon as they could fend for themselves. These patterns began to undergo profound changes in the eighteenth century. Parents—especially mothers—became more emotionally attached to their offspring. Society recognized that children had to be educated and nurtured, and that they needed not only a sphere of their own—a bed of their own—but also clothing, toys and schooling designed for children.

The conditions for such changes, in terms of resources and motivation, were most favorable in the middle class, which regarded love as the element that held families together and as a central characteristic of family life. But the ideal did not always correspond to reality. The nineteenth century was an era of transition, in which most middle-class marriages fell somewhere between arranged marriages and love matches. In the business class, marriages were often economically motivated—the woman's dowry had to correspond to the man's economic status. But, as Peter Gay has shown, romantic love, and even grand passion, were not uncommon in bourgeois marriages of the Victorian era.

The bourgeois ideal of the family as an emotional sphere cut off from the outside world was accompanied by the rise of the ideology of "separate spheres," according to which the public sphere was the man's sphere, whereas the private sphere was the domain of the woman, who could find her greatest fulfillment as wife and mother. The idleness of the wife, which became an important status symbol, was for most people a myth. Lower-middle-class families could not afford this luxury.

In some families, the pretense of ladylike idleness was preserved while the wife took in work, hidden from society's watchful eye. In addition, most bourgeois women had to do a fair amount of housework. Though this labor was unpaid, performed "out of love," it too was shamefacedly concealed.

Although the bourgeois family became the model for all of German society in the nineteenth century, nonbourgeois segments of society were usually not able to put the ideal into practice. Though factory workers and cottage workers married for love, emotional bonds greatly suffered under the burden of economic deprivation. The intimacy of the family was often disrupted by the presence of boarders. Proletarian women and their teenage children were forced into gainful employment to supplement family income. Among peasants and artisans, older (pre-bourgeois) forms of family life survived well into the twentieth century. In selecting a spouse, peasants thought primarily of land acquisition, whereas artisans thought primarily of professional and economic advancement. The family was a working unit organized and directed by the father. Women and children were generally regarded as farmhands or assistants. Teenage children were sent off to work in other households in hopes of instilling discipline in them.

Broader demographic developments also had a major impact on the German family. Between the 1870s and the 1930s, industrialization and urbanization brought about a shift to low birth and death rates. Fertility declined by about 60 percent, plunging to about 15 to 20 live births per 1,000 inhabitants per year in the Weimar period, largely as a result of family planning within marriage. Fertility rates declined earlier in the middle class than in the working class. For example, officials and salaried employees in big cities who married before 1905 averaged three children, whereas urban factory workers marrying in the same era averaged four.

In the 1950s, a "restoration" of traditional bourgeois family life occurred in West Germany (much as in the United States), but by the mid-1960s the bourgeois family was in the grips of a process of dissolution. Growing individualism and women's liberation led to a decline in marriage and fertility rates. The birth rate fell to nine per 1,000 inhabitants in 1978, though a moderate rebound occurred in the 1980s. The birth rate declined to a similar level in East Germany, but the ensuing growth phase (starting in 1975) was stronger, thanks in large part to the government's pro-natalist policy. State interventionism, through the virtual state monopoly on day-care and youth organizations, largely destroyed the bourgeois family in East Germany. Much as in other industrialized countries, bourgeois patterns of family life became the norm for most of German society by the 1960s, only to suffer a decline in the 1970s and 1980s.

Dolores L. Augustine

See also Bourgeoisie; Childbirth and Motherhood; Domestic Industry; Federal Republic of Germany: Women; Fertility; German Democratic Republic: Women; Infants, Children, and Adolescents; Marriage and Divorce; Women; (Bourgeois) Women's Movement; Women's Occupations; Working Conditions; Youth

References

Aries, Philippe. *Centuries of Childhood: A Social History of Family Life*. New York, NY: Knopf, 1962.

Evans, Richard J. and W.R. Lee, eds. *The German Family: Essays on the Social History of the Family in Nineteenth- and Twentieth-Century Germany*. London: Croom Helm, 1981.

Frevert, Ute. *Women in German History: From Bourgeois Emancipation to Sexual Liberation.* Oxford: Berg Publishers, 1989.

Gay, Peter. *The Bourgeois Experience.* Vol. 1: *The Education of the Senses.* Vol. 2: *The Tender Passion.* New York, NY: Oxford University Press, 1984 and 1986.

Kaplan, Marion. *The Making of the Jewish Middle Class: Women, Family, and Identity in Imperial Germany.* New York, NY: Oxford University Press, 1991.

Knodel, John. *The Decline of Fertility in Germany, 1871–1939.* Princeton, NJ: Princeton University Press, 1974.

Rosenbaum, Heidi. *Formen der Familie: Untersuchungen zum Zusammenhang von Familienverhältnissen, Sozialstruktur und sozialem Wandel in der deutschen Gesellschaft des 19. Jahrhunderts.* Frankfurt am Main: Suhrkamp, 1982.

Fassbinder, Rainer Werner (1945–82)

High-school dropout, unsuccessful applicant to the Berlin Film Academy, stage and film actor, avant-garde theater director and dramatist, critic and essayist, Rainer Werner Fassbinder taught himself how to make films and went on to become the most prolific film maker in Germany, producing 42 feature films or series for the cinema and television between 1969 and 1982—mostly based on scripts he wrote or co-authored.

Fassbinder's early films grew out of his stage productions, which provided the stable ensemble of actors and technicians that continued to work with him in various constellations for an entire decade. The early films were characterized by low budgets and experimental, avant-garde aesthetics. *Katzelmacher,* 1969, typifies the early features in its critique of middle-class boredom that generates intolerance, hate, and violence and in its use of an irritating naturalism. A crucial turning point came in 1970–71 when Fassbinder "discovered" the Hollywood melodramas of the German emigré director Douglas Sirk (alias Detlef Sierck, 1897–1987), which enabled him to translate the thematic and formal elements of entrapment in the early films into a more accessible film genre. The psychological realism, stylized exaggeration, and representation of powerful emotions in *Ängste essen Seele auf* (produced as *All Fear Eats the Soul*), 1973, for example, build on melodramatic elements, but the film also reverses the genre's conventional triumph of good over evil in order to make an overt political statement. This formula fit Fassbinder's polemical tendencies, allowing him to portray victims of oppression and self-delusion in German society—foreign workers, homosexuals and lesbians, working-class people, terrorists, criminals.

By the mid-1970s Fassbinder had established his international reputation and began to produce large-scale prestige films that sought to present an epic history of Germany since the mid-nineteenth century. The most popular and critically successful was *Die Ehe der Maria Braun* (produced as *The Marriage of Maria Braun*), 1979, an allegory about the emotional and psychological price extracted by West Germany's economic recovery in the 1950s.

Fassbinder's death by drug overdose in 1982 symbolically marked for many the exhaustion and demise of the New Ger-

Rainer Werner Fassbinder. Courtesy of Inter Nationes, Bonn.

man Cinema. Like no other postwar director he understood how to use the opportunities of the state subsidy system as well as the dynamics of the collective process of film production to explore his creative vision and to provoke controversy.

Marc Silberman

See also Cinema; Drama; Theater

References

Arnold, Heinz Ludwig, ed. "Rainer Werner Fassbinder." *Text + Kritik* 103 (July 1989).

Fassbinder, Rainer Werner. *The Anarchy of Imagination: Interviews, Essays, Notes.* Ed. Michael Töteberg and Leo A. Lensing. Trans. Krishna Winston. Baltimore: The Johns Hopkins University Press, 1992.

———. *Fassbinders Filme.* Ed. Michael Töteberg. Frankfurt am Main: Verlag der Autoren, 1990 *ff.* (Vol. 1, *Die Kinofilme 1*, appeared under the imprint of Schirmer/Mosel Verlag, 1987; Verlag der Autoren also published Fassbinder's *Sämtliche Stücke*, 1991.)

———. *Filme befreien den Kopf: Essays und Aufsätze.* Ed. Michael Töteberg. Frankfurt am Main: Fischer, 1984.

Hayman, Ronald. *Fassbinder Film Maker.* London: Weidenfeld and Nicolson, 1984.

Iden, Peter et al. *Rainer Werner Fassbinder.* Munich: Carl Hanser Verlag, 1985. (Includes English language bibliography.)

Katz, Robert. *Love is Colder than Death: The Life and Times* of *Rainer Werner Fassbinder*. New York, NY: Random House, 1987.

Rainer Werner Fassbinder Foundation. *Rainer Werner Fassbinder Werkschau*. Exhibition Catalog. Berlin: Argon Verlag, 1992.

Schattuc, Jane. *Television, Tabloids, Tears: Fassbinder and Popular Culture*. Minneapolis, MN: University of Minnesota Press, 1995.

Fatherland Party (Vaterlandspartei) (1917–18)

The Vaterlandspartei (Fatherland Party) was a short-lived attempt to rally extreme annexationist opinion into a united "national opposition" during the final stage of the First World War and thereby to create the framework for a united party of the political Right. Launched in September 1917 under the chairmanship of the recently dismissed Admiral Alfred von Tirpitz (1849–1930), it assembled a familiar coalition of antidemocratic voices, identified with the anti-socialist and protectionist *Sammlung* (informal coalition) of 1897–98. Though officially limited to questions of foreign policy, and disavowing any relationship to domestic issues of economic and social policy or the proposal for Prussian suffrage reform, the Vaterlandspartei nonetheless inevitably challenged the established forms of right-wing party allegiance. By September 1918, it had organized some 800,000 members into 2,536 local branches, and the logic of this independent activity necessarily disputed the existing parties' legitimacy. It seemed to achieve the culmination of a long-standing desire for unity in the Right, standing in a direct line with earlier moments of coalescence, from the Bismarckian coalition of "iron and rye" of 1879, to the *Sammlungspolitik* (coalition politics) of 1897–98, to the *Kartell der schaffenden Stände* (Cartel of the Producing Estates) of 1913.

However, there were key differences. First, traditional aristocratic conservatives and conservative Center Party representatives, both of whom were crucial to the earlier fronts of 1879 and 1897–98, were notable by their absence. The conservative presence in the Vaterlandspartei was confined to a combination of bourgeois conservatives and Agrarian Leaguers. Second, unlike in 1879 and 1897–98, the organized petty bourgeoisie, or *Mittelstand,* was prominently represented in the party, and the party's dominant ideological tone was set by Pan-Germans and other radical nationalists. Finally, the leading role in the Vaterlandspartei's formation was played not by the older-style notables of *Sammlungspolitik* but by two right-wing politicians of a new type, the bourgeois conservative civil servant son of a famous liberal, Wolfgang Kapp (1858–1922), and the equally bourgeois provincial lawyer and Pan-German League chairman Heinrich Class (1860–1954).

The party disappeared in the confusion of the Revolution of 1918 and Germany's military defeat, and disbanded on December 10, 1918.

Geoff Eley

See also Agrarian Leagues; Class, Heinrich; Conservatism; Nationalism; Radical Nationalism; Radical Right; Revolution of 1918–19; *Sammlungspolitik*; Tirpitz, Alfred von; World War I

References

Eley, Geoff. *Reshaping the German Right: Radical Nationalism and Political Change after Bismarck*. Ann Arbor, MI: The University of Michigan Press, 1991.

Retallack, James N. *Notables of the Right: The Conservative Party and Political Mobilization in Germany, 1876–1918*. Boston, MA: Allen and Unwin, 1988.

Stegmann, Dirk. *Die Erben Bismarcks: Parteien und Verbände in der Spätphase des Wilhelminischen Deutschlands: Sammlungspolitik 1897–1918*. Cologne: Kiepenheuer & Witsch, 1970.

———. "Zwischen Repression und Manipulation: Konservative Machteliten und Arbeiter- und Angestelltenbewegung 1910–1918." *Archiv für Sozialgeschichte* 12 (1972), 351–432.

Faulhaber, Michael von (1869–1952)

Archbishop of Munich from 1917, Michael von Faulhaber attained international fame as a prophetic warner against threats to his faith and church, real and imagined, from every quarter: "One of the last princes of the Church and one of the great bishops of this century" (Ludwig Volk). Faulhaber's opposition to Nazism was compromised by excessive regard of Adolf Hitler's mantle of legality and by the führer's skill in treating Faulhaber as a fellow sovereign.

The third of seven children of a Franconian baker and farmer, Faulhaber was born on March 5, 1869. Following his *Abitur* (senior matriculation) in a minor seminary (1888) and compulsory military service, which kindled a brief interest in an army career, he was ordained priest for the Würzburg diocese on August 1, 1892. Combining pastoral work with further study, he gained the doctorate in 1896 and a brilliant Roman *Habilitation* (post-doctoral thesis) in 1899. As professor of the Old Testament in Strassburg (then German territory) from 1903, Faulhaber became known beyond his university as a gifted orator.

Named bishop of Speyer at the end of 1910, he added the duties of military bishop for the Bavarian army in 1914. In 1917 he became archbishop of Munich and in 1921 cardinal. The collapse of the Bavarian Wittelsbach monarchy in 1918 deeply shocked Faulhaber, who managed almost effortlessly, however, to fill the resulting void in Bavarian popular sentiment.

Faulhaber's patriarchal social views and inability to understand politics as the art of the possible made him mistrust both the Weimar Republic and the Center Party, which supported it. In 1930, however, he branded National Socialism "a heresy irreconcilable with the Christian world view." In 1933, his four Advent sermons defending the "Jewish" Old Testament against Nazi attacks attracted wide notice. He was the principal author of Pope Pius XI's encyclical *Mit brennender Sorge* (March 14, 1937), a scathing denunciation of Nazi crimes.

Faulhaber qualified his denunciations of the regime in order to avoid an open break, and in the belief (which even the smashing of his windows during the Crystal Night [*Kristallnacht*] of November 1938 could not dispel) that the worst excesses were the work of underlings, and that Hitler as legal head of state was susceptible to reasoned appeals. Like many anti-Nazi Germans of conservative views, Faulhaber could never really believe that his beloved fatherland was governed by criminals.

Though 76 when the war ended, he threw himself energetically into reconstruction of his devastated city while protesting the injustices of the American de-Nazification policy and the undermining of Catholic schools. On June 12, 1952, as he walked in the Munich Corpus Christi procession, death snatched from his hand the pastoral staff he had wielded "without a sabbath rest" (Faulhaber's words) for 35 years.

John Jay Hughes

See also Catholicism, Political; Center Party; National Socialist Germany; Resistance; Roman Catholic Church

References

Buscher, F.M. and M. Phayer. "German Catholic Bishops and the Holocaust, 1940–1952." *German Studies Review* 11 (October 1988), 463–85.

Conway, John S. *The Nazi Persecution of the Churches.* London: Weidenfeld and Nicholson, 1968.

Gallin, Mary A. "The Cardinal and the State: Faulhaber and the Third Reich." *Journal of Church and State* 12 (1970), 385–404.

Helmreich, E.C. *The German Churches under Hitler.* Detroit, MI: Wayne State University Press, 1979.

Lewy, Guenter. *The Catholic Church and Nazi Germany.* New York, NY: McGraw-Hill, 1964.

Oppen, Beate Ruhm von. "Revisionism and Counter-Revisionism in the Historiography of the German Church Struggle." *The German Church Struggle and the Holocaust.* Ed. F.H. Littell and Hubert G. Locke. Detroit, MI: Wayne State University Press, 1974.

Federal Republic of Germany

Created out of the three western zones of occupation, the Federal Republic of Germany (FRG) represents, in many respects, a remarkable success story. Part of a militarily defeated and politically divided country, with a "provisional" political system conditioned by the Western Allies, the FRG nevertheless developed into a secure and stable democracy that most citizens came to support in principle. Renouncing the Nazi heritage of expansionism, militarism, and aggression, the territorially much-reduced FRG developed into a "post-nationalist" protagonist of emerging Western European processes of integration. In the heart of Europe, at the center of Cold War tensions, the West German system eventually won the battle for the terms of German unity; when the Communist system collapsed in the German Democratic Republic (GDR), most East Germans opted for rapid unification with the West.

Yet, in the shadow of Auschwitz, the outward successes of the FRG were accompanied by undercurrents of uncertainty over its national identity and bought at a price of considerable social inequality. The new Germany since 1990 has had to contend not only with the economic and ecological legacies of the former GDR, but also with ambiguous aspects of the West German heritage.

The constitution of the FRG was designed with an eye to the weaknesses of the Weimar Republic. The stability and success of the West German democracy, in contrast to its ill-fated forbear, owes much to constitutional safeguards: the largely ceremonial role of the president, the 5-percent hurdle for parties to gain national representation, the "two-vote system" combining proportional representation with constituency representatives, the ban on anticonstitutional, antidemocratic parties, and the "constructive vote of no confidence" ensuring a relatively smooth political succession. Together, these measures have helped to ensure the emergence of a system with two major parties, the allied conservative Christian parties—the Christian Democratic Union (CDU) and Christian Social Union (CSU)—and the Social Democratic Party (SPD), and one smaller party, the Free Democratic Party (FDP), which effectively held the balance of power. The only major changes of government in the FRG's history—in 1969 and 1982—occurred when the FDP shifted its allegiance from the CDU/CSU to the SPD and then back again.

The extraordinarily rapid economic success of West Germany's early years, fueled by Marshall Plan aid in the context of the more general postwar economic recovery and assisted by the supply of cheap and mobile labor in the form of refugees from the east, helped to give the new political system a degree of pragmatic legitimacy in the views of most citizens. Moreover, the first chancellor, Konrad Adenauer (chancellor 1949–63), incorporated former Nazis into the new democracy: building for a better future took precedence over raking the ashes of the past. Communists were squeezed out of the system entirely (the German Communist Party [KPD] was banned in 1956), and the Social Democrats revised their radical program to become a more moderate centrist party in 1959. Former "nominal" Nazis joined the political establishment of conservatives in a new consensus that contrasted markedly with the political fragmentation and revisionism of the Weimar years. At the same time, in the Cold War era, West Germany became a key ally in the Western military and economic systems. It entered NATO in 1955, and became a founding member of the European Economic Community in 1957.

The apparently self-satisfied, prosperous West German society that emerged during the Adenauer era faced challenges from left and right in the transitional period of the mid- and late 1960s. The faltering of economic growth under Adenauer's successor, former Economics Minister Ludwig Erhard (1897–1977; chancellor 1963–66), was followed by worrisome, if ultimately marginal, local electoral successes for the right-wing Nationaldemokratische Partei Deutschland (NPD; National Democratic Party). The rise of the New Left and of youth revolts in the Western world generally was peculiarly refracted in West Germany by confrontation with the Nazi heritage of the parental generation, while a developing "extra-parliamentary opposition" responded to the Grand Coalition government headed by the conservative chancellor Kiesinger in 1966–69. But the storms of the later 1960s heralded a new era: the *Ostpolitik* (eastern policy) of Willy

Brandt's (1913–92) SPD/FPD coalition (1969–74) inaugurated a period of East-West detente and the improvement of human contacts between the FRG and the GDR, while the economic strength and political stability of West Germany proved a secure anchor in face of political challenges from terrorist groups and of economic recession in the 1970s and 1980s.

The transition from Brandt's successor Helmut Schmidt (1913– ; chancellor 1974–82) to the conservative Chancellor Helmut Kohl paved the way for a controversial reassertion of German national pride and demands to let the past be finally relegated to history. At the same time, the growth of new social movements, such as the peace movement and the unexpected electoral successes of the new Green Party, proved important in challenging the agendas of the major political parties at the national level and introducing variety in possible coalition formations in *Land* parliaments. The rise of neo-nation-

alist parties (the Deutsche Volks Union [DVU] and Republicans) on the right-wing fringes of politics and an increasing proportion of Germans expressing a sense of political disillusionment signified further shifts in the political landscape. But Chancellor Kohl's historical reputation was secured as the driving force for rapid unification following the collapse of Communism in the GDR, and as the 'unity chancellor' of 1990.

The FRG became internationally renowned for its legendary German efficiency, stable currency, and economic success combined with environmental awareness, while its decentralized federal system provided something of a model in an era in which emerging supra- and international entities were linked to a focus on regional devolution and local loyalties. The FRG could rightly claim that in many respects it had cast off the shadows of its problematic past: gone were the marching jackboots, the militarism of the Prussian army, the social

Germany, 1990

pretensions of the old landed aristocracy, the fears of a frightened petty bourgeoisie, the specter of a revolutionary proletariat. In their place appeared to be social partnership, paternalistic employers, moderate and well-organized trade unions, and the realization of German national interests abroad through economic strength and international cooperation rather than military invasion. Most West Germans appeared to have learned only too well the "lessons of history," evincing the most pacifist and least nationalist attitudes of any Western European country. In this sense, 1945 marked a crucial break in German history. But 1945 was not entirely the *Stunde Null* (zero hour) so often proclaimed, and there were ambiguous legacies for subsequent democracy.

The political watershed of 1945 did not represent any concomitant break in economic and social inequalities. With rapid urbanization and the growth of new technologies and of the service industries, the social structure of the FRG changed markedly. The proportion of agricultural and blue-collar sectors declined, the economic emphasis shifted from the heavy industries of the Ruhr to the high-tech production of the southwest, and the growth of communications fostered a degree of Westernization, cultural homogenization, and decline in regional differences. Although Germans as a whole became the most well-paid workforce in Europe, the importance of social background as a key determinant of educational achievement and adult occupation was not diminished. Despite changes in the cultural climate, the place of women remained, if no longer so much in the church and kitchen, certainly in the home and in part-time and less well-paid employment. Domestic labor remained largely the woman's responsibility; for many working women, "emancipation" simply meant a double burden.

The proclaimed affluent society rested on an often unnoticed degree of deprivation for minorities. Following the erection of the Berlin Wall in 1961, the supply of refugee labor from the GDR dried up; it was replaced by an initially welcome influx of cheap labor from Mediterranean countries (euphemistically termed "guest workers" or *Gastarbeiter*). With the economic recession after the oil crisis of 1973, the guests rapidly found that they were less than welcome: by the 1980s, they and their children were very much second-class residents, an economic underclass supporting the affluent society. Their situation was compounded by unique features of German nationality laws.

The unwillingness to recognize post-1945 political boundaries as permanent left the definition of German citizenship in the FRG essentially ethnic, rooted in "German blood." Refugees from former German territories in the east as well as the GDR had automatic rights to citizenship in the FRG. But it was less easy for ethnic "foreigners" to attain German citizenship, and little attention was paid to issues of assimilation or integration in a multicultural society. This ethnic entitlement to citizenship was combined with uniquely liberal asylum laws—an intrinsically laudable attempt at reparation for Auschwitz. The combination, however, proved somewhat problematic in the 1980s, and was dramatically exacerbated by the rapidly increasing numbers of asylum seekers and economic migrants following the fall of the Iron Curtain. The rise of extremist neo-Nazi attacks on asylum-seekers' hostels, on Turkish residents, on Jews, and on other "foreigners" and the desecration of Jewish cemeteries and memorials indicated that the ghosts of the past had been hardly laid to rest. The Germany of the 1990s is facing tough questions about the definition of citizenship in an era of increased international mobility, when old considerations may no longer be pertinent.

The FRG is of major significance in German history, in that it has represented a stable, economically productive, democratic state, able to respond flexibly to domestic tensions and to mediate between East and West. The implications of the dramatic changes inaugurated by the new watershed of 1989–90 remain to be seen. The problem of defining an acceptable German patriotism, combined with a clear sense of international responsibilities, remains, but the balance between commitment to regional identities and a more general set of political values anchored in a federal democracy appear to represent a viable framework, a promising solution to some of the long-term patterns and problems of the history of German states in central Europe.

Mary Fulbrook

See also Adenauer, Konrad; American-German Relations; Anglo-German Relations; The Basic Law; Basic Treaty; Berlin; Berlin Blockade; Berlin Wall; Brandt, Willy; Bundesbank; Chancellor's Office; Christian Democratic Union; Christian Social Union; Citizenship and Foreigners; Codetermination; The Cold War and Germany; Economic Miracle; The Economics of German Reunification; Elections; Erhard, Ludwig; Federal Republic of Germany: Armed Forces; Federal Republic of Germany: Economy; Federal Republic of Germany: Foreign Policy; Federal Republic of Germany: Internal Security; Federal Republic of Germany: Judicial System; Federal Republic of Germany: Literature; Federal Republic of Germany: Political Radicalism and Neo-Nazism; Federal Republic of Germany: Political Terrorism; Federal Republic of Germany: Postwar Refugee and Expellee Organizations; Federal Republic of Germany: Women; Feminism in the Federal Republic of Germany; Franco-German Relations; Free Democratic Party; German-German Relations; Grand Coalition; Israeli-German Relations; Kiesinger, Kurt Georg; Kohl, Helmut; Local Government; Minorities: Ethnocultural and Foreign; NATO and Germany; *Ostpolitik*; Parliamentary System; Parties and Politics; Postwar European Integration and Germany; Postwar Reconstruction; Presidency; Refugees; Reunification; Schmidt, Helmut; Science in the Postwar Germanys; Social Democratic Party, 1919–90; Soviet-German Relations; State and Economy; Trade Unions, 1945–90

References
Berghahn, Volker. *Modern Germany.* 2nd ed. Cambridge: Cambridge University Press, 1987.

Bracher, Karl Dietrich, Theodor Eschenburg, Joachim C. Fest, and Eberhard Jäckel, eds. *Die Geschichte der Bundesrepublik Deutschland.* 6 vols. Stuttgart: Deutsche Verlags-Anstalt; Wiesbaden: F. A. Brockhaus, 1983–87.

Diefendorf, Jeffry M., Axel Frohn, and Herman-Josef Rupieper, eds. *American Policy and the Reconstruction of West Germany, 1945–1955.* Washington, DC: German Historical Institute and New York, NY: Cambridge University Press, 1993.

Fulbrook, Mary. *The Divided Nation: A History of Germany, 1918–1990.* New York, NY: Oxford University Press, 1992.

———. *The Two Germanies, 1945–1990: Problems of Interpretation.* Basingstoke: Macmillan, 1992.

Heineman, Elizabeth. "The Hour of the Woman: Memories of Germany's 'Crisis Years' and West German National Identity." *American Historical Review* 101 (April, 1996), 354–95.

Smith, Gordon et al., eds. *Developments in German Politics.* Basingstoke: Macmillan, 1992.

Turner, Henry Ashby. *Germany from Partition to Unification.* 2nd ed. New Haven, CT: Yale University Press, 1993.

Federal Republic of Germany: Armed Forces (Bundeswehr)

The Bundeswehr has always been a case study in ambivalence. The linchpin of Europe's conventional defense, it existed in a society uncomfortable with the concept and the reality of armed forces. The fear of nuclear devastation and the desire to show that Germany's past has been overcome meant that the Bundeswehr's democratic orientation was considered at least as important as its operational efficiency.

German rearmament seemed unthinkable in the aftermath of World War II, even as the Grand Alliance collapsed into two hostile camps. Chancellor Konrad Adenauer, however, argued that if the newly created Federal Republic was to become part of a reconstituted Europe, it must be given a military stake in the new order. This position was unpopular across a broad spectrum of West German society, because not until the outbreak of the Korean War in 1950 were the Bundeswehr's foundations established—a conscript-based force, thoroughly under parliamentary control, unidentified with any political party or interest group.

Although Wehrmacht veterans were initially integrated into the new structure, the Bundeswehr took pains to keep out of leadership positions anyone whose attitudes or behavior were too reminiscent of the Hitler era. From the beginning, the political system accepted responsibility for the military leaders. Six hundred and one candidates were initially considered for senior posts; 101 were rejected or withdrew their applications. Far more careers have been broken for indiscretion than for incompetence.

The Bundeswehr has stayed out of politics, steering clear of efforts to influence either foreign or domestic policy. The limits of the anti-socialism of the Imperial and Weimar eras were all too clear. Instead of building walls, the Bundeswehr sought common denominators. Military service in the Federal Republic was intended to shape civic character by developing and reinforcing a democratic consciousness. The concept of *Innere Führung* (internal governance) is easier to describe than to define. It invokes soldiers to act as autonomous moral beings, able to balance the claims of subordination against the demands of conscience. *Innere Führung* also stresses a dialectic of rights and responsibilities, emphasizing involved participation in the armed forces and the state those forces serve.

Despite concern about increasing numbers of conscientious objectors, recruit shortages resulting from falling birth rates, and draftees' suitability for modern, high-tech war, the Bundeswehr has remained conscript-based. Like West German society, the Bundeswehr has become bureaucratized and credentialized, to the point where critics challenge its ability to fight. The Bundeswehr has also coped with increasing success with Germany's military past—not least because in the four decades of their existence, the Federal Republic's armed forces developed viable traditions of their own.

The Basic Law of the Federal Republic forbids preparations for aggressive war, but allows membership in a collective organization to maintain peace. The Bundeswehr's only role is to defend West Germany in a NATO context. It can not be deployed outside the NATO area. It is allowed neither chemical nor nuclear weapons—though these are hardly regarded as deprivations by a force expecting to fight only on its home ground. The Bundeswehr needs to be strong enough to support specific West German and NATO policies without having to choose between them. It needs to present a benign face to its alliance partners. It needs, above all, to contribute to the containment of any future European conflict at sub-nuclear levels. In these contexts, the Bundeswehr developed as a mid-level conventional force based on twelve combat divisions, an air force whose tactical role belied its official independence, and a navy with limited coastal capacities. Prior to reunification, its strength was just short of half a million: 340,000 in the army, 106,000 in the air force, and 36,000 in the navy, with over 11,000 more inter-service staff.

For political and strategic reasons, the Bundeswehr insisted, the Federal Republic had to be defended on its frontiers. West Germany was too small for operational maneuvers of the kind practiced on the Russian steppe. Instead, the Bundeswehr drew on Wehrmacht experience at the tactical level to argue that conventional military forces properly trained, equipped, and commanded could stop an attack by quick ripostes, counterattacks at brigade and battalion levels undertaken without references to higher headquarters. Ideally there would be no single decisive point inviting the use of nuclear weapons. The enemy would be slowed, then halted, by a death of a thousand cuts.

The effect of the doctrine against the Warsaw Pact was never tested. Instead, the Bundeswehr of the 1990s faces the task of absorbing the former German Democratic Republic's National People's Army while finding new missions to replace the one on which its existence had depended.

Dennis E. Showalter

See also Adenauer, Konrad; Blank, Theodor; Baudissin, Wolf von; The Cold War and Germany; Disarmament; Federal Republic of Germany: Foreign Policy; Heusinger, Adolf; Maizière, Ulrich de; NATO and Germany; Postwar European Integration and Germany; Rearmament; Schmidt, Helmut; Strauss, Franz Josef

References

Abenheim, Donald. *Reforging the Iron Cross: The Search for Tradition in the West German Armed Forces.* Princeton, NJ: Princeton University Press, 1988.

Clemens, Clay. "Opportunity or Obligation? Redefining Germany's Military Role Outside of NATO." *Armed Forces and Society* 19 (1993), 231–51.

Lider, Julian. *Essays on West German Military Thought.* 3 vols. Stockholm: Swedish Institute of International Affairs, 1983–84.

Militärgeschichtliches Forschungsamt, *Anfänge westdeutscher Sicherheitspolitik 1945–1956.* Vols. 1 and 2. Munich: Oldenbourg, 1982–90.

Showalter, Dennis. "The Bundeswehr of the Federal Republic of Germany." *The Defense of Western Europe.* Ed. Lewis H. Gann. Dover, NH: Auburn House, 1986.

Federal Republic of Germany: Economy

At the conclusion of World War II, German recovery had to occur across four (American, British, French, and Soviet) occupation zones. Until 1948, the highly centralized economic controls of the Nazi regime were not dismantled. Then the Allies transferred sovereignty in the Western occupation zones back to the Germans. Ludwig Erhard (1897–1977) became the first minister of economics. His policies decentralized the economy and introduced a currency reform. These policies and the prevailing circumstances produced West Germany's Economic Miracle (*Wirtschaftswunder*).

With defense expenditures modest relative to those of the superpowers, and with correspondingly minor government outlays, the Federal Republic of Germany (FRG) achieved its postwar expansion in part by the prudent use of fiscal surpluses. Since private savings were modest, these surpluses were channeled through banks or direct credits to business for investment purposes. The degree of concentration in German business remained surprisingly high, despite anti-monopoly legislation. Moreover, the role of banking in corporate finance was considerable, with significant cooperation between the directorates of banks and industrial corporations.

The role of nationalized industries in the FRG is significant. Nationalized firms include various public utilities, among them the postal and telephone systems, and more than 3,000 firms, including some large ones such as Volkswagen. Some privatization in recent years has not changed this basic picture.

As the momentum from the initial recovery period was dissipating, the onset of the European Coal and Steel Community, and its successor, the European Economic Community, provided additional stimulus to economic growth through the trade sector. The hope of the founding "Europeans," Jean Monnet, Walter Hallstein (1901–82), and others, was that interdependence in economic affairs would assure more peaceful conditions, and also ultimately provide the impetus for political integration. From the perspective of the 1990s, this dream and German support for it were not in vain. For the Europe of the 1950s and 1960s, it also meant huge

Anticipated Currency Reform, 1948. Courtesy of Inter Nationes, Bonn.

increases in the volume of intra-European international trade. No country benefited from this more than Germany.

Penetrating Western and Eastern European markets, and then many other parts of the world, made Germany the global trading leader. In recent years, the Germans have challenged the United States, with its far larger economy, for the leading position in terms of the value of total exports. It has long had the highest value of per capita exports.

Economic policy has been conservative, with clear priority given to avoiding inflation. The 1969 Brandt coalition government of Social and Free Democrats brought Karl Schiller (1911–95) to the economics ministry, but this produced little neo-Keynesian deficit spending. It did create "concerted action," a system of negotiations involving government, labor, and industry designed to moderate inflationary wage increases. Of more impact on the economy was the use of investment and tax allowances to encourage housing construction, tax credits, and depreciation allowances for ship construction, plus tax exemptions to stimulate savings.

West German workers, pacified early in the recovery period by codetermination laws that gave them some participation in corporate governance, were willing for a number of years to forgo rapid wage increases. As the social pie grew, however, they ultimately became the highest-paid employees in the world.

The fruits of economic growth have been widely shared in West German society. Yet extensive social programs in recent years have led to rapidly growing federal budgets as health-care costs and other social programs have escalated rapidly. State outlays as a share of GNP rose from 32.5 percent in 1960 to roughly 50 percent by 1990.

The most important recent chapter of German economic history began with the opening of the Berlin Wall in late 1989, which led rapidly to German reunification on October 3, 1990. The implications of reunification were dramatic: the economic transformation of the five East German states required massive fiscal transfers from the federal budget. On the positive side, this expenditure provided substantial economic stimulus to West German suppliers. Less positively, transfers (in excess of 100 billion deutsche marks annually in the first years of reunification) were funded largely by money creation, generating concern about the threat of rapid inflation.

The new federal states in the east were tormented at the beginning of the 1990s with extensive unemployment as the subsidization of inefficient enterprises ceased and excessively large payrolls could no longer be maintained. The FRG had committed itself irrevocably to supporting the politico-economic transformation of East Germany.

Phillip J. Bryson

See also Allied High Commission to Germany; Banking; Bundesbank; Cartels; Codetermination; Currency; Economic Miracle; The Economics of German Reunification; Erhard, Ludwig; Exports and Foreign Trade; Federation of German Industry; Postwar European Integration and Germany; Schiller, Karl; Schmidt, Helmut; State and Economy; Strikes; Trade Unions, 1945–90; Wages; Working Conditions

References

Arndt, Hans-Joachim. *West Germany: The Politics of Non-Planning.* Syracuse, NY: Syracuse University Press, 1966.

Lampert, H. *Die Wirtschafts- und Sozialordnung der Bundesrepublik Deutschland.* 6th ed. Munich: Verlag G. Olzog, 1978.

Smyser, W.R. *The Economy of United Germany.* New York, NY: St. Martin's Press, 1992.

Stolper, Gustav, Karl Häuser, and Knut Borchardt. *The German Economy: 1870 to the Present.* New York, NY: Harcourt, Brace & World, 1967.

Thalheim, Karl, ed. *Materialien zum Bericht zur Lage der Nation im geteilten Deutschland 1987.* Bonn: Bundesministerium für innerdeutsche Beziehungen, 1987.

Wallich, Eli. *Mainsprings of the German Revival.* New Haven, CT: Yale University Press, 1955.

Federal Republic of Germany: Foreign Policy

West German foreign policy may be divided into four periods: from occupation to sovereignty (1945–55); the western policy (1955–60s), the eastern policy or *Ostpolitik* (1960s–80s), and Germany since unification (1990 on).

During the initial phase, West Germany's foreign policy was largely determined by the West, particularly the United States, which wanted to create a West German political and economic entity compatible with the principles of Western democracy and free enterprise. For that reason, the United States initiated a currency reform in the Western zones of occupied Germany (1948), which were also included in the European Recovery Program. Both the currency reform and the Marshall Plan aid contributed to West Germany's socioeconomic and political stability.

Konrad Adenauer, the first West German chancellor, was determined to firmly integrate the Federal Republic of German (FRG) into the West. His decision to establish close ties with the West guaranteed economic prosperity for the new West German state, security against potential Soviet encroachment, and the FRG's eventual sovereignty. It also led to the FRG's economic integration with Western Europe. West Germany joined the European Coal and Steel Community (ECSC) in 1951 in order to reduce trade barriers and stimulate the production of steel among six Western European countries.

Mounting East-West conflicts, such as the Berlin Blockade (1948–49), the Korean War (1950–53), and the uprising of the East Germans against their unpopular regime (1953) accelerated West Germany's integration into the West. Adenauer supported the Western Allies proposals of West German rearmament and integration into NATO, particularly after France rejected creation of the European Defense Community (1954). His efforts and those of the United States and Great Britain led to West Germany joining NATO (1955), which in turn provided the FRG with sovereignty, a goal for which Adenauer had striven since the creation of the Federal Republic.

During the second phase of West Germany's foreign policy, Adenauer continued his policy of integration. By signing the Treaty of Rome (1957), West Germany supported enhanced economic European integration and the creation of the European Economic Community. Late in his political career, Adenauer crowned his Western-oriented policy with the signing of the French-German Treaty of Friendship and Reconciliation (1963) with French President Charles de Gaulle.

Although Adenauer succeeded in fully integrating the FRG into the West, he was not able to advance unification between the two German states. His expectation that a Western-oriented "policy of strength" would lead to unification was not realized. He and the West rejected Soviet offers in the 1950s to grant German unification on the condition that a united Germany would have to accept neutrality and demilitarization.

After Adenauer's resignation (1963), foreign policy became more flexible. His successors realized that the FRG experienced increasing diplomatic isolation, largely caused by the Hallstein Doctrine, a policy in which the FRG severed diplomatic relations with any country (except the Soviet Union) that recognized East Germany. With Willy Brandt (1913–92) as foreign minister (1966–69) in the Grand Coalition government and as chancellor (1969–74) of a liberal-left coalition, West Germany initiated its *Ostpolitik*, or eastern policy. Its objective was to improve relations with Eastern Europe in general and East Germany in particular for the major purpose of increasing humanitarian contacts between Germans and of attaining stability for West Berlin, which had been isolated by the Berlin Wall. Brandt and those who supported Bonn's *Ostpolitik* realized that the policy could be executed only by maintaining its strong alliance with the West.

The Brandt administration, by signing treaties with the Soviet Union and Poland (1970), accepted the status quo of Europe, thus acknowledging Germany's territorial losses to Poland and the Soviet Union. A Four-Power Agreement signed by the former Allied occupation powers (1971) guaranteed West Berlin's de facto link to West Germany. These treaties and the Basic Treaty (1972), according to which West Germany agreed to recognize the German Democratic Republic (GDR), paved the road to the Helsinki Agreement (1975) signed by 33 European countries, the United States, and Canada, an agreement hailed by many as the climax of the detente process which had started in the 1960s.

Foreign policy during the 1970s and the 1980s was based on alliance with the West and continued detente with the East, particularly improvement of relations with the GDR. Chancellors Helmut Schmidt (1913–) and Helmut Kohl (1930–) strengthened the FRG's ties with the West while still pursuing *Ostpolitik*.

With German reunification, the foreign policy of unified Germany has taken on a new dimension. While maintaining its link with the West, the Federal Republic was forced to intensify its *Ostpolitik* owing to the disintegration of the USSR and the accompanying instability in the East. Whereas NATO is still a major prerequisite for military stability in Europe, Germany's major objective is to integrate the central and eastern European countries into a larger European framework. To alleviate the fear of a "Fourth Reich," West German foreign policy has aimed at further-

ing European integration through existing institutions, such as the European Union, NATO, and the Conference on Security and Cooperation in Europe (CSCE).

Wolfgang Schlauch

See also Adenauer, Konrad; American-German Relations; Anglo-German Relations; Bahr, Egon; Brandt, Willy; Brentano, Heinrich von; The Cold War and Germany; Franco-German Relations; Genscher, Hans-Dietrich; Hallstein, Walter; *Ostpolitik*; Postwar European Integration and Germany; Schröder, Gerhard; Soviet-German Relations

References

Ash, Timothy Garton. *In Europe's Name: Germany and the Divided Continent.* New York, NY: Random House, 1993.

Bark, Dennis, L. and David R. Gress. *A History of West Germany.* 2nd ed. Oxford: Blackwell, 1993.

Hanrieder, Wolfram F. *Germany, America, Europe: Forty Years of German Foreign Policy.* New Haven, CT: Yale University Press, 1989.

———. *West German Foreign Policy, 1949–1963: International Pressure and Domestic Response.* Palo Alto, CA: Stanford University Press, 1967.

———, ed. *West German Foreign Policy, 1949–1979.* Boulder, CO: Westview Press, 1980.

Merkl, Peter H. *German Foreign Policies, East and West: On the Threshold of a New Era.* Santa Barbara, CA: ABC-Clio, 1974.

Moreton, Edwina, ed. *Germany between East and West.* Cambridge: Cambridge University Press, 1987.

Morgan, Roger P. *The United States and West Germany, 1945–1973: A Study in Alliance Politics.* London: Oxford University Press, 1974.

Richardson, James L. *Germany and the Atlantic Alliance: The Interaction of Strategy and Politics.* Cambridge, MA: Harvard University Press, 1966.

Whetten, Lawrence L. *Germany, East and West: Conflicts, Collaboration and Confrontation.* New York, NY: New York University Press, 1980.

———. *Germany's Ostpolitik: Relations between the Federal Republic and the Warsaw Pact Countries.* London: Oxford University Press, 1971.

Federal Republic of Germany: Internal Security

Any democratic state must protect itself from individuals and groups intent on destroying it but at the same time must guarantee maximum civil liberties to its population. The Federal Republic of Germany's (FRG) Basic Law (its de facto constitution) stipulates 20 basic rights, such as freedom of speech, press, religious belief, and movement. It also includes provisions, based on the concept of "militant democracy," to prevent a repetition of the Weimar Republic's collapse in 1933. Articles 9, 18, and 21 grant the government the right to deprive political parties, associations, and individuals of their freedoms and rights if they abuse these rights in order to destroy the "free and democratic basic order."

Article 21 stipulates that parties judged by their "aims or the behavior of their adherents to impair or abolish the free order or to endanger the existence of the Federal Republic shall be unconstitutional." Based on this provision, the Federal Constitutional Court in the 1950s banned the German Communist Party and the neo-Nazi Socialist Reich Party.

The Bundestag also enacted over the decades laws dealing with national security, many of them contested for unduly restricting individual rights. In 1968, after years of heated discussions in the country, the Bundestag passed the National Emergency Act (*Notstandsgesetz*), which ended the reserved emergency powers of the Allied occupation authorities. Its provisions refer to a "state of defense" and a "state of tension" against an external enemy and a "state of internal emergency" (for instance, a natural catastrophe or an endangering of the democratic order), in which individual rights would be limited. No chancellor has ever had to make use of the act.

The police, supported by the Federal Criminal Investigation Bureau, is charged with the maintenance of public order. In 1950, the federal and *Länder* offices for the protection of the constitutions (*Verfassungsschutz*) were established to keep subversive activities in the FRG under observation. According to statute, the offices, supervised by the ministries of the interior, are responsible for compiling dossiers on left- and right-wing extremists and their organizations' attempts to undermine the democratic system. Critics insist that the offices have exceeded their legal restrictions, for instance by illegal wiretapping and making use of thousands of informers whose information often is based on hearsay evidence, malice, or mistaken identities.

Government agencies also have expanded their network of data banks to collect information on every FRG resident as a means of enhancing internal security. National and state parliaments have created the posts of commissioners for data protection and passed legislation restricting the use of information in the data banks. Nevertheless, critics have been concerned about the misuse of data and the names of innocent persons stored in intelligence computer systems.

In the early 1980s, the Green Party and citizens' initiatives protested the upcoming 1980 census, postponed for budgetary reasons until 1983. They objected to provisions in the law that would permit police and security agencies to compare the census data with individuals' registration data already on file with local authorities. The Federal Constitutional Court, upon petition, ruled that the census bill's provisions endangered the individual's right to privacy. Government and the Bundestag thereupon revised the bill; a census was held in 1987.

In the late 1960s, the Baader-Meinhof Group and other leftist terrorist groups formed to fight a capitalist government they viewed as repressive. The government, reacting to the popular fear and near-hysteria engendered by the media, called for more law and order to crush the groups responsible for assassinations, arson, bank robberies, and other illegal acts. The Bundestag passed a series of sweeping antiterrorist laws, some of which, however, limited the rights of all residents—e.g., one act granted the police the right to search all apartments in a building in which a terrorist might be hiding. In 1976, an amendment to the penal code, repealed in the 1980s, instituted censorship of materials recommending unlawful violent acts. The law led to harassment of radical bookstore owners and to cancellation of provocative plays and films on television.

As of 1967, new social movements, concerned with ecology and peace against nuclear energy, protested government policies, partly by political demonstrations. Most demonstrations were peaceful, but some turned confrontational when leftist anarchists, wearing masks to hide their identity, infiltrated them. In 1985, the Bundestag passed a law prohibiting individuals from wearing masks and/or carrying "protective" weapons. Police could require demonstrators to disperse if there was an imminent danger of violence.

Government intelligence agencies have kept watch over left-wing radical parties and groups. These parties, claiming to uphold the democratic order, have received some voter support in municipal and state elections, especially in periods of recession, but have not constituted an immediate threat to the system. Government agencies are more concerned with the small right-wing and neo-Nazi groups that have engaged in violence against foreigners, homosexuals, and leftists.

To sum up: the FRG governments have preserved internal security from 1949 to 1990 despite challenges from leftist and rightist extremists. In the process, however, they have on numerous occasions infringed on the civil liberties of all residents. Since unification, the failure to take action or to be informed about the newest wave of right-wing, antiforeigner unrest has cast doubts on the intentions of the police's political masters and on the capabilities of the system.

Gerard Braunthal

See also Baader-Meinhof Group; The Basic Law; Censorship; Citizenship and Foreigners; Civil Service; Crime; Extra-Parliamentary Opposition; Federal Republic of Germany; Judicial System; Federal Republic of Germany: Political Radicalism and Neo-Nazism; Federal Republic of Germany: Political Terrorism; German Democratic Republic: State Security; The Greens: Movement, Party, Ideology; Information Processing; Radical Right; Violence

References

Atlantic Brücke. *Civil Liberties and the Defense of Democracy against Extremists and Terrorists: A Report on the West German Situation.* Freiburg: Rombach, 1980.

Becker, Jilian. *Hitler's Children: The Story of the Baader-Meinhof Terrorist Gang.* Rev. ed. London: Panther, 1978.

Bertrand Russell Peace Foundation. *Censorship, Legal Defence and the Domestic Intelligence Service in West Germany: Conclusions of the Final Session of the Third Russell Tribunal.* Nottingham: Russell Press, 1979.

Braunthal, Gerard. "Public Order and Civil Liberties." *Developments in West German Politics.* Ed. Gordon Smith, William E. Paterson, and Peter H. Merkl. Houndmills: Macmillan, 1989.

Cobler, Sebastian. *Law, Order, and Politics in West Germany.* Middlesex: Penguin Books, 1978. Trans. Francis McDonagh. Revised from *Die Gefahr geht von den Menschen aus.* Berlin: Rotbuch, 1976.

Federal Republic of Germany: Judicial System

The German judiciary embraces a single countrywide system of courts. It consists of regular courts and four sets of special courts. The regular courts hear ordinary civil and criminal suits as well as cases dealing with commercial law. Separate labor, administrative, social, and tax courts exercise jurisdiction in their specialized domains. Like the regular courts, these tribunals are organized into integrated judicial hierarchies. All trial and intermediate appellate courts are *Land* (state) courts, whereas the final court of appeal within each hierarchy is a federal tribunal. Federal statutes determine the structure, procedure, and authority of these courts. Except for the final courts of appeal at the federal level, however, all the courts are administered, financed, and staffed by the individual *Länder* (states).

The regular courts of ordinary jurisdiction exemplify the basic structure of the judiciary. Local courts (*Amtsgerichte*) line the bottom of the judicial pyramid. Numbering about 800, staffed by more than ten times as many judges, and readily available throughout the country, they administer small civil claims and petty criminal matters. They also act as juvenile and family courts. Finally, they exercise jurisdiction over noncontentious matters such as maintaining land registers, drafting wills, and administering estates. Local courts are single-judge tribunals, but they may include twenty or more judges, each constituting a specialized division within the court. The number of judges assigned to a local court depends on the size of its docket and the population of the area it serves.

Landgerichte (district courts) occupy the next level of the regular judiciary. Numbering around 100, they try criminal and civil cases beyond the jurisdiction of local courts and also manage cases arising under the commercial code. Unlike general trial courts of original jurisdiction in the United States, where single judges preside, German district courts are collegial tribunals. Three professional judges hear each case. When trying criminal cases, however, in what is called the *Grosse Strafkammer* (Upper Criminal Court), the court consists of three professional judges and two lay judges. In commercial cases, one professional judge is joined by two lay judges with business backgrounds. The district court serves as an appellate tribunal in criminal appeals from the lower courts. The *Kleine Strafkammer* (Lower Criminal Court), made up of one professional judge and two lay judges, hears these appeals.

The *Oberlandesgericht* (Court of Appeal) is a regional court that hears appeals on matters of law from lower courts. Most *Länder* have one such tribunal but the more populous states have as many as three. These courts sit in divisions called senates, each consisting of three judges. The *Bundesgerichtshof* (Federal Supreme Court), the court of last resort, is at the apex of the regular judiciary. It has 120 judges who sit in 5-judge senates. A president presides over each senate. The court as a

whole consists of twelve civil senates, five criminal senates, and seven additional senates specializing in particular subject areas. The president of the full court is responsible for its internal administration. In nonjudicial matters he is subject to the supervisory authority of the Federal Ministry of Justice.

The special courts have a similar structure. Cases involving labor law, tax law, or social security law, as well as a wide range of disputes arising out of the relations between citizens and public administrative authorities, are initiated in courts of original jurisdiction corresponding to the regular district courts. In each of these courts, lay judges experienced in the subject matter under consideration serve in an equal capacity with professional judges. The highest court of appeal in each of these areas are, respectively, the *Bundesarbeitsgericht* (Federal Labor Court), the *Bundesfinanzgericht* (Federal Tax Court), the *Bundessozialgericht* (Federal Social Court), and the *Bundesverwaltungsgericht* (Federal Administrative Court). Like the federal supreme court, these federal high courts, each headed by a president, are divided into senates of five judges each.

The country's highest tribunal is the *Bundesverfassungsgericht* (Federal Constitutional Court). Like the Bundestag and Bundesrat, however, the federal constitutional court, which sits in two senates of eight judges each, is an independent and coequal branch of the national government—it is not part of the regular judiciary. It alone is empowered to declare statutes unconstitutional under the Basic Law. Its jurisdiction includes the authority to hear constitutional disputes between levels and branches of government and, at the request of a state or the federal government, to decide whether a political party should be banned as unconstitutional. Its decisions are binding on all courts, all legislatures, and all executive officials at both state and federal levels.

The judges who preside over the judiciary are highly trained legal professionals. If law graduates choose to become judges, they enter a probationary period of three years, upon the successful completion of which they receive a judgeship with lifetime security and tenure (up to the mandatory retirement age of 68). In 1994, Germany had some 19,000 judges, nearly all of whom served on regular and special courts below the federal level. Although independent and subject only to the law, these judges are recruited, trained, and supervised by the *Land* justice ministries. All federal judges are recruited at the national level. The 16 judges of the federal constitutional court are the only members of the judiciary who serve for limited terms of office. The Bundestag and Bundesrat each chooses half of the justices for nonrenewable terms of 12 years.

Donald P. Kommers

See also The Basic Law; Civil Service; Constitutions; German Democratic Republic: Judicial System; Labor Laws; Law, German Conception of; Legal Profession; Third Reich: Legal Profession; Trade Unions, 1945–90

References
Forrester, Ian S. and Hans-Michael Ilgen. *The German Legal System.* South Hackensack, NJ: Fred B. Rothman, 1972.

Foster, Nigel. *German Law and Legal Systems*. London: Blackstone Press, 1993.

Kommers, Donald P. *The Federal Constitutional Court.* Washington, DC: American Institute for Contemporary German Studies, Johns Hopkins University, 1994.

———. *Judicial Politics in West Germany*. Beverly Hills, CA: Sage, 1976.

Richert, John P. *West German Lay Judges*. Tampa, FL: University Presses of Florida, 1983.

Federal Republic of Germany: Literature

It could be argued that the question of nationalism in the literature of the Federal Republic of Germany (FRG) until 1990 is irrelevant. Many writers who had survived the Third Reich within its borders and supported Hitler soon fell into oblivion as a result of their country's political collapse and the ensuing "reeducation" measures taken by the Allies. Others who emerged from "inner emigration" or who were just beginning their careers as writers strove for a renewal of German literature based on general humanitarian, rather than national, characteristics. The majority of exile writers did not return immediately after the war, or they resettled in the Soviet zone, which in 1949 became the German Democratic Republic (GDR).

The widespread desire of German readers and writers to become current with international trends in literature led to the popularity of American, English, Spanish, and other authors who previously were banned or neglected. The influence of Ernest Hemingway in particular may be noticed in the short stories of Wolfgang Borchert (1921–47), Heinrich Böll (1917–85), Hans Bender, and Wolfdietrich Schnurre. Modern culture in general has a tendency to cross national boundaries, and the FRG soon emerged as the leader in the publication of German-language literature, including works written in Austria, Switzerland, and the GDR. The social historian and cultural critic Theodor W. Adorno (1903–69) wrote in 1950, soon after his return from American exile, that in view of today's wide range of intellectual influences, modern cultures can no longer be defined along national lines.

Nevertheless, one may observe certain national characteristics in the literature of the FRG. The need for a new beginning of German culture and literature was proclaimed in the journal, *Der Ruf* (The call), which Hans Werner Richter and Alfred Andersch (1914–80) had founded as prisoners of war in the United States and later continued to publish in Germany until it was forbidden by the Allies for its excessively liberal outlook. It was also upon Richter's initiative that, beginning in 1947, a group of young German writers founded the Gruppe 47, which met annually and awarded prizes for the best unpublished works presented at their meetings. Böll, Günter Eich (1907–72), Ilse Aichinger, Günter Grass (1927–), Ingeborg Bachmann (1926–73), Peter Weiss (1916–82), and Martin Walser (1927–), all at one time or another, belonged to this group.

While young German writers tried to find a new way of depicting reality by weighing each word for its ability to express the truth, debates arose about the works of some previously established writers that were being published for the first

Günter Grass. Courtesy of Inter Nationes, Bonn.

time in Germany. For example, the novel *Dr. Faustus* by Thomas Mann (1875–1955) was published in 1947 and added much momentum to the discussion about Germany's collective guilt. The great popularity of the play *Des Teufels General* (published as *The Devil's General*), 1947, by Carl Zuckmayer (1896–1977) must in part be attributed to the audience's identification with the play's hero, a German general in Hitler's Luftwaffe whose dislike of Hitler is only surpassed by his love of flying airplanes. The feelings of a great number of German people were reflected in Ernst von Salomon's (1902–72) *Der Fragebogen* (published as *The Questionnaire*), 1951, an expanded answer to the questionnaire with which the Allies tried to determine the amount of Germans' involvement in Nazi activities. Even the apparent lack of an answer to the protagonist's problems in the play by a young German author, Borchert's *Draussen vor der Tür* (published as *The Man Outside*), 1947, may have confirmed Germans in their desire to forget the past.

For many German readers literature after the war was a way of escaping the dire realities of daily survival and of rebuilding their wartorn country. Their tendency to forget was also aided politically with the implementation of the Marshall Plan in 1947 and the ensuing Economic Miracle. Lyrical poetry and apolitical literature in general were popular in the 1950s. Key figures were Gottfried Benn (1886–1956), who after a long period of professional isolation found eager readers and listeners for his "static poems," and Rudolf Hagelstange, whose sonnets were aimed at a revival of classical forms and values. Another popular genre during this period was the *Hörspiel* (radio play), allowing for the expression of dreams and other unrealistic situations (Eich, Bachmann, Wolfgang Hildesheimer). German authors also responded to the escapist propensity of their readers with novels and stories depicting imagined situations (Hermann Kasack, Hans Erich Nossack), literary conjectures (Uwe Johnson [1934–84], Arno Schmidt [1914–79]), magic realism in prose form

(Aichinger, Elisabeth Langgässer [1899–1950]), the drama of the absurd (Grass, Hildesheimer), and so-called "concrete" poetry (Helmut Heissenbüttel, Franz Mon).

Nevertheless, during this period of general escapism, individual writers made a strong effort at coming to terms with their national past. Walser, who had already lampooned German society for its vain snobbery, political corruption, and professional opportunism in his novels *Ehen in Philippsburg* (Marriages in Philippsburg), 1957, and *Halbzeit* (Half-time), 1960, directly confronted Germans with their ostensibly painless switch from National Socialism to Western capitalism in a trilogy of dramas beginning with *Eiche und Angora* (Oak and angora), 1961. Andersch recounted his renouncement of German nationalism in his autobiographical novel, *Die Kirschen der Freiheit* (The cherries of freedom), 1953, and combined his coping with the past with a critique of contemporary West German society in *Sansibar oder der letzte Grund* (published as *Flight to Afar*), 1957. In several of his prose works Böll depicted parallels between the racial and political dualism of the Third Reich and the social inequalities of the Economic Miracle. Grass reminded his people of their infamous Nazi past in such novels as *Die Blechtrommel* (published as *The Tin Drum*), 1959, and *Hundejahre* (published as *Dog Years*), 1963. Another author who delved into Germany's immediate past and tried to extract a "German lesson" from it for the present was Siegfried Lenz (1926–) with his novel *Die Deutschstunde* (published as *The German Lesson*), 1968. The opportunistic practices of the Bonn political establishment were exposed in Wolfgang Koeppen's (1906–96) *Das Treibhaus* (The hot house), 1953. In trying to stem the political and cultural restoration of the first two decades of the FRG, these authors made their readers aware of what the German psychologists Alexander (1909–82) and Margarete Mitscherlich (1917–) called the need to overcome their "inability to mourn" and their "loss of historical consciousness."

During the 1960s, a sequence of political and social events led to the gradual change of public opinion: the 1962 trial of the news magazine *Der Spiegel* (The mirror) concerning its alleged betrayal of government secrets; the formation of an *ausserparlamentarische Opposition* (APO; extra-parliamentary opposition), of which the Sozialistischer Deutscher Studentenbund (SDS; Socialist German Students Federation) made headlines in 1967 when it demonstrated against the escalation of the war in Vietnam, the shah of Iran's visit to Germany, and the emergency laws enacted by the German government; the depression of 1966–67, marking the end of the Economic Miracle and increasing unemployment; the intellectuals' critique of the overcrowded German universities and the need to reform the entire school system; and the stationing of atomic weapons on German soil.

These factors also led to new developments in literature. Already in 1956, the year after Germany joined NATO, Richter and other writers of the Gruppe 47 had formed the Grünwalder Kreis in order to protest against growing militarism and neo-Fascism in the FRG. However, writers who had once been considered political were gradually losing esteem in favor of more radical new writers who were proclaiming

revolutionary action, among them Max Bense, Oswald Wiener, Alexander Kluge (1932–), Rolf Dieter Brinkmann, and Wolfgang Wondratschek. In 1968, Hans Magnus Enzensberger (1929–) declared "the death of literature" and left an American college mid-semester to go to Cuba, where he collected the material for his play *Das Verhör von Habana* (published as *The Interrogation of Havana*), 1970, about the failed American invasion of the Bay of Pigs.

During the 1960s, a wave of political documentary drama swept the FRG, including plays by Rolf Hochhuth (1931–) (*Der Stellvertreter* [published as *The Deputy*], 1963), about the Pope's lack of intervention in the Nazis' genocide of the Jews), Heinar Kipphardt (*J. Robert Oppenheimer*, 1964, about the invention and the effects of the atomic bomb), Peter Weiss (1916–82) (*Die Ermittlung* [published as *The Investigation*], 1965, about the 1965 Auschwitz trial in Frankfurt), and Tankred Torst (*Toller*, 1968, about the writer by the same name and his participation in the Bavarian Soviet Republic of 1919). Other authors (e.g., Max von der Grün, Günter Wallraff, Erika Runge) exposed the hard conditions of blue-collar workers, including the millions of foreign workers. A number of authors, particularly Grass, actively participated in the political campaign that resulted in the election of Willy Brandt (1913–92) to the office of chancellor in 1969.

The wave of political activism spread into the early 1970s, with young new writers (Rainer Werner Fassbinder [1945–82], Martin Sperr, Franz Xaver Kroetz) calling attention to the social problems of minority groups and German rural inhabitants. However, the 1970s also marked a turn toward the private sphere and a newly discovered inwardness in FRG literature. Handke, Koeppen, Walter Kempowski (1929–), Elisabeth Plessen, and others brought about a new subjectivity in literature by replacing national concerns with matters of the private realm.

Postmodernist thought in culture and philosophy, which prescribed no specific rules for either the contents or the form of a literary work, had a profound influence on the literature of the 1980s. The "strong thinking" proclaimed by the most significant cultural philosopher of the FRG, Jürgen Habermas (1929–), who was also an important spokesman for enlightened reasoning and antinationalism, was replaced by the "weak thinking" of a literary fundamentalism that lacked critical perspective. In the verses of such song writers as Udo Lindenberg, as well as the prose works of authors such as Botho Strauss (1944–) and Herbert Achternbusch, the reader is free to choose from a large variety of ostensibly meaningless literary expressions, ranging from an appeal for favoring simple pleasures to black humor about the environmental catastrophe affecting the FRG and the rest of the world. Germany's reunification in 1990 marked the end of a separate stream of literary development in the FRG (as opposed to that of the GDR) and set the stage for a new all-German national literature.

Helmut F. Pfanner

See also Andersch, Alfred; Bachmann, Ingeborg; Benn, Gottfried; Böll, Heinrich; Borchert, Wolfgang; Eich, Günter;

Enzensberger, Hans Magnus; Extra-Parliamentary Opposition; Fassbinder, Rainer Werner; Feminist Writing; *Germanistik;* Grass, Günter; Habermas, Jürgen; Handke, Peter; Hochhuth, Rolf; Kempowski, Walter; Kluge, Alexander; Koeppen, Wolfgang; Langgässer, Elisabeth; Lenz, Siegfried; Mann, Thomas; Mitscherlich, Alexander; Mitscherlich, Margarete; Radio Plays; Salomon, Ernst von; Schmidt, Arno; Strauss, Botho; Wallraff, Günter; Walser, Martin; Weiss, Peter; Working-Class Literature; Zuckmayer, Carl

References

Demetz, Peter. *Postwar German Literature: A Critical Introduction.* New York, NY: Pegasus, 1970.

Durzak, Manfred, ed. *Die deutsche Literatur der Gegenwart: Aspekte und Tendenzen.* 3rd ed. Stuttgart: Reclam, 1976.

Glaser, Hermann. *Die Kulturgeschichte der Bundesrepublik Deutschland.* 3 vols. Munich: Carl Hanser, 1989.

Grimminger, Rolf, ed. *Hansers Sozialgeschichte der deutschen Literatur vom 16. Jahrhundert bis zur Gegenwart.* Vol. 10. Munich: Carl Hanser, 1987.

Jens, Walter. *Deutsche Literatur der Gegenwart: Themen, Stile, Tendenzen.* New ed. Munich: R. Piper, 1973.

Lattmann, Dieter, ed. *Kindlers Literaturgeschichte der Gegenwart: Autoren: Werke, Themen, Tendenzen seit 1945. Die Literatur der Bundesrepublik Deutschland,* vols. 1 and 2. Rev. ed. Frankfurt am Main: Kindler, 1980.

Literatur in der Bundesrepublik Deutschland bis 1967. Ed. Ludwig Fischer. Munich: Carl Hanser, 1986.

Moos, Detlev et al., eds. *Kulturelles Leben in der Bundesrepublik Deutschland.* Bonn: Inter Nationes, 1992.

Moser, Dietz-Rüdiger, ed. *Neues Handbuch der deutschen Gegenwartsliteratur seit 1945.* Munich: Nymphenburger, 1990.

Reich-Ranicki, Marcel. *Deutsche Literatur in West und Ost: Prosa seit 1945.* Munich: R. Piper, 1963.

Schnell, Ralf. *Die Literatur der Bundesrepublik: Autoren, Geschichte, Literaturbetrieb.* Stuttgart: J.B. Metzler'sche Verlagsbuchhandlung, 1986.

Schütz, Erhard and Jochen Vogt. *Einführung in die deutsche Literatur des 20. Jahrhunderts.* Vol. 3: *Bundesrepublik und DDR.* Opladen: Westdeutscher Verlag, 1980.

Urbanek, Walter. *Deutsche Literatur: Das 19. und 20. Jahrhundert: Epochen, Gestalten, Gestaltungen.* 2nd rev. ed. Bamberg: C.C. Buchners Verlag, 1971.

Federal Republic of Germany: Political Radicalism and Neo-Nazism

Most Western democracies have extreme right-wing parties and other social movements that express nationalist, racist, xenophobic, and aggressive sentiments. What distinguishes the Federal Republic of Germany (FRG) is not the size or ferocity of its groups but rather the fact that, half a century ago, such a movement—National Socialism—went berserk, starting wars and slaughtering "racial inferiors." Given this past experience, any recurrence of such groups in Germany makes observers nervous—a fact that many Germans resent.

Public opinion surveys in postwar Germany suggest that perhaps one in four Germans endorsed Nazism and twice that many found it tolerable. The obvious failure of Nazism itself and strong educational campaigns moved many Germans toward democracy, and the FRG's political and social successes made such a form of government seem best for Germans. Real social change cut the number of hardcore Nazis—those accepting great chunks of its ideological baggage—to about one in six in 1950, one in twelve a decade later, and below one in twenty after 1970. The current ratio of 2 to 4 percent in Germany is not greater than in the United States, Great Britain, or France.

Post-1945 Germany has nevertheless had more than its share of extreme right-wing political groups. The German Rightist Party (Deutsche Rechts-Partei; DRP) in the British zone and the Economic Reconstruction Alliance (Wirtschaftliche Aufbauvereinigung; WAV) in the American zone were only two of the larger among those emerging as early as late 1945. Conflict among "true believers" about Hitler's goals and policies, and competition in an electoral system that denies seats to members of parties not crossing a 5-percent hurdle, nevertheless meant poor showings in the first national election of August 1949.

Some extreme right-wingers soon agreed to coalesce under a new Socialist Reich Party (Sozialistische Reichspartei; SRP), founded in October 1949. Its leaders openly supported Hitler and the Third Reich, sought to propagate a new stab-in-the-back myth, belittled talk of a Holocaust under Nazism, and eventually adopted Hitler's organizational principle, the *Führerprinzip,* as their own. After some modest and ever-diminishing successes in provincial elections, the SRP, with its anticonstitutional stance, was banned by the federal constitutional court in October 1952.

Regrouping the floundering extreme right-wing parties took a dozen years, until rightists came up with the National Democratic Party (Nationaldemokratische Partei Deutschlands; NPD) in November 1964. The NPD avoided the constitutional trap that befell the SRP. It also had the good fortune of encountering troubles in the FRG's economy, which it used successfully for its own partisan purposes. Even so, after some sharp gains in provincial elections, the NPD obtained only 4.3 percent in the national election of September 1969. The party slowly declined. Although it continues to exist today, its political significance is minuscule.

By the early 1970s, it almost seemed as if neo-Nazism in the FRG, and perhaps even right-wing extremism, were dead. But in fact such sentiments remained alive among a small minority; and reminders of the dangers took place from time to time. In September 1980, a member of the Hoffmann Defense Sport Group (Wehrsportgruppe Hoffmann) planted a bomb that killed 13 and wounded 219 visitors to Munich's Octoberfest. (The Sport Group was later banned.) A plethora of such splinter groups and sometimes tragic events notwithstanding, right-wing extremists seemed interested more in self-preservation than making political gains.

The most successful among current extreme right-wing groups, the Republicans (Die Republikaner; REP), originated in Bavaria in November 1983. Early tries at provincial elections failed. In West Berlin's election of January 1989, however, the REPs found the issue that could win: the FRG's growing number of foreign immigrants. While other parties pussyfooted around the issue, the REP faced it head on—stating clearly that Germany was not and should not become an immigrant state, that foreigners seeking "political refuge" were abusing the privilege, that the numerous foreign workers, asylum seekers, and others entering the FRG were destroying the economy and the well-being of the German people. This open confrontation with government policy netted the REP 7.5 percent of the vote and 11 parliamentary seats.

The election in West Berlin, followed in June 1989 by the European parliamentary election in which the REP gained 7.1 percent of the German vote, gave the REP and other right-wing extremists a clear notion of the major parties' vulnerability. The REP itself soon split and lost members, without, however, dissolving. Meanwhile, skinheads, undertrained and unemployed youths in the FRG's new eastern provinces, and others picked up the REP chant of "Germany for the Germans" and used it to voice their own, often inchoate, grievances. It gave them the "right" to beat up foreign workers, firebomb residences of asylum seekers, display Nazi symbols, and daub Jewish gravestones with swastikas.

Such protest against government policy was fueled by the government's inability—some saw an unwillingness—to move quickly either to resolve what many Germans saw as a serious immigration problem, to stop criminal behavior, or to provide more employment opportunities in the FRG's depressed areas. Public opinion surveys found substantial numbers of Germans who, until the more deadly firebombings occurred, condoned the activities of the REP, skinheads, and others as a means to force the government to deal with important issues.

By late summer 1992, the German and the world press was expressing alarm with the antiforeign violence reported to be taking place in Germany. The end of that year saw important government policies aimed at mitigating the cause of this violence, improved training procedures to protect foreigners—and, indeed, all people—and private and public efforts to create a positive climate of opinion toward immigrants, asylum seekers, and other foreigners. In March 1993, however, at communal elections in Hesse the REP garnered 8.3 percent of the vote.

Optimists believe that the immediate problem can be resolved, albeit at some cost because of the government's slow intervention. Pessimists see a slowly growing number of hardcore extremists, as opposed to disgruntled citizens expressing their opposition. But the reality—that a small percentage of people generate and respond positively to the lures of right-wing extremism—will remain, for Germany and other countries.

Richard Merritt

See also Baader-Meinhof Group; Extra-Parliamentary Opposition; Federal Republic of Germany: Internal Security; Fed-

eral Republic of Germany: Political Terrorism; Minorities: Ethnocultural and Foreign; Parties and Politics; Students; Universities; Violence

References

Nagle, John David. *The National Democratic Party: Right Radicalism in the Federal Republic of Germany.* Berkeley, CA: University of California Press, 1970.

Stöss, Richard. *Politics against Democracy.* Providence, RI: Berg Publishers, 1992.

Tauber, Kurt P. *Beyond Eagle and Swastika: German Nationalism since 1945.* Middletown, CT: Wesleyan University Press, 1967.

Federal Republic of Germany: Political Terrorism

The first political terrorist groups in the FRG emerged on the left from militant by-products of the decaying extra-parliamentary opposition (*ausserparlamentarische Opposition*, APO). At its peak (from April to early summer 1968), the APO occasionally used violence against material objects as a protest sign (e.g., arson in department stores). With the APO in decline, some circles of the militant West Berlin subculture (Blues) used terror in order to recruit a revolutionary front, to liberate imprisoned comrades, and as a device of self-realization. The militant circles of the APO continued to decline until 1970. In the process, they spawned a core of individuals from which terrorist groups emerged. A circle around the arsonists Andreas Baader and Gudrun Ensslin founded the Red Army Faction (RAF) in 1970, proclaiming that they would organize a military assault on the state. In 1972, sections of the Blues formed the Second of June Movement, which also adopted the strategy of attacking the state apparatus. Right-wing terrorism began around 1976, after militant and legalistic right-wing extremist forces became polarized during the 1970s. After electoral success in the second half of the 1960s, the right-wing National Democratic Party (NPD) failed to enter the federal parliament in the 1969 elections. An increasing number of militant right-wing extremist, mainly neo-Nazi groups, were then established in the first half of the 1970s.

The capitalist economic order served as the target of social revolutionary left-wing terrorism. Whereas the RAF, regarding itself as an avant garde, opened the collectively planned military assault on the state apparatus, the Second of June Movement criticized the RAF's ascetic and calculated use of terror and tried to mobilize spontaneous revolutionary forces. Initially, the RAF focused its attacks on the American army in Germany because of American military action in Vietnam. The RAF also criticized the FRG as a loyal ally of the United States. In June 1972, FRG authorities had the leading figures of the RAF imprisoned. The Second of June Movement, which criticized Great Britain's role in Northern Ireland, concentrated its attacks on British institutions (an assault on a British yacht club resulted in an unintended death).

The Revolutionary Cells (RZ), founded in 1973, rejected the RAF's transition to military warfare against the state, accepted terror as a tactical device, and restricted themselves to the pre-revolutionary organization of the revolutionary forces, which were regarded as being too weak for a military confrontation. The RZ attacked predominantly material objects but also resorted to kneecappings and assassinations. Between 1974 and 1977, the RZ turned to kidnapping prominent individuals in order to liberate imprisoned comrades. The ex-members of the disintegrating Second of June Movement merged with the RAF, while others joined the RZ or reinforced the "autonomous" scene that emerged at the beginning of the 1980s. This was a movement of nonorganized streetfighters, some of whom accepted terror as a device for the self-expressive realizations of a revolutionary identity.

After 1974, the RAF abandoned theories about a latent revolutionary situation, and by the end of the 1970s proceeded to combat assumed global consolidation strategies of Western industrialized states by the selected assassination of key exponents of these strategies. During the 1980s, the RAF consolidated its international connections with allied terrorist groups and started tactical cooperation with the East German state security service (Stasi). Reflecting their lack of success and the changing world order (decline of state socialism), the RAF provisionally renounced its strategy of armed struggle in April 1992 and has since been seeking a new orientation, exploring cooperation with all militant forces. The authorities lack hard evidence about the perpetrators of left-wing terrorist acts since 1984, recently calling the present existence of the RAF into question.

Terrorism on the right rejects the concept of a democratic state ruled by constitutional law and aims at the seizure of the authority of the state in order to realize authoritarian values regarded as national and binding. Between 1976 and 1982, five ephemeral right-wing terrorist groups emerged, each of which decayed after the arrest of core members. The Kühnen-Schulte-Wegener Group (1977–78) emerged from neo-Nazi circles and sought to attack the military, the Berlin Wall, transit traffic through the GDR, and the concentration camp memorial in Bergen-Belsen. It failed to outlive the preparatory logistical phase. The Otte Group (1976–78) sought to prepare the seizure of power by neo-Nazi groups with the help of attacks on public buildings, public figures, the inner-German border, transit traffic, and members of the legal profession. In 1977, the group successfully carried out an assault on the county court in Hannover. The Deutsche Aktionsgruppen (German Action Groups), 1980, attacked institutions for asylum seekers (two deaths) and memorials dedicated to the persecution of Jews under Nazism. In late 1980, members of the paramilitary group Wehrsportgruppe Hoffman (Defense Sport Group), preparing a national revolution, shot the Jewish publisher Lewin and his partner. The Hepp-Kexel Group (1982–83) successfully attacked United States army institutions. This marks the peak to date of right-wing violence. Other than attacks by individuals, no new terrorist groups appeared between 1983 and 1990. The increasing use of terror against foreigners since 1991 does not generally appear to have the strategic aim of seizing power and can therefore not be classified as political terrorism. Since 1992, the term ter-

"Wanted list" of terrorists. Courtesy of Inter Nationes, Bonn.

rorism nevertheless has been widely used to characterize these xenophobic assaults.

Frank Krause

See also Baader-Meinhof Group; Extra-Parliamentary Opposition; Federal Republic of Germany: Political Radicalism and Neo-Nazism; Minorities: Ethnocultural and Foreign; Radical Right; Students; Violence

References

Aust, Stefan. *The Baader-Meinhof Group: The Inside Story of a Phenomenon.* London: Bodley Head, 1987.

Becker, Julian. *Hitler's Children: The Story of the Baader-Meinhof Terrorist Gang.* Philadelphia, PA: Lippincott, 1977.

Hoffman, Bruce. *Right-Wing Terrorism in West Germany.* Santa Monica, CA: Rand Corporation, 1986.

Federal Republic of Germany: Postwar Refugee and Expellee Organizations

Beginning with Germany's unconditional surrender, and sanctioned by the decisions reached at Potsdam in July–August 1945, roughly 12 million Germans became part of Europe's largest population transfer. As an immediate consequence, numerous refugee and expellee organizations emerged within the Western occupation zones. Discouraged by the occupying powers from engaging in political activities, hundreds of informal groups and clubs, church and cultural organizations, and special-interest groups provided support and unity for the growing numbers of refugees and expellees. After 1949, their interests were represented by the Bloc of Expellees and Disenfranchised (BHE).

Distinctly different from displaced persons (DPs), expellees and refugees cooperated in the creation of organizations representing their interests. The official distinction between expellees and refugees rested upon the individual's legal place of residence as of September 1, 1939. Expellees were those people who resided in eastern German territories under foreign administration after 1945 (defined by Germany's borders as of December 31, 1937), in the Saar Basin, or in other countries. Refugees, on the other hand, were those persons who resided within the Soviet occupation zone after 1945. Collectively, refugees and expellees numbered roughly eight million persons (16 percent of the West German population) in 1950.

Though an attempt to create a national organization originated in the British zone in 1948, only after May 1949—when the new West German Basic Law took effect—did expellee-refugee political activity commence on the state and national levels. "Homeland provincial societies" (*Landsmannschaften*) at the state level were united in August 1949 in a national organization, the United East German Provincial Societies, headed by Hans Lukaschek. While assisting in the location of family members and integration into West Germany, these societies also worked to keep alive a knowledge of their respective homelands' history, culture, and language (dialect) by encouraging a sense of unity among the members. The political outlook of these societies differed, ranging from the liberal to the clearly nationalistic. Nevertheless, they all shared the desire to preserve their cultural heritage in anticipation of their eventual return to their *Heimat* (homeland).

The homeland provincial societies and associated groups were divided around four regional affiliations: northeastern Germany, Silesia, the Sudetenland, and southeastern Europe (Russia and the Balkans). Those associated with northeastern Germany represented smaller regional groups: East Prussia, West Prussia, Pomerania, East Brandenburg, the Baltic, and Poland (the area around Danzig).

Whereas East Prussians united within their own *Landsmannschaft*, West Prussians, largely from the former free city of Danzig, organized their own society, the Bund der Danziger. Expellees from territories transferred to Poland divided themselves into three groups: those from central Poland (Landsmannschaft Weichsel-Warthe), East Brandenburg (Landsmannschaft Berlin-Mark Brandenburg), and Pomerania. Ethnic Germans from Poland numbered approximately 300,000, from East Brandenburg 130,000, and from Pomerania 900,000. Led initially by Herbert von Bismarck, Pomeranians created their own national parliament and Pommersche Landsmannschaft. Preserving Pomeranian cultural interests were the Hans-Lange-Bund (Hans Lange Federation) and the Gesellschaft für Pommersche Geschichte, Altertumskunde und Kunst (Society for the History, Archaeology, and Art of Pomerania).

Additional societies represented refugees from Saxony, Saxony-Anhalt, Mecklenburg, and Thuringia. These various *Landsmannschaften* were united in Walter von Keudell's United Homeland Provincial Societies of Central (East) Germany (Vereinigte Landsmannschaften Mitteldeutschlands).

Silesian Germans were divided among those whose identity was linked with Upper Silesia (ceded to Poland after World War I) and Lower Silesia (transferred to Polish authorities after World War II). The preservation of cultural traditions remained strong within every group. The Kulturwerk Silesia (Silesian Cultural Association) espoused a romanticized vision of its past rather than cultivating the typical optimistic hope of returning to the *Heimat*.

Sudeten Germans campaigned first during the Weimar era for the annexation of the Sudetenland to Germany. The largest single group of expellees (just under two million), the Sudeten Germans established a collection of institutions to protect their heritage and promote their political agenda in West Germany. Building upon their previous experience as a unique ethnic minority, their scholars organized the Sudetendeutsches Archiv (Sudeten German Archive) and Collegium Carolinum in Munich, along with various historical, research, and political associations to promote Sudeten German interests. Unlike the more pessimistic Kulturwerk Silesia, Sudeten Germans blended a sense of nationalism within a romantic vision of their history.

The most diverse group of ethnic Germans came from the southeast. Of the half-million expellees in this group, large numbers came from Hungary, Slovakia, Romania, Yugoslavia, and the Soviet Union. These groups formed their own societies and cultural organizations.

Alongside Lukaschek's cultural-political organization, Linus Kather gathered special-interest groups in April 1949 in the Central Association of Expelled Germans (Zentralverband vertriebener Deutscher). In 1959, these two organizations merged in the Federation of Expellees (Bund der Vertriebenen).

Early in 1950, Waldemar Kraft founded the Bloc of Expellees and Disenfranchised (BHE) as a national political party acting as an umbrella organization for all organizations representing expellees and refugees. Better known as the Gesamtdeutscher Block-Bund der Heimatvertriebenen und Entrechteten (GB/BHE; all-German Bloc Federation of Expellees and the Disenfranchised), it placed 28 representatives in the Bundestag and 33 in the various *Länder* (state) parliaments in 1954. By 1959, the supporters of the GB/BHE had been largely drawn into the ranks of the center-right parties, primarily the Christian Democratic Union (CDU).

Expellees and refugees continued, nevertheless, to influence West German politics. Chancellor Willy Brandt's (1913–92) *Ostpolitik* (eastern policy) appeared as a direct threat to the recovery of lost eastern territories, especially in view of the treaties that the FRG signed with Poland and Czechoslovakia in the 1970s. Conservative politicians tapped this unrest, arguing that no agreement could be viewed as definitive pending a final peace settlement. With the fall of Communism in 1989 and the reaffirmation of German-Polish borders along the Oder-Neisse line on November 14, 1990, expellee and refugee groups again argued that their interests had been ig-nored. In response, Chancellor Helmut Kohl, in his presen-tation to the Bundestag on June 1, 1995, acknowledged the suffering of all expellees and refugees. Acknowledging the fi-nality of the lost territories, Kohl encouraged expellees and refuges to preserve their culture and traditions as well as to husband their personal memories. As Kohl pointed out, their unforgettable heritage included the contributions of Immanuel Kant and Lovis Corinth from East Prussia, Heinrich von Stephen from Pomerania, and Joseph von Eichendorff and Gerhart Hauptmann from Silesia.

David D. Meier

See also Citizenship and Foreigners; Federal Republic of Ger-many; Migration; Minorities: Ethnocultural and Foreign; Parties and Politics; Polish-German Relations (after 1945); Refugees

References

Lattimore, Bertram Gresh, Jr. *The Assimilation of German Expellees into the West German Polity and Society since 1945: A Case Study of Eutin, Schleswig-Holstein.* The Hague: Martinus Nijhoff, 1974.
Schönberg, Hans W. *Germans from the East: A Study of Their Migration, Resettlement and Subsequent History.* The Hague: Martinus Nijhoff, 1970.
Theisen, Alfred. "Die Vertreibung der Deutschen—Ein unbewältigtes Kapitel europäischer Zeitgeschichte." *Aus Politik und Zeitgeschichte* B7–8 (February 10, 1995).

Federal Republic of Germany: Women

The end of the Nazi regime and Germany's unconditional surrender in 1945 offered a unique chance for a new begin-ning in gender politics. According to the Basic Law of 1949, "men and women are equal." But that law constructed legal tensions between the postulate for gender equality on the one side and the protection of the family and the freedom of con-tract between employers and employees on the other. These tensions were basically solved at women's expense ("housewife marriage," low wages for women, inferior social status of women). Only in the 1970s, with the advent of the women's movement and more liberal politics, did the situation start to change. At present, the diversity of women's lives reflects the inability of industrial societies to equally distribute paid and unpaid labor among women and men and to reconcile pro-duction and reproduction. The unification of Germany has further complicated conditions.

Immediately after the war, the German population con-sisted of 7.3 million more women than men. In 1950, nearly one-third of the 15 million households were headed by single women: widows, single mothers, and divorced women. The impact of war and its destruction had strengthened women's economic position, yet since life basically consisted of survival work, this advantage existed only in the traditional fields of housewifery and mothering. It became evident in the 1950s that this was not a position from which political influence

could be obtained. It was widely believed after the war that women should be entitled to the same rights as men. But hardly anyone knew what gender equality should encompass. Some, in particular the churches, adhered to a "separate but equal" formula in which equality meant partnership under men's authority and legal hegemony. Others thought it meant legal equality between men and women, but a continuance of women's positions as primary caretakers of the family. This was the dominant position, shared by the Social Democratic Party and the union leaders, who at that time were busy fighting for a sufficient male-headed family income. The division of Ger-many and the example of women's "forced emancipation" and integration into the labor force in East Germany further re-duced the prospects of any serious and profound changes of women's place in West German society. Traditional definitions of "women's place" were equated with the values of the "free Western world." The so-called woman's question was thus subordinated to the priorities of the national question and the evolving Cold War.

Against massive resistance, and mainly due to the efforts of Elisabeth Selbert (1896–1986), a member of the Social Democratic Party who mobilized women's public opinion, the Basic Law finally established in its Article 3 that "men and women are equal." This meant that the Civil Code of 1900 had to be redrawn. In 1957, parliament passed the Act on Equal Rights for Men and Women. Men's legal preponderance in most issues related to marriage was abolished. Women gained the right in principle to engage in paid work (previ-ously they had had to ask for their husbands' permission). The husband's right of disposal over the wife's property (a legacy of the Civil Code) was also abolished. But Articles 1356 and 1360 of the Civil Code stated that women's contribution to the support of their families consisted mainly of doing the housework, and that women were allowed to go out to work only if this option did not interfere with their duties as moth-ers and wives. The Act on Equal Rights for Men and Women of 1957 legalized what came to be called the "housewife mar-riage," in which the role of woman was defined as combining duties of marriage and family. In 1977, parliament, led by the Social Democratic-liberal coalition, passed a new law that en-abled men and women to determine their family and work ar-rangements freely for themselves (the "partnership marriage").

Inherent in the Basic Law was a tension between the principle of gender equality and the principle of freedom of contract, which was guaranteed to employers and workers. This made women systematically into second-class workers, because their labor market availability is (at least potentially) more limited than men's. Only if the impact of the freedom of contract was too obviously damaging to women, for ex-ample, when female workers were pregnant, did the political and the legal system intervene and issue protective legislation. Second, the Basic Law also put the family under its special protection. This meant that the concepts of women as inde-pendent human beings and as potential mothers would be under a permanent tension that could not be solved within the existing legal and political, as well as social and economic, system. In the 1940s and 1950s, politics that were aimed at protecting families clearly defined women's social and political status.

Despite massive exposure to traditional gender ideology, women were driven into the work force, first through the severe downward mobility of the 1940s and later through the promises of the Economic Miracle. Between 1950 and 1975, the rate of female employment increased from 47.4 percent to 54.0 percent. This rise seems moderate if compared to the German Democratic Republic, where female employment increased from 52.4 percent to 81.5 percent between 1950 and 1975.

Even more striking is the change in the internal structure of the female labor force. First, the share of married women in the labor force rose constantly, from 25 percent in 1950 to 42 percent in 1982. Nearly 90 percent of women married to an industrial worker were in gainful employment outside the home. This shows the class character of the debate on women's work, which was saturated with middle-class ideology on gender roles.

The second major change that occurred was a shift in the sectors in which women were employed. Between 1950 and 1985, the percentage of working women in agriculture declined from 34 percent to 7 percent, while the percentage employed in the service sector (industries and professions) rose from 12 percent to 32 percent. The continued expansion of women's, and especially married women's, labor clearly conflicted with the discourse about women's place in society. By the notion of female work as only *supplementary* to the family income, the constant expansion of female work outside the home could take place without endangering the stability of traditional role models. The burden of work and family had to be shouldered by women, whose life situations were at best ambiguous, at worst torn.

Single women were in a particularly difficult position, as their wages were especially low—in the 1950s, industrial wages for women were 45.7 percent lower and white-collar wages were 43.7 percent lower than respective male wages. Families headed by women were especially badly off. But married women were also in a difficult position. If they worked while their children were still young, they were accused of neglecting their families and blamed for all kinds of societal ills. As soon as the children were older, women were expected to pick up at least a part-time job. This meant mothering and working in the limits of the "three-phase-model," with all its restrictions on income and professional advancement. If women chose to stay home altogether, the potential costs might become apparent only late in life, when the housewife syndrome (having done nothing but work at home) might fully develop and give the homemakers a sense of uselessness. Depression was quite common for those women. Gender norms in the 1950s and 1960s were neither consistent nor livable for many women, and they caused severe friction in women's (and thus also in men's) lives.

In the last 20 years, with the advent of the new women's movement, women have found some reprieve. Women have found a language for their concerns and their awareness of gender inequality has increased. Ever since, women's life choices have become more complex, if not necessarily easier. The unification of Germany has had complex ramifications for women, east and west. The divergent model of women's lives in the former German Democratic Republic is about to be adjusted to the Western model. Unemployment for women, claims on the social system (rents, unemployment benefits), and the abortion issue have been the most visible signs of the incompatibility of a market economy and a state socialist system. Women's issues are on the one hand particularly interesting for a comparison of these two systems (including a systematic reflection about women's place in industrial society). Simultaneously, the "woman question" again is in danger of being subordinated to the larger national and economic issues of unification.

Hanna Schissler

See also Childbirth and Motherhood; Family; Feminism and Anti-Feminism; Feminism in the Federal Republic of Germany; Fertility; German Democratic Republic: Women; Infants, Children, and Adolescents; Marriage and Divorce; Women; Women's Occupations; Working Conditions; Youth

References

Beck, Ulrich and Elisabeth Beck-Gernsheim. *Das ganz normale Chaos der Liebe.* Frankfurt am Main: Suhrkamp, 1990.

Bundesministerium für Frauen und Jugend, ed. *Frauen in der Bundesrepublik Deutschland.* Bonn: Bundesministerium für Frauen und Jugend, 1992.

Castell Rüdenhausen, Adelheid, zu. "Die demographischen Konsequenzen des Ersten und Zweiten Weltkriegs für das Deutsche Reich, die Deutsche Demokratische Republik und die Bundesrepublik Deutschland." *Zweiter Weltkrieg und sozialer Wandel.* Ed. Waclaw Dlugoborski. Göttingen: Vandenhoek & Ruprecht, 1981.

Cole, Helena, Jane Caplan, and Hanna Schissler. *The History of Women in Germany from Medieval Times to the Present: Bibliography of English-Language Publications.* Washington, DC: Reference Guides of the German Historical Institute, 1990.

Delille, Angela and Andrea Grohn, eds. *Perlonzeit: Wie die Frauen ihr Wirtschaftswunder erlebten.* Berlin: Elephantenpress, 1985.

Frevert, Ute. *Women in German History: From Bourgeois Emancipation to Sexual Liberation.* Oxford: Berg, 1993.

Gerhardt, Uta and Yvonne Schütze, eds. *Frauensituation: Veränderungen in den letzten zwanzig Jahren.* Frankfurt am Main: Suhrkamp, 1988.

Heineman, Elizabeth. "The Hour of the Woman: Memories of Germany's 'Crisis Years' and West German National Identity." *American Historical Review* 101 (April, 1996), 354–95.

Kolinsky, Eva. *Women in West Germany: Life, Work and Politics.* Oxford: Berg, 1989.

Möding, Nori. "Die Stunde der Frauen? Frauen und Frauenorganisationen des bürgerlichen Lagers." *Von Stalingrad zur Währungsreform: Zur Sozialgeschichte des Umbruchs in Deutschland.* Ed. Martin Broszat et al. Munich: Oldenbourg, 1989.

Moeller, Robert G. *Protecting Motherhood: Women and the Family in the Politics of Postwar West Germany.* Berkeley, CA: University of California Press, 1993.

Poiger, Uta. "Rock 'n' Roll, Female Sexuality, and the Cold War Battle over German Identities." *Journal of Modern History* 68 (September, 1996), 577–616.

Statistisches Bundesamt, ed. *Frauen in Familie, Beruf und Gesellschaft.* Stuttgart: Kohlhammer, 1987.

Willenbacher, Barbara. "Zerrüttung und Bewährung der Nachkriegsfamilie." *Von Stalingrad zur Währungsreform: Zur Sozialgeschichte des Umbruchs in Deutschland.* Ed. Martin Broszat et al. Munich: Oldenbourg, 1989.

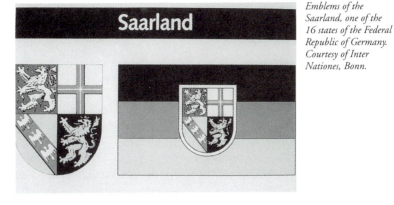

Emblems of the Saarland, one of the 16 states of the Federal Republic of Germany. Courtesy of Inter Nationes, Bonn.

Federalism

As an organizational principle for Germany, federalism became effective only in the nineteenth century. The struggle between the German states and a German central government, however, predates that century by many generations. The example of the hypercentralization of the Nazi period notwithstanding, German history since at least 1648 has been characterized by a pervasive desire to maintain as decentralized a polity as possible. But any German central government was expected to possess sufficient internal cohesion and coercive power to protect the national interest both within and without Germany's borders. The great conundrum for the Germans in the modern age has thus been how to create a central government capable of providing these services while allowing the individual states to retain their organically developed individuality.

With the creation of Imperial Germany in 1871 under Chancellor Otto von Bismarck's leadership, the question of Germany's organizational shape became acute. Despite Prussia's economic and political hegemony, the empire still possessed a great variety of geographic, cultural, and historical regional differences. There existed, for example, large and politically potent Roman Catholic minorities in Bavaria, Westphalia, and Silesia. While the latter regions were constitutionally part of Prussia, Bavaria remained an independent-minded state that could well rally Catholics elsewhere to Prussia's discomfiture. To obviate such a possibility and to help reconcile Bavaria, Baden, Württemberg, and other Roman Catholic states to the empire, a federal constitution was adopted.

Drawing on the constitutional arrangements of the short-lived North German Confederation (1867–71), the constitution of 1871 attempted to secure Prussia's dominance while ensuring the other states' continued political viability. Crucial from Prussia's view was the personal union of Prussian minister-president, Imperial chancellor, and Imperial minister for foreign affairs in Bismarck. In addition, the states' collective expression of Imperial sovereignty in the Federal Council (Bundesrat) was effectively controlled by Prussia's voting majority. Nevertheless, many prerogatives remained with the states, or at least the larger ones such as Bavaria, which retained its own postal and railway systems as well a military establishment, diplomatic representation, and other rights.

Though many wholly or partially symbolic privileges were granted to the states, the crucial issue of their financial independence from the empire (via Imperial tax laws) remained unresolved. Indeed, this issue proved to be a standing problem between the central government and the states throughout the Imperial period.

The collapse of the empire in 1918 renewed the constitutional debate in Germany. The declaration of the Weimar Republic did not end it. Instead, the new Republic's unitary constitution reduced the Bundesrat—renamed the Reichsrat after 1918—to constitutional insignificance relative to the Reichstag. The states themselves were reduced in constitutional importance as well, though Prussia remained by far the most significant of them. Centrist parties such as the Social Democrats, the Liberals, and the German National People's Party considered this a salutary change. Others, however, such as the Bavarian People's Party and parts of the Catholic Center, resisted the change. Indeed, the republic's entire 14 years saw constant wrangling over possible revisions to the constitution. These battles contributed to the national political paralysis of which the Nazis eventually took keen advantage.

Emerging in 1945 from the catastrophe of dictatorship and war, Germans in the Western zones of occupation soon found themselves confronted again with the issue of federalism. By consensus, and with a certain pressure from the Allies, West German leaders officially recognized the value of a federal order in preserving Germans' freedom while maintaining the rights of the states (*Länder*) and the power of a central government. Acting effectively to establish a workable federal system, these leaders formulated a provisional constitution for their zones of occupation between 1945 and 1949. Based primarily on the historical experience of the Germans themselves, this Basic Law established a functional federal structure for the 11 states of the Federal Republic of Germany in 1949. Legislative, judicial, and administrative powers were divided between the central government and the states. In addition, a workable (though still troublesome) division of tax revenues was created to finance the national government while assuring the states a secure financial existence.

Though initially rejected by Bavaria as insufficiently federalist, the Basic Law offered a major contribution: it guaranteed the coexistence between a powerful German central government and all of the self-assertive individual states. None of the turmoils of the postwar era succeeded in destabilizing this arrangement. On the contrary, this federal order was ordained

to be a non-negotiable condition of Germany's eventual re-unification in the revolutionary year 1989. Under it, five new states were created from the territory of the former German Democratic Republic. Their subsequent incorporation into the Federal Republic in October 1990 (bringing the number of states to sixteen) demonstrated clearly the desirability of the continuation of federalism in Germany.

David R. Dorondo

See also The Basic Law; Baden-Württemberg; Bavaria; Bavarian People's Party; Berlin; Bonn; Brandenburg; Bremen; Center Party; Constitutions; Hamburg; Hesse; Lower Saxony; Mecklenburg-Vorpommern; North Rhine-Westphalia; Parliamentary System; Parties and Politics; Rhineland-Palatinate; The Saar; Saxony; Saxony-Anhalt; Schleswig-Holstein; Thuringia

References

Dorondo, D.R. *Bavaria and German Federalism: Reich to Republic, 1918–33, 1945–49.* New York, NY: St. Martin's, 1992.

Gunlicks, Arthur B., ed. "Federalism and Intergovernmental Relations in West Germany: A Fortieth Year Appraisal." *Publius: The Journal of Federalism* 19 (1989). Special Edition.

Hicks, Ursula K. *Federalism: Failure and Success: A Comparative Study.* London: Macmillan, 1978.

Laufer, Heinz. *Das Föderative System der Bundesrepublik Deutschland.* 5th ed. Munich: Bayerische Landeszentrale für politische Bildungsarbeit, 1985.

Pinney, Edward L. *Federalism, Bureaucracy, and Party Politics in Western Germany: The Role of the Bundesrat.* Chapel Hill: University of North Carolina Press, 1963.

Wheare, K.C. *Federal Government.* 3rd ed. London: Oxford University Press, 1953.

Windell, George G. "The Bismarckian Empire as a Federal State, 1866–1880: A Chronicle of Failure." *Central European History* 2 (1969), 291–311.

Federation of German Industry

In October 1949, 32 German industrial associations founded the Federation of German Industry (Bundesverband der deutschen Industrie; BDI). The national federation represents their interests at the regional, national, and increasingly, at the international levels.

The BDI is the successor organization to associations formed since the beginning of the Industrial Revolution. In 1876 the Central Association of German Industrialists was founded, rivaled after 1895 by the League of Industrialists. In 1919 the two organizations merged to form the powerful National Association of German Industry, which remained in existence until 1933, when the Hitler regime established its own industrial organization.

After World War II, the Western Allies delayed granting permission to the discredited industrialists, some of whom had helped to finance the Nazi party before 1933, to form a new national "peak" organization. Only when West Germany became a sovereign state in 1949 could the industrial associations, representing all industrial sectors ranging from automobiles to steel to sugar, form the BDI. It currently is the coordinating organization of 34 affiliated associations (the number has varied since 1949 because of additions and mergers). The associations in turn are made up of 500 suborganizations comprising 80,000 private industrial firms with a labor force of about 7 million, to which must be added those firms privatized since 1990 in East Germany.

The BDI represents the economic interests of German industry vis-à-vis the government, the Bundestag, political parties, and supranational organizations such as the European Community. Its headquarters in Cologne serves as the organization lobbying the federal government in Bonn. It has also established liaison offices in the German *Länder* (states), Brussels, London, Washington, and Tokyo.

BDI policies are made by its president, the presidential board, the executive committee's administrative office, and numerous specialized committees and working groups. Policies are coordinated with other business organizations (especially the Diet of German Industry and Commerce and the Federation of German Employers' Associations, which engage in collective bargaining with trade unions) and banking, insurance, and agricultural associations. The BDI is a member of the Council of European Industrial Associations.

As an interest and lobbying group, the BDI has had considerable success in molding public opinion through the Institute for German Industry and the media. It has maintained close contact with conservative governments (and almost as successfully with Social Democratic–led governments), with the Ministry of Economics, and with deputies who support its efforts. As a consequence, much legislation consonant with its goals is passed and unfavorable legislation is blocked. Occasional divisions within the industrial community, however, temper the power of the BDI in such questions as investment, trade, and cartel policies. Even when the BDI is united, the government may resist its policy recommendations, as in the case of increasing support for private investments in eastern Germany.

Gerard Braunthal

See also Balke, Siegfried; Beitz, Berthold; Berg, Fritz; Cartels; Central Association of German Industrialists; Coal Industry; Codetermination; Flick Family; Friedrich, Otto; Krupp: Family and Firm; Pressure and Special Interest Groups; Ruhr Region; The Saar; Silverberg, Paul; Sohl, Hans-Günther; Steel Industry

References

Alemann, Ulrich von and Rolf G. Heinze. *Verbände und Staat: Vom Pluralismus zum Korporatismus.* Opladen: Westdeutscher Verlag, 1979.

Braunthal, Gerard. *The Federation of German Industry in Politics.* Ithaca, NY: Cornell University Press, 1965.

Brodach, Georg. *Der Bundesverband der Deutschen Industrie.* Düsseldorf: Droste, 1987.

Hartmann, Heinz. *Authority and Organization in German Management.* Princeton, NJ: Princeton University Press, 1959.

Lochner, Louis P. *Tycoons and Tyrants: German Industry from Hitler to Adenauer.* Chicago, IL: Regnery, 1954.

Simon, Walter. *Macht und Herrschaft der Unternehmerverbände: BDI, BDA und DIHT im ökonomischen und politischen System der BRD.* Cologne: Pahl-Rugenstein, 1976.

Stein, Gustav, ed. *Unternehmer in der Politik.* Düsseldorf: Econ-Verlag, 1954.

Varain, Heinz Josef. *Interessenverbände in Deutschland.* Cologne: Kiepenheuer und Witsch, 1973.

Fehrenbach, Konstantin (1852–1926)

The conservative south German democrat Konstantin Fehrenbach was one of the leading personalities of the Catholic Center Party in the first quarter of the twentieth century. He represented the Center Party in the Reichstag from 1903 until his death and exerted considerable influence on his party's politics. As the last president of the Reichstag in Imperial Germany and as president of the 1919 Weimar National Assembly, he symbolized continuity in the transition from empire to republic. His appointment as chancellor of the first bourgeois government of the Weimar Republic (1920–21) was, however, hardly more than an interim solution.

Born as the son of an elementary-school teacher in a small Black Forest village, Fehrenbach entered politics after studying theology and law. In 1885 he became a member of the Baden parliament; he was elected to the Reichstag for the Center Party in 1903. During World War I, which he considered to be a defensive conflict, he rose to chair of the budget committee (Vorsitzender des Hauptausschusses) and was elected president of the Reichstag in June 1918. After November 1917, he presided over the Inter-Party Caucus, the informal committee representing the Center, the Social Democrats (SPD), and the Liberals in the Reichstag. Like the majority of the bourgeois politicians, he was overtaken by the Revolution of 1918.

Toward the end of the war, he recognized the necessity of political reforms that would transform the Prussian-German authoritarian state into a parliamentary democracy. His demands during the revolutionary weeks that the old Reichstag be convened remained fruitless. In February 1919, the Weimar National Assembly elected him as president. After the Weimar coalition had lost its majority in the June 1920 election and the SPD had gone into opposition, the sixty-eight-year-old Fehrenbach assumed the office of chancellor of a minority government consisting of the Center, the German Democratic Party (DDP), and the German People's Party (DVP); it was, however, a transitional coalition.

Fehrenbach was an honest broker, a man who believed in consensus and who strove for a balancing of interests. His strength lay in rhetoric and representation, not in daily politics or trailblazing political strategy. He left no lasting legacy after his term of office, which lasted barely one year. He was not the strong chancellor required by the political situation. His term of office was characterized by domestic crises and external pressures, especially by the burden of reparation payments, which eventually led to Fehrenbach's resignation under the pressure of the London Ultimatum, which forced Germany to accept the schedule of reparation payments determined by the Allies. His government resigned in May 1921. Two years later, Fehrenbach became Center Party parliamentary whip, a position he held until his death.

Walter Mühlhausen

See also Catholicism, Political; Center Party; Chancellor's Office; Weimar Germany

References

Becker, Josef. "Konstantin Fehrenbach (1852–1926)." *Zeitgeschichte in Lebensbildern: Aus dem deutschen Katholizismus des 20. Jahrhunderts.* Ed. Rudolf Morsey. Mainz: Matthias-Grünewald, 1973.
Wulf, Peter. "Konstantin Fehrenbach (1852–1926)." *Die deutschen Kanzler. Von Bismarck bis Schmidt.* Ed. Wilhelm von Sternburg. Königstein: Athenäum, 1985.
———, ed. *Akten der Reichskanzlei, Das Kabinett Fehrenbach, 25. Juni 1920 bis 4. Mai 1921.* Boppard: H. Boldt, 1972.

Feminism and Anti-Feminism, 1871–1918

The term "feminism," which came into general use around 1900, usually designates the variety of organizations and campaigns aimed at improving the status of women. As feminism developed into a mass movement, anti-feminism arose among defenders of traditional forms of male dominance.

The first national feminist organizations were the General German Women's Association (Allgemeiner deutscher Frauenverein; ADF), founded in 1865, and the Lette Association (Lette-Verein, named for its founder, Wilhelm Adolf Lette), established in 1866. Both were affiliations of diverse women's organizations operating in all of the German states. Whereas the Lette-Verein concentrated on practical work, the ADF explicitly championed the emancipation of women. The work of feminist organizations was limited by the Prussian Law of Association (*Vereinsgesetz*) of 1850, which prohibited the participation of women in political parties or activities. The first feminist groups worked toward the educational and professional advancement of women rather than toward political rights such as suffrage.

In 1888, a group of feminist activists led by Minna Cauer (1841–1922) founded a new organization, the Association for Women's Welfare (Verein Frauenwohl), which called for more assertive strategies and openly advocated suffrage. Women favoring this approach become known as "radicals"; defenders of the traditional approach called themselves "moderates." A new "umbrella" feminist organization formed in 1893, the Federation of German Women's Associations (Bund deutscher Frauenvereine; BDF), included both radical and moderate groups, but the tension between the two wings of the movement continued.

Members of the radical wing within the BDF led a highly publicized petition campaign against the family law provisions of the new civil code in 1896. Radicals also led the German branch of the International Abolitionist Federation, centrally organized in 1904 under the leadership of Katherina Scheven, which denounced state-regulated prostitution as the officially sanctioned sexual exploitation of women. In 1899, another "umbrella" organization, the Federation of Progressive Women's Associations (Verband fortschrittlicher Frauenvereine) was formed to include the radical groups, most of which also continued as affiliates of the BDF.

Under the leadership of radical feminist Marie Stritt from 1899 to 1910, the BDF endorsed some radical positions. However, the growth and diversification of the organization's membership, which after 1908 included the conservative German Protestant Women's League, strengthened the influence of the moderates. In 1908, a proposal by the BDF's legal committee to recommend complete abolition of the law against abortion was voted down by the majority of members. In 1910, the moderate Gertrud Bäumer (1873–1954) replaced Stritt.

A major issue for the feminist movement was the relationship between bourgeois and socialist women's organizations. In the 1890s, a socialist women's movement emerged under the leadership of Clara Zetkin (1857–1933). The majority of socialist women, who worked to advance the influence of working-class women within the Social Democratic Party, rejected cooperation with bourgeois feminists in favor of solidarity with male workers. The charter of the overwhelmingly middle-class BDF, which limited membership to nonpartisan groups, provided a pretext to exclude socialist organizations. Despite the efforts of some individuals to promote cooperation across class lines, the split between bourgeois and socialist women reduced the effectiveness of the feminist movement.

In 1902, a new organization, the German Society for Women's Suffrage (Deutscher Verein für Frauenstimmrecht), was founded by radicals Lida Gustava Heymann (1868–1943) and Anita Augspurg (1857–1943). The suffrage movement benefited in 1908 from the ending of former limits by the Prussian Law of Association and the identifying of new rights by the Reich Law of Association; women were now free to join parties and engage in political activities. But the movement was soon divided between those who favored the enfranchisement of women on the same terms as men and those who advocated universal suffrage for both sexes, and thus the abolition of property qualifications, such as those imposed by the Prussian three-class system. Women's suffrage was granted by the Weimar Republic in 1918, partly as a reward for German feminists' active role in supporting the war effort through the National Women's Service (Nationaler Frauendienst).

Anti-feminism arose as an explicit defense of male supremacy against the feminist challenge. Anti-feminists developed theoretical arguments; philosophers as early as Arthur Schopenhauer (1788–1860) and Otto Weininger (1880–1903) proclaimed the intellectual, and physicians such as Theodor Bischoff (1807–82) and Paul J. Möbius (1853–1907) the physical, inferiority of women to men. Most male professional organizations and labor unions, fearing competition from lower-paid female labor, vigorously opposed the entry of women into their occupations. Moral-reform societies, such as the "morality leagues" (Sittlichkeitsvereine), the first of which was founded in 1885, and the German League in Opposition to Women's Emancipation (Deutscher Bund zur Bekämpfung der Frauenemanzipation), founded in 1912, warned of the dangers to family life and religious belief posed by changes in the status of women.

Ann T. Allen

See also Abortion; Bäumer, Gertrud; Cauer, Minna; Childbirth and Motherhood; Family; Feminism and Anti-Feminism, 1918–45; Infants, Children, and Adolescents; Heymann, Lida Gustava; Marriage and Divorce; Morality; Sex Reform and Birth Control; Women, 1871–1918; (Bourgeois) Women's Movement; Women's Occupations; Zetkin, Clara

References

Clemens, Barbel. *Menschenrechte haben kein Geschlecht: Zum Politikverständnis der bürgerlichen Frauenbewegung.* Pfaffenweiler: Centaurus-Verlagsgesellschaft, 1988.

Evans, Richard J. *The Feminist Movement in Germany, 1894–1933.* London: Sage, 1976.

Greven-Aschoff, Barbara. *Die bürgerliche Frauenbewegung in Deutschland, 1894–1933.* Göttingen: Vandenhoeck & Ruprecht, 1981.

Stoehr, Irene. *Emanzipation zum Staat? Der Allgemeine Deutsche Frauenverein-Deutsche Staatbürgerinnenverband (1893–1933).* Pfaffenweiler: Centaurus-Verlagsgesellschaft, 1990.

Weiland, Daniela. *Geschichte der Frauenemanzipation in Deutschland und Österreich: Biographien, Programme, Organisationen.* Düsseldorf: ECON Taschenbuch-Verlag, 1983.

Feminism and Anti-Feminism, 1918–45

The subject of feminism and anti-feminism in early-twentieth-century Germany poses difficulties of definitions. Many leaders of the German women's movements in the Weimar Republic, for instance, espoused notions that are hard to differentiate from those of their self-defined anti-feminist contemporaries: they insisted on the importance of marriage and motherhood and stressed women's "innate" differences from men.

The Weimar Republic brought with it the enfranchisement of women and the principle of legal equality between the sexes. Such advances had an ambiguous effect on the socialist and the bourgeois women's movements. All parties now wooed female voters, and put female candidates—often members of the women's movements—on their election lists. Yet female politicians were restricted to "women's issues," such as social policy, education, health care, and maternal and child welfare. Some important legislative victories in these realms were achieved—only to have their implementation compromised by the "larger" questions of political and fiscal policy managed by the male parliamentarians. Meanwhile, ironically, the conservative parties that had traditionally opposed women's suffrage were able to claim more female votes than the SPD, which had most vocally supported it—the majority of German women revealed themselves to have either moderate or conservative political views.

Within the ruling Social Democratic Party (SPD), a more conservative attitude about gender relations reasserted itself. Having been reintegrated into the SPD after the 1908 Reich Association Law made women's political activity legal again, the socialist women's movement was forced to confine itself to recruitment drives and social work; in disgust at this anti-feminism and the SPD's wartime militarism, socialist feminist leaders such as Luise Zietz (1865–1922) and Clara Zetkin (1857–1933) switched to the Independent Social Democrats (USPD), while more reformist socialist women such as Marie Juchacz (1879–1956) took over—thus paving the way for cooperation with bourgeois feminists.

Provoked in part by the rise of organized anti-feminism in the prewar years, bourgeois feminists increasingly came to resemble their opponents, directing middle-class women away from career aspirations and back into housework or at best unremunerated social work and vociferously encouraging a rise in the German birth rate. The umbrella organization of bourgeois feminists, the Federation of German Women's Associations (BDF) under the leadership of Gertrud Bäumer (1873–1954), came out of the war with its prewar tendencies toward patriotic nationalism even further solidified. The BDF continued to grow (from at most 280,000 prewar members to a Weimar peak of about 750,000) as more and more women's organizations (especially housewives' and white-collar organizations) joined it. Increasingly the BDF's public stances reflected the right-wing (and even racist) views of its new members.

The radical bourgeois feminists who had been expelled from the BDF during the war for their pacifism, continued—despite their shrinking numbers—to campaign for feminist causes. Some German feminists—such as Anita Augspurg and Lida Gustava Heymann (1868–1943)—played leadership roles in the International Women's League for Peace and Freedom. Others, such as Helene Stöcker (1869–1943) and Alice Rühle-Gerstel, working together especially with Communist activists and sympathetic members of the medical profession, joined male sex reformers in pushing for a change in the abortion law, making knowledge about sexual technique and contraception more readily available, and insisting on women's rights to sexual pleasure and control over their own fertility. Nevertheless, since sex reformers often interwove these arguments with eugenic ones that stressed the benefits of "healthy" sexuality for family and nation, this movement too had ambiguous ramifications.

Nazi ideologues had never made a secret of their hostility to the women's movements. They stressed the woman's role as breeder and subordinate partner, responsible for a separate female sphere. The ground for these kinds of claims had been well-prepared by politically far more moderate forces. Many women found the Nazis' gender program and their overall political strategy appealing—approximately as many women as men gave the Nazis their vote in the early 1930s. While the BDF dissolved itself rather than face "coordination" by the Nazis, many of its member organizations dutifully expelled their Jewish members and integrated themselves into the elaborate hierarchy of Nazi women's associations run by Gertrud Scholtz-Klink (1902–).

Socialist, Communist, and pacifist feminists were driven into exile or imprisoned in concentration camps like their male counterparts; sex reform organizations were crushed and their leaders persecuted; millions were tortured and murdered in the name of a society organized around "eugenic" principles. But in a painfully paradoxical twist, this virulently racist and anti-feminist regime did much to facilitate many women's escape from domesticity into participation and recognition in public life (and their acquisition of organizational skills) through the millions of minor leadership posts and honorary offices available in its elaborate network of girls' and women's groups and programs.

Dagmar Herzog

See also Bäumer, Gertrud; Childbirth and Motherhood; Eugenics; Family; Feminism in the Federal Republic of Germany; German Democratic Republic: Women; Heymann, Lida Gustava; Homosexuality and Lesbianism; Infants, Children, and Adolescents; Juchacz, Marie; Marriage and Divorce; Scholtz-Klink, Gertrud; Sex Reform and Birth Control; Women, 1918–45; (Bourgeois) Women's Movement; Women's Occupations; Zetkin, Clara; Zietz, Luise

References

Boak, Helen. "Women in Weimar Germany: The 'Frauenfrage' and the Female Vote." *Social Change and Political Development in Weimar Germany.* Ed. Richard J. Bessel and Edgar J. Feuchtwanger. London: Croom Helm, 1981.
———. "Women in Weimar Politics." *European History Quarterly* 20 (1990), 369–99.
Bridenthal, Renate et al., eds. *When Biology Became Destiny: Women in Weimar and Nazi Germany.* New York, NY: Monthly Review Press, 1984.
Evans, Richard. *The Feminist Movement in Germany 1894–1933.* London: Sage, 1976.
Frevert, Ute. *Women in German History: From Bourgeois Emancipation to Sexual Liberation.* Oxford: Berg, 1989.
Gerhard, Ute. *Unerhört: Die Geschichte der deutschen Frauenbewegung.* Reinbek bei Hamburg: Rowohlt, 1990.
Grossmann, Atina. "The New Woman and the Rationalization of Sexuality in Weimar Germany." *Powers of Desire: The Politics of Sexuality.* Ed. Ann Snitow et al. New York, NY: Monthly Review Press, 1983.

Feminism in the Federal Republic of Germany

The "new feminism" refers to a movement that began in the late 1960s and is still influential today. Feminists have tried to improve women's status and fight discrimination in many areas of political, economic, and social life. Although they have often disagreed about priorities and means, the movement has been influential in German politics; it has also deeply affected the lives of feminists and women who came of age in environments that had already been altered by feminism.

Feminist activity in the Federal Republic predated the emergence of "new feminism" in the late 1960s. Many "old feminists"—women who had been active in the pre-Nazi-era feminist movement—were influential in the political life of the early Federal Republic. Some younger women who disclaimed the label "feminist" nevertheless worked to improve women's status. Among them was Elisabeth Selbert (1896–1986), whose efforts resulted in the inclusion of an equal-rights clause in the Federal Republic's Basic Law. In the 1950s, union women successfully fought separate (and lower) wage classifications for women, and women involved in the peace movement identified sex-specific motivations for their work. Although none of this activity constituted a feminist movement, it indicates a history of female organizing in the interests of women that predated the "new feminism."

In 1968, some female student radicals rejected the sexism they perceived within their organizations and the low priority the students' movement afforded women's concerns. Although such women often continued to identify themselves as Marxists, they established women's councils in West Berlin and Frankfurt. The movement soon split, however, between women who understood their oppression to be an outgrowth of capitalist exploitation and those who saw patriarchy—a system whereby sex, not class, is the basis of privilege—as the central problem.

Feminism expanded beyond the radical student population in 1971, when 374 women published acknowledgements of their abortions and turned the movement's focus to West

Germany's restrictive abortion laws. For the next several years, abortion dominated the movement's agenda. In 1975, the Bundestag passed liberal abortion legislation, only to see it overturned the following year by the Federal Constitutional Court. Efforts for reformed abortion legislation continued, but feminists experienced the court's decision as a severe setback.

After 1975, feminist energies, although plentiful, were less unified than in the earlier years of the movement. An initiative for wages for housework found a deeply mixed response among feminists: some welcomed the opportunity to recognize women's unpaid labor, whereas others feared ghettoizing women in traditional, low-status roles. Through consciousness-raising groups many women explored the relationship of their personal experiences to what they increasingly perceived as systematic sexism. Hundreds of feminist institutions, such as bookstores, women's centers, lesbians' organizations, and homes for battered women, found root. The periodicals *Emma*, published by Alice Schwarzer, and the now-defunct *Courage*, published by a West Berlin collective, became the quasi-official voices of the movement.

Many feminists believed (and believe) that women's interests can find voice only in "autonomous" institutions free from association with established, mixed-sex organizations. Others, however, have worked to end the long-standing male domination of such institutions as labor unions and political parties. As a result of feminist influence, the Green Party fields equal numbers of women and men as candidates, and the Social Democratic Party plans to present candidates lists that are at least 40 percent female by 1998.

Reunification presented both opportunities and challenges to the feminist movement. The abortion issue was suddenly reopened, and feminist pressure prevented legislators from abolishing the liberal access to abortion that East German women had enjoyed. Once again, however, the federal constitutional court ruled to limit women's access to abortion. East German feminists contributed experience and knowledge about the problems facing East German women, only to face difficulties finding a place in West German feminist organizations as they migrated West or as their own institutions folded under political and financial pressures.

The feminist movement has not been able to alter such fundamental elements of women's disadvantage as low representation in political life and high representation in poorly paid employment. Nevertheless, it has profoundly shaped women's expectations, and it has made feminist issues a routine feature of political discourse. Although the movement has not yet accomplished all its goals, it has probably had a deeper influence than the nineteenth-century feminist movement that preceded it.

Elizabeth Heineman

See also Abortion; Childbirth and Motherhood; Family; Federal Republic of Germany: Women; German Democratic Republic: Women; Infants, Children, and Adolescents; Marriage and Divorce; Schwarzer, Alice; Selbert, Elisabeth; Sex Reform and Birth Control; (Bourgeois) Women's Movement; Women's Occupations

References
Altbach, Edith H. et al., eds. *German Feminism: Readings in Politics and Literature*. Albany, NY: State University of New York Press, 1984.
Fabel, Christel and Traute Meyer, eds. *Unterm neuen Kleid der Freiheit das Korsett der Einheit: Auswirkungen der deutschen Vereinigung für Frauen im Ost und West*. Berlin: Edition Sigma, 1992.
Frevert, Ute. *Women in German History: From Bourgeois Emancipation to Sexual Liberation*. Trans. Stuart McKinnon-Evans. Oxford: Berg, 1989.
Herve, Florence, ed. *Geschichte der deutschen Frauenbewegung*. Cologne: PapyRossa, 1990.
Kolinsky, Eva. *Women in West Germany: Life, Work and Politics*. Oxford: Berg, 1993.
Nave-Herz, Rosemarie. *Die Geschichte der Frauenbewegung in Deutschland*. Hannover: Niedersächsische Landeszentrale für politische Bildung, 1989.
Schenk, Herrad. *Die feministische Herausforderung: 150 Jahre Frauenbewegung in Deutschland*. Munich: Beck, 1980.
Wiggershaus, Renate. *Geschichte der Frauen und der Frauenbewegung in der Bundesrepublik Deutschland und in der Deutschen Demokratischen Republik nach 1945*. Wuppertal: Peter Hammer Verlag, 1979.

Feminist Writing

Understandings of what constitutes "feminist writing" vary according to historically conditioned changes in what is meant by "feminism." In the broadest sense, the term includes a variety of responses to culturally constructed theories of women's inferiority.

In nineteenth-century approaches to the "women's question," German feminists, unlike Anglo-American suffragists who sought the vote by emphasizing women's equality with men, tended to stress biological differences between the sexes, arguing for the right of women to work and education on the basis of their unique moral and cultural contributions to society. The first German women's movement is generally traced back to Louise Otto-Peters (1819–95), who emphasized the importance of women's involvement in matters of the state in the first German feminist journal, her *Frauen-Zeitung* (Women's journal), 1849–52, as well as in her later *Neue Bahnen* (New paths), 1866–95 and *Das Recht der Frauen auf Erwerb* (Women's right to paid work), 1866. The first generation of German feminists also includes writers such as Fanny Lewald (1811–99), who advanced arguments for fairer treatment of women in fiction and nonfiction. Of particular interest as a document of the times is her autobiography, *Meine Lebensgeschichte* (The education of Fanny Lewald), 1861–62. Mathilde Franziska Anneke (1817–84), another early journalist and author of a famous pamphlet, *Das Weib im Conflict mit den sozialen Verhältnissen* (Woman's conflict with social conditions), 1847, emigrated to the United States, where she wrote her *Memoiren einer 1848erin* (Memoirs of one of the 1848ers), 1853, and joined American feminists such as Elizabeth Cady Stanton and Susan B. Anthony in advocating equal rights and suffrage for women.

The organized women's movement began with the founding of the Allgemeiner Deutscher Frauenverein (German Women's Association) in 1865 by Otto-Peters and others. Soon thereafter, the Lette-Verein focused more narrowly on job training for women. In addition to the organizational activities of the bourgeois women's movement, a radical wing, led by women whose names are more familiar today, developed. Clara Zetkin (1857–1933) published her important treatise *Die Arbeiterinnen- und Frauenfrage der Gegenwart* (The question of women and women workers in the present) in 1899 and edited *Die Gleichheit* (Equality), the journal of socialist feminists, from 1891 to 1917. Lily Braun (1865–1916) paid particular attention to economic and social issues affecting women in her book *Die Frauenfrage: Ihre geschichtliche Entwicklung und wirtschaftliche Seite* (The women's question: historical development and economic aspects), 1901, and subsequently employed the form of a novel to publish her best-known work, *Memoiren einer Sozialistin* (Memoirs of a female socialist), 1909–11. Although she refrained from participation in women's movement organizations, Hedwig Dohm maintained contacts with activists of various persuasions, addressing gender issues of her day in more than a dozen volumes of dramatic and fiction writing in addition to her most famous feminist tracts: *Die wissenschaftliche Emanzipation der Frau* (A scientific approach to the emancipation of woman), 1874, and *Die Anti-feministinnen* (The [female] anti-feminists), 1902. By the turn of the century, a more conservative wing of the movement had emerged, represented most prominently by Helene Lange (1848–1930), whose *Handbuch der Frauenbewegung* (Handbook of the women's movement), 1901–06, was particularly critical of Lily Braun's *Die Frauenfrage*. Gertrud Bäumer (1873–1954), who worked with Lange, continued publishing their journal, *Die Frau* (The woman), even in the Third Reich.

In 1949, both newly established German states included a statement of equal rights for men and women in their respective constitutions. In its attempt to integrate women into the building of a socialist society, the German Democratic Republic (GDR) stressed the legacy of Marx, Engels, August Bebel (1840–1913), Clara Zetkin, and Rosa Luxemburg (1870–1919), asserting that woman's position in society is anchored in her participation in the process of production and that the class struggle, not the battle of the sexes, is decisive for her emancipation. An organized women's movement did not emerge in the officially controlled public sphere of the GDR. Writers, even those who were much admired by Western feminists, carefully avoided the appellation "feminist." A mass women's organization, the Demokratischer Frauenbund Deutschlands (DFD; Democratic Women's Federation of Germany), and its magazine, *Für Dich* (For you), encouraged conformity, not challenges to the status quo. A legally anchored right to work, access to extensive childcare facilities, legalized abortion (since 1972), and generous maternity-leave policies supported the participation of more than 90 percent of women in the workforce.

The representation of women in powerful state and party offices was, however, low. In this situation, women's issues were often first addressed in literary works, sometimes in bold ways, which led to the considerable popularity of GDR women writers with Western feminists. After an initial stage in the 1950s in which writers participated in official efforts to attract women to the workplace, a more critical phase ensued as a new generation of writers, such as Christa Wolf (1929–) and Brigitte Reimann, addressed the contradictions encountered by women in their new experiences. Christa Wolf's *Nachdenken über Christa T.* (published as *The Quest for Christa T.*), 1968, and Irmtraud Morgner's complex, fantastic *Leben und Abenteuer der Trobadora Beatriz* (Life and adventures of the Trobadora Beatriz), 1974, and its 1983 sequel, *Amanda*, are the most important works in this vein.

A new genre of "documentary literature," such as Sarah Kirsch's (1935–) *Die Pantherfrau: Fünf unfrisierte Erzählungen aus dem Kassetenrecorder* (published as *The Panther Woman: Five Unretouched Stories from the Tape Recorder*), 1973, and Maxie Wander's *Guten Morgen, du Schöne* (Good morning, my lovely one), 1977, emerged almost simultaneously. Wolf's *Kein Ort: Nirgends* (published as *No Place on Earth*), 1979, and *Kassandra* (published as *Cassandra*), 1983, have also enjoyed wide reception as "feminist" texts, but equally important are her essayistic attempts to enlarge the canon of writers who can be regarded as "feminist" by pointing back to writers such as Bettina von Arnim (1785–1859) and Karoline von Gunderode (1786–1806), as well as her own older contemporaries, Anna Seghers (1900–83) and the Austrian Ingeborg Bachmann (1926–73).

In the years after World War II, few West German texts could be identified as "feminist" until the discontent of women working in the political New Left, particularly in the Socialist German Students' Federation (SDS), resulted in the formation of the Action Council for Women's Liberation in West Berlin in 1969. Their protest against patriarchal relations in politics as well as in private life gained wider support around issues of child care and sexuality. Important also was the 1971 campaign against the long-standing German anti-abortion law (Paragraph 218), that appeared in a popular German magazine, *Stern*, and included testimony from prominent women, doctors, and academicians. In 1975, the "International Year of the Woman," the first feminist film (*REDUPERS—The All-Around Reduced Personality*) was made by Helke Sander, who also established the first feminist film journal, *Frauen und Film*. Influenced by developments and texts in the United States women's movement, feminist consciousness-raising groups, women's centers, cafés, publishing houses, and bookstores began to spring up.

Among younger women, the first yearbook published by the Frankfurt women, *Frauenjahrbuch '75* (Women's yearbook '75), had a galvanizing effect, as did *Der kleine Unterschied und seine große Folgen* (A minor difference and its major consequences), published by Alice Schwarzer (1942–), who also in 1977 founded *Emma*, the mass-circulation journal of the movement. The first major West German attempt to articulate women's subjective experience in literary form, Verena Stefan's *Häutungen* (published as *Shedding*), 1975, also addressed the challenges of finding a language for women's writing that was not rooted in a male, heterosexual world view.

At about the same time, Margot Schroeder approached the problem from a working-class perspective in her *Ich stehe meine Frau* (Taking it like a woman), 1975. As new texts by women were changing the literary scene in Germany, scholars also undertook research that opened the long-neglected history of writing by women in the German language. More recent developments in feminist theory now enable contemporary readers to identify texts from many centuries that yield new insights when subjected to feminist analysis, thus vastly enlarging the corpus of what is currently understood as "feminist writing."

Patricia Herminghouse

See also Abortion; Bachmann, Ingeborg; Bebel, August; Braun, Lily; Feminism and Anti-Feminism; Feminism in the Federal Republic of Germany; *Germanistik;* Kirsch, Sarah; Lange, Helene; Luxemburg, Rosa; Otto-Peters, Louise; Schwarzer, Alice; Seghers, Anna; Wolf, Christa; Zetkin, Clara

References
Allen, Ann Taylor. *Feminism and Motherhood in Germany, 1800–1914.* New Brunswick, NJ: Rutgers University Press, 1991.
Altbach, Edith Hoshino et al., eds. *German Feminism: Readings in Politics and Literature.* Albany, NY: State University of New York Press, 1984.
Evans, Richard J. *The Feminist Movement in Germany, 1894–1933.* London: Sage, 1978.
Frevert, Ute. *Women in German History: From Bourgeois Emancipation to Sexual Liberation.* Oxford: Berg, 1989.
Pore, Renate. *A Conflict of Interest: Women in German Social Democracy, 1919–1933.* Westport, CT: Greenwood Press, 1981.
Quatert, Jean H. *Reluctant Feminists in German Social Democracy, 1885–1917.* Princeton, NJ: Princeton University Press, 1979.

Fertility

The German birth rate has declined from 38.5 births per 1,000 population in 1870 to barely over 10 per 1,000 per year recently. The falling German birth rate has caused two periods of near panic among nationalists, one in the 1890s and the other today. In the generation before World War I, German writers worried that the higher fertility of the Slavic populations to the east of Germany would permit them to overwhelm the outnumbered Germans. These fears were reinforced by social Darwinism, which applied Darwinian ideas of "survival of the fittest" to the competition among national states. If the Germans were not reproducing, would they survive? These fears played an important part in the rise of antimodernism before World War I and to the climate of opinion that later helped the Nazi Party to power. Similarly in the Federal Republic in the 1980s and 1990s, conservatives have worried that the increasing numbers of "foreigners" and their higher birth rates will undermine "German" civilization.

Germany was not unique. The German population passed through the common "fertility transition," the pattern of declining death and birth rates that moved across Europe from west to east in the late nineteenth and early twentieth centuries. Historians would very much like to know why this happened, but unfortunately professional demographers have virtually abandoned any attempt to explain these movements in the terms that historians recognize. Previously, demographers were the last remaining adherents of modernization theory, and elaborate attempts were made to correlate "modernization" variables with fertility. These attempts were not notably successful. In the currently prevailing paradigm of demographic research, social and economic factors are no longer seen as having any direct effect on fertility. Instead, they must operate through a limited set of behavioral variables, the so-called "proximate" determinants of fertility, which determine exposure to intercourse, control of conception, and rates of successful parturition. Most studies therefore simply concentrate on showing how the proximate variables have changed over time, and the results predictably are largely descriptive.

Average levels of fertility in Germany rose from the 1860s to the 1870s. Birth rates of upper-class families may have begun to decline early in the nineteenth century, and the average birth rate was falling after 1875. Infant mortality rose until 1860 and then declined. The decline in total fertility ratios set in during the 1880s in western Germany. The decline then moved eastward through the 1930s. Knodel and others found consistent patterns in fertility and in the timing of the decline. Rural areas consistently had higher fertility rates than urban districts—this was the fact that publicists such as Karl Oldenburg seized on in the 1890s. However, fertility did decline in rural areas, but the decline began later and proceeded more slowly than in the urban districts in each region. In addition, small cities showed higher fertility rates than large cities, and the decline began later.

Regarding social variables, the fertility of workers was consistently higher than that of managers in all sectors of the economy. As might be expected from the rural/urban comparison, the agricultural population's fertility was higher than that of the industrial population. A less intuitive result was that the industrial population had a higher fertility than the population employed in services—indeed, service workers had lower fertility rates than agricultural workers around the census year of 1907. In addition there are figures that suggest that, within social classes, wealthier families had fewer children than less-wealthy families.

With regard to possible explanations, attempts to connect the decline in fertility with the process of industrialization have proved largely unsuccessful. There is an obvious global correlation—as Germany industrialized the birth rate declined—but explanatory models break down at lower levels when applied to specific districts or social groups—Marschalck insists that the decline in fertility of all social groups between 1900 and 1930 demonstrates that there were no "leading classes" and therefore no demonstration effect, as might be inferred from Knodel's study. The decline in birth rates began before the decline in infant mortality, and the number of adult children per family declined, so decisions to have fewer children were not a response to declining death rates. As for the proximate variables affecting exposure to intercourse and completion of pregnancy, there was little or no change in the percentage of women who married or in their age at marriage, and therefore little change in exposure to intercourse. The fact that more women were in waged work outside the home may have increased awareness of contraception and abortion. Shorter argues that abortion, though illegal, was common and increasing. It is reasonably certain that abortions were often recorded as accidental miscarriages among factory workers in the 1920s, a deception that not only avoided criminal penalties but also entitled the women to compensation. It was easier to obtain an abortion in a large city, and this may in part explain the lower birth rates and earlier decline in fertility in urban centers.

In the postwar years, the demographic transition was considered a "European" phenomenon lasting around 70 years, with birth rates stabilizing at a new lower level. This has not proved to be the case. The demographic transition is now being replicated, but much more rapidly, in East and Southeast Asia. In addition, European fertility began to decline yet again in the 1960s. The West German birth rate dropped from 17.4 per 1,000 in 1960 to 10.5 in 1987, and the East German birth rate from 17.0 to 13.3. We of course do not know what will happen in the future, but France—which suffered its own panic at the thought of high German birth rates before World War I and which was cited by German authors as an example of a degenerate race because of its historically low birth rate—now has one of the highest levels of fertility in Europe.

Frank B. Tipton

See also Abortion; Childbirth and Motherhood; Family; Federal Republic of Germany: Women; German Democratic Republic: Women; Health; Infants, Children and Adolescents; Marriage and Divorce; Women

References

Eversley, David, and Wolfgang Kollmann, eds. *Population Change and Social Planning: Social and Economic Implications of the Recent Decline in Fertility in the United Kingdom and the Federal Republic of Germany.* London: Edward Arnold, 1982.

Knodel, John E. *The Decline of Fertility in Germany, 1871–1939.* Princeton, NJ: Princeton University Press, 1974.

Marschalck, Peter. "The Age of Demographic Transition: Mortality and Fertility." *Population, Labour, and Migration in 19th and 20th-Century Germany.* Ed. Klaus J. Bade. Leamington Spa: Berg, 1987.

———. *Bevölkerungsgeschichte Deutschlands im 19. und 20. Jahrhundert.* Frankfurt am Main: Suhrkamp, 1984.

Shorter, Edward. *A History of Women's Bodies.* Harmondsworth: Penguin, 1982.

Festivals

The numerous German festivals may be divided into the nationally celebrated annual festivals, often with origins in the church calendar, pageants commemorating historical events or folklore, and locally based food, wine, and beer festivals.

National Festivals

Easter is a curious intermingling of Christian and pre-Christian celebrations in which superstition and faith go hand in hand. Most homes are decorated with an "Easter tree"—flowering branches in a vase—from which dangle small wooden eggs, wooden hares from the Erzgebirge, and decorated blown hens' eggs. The Sunday before Easter, Palm Sunday, is celebrated in church in much the same way as in other countries. "Green Thursday," the day before Good Friday, is celebrated in various ways, from taking a bath to eating green food, such as spinach, kale, cress, leek, chives, and other herbs.

Many rural communities possess big wooden Good Friday rattles, in appearance rather like football rattles. Besides being known as *Karfreitag* (Sorrowful Friday) it is also known as Quiet Friday. On this solemn day no church bells are rung in Roman Catholic areas. Some children believe that the bells have been sent to Rome to be consecrated. The male members of the community summon the villagers to the church services by making as much noise as possible with their rattles.

In the days before Easter Saturday children collect wood for the traditional Easter Saturday bonfire. The highlight for many families is waking up to beautifully decorated Easter breakfast tables on Sunday. Specially dyed and decorated eggs are a must, as are special breads. Children look forward to searching for small chocolate and marzipan Easter eggs, which they believe the Easter Hare has hidden either around the house or in the garden.

May Day is heralded in Heidelberg by the students' "May singing" on April 30 and is celebrated (as in some other countries) with a public holiday, parades, and public speeches. Ascension Day, forty days after Easter, is also known as Men's Day, when men don straw boaters and carry cane walking sticks and go on outings and drinking parties. Ten days later, Whitsuntide is celebrated. In some areas, "Whitsun bunches," bunches of birch, are put in vases and the peonies, or "Whitsun roses," are in blossom. In Münster, wooden hoops decorated with lamps and colored eggs are hung between the houses, with a dove, the "Whitsun bird," in the middle of the hoops.

November 11 is known as St. Martin's Day. The Martin's Goose can still be seen on menus as the day was originally celebrated by eating goose, supposedly because St. Martin had tried to hide in a flock of geese. At dusk, children parade through the streets holding lanterns containing candles and singing Martinmas songs. Special bread in the shape of a man holding a clay pipe is baked for St. Martin's Day.

The remaining church festivals of the year are more serious. The Protestant Church celebrates Reformation Day on October 31, commemorating how in 1517 Martin Luther nailed his 95 theses to the church door in Wittenberg, thereby sparking the Reformation. November 1 is All Saints' Day and honors all the saints who have not been assigned a day of their it flows free for all from the village fountain). Even where no festival is held, new wine is on sale in all the restaurants, served in the Stuttgart area with the traditional onion tart. The Dürkheim Sausage Fair, held for eight days each September, ranks as the largest and best known of the wine festivals. It prides itself on never closing and on its wheelbarrow-shaped wine booths. The world-famous Octoberfest in Munich is over 170 years old. Several million liter-size glasses of beer are served by dirndl-clad waitresses to the accompaniment of brass bands. Like many festivals, the Octoberfest is combined with a big fun fair. Fun fairs also play an important part at the church festival fairs (*Kirmes, Kirchweih*) and the sharpshooting festivals. Traditional food is on sale, including large heart-shaped gingerbreads containing messages of love to be worn around one's neck on a long ribbon.

Jennifer M. Russ

See also Carnival; Christmas; Customs; Folklore; *Heimat*; National Holidays; National Identity; Nationalism; Patriotic Literature

References

Beitl, Richard. *Wörterbuch der deutschen Volkskunde.* 3rd ed. Stuttgart: Kröner, 1974.

Russ, Jennifer M. *German Festivals and Customs.* London: Oswald Wolff, 1982.

Schönfeldt, Sybil Gräfin. *Das Ravensburger Buch der Feste und Bräuche.* Ravensburg: Otto Maier, 1980.

Weber-Kellermann, Ingeborg. *Saure Wochen, Frohe Feste: Fest und Alltag in der Sprache der Bräuche.* Munich: C.J. Bucher, 1985.

Feuchtwanger, Lion (1884–1958)

In his eminently successful novels, Lion Feuchtwanger searched for the truth in historical situations, which he tried to interpret with political application to the present. He situated his plots in times of important historical changes and simultaneously tried to distance himself from the events and the characters he depicted in order to demonstrate the significant lines in the course of history.

Feuchtwanger was born into a well-to-do Munich Jewish industrialist family. His first literary ambition was to become a dramatist, at which he was quite successful, with several plays being performed on German stages. One of his best plays from this period, *Thomas Wendt*, 1920, was a reflection of the German intellectuals' role in the 1919 Munich Soviet Revolution; here he tries to create a "dramatic novel," thus anticipating the similar mix of genres in Bertolt Brecht's epic theater. Feuchtwanger and Bertolt Brecht (1898–1956) became close friends during this time and collaborated on various literary projects throughout their lives.

It took Feuchtwanger three years to find a publisher for his most successful work, the novel *Jud Süss* (Jew Süss), 1925. The protagonist, Joseph Süss Oppenheimer, places himself into the service of an eighteenth-century German provincial ruler. Although at first successful, he ultimately fails to become fully integrated into German society and is cruelly executed.

Bad Hersfeld summer festival. Courtesy of German Embassy, Ottawa.

own. The following day, All Souls' Day, is important to Roman Catholics, who make supplication for the souls in purgatory on that day. If possible, people like to return to their home towns or villages to visit the graves of their relatives. Remembrance Sunday takes place two Sundays before the beginning of Advent. Services are held at war memorials to remember those who died in the wars. On the following Sunday, Totensonntag, (Memorial Day—literally, Sunday for the dead) Protestants visit the graves of their dead.

Local Pageants

Well-known local pageants include the Walpurgis Night celebrations in the Harz mountains, the Princely Wedding at Landshut, Spearing the Dragon at Fürth im Wald, the Master Draught at Rothenburg-on-the-Tauber, the Women of Weinsberg, the Fishermen's Jousting Match at Ulm, the Pied Piper Play at Hameln, the Tänzel Festival at Kaufbeuren, the Schäffler Dance in Munich, the Children's Reckoning at Dinkelsbühl, the Shepherds' Race at Markgröningen, the Pandours Pageant at Waldmünchen, the Till Eulenspiegel Festival at Mölln, and, once every ten years, the Passion Plays at Oberammergau.

Wine and Beer Festivals

The main wine-growing areas hold *Winzerfeste* (wine growers' festivals) in late summer. Rüdesheim, for example, chooses a wine queen and enjoys band concerts, festival plays, and dances by the vintners. Wine flows freely (in some localities

However, before his death he realizes that he has not taken the right course by entering Germany's arena of political action and opts for a contemplative life. The success of this book and its film adaptation was so immense that even the Nazis exploited its popularity in a 1940 anti-Semitic propaganda film of the same title.

In 1925 Feuchtwanger moved to Berlin, where he found the necessary distance to write the novel that related his experiences with the nationalistic powers in Munich. *Erfolg* (published as *Success*), 1930, subtitled "Three Years in the History of a German Province," was the first German novel to take a critical look at Adolf Hitler's political threat. The nationalistic press of Germany reacted vehemently to *Erfolg*. The *Völkischer Beobachter* (People's observer), the Nazi newspaper published in Munich, promised Feuchtwanger a "passport for emigrants" (i.e., they would run him out of the country if given the chance) as early as October 17, 1931. Thus, the author was fortunate to be on a lecture tour in the United States when Hitler became chancellor. He never saw his homeland again, living in Sanary-sur-mer on the French Riviera from 1933 to 1940 and thereafter, until his death in 1958, in the United States, primarily in Pacific Palisades, California.

Although Feuchtwanger did not experience the typical hardships of many exiles, such as lack of finances, he was interned behind bars in France after the outbreak of World War II in 1939 and again in the course of the German-French hostilities of 1940. In addition, he was unable to gain American citizenship due to his reputation as a Communist sympathizer. He also could not write the fourth and last novel in the *Der Wartesaal* (The waiting room) series of which *Erfolg* was the first one. The second of the *Wartesaal* novels, *Die Geschwister Oppermann* (published as *The Oppermanns*, 1934), 1933, relates the story of a Jewish family in Berlin during the years immediately prior to and following Hitler's takeover in Germany. The third novel in the series, *Exil* (published as *Paris Gazette*), 1940, looks at the German exile community of Paris and contains a more direct call for a fight against Nazism. The author also reacted negatively to provincial thinking and irrational fears in his host country in his prose drama *Wahn oder der Teufel von Boston* (Illusion; or the devil in Boston), 1948, a portrayal of the Salem witch trials written during the height of anti-Communist phobia in the United States.

In all of his works, Feuchtwanger strongly criticized nationalistic thinking, especially in its extreme form of fascism, and became an avid spokesman of reason.

Helmut F. Pfanner

See also Anti-Semitism; Exile Literature; Federal Republic of Germany; Jews; Novel; Theater; Weimar Germany: Literature

References

Dietschreit, Frank. *Lion Feuchtwanger*. Sammlung Metzler. Vol. 245. Stuttgart: J.B. Metzler'sche Verlagsbuchhandlung, 1988.

Jeske, Wolfgang and Peter Zahn. *Lion Feuchtwanger oder der arge Weg der Erkenntnis: Eine Biographie*. Stuttgart: J.B. Metzler'sche Verlagsbuchhandlung, 1984.

Kahn, Lothar. *The Life and Work of Lion Feuchtwanger*. Cranbury: Associated University Presses, 1975.

Köpke, Wulf. *Lion Feuchtwanger*. Autorenbücher, vol. 35. Munich: C.H. Beck, 1983.

John M. Spalek, ed. *Lion Feuchtwanger, The Man, His Ideas, His Work: A Collection of Critical Essays*. Los Angeles, CA: Hennessey and Ingalls, 1972.

The Fischer Controversy

The Fischer controversy, named after its originator, Professor Fritz Fischer (1908–) of the University of Hamburg, was the most important historiographical debate in post-Nazi Germany before the *Historikerstreit* (historians' debate). Fischer's work centered on the origins of World War I but had wider implications.

The controversy was unleashed by the theses in his book *Griff nach der Weltmacht* (published as *Germany's Aims in the First World War*), 1961, and reaffirmed in *Krieg der Illusion* in 1969 (published as *War of Illusions: German Policy 1911 to 1914*). In his studies Fischer demonstrated that the German Empire exploited the crisis over the June 28, 1914 assassination of the Austrian Archduke Franz Ferdinand at Sarajevo in order to bring about a reckoning with Russia and France, with the objective of redrawing the map of Central Europe (*Mitteleuropa*) and also of the colonial world (*Mittelafrika*) in Germany's favor.

Fischer reexamined the July-August crisis of 1914 and concluded that Germany had manipulated the situation to challenge the Triple Entente of Great Britain, France, and Russia, whereby Berlin hoped that Russia would shrink from coming to Serbia's aid. This would have had the effect of demonstrating the ineffectuality of the Entente, but if Russia stood by Serbia (in which event France was obliged to support Russia), then Germany was ready to implement the Schlieffen Plan for a two-front war. Although the possibility of a British military intervention on the side of France was appreciated, the German war planners did not believe that it would make any difference to the outcome. When this plan appeared to be on the point of success, in early September 1914 in France, the Reich government developed a memorandum of war aims (the September Program) that included vast annexations at the expense of Russia, France, and Belgium.

All these findings appeared to confirm the imputation of sole war guilt imposed on Germany and her allies in the Treaty of Versailles, namely that Germany had planned for a war and at the opportune moment brought it about with concrete objectives already in mind. Fischer thus effectively started a methodological revolution in German historical scholarship with far-ranging consequences. Not only did he show that policy was the result of the inputs of many influential pressure groups combined with the dominant statist and imperialist ideologies of the time, but he insisted that the rise of the Third Reich and the war aims of Nazi Germany had to be seen in connection with the imperialistic objectives of Wilhelmine Germany. As well as the innovatory methodology of Fischer's work, it was this projection of a continuity between the kaiser's Germany and that of Adolf Hitler that many contemporaries felt to be unjustified and that angered conservative German scholars, especially Gerhard Ritter. Fischer, however, has held his ground and won over some of his former opponents. His work stands as a witness to the triumph of liberal and cosmopolitan values in modern Germany as opposed to the former nationalist and antidemocratic political culture.

John A. Moses

See also Bethmann Hollweg, Theobald von; *Historikerstreit*; History; *Sonderweg*; World War I

References

Berghahn, Volker. *Germany and the Approach of War in 1914.* 2nd. ed. New York, NY: St. Martin's Press, 1993.

Bucholz, Arden. *Moltke, Schlieffen and Prussian War Planning.* New York, NY: Berg Publishers, 1991.

Farrar, Lancelot. *The Short War Illusion—German Policy, Strategy and Domestic Affairs, August–December 1914.* Santa Barbara, CA: Clio, 1973.

Fischer, Fritz. *From Kaiserreich to Third Reich.* Trans. Roger Fletcher. London: Allen and Unwin, 1986.

———. *Germany's Aims in the First World War.* London: Chatto and Windus, 1967.

———. *Hitler war kein Betriebsunfall.* Munich: Beck, 1990.

———. *War of Illusions: German Policies from 1911 to 1914.* London: Chatto and Windus, 1975.

Kocka, Jürgen. *Facing Total War: German Society 1914– 1918.* Leamington Spa: Berg Publishers, 1984.

Moses, John A. *The Politics of Illusion: The Fischer Controversy in German Historiography.* London: George Prior Publishers, 1975.

Schöllgen, Gregor, ed. *Escape into War? The Foreign Policy of Imperial Germany.* Oxford: Berg Publishers, 1990.

Fischer, Emil (1852–1919)

Emil Fischer, the first German-born winner of the Nobel Prize in Chemistry (1902), was among the leading organic chemists of his time. He produced work of both industrial and scientific importance in areas ranging from dyestuffs to biologically important molecules. He also shaped the modernization of German scientific research institutions before and during World War I.

Born in Euskirchen in the Rhineland, Fischer obtained his doctorate in chemistry at the University of Strassburg (1874). After becoming associate professor under his mentor Adolf Baeyer in Munich (1879), Fischer advanced rapidly through successive full professorships in the universities of Erlangen (1882), Würzburg (1886), and Berlin (1892). His marriage (1887) to Agnes Gerlach (d. 1895) produced three sons, but only Hermann O. L. Fischer (1888–1960) survived World War I.

Fischer's most significant early work (with his cousin Otto Fischer) clarified the structure of the important rosaniline dyestuffs and forged an enduring, profitable relationship with the German dye industry. During the 1880s he

moved toward biochemistry, studying the sugars and purines (whose synthesis won him the Nobel Prize and also led to the industrial production of synthetic caffeine, barbiturates, and other pharmaceuticals). After 1899, Fischer's large research group studied the amino acids and synthesized many protein-like polypeptides, then turned to nucleic acids, depsides, and fats.

In Berlin, Fischer assumed August Wilhelm von Hofmann's (1818–92) mantle as Germany's most influential chemist in professional and institutional affairs. His new teaching institute (1900) was the largest and most modern of its time. From 1905 he, Walther Nernst (1864–1941), and (briefly) Wilhelm Ostwald (1853–1932) worked to establish a national chemical research institution, culminating in the first two research institutes (1912) of the Kaiser Wilhelm Society. Respected in both business and bureaucratic circles, Fischer became a vice-president of the society and shaped its scientific policy, emphasizing the interaction of chemistry and biology.

From August 1914, Fischer worked to organize scientific support for the German war effort, promoting the use of chemical substitutes for materials in short supply and eventually heading a section of the Kaiser Wilhelm Stiftung für kriegstechnische Wissenschaft (Kaiser Wilhelm Foundation for Military Technology), 1917–18; he became, however, increasingly disillusioned with Germany's leadership. His post-

Emil Fischer. Courtesy of German Information Center, New York.

war efforts toward the recovery of German scientific institutions were cut short by his death (July 1919).

Fischer's lifework had great intellectual and institutional significance, advancing modernization in both areas by promoting the integration of chemistry and biology as well as the integration of science, industry, and government.

Jeffrey A. Johnson

See also Baeyer, Adolf von; Chemistry, Scientific and Industrial; Hofmann, August Wilhelm von; Kaiser Wilhelm/Max Planck Societies and Institutes; Nernst, Walther; Ostwald, Wilhelm

References

Fruton, Joseph S. *Contrasts in Scientific Style: Research Groups in the Chemical and Biological Sciences.* Philadelphia, PA: American Philosophical Society, 1990.

Johnson, Jeffrey Allan. *The Kaiser's Chemists: Science and Modernization in Imperial Germany.* Chapel Hill, NC: University of North Carolina Press, 1990.

Fischer, Oskar (1923–)

Minister of foreign affairs of the German Democratic Republic (GDR) from 1975 to 1990, Oskar Fischer was born on March 19, 1923, in Asch, Czechoslovakia. His father was a worker and a Communist Party functionary. After completing school, Fischer became apprenticed to a tailor. Between 1941 and 1944, he served as a corporal in the Wehrmacht and became a Soviet prisoner of war until 1946. Returning to Czechoslovakia, he worked in a quarry before being expelled to Germany in 1947.

Fischer's career as a Communist Party functionary started in 1947 when, while already a member of the Socialist Unity Party (SED), he became the chairman of the Free German Youth (Freie Deutsche Jugend; FDJ) in the small town of Spremberg. From 1951 to 1955, he worked in the Central Council of the FDJ—the highest body of the youth organization. During this time, he became a close associate of FDJ Chairman Erich Honecker (1912–94).

In 1955, Fischer entered the diplomatic service of the GDR as ambassador to Bulgaria, a post he held until 1959. Upon his return to Berlin, he officiated in the Central Committee of the SED from 1960 to 1962. During the following three years he studied at the highest Communist Party of the Soviet Union (CPSU) educational level in Moscow and received a social-science diploma. In 1965, Fischer became a deputy of the minister of foreign affairs in charge of East German relations with the Eastern Bloc countries.

In 1975, when Foreign Minister Otto Winzer left office because of illness, Fischer took over his position. Fischer had been Honecker's confidant since the FDJ days. As foreign minister, Fischer mainly served Honecker in promoting his foreign policy. From 1975 to 1989, he officiated as a member of the SED's Central Committee, and between 1976 and 1990 he sat in the parliament (Volkskammer).

Fischer earned a reputation as a moderate politician. After the collapse of the SED regime, he was one of the few SED ministers to remain in office in the Modrow government. Following the first free elections in the GDR, held on March 18, 1990, he vacated his office on April 12, 1990 to Markus Meckel, the new foreign minister. Fischer, who is married and has two children, is currently a pensioner.

Heinrich Bortfeld

See also Free German Youth; German Communist Party; German Democratic Republic: Foreign Relations; Honecker, Erick; Socialist Unity Party

References

Schulz, Eberhard, Hans-Adolf Jacobsen, Gert Leptin, and Ulrich Scheuner. *GDR Foreign Policy.* Armonk, NY: M.E. Sharpe Inc., 1982. (Translation, by Michel Vale, of portions of *Dreijahrzehnte Aussenpolitik der DDR.* Munich: Oldenbourg Verlag, 1980.)

Fischer, Ruth (1895–1961)

Ruth Fischer (born Elfriede Eisler) was prominent in the German Communist Party (KPD) from 1919 to 1926. Although a staunch left-wing exponent of proletarian internationalism, she played the German national card during the crisis precipitated by France's occupation of the Ruhr during January 1923. Thereafter she tried, but failed, to prevent the subordination of German Communism to Soviet interests.

Elfriede Eisler was born into an academic family in Leipzig on December 11, 1895. A student of philosophy and economics at Vienna University, she joined the Austrian Social Democrats during World War I and was a founding member of the Austrian Communist Party. As Ruth Fischer she returned to Berlin in 1919 and became a leading left-winger in the Communist Party there before joining the Central Committee in early 1923. The right-wing leadership (Heinrich Brandler [1881–1967], August Thalheimer) was advocating a revolutionary national struggle against the French, but the left (Fischer, Arkadi Maslow) feared that resulting compromises with the nationalist radical right would dilute the class struggle.

In May, the Comintern settled the matter in the right's favor and Fischer was prominent among erstwhile left-wing internationalists who joined the largely unsuccessful campaign to forge links with right-wing radicals, including Nazis. Simultaneous attempts to collaborate with left-wing Social Democrats culminated in disaster (November 1923), leading to the replacement of Brandler by Fischer as party leader (April 1924). She was immediately involved in a national struggle of a different sort, defending the KPD against Soviet attempts to assert hegemony over all Communist parties, but her failure led first to her dismissal as party leader (November 1925) and then to her expulsion from the KPD (August 1926).

By 1929 she had left politics altogether to become a social worker in Berlin, but fled to France (1933) and then the United States (1940). After the war she returned to Paris as an American citizen. There she wrote several books on Communism and Communist leaders before her death in 1961.

Fischer, like many early German Communist leaders, had

devoted considerable energy to an almost hopeless task. The inherent unpopularity of Communism led her, among others, to dabble unsuccessfully with a lethal cocktail of revolutionary socialism and nationalism. Subsequently she failed to maintain a distinctively German form of Communism, for many of her colleagues saw the sole hope for political survival in a tight alliance with Moscow.

Conan Fischer

See also Brandler, Heinrich; Drama; German Communist Party; Levi, Paul; Social Democratic Party, 1919–90; Thälmann, Ernst; Weimar Germany

References

Degras, Jane, ed. *The Communist International 1919–1943: Documents.* 2 vols. London: Oxford University Press, 1971.

Fischer, R. and A. Maslow. *Abtrünnig wider Willen: aus Briefen und Manuskripten des Exils.* Munich: R. Oldenbourg, 1990.

———. *Stalin and German Communism: A Study in the Origins of the State Party.* Cambridge, MA: Harvard University Press, 1948.

Fowkes, Ben. *Communism in Germany under the Weimar Republic.* London: Macmillan Press, 1984.

Rosenberg, Arthur. *The History of the German Republic.* London: Methuen, 1936. Reprint, New York, NY: Russell and Russell, 1965.

Fischer, Samuel (1859–1934)

Samuel Fischer, one of the most prominent German publishers of the twentieth century, mediated new literary movements and fostered the development of literary institutions to link production and dissemination. Fischer wanted to be known as a publisher of the literary avant garde.

After a brief publishing partnership (Steinitz & Fischer), Fischer established his own firm, S. Fischer Verlag, in 1886 in Berlin. During the next 15 years, he published Scandinavian literature in German translations (in the series *Nordische Bibliothek* [Nordic library]) and numerous works by German dramatists in the vanguard of the naturalist movement. In 1889, Fischer was instrumental in founding a new society that organized contemporary stage productions, and he published the first issue of its journal (*Freie Bühne* [Free theater]) the following year. By 1900, S. Fischer Verlag was considered the preeminent publisher of contemporary drama, including works by Gerhart Hauptmann (1862–1946), Hugo von Hofmannsthal (1874–1929), Henrik Ibsen, and Arthur Schnitzler (1862–1931).

During the first decade of the twentieth century, the trend toward poetry and prose, rather than drama, added a new dimension to the publishing program. The modern German novel, as exemplified in the works of Hermann Hesse (1877–1962), Thomas Mann (1875–1955), and Jakob Wassermann, established a literary profile that became inextricably linked with the image of the publishing house. In 1908, Fischer introduced a series of inexpensive pocket books (*Fischers Bibliothek*

zeitgenössischer Romane [Fischer's library of contemporary novels]) in order to reach new readers and markets.

Despite the skepticism of many of his contemporaries, Fischer was also intrigued by the possibilities of film and the transferral of literature into the film medium, although such media "tie-ins" were in their infancy. His interest in the new media of "modernity," and in the aesthetics of their communication (as in the literature of expressionism), was also reflected in the publication of works by Otto Flake and Alfred Döblin (1878–1957).

In the 1920s, Fischer expanded the publishing program and restructured the production of literary editions. In addition to an author's collected works, the individual works were reprinted and published simultaneously in special editions or thematic collections. Fischer introduced this concept with the works of Thomas Mann, whose critical acclaim and reception during the Weimar Republic culminated in the Nobel Prize in 1929, and successfully repeated it for the works of Jakob Wassermann and Hermann Hesse. By his seventieth birthday in 1929, Fischer and his publishing house had become a literary institution that continued to come up with new emphases, such as publication of authors in German translations (Joseph Conrad, John Dos Passos, Eugene O'Neill, George Bernard Shaw, and Walt Whitman).

Mark W. Rectanus

See also Bestsellers, Contemporary; Books; Döblin, Alfred; Hauptmann, Gerhart; Hesse, Hermann; Hofmannsthal, Hugo von; Mann, Thomas; Publishing and the Book Trade; Rowohlt, Ernst; Schnitzler, Arthur; Ullstein Publishing

References

Mendelssohn, Peter de. *S. Fischer und sein Verlag.* Frankfurt am Main: S. Fischer Verlag, 1970.

Stach, Rainer. *100 Jahre S. Fischer Verlag 1886–1986: Kleine Verlagsgeschichte.* 2nd ed. Frankfurt am Main: S. Fischer Verlag, 1991.

Flick Family

Virtually unknown at the beginning of the twentieth century, the Flick family became one of Germany's most influential industrial and financial actors during World War I. The history of the Flick "empire" illustrates the sometimes troubled connection between business and politics in Germany, strands of continuity in German elites despite political upheaval, and the gradual shift in industrial power away from heavy industry and toward consumer goods and technology intensive industries.

Friedrich Flick (1883–1972) dominated the family's fortunes for most of the twentieth century. After an apprenticeship as a salesman at the Bremer Iron Works in 1902, Flick studied at the *Handelshochschule* (commercial college) in Cologne, where he received his diploma in 1906. He then moved quickly up the ranks in various iron and steel concerns, becoming a member of the managing board of the Charlottenhütte in 1915.

Flick's meteoric rise to industrial power and political prominence took place in the context of World War I and the severe inflation that followed. Already in 1915, he had begun buying shares in the Charlottenhütte. Windfall profits from the war provided Flick with the leverage to gain credit during the immediate postwar period, which he used to enlarge his empire substantially during the period of inflation through 1924. He focused for the most part on holdings in heavy-industry firms.

During the 1920s, Flick was involved in the creation of the Vereinigte Stahlwerke, the massive steel concern that would be broken up by Allied trust-busters after 1945. During the Nazi period, political flexibility enabled Flick to further his gains and his holdings: not initially a supporter of the party, Flick became closely involved with the *Freundeskreis* (circle of friends) Himmler and other organizations that linked the party and the business community. He participated actively in rearming Germany in preparation for the upcoming war and in taking over industrial concerns in conquered territories. When German defeat became imminent by 1944, however, Flick began preparations for the postwar period by reorganizing his holdings and turning over nominal control over most of them to two of his sons.

Partly because of his actions during the war, and partly because he symbolized for the Allies the complicity of the German business community in the excesses of the Nazi regime, Flick was tried at Nuremberg in 1947. He was found guilty of using slave labor, plundering foreign industry, and supporting the SS and was sentenced to seven years' imprisonment. Flick lost about two-thirds of what he owned because the firms were located in central and eastern Germany and were taken over by the East German, Polish, and Soviet governments. He directed his remaining holdings from Landsberg prison. Released in August 1950, Flick immediately took formal control of his now more limited empire.

Having lost much of his previous holdings, especially those in heavy industry, Flick took advantage of the situation to diversify and reorient his affairs during the 1950s and 1960s. With the aid and advice of prominent bankers, such as Hermann Josef Abs, Flick expanded his empire to include significant parts of Feldmühle AG (consumer goods and paper products), Dynamit AG (chemicals and explosives), Buderus (foundry and metalworking), Daimler-Benz, and Krauss-Maffei (armaments). At the same time, his holding firm continued in the previously established pattern: it was always a closely held family concern and never issued stock publicly.

These same years saw the cultivation of his successor, Friedrich Karl Flick (1927–). The elder Flick's third son, Friedrich Karl Flick continued aspects of his father's tradition: by the 1980s, the younger Flick headed a far-flung industrial empire that included more than 60 firms, about 43,000 employees, and an annual turnover of 9 billion deutsche marks; the younger Flick, like his father, became embroiled not only in business but also in governmental affairs. The firm was involved in a major scandal in the early 1980s involving donations to political parties.

Friedrich Karl Flick also epitomized new directions in German business. He studied business at the University of Munich through 1951, eventually participating in a doctoral seminar (he took his doctorate in economic and social science at the University of Cologne in 1965). More importantly, the younger Flick developed close contacts with American industrial interests. From 1954 to 1956, he worked at the Grace National Bank in New York City and later became involved in W.R. Grace Corporation, eventually holding more than 27 percent of Grace's share capital. Along with this internationalization of Flick interests, Friedrich Karl Flick continued his father's postwar reorientation of the firm away from heavy industry after taking over his father's position as head of the Flick holding company (Friedrich Flick Industrieverwaltung KG) in 1972.

Despite these concessions to postwar development, the Flick holding company remained a family firm, the largest in Germany. The scandal of the mid-1980s played a role in bringing the Flicks' extraordinary empire to an end. In December 1985, Flick announced the sale of his firm for approximately 5 billion deutsche marks (about $1.98 billion at the time) to the Deutsche Bank, which renamed it Feldmühle Nobel AG.

Raymond Stokes

See also Abs, Hermann; Cartels; Daimler-Benz AG; Deutsche Bank; Four-Year Plan; Inflation; Steel Industry; Third Reich: Industry

References

Feyerabend, Joachim. *Die leisen Milliarden: Das Imperium des Friedrich Karl Flick.* Düsseldorf: Econ, 1984.

Horster-Philipps, Ulrike. *Im Schatten des grossen Geldes: Flick-Konzern und Politik, Weimarer Republik, Drittes Reich, Bundesrepublik.* Cologne: Pahl-Rugenstein, 1985.

Turner, Henry Ashby. *German Big Business and the Rise of Hitler.* New York, NY: Oxford University Press, 1985.

Folklore

The German word for folklore, *Volkskunde*, appeared in various writings of the late eighteenth century, but semantically it was used in a diffuse way. The discipline itself cannot trace its beginnings to any particular time, nor can it make reference to a single founder. Johann Gottfried Herder (1744–1803) provided a romantic-nationalistic stimulus through his concept of *Naturpoesie* (natural poetry), which in time led directly to feverish collecting and publishing activity best exemplified by the Brothers Grimm.

Scholars who followed arrived at a limited and ideologically romanticized conceptualization of the German peasant as the embodiment of the *Volk*. This stereotype of the *Volk*, coupled with a bourgeois yearning for a lost past, resulted in an equally unrealistic concept of a *Volkskultur* (people's culture). By the last quarter of the nineteenth century, canonical categories for investigation were developed, formal societies to further this study were founded, and specific organs for the dissemination of the research were being published.

In 1890, Karl Weinhold founded the Berliner Verein für

Volkskunde (Berlin Association for Folklore), which published the *Zeitschrift des Vereins für Volkskunde* (Journal of the association for folklore), 1891, soon followed by many regional societies and journals. In the lead article of the new journal, a vigorous statement on nationalism appeared. Weinhold championed an alleged impartiality in all national questions. This principle was built on the ideological concept of the *Volk* and would continue until well past the middle of the twentieth century. *Volkskunde* and the views of its practitioners thereby left themselves open for ideological abuses.

In the first two decades of this century, most of the discussion and debate among folklorists centered on the idea of the continuity of a *Volksseele* (folk soul), and most specifically on whether this was primarily productive or reproductive, i.e., creative or receptive. Eduard Hoffmann-Krayer introduced the concept of a *vulgus in populo*, and coined the phrase *das Volk produziert nicht, es reproduziert*. Adolf Spamer tried to expand this concept of the folk by looking at other lower classes who seemed to exemplify a primitive life that was premoral, prelogical, or precultural.

It was, however, Hans Naumann who drew the attention of folklorists in Germany and throughout the Western world with his interpretations of the folk and their traditions. Cultural goods produced by the folk he conceived of as "primitive communal goods" (*primitives Gemeinschaftsgut*), which were to be distinguished from *gesunkenes Kulturgut*, traditional materials that had "sunk down" from higher strata of society. A storm of controversy surrounded Naumann for the rest of his life, and he found himself first accepted by the new Nazi regime, only to be thrown out of the party later because of his divergent view of the much-heralded German *Volk*.

German *Volkskunde* from 1933 until the present day has stood in a shadow cast by the Nazi perversions of the discipline between 1933 and 1945. Ostensible scholars became the handmaidens of a perverted nationalistic regime that used folklore and folklorists for its own ends. Departments of *Volkskunde* were established, institutes were founded, and others were compromised through "political coordination" (*Gleichschaltung*). The discipline was further usurped by the two major competing umbrella organizations, the Rosenberg Bureau under Alfred Rosenberg (1893–1946) and the SS Office of Ancestral Inheritance (SS Ahnenerbe) managed by Heinrich Himmler (1900–45). Elements of this perversion still haunt contemporary *Volkskunde* departments as well as individual folklorists. In the recent past, folklorists from both West and East Germany, as well as Austrian scholars, began to undertake detailed studies to overcome the Nazi past of their discipline.

Since 1945, several thrusts have become apparent in *Volkskunde*. The traditions of large numbers of displaced persons were studied by German folklorists, particularly by Johannes Künzig in the Institut für Ostdeutsche Volkskunde (Institute for East German Folklore). He worked intensively with ethnic Germans (*Volksdeutsche* referred to as *Heimatvertriebene*) who had been forced to return to Germany ("*Heim ins Reich*" [home into the Reich]) during the war or who had fled or been expelled after the war after Poland was divided in 1939, from settlements throughout the Balkans, Russia, and the Baltic States.

In the 1960s, as a result of militant confrontations at West German universities, folklorists called for an applied social-scientific orientation to the discipline and proclaimed a two-sentence doctrine called the Falkenstein Formula: "*Volkskunde* analyzes the transmission of cultural values (including their causes and the processes that accompany them) in their objective and subjective form. The goal is to contribute to solving sociocultural problems." At universities in West and East Germany, several schools of study were developing. The earliest was the so-called Munich School under the influence of Hans Moser and Karl-Sigismund Kramer. These scholars demystified the discipline by digging deeper into historical sources as a basis for studying the everyday life of the lower classes of society. A strong interest developed in the study of *Folklorismus* (second-hand folk culture, or "new" traditions not necessarily based on old ones). A Marxist-Leninist *Volkskunde* was also promoted in the German Democratic Republic, where there was a keen and abiding interest in the folk culture of the working classes. Finally, the Tübingen School, under the leadership of Hermann Bausinger, took leave of unrealistic concepts of the past and the *Volk* and worked toward a theoretically applied social science that it called "empirical cultural science."

James R. Dow

See also Anthropology; Federal Republic of Germany: Postwar Refugee and Expellee Organizations; *Heimat*; Himmler, Heinrich; National Identity; National Socialism; Nationalism; Patriotic Literature; Rosenberg, Alfred; *Völkisch* Ideology

References

Bausinger, Hermann, Utz Jeggle, Gottfried Korff, and Martin Scharfe. *Grundzüge der Volkskunde.* 2nd ed. Darmstadt: Wissenschaftliche Buchgesellschaft, 1978.

Brednich, Rolf Wilhelm, ed. *Grundriss der Volkskunde: Einführung in die Forschungsfelder der Europäischen Ethnologie.* Berlin: Dietrich Reimer Verlag, 1988.

Dow, James R. and Hannjost Lixfeld, eds. *Folklore and Fascism: The Reich Institute for German Folklore.* Bloomington, IN: Indiana University Press, 1994.

———, eds. *German Volkskunde: A Decade of Theoretical Confrontation, Debate, and Reorientation (1967–1977).* Folklore Studies in Translation. Bloomington, IN: Indiana University Press, 1986.

Jacobeit, Wolfgang, Olaf Bockhorn, and Hannjost Lixfled, together with James R. Dow, eds. *Völkische Wissenschaft: Gestalten und Tendenzen der deutschen und österreichischen Volkskunde in der ersten Hälfte des 20. Jahrhunderts.* Vienna: Böhlau Verlag, 1994.

Naumann, Hans. *Grundzüge der deutschen Volkskunde.* Wissenschaft und Bildung: Einzeldarstellungen aus allen Gebieten des Wissens, vol. 181. Leipzig: Quelle & Meyer, 1922.

———. *Primitive Gemeinschaftskultur: Beiträge zur Volkskunde und Mythologie.* Jena: Eugen Diedrichs, 1921.

Fontane, Theodor (1819–98)

Born into a family of largely Huguenot descent on December 30, 1819 in Neuruppin, Theodor Fontane initially followed—with apparent competence but little enthusiasm—his father's profession, that of pharmacist. His true talent, however, lay in writing, and while still in his early twenties he wrote a number of popularly acclaimed historical ballads. As a result, he was invited in 1844 to join a distinguished Berlin literary group, the *Tunnel über der Spree* (published as *Tunnel over the Spree*).

Abandoning pharmacy, he went to England as a newspaper correspondent in 1852, and in 1855 became editor of an Anglo-German news agency that had the financial backing of the Prussian government. It was not his first experience with state service, since he had earlier held an appointment in the press section of the Prussian ministry of the interior. But he was no happier as a bureaucrat than as a pharmacist, and in 1859 he returned to Berlin to become a professional writer. In part, this meant working as a journalist; he joined the staff of the Conservative *Kreuzeitung*, for which he covered all three of Bismarck's wars. In 1870, after his return from the French theater of war (where he had been captured by the French and briefly held on the erroneous suspicion of espionage) he moved to the Liberal newspaper *Vossische Zeitung—Tante Voss* as he called it—to become its theater critic. But in even larger part it meant the writing of novels and travel books. Among the latter, the four volumes of his *Wanderungen durch die Mark Brandenburg* (published as *Travels through the Mark Branden-*

burg), 1862–82, with their unique combination of scenic description, personality sketches, and historical anecdotes and background, remain the most notable. They also were the most successful. But his novels made an equal mark with readers and critics. Some that stand out are *Irrungen Wirrungen* (published as *Delusions, Confusions*), 1888, *Frau Jenny Treibel* (1892), *Effi Briest* (1895), and his late masterpiece, *Der Stechlin*, 1899. These books have enjoyed a remarkable lifespan—they can still be read for the pleasure they give and for the sharply yet sympathetically observed insights into the worlds of contemporary Berlin society and of the Prussian squirearchy.

Joachim Remak

See also Imperial Germany: Literature; Journalism; Novel; Prussia; Realism (Literary)

References

Ahrens, Helmut. *Das Leben des Romanautors, Dichters und Journalisten Theodor Fontane.* Düsseldorf: Droste, 1985.

Fontane, Theodor. *Sämtliche Werke.* 19 vols. Ed. Walter Keitel. Munich: Hanser, 1962–88.

Nürnberger, Helmuth. *Theodor Fontane in Selbstzeugnissen und Bilddokumenten.* Reinbek: Rowohlt, 1968.

Remak, Joachim. *The Gentle Critic: Theodor Fontane and German Politics, 1848–1898.* Syracuse, NY: Syracuse University Press, 1964.

Theodor Fontane. Courtesy of Inter Nationes, Bonn.

Food

Food emerged as a crucial and often dynamic issue in Germany because of persistent population growth, urbanization, and growing dependency on foreign feed and foodstuffs. During and immediately after both world wars, in 1916–23 and again in 1945–48, Germany suffered from severe food shortages that brought its population to the brink of malnutrition, social despair, and physical exhaustion. Efforts to resolve the food issue led to a fundamental clash of producer and consumer interests as well as of city and countryside.

After 1871, the spread of capitalistic agriculture, modernized transportation systems, and an agricultural revolution allowed Germany to meet a growing urban demand for food. The Bismarckian tariffs after 1879, reflecting national protection of producer interests and the influence of the "bacterial revolution" in public health, proved unable to satisfy a growing demand for meat, leading to series of riots and unrest in the 1890s. While Chancellor Leo von Caprivi's (1831–99) tariff reform helped to mitigate the problem, after 1907 the Bülow tariffs resulted in repeated crises on the meat markets and ominous signs of deteriorating standards of living in some urban areas. Under pressure from urban leaders, the Reich commissioned a major study of the problem on the eve of World War I, the *Fleischenquete* (meat inquiry) of 1913. Military strategists also confronted the problem, which was one reason for their doctrine of a short war.

Both world wars saw Germany suffer under naval blockade. Bread rationing was begun in January 1915 and eventually controls were extended to nearly all food groups. The disastrous "turnip winter" of 1916–17 caused a collapse of public health and widespread discontent with the war. Only the stabilization of the mark in 1924 ended the prolonged crisis over the food supply. Similarly during World War II, the Third Reich tried to promote economic autarky and ruthlessly exploited occupied areas in order to preserve the German standard of living, only to collapse into chaos lasting from the end of the war until the coming of the Marshall Plan in 1948.

The food problems helped to promote the "stab-in-the-back" legend (*Dolchstosslegende*) after 1918 and were linked to political anti-Semitism among the masses from the 1890s onwards. Eventually, Germany was able to solve its food problems by peaceful economic integration within the EEC. German agriculture now provides ample supplies for the consumer. Belated use of refrigeration since 1914 has also helped, as have changes in diet and custom.

Concern over sanitation and quality of food products developed in the wake of the "bacterial revolution," but beyond local ordinances, national intervention on behalf of the quality of food for the consumer has come largely through policing *Ersatz* (substitute) products, enforcing sanitation codes, and reliance on *Selbstverwaltung* (self-administration).

William Mathews

See also Agriculture; Postwar Reconstruction; Protectionism; World War I; World War II

References

Barkin, Kenneth D. *The Controversy over German Industrialization 1890–1902*. Chicago, IL: University of Chicago Press, 1970.

Beckstein, Hermann. *Städtische Interessenpolitik: Organisation und Politik der Städtetage in Bayern, Preussen und im Deutschen Reich 1896–1923*. Düsseldorf: Droste Verlag, 1991.

Croon, Helmut. "Die Versorgung des Ruhrgebietes im 19. und 20. Jahrhundert." *Jahrbuch für Nationale Ökonomie und Statistik* 179 (1966), 1356–68.

Farrar, L.L. *The Short-War Illusion: German Policy, Strategy and Domestic Affairs August–December 1914*. Santa Barbara, CA: ABC Clio, 1973.

Feldman, Gerald D. *The Great Disorder: Politics, Economics and Society in the German Inflation, 1914–1924*. Oxford: Oxford University Press, 1993.

Das Fleischenquete 1912/13: Verhandlungen der Gesamtkommission und Zusammenstellung des Sachverständigen. Berlin: Reichsdruckerei, 1913.

Mason, Tim. "The Legacy of 1918 for National Socialism." *German Democracy and the Rise of Hitler: Essays on Recent German History*. Ed. A.J. Nicholls and E. Matthias. New York, NY: St. Martin's, 1971.

Offer, Avner. *The First World War: An Agrarian Interpretation*. Oxford: Clarendon Press, 1989.

Perkins, J.A. "The Agricultural Revolution in Germany, 1850–1914." *Journal of European Economic History* 10 (1981), 71–129.

Teuteberg, Hans and Wiegelmann. *Der Wandel der Nahrungsgewohnheiten unter dem Einfluss der Industrialisierung*. Göttingen: Vandenhoeck & Ruprecht, 1972.

Forckenbeck, Max von (1821–92)

Born in Münster on October 21, 1821, Max von Forckenbeck studied law at the universities of Giessen and Berlin between 1839 and 1842, entering state service in law in 1847. Forckenbeck participated in the Revolution of 1848, chairing the Democratic-Constitutional Association in the city of Breslau in Silesia. His chairmanship defined Forckenbeck as a liberal and as a leader. Organizations like this were almost entirely moderate in their actions; that is, they were "liberal" in the sense that they were not radical. When the revolution failed in 1849, Forckenbeck returned to state service as a lawyer in Elbing.

Like most participants in the Revolution of 1848 who did not emigrate, Forckenbeck quietly pursued his state career in the 1850s. Galvanized into action by the events of 1858, notably the New Era inspired by Wilhelm's regency in Prussia and events in Italy, Forckenbeck won election to the Prussian Lower House of Parliament. During the 1862–66 constitutional conflict between Prussian parliament and King Wilhelm I over the government's use of revenues granted conditionally by parliament, Forckenbeck played a key role as chair of the budget committee and as a powerful member of the Fortschrittspartei (Progressive Party).

The conflict derived from Otto von Bismarck's insistence that the Prussian state could govern without parliamentary approval of annual budgets, in violation of the 1849 constitution decreed by King Friedrich Wilhelm IV. Dominated by the Progressives, the Lower House refused to approve any budget from 1862 to 1866. Unfortunately for the Progressives, the conflict ended with Bismarck's successful war in 1866 against Austria and several smaller German states, among them Bavaria, Saxony, and Hannover. Enjoying political popularity at the conclusion of the war, Bismarck asked for and received retroactive parliamentary approval of his budgetary actions since 1862. Key votes for this "compromise" came from the right wing of the Progressive Party, which split off and formed a new party, the National Liberal Party.

Forckenbeck was one of the key founders and leaders of the National Liberals, as befitted the man who was president of the Lower House in August 1866. The original policy of the National Liberal Party was to support Bismarck's policy of unifying Germany, and Forckenbeck promoted that policy in the Prussian Landtag (state legislature) and, after election in 1867, in the Reichstag as well. In 1873, Forckenbeck won election as *Oberbürgermeister* (lord mayor) of Breslau and became its representative in the Upper House. In 1874, he replaced Eduard Simson as president of the Reichstag. Although a determined opponent of Bismarck in the early 1860s, Forckenbeck proved open to compromise in the later 1860s and 1870s. In 1878, Forckenbeck was one of a small number of National Liberals whom Bismarck considered as possible ministers. But a new conflict erupted between the National Liberals and Bismarck over tariff policy and the Social Democratic Party, and Forckenbeck resigned from the party in 1879. The conflict eventually led to secession in 1881 of the left wing of the National Liberal Party. Forckenbeck joined that group and stayed with it when it changed its name to the Freisinnige (free-thinking, literally, liberal-minded) in 1884, but he played less and less of a role as leader. Max von Forckenbeck died on May 26, 1892 in Berlin.

James F. Harris

See also Bismarck, Otto von; Liberalism; National Liberal Party; Prussia

References

Phillipson, Martin. *Max von Forckenbeck: Ein Lebensbild.* Leipzig: H. Seemann Hachfolger, 1898.
Sheehan, James J. *German Liberalism in the Nineteenth Century.* Chicago, IL: University of Chicago Press, 1978.

Foundations and Research Institutes (*Stiftungen und Institute*)

Germany has many public foundations and institutes. Some date to the Middle Ages, when charitable organizations, such as old-age homes and hospitals, were created by rich patrons such as the Fuggers in Augsburg. Academies of sciences have existed since the seventeenth century to attract leading scholars. In the nineteenth and twentieth centuries, foundations and research institutes have proliferated in Germany with a variety of emphases and functions.

Among the larger educational institutes and foundations that support research are the Robert Bosch Foundation, Stuttgart (education, research, and charities), the Alfred Krupp von Bohlen und Halbach Foundation, Essen (education, international cooperation, charities), the Fraunhofer Society (technology transfer in 33 institutes with 3,000 researchers), the Academies of Sciences (large-scale publications and special projects), the Friedrich Naumann Foundation, Bonn (tied to the liberal Free Democratic Party [FDP] and supportive of educational and research projects), the Fritz Thyssen Foundation (international relations, humanities, medicine, economic development), and the German Research Council (Deutsche Forschungsgemeinschaft; encourages research in 172 fields by competitions for approximately 1 billion deutsche marks). Included here for more detailed treatment are the Alexander von Humboldt-Stiftung, the Deutscher Akademischer Austauschdienst, the Friedrich Ebert-Stiftung, the Goethe Institutes, the Konrad Adenauer-Stiftung, and the Volkswagen-Stiftung.

Dieter K. Buse and Juergen C. Doerr

See also Adenauer, Konrad; Archives; Bosch, Robert; Ebert, Friedrich; Education; German as an International Language; Kaiser Wilhelm/Max Planck Societies and Their Institutes; Krupp: Family and Firm; Universities; Volkswagen; Zeiss, Carl: Firm and Foundation

References

Massow, Valentin. *Wissenschaft und Wissenschaftsförderung in der Bundesrepublik Deutschland.* Bonn: Inter Nationes, 1986. English translation: *Organization and Promotion of Science in the Federal Republic of Germany.* Bonn: Inter Nationes, 1983.

Alexander von Humboldt Foundation

The Alexander von Humboldt Foundation grants research fellowships and research awards to academically trained and highly qualified persons of foreign nationality regardless of their sex, race, religion, or ideology to enable them to carry out research projects in Germany and maintain the academic contacts that result. It is an incorporated, nonprofit foundation in private law with registered offices in Bonn. Additionally, the foundation has a liaison office in Washington, DC, and a representative in Berlin.

The foundation was established in Berlin in 1860 with the idea of financing foreign research by German academics. It is named after the eminent German scientist and explorer Alexander von Humboldt (1769–1859). In 1925, the foundation was reestablished with the aim of supporting foreign researchers and doctoral candidates engaged in studies in Germany. In 1953, the foundation went through its most recent developmental stage, which established the present-day Alexander von Humboldt Foundation. Funding comes from the Federal Republic of Germany (FRG), represented by the Federal Minister for Foreign Affairs.

The Humboldt Foundation grants:

- Humboldt research fellowships for highly qualified foreign scholars holding doctorates, up to the age of 40, from all countries and disciplines. These fellowships are designed to enable these scholars to undertake long-term research projects (one to two years) in Germany.
- Humboldt research awards for internationally recognized foreign scholars in all disciplines and from all countries. Research awardees are invited to German research institutes.
- Feodor Lynen research fellowships for highly qualified German scholars holding doctorates, up to the age of 38. Feodor Lynen fellows carry out research projects at institutes of former Humboldt guest researchers abroad.
- Funding for various collaborative research projects on a European and worldwide scale.

During their stays in Germany, Humboldt guest researchers participate in German-language courses, introductory meetings, symposia, study tours, and annual meetings. The Alexander von Humboldt Foundation maintains contact after the return of its guest researchers to their home countries. The follow-up program is designed according to the professional wishes of the Humboldt fellows and awardees. Some 85 percent of them have benefited from renewed sponsorship through invitations to short-term research stays in Germany, donations of academic literature and scientific equipment for countries with low foreign currency reserves, and grants for attending academic conferences and for printing costs. The foundation also organizes and supports meetings in Germany and abroad.

Since 1953, the foundation has sponsored over 16,000 scholars and scientists from 120 countries. In 1992, two-thirds of the Humboldt fellows were natural scientists, 21 percent scholars of the humanities, and 13 percent engineering scientists. Various selection committees with a total of some 100 renowned German scholars decide on the applications for the various programs.

A board of governors oversees the work of the foundation and makes general policy decisions. A secretary general heads the professional administrative staff of the foundation. In 1992, some 96 percent of the foundation's budget originated from federal governmental sources. Additional funding is provided by private foundations and donations. The total budget for 1992 amounted to 88.1 million deutsche marks.

Georg Schütte

References

Alexander von Humboldt-Stiftung. *Alexander von Humboldt-Stiftung 1953–1993: 40 Jahre im Dienst von Wissenschaft und Forschung; 40 years in the Service of Science and Research.* Bonn, Germany: Alexander von Humboldt-Stiftung. 1993.

Botting, Douglas. *Humboldt and the Cosmos.* London: Michael Joseph, 1973.

Maass, Kurt-Jürgen. *Bridges for Research: Range and Impact of the Humboldt Foundation.* Bonn: Humboldt, 1989.

DAAD (German Academic Exchange Service)

The Deutscher Akademischer Austauschdienst (DAAD) is an academic exchange and support organization jointly founded by the institutions of higher education in the Federal Republic of Germany (FRG). Its function is the promotion of higher-education relations abroad, especially through the exchange of students and academics. It is a registered association under private law and was founded in 1925 by the German universities, dissolved in 1945, and refounded in 1950. DAAD membership comprises the institutions of higher education and their student unions or associations. In 1988, membership was extended to include the *Fachhochschulen* (practically oriented higher-education institutions). Since German unification in 1990, the East German institutions of higher education have also become members of DAAD. The number of member institutions currently runs to 214.

DAAD at present has 398 staff members (of whom 80 are abroad). DAAD's head office is located in Bonn. It has branch offices in London, Paris, New York, Tokyo, Cairo, New Delhi, Rio de Janeiro, San José (Costa Rica), and Moscow. These branch offices maintain close contacts with the national authorities, higher education organizations, and the institutions of higher education in the host country and participate in the conception and implementation of exchange programs.

The DAAD has the following functions:

- The allocation of scholarships to foreign and German students, student trainees, junior academic staff, and professors in order to promote international experience in education and research;
- Recruitment, placement, and support of German academic teaching staff from all disciplines for short or long-term teaching assignments at foreign institutions of higher education (especially *Lektors*, young academics who teach German language and literature and contemporary German studies);
- Provision of information on study and research opportunities at home and abroad through leaflets and brochures, oral and written advice to individuals, and information visits;
- Maintenance of follow-up contact with former scholarship holders, especially those abroad, through a reinvitation program, follow-up meetings, and publications, for instance the *DAAD Letter.*

Eligibility for the 198 different DAAD programs extends to all countries and disciplines. The programs range from short visits by academics and scientists to one-semester or one-year scholarships for students to scholarships of up to several years' duration for doctoral studies. In 1992, a total of 44,798 students, scientists, and academics were supported, of whom 20,494 were foreigners.

DAAD programs focus on the individual applicant; that is, on the person and not on the project. Decisions on support applications are generally made by independent academic selection committees, comprising more than 500 honorary academic staff. The prime criterion is the applicant's scientific ability, or the quality of his or her project. Experience has led DAAD not to award student scholarships for first-year students or to fund a full course of higher-education study.

DAAD operates mainly on public funding, provided principally by the German government, the European Community, the Donors' Association for the Promotion of Science, and other foundations. The total budget for 1992 amounted to around 345 million deutsche marks.

The following selection of DAAD publications for foreigners may be obtained from the DAAD branch offices or the German foreign missions: "Studying in Germany" three booklets; "General Information, Universities, *Fachhochschulen*"; "Degree courses at Institutions of Higher Education in the FRG"; "Summer Courses in the FRG—Language, Literature, Music, Contemporary German Studies" (annually in December); "German as a Foreign Language—Courses Offered" (in German).

Heinz-Jürgen Vogels

Friedrich-Ebert-Stiftung

The Friedrich-Ebert-Stiftung (FES) is a nonprofit, private educational institution, committed to the concepts and basic values of democratic socialism and the labor movement. Founded in honor of the first president of the Weimar Republic, Friedrich Ebert (1871–1925), in 1925, it was prohibited by the Nazis in 1933 and reestablished in 1947. Though affiliated with the Social Democratic Party (SPD), much of its funding comes from the federal government.

With its worldwide activities, the FES has the following aims: political and civic education in a democratic spirit for people from all walks of life; fostering international understanding and partnership with developing countries; subsidizing scholarships for German and non-German students of exceptional academic talents as well as young German and foreign graduates; scholarly research conducted in its own research institute; supporting external research projects in its own library and archives; and fostering the arts and culture as elements of democracy. The FES staff totals 760 employees. FES programs include:

- The Academy of Political Education, with its own education centers, which concentrates on the following themes: problems of unified Germany; creation of a united Europe; the history of social democracy; protection of the environment; women's issues; development aid policy; and economic and social problems.

- The granting of scholarships to students and young graduates of all disciplines, from Germany and abroad; assisting studies through seminars and other functions; follow-up support at universities through trustee lecturers; special programs for young graduates from the People's Republic of China and the United States; scholarship programs for postgraduates from Eastern and Southeastern Europe; follow-up support for former scholarship holders.

- Assistance rendered to partners in trade unions, politics, the sciences, and culture through development projects in cooperatives and economic promotion, media and communication, trade union and social education and training, practice-related research, and scientific consulting in Third-World countries.

- Research in social and contemporary history, social and economic sciences with specialized areas of economic policy, labor and social studies, women's issues, policy toward foreigners, international research cooperation, and foreign policy.

- Research on the life and work of Marx and Engels at the FES study center in Karl Marx's birthplace in Trier.

- Collection of materials (2,000 meters of papers) on the history of the German and international labor movement in the Archiv der sozialen Demokratie (Archives of Social Democracy). The library, having more than 340,000 volumes, functions as a central library for supplying literature on the German and international labor movement and participates in the German and international lending network.

Dieter Dowe and Klaus Reiff
(Translation, Diet Simon)

Goethe Institutes

The Goethe Institute, Bonn, has the primary responsibility of promoting the German language and culture abroad and of promoting cultural cooperation. The present organization was founded in 1952.

After the disastrous Nazi years, the first step in promoting German was to reestablish relations with foreign German scholars and teachers of German. In 1953, the institute conducted the first summer courses for Danish and American teachers. That same year the first language courses for foreigners without previous instruction began in Bad Reichenhall. Within a year, three further institutes were opened in response to demand. In 1954, the Goethe Institute took over privately sponsored courses in Athens, Salonika, Turin, Bangkok, and Beirut. This was the beginning of activities abroad.

By 1992, some 167 Goethe Institutes were in operation, 151 outside the Federal Republic. Over 31,000 individuals participated in courses facilitated by the institute. In 1992, the German Foreign Office covered about 85 percent of the Institute's expenditures of some 358 million deutsche marks; the remainder was paid for from fees charged participants and from other income.

Goethe Institute activities may be divided into three main categories: 1) furthering international cultural cooperation; 2) providing resource centers such as libraries with information on German history, culture, and society; and 3) promoting familiarity with the German language. Cooperative cultural programs envisioned to further mutual understanding may include film presentations, theater performances, exhibitions, concerts, lectures, symposia, and other means for explaining German culture and society. The holdings of libraries and other types of resource centers include not only various types of books, but magazines, newspapers, films, videos, compact disks, and cassettes. In countries in which knowledge of German is slight, these resources may be made available in the language of the guest country. Promotion of the German language is pursued by (1) facilitating the teaching of German in the school system of the guest country; (2) offering German language courses; and (3) helping German-speaking groups to maintain their familiarity with the German language.

During the 1970s and 1980s, the Goethe Institutes had a competitor in the German Democratic Republic's (GDR) Schiller Institutes. Just as the West German institutes fostered their own understanding of history and culture, emphasizing the positive aspects and contributions of Germany's past, especially in propagating its views in the Western world, the East Germans emphasized the labor and Communist tradition as well as the GDR's special attributes, especially in propagating their views in the Third World. Occasionally, the Goethe Institute's conservative policies have led to scandal, for instance, its trying to limit dissemination of radical or satirical aspects of West German culture.

Juergen C. Doerr

Konrad Adenauer-Stiftung

The Konrad Adenauer-Stiftung (foundation) is a self-funded organization that is politically and ideologically linked to the

Christian Democratic Union (CDU) political party. Legally, organizationally, and financially, however, it is independent of the party.

In its work in Germany and abroad, the Adenauer Foundation is committed to the principles of Christian Democracy. At the initiative of Konrad Adenauer, the Eichholz Education Center was opened in 1956. In 1964, it was renamed after Adenauer, whose political ideals and goals it seeks to promote.

The foundation pursues, exclusively and directly, nonprofitmaking objectives. It envisions its tasks to be providing political education; researching and documenting the historical development of Christian Democracy (the foundation has created an important archive at its Sankt Augustine headquarters); elaborating, through research and the provision of advice, the scientific foundations for political action; furthering the unification of Europe; cultivating international understanding by supplying information, arranging meetings, and providing aid through development projects and programs; giving ideological and material assistance to democrats suffering political persecution; helping with the scientific training of talented young people of suitable character; and promoting culture and the arts.

The foundation's income comprises grants from the state, donations, contributions from participants, and the proceeds of the sale of publications. Its 1993 budget amounted to 225 million deutsche marks. The biggest single expenditure, accounting for almost 50 percent, is the promotion of projects in development cooperation. The foundation employs some 500 people, 85 of them abroad.

The organs of the Konrad Adenauer Foundation are the general meeting, the executive committee, and the board of trustees. The foundation comprises the following departments: research and consultancy, international cooperation, political education, and scientific services and administration.

Frank Priess

Volkswagen-Stiftung

The Volkswagen-Stiftung (foundation) is a private foundation that fosters research and education. Funds are supplied to academic institutions, not individuals, and are not designed to replace public funding. At present, the capital amounts to over 3 billion deutsche marks; in 1992 about 160 million deutsche marks were spent. Between 1962 and 1992 the foundation supported over 20,000 projects and dispensed nearly 4 billion deutsche marks.

The Volkswagen Foundation emerged out of an agreement between the Federal Republic and the state of Lower Saxony because of the lack of clarity on the ownership of the automobile firm after World War II. The firm was transformed into a public company; 60 percent of its stock was sold in the stock market, 20 percent remained in the possession of the Federal Republic, and 20 percent stayed in Lower Saxony. The profits of the state-owned shares revert to the foundation to support its projects. These include symposia and summer schools, foreign research, and many large-scale special projects. At present, major topics include prehistory, twentieth-century

dictatorships, new communications information, economic systems transformations, environmental studies to reduce waste, modeling of complex social relationships, and metal particles in organic systems. Foreigners may apply to the foundation, but only for projects to be conducted in cooperation with German academics.

Dieter K. Buse

Founding Years (*Gründerjahre*) (1871–73)

The explosive surge of economic activity following German unification achieved renown as a time of unbridled capitalism, frenzied speculation, and scandal. Epitomized by the founding (*Gründung*) of more than 900 joint-stock companies between 1871 and 1873 as well as by the founding of the German Empire, the *Gründerzeit* (Founders' Era) represents an important stage in Germany's development as a leading economic and political power. The boom mentality of the *Gründerjahre*—and the spectacular crash of 1873 that ended it—reverberated through political, social, and cultural realms, profoundly influencing the self-perception of Germans.

Although the elements of Germany's economic ascendancy had formed in the two decades preceding unification, the Franco-Prussian War and its aftermath accelerated the structural changes that inaugurated urbanization, industrialization, railway building, and financial consolidation. Wartime armaments orders stimulated an upsurge in heavy industry. More important, the enormous five-billion-franc war indemnity paid by France beginning in 1871 flooded the economy with capital in the form of paid-off war debts, military pensions, and rearmament orders. The growing involvement of German manufacturers in the world market drove dozens of family-owned companies to expand into joint-stock companies in order to compete. New companies quickly followed, assisted by the readiness of Berlin banks, old and new, to provide the capitalization and of the stock market to issue new stock offers. Sensational prospectuses with promises of doubling or tripling investments lured thousands to commit vast fortunes or meager savings. Berlin's rapid expansion as the new capital added another dimension to the furor: an orgy of speculation in the surrounding agricultural lands ensued.

Warnings about the precariousness of the boom mounted. In February 1873, Liberal deputy Eduard Lasker (1829–84) cast a further pall with his speeches to the Prussian Chamber cataloguing unethical involvement of high officials in Bethel Strousberg's Pomeranian railway project. A worldwide financial crisis beginning in the spring of 1873 in New York and Vienna, instigated the German crash. The concomitant crisis of overproduction extended to virtually all German industries, resulting in a chain of bankruptcies and bank failures in the fall of 1873. The crash and the succeeding depression left a deep scar on the German psyche, as was first suggested in Friedrich Spielhagen's bestselling novel *Sturmflut*, 1877, which not only captured the intricate economic maneuvers and scramble for unlimited wealth of the *Gründerjahre* but interpreted the "stormflood" of the collapse as evidence of a serious national moral failure. Such conclusions gave strong impetus to an anti-capitalist mythology that emerged as a counterpoint to the exuberant values associated with the *Gründermentalität* (founders' mentality).

The *Gründerjahre*, far from culminating in a return to traditional ways or a collapse of the industrial system, cemented capitalistic development in Germany, restructured its activity, and saw the founding of numerous lasting enterprises. The psychological price for German identity, however, was high.

Katherine Roper

See also Anti-Semitism; Banking; Bismarck, Otto von; Depression, 1873–95; Franco-German Relations; Imperial Germany; Industrialization; Jews, 1871–1933; *Kulturkampf*; Lasker, Eduard; Liberalism; National Liberal Party; Protectionism; State and Economy

References

Böhme, Helmut. *Deutschlands Weg zur Grossmacht: Studien zum Verhältnis von Wirtschaft und Staat während der Reichsgründungszeit (1848–1881)*. 2nd ed. Cologne: Kiepenheuer & Witsch, 1972.

Glagau, Otto. *Der Börsen- und Gründungs-Schwindel in Berlin*. Leipzig: Paul Frohberg, 1876.

Gommel, Richard. "Entstehung und Entwicklung der Effecktenbörse im 19. Jahrhundert bis 1914." *Deutsche Börsengeschichte*. Ed. Hans Pohl. Frankfurt am Main: Fritz Knapp, 1992.

Hermand, Jost. "Grandeur, High Life und Innerer Adel: 'Gründerzeit' im Europäischen Kontext." *Monatshefte für deutschen Unterricht, deutsche Sprache und Literatur*. 69 (1977), 189–206.

Lange, Annemarie. *Berlin zur Zeit Bebels und Bismarcks: Zwischen Reichsgründung und Jahrhundertwende*. Berlin: Dietz, 1972.

Mork, Gordon R. "The Prussian Railway Scandal of 1873: Economics and Politics in the German Empire." *European Studies Review* 1 (1971), 35–48.

Müller-Jabusch, Maximilian. *So waren die Gründerjahre*. Düsseldorf: Becker & Wrietzner, 1957.

Four-Year Plan (1936–42)

Launched in September 1936 pursuant to Hitler's command that the German economy be made "capable of war" within four years, the Four-Year Plan was a program of channeling German capital, goods, and labor into the production of arms and substitutes for imported raw materials. As originally conceived, the plan was not intended to make the Reich economically self-sufficient or blockade-proof for an appreciable length of time, but to free and apply sufficient resources to enable the regime to escape from Germany's material deficiencies through conquest. Despite initial confusion in the selection and prioritizing of the project, which prompted decisions in 1938 to narrow the plan's focus and extend it by two years, it largely succeeded in this goal. At least 15 billion reichsmarks expended under the auspices of the plan yielded more than 300 new productive installations and a doubling or more of German output of synthetic fibers, explosives, zinc, lignite, oil, light metals, plastics, electric power, and iron ore. Raw-material shortages did not prove significantly detrimental to German war production or military operations until 1944.

Presided over by Hermann Göring (1893–1946) and a somewhat haphazard organization in Berlin, the plan was a characteristic creation of the Third Reich. Though its inauguration amounted to a decisive step in the subordination of German industry and the economy in general to the regime's political purposes, the Plan neither created a comprehensive central bureaucracy with undisputed powers to set output targets and assure their fulfilment, nor operated through the disbursement of public funds (other than occasional loans for construction at particular sites). Instead, building on a network of government controls established over the preceding three years, Göring pulled together a series of staffs to coordinate policies related to agriculture and labor with the appropriate ministries. They dictated prices, allotments of foreign exchange, and the distribution of raw materials; they identified opportunities for the expansion of production on the basis of natural resources available within Germany. Each staff was backed by Göring's personal authority and directed by a military officer or a veteran Nazi. The staffs assembled their personnel from the state and party bureaucracies and from the ranks of relevant private industries, with which the plan then worked closely in selecting products and locations for development. Funding for the designated installations was usually drawn from the profits of the participating firms themselves, and alternative investments were foreclosed by denying the requisite government permissions to purchase supplies or to recruit additional workers.

When such measures, reinforced by annual increases in the corporate tax rate by 5 percent during the period 1936–40, did not suffice to encourage appropriate private initiatives, the plan fostered new, rival producers of import substitutes, either state-owned or formed by compulsory participation of private enterprises. Such entities included the Reichswerke Hermann Göring (established to produce steel from relatively poor-quality German iron ore), ten regional manufacturers of synthetic fibers, and Brabag, a maker of fuel from German brown coal.

Through a system of controls, compulsion, and competition, the Four-Year Plan succeeded in channeling some 50 percent of all industrial investment in Germany toward privileged areas of output during the period 1936–42. However, because Göring never exercised plenary power over the allocation of labor and ferrous metals from other ministries and the Wehrmacht, supplies of these essential commodities nearly always fell short of what his projects required. The plan therefore constantly lagged behind its ever-more-demanding targets and timetables, and its successes were increasingly overshadowed by its shortfalls. Fuel production proved the plan's most embarrassing failure: despite consuming roughly 40 percent of total investments, output peaked at only 45 percent of the goal.

After the outbreak of war, Göring's staffs focused on the completion of those installations judged to be finishable within one year, then on the exploitation and spoilation of occupied Europe, largely through state-controlled firms tied to the Four-Year Plan such as the Reichswerke and Kontinentale Oel. When the Reich's military situation dictated a change in 1942 toward a total coordination of economic resources behind the war effort, Göring and the Four-Year Plan apparatus were shunted aside by Albert Speer (1905–81) and his new Ministry of Armaments.

Largely the creature of Göring's ambitious management style, the Four-Year Plan rose and fell with him in the Third Reich. Contrary to historiographical legend, it was not dominated by the I.G. Farben chemicals corporation, whose factories contributed less than one-quarter of all funds disbursed under the plan and whose employees composed a similar share of the officials in only one subdivision of the plan's central offices. Neither did the plan's existence attest to the preponderant influence of the chemical and electrical industries in the Nazi economy; so far as statistics permit reliable estimates, it appears that the German metals industry benefited more than any other industrial sector from the plan.

Peter Hayes

See also Armaments Policy; Göring, Hermann; Hitler, Adolf; I.G. Farbenindustrie AG; National Socialist Germany: Foreign Policy; National Socialist Germany: Military; Rearmament; Schacht, Hjalmar; Speer, Albert; Third Reich: Industry

References

Hayes, Peter. *Industry and Ideology: IG Farben in the Nazi Era.* New York, NY: Cambridge University Press, 1987.

Overy, Richard. *Goering: The "Iron Man."* Boston, MA: Routledge & Kegan Paul, 1984.

Petzina, Dietmar. *Autarkie Politik im Dritten Reich.* Stuttgart: Deutsche Verlags Anstalt, 1968.

Volkmann, Hans-Erich. "The National Socialist Economy in Preparation for War." *Germany and the Second World War.* Ed. Militärgeschichtliches Forschungsamt. Vol. 1: *The Build-up of German Aggression.* Ed. Wilhelm Deist et al. Oxford: Clarendon Press, 1990.

Franck, James (1882–1964)

By his contributions to experimental atomic and molecular physics, James Franck played a significant role in the development of quantum physics.

Franck grew up in a Jewish family in Hamburg. In 1901 he began his studies at the University of Heidelberg. His subject was mainly chemistry, but his interests shifted to physics when he moved to Berlin in the following year. Franck started his dissertation under E. Warburg on the mobility of ions and finished it under Warburg's successor, Paul Drude (1863–1906), in 1906. After a few months as *Assistent* (assistant) in Frankfurt he returned to Berlin, becoming *Assistent* to Drude's successor, Heinrich Rubens (1865–1922). In 1911, he completed his *Habilitation* (university teaching qualification thesis). Then Franck began a cooperation with Gustav Hertz on

James Franck. Courtesy of German Information Center, New York.

ionization potentials. In 1914, they published the remarkable result that only electrons with a kinetic energy of more than 4.9 eV can impart energy to mercury atoms. At that time Franck and Hertz still did not know Bohr's theory and interpreted this energy as an ionization rather than an excitation potential. In 1926, they jointly received the physics Nobel Prize for this discovery.

After the outbreak of World War I, Franck joined the army voluntarily but later had to return to civilian life because of illness. In 1917, he became head of the physics division of the Kaiser Wilhelm Institute (KWI) for physical chemistry. In 1921 he accepted a chair for experimental physics in Göttingen. A major part of his research was devoted to excitations of molecules. Franck found a rule concerning their spectra, which, after its wave-mechanical formulation by Edward Condon (1902–74), became known as the Franck-Condon principle.

Franck was the designated successor of Walther Nernst (professor of experimental physics) and Fritz Haber (director of the KWI of physical chemistry) in Berlin. The political events of 1933, however, made this impossible. Due to an exception in the racial laws for combatants of the war, Franck could have stayed in his position in Göttingen. But he resigned as a public protest against the new policy of discrimination. After a year in Copenhagen, Franck emigrated to the United States. There, photosynthesis became the central subject of his research. From 1935 until 1938, he held a professorship at Johns Hopkins University in Baltimore and subsequently at the University of Chicago. During World War II, he joined the nuclear weapons program in the metallurgical laboratory in Chicago. After the defeat of Germany, Franck warned in a memorandum to the American government of the dangers of using the atomic bomb (the Franck Report).

As one of the professors in Göttingen, Franck took an essential part in the manifold cooperations among experimentalists, theorists, and mathematicians that made Göttingen one of the most important and attractive research centers of modern physics from the 1920s to 1933.

Stefan L. Wolff

See also Atom Bomb (German Development of); Kaiser Wilhelm/Max Planck Societies and Their Institutes; Physics

References

Beyerchen, Alan D. *Scientists under Hitler: Politics and the Physics Community in the Third Reich.* New Haven, CT: Yale University Press, 1977.

Jungk, Robert. *Brighter than a Thousand Suns: A Personal History of the Atomic Scientists.* Trans. James Cleugh. New York, NY: Harcourt Brace, 1958.

Kuhn, H. G. "Franck, James." *Dictionary of Scientific Biography* 5 (1972), 117–18.

———. "James Franck 1882–1964." *Biographical Memoirs of Fellows of the Royal Society* 11 (1965), 53–74.

J. Lemmerich. *Max Born, James Franck: Physiker in ihrer Zeit: Der Luxus des Gewissens.* Berlin: Staatsbibliothek Berlin, 1982.

Franco-German Relations

Between 1870 and 1990, relations between France and Germany were completely reversed. After three ravaging wars (1870–71, 1914–18, 1939–45) the former arch-enemies signed a friendship treaty in 1963. Today they are the driving force toward European unification.

The cultural relations between the two countries were as intense as they were contradictory. While the French feared, from a political perspective, Prussian "virtues," they were at the same time fascinated by German music, literary works, and philosophy. The Germans, for their part, admired the elegance and manners of the French as expressed in their literature, visual arts, painting, and architecture. Travelers (and also German emigrants who, like Heinrich Heine or Karl Marx [1818–83], fled to Paris), functioned as mediators. Political developments were, however, barely influenced by this mutual regard, which would later be manifested in the respective recognition of French engineering achievements and admiration for the solidity of German industrial products.

In the nineteenth century Germany consisted of a multitude of individual states. The attempt to effect national unification in 1848 on the French model failed. Prussia, which rejected the "greater German" (*Grossdeutsch*, inclusive of Austria) ideal of the revolution, preferred instead the "small German" (*Kleindeutsch*, exclusive of Austria) solution. Prussia's victory over Austria and the creation of the North German Confederation in 1867 caused consternation in France. On July 19, 1870 Napoleon III declared war on the Prussian-dominated confed-

eration, but was captured along with his army near Sedan on September 2, 1870. While German troops were still besieging Paris, in Versailles Wilhelm I was pronounced kaiser of the new German Empire on January 26, 1871.

The reparations that France accepted in the Treaty of Frankfurt (October 10, 1871) were retired rapidly because of Europe's economic boom. On the other hand, the French felt the loss of Alsace-Lorraine deeply. Chancellor Otto von Bismarck kept France isolated by forming alliances with Russia, Austria-Hungary, and Italy. In his trade and colonial policy, however, he supported Paris. Loans preceded France's Military Convention with Russia (August 17, 1892). As had been expected in Berlin, France came into conflict with Great Britain concerning colonial policy, but this did not prevent closer relations from developing.

France's 1904 Entente Cordiale with Great Britain challenged Germany's claim to hegemony. Germany unsuccessfully sought to stop French expansion in Morocco in 1905 and 1911. Instead of shattering the Entente, Germany's gunboat diplomacy of 1907 encouraged Russia to join, forming the Triple Entente.

Germany now felt encircled. The assassination at Sarajevo (June 26, 1914) provided the pretext for attacking Russia. Because Germany's own military strategy demanded a victory in the west, Imperial Germany declared war on France on August 3. Instead of the hoped-for quick triumph, the offensive ground to a halt at the Marne (September 6, 1914). A costly three-front war began for the Empire. With the armistice of November 11, 1918 France had Alsace-Lorraine restored; Allied troops occupied the Rhineland.

At the Paris peace negotiations in 1919, France demanded security from Germany but could not secure an alliance with the United States and Great Britain. Because its industry was dependent upon German coal, France could not force full reparations despite the Ruhr occupation (January 11, 1923), whereupon France changed its diplomatic course. At Locarno (October 16, 1925), Germany accepted its new western boundary (minus Alsace-Lorraine) as permanent and was consequently accepted into the League of Nations (September 8, 1926). Despite the high degree of agreement between foreign ministers Aristide Briand and Gustav Stresemann, the conclusion of a trade agreement (August 17, 1927), cultural exchanges, and the early withdrawal of troops from the Rhineland (June 30, 1930), the Franco-German detente remained brief.

Germany's customs union project with Austria (1930), the reparations moratorium, and Hitler's appointment as chancellor (January 30, 1933) reawakened old fears, particularly because France now also succumbed to the worldwide economic crisis and was shaken by internal disturbances. As a result of the German-Polish non-aggression pact, France in 1934 lost a longtime Eastern European partner. Despite French agreements with Italy (January 7, 1935) and the USSR (May 2, 1935), Great Britain remained France's most important partner. But Britain did not provide the expected support when Germany, contrary to treaty terms, reoccupied the Rhineland (March 7, 1936).

A new danger arose when Hitler took Franco's side in the Spanish Civil War (1936–1939). Italy joined Hitler in the Rome-Berlin Axis (1936) when France failed to support Italy's colonial aspirations in Africa. Germany did, whereupon Italy abandoned Austria to Germany. In order to gain time for rearmament, France's premier, Eduard Daladier, after the annexation of Austria (March 12, 1938), was willing to give up not only some of the social advances of the Popular Front government, but also, at the Munich Conference (September 29–30, 1938), France's ally Czechoslovakia.

When Hitler attacked Poland on September 1, 1939, France and Great Britain declared war on Germany but did not attack. The resulting "phony war" undermined the morale of the French. Upon the German attack of May 10, 1940, France's military resistance collapsed within a few weeks. In vain did General Charles de Gaulle in London demand, on June 18, 1940, the continuation of the war. Following the armistice (June 22, 1940), large areas of France were occupied and the economy and the people were put in the service of the German war effort. Marshall Pétain and Pierre Laval held the French Republic responsible for the debacle. With the authorization of the National Assembly meeting in Vichy, they created, in the name of the "national revolution," a new French state. The resistance to the "collaboration" agreed to by Pétain and Hitler at Montoire on October 24, 1940, expanded into a civil war as the Germans, after the Allied landing in North Africa on November 11, 1942, occupied the free zone of Vichy.

First, in London, later in Algiers, General de Gaulle had to fight for recognition as leader of the Free French. Just prior to the Normandy landings (June 6, 1944) he proclaimed his Liberation Committee to be the provisional government of France. After his triumphant entry into Paris (August 25, 1944) de Gaulle pushed his troops forward, as he considered the occupation of German territory as an important negotiating pawn. Upon the capitulation of the Third Reich (May 7–9, 1945) France received on June 5, 1945 its own occupation zone, but was not invited to the Potsdam Conference (July 17–August 2, 1945). De Gaulle and his successors failed to persuade the United States and the Soviet Union of their views on the "German Question" at the 1947 Moscow foreign ministers' conference. Only much later did it become clear that despite the perception that the French occupation had been severe, France's cultural-reorientation policy and the introduction of a progressive social policy provided decisive impulses for a democratic renewal in Germany.

The division of Germany, which seemed sealed in 1949 with the establishment of the Federal Republic of Germany (FRG) and the German Democratic Republic, approximated French views of tying Germany down. French foreign minister Robert Schuman proposed on May 9, 1950 a European Coal and Steel Community, which was to become the precursor of the European Economic Community (March 25, 1957). France rejected (August 30, 1954) a defense community that would include Germany but then agreed to partial sovereignty for, as well as acceptance into NATO of, the Federal Republic, (May 5, 1955). In 1957, the Saar was returned to Germany after its population had rejected special status and France had given up its claims. Economically, France and the Federal Republic (FRG) now increasingly cooperated. In 1958, at the height of the Algerian war (1954–62), General de Gaulle again took over the government.

As FRG Chancellor Konrad Adenauer developed his vision of a Franco-German partnership, a struggle ensued in Bonn between "Gaullists" and "Atlanticists." In order not to burden relations with the United States, the Bundestag inserted a preamble into the Franco-German Treaty of Friendship of January 22, 1963, whereby the treaty lost its political significance for de Gaulle. The practical aspects of the treaty, however (youth exchanges, language learning), contributed significantly to the reconciliation of the two countries.

While the FRG became one of the seven leading industrial countries of the world, politically it was a prisoner of the East-West conflict. When the Brandt government sought to find a way out of this dilemma at the close of the 1960s, French President Georges Pompidou in response agreed to the entry of Great Britain into the European Economic Community (January 22, 1972). The mistrust disappeared as Bonn made it clear through its engagement in the European Community that fears of a turn to the East on the Rapallo (1922) model were unjustified. Chancellor Helmut Schmidt (1913–) and French President Giscard d'Estaing provided further important impulses toward European integration by introducing European elections (September 20, 1976) and a common monetary system (March 13, 1979). President François Mitterrand and Chancellor Helmut Kohl continued this policy.

The disintegration of the Berlin Wall only temporarily endangered the close friendship that had been symbolically enhanced by the handshake at Verdun in 1984. Fears of a renaissance of a too-powerful Germany that were expressed during the Two-plus-Four negotiations were effectively countered when Bonn officially recognized the Oder-Neisse boundary and unequivocally committed itself to Western Europe. With the creation of the first Franco-German army brigade parallel to the conclusion of German unification on October 3, 1990, Paris and Bonn reinforced as equal partners their determination to pursue in cooperation the further integration of Europe.

Stefan Martens

See also Adenauer, Konrad; American-German Relations; Anglo-German Relations; Expulsion and Exile of Scientists and Scholars; Federal Republic of Germany: Foreign Policy; Imperial Germany: Foreign Policy; Italian-German Relations; National Socialist Germany: Foreign Policy; Postwar European Integration and Germany; Ruhr Crisis; The Saar; Schuman Plan; Stresemann, Gustav; Versailles, Treaty of; Weimar Germany: Foreign Policy; World War I; World War II

References

Azema, Jean-Pierre. *From Munich to Liberation 1938–1944.* Cambridge: Cambridge University Press, 1984.
Bariety, Jacques and Raymond Poidevin. *Les relations*

franco-allemandes 1815–1975. Paris: Armand Colin, 1977.

LeGloannec, Anne-Marie. "France, Germany, and the New Europe." *The Germans and Their Neighbors*. Ed. Dirk Verheyen and Christian Søe. Boulder, CO: Westview Press, 1993.

McCarthy, Patrick, ed. *France and Germany 1983–1993: The Struggle to Cooperate*. London: Macmillan, 1993.

Mitchell, Allan. *The Divided Path: The German Influence on Social Reform in France after 1870*. Chapel Hill, NC: University of North Carolina Press, 1991.

———. *The German Influence in France after 1870: The Formation of the French Republic*. Chapel Hill, NC: University of North Carolina Press, 1979.

———. *Victors and Vanquished: The German Influence on Army and Church in France after 1870*. Chapel Hill, NC: University of North Carolina Press, 1984.

Frank, Hans (1900–46)

Hans Frank, chief Nazi jurist and governor-general of occupied Poland during World War II, was not one of the truly powerful men of the Third Reich. Yet he bears much of the responsibility for the bloody German terror regime in Poland. His function as Nazi jurist was insignificant in comparison to his role as governor-general. The first phase of his political career demonstrated the typical development of a middle-class intellectual, who, after some initial uncertainty, joined the Nazi movement and pursued a career in the party.

Hans Frank was born on May 23, 1900, in Karlsruhe, the son of a lawyer. He attended a gymnasium in Munich, intermittently also in Prague. The information concerning his early political activities upon attaining his *Abitur* (senior matriculation) in 1918 is incomplete, but reflects his uncertain political orientation. In September 1923, Frank, who was studying political economy and law, joined the Sturmabteilung (SA); a month later he became a member of the Nazi Party. He participated in the Hitler *Putsch* of November 9, 1923, but in late 1926 he temporarily left the party because of Hitler's position concerning the South Tyrol problem.

Frank rejoined the Nazi Party some time in 1927 or 1928 and then began his career as a jurist in the party and the state bureaucracy. He defended members of the party in many legal battles. Above all, he gained fame and historical significance through the Leipzig high treason trials of a number of Reichswehr officers. At this time, Hitler firmly pursued his strategy of attaining power legally and through Frank, who served as a witness, the trial proved to be an effective public forum for asserting this strategy under oath. A special relationship of trust developed between Hitler and Frank, which possibly explains Frank's survival in the office of governor-general despite extensive conflicts. In October 1939, he was named chief of the General Government, that area of central Poland under a separate German administration. Frank created here, as did the *Gauleiter* (district leader) in the annexed western parts of Poland, a terror regime that exemplified most clearly the new "ideological war of extermination."

Frank chose Krakow as his seat of government using the Wawel, the old Polish royal palace, as his official residence. His activities as governor-general were shaped, above all, by his efforts to assert himself in his conflicts with Reich officials, especially Heinrich Himmler's (1900–45) SS. Although he was formally directly responsible to Hitler, in practice his position was continuously being undermined. He thus sought to find compensation for his declining authority. His unique diary (*Diensttagebuch*), which he kept from 1939 to 1945 and whose 38 volumes remained intact, provides extensive information on his efforts. In Poland Frank sought, to the point of being ludicrous, to imitate his much-adored führer.

The coexistence of cynicism and brutality on the one hand and middle-class cultural pretension on the other is particularly noticeable in Frank's case. His limitless need for prestige and his extravagant German cultural activities (with his own state theater, symphony orchestra, and German journals) adds to the portrait of the "butcher of Poles"—who shared responsibility for the extermination of the Polish intelligentsia—particularly macabre features.

Among the major war criminals sentenced to death at Nuremberg, he was one of the few who from the beginning admitted his guilt. In his autobiographical notes, "In the Face of the Gallows," he, however, reversed this admission. He was unable to the end to separate himself from Hitler.

Christoph Klessmann

See also Anti-Semitism; Concentration Camps; Himmler, Heinrich; Hitler, Adolf; National Socialist Germany; Nuremberg Trials; Polish-German Relations, 1933–45; Schutzstaffel; Third Reich: Legal Profession

References

Fest, Joachim. *The Face of the Third Reich: Portraits of the Nazi Leadership*. London: Weidenfeld and Nicolson, 1970.

Klessmann, Christoph. "Hans Frank." *The Nazi Elite*. Ed. Ronald Smelser and Rainer Zitelmann. Trans. Mary Fischer. Houndmills: Macmillan, 1993.

Frank, Walter (1905–45)

Karl Paul Walter Frank's career as a historian represented the Nazi debasement of German scholarship. Frank was born in Fürth on February 12, 1905. Prior to his graduation (*Abitur*) the family moved from Munich to Nuremberg, where Frank became active in the Grossdeutscher Jugendbund (Greater Germany Youth Federation), which fostered *völkisch* (folkish-racist) and Christian ideas. Beginning in 1923, Frank attended classes at the University of Munich taught by the geopolitician Karl Haushofer and the historian Karl Alexander von Müller, under whom he wrote his dissertation on Adolf Stoecker (1835–1909).

Frank planned to become the "historian of the German revolution," yet he never joined the Nazi Party, although his wife, Maria, and close associates became members. In the late 1920s, he wrote for the Nazi newspaper, *Völkischer Beobachter* (People's observer), participated in several party conventions, and kept close contacts with Rudolf Hess (1894–1987) and Baldur von Schirach (1907–74).

In 1922, the young Frank had met and idolized General Erich Ludendorff (1865–1937), but he later claimed that even in the 1920s he saw only Adolf Hitler as future political leader. In the late 1920s, Frank submitted a series of articles directed against pacifism, internationalism, the cowardly bourgeoisie, liberal parliamentarianism, and the corrupt Weimar Republic to Alfred Rosenberg (1893–1946), with whom he would later quarrel bitterly. In 1935, with two studies to his credit, Frank, only 30 years old, was appointed head of the Reich Institut für Deutsche Geschichte (Reich Institute for German History) in Berlin.

At the University of Munich, Frank had written his dissertation, *Hofprediger Adolf Stoecker und die christlichsoziale Bewegung* (Adolf Stoecker and the Christian social movement), which was published in 1928. In a review, Friedrich Meinecke (1862–1954) commented favorably, though distancing himself in some matters. Helmut Heiber has voiced his astonishment that Meinecke had not recognized Frank's "sympathy for Stoecker's anti-Semitism." In 1933 Frank published his second major work, *Nationalismus und Demokratie im Frankreich der dritten Republik* (published as *Nationalism and Democracy in the Third French Republic*), which he had researched in Paris. A review in the *Historische Zeitschrift* (Historical journal) by Otto Becker was quite positive. Frank's admiration of E. Drumont, the anti-Semitic author of *La France Juive* (The French Jew), of Maurice Barrès, the *völkisch* (racist) writer, and of Charles Maurras, the propagator of the dominance by an elite and of the *Camelots du roi* (knights of the king), was the more startling, as they were all prophets of a war of revenge against Imperial Germany.

During his career, Frank became embroiled in drawn-out disputes with distinguished historians—accusing them of lukewarmness, if not hostility, toward Nazi philosophy—as well as feuds with prominent Nazis and even a dispute with his young collaborator Wilhelm Grau at the Reich Institute. An extremist on the Jewish question, Frank often acknowledged himself as a disciple of the pornographic Jew-hater Julius Streicher (1885–1946) and boasted to have been a loyal participant in the mass assemblies of the *Frankenführer*. Judaism, he wrote, "is one of the great negative principles of world history," a "parasite." Frank's feud with Grau ultimately involved men close to Hitler. Grau, the author of *Antisemitismus im späten Mittelalter* (published as *Antisemitism in the Late Middle Ages*), 1934, had been made a leading specialist for the Jewish question at the institute, but had gone his own way. He wrote a memoir for Hitler, stressing the need to solve German Jewish policy by winning adherents for Nazi Jewish policies abroad. When Frank learned of Grau having submitted his proposals to the Chancellery without informing him, he denounced Grau's "*Fronde*" against himself. In the end, Frank lost his prestigious post as head of the *Reich Institute*.

On August 9, 1945, in the wake of Hitler's suicide and the destruction of the Third Reich, Frank revealed to his wife that he intended to commit suicide and secured her help in taking his own life.

Alfred D. Low

See also Hess, Rudolf; History; Meinecke, Friedrich; National Socialist Germany; Schirach, Baldur von; Stoecker, Adolf; Streicher, Julius

References

Frank, Walter. *Hofprediger Adolf Stöcker und die christlich-soziale Bewegung.* 2nd ed. Hamburg: Hanseatische Verlagsanstalt, 1935.

———. *Nationalismus und Demokratie im Frankreich der dritten Republik (1871 bis 1918).* Hamburg: Hanseatische Verlagsanstalt, 1933.

Heiber, Helmut. *Walter Frank und sein Reichsinstitut für Geschichte des Neuen Deutschlands.* Stuttgart: Deutsche Verlags-Anstalt, 1966.

Iggers, George G. *The German Concept of History: The German Tradition of Historical Thought from Herder to the Present.* Middletown, CT: Wesleyan University Press, 1968. 2nd ed. 1984.

The Frankfurt School (1923–50)

This name has been given to the group of left-wing intellectuals who gathered around the privately funded Institut für Sozialforschung (institute for social research). In its early years, this group was affiliated with the University of Frankfurt am Main. Among the major figures of the institute were Max Horkheimer (1895–1973), Theodor W. Adorno (1973–69), Herbert Marcuse (1898–1979), Leo Lowenthal (1900–93), Walter Benjamin (1892–1940), Erich Fromm (1900–80), and Jürgen Habermas (1929–). During the Weimar Republic, and throughout the period of exile and war, these intellectuals engaged in interdisciplinary work in areas as diverse as philosophy, literary criticism, psychology, political science, and economics. These scholars endeavored to develop a "critical theory" of society.

The diversity and complexity of the work of critical theory have resulted in its being characterized variously as a radical sociology, as a highly complex form of cultural criticism in which the insights of Sigmund Freud (1856–1939), Friedrich Nietzsche (1844–1900), and Karl Marx (1818–83) are entwined, and as a form of philosophical speculation deeply informed by German idealism and, perhaps more indirectly, by aspects of Jewish thought. The proponents of critical theory perceived themselves as responding to the concrete historical and social conditions of their own time. Their probing had an open-ended inquiry, expressed through a dialogue with philosophical systems and with a range of other thinkers, that must not be undervalued.

The roots of critical theory are to be found in the philosophy of Immanuel Kant (1724–1804) and the critique of political economy developed by Marx. Together, these traditions posed a challenge to scientific thought and rationality from the standpoint of a social theory that offered ethical enlightenment. It also posed a challenge to capitalist society as an irrational and crisis-laden system that frustrates human freedom and fulfillment. The confrontation between "idealism" and "materialism" precipitated the fundamental dilemma that critical theory sought to address: the relationship of theory and practice.

By postulating reason as an active faculty that produces reality, Kant tried to resolve the contradictions in Enlightenment rationality, for example between freedom and necessity and between individuality and communality. His system, however, separated moral from scientific reason and ideal from material reality. Georg Hegel (1770–1831) attempted to bridge this gap by locating reason in history. In his view, reason resides in the progressive, dialectical unfolding of real (i.e., objective) institutions that developed historically. Hegel became convinced that historical contradictions had been virtually resolved by the Prussian constitutional monarchy that was introduced during his lifetime. Marx perceived the illogic that beset the Enlightenment as contradictions inherent in capitalism.

Upon just this point, Marx's view departed from Hegel's. For Marx, the critique of rationality had to transcend philosophy by involving the critique of political economy. Among the elements of Marxian dialectics that largely influenced members of the institute was that of the critique of ideology. Marx wanted to expose any doctrine or belief that supported or justified the political or economic domination of one class by another.

The optimistic aspect of Marx's analysis, however, was achieved at the expense of the individual, who lost his identity, becoming absorbed into a certain "class." The critical theorists, therefore, regarded Marx's analysis as necessary but not sufficient. In the writings of Sigmund Freud they discovered a psychological theory that explained the persistence of social forms that obstructed the achievement of an ideology of enlightened social and cultural change. In Freud's view, reason itself operates through mechanisms of repression and domination.

In the writings of Max Weber (1881–1962), the critical theorists found a sociological counterpart to Freudian psychology. According to Weber, under modern conditions reason is reduced to a mere instrumentality. The calculation of its means and ends he termed "purposive rationality." The domination of this form of rationality over all others, (e.g., practical and critical reason) is the theme of Horkheimer and Adorno's *Dialektik der Aufklärung* (published as *Dialectic of Enlightenment*), 1947, written in the United States.

In the years of exile (1933–47), the members of the institute, many of whom fled to the United States, carried out, both jointly and independently, studies that examined the relation between culture and totalitarianism. Work in critical theory is currently carried on by Habermas and those associated with him, known as the "second generation" of the Frankfurt School.

Paul Kelley

See also Adorno, Theodor; Benjamin, Walter; Fromm, Erich; Habermas, Jürgen; Horkheimer, Max; Lowenthal, Leo; Marcuse, Herbert; Marx, Karl; Neumann, Franz; Weber, Max

References

Adorno, T.W. *Esthetic Theory*. Trans. C. Lenhardt. New York, NY: Routledge, 1984.

———. *Negative Dialectics*. Trans. E.B. Ashton. New York, NY: Seabury, 1973.

Arato, A. and E. Gebhardt. *The Essential Frankfurt School Reader*. New York, NY: Continuum, 1982.

Benjamin, W. *Illuminations*. Trans. H. Zohn. New York, NY: Schocken, 1969.

———. *Reflections: Essays, Aphorisms, Autobiographical Writings*. Trans. E. Jephcott. New York, NY: Harcourt Brace Jovanovich, 1978.

Held, D. *Introduction to Critical Theory: Horkheimer to Habermas*. Berkeley, CA: University of California Press, 1980.

Horkheimer, M. *Critical Theory*. Trans. J. Cumming. New York, NY: Seabury, 1972.

———. *The Eclipse of Reason*. New York, NY: Continuum, 1974.

Horkheimer, M. and T.W. Adorno. *Dialectic of Enlightenment*. Trans. J. Cumming. New York, NY: Seabury, 1972.

Ingram, D. *Critical Theory and Philosophy*. New York, NY: Paragon House, 1990.

Jay, M. *The Dialectical Imagination: A History of the Frankfurt School and the Institute for Social Research, 1923–1950*. Boston, MA: Little, Brown, 1973.

Lowenthal, L. *Literature, Popular Culture and Society*. Englewood Cliffs, NJ: Prentice-Hall, 1961.

Frankfurter Allgemeine Zeitung (FAZ; 1949–)

The *Frankfurter Allgemeine Zeitung* (*FAZ*; Frankfurt general newspaper) is Germany's leading national daily. The paper has earned its reputation as the authority in the coverage of politics, business, and financial news. It is conservative by nature. With a daily run of 429,396 copies (1991), *FAZ* is available throughout all of the German states. Moreover, 43,705 copies are shipped daily to 147 countries, making *FAZ* a credible voice of Germany throughout the world. The paper has its headquarters in Frankfurt am Main, Germany's and Europe's financial capital, where it also originated on November 1, 1949. Barely 9,000 subscriptions were sold during its first year, yet *FAZ* received immediate backing from West Germany's newly emerging industrialists. They were looking for a paper in the tradition of the venerable *Frankfurter Zeitung*, which the Nazis closed down on August 31, 1943 after more than 80 years of publishing.

Dr. Paul Sethe, former political editor of the *Frankfurter Zeitung*, Professor Erich Welter, long-time contributor to the *Frankfurter Zeitung*, and other renowned journalists joined in forming the *Frankfurter Allgemeine: Zeitung für Deutschland*. The paper's startup capital was raised by German industrialists, who also assisted in creating the paper's legal framework, which is unique in the publishing field. Paragraph 2 of the corporate charter of the Frankfurter Allgemeine Zeitung GmbH (December 12, 1949; since April 22, 1959, FAZIT Stiftung) states that the paper is to be totally independent from government, political parties, and special interest groups. It is the publishers' sole responsibility to determine the intellectual, political, and economic line of the paper.

Since its inception, *FAZ* has adhered to this directive. Today, five publishers determine by consensus the editorial direction of the daily, assuring its standard of reporting. At first glance, FAZ reflects a well-balanced arrangement of three principal areas of coverage. Politics, business, and feuilleton each claim a separate daily section of the paper. Additional departments are inserted throughout the week. The *Frankfurter Allgemeine Magazin,* for example, inserted every Friday since March 7, 1980, has received numerous national and international awards and citations for its artistic standards, its layout and design, the high level of its photography, and the quality of its essays. Saturday's insert, *Bilder und Zeit* (Pictures and period), constitutes a forum for intellectual and literary life in Germany and elsewhere. Essays, editorials, short stories, and poems, contributed by historians, philosophers, writers, literary and art critics, social scientists, and other scientists, invite reflection as well as further discussion. For readers residing in the city of Frankfurt and for those in the larger Rhine-Main region, a complete regional paper, the *Rhein-Main-Zeitung für Frankfurt,* is inserted daily into *FAZ.*

The paper's reputation rests primarily on its thorough coverage of the world of business and finance. It analyzes economic policies, investigates economic trends, debates monetary policies, and discusses trade union and wage policies. Market conditions, the economic climate, and economic cycles receive expert coverage. It is not surprising that 58 percent of middle and upper management consult *FAZ* daily. Politics and business are expertly intertwined. To accomplish this local, regional, national, and international scope of news coverage, *FAZ* employs a full-time editorial staff of 202 editors and over 500 freelance journalists. The paper maintains news bureaus in every capital of the *Länder* (states), Bonn and Frankfurt in particular. Moreover, *FAZ* correspondents are also placed in Berlin, Munich, Hamburg, Düsseldorf, Stuttgart, Bremen, Hannover, Cologne, Mainz, Nuremberg, Karlsruhe, and Wiesbaden. Ninety-one foreign correspondents—in *FAZ* bureaus in Brussels, London, New York, Paris, and Washington, as well as in capitals throughout Eastern and Western Europe, Africa, and Asia—assure accurate and timely coverage of international news. These bureaus constitute an infrastructure for news gathering that has few if any equals. In 1963, the faculty of the School of Journalism at Syracuse University voted *FAZ* among the world's ten best papers. They ranked it as number two, followed by *The New York Times* and *The Christian Science Monitor.*

Manfred K. Wolfram

See also Bild Zeitung; Die Welt; Die Zeit; Federal Republic of Germany; Journalism; Liberalism; Magazines; Press and Newspapers; *Süddeutsche Zeitung*

References

"Dokumentation 'Alles über die Zeitung.'" Frankfurt am Main: Verlag Frankfurter Allgemeine Zeitung GmbH, 1993.

Korda, Rolf Martin. "Für Bürgertum und Business: Die Frankfurter Allgemeine Zeitung." *Porträts der deutschen Presse: Politik und Profit.* Ed. Michael Wolf Thomas. Berlin: Volker Spiess, 1980.

Free Democratic Party (FDP)

Despite its slim electoral base, the liberal Free Democratic Party (FDP) has played a crucial role in the politics of the Federal Republic. Between 1949 and 1990, the FDP was a member of the West German government longer than any other party. The small party's influence on the policy direction and governing style in Bonn varied with time and circumstance, but it was often considerable.

The FDP was founded in December 1948 as a fairly loose union of several regional liberal parties that had sprung up in the Western occupation zones of Germany. Theodor Heuss (1884–1963) was the first leader of the new party. He and two of his successors, Thomas Dehler (1897–1957) and Reinhold Maier (1889–1971), had been active liberals in the Weimar Republic. Although it is a postwar party, the FDP regards itself as heir to the country's much older liberal tradition, and it long showed traces of the political dualism that had kept German liberalism organizationally and ideologically divided after the middle of the nineteenth century.

Beneath its loose formal unity, the early FDP harbored a motley collection of individuals and groups, some with a more "democratic" or "progressive" tendency and others with a more "national" or "economic" orientation. These left and right wings have become increasingly blurred and now operate more as internal cross-pressures rather than as clearly distinct factions. A small national remnant lost out to the proponents of a new *Ostpolitik* (eastern policy) in the late 1960s when Walter Scheel (1919–) replaced Erich Mende (1916–) as party leader.

Today, strong neoliberal market views coexist in the FDP with a distinctive civil libertarian outlook. Reformist concerns found expression in the Freiburg Theses of 1971, but these social-liberal intentions were later modified in programs that reemphasized a market orientation, such as the Kiel Theses (1977) and the Liberal Manifesto (1985). Electorally, the FDP has sought to address the economic and cultural concerns of the "old" (entrepreneurial) and the "new" (professional) middle class among the voters. It has long taken a rhetorical stand against what it calls the socialism of the Social Democrats (SPD) and the conservatism or clericalism of the Christian Democrats (CDU/CSU), suggesting that both of its large rivals are really statist in promoting their respective goals of greater social equity and greater social order. Whenever feasible, the small party has linked its electoral appeal to a well-known leader, such as the longtime foreign minister Hans-Dietrich Genscher (1927–). For many years, its strong advocacy of policies that encouraged private enterprise was personified by Otto Lambsdorff (1926–).

The FDP has always been a relatively small party, with an average support of slightly less than 10 percent of the party vote in federal elections. Its parliamentary survival is therefore dependent on an electoral system that gives proportional representation to any party that wins at least 5 percent of the vote. Unlike numerous other small post-1945 parties, the FDP was able to survive the electoral "nutcracker effect" that resulted in a consolidation of the West German party system during the 1950s.

Between 1961 and 1983, the FDP was the only "third" party in the Bundestag. There it functioned as a balancer or majority maker, serving in governments with the CDU/CSU (1949 to 1956, 1961 to 1966, and after 1982) or the SPD (1969 to 1982). Although the FDP lost its exclusive pivotal position in 1983 when the new Green Party entered the Bundestag, it continued to be a necessary building block in any majority coalition that did not include both of the large parties. As a result of the delicate power balance in the Bundestag and its own determined coalition strategy, the FDP served only two relatively short stints in the parliamentary opposition in Bonn. It was a member of all but three of sixteen cabinets before reunification, including every one after 1969.

The FDP has occupied some important federal ministries for long periods of time, including those controlling foreign affairs, economics, and justice. Two of the first six federal presidents (Heuss and Scheel) were FDP leaders. No Free Democrat has ever headed a government in Bonn, but each West German chancellor had his term in office decisively affected by the FDP's offer, withdrawal, or refusal of support for his government. It was the FDP that provided the parliamentary margins that brought to power chancellors Konrad Adenauer (1876–1967) in 1949, Willy Brandt (1913–92) in 1969, and Helmut Kohl (1930–) in 1982, or that ended the governments of chancellors Ludwig Erhard (1897–1977) in 1966, Kurt Georg Kiesinger (1904–88) in 1969, and Helmut Schmidt (1913–) in 1982.

Whenever possible, the FDP tries to play a similar role in coalition politics at the state level. Here it reached its high point in the early 1960s, when for a time it was included in nine of the eleven state cabinets. In later years, the balance of power shifted, and the liberal state parties could be found more frequently in the opposition or sometimes without parliamentary representation at all. In each of the 11 West German *Länder* (states), except for Baden-Württemberg, the FDP failed to win 5 percent of the vote on one or more occasions. So far, it has always been able to return to the Landtag (state legislature) in a later election, but the fear of political mortality haunts the small party.

In justifying its disproportional role as junior cabinet member in Bonn and some state capitals, the small party has developed a claim to function as a kind of flywheel or "check and balance" within the government. It argues in effect that its presence in the cabinet serves to guard against a dangerous concentration of power in the hands of a single governing party—a condition that Free Democrats refer to ominously as *Alleinherrschaft* (autocratic rule). This "functional" argument for coalition government with a liberal additive seems to appeal to West German voters, a fact that has become increasingly important in the small party's self-presentation.

In August 1990, less than two months before national reunification, the Free Democrats became the first of the West German parties to unite with their East German counterparts. By its "friendly takeover" of two of the formerly privileged "bloc parties" in the German Democratic Republic (the Liberal Demokratische Partei Deutschlands [LDPD; Liberal Democratic Party of Germany] and the National-Demokratische Partei Deutschlands [NDPD; National Democratic Party of Germany]), the FDP temporarily tripled its membership and appeared to acquire considerable material resources as well. The FDP also absorbed two much smaller East German oppositional groupings, the Ost [East]-FDP and the German Forum Party (an offspring of New Forum). These tiny parties, which had been hurriedly formed with the guidance and patronage of West German liberals at the beginning of 1990, were primarily important for adding a symbolic element of democratic legitimacy to the hurried party merger.

In the first elections in the new eastern states in October 1990, the FDP entered all five parliaments and became a member of four coalition cabinets. Less than two months later, in the first all-German Bundestag election of December 1990, the FDP won 11 percent of the overall party vote. Its performance in the area of the former East Germany was even better, with 12.9 percent. This superb result ensured the FDP's continuation in the Bonn government during the first years after national reunification. It soon became an open question, however, whether its position of special leverage in the party system could be sustained in the wake of electoral reactions to the wrenching changes that followed.

Christian Søe

See also Dehler, Thomas; Genscher, Hans-Dietrich; Hamm-Brücher, Hildegard; Heuss, Theodor; Lambsdorff, Otto; Liberalism; Maier, Reinhold; Mende, Erich; Pfleiderer, Karl Georg; Scheel, Walter

References

Braunthal, Gerard. "The Free Democratic Party in West German Politics." *The Western Political Quarterly* 13 (June 1960), 332–48.

Kaack, Heino. "The FDP in the German Party System." *Germany at the Polls: The Bundestag Election of 1976.* Ed. Karl H. Cerny. Washington, DC: American Enterprise Institute, 1978.

Kirchner, Emil J. and David Broughton. "The FDP in the Federal Republic of Germany: The Requirements of Survival and Success." *Liberal Parties in Western Europe.* Ed. Emil J. Kirchner. Cambridge: Cambridge University Press, 1988.

Søe, Christian. "The Free Democratic Party." *West German Politics in the Mid-Eighties.* Ed. H.G. Peter Wallach and George K. Romoser. New York, NY: Praeger, 1985.

———. "'Not Without Us!' The FDP's Survival, Position, and Influence." *The Federal Republic of Germany at Forty.* Ed. Peter H. Merkl. New York, NY: New York University Press, 1989.

Free German Trade Union Federation

The Freier Deutscher Gewerkschaftsbund (FDGB; Free German Trade Union Federation), East Germany's trade union, was the country's largest mass organization and enjoyed a monopoly position under the control of the Socialist Unity Party (SED). It embraced all workers and members of the intelligentsia, but excluded the armed forces, cooperative farmers, and the self-employed.

Sixteen unions (organized along industrial rather than craft lines) were members of the FDGB. Eight of these were for workers in food and retail trade, state agriculture, education, health, science, the arts, armed forces (civilian employees only), and government and public service. The remainder represented East German industry. The Federation was headed by a 26-member presidium under the direction of Harry Tisch (1927–), who was also a member of the Politbüro. The FDGB was represented in every enterprise and institution as well as in party and government bodies. It had, for example, 68 of the 500 seats in the People's Chamber.

Since in the Marxist-Leninist system the representative and advocate of the worker is the Communist Party, trade unions play a somewhat different role. The FDGB's functions included the implementation of party policy, especially the execution of state production plans, the organization of "socialist competition" to enhance productivity, the reduction of waste and inefficiency, and the encouragement of technical progress and worker discipline. In the planning process, the FDGB rubber-stamped the wage structures established by the Council of Ministers. The federation protected workers by ensuring, for example, that enterprise managers were in compliance with health and safety regulations. Finally, it administered the social-security system.

According to socialist ideology, the federation did not need to be involved in strikes. This traditional privilege of labor in contemporary capitalism, featured in the constitution of 1949, had disappeared in the constitution of 1968. By this latter date, it had become apparent that a strike in a workers' state could only represent workers striking against themselves. In spite of these general limitations, however, the economic reform of 1963 and the SED's Eighth Party Congress in 1971 strengthened the Federation's powers. This became apparent as the code of labor law (*Arbeitsgesetzbuch*) extended labor's rights of codetermination and permitted it greater cooperation in political and planning activities. In the later years of the German Democratic Republic, it became a partner, albeit a weak one, of the party and state apparatus.

Whereas the East German labor force was not protected against the inconveniences and hazards of industrial and agricultural conditions in East Germany (noise, pollution, unsafe conditions, extensive shift work), it was not subjected to a stressful work pace, and legal sanctions provided protection against unwarranted dismissal. Workers enjoyed a high degree of job security.

Phillip J. Bryson

See also German Democratic Republic; Reunification; Socialist Unity Party; Tisch, Harry; Trade Unions

References

Berger, M., V. Kurzweg, and J. Prang. *Zur Kultur- und Bildungsarbeit des FDGB: Positionen—Probleme—Aufgaben.* Berlin (East): Verlag Tribüne, 1986.

Jeffries, Ian and Manfred Melzer, eds. *The East German Economy.* London: Croom Helm, 1987.

Lexikon Wirtschaft: Arbeit—Bildung—Soziales. Berlin (East): Verlag Die Wirtschaft, 1982.

Zimmerman, Hartmut. "Die Arbeitsverfassung der DDR." *Materialien zum Bericht zur Lage der Nation im geteilten Deutschland.* Ed. Karl Thalheim. Bonn: Bundesministerium für innerdeutsche Beziehungen, 1987.

———. *Freier Deutscher Gewerkschaftsbund (FDGB): DDR Handbuch.* Vol 1. Ed. Hartmut Zimmerman et al. Cologne: Verlag Wissenschaft und Politik, 1985.

Free German Youth (Freie Deutsche Jugend; FDJ)

The Free German Youth (FDJ), founded on March 7, 1946 in the city of Brandenburg (after Soviet approval), was the successor organization of some anti-Fascist youth committees that had been active in the Soviet zone since the summer of 1945. The FDJ was not founded as the youth organization of the Socialist Unity Party (SED) but as a democratic, anti-Fascist movement of all young people, no matter what their political or religious belief or affiliation. The main targets were fighting for peace, Germany's unity, the right to work, education, and recreation. Erich Honecker (1912–94) became its first chairman.

The gradual transformation of the FDJ into a socialist youth organization was under way in the late 1940s and early 1950s. In 1952, the new FDJ constitution acknowledged the leadership position of the SED and the ideology of Marx, Lenin, and Stalin. The basic organizational principle became "democratic centralism." From this time, the FDJ was part of the East German mass organizations led and supervised by the SED. The FDJ declared itself to be a socialist youth organization with avant-garde character. It became the "reserve and aid to the party." The FDJ, and the affiliated Ernst Thälmann Young Pioneers for children ages 6 to 13, were the only youth organizations permitted in the German Democratic Republic (GDR).

Membership to the FDJ was open, but it mostly appealed to young people aged 14 to 25. Membership in the 1980s was around 2,300,000, or almost 80 percent of all youth of that age. The publication organ was *Junge Welt* (Young world).

The organizational structure of the FDJ followed the usual GDR model. Every school, industrial enterprise, and university had an FDJ organization. In the 1980s there were around 30,000 basic organizations. The highest body was the Parliament, which met once every five years. In fact, however, political control was exercised by the Bureau of the Central Council, chosen by the *Politbüro* of the SED. The officials within the FDJ constituted a supply of young cadres for the SED and the state bureaucracy. For example, Egon Krenz, chairman of the FDJ from 1974, became a member of the SED *Politbüro* nine years later.

The FDJ's 1976 statute depicted the movement as an "active helper and reserve force" of the SED. The FDJ strove to mold young people as "socialist personalities," whether at work, in school, or in their leisure time. Almost 10,000 youth clubs catered to leisure interests, mostly for enjoying music and dance. There were, however, special youth projects to tie young people to the state's economic and social objectives. Such was the FDJ's Berlin Initiative as part of the capital's rebuilding program, or the Young Inventors' Fairs, launched in 1957, to demonstrate young people's scientific achievements. The FDJ was an active participant in pre-military training programs and played an active role in ideological education (*FDJ-Studienjahr* [FDJ study year]).

The official character of the FDJ, its ritualism, its political meetings and mass demonstrations, and a change of values that favored Western style, music, and fashion led to much dissatisfaction among young FDJ members during the 1980s. With the collapse of the SED and the GDR in late 1989, the FDJ sank into a deep crisis. The chairman, Eberhard Aurich, the successor of Egon Krenz, tried to revitalize the FDJ. At the 12th meeting of the Central Council on November 7, 1989, the leadership tried to get rid of ideological ballast and to attain independence from the SED. The attempt failed. The FDJ thereupon became discredited as a puppet organization obedient to the SED. Hundreds of thousands of young people resigned. At the 13th session, Aurich and the entire Central Council stepped down. According to the new statute, the FDJ acclaimed itself as a socialist, democratic, anti-fascist, and independent youth organization. The FDJ surrendered its right to speak for all young people. It eliminated the paragraph from the 1976 statute that proclaimed the FDJ as the "helper and cadre reserve of the SED." At the 14th session on December 14, 1989, the new leadership proclaimed the demise of the old FDJ. The new FDJ desired to be just another youth organization among others, but the changes came too late.

The FDJ failed to get a seat to participate in the "*Runde Tisch*" (Round Table) meetings held by a variety of GDR organizations to discuss the future of the GDR. At the Brandenburg congress in late January 1990, 1,785 delegates tried to renew the FDJ as a leftist youth organization with a new program and statute. At this session, the FDJ was nearly dissolved. Frank Turkowsky stepped down and Birgit Schröder became the new chair. Two months later, in March 1990, the Young Pioneers organization dissolved itself. By mid-1990, only 20,000 FDJ members were left, and 6,000 out of the 7,500 functionaries had been dismissed. The "new" fdj (which is no longer capitalized), is a marginal organization with a few thousand Leninist-oriented members. It has no influence either in politics or among most young people. Many, however, regret the loss of leisure-time opportunities that the 10,000 FDJ youth clubs once provided. Half of them are closed.

Heinrich Bortfeld

See also German Democratic Republic; Honecker, Erich; Krenz, Egon; Socialist Unity Party; Youth; Youth Movements

References

Broszat, Martin and Hermann Weber, eds. *SBZ-Handbuch*. Munich: R. Oldenburg, 1990.

Zimmermann, Hartmut, ed. *DDR Handbuch*. 3rd ed. Cologne: Verlag Wissensschaft und Politik, 1984.

Freisler, Roland (1893–1945)

The head of the People's Court, Roland Freisler, was born on October 1, 1893, in Celle, Lower Saxony, the son of a Prussian civil servant. After receiving his *Abitur* (senior matriculation) in Kassel, he studied law in Jena. His studies were interrupted by World War I—he served on the eastern front, was taken captive by the Russians in 1915, and spent several years in Siberia where he learned Russian and, according to unsubstantiated rumors, became a Communist and possibly a commissar. In 1920 he returned to Germany, and he obtained a doctorate in law in 1921. He established a law practice, first in Karlsbad, then in Kassel. In 1925 he joined the Nazi Party; he became city councillor in Kassel, then deputy to the Prussian legislature in 1932 and, in March 1933, a member of the Reichstag.

Freisler became state secretary in the Prussian Department of Justice and, after its dissolution in 1934, he occupied the identical post in the Reich Department of Justice. He was an unflinching proponent of National Socialist ideology and of a "National Socialist administration of justice." He presided over a number of professional committees and commissions, worked on the reform of the criminal law, and became director of the Department of Criminal Law at the Academy of German Law which had been founded by Reich Legal Director Hans Frank. On January 20, 1942, he represented the Department of Justice at the Wannsee conference on the "final solution of the Jewish question." Freisler, however, found his true calling when he became president of the Nazi tribunal or People's Court (Volksgerichtshof) on August 20, 1942.

There "Raging Roland" was in his element, especially in proceedings against the members of the Resistance. Even though the military was in charge of most of these trials, Adolf Hitler had insisted that the resisters should be brought before the People's Court. He equated Freisler with A. Vyshinsky, the chief prosecutor of the Moscow show trials from 1936 to 1938. Freisler fully lived up to these expectations. As presiding judge he reduced all other participants in the trial, even his associates, to mere extras. He humiliated, insulted, and mocked the accused. Freisler died on February 3, 1945, during an air raid on Berlin.

When Freisler is portrayed as the incarnation of all crimes committed in the name of the law during the Third Reich, it is easily forgotten that he was considered a brilliant legal thinker. Hundreds of his articles, speeches, and memoranda indicate that he was a hard-working, intelligent, and well-read leader in shaping the National Socialist legal system, an expert whom law professors were fond of citing. The historian Michael Freund considers it symptomatic that the Germans chose not a servile subordinate but a highly gifted jurist for the presidency of their revolutionary tribunal: "Even for mechanized mass murder they demanded a high mark in the bar exam."

Ingo Müller

See also Frank, Hans; Judicial System of Imperial and Weimar Germany; Law, German Conception of; Legal Profession; Third Reich: Legal Profession; People's Court; Resistance

References

Buchheit, Gert. *Richter in roter Robe: Freisler, Präsident des Volksgerichtshofes.* Munich: List, 1968.
Müller, Ingo. *Hitler's Justice.* Trans. Deborah Schneider. Cambridge, MA: Harvard University Press, 1991.
Ortner, Helmut. *Der Hinrichter: Roland Freisler, Mörder im Dienste Hitlers.* Vienna: Zsolnay, 1993.

Freud, Sigmund (1856–1939)

Sigmund Freud was the founder of psychoanalysis, a theory of human behavior and a method of therapy that views mental dysfunction as a psychological phenomenon based on unconscious conflict between sexual instinct and social norms. This opposed the prevailing psychiatric conception that attributed psychological disturbances to physiological disorders of the brain and nervous system. Freud's thinking evolved through a voluminous series of case studies and monographs, chief among which are *Studien über Hysterie* (Studies in hysteria), 1895, with Joseph Breuer, *Die Traumdeutung* (published as *The Interpretation of Dreams*), 1900, *Drei Abhandlungen zur Sexualtheorie* (Three essays on sexuality), 1905, *Jenseits des Lustprinzips* (published as *Beyond the Pleasure Principle*), 1920, *Massenpsychologie und Ich-Analyse* (Group psychology and analysis of the ego), 1921, *Das Ich und das Es,* 1923, *Hemmung, Symptom, und Angst,* 1926, and *Das Unbehagen in der Kultur* (published as *Civilization and its Discontents*), 1930.

Freud was born in Freiberg, Moravia, and was educated in Vienna. He died in London in 1939 after emigrating there in the wake of the Austrian *Anschluss* in 1938. At university he studied biology and medicine under Ernst Brücke. Barred from a university research career by a quota for Jews, he subsequently specialized in clinical neurology and in 1885 traveled to Paris to study with Jean Martin Charcot, who was treating hysteria with hypnosis. Unlike Charcot, Freud became convinced that hysteria was psychological rather than somatic in origin. Back in Vienna, Freud turned away from hypnotic catharsis toward treatment by free association. Freud surmised that the repression of the patient's unconscious sexual conflicts could be lifted only by means of a conscious "working through" of the material by the patient under the unique conditions of psychoanalytic treatment.

Freud believed that neurosis may be traced to childhood sexual fantasies and that dreams are the "royal road" to the unconscious. The central emotional struggle, according to Freud, is the Oedipus complex. Freud later posited the existence of an aggressive instinct alongside the sexual and also came to devote more attention to the functioning of the ego and superego in their struggle with the id, the repository of instinct. His works on slips of the tongue and pen (1904) and on jokes (1905), along with his introductory lectures on psychoanalysis (1922, 1933), helped to popularize his ideas. He attracted a devoted group of followers, some of whom over time diverged or broke away from psychoanalytic orthodoxy.

Freud was a conservative nineteenth-century bourgeois who, while sympathizing with the individual's struggle against society, viewed sublimated sexual energy as positive, the basis for the achievements of civilization.

Freud's thought was given a mixed reception in Germany. Many psychiatrists expressed varying degrees of interest in psychoanalysis, but many rejected it for being unscientific according to the physicalist standards of German psychiatry. And although Freud's ideas sparked significant popular interest, in both professional and popular circles there was also (often anti-Semitic and racist) revulsion at Freudian "pansexualism." Karl Abraham of Berlin was the most prominent early disciple of Freud in Germany and made contributions to the psychoanalytic study of character. Otto Fenichel published the first comprehensive summary of psychoanalytic thought from exile in the United States in 1934. Fenichel, Siegfried Bernfeld, Wilhelm Reich, and members of the Frankfurt Institute for Social Research, such as Erich Fromm (1900–80) and the sociologist Max Horkheimer (1895–1973), attempted in the 1920s to synthesize Marxist and Freudian theory. Karen Horney was another of the many neo-Freudians—or cultural Freudians—in Germany who emphasized ego functions over sexual drives.

Many Freudians, most of them Jews, were driven out of Germany by the Nazis. During the Third Reich, Freudianism was variously attacked, suppressed, camouflaged, preserved, adulterated, or employed by organized psychiatry and psychotherapy. After the war, Freud reemerged as a scientific and cultural resource in the Federal Republic, though one in competition with other approaches in the rapidly professionalizing venues of applied psychology. In the German Democratic Republic, Ivan Pavlov and others supplanted Freud. In both states, anti-Freudian psychiatry had been weakened as a result of its involvement in Nazi eugenics.

Geoffrey Cocks

See also Adler, Alfred; Frankfurt School; Fromm, Erich; Horkheimer, Max; Jung, Carl; Psychiatry; Psychoanalysis; Psychology

References

Freud, Sigmund. *The Standard Edition of the Complete Psychological Works of Sigmund Freud.* 24 vols. Ed. and trans. James Strachey. London: Hogarth Press, 1953–74.
Gay, Peter. *Freud: A Life for Our Time.* New York, NY: W.W. Norton, 1988.
Jones, Ernest. *Sigmund Freud: Life and Work.* 3 vols. New York, NY: Basic Books, 1953–57.

Freyer, Hans (1887–1969)

Hans Freyer was among the most articulate social thinkers associated with the movement for a "conservative revolution" in the 1920s and one of the more respected voices of German conservatism during the first decade and a half of the Federal Republic.

Born into the lower reaches of the *Bildungsbürgertum* (cultivated bourgeoisie) in 1887, Freyer was deeply stamped by the disillusionment with bourgeois society characteristic of the *Jugendbewegung* (youth movement), and his experience as a decorated officer during World War I suggested a more illiberal alternative. In 1924, Freyer was appointed to one of first chairs of sociology in Germany, at the University of Leipzig. In the following years, he straddled the roles of social scientist and radical conservative ideologist. His writings drew upon the more pessimistic assessments of capitalist society in the work of Karl Marx (1818–83), Ferdinand Tönnies (1855–1936), Max Weber (1864–1920), and Georg Simmel (1858–1918), and spelled out the logic of a radical brand of sociology that appealed to politically engaged academic intellectuals on both the left and right. In 1931, Freyer published a booklet, *Revolution von rechts* (Revolution from the right), which interpreted the rise of Nazism as evidence of a deep-seated revolt against "bourgeois society" and the Weimar polity and appealed to his readers of the educated middle class to add their weight to the movement.

In 1933 and 1934, Freyer and like-minded intellectuals rose to important posts in the academy, in cultural institutions, and in government. Freyer was appointed head of a renowned institute of historical research and was elected president of the German Sociological Association. His experience from 1934 to 1938, however, led to a gradual disillusionment with National Socialism and with totalitarian solutions to the problems of modernity. Yet like many conservative Germans disabused of their hopes for the Third Reich, Freyer continued to serve the regime. From 1938 through 1945, he lived in Budapest as visiting professor of German studies and as director of a German scientific institute: both positions were creations of the German Foreign Office, intended to boost the prestige of the regime abroad.

After the war, during the Sovietization of the University of Leipzig, Freyer lost his professorship. He moved to the Western zone in 1948 but was unable to secure a university post, due in part to his role in legitimating the rise of National Socialism. After working for several years as an editor of the Brockhaus encyclopedia, Freyer was appointed emeritus professor of sociology in Münster, where he taught through the mid-1960s.

Chastened by the experience of totalitarianism, Freyer formulated a brand of conservative social theory that remained skeptical of the claims of modern liberal-democratic society but was reconciled to its inevitability. It rather sought to bolster the cultural and social "forces of conservation," which lay largely outside the realms of politics and economic production. His books *Weltgeschichte Europas* (published as *Europe's World History*), 1948, and *Theorie des gegenwärtigen Zeitalters* (Theory of the current age), 1955, combined sociological, philosophical, and historical reflection and articulated the resigned reconciliation of German intellectual conservatives with pluralistic liberal democracy. Some of the most influential West German sociologists and historians of the 1950s and 1960s were Freyer's former students, and his writings played a role in the development of a more sociologically informed historiography in the Federal Republic.

Jerry Z. Müller

See also Conservatism, 1918–45; History; National Socialism; Professions; Sociology

References

Müller, Jerry Z. *The Other God that Failed: Hans Freyer and the Deradicalization of German Conservatism.* Princeton, NJ: Princeton University Press, 1987.

Freytag, Gustav (1816–95)

Gustav Freytag was a noted author, journalist, and cultural historian. Best known for the novel *Soll und Haben* (Debt and credit), 1855, the multivolume cultural history *Bilder aus der deutschen Vergangenheit* (Scenes from the German past), 1859–67, and the handbook on drama *Die Technik des Dramas* (The technique of the drama), 1863, Freytag also edited the influential journal *Die Grenzboten* (The border messengers) from 1848 to 1870. His play *Die Journalisten* (The journalists), 1854, was a favorite on the German stage, and *Die Ahnen* (The ancestors), 1872–80, offered an ambitious cycle of six novels depicting German history from the Romans to the present.

Born in Kreuzburg, Silesia, Freytag studied in Breslau (now Wroclaw, Poland) and Berlin, earned a doctorate in 1838, and lectured on German literature at the university in Breslau until 1844. In his later career as an author and journalist, he retained the commitment to advance German culture. A typical representative of bourgeois liberal nationalism, Freytag advocated German unity under Prussian leadership, excluding Austria. In 1867, he was a representative for one session in the North German Parliament, and during the Franco-Prussian War he accompanied Crown Prince Friedrich on his campaigns. As editor of *Die Grenzboten* and as a close friend of Ernst II, Duke of Sachsen-Coburg and Gotha and founder in 1853 of the National-liberaler Verein (National Liberal Association), Freytag had various opportunities to promote German political and cultural unification. Not only a political medium for the national-liberal ideology, *Die Grenzboten* was also the forum for discussions about literary realism at mid-century. From 1871 to 1873, Freytag contributed to the journal *Im Neuen Reich* (In the new Reich).

Freytag's best-known novel is *Soll und Haben*, which contrasts the success story of a middle-class hero to the financial ruin of a representative family of the German nobility and to the moral disintegration of the major Jewish character. Later criticized for being anti-Semitic and chauvinistic, the novel was praised as being "realistic" in the mid-1850s. Freytag's next novel, *Die verlorene Handschrift* (The lost manuscript), 1864, and the six novels of *Die Ahnen* never achieved the popularity and critical acclaim of *Soll und Haben*.

Die Ahnen presents a fictional chronicle of German history; the volumes of *Bilder aus der deutschen Vergangenheit* trace the major periods of German cultural history with a mixture of essays, biographical sketches, and anecdotal vignettes. Freytag also provided posterity with a valuable collection of political pamphlets from the Reformation through the Thirty Years' War, now housed in the Municipal and University Library of Frankfurt am Main.

Nancy Kaiser

See also Anti-Semitism; History; Imperial Germany: Literature; Journalism; Liberalism; National Liberal Party; Nationalism; Novel

References

Bramsted, Ernest. *Aristocracy and the Middle-Classes in Germany: Social Types in German Literature 1830–1900.* London: P.S. King & Son, Ltd. 1937. Reprint: Chicago, IL: University of Chicago Press, 1964.

Carter, T.E. "Freytag's *Soll und Haben*: A Liberal National Manifesto as a Best-Seller." *German Life and Letters* 21 (1967–68), 321–29.

Gelber, Mark. "An Alternate Reading of the Role of the Jewish Scholar in Gustav Freytag's *Soll und Haben*." *Germanic Review* 58 (1983), 83–88.

———. "Die literarische Umwelt zu Gustav Freytags Soll und Haben und die Realismustheorie der Grenzboten." *Orbis Litterarum* 39 (1984), 38–53.

Holz, Claus. *Flucht aus der Wirklichkeit: "Die Ahnen" von Gustav Freytag: Untersuchungen zum realistischen historischen Roman der Gründerzeit 1872–1880.* Frankfurt am Main: Lang, 1983.

Kaiser, Nancy. "Cohesion and Integration: Reading as Reaffirmation (*Soll und Haben*)." *Social Integration and Narrative Structure: Patterns of Realism in Auerbach, Freytag, Fontane, and Raabe.* Ed. N. Kaiser. Berne: Lang, 1986.

Lindau, Hans. *Gustav Freytag.* Leipzig: Hirzel, 1907.

Sammons, Jeffrey. "The Evaluation of Freytag's *Soll und Haben*." *German Life and Letters* 22 (1968–69), 315–24.

Tatlock, Lynne. "Realist Historiography and the Historiography of Realism: Gustav Freytag's *Bilder aus der deutschen Vergangenheit*." *German Quarterly* 63 (1990), 59–74.

Frick, Wilhelm (1877–1946)

Wilhelm Frick served as minister of the interior (1933–43) and protector of Bohemia and Moravia (1943–45). With a doctorate of law from Göttingen University (1901), and unable to serve in World War I, Frick established himself in Munich's police department (1904–25). From that position he helped to protect the Nazi Party from police action, most notably at the time of the Beer Hall *Putsch* (November 1923). He became one of the Nazi Party's first Reichstag deputies (1924) and later its parliamentary leader (1925). When elected minister of the interior and education in the province of Thuringia (December 1929), he became the first Nazi to hold ministerial rank. He banned jazz music, introduced pro-Nazi prayers in schools, secured a chair at Jena University for the racial theorist H.F.K. Günther (1891–1968), and purged the province's police force.

With the seizure of power by the Nazis in January 1933, Frick joined Adolf Hitler's cabinet. As Reich minister of the interior, he was responsible for much of the legislation that marked Nazism's *Gleichschaltung* process (the coordination of the entire country along Nazi lines), for example the Enabling Act of March 1933, which laid the legal foundation for Hitler's dictatorial rule.

Frick worked doggedly at creating a centralized Nazi state administered by a professional civil service. Consequently, the Law for the Reconstruction of the Reich of January 30, 1934 abolished provincial parliaments and declared Reich governors (who were generally also *Gauleiter* [district leaders]) subject to his ministry's authority. Unfortunately for Frick, the local party bosses paid scant attention to his legislation and his plans never became reality.

Frick's attempt to control Germany's police proved equally unsuccessful. On two occasions (January 1934 and January 1935) he tried in vain to regulate Himmler's arbitrary use of "protective custody." Frick's failure became total when Hitler appointed Himmler chief of police on June 17, 1936. Himmler later replaced Frick as Reich minister of the interior in August 1943.

Frick was essentially a civil servant who liked order and respected written regulations. He was hopelessly out of tune with the reality of the Third Reich. His enemies despised him as a political weakling. Nevertheless, Frick was sentenced to death by the court at Nuremberg in October 1946.

Martyn Housden

See also Civil Service; Coordination; Günther, Hans; Himmler, Heinrich; Hitler, Adolf; National Socialism; Nuremberg Trials

References

Broszat, Martin. *The Hitler State.* London: Longman, 1981.

Das Deutsche Führerlexikon 1934/5. Berlin: Otto Stollberg, 1934.

Neliba, G. *Wilhelm Frick: Der Legalist des Unrechtsstaates.* Paderborn: Schöningh, 1992.

Orlow, D. *The History of the Nazi Party.* 2 vols. Pittsburgh, PA: University of Pittsburgh Press, 1969.

Peterson, E.N. *The Limits of Hitler's Power.* Princeton, NJ: Princeton University Press, 1969.

Fried, Erich (1921–88)

Erich Fried was known initially for his translations of the work of Dylan Thomas, William Shakespeare, and T.S. Eliot, among others, but he gradually established a reputation as a poet in his own right. His literary work was often political and characterized by a keen sensitivity to the use—and misuse—of language. Although Fried was known principally as a poet and translator, he also wrote radio plays, short stories, and one novel, *Ein Soldat und ein Mädchen* (A soldier and a girl), 1960. Formal recognition came late in Fried's life. For his poetry and Shakespeare translations he was awarded the Georg Büchner Prize (1987), the most prestigious West German prize for literature.

Fried was born in Vienna in 1921 into an assimilated Jewish family. Following the *Anschluss* of Austria he was forced into exile in London. His poems written in wartime London were conventional in form and anti-Nazi in content. After 1945, he worked for the BBC German Service before becoming a professional writer. He soon abandoned political poetry written in traditional form in favor of experiments with half-rhyme and puns. The poems of this period betray a deep sense of unease. *Gedichte* (Poems), 1958, and *Warngedichte* (Warning poems), 1964, center around the fear of another war and Fried's attempt to come to terms with the Holocaust. Similarly, Fried's *Ein Soldat und ein Mädchen* draws on the experiences of Nazism and provides a psychological exploration of the origins of human brutality. In this novel and in his later short prose pieces Fried employed a technique of word association, but with less success than in his poetry.

In the 1960s, Fried returned to the realm of politics and became increasingly involved in the West German student movement. In *. . . und Vietnam und . . .*, 1966, he combined the skillful use of punning with criticism of the Vietnam war. In the controversial publication, *Höre, Israel!*, 1974, Fried attacked Zionist expansionism and drew parallels between Israeli and Nazi behavior. His position on the political left made Fried an unwelcome commentator on developments in the Federal Republic. *So kam ich unter die Deutschen* (That is how I came to be among the Germans), 1977, concerns the events surrounding the Baader-Meinhof terrorists. Fried feared that the state might compromise justice and democracy and he perceived a frightening similarity between the Federal Republic of Germany and Nazi Germany. His poetry took a variety of different forms, but he frequently employed unique rhetoric that led the reader to reach unexpected conclusions. Fried's work may have been influenced by his political position, but his poetry was never marred by recourse to dogmatic party politics.

In the 1970s and 1980s, Fried became extremely productive, publishing up to three volumes of poetry each year. He dealt with subjects as varied as Third-World poverty, the situation in Nicaragua and Austria, the arms race, and the dogmatism of the German left wing. Fried also dwelled increasingly on the past, on National Socialism, and on the war. This preoccupation became evident in titles such as *Gegen das Vergessen* (Against forgetting), 1987, and *Unverwündenes*, 1988.

Fried has been praised for writing some of the best, and accused of writing some of the worst, German poetry. His determination to criticize contemporary political and moral ills frequently served as the reason for the hostile response he received. Only in his work as a translator was Fried the object of nearly unanimous praise. By the time of his death in 1988, Fried was one of the most important poets writing in German, and—much like Heinrich Böll (1917–85)—he had become the unwelcome conscience of the German nation in Austria and the Federal Republic.

Steven W. Lawrie

See also Baader-Meinhof Group; Extra-Parliamentary Opposition; Federal Republic of Germany: Literature; Holocaust; Memory, Collective; Poetry; Radio Plays

References

Fried, Erich. *Gesammelte Werke in vier Bänden.* Ed. Volker Kaukoreit and Klaus Wagenbach. 4 vols. Berlin: Wagenbach, 1993.

———. *Shakespeare.* 4 vols. Berlin: Wagenbach, 1989.
Heimann, Angelika. *"Bless thee! Thou art translated": Erich Fried als Übersetzer moderner englischsprachiger Lyrik.* Amsterdam: Münchener Studien zur neueren englischen Literatur, 1987.
Kaukoreit, Volker. "Auswahlbibliographie." *Erich Fried.* Ed. Heinz Ludwig Arnold. Munich: *Text + Kritik*, 1986.
———. *Vom Exil bis zum Protest gegen den Krieg in Vietnam: Frühe Stationen des Lyrikers Erich Fried: Werk und Biographie 1938–1966.* Darmstadt: Verlag Jürgen Hausser, 1991.
Lampe, Gerhard. *"Ich will mich erinnern an alles was man vergisst": Erich Fried: Biographie und Werk.* Cologne: Bund-Verlag, 1989.

Friedrich (Frederick) III (1831–88)

When asked to comment on the death of Emperor Friedrich III in 1888, Liberal British Prime Minister William Gladstone called him "the Barbarossa of German liberalism." Many German liberals felt the same way. He was born on October 18, 1831, and was the only son of Kaiser Wilhelm I. As a young man, his political views were very much in line with the conservative court in Berlin. This changed after his 1858 marriage to Princess Victoria, the eldest daughter of Queen Victoria of England. The princess was determined to convert her husband to British-style liberalism; a major goal was to have the powers of parliament increased at the expense of the Prussian monarchy. After his marriage, Friedrich appeared to follow his wife's lead: he began to foster ties with prominent liberals and rejected the conservative domestic and foreign policies of Chancellor Otto von Bismarck. But when Friedrich came to the throne in 1888, he was mortally ill with cancer and reigned for only three months.

Friedrich's biographers, along with a majority of historians of nineteenth-century Germany, believe that liberalism would have triumphed had it not been for his untimely illness and death. However, the unpublished correspondence between Friedrich and his wife paints a different picture. Far from being a pliant man who heeded his wife's wishes, he firmly resisted Victoria's attempts to convince him to support increasing the powers of parliament at the expense of the monarchy. Friedrich was first and foremost a constitutional liberal, and agitated on behalf of the preservation of constitutionalism when conservatives threatened it with extinction. His approach to reform was cautious: he favored adoption of liberal reforms only within the framework of the constitutional status quo.

To the immense chagrin of Victoria, her husband's hostile attitude toward Bismarck's policies changed when the latter assured him in 1870 that he would pursue German unification in a liberal-constitutional framework. But Friedrich's hopes for a liberal Germany were dashed by Bismarck's alliance with anti-liberal forces in 1879. He became subject to fits of depression and feelings of hopelessness. Nonetheless, he continued to warn Bismarck that he would not work with a chancellor who subverted the constitution during his coming reign.

Friedrich's liberal constitutionalism therefore played a decisive role in ensuring the survival of constitutionalism in Germany. Yet it is also true that some accounts on the extent of his liberal views have been exaggerated. The person most responsible for this was his wife. After Friedrich's death, Victoria, in her letters and correspondence, made the late emperor the progressive liberal he never was in life. Her agitation on behalf of her husband's alleged liberal views fostered the legend of Friedrich III. The legend, in the end, ultimately obscured Friedrich's true contributions as a constitutional liberal.

Patricia Kollander

See also Anglo-German Relations; Bismarck, Otto von; Constitutions; Liberalism; Wilhelm I; Wilhelm II

References
Dorpalen, Andreas. "Emperor Frederick III and the German Liberal Movement." *American Historical Review* 54 (October 1948), 1–31.
Heere, Franz. *Kaiser Friedrich III: Deutschlands liberale Hoffnung.* Stuttgart: Deutsche Verlags-Anstalt, 1987.
Kollander, Patricia. *Frederick III: Germany's Liberal Emperor.* Westport, CT: Greenwood Press, 1995.
Poschinger, Margarethe von. *Frederick III, German Emperor: 1831–1888.* London: Chapman, 1902.

Friedrich, Otto A. (1902–75)

Otto Friedrich, a prominent industrialist during the 1940s and 1950s, served as president of the German Employers' Federation between 1969 and 1973.

Born in Marburg on July 3, 1902, Friedrich grew up in an upper-middle-class family. After a few years of studies at Vienna, Heidelberg, and Berlin in the early 1920s, he went to the United States, where his brother Carl Friedrich, soon to become an influential political scientist, had just obtained a position at Harvard University. Otto Friedrich worked for Goodrich in Ohio before being sent back to Germany in 1929 as the company's agent in the Weimar Republic. Having worked for various rubber-cartel organizations in the 1930s, Friedrich joined the board of Phoenix Rubber in 1939 and in World War II rose to the position of Deputy Commissioner for Rubber in the Nazi war economy.

Thanks to his good contacts with the British and American occupation authorities, Friedrich came through the defeat of 1945 and his de-Nazification procedures well and became Phoenix's head in 1949. He rose quickly in the hierarchy of entrepreneurs as a member of the presidium of the Federation of German Industry. He acted as an advisor to the Bonn government during the Korean War and became a close ally of Economics Minister Ludwig Erhard (1897–1977). In 1966, he became a partner in Friedrich Flick's powerful industrial empire before he was elected president of the German Employers' Federation in 1969.

Partly influenced by his brother, who worked as an advisor to United States Military Governor Lucius D. Clay, Friedrich represented the modern and liberal entrepreneur. He had many intellectual interests and was a good speaker. This enabled him to become an influential spokesman among West Germany's entrepreneurs, who were trying to reconstruct an ideological position for themselves after the political, economic, and moral disaster of National Socialism.

Volker R. Berghahn

See also American-German Relations; Erhard, Ludwig; Federation of German Industry; Flick Family; State and Economy

References
Berghahn, V.R. *The Americanization of West German Industry: 1945–1973.* New York, NY: Cambridge University Press, 1986.
Berghahn, V.R. and P.J. Friedrich. *Otto A. Friedrich: Ein politischer Unternehmer, 1902–1975.* Frankfurt am Main: Campus Verlag, 1993.
Friedrich, O.A. *Das Leistungsprinzip in unserer Zeit.* Berlin: Beuth, 1974.
———. *Das Leitbild des Unternehmers ändert sich.* Stuttgart: Seewald Verlag, 1959.

Frings, Joseph (1887–1978)

Archbishop of the Diocese of Cologne (1942–69), cardinal after 1946, and chair of the Fulda Conference of German Bishops (1945–65), Joseph Frings shaped the reconstruction of the German Roman Catholic Church. He decisively influenced the course of the Second Vatican Council (1962–65).

Born February 6, 1887, in Neuss, North Rhine–Westphalia, Frings grew up in a large, pious, affluent industrialist's family. He decided early to serve the Church and attended universities at Innsbruck (1905), Bonn, Rome, and Freiburg im Breisgau, where he attained his doctorate in theology in 1916. Preferring pastoral to theological church work, he was ordained in 1910. His experiences as priest and pastor in urban and rural parishes (1910–37), and as teacher and *Regens* (regent) at the Theological Seminary, Bensberg, until 1942 explain Frings's lifelong commitment to the affairs of the Catholic working class. As archbishop, Frings opposed the Nazi regime and publicly criticized Nazi measures and brutalities through pastoral letters and pulpit sermons. During the early postwar years his outspokenness earned Frings popularity with Germans but opprobrium from Allied officials for his criticism of their anti-German measures such as severe restrictions on food, energy, and housing, and the dismantling of factories.

Using the Fulda Conference, Frings guided the renewal and development of the Roman Catholic Church, which, instead of soul-searching over past omissions and commissions, confronted the harsh issues of survival by providing material and spiritual sustenance for millions of homeless persons. Frings's modernization measures regarding church administration, lay participation, episcopal democracy, and transformation of the liturgy anticipated the Second Vatican Council. By establishing, first, an episcopal partnership between Cologne and Tokyo in 1954; then *Misereor* (an organization to support Catholic colleges in the Third World by subsidizing education and missionary work) in 1959; and lastly *Adveniat* (an organization doing work similar to *Misereor*) in 1961, Frings opened German Catholicism to world problems. At the Second Vatican Council, Frings's interventions, on October 13, 1962 and November 8, 1963, shaped the council's course. He demanded free elections, open procedures, and the right to be heard. He expressed the sentiments of international progressive Roman Catholicism, which, he believed, the council would renew worldwide.

Always unassuming and not an original thinker, Frings nonetheless was a German Roman Catholic Church leader of great significance and world stature. He resigned his offices in 1969 and died on December 17, 1978 in Cologne.

E.R. Zimmermann

See also Catholicism, Political; Christian Democratic Union; Federal Republic of Germany; Postwar Reconstruction; Roman Catholic Church

References

Frings, Kardinal Josef. *Für die Menschen bestellt: Erinnerungen des Alterzbischofs von Köln.* Cologne: J.P. Bachem, 1974.

Froitzheim, Dieter, ed. *Kardinal Frings: Leben und Werk.* Cologne: Wieland Verlag, 1979.

Helmreich, Ernst Christian. *The German Churches under Hitler: Background Struggle and Epilogue.* Detroit, MI: Wayne State University Press, 1980.

van Elten, Josef, ed. *Pro Hominibus Constitus.* Gedenkausstellung des Historischen Archivs des Erzbistums Köln zum 100. Geburtstag von Josef Kardinal Frings am 6. Februar 1987. Katalog. Cologne: J.P. Bachem, 1987.

Frisch, Max (1911–91)

Although Max Frisch was formally trained as an architect, his importance as a modern Swiss cultural figure rests entirely on his literary contributions as a dramatist and prose author. Born in Zürich in 1911, Frisch briefly studied literature and art history at the University of Zürich until financial problems caused by his father's death led him to pursue his living as a journalist. After only a few years, he abandoned journalism to follow in his father's footsteps by studying to be an architect, a profession he attempted to combine with his writing until the early 1950s. More important than any building he designed was his criticism of the dominant sentimental, provincial paradigms of postwar Swiss architecture. This critical attitude toward tradition was also a hallmark of his literary work.

Frisch first gained attention as an author in 1950 with the publication of his *Tagebuch 1946–1949* (Sketchbook), which in dealing with the immediate postwar situation also contained the germs of much of his later work—including the use of the diary form. A famous trilogy that took up the complex theme of the troubled relationship between the individual and the social order began with his novel *Stiller* (published as *I'm not Stiller*) in 1954. The searching exploration of the problem of identity begun in this work continued in *Homo Faber,* 1957, and *Mein Name sei Gantenbein,* 1964, which, as a tril-

ogy, are generally considered to be Frisch's chief achievement in the realm of fiction. A 1975 novel, *Montauk*, with much more pointed autobiographical allusions, explores the encounter of an aging narrator (a writer, suggestively named Max) with a young woman during a visit to New York. The introspective confrontation with the past reached another high point in *Der Mensch erscheint im Holozän* (published as *Man in the Holocene*), 1979, this time from the perspective of old age.

Frisch's first dramatic success, *Nun singen sie wieder* (published as *Now They Sing Again*), 1946, was quickly followed by two others dealing with the question of postwar guilt: *Die chinesische Mauer* (published as *The Chinese Wall*), 1947, and *Als der Krieg zu ende war* (When the war was over), 1948. Frisch's conviction that the question of guilt was not to be limited to finger-pointing at Germany was made powerfully in one of his best-known plays, *Andorra,* 1961, a parable of anti-Semitism set in a fictional small country. Of Frisch's plays, *Biedermann und die Brandstifter* (published as *The Firebugs*), 1958, another warning parable that also clearly reveals the influence of Bertolt Brecht (1898–1956), has enjoyed the most enduring success.

Frisch's critical reflections on his own society can also be clearly traced in a second *Tagebuch 1966–1971* (published as *Sketchbook*), 1972, as well as in his *Wilhelm Tell für die Schule* (William Tell: a school text), 1971, in which he continues the critique of a mythical sort of Swissness that characterized his position from the beginning. In his old age, he continued to speak out against threats to humankind and human dignity, feeling ever more alienated by unenlightened developments in Swiss and world politics. A final volume of his essays, *Schweiz als Heimat?* (Switzerland as home), 1990, appeared just before his death on April 4, 1991.

Patricia Herminghouse

See also Brecht, Bertolt; Drama; Federal Republic of Germany: Literature; Novels

References

Butler, Michael. *The Novels of Max Frisch.* London: O. Wolff, 1976.

———. *The Plays of Max Frisch.* London: Macmillan, 1985.

Kieser, Rolf, ed. *Frisch, Max: Novels, Plays, Essays.* New York, NY: Continuum, 1989.

Koepke, Wulf. *Understanding Max Frisch.* Columbia, SC: University of South Carolina Press, 1991.

Probst, Gerhard F. and Jay F. Bodine, eds. *Perspectives on Max Frisch.* Lexington, KY: University Press of Kentucky, 1982.

Fritsch, Katharina (1956–)

Sculptor Katharina Fritsch was born in 1956 in Essen and currently lives in Düsseldorf. Her art seems to invite labeling, yet its apparent unambiguity fades quickly as attempts are made to place her work into categories such as conceptual art or sculpture, minimalism or hyper-realism, surrealistic ready-made art or postmodern strategy.

Katharina Fritsch is a typical representative of the German postwar generation that matured during the era of the Economic Miracle. This generation was too young for the 1968 students' revolt but it finally found itself in the 1980s, which were characterized by pluralism and cynicism. Though generations are always anchored in their historical context, traditional concepts have increasingly lost their validity. Consequently Fritsch and others of her generation are attempting to reassess and revise reality without, however, providing an unequivocal epistemology (*Welterklärungsmuster*). At the end of the twentieth century, women have started to partake actively in this process.

After her studies (1977–81) with professor Fritz Schwegler at the *Kunstakademie* (Academy of Art) in Düsseldorf, which had acquired renown through the legendary Joseph Beuys (1921–86), Fritsch participated in numerous national and international exhibitions (e.g., *Von hier aus*, Düsseldorf, 1984; *Europa und Amerika*, Cologne, 1986; *Skulptur Projekte Münster*, Münster, 1987; *Binationale Deutsche Kunst der späten 80er Jahre*, Boston, 1988); in 1989 she had her first personal show. In 1994, she was the recipient of the Coutts Contemporary Art Foundation Prize.

Fritsch's artistic vocabulary relates to well-known and familiar spheres and themes. She reproduces singularly, or in extensive ensembles, common objects in plastic, wax, or plaster: pots, cheese, bowls, vases, scarves, books, and cars. A precise reconstruction of a department store rummage table (1987–89) and the true polyester replica of an elephant, painted green and placed on a wooden pedestal (1987) are part of her system of references. Of course, Fritsch investigates the inherent reality (*Realitätscharakter*) of all matters that are subject to a collective code of recognition. The perfection of her serialized production attains, however, such a high standard that it becomes manifestly the simulation of reality. Being herself the protagonist of this reality, Fritsch brings various articles of a catalogue of merchandise into play whose position, between fetish and articles of mass production, develops a kind of borderline syndrome. This becomes particularly evident in *Warengestell mit Madonnen* (Shelf with merchandise and madonnas), 1987–89, whose cylindrical placement is reminiscent of a display of laundry detergent. *Bücherregal* (Book shelves), produced in 1986 and consisting of 200 books without any print whatsoever but bound in leather, is similarly perverted.

As arbitrary as the choice of objects may seem initially, their cultural definition becomes clearly evident. Fritsch traces with the simplest means a "collective biography," a semantic of collective memory units, which is composed of fragments of subjective history and which manifests itself in the commercial aspect of all matter. For example, in *Warengestell* (which was rearranged and needs to be dated 1989–90 rather than 1970–84), objects are placed in rows on glass panes that correspond to layers of the conscious and the subconscious mind.

Fritsch uses a deliberate structuralist method that consists of the reconstruction of an object in such a way that aspects come to the surface that were invisible or, as it were, unintelligible in the natural object. Another concrete example

of this approach is the *Tischgesellschaft*, consisting of 32 identical models of a male prototype grouped around a long table: members of a secret fraternity in a faceless society whose communication patterns follow strict regulations. This same theme is portrayed on a different level in the installation *Rattenkönig* (Rat king) of 1993 in the Dia (Slide) Center for the Arts in New York. The 8.54-foot-high figures, which are inextricably intertwined through their tails, represent an indissoluble association of need, which in the final analysis is doomed to insanity and ruin. In this work, Fritsch's art has found its most intense expression.

Ellen Maurer

See also Artists; Beuys, Joseph; Painting; Sculpture; Trockel, Rosemarie

References
BiNationale. Exhibition catalog. Düsseldorf and Boston: DuMont, 1988.
Blase, Christoph. "On Katharina Fritsch." *Artscribe.* No. 68 (March–April 1988).
Koether, Jutta. "Katharina Fritsch—Elephant: Zur Ausstellung im Kaiser-Wilhelm-Museum, Krefeld." *Parkett.* 13 (1987), 90–91.
Locker, Ludwig. "Architektonische Aspekte in der Düsseldorfer Gegenwartskunst." *Arte factum.* 12 (Feb.–March 1986), 2–9.
Puvogel, Renate. "Katharina Fritsch, Rosemarie Trockel, Anna Winteler." Kunstforum *International* 97 (November-December 1988), 313–17.
Westfälischer Kunstverein. *Katharina Fritsch 1979–1989.* Münster: Verlag der Buchhandlung Walther König, 1989.

Fritsch, Theodor (1852–1933)
One of the most prolific anti-Semitic publishers of the Imperial and Weimar eras, Theodor Fritsch is best known as editor of the *Handbuch der Judenfrage* (Handbook on the Jewish question), 1903, and an anti-Semitic journal with intellectual pretensions, *Hammer: Blätter für deutschen Sinn* (Hammer: papers for Germanness), 1902–40. The "old master," as he was called, lived long enough to see the Nazi seizure of power and to be eulogized by the Nazi elite.

Born to peasant parents in Prussian Saxony, Fritsch became a milling engineer, founded an organization for small-scale millers, and published its newspaper (1879); the proceeds of this venture financed his anti-Semitic activities. He entered the anti-Semitic movement through *Mittelstand* (lower-middle-class) reform politics, helping to establish anti-Semitic associations in Dresden and Leipzig in the early 1880s. In 1885 he started a newspaper, the *Antisemitische-Korrespondenz* (Anti-semitic correspondence), which became one of the main organs of the parliamentary anti-Semites.

But Fritsch, who was unable to make an effective speech in public, never favored parliamentarizing the movement. Viscerally antidemocratic, he had no faith in the judgment of the German masses, and eventually advocated a constitutional dictatorship. In 1894 he dropped out of party politics and devoted himself to what he saw as his own special mission—the nonpartisan anti-Semitic indoctrination of all sectors of German society. Writing under his own name and the pseudonyms Theodor Kämpfer, F. Roderich Stoltheim, Fritz Thor, and Thomas Frey, he pursued this goal for the next 40 years with massive publications of books and pamphlets, including an early version of *The Protocols of the Elders of Zion*, 1924, and a translation of Henry Ford's *The International Jew*, 1922.

Typically, Fritsch sent out half the edition of one of his works free of charge to youth groups, influential individuals, Sunday schools, and various nationalist organizations; the interest thus drummed up usually sufficed to sell the other half and then finance a new edition. He combined deep hatred of Jews with a condemnation of most modern developments. Contemptuous of the kaiser, the Reichstag, education, and the press, he preached a "revolution of Germanic values" that would include tax reform, elevation of the *Mittelstand*, vegetarianism, abstinence, and a return to the land. Only then could suitable legislation deny Jews the power to rule over Germans. After the 1912 Reichstag elections he began calling openly for "a holy *Fehme* (feud) of dedicated men" to kill off the leaders of an expected socialist revolution. The German collapse of 1918 confirmed his direst predictions of doom, and he remained militantly pessimistic about Germany's future even after the rise of Hitler and the Nazi Party, about which he also remained skeptical through the late 1920s.

Fritsch's 50 years of indefatigable propagandizing against Jews contributed to winning anti-Semitism a secure place in German political culture. Earlier than most, he saw that parliamentary politics offered little prospect of "solving the Jewish question," a conclusion shared and acted upon by Adolf Hitler.

Richard S. Levy

See also Anti-Semitism

References
Hartung, G. "Pre-Planners of the Holocaust: The Case of Theodor Fritsch." *Why Germany? National Socialist Antisemitism and the European Context*. Ed. John Milfull. New York, NY: Berg, 1992.
Müller, Josef. *Die Entwicklung des Rassenantisemitismus in den letzten Jahrzehnten des 19. Jahrhunderts. Historische Studien*, vol. 372. Berlin: Ebering Verlag, 1940.
Phelps, Reginald. "Theodor Fritsch und der Antisemitismus." *Deutsche Rundschau* 87 (1961), 442–49.

Fritsch, Werner von (1880–1939)

Colonel-General Werner von Fritsch, the commander-in-chief of the German army from 1934 to 1938, had a major share in the development of a modern and highly technical army.

Fritsch was born into an old Prussian military family on August 4, 1880. He joined the army in 1898. From 1907 to 1910, he trained to be a general-staff officer. During World War I, he served as a general-staff officer in various commands. During his time at Border Defense Command North, he developed a close friendship with General Seeckt. From 1920 to 1922, Fritsch worked in the Army Ministry. Later, he served in various staff and command positions before being made commander of the Third Division in 1932.

His family required "strict discipline," and Fritsch was a military man by conviction. Both combined to make him a highly gifted military commander. His unpolitical stance was a result of his upbringing and of Seeckt's guidance. It was by President Hindenburg's express wish, somewhat against Hitler's intentions, that Fritsch was made chief of Army Command on February 1, 1934 (commander in chief, army, from 1935). At the same time, he was promoted to full general. Fritsch did not object to National Socialism, but rather hoped to make its more "valuable" elements part of the army tradition. Fritsch did not realize the ulterior motives of the Nazi ideology and hoped to absorb it into the nationalist concepts of the army command. He intended to revert to Seeckt's principles, and tried to keep Nazi, SA, and SS influence out of the army. This was not so much a rejection of Nazi ideology but a result of his aim to keep the army out of politics.

As a military expert, he succeeded in converting the army from a small cadre into a large conscript army. Differing from Hitler, he believed in continuous buildup without undue haste. His marked character had great influence over the army's officer corps, making him the symbol of the non-Nazi officers. Due to his upbringing, he remained loyal to Hitler, who promoted him to colonel-general on April 1, 1936. When Hitler revealed his expansionist plans to the armed forces' commanders in 1937, Fritsch believed he could dissuade Hitler with technical objections. As a consequence, he fell from grace.

When Hitler decided in 1938 to take over the armed forces' high command himself as a result of the Blomberg Affair, Fritsch was sacked, too. A charge of homosexuality was trumped up, based on forged evidence. Without any neutral investigation, and despite Fritsch's protestations of innocence, Hitler accepted the commander in chief's demise. Fritsch never realized that Hitler was part of the plot. A court-martial cleared Fritsch on all counts, but due to the simultaneous annexation of Austria, this finding never made an impact on the public. Hitler refused to reinstate Fritsch and only made him an honorary colonel of his former regiment. Fritsch took part in the Polish campaign with this regiment and was killed in action near Warsaw on September 22, 1939.

Klaus Schönherr

See also Beck, Ludwig; Blomberg, Werner von; Himmler, Heinrich; Hindenburg, Paul von; Hitler, Adolf; National Socialist Germany: Military; Resistance; Seeckt, Hans von

References
Deutsch, Harold C. *Hitler and His Generals: The Hidden Crisis, January-June 1938*. Minneapolis, MN:

University of Minnesota Press, 1974.

Janssen, Karl-Heinz. *Der Sturz der Generäle: Hitler und die Blomberg-Fritsch-Krise 1938.* Munich: Beck, 1994.

Kielmansegg, Johann A. Graf von. *Der Fritschprozess 1938.* Hamburg: Hoffmann & Campe, 1949.

Mellenthin, Friedrich W. von. *German Generals of World War II: As I Saw Them.* Norman, OK: University of Oklahoma Press, 1977.

O'Neill, Robert. "Fritsch, Beck and the Führer." *Hitler's Generals.* Ed. Correlli Barnett. London: Weidenfeld and Nicolson, 1989.

Fromm, Erich (1900–80)

After receiving his doctorate in sociology from the University of Heidelberg in 1923, Erich Fromm trained as a psychoanalyst in Berlin and then helped to establish the Frankfurt Psychoanalytic Institute, where he practiced from 1927 to 1932. In 1933, he took up residence in the United States. From 1934 to 1938, he was director of social psychology at the Frankfurt Institute for Social Research (Frankfurt School), then temporarily housed at Columbia University. As a result of disagreements with several of his Frankfurt School colleagues, Fromm left the institute in 1938. For the next several years he taught, continued his work in psychoanalysis, and published many articles and the widely read *Escape from Freedom,* 1941. For the next two decades, Fromm helped to establish and/or direct several psychoanalytic institutes, including the Mexican Institute of Psychoanalysis. In 1960, he joined the American Socialist Party and in 1969 was made president of the International Forum of Psychoanalysis.

After 1929, Fromm's increasing disagreement with orthodox Freudian psychoanalytic theory—specifically with Freud's insistence on the centrality of libido and the Oedipus complex—and his developing sense of the social determinants of personality resulted in his attempt to synthesize psychoanalytic theory and Marxian materialist theory. He believed that, while Marxian materialist theory correctly grasped the relationship between ideology and socioeconomic base, the addition of a modified psychoanalytic theory could provide insights into the social production of dominant modes of thought and personality. His concept of "social character" attempted to preserve psychoanalytic theory's insistence on the internal, biological determinants of individual personality while allowing for the uniformities imposed by a given society's mode of production. In his Freudian Marxist approach, Fromm came to emphasize more and more the increasing alienation experienced by people in the twentieth century. He decried the growing materialism of Western society, the ability of capitalism to penetrate practically every level of human interaction, and, in the face of these developments, the increasing irrelevance of a bureaucratized psychoanalytic movement.

Fromm's writings continue to be of interest to anyone studying the relationship between individual personality and society. His attempt to synthesize psychoanalytic theory and materialist theory contributed to the development of a major component of the work of the Frankfurt School. While main-taining this focus, his later writings emphasized the need to reestablish the human powers of love and reason in a genuine "relatedness" among people.

James Moran

See also Frankfurt School; Freud, Sigmund; Marx, Karl; Psychoanalysis; Sociology

References

Burston, D. *The Legacy of Erich Fromm.* Cambridge, MA: Harvard University Press, 1991.

Fromm, E. *The Anatomy of Human Destructiveness.* Greenwich, CT: Fawcett Premier Books, 1973.

———. *The Art of Loving.* New York, NY: Bantam Books, 1970.

———. *Beyond the Chains of Illusion: My Encounter with Marx and Freud.* New York, NY: Simon and Schuster, 1962.

———. *The Crisis of Psychoanalysis: Essays on Freud, Marx, and Social Psychology.* Greenwich, CT: Fawcett Premier Books, 1970.

———. *Escape from Freedom.* New York, NY: Avon Books, 1965.

———. *Man for Himself.* Greenwich, CT: Fawcett Premier Books, 1947.

———. *Marx's Concept of Man.* New York, NY: Frederick Ungar, 1961.

———. *The Sane Society.* Greenwich, CT: Fawcett Premier Books, 1955.

———. *Sigmund Freud's Mission: An Analysis of His Personality and Influence.* New York, NY: Harper and Row, 1972.

Fuchs, Anke (1937–)

This Social Democratic Party (SPD) official was born July 5, 1937, in Hamburg. The daughter of the city's mayor, Paul Nevermann, Anke Fuchs grew up in a family with a strong Social Democratic tradition. Her brother, Knut Nevermann, became a well-known politician in the APO (extra-parliamentary opposition). She joined the SPD youth organization, The Falcons, while attending school and became a member of the SPD in 1956, shortly before her graduation. She studied jurisprudence and wrote examinations of the highest quality.

In 1964, Anke Fuchs began to work in various trade unions (e.g., the German Trade Union Federation [DGB] and IGMetall). In 1971, she became a member of the Hamburg state legislature. She was primarily interested in the rights and equal treatment of workers and employees—especially of female workers and employees. In 1977, the federal minister for labor and social policy, Herbert Ehrenberg, made her his secretary for insurance, health, and rehabilitation, and later she was also responsible for the Department of Labor's market policy and unemployment benefits.

In 1979, she became a member of the SPD executive (*Vorstand*), and in 1980 she successfully ran for the Bundestag. Chancellor Helmut Schmidt (1913–) made her his minister for youth, family, and health. After the demise of the Schmidt-Genscher coalition government she remained in the Bundestag and made a name for herself as a resolute speaker for the opposition on all social-policy matters. Since 1987, she has been the general secretary of the Social Democratic Party, responsible for party policy and election programs.

Sabine Hering

See also Schmidt, Helmut; Social Democratic Party; Trade Unions, 1945–90

References

Besters, Hans and Anke Fuchs, eds. *Bevölkerungspolitik und Generationenvertrag.* Baden-Baden: Nomos-Verlagsgesellschaft, 1980.

Farthmann, Friedhelm and Anke Fuchs, eds. *Landesforum Schichtarbeit.* Recklinghausen: Verlag Neue Gesellschaft, 1979.

Fuchs, Anke. *Mut zur Macht: Selbsterfahrung in der Politik.* Hamburg: Hoffmann & Campe, 1991.

Fuchs, Anke and Herbert Ehrenberg. *Sozialstaat und Freiheit.* Frankfurt am Main: Suhrkamp, 1981.

Funk, Walther (1890–1960)

Walther Funk was a minor functionary of the Nazi Party until he was suddenly promoted into the limelight in 1938 as minister of economics to succeed Hjalmar Schacht (1877–1970). In January 1939, he was also appointed head of the Reichsbank. Throughout the war, he was the senior civilian minister responsible for German economic affairs.

Funk was born in Trakehnen, East Prussia, into a family of businessmen. He attended the University of Berlin, was drafted into the army in 1916 but discharged on grounds of ill health, and became a journalist on the business newspaper *Berliner Börsenzeitung* (Berlin financial paper). Between 1922 and 1932 he was the paper's editor. His strong economic nationalism and fierce anti-Marxism drew him toward the radical right. In 1931, his contacts with Gregor Strasser (1892–1934) led him to join the Nazis, and in 1932 he became Strasser's economic adviser, strongly favoring a domestically induced economic revival through public works. With Strasser's fall from grace in December 1932, Funk became a private economic advisor to Hitler.

In March 1933, Funk was appointed press chief for the Hitler government and under secretary of state in Joseph Goebbels's (1897–1945) Propaganda Ministry. Although his homosexuality and his heavy drinking habit were well known, he was chosen to succeed Schacht as minister of economics. His appointment allowed Hermann Göring (1893–1946), as head of the Four-Year Plan, to dominate the Economics Ministry. Funk was appointed plenipotentiary for war economy in 1939, a role where he was again under Göring's close influence. In January 1939, Funk was chosen to succeed Schacht as head of the Reichsbank.

Funk enjoyed wide economic responsibilities, but he relied heavily on the help of his professional subordinates in the ministry and at the Reichsbank. He was unhappy about state intervention in the economy, but during his period of office a virtual command economy was established. He disliked Party interference in economic affairs, but in 1942 he had to accept the right of the Party regional economic offices to oversee much regional economic and industrial policy. He did favor the creation of a larger, German-dominated economic bloc in Europe and was a prominent champion of the New Order brought about by German victories. His weak personality, poor health, and administrative indolence contributed to the ineffective mobilization of the German civilian economy between 1939 and 1942. Although Albert Speer (1905–81) invited Funk to be a member of the new Central Planning Board in March 1942, his responsibilities in the economic field dwindled as power passed to special commissioners and plenipotentiaries.

Funk was arrested at the end of the war and indicted at the main Nuremberg Tribunal. As president of the Reichsbank he had authorized special accounts to hold the gold and valuables seized from Europe's Jewish populations. He was found guilty of crimes against peace and against humanity and sentenced to life imprisonment. Released in poor health in 1957, he died in Düsseldorf on May 31, 1960.

Richard J. Overy

See also Banking; Four-Year Plan; Goebbels, Joseph; Göring, Hermann; Nuremberg Trials; Schacht, Hjalmar; State and Economy; Strasser, Gregor; Third Reich: Propaganda and Culture

References

Boelcke, Willi A. *Die deutsche Wirtschaft 1930–1945: Interna des Reichswirtschaftsministeriums.* Düsseldorf: Droste Verlag, 1983.

———. *Die Kosten von Hitlers Krieg.* Paderborn: Ferdinand Schöningh, 1985.

Overy, Richard J. *Goering: The "Iron Man."* London: Collins, 1976.

Fürstenberg, Carl (1850–1933)

Carl Fürstenberg was a major financier in the Imperial period, the decisive force in one of the largest Berlin banks, the Berliner Handels-Gesellschaft. He was active in international high finance, as well as in the financing of German industry.

Born the son of a Jewish merchant in Danzig, Fürstenberg received an elementary-school (*Volksschule*) education. In 1868, after a commercial apprenticeship, he left Danzig for Berlin, where he worked his way up to the pinnacle of the banking world. In 1883, he became a top executive of the Berliner Handels-Gesellschaft.

Fürstenberg did much to expand the scope of the bank's activities abroad. Before World War I, he negotiated loans for Austria-Hungary, Italy, and Serbia. When the Serbian government fell behind in loan payments, he helped to reorganize Serbian finances. In cooperation with financial circles in Vienna and Paris, he expanded his bank's financial dealings in the Balkans, particularly through trading in government bonds. Thanks to his efforts, his institution was named "Imperial Russian banker" and was put in charge of a part of Russian state finances (1890). He saw the German government's decision to cut off loans to Russia at the turn of the century as a serious mistake. He tried to pursue financial relations with Russia until 1914.

After the Treaty of Rapallo (1922), Fürstenberg became the first Western banker to provide the Soviet Union with large loans. He participated in the founding of several firms abroad, including the Banca Commerciale Italiana of Milan, and had extensive business dealings abroad. With the onset of the Great Depression, these international connections were largely severed.

Fürstenberg's activities in Germany were also of considerable importance. His bank participated in the development of Berlin. He played a major role in the financing of industry (particularly heavy industry and shipbuilding), and he sat on the boards of many of the corporations in which his bank owned an interest, including AEG, while eschewing the role of "amateur industrialist," i.e., participating only as a financial but not an industrial advisor.

Possessing the full confidence of the owners, Fürstenberg was largely responsible for the tremendous financial successes of the Berliner Handels-Gesellschaft, which he organized as a centralized institution without branch offices. More importantly, he played a major role in the financing of industry in Germany and abroad, contributing to the fruitful cooperative relationship between industry and banking. A businessman through and through, he shied away from political activity of any kind. Fürstenberg's memoirs, ghost-written by his son, Hans Fürstenberg, contain a comprehensive picture of the business world and high society in Wilhelmine Germany.

Dolores L. Augustine

See also AEG AG; Banking; Jews, 1869–1933; Rapallo, Treaty of; State and Economy

References

Augustine, Dolores L. *Patricians and Parvenus: Wealthy Business Families in Wilhelmine Germany.* Oxford: Berg Publishers, 1994.

Fürstenberg, Carl. *Die Lebensgeschichte eines deutschen Bankiers, 1870–1914.* Berlin: Ullstein Verlag, 1931.

Fürstenberg, Hans. *Erinnerungen: Mein Weg als Bankier und Carl Fürstenbergs Ältersjahre.* Düsseldorf : Econ-Verlag, 1968.

Mosse, Werner. *The German-Jewish Economic Elite, 1820–1935: A Socio-Cultural Profile.* New York, NY: Oxford University Press, 1989.

Furtwängler, Wilhelm (1886–1954)

An eminent conductor, Gustav Heinrich Ernst Martin Wilhelm Furtwängler had long-term positions with such orchestras as the Berlin Philharmonic, Vienna Philharmonic, and Leipzig Gewandhaus and made guest appearances with the New York Philharmonic, the Philharmonia Orchestra of London, and at Covent Garden, among many others. Furtwängler's reputation has been clouded by what appears to be an ambivalent attitude toward the Nazi governments of the 1930s and 1940s. Nevertheless, his legacy as conductor, as Romantic interpreter of the nineteenth-century German masters, remains unchallenged. He also composed orchestral and chamber music (above all, three symphonies) and published five books (largely autobiographical), the most important of which is *Gespräche über Musik* (Concerning music), 1949.

Furtwängler's training was initially in composition (under Beer-Walbrunn, Rheinberger, and Schillings) and piano (under Ansorge). Financial and artistic needs led him after 1908 to pursue a career in conducting, which followed the normal apprenticeship: rehearsal conductor, two years as repetiteur (assistant conductor) in Munich, a year as third conductor (Strassburg), four years as conductor of a small orchestra (Lübeck), and five years at the head of a larger opera orchestra (Mannheim). By the end of this period (1920), he had emerged as a leading young talent, and thus in 1922 received a call to Berlin, as successor to Nikisch at the Gewandhaus and the Berlin Philharmonic. The latter orchestra would serve as a home base throughout the rest of Furtwängler's career.

Nazi interference in orchestral matters caused Furtwängler to resign all of his posts in 1934, but he was eventually convinced not to give up his profession altogether and continued to conduct throughout the war years in Germany and Austria. Furtwängler's failure to take more decisive steps to reject the Nazi government had to do with a deeply rooted love for his German homeland and a total immersion in the world of art. He did escape to Switzerland in January of 1945, but he returned to Germany in 1946 and was cleared of collaboration charges by the Allies. While he resumed his former conducting activities in Germany in 1947, sympathies were against Furtwängler in the United States—he was required to withdraw from the competition for music director of the Chicago Symphony Orchestra in 1949. His last years were marked by deafness and other health-related problems, but they also brought forth definitive recordings of such works as Wagner's *Tristan und Isolde* and *Die Walküre* and symphonies by Brahms, Bruckner, and Schumann.

Some musicians call Furtwängler the most important German conductor of the first half of the twentieth century. He certainly entered into the spirit of the German Romantic repertory better than any other conductor of his day. Such technical elements as the impreciseness of beat and the spontaneity of tempi are but contributing factors to the mysticism that Furtwängler brought to the experience of conducting the beloved masterpieces of the late eighteenth, nineteenth, and early twentieth centuries.

James Deaville

See also Conductors; Karajan, Herbert von; National Socialist Germany; Orchestras

References

Gillis, Daniel, ed. *Furtwängler Recalled.* Zürich: Artemis Verlag, 1965.

Olsen, Henning Smidth. *Wilhelm Furtwängler: A Discography*. Copenhagen: Nationaldiskotheket, 1970.

Schonzeler, Hans-Hubert. *Furtwängler*. London: Duckworth, 1990.

Shirakawa, Sam H. *The Devil's Music Master: The Controversial Life and Career of Wilhelm Furtwängler*. New York, NY: Oxford University Press, 1992.

Wessling, Berndt W. *Furtwängler: Eine kritische Biographie*. Stuttgart: Deutsche Verlags-Anstalt, 1985.

G

Gadamer, Hans-Georg (1900–)

Hans-Georg Gadamer, an accomplished scholar and historian of philosophy, particularly ancient philosophy and German idealism, is best known for his original contributions to philosophical hermeneutics. Technically, hermeneutics has to do with methods and procedures for the interpretation of texts. More broadly, hermeneutical theories address the relations between text and reader, the cultural factors that shape textual interpretation, and the function of language in the formation of worldviews. With Gadamer's work, particularly his seminal *Wahrheit und Methode* (published as *Truth and Method*), 1960, hermeneutics is refined into a full-scale analysis of the role of traditions and cultural forms in the ongoing process of human self-understanding.

One of the main themes of *Truth and Method* is the historical and cultural grounding of human reason. Reason, particularly as applied to humanistic and ethical issues, is not simply a universal and value-neutral tool. Rather, reason works within formats shaped by cultural attitudes and traditions. On the negative side, this means that the individual use of reason is informed by interpretative structures that may bias one's orientation—part of the task of philosophical hermeneutics is to disclose these structures so that they can be subjected to critique and transformation. On the positive side, Gadamer argues that cultural forms provide the basis for thought, i.e., that reason develops in a dialogical relation with the insights of cultural heritages. Gadamer employs the expression *Horizontverschmelzung* (fusion of horizons) to describe the critical and dialogical encounter between reader and text or tradition in which new insights emerge. This fusion can also be understood as a meeting of past and present, since the interpreter will be shaped by contemporary attitudes that may be revealed and interrogated in the encounter with the format opened by the cultural world of the text.

Gadamer's dialogical model of understanding, as indicated in his description of the text as a "Thou" that can challenge us as we seek to understand it, has explicitly ethical connotations. Dialogue involves awakening us to the distort-

Hans-Georg Gadamer. Courtesy of German Information Center, New York.

ing biases that shape our worldviews and hence our attitudes to others. It reveals that self-knowledge depends on an openness to others and a capacity to listen to alternative views.

Gadamer emphasizes the role of renewed appropriations of cultural history in the task of promoting human understanding. He indicates not only the need for the preservation of traditions but also for their continued interrogation. By demonstrating that the past lives only through the present, and that it is distorted in any rigid appropriation, Gadamer provides us with tools to differentiate between nurturing our cultural heritage and some of the more problematic aspects of, for example, nationalism. Our groundedness in traditions that provide symbolic and conceptual models is a source of experiential richness and potential wisdom, what Gadamer terms a *sensus communis*. However, Gadamer argues, we are historically formed beings who live in a continually changing, pluralistic world. The static and exclusive appropriation of tradition, often found in nationalism, denies the pluralism of human historical existence and abrogates creative dialogue.

James DiCenso

See also History; Human Sciences; *Kultur*; Philosophy; Understanding

References
DiCenso, James. *Hermeneutics and the Disclosure of Truth: A Study in the Work of Heidegger, Gadamer, and Ricoeur*. Charlottesville, VA: University of Virginia Press, 1990.

Warnke, Georgia. *Gadamer: Hermeneutics, Tradition, and Reason*. Palo Alto, CA: Stanford University Press, 1987.

Weinsheimer, Joel. *Gadamer's Hermeneutics*. New Haven, CT: Yale University Press, 1985.

Galen, Clemens August von (1878–1946)

Famed in his lifetime as "The Lion of Münster" for his public protests against Nazi crimes, Cardinal Galen possessed courage that "consoled and upheld millions of Germans, thus saving the honor of the German people" (from the grant of the Freedom of the City of Münster to its bishop and newly created cardinal, March 15, 1946).

Clemens Galen was born on March 16, 1878, the eleventh of thirteen children of Westphalian Catholic aristocrats (he inherited the title of count). After theological studies in Freiburg, Innsbruck, and Münster, he was ordained a priest on May 28, 1904. For three decades he worked as a parish priest in Münster and Berlin.

A conservative nineteenth-century patriot with patriarchal social views, Galen mistrusted the Weimar Republic (founded, he believed, on the legendary "stab in the back" of November 1918) and the Center Party. His simple faith and childlike piety had little room for postwar Catholic renewal efforts such as the liturgical and youth movements. His appointment as bishop of Münster on September 5, 1933, which was greeted with astonishment and skepticism by political Catholics, was probably due to the hope of cooperation with the regime which, in the Concordat of July 20, 1933, had pledged to respect church rights. Uniformed Nazis with swastika flags attended Galen's consecration in Münster on October 28, 1933.

The honeymoon was brief. In 1934, the *Gauleiter* (regional director) of Oldenburg complained that Galen's Lenten pastoral manifested "hatred of National Socialism in every sentence." Numerous protests against Nazi lawlessness followed, culminating in three famous sermons preached in July and August 1941 fiercely denouncing the "euthanasia" of the mentally ill. Underground copies circulated immediately throughout Germany and were dropped from the air by Allied planes.

Postwar research has disclosed that Galen was restrained from denouncing the persecution of the Jews by Jewish leaders in Münster, who feared reprisals. From 1936 he reckoned with arrest, after 1941 with martyrdom. Nazi documents record the decision to hang Galen after "final victory."

In March 1946, Pope Pius XII, who during the war had privately commended Galen for his courage, made him a cardinal, together with his fellow bishops Frings of Cologne and Preysing (Galen's cousin) of Berlin.

A patriot to the end, Galen had publicly branded the entry of British troops into Münster "a day of shame for our city." After the war he denounced the British occupation authorities for inhumanity. On March 22, 1946, death spared him further confrontation with a world that had he could not understand.

John Jay Hughes

See also Catholicism, Political; Center Party; Euthanasia; National Socialist Germany; Racism; Resistance; Roman Catholic Church; Vatican-German Relations

References
Buscher, F.M. and M. Phayer. "German Catholic Bishops and the Holocaust." *German Studies Review* 11 (October 1988), 463–85.

Conway, John S. *The Nazi Persecution of the Churches*. London: Weidenfeld and Nicholson, 1968.

Conzemius, V. "Pius XII and Nazi Germany." *Historical Studies* 7 (1969), 97–124, esp. 115 and 121.

Helmreich, E.C. *The German Churches under Hitler*. Detroit, MI: Wayne State University Press, 1979.

Portmann, H. *Cardinal von Galen*. Trans. R.L. Segwick. London: Jarrolds, 1957.

Gardens and Landscape Architecture

German concepts about garden design have often reflected political attitudes. Recent designs have shown evidence of democratic and modern ideas about gardens and society as well as nationalistic and racist thinking in the field of landscape architecture.

During the nineteenth century the imitation of the English landscape garden on a small scale was a main characteristic of garden design in Germany. This was exemplified in books such as Carl Ritter's *Schlüssel zur praktischen Gartenkunst* (Key to practical garden design), 1836. As a result of industrialization and economic prosperity after the foundation of the German Empire in 1871, an increasing demand for villa gardens emerged. The English landscape garden, a model for the middle-class house garden, did not correspond to this interest in gardens that were to serve various outdoor social activities. Influenced by the English arts and crafts movement, a new formal garden aesthetic emerged. The garden itself was defined as an extension of the housing space. The architect Hermann Muthesius (1861–1927) and landscape architects such as Friedrich Bauer (1872–1937) and Hermann Koenig (1883–1961) were prominent proponents of formal garden design.

During the Weimar Republic, the dialogue on the future of garden design gained a more democratic quality. Landscape architects such as Georg Bela Pniower (1896–1960), Leberecht Migge (1881–1935), and Hans Friedrich Pohlenz designed gardens that corresponded to the social, economic, and aesthetic needs of their middle-class clients. They also experimented with modernist and avant-garde expressions in gardens.

Nationalistic trends influenced, from the very outset, the search for new concepts in garden design. Imperial Germany's push for a position of world power, and national pride among the bourgeoisie, found expression in garden design. Landscape architects began to devise a "German" garden that could be distinguished from the gardens of other peoples. The book *Deutsche Gartenkunst* (German garden design), 1902, by Carl Hampel, exemplified this thinking. Gardens designed for exhibitions and professional competitions were often designated as "Der Deutsche Garten." For over 20 years, starting in 1900, the landscape architect Willy Lange (1864–1941) developed an elaborate ideological basis for such a nationalistic, "truly" German garden design—the natural garden. Lange's ideas were based on the assertion that close connections exist between nature, landscapes, and the German people. His concepts of natural gardens, as well as those of his followers, were attempts to fight modern and international trends. With his article "Garten und Weltanschauung" (Garden and worldview), published in the magazine *Gartenwelt* in 1904, Lange vehemently rejected the idea that "art could be international." In an influential book, *Gartengestaltung der Neuzeit* (Contemporary garden design), 1907, Lange stated the need for "German nature that must provide all ideas for the design of gardens."

After 1933 landscape architects such as Alwin Seifert (1899–1972) and Hans Hasler (1896–1976), the latter with his book also named *Deutsche Gartenkunst,* 1939, turned concepts of natural garden design into a doctrine in accordance with the Nazi ideology of "blood and soil." Articles such as "Plant Sociology and the Blood and Soil Rooted Garden," published in 1936 by Albert Krämer in the magazine *Gartenkunst,* provide evidence of Nazi ideas about gardens. All discussions about alternative trends in garden design ended. Progressive landscape architects such as Pniower, who had promoted modern and democratic garden ideas, were forbidden to practice.

German postwar garden design was marked by mediocrity; it was dominated by those landscape architects who had made their career during the Nazi period.

Gert Gröning

See also Architecture; Bourgeoisie; Country Life; National Socialism; Parks, Public; Zoological Gardens

References

Allinger, Gustav. *Der deutsche Garten: Sein Wesen und seine Schönheit in alter und neuer Zeit.* Munich: F. Bruckmann, 1950.

Gröning, Gert and Joachim Wolschke-Bulmahn. *1887–1987: DGGK, Deutsche Gesellschaft für Gartenkunst: Ein Rückblick auf 100 Jahre DGGK.* Berlin: Boskett Verlag, 1987.

Wolschke-Bulmann, Joachim. "'The Peculiar Garden'— The Advent and the Destruction of Modernism in German Garden Design." *Masters of American Garden Design: The Modern Garden in Europe and the United States.* Ed. Robin Karson. New York, NY: Garden Conservancy, 1994.

Wolschke-Bulmann, Joachim and Gert Gröning. "The Ideology of the Nature Garden. Nationalistic Trends in Garden Design in Germany During the Early Twentieth Century." *Journal of Garden History* 12 (1992), 73–81.

Gehlen, Arnold (1904–76)

Arnold Gehlen was a philosopher and sociologist. In his most influential work, *Mensch, seine Natur und seine Stellung in der Welt* (published as *Man: His Nature and Place in the World*), 1940, Gehlen argues that humans are by nature agents, neither metaphysically nor biologically determined; they are creators of culture. Gehlen's writings focus on the institutions constructed by human beings in their attempt to counteract the relative lack of instinctual endowment that would guide their conduct. Gehlen regarded institutions as essential for stable and predictable social conduct. Among Gehlen's other important works are *Urmensch und Spätkultur* (Early humans and recent culture), 1956, *Seele im technischen Zeitalter* (published as *Man in the Age of Technology*), 1957, and *Moral und Hypermoral* (Morality and hypermorality), 1965.

Gehlen studied philosophy, art history, and German philology in Cologne and Leipzig, where he was the assistant of the sociologist Hans Freyer (1887–1969). He became a professor at the University of Königsberg (1938) and at the University of Vienna (1940). After World War II, Gehlen taught at Speyer and at the Technical University of Aachen. He was awarded the Konrad Adenauer Prize in 1971.

Gehlen's "philosophical anthropology" interrelates biological, cultural, and philosophical aspects of human nature. The sociological and social-psychological writings of his last decades focus on problems of industrial society and modern culture. Modern societies represent a new stage in the emergence of human historical cultures, one that is beyond the grasp of a theory such as the Marxian attempt to combine an all-encompassing theory of society with a political action program. Gehlen sought a sober acknowledgement of the facts of modern culture by those actively participating in the organization of public and corporate power. Modern social institutions should be appraised realistically, he argued, and policies must be designed on this background.

Gehlen had an enormous respect for technology and industry as collective achievements of modern society. He used the term "cultural crystallization" (borrowed from Pareto) in order to identify the situation of modernity as *post-histoire.* This situation arises when all the possibilities inherent in a cultural domain have been developed, so that changes in their basic elements, in their premises and fundamental ideas, become increasingly unlikely—modernity no longer possesses the cultural capacity to produce global ideologies or world views. Gehlen's philosophical anthropology was developed in a sociological direction in the work of Niklas Luhmann.

Volker Meja

See also Anthropology; Freyer, Hans; Philosophy; Sociology; Technology

References

Fonk, P. *Transformation der Dialektik: Grundzüge der Philosophie Arnold Gehlens.* Würzburg: Königshausen und Neumann, 1983.

Gehlen, Arnold. *Gesamtausgabe.* 4 vols. Ed. L. Samson and K.S. Rehberg. Frankfurt am Main: Klostermann, 1978 *ff.*

———. *Man: His Nature and Place in the World.* New York, NY: Columbia University Press, 1988 [1940].

———. *Man in the Age of Technology.* New York, NY: Columbia University Press, 1980 [1957].

———. *Moral und Hypermoral.* Frankfurt am Main: Athenäum, 1969.

———. *Studien zur Anthropologie und Soziologie.* Neuwied: Luchterhand, 1963.

———. *Urmensch und Spätkultur.* Frankfurt am Main: Athenäum, 1956.

Samson, L. *Naturteleologie und Freiheit bei Arnold Gehlen. Systematisch-historische Untersuchungen.* Freiburg: Alber, 1976.

Genscher, Hans-Dietrich (1927–)

On his retirement as cabinet minister in May 1992, Hans-Dietrich Genscher could look back on a remarkable record as government member and party politician in the Federal Republic. It included eighteen years as foreign minister (1974–1992) and five years as interior minister (1969–1974). He had been leader of the Free Democratic Party (FDP) during an unusually challenging decade (1974–85), and he continued to be widely regarded as its most important and popular politician.

Genscher played a major and, at first, controversial role in the relaxation of Western policy toward the Soviet Union in the 1980s. He early emphasized the need to establish non-military and cooperative security structures between East and West. While he did not anticipate the developments that led to the rapid unification of Germany, his security approach undoubtedly made it easier for Mikhail Gorbachev to abandon the Brezhnev Doctrine.

Genscher was born in 1927 near Halle. He served briefly in the military and returned home to what had become the Soviet occupation zone. He studied law in East Germany before fleeing to the West in 1952. After completing his legal training, he embarked on a career in the FDP. He rose quickly to become federal party manager, then was elected to the Bundestag in 1965. Here he became parliamentary whip and joined the reformers around Walter Scheel.

When the FDP entered a government coalition with the Social Democrats (SPD) in 1969, Interior Minister Genscher soon acquired a reputation as problem-solver

rather than reformer. His most demanding task became finding measures against the wave of political terrorism by left-wing extremists.

Genscher had little preparation for the Foreign Office, which he took over from Scheel in 1974. Initially, he was overshadowed by Chancellor Helmut Schmidt (1913–), but Genscher rapidly gained a solid grasp of foreign affairs. He supported Schmidt's "mini-detente" toward Eastern Europe as well as the controversial "dual track" decision to station intermediate range nuclear forces in West Germany in response to a previous Soviet build-up in the East.

In 1982 Genscher led his party out of its long partnership with the SPD and into a new government coalition with the Christian Democrats under Chancellor Helmut Kohl. Although widely accused of political betrayal, Genscher eventually became a symbol of continuity and moderation in foreign policy. This may well have saved his party, but when the FDP was tainted by a political finance scandal (the Flick Affair), Genscher stepped down as party leader in early 1985. This fortuitous decision left him free to concentrate on foreign policy just as Gorbachev emerged as a reformist Soviet leader.

Genscher's international reputation came primarily from his direction of Bonn's foreign policy after the mid-1980s. At least until reunification, Chancellor Kohl interfered only rarely with Genscher's strategy of providing support for evolutionary change in Eastern Europe. When the Soviet Bloc began to crumble rapidly in 1989, Genscher was caught by surprise.

Hans-Dietrich Genscher. Courtesy of German Information Center, New York.

Kohl first pushed boldly for reunification, but Genscher played a major role both in working out the international agreements and in reducing the fears of Germany's many neighbors over this major shift in the balance of power.

Reunification was a source of great personal joy for Genscher. He was enormously popular in his East German homeland, and he played a crucial role in his party's excellent performance there in the first all-German Bundestag election in December 1990.

Christian Søe

See also Federal Republic of Germany: Foreign Policy; Free Democratic Party; German-German Relations; Kohl, Helmut; Lambsdorff, Otto; Reunification; Scheel, Walter; Schmidt; Helmut

References

Garton Ash, Timothy. *In Europe's Name: Germany and the Divided Continent.* New York, NY: Random House, 1993.

Genscher, Hans-Dietrich. *Unterwegs zur Einheit: Reden und Dokumente aus bewegter Zeit.* Berlin: Siedler, 1991.

Pond, Elizabeth. *Beyond the Wall: Germany's Road to Unification.* Washington, DC: The Brookings Institution, 1993.

Schulze, Helmut R. and Richard Kiessler. *Hans-Dietrich Genscher: Ein deutscher Aussenminister.* Munich: C. Bertelsmann, 1990.

Søe, Christian. "Hans-Dietrich Genscher." *Political Leaders of Contemporary Western Europe.* Ed. David Wilsford. New York, NY: Greenwood Press, 1994.

Szabo, Stephen. *The Diplomacy of German Unification.* New York, NY: St. Martin's, 1992.

Geography (Human)

The decades following the defeat of France and the founding of the German Empire in 1871 witnessed the institutionalization of human geography within the structure of higher and lower education in Germany. At the same time, Germany emerged as one of the leaders of geographical science internationally. The strong interest in human geography related to national and political as well as purely academic concerns. Geography's involvement in extra-academic issues became increasingly clear after 1918 and, especially, 1933. The defeat in 1945 acted as a caesura of sorts, allowing a rethinking and reorientation of research and giving German geographers the opportunity to build their discipline once again.

The reorganization of education in Germany that took place during the Empire proved remarkably salutary for the discipline of geography. While prior to 1874 the subject had been taught at only three universities, the government in Berlin resolved in that year that geography was to be represented at each Prussian university. Within a decade, 15 new chairs had been established across the country. This dramatic expansion in higher education was matched by the broad introduction of geography into the curriculum of grammar schools and high schools. Such unprecedented interest in this heretofore rather unfamiliar subject was stimulated by a number of factors. Not least of these was the Franco-Prussian War itself, which had demonstrated the usefulness of general geographical knowledge and in particular an appreciation of cartography. Equally important, however, was the nationalist *Bildungswert* (educational value) that the government and influential educators perceived in the discipline, for geography was seen by many as an ideal way to teach national values. On the one hand, it would train German youth in *Heimatkunde* (civics), through which they would learn to know and value their fatherland, while on the other it would provide a perspective to help them appreciate their country's increasingly important international position as a world power.

As this institutionalization was taking place, human geography was being intellectually and methodologically recast. The inspiration for this came above all from Friedrich Ratzel (1844–1904). Ratzel, whose training was in zoology, had been heavily influenced by German Darwinists such as Ernst Haeckel (1834–1919) and Moritz Wagner, and made it his life's work to apply the insights he took from them to the study of human society. The resulting perspective he called "human geography," or *Anthropogeographie.* The focus of this new discipline—the complex pattern of interactive relationships between human (*Mensch*) and society (*Gesellschaft*) on one hand and Earth (*Erde*) on the other—had been apparent in the work of Ratzel's geographical predecessors, most notably Carl Ritter and Alexander von Humboldt. What was new was that Ratzel discarded their teleological Romanticism and turned instead to the concepts and methods of the evolutionary natural sciences, in order to make the study of human geography rigorously scientific.

The subsequent development of Ratzel's *Anthropogeographie* directed research into two general arenas. This remained characteristic of German geography down to 1945. One area, *Länderkunde* or regional geography, examined the manner in which the interaction between physical milieu and human culture operated to parcel the earth's surface into discrete regions. The great methodologist of this approach was Ratzel's student Alfred Hettner. The scale of investigation could vary, and included studies on virtually every major part of the globe, the European continent, and finally the greater German culture area itself. In regard to the latter, Joseph Partsch and Hugo Hassinger in particular made important geographical contributions to the emerging vision of *Mitteleuropa* (a unified central Europe).

The study of world regions was an important part of so-called *Kolonialgeographie* (colonial geography), which in turn represented a major area of geography's involvement in national political life before 1918. Virtually every major academic geographer had considerable field experience in Latin America, Africa, or Asia, which put them in a unique position to publicize and explain to their countrymen the national importance of these unfamiliar regions. Moreover, geographers were active in the colonial movement not only as scholars but organizationally as well, playing major roles in colonial advocacy leagues such as the Gesellschaft zur Erforschung

Zentralafrikas (Society for Research on Central Africa; F. von Richthofen), or the Kolonialverein (Colonial Society; F. Ratzel, T. Fischer, A. Kirchhoff).

The second focus in German *Anthropogeographie* was *Kulturgeographie,* or cultural geography. The object of study here was the *Kulturlandschaft,* or cultural landscape, which was formed through prolonged human habitation in a given natural environment. Village patterns, house structures, field types, crop and other vegetational patterns, and communication routes were all part of the distinctive stamp or imprint of a culture on its milieu; in effect, this imprint became a material artifact of the culture. Among the outstanding pioneers of German cultural geography were A. Meizen, R. Gradmann and O. Schluter, all of whom made major contributions to the historical reconstruction of the European and German *Kulturlandschaft.*

The strongly patriotic and *völkisch* (racist) interest that underlay this work was muted in the period before World War I, but became more direct and emphatic during the 1920s. This was particularly apparent in the notion of *Volks- und Kulturboden* (race and cultural basis) formulated by A. Penck and N. Krebs. As part of the post-Versailles disputes about Germany's proper national boundaries, Penck used the evidence of historical-cultural landscapes to argue that areas could be German "cultural territories" (and therefore legitimately German land) even if they were not presently inhabited by ethnically German population. And, in a display of chauvinistic *völkisch* nationalism, the Hamburg geographer Siegfried Passarge argued for the relevance of landscape science to radical anti-Semitism with a study of *Das Judentum als landschaftskündlich-ethnologisches Problem* (Jewishness as a geographic and ethnological problem), 1929.

In a rather different direction, a novel research interest in economic geography emerged in the 1920s in the work of W. Credner, A. Ruhl, L. Waibel, and others. On the one hand, they attempted to apply the traditional notion of geographical regions to economic activities and organization, leading to Waibel's concept of the *Wirtschaftsformation* (economic formation). Along with this, however, went a new interest in so-called location theory, in other words the spatial expression of economic and social activities. The culminating contribution in this field was W. Christaller's celebrated "central-place theory," first proposed in the early 1930s and remaining still today as one of the outstanding theoretical contributions to geographical science in the twentieth century. The implications of Christaller's work for regional planning were immediately appreciated—not least by the Nazi government, which set Christaller and others to work after 1939 planning for new settlement patterns in the occupied territories of Poland and Ukraine in anticipation of German settlement of the region.

The year 1945 was a catharsis for German geography, as for many other academic disciplines. While the postwar period by no means saw a decline in geographical science in Germany, there was a very fundamental reorientation. The deemphasis of those elements that had operated in some way in the penumbra of *völkisch* and/or nationalist inspiration resulted in a general decline in *Anthropogeographie* and *Kulturgeographie,* and in cultural landscape studies in particular. The previously strong links between geography and *Heimatkunde* were played down, and for the first time geography in Germany began to be strongly influenced by developments in other countries, in particular Great Britain, France, and the United States. From the 1950s through the 1970s, the main direction of these influences was toward the transformation of geography into a nomothetic social science, in effect a science of spatial relations that was distinctly positivist and quantitative. As well, entirely new sub-fields of study appeared, including social geography and population geography. Thanks to the connections between Karl Haushofer's *Geopolitik* and certain elements of the Nazi movement—highly overrated after the war but notorious nonetheless—political geography went into a marked decline after the war. It has undergone a renaissance of sorts in recent years, as it has tended to focus on local issues and electoral geography rather than international relations.

Mark Bassin

See also Anthropology; Anti-Semitism; *Bildung und Bildungsbürgertum;* Colonies and Colonial Society; Geology; Geopolitics; Haeckel, Ernst; *Heimat;* Imperialism; National Identity; National Socialism; Nationalism; Political Cartography; Ratzel, Friedrich; Universities; *Völkisch* Ideology

References

Bassin, Mark. "Imperialism and the Nation-State in Friedrich Ratzel's Political Geography." *Progress in Human Geography* 11 (1987), 473–495.

Ehlers, Eckart. *40 Years After: German Geography: Developments, Trends, and Prospects 1952–1992.* Bonn: Geographische Institute, 1992.

"Geographie und Nationalsozialismus. 3 Fallstudien." *Urbs et Regio* 51 (1989).

Heske, Henning. *"Und Morgen der ganzen Welt": Erdkundeunterricht im Nationalsozialismus.* Giessen: Focus, 1988.

Roessler, Mechtild. *"Wissenschaft und Lebensraum": Geographische Ostforschung im Nationalsozialismus.* Hamburger Beitraege zur Wissenschaftsgeschichte, vol. 8. Berlin: Dietrich Reimer, 1990.

Schulte-Althoff, Franz-Josef. *Studien zur politischen Wissenschaftsgeschichte der deutschen Geographie im Zeitalter des Imperialismus.* Paderborn: Schöningh, 1971.

Schultz, Hans-Dietrich. *Die deutschsprachige Geographie von 1800 bis 1970: Ein Beitrag zur Geschichte ihrer Methodologie.* Abhandlungen des Geographischen Instituts (Anthropogeographie), vol. 29. Berlin: Selbstverlag des Geographischen Instituts der FU Berlin, 1980.

Troll, Carl. "Geographical Science in Germany during the Period 1933–1945: A Critique and a Justification." *Annals of the Association of American Geographers* 39 (1949), 100–137.

Geology

In 1871, many in Germany still understood geology as the science of collecting petrified curiosities relating to the Earth. Since then, it has become the historical explanation of the origin, development, and nature of the Earth and its proximate cosmic neighborhood. At the beginning of the nineteenth century, some educated Europeans still believed that the Earth had an age of approximately 6,000 years. Now it is believed to be nearly five billion years old, and German scientists contributed to that new understanding.

German contributions to the study of the Earth, its creation, and its changes were especially pronounced during the eighteenth and early nineteenth centuries. During the early twentieth century, a German meteorologist developed the startling theory of plate tectonics to explain the present condition of the Earth's continents by studying their past configuration.

Among the German contributors to geological understanding, Georgius Agricola (1494–1555) has been termed the father of mineralogy, especially for his study *De re metallica*, which illustrated the relationship between ores and geological formations. In the Enlightenment, G.W. Knorr (1705–61) and J.E.I. Walch (1725–78) published *Merkwürdigkeiten der Natur* (Noteworthy traits of nature) and *Naturgeschichte der Versteinerungen* (The natural history of petrification), in keeping with the attempts to classify varieties of rocks as well as relationships in nature. Simultaneously, regional studies defined the geology of German lands, for instance, those by G.C. Füchsel of Thuringia and J.F.W. Charpentier of Saxony. Among the most important of these classifiers was Abraham Gottlob Werner (1749–1817), who became a professor at one of Germany's main institutes of applied geological studies, the Freiburg Mining Academy. In addition to a systematic classification of rocks, he developed the now-discarded theory that all rocks were formed by precipitation from a universal ocean (Neptunism). His disciple Leopold von Buch (1774–1853) and Alexander von Humboldt (1769–1859) disputed Werner's view and favored a perspective in which the interaction of the crystalline crust of the earth and its molten interior shaped the Earth by volcanic action (Plutonism). Humboldt tried to account for all geographic, geological, and biological forms in his *Cosmologie*.

Such attempts at a comprehensive explanation of nature and of the Earth were doomed to failure, because of the limited understanding of processes of change and because of the multitude of rock and fossil discoveries which did not fit with theories of continuity or catastrophe. However, German authors provided some of the most comprehensive descriptive accounts: Hermann Credner (1841–1913), with *Elemente der Geologie* (Elements of geology), 1872, and E. Suess (1831–1914), with *Das Antlitz der Erde* (The face of the earth), 1883.

The development of modern physics and chemistry after 1900 showed the Earth to be a large physical and chemical laboratory. The first geologist to emphasize this was G. Bischof in his *Elemente physikalische und chemische Geologie*, (Textbook of physical and chemical geology), 1854–59. He analyzed especially the weathering of rocks (magmatites, sediments, and metamorphites).

In keeping with the search for a comprehensive explanation, in 1915 the meteorologist Alfred Wegener published *Die Entstehung der Kontinente und Ozeane* (published as *The Origin of Continents and Oceans*). His ideas were based on a convection theory—a molten interior to the Earth with the continents floating as plates on it. His theory was controversial, because it emphasized continents adrift and tried to show how all the continents had been one land mass moving away from the Earth's poles. He lacked a proper mechanism to explain the changes, and because of the anti-German attitudes among many Western scientists during the 1920s, Wegener's theory was originally rejected. Since the 1960s, it has been widely accepted, although some geologists believe that vertical movement (volcanoes, erosion) is more important than drift to explain change.

German scientists made many contributions to hydrology, to geological mapping via zeppelins, to understanding the movement of radium, to regional knowledge of rock formations, and to many other scientific fields. National Socialist pseudo-science undercut the discipline, and it has only slowly regained international contacts and stature since World War II.

Robert Lauterbach

See also Biology; Chemistry, Scientific and Industrial; Physics

References
Credner, H. *Elemente der Geologie*. Leipzig: W. Englemann, 1912.
Geikie, Archibald. *The Founders of Geology*. 2nd ed. New York, NY: Dover Publications, 1962.
Lauterbach, R. *The World of Geology*. Leipzig: Edition Leipzig, 1976.
Schneiderhöhn, H. *Erzlagerstätten*. Jena: G. Fischer, 1962.
Wood, Robert Muir. *The Dark Side of the Earth: The Battle for the Earth Sciences 1800–1980*. London: Allen and Unwin, 1986.
Zittel, Karl Alfred. *History of Geology and Palaeontology*. New York, NY: Hafner Publisher, 1962.

Geopolitics (*Geopolitik*)

The origins of modern German geopolitics are to be found in the work of the geographer Friedrich Ratzel (1844–1904), who in the final two decades of the nineteenth century developed a theory of the political state as an integral geographical "organism." Like biological organisms, the vital needs of the state were determined by fixed natural laws, in accordance with which it both grew and declined. In particular, Ratzel postulated that in order to sustain a natural process of vigorous development and maturation, the state organism needed to be nourished constantly with ever-increasing amounts of territory. To name this need for territory, which he argued human society shared with animal and plant populations, he coined the term *Lebensraum* (living space). Ratzel's ideas on state expansion had taken shape in the context of Wilhelmine Germany's belated move to compete with other Western powers for colonial acquisitions, and thus Germany's vital

Lebensraum was in his view to be found in the non-European world. In the years following his death, Ratzel's rather disparate ideas were organized and systematized in numerous works by the Swedish political scientist Rudolf Kjellén (1846–1922), who christened this new framework *Geopolitik*.

It was only after the trauma of defeat in 1918 and the readjustments of borders at Versailles that Germany's truncated and still-threatened living space became a national preoccupation. Now, however, *Lebensraum* was understood in an exclusively European framework. Due largely to the efforts of the geographer Karl Haushofer (1869–1946), a retired Bavarian general, *Geopolitik* emerged as a popular field for academic study and political debate in the 1920s. Haushofer's widely circulated journal, *Zeitschrift für Geopolitik*, founded in 1924, immediately became a major forum for radical conservative and revanchist sentiment. Well-connected and enormously ambitious, Haushofer promoted his new discipline indefatigably, claiming that the "science" of *Geopolitik* offered a basis on which to formulate national and foreign policy. In effect, *Geopolitik* could serve as a torch to illuminate Germany's way back to territorial integrity, rightful borders, and national well-being. Through Rudolf Hess (1894–1987), a former student of his who had fought under him during the war, Haushofer had some limited access to the upper echelons of the Nazi Party itself. Throughout the 1930s, he made every effort to ingratiate himself with the new regime. After the war much was made by the occupying forces of the alleged influence of Hitler's "geographical wizard."

It would seem, however, that despite all appearances—Hitler's references in *Mein Kampf* to Germany's need for *Lebensraum*, the obvious fact that German foreign policy during the war was indeed founded on this quest, and Haushofer's entirely transparent ambitions that geopolitics should become, as he put it, "das geographische Gewissen des Staats" (the geographic conscience of the state)—his *Geopolitik* nonetheless never exerted any appreciable influence on Nazi doctrine. The Nazis remained implacably hostile to his "geographical-materialist" leanings, which they were (rightly) convinced made him rather less of a pure racist than they demanded. Their suspicions to this effect were merely enhanced by the fact that his wife was half Jewish.

No less importantly, Haushofer's vociferous urging throughout the 1930s of a continental German-Soviet alliance against the maritime powers of Great Britain and North America, inspired by the English geographer Halford Mackinder's "heartland theory," was entirely at odds with the Nazis' deepest intentions to defeat Bolshevism, conquer the Slavic East, and secure their own *Lebensraum* there. For these reasons, Haushofer increasingly fell out of favor after 1933; ultimately some of his works were even banned. Interrogated after 1945 by the occupation forces and convinced (wrongly) that he would be among those charged in the Nuremberg proceedings, he and his wife took their lives together in 1946.

The association of *Geopolitik* with National Socialism ensured a taboo that effectively kept it out of academic geography both in the Federal Republic and the German Democratic Republic (GDR). Only during the last decade has there been a resurgence of interest in "politische Geographie" in the universities, which is however extremely careful to distinguish itself from the organicism and concern for *Lebensraum* of the Ratzelian tradition. On the other hand, the international strategic realignments of the 1980s—most notably the debate over the stationing of middle-range nuclear weapons in Western Europe—made geopolitics a buzzword of sorts in public political discourse in Europe and North America.

This was especially apparent in France (where, in a bizarre twist, translations of Ratzel and Haushofer enjoyed considerable popularity), and there was some evidence of this in West Germany as well. A continuity of sorts, if only symbolic, with pre-1945 *Geopolitik* is suggested by the fact that recent German works along these lines, such as H. Jordis von Lohausen's *Mut zur Macht: Denken in Kontinenten* (Courage regarding power: thinking in continents), 1979, are published by Vowinckel, the same press that Haushofer used.

Mark Bassin

See also Anthropology; Anti-Semitism; Colonies and Colonial Society; Geography (Human); Geology; Haeckel, Ernst; Hess, Rudolf; Imperialism; National Socialism; Nationalism; Ratzel, Friedrich; Universities; *Völkisch* Ideology

References
Bakker, G. *Duitse Geopolitiek 1919–1945: Een imperialistische ideologie.* Assen: Van Gorcum, 1967.

Bassin, Mark. "Race *contra* Space: The Conflict between German *Geopolitik* and National Socialism." *Political Geography Quarterly* 6 (1987), 115–34.

Jacobsen, Hans-Adolf, ed. *Karl Haushofer: Leben und Werk.* 2 vols. Schriften des Bundesarchives, vol. 24. Boppard-am-Rhein: H. Boldt, 1979.

Korinman, Michel. *Quand l'Allemagne pensait le monde: Grandeur et décadence d'une géopolitique.* Paris: Fayard, 1990.

Kost, Klaus. *Die Einflüsse der Geopolitik auf Forschung und Theorie der Politischen Geographie von ihren Anfängen bis 1945.* Bonn: Bonner Geographische Abhandlungen, 1988.

Zoppo, C. and C. Zorgbibe, eds. *On Geopolitics: Classical and Nuclear.* NATO ASI Series D, no. 20. Dordrecht: Martinus Nijhoff, 1985.

George, Stefan (1868–1933)
Stefan George is one of the most important and most controversial modern German poets. After high school he traveled extensively in Italy, France, and Spain. While in Paris, he met Stéphane Mallarmé (1842–98) and began translating Baudelaire and the French symbolists. Back in Germany, he tried to found a circle similar to Mallarmé's Mardis, but failed to persuade Hofmannsthal to collaborate. Later, he joined the Kosmiker-Kreis (Ludwig Klages [1872–1956], Ludwig Derleth [1870–1955], and Karl Wolfskehl [1869–1948]) in Munich and eventually founded his own circle, the George-Kreis (Friedrich Gundolf [1880–1931], Ernst Morwitz

[1887–1971], and the brothers Waldemar [1898–1939] and Bernhard Victor von Uxküll-Gyllenband [1899–1918]). In 1933 he was offered an honorary position in Nazi cultural politics, which he turned down. Despite certain common convictions, George did not become a supporter of the new regime, which he thought populist and vulgar. He moved to Switzerland, where he died in December 1933.

George's poetry is formally strict, reflecting the influence of Baudelaire and the Parnassus tradition rather than the French symbolists. His cycles are tectonically constructed, and form is independent of the content and very regular. His preferred stanza, which consists of four lines with five accents and arses, became known as *George-Strophe*. In his attempt to make poetry as distinct from everyday language as possible, he used obscure and archaic words, neologisms, nominalizations, and elliptical syntax. His punctuation and spelling are idiosyncratic and his elitist approach also manifests itself in the exclusive presentation of his books (special typeface designed by his friend Melchior Lechter [1865–1937], expensive paper, few copies). The symbolist emphasis on the sound quality of words is formalized according to the architecture of the poems rather than their content.

In his early works, *Hymnen* (Hymns), 1890, *Algabal,* 1892, and *Das Jahr der Seele* (The year of the soul), 1897, art is perceived as an orderly, elevated, and safe haven against a vulgar and threateningly chaotic world. In *Algabal* a loss of sense of reality and fertility is acknowledged as the price for this security, which leads to a more positive view of nature in *Das Jahr der Seele*, reflecting the "*Grosse Ja*" (Big yes) of Nietzsche's later philosophy. In his middle years, his poetry became increasingly didactic in tone, as he gathered disciples in a close-knit esoteric circle. In *Der siebente Ring* (The seventh ring), 1907, he ordained himself prophet of the god Maximin, making poetry a quasi-religion. The problems caused by his rather despotic ways with his disciples show clearly in *Der Stern des Bundes* (The star of the Bundes), 1914. In his last cycle, *Das neue Reich* (The new empire), 1928, his tone changed to a more lyrical, less pompous style.

From 1892 to 1919, George published the *Blätter für die Kunst* (Pages for art) as a forum for *Geistige Kunst* (spiritual art), i.e., anti-naturalistic literature. George's translations of poetry from seven languages, among them Dante's *Commedia*, Baudelaire's *Fleurs du mal,* and Shakespeare's sonnets, inspired George's own writing, but they are also of significant literary value in their own right.

Julia Hughes

See also Imperial Germany: Literature; Myth; Nietzsche, Friedrich; Poetry; Symbolism; Weimar Germany: Literature

References

David, Claude. *Stefan George: Sein dichterisches Werk.* Trans. Alexa Remmen and Karl Thiemer. Munich: Hanser, 1967.

George, Stefan. *Sämtliche Werke in 18 Bänden.* Stuttgart: Klett-Cotta, 1982 *ff.*

Landmann, Georg Peter, ed. *Der George-Kreis: Eine Auswahl aus seinen Schriften.* 2nd ed. Stuttgart: Kiepenheuer und Witsch, 1980.

———. *Stefan George und sein Kreis: Eine Bibliographie.* 2nd ed. Hamburg: Hauswedell, 1976.

Schönauer, Franz. *Stefan George.* Romono 44. Reinbek: Rowohlt, 1979.

Winkler, Michael. *George-Kreis.* SM 110. Stuttgart: Metzler, 1972.

———. *Stefan George.* SM 90. Stuttgart: Metzler, 1970.

German Army League (1912–35)

As Imperial Germany flaunted its recently acquired colonial empire and challenged its European rivals for economic primacy, it simultaneously began to flex its military muscles. What the Navy League did to popularize and expand the German fleet, the German Army League (Deutscher Wehrverein) sought to do for the army. Founded in January 1912, the Army League, the last in a series of popular nationalist associations that emerged after 1890, devoted itself to inculcating Germans with the martial spirit and raising their level of national consciousness.

Assisted by a combination of foreign (Agadir, Balkans crisis, French Army Bills) as well as domestic tensions (the rapid expansion of the Social Democrats), the Army League became the second largest of the many ultranationalist groups, with a membership of roughly 350,000 by 1914. The League stressed the importance of the army as the "school of the nation," a community in which theoretically the bonds of military preparedness and sacrifice would supersede the sectionalism of class and religious division. Its leaders, especially its firebrand president, August Keim (1845–1926), used the league as a platform from which to assail the government for its reluctance to expand the army and to improve its efficiency. Justifying the league's objectives by the popular appeal they elicited and by the worrisome military expansion of Germany's European rivals, Keim and his fellow executive members Eduard von Liebert, Karl Litzmann, Dietrich Schäfer, and Kurd von Strantz demanded that the government accept the Army Bills of 1912 and 1913 in their revised versions.

While both bills indeed were passed by the Reichstag, one should not overestimate the league's influence as a popular nationalist phenomenon. By 1913, stagnating membership and delinquent dues signaled the limits of the ultranationalist gospel; the outbreak of World War I and the subsequent rush to the colors only accelerated that trend. With the departure of a number of its leaders for military administration, and with the subsequent attrition of its membership through death and indifference, the Army League barely clung to life by war's end. Its survival until 1935 was more a testimony to the commitment of a diehard few than to the broader resonance of its popular nationalist appeal.

Marilyn Shevin-Coetzee

See also Imperial Germany: Army; Imperial League against Social Democracy; Keim, August; Militarism; Navy League; Pan-German League; Radical Nationalism; Radical Right

References

Shevin-Coetzee, Marilyn. *The German Army League: Popular Nationalism in Wilhelmine Germany.* New York, NY: Oxford University Press, 1990.

German as an International Language

If German served for communication only between Germans and Austrians, or between German-speaking Swiss, then it could hardly be called an international language. A language can only seriously be called international when it is used by native speakers of other languages. If such speakers of different languages are citizens of the same country then the language is interlingual but not really international. Such language use can be asymmetrical (between native speakers and non-native speakers), or it can function as a lingua franca between non-native speakers of different languages.

Following these conceptual distinctions, it is possible to rank languages according to their international use. One would have to record all speech events and language contacts if one wanted to establish an exact classification of the languages according to their degree of internationality. As this is impossible, the examination of segments of language use must suffice, or one must be content with mere indicators of the degree of international use. A reasonably reliable picture arises if various figures are brought together.

A language's degree of internationality is dependent on a multitude of factors. Three of these will be examined here. The spread of a language over different nations enhances its degree of international use. If a language has official status in many countries ("official-status strength") it has at the same time better chances of receiving official status within international organizations. Also, the number of native speakers of a language, its "numerical strength," promotes its international use. The international languages almost always belong to the group of the "big languages" among the roughly 5,000 languages in the world. The "economic strength" of a language, or rather of its language community, is another factor which influences a language's international standing. It is calculated as the gross national product (GNP) of all the native speakers of the language. The size of the market accessible through the language is related to its economic strength, for it is well established that someone who knows the language of her/his market has better chances to sell her/his product

there. Economic strength also correlates closely with the technological standards of the language community, which makes the learning of such a language even more attractive. Table 1 gives an overview of the three factors. The figures are certainly correct in their overall tendency, even though their exact calculation can cause problems.

German ranks higher according to economic strength than according to its official-status or numerical strength. In comparison, a number of languages which are numerically stronger are economically weaker and therefore show an overall lower international standing by country.

German has often been referred to in studies of "world languages"—languages that are used internationally worldwide—as an important language of science. This view corresponds to the traditional belief that German is the language of science, French the language of diplomacy, and English the language of trade. It suggests that in order to examine the internationality of languages it can be useful to distinguish between different "domains" of communication.

The reputation of German as a language of science is not a figment of the imagination. At the beginning of the twentieth century it was certainly common for scientists of various disciplines to study German in order to get access to the newest scientific developments. Natural scientists from many different countries studied at German universities. Likewise, German textbooks, often in the original, were used at foreign universities. For a couple of decades, the number of scientific publications was higher in German than in English. However, this trend has changed thoroughly in the course of this century. English has by far outstripped German and is now undisputedly the most important language of science. For two reasons, among others, German could not retain its superiority as a language of science. First, Germany and Austria were ruined as a result of World War I. France met much the same fate though it was among the victorious powers. After the war Germany no longer possessed the resources necessary to sustain scientific leadership. Second, Nazism was responsible for the persecution of a great number of German-speaking scientists, not only Jews, and caused a further war catastrophe for the German-speaking countries. The United States remained untouched by these devastations, and even benefited from the immigration of European scientists, taking the scientific lead. An indication of this

Table 1. Official-status, Numerical, and Economic Strength of the Highest-Ranking Languages (around 1990)

Official-status Strength (Number of countries)		Numerical Strength (in millions)		Economic Strength (in trillions of US $)	
English	63	Chinese	700	English	4.271
French	34	English	391	Japanese	1.277
Spanish	23	Spanish	211	German	1.090
Arabic	22	Hindi-Urdu	194	Russian	.801
German	7	Russian	154	Spanish	.738
		Portuguese	120	French	.669
		German	119	Chinese	.44

Table 2. Proportion of German and English in Natural Science Publications as Compared to Shares of German- and English-speaking Countries in Nobel Prizes of Science.

	1910	1920	1930	1940	1950	1960	1970	1980
Percentage of scientific publications in German								
	33.7	44.0	33.0	27.3	21.2	15.2	10.2	11.9
Percentage of scientific publications in English								
	30.7	33.3	46.3	48.6	53.3	50.6	55.6	64.1
Percentage of Nobel Prize winners in natural sciences who are German-speaking								
	36.1	33.3	33.3	37.1	19.4	5.8	9.5	9.0
Percentage of Nobel Prize winners in natural sciences who are English-speaking								
	16.7	16.7	33.3	45.7	61.1	73.1	66.1	77.6

development is the number of Nobel Prize winners from the various language communities. Table 2 gives an overview of the number of English and German scientific publications as well as the share in the Nobel prizes of science that the English- and German-speaking countries reaped during this century. The two sets of figures show a parallel development.

German now plays a similarly modest role as a language of science, as does French, Japanese, and Russian. However, it still belongs to the circle of important international scientific languages, even if the difference from English is spectacular. English is, however, not as dominant in the humanities and social sciences as it is in the natural sciences.

German still plays a significant role as a language of science in some of its neighboring countries, more so in Eastern than in Western Europe. German has for a long time served as the dominant lingua franca of Eastern Europe. It developed this role as a consequence of the expansion of the Austrian Empire, for which Emperor Joseph II declared German the sole official language at the end of the eighteenth century. Numerous settlers from German-speaking countries strengthened the position of German all over Eastern Europe as they maintained their language after emigration.

However, the role of German as a bridge language in Eastern Europe suffered from the consequences of Nazism and World War II. Many of the German-speaking settlers were expelled after the war and Russian was made the compulsory first foreign language in all Eastern European schools. Only with the dissolution of the Soviet Union were the foreign-language curricula in schools revised. Schoolchildren were now offered the possibility to choose from various foreign languages, mainly English, German, French, and Russian. As a consequence of this development, Russian has lost its dominant position in favor of English and German. In some countries, such as the Czech and Slovak republics and Hungary, German competes with English for the position as the favorite foreign language at the elementary level. English is, however, preferred everywhere at secondary and tertiary level to German. This corresponds to the dominant role of English as a language of science.

The main reason for the attractiveness of German as a foreign language is its importance as a language for business. It enhances connections with the attractive markets of the German-speaking countries.

During the past hundred years German has changed from a world language of science to a regional business language. The German-speaking countries are interested in maintaining the international presence of their language. Every country profits from a strong international standing of its language, which eases communication with other countries and requires less learning of foreign languages. With the opening of Eastern Europe the German language has been influenced by conflicting forces. It has, on the one hand, profited from the decline of Russian, yet on the other hand has come under far stronger competition from English, a threat that Russian never posed. Due to ideological reasons the old Soviet system ensured that the spread of English was limited. The fall of the Soviet system meant that such limitations have now vanished, and the appeal of the "world language" has proven to be strong, especially among the young. It is difficult to predict how the international standing of German will develop under these circumstances.

Ulrich Ammon

See also Biochemistry; Chemistry, Scientific and Industrial; Diplomatic Corps and Diplomacy; Exports and Foreign Trade; Kaiser Wilhelm/Max Planck Societies and Their Institutes; Physics; Psychiatry; Psychoanalysis; Psychology; Science and National Socialism; Science in the Postwar Germanys

References

Ammon, Ulrich. *Die deutsche Sprache in Deutschland, Österreich und der Schweiz. Das Problem der nationalen Varietäten.* Berlin: de Gruyter, 1995.

———. *Die internationale Stellung der deutschen Sprache.* Berlin: de Gruyter, 1991.

———"German as an International Language." *International Journal of the Sociology of Language* 83 (1990), 135–170.

Bericht der Bundesregierung über die deutsche Sprache in der Welt. (Bundestagsdrucksache 10/3784.) Bonn: Bundesregierung, 1985.

Skudlik, Sabine. *Sprachen in den Wissenschaften: Deutsch*

und Englisch in der internationalen Kommunikation.
Tübingen: Narr, 1990.

Sturm, Dietrich, ed. *Deutsch als Fremdsprache weltweit.*
Munich: Hueber, 1987.

German Christians

The name "German Christians" (*Deutsche Christen*) was given to
the pro-Nazi sections of the German Evangelical Church, which
achieved prominence in the early years of Nazi rule after 1933.
Their supporters were largely drawn from the ranks of the
younger pastors, who were discontented with the traditional
orthodoxies of Lutheranism and its heavily bureaucratic estab-
lishmentarianism. They adopted highly nationalistic political
views, calling for a restoration of Germany's national prestige
through active participation in the Nazi Party. Under the leadership of such prominent theologians as Emanuel Hirsch and
Paul Althaus, they sought to find theological justification for a
German nationalist interpretation of Christianity, in particular opposing any Universalist or Jewish traditions, and believed
that Luther's reformation would finally be completed by a national and spiritual reassertion of German power and strength.

In 1933, led by astute opportunists such as Ludwig
Müller and Joachim Hossenfelder, German Christians succeeded, with Adolf Hitler's open support, in securing victory
in the July church elections and took control of the majority
of the provincial church administrations. Their extremist
wing, however, led by a group of pastors from Thuringia,
aroused widespread opposition to their demands for the eradication of all Jewish personnel and influences, including the
abolition of the Old Testament and the recognition of Hitler
as the "redeemer" of German national life.

Despite the fact that Ludwig Müller was made Reich
bishop in September 1933, these radical views gave rise to the
Confessing Church, which defended the church's autonomy
from Nazi encroachments. The evident split in the Protestant
ranks led to the "German Christians" being abandoned by the
Nazi leadership, and their influence markedly declined in
subsequent years. Despite its appeal to nationalistic idealism
in 1933, the movement was characterized by a lack of theological depth and the propagation of an opportunistic pro-
Nazi activism and became totally discredited by 1945.

John Conway

See also Barth, Karl; Confessing Church; National Socialist
Germany; Niemöller, Martin; Protestantism and the Protestant Church; *Völkisch* Ideology

References

Conway, John. *The Nazi Persecution of the Churches.* New
York, NY: Basic Books, 1968.

Ericksen, Robert P. *Theologians under Hitler.* New Haven,
CT: Yale University Press, 1985.

Meier, Kurt. *Die Deutschen Christen: Das Bild einer
Bewegung im Kirchenkampf im Dritten Reich.*
Göttingen: Vandenhoeck & Ruprecht, 1964.

Scholder, Klaus. *The Churches and the Third Reich.* 2 vols.
London: SCM Press, 1987–88.

German Communist Party (Kommunistische Partei Deutschlands; KPD) (1919–41)

The product of a schism within Germany's socialist movement, the Communist Party (KPD) became an implacable
enemy of the Weimar Republic and of the republican Social
Democrats. With time, the KPD's relative weakness drove it
into ever closer dependence on the Soviet Union, whose interest it came to serve (1925–41). Violent confrontations with
the Nazis ended once Hitler had seized power and many Communist activists had been incarcerated.

The infant KPD (founded January 1, 1919) comprised
a coalition of left-wingers hostile to the imminent creation
of a parliamentary republic. Its adherents, however, had diverse, even contradictory, aims. Led by former left-wing
Social Democrats (Rosa Luxemburg [1870–1919], Karl
Liebknecht [1871–1919]) who had opposed the war from
within the Spartacus League and now advocated a program
of nonviolent mass education of the working class, most of
the KPD's following tended more to anarchosyndicalism
(e.g., the International Communists of Germany) or even
proposed a revolutionary war of national liberation against
the victorious, capitalist Allies (e.g., the National Communists). This activist following staged or joined a series of insurrections against the emerging republican order. These
efforts failed and, ironically, cost the lives of the more cautious Luxemburg and Liebknecht. A power struggle developed between moderates and radicals. The former, who
advocated participation in elections and the trade-union
movement and even some cooperation with the Social
Democrats, prevailed and, supported by the Comintern, expelled many of the radicals.

Lost were the syndicalists and "national Communists"
who formed the short-lived Communist Workers' Party of
Germany (KAPD; April 5, 1920), but won was much of the
Independent Social Democratic Party (December 1920),
which provided the KPD with a membership of 300,000 and
considerable influence in the trade unions. However, the tensions between gradualists and insurrectionists, between advocates of class struggle and of national revolutionary struggle,
remained unresolved and were complicated by the KPD's
membership in the Comintern, which allowed increasing
Soviet intervention in the party's strategy and affairs.

These contradictions culminated in disaster during the crisis precipitated by France's occupation of the Ruhr region (1923).
The KPD vacillated between exploiting the ensuing chaos to
precipitate class struggle and forging a broad radical-nationalist
alliance, between confrontation and cooperation with the Social Democrats, between participation in and opposition to the
trade unions. All potential allies became antagonized, disillusioned members deserted the party to leave just 130,000, and
the KPD lost any significant influence in the trade unions.

Within the party itself, moderates such as Heinrich
Brandler (1881–1967) and left-wingers opposed to Soviet
domination such as Ruth Fischer (1895–1961) were removed
from office and eventually expelled. Ernst Thälmann (1886–
1944), who was unswervingly loyal to Moscow, was formally
appointed leader (November 1925) and rapidly completed the

reorganization of the party on Bolshevik lines. He did Moscow's bidding in policy matters and by 1929, with all notable moderates expelled, the KPD had effectively become the German branch of the Comintern. As such, it participated vigorously in the offensive against "Social Fascism," by which it meant the Social Democrats. Germany's Social Democrats were regarded as over-tolerant of the capitalist order and as dangerously sympathetic to the Western powers, thereby threatening the special understanding forged between the USSR and Germany in the treaties of Rapallo (May 1922) and Berlin (April 1926). Ordinary Social Democrats were to be converted to Communism, and the party and trade union bureaucracies were to be destroyed by a united front from "below."

The increasingly powerful Nazi movement posed far greater ideological and practical problems, however. The KPD viewed the Nazis' rejection of the Versailles settlement and of the republic positively, but it deplored their collaboration with elements of the old Imperial establishment and their ethnic brand of socialism. It feared their attraction of a mass constituency, including many workers, and demanded both a negative and a positive response. Street battles erupted between the Communist Red Front and the Nazi Sturmabteilung (SA), but at the same time the KPD appealed to ordinary Nazis, as it had to Socialists, over the heads of their leaders and tried to steal the Nazis' nationalist thunder (Neumann Program, September 1930).

As in 1923, the KPD's strategy lacked overall coherence and inner conviction. It gained new support, but not in decisive numbers and seldom from the Social Democrat–dominated factories or trade unions as it had desired. The KPD also failed to stem the growth of the Nazi movement. When Adolf Hitler came to power (January 31, 1933) the KPD suffered arrests, desertions, and prohibition. At its Brussels congress (1935) the KPD called off its war against the Social Democrats and proposed an "Anti-Fascist Popular Front," and the "Bern" congress, held outside Paris (1939), declared unity with all socialist parties. These events, however, had little practical impact within Germany, where the party was restricted to uncoordinated, unarmed, low-level resistance by small pockets of members. Those leaders who escaped arrest or death sought asylum in the USSR; some, such as Walter Ulbricht (1893–1973), returned after the war.

The KPD had failed to "square the circle." Its proletarian internationalism would have had to be spiced with German nationalism to broaden its appeal even in proletarian circles, while most Germans appreciated that this internationalism meant little more than subservience to Soviet national interest. Its increasingly Bolshevik brand of socialism also had limited appeal in a country where socialists either identified with the libertarian achievements of 1789 and 1848 or later with the populist ethnic nationalism of the Nazis.

Conan Fischer

See also Brandler, Heinrich; Fischer, Ruth; German Democratic Republic; Independent Social Democratic Party; Liebknecht, Karl; Luxemburg, Red Orchestra; Resistance; Rosa; Pieck, Wilhelm; Social Democratic Party; Socialist Unity Party; Soviet-German Relations; Spartacus League; Sturmabteilung; Thälmann, Ernst; Ulbricht, Walter; Zetkin, Clara

References

Bahne, S. *Die KPD und das Ende von Weimar.* Frankfurt am Main: Campus Verlag, 1976.

Barclay, David E. and Eric Weitz, eds. *Between Reform and Revolution: German Socialism and Communism from 1840–1990.* Providence, RI: Berghan Books, 1998.

Degras, J. *The Communist International 1919–1943: Documents.* Vols. 1–3. London: Oxford University Press, 1971.

Duhnke, K. *Die KPD von 1933 bis 1945.* Cologne: Kiepenheuer & Witsch, 1972.

Fischer, C. *The German Communists and the Rise of Nazism.* London: Macmillan, 1991.

Flechtheim, O.K. *Die KPD in der Weimarer Republik.* Frankfurt am Main: Europäische Verlagsanstalt, 1976.

Fowkes, B. *Communism in Germany under the Weimar Republic.* London: Macmillan, 1984.

Merson, A. *Communist Resistance in Nazi Germany.* London: Lawrence and Wishart, 1985.

Rosenberg, A. *The History of the German Republic.* London: Methuen, 1936.

Rosenhaft, E. *Beating the Fascists? The German Communists and Political Violence, 1929–1933.* Cambridge: Cambridge University Press, 1983.

Weitz, Eric D. *Creating German Communism, 1890–1990: From Popular Protests to Socialist State.* Princeton, NJ: Princeton University Press, 1997.

German Conservative Party (1876–1918)

The Deutsch-Konservative Partei (DKP; German Conservative Party) was founded half a decade after the establishment of the empire as an attempt to overcome debilitating rivalries that had splintered the conservative movement under Otto von Bismarck. Fiercely resistant to such Bismarckian innovations as national unification, the *Kulturkampf* against the Catholic Church, the reform of rural government, and liberal economics, Conservatives reluctantly and incompletely papered over their internal divisions. Yet this party, dominated by aristocrats and others close to the Prussian throne, was ill-equipped to meet new political challenges in a national—not just Prussian—setting.

The DKP was known as the party of "throne and altar," meaning that it rigorously defended the prerogatives of the Prussian monarchy, the state, and the (Protestant) church. It drew the bulk of its voters from sparsely populated agricultural areas in Prussia's eastern provinces (for example, Pomerania and Brandenburg). Nonetheless, to classify the party as "merely" monarchist and agrarian, or to suggest that the party remained in 1914 as it had been in the 1870s and 1880s, is to miss one of the most important features of Conservative Party history. Although historians disagree about the exact manner in which the rise of an independent agrarian movement in the early 1890s transformed the DKP, they agree that from that point on, the party's loyalty to the state—or more precisely, to those who determined state policy—was extremely problematic. When anti-Semitism, economic self-interest, and chauvinistic nationalism made inroads among the party's functionaries and voters, government ministers and even the kaiser came to the conclusion that the formerly reliable Conservative Party had "lost its way." As Chancellor Bethmann Hollweg declared shortly before the war, the party was being led down "demagogic paths" by "dictatorial" leaders who believed that they had to appeal to the masses for popularity.

Although the DKP, like all other parties, sought popularity and power, neither mass democracy nor dictatorship were ever Conservative goals. It was the narrow three-class Prussian franchise that helped to maintain the DKP's steady representation of 120–150 deputies in the Prussian *Landtag* (state legislature) from the 1880s onward. In other state parliaments, whose deputies were elected under a variety of franchise laws, the Conservatives generally did less well: in southwestern Germany, the party's political significance was almost nil. In national elections, the party's fortunes declined steadily. In the Reichstag elections of 1887, the Conservatives reached the high-water mark of 80 seats (with 15.2 percent of the popular vote) largely because they were allied with Free Conservatives and National Liberals in many districts. From 1893 onward, the Conservatives gained crucial campaign assistance from the Agrarian League, which supplemented their traditional political style with considerable money, rhetorical skill, and organizational expertise. Yet the Reichstag elections of 1898, when the League launched its first full-scale campaign, brought the Conservatives their most dramatic losses: their caucus fell from 72 to 56 members. By 1912, the DKP had been reduced to 43 Reichstag members, elected with just 9.2 percent of the popular vote.

During the war, the party was again buffeted by the same strains and paradoxes that characterized its whole history: how to reconcile the demands of mass politics with an ideology that cherished the quiet back-room politics of a bygone era? Between 1914 and 1918, this dilemma pitted such cool and aloof leaders as Ernst von Heydebrand (1851–1924) and Kuno von Westarp against young "red-hots" in the party's rank and file who advocated extreme Pan-German demands, for instance extensive annexations in the east and west. Thus the party was pushed toward (or backed into) intransigent positions that equated the war cry of "no surrender" on the battlefield with "no compromise" at home. Until November 1918, the Conservatives did everything possible to resist constitutional reform—in particular, revision of the Prussian franchise and the introduction of ministerial responsibility in the Empire. Little wonder, then, that when the war-weary masses rebelled against a delegitimized state and when the Kaiser fled to exile in Holland, the party that had defended statism, monarchism, and authoritarian rule was crushed under the weight of outraged public opinion. The DKP virtually self-destructed. On November 11, 1918, Westarp wrote to Heydebrand that there was only one option left: "I am going on vacation for a while. There is nothing the Conservative Party can do."

James Retallack

See also Agrarian League; Bismarck, Otto von; Conservatism; German National People's Party; Heydebrand, Ernst von; Imperial and Free Conservative Party; Imperial Germany; *Kulturkampf*; Prussia

References

Hartwig, Edgar. "Konservative Partei (KoP) 1848–1918." *Lexikon zur Parteiengeschichte 1789–1945.* 4 vols. Ed. Dieter Fricke et al. Leipzig: VEB Bibliographisches Institut, 1985. Vol. 3, 283–309.

Jones, Larry Eugene and James Retallack, eds. *Between Reform, Reaction, and Resistance: Studies in the History of German Conservatism from 1789 to 1945.* Oxford and Providence, RI: Berg, 1993.

Puhle, Hans-Jürgen. *Agrarische Interessenpolitik und preussischer Konservatismus im wilhelminischen Reich 1893–1914: Ein Beitrag zur Analyse des Nationalismus in Deutschland am Beispiel des Bundes der Landwirte und der Deutsch-Konservativen Partei.* 2nd ed. Bonn/Bad-Godesberg: Neue Gesellschaft, 1975.

Retallack, James. "Anti-Semitism, Conservative Propaganda, and Regional Politics in Late Nineteenth-Century Germany." *German Studies Review* 11 (1988), 377–403.

———. *Notables of the Right. The Conservative Party and Political Mobilization in Germany, 1876–1918.* London and Boston: Unwin Hyman, 1988.

Westarp, Kuno Count von. *Konservative Politik im letzten Jahrzehnt des Kaiserreichs.* 2 vols. Berlin: Deutsche Verlagsgesellschaft, 1935.

German Democratic Party (1918–33)

The German Democratic Party (Deutsche Demokratische Partei; DDP) was most closely identified with the Weimar Republic. Founded at the height of the Revolution of 1918 in response to an appeal from Theodor Wolff (1868–1943) and Alfred Weber (1868–1958), the DDP emerged from the January 1919 elections to the Weimar National Assembly as the largest nonsocialist and nondenominational party in Germany and played a major role in establishing the constitutional foundations of postwar German democracy.

Inspired by the intellectual legacy of its first national chairman, Friedrich Naumann (1860–1919), the DDP sought to unite the more progressive elements of the middle classes and the working class into a powerful phalanx committed to the creation of a viable parliamentary democracy. The party's effectiveness at Weimar, however, was severely compromised not only by a bitter internal conflict over acceptance or rejection of the Treaty of Versailles but also by a lack of consensus in the realm of social and economic policy. As a result, the party suffered a resounding defeat in the June 1920 Reichstag elections and saw its share of the popular vote decline from 18.6 percent in 1919 to 8.3 percent in 1920.

The DDP's fate as a viable political force was effectively sealed by the runaway inflation of the early 1920s. The inflation did much to intensify the general level of antagonism within the party and brought about the virtual collapse of the DDP's national organization. Carl Petersen (1868–1933),

Naumann's successor as DDP national chairman, was singularly unsuccessful in his efforts to steer a clear course behind which the various social groups constituting the DDP's material base could unite, with the result that the party experienced an even more devastating defeat in May 1924—its share of the popular vote fell to 5.7 percent. Despite a modest recovery in December 1924, the DDP's decline continued unabated throughout the second half of the 1920s as more and more erstwhile Democrats abandoned the party in favor of special-interest parties such as the Business Party of the German Middle Class (Wirtschaftspartei des deutschen Mittelstandes), the Reich Party for People's Justice and Revaluation (Reichspartei für Volksrecht und Aufwertung), and the German Peasants' Party (Deutsche Bauernpartei). The DDP received only 4.8 percent of the popular vote in the May 1928 Reichstag elections. Nonetheless, the DDP remained a staunch defender of Germany's republican system and never wavered in its support of the foreign policy identified with Gustav Stresemann (1878–1929).

After the 1928 Reichstag elections, Erich Koch-Weser (1875–1944), DDP national chairman since January 1924, became increasingly concerned over his party's future and began to explore a merger with other moderate bourgeois groups. Koch-Weser's efforts reached a dramatic climax in July 1930 with the founding of the German State Party (Deutsche Staatspartei; DStP). Although the DStP never fulfilled its promise as a party of national consolidation and suffered an embarrassing defeat in the September 1930 Reichstag elections, the DDP officially dissolved itself in November 1930 and urged its members to join the DStP. For its own part, the DStP never recovered from the acrimony that had surrounded its founding and experienced a string of electoral defeats over the course of the next several years before it formally dissolved itself in the summer of 1933.

Larry Eugene Jones

See also Inflation and Hyperinflation; Koch-Weser, Erich; Liberalism; Naumann, Friedrich; Rathenau, Walther; Weber, Alfred; Weimar Germany; Wolff, Theodor

References

Albertin, Lothan. *Liberalismus und Demokratie am Anfang der Weimarer Republik: Eine vergleichende Analyse der Deutschen Demokratischen Partei und der Deutschen Volkspartei.* Düsseldorf: Droste, 1972.

Frye, Bruce B. *Liberal Democrats in the Weimar Republic: The History of the German Democratic Party and the German State Party.* Carbondale, IL: Southern Illinois University Press, 1985.

Hess, Jürgen C. *"Das ganze Deutschland soll es sein": Demokratischer Nationalismus in der Weimarer Republik am Beispiel der Deutschen Demokratischen Partei.* Stuttgart: Klett-Cotta, 1978.

Jones, Larry Eugene. *German Liberalism and the Dissolution of the Weimar Party System, 1919–1933.* Chapel Hill, NC: University of North Carolina Press, 1988.

Schneider, Werner. *Die Deutsche Demokratische Partei in der Weimarer Republik 1924–1930.* Munich: Fink, 1978.

Stephan, Werner. *Aufstieg und Verfall des Linksliberalismus 1918–1933: Geschichte der Deutschen Demokratischen Partei.* Göttingen: Vandenhoeck & Ruprecht, 1973.

Wegner, Konstanze, ed. *Linksliberalismus in der Weimarer Republik: Die Führungsgremien der Deutschen Demokratischen Partei und der Deutschen Staatspartei 1918–1933.* Düsseldorf: Droste, 1980.

German Democratic Republic

The German Democratic Republic (GDR), founded in October 1949 and also known as "East Germany," perceived itself to be, in contrast to the Federal Republic of Germany (FRG), a "new Germany" in the tradition of the anti-fascist resistance. It rejected all legal and political liability for the Third Reich. Its development was dialectically influenced on the one hand by transformation to a people's democracy (adjusting to Soviet state and party organization) and on the other by maintaining loyalty, at least for the moment, to the German nation. The "construction of socialism," which had been pushed through at the second party conference of the ruling Socialist Unity Party (SED) in 1952, was accompanied by serious crises. The workers' uprising of June 17, 1953, made clear the fragile basis of support for the SED regime. Only with the construction of the Berlin Wall on August 13, 1961, was the mass flight of the population stopped. On this basis it was possible for the GDR, after the 1960s, to develop internal stability and to work actively toward the modernization of its economic and political system. On this basis it also provided broader latitude for individuals, even if it maintained insulation from West Germany as before.

The SED invariably rejected the repeated claim of the FRG to be the sole political representative of the Germans. Until the mid-1960s, it propagated reunification on the basis of a socialist order. With the beginnings of the new eastern and German policies of the Brandt-Scheel government in 1969, the SED (after the removal of Walter Ulbricht [1893–1973] in 1971), under the direction of its general secretary Erich Honecker (1912–94), pulled back decisively from its "national" goals and sought international recognition of the GDR as a second German state. The Basic Treaty of 1972 accepted the existence of two German states but refused recognition of the GDR under international law and insisted on the unity of the German nation.

Worker demonstrations, East Berlin, June 17, 1953. Courtesy of German Embassy, Ottawa.

Measured by the standards of the Warsaw Pact states, the GDR undoubtedly achieved a number of economic and social successes. But in the long run, the costs of the extensive social policy were prohibitive and were one of the reasons for the economic ruin of the GDR.

Since, in contrast to the other East European "socialist sister-states" with their national communist parties, the SED could not serve as a medium for integration, the GDR was consistently (and against its will) connected to the FRG, from which it steadily sought to distance itself by propagandistic means. Through its participation in inter-German trade, the GDR indirectly benefited from the advantages of the European Community. Under the influence of the intense armaments race of the superpowers and the resulting dangers for all European states, the GDR, alongside its delimitation efforts, undertook more intensive attempts at cooperation and recognition of a common German past.

The SED regime contributed toward its own demise when it clearly distanced itself from the reforms associated with Mikhail Gorbachev's *perestroika* and when it increasingly isolated itself from the population by extending the state security service and oppressing all dissident groups. The growing economic crisis, magnified by sizable debts in the West, and the ecological disaster (poisoning of the soil, air pollution, disintegration of the cities) irreversibly undermined the basis of support for SED rule so that, with the collapse of the Berlin Wall on November 9, quick union with the FRG seemed to be the only salvation for the population.

In the FRG in the 1950s, the GDR was essentially ignored as a "state that should not be" (Ernst Richert). After the 1960s, however, political and historical research freed itself from the clichés of the Cold War. During the last two decades, Western research took for granted the existence of two German states, analyzed GDR history independently of West German developments, and despite some differences, frequently presented an optimistic portrait of the domestic conditions in the SED dictatorship. Since unification, east and west German historians and political scientists have undertaken to correct in different ways the "false GDR picture."

Christoph Klessmann

See also Ackermann, Anton; Anti-Fascism; Axen, Hermann; Basic Treaty; Berlin; Berlin Blockade; Berlin Wall; The Economics of German Reunification; Fischer, Oskar; Free German Trade Unions Federation; Free German Youth; German Communist Party; German Democratic Republic: Arts and Politics; German Democratic Republic: Churches; German Democratic Republic: Collapse; German Democratic Republic: Constitutions; German Democratic Republic: Economy; German Democratic Republic: Education; German Democratic Republic: Foreign Relations; German Democratic Republic: Government System; German Democratic Republic: Judicial System; German Democratic Republic: Literature and Literary Life; German Democratic Republic: Marxism-Leninism; German Democratic Republic: Media; German Democratic Republic: National People's Army; German Democratic Republic: Nationalism; German Democratic Republic: Opposition; German Democratic Republic: Political Culture; German Democratic Republic: Political Party System; German Democratic Republic: Sports; German Democratic Republic: State Security; German Democratic Republic: Technical Intelligentsia; German Democratic Republic: Women; German-German Relations; German-Soviet Relations; Gorbachev and the German Question; Grotewohl, Otto; Hager, Kurt; Honecker, Erich; Honecker, Margot; Maizière, Lothar de; Mielke, Erich; Mittag, Günter; Modrow, Hans; *Ostpolitik*; Party of Democratic Socialism; Pieck, Wilhelm; Reunification; Science in the Postwar Germanys; Sindermann, Horst; Socialist Unity Party; Stalin Notes; Stoph, Willi; Tisch, Harry; Ulbricht, Walter; Verner, Paul; Wolf, Markus

References

Barclay, David E. and Eric Weitz, eds. *Between Reform and Revolution: German Socialism and Communism from 1840–1990*. Providence, RI: Berghan Books, 1998.

Childs, David. *The GDR: Moscow's German Ally*. 2nd ed. London: Unwin Hyman, 1988.

———. *The Stasi: The East German Intelligence and Security Service*. New York, NY: New York University Press, 1996.

Dennis, Mike. *German Democratic Republic: Politics, Economics and Society*. London: Pinter Publishers, 1988.

Fulbrook, Mary. *Anatomy of a Dictatorship: Inside the GDR, 1949–1989*. New York, NY: Oxford University Press, 1995.

Klessmann, Christoph. *Die doppelte Staatsgründung: Deutsche Geschichte 1945–1955*. Göttingen: Vandenhoeck & Ruprecht, 1982.

———. *Zwei Staaten, eine Nation: Deutsche Geschichte, 1955–1970*. Göttingen: Vandenhoeck & Ruprecht, 1988.

Kopstein, Jeffrey. *The Politics of Economic Decline in East Germany, 1945–1989*. Chapel Hill, NC: University of North Carolina Press, 1997.

Maaz, Hans-Joachim. *Behind the Wall: The Inner Life of Communist Germany*. Trans. Margot Bettauer Dembo. New York, NY: W.W. Norton, 1995.

McCauley, Martin. *The German Democratic Republic since 1945*. London: Macmillan, 1983.

Naimark, Norman M. *The Russians in Germany: A History of the Soviet Zone of Occupation, 1945–1949*. Cambridge, MA: Belknap Press, 1995.

New Hampshire Symposium on the German Democratic Republic. *Studies in GDR Culture and Society*. 11 vols. 1980–93. Washington, DC: University Press of America.

Thomaneck, J.K.A. and James Mellis, eds. *Politics, Society and Government in the German Democratic Republic: Basic Documents*. Oxford: Berg, 1989.

Wallace, Ian. *East Germany: The German Democratic Republic*. Oxford: Clio, 1987.

Weitz, Eric D. *Creating German Communism, 1890–1990: From Popular Protests to Socialist State*. Princeton, NJ: Princeton University Press, 1997.

German Democratic Republic: Arts and Politics

The painting, graphics, and sculpture of postwar East Germany had their roots in the Nazi period, in the Weimar Republic, and in the traditions of earlier periods such as the realism of nineteenth-century painting. During the first major postwar exhibition of art in Dresden in 1946, artists from West and East Germany exhibited their works. Expressionists, members of ASSO (Association of Revolutionary Artists of Germany, 1928–1933), as well as artists identified with other prewar artistic movements were represented. Barlach, Beckmann, Grosz, Heckel, Kirchner, Kokoschka, Schlemmer, and Schmidt-Rottluff were among the artists exhibited. The early openness for a variety of artistic styles was reinforced at the First Central Cultural Congress of the German Communist Party (KPD).

At the same time, however, there were already signs of a more confining conception of the role of art, stemming from the Soviet Union and intensified by the Cold War. Accusations of formalism—the negative counterpart to socialist realism—grew out of efforts at establishing an independent identity and separating the German Democratic Republic (GDR) from western "bourgeois" developments. Control over art grew especially severe as Stalinism came to be implemented, even though artistic development in East Germany took a somewhat different turn than in the Soviet Union.

Artists faced a number of dilemmas. The first involved conceptions about the function of art; modern art not only reflected the individual experience of artists but also tended to look critically at society, focusing on suffering or fragmentation. Supporting the new socialist political elite was thus at odds with many artists' self-conception. A second contradiction concerned the audience. Art in the new society was to be accessible to working people, yet it was the esoteric standards of earlier modern art that defined artistic integrity. The third dilemma was that exchanging the security of public support for the marginal economic existence of old also entailed control by the state as patron.

The *Second German Art Exhibition* in 1949 was dominated by socialist realism, though there was a small representation of expressionists. By 1953, the *Third Exhibition* was filled with agitation art, naturalist illustration, and socialist realism similar to work in the Soviet Union. Stereotyped symbols such as flags, peace doves, and clasped hands predominated. The cultural scene was bleak throughout the Ulbricht era (until 1971), even if there were still controversies about the role of art. In 1971, Erich Honecker declared a new principle: provided one started from the standpoint of socialism, there could be no taboos in art and literature.

As in the Soviet Union, the Ministry of Culture and the Union of Artists (Verband Bildender Künstler; VBK) shaped the institutional world of GDR art. Both were linked to the leading party, the Socialist Unity Party (SED). It was not impossible to work as an artist outside the union, but it was much more difficult to gain access to jobs and studios, participate in major exhibitions, pay for materials, travel abroad, or earn as much when selling work (because of the higher tax on self-employed, non-union artists).

Eighty percent of the artists in the GDR joined the VBK, beginning as candidates after graduating from art school. The union enforced official policy on the arts, but, in addition, it played a mediating role between official policy and the demands of the artists. Ideology was not the only bone of contention in the ensuing conflicts. The desire to maintain positions of power equally reinforced traditional and constricted notions of art. Willi Sitte, who became president of the union after the changes in 1971, and who was seen as a symbol of stagnation in the late 1980s, lost his leadership position in 1988. Similar changes occurred at the district levels of the union.

Since the 1970s, works shown in the GDR included those in the tradition of late impressionism, some constructivist and surrealistic works, as well as pictures based on montage and collage. There was a growing interest in depicting problematic aspects of everyday life, including expressions of isolation and alienation as well as some selected social issues—for example, pollution and war. By the 1980s, a number of interesting galleries represented a variety of styles, and some interesting experimental work existed, as well as collaborative arrangements among artists and writers or artists and musicians. Some innovative work was also shown at the national exhibitions in Dresden. More artists were allowed to travel to the West, especially to West Germany, where there was a great interest in GDR art. At the same time, controls remained on what was acceptable and clampdowns on certain exhibitions and other cultural events continued. Between 1982 and 1987, some excellent artists left Dresden for the west. The number has been estimated to be comparable to an earlier emigration of artists in the 1950s, when movement was easier.

When the political system broke down, GDR artists were active in protests, newly formed political groups, and new parties. Unification of the two Germanys thus brought tremendous opportunities for artists but also new insecurity. Though a number of galleries remained, artists could no longer count on extensive support from the state and had to face competition in the international art world. Above all, their place in culture and society changed. Against the background of official expectations, GDR painters and sculptors could play a subtly oppositional role in culture and society, especially in the 1970s and 1980s. Both the pressure to conform and the chance of a more autonomous expression of meaning have been swept away by the social and political changes brought by unification.

Marilyn Rueschemeyer

See also Artists; Biermann, Wolf; Cremer, Fritz; German Democratic Republic; German Democratic Republic: Government System; German Democratic Republic: Literature; German Democratic Republic: Marxism-Leninism; German Democratic Republic: Media; German Democratic Republic: Nationalism; German Democratic Republic: Opposition; German Democratic Republic: Political Culture; German Democratic Republic: Technical Intelligentsia; *Germanistik;* Penck, A.R.; Socialist Unity Party; Wolf, Christa

References

Feist, Günter, with Eckhart Gillen. *Stationen eines Weges.* Berlin: Museumspaedagogischer Dienst and Verlag Dirk Nishen, 1988.

Kober, Karl Max. "Art Exhibits and Art Galleries: Their Role in Art Appreciation and the Perception of Art." *Journal of Popular Culture* 18 (Winter 1984), 125–43.

Rueschemeyer, Marilyn. "State Patronage in the German Democratic Republic: Artistic and Political Change in a State Socialist Society." *The Journal of Arts, Management and Law* 20 (Winter 1991), 31–55.

Rueschemeyer, Marilyn, Igor Golomshtok and Janet Kennedy. *Soviet Emigre Arts: Life and Work in the USSR and the United States.* New York, NY: M.E. Sharpe, 1985.

Thomas, Karin. *Die Malerei in der DDR 1949–1979.* Cologne: Dumont Buchverlag, 1980.

German Democratic Republic: Churches

The German Democratic Republic (GDR) hoped to remove religion as a sociopolitical force in its citizens' lives. The GDR leaders attacked it as an opiate of the masses, punished the openly religious, and weakened church leadership. The initial phase of this process propagandized and harassed clerics and church workers and, by ending church taxes, put churches into dire economic straits. A second phase, beginning in 1952, pressured individuals, for example by making children's education and advancement contingent on joining the explicitly antireligious Free German Youth. Beginning around 1960, the GDR eased its heavy-handedness to focus on dividing its churches from those in West Germany; by the 1980s, it aimed at a modus vivendi between church and state.

Organizational structures were crucial in helping the Roman Catholic Church survive this onslaught. The Catholic Church was flexible. Its relatively low membership in the GDR, past experience with religious persecution in Prussia, and a rigid hierarchy linked to Rome inured Catholics to adversity. Even at the cost of individual suffering it insisted on internal control over the Church's structure and personnel and the communicants' personal responsibility to the Church. If, however, the state wanted to rearrange dioceses to sharpen the distinction between East and West German Catholics, then churchmen in Rome and Berlin could easily agree—provided that changes enhanced the right of Catholics in both countries to pursue their faith.

Jews faced an especially difficult situation in the GDR. The Holocaust reduced Germany's 590,000 Jews (1931) to 4,639 East German Jews in 1946 and three to four times that many in West Germany. The GDR originally lionized Jews as victims of Nazism. But Stalin's Jewish purges in 1952 led to a breakup of Jewish communities and three decades of governmental attacks aimed ostensibly at "Zionists." Their relative isolation in society nevertheless permitted the autonomous Jewish communities to survive, and by 1988, the 360 mostly elderly Jews remaining in the GDR looked forward to a more enlightened state policy.

In 1948, the Evangelical Church in Germany (EKD), succeeded the Confessing Church, a revolutionary brotherhood of Protestant clerics who had resisted the established church's support of Nazism. It included Protestant dioceses in East and West Germany. Its leadership during the 1950s, however, unquestionably equated the GDR with godless Communism and dictatorial Nazism.

By 1968, GDR pressure led the eastern dioceses to separate into the Federation of Evangelical Churches (BEK). A similar effort to split the Evangelical Church in Berlin-Brandenburg, which included West Berlin, resulted in a stand-off. The principle of unity remained intact, but each side had its own bishop and synod. The GDR found the BEK easier to deal with and moved toward better relations. But, during the revolutionary period of 1989–90, the same Protestant leaders in the GDR provided meeting places and other support for the advocates of change.

The GDR's incorporation into the Federal Republic in 1990 enabled the three main churches to restore their previous structures.

Richard Merritt

See also German Democratic Republic: Marxism-Leninism; German Democratic Republic: Media; German Democratic Republic: Nationalism; German Democratic Republic: Opposition; German Democratic Republic: Political Culture; Reunification; Socialist Unity Party

References

Goeckel, Robert F. *The Lutheran Church and the East German State: Political Conflict and Change under Ulbricht and Honecker.* Ithaca, NY: Cornell University Press, 1990.

Merritt, Richard L. "Politics of Judaism in the GDR." *Studies in GDR Culture and Society.* Ed. Margy Gerber et al. Lanham, MD: University Press of America, 1989.

Solberg, Richard W. *God and Caesar in East Germany: The Conflicts of the Church and State in East Germany since 1945.* New York, NY: Macmillan, 1961.

German Democratic Republic: Collapse (1989–90)

Although the assorted factors contributing to the demise of the German Democratic Republic (GDR) can be traced in that country's earlier history, the actual collapse of its government and political system unfolded with great rapidity. As the other countries of the region were grappling with the quest for a new system to replace the Communist one, that struggle was averted in the GDR by its precipitate absorption into the Federal Republic of Germany. In September 1989, thousands of East Germans abroad in neighboring countries began a massive exodus, first over the newly opened border between Hungary and Austria, then through West German embassies in Prague and Warsaw. Helpless to stem the flight of its citizens, the ruling party and government began a process of accommodation. The general secretary of the Socialist Unity Party (SED) and president of the GDR Council of State, Erich Honecker (1912–94), was deposed in October; the GDR borders were opened in November as the government and *Politbüro* resigned; in December the whole party leadership resigned as the SED renounced its constitutionally sanctioned leading role, renaming itself the Party of Democratic Socialism (PDS).

As the exodus continued in early 1990, and as the bankruptcy of the PDS regime became ever more conspicuous, there was, simultaneously, increasing talk of reunification and sober reflection on what a transformed GDR might look like. The New Forum, more a nationwide discussion group than a political party, was the principal locus for deliberation on renewal. The numerous political parties that were forming in late 1989 and early 1990 advanced toward March elections with some version of reunification high on the agenda. On March 18, the electorate chose annexation, voting the GDR out of existence. The Alliance for Germany, predominantly a counterpart of the West German Christian Democratic Union (CDU), emerged as the major electoral winner, and in April, the first non-Communist government of the GDR took office under the leadership of Lothar de Maizière (1940–). This was only an interlude, for in July an economic and currency union prefigured the complete absorption of the GDR. The process was completed in October with the treaty uniting the two countries. West German chancellor Helmut Kohl and his CDU-controlled government in Bonn provided direction and funds as the process unfolded throughout 1990.

The bare chronology conceals almost as much as it reveals, for such a recital affords little sense of the immensity of emotional outpouring or the conflict and manipulation that animated the process. No account should omit the enthusiasm of the population as expressed in mass demonstrations in Berlin and Leipzig or in celebration at the opening of the Berlin Wall late in 1989. Nor should one overlook two developments that were all but forgotten in the overwhelming tempo of reunification: the belated attempt by the SED to reform itself under new leadership and the surge of sentiment favoring a renewed GDR under a democratic form of socialism in which national pride would not be overshadowed by contempt for the corrupt SED regime. And, as developments subsequent to the union of East with West Germany make clear, it is important to note the sheer difficulty of joining two countries with such disparate historical experiences lasting a generation and a half. Had the reforming impulse manifested itself earlier, as it did in neighboring countries, the GDR might have entered upon reunification as a full partner rather than as the object of effective annexation.

Lyman H. Legters

See also Axen, Hermann; Basic Treaty; Berlin; Berlin Wall; The Economics of German Reunification; Fischer, Oskar; German Democratic Republic: Arts and Politics; German Democratic Republic: Churches; German Democratic Republic: Constitutions; German Democratic Republic: Economy; German Democratic Republic: Foreign Relations; German Democratic Republic: Government System; German Democratic Republic: Literature and Literary Life; German Democratic Republic: Marxism-Leninism; German Democratic Republic: Media; German Democratic Republic: National People's Army; German Democratic Republic: Nationalism; German Democratic Republic: Opposition; German Democratic Republic: Political Culture; German Democratic Republic: Political Party System; German Democratic Republic: State Security; German Democratic Republic: Technical Intelligentsia; German-German Relations; Gorbachev and the German Question; Honecker, Erich; Maizière, Lothar de; Mielke, Erich; Mittag, Günter; Modrow, Hans; *Ostpolitik*; Party for Democratic Socialism; Reunification; Socialist Unity Party; Soviet-German Relations; Stoph, Willi; Tisch, Harry, Wolf, Markus

References

Borneman, John. *After the Wall; East Meets West in the New Berlin*. New York, NY: Basic Books, 1991.

Darnton, Robert. *Berlin Journal, 1989–1990*. New York, NY: W.W. Norton, 1991.

Garton Ash, Timothy. *The Magic Lantern*. New York, NY: Random House, 1990.

Jarausch, Konrad. *The Rush to German Unity*. New York, NY: Oxford University Press, 1994

Keithly, David M. *The Collapse of East German Communism*. Westport, CT: Praeger, 1992.

McAdams, A. James. *Germany Divided: From the Wall to Reunification*. Princeton, NJ: Princeton University Press, 1993.

Maier, Charles S. *Dissolution: The Crisis of Communism and the End of East Germany*. Princeton, NJ; Princeton University Press, 1997.

German Democratic Republic: Constitutions

A constitution in the Western, liberal tradition limits the power of the people's representatives, guarantees fundamental rights, serves as an authoritative document superior to ordinary law, and establishes a political community in perpetuity. The constitutions of the German Democratic Republic (GDR) failed to embody these elements of limited government. Instead, as in other Marxist-Leninist states, the constitution vested uncontrolled power in the people's representatives, renounced the concept of individual rights, placed the state in the service of ordinary law, and viewed the constitutional text as the momentary expression of a given stage in the evolution of socialist society.

The 1949 constitution, adopted by the East German parliament shortly after the GDR's founding, blended Western parliamentary institutions with socialist influences. Many of its provisions on the organization of the state, like those of the Federal Republic's Basic Law, imitated the Weimar constitution of 1919. Like the Basic Law, the GDR's first constitution provided for a president and two legislative chambers (a People's Chamber and a Chamber of State Representatives), included a bill of individual rights, and left the way open to reunification. On the socialist side, the constitution contemplated the nationalization of all natural resources and major industries, the development of a state economic plan, and the expropriation of private property.

Within a short time, however, the constitution turned into little more than a sham. The Socialist Unity Party (SED) proclaimed the GDR a socialist state and transformed itself into the state's major ruling party. Constitutional amendments eliminated the state parliaments, abolished the office of the president, and replaced the latter with a Council of State that superseded the People's Chamber in importance. Unsurprisingly, the first secretary of the SED, at that time Walter Ulbricht (1893–1973), became the council's chairman. Basic rights and liberties, too, turned out to be illusory in the absence of an independent judiciary.

Claiming that the existing constitution no longer accorded "with the relations of socialist society and the present level of historical development," Ulbricht demanded a new constitution at the SED's 1967 Party Congress. Accordingly, the 1968 constitution defined the GDR as "a socialist state of the German nation" and proudly proclaimed that "the exploitation of man by man is abolished forever." Celebrating the GDR's "fraternal ties" with the Soviet Union, it also announced a new principle of social organization: "From each according to his abilities, to each according to his work." To achieve these ends, the constitution declared that the country would henceforth operate "under the leadership of the working class and its Marxist-Leninist party," the SED. The constitution reinforced the principle of single-party rule by declaring that the "sovereignty of the working people . . . is implemented on the basis of democratic centralism [which] is the fundamental principle of the state structure" (Article 47 [2]).

On the initiative of Erich Honecker (1912–94), who replaced Ulbricht as first secretary of the SED in 1971, several constitutional amendments, adopted in 1974, changed vital parts of the 1968 constitution. The amendments retained the structure of socialism, but now defined the GDR as a "socialist state of workers and farmers." By dropping all references to the German nation, the constitution was asserting the GDR's autonomy and the impossibility of a reunited Germany on anything other than socialist principles. In addition, the 1974 amendments consolidated the powers of the SED's first secretary and proclaimed the GDR's "eternal and irrevocable connection to the Soviet Socialist Republic."

Three phases thus marked the constitutional development of the GDR. Having started as a democratic republic in 1949, it became a socialist state of the German nation in 1968, and came to rest as a socialist state of workers and farmers in 1974. In 1990, however, the world witnessed the collapse of the GDR and its absorption into the constitutional system of the Federal Republic.

Donald P. Kommers

See also Constitutions; German Democratic Republic; German Democratic Republic: Judicial System; German Democratic Republic: Political Culture; Honecker, Erich; Socialist Unity Party; Ulbricht, Walter

References

Childs, David. *The GDR: Moscow's German Ally*. London: George Allen and Unwin, 1983.
East Germany. Washington, DC: U.S. Government Printing Office, 1988.
Markovits, Inga. "Law or Order—Constitutionalism and Legality in Eastern Europe." *Stanford Law Review* 34 (1982), 513.
———. "Pursuing One's Rights under Socialism." *Stanford Law Review* 38 (1986), 689.
McCardle, Arthur W. and A. Bruce Boenau. *East Germany*. Lanham, MD: University Press of America, 1984.
Merkl, Peter H. *German Reunification in the European Context*. University Park, PA: Pennsylvania State University Press, 1993.
Scharf, C. Bradley. *Politics and Change in East Germany: An Evaluation of Socialist Democracy*. Boulder, CO: Westview Press, 1984.

German Democratic Republic: Economy

The postwar status of East Germany was initially that of Soviet occupation zone. Actual war damage was less than in West Germany, but from 1946 to 1948 reparation and occupation costs represented an estimated 25 percent of social product. Large-scale Soviet dismantling of East German industry also hampered reconstruction.

In some industrial fields, East Germany was more advanced than West Germany, but chemicals, iron, and steel were only weakly developed in the region. The economic imbalances, the disadvantaged postwar recovery, and the necessity of learning how to make a new centralized planning system function all resulted in a more protracted recovery than in West Germany, where Marshall Plan assistance and friendly export markets helped facilitate the process.

The GDR, which was founded on October 7, 1949, adopted the Soviet political system and central-planning model. Over the years, the East Germans gained the reputation in Eastern Europe of being very competent planners and organizers. Their system was somewhat simpler to coordinate and manage than that of the huge Soviet Union, but it was affected by the same impediments all central-planning systems shared. First, the lack of scarcity prices that would reflect both costs of production and consumer demands caused queuing and shortages, because prices for necessities were set below market-clearing levels. Also, the central planning organs established what would be produced by what enterprises, financed the commodities, and determined who would receive them at what prices. This resulted in immense information requirements, which prevented the center from accessing the available information at the enterprise level, which in turn made it impossible to develop consistent plans and to oversee their implementation.

The attempt to guarantee full employment and the temptation for enterprises to hoard labor (since the state subsidized the enterprise payroll) meant that inefficiency was very high and productivity correspondingly low.

The specific institutional responses to the above conditions included the propensity to avoid the adoption of new technologies and an inability to participate internationally in a rational division of labor and specialization with either capitalist or other socialist nations in normal foreign trade.

By 1963, the socialist countries were seeking to liberate their economies from the inefficiencies of central planning. In a pilot experiment, the GDR adopted a set of economic reforms based on the conceptions of Soviet economist Evsei Liberman. The reforms, designed to offer greater independence and incentives to production units, initially seemed to have some effect. By 1970, however, the planning bureaucracy had succeeded in undermining the reform effort, which had not gone far enough nor functioned well. Internal conflicts between the indirect controls and the remaining central controls paralyzed the system. Moreover, the partial loss of control over the investment process made the center feel it had lost control over the development of the economy. The crisis of the reform movement coincided with the decline of Walter Ulbricht (1893–1973) as first secretary of the party and the ascension of Erich Honecker (1912–94) to that position. It also coincided with the decline of reform efforts in the Soviet Union and the ascension of Leonid Brezhnev.

As the GDR returned to traditional planning techniques, Honecker attempted to establish a new social contract with the workers. He described this plan as the "Unity of Social and Economic Policy," an explicit promise that, should the workers be productive, they would receive the fruits of their efforts in terms of enhanced availability of public and private goods. In practice this implied a substantive increase of resources for the consumer and a serious reduction for investment.

By the beginning of the 1980s, a new economic initiative had been launched—the establishment of the combine (*Kombinat*) system. This was an attempt to tighten the central organization through the establishment of huge, vertically and horizontally integrated industrial combines under a director general (DG). This manager of what was essentially a national monopoly, working directly with the relevant minister, had extensive power in managing all the associated enterprises. The DG simultaneously managed the most high-profile enterprise in that industry, thereby gaining access to information pertaining to real prices and production requirements and achieving collegiality with other managers under the DG's supervision.

The new system seemed to function well until about 1985, when a gradual decline in effectiveness was observed. The lack of adequate investments and an inept structural policy for industry led to serious industrial decay and distortion. The policy, attributed to Honecker's *Politbüro* economics specialist, Günter Mittag (1926–94), emphasized "key industries" (*Schlüsseltechnologien*), and it provided more resources for their development than they could profitably utilize while withholding from other industries the resources needed to remain viable. The extent of the industrial decline was not made apparent until the disastrous flight of labor and the opening of the Berlin Wall in November 1989.

Phillip J. Bryson

See also The Economics of German Reunification; German Democratic Republic: Technical Intelligentsia; Mittag, Günter; Reunification; Socialist Unity Party

References

Bryson, Phillip J. and Manfred Melzer. *The End of the East German Economy: From Honecker to Reunification.* New York, NY: St. Martin's Press, 1991.
Deutsches Institut für Wirtschaftsforschung, ed. *Handbuch DDR-Wirtschaft.* 4th ed. Reinbek bei Hamburg: Rowohlt Taschenbuch Verlag, 1984.
Gutmann, Gernot, ed. *Das Wirtschaftssystem der DDR.* Stuttgart: Gustav Fischer Verlag, 1983.
Jeffries, Ian and Manfred Melzer. *The East German Economy.* London: Croom Helm, 1987.
Leptin, Gert and Manfred Melzer. *Economic Reform in East German Industry.* Oxford: Oxford University Press, 1978.
Schulz, Gerhard, Karl-Heinz Stiemerling and Günter Pöggel, eds. *Die Volkswirtschaft der DDR.* Berlin [East]: Verlag Die Wirtschaft, 1979.
Thalheim, Karl C., ed. *Materialien zum Bericht zur Lage der Nation im geteilten Deutschland 1987.* Bonn: Bundesministerium für innerdeutsche Beziehungen, 1987.

German Democratic Republic: Education

Education policy was central to the Marxist-Leninist policies of the ruling Socialist Unity Party (SED) in the German Democratic Republic (GDR). The SED used education as an ideological tool to educate its population to socialism and to provide better chances for working-class children. Following the Soviet model, the SED created a mass, uniform system with a highly centralized structure, in which education at all levels was to be brought close to the world of work and the needs of the economy.

The joint statement of the three wartime allies of August 2, 1945 at the Potsdam Conference ordered the removal of all Nazi influence from the education system in Germany. It was immediately put into effect by the Soviet Union in its zone of occupation through a decree on August 25. As a result, more than two out of three teachers were dismissed by 1949. The different ideological emphasis compared with the Western zones became immediately clear in the other changes ordered in the decree: it created six-month teacher-training programs to replace the dismissed teachers, it abolished private schools and religious education, and it created a central administration to supervise the systems in the individual states (until their abolition in 1952).

The radical nature of the changes in the Soviet zone was underlined by the May 22, 1946 Law on the Democratization of the German School, which abolished the existing pattern of schools and introduced eight-year comprehensive schools (*Einheitsschulen*) for children from the age of 6 to 14. These were followed by two-year middle schools, and four-year upper schools for those pupils who planned to take the *Abitur*, the graduation exam that gives access to higher education. The universities were less affected by change at this stage, but for the rest of the system, the major changes were already in place by the founding of the GDR in 1949.

The changes introduced to the system after 1949 built on the radical alterations of 1946. In 1959, the three-stage, ten-year general polytechnical upper school (POS), became the norm. It gradually replaced the eight-year and middle school during the 1960s. All children, except the exceptionally gifted, attended these schools from the age of 6 to 16. By 1974, 90 percent of children were remaining to the age of 16.

Academically gifted children, about 13 percent of the age group, transferred to the extended upper school (EOS), and took the *Abitur* at 18. Other children attended different forms of vocational school for one-, two-, or three-year courses in which they gained practical qualifications. In the three-year courses, students attained a practical qualification and the *Abitur*.

The school system in the GDR stressed the close relationship between school and work. In 1946, the curriculum allocated 10–12 hours of work per week. In 1958, polytechnical education on the Soviet model became more systematized in the upper stage of the POS by combining some form of vocational training with theoretical work on economic processes. In 1967, this system was gradually phased out in favor of a more general approach, in which pupils were given an introduction to socialist production processes and visited the workplace for about four hours each week. It no longer provided a specialized introduction to a particular trade.

Preschools became a priority in a country where, by the late 1980s, nearly nine out of ten women of working age were employed. The government provided day care for children up to age three, and established kindergartens (for ages three to six), many of which were situated at the workplace. By 1989, over 80 percent of children attended day cares, and over 90 percent attended kindergartens. The last year of kindergarten served as a preparation for the POS, and all children were encouraged to attend.

In order to provide greater access to higher education for working-class students without the *Abitur*, worker and peasant faculties (ABF) were added to three-year bridging courses, which functioned until 1963, by which time 34,000 students had reached university. By 1960, the number of working-class students had increased from 5 percent in 1949 to 50 percent, but during the 1960s the children of the intelligentsia started to gain a higher proportion of places, because the authorities placed less emphasis on social background when selecting students. In 1951, the Higher Education Reform Act established a two-year foundation stage at universities and also made the study of Marxism-Leninism compulsory. Fees were waived, but all students had to work during vacations in industry or agriculture. Between 1951 and 1954, 25 new technical institutions of higher education were created and the number of students doubled. In 1968, universities underwent a structural reform that abolished the traditional faculty structure and divided institutes and universities into 190 sections. At the same time, research projects were brought closer to the requirements of the economy, and the amount of pure research became severely restricted. Universities came directly under the control of the Ministry of Higher Education, which destroyed the traditional independence of learning and research.

After unification in 1990, the former GDR adopted the education system of West Germany, although the pattern of schools varies from state to state. Some states retained a number of comprehensive schools, but in most states, a two- or three-tier system exists. The centralized administration of education has disappeared, and schools and universities have reverted to control by the individual states.

Peter Barker

See also Free German Youth; German Democratic Republic: Arts and Politics; German Democratic Republic: Churches; German Democratic Republic: Sports; German Democratic Republic: Technical Intelligentsia; Honecker, Margot; Socialist Unity Party

References

Annweiler, Oskar, ed. *Vergleich von Bildung und Erziehung in der Bundesrepublik Deutschland und in der Deutschen Demokratischen Republik.* Cologne: Verlag Wissenschaft und Politik, 1990.

Bildung und Erziehung in der DDR im Umbruch. Bonn: Verlag Neue Gesellschaft, 1989.

Friedrich-Ebert-Stiftung, ed. *Das Bildungswesen in der DDR.* Bonn: Verlag Neue Gesellschaft, 1985.

Hearnden, Arthur. *Education in the Two Germanies.* Oxford: Basil Blackwell, 1974.

Moore-Rinvolucri, Mina. *Education in East Germany.* Hamden, CT: Archon Books, 1973.

German Democratic Republic: Foreign Relations

The Soviet Union's formal cession of foreign-affairs sovereignty to the German Democratic Republic (GDR) in the mid-1950s marks the beginning of the smaller German state's drive to gain foreign diplomatic recognition in competition with a West German leadership that denied its rival's statehood. The normalization of East Germany's relations with West Germany in 1972 and the GDR's accession to United Nations membership in 1973 were of decisive importance in obtaining the diplomatic prestige and opportunities for broader economic links sought by the Communist regime. East German foreign policy thereafter aimed at the ultimately unattainable goal of utilizing the GDR's international presence to strengthen its vulnerable domestic economy and to effectively instill a sense of GDR nationhood among the populace.

With the breakdown of East-West negotiations on the German question and the subsequent incorporation of two German states into hostile military alliances in 1955, the postwar contours of East German foreign policy were formed. From the beginning, the Socialist Unity Party (SED) leadership under first secretary Walter Ulbricht (1893–1973) recognized the critical role of its external policies in establishing the legitimacy of a state maintained by force of Soviet arms and engaged in a permanent competition with the larger Federal Republic of Germany (FRG) to win the fealty of the GDR population.

Early East German diplomatic initiatives were closely aligned with those of the Soviet mentor and aimed at the achievement of negotiating parity with West Germany. After the erection of the Berlin Wall in 1961 further solidified Soviet commitment to the permanency of an East German state, the Ulbricht leadership combined efforts to consolidate GDR economic life with a program seeking broader diplomatic recognition. Success was attained in this latter effort mainly in the forging of such links with Soviet allies in Eastern Europe as well as some nonaligned countries in the developing world throughout the decade.

The next critical phase in East Germany's foreign activities followed from Erich Honecker's (1912–94) replacement of Ulbricht as SED first secretary in 1971 and the signing of the 1972 Basic Treaty with West Germany. The latter document fell somewhat short of East Berlin's goal of full diplomatic recognition by Bonn but expedited GDR membership in the United Nations and the adoption of official ties with the rest of the world. Honecker thereafter moved to forestall the possible unsettling effects of greater East German–West German popular contacts promoted by the Basic Treaty, such as cross-border travel, by binding the GDR more tightly to its Soviet ally in treaties of friendship and scientific and technical collaboration. GDR training of military and security personnel in Soviet-allied states, notably in Africa, constituted an additional dimension of cooperation with Moscow. However, the GDR elite also moved to extend economic ties beyond the Soviet-led Council of Mutual Economic Assistance (CMEA) to secure Western financial credits and improve the quality of its exports.

Significant East German departures from Soviet foreign policy began to surface in the fateful 1980s, the most consequential of which was Honecker's initially lukewarm and later defiant response to Mikhail Gorbachev's calls for socialist restructuring and renewal. The Soviet general secretary's inability, or unwillingness, to impose a reform scheme on an aging SED allowed the latter to pursue its eventually self-defeating blockage of domestic reform that contributed to the GDR's popular revolution in 1989.

East German foreign policy was an essential element of the ruling elite's desperate effort to foster its citizens' identification with a separate, socialist GDR. SED decisionmakers saw both a higher level of foreign trade and finance and expanded diplomatic recognition, among other programs, as vital means to this end. Yet GDR trade remained heavily CMEA-oriented in the presence of repeated Soviet demands for increased East German industrial deliveries, while the Honecker leadership's steps toward cooperative ventures with the West were timid in comparison to those taken by its socialist allies. There is equally little evidence that East Germany's securing of broad diplomatic recognition strengthened the SED's nation-building exertions, as Honecker's failure to address political and economic reform in the late 1980s tilted the national question in favor of the FRG.

Ernest D. Plock

See also Basic Treaty; Berlin; Berlin Wall; The Cold War and Germany; Fischer, Oskar; German-German Relations; Gorbachev and the German Question; Honecker, Erich; *Ostpolitik*; Socialist Unity Party; Soviet-German Relations; Ulbricht, Walter

References

Deutsches Institut für Zeitgeschichte. *Dokumente zur Aussenpolitik der Deutschen Demokratischen Republik.* Berlin: Rütten & Loening, 1987.

Frey, Erich G. *Division and Detente: The Germanies and Their Alliances.* New York, NY: Praeger, 1987.

Gedmin, Jeffrey. *The Hidden Hand: Gorbachev and the Collapse of East Germany.* Washington, DC: AEI Press, 1992.

Jacobsen, Hans-Adolf, Gert Leptin, Ulrich Scheuner, and Eberhard Schulz, eds. *Drei Jahrzehnte Aussenpolitik der DDR.* Munich: R. Oldenbourg Verlag, 1980.

McAdams, A. James. *East Germany and Detente: Building Authority after the Wall.* Cambridge: Cambridge University Press, 1985.

Phillips, Ann L. *Soviet Policy toward East Germany Reconsidered: The Postwar Decade.* New York, NY: Greenwood Press, 1986.

Weber, Hermann. *Geschichte der DDR.* Munich: Deutscher Taschenbuch Verlag, 1985.

Wettig, Gerhard. *Die Sowjetunion, die DDR und die Deutschlandfrage.* Bonn: Bonn Aktuell GmbH, 1976.

Winters, Peter Jochen. "Die Aussenpolitik der DDR." *Handbuch der deutschen Aussenpolitik.* Ed. Hans-Peter Schwarz. Munich: Piper & Co. Verlag, 1975.

German Democratic Republic: Government System

As in other Communist systems, all important political decisions in the German Democratic Republic (GDR) were made by the leadership of the ruling party, in this case the Socialist Unity Party (SED). Bodies belonging to the formal government were charged with, at best, secondary decisions and with implementing the party's policies.

Under the 1968 constitution, revised in 1974, the GDR's governmental institutions resembled, on paper, those of Western parliamentary systems. The "highest organ of state power" was the People's Chamber (Volkskammer), a unicameral legislature whose members were elected without opposition. The members included representatives of the SED, the four small "bloc parties" allied to it, and several "mass organizations," including the Free German Youth and the Federation of Free German Trade Unions. The Volkskammer met for only a few days each year and only once (prior to the upheaval of late 1989) did it depart from its practice of making all decisions unanimously.

The government's executive, the Council of Ministers, and its chairman (often referred to as the GDR's prime minister) were nominally chosen by and responsible to the Volkskammer. The most important responsibility of this body of some 40 members was the day-to-day management of the economy, particularly through the State Planning Commission and the large number of economic ministries. Serving as collective head of state was the State Council; its chairman was in effect the country's ceremonial president. The National Defense Council was responsible for defense matters and was supposed to assume full legislative and executive powers in the case of an internal or external emergency.

The GDR was divided into 15 regions, which in turn were subdivided into districts and communes; each elected its own parliament, from which an executive council was chosen. The powers of these bodies were modest compared both to those of the central government and to those of the regional party organizations. The country's judicial system was also hierarchically organized, from the district level to the national Supreme Court, which in turn stood under the supervision of the State Council. As this structure suggests, the judiciary was firmly subordinated to the country's political authorities.

The GDR's military forces were probably second in importance within the Warsaw Pact only to Soviet forces; in addition to some 175,000 regular troops, the country maintained border guards and militia-like factory "combat groups." Still more important for the purposes of social control was the State Security Service (SSD), popularly known as the Stasi; in addition to carrying out extensive espionage and counterespionage activities, the SSD penetrated virtually all GDR institutions and groups, including those of actual or potential dissidents, with the help of an extensive network of secret informers.

The crisis of October and November 1989 dramatically altered the character, though not the basic form, of the GDR's government; the Volkskammer and the Council of Ministers quickly assumed the genuine policymaking authority that the SED had lost. A new government led by the reform Communist Hans Modrow (1928–) was elected by the parliament on November 13; the formation of a government-opposition round table in December led within a few weeks to opposition members joining the government. Democratic elections in March 1990 brought the formation of a conservative-led government under Lothar de Maizière (1940–), a Christian Democrat, that presided over the process that culminated in German unification on October 3.

Thomas A. Baylis

See also Ackermann, Anton; Axen, Hermann; Berlin; Free German Trade Union Federation; Free German Youth; German Communist Party; German Democratic Republic: Arts and Politics; German Democratic Republic: Churches; German Democratic Republic: Constitutions; German Democratic Republic: Economy; German Democratic Republic: Judicial System; German Democratic Republic: Marxism-Leninism; German Democratic Republic: Media; German Democratic Republic: National People's Army; German Democratic Republic: Nationalism; German Democratic Republic: Opposition; German Democratic Republic: Political Culture; German Democratic Republic: Political Party System; German Democratic Republic: Sports; German Democratic Republic: State Security; German Democratic Republic: Technical Intelligentsia; German-German Relations; Grotewohl, Otto; Hager, Kurt; Honecker, Erich; Honecker, Margot; Mielke, Erich; Pieck, Wilhelm; Socialist Unity Party; Stoph, Willi; Ulbricht, Walter

References

Glaessner, Gert-Joachim. *Die andere deutsche Republik.* Opladen: Westdeutscher Verlag, 1989.

Krisch, Henry. *The German Democratic Republic: The Search for Identity.* Boulder, CO: Westview Press, 1985.

Neugebauer, Gero. *Partei und Staatsapparat in der DDR.* Opladen: Westdeutscher Verlag, 1978.

German Democratic Republic: Judicial System

In a constitutional democracy, such as the Federal Republic of Germany (FRG), the judiciary is independent of legislative and executive authority. In the German Democratic Repub-

lic (GDR), however, the judiciary was subordinated to the regime's political goals. The entire system of judicial administration, from its reorganization in 1952 until 1990, served to uphold socialist principles and to protect and defend the policies of the existing state. Indeed, the basic rights of citizens derived from "socialist legality" and the political power of the people's state. In this way justice and politics would join together in perfect unity.

The GDR reorganized and simplified its judiciary in 1952 in response to a new system of administrative districts created to replace the five territorial states (*Länder*). A single, three-tiered system of regular courts replaced the old mixed system of regular and specialized courts inherited from the past. Each tier corresponded with a particular level of government. At the bottom level sat the local courts (*Kreisgerichte*). In the 1980s, over 900 professional judges staffed 234 such courts. Local courts exercised limited criminal and civil jurisdiction and served as labor and family courts as well. One professional judge and two lay judges presided over each case tried at this level.

District courts (*Bezirksgerichte*) convened at the next level. One such tribunal sat in each of the GDR's 15 administrative districts. Presided over by 285 judges, these courts served in appellate and trial capacities, hearing appeals from local courts and exercising original jurisdiction over serious civil and criminal offenses. Treason and other major political crimes formed the hard core of the district court's criminal jurisdiction. Headed by a director and organized into criminal, civil, labor, and family divisions, each of these courts did most of its appellate work in panels of three professional judges. Lay judges, however, participated in appeals in labor cases.

At the top of this hierarchy stood the Supreme Court (*Oberstesgericht*), which by 1985 consisted of 47 judges headed by a president. Organized into specialized divisions grouped under criminal, civil, labor, and family departments, the Supreme Court served mainly as an appellate tribunal. Its appellate work included hearing appeals from military courts. But it also functioned as a court of cassation: at the request of the procurator general, an executive official charged with administrative control over all lower and district courts, the Supreme Court could revise or annul any judgment of any court in the regular judiciary, a frequent occurrence in criminal cases. Finally, the Supreme Court served in a quasi-legislative capacity, occasionally handing down directives on legal matters unrelated to pending cases on direct appeal. Ultimately responsible to the People's Chamber, the Supreme Court lacked the independence of equivalent high courts in the Federal Republic.

The GDR's regular court system had far fewer judges and heard far fewer cases than equivalent tribunals in the FRG. One reason was East Germany's system of conflict commissions, later known as social courts. Staffed entirely by laypersons, several thousand of these courts existed in neighborhoods, factories, and agricultural cooperatives. Following informal methods of conflict resolution, social courts sought to reconcile opposing sides in civil disputes and to serve as instruments of education and social discipline in petty criminal cases. In 1982, according to one report, "a total of 292,111 persons, all of them nonlawyers, served on the social courts of the country." The decisions of these courts were appealable to the district courts, although reportedly persons appearing before them seldom chose that option.

GDR judges were not as highly trained as were their counterparts in the FRG. Students wishing to pursue careers in the judiciary would, after careful screening for their political reliability, embark on four years of legal education in East Berlin's Humboldt University. Upon the successful completion of a course of studies laden with Marxist-Leninist ideology and oriented toward the defense and promotion of socialist legality, they would receive the degree of *Diplomjurist*, thus qualifying them for an appointment to the regular judiciary. Following a short apprenticeship, they would qualify for election to the regular judiciary.

In the GDR, all judges below the level of the Supreme Court were elected for five-year terms by the legislative assembly of the governmental subdivision in which their courts were located. Judicial and executive officials selected candidates who ran unopposed in these elections. Most could count on reelection, and most judges remained on the bench until their retirement. The national parliament elected the members of the Supreme Court. Most East German judges were members of the Socialist Unity Party (SED); in their judging, they were expected to follow the principles that the party represented. Many of these judges lost their positions when the two German states united in 1990. Those who had compromised themselves politically while serving on the East German bench were permanently barred from regaining their judgeships.

Donald P. Kommers

See also German Democratic Republic; German Democratic Republic: Constitutions; German Democratic Republic: Political Culture; German Democratic Republic: State Security; Honecker, Erich; Mielke, Erich; Socialist Unity Party; Ulbricht, Walter

References

Feth, Andrea. *Hilde Benjamin: Eine Biographie.* Berlin: Arno Spitz, 1997.

Hazard, John Newbold. *The Communists and Their Law: A Search for the Common Core of the Legal Systems of the Marxian Socialist States.* Chicago, IL: University of Chicago Press, 1969.

Markovits, Inga. "Last Days." *California Law Review* 55 (1992), 80.

Meador, Daniel John. *Impressions of Law in East Germany.* Charlottesville, VA: University Presses of Virginia, 1983.

Schroeder, Friedrich-Christian. "The Rise and Fall of the Criminal Law of the German Democratic Republic." *Criminal Law Forum* 217 (1991), 2.

German Democratic Republic: Literature and Literary Life

Because of the sociopolitical context in which it existed, the literature of the German Democratic Republic (GDR) is less easy to define than the geographic descriptor would suggest. GDR literature, as it is usually termed, can be said to include not only works written by authors residing within the boundaries of East Germany but also much of what has been written by those who left or were expelled from the GDR (particularly in the wake of the cultural-political repression of the late 1970s), most famous among them the poet-singer Wolf Biermann. To the extent that these emigré writers—among them Jurek Becker (1937–97), Sarah Kirsch (1935–), Reiner Kunze (1933–), and Günter Kunert (1929–)—continued to ground their writing in the GDR experience, they may be regarded as belonging to GDR literature. Likewise, writers who took up residence in the GDR, such as those who settled there after years of exile outside National Socialist Germany, also contributed to GDR literature. Among these are Johannes R. Becher (1891–1958), Stephan Hermlin (1915–97), Stefan Heym (1913–), Anna Seghers (1900–83), Friedrich Wolf, and Arnold Zweig (1887–1968), as well as younger writers who later emigrated to the GDR from West Germany, including Biermann.

The issue is further complicated by the fact that some GDR writers, such as Christa Wolf (1929–) and Heiner Müller (1929–95), have often been acclaimed simply as "German" writers, owing to the critical nature and extreme complexity of their texts, which limited their accessibility to average citizens in the GDR. The still-unresolved question of whether there are two (East and West) German literatures, four (including Austria and Switzerland), or only one has recurred frequently in the postwar period.

Anna Seghers. Courtesy of Inter Nationes, Bonn.

Like their peers in other Eastern Bloc states, GDR writers stood in an explicit relationship to their state. Within the GDR, a highly centralized, hierarchical system exerted control from the Central Committee of the Socialist Unity Party down through the publishing houses, bookstores, libraries, and cultural institutions such as theaters, journals, and clubs. Beyond such extensive scrutiny and censorship, there was also a system of rewards which sustained authors with salaried positions, generous royalties, prizes, and social privileges. Highly subsidized books, theater performances, and museums were well within the financial means of GDR citizens, who were particularly alert to the nuances and shifts of cultural policy, which could be detected in literary texts. But GDR writers also had access to western German-language media, which readily publicized texts that were regarded as dissident or critical of the GDR.

The GDR's investment in culture implied considerable faith in the power of literary works to influence readers' support for the agenda of the state. For this reason, chronologies of GDR literature are often organized according to developments in the political sphere. Although not all literary historians agree on the exact divisions, there is a tendency to characterize the earliest publications of the returning exile writers as "anti-fascist" literature. To this group belong most notably Anna Seghers's *Das siebte Kreuz* (published in English as *The Seventh Cross,* 1942; published as the first novel in the Soviet Occupation Zone, 1946), and Bruno Apitz's much later *Nackt unter Wölfen* (Naked among wolves), 1958, both of which were sold in millions of copies, and the poetry of Johannes R. Becher and Bertolt Brecht (1898–1956).

With the founding of the GDR in 1949, emphasis shifted to the establishment of a viable socialist system of production in an economy devastated by the dismantling of its industries by the Soviet Union in reparation for war losses and by the lack of an adequate male workforce. For the next decade, prose and drama tended to idealistic depictions of the satisfaction and achievements of those, particularly women, who entered the industrial or agricultural workforce, often guided by a fatherly party secretary. Writers who had been active in the German labor and socialist movements before 1933 provided some of the founding texts of this phase, including Eduard Claudius (*Menschen an unserer Seite* [People at our side], 1951), Elfriede Brüning (*Regine Haberkorn,* 1955) and Otto Gotsche (*Tiefe Furchen* [Deep furrows], 1949). Soon a new generation began to address the tensions and conflicts of the rebuilding process.

At the Bitterfeld Conference of 1959 writers were enjoined to learn more about what was being accomplished in factories and on farms and workers themselves were urged to write about their own experiences. Writers such as Dieter Noll (*Die Abenteuer des Werner Holt* [The adventures of Werner Holt], 1960, 1963), Brigitte Reimann (*Ankunft im Alltag* [Arrival at the everyday], 1961), Erwin Strittmatter (*Ole Bienkopp* [Old Bienkopp], 1963), Erik Neutsch (*Spur der Steine* [Traces of stones], 1964), and Peter Hacks (*Die Sorgen und die Macht* [The sorrows and the power], 1960; *Moritz Tassow,* 1965) emerged, as did other more well-known writers whose literary debuts fell in these years: Volker Braun (1939–), Heiner Müller (1929–95), Hermann Kant (1926–), and Christa Wolf.

Following the building of the Berlin Wall in 1961, the GDR seemed well on its way to developing a distinct literary tradition. This perception enjoyed support in the West with the apparent move to liberalization that marked the replacement of the repressive Walter Ulbricht (1893–1973) by Erich Honecker (1912–94) in 1971 and political recognition of the GDR in the wake of Willy Brandt's (1913–92) *Ostpolitik* (eastern policy) of the early 1970s. By the late 1960s, a body of literature in a more subjective, critical vein had begun to emerge. Of these works, Christa Wolf's 1968 *Nachdenken über Christa T.* (published as *The Quest for Christa T.*) marks a watershed. With its initial circulation cut short, the book was only released to a general readership after Honecker promulgated less restrictive policies on censorship in 1971. Until the uproar that followed reprisals against Wolf Biermann in 1976, GDR literature enjoyed a brief period of relative openness, marked by the appearance of controversial works such as Volker Braun's "Unvollendete Geschichte" (Unfinished story), 1975, Irmtraud Morgner's *Leben und Abenteuer der Trobadora Beatriz* (Life and adventures of the troubador Beatriz), 1974, and Christa Wolf's *Kindheitsmuster* (published as *Patterns of Childhood*), 1976.

Subsequent to Biermann's expulsion and protests against the state's action by some writers, more than 70 writers and performing artists left the GDR. The literary scene once again became more restrictive until Mikhail Gorbachev's policies of *glasnost* in the Soviet Union led writers to criticize openly the system of censorship that curtailed freedom of expression in the GDR. With increasing boldness after 1987, they spoke out on behalf of their fellow citizens against failed policies and abuses of state power. Their protests culminated in the events of fall 1989.

Subsequent to the demise of the GDR, critical assessments of its literature have been complicated both by the resistance of some writers, committed socialists, who would have preferred a reformed GDR to unification with the west and by ongoing revelations of others' complicity as informers to the state secret police (Staatssicherheitsdienst). Criticism of the role assumed by writers was particularly acute in the controversy that swirled around Christa Wolf's *Was bleibt* (What remains), 1990, most of which had been written, but not published, in 1979. The question of whether or how GDR literature can or should be integrated into postwar German literary history is not likely to be resolved before the end of the twentieth century.

Patricia Herminghouse

See also Becher, Johannes Robert; Becker, Jurek; Biermann, Wolf; Books; Braun, Volker; Brecht, Bertolt; Federal Republic of Germany: Literature; Feminist Writing; German Democratic Republic: Arts and Politics; German Democratic Republic: Nationalism; German Democratic Republic: Political Culture; *Germanistik;* Hermlin, Stephan; Heym, Stefan; Kant, Hermann; Kirsch, Sarah; Kunert, Günter; Kunze, Reiner; Libraries; Müller, Heiner; Seghers, Anna; Wolf, Christa; Zweig, Arnold

References

Emmerich, Wolfgang. *Kleine Literaturgeschichte der DDR. 1945–1988*. Frankfurt am Main: Luchterhand, 1989.

Fox, Thomas C. *Border Crossings: An Introduction to East German Prose*. Ann Arbor, MI: University of Michigan Press, 1993.

Hallberg, Robert von. *Literary Intellectuals and the Dissolution of the State: Professionalism and Conformity in the GDR*. Trans. Kenneth J. Northcott. Chicago, IL: University of Chicago Press, 1996.

Kane, Martin, ed. *Socialism and the Literary Imagination*. New York, NY: Berg, 1991.

Reid, J.H. *Writing without Taboos: The New East German Literature*. New York, NY: Berg, 1990.

German Democratic Republic: Marxism-Leninism

The official Soviet ideology, known as Marxism-Leninism, was taken over without significant modification by the ruling elements of the German Democratic Republic (GDR). Throughout the nearly four decades of that country's existence, Marxism-Leninism was systematically propagated and enforced as the doctrinal basis for the socialization of youth, the administration of public affairs, and the attempted development of national identity.

Marxism-Leninism, as it evolved in the Soviet Union after 1917, purported to supply a complete system of thought and belief, an ideological point of reference covering all aspects of public life: the social order, economy, science, art, and the understanding of historical development. Like the other client states of the Soviet Union, the GDR espoused the doctrine and did so with noteworthy loyalty and rigidity, following the Soviet example with utmost care in its style of indoctrinating young people and regulating cultural life. Marxism-Leninism was not only a guide to official policies in political and economic affairs but also a set of rules for intellectual activity and personal morality.

Although the GDR—as the partial homeland of original Marxist thought—might have been expected to evince a more sophisticated grasp of the Marxian tradition, it was notable for the absence of any significant dissenting or critical variants of the reigning ideology. Those thinkers capable of such dissent, Ernst Bloch (1885–1977) or Rudolf Bahro for example, either emigrated or were expelled. Others, such as the playwright Bertolt Brecht (1898–1956), tended to keep their misgivings to themselves. Unlike Poland, Hungary, or Czechoslovakia, the GDR thus failed to produce a significant Marxian challenge to the official perversion of Marxism.

The GDR did succeed in generating a measure of national pride and identity, a fact that became visible as the regime collapsed and before the tide of reunification became irresistible. But such national self-awareness as there was owed little to the official Marxism-Leninism upheld by the regime. Indeed, while at this stage some loyalty to socialism and its policies existed, the official ideology was as thoroughly discredited as the ruling group that had espoused it.

Lyman H. Legters

See also Ackermann, Anton; Axen, Hermann; German Democratic Republic; German Democratic Republic: Arts and Politics; German Democratic Republic: Churches; German Democratic Republic: Collapse; German Democratic Republic: Economy; German Democratic Republic: Education; German Democratic Republic: Government System; German Democratic Republic: Political Culture; German Democratic Republic: Political Party System; German Democratic Republic: Opposition; Honecker, Erich; Socialist Unity Party; Ulbricht, Walter

References

Gerber, Margy, ed. *Studies in GDR Culture and Society 6*. Lanham, MD: University Press of America, 1986.

Holmes, Leslie. "The Significance of Marxist Dissent to the Emergence of Postcommunism in the GDR." *The Road to Disillusion*. Ed. Raymond Taras. Armonk, NY: M.E. Sharpe, 1992.

Ludz, Peter Christian, ed. *Soziologie und Marxismus in der Deutschen Demokratischen Republik*. Vol 1. Neuwied: Luchterhand, 1972.

McCauley, Martin. *Marxism-Leninism in the German Democratic Republic*. London: Macmillan, 1979.

German Democratic Republic: Media

The media in the GDR were primarily instruments of ideological control, with the dissemination of news and entertainment always subordinated to considerations of political suitability. Centralized coordination, both of the media themselves and of the material that went into them, was designed to ensure a watertight system of guided opinion-formation. However, the widespread viewing of West German television and listening to radio (where not blocked) was a major challenge to these principles.

The GDR media system legitimated itself by rejecting Western notions of neutrality and pluralism: all public communication, it asserted, is inherently partisan, and predominantly reflects and consolidates the interests of the ruling class. Given the Communists' uniquely correct insight into the workings of history, it was their responsibility to ensure that their particular view, and no others, should be purveyed by the media in a country where the class they represented had come to power. Although Article 27 of the constitution contained an explicit guarantee of freedom of expression and of the press and broadcasting, this amounted to little more than the ruling Socialist Unity Party's (SED's) right to determine what could and could not be published, as Article 1 had already defined the GDR as a "socialist" state "under the leadership of the working class and its Marxist-Leninist Party."

The function of the media was, according to a frequently cited observation of Lenin's, essentially threefold: to act as "collective propagandist," "collective agitator," and "collective organizer." In the GDR, the media were accordingly noncommercial operations, and a complex system of control and coordination touched every level of their activities. At the top was the government's press office, which in its turn was effectively subordinated to the Central Committee and *Politbüro* of the SED. All magazines and newspapers had to be licensed by the press office: in fact, the press landscape hardly changed after the basic pattern was established in the 1950s. More important was the issuing of daily, weekly, and longer-term directives to editors on what was to be covered in their papers, something that was in any case also determined by the fact that there was only one news agency, the state-controlled ADN, to which they could subscribe. Compliance on the part of editors and journalists could be ensured by the care with which they were selected and trained—usually at the University of Leipzig's School of Journalism—before being allowed to qualify.

Western newspapers and magazines were to all intents and purposes unobtainable. Any differences between the 40 or so daily papers in the GDR lay not in ideology but in their attempts to address different geographical and social interests within the population. The central organs of the parties and mass organizations—including, most prominently, the SED's newspaper *Neues Deutschland* (New Germany), with a circulation of just over one million—appeared in Berlin. More popular (largely because of their local coverage) were the *Bezirkszeitungen* (regional newspapers), also owned by the SED, that appeared in the country's 14 administrative districts. Although strictly speaking only 17 dailies belonged to the SED, all—like the parties and organizations they represented—were ultimately beholden to the party's version of Marxism-Leninism. The same was true of the GDR's magazine press, where no opportunity was lost to drive home political points in every possible context.

The structures of broadcasting in the GDR were highly centralized, with two television channels and three main radio services for the whole country, all subject to the same ideological constraints as the press. However, West German broadcasts could be received over most of the GDR and were immensely popular. In the Honecker years, the authorities more or less condoned the consumption of Western television and radio shows but attempted to recapture viewers by increasing the entertainment element in their own programs. Their news bulletins remained as wooden as ever, however, and attracted only a minimal audience.

After the *Wende* ("turn" [of 1989]), the GDR media landscape was rapidly transformed—partly through the lifting of state control, partly through the importation of West German newspapers and magazines, and partly through the appearance of numerous new organs. By the time of unification one year later, most of the latter had disappeared again, together with the citizens' movements they largely represented, and the curiosity value of the West German press was fading. In the end, the old patterns of readership proved remarkably resilient, and a substantial number of GDR titles survived, now shorn of their Marxist ideology and bought up by Western companies, to preserve a distinct press landscape in the east of the united Germany. The GDR broadcasting system, on the other hand, was dismantled and replaced with regional services on the West German pattern.

John Sandford

See also German Democratic Republic; German Democratic Republic: Arts and Politics; German Democratic Republic: Education; German Democratic Republic: Marxism-Leninism; German Democratic Republic: Political Culture; Socialist Unity Party

References

Holzweissig, G. *Massenmedien in der DDR.* Berlin: Verlag Gebr. Holzapfel, 1989.

Sandford, John. *The Mass Media of the German-Speaking Countries.* London: Oswald Wolff; Des Moines, IA: Iowa University Press, 1976.

———. "The Transformation of the Media in East Germany since the *Wende.*" *Journal of Area Studies* 13 (1993), 25–36.

German Democratic Republic: National People's Army (Nationale Volksarmee)

The National People's Army (Nationale Volksarmee; NVA) of the German Democratic Republic (GDR) existed officially from January 18, 1956, until October 3, 1990. Some paramilitary predecessor organizations of the NVA came into existence a decade earlier. Selected NVA veterans continued service in the Bundeswehr after unification in 1990. In its heyday, from the late 1960s until the mid-1980s, the 175,000-strong NVA acquired a reputation as the most effective and powerful armed force in the Warsaw Pact besides the Soviets themselves. Although the NVA shared certain superficial similarities with the Bundeswehr with regard to the chronology of its creation and its subordination to multinational alliances, the political-strategic character of the NVA, as well as its institutions of leadership, command, and obedience, differed markedly from its counterpart in West Germany. The civil-military demarcation between external and internal security was far less distinct in the GDR than in the FRG. The NVA was the army of a Communist party, that is, "an army of the socialist type," organized according to a Marxist-Leninist doctrine of society and arms. The founders of the NVA emulated Soviet military institutions regarding strategy, operations, inner structure, and equipment.

The NVA was fully integrated in the command structures of the Combined Armed Forces Command of the Warsaw Pact, created in 1955. Soviet advisors served in all echelons of the NVA as liaisons and observers. Final say in matters of strategy and operations that would affect the NVA in combat rested with them.

The creation of military units in the Soviet Zone of Occupation (SBZ) began in the last half of 1945. The armed organizations comprised the Kasernierte Volkspolizei (KVP; Barracks-quartered Police), whereas the Deutsche Grenzpolizei (German Border Police) formed the cadres from which the NVA emerged a decade later. These troops participated, with mixed results, in the suppression of the June 17, 1953 workers' revolt. This outcome weakened Soviet faith in the efficacy of their military preparations in the GDR. On January 18, 1956, as the Bundeswehr began mustering its first troops, the GDR Volkskammer (People's Chamber) enacted a law for the creation of the NVA and a Ministry of National Defense (MfNV).

The first units of the NVA paraded through East Berlin on May 1, 1956, in a familiar field-gray uniform based on those of the Reichswehr and Wehrmacht. This image was chosen to appeal to national sensibilities and to offer a contrast to the Yankee look-alikes of the new Bundeswehr. The NVA was organized into land, air, air defense, and naval forces, as well as a large contingent of border troops. The Ministry of National Defense took up residence in an old Luftwaffe base in Strausberg, beyond the eastern city limits of Berlin. Military district headquarters (corps/territorial HQ) appeared in Neubrandenburg in the north and Leipzig in the south. Other armed organizations integrated into the Ministry of National Defense included the military units of the Ministry for State Security (MfS), the workers' militias, and the readiness police.

The role of the NVA-border troops in the erection of the Berlin Wall in August 1961 occupied a place of special honor in the military ethos of the GDR. This event represented the army's "baptism of fire" against a diplomatic-subversive assault by the imperialists of NATO. Until 1973, the border troops remained within the ranks of the NVA. Even in their subsequent semi-independent form as the elite Grenztruppen der DDR (Border Troops of the GDR) they remained prepared for the tactical offensive in crisis and war in conjunction with the NVA field army.

After an initial phase as a volunteer force, the NVA introduced conscription in 1962. After pre-military training in schools and youth organizations (Freie Deutsche Jugend [FDJ; Free German Youth] and the Gesellschaft für Sport und Technik [GST; Society for Sport and Technology]), young men served an 18-month term in the land, air, or naval forces. The SED controlled each soldier through a system of interlocking party-military institutions as well as iron military discipline. The NVA soldier was a tiny part of the overall Soviet mobilization system that boasted a lightning reaction time. The East German units stood at the ready within a network of headquarters and field forces controlled from headquarters in Moscow. Garrison life was hard on officer and soldier alike. Demands of constant combat readiness based on an ideological foundation revived barracks-square abuses that had existed before 1945. These practices left a deep impression on an East German civilian population that found no joy in soldiering.

Nearly all officers, and half of the noncommissioned officers, were members of the SED. Without the party badge, progress in a soldier's career became impossible; continued party discipline remained essential. The NVA began the process of officer recruitment among young men of early high-school age. Those selected soon received social and material benefits, as the SED treated the NVA officer corps as a privileged elite. Outstanding among the multifaceted institutions of SED control in arms was the Main Political Administration (Politische Hauptverwaltung). Its chain of command reached from the company level into the SED's Central Committee. The MfS operated throughout the armed forces as the Verwaltung 2000 (Administration 2000). Its agents and their network of informers were present in most headquarters staffs.

Soviet/Warsaw Pact strategy and doctrine required that the NVA be constantly poised for an operational counter-offensive against NATO. Some 85 percent of front-line units had to be ready for war within two hours' time. Until 1988, NVA units trained to mount a major offensive operation against

Helicopters of former National People's Army being refitted for civilian purposes. Courtesy of German Embassy, Ottawa.

the FRG, Denmark, and the Benelux states. Such operations would have included extensive Soviet tactical/operational nuclear strikes against NATO targets. NVA units, together with other Warsaw Pact forces, were to destroy NATO forward forces in situ, devastate the U.S.-FRG-Benelux rear area, and erect a military government in the vanquished FRG.

From the mid-1980s until 1989, the economic and social decline of the GDR undercut its ability to maintain the burden of constant readiness in the military sphere. Once the upheaval of late 1989 struck the SED regime, the draftees deserted the army to leave behind an officer corps disillusioned with the SED. The FRG abolished the NVA on October 3, 1990 and offered temporary service in the Bundeswehr to some 90,000 soldiers, of whom 24,000 were officers. By 1994, 3,200 of these former NVA officers received permanent Bundeswehr commissions, and 7,800 term appointments as Bundeswehr NCOs and soldiers.

Donald Abenheim

See also Federal Republic of Germany: Armed Forces; German Democratic Republic; German Democratic Republic: Foreign Relations; German Democratic Republic: Marxism-Leninism; German Democratic Republic: Nationalism; German Democratic Republic: Opposition; German Democratic Republic: Political Culture; German Democratic Republic: Political Party System; German Democratic Republic: Sports; German Democratic Republic: State Security; Grotewohl, Otto; Honecker, Erich; Mielke, Erich; Socialist Unity Party; Soviet-German Relations; Stoph, Willi; Ulbricht, Walter; Wolf, Markus

References

Backerra, Manfred, ed. *NVA: Ein Rückblick für die Zukunft: Zeitzeugen berichten über ein Stück deutscher Militärgeschichte.* Cologne: Markus Verlag, 1992.

Bald, Detlef, ed. *Die Nationale Volksarmee: Beiträge zu Selbstverständnis und Geschichte des deutschen Militärs von 1945–1990.* Baden-Baden: Nomos, 1992.

Baron, Udo. *Die Wehrideologie der Nationalen Volksarmee der DDR.* Bochum: Brockmeyer, 1993.

Farwick, Dieter, ed. *Ein Staat, Eine Armee: Von der NVA zur*

Bundeswehr. Frankfurt am Main and Bonn: Report Verlag, 1992.

Forster, Thomas M. *The East German Army: The Second Power in the Warsaw Pact.* London: Allen and Unwin, 1980.

Giessmann, Hans-Joachim. *Das unliebsame Erbe: Die Auflösung der Militärstruktur der DDR.* Baden-Baden: Nomos, 1992.

Naumann, Klaus. *NVA: Anspruch und Wirklichkeit.* Bonn: Mittler, 1993.

Schönbohm, Jörg. *Zwei Armeen und ein Vaterland: Das Ende der Nationalen Volksarmee.* Berlin: Siedler, 1992.

German Democratic Republic: Nationalism

A problematical aspect of the German Democratic Republic (GDR) is the question of nationalist feeling on the part of the population and nationalist appeals by the leadership. Until the signing of the Basic Treaty between the two Germanys, the GDR leadership wavered between encouraging a separate GDR nationalism, based partly on "anti-fascism" and social revolution, and competing with the Federal Republic to shape an all-German nationalism. The GDR was heralded as a positive development in German history—"the first workers' and peasants' state on German soil"—the goal of a socialist Germany was not abandoned, and the West Germans and western Allies were blamed for German partition.

When treaty relations between the two German states were established in 1972–73, the GDR adopted a policy of *Abgrenzung* (demarcation) that stressed a separate identity for the GDR based on the national consciousness of a socialist nation. This socialist nation (encompassing all the people of the GDR) was to feature growing political unity at home and socialist internationalism abroad. Although said to be rooted in German history, especially in the struggles of the German people for social justice, and to share cultural and folkloric elements with West Germany (and, indeed, with other German-speaking nations), the socialist nation of the GDR was declared to be a separate and superior manifestation of nationalism.

While this notion remained official doctrine between 1971 and 1989, the leadership never mastered the task of explaining how two culturally and historically related nations could be so different, based solely on their social and economic circumstances. A major effort in this regard was the rehabilitation of "reactionary" elements of the German past, beginning with Frederick the Great; eventually almost all of German history except for the Nazi period was accorded a suitable place in the "national" heritage of the GDR. This effort (like that of other Eastern European regimes) to buttress a social identity with nationalist underpinnings could not overcome the West German claim to represent German nationality.

One cannot give a definitive answer to the question of whether this complex set of attitudes was absorbed by the people of East Germany. The increase in applications to leave the GDR throughout the 1980s, culminating in the mass exodus of 1989, suggests that many GDR citizens felt no nationalist constraints in going to the West. Survey data from before as well as after the *Wende* ("turn" [of 1989]), indicate that young people's identification with the GDR sharply de-

creased from about 1986 onward. These data include such aspects of loyalty as performing military service, confidence that socialism would shape the world's future, and adherence to the official ideology. GDR allegiance was based largely on a bundle of attitudes that centered on social security and habit (*Geborgenheit*): a complex of family, friends, and locality.

The unrest of 1989 produced a brief increase in allegiance to the GDR; however, for all but a small group of intellectual activists (who later formed the core of Bündnis 90 [Alliance (19)90]), this feeling was overtaken by and submerged in an all-German euphoria (*"Wir sind ein Volk"* [we are one people]). GDR nationalism, as such, did not survive German unification; a "GDR awareness," however, has survived in the former East Germany. It is compounded of social and economic grievance, contrariness in the face of West German arrogance, and recognition of the differences that the 40 years of the GDR wrought in people's daily life.

Henry Krisch

See also German Democratic Republic; German Democratic Republic: Arts and Politics; German Democratic Republic: Churches; German Democratic Republic: Collapse; German Democratic Republic: Economy; German Democratic Republic: Education; German Democratic Republic: Government System; German Democratic Republic: Marxism-Leninism; German Democratic Republic: Opposition; German Democratic Republic: Political Culture; German Democratic Republic: Political Party System; *Germanistik;* History; Honecker, Erich; National Identity; Nationalism; Reunification; Socialist Unity Party; Ulbricht, Walter

References

Buse, Dieter and Juergen C. Doerr, *German Nationalisms: A Bibliographic Approach.* New York, NY: Garland, 1985.

Grunenberg, Antonia. "Zwei Deutschlands—zwei Identitäten?" *Die DDR in der Ära Honecker.* Ed. Gert-Joachim Glaessner. Opladen: Westdeutscher Verlag, 1988.

Kosing, Alfred. *Nation in Geschichte und Gegenwart.* Berlin: Dietz Verlag, 1976.

Lepsius, M. Rainer. *Demokratie in Deutschland: Soziologisch-historische Konstellationsanalysen.* Göttingen: Vandenhoek & Ruprecht, 1993.

Meier, Helmut and Walter Schmidt. *Erbe und Tradition: Geschichtsdebatte in der DDR.* Cologne: Pahl-Rugenstein, 1989.

Meuschel, Sigrid. "Auf der Suche nach Madame L'Identité? Zur Konzeption der Nation und Nationalgeschichte." *Die DDR in der Ära Honecker.* Ed. Gert-Joachim Glaessner. Opladen: Westdeutscher Verlag, 1988.

Riege, Gerhard and Hans-Jürgen Kulke. *Nationalität: Deutsch. Staatsbürgerschaft: DDR.* Berlin: Staatsverlag der DDR, 1980.

German Democratic Republic: Opposition

If the notion of opposition is understood loosely to include disaffection, power struggles, and passive resistance, then the German Democratic Republic (GDR) had much of it. But if the concept is defined more narrowly and precisely as organized efforts to change the prevailing sociopolitical system as well as its ruling personnel, then the GDR made a rather poor showing over its 40-year history. Such opposition may originate from within the ruling party or outside of it: the GDR had only a negligible taste of the former, but a more significant experience of the latter.

Certainly, the Socialist Unity Party (SED) had its internecine struggles. The farmers were discontented with collectivization, the workers disaffected by official exploitation, and the intellectuals alienated by censorship. It is conceivable that these negative reactions to official policy might have been galvanized into genuine opposition but for the relatively easy escape route, taken by thousands before 1961 (when the Berlin Wall was erected), to West Germany and West Berlin. The most dramatic show of unrest in the GDR before 1989—the workers' uprising of 1953—was a spontaneous demonstration; although it generated wide-ranging political demands as it evolved, no organization existed to pursue them beyond the demonstration itself.

In the aftermath of that uprising and against the backdrop of a somewhat relaxed Stalinism, a small group of intellectuals, the so-called Harich-Janka Group, did appear from within SED ranks. That was the GDR's nearest approximation of the reform movements of Hungary, Poland, and Czechoslovakia a few years later. But it had no significant influence in the upper reaches of the SED and was easily vanquished. A number of individual dissidents also appeared subsequently. They were all committed socialists advocating fundamental change in a democratic and humane direction. The most notable of these were the scientist Robert Havemann (1910–82), who eventually aligned himself with the peace movement, the balladeer Wolf Biermann (1936–), who was expelled from the GDR, and Rudolf Bahro, a Marxist critic of Stalinism who was forced to emigrate.

Late in the 1970s, as the GDR intensified the military training of its youth, a movement began to crystallize from within church circles with the modest objective of countering the militarizing tendency. From such small beginnings arose the most significant challenge the GDR ruling group ever faced. The churches were the only independent institutions available to underpin an oppositional force, and this fact permitted the East German peace movement to survive all efforts by the state to neutralize it. By reclaiming the advocacy of peace from the slogans of the regime, the movement laid the basis for recapturing a whole arena of public discussion from state monopoly. During the 1980s, it staged demonstrations for peace that were without precedent in the GDR after 1953. The Berlin Appeal of 1982 for an authentic peace policy, initiated by Pastor Rainer Eppelmann, signaled a broadening of the movement that continued through the decade.

The broadening included a growing network of European peace groups that helped to sustain the movement in the GDR and the emergence of a distinct women's peace initiative headed by Barbel Bohley and Ulrike Poppe. By 1989 the autonomous peace movement, rooted in the churches but by no means always supported by the official church hierarchies,

provided a major part of the impetus for the transformation of the GDR.

The SED itself played a role in the belated attempt to reform the system. After the Honecker era, it became possible for SED leaders to emerge, Gregor Gysi and Hans Modrow (1928–) in particular, who were committed to democratic change. These gestures came too late to restore the party's credibility and too late as well to stem the tide of reunification.

Lyman H. Legters

See also Biermann, Wolf; German Democratic Republic; German Democratic Republic: Arts and Politics; German Democratic Republic: Churches; German Democratic Republic: Collapse; German Democratic Republic: Economy; German Democratic Republic: Education; German Democratic Republic: Government System; German Democratic Republic: Marxism-Leninism; German Democratic Republic: Opposition; German Democratic Republic: Political Culture; German Democratic Republic: Political Party System; German Democratic Republic: State Security; Havemann, Robert; Honecker, Erich; Modrow, Hans; Reunification; Socialist Unity Party; Ulbricht, Walter

References

Allen, Bruce. *Germany East: Dissent and Opposition.* Montreal: Black Rose Books, 1991.

Baring, Arnulf. *Der 17. Juni 1953.* Cologne: Kiepenheuer & Witsch, 1965.

Fricke, Karl Wilhelm. *Opposition und Widerstand in der DDR.* Cologne: Verlag Wissenschaft und Politik, 1984.

Holmes, Leslie. "The Significance of Marxist Dissent to the Emergence of Postcommunism in the GDR." *The Road to Disillusion.* Ed. Raymond Taras. Armonk, NY: M.E. Sharpe, 1992.

German Democratic Republic: Political Culture

East German political culture existed on several levels: an official, dominant pattern and several subcultural orientations. In the 41 years of the German Democratic Republic (GDR) as a political entity, the divergence between them grew; the political upheaval of 1989 dynamically resolved the resulting tension.

The pattern of East German political orientation resembled that in the Western zones after 1945. Their pattern was marked by authoritarian attitudes, avoidance of social conflict, approval of a highly integrated social order, and disdain for the turmoil of democracy. These inherited traits from the Imperial period had helped to undermine the Weimar Republic and were reinforced and broadcast to a subservient population by the Nazi regime.

The GDR leadership responded ambivalently to this political culture. Overtly, it propagated an ethos of revolutionary vanguard politics, which meant that it maintained and encouraged conformist, collectivist, and authoritarian political attitudes. It also paid lip service to, and to some extent provided, an ethos of participation. But it maintained the political system by inculcating a sense of hierarchy and order. This was especially true for all those holding (or aspiring to hold) *nomenklatura* (bureaucratic) positions in the party, state, and social bureaucracies.

This bifurcated official political culture prolonged and intensified the division between public and publicly-espoused attitudes and those only spoken in private. During periods of political calm, this political culture helped the regime to secure displays of public support, which reinforced the "privateness" of dissenting attitudes. In a crisis, however, this policy weakened the regime by deceiving it as to the extent of popular disaffection. Many people deliberately withdrew from voicing public commitments by "hiding" in societal niches, such as small clubs (e.g., pigeon fanciers, personal discussion and reading clubs, corner-pub groups) with no organizational structure. The supposedly supportive attitude of many GDR citizens was therefore only a pro forma gesture.

In the Honecker era, the regime apparently became aware of the hollowness of its official political culture. Without abandoning its revolutionary mission, it extended and buttressed supportive attitudes by extending the scope of its popular appeal. The GDR leadership accepted consumerism as a societal goal; it sought to confirm the legitimacy of its national credentials by identifying itself with much of German historical tradition. It cautiously attempted to coopt at least some of the ingredients of the international youth culture. These, however, were values shared with West Germany and as such they were unlikely to strengthen support for the GDR.

During the 1980s, the GDR had its dominant political culture challenged by the emergence of dissenting public patterns of engagement with vital issues that differed from official positions. Ironically, these new attitudes resulted from the relative success which the regime enjoyed in having modernized its political and social structure. A well-educated generation of socially involved people raised in the GDR began to display attitudes resembling those that had emerged in West Germany in the 1960s. The GDR public became interested in new social issues, such as ecology, feminism, and the Third World. It turned skeptical on such issues as peace, nuclear energy, and the GDR's military influence in society. It grew dissatisfied with the officially promulgated socialist goals of personal and public life.

Most importantly, the East German public demanded autonomous political participation. This participatory political culture drew heavily from the educated urban social strata, but was by no means limited to them. This public forum began with efforts to establish a movement for nuclear disarmament alongside of, but autonomous from, the official peace organizations; later its interest spread to other vital issues. Organizationally, it functioned under the auspices of the Evangelical Church, where it remained for logistical support and for communal reasons. Later its activities spread to other unauthorized groups, to universities and academies, and to informal social circles. By 1989, the movement had gone from demands for spontaneous involvement in vital issues to political demonstrations and monitoring the political life of party functionaries.

This shift in political culture reflected evolving attitudes rather than the rejection of the GDR's social and economic goals. This is indicated by the upsurge in protest against the regime's active hostility to Gorbachev's reforms, and the fact that many of the dissenters of 1988–89 demanded the creation of a reformed, but still socialist, GDR.

Henry Krisch

See also German Democratic Republic; German Democratic Republic: Arts and Politics; German Democratic Republic: Churches; German Democratic Republic: Collapse; German Democratic Republic: Economy; German Democratic Republic: Education; German Democratic Republic: Government System; German Democratic Republic: Marxism-Leninism; German Democratic Republic: Media; German Democratic Republic: Opposition; German Democratic Republic: Political Party System; German Democratic Republic: State Security; Honecker, Erich; Reunification; Socialist Unity Party; Ulbricht, Walter

References

Berg-Schlosser, Dirk and J. Schissler, eds. *Politische Kultur in Deutschland.* Opladen: Westdeutscher Verlag, 1987.

Bürklin, Wilhelm. "Perspektiven für das deutsche Parteiensystem: Politische Konfliktlinien und die sozialdemokratische Kultur." *Deutschland: Eine Nation—doppelte Geschichte.* Ed. Werner Weidenfeld. Cologne: Verlag Wissenschaft und Politik, 1993.

Feist, Ursula. "Zur politischen Akkulturation der vereinten Deutschen . . ." *Aus Politik und Zeitgeschichte* 11–12 (1991), 21–32.

Krisch, Henry. "Changes in Political Culture and the Transformation of the GDR, 1989–1990." *The German Revolution of 1989: Causes and Consequences.* Ed. Gert-Joachim Glaessner and Ian Wallace. Oxford: Berg, 1992.

Rytlewski, Ralf. *Political Culture in Germany.* New York, NY: St. Martin's Press, 1993.

———. *Politische Kultur in der DDR.* Stuttgart: Kohlhammer, 1989.

German Democratic Republic: Political Party System

The Socialist Unity Party (Sozialistische Einheitspartei Deutschlands; SED) dominated East German political life from its creation in 1946 until the crisis of fall 1989. Four other parties, however, maintained a legal existence throughout the years of Communist rule: the Christian Democratic Union (CDU), the Liberal Democratic Party (LDPD), the Democratic Peasants' Party (DBD) and the National Democratic Party (NDPD). All four of these "bloc parties" acknowledged the "leading role" of the SED in the German Democratic Republic (GDR) and gave unqualified support to its policies. As members of the GDR's "National Front," their candidates for public office ran on an unopposed joint slate with candidates representing the SED and several SED-controlled mass organizations. Their function seems to have been to enlist the support of groups outside the traditional working class for the SED's policies and to allow members of such groups to satisfy regime demands for political activism without actually joining the ruling party.

East Germany's Soviet occupiers initially recognized four parties in mid-1945: the German Communist Party (KPD), the Social Democratic Party (SPD), the CDU, and the LDPD. The first two merged into the SED in 1946, partly because of Communist and Soviet pressure but also in response to the widespread feeling in both parties that the division between them had substantially contributed to the Nazi seizure of power. The CDU and LDPD both began as independent "bourgeois" parties that often criticized Communist policies, but by the late 1940s, after many of their leading members had been forced into exile or arrested, they had been reduced to subservience to the SED. The NDPD and DBD were created in April 1948 under the aegis of the ruling party, the first to integrate former Nazis and military officers into the new order and the second to bring in independent peasants.

The SED saw itself as a classic Leninist party, organized according to the principles of "democratic centralism" and charged with mobilizing and leading East German society in the construction of Soviet-style socialism. With some 2.3 million members (1986)—roughly one for every five adults—the party penetrated every sector of society; it assumed primary responsibility for political education and indoctrination, the recruitment of personnel for all important positions in society, and the supervision of the work of all state organs, economic institutions, and mass organizations. The party's *Politbüro* (22 members and 5 candidate members) made the country's major policy decisions; the powerful party bureaucracy, headed by a Secretariat of 11 members, supervised implementation.

Of the bloc parties, the CDU, with some 125,000 members, was probably the most important; it sought to enlist the support of believing Christians for the regime's version of socialism and in particular for its "peace" policies. The LDPD (83,000 members) represented the GDR's remaining "middle class"—its small private sector along with some professionals and members of the intelligentsia. The DBD (106,000 members) and NPDP (90,000 members) were probably most important in the GDR's early years in supporting agricultural collectivization and diluting the potential of the CDU and LDPD.

With the collapse of Communist rule, the SED purged itself of most of its former leaders and renamed itself the Party of Democratic Socialism (PDS); as such, it became an important opposition force in the eastern *Länder* (states). Generally, however, the new party system that emerged prior to the GDR's first free elections in March 1990 was dominated by Western parties, most notably the West German CDU, which absorbed its East German namesake. Former East German CDU members, and a few from the LDPD (which merged with the West German Free Democrats), took a number of important positions in the new GDR government and in the state governments formed in October 1990. Parties based on the GDR's dissident movement fared badly in the elections, but some survived as part of the Bündnis 90 (Alliance [19]90).

Thomas A. Baylis

See also German Democratic Republic; German Democratic Republic: Arts and Politics; German Democratic Republic: Churches; German Democratic Republic: Collapse; German Democratic Republic: Economy; German Democratic Republic: Government System; German Democratic Republic: Marxism-Leninism; German Democratic Republic: Opposition; German Democratic Republic: Political Culture; German Democratic Republic: State Security; Honecker, Erich; Party of Democratic Socialism; Reunification; Socialist Unity Party; Ulbricht, Walter

References
Childs, David. *The GDR: Moscow's German Ally.* London: Unwin Hyman, 1988.
Fortsch, Eckard. *Die SED.* Stuttgart: W. Kohlhammer Verlag, 1969.
Glaessner, Gert-Joachim. *Die andere deutsche Republik.* Opladen: Westdeutscher Verlag, 1989.
Krisch, Henry. *The German Democratic Republic: The Search for Identity.* Boulder, CO: Westview Press, 1985.
McCauley, Martin. *Marxism-Leninism in the German Democratic Republic.* London: Macmillan, 1979.
Neugebauer, Gero. *Partei und Staatsapparat der DDR.* Opladen: Westdeutscher Verlag, 1978.

German Democratic Republic: Sports

Sport performed many functions in the German Democratic Republic (GDR). The successes of the country's athletes and a high level of popular participation in sport were to demonstrate the superiority of the socialist system over capitalism, thereby reducing the legitimacy deficit of the East German state. In addition, sport contributed to women's health in childbirth and to the development of desirable features of the "socialist personality," such as discipline, honesty, and a willingness to defend the homeland. At one time fully integrated into the system of "real existing socialism," the elaborate ideological and administrative structure of East German sport was rapidly dismantled after unification.

The large mass organizations, such as the unions (Freier Deutscher Gewerkschaftsbund [FDGB; Free German Trade Union Federation]), the youth (FDJ; Free German Youth) and the women (Democratischer Frauenbund Deutschlands [DFD; Democratic Women's Federation of Germany]), as well as the army (NVA) and the Ministry of Education, were enmeshed in a complex organizational network that required close cooperation with the main central sports organs, the State Secretariat for Physical Culture and Sport and the German Gymnastics and Sports Association (DTSB). The former was responsible for drawing up the annual and long-range sports plans, the development of sports science and research, and the training of cadres. The DTSB, founded in 1957 as the successor to the German Sports Committee established in 1948, was the key central organ, with a series of close-knit national, regional, and local administrative units. Its members (1,295,305 in 1958, 3,658,671 in 1988) were spread across 10,674 "sports communities" in factories, agricultural and craft cooperatives, universities, technical colleges, the army, the police, and residential areas. The sports communities were usually subdivided into "sections" (which provided facilities for intensive training), and "general sports groups" for members with less specialized needs.

Another link in the system was the Society for Sport and Technology (GST), which was mainly responsible for the pre-military training of youths from the age of 14. Formal instruction at educational institutions was not neglected: most students at school, college, and university enjoyed at least two hours per week of curricular sport.

One striking feature of mass sport in the GDR was its competitive orientation. The famous children's and youth Spartakiads held each year at the local level and biennially at the regional and national levels stimulated a high level of performance and participation. The Joint Sports Program of the DTSB, FDGB, and FDJ encouraged not only active relaxation in the form of walking and swimming but also the competitive spirit of participants. The key element was the insignia, "Ready to Work and Defend the Homeland." Over four million people qualified for one of the bronze, silver, and gold medals in 1983.

Despite these relatively high levels of sports and recreational activity, the Socialist Unity Party (SED) leadership failed to fulfill its goal of "Everyone in every place, several times a week [do] sport." Employed women, shift workers, and apprentices, in particular, exhibited low participation rates. In addition to the pressure of work and the attraction of alternative leisure pursuits, many East Germans deliberately abstained from institutionalized sport, as they regarded sport as essentially a personal or a family activity. A relative shortage of equipment and accommodation for adults was another significant constraint. The authorities enjoyed more success in high-performance sport. Elite sport was promoted from 1954 onward and with renewed vigor after the entry of a separate GDR team in the 1968 Mexico City Olympics. The GDR's "diplomats in tracksuits" were utilized by the SED as one of the main weapons with which to break the country's diplomatic isolation.

The medal tally testifies to the success of SED policy: whereas the GDR's athletes gained 25 medals (9 gold) at the 1968 Olympics, they won 102 (37 gold) in Seoul in 1988. The secret of success lay in the clear definition of goals, a vast organizational network geared to these goals, and the widespread use of performance-enhancing drugs. Medal-intensive sports, such as track and field, swimming, and gymnastics were designated as prime targets, and highly gifted children were selected early in their school life and developed at one of the 24 elite boarding sport schools. Talented athletes were concentrated in about 30 large, well-endowed sports clubs, such as SC Dynamo Berlin. The Sport and Physical Culture College in Leipzig became world-famous for its systematic training of top coaches and instructors. Powerful incentives were offered to the elite: foreign travel, payments in Western currency, and good career opportunities.

Drugs, notably anabolic steroids, were used to a high degree. The scientific center of the vast top-secret doping project was the Research Institute for Physical Culture and Sport in Leipzig, which had about 600 scholars. Partner institutions included the Academy of Sciences and industrial institutes such as Jenapharm. For about a quarter of a century, the Leipzig institute, in conjunction with sports club officials and trainers, was responsible for the systematic doping not only of many leading athletes, such as the sprinters Marlies Gohr and Marita Koch, the shotputters Udo Beyer and Ulf Timmermann, and the long-jumper Heike Daute-Drechsler, but also of many talented children.

Michael Dennis

See also German Democratic Republic; German Democratic Republic: Arts and Politics; German Democratic Republic: Education; German Democratic Republic: Government System; German Democratic Republic: Marxism-Leninism; German Democratic Republic: Media; German Democratic Republic: Political Culture; Honecker, Erich; The Olympic Games; Reunification; Socialist Unity Party; Ulbricht, Walter

References

Berendonk, Brigitte. *Doping: Von der Forschung zum Betrug.* Reinbek bei Hamburg: Rowohlt Taschenbuch, 1992.

Fuchs, Ruth and Klaus Ulrich. *Lorbeerkranz und Trauerflor, Aufstieg und "Untergang" des Sportwunders DDR.* Berlin: Dietz, 1990.

Gilbert, Doug. *The Miracle Machine.* New York, NY: Coward, McCann and Geoghegan, 1980.

Holzweissig, Gunter. *Diplomatie im Trainingsanzug.* Munich: R. Oldenbourg, 1981.

Kleine Enzyklopädie Körperkultur und Sport. Leipzig: Bibliographisches Institut, 1979.

Knecht, Willi. *Das Medaillenkollektiv.* Berlin: Holzapfel, 1978.

Voigt, Dieter. *Soziologie in der DDR: Eine exemplarische Untersuchung.* Cologne: Wissenschaft und Politik, 1975.

German Democratic Republic: State Security (MfS)

In February 1950, four months after the formation of the German Democratic Republic (GDR), a statute passed by the People's Assembly established the Ministry for State Security (MfS), an intelligence-gathering agency that eventually proliferated into an omnipresent and invasive organization, one that generated such apprehension and hostility among GDR citizens that these resentments may well have precipitated the collapse of the Honecker government in 1989.

The single brief paragraph of the legislation that created the MfS failed to explain the mission of the Ministry. Nor, aside from a few references to the MfS in other statutes, such as the GDR criminal procedural code, police law, and military law, was the legal basis for MfS activities specified. Internal orders and regulations were for the most part held strictly confidential; only after socialist rule ended in 1989 could the exact nature of the MfS be ascertained.

The official political dictionary of the GDR designated the MfS as an organ of the Council of Ministers of the GDR, with special tasks pertaining to security and administration of justice for the dependable protection against all hostile attacks on the sovereignty and territorial integrity of the GDR or against the socialist accomplishments or peaceful life of its people.

The "friend/enemy" dichotomy that the GDR government persistently and vehemently promulgated not only justified the existence of the MfS but also led to the use of the ministry to invade and document virtually every aspect of citizens' lives in the effort to identify every "enemy" and prevent his or her undermining the GDR. One consequence of the deliberately fostered atmosphere of constant threat was that the MfS followed a "need to know" secrecy policy that was so strict that only the minister had full knowledge of MfS operations.

Three people held the office of minister of the MfS: Wilhelm Zaisser from 1950 to 1953, Ernst Wollweber from 1953 to 1957, and Erich Mielke (1907–) from 1957 to 1989. The MfS had 13 principal divisions and 20 independent sections as well as other administrative groups. The minister directly supervised the central office for evaluation of information, personnel and training, incarceration, and other administrative sections. Four deputies to the minister each directed particular operations, such as espionage, communications, domestic observation, and economic activity. To an astounding degree, the activities of individual personnel were unknown to others within the MfS.

In practice, the MfS performed functions of domestic intelligence (counterespionage), foreign intelligence (espionage), and maintenance of the security of state personnel and foreign dignitaries. At its zenith, in the fall of 1989, the MfS had about 99,000 full-time employees and a financial allocation that represented approximately 1.3 percent of the GDR's annual budget.

Units engaged in domestic intelligence claimed by far the largest allocation of personnel. MfS leaders were ordered to achieve a total (*flächendeckend*) system of surveillance, including the ability to monitor all mail and telephone communications. Eventually, the MfS compiled dossiers on approximately 6,000,000 GDR citizens out of a total population of 17,000,000. An allegation of "crime against the state," a broad and vaguely worded statutory category, could trigger investigation by the MfS instead of the usual police detective units, pretrial detention in special MfS jails, prosecution by MfS lawyers, trial by specially chosen judges, and incarceration in particular prisons.

An army of "unofficial workers" (IMs) enormously enhanced the effectiveness of domestic surveillance. These informed on their fellow citizens without being official employees of the MfS. Anywhere between 109,000 and 500,000 people were drawn into this service for widely varying reasons—from ideological conviction to simple greed. The IMs enabled the MfS to monitor suspected individuals and incipient dissentient groups. The uncertainty regarding the identity of IMs undermined normal relationships of trust in GDR society.

Estimates of the number of active MfS personnel in the Espionage Department vary from 4,000 to 6,000. Under Markus Wolf (1923–) from 1958 to 1987 and Werner Grossmann from 1987 to 1989, the Espionage Department placed GDR intelligence agents abroad and recruited foreign citizens to spy against their own countries. The principal ex-

ternal targets were the Federal Republic of Germany and West Berlin, the United States, and other NATO countries. The Espionage Department, an integral part of the MfS, allegedly extended its spying activities domestically and thereby substantially enhanced the repressiveness of the SED regime.

In addition to MfS counterespionage and espionage personnel, about 11,000 people served in the Feliks Dzierzynski Watch Regiment, an armed unit affiliated with the MfS. Housed in its own Berlin barracks, the regiment functioned as reserve troops for emergencies. They also protected persons and MfS installations, such as jails. In the fall of 1989, when the GDR government appeared to be losing control over demonstrators, it called in the Watch Regiment.

Often referred to as the "Stasi" (a combination of the first two syllables of the German words for "state" and "security"), the MfS was the "sword and shield" of the ruling political party of the GDR, the Socialist Unity Party (SED). No mere figure of speech, the phrase clarified the domination of the MfS by the SED. The Section for Security Questions of the Central Committee of the SED directed and monitored the MfS. After 1950, the minister of the MfS was also an SED *Politbüro* member. Erich Mielke and Erich Honecker (1912–94) allegedly determined MfS policy and operations on their own.

On November 4, 1989 (within a few days of the collapse of the Honecker government), Mielke resigned as minister of the MfS. The new political leader of the GDR, Hans Modrow (1928–), announced the planned abolition of the MfS on November 17. A new organization, the Office for National Security (AfNS) replaced the MfS under Wolfgang Schwanitz, a former deputy of the minister of state security, but public protests forced the dissolution of this agency as well. Thus, until October 1990, the GDR lacked a foreign or domestic intelligence service. After bitter debates, the government established an archive in Berlin to house surviving MfS documents. The authorities recognized the right of each person to see his or her own file.

The MfS was perhaps the most effective organization in the GDR. Former MfS personnel (including Mielke) and scholars have argued that the MfS was realistically informed about events and the opinions of GDR citizens and that this information was honestly and routinely forwarded to the highest political leadership. Furthermore, MfS personnel appear to have offered substantial constructive criticism of GDR policies and tendered recommendations for policy changes to the SED leadership.

The MfS has continued as a focus of dissension in Germany. As information concerning secret informants has emerged, friends and families have been traumatized amid allegations of spying and betrayal. Political careers have been aborted by accusations easily made but often difficult to disprove. Mutual accusations of past acts of espionage between the GDR and the FRG continue to exacerbate grievances between the two areas. And for many East Germans, the MfS serves as a handy scapegoat for the repressive policies of the defunct GDR regime.

Nancy T. Wolfe

See also German Democratic Republic: Judicial System; German Democratic Republic: Marxism-Leninism; German Democratic Republic: Media; German Democratic Republic: National People's Army; German Democratic Republic: Nationalism; German Democratic Republic: Opposition; German Democratic Republic: Political Culture; German Democratic Republic: Political Party System; Honecker, Erich; Honecker, Margot; Maizière, Lothar de; Mielke, Erich; Modrow, Hans; Party of Democratic Socialism; Reunification; Socialist Unity Party; Stoph, Willi; Wolf, Markus

References

Childs, David. *The Stasi: The East German Intellligence and Security Service*. London: Macmillan, 1996.

Fricke, Karl Wilhelm. *MfS intern: Macht, Strukturen, Auflösung der DDR-Staatssicherheit: Analyse und Dokumentation*. Cologne: Verlag Wissenschaft und Politik, 1991.

Gauck, Joachim. *Die Stasi-Akten: Das unheimliche Erbe der DDR*. Reinbeck bei Hamburg: Rowohlt Taschenbuch Verlag, 1991.

Gellately, Robert. "Denunciations in Twentieth-Century Germany: Aspects of Self-Policing in the Third Reich and the German Democratic Republic." *Journal of Modern History* 68 (December, 1996), 931–967.

Gill, David und Ulrich Schröter. *Das Ministerium für Staatssicherheit*. Berlin: Rowohlt, 1991.

Wolfe, Nancy. *Policing a Socialist Society: The German Democratic Republic*. Westport, CT: Greenwood Press, 1992.

German Democratic Republic: Technical Intelligentsia

Both the Socialist Unity Party (SED) regime and Western analysts viewed the German Democratic Republic's (GDR) technical intelligentsia as a social stratum of critical importance in determining the country's economic fortunes. The technical intelligentsia was normally distinguished from the cultural or artistic intelligentsia; broadly defined, it numbered some 1.3 million persons, those with a university or *Fachschule* (technical school) education in the natural sciences, engineering, economics, management, agronomy, or other technical fields. Since early in the GDR's history, the regime understood that the creation of its own "socialist" technical intelligentsia was vital to its long-term survival, and it reshaped the country's system of higher education partly with this goal in mind. By the 1970s, some 80 percent of *Fachschule* students and 70 percent of university and *Hochschule* (academy) students were studying scientific and technical subjects. The new intelligentsia gradually replaced the old "bourgeois" specialists, to whom the regime had accorded special privileges and high incomes in an effort to secure their services and loyalty.

The SED never fully settled the question of the place of the technical intelligentsia in the GDR's emerging "socialist" social structure, despite the stratum's large numbers and economic importance. In the 1950s, and again in the 1970s, official doctrine emphasized the need to recruit the technical intelligentsia largely from the working class and to bring the technical specialists and workers closer together (*Annäherung*) in their work, status, and rewards. During the economic reform in the 1960s, however, the regime sought to single out the technical intelligentsia for special recognition and compensation because of its pivotal role in advancing the "scientific-technical revolution." A number of GDR sociologists, such as Manfred Lötsch, returned to this theme in the 1980s, urging greater social differentiation and the conscious recruitment and nurturing of a scientific and technical elite—particularly the top 20,000–30,000 engaged in research and development—regardless of its members' class background. Although some of these recommendations were followed, Lötsch nevertheless later complained that one of the principal reasons for the GDR's demise was the unwillingness of the political leadership to give proper recognition to the intelligentsia. It is noteworthy, however, that only a few members of the technical intelligentsia, notably natural scientists, were among the leaders of the opposition groups that helped to bring down the East German regime.

During the 1960s, the number of members of the GDR's political leadership bodies—the Council of Ministers, the SED Central Committee, and the *Politbüro*—who had an advanced education in technical subjects grew dramatically. The influential West German sociologist Peter Ludz argued that an "institutionalized counter-elite" of technical experts was challenging the power of the traditional party leadership and might ultimately alter the very nature of Communist rule. Although individuals with technical backgrounds, such as Günter Mittag (1926–94), Werner Jarowinsky, Gerhard Schürer, and Günther Kleiber, did rise to leading positions, they remained far outnumbered by the aging representatives of the party bureaucracy, propaganda apparatus, and security establishment. Mittag himself, identified by Ludz and others as a leading partisan of economic reform in the 1960s, became the dogmatic czar of the GDR's centralized command economy, and many of his colleagues later blamed him for decisions that had led to economic failure. Other "technocrats," particularly Schürer, sought to persuade the *Politbüro* to change its disastrous economic course, but in vain.

Thomas A. Baylis

See also Free German Trade Union Federation; German Democratic Republic: Collapse; German Democratic Republic: Economy; German Democratic Republic: Education; German Democratic Republic: Government System; German Democratic Republic: Political Culture; German Democratic Republic: Political Party System; German Democratic Republic: Women; Grotewohl, Otto; Hager, Kurt; Honecker, Erich; Mittag, Günter; Science in the Postwar Germanys; Socialist Unity Party; Stoph, Willi; Tisch, Harry; Ulbricht, Walter

References

Baylis, Thomas A. *The Technical Intelligentsia and the East German Elite*. Berkeley, CA: University of California Press, 1974.

Belwe, Katharina. "Sozialstruktur und gesellschaftlicher Wandel in der DDR." *Deutschland-Handbuch: Eine doppelte Bilanz 1949–1989.* Ed. Werner Weidenfeld and Hartmut Zimmermann. Bonn: Bundeszentrale für politische Bildung, 1989.

Erbe, Günter. *Arbeiterklasse und Intelligenz in der DDR.* Opladen: Westdeutscher Verlag, 1982.

Ludz, Peter C. *The Changing Party Elite in East Germany.* Cambridge, MA: MIT Press, 1972.

Meyer, Gerd. *Die DDR-Machtelite in der Ära Honecker.* Tübingen: Francke Verlag, 1991.

German Democratic Republic: Women

Women's roles in the German Democratic Republic (GDR) were characterized by a contradictory situation. Women were beneficiaries of a system that removed patriarchal German family laws, improved the education of girls and women, opened professional jobs, and provided an extensive net of child-care facilities. Yet they were also instrumentalized as objects of the paternalistic state-socialist regime, which severely limited women's choices and opportunities in society and curtailed their voice as citizens in the political community. Women's attitudes toward the GDR state were therefore ambivalent.

Two features exemplify women's ambiguous position in GDR society: the high percentage of working women and the official emphasis on the family. The Socialist Unity Party (SED) regime mobilized women to participate in the labor force because of a chronic labor shortage and provided comprehensive child-care facilities. Women's employment increased steadily. In 1989, 83 percent of all women between the ages of 16 and 60 worked outside the home. According to data published by the German Institute for Economic Research, women in the GDR contributed 40 percent to household income before unification. In comparison, women in the Federal Republic of Germany (FRG) contributed about 18 percent.

Contrary to the official position proclaimed by the SED that equal rights existed, discrimination persisted. For example, women's wages among industrial and construction workers were 12 percent lower than that of men, even if they performed the same tasks. Discriminatory practices in hiring and promotion were widespread. Women were more often employed in typically female occupations such as nursing, teaching, and retail sales, and they were concentrated in lower-level positions.

Family policy strongly emphasized the important role of women as mothers. Generous maternity-leave policies (paid one-year leave of absence after childbirth), financial support for families, and other benefits for women were introduced in the mid-1970s to prevent birth rates from further declining, with modest results. Because most mothers worked, the dual burden of work and family responsibilities plagued many women. Given the support for single mothers, as well as the relatively simple arrangement for a divorce, the rate of single mothers was increasing steadily. About one-third of all children were born out of wedlock in 1989.

Despite the official rhetoric, women did not share political power, with some few exceptions. However, women played a major role in the small but important opposition against the Communist regime. In 1982, a pacifist group called Women for Peace was formed to protest a new military draft law. Women were active in the emerging human-rights groups, such as the Initiative for Peace and Human Rights, as well as in environmental groups, some of which formed under the shelter of the Protestant church in the 1980s. Several of the activists later took leading roles in the opposition that formed shortly before the collapse of the Communist regime. Mobilization of women was highest in the fall and winter of 1989, leading to the formation of an umbrella organization, the Independent Women's Association (UFV), which was represented at the roundtable as the SED regime collapsed.

Despite the active role of women in the opposition and their mobilization in the final months of the GDR, women's groups were quickly marginalized before unification in 1990. The legacies of Communist rule, under which feminists had been silenced, the increasing influence of West German political parties, the de facto marginal role of "third way" proponents, and the powerful push toward a market-based economy created an unfavorable climate for grass-roots–based, communitarian, civil-rights–oriented women's groups. Nearly 50 percent of all women voted for the conservative Christian Democratic Union-led Alliance for Germany in the first (and last) free elections held in the GDR in March 1990.

Among the many paradoxes produced by the collapse of Communist rule throughout eastern Europe is the fact that political liberalization did not immediately enhance women's role and status. The collapse of the SED regime in 1989–90 opened new and unexpected opportunities for women in education and in the realm of activities on the local level. It also created a social and economic crisis for many women, particularly single mothers, divorced women, and women over 45 seeking a new job. A new conservativism—from a more restrictive abortion law to a reemphasis of women's traditional roles in the family—has characterized the post-unification years. So far, German unification has been a mixed blessing for women, but limited nostalgia persists for the GDR.

Christiane Lemke

See also Abortion; Family; Federal Republic of Germany: Women; Feminist Writing; German Democratic Republic: Judicial System; German Democratic Republic: Literature and Literary Life; German Democratic Republic: Marxism-Leninism; German Democratic Republic: Media; German Democratic Republic: National People's Army; German Democratic Republic: Nationalism; German Democratic Republic: Opposition; German Democratic Republic: Political Culture; German Democratic Republic: Political Party System; Honecker, Erich; Honecker, Margot; Socialist Unity Party

References

Dölling, Irene. "Between Hope and Helplessness: Women in the GDR after their 'Turning Point.'" *Feminist Review* 39 (1991), 3–15.

Goldman, Guido et al., eds. "Gender and Germany." Special issue of *German Politics and Society.* 24/25 (Winter 1991–92).

Lemke, Christiane, ed. *The Quality of Life in the German Democratic Republic: Changes and Developments in a State Socialist Society*. Boulder, CO: Westview, 1989.
———. "Women and Politics in the New Federal Republic of Germany." *Women and Politics World Wide*. Ed. Barbara Nelson and Najma Chowdhury. 2 vols. New Haven, CT: Yale University Press, 1994.
Nickel, Hildegard Maria. "Women in the GDR and in the New Federal States. Looking Backwards and Forwards." Special issue of *German Politics and Society*. 24/25 (Winter 1991–92), 34–52.

German-German Relations

Relations between the Federal Republic of Germany (FRG) and the German Democratic Republic (GDR), from the foundation of the two states in 1949 to reunification in 1990, were of "a special sort." During the first decade, no official political relations, only private connections, existed between the two Germanys, because the FRG claimed, on moral and political grounds, to be the sole legitimate German state and representative of the German people (*Alleinvertretungsrecht*). Only during the 1960s did negotiations on the political level as well as among parties, organizations, and institutions commence.

The legality of inter-German contacts became a subject of debate. In contrast to the FRG, which adhered to the concept of a "special relationship" between the two German states, the GDR emphasized the legitimacy of its foreign relations according to international law. The 1972 Basic Treaty

West and East German border guards watching the dismantling of the Berlin Wall, November 1989. Courtesy of German Embassy, Ottawa.

(Grundlagenvertrag) between the GDR and the FRG produced an agreement to recognize each other as states but not necessarily as different nations. The FRG, however, remained a foreign country for Honecker. Although the East German state, until 1967, possessed a Ministry for Foreign Trade and Intra-German Relations (Ministerium für Aussenhandel und innerdeutsche Beziehungen), like the West German Ministry for Intra-German Relations (Bundesministerium für innerdeutsche Beziehungen, until 1969 the Ministerium für gesamtdeutsche Fragen [Ministry for Inner German Questions]), the GDR nevertheless rejected the concept of "intra-German" as "revanchist."

In contrast to economic relations, which existed without interruption after the end of the war, contacts on the political level remained blocked until the end of the 1960s. Only Willy Brandt's (1913–92) 1969 offer to accept the principle of the existence of two German states led, after lower-level consultations and the meetings of Brandt and GDR Prime Minister Willi Stoph (1914–) in Erfurt and Kassel (1970), to the conclusion of the Basic Treaty with the GDR in 1972. Preceding this contract and the Quadripartite Agreement on Berlin in 1971, 30 smaller agreements were reached, concerning, for example, Berlin transit, travel, and visiting rights; an exchange of territory (*Gebietsaustausch*), navigation, postal, and train service; as well as refuse removal and indemnification (*Schadenausgleich*). After the 1972 agreement, more than one hundred additional agreements were concluded.

The stability of intra-German relations became manifest during the international crisis following the Soviet invasion of Afghanistan in 1979. Despite great tensions—in January 1980 Chancellor Schmidt cancelled a meeting with Honecker—a dialogue was still possible, even if it took place in a tense atmosphere, as for example during Schmidt's visit to East Germany in December 1980. It is evident from Honecker's visit to West Germany in 1987 and the agreements that were subsequently signed that neither side anticipated the rapid implosion of the GDR that occurred in 1989–90. As late as 1988, negotiations were started on the construction of a high-speed train line between Berlin and Hannover.

Cultural relations developed in accordance with the political situation; only with the Basic Treaty did both sides agree to cooperate in cultural matters. The GDR leadership's fear of "subversion" by Western democratic ideas, the West German demand that art objects from the Prussian Cultural Foundation (Stiftung preussischer Kulturbesitz) be returned, and the expulsion of artists who fell into disfavor with the GDR regime after the mid-1970s impeded better relations. Only the Schmidt-Honecker meeting in 1981 made mutual art exhibitions possible. In 1986, the GDR's proposal that the demand for the return of artworks should be put on hold opened the way for the signing of an agreement on cultural collaboration, which in turn increased cultural exchanges, especially guest performances of West German artists on GDR territory.

In sum, the "basis for the continuing unity of the German nation" (the Unification Agreement of 1990), was made possible by the political negotiations furthered by both states but, above all, by the uninterrupted cultural ties between them.

Bernd Stöver

See also Adenauer, Konrad; Bahr, Egon; Basic Treaty; Brandt, Willy; Federal Republic of Germany: Foreign-Relations; Genscher, Hans-Dietrich; Honecker, Erich; Kohl, Helmut; *Ostpolitik*; Reunification; Scheel, Walter; Schmidt, Helmut; Socialist Unity Party; Soviet-German Relations; Stoph, Willi; Ulbricht, Walter

References

Dean, Jonathan. "Changing Security Dimensions of the Inter-German Relationship." *The Two German States and European Security.* Ed. F. Stephen Larrabee. New York, NY: St. Martin's Press, in association with The Institute for East-West Security Studies, 1989.

Frey, Eric G. *Division and Detente: The Germanies and Their Alliances.* New York, NY: Praeger Publishers, 1987.

Hacke, Christian. "Die Deutschlandpolitik der Bundesrepublik Deutschland." *Deutschland-Handbuch: Eine doppelte Bilanz 1949–1989.* Ed. Werner Weidenfeld and Hartmut Zimmermann. Munich: Carl Hanser Verlag, 1989.

Keithly, David M. *Breakthrough in the Ostpolitik: The 1971 Quadripartite Agreement.* Boulder, CO: Westview Press, 1986.

Kuppe, Johannes. "Die deutsch-deutsch Beziehungen aus der Sicht der DDR." *Deutschland-Handbuch: Eine doppelte Bilanz 1949–1989.* Ed. Werner Weidenfeld and Hartmut Zimmermann. Munich: Carl Hanser Verlag, 1989.

Nawrocki, Joachim. *Die Beziehungen zwischen beiden deutschen Staaten.* Berlin: Holzapfel, 1986.

Plock, Ernest D. *The Basic Treaty and the Evolution of East-West German Relations.* Boulder, CO: Westview Press, 1986.

———. *East German–West German Relations and the Fall of the GDR.* Boulder, CO: Westview Press, 1993.

Potthoff, Heinrich. *Bonn und Ost Berlin 1969–1982.* Bonn: J.H.W. Dietz, 1997.

German-Jewish Organizations (1871–1943)

In Imperial Germany and in the Weimar Republic, in the golden years of the much-discussed "German-Jewish symbiosis," countless organizations emerged representing Jewish interests and maintaining a Jewish identity. They were established on all levels—national and regional, communal and religious, political and social, philanthropic and professional—reflecting the manifold landscape of German Jewry. This Jewish "organizational renaissance" took place not only against the backdrop of the general advent of pressure and interest groups symptomatic of modern society but also and primarily as a response to anti-Semitism.

In 1871, after a century of debate, Jews were granted political equality. Very soon, vehement anti-Semitic campaigns were launched, designed to prevent social integration

and revoke the emancipation. This new, modern anti-Semitism, with its political and racial undertones, contributed to continued Jewish cohesion and forced Jews to defend their positions and to define their identities. Banned from general student associations, Jewish students were the first to form their own fraternities. Youth and sporting organizations attracted a considerable membership. B'nai B'rith lodges were formed, numbering 103 individual lodges with 15,000 members in the late 1920s. 50,000 joined the jüdischer Frauenbund (League of Jewish Women), founded in 1904. The Centralverein deutscher Staatsbürger jüdischer Glaubens (CV; Central Association of German Citizens of the Jewish Faith) was the largest organization, with a membership of 60,000 by 1932, representing half of Jewish families. Established in 1893 primarily as a defense organization against anti-Semitism, the CV felt compelled to take up the unequal fight against the rising tide of Nazism. From the very outset, it spoke out and acted in the name of the liberal and acculturated middle-class Jews who regarded themselves as both Germans and Jews and who firmly believed in their seemingly symbiotic community.

Zionists adopted a different program and approach. Conflict with the CV was inevitable and manifested itself in numerous disputes. Convinced that assimilation and acculturation would not solve the "Jewish question," Zionists propagated Jewish nationalism and settlement in Palestine aiming at the establishment of a Jewish state. The Zionistische Vereinigung für Deutschland (ZVFD; Zionist Federation of Germany), founded in 1897, remained a minority until 1933, mobilizing some 20,000 followers by World War I. German patriotism and the attempt to combat anti-Semitism characterized the policy of the Reichsbund Jüdischer Frontsoldaten. Created in 1919, the League of Jewish Veterans repeatedly drew attention to the contributions and sacrifices German Jews had made during World War I. Its membership reached 50,000. Some 3,000 Jews joined the Verband nationaldeutscher Juden (VnJ; League of German Nationalist Jews), an explicit right-wing organization strongly opposed to Zionism and the liberal tendencies of the CV.

When in 1933 the Nazis seized power, representatives of the opposing German-Jewish organizations raised their voices, declaring loyalty to the German people and readiness to reach some sort of modus vivendi with the new "legal" government. A new umbrella organization came into being, the Reichsvertretung der deutschen Juden (Reich Representation of German Jews). Under the leadership of Leo Baeck (1873–1956) and Otto Ilirisch, it made great efforts to protect and maintain Jewish life and continued existence in Germany.

But step by step, Nazi persecution and expulsion destroyed the foundations of the Jews' existence; gradually, Jewish organizations and institutions vanished. In early 1939, the Reichsvertretung was transformed into the Reichsvereingung der Juden in Deutschland (Reich Assocation of Jews in Germany), embracing all "racial Jews" and placed under the direct supervision of the Gestapo. Its tasks encompassed social-welfare measures, retraining, and emigration as well as the preparation for the self-dissolution of German Jewry envisaged for 1943. The Reichsvereinigung was, however, like the Jewish councils in occupied Europe, compelled to furnish bureaucratic-administrative assistance in helping to carry out the ghettoization and "evacuation" of Jews.

Having fulfilled its function, the Reichsvereinigung was officially abolished in 1943. The last leaders were deported to the Theresienstadt ghetto; remaining assets, including properties, were confiscated and taken over by the treasury on June 10, 1943. On that day, the last German-Jewish organization ceased to exist.

Konrad Kwiet

See also Anti-Semitism; Baeck, Leo; Holocaust; Israeli-German Relations; Jewish Women, League of; Jews

References

Benz, W., ed. *Die Juden in Deutschland, 1933–1945: Leben unter nationalsozialistischer Herrschaft.* Munich: Beck, 1993.

Breuer, M. *Modernity within Tradition: The Social History of Orthodox Jewry in Imperial Germany.* Trans. Elizabeth Petuchowski. New York, NY: Columbia University Press, 1992.

Gay, Ruth. *The Jews of Germany: A Historical Portrait.* New Haven, CT: Yale University Press, 1992.

Lamberti, Marjorie. *Jewish Activism in Imperial Germany.* New Haven, CT: Yale University Press, 1978.

Niewyk, D.L. *The Jews in Weimar Germany.* Baton Rouge, LA: University of New Orleans Press, 1980.

Paucker, A. *Der jüdischer Abwehrkampf gegen Antisemitismus und Nationalsozialismus in den letzten Jahren der Weimar Republik.* Hamburg: Leibniz-Verlag, 1969.

Pulzer, Peter. *Jews and the German State: The Political History of a Minority 1848–1933.* Oxford: Blackwell, 1992.

Reinharz, Y., ed. *Dokumente zur Geschichte des deutschen Zionismus, 1882–1933.* Tübingen: Mohr, 1981.

———. *Fatherland or Promised Land: The Dilemma of the German Jews, 1893–1914.* Ann Arbor, MI: University of Michigan Press, 1975.

Reinharz, Y. and W. Schatzberge, eds. *The Jewish Response to German Culture: From the Enlightenment to the Second World War.* Hanover, NH: University Press of New England, 1986.

Richarz, M., ed. *Jewish Life in Germany: Memoirs from Three Centuries.* Bloomington, IN: University of Indiana Press, 1991.

Volkov, Shulamit. *Jüdisches Leben und Antisemitismus im 19. und 20. Jahrhundert.* Munich: C.H. Beck, 1990.

German Labor Front (1933–45)

The German Labor Front (Deutsche Arbeits Front; DAF) was a totalitarian mass organization created in 1933 by the Nazi regime to mobilize, supervise, integrate, and control Germany's workers through a mixture of carrot and stick. Led by a fanatic Hitler loyalist, Robert Ley (1890–1945), it was intended to be a major tool to wean the workers from Marxism, make German patriots of them, and provide them with mechanisms for vocational training and upward mobility, as well as to create a future German racial and social utopia.

In May 1933, the Nazis smashed the German trade-union movement, confiscated its wealth and property, and created the German Labor Front because they feared that, left to themselves, the workers would always be susceptible to the blandishments of underground Communists and socialists. The DAF's formative stages were confusing. Various trends appeared within its structure and leadership, including Nazi trade unionism and petty-bourgeois dreams of a recreated medieval society of estates. Under Ley's leadership, however, the DAF gradually evolved into a totalitarian mass organization encompassing labor and management, with an eventual membership of 23 million. It became a major bureaucratic player in the competitive jungle that was the Nazi regime, challenging government ministries, big corporations, and other party agencies with the goal of becoming a Nazi "super-agency" in social and economic policy. The idea was to integrate the German worker into a racially based social utopia characterized by upward mobility and generous social benefits—the costs to be defrayed by the enslavement and exploitation of "inferior" races.

The Labor Front's many initiatives and programs reflect these Nazi utopian dreams as well as the more immediate task of harnessing German workers for Hitler's war preparations by heightening their skills and productivity and making them more amenable to discipline.

With respect to the carrot, the DAF developed plans to allow the productive worker to become a consumer through a number of "people's" (*Volks*) products, including the people's radio, people's refrigerator, people's bungalow, and, most famously, the people's car (Volkswagen). Most of these products remained in the planning stages as the war drastically curtailed their production. The Nazis also tried to organize the workers' time outside the workplace. Recognizing the utility of regulated leisure, the DAF founded one of its most important sub-organizations, the so-called Strength through Joy, which provided a myriad of leisure and vacation possibilities for workers, ranging from inexpensive concert and theater tickets to vacations in the Alps. Cleverly playing on the technique of uplifting through social leveling, the DAF appropriated many of these leisure pursuits, such as ocean cruises and tennis lessons, from the enjoyments of the upper classes. Social leveling, at least at the psychological level, also involved other DAF institutions such as the Court of Social Honor, before which an employer could be hauled if he insulted a worker, as well as "comradeship evenings," when bosses had to provide an evening of gratis beer and sausages while socializing with their employees.

The DAF also played an important role in combining workers' skills and productivity with social mobility. Germany had one of the world's best vocational education systems, which enabled workers to climb from unskilled to semiskilled to skilled status with the expectation that they could, eventually, aspire to bourgeois levels in society. Highly organized annual competitions provided additional impetus for skill and productivity enhancement.

Simultaneously, the regime regimented the workers through disciplined factory militias and, ultimately, through its close cooperation with the SS and the Gestapo. After the war broke out, the carrot aspects of DAF activities increasingly tended to languish, while the stick, including draconian discipline and 70-hour weeks, assumed enhanced importance.

Although many of the DAF programs seem progressive, they were also instruments to prepare and wage total war and were exclusive to members of a putative master race. They were also conceivable in the long run only if based on the exploitation of conquered peoples whose only place in the Thousand-Year Reich was that of helots.

The German Labor Front must be viewed as an organized expression of a radicalized racial nationalism and an instrument to mollify, but really to control and manipulate, millions of working people and convince them to produce for the regime in exchange for the promise of life in a future national-racial utopia.

Ronald Smelser

See also Gestapo; Hitler, Adolf; Leipart, Theodor; Ley, Robert; National Socialist Germany; National Socialist Factory Cell Organization; Nationalism; Schutzstaffel; Strength through Joy; Trade Unions, 1871–1945; Volkswagen; Workers and National Socialism

References

Mason, Timothy. *Social Policy in the Third Reich: The Working Class and the National Community.* Oxford: Berg Publishers, 1993.

Smelser, Ronald. "How 'Modern' Were the Nazis? DAF Social Planning and the Modernization Question." *German Studies Review* 13 (May 1990), 285–302.

———. *Robert Ley: Hitler's Labor Front Leader.* Oxford: Berg Publishers, 1988.

German National People's Party (Deutschnationale Volkspartei; DNVP)

Organized in the winter of 1918–19, the German National People's Party (DNVP) included various right-wing groups opposed to the Weimar Republic. After an initial period of ideological opposition, the party compromised its position and participated in the government. The election of Alfred Hugenberg (1865–1961) as chairman in 1928 placed the most reactionary elements in control of the party and helped to make possible the first Nazi cabinet.

To become more broadly based than any of the reactionary parties of the Wilhelmine era, the DNVP sought to rally not only industrialists, *Junkers,* and military leaders but also professional people, craftsmen, white-collar workers, anti-Semites, and newly enfranchised women. With its varied constituencies, the party seemed more like a rightist confederation than a unified bloc. Support for the monarchy and opposition to the Treaty of Versailles and the Weimar constitution left the party in ideological opposition during the first years of the Republic, but the need for a pragmatically con-

servative group increased its appeal after 1923. In August 1924, the party's split vote on the Dawes Plan underlined differences between realists and ideologues.

From 1924 to 1928, the party tepidly supported the Republic by participating in right-of-center cabinets. Meanwhile, Hugenberg and the radicals narrowly seized control of the organization. The new leadership sought to mold the party into an ideological bloc rather than the coalition led by previous party leaders. The Young Plan presented them with the opportunity to forge an alliance, a *Sammlung,* of all radical right-wing groups, including the Nazi Party, behind a plebiscite against war guilt and reparations. The attempt to do so alienated relatively moderate German Nationals, who seceded from the party. The plebiscite failed, and the vast publicity given to the politics of dissent coupled with the advent of the Great Depression saw the masses flock not to the DNVP but to the Nazi Party.

From 1930 to 1932, Hugenberg unsuccessfully sought to influence Hitler. An attempt at Bad Harzburg in 1931 to rally support for a joint presidential candidate failed. Conflict between the two parties centered not merely on tactics, but on the role of socialism in National Socialism. Despite his misgivings, Hugenberg in January 1933 joined the Hitler cabinet of "national opposition" and took control of four major economic ministries. For the elections of March 1933, the DNVP nominally collaborated with other non-Nazi nationalists in the "Battle Front: Black-White-Red." German Nationalists won only 52 seats, but voted with the Nazis to secure Hitler's majority in the Reichstag. Unable to alter Nazi policy, Hugenberg resigned from the cabinet and the party dissolved itself in June 1933.

John A. Leopold

See also Conservatism; Dawes Plan; German Conservative Party; Hugenberg, Alfred; Jung, Edgar; National Socialism; Nationalism; Nationalist Women's Associations; (German) Protestant Women's League; Reparations; Versailles, Treaty of; Weimar Germany; Young Plan

References

Grathwohl, Robert. *Stresemann and the DNVP.* Lawrence, KS: Regents Press of Kansas, 1980.

Hertzman, Lewis. *DNVP: Right Wing Opposition to the Weimar Republic 1918–1924.* Lincoln, NE: University of Nebraska Press, 1963.

Jones, Larry Eugene and James Retallack, eds. *Between Reform, Reaction, and Resistance: Studies in the History of German Conservatism from 1789 to 1945.* Providence, RI: Berg, 1993.

Leopold, John A. *Alfred Hugenberg: The Radical Nationalist Campaign Against the Weimar Republic.* New Haven, CT: Yale University Press, 1977.

German People's Party (1918–33)

The German People's Party (Deutsche Volkspartei; DVP) was founded on November 23, 1918, after efforts to reach an accommodation with the leaders of the newly-founded German

Democratic Party (Deutsche Demokratische Partei; DDP) had broken down.

The driving force behind the DVP was Gustav Stresemann (1878–1929), the former parliamentary leader of the National Liberal Party (Nationalliberale Partei; NLP), who had been excluded from a leadership position in the DDP on account of his annexationist activities during World War I. Stresemann managed to rally what still remained of the NLP organization to the support of the DVP, which received 4.4 percent of the popular vote in the January 1919 elections to the Weimar National Assembly. At Weimar, the DVP voted against acceptance of the Treaty of Versailles and failed to support ratification of the Weimar constitution despite its obvious sympathy for many of the new constitution's provisions. As a result, the DVP proved a major beneficiary of the dramatic swing to the right that characterized German political life in the second half of 1919 and emerged from the June 1920 Reichstag elections with 13.9 percent of the popular vote and 62 seats.

In terms of its basic ideology, the DVP portrayed itself as the heir to the national and liberal traditions of the prewar NLP. In terms of its social composition, the DVP recruited the bulk of its electoral support from three vocational groups: the independent middle class, the white-collar population, and the professional civil service. The party also received massive financial support from German heavy industry, which through men such as Hugo Stinnes (1870–1924) and Albert Vögler (1877–1945) exerted enormous influence upon party affairs after 1920. The DVP's victory in the 1920 elections paved the way for its entry into the national government, and in 1922 it signaled its acceptance of the republican system of government.

Stresemann's appointment as chancellor in August 1923 only aggravated the internal divisions within the party and precipitated an ill-fated secession of its right wing in the form of the National Liberal Association (Nationalliberale Vereinigung). The effects of this split could be seen in the outcome of the May 1924 Reichstag elections, when the DVP lost 900,000 votes and saw its share of the popular vote slip to 9.2 percent. Although the DVP experienced a modest recovery in the December 1924 elections, the DVP continued to lose voters to special-interest parties throughout the 1920s and saw its share of the popular vote decline to 8.7 percent in 1928 and 4.6 percent in 1930.

With Stresemann's death in October 1929, the party lost the one person capable of holding it together in the face of deepening internal strife. His successors at the party helm, Ernst Scholz (1874–1932) from December 1929 to November 1930 and then Eduard Dingeldey (1886–1942) until the DVP's official dissolution, found themselves exposed to increasingly heavy pressure from the party's industrial wing for the establishment of closer ties with Germany's antiparliamentary right. In October 1931, the DVP formally broke with the cabinet of Heinrich Brüning (1885–1970) and allied itself with the forces of the so-called "national opposition." This, however, did little to stem the DVP's decline in the July and November 1932 Reichstag elections, and in March 1933 it received a mere one percent of the popular vote. Although it publicly endorsed the goals of the Hitler government, the DVP could not escape the fate that befell Germany's other political parties and formally dissolved itself in July 1933.

Larry Eugene Jones

See also German Democratic Party; Liberalism; National Liberal Party; National Socialism; Nationalism; Stinnes, Hugo; Stresemann, Gustav; Versailles, Treaty of; Weimar Germany

References

Albertin, Lothan. *Liberalismus und Demokratie am Anfang der Weimarer Republik: Eine vergleichende Analyse der Deutschen Demokratischen Partei und der Deutschen Volkspartei.* Düsseldorf: Droste, 1972.

Döhn, Lothar. *Politik und Interesse: Die Interessenstruktur der Deutschen Volkspartei.* Meisenheim an Glan: Hain, 1970.

Hartenstein, Wolfgang. *Die Anfänge der Deutschen Volkspartei 1918–1920.* Düsseldorf: Droste, 1962.

Jones, Larry Eugene. *German Liberalism and the Dissolution of the Weimar Party System, 1919–1933.* Chapel Hill, NC: University of North Carolina Press, 1988.

Thimme, Roland. *Stresemann und die Deutsche Volkspartei 1923–1925.* Lübeck: Matthiesen, 1961.

Turner, Henry Ashby Jr. *Stresemann and the Politics of the Weimar Republic.* Princeton, NJ: Princeton University Press, 1963.

Germanistik

Germanistik, the study of the German language and of literature, arose as a discipline at the beginning of the nineteenth century. In response to a crisis of scholarship, *Germanistik* evolved beyond a learned contemplation of literature. Further, *Germanistik* emerged in response to the need for a discipline that would build a German national culture as a substitute for the missing political nation and would impart a sense of national consciousness as advocated by Johann Gottfried Herder.

Examination of Germany's cultural past was supposed to rehabilitate the struggle for national unity, to demonstrate the continuity of German cultural development, to compensate for the desolation of contemporary materialism, and to legitimize the German claim to a future as a nation. Thus, *Germanistik* took on the form of literary history. The self-appointed political-national mission made the discipline unique in the landscape of national literary studies and distinguished it from German philology as practiced on foreign soil.

At the first meeting of German philologists in 1846, Jacob Grimm introduced the term "*Germanistik*," which for him was the study of German law, history, and language. In that sense, *Germanistik* originally combined several disciplines, and thus began as cultural studies. Today, *Germanistik* includes ancient and medieval as well as modern literary criticism and the study of the German language. The term "*Literaturwissenschaft*" (literary studies) may be found first in 1828, but became widely used only in the twentieth century.

The origins of *Germanistik* depend on whether the focus is on its major component parts such as philology, the history of literature, and literary criticism. The *Deutsche Grammatik*

(German grammar), 1819, of Jacob Grimm or the five volumes of the *Geschichte der poetischen Nationalliteratur der Deutschen* (History of the poetic national literature of the Germans), 1835–42, by Georg Gottfried Gervinus have generally been considered as the starting point of the discipline. Karl Lachmann (philology) or the Schlegel brothers and Herder are also cited among the founding fathers. There are no founding mothers; for the most part, women were engaged neither in the study of literary history nor in literary criticism. This situation has changed, but only slowly, in the second half of the twentieth century.

The evolution of *Germanistik* can be considered on three levels: the textual (concerned with literary history, textual analysis, and theory), the social (concerned with institutions) and the educational (concerned with the public and the teaching of German language and literature). Although the development of the discipline was discontinuous and unequal in the three spheres, five phases may be distinguished:

From the beginning of the nineteenth century to 1848

At first, the primary considerations in the evaluation of literature were political. This was the epoch of popular literary histories as well as philological works and magazines (e.g., the *Zeitschrift für deutsches Altertum* [1841], the oldest German publication still in circulation).

Literary studies served the promotion of a democratic, anti-feudal society and were characterized by political commitment, especially in 1837, when the "Göttinger Sieben" (Göttingen seven [a group of professors]) protested arbitrary aristocratic rule, and in 1848, when numerous *Germanisten* participated in the Frankfurt Paulskirche Parliament. As in other disciplines, a gradual institutionalization of *Germanistik* occurred. The first step was the creation of a nonremunerated extraordinary professorship at the University of Berlin for Friedrich Heinrich von der Hagen in 1810. In 1837, the first conference of German philologists and teachers took place in Göttingen; they were joined in 1844 by the Orientalists. In 1846, Grimm organized the first meeting of German philologists in Frankfurt. This session and the subsequent ones (1847 in Lübeck, 1848 in Frankfurt) had a largely political agenda. During this phase, national values replaced the previous humanist orientation.

1848 to 1870

The failed Revolution of 1848–49 had a profound influence on German philology and its function. The national was abandoned; the previously dominant groups of the liberal-democratic movement were disillusioned and replaced by scholars with a philological orientation. Hence, textual analysis was depoliticized. In 1861, the Assembly of German Philologists, Teachers and Orientalists established a German section. *Germanistik* now focused on classical philology. As the discipline developed its parameters and its terminology, it became increasingly esoteric. The discipline remained apolitical until the next major national watershed in 1870; its increasingly esoteric isolation resulted in a legitimization crisis. Nevertheless, professorships in German philology, already requested at the end of the

Title page of Deutsches Wörterbuch *by Jacob and Wilhelm Grimm. Courtesy of German Embassy, Ottawa.*

eighteenth century, finally were granted. With the introduction of the *Habilitation* (university teaching qualification thesis) in 1869 in Kiel, scholarship acquired the status of a profession.

1870 to the 1920s

Germanistik's narrow political and philological focus, which persisted after the founding of the empire in 1871, sought to confer cultural legitimation upon the new nation. Subsequently, a paradigm shift toward positivism occurred, developed by Wilhelm Scherer and based on the philosophy of August Comte. As a response to the crisis in *Germanistik*, which had occurred during the second phase, and inspired by the founding of the empire as well as by the success of the natural sciences, Scherer, in *Die Geschichte der deutschen Literatur* (History of German literature), 1880–83, sought to develop a system of national ethics on a scientific-empirical basis. The etiology (genesis) of a literary work became of paramount concern. It was analyzed in terms of facts (the inherited, learned, and experienced); the basic category of analysis was causality. The striving for scientific precision, which could not be realized, led, however, to a number of critical historical editions, linguistic writings, studies (especially in the Scherer school), and authors' biographies, which tended to overemphasize biographical detail.

The phase of institutionalization and expansion as a scientific discipline terminated during this period: the first chairs for "new German literary history" were established in 1868 for Karl Tomaschek in Vienna, in 1874 for Michael Bernays in Munich, and in 1877 for Scherer in Berlin. German philology continued to research and explore intellectual life; its nation-building function was strengthened but was now oriented toward Chancellor von Bismarck's national ideal. Consequently, the teaching of German language and literature in secondary schools became increasingly significant, and the formerly distinct traditions of the textual, social, and educational merged.

From the 1920s to the 1960s

These years were characterized by the primacy of the liberal-arts tradition and the rejection of positivism, but within a national set of values. The phenomenon of genius, intellect, and the context of experience and learning formed the focal points. Already in the third phase and parallel to positivism, Wilhelm Dilthey (1833–1911) (*Das Erlebnis der Dichtung,* 1906 [published as *Poetry and Experience,* 1985]), emphasized the independence of the discipline from the natural sciences and pointed out that it was the task of the liberal arts (*Geisteswissenschaft*) to understand rather than to explain causal links. The hermeneutic work endeavored to reproduce the author's spirit as a whole in order to achieve a total comprehension of the other. This generated an interest in the history of ideas (Hermann August Korf) and the history of issues (*Problemgeschichte*). The increasing mystification of the genius (Friedrich Gundolf) prepared the intellectual terrain for the ideas of Nazism. Simultaneously, the nationalistic discourse of the discipline was intensified by studies on "racial" and "tribal" questions (Joseph Nadler and Adolf Bartels), so the political changeover in 1933 did not necessitate a paradigm shift. Only the function of *Germanistik* changed: it became an "instrument of warfare." Its task remained to prove, and to teach, the superiority of all matters German. Literature was assumed to serve the quintessential expression of Germanness. At this point *Germanistik* reached its nadir.

The events of 1945 failed to bring about a dramatic alteration; in the Federal Republic of Germany (FRG), the educational system changed only on the functional level. The staff remained essentially the same, and even the textual system did not deviate significantly. In both Germanys, *Germanistik* focused on the classics and neglected modern literature. It rejected any kind of history that the discipline was not ready to confront. The autonomous "linguistic masterpiece" (Wolfgang Kayser) became the focal point of literary analysis. Interpretation based on the text alone (Emil Staiger), influenced by "New Criticism" and the *explication de texte,* determined *Germanistik* in the FRG. In the German Democratic Republic (GDR) Georg Lukács's (1885–1971) materialistic-sociological methodology, emphasizing the relationship between literature and societal developments, prevailed.

1960s to date

In the GDR, the late 1950s marked a turning point. Triggered by the Twentieth Congress of the Communist Party in the USSR and the Hungarian rebellion in 1956, which virtually illegitimized references to Lukács overnight, the 1959 Bitterfeld Conference moved contemporary literature into the limelight, and socialist realism became obligatory. Because of these changes several professors, including Hans Mayer, left

the GDR, as *Germanistik* was assigned the task of providing the country with a cultural-political tradition founded largely on *Vormärz* (pre-1848) literature. Hence, one of the most significant undertakings of GDR philology was to compile a multivolume history of literature. As in the early nineteenth century, literary history was to legitimize the nation or state—this time the GDR. As in the FRG, few attempts were made to come to terms with the Nazi past, and the discipline failed in both parts of Germany to study its own history.

In the FRG, the year 1966 marked a much more radical turning point than in the GDR. At the 1966 Convention of German Philologists in Munich a new generation of philologists started criticizing the continuity of the discipline throughout the rise and fall of Nazi Germany. The ensuing public discussion resulted in a paradigm shift with regard to methodology, literary canon, and political mission. Gradually, *Germanistik* changed into a cultural discipline with a multiplicity of new discourses, such as the poststructuralist, sociohistorical, reader-response, functional, psychoanalytical, system-theoretical, feminist, and hermeneutical varieties. Philologists became more receptive to interdisciplinary collaboration. Feminist literary criticism became one of the most significant operative forces in the paradigm shift, which has been particularly innovative in theory and has brought about fundamental changes in the literary and the thematic canon.

Since turning away, around 1966, from a relatively homogeneous, patriarchal discipline that functioned for a time without any major internal resistance or contradictions, *Germanistik* has been in a state of crisis. This crisis, which manifests itself in overcrowded lecture halls, budget cuts, and widespread unemployment, has become a subject in its own right within the discipline. Simultaneously, it seems that *Germanistik* has discarded its nationalistic mission. The currents of the 1960s have paved the way for the internationalization of *Germanistik,* which has reduced the traditional and fatal isolation of the discipline.

Claudia I. Mayer-Iswandy

See also Dilthey, Wilhelm; Education; Federal Republic of Germany: Literature; Folklore; German Democratic Republic: Literature and Literary Life; History; Human Sciences; Imperial Germany: Literature; *Kultur;* Language; Literary Criticism; Lukács, Georg; National Identity; National Socialist Germany: Literature; Nationalism; Patriotic Literature; Philosophy; Professions; Teaching; Weimar Germany: Literature

References

Brackert, Helmut. "Zur Geschichte der Germanistik bis 1945." *Literaturwissenschaft: Ein Grundkurs.* Ed. Helmut Brackert and Jörn Stuckrath. Reinbek bei Hamburg: Rowohlt Taschenbuchverlag, 1992.

Conrady, Karl Otto. "Miterlebte Germanistik: Ein Rückblick auf die Zeit vor und nach dem Münchner Germanistentag von 1966." *Diskussion Deutsch* 19 (1988), 126–43.

Dünninger, Josef. "Geschichte der deutschen Philologie." *Deutsche Philologie im Aufriss.* Vol. 1. Ed. Wolfgang Stammier. Berlin: Erich Schmidt Verlag, 1957.

Fohrmann, Jürgen and Wilhelm Vosskamp, eds. *Wissenschaft und Nation: Zur Entstehungsgeschichte der deutschen Literaturwissenschaft*. Munich: Wilhelm Fink Verlag, 1991.

Germanistik—eine deutsche Wissenschaft: Beiträge von Eberhard Lammert, Walter Killy, Karl Otto Conrady und Peter v. Polenz. Frankfurt am Main: Suhrkamp Verlag, 1967.

Götze, Kark-Heinz. "Die Entstehung der deutschen Literaturwissenschaft als Literaturgeschichte: Vorgeschichte, Ziel, Methode und soziale Funktion der Literaturgeschichtsschreibung im deutschen Vormärz." *Germanistik und deutsche Nation 1806–1848: Zur Konstitution bürgerlichen Bewusstseins*. Ed. Jörg Jochen Müller. Stuttgart: Metzler Verlag, 1974.

Hermand, Jost. "Neure Entwicklungen zwischen 1945 und 1980." *Literaturwissenschaft: Ein Grundkurs*. Ed. Helmut Brackert and Jörn Stuckrath. Reinbek bei Hamburg: Rowohlt Taschenbuchverlag, 1992.

Jonata, Johannes, ed. *Eine Wissenschaft etabliert sich 1810–1870: Texte zur Wissenschaftsgeschichte der Germanistik*. Tübingen: Max Niemeyer Verlag, 1980.

Lunding, Erik. "Literaturwissenschaft." *Reallexikon der deutschen Literaturgeschichte*. Ed. Werner Kohlschmidt and Wolfgang Mohr. Berlin: Walter de Gruyter Verlag, 1965.

Reiss, Gunter, ed. *Materialien zur Ideologiegeschichte der deutschen Literaturwissenschaft: Von Wilhelm Scherer bis 1945*. 2 vols. Tübingen: Max Niemeyer Verlag, 1973.

Seeba, Hinrich C. "Nationalliteratur: Zur Ästhetisierung der politischen Funktion von Geschichtsschreibung." *Kontroversen, alte und neue*. Vol. 5: *Akten des VII. Internationalen Germanisten-Kongresses Göttingen 1985*. Ed. Franz Josef Worstbrock. Tübingen: Niemeyer Verlag, 1986.

Weigel, Sigrid. "Geschlechterdifferenz und Literaturwissenschaft." *Literaturwissenschaft: Ein Grundkurs*. Ed. Helmut Brackert and Jörn Stuckrath. Reinbek bei Hamburg: Rowohlt Taschenbuchverlag, 1992.

Weimar, Klaus. "Zur Geschichte der Literaturwissenschaft. Forschungsbericht." *Deutsche Vierteljahrsschrift für Literaturwissenschaft und Geistesgeschichte* 50 (1976), 298–364.

Germany Treaty (*Deutschlandvertrag*) (1952, 1954)

The *Deutschlandvertrag* was the name given to the contractual agreements that ended the Allied occupation of West Germany and restored "practical" sovereignty to the Federal Republic. The Cold War and the division of Germany led the three Western powers—the U.S., Great Britain, and France—and the German government to recognize that, although the occupation should end, a conventional peace settlement and military withdrawal was not in their interest. The Western foreign ministers agreed in September 1951 to negotiate the contractual agreements along with the participation of German forces in the European Defense Community (EDC). The lengthy and intricate agreements covered the whole spectrum of issues arising out of the occupation. Among the most im-

portant were the convention on the rights and obligations of Allied forces in the Federal Republic, the financial arrangements covering these forces, the arbitration tribunal to adjudicate issues between the Western powers and the FRG, and a series of transitional provisions dealing with topics such as war criminals, decartelization, internal and external restitution, displaced persons and refugees, foreign interests in Germany, and civil aviation. Controversy arose over the Allied insistence on the right to declare a state of emergency and assume full authority. The final treaty specified the conditions under which such a state of emergency could be proclaimed and provided for the full consultation with the German government.

The *Deutschlandvertrag* was signed on May 26, 1952 in Bonn, one day after the EDC treaties were signed in Paris. The controversy over German rearmament delayed the ratification of the treaties until August 1954, when the French Assembly defeated the EDC. To restore the political strength of the Adenauer government, which had staked its position on the approval of the EDC and contractual agreements, the American secretary of state, John Foster Dulles, insisted on a "sweeping and generous" revision of the *Deutschlandvertrag*. Although retaining their reserved rights to questions relating to Berlin and the unification of Germany, the Allies agreed to change their right to station forces from the category of a reserved right to that of an agreed treaty right, and revised the "state of emergency" clause, agreeing to allow this power to lapse when the German government enacted the appropriate legislation. Along with agreements allowing Germany to join the Western European Union and NATO, the revised treaty was signed in September 1954 and came into effect on May 5, 1955. The *Deutschlandvertrag* remained in effect until the Moscow treaties of September 1990, which constituted the final peace settlement of World War II.

Thomas Schwartz

See also Adenauer, Konrad; Allied Occupation Statute; American-German Relations; American Occupation; Anglo-German Relations; British Occupation Policy; The Cold War and Germany; Diplomatic Corps and Diplomacy; Federal Republic of Germany: Foreign Policy; Franco-German Relations; NATO and Germany; Postwar European Integration and Germany

References
Rupieper, Hermann-Josef. *Der besetzte Verbündete: Die amerikanische Deutschlandpolitik 1949–1955*. Opladen: Westdeutscher Verlag, 1991.

Schwartz, Thomas. *America's Germany: John J. McCloy and the Federal Republic of Germany*. Cambridge, MA: Harvard University Press, 1991.

Gerstenmaier, Eugen (1906–86)

Eugen Gerstenmaier was born on August 25, 1906 into an artisan family in the Swabian town of Kirchheim and died on March 13, 1986. He served in the External Affairs Office of the German Evangelical Church from 1936 until his arrest on

July 20, 1944. In 1939, he was given an additional post in the Information Department of the German Foreign Ministry. Gerstenmaier fostered contact between the national church and the ecumenical movement abroad, participated in the discussions of the Kreisau Circle, and contributed to the July 20, 1944, conspiracy against Hitler's life.

Gerstenmaier studied theology at Rostock, where in 1934 he was arrested for opposing Nazi religious policy—even though his licentiate thesis would later affirm the nation as an expression of divine revelation, implying the subordination of the German church to the national mission. After a brief stint in the Württemberg Landeskirche (regional church), Gerstenmaier entered the Church External Affairs Office, where he was responsible for maintaining relations with foreign churches. There he consistently opposed separate representation for the Confessing Church in the ecumenical movement, arguing that the national church was the best front for anti-Nazi religious action.

In 1939, Gerstenmaier was posted in the Foreign Office as a scientific advisor, assigned to exploit the church's foreign contacts for the German cause. There he was introduced to the conspiracy by Adam von Trott zu Solz (1909–44). Throughout the war, he fully supported the removal of Hitler by force, even assassination. By 1942, Gerstenmaier was active in the Kreisau Circle as an expert on church-state relations and social questions, where he opposed a conservative political restoration.

In the July 20, 1944 coup attempt, Gerstenmaier was one of the coordinators of the Berlin *Putsch*. Designated "military plenipotentiary for cultural and church affairs," he was arrested that evening and only narrowly escaped execution on the spot. Gerstenmaier was tried for high treason but avoided the death sentence by portraying himself as a naïve clergyman.

After the war, Gerstenmaier developed the Evangelical aid program (*Hilfswerk*) to alleviate problems of homeless refugees, destroyed church buildings, and dislocated parish life. Gerstenmaier was *Hilfswerk* chairman until 1957. A popular CDU deputy in the West German Bundestag, he headed its Foreign Affairs Committee and served four terms as Bundestag speaker, from 1954 to 1969. Gerstenmaier opposed Adenauer's rigid foreign-policy stance. He favored arms reductions, negotiations with the Soviet Union, and the possibility of a unified, neutral Germany. Gerstenmaier's career ended scandalously because of his inflated claims for restitution of wartime losses.

Kyle Jantzen

See also Adenauer, Konrad; Christian Democratic Union; National Socialist Germany; Protestantism and the Protestant Church; Refugees; Resistance; Trott zu Solz, Adam von

References
Gerstenmaier, E. "The Church Conspiratorial." *We Survived.* Ed. E. Boehm. New Haven, CT: Yale University Press, 1949.
———. *Reden und Aufsätze.* 2 vols. Stuttgart: Evangelisches Verlagswerk, 1956 and 1962.
———. *Streit und Friede hat seine Zeit: ein Lebensbericht.* Frankfurt am Main: Propyläen, 1981.
Schlabrendorff, Fabian von, ed. *Eugen Gerstenmaier im Dritten Reich: Eine Dokumentation.* Stuttgart: Evangelisches Verlagswerk, 1965.

Gessler, Otto (1875–1955)

Otto Gessler was a jurist, a Bavarian professional civil servant, and a politician in the Weimar Republic. During World War I he was mayor of Nuremberg (1914–19), in 1919–20 he was federal minister for reconstruction, and from 1920 to 1928 he was minister of defense. He was a member of the German Democratic Party until 1927, and a one-term member of the Reichstag (1920–24). After World War II he served as president of the German Red Cross (1950–52).

Gessler is remembered as the highly controversial defense minister of a republic he never loved; emotionally, he remained attached to the Bavarian Wittelsbach monarchy. He viewed Weimar as a mere "party state." In his constitutional-reform proposals he wanted to curtail the authority of the parliament and increase the powers of the president. As defense minister, he quite consciously tried to keep party politics and parliamentary influence out of the army, and allowed General Hans von Seeckt (1866–1936), chief of the Army Command, to exercise full control of military policy.

Gessler did not believe himself qualified to lead in military matters, and did not wish to play a military role. Not surprisingly, his left-wing critics, including many Democrats, took a grim view of his failure to create a reliable republican army. And they had good reasons for complaining that for years Gessler deliberately misled parliament and his own party in trying to cover up German secret rearmament and evasions of the Versailles treaty terms. Whether he was a willing partner of the army leaders in these matters and a parliamentary shield for the army or a dupe, himself deceived and dominated by General Seeckt, is a question that still divides historians. When in 1926 he finally dismissed the independent-minded general, it was largely for personal reasons.

Gessler was a profoundly patriotic man who believed in Germany's right to build up an adequate defensive military force, by circumventing Versailles if there was no other way. In 1927, increasing criticism by his fellow Democrats finally forced him out of the party, and a year later a scandal led to his resignation as defense minister.

Attila Chanady

See also Ebert, Friedrich; German Democratic Party; Seeckt, Hans von; Weimar Germany; Weimar Germany: Army

References
Carsten, Francis L. *The Reichswehr and Politics: 1918–1933.* Oxford: Oxford University Press, 1966.
Frye, Bruce B. *Liberal Democrats in the Weimar Republic: The History of the German Democratic Party and the German State Party.* Carbondale, IL: University of Southern Illinois Press, 1985.
Gessler, Otto. *Reichwehrpolitik in der Weimarer Zeit.* Ed.

Kurt Sendtner. Stuttgart: Deutsche Verlags-Anstalt, 1958.

Schneider, Werner. *Die Deutsche Demokratische Partei in der Weimarer Republik 1924–1930*. Munich: Fink, 1978.

Schustereit, Hartmut. "Unpolitisch-Überparteilich-Staatstreu: Wehrfragen aus der Sicht der Deutschen Demokratischen Partei 1919–1930." *Militärgeschichtliche Mitteilungen* 16 (1974), 131–72.

Stephan, Werner. *Aufstieg and Verfall des Linksliberalismus 1918–1933. Geschichte der Deutschen Demokratischen Partei*. Göttingen: Vandenhoeck & Ruprecht, 1973.

Gestapo (Geheime Staatspolizei) (1933–45)

Gestapo was the acronym for the political police of the Third Reich. For them, political crime extended beyond opposition to the state and Nazi ideology to anything detrimental to the "racial purity" of the German people. This redefinition grew from Nazism, a xenophobic fusion of state nationalism, cultural nationalism, and the pseudo-scientific racism of the age. The ideology demanded national strength through homogeneity; the Gestapo was to control and eliminate heterogeneity.

Political police specialize in crimes against the state: espionage, sabotage, assassination, conspiracy to overthrow the government, and illegal political organizations. To expand beyond that conventional definition, in 1933 the Nazi governments in every state sought to establish ideologically correct political police forces. After Heinrich Himmler (1900–45), *Reichsführer* of the Schutzstaffel (SS), became chief of the Bavarian Political Police, it evolved along with the SS-controlled concentration camp at Dachau into a model for the future police state. However, the largest such force was the Prussian Geheime Staatspolizei (Gestapo), created by Prime Minister Hermann Göring (1893–1946).

By April 1934, Himmler had become nominal commander of the political police in each state and inspector of the Prussian Gestapo. All political police were then coordinated through his Office of the Commander in the Berlin Gestapo Office. Command fell to Reinhard Heydrich (1904–42), also chief of the Sicherheitsdienst (SD). By 1936, Himmler had built a model that fulfilled Adolf Hitler's needs, so Hitler appointed him chief of all German police.

To create an ideologically guided police, Himmler tried to fuse them with his Schutzstaffel (SS). Since 1933, Nazis, mostly Sturmabteilung (SA) or SS men, had entered the ranks of the political police. Many detectives reciprocated, joining Nazi organizations. By the summer of 1935, 21 percent of the Gestapo were SS members. Between 1935 and 1936, Himmler coordinated the penetration, designating the SD as the branch for all SS men in the Gestapo. After 1936, despite disruption by wartime pressures, SS officers commanded almost every office of the Gestapo, and total SS penetration ran as high as 77 percent in some units.

By the end of the regime, the Gestapo numbered over 32,000, divided into three categories: 9 percent administrative and juridical civil servants, 48 percent police detectives, and 42 percent police employees. All ranks had been inflated by emergency wartime supplements, while training and quality had suffered to facilitate SS penetration. Nevertheless, the Gestapo never achieved a size comparable to its overextended mission. The relative significance of Gestapo spies, reports from the vast network of party and state agencies, and public cooperation is a current focus of research on the operation of the police state.

The Gestapo exercised totalitarian police state powers. By 1936, its actions were almost totally immune to external review. By 1939, under the guise of "national security," it could whisk away any but the most prominent opponents. It controlled or eliminated "biological enemies" of the *Volk*, delivering these "racial criminals" from occupied Europe to their fates in the concentration camps and, in some cases, executing them on the spot. Gestapo men commanded *Einsatzkommandos*, teams for mass extermination on the eastern front. As slave laborers flooded Germany, Gestapo energy turned increasingly to monitoring their personal relationships with the *Volk*.

Nationalist sentiments apparently played a minimal role in overt public support of the Gestapo. However, arguments for national security helped create the passive acceptance of the police state. Modern nationalism and fear of undermining the strength of one's nation create overwhelming pressures for excessive social-political conformity and fear of being perceived as an enemy of the nation. Consequently, such an "enemy" seems to have sacrificed all rights and to deserve any fate, even one that otherwise violates all norms.

Although extensive scholarly literature on the SS and police states outlines the history of the Gestapo, no single, reliable monograph focuses on it. Robert Gellately's *The Gestapo and German Society*, 1990, the best brief historical overview in English, opens valuable social perspectives on operations during the war years. Among the uneven journalistic histories, the most recent is Jochen von Lang's *Die Gestapo: Instrument des Terrors* (The Gestapo: instrument of terror), 1990. The most scholarly overview, Johannes Tuchel and Reinhold Schattenfroh's, *Zentrale des Terrors: Prinz-Albrecht-Strasse 8, Das Hauptquartier der Gestapo* (Center of terror: Prinz-Albrecht-Strasse 8, the headquarters of the Gestapo), 1987, focuses on the central headquarters in Berlin. For early organizational development and the political struggle that shaped it, there are George C. Browder's *The Foundations of the Nazi Police State: The Formation of Sipo and SD*, 1990; Shlomo Aronson's *Reinhard Heydrich und die Frühgeschichte von Gestapo und SD* (Reinhard Heydrich and the early history of the Gestapo and security service), 1971; and Christoph Graf's *Politische Polizei zwischen Demokratie und Diktatur* (Political police between democracy and dictatorship), 1983. Numerous publications of Gestapo reports have focused primarily on its victims, although several volumes now document the field-level work of the Gestapo itself.

George C. Browder

See also Einsatzgruppen; Gisevius, Hans Bernd; Göring, Hermann; Heydrich, Reinhard; Himmler, Heinrich; Hitler, Adolf; National Socialist Germany; Policing; Schutzstaffel

References

Browder, George. *Hitler's Enforcers: The Gestapo and the SS Security Service in the Nazi Revolution.* New York, NY: Oxford University Press, 1996.

Gellately, Robert. *The Gestapo and German Society.* Oxford: Clarendon Press, 1990.

———. "Rethinking the Nazi Terror System: Historiographical Analysis." *German Studies Review* 14 (1991), 23–38.

———. "Situating the 'SS State' in a Social-Historical Context: Recent Histories of the SS, the Police, and the Courts in the Third Reich." *Journal of Modern History* 64 (1992), 338–365.

Gierke, Anna von (1874–1943)

Anna von Gierke, the daughter of noted legal scholar Otto von Gierke, helped to create the profession of social work in Germany and became a prominent female politician and Reichstag delegate.

Gierke was recruited into volunteer work by Hedwig Heyl (1850–1934) at the Charlottenburger Jugendheim (Charlottenburg youth center), an after-school center for girls that Heyl had founded in 1892. The institution, of which Gierke soon became the head, was supported by a group of Charlottenburg citizens, the Verein Jugendheim (Youth Center Association). After courses at the Pestalozzi-Froebel House, an institution training child-care and youth workers, she opened an after-school program for boys in 1901. A day-care program for preschool children was added in order to enable girls who were responsible for younger brothers and sisters to attend the center. Gierke gained the support of the Charlottenburg city government for a school-lunch program in 1907. These programs were intended for children of low-income, working mothers. Gierke persuaded the school system to employ social workers to select eligible children. By 1920 the Verein Jugendheim under Gierke's leadership supported 20 day-care and after-school centers in Charlottenburg.

Gierke became a nationally known advocate of social-work training for women. She created a *Sozialpädagogisches Seminar* (social-work seminar) that combined practical work in the youth centers with theoretical training. She also became a prominent advocate of governmental involvement in child welfare. Many of the services that the Youth Center provided were taken over by the Charlottenburg city government in the 1920s.

Gierke gained influence in the women's movement through her prominent position in the Reichsverband deutscher Hausfrauenvereine (National Federation of German Housewives' Associations). She was elected to the Reichstag as a delegate of the conservative German National People's Party (DNVP) in 1919. However, she served only one term; as the daughter of a Jewish mother, she objected to the growing anti-Semitism of the DNVP, from which she soon resigned. After the Nazi seizure of power in 1933, she was removed from her position as head of the Youth Center, which was dissolved in 1934. She continued to live in Berlin, where she joined the Confessing Church (a group within the Protestant churches that opposed National Socialism) and helped Jews to live in hiding and to escape to other countries.

Anna von Gierke contributed to the formation of the German welfare state by creating social-service agencies to meet the needs of disadvantaged children and by advocating the widening of such services by both governmental and private agencies.

Ann T. Allen

See also Anti-Semitism; Childbirth and Motherhood; Confessing Church; German National People's Party; Social Reform; (Bourgeois) Women's Movement; Youth; Youth Movement

References

Allen, Ann T. *Feminism and Motherhood in Germany, 1800–1914.* New Brunswick, NJ: Rutgers University Press, 1991.

Baum, Marie. *Anna von Gierke: Ein Lebensbild.* Weinheim: Beltz Verlag, 1954.

Brehmer, Ilse, ed. *Mütterlichkeit als Profession?* Pfaffenweiler: Centaurus, 1990.

Zeller, Susanne. *Volksmutter: Frauen im Wohlfahrtswesen der zwanziger Jahre.* Düsseldorf: Schwann Verlag, 1987.

Gisevius, Hans Bernd (1904–74)

Hans Bernd Gisevius, the son of a jurist, was born in Arnsberg on June 14, 1904. He studied law, passed the necessary examinations, and entered the Prussian civil service in July 1933. In August Gisevius was transferred to the Geheime Staatspolizei (Gestapo; Secret State Police). Since he was not a Nazi, Gisevius was not given a warm welcome by his chief, Rudolf Diels, and in December he was transferred to the Reich Interior Ministry.

Gisevius became active in the conspiracy to overthrow Hitler in 1938. In 1939 he was conscripted into the German military as a member of the Abwehr, the military counterintelligence unit. There Gisevius joined the group of anti-Nazis led by Admiral Wilhelm Canaris (1887–1945) and Lieutenant-Colonel Hans Oster (1888–1945). As an Abwehr agent he was appointed German vice-consul in Zürich, Switzerland (1940–44). As a representative of the Resistance he often met with Allen Welsh Dulles (1893–1969) of the American Office of Strategic Services located in Bern. Between January 1943 and July 1944, Gisevius provided Dulles with information, documents, and letters regarding Resistance activity in Germany. He also conveyed information in 1943 on the German military's V-1 and V-2 rocket program and its base at Peenemünde.

On July 9, 1944, Gisevius returned to Germany to participate in the July 20, 1944 assassination attempt on Hitler. After its failure, Gisevius hid in Berlin until Dulles was able to provide him with a false passport. This enabled Gisevius to take refuge in Switzerland in January 1945. After being called as a witness for the prosecution in the Nuremberg Military Tribunal in April 1946, he published his controversial memoirs, *Bis zum bitteren Ende* (published as *To the Bitter End*, 1948),

1946. Gisevius then spent several years in the United States and West Berlin before finally settling in Switzerland. He died in Baden on February 23, 1974.

Gisevius's contribution to the Resistance resides mainly in his actions as a link to the West. His position in Switzerland provided the Resistance with a line of communication to the Allies.

Kenneth Reynolds

See also Canaris, Wilhelm; Gestapo; National Socialist Germany; Oster, Hans; Policing; Resistance

References

Dulles, Allen Welsh. *Germany's Underground*. New York, NY: Macmillan, 1947.
Gisevius, Hans Bernd. *To the Bitter End*. London: Jonathan Cape, 1948.
Hoffmann, Peter. *The History of the German Resistance, 1933–1945*. Cambridge, MA: MIT Press, 1977.

Globke, Hans (1898–1973)

As a civil servant, first in Prussia, later in the Reich Ministry of the Interior (1929–45), and then as advisor to Chancellor Konrad Adenauer, Hans Globke exercised much influence and represented the continuity of state personnel despite the change in political regimes.

Holding special responsibility for nationality affairs, Globke helped implement the racialist Nuremberg Laws of 1935 which excluded "non-Aryans" from German citizenship. He co-authored an official commentary on those laws.

Despite this background, Globke worked closely with Chancellor Adenauer from 1949, serving as state secretary in the Chancellery from 1953 to 1963. Since Adenauer was also responsible for foreign and defense policy, the secretaryship was a position of considerable power; Adenauer and Globke built it into an office that served the chancellor directly rather than the cabinet as a whole. Globke's duties included reviewing the monthly ministerial reports, setting the agenda for the cabinet meetings (which he also attended), and supervising both the Federal Press Office and the internal security system headed by General Gehlen. He was a skilled and discreet civil servant with a deep personal loyalty to his chancellor.

The degree to which Globke used his position to help place ex-Nazis into positions of authority remains unclear. Finding capable and experienced civil servants when the German state was refounded after World War II was a problem. A list of potential high officials for a ministry of the interior drawn up in 1948 contained only one non-Nazi out of 26, and 15 had, like Globke, worked for the Nazi Ministry of the Interior.

Along with the senior diplomat Herbert Blankenhorn (1904–91), Globke was accused in the early 1950s by the Social Democrats of having too faithfully served the Nazi regime. In September 1960 the news magazine *Der Spiegel* pointed out that Globke had direct contacts with Adolf Eichmann with regard to the release of a shipment of Jews from Macedonia. An East German investigation brought forth more details of his part in providing legitimization for actions against Jews and foreigners. He was forced to resign after the East German Supreme Court convicted him in absentia as a Nazi criminal in 1962.

Jane Caplan

See also Adenauer, Konrad; Chancellor's, Office; Civil Service; National Socialist Germany

References

Adenauer, K. *Memoirs*. London: H. Regnery, 1966.
German Democratic Republic. *On the Criminal Past of Globke: Adenauer's State Secretary and the Extermination of the Jews*. Berlin: Committee for German Unity, 1960.
Gotto, Klaus, ed. *Der Staatssekretär Adenauers: Persönlichkeit und politisches Wirken Hans Globkes*. Stuttgart: Klett-Cotta, 1980.
Hiscocks, Richard. *The Adenauer Era*. Philadelphia, PA: J.B. Lippincott Co., 1966.
Johnson, Nevil. *Government in the Federal Republic of Germany*. Oxford: Pergamon Press, 1973.
Köhler, Henning. *Adenauer: Eine politische Biographie*. Berlin: Propyläen, 1994.
Nationale Front des demokratischen Deutschlands. *Brown Book: War and Nazi Criminals in West Germany: State, Economy, Administration, Army, Justice, Science*. Dresden: Verlag im Bild, 1965.
Schwarz, Hans-Peter. *Adenauer*. 2 vols. Providence, RI and Oxford: Berghahn Books, 1995–1997.

Goebbels, Joseph (1897–1945)

Goebbels became the first minister for popular enlightenment and propaganda in 1933, a position he retained throughout the Third Reich. In 1944 he was appointed Reich trustee for total war and in Hitler's final act of state was named Reich chancellor.

Paul Joseph Goebbels was born on October 29, 1897 at Rheydt in the Rheinland, and after attending the universities of Bonn, Freiburg, Würzburg, and Munich he settled in Heidelberg, where in November 1921 he took a Ph.D. with the thesis "Wilhelm Scheutze: A Contribution to the History of the Romantic Theater." He was also acquiring literary ambitions, and in 1921 he completed *Michael: Ein deutsches Schicksal* (Michael: a German destiny), a novel written in the form of a diary and based on his adventures as a student. (This novel would not be published until 1929 when Eher Verlag, the Nazi Party publisher, accepted it.)

After failing to become a journalist with the local newspaper, *Berliner Tageblatt*, Goebbels entered politics in 1924 when he was appointed private secretary to Franz von Wiegershaus, the Elberfeld nationalist politician and Prussian parliamentary deputy. Toward the end of 1924 his work brought him into contact with prominent Nazis, and in 1925, when the Nazi Party was reformed after Adolf Hitler's release from prison, Goebbels was appointed manager of the Gau (district) Rheinland-Nord and secretary to Gregor Strasser

(1892–1934), the north and west German party leader.

In November 1926 Goebbels became *Gauleiter* (district leader) of Berlin and began immediately to reshape the party organization in the German capital with the aid of a new weekly newspaper, *Der Angriff* (The attack), set up to attack political opponents and the Weimar system. Hitler subsequently appointed him head of party propaganda in 1928. In the electoral contests between 1928 and 1933, in which the Nazis made their electoral breakthrough and eventually gained power, Goebbels was the campaign manager who skillfully orchestrated the distinctive Nazi propaganda. These campaigns are described by Goebbels in *Der Kampf um Berlin* (The struggle for Berlin), 1932, and *Vom Kaiserhof zur Reichskanzlei* (From Kaiserhof to the Reich Chancellery), 1934. Once in power Goebbels became minister for the new Ministry for Popular Enlightenment and Propaganda, which came into being on March 13, 1933. As minister of propaganda, Goebbels aggressively used the mass media—indeed, all forms of communication—on a scale that made propaganda a major instrument of political control at home and of foreign policy abroad.

Goebbels would have liked to have extended his position beyond propaganda and to have had a greater say in shaping Nazi policy, particularly the organization of the German war effort. However, despite his best endeavors to persuade Hitler, his views on the occupation policy in Russia and the mobilization of the civilian population continued to be ignored. Nevertheless, he remained an implacable supporter of the führer even when the war turned against Germany. After defeat at Stalingrad and Hitler's refusal to broadcast or appear in public, it was Goebbels who became the major political speaker in an attempt to uphold morale and radicalize the home front.

After the failed attempt on Hitler's life in July 1944, Goebbels was finally given the powers he wanted as Reich trustee for total war. However Goebbels' efforts and propaganda could not compensate for the worsening military situation. In the final stage of the war, he moved into the Hitler bunker with his wife, Magda, and their six children. Of the original group who had come to power with Hitler in 1933, Goebbels alone retained his confidence; he was named Reich chancellor in Hitler's final act of state. In the ruins of the Chancellery, Goebbels helped his wife to kill his children and then shot her and himself.

As a propagandist, Goebbels was a master with few equals. Nazi propaganda was dictated by emotion, prejudice, hatred, and passion. His two most notable propaganda achievements were the projection of the "führer myth" and the orchestration of the Nazi Party rallies. Probably more than any single individual Goebbels is responsible for the pejorative associations that are commonly associated with the term propaganda.

David Welch

See also Anti-Semitism; Berlin; Göring, Hermann; Himmler, Heinrich; Hitler, Adolf; Journalism; National Socialism; National Socialist Germany; National Socialist Germany: Art; Prussian Art Academy; Strasser, Gregor; Third Reich: Film; Third Reich: Propaganda and Culture

References

Bramsted, Ernst. *Goebbels and National Socialist Propaganda 1925–45.* East Lansing, MI: Michigan State University Press, 1965.

Fröhlich, E., ed. *Die Tagebücher von Joseph Goebbels: Sämtliche Fragmente.* 4 vols. Munich: K.G. Baur, 1987.

Heiber, Helmut. *Goebbels.* New York, NY: Hawthorn Books, 1973.

Lemmons, Russel. *Goebbels and Der Angriff.* Lexington, KY: University of Kentucky Press, 1994.

Reuth, Ralf Georg. *Goebbels.* Trans. Krishna Winston. New York: Harvest, 1994.

Taylor, R. "Goebbels and the Function of Propaganda." *Nazi Propaganda: The Power and the Limitations.* Ed. D. Welch. London: Croom Helm, 1983.

Welch, David A. *The Third Reich: Politics and Propaganda.* London: Routledge, 1993.

Goerdeler, Carl (1884–1945)

Carl Friedrich Goerdeler was a decisive figure in the German Resistance. He gathered adherents among various parties but retained a conservative and nationalist outlook.

Goerdeler was born in Schneidemühl, West Prussia, on July 31, 1884. His father became county court judge in Marienwerder a few years later. Goerdeler studied law in Tübingen and Königsberg, but he found administration and the economy more challenging than a judicial career. During World War I, he served as administrator of finance in the occupied regions of Belorussia and Lithuania. When West Prussia faced separation from the Reich because of the Treaty of Versailles, many were prepared to create an independent state in the East if necessary. In 1919, this movement for national defense brought Goerdeler back to West Prussia, where he aimed not only at blocking an invasion by the Polish army but, with the help of German troops in the region, at the removal or destruction of the new Polish state. These volunteers were defeated. In his subsequent judgment, he had grown up in "a nationalism of a narrow type," which he only discarded later, when he had come to know many foreigners.

As *Oberbürgermeister* of Leipzig after 1930, he became a widely known local politician as well as frequent writer in public administration. Goerdeler was a man of tremendous energy and independence. His duties brought him closer to the German populace, including the working class and its trade-union representatives. He shared the nationalist prejudices of the conservative German National People's Party, embraced an authoritarian concept of the state, and had little interest in the parliamentary constitutions of Western democratic governments. He did not share the biases of prominent capitalists against the social aspirations of the workers. He had a strong personality, possessed great persuasiveness, deeply believed in the power of reason, and was moved by a strong moral conscience. He showed no confidence in the Franz von Papen (1879–1967) cabinet or in General Kurt von Schleicher

(1892–1934), but his own hopes for a more significant political role in the Weimar Republic did not materialize.

Like many other German contemporaries, he took a long time to comprehend the demonic character of Nazism, though he was repelled by its noisy, violent propaganda. His biographer, Gerhard Ritter, found little evidence in Goerdeler's papers of an early clear-cut opposition to the Third Reich. As late as 1937, he maintained that in times of emergency dictatorship may have its justification. After Hitler's seizure of power, Goerdeler refused to raise the swastika above the Leipzig city hall and personally protected Jewish shopkeepers against plundering stormtroopers. On the other hand, he at first trustingly cooperated with the Nazis and entertained a personal relationship with Hitler despite his liberal policy as a controller of prices. Goerdeler's championship of "price discipline, not price dictate," and his opposition to a planned economy, seemed to assure his job. But when the party congress of September 1936 proclaimed the Four-Year Plan, Goerdeler, though recently reelected in Leipzig for a 12-year term, was increasingly challenged. While he was abroad, the Nazi Party removed the Mendelssohn-Bartholdi Monument, which had honored the great Jewish composer. After his return, Goerdeler resigned in protest.

Thereupon Goerdeler traveled extensively abroad. His journeys took him to many European countries, the Middle East, North Africa, and the United States. His reports were transmitted to Krupp, Göring, Schacht, and many prominent generals; some went to the Chancellery. He wanted to show that the Western governments were ready for compromise, although he discerned a limit to their willingness to support German expansion and conquest. Despite some informed observations, he was not entirely free of illusions and he overestimated his influence. He was perturbed about the indifference with which people abroad accepted the news of the cruelties of the Hitler regime, seeing in National Socialism only a bulwark against the peril of a Communist world revolution. Still, in his talks with English statesmen, Goerdeler came rather close to suggesting the policy of "appeasement at any price," a course hardly likely to stiffen the hoped-for resistance against Hitler's expansionism.

On the eve of World War II, Goerdeler privately criticized Western statesmen for failing to resist the aspirations of Hitler, an "unscrupulous adventurer and world conqueror." During the war he protested against the mutilations and murders of citizens of alien nations. He privately accused Hitler of "having sullied the German name through horrible crimes," pointing especially to the brutal maltreatment of the Poles and "the deliberate beastly extermination of the Jews." He voiced the fear that Germany would face a second, worse Versailles.

Several weeks after the failed attempt to overthrow and kill Hitler in July 1944, the authorities ordered Goerdeler's arrest. In September 1944, Goerdeler was sentenced to death, but it was not until February 2, 1945, that the sentence was carried out. Though he had uttered doubts about political murder, including that of the tyrannical führer, he did not deny his own responsibility since he had known of the impending plot. In the words of his biographer, "that he, the main organizer of the German Resistance movement, showed sharp opposition to the assassination of Hitler was a bitter pill for all who approved of the ethical right of this deed."

Alfred D. Low

See also National Socialist Germany; Resistance

References

Klemperer, Klemens von. *German Resistance against Hitler.* Oxford: Clarendon Press, 1992.

Ritter, Gerhard. *The German Resistance: Carl Goerdeler's Struggle Against Tyranny.* Trans. R.T. Clark. Freeport, NY: Books for Libraries Press, 1970.

Rothfels, Hans. *The German Opposition to Hitler: An Appraisal.* Chicago, IL: Henry Regnery, 1963.

Gorbachev and the German Question

The spread and the collapse of the Soviet empire was inseparable from the division and reunification of Europe, and the division and reunification of Germany was at the center of the process. During most of the Brezhnev era (1964–82) and throughout the 1980s, the USSR officially regarded the German question as closed. Only after the beginning of 1990—under the pressure of internal Soviet exhaustion and the breakup of the Soviet empire—did Soviet diplomacy become a promoter of German unity.

When Mikhail Gorbachev became general secretary of the Communist Party of the Soviet Union on March 11, 1985, he did not appear to have in mind a new approach to the German question. During the state visit of the Federal Republic of Germany's (FRG) President Richard von Weizsäcker (1920–) on July 6–11, 1987—the first visit by a West German head of state to the USSR in 13 years—Moscow did not agree to any concrete concessions on unification, but the Soviet leaders acknowledged that in the long term ("a hundred years") history would decide the matter. By contrast, the atmosphere during Chancellor Helmut Kohl's working visit to Moscow on October 24–27, 1988, his first in five years, reflected a more flexible Soviet attitude toward improving bilateral relations. However, concerning the German question, Gorbachev warned about shaking up the status quo or fostering any unrealistic strategies.

The days that Gorbachev spent in the FRG (from June 12 to 15, 1989), set the seal on the special relationship with the FRG. Gorbachev accepted in the Joint Declaration the right of self-determination for all peoples and states. This created a corresponding unease in East Berlin, despite the efforts made to reassure the German Democratic Republic (GDR) that its future was not in question. Because of the increasing opposition of the GDR's leadership to Gorbachev's *perestroika* and Moscow's need for economic support from West Germany, there was a tendency in Moscow to make the fate of the GDR less an overriding preoccupation than in the past. This reserve placed more responsibility on the shoulders of the Socialist Unity Party (SED) *Politbüro*. After Hungary opened its borders with Austria on September 11, 1989, tens of thousands of GDR citizens left East Germany via Hungary and by occupying FRG embassies in Prague and Warsaw. On October 7, 1989, after attending the GDR's fortieth-anniversary celebrations, Gorbachev cautiously demanded reforms in East Germany (like the ones in the USSR, Poland, and Hungary), which led to the removal of Erich Honecker's (1912–94) circle in the GDR leadership.

On November 9, 1989, Honecker's successor, Egon Krenz, opened the Berlin Wall, leading to a rapid destabilization of the GDR and to street demonstrations demanding the unification of the two Germanys. Making a virtue of necessity, Gorbachev, at the end of January 1990, adopted the role of promoter of German unity. His meetings with Chancellor Kohl on July 15–16, 1990 in Moscow and Arkhyz marked the culmination of a negotiating process over conditions for solving the German question. In an unexpected concession, Gorbachev agreed that Germany could not only unify—this was already conceded in the ongoing Two-plus-Four talks—but could also choose its military alliance.

At the last Two-plus-Four meeting, held in Moscow on September 12, 1990, the "Treaty on the Final Settlement for Germany" was signed. The conclusion of the treaty brought an end to four-power rights. A united Germany renounced all territorial claims. It confirmed its existing promises not to manufacture, possess, or deploy nuclear, biological, or chemical weapons. German troops would be cut by over 42 percent, to a total of 370,000 men. Until the evacuation of Soviet troops was completed, only forces from the German territorial army would be stationed on former East German territory.

Additional agreements were signed between Moscow and Bonn: the Treaty on Good Neighborliness, Partnership, and Cooperation; the Treaty on the Stationing and Withdrawal of Troops; the Transition Treaty; and the Treaty on Wide-Ranging Economic, Industrial, Scientific, and Technological Cooperation. The Supreme Soviet ratified these agreements on March 4 and April 2, 1991 in Moscow, but only after harsh opposition by conservative forces.

The financial costs of unification were enormous. Germany had to pay for Soviet troop withdrawals, which concluded at the end of August 1994. The estimated costs exceeded 15 billion deutsche marks (DM). Until mid-1993, Germany had contributed to the Soviet Union or its successor countries a total of 81 billion DM, or more than 55 percent of Western aid.

Fred Oldenburg

See also Federal Republic of Germany: Foreign Policy; German Democratic Republic: Collapse; German Democratic Republic: Foreign Relations; Honecker, Erich; Kohl, Helmut; Reunification; Soviet-German Relations

References

Laird, Robin F. *The Soviets, Germany, and the New Europe.* Boulder, CO: Westview Press, 1991.
Malcolm, Neil, ed. *Russia and Europe.* London: Pinter, 1993.
McAdams, James A. *From the Wall to Reunification.* Princeton, NJ: Princeton University Press, 1992.
Sodaro, Michael J. *Moscow, Germany, and the West from Khrushchev to Gorbachev.* Ithaca, NY: Cornell University Press, 1990.

Göring, Hermann Wilhelm (1893–1946)

Hermann Göring was a leading member of the Nazi Party by the late 1920s. He became a Reichstag deputy in 1928, president of the Reichstag in 1932, and following the Nazi assumption of power in 1933 became first minister of aviation (1933), then commander in chief of the German air force (1935). A year later, in October 1936, he was appointed plenipotentiary for the Four-Year Plan. In 1939, Hitler designated him his chosen successor, and in 1940 he was promoted to the rank of Reich marshal, the highest military office in Germany. Throughout the Third Reich he played a central role in military and economic affairs.

Göring was born in Bavaria, the son of a consular official. He became a professional soldier before World War I, and during the war joined the air force, rising by 1918 to command the famous Richthofen Squadron. After the war he found it difficult to settle down to civilian life, and in 1922 joined the fledgling Nazi Party. He became head of its paramilitary wing, the SA, and was wounded in the failed Beer Hall *Putsch* of November 1923. After a period in exile in Italy he returned to Germany, where he rejoined the party. Hitler chose him as one of the first 12 Nazi Reichstag deputies in 1928 because of his links with traditional nationalist and conservative circles. He became president of the Reichstag following the success of the Nazi Party in July 1932, when it became the largest party. He played some part in the final intrigues that led to Hitler's assumption of power in January 1933 and was rewarded by a seat in the cabinet and the job of interior minister in Prussia. He set about establishing a secret police force, the Gestapo, and authorized the first concentration camps. In 1934, these police responsibilities were given to Heimrich Himmler, and Göring devoted his energies to building up the German air force, which became the most technically advanced and successful air force in the world by 1940.

In October 1936, Hitler chose Göring to head the Four-Year Plan organization, established to oversee the transformation of the German economy for war preparation. He used the office as an instrument to extend his influence over wide areas of economic and military life. He interfered where he could in foreign affairs, though his advice to Hitler to be more prudent until Germany was fully armed was only heeded once, during the Czechoslovakian crisis in September 1938. During the war, Göring assumed much of the responsibility for managing the war economy as well as commanding the air force. The two tasks proved too onerous. By 1941, the war economy was debilitated by a lack of central control and by much political infighting, in which Göring was conspicuously involved. The air force suffered from a lack of clear planning and direction. By the middle of the war it was short of aircraft and crewmen, its technical development in chaos. In 1942, Göring was excluded from most of his economic responsibilities by Hitler, who also came to exercise increasing influence over the use and development of the air force. By the end of the war, Göring, famous for his personal greed, corruption, and flamboyance, was no longer a significant political figure. He was tried as a war criminal at Nuremberg, found guilty, and sentenced to death. He committed suicide on the eve of his execution, on October 14, 1946.

Richard J. Overy

See also Air Force; Concentration Camps; Four-Year Plan; Gestapo; Goebbels, Joseph; Himmler, Heinrich; Hitler, Adolf; Milch, Erhard; National Socialism; National Socialist Germany; Nuremburg Trials; Prussia; World War I; World War II

References
Hoyt, Edwin P. *Goering's War.* London: Robert Hale, 1990.
Kube, Alfred. *Pour le mérite und Hakenkreuz: Hermann Göring im Dritten Reich.* Munich: Oldenbourg, 1986.
Martens, Stefan. *Hermann Göring: "Erster Paladin des Führers" und "Zweiter Mann im Reich."* Paderborn: Ferdinand Schöningh, 1985.
Overy, Richard J. *Goering: The "Iron Man."* London: Routledge, 1984.
Taylor, Telford. *The Anatomy of the Nuremberg Trials.* London: Bloomsbury, 1993.

Grand Coalition

In the German and Austrian contexts, a "Grand Coalition" refers to a governing alliance of the two largest parties, Christian Democrats (CDU) and Social Democrats (SPD). For Germany this type of coalition has occurred only once at the national level (during the years 1966–69) although a few early postwar governments at the *Land* (state) level provided precedents and the pattern has recurred recently.

The two underlying factors that led to this unusual power-sharing in 1966 were the gradual concentration of popular support within the two populist parties and the gradual depolarization of partisan divisions, sometimes referred to as the "end of ideology." The more immediate circumstances leading to this coalition included Germany's first postwar recession, a decline in popular satisfaction with the Ludwig Erhard (1897–1977) government (despite its resounding victory in the 1965 election), and squabbling among the governing coalition parties. This culminated in the forced resignation of Erhard and the election of his successor, Kurt Georg Kiesinger (1904–88), who advocated a governing arrangement with the SPD.

For the CDU, the Grand Coalition offered a needed period of consolidation. From the Social Democratic perspective, as expressed by the party's chief strategist, Herbert Wehner (1906–90), the coalition provided an opportunity for the SPD to build popular trust and credibility as a party of government.

The Christian Democratic–Social Democratic coalition comprised approximately 90 percent of the seats in the Bundestag, and therefore created an "end of opposition" effect. The absence of vigorous opposition was interpreted by critics as a threat to German parliamentary democracy. In fact,

the Grand Coalition amounted to a relatively short transitional phase. The Kiesinger-led government, with SPD leader Willy Brandt (1913–92) as foreign minister, enjoyed some considerable policy success, both in initiating *Ostpolitik* (eastern policy) and a new debate in foreign affairs and in economic management that led the Federal Republic out of recession. The government's economic strategies were guided by the cooperation between Franz Josef Strauss (1915–88) (CSU) as minister of finance and Karl Schiller (1911–95) (SPD) as minister of economics. However, it was the SPD that reaped the greatest political benefits from economic recovery. Significant reforms in federal fiscal relations were also introduced under the Grand Coalition.

The immediate consequence of the Grand Coalition was political. This three-year period enhanced the legitimacy of the SPD as a party competent to govern. The formation of a Social-Liberal (SPD and Free Democrats) coalition following the 1969 elections signified a period of gradualist policy innovation in both domestic and foreign affairs.

After 1969 the Grand Coalition alternative in federal politics faded as a viable option. However, in the post-unification era, the model has found new application regionally, in Berlin after 1990 and in Baden-Württemberg following the 1992 *Land* elections.

William M. Chandler

See also Brandt, Willy; Christian Democratic Union; Erhard, Ludwig; Federal Republic of Germany; Kiesinger, Kurt Georg; Parliamentary System; Parties and Politics; Schiller, Karl; Schmidt, Helmut; Social Democratic Party, 1919–90; Strauss, Franz Josef; Wehner, Herbert

References
Bark, Dennis L. and David R. Gress. *Democracy and Its Discontents: A History of West Germany.* Vol. 2, 2nd ed. Oxford: Blackwell, 1993.
Hancock, Donald. *West Germany: The Politics of Democratic Corporatism.* Chatham: Chatham House, 1989.
Hildebrand, Klaus. *Von Erhard zur Grossen Koalition, 1963–1969.* Geschichte der Bundesrepublik Deutschland, vol. 4. Ed. Karl-Dietrich Bracher, et al. Stuttgart: Deutsche Verlagsanstalt; Wiesbaden: F.A. Brockhaus, 1983–87.
Hofmann, Robert. *Geschichte der deutschen Parteien.* Munich: Piper, 1993.
Jesse, Eckhard. *Die Demokratie der Bundesrepublik Deutschland.* 7th ed. Berlin: Colloquium, 1988.

Grass, Günter (1927–)

This German writer and artist has published numerous works of literature, essays, commentaries, interviews, letters, speeches, even collections of drawings and paintings. The winner of major literature prizes, Günter Grass is an honorary member of the American Academy of the Arts and Sciences, was president of the Berlin Academy of Arts (1983–86), and has received honorary doctorates from Kenyon College in Ohio (1965) and Harvard University in Massachusetts (1976).

Grass's first novel, *Die Blechtrommel* (published as *The Tin Drum*), 1959, is one of the most famous works of contemporary world literature. It was followed by *Katz und Maus* (published as *Cat and Mouse*), 1961, and *Hundejahre* (published as *Dog Years*), 1963. All three works of this "Danzig Trilogy" deal with the problems of *Vergangenheitsbewältigung*, i.e., coming to terms with the past of Nazism and its heinous crimes against the Jewish and Polish people.

Örtlich betäubt (published as *Local Anesthetic*), 1969, criticizes the fanatic Nazi past as well as the radical elements in some ideologies of the 1960s. *Aus dem Tagebuch einer Schnecke* (published as *From the Diary of a Snail*), 1972, is Grass's campaign novel. It reflects his sympathy for the Social Democratic Party under Willy Brandt (1913–92), one of his best friends. *Der Butt* (published as *Adventures of a Flounder*), 1977, presents a satirical history of the war between the sexes. *Das Treffen in Telgte* (published as *Meeting at Telgate*), 1979, is a fictitious meeting between German Baroque poets. By this time, Grass's concept of a *Kulturnation* has emerged: for him cultural heritage determines national identity.

Grass's literary and artistic creations during the 1980s consisted of such works as *Kopfgeburten oder Die Deutschen sterben aus* (published as *Headbirths, or the Germans are Dying Out*), 1980, *Die Rättin* (The rat), 1986, *Zunge zeigen* (Show your tongue), 1988, and *Totes Holz* (published as *Dead Wood*), 1990. Among the most important issues for Grass are global problems, such as the nuclear arsenal, the population growth in developing countries, and the alarming increase in environmental pollution; these issues he treats in depth in *Die Rättin*.

Grass repeatedly addresses the struggles of the Third World. His first trip to India and China resulted in *Kopfgeburten*, his second trip to India in his travelogue *Zunge zeigen*, in which drawings of "pavement dwellers" accompany a depressing literary account of lives without hope.

Totes Holz focuses on Europe's dying forests through drawings, aphorisms, quotations from scientific reports, short parody, and prose. Finally, in *Unkenrufe* (published as *The Call of the Toad*), 1992, he goes beyond the bleak imagery of the 1980s. Here German-Polish relations and the reunification of the two Germanys are woven into a fictive love story. Grass's international fame is underscored by the fact that all his literary works have been translated into English.

Mark M. Gruettner

See also Federal Republic of Germany: Literature; Novel; Social Democratic Party, 1919–90

References
Labroisse, Gerd, ed. *Günter Grass: Ein europäischer Autor?* Amsterdam: Rodopi, 1992.
Lawson, Richard H. *Günter Grass.* New York, NY: Ungar, 1985.
O'Neill, Patrick, ed. *Critical Essays on Günter Grass.* Boston, MA: Hall, 1987.
———. *Günter Grass: A Bibliography: 1955–1975.* Toronto: University of Toronto Press, 1976.
Reddick, John. *The "Danzig Trilogy" of Günter Grass.* New York, NY: Harcourt, 1975.
Vormweg, Heinrich. *Günter Grass.* Hamburg: Rowohlt, 1986.

The Greens: Movement, Party, Ideology

Profound and overlapping changes in values, in society, and in the economy since the end of World War II provided fertile soil for the creation of the Greens as an ecological movement and political party. The changes are most evident in the two generations raised during the Economic Miracle and reintegration of the Federal Republic into the family of nations. These young Germans share a "postmaterialist" set of values, characterized by concern for the environment and self-actualization, for women's rights and the quality of life, for individual liberties and participatory democracy. The student movement, ecological limits to growth, and economic stagflation gave rise in the 1970s to citizens' initiatives and popular movements of the groups (composed primarily of postmaterialists opposed to nuclear power and weapons, patriarchy, and "the establishment") that would form the core of the Greens.

Green political activity first sprang up in villages, towns, and cities, and spread by the mid-1970s to the state level. Green Party activists and voters are distinctive: young, highly educated, left-leaning, libertarian, and disposed toward employment in education and the social services. Indeed, in its early days, the ecologists were known as the "party of the teachers." A coalition of several Green organizations was formed to contest the first European Parliament elections in 1979; it garnered 3.2 percent of the vote and several million deutsche marks (provided by German electoral law and used to help build the grass-roots party over the next few years). Autumn 1979 and winter 1980 saw the construction of the initial Green program and the creation of the federal-level party.

After gaining representation in local councils and state parliaments, the Greens entered the Bundestag after the 1983 elections with 5.6 percent of the vote (27 seats). The Greens held the balance of power in Hamburg for a while, and later participated in coalition governments with the Social Democrats (SPD) in Hesse and Lower Saxony. The party received 8.3 percent of the vote in the 1987 Bundestag elections (44 seats). The party has been plagued throughout its brief history by factionalism—the conflict between "realists" (those open to cooperation with other parties) and "fundamentalists" (those opposed to compromise with the establishment) paralyzed the Greens during the mid- to late-1980s. Coupled with its initial opposition to and grudging acceptance of reunification, this unveiled fractiousness left the western party in the 1990 elections with less than the 5 percent of the vote necessary for representation in the new all-German parliament (although the coalition of eastern Greens and civil-rights groups gained seats). The party appears to be on the mend since the fundamentalists left to form their own party in 1991 and has steered a decidedly realist course since then.

Green ideology is summed up by the four pillars of the original Green program: ecology, nonviolence, grass-roots democracy, and social responsibility. Green theorists recom-

Petra Kelly, prominent member of Greens. Courtesy of Inter Nationes, Bonn.

mend an "ecological restructuring" of the German economy to reduce pollution and wasteful use of natural resources. Green opposition to the incomplete sovereignty and militarization of the Federal Republic led to calls for withdrawal from NATO, a position met by charges of "neutralist nationalism," *Sonderweg* (special path), and anti-Americanism. Preferences for participatory democracy and against bureaucratization led the party to adopt consensus decisionmaking, decentralization, feminism, and opposition to hierarchy as central principles. The Green utopia is one of wide-ranging civil liberties for all citizens, a global redistribution of wealth from north to south, disarmament, sustainable development, and harmony with nature.

The future prospects of the Greens as an ideological and political alternative appear moderately bright. Their hesitance about the rush toward reunification now seems justified in light of the resurgence of xenophobia and right-wing extremism brought on by the wrenching economic difficulties in the former German Democratic Republic (GDR) and the influx of asylum-seeking foreigners. The moves in the early 1990s toward greater accountability on the part of Green elected officials, toward more effective organization, and toward structures representative of the party's grass roots bode well as ecological issues assume greater prominence in Germany and around the world.

Steven J. Breyman

See also Ecology; Federal Republic of Germany; Kelly, Petra; Nuclear Power and the Nuclear Industry; Pacifism and the Peace Movement; Parties and Politics

References

Capra, Fritjof and Charlene Spretnak. *Green Politics: The Global Promise*. New York, NY: Dutton, 1984.

Frankland, E. Gene and Donald Schoonmaker. *Between Protest and Power: The Green Party in Germany*. Boulder, CO: Westview, 1992.

Hulsberg, Werner. *The West German Greens*. London: Verso, 1987.

Inglehart, Ronald. *Culture Shift in Advanced Industrial Society*. Princeton, NJ: Princeton University Press, 1990.

Porritt, Jonathan. *Seeing Green: The Politics of Ecology Explained*. New York, NY: Blackwell, 1985.

Grimm, Hans (1875–1959)

A journalist and writer of the Weimar era, Grimm is best known for his novel *Volk ohne Raum* (People [nation] without space), 1926, which was immensely popular on the political Right.

Born in Wiesbaden, Grimm came from an academic family, but in his twenties he was forced to follow a mercantile career in South Africa. The Boer War strengthened Grimm's rightist nationalism and convinced him that Germany needed a larger colonial empire to assure the future of the *Volk*. He returned to Germany as a journalist in 1910, served in World War I, and decided after the war to become a novelist to propagate his political message of traditionalism versus modernism and the need for "breathing space" as a requirement for the development of a German psyche. *Volk ohne Raum*, a long novel with modest literary merit, achieved popularity mainly because of that message. It persuaded the Nazis to publicize the novel and its author, although Grimm never became a party member.

Volk ohne Raum follows its hero, Cornelius Friebott, through apprenticeship as a cabinetmaker, military service, industrial employment, emigration to South Africa and then to German Southwest Africa, political enlightenment, return to Germany, and assassination after World War I. The novel sounds such themes as the decadence of traditional culture; the dangers of urban industrial society, Social Democrats, and Jews; and the need for wide-open spaces in colonies as venues where the German character can be modeled. Although Grimm never used the term, his novel gives a comprehensive treatment of what the idea of *Lebensraum* came to mean in Nazi political thinking.

Woodruff D. Smith

See also Journalism; Nationalism; National Socialist Germany; *Völkisch* Ideology

References

Geissler, Rolf. *Dekadenz und Heroismus: Zeitroman und völkischnationalsozialistische Literaturkritik*. Stuttgart: Deutsche Verlags-Anstalt, 1964.

Ridley, Hugh. "Colonial Society and European Totalitarianism." *Journal of European Studies* 3 (1973), 147–59.

Smith, Woodruff D. "The Colonial Novel as Political Propaganda: Hans Grimm's *Volk ohne Raum*." *German Studies Review* 6 (1983), 215–35.

———. *The Ideological Origins of Nazi Imperialism.* New York, NY: Oxford University Press, 1986.

Groener, Wilhelm (1867–1939)

As a senior military leader in World War I and as defense minister in the Weimar Republic, Wilhelm Groener played a major role in German military strategy over a period of several decades. Groener is best remembered for taking over Ludendorff's post as first quartermaster general in October 1918 and for convincing Kaiser Wilhelm II of the need to abdicate and accept Allied armistice terms.

Groener was born in Württemberg in 1867. He came from a humble background: his father was a noncommissioned officer in the Württemberg army. Groener was recognized early for his brilliance. He won the Kaiser's Prize for the top officer examination score, and was commissioned in the Württemberg army in 1886. Groener served most of his career in the General Staff and the elite Railroad Section, which bore the responsibility for planning the details of mobilization and army deployment.

From 1914 to 1917, Groener served in turn as chief of army railroads, chief of the Reich food office, and the General Staff's representative to the Bundesrat. During 1917 and 1918, he served as commander of the Thirty-third Infantry Division and of the first Army Corps and as chief of staff of Army Group Kiev. When the military situation collapsed, Groener took over Ludendorff's post as first quartermaster general in October 1918.

After the armistice in November 1918, Groener was responsible for safely withdrawing the army to Germany. As commander of General Headquarters, Groener was responsible for organizing a provisional army, restoring discipline, and suppressing Communist rebellions in Germany. Through a secret pact with Friedrich Ebert (1871–1925) on November 10, 1918, Groener assured the survival of the General Staff as the central institution of the military establishment in return for supporting the civilian socialist government.

Before retiring from the army in 1919, Groener helped to gain acceptance of the Treaty of Versailles in Germany. Groener served the Weimar Republic as transport minister (1920–23) and defense minister (1928–32). As defense minister, Groener supported military modernization programs and led Germany's first postwar rearmament efforts with an armored cruiser program for the navy.

Groener was one of the most capable German military leaders of his time. Although conservative by nature, he loyally and effectively served the Weimar Republic as a minister. During a short term as interior minister in 1932, he attempted to ban the Nazi stormtrooper (SA) organization.

James S. Corum

See also Ebert, Friedrich; Hindenburg, Paul von; Revolution of 1918–19; Schleicher, Kurt von; Seeckt, Hans von; Weimar Germany: Army; World War I

References

Carsten, Francis L. *The Reichswehr and Politics, 1918–1933.* Oxford: Oxford University Press, 1966.
Groener, Wilhelm. *Lebenserrinerungen: Jugend, Generalstab, Weltkrieg.* Göttingen: Vandenhoeck & Ruprecht, 1957.
Groener-Geyer, Dorothea. *General Groener: Soldat und Staatsmann.* Frankfurt am Main: Societäts-Verlag, 1955.
Hürter, Johannes. *Wilhelm Groener: Reichswehrminister am Ende der Weimarer Republik (1928–1932).* Munich: R. Oldenbourg, 1993.
Rakenius, Gerhard W. *Wilhelm Groener als Erster Generalquartiermeister: Die Politik der Obersten Heeresleitung 1918/19.* Boppard: Boldt Verlag, 1977.

Gropius, Walter (1883–1969)

Walter Gropius belongs to the group of outstanding architects, designers, and teachers of the first half of the twentieth century. His major works include the Fagus Factory in Alfeld/Hannover (1911), the Bauhaus Building (1925–26), the Employment Office Building (1928–29) and the Settlement of Törten (1926–28) in Dessau. Gropius was the founder and the first director of the school of design known as the Bauhaus.

Gropius was a descendant of an old Berlin family of architects. After interrupted architectural study and a short military service he became a member of the architect's office of Peter Behrens (1868–1940). After 1908, Gropius was searching for a new expression in architecture, design, and town planning to create a new cultural basis for industrial society. In applying the latest technological discoveries, Gropius favored simple, clear forms to demonstrate the structure and the practical use of a building or an object. In the Fagus Factory and the Office Building at the Werkbund exhibition in Cologne (1914), he replaced the traditional ornamental façade with a transparent steel and glass curtain wall. The upsetting experience of World War I stimulated Gropius to adopt utopian reform ideas. His architectural designs showed expressionistic influences. In 1919, Gropius founded the Bauhaus in Weimar as a crafts-oriented reform institute. In 1923, Gropius reformulated his thoughts regarding the role of industry and gave the school a new slogan: "Art and technology—a new unity."

For Gropius, the designing process started with the search for the "character of an object." This process would be expedited by advanced technology, the demands of material practice, and the quest for prototypes for mass production. He believed that the development of settlement housing would make a contribution to solving the social problems created by the housing shortage.

In 1934, after the Nazi takeover, Gropius went to England, whence he followed the call to Harvard University in the US. Until 1952, Gropius was the chairman of the Department of Architecture, Graduate School of Design, Harvard University. A brief collaboration with Marcel Breuer was followed by a period of designing and planning prefabricated houses in collaboration with Konrad Wachsmann (1942–52). In 1945, jointly with former students and assistants, Gropius founded The Architects' Collaborative. They designed and built numerous buildings in the United States and Europe.

Between 1948 and 1950, Gropius was the president of the Congrés Internationaux d'Architecture Moderne.

Gropius influenced a whole generation of architects and designers in all industrial countries. He is renowned as one of the most important pioneers in modern architecture and design.

Wolfgang Thöner

See also Architecture and Urban Design; Bauhaus; Behrens, Peter; Expulsion and Exile of Scientists and Scholars; Mies van der Rohe, Ludwig; Werkbund

References

Claussen, Horst. *Walter Gropius: Grundzüge seines Denkens.* Hildesheim: Olms, 1986.

Isaaks, Reginald R. *Walter Gropius: Der Mensch und sein Werk.* 2 vols. Berlin: Gebr. Mann Verlag, 1983 and 1984.

Nerdinger, Winfried. *Walter Gropius: The Architect Walter Gropius: Drawings, Prints, Photographs, Complete Project Catalog.* Berlin: Gebr. Mann Verlag, 1985.

O'Neal, William B. *A Bibliography of Writings by and about Walter Gropius.* Charlottesville, VA: University of Virginia Press, 1966.

Probst, Hartmut and Christian Schädlich. *Walter Gropius.* 3 vols. Berlin: VEB Verlag für Bauwesen, 1985–87.

Wilhelm, Karin. *Walter Gropius: Industriearchitekt.* Braunschweig: Vieweg & Sohn, 1983.

Grosz, George (Georg Ehrenfried Gross) (1893–1959)

One of the most famous artists of the Weimar Republic, George Grosz was notorious for acerbic drawings and paintings that depicted German society dominated by brutal military figures, porcine capitalists, lecherous bourgeois types, grotesque prostitutes, and downtrodden workers—stereotypes that for many observers became virtual symbols of the republic. An aggressive Berlin Dadaist who joined the German Communist Party (KPD), Grosz was brought to trial repeatedly for his revolutionary and critical drawings. After a highly visible career in Germany, Grosz emigrated to the United States shortly before the Nazi takeover (1933).

Grosz studied art in Dresden (1909–11), Berlin (1912–14), and Paris (1913). Between two brief, troubled tours of military service (1914–15, 1917), Grosz collaborated with Wieland Herzfelde (1896–1988) and John Heartfield (1891–1968) on antiwar activities and publications, including Grosz's first two portfolios of drawings. Grosz's belligerent antiwar and anti-art actions and drawings were at the center of Berlin dada (1917–20). Radicalized by the Revolution of 1918, Grosz joined the November Group (1918), the KPD (1919), the Red Group (1924), and the Association of Revolutionary German Artists (1928) and collaborated on the Communist satirical journals *Jedermann sein eigener Fussball* (Everyone his own football), 1919, *Die Pleite* (Bankruptcy), 1919–24, *Der blutige Ernst* (Bloody Earnest), 1919–20, *Der Gegner* (The opponent), 1919–24, and *Der Knüppel* (The cudgel), 1923–27.

Georg Grosz with sketch (below). Courtesy of Inter Nationes, Bonn.

Grosz's bitter anticapitalist, antimilitary drawings appeared in portfolios and inexpensive books, including *Gott mit uns.* (published as *God with Us*), 1920, *Das Gesicht der herrschenden Klasse* (published as *The Face of the Ruling Class*), 1921, *Im Schatten* (In the shadows), 1921, *Mit Pinsel und Schere* (With scissors and paintbrush), 1922, *Die Räuber* (The robbers), 1922, *Abrechnung folgt!* (published as *Reckoning Follows!*), 1923, *Ecce Homo*, 1922–23, and *Hintergrund* (Background), 1928. With Herzfelde, he analyzed the role of contemporary artists in *Die Kunst ist in Gefahr* (published as *Art Is in Danger*), 1925. Active with International Workers' Aid, he traveled to the Soviet Union, where he met Lenin, Lunacharsky, and Zinoviev (1922), and traveled to France with friends (1925, 1927). His first major exhibition was held by Hans Goltz in Munich (1920); Alfred Flechtheim became his dealer in 1923. By the mid-1920s, Grosz turned to oil painting, portraiture, and socially critical drawings in *Der Spiesser-Spiegel,* (published as *The Philistine-Mirror*)1925, *Das neue Gesicht der herrschenden Klasse* (published as *The New Face of the Ruling Class*), 1930, *Über alles die Liebe* (published as *Above All Love*), 1930, and in the liberal journals, *Simplicissimus,* 1926–32, *Querschnitt* (Crosscut), 1921–1933, *Das Illustrierte Blatt* (The illustrated page), 1926–31, and *UHU* (1932).

The Weimar government brought Grosz to trial for defamation of the Reichswehr (1921), offending the morals of the German people (1923), and blasphemy (1928–30). Grosz emigrated before the Nazis revoked his citizenship (March 1933) and confiscated 285 of his works, some of which were included in the *Degenerate Art* exhibition (1937–39). In America, Grosz's rich drawings of New York's urban scene were balanced by his anguished paintings and drawings of Hitler's devastation of Europe, including a 1936 portfolio, *Interregnum.* After the war he received many honors in West Germany.

Beth Irwin Lewis

See also Artists; Dada; Decadence; Expressionism (Visual Arts); German Communist Party; Heartfield, John; Herzfelde, Wieland; Painting; Revolution of 1918–19; Weimar Germany

References

Dückers, Alexander. *George Grosz: Das druckgraphische Werk.* Frankfurt am Main: Propyläen Verlag, 1979.

Flavell, M. Kay. *George Grosz: A Biography.* New Haven, CT: Yale University Press, 1988.

Grosz, George. *Ein kleines Ja und ein grosses Nein.* Hamburg: Rowohlt Verlag, 1955. Paperback edition, 1974. English edition: *The Autobiography of George Grosz: A Small Yes and a Big No.* Trans. Arnold J. Pomerans. London: Alison and Busby, 1982.

Grosz, George and Wieland Herzfelde. *Die Kunst ist in Gefahr.* Berlin: Malik Verlag, 1925. English edition: *Art Is in Danger! Art on the Line.* Trans. Paul Gorrell. Willimantic, CT: Curbstone Press, 1987.

Herzfelde, Wieland and Hans Marquardt, ed. *Pass auf! Hier kommt Grosz: Bilder, Rhythmen und Gesänge 1915–*

1918. Leipzig: Verlag Philippe Reclam jun., 1981.

Hess, Hans. *George Grosz.* New York, NY: Macmillan and Studio Vista, 1974. Reissue: New Haven, CT: Yale University Press, 1985.

Knust, Herbert, ed. *George Grosz: Briefe 1913–1959.* Reinbek bei Hamburg: Rowohlt Verlag GmbH, 1979.

Lewis, Beth Irwin. *George Grosz: Art and Politics in the Weimar Republic.* Madison, WI: University of Wisconsin Press, 1971. Paperback edition with revised bibliography: Princeton, NJ: Princeton University Press, 1991.

Schneede, Uwe M. *George Grosz: Der Künstler in seiner Gesellschaft.* Cologne: Verlag M. DuMont Schauberg, 1975. English edition: *George Grosz: The Artist in Society.* Woodbury, NY: Barrons, 1985.

———. *George Grosz: Leben und Werk.* Stuttgart: Verlag Gerd Hatje, 1975. English edition: *George Grosz: Life and Work.* New York, NY: Universe, 1979.

Grotewohl, Otto (1894–1964)

From 1949 to 1960, Otto Grotewohl served as prime minister of East Germany. Grotewohl was born on March 11, 1894 in Braunschweig, the son of a worker. After attending school, he apprenticed as a bookprinter. He worked in this job until World War I started. In 1908, he joined the socialist workers' youth movement, and in 1912 he became a member of the Social Democratic Party (SPD). From 1914 to 1918 he served as a soldier. He joined the Independent Social Democratic Party (USPD) in 1918, and during the Revolution of 1918 headed a workers' and soldiers' council. During the Weimar Republic he mainly worked in the Braunschweig area, where from 1921 to 1924 he was a member of a state insurance company and, from 1925 to 1933, its president. During this time, he was a member of the Reichstag. During the Nazi period he belonged to an illegal Social Democratic group. In 1938 and 1939, he was in imprisonment on remand. From 1940 to 1945 he managed a small business in Berlin.

In 1945, Grotewohl became the chairman of the Central Council of the SPD, together with Max Fechner and Erich W. Gniffke. He was one of the signers of an agreement with the Communist Party for coordinated activity. He took major responsibility for the forced merger of the German Communist Party (KPD) and the SPD into the Socialist Unity Party (SED) in the Soviet zone during April 1946. From then until 1954, he shared the leadership of the SED with the Communists Wilhelm Pieck (1876–1960) and Walter Ulbricht (1893–1973). With the foundation of the German Democratic Republic (GDR) in October 1949, he became its first prime minister, but was more of a figurehead than a wielder of power.

In November 1960, he fell ill and had to retreat from political life. He died on September 21, 1964.

Heinrich Bortfeld

See also German Communist Party; German Democratic Republic; German Democratic Republic: Political Party System; Pieck, Wilhelm; Schumacher, Kurt; Social Democratic Party, 1919–90; Socialist Unity Party; Ulbricht, Walter

References

Krisch, Henry. *German Politics under Soviet Occupation.* New York, NY: Columbia University Press, 1974.

McCauley, Martin. *The German Democratic Republic since 1945.* London: Macmillan, 1983.

Sandford, Gregory. *From Hitler to Ulbricht: The Communist Reconstruction of East Germany, 1945–46.* Princeton, NJ: Princeton University Press, 1983.

Vosske, Heinz. *Otto Grotewohl: Biographischer Abriss.* Berlin: Dietz, 1979.

Gründgens, Gustaf (1899–1963)

A stage and screen actor known for intelligence, irony, and precise, musical diction, Gustaf Gründgens was also an accomplished director and theater manager, specializing in classics by Goethe, Schiller, and Shakespeare. He presented modern works by, among others, Brecht, Eliot, and Shaw. Gründgens was especially renowned as Mephistopheles in Goethe's *Faust,* for which he first gained fame at Berlin's Prussian State Theater in 1932–33. The popular identification of Gründgens with the devil personified also derived from Klaus Mann's (1906–49) novel *Mephisto,* 1936, the basis for the 1981 film by István Szabó, in which the fictional opportunistic actor Hendrik Höfgen, a much-disputed Gründgens characterization, rises to theatrical power under the Nazis.

Born in Düsseldorf, Gründgens studied there in 1919–20 under Louise Dumont. He next worked in Halberstadt and Kiel before beginning to make a name for himself by acting, and at times by directing, in the Hamburger Kammerspiel (Chamber Theater). He became friendly with Thomas Mann's (1875–1955) children, touring with Klaus and Erika Mann and Pamela Wedekind in the Revue zu Vieren (Four: a revue). Although his homosexual affairs were not secret, Gründgens twice married, first to Erika Mann in 1925; they were separated by 1928 and divorced in 1933. In 1928, Gründgens was called to Berlin, where he worked in Max Reinhardt's (1873–1943) Deutsches Theater, began directing operas, and became known for portraying sophisticated gangsters and dandies such as the white-gloved kingpin of the Berlin underworld in Fritz Lang's classic film *M,* 1931.

Actress Emmy Sonneman, the girlfriend and later wife of Nazi leader and Prussian premier Hermann Göring (1893–1946), probably recommended Gründgens to be superintendent of the Prussian State Theater. He reluctantly accepted the post in 1934, and until its closing in 1944, Gründgens's (and Göring's) stage, independent of Goebbels's Propaganda Ministry, specialized in the classics. Four of Gründgens's five directorial films also derive from the Nazi years, including *Zwei Welten* (Two worlds), in which official Nazi ideology is said to be undermined by homoeroticism.

After the war, Gründgens was soon cleared of any punishable Nazi activity and enjoyed a distinguished career acting, directing, and managing theaters in Düsseldorf and Hamburg. His classic Mephistopheles, based on the Hamburg stage version of 1957, is preserved in the film *Faust,* 1960. Opinion remains divided as to whether his activities under the Nazis provide evidence of his noble commitment, against great odds, to the classics and to his craft, or, as Klaus Mann claimed in his autobiography, that he "prostitute[d] his talent for the sake of tawdry fame and transitory wealth." Both positions contain some truth: not a Nazi, he did what he could to preserve his and his theater's dignity; he benefited from the Nazis' patronage, and they gained legitimacy from his work. Gründgens's death while in the Philippines on a world tour has been called a suicide.

Peter Chametzky

See also Göring, Hermann; National Socialist Germany; Reinhardt, Max; Theater

References

Dumont-Lindemann-Archiv, Theatermuseum der Stadt Düsseldorf. *Gustaf Gründgens: Eine Dokumentation des Dumont-Lindemann Archivs.* Munich: Albert Langen, 1981.

Gründgens, Gustaf. *Wirklichkeit des Theaters.* Frankfurt am Main: Suhrkamp, 1963.

Holba, Herbert. *Gustaf Gründgens: Filme.* Vienna: Verlag des Dokumentationszentrums Action, 1978.

Hull, David Stewart. *Film in the Third Reich: Art and Propaganda in Nazi Germany.* New York, NY: Simon and Schuster, 1969.

Luft, Friedrich. *Gustaf Gründgens.* Berlin: Rembrandt, 1960.

Mann, Klaus. *Mephisto.* Amsterdam: Querido, 1936.

———. *The Turning Point.* New York, NY: Markus Wiener, 1984 [1942].

Muhr, Alfred. *Mephisto Ohne Maske: Gustaf Gründgens, Legende und Wahrheit.* Munich: Langen-Müller, 1981.

Riess, Curt. *Gustaf Gründgens: Eine Biographie.* Hamburg: Hoffmann & Campe, 1965.

Rischbieter, Henning. *Gründgens: Schauspieler, Regisseur, Theaterleiter.* Velber bei Hannover: Erhard Friedrich Verlag, 1963.

Spangenberg, Eberhard. *Karriere eines Romans: Mephisto, Klaus Mann, und Gustaf Gründgens.* Munich: Ellermann Verlag, 1982.

Guardini, Romano (1885–1968)

Born in Verona, Italy, Romano Guardini was ordained as a Roman Catholic priest in 1910 in Mainz and became a German citizen in 1919. He attended to the pastoral needs of his diocese immediately after his ordination. In 1912, he began his theological studies, which culminated with his Habilitation (university teaching qualification thesis) in 1922 at Bonn University. His work in theology and philosophy was instrumental in his obtaining the chair of philosophy of religion and the Christian *Weltanschauung,* first at Tübingen (1945–48) and then at Munich (1948–68).

Guardini's obsession with the truth of revelation produced stimulating lectures on ethics without a nuanced knowledge of the ethics textbooks and lectures on the New Testament and without an expertise in exegetical techniques. His own work was based on the foundation that the Church and revelation were unconditional. He had no wish to explore what had been said about Christian truth, but rather wanted to find that truth. In this search, he insisted, the foremost problems in the modern era are the ideas that the truth-faith relationships can be uncovered through historico-critical and linguistic methodologies or that they can be exposed by reflecting on psychological needs. He was adamant that faith, i.e., truth, is rooted firmly in revelation.

Guardini's reflections focused on the needs of his era. Guardini's lecture, "Vom Sinn der Kirche" (the purpose of the church), 1922, for example, articulated an organic ecclesiology that became a crucial point for Vatican II. In essence, the Church, viewed as the Body of Christ, served as the foundation for the development of human freedom with a more pluralistic understanding. Paradoxically, in obeying the Church humans would gain full freedom. From this ecclesiology, Guardini deduced a vital and dynamic Christology during the Third Reich period and ended this phase of his career with *Das Christusbild der paulinischen und johanneischen Schriften* (The Christ image in the New Testament), 1961. He viewed Jesus as the embodiment of all the opponents of the oppressive regimes that have plagued the twentieth century. Guardini's view of "person" as the mystery that develops through dialogue with the God who summons humanity to fulfill its potential has been crucial for modern moral theologians. This work has reinforced the post–Vatican II Catholic Church's stress on the dignity of the person as the crucial criterion in evaluating humanity's sociopolitical environment.

Donald J. Dietrich

See also Biblical Criticism; Küng, Hans; Protestant Theology; Rahner, Karl; Roman Catholic Church; Philosophy

References
Biser, Eugen. "Wer war Romano Guardini." *Stimmen der Zeit* 203 (1985), 435–88.

Borsig, Hover. *Zeit der Entscheidung: Zu Romano Guardinis Deutung der Gegenwart.* Fridingen: Borsing Verlag, 1990.

Gerl, Hanna Barbara. *Romano Guardini, 1885–1968: Leben und Werk.* Mainz: Matthias Grünewald, 1985.

Mercken, Hans. *Christliche Weltanschauung als Problem: Untersuchungen zur Grundstruktur im Werk Romano Guardinis.* Paderborn: F. Schöningh, 1988.

Ratzinger, Joseph Kardinal. *Wege zur Wahrheit: Die bleibende Bedeutung von Romano Guardini.* Düsseldorf: Patmas Verlag, 1985.

Schmucker-von Koch, Joseph. *Autonomie und Transzendenz: Untersuchungen zur Religionsphilosophie Romano Guardinis.* Mainz: Matthias Grünewald, 1985.

Guderian, Heinz (1888–1954)

Guderian was the creator of the German *Panzer* (tank) force. During World War II, he was one of its ablest commanders. Despite several disagreements with Hitler on the conduct of the war, he was the Third Reich's last chief of the Army General Staff.

Guderian was born into a military family. He joined the cadet corps, became an officer in an infantry battalion in 1908, and served in World War I in a signals unit and in the General Staff. During the Weimar Republic he was taken into the Reichswehr and assigned the task of organizing highly mobile units. Guderian discovered the potential of the tank, which had been developed toward the end of the war. However, unlike the French, Guderian did not regard the tank as an infantry support weapon. Rather, he expected tanks to provide operational mobility that would enable German units to pierce enemy lines and then operate in the opponent's rear. Therefore, he designed light tanks with a long operating range and generous radio equipment. Unlike his British counterpart, General John F.C. Fuller (1878–1966), Guderian did not plan to muster an all-armored force; rather, he wanted the other arms branches, notably infantry, artillery, and engineers, to be motorized sufficiently to keep up with an advancing tank force.

Guderian's plans met with opposition from conservative officers, among whom numbered Lieutenant General (later Colonel General) Ludwig Beck (1880–1944). Nevertheless, by 1933 Guderian had laid the theoretical groundwork for fully integrated, operationally capable tank forces. In 1935, he was made commander of the Second Panzer Division. Promoted to full general in 1938, he commanded an army corps during the Polish campaign. Due to the success of the *Panzer* divisions, Guderian was given command of the first *Panzer* army ever to be assembled. He led it during the campaign in France in May and June 1940, often exceeding his orders and advancing farther than he was supposed to. The eventual success of the campaign and the crushing defeat of France were due both to the application of these ideas and Guderian's personal involvement in their execution.

During the war against the Soviet Union, Guderian increasingly resented Hitler's personal interference with tactical details. In particular, Guderian objected to the kind of static warfare that Hitler demanded and that Guderian had always condemned. In December 1941, he resigned his command. In February 1943, Hitler recalled him as inspector general of the *Panzer* forces. After the attempted coup against Hitler, which Guderian condemned, he was made chief of the Army General Staff, working directly under Hitler as commander in chief. Guderian was a member of the Court of Honor, which expelled the conspirators of July 20, 1944 from the army so that they could be tried by the Nazi Party's Volksgerichtshof (People's Court).

Guderian was taken prisoner by the Americans, who dropped plans for prosecuting him for alleged war crimes. He lived in seclusion until his death in Schwangau, Bavaria, on May 14, 1954.

Winfried Heinemann

See also National Socialist Germany: Military; World War II

References
Guderian, Heinz. *Achtung—Panzer! The Development of Armoured Forces, Their Tactics and Operational Potential.* Trans. Christopher Duffy. London: Cassell, 1992.

———. *Panzer Leader*. New York, NY: Dutton, 1952.

Heinemann, Winfried. "The Development of German Armoured Forces 1910–40." *Armoured Warfare*. Ed. J. Paul Harris and F.H. Toase. London: Batsford, 1990.

Macksey, Kenneth John. *Guderian: Panzer General*. London: Macdonald & James, 1975.

Meyer, Georg. "Generaloberst Guderian: Zur Erinnerung an seinen 100. Geburtstag." *Militärgeschichtliches Beiheft zur Europäischen Wehrkunde/ Wehrwissenschaftliche Rundschau* 3 (1988).

Günther, Hans Friedrich Karl (1891–1968)

Hans F.K. Günther was the leading popularizer of pseudo-scientific racism in Germany after World War I. Trained as a philologist, Günther expounded racialist doctrine as a means of reviving German pride and power after defeat in the war. His *Rassenkunde des deutschen Volkes* (Ethnology of the German people), first published by J.F. Lehmann in 1922, appeared in 16 expanded and revised editions and sold over 120,000 copies by 1942. An abridged version, *Kleine* (little) *Rassenkunde des deutschen Volkes*, published in 1929, sold 295,000 copies by 1942. These books were popularly known as the *Rassen-Günther* and the *Volks-Günther*, respectively.

Günther defined a race loosely as a group of people whose combination of hereditary physical and psychological traits is distinct from any other group's. Using a number of questionable sources, including the works of French anthropologists Joseph Deniker (1852–1918) and Georges Vacher de Lapouge (1854–1936), Günther identified six racial types among the German peoples, of which the "Nordic" type was both the most representative and of the highest quality. He collated a wide variety of anthropological data, including cephalic measurements to describe his racial "ideal types," but his valuations were based on subjective aesthetic and political criteria. To the Nordic race he attributed not only superior physical beauty but also the heroic qualities valorized in fascist and *völkisch* (racist) ideology.

A proponent of Social Darwinism and "racial hygiene" (eugenic measures to improve the race), Günther popularized the notion of *Aufnordung* (Nordicizing) the German nation to counteract the alleged *Entnordung* (de-Nordicizing) of the present degenerate age, the origins of which he traced to the French Revolution and the spread of humanitarian values that fostered the preservation of the weak and the sick. He urged Germans to recreate themselves as a Nordic race by strengthening their Nordic elite, raising the birth rate in Nordic families, and adopting a Nordic Protestant faith. He advocated legislation to support the landed population, reverse the trend toward urbanization, and reinforce "natural" hierarchies in the state. He urged the exclusion of Jews, whom he denounced as rootless carriers of liberal individualism, moral relativism, and democratic subversion.

Although Günther did not join the Nazi Party until 1932, his social and political values coincided with Nazi ideology. In 1930, the Nazi interior minister of the state of Thuringia, Wilhelm Frick (1877–1946), appointed Günther to a newly created chair of social anthropology at the University of Jena over the objections of the faculty senate. In 1935 he received an appointment at the University of Berlin, and from 1939 to 1945 he taught at the University of Freiburg, the city of his birth. Nazi ideologist Alfred Rosenberg (1893–1946) and Reich Farmers' Leader R. Walther Darré (1895–1953) defended Günther against critics who charged that his emphasis on the superiority of the Nordic race and the mixed racial composition of the German people would undermine national unity. He received many honors and awards, including the Nazi Party Science Prize in 1935, the Goethe Medal for Art and Science in 1941, and the Golden Party Badge. As a member of the Council of Experts for Population and Race Policies he helped to approve compulsory sterilization laws.

After the war, Günther was barred from teaching, but he continued to publicize his racist ideas in modified form. As late as 1967, he continued to call for *Aufartung* (the upgrading of the species) and lamented the alleged counterselective forces undermining the health of the white races of Europe. He viewed the postwar era as the triumph of mass society in its American and Soviet forms and deplored the attendant loss of aristocratic values and racial consciousness.

Rod Stackelberg

See also Anthropology; Anti-Semitism; Eugenics; Frick, Wilhelm; Racism; Rosenberg, Alfred; Social Darwinism; *Völkisch* Ideology

References
Becker, Peter Emil. *Wege ins Dritte Reich*. Teil II. *Sozialdarwinismus, Rassismus, Antisemitismus und völkischer Gedanke*. Stuttgart: Georg Thieme Verlag, 1990.

Lutzhöft, Hans-Jürgen. *Der Nordische Gedanke in Deutschland 1920–1940*. Stuttgart: Ernst Klett Verlag, 1971.

Proctor, Robert N. *Racial Hygiene: Medicine under the Nazis*. Cambridge, MA: Harvard University Press, 1988.

Weindling, Paul. *Health, Race and German Politics Between National Unification and Nazism, 1870–1945*. Cambridge: Cambridge University Press, 1989.

Weingart, Peter, Jürgen Kroll, and Kurt Bayertz. *Rasse, Blut und Gene: Geschichte der Eugenik und Rassenhygiene in Deutschland*. Frankfurt am Main: Suhrkamp Verlag, 1988.

zur Mühlen, Patrik von. *Rassenideologien: Geschichte und Hintergründe*. Berlin: Dietz Verlag, 1977.

Gypsies

More than 500,000 Gypsies, more accurately called Roma and Sinti, fell into the hands of the Nazis and their collaborators. Over 250,000 perished. Other estimates indicate losses of a much higher proportion.

The tragedy of the Gypsies—long neglected by society and researchers—bear some striking similarities to the history of the Jews and the Holocaust. Having originated from northwest India, Gypsies reached Europe in the twelfth or thirteenth century. As strangers and vagabonds they were punished for their distinctiveness and otherness, almost everywhere subjected to defamation and discrimination. Enlightened, modern societies declared their readiness to assimilate Gypsies—on the condition that they abandon their traditions and identity, renouncing their nomadic way of life.

The Nazis offered their own solution to the "Gypsy problem." Gypsies were classified as "asocials" and persecuted on racial grounds. Under the guidance of the Criminal Police, the Zentralstelle zur Bekämpfung des Zigeunerunwesens (Central Office to Combat the Gypsy Menace) was established: registration, with classifications of full Gypsy, three-quarter Gypsy, half Gypsy, quarter Gypsy, and non-Gypsy followed. A bureaucratic apparatus emerged, collecting and evaluating genealogical and anthropological data, and preparing laws and measures for the implementation of the racial doctrines and genocidal strategies. Already prior to 1939, the incarceration into special "Gypsy camps" and concentration camps had begun. After the outbreak of the war German and Austrian gypsies were detained in Jewish ghettos and camps set up in occupied Poland. From summer 1941 the mobile SS *Einsatzgruppen* as well as regular units of the German Order Police and the army distinguished themselves through the execution of Gypsies arrested in the occupied territories of the Soviet Union and southeastern Europe: some 20,000 Gypsies were deported to Auschwitz. It is estimated that more than 14,000 of these were gassed in Birkenau.

After the war, suspicion, prejudice, and stereotypes, continued to dominate attitudes and policies towards the survivors and their descendants. At first as "displaced persons," then as unwelcome vagabonds, they rebuilt their families and tried to preserve their identity. It took some time before some Sinti and Roma were recognized to be victims of Nazi perse-cution and as such entitled to restitution. It is only very recently that initial efforts have been made to recognize and to address the dimension of the Gypsy tragedy, a tragedy which against the background of the current dramatic events in Eastern and southeastern Europe seems to be reemerging.

Konrad Kwiet

See also Auschwitz; Concentration Camps; *Einsatzgruppen*; Holocaust; National Socialist Germany; Racism; *Völkisch* Ideology

References

Kenrick, D. and G. Puxton. *The Destiny of Europe's Gypsies.* London: Chatto, 1972.

Milton, S. "The Context of the Holocaust." *German Studies Review* 13 (1990), 60–83.

———. "Nazi Policies Towards Roma and Sinti, 1933–1945." *Journal of the Gypsy Lore Society* 5 (1992), 1–18.

Müller-Hill, B. *Murderous Science: Elimination by Scientific Selection of Jews, Gypsies, and Others: Germany 1933–1945.* Oxford: Oxford University Press, 1988.

Zimmermann, M. *Rassenutopie und Genozid. Die national-sozialistische "Lösung der Zigeunerfrage."* Hamburg: Christians Verlag, 1996.

———. *Verfolgt, vertrieben, vernichtet: Die national-sozialistische Vernichtungspolitik gegen Sinti und Roma.* Essen: Klartext, 1989.

Züich, T., ed. *In Auschwitz vergast, bis heute verfolgt: Zur Situation der Roma (Zigeuner) in Deutschland und Europa.* Reinbek bei Hamburg: Rowohlt, 1979.

H

Haase, Hugo (1863–1919)

One of ten children of a relatively prosperous East Prussian Jewish family, Hugo Haase studied law in Königsberg and established a successful practice there before becoming actively involved in politics. Elected to the Königsberg city council (1894–1910), Haase eventually became a leader of the Social Democratic Party (SPD) at the national level. He served in the Reichstag (1897–1907, 1912–19), and was elected co-chair of the SPD in 1911 and co-chair of the party's Reichstag delegation in 1912. He was chosen for leadership in large measure because he combined a principled adherence to the orthodox interpretation of Marxist theory, which dominated the SPD at the time, with a relatively conciliatory personality. He set himself against the majority of his colleagues when war broke out in 1914 by rejecting the argument that Germany was merely defending itself. His opposition became increasingly public as the war progressed, leading to a formal schism within the Reichstag delegation in 1916 and then the establishment of the Independent Social Democratic Party (USPD) in 1917.

Haase served as co-chair of the antiwar Social Democratic Working Group in the Reichstag and then of the USPD and its Reichstag delegation. Although considered a moderate within the USPD, Haase, like the new party as a whole, became increasingly revolutionary as the war dragged on. He rejected the constitutional reforms initiated in October 1918 by the government with the support of the SPD, and he helped to set the stage for the revolution that overthrew the empire in November.

After the kaiser's abdication Haase emerged as co-chair—with Friedrich Ebert (1871–1925)—of the new revolutionary government, only to find himself and his party hopelessly outmaneuvered by Ebert and the SPD he now headed. Returning to opposition at the end of December 1918, Haase struggled to move Germany toward democratic socialism while resisting the efforts of the newly established Communist Party to further divide the left. He died in November 1919, the victim of an assassin's bullet.

Kenneth R. Calkins

See also Ebert, Friedrich; Imperial Germany; Independent Social Democratic Party; Revolution of 1918–19; Social Democratic Party, 1871–1918

References

Calkins, Kenneth. *Hugo Haase: Democrat and Revolutionary.* Durham, NC: Carolina Academic Press, 1979.

Haase, Ernst. *Hugo Haase.* Berlin: J.J. Ottens, 1929.

Krause, Hartfrid. *USPD.* Frankfurt am Main: Europäische Verlagsanstalt, 1975.

Morgan, David. *The Socialist Left and the German Revolution.* Ithaca, NY: Cornell University Press, 1975.

Prager, Eugen. *Geschichte der USPD.* Glashütten im Taunus: Detlev Auvermann, 1970.

Haber, Fritz (1868–1934)

One of the most significant German physical chemists of the twentieth century, Haber is best known for the synthesis of ammonia, (for which he won the 1918 Nobel Prize in chemistry), for directing German chemical warfare during World War I, and for his role in developing German scientific institutions.

Born in Breslau (now Wroclaw, Poland), Haber obtained a doctorate in Berlin in 1891. After postdoctoral work in Zürich and Jena, he went to the Karlsruhe Technische Hochschule (technical university), where he rose from teaching assistant (1894) to full professor and director of the institute for physical chemistry (1906) and produced the first practical process for synthesizing ammonia using heat and pressure. Commercially developed by Carl Bosch's (1874–1940) group at the BASF corporation, the Haber-Bosch process became a key source of nitrates for fertilizers and for explosives during World War I.

In 1912, Haber became first director of the Kaiser Wilhelm Institute for Physical Chemistry and Electrochemistry in Berlin-Dahlem. In early 1915, Haber proposed supplementing scarce German ammunition through the large-scale use of poison gas. Appointed captain in the Prussian Army, Haber directed the German chemical warfare branch until 1918; research and development were centered in his institute.

In 1901, Haber had married Clara Immerwahr, the first woman to receive a chemistry doctorate from the University of Breslau (1900); they had one son. Clara committed suicide (May 1915), at least partly in protest against Haber's war work. His second marriage, to Charlotte Nathan (1917), produced a daughter and a son but ended in divorce (1927). In 1916–17, Haber also helped to organize the short-lived Kaiser Wilhelm Stiftung für Kriegstechnische Wissenschaft (Foundation for Military Technology) to coordinate academic-based military scientific research.

After the war, Haber helped to organize government-funded research grants to academic science through the Notgemeinschaft der deutschen Wissenschaft (Emergency Society for German Science and Scholarship). He worked effectively to restore Germany's international scientific standing and exerted scientific leadership in the Kaiser Wilhelm Society, where his innovative interdisciplinary colloquium attracted international attention; however, he also unsuccessfully pursued a futile project to extract gold from seawater to pay German reparations.

In 1933, despite his Jewish origins, Haber was exempted from immediate dismissal by the Nazis thanks to his prewar official rank and wartime service, but he resigned rather than dismiss his "non-Aryan" subordinates. Intending to follow Chaim Weizmann's invitation to settle in Palestine, Haber died en route in Switzerland.

Haber exemplifies the tragic duality of the technologically oriented scientist who unleashes forces both creative and destructive.

Jeffrey A. Johnson

See also Anti-Semitism; BASF; Bosch, Carl; Chemistry, Scientific and Industrial; Inventions; Jews, 1869–1933; Kaiser Wilhelm/Max Planck Societies and Their Institutes; World War I

References
Goran, Morris H. *The Story of Fritz Haber.* Norman, OK: University of Oklahoma Press, 1967.

Johnson, Jeffrey Allan. *The Kaiser's Chemists: Science and Modernization in Imperial Germany.* Chapel Hill, NC: University of North Carolina Press, 1990.

Nachmansohn, David. *German-Jewish Pioneers in Science, 1900–1933.* New York, NY: Springer-Verlag, 1979.

Stern, Fritz. *Dreams and Delusions: The Drama of German History.* New York, NY: Alfred A. Knopf, 1987.

Habermas, Jürgen (1929–)

Habermas has been professor of philosophy at the Johann Wolfgang Goethe Universität in Frankfurt since 1983. From 1971 to 1983 he directed the Max Planck Institute for Research into the Life Conditions of the Scientific-Technical World in Starnberg. As professor in Frankfurt and Heidelberg before 1971 and with frequent visiting professorships in the United

Jürgen Habermas. Courtesy of German Information Center, New York.

States, Habermas served as the foremost representative of the Frankfurt School of Social Thought (Frankfurter Schule).

A prominent political and social critic in West Germany from the 1960s to the present, Habermas has frequently criticized the lack of democratic attitudes in German politics after World War II. Habermas initiated the famous historians' dispute (*Historikerstreit*) in 1986 by attacking the neo-nationalism of some major West German historians writing on Nazism and the two world wars. Habermas is a prolific writer whose influence reaches around the world. His works have been translated into several languages and are discussed in many countries. He has contributed to the disciplines of philosophy, sociology, social psychology, political science, and political theory. His major work is *Theorie des kommunikativen Handelns* (published as *Theory of Communicative Action*), 1981.

Habermas draws on the tradition of German Idealism, Karl Marx (1818–83), and his predecessors in the Frankfurt School, as well as on modern Anglo-American philosophy and the history of sociological theory, in order to argue a new position: the rational and humane organization of modern societies is a consequence of the development of structures of communication. Societal differentiation, or the freedom to form various and complex personal and group identities, is a major achievement of modern societies, as long as these societies remain sufficiently integrated. Habermas regards democracy as a developmental process, which can lead to more democracy in the course of evolution, assuming that the will to create a society liberated from unnecessary force, suffering, and domination (control) persists. In Habermas's view, public argumentation, and the treatment of utterances made in language as claims on which one can take a position, act as major foundations for the further development of democratic attitudes. Thereby, the free and cooperative expression of needs and interests is facilitated. Social and political institutions are judged on whether they are adequate to human needs and desires in terms of criteria derived from this theoretical position.

Habermas is one of the outstanding philosophers of the last decades and the first major German social and political theorist to have gained wide international acclaim as an investigator of democracy. His contributions to modern philosophy and his instigation of a series of major debates in contemporary philosophy and sociology also deserve attention.

Dieter Misgeld

See also Adorno, Theodor; Benjamin, Walter; Frankfurt School; Fromm, Erich; *Historikerstreit*; Horkheimer, Max; Lowenthal, Leo; Marcuse, Herbert; Marx, Karl; Neumann, Franz; Philosophy; Political Science; Sociology

References

Dews, P., ed. *Habermas: Autonomy and Solidarity: Interviews with Jürgen Habermas.* London: Verso, The Imprint of New Left Books, 1986.

Habermas, J. *Communication and the Evolution of Society.* Trans. T. McCarthy. Boston, MA: Beacon, 1979.

———. *Knowledge and Human Interests.* Trans. J.F. Shapiro. Boston, MA: Beacon, 1971.

———. *Legitimation Crisis.* Trans. Th. Mc.Carthy. Boston, MA: Beacon, 1975.

———. *The New Conservatism: Cultural Criticism and the Historians' Debate.* Ed. and trans. S. Weber-Nicholsen. Cambridge, MA: MIT Press, 1989.

———. *The Philosophical Discourse of Modernity.* Trans. F.G. Lawrence. Cambridge, MA: MIT Press, 1987.

———. *Philosophical Political Profiles.* Trans. F.G. Lawrence. Cambridge, MA: MIT Press, 1983.

———. *The Structural Transformation of the Public Sphere: An Inquiry into a Category of Bourgeois Society.* Trans. T. Burger. Cambridge, MA: MIT Press, 1989.

———. *Theory and Practice.* Trans. J. Viertel. Boston, MA: Beacon, 1973.

———. *Theory of Communicative Action.* 2 vols. Trans. T. McCarthy. Boston, MA: Beacon, 1984.

McCarthy, T. *The Critical Theory of Jürgen Habermas.* Cambridge, MA: MIT Press, 1978.

Haeckel, Ernst (1834–1919)

Ernst Haeckel, professor of zoology at the University of Jena from 1861 to 1919, was the most influential popularizer of Darwinism in Germany. His widely-read *Natürliche Schöpfungsgeschichte* (published as *History of Creation*), 1868, popularized the ideas of his major scholarly work, the two-volume *Generelle Morphologie der Organismen* (General morphology of organisms), 1866, which offers a comprehensive explanation of the development of organisms based on Darwin's principle of natural selection. Haeckel's hypothesis of the absolute unity of organic and inorganic nature transcended Darwin's more cautious theories and anticipated the philosophy of "monism," publicized by Haeckel in 1899 in his best-selling *Die Welträtsel* (The riddle of the universe). Having advocated "monism" as a unified worldview based on evolutionary biology rather than religion, Haeckel co-founded the *Deutscher Monistenbund* (German Monist Society) in 1906. Haeckel's works and indefatigable publicistic activity contributed greatly to the dissemination of the view that all ethical, social, and political problems could be solved by the application of biological laws. Assuming a natural hierarchy of organisms and the inevitability of struggle, this biological worldview came to be increasingly linked to the cause of authoritarian and racist nationalism in Germany.

The scientific reputation of Haeckel rests on his innovative contributions to marine biology in a number of pioneering monographs on deep-sea organisms. In these, accompanied by his own expertly drawn illustrations, he identified hundreds of previously unknown species. His general works have stood the test of time less well. His aesthetic view of nature, the speculative quality of many of his hypotheses (such as his biogenetic law, according to which every organism recapitulates in its own development the stages of its evolutionary history), and his transformation of Darwinism into an all-explanatory cosmology show the lingering influence of Romantic *Naturphilosophie* (philosophies of nature).

Although Haeckel attacked established religions in the name of science, his monism resembled a form of nature mysticism by imputing a soul even to inorganic matter. Coming to professional maturity in the age of German unification, Haeckel viewed society as a complex and highly differentiated organism that could be effectively governed only according to the integrative principles revealed by the study of biology. He also believed in the superiority of the "Indo-Germanic" race. His shift in political sympathies from liberal radicalism to an increasingly quiescent and hierarchical nationalism parallelled Germany's transition to *Weltpolitik* (world power) and the growth of pan-Germanism at the end of the century. Several of his former students became active in the eugenic racial-hygiene movement in the 1900s. Daniel Gasman's biography, however, overstates the affinity of Haeckel's views to those of Nazism. In his own lifetime Haeckel was unable to find acceptance for his evolutionary doctrines because their progressive implications were rejected by the adherents of *völkisch* (racist) ideology.

Rod Stackelberg

See also Biology; Nationalism; Pan-German League; Racism; Social Darwinism; *Völkisch* Ideology; *Weltpolitik*

References

Gasman, Daniel. *The Scientific Origins of National Socialism: Social Darwinism in Ernst Haeckel and the Monist League.* London: Macdonald, 1971.

Kelly, Alfred. *The Descent of Darwin: The Popularization of*

Darwinism in Germany, 1860–1914. Chapel Hill, NC: University of North Carolina Press, 1981.

Weindling, Paul. *Health, Race and German Politics between National Unification and Nazism, 1870–1945*. Cambridge: Cambridge University Press, 1989.

Hager, Kurt (1912–)

Kurt Hager was a member of the German Democratic Republic's (GDR) Socialist Unity Party (SED) *Politbüro* and was Central Committee secretary for culture and science (*Kultur und Wissenschaft*). He was recognized as chief party ideologist from the mid-1960s.

Hager, whose father worked as a domestic servant, grew up near Stuttgart and was among the best-educated of the first generation of SED leaders. He studied philosophy at the *Oberrealschule* (high school preparing for admission to technical institutes) in Stuttgart, became a member of the German Communist Party at age 18, and fought in the Spanish Civil War. The World War II years were spent in exile in the West, where he worked as a jounalist.

Upon joining the SED in 1946, Hager began a career in the party apparatus that focused on cultural and scientific affairs. He held numerous positions, among them deputy editor of the newspaper *Vorwärts* (Forward) 1946–48, director of the department for propaganda (from 1949), and director of the Department of Science and Universities of the Central Committee of the SED (from 1952). In 1949, he was appointed to a chair in philosophy at the Humboldt University in East Berlin, although he never lectured there. After 1955, he was Central Committee secretary for culture and science. From 1958 to 1963, he was a candidate and thereafter a full member of the *Politbüro*. After 1976, he was a member of the State Council.

In the 1970s and early 1980s, Hager played a key role in defining East German domestic policy. After Honecker replaced Ulbricht in 1971, Hager denounced some key features of Ulbricht's concept of socialism, which had been a source of tension with the Communist Party of the Soviet Union. Ulbricht had emphasized a particularly German, scientific-technocratic socialist society in which class conflict no longer played the prominent role. Hager returned to the traditional categories of analysis. In cultural policy, however, he advocated a more pluralistic style in expressing socialist values than Ulbricht had tolerated.

On the issue of German-German relations, his tenure as ideology chief was marked by emphasis on the distinct and separate character of the GDR (in effect abandoning the goal of German unification under socialism). He supported rapprochement with West Germany but interpreted the principles outlined in the SED-Social Democratic Party paper, "Conflicting Ideologies and Common Security," 1987, very narrowly.

From the mid-1980s, Hager slowly lost influence. Nonetheless, his expressed opposition to Gorbachev-type reforms in the GDR is often cited as reflecting the sclerosis in the highest echelons of the SED.

Ann L. Phillips

See also German Democratic Republic; German Democratic Republic: Arts and Politics; German Democratic Republic: Education; German Democratic Republic: Marxism-Leninism; German Democratic Republic: Media; German Democratic Republic: Technical Intelligentsia; German-German Relations; Honecker, Erich; Socialist Unity Party; Ulbricht, Walter; Universities

References

Hager, Kurt. *Der dialektische Materialismus—die theoretische Grundlage der Politik der SED*. Berlin: Dietz Verlag, 1959.

———. *Gesetzmässigkeiten unsere Epoche, Triebkräfte und Werte des Sozialismus: Rede auf der Gesellschaftswissenschaftlichen Konferenz des Zentralkomitees der SED am 15 und 16 Dezember 1983*. Berlin: Dietz Verlag, 1984.

———. *Kontinuität und Veränderung: Beiträge zu Fragen unserer Zeit*. Berlin: Dietz Verlag, 1988.

———. *Marxistische-leninistische Philosophie und ideologischer Kampf*. Berlin: Dietz Verlag, 1970.

———. *Sozialismus und wissenschaftlich-technische Revolution*. Berlin: Dietz Verlag, 1973.

———. *Wissenschaft und Wissenschaftspolitik im Sozialismus: Vorträge, 1972 bis 1987*. Berlin: Dietz Verlag, 1987.

Krenz, Egon. *Wenn Mauern Fallen: Die friedliche Revolution*. Vienna: Paul Neff, 1990.

Schabowski, Günter. *Das Politbüro*. Reinbek bei Hamburg: Rowohlt, 1990.

Spittman, Ilse, ed. *Die SED in Geschichte und Gegenwart*. Cologne: Verlag Wissenschaft und Politik, 1987.

Hahn, Otto (1879–1968)

Otto Hahn, a pioneer in experimental radiochemistry and nuclear chemistry, co-discovered nuclear fission (1938–39), although his associates did not share his 1944 Nobel Prize. Hahn also played a prominent role in the postwar reorganization of German research institutions.

Born in Frankfurt am Main, Hahn earned a doctorate (1901) and worked as assistant in organic chemistry in Marburg, then assisted the inorganic chemist Sir William Ramsay in London (1904). Though unfamiliar with the new field of radiochemistry, Hahn discovered radiothorium, a radioactive isotope of thorium, and Ramsay recommended him to physicist Ernest Rutherford in Montreal (1905–06), then to Emil Fischer (1852–1919) in Berlin, where he became *Privatdozent* (assistant professor) and then titular professor (1910). In 1907, he began a long-lasting collaboration with physicist Lise Meitner (1878–1968). Their research helped to elucidate the complex patterns of radioactive emission and decay by which unstable radioactive elements are transformed into more stable elements. Hahn also profited when mesothorium, one of his discoveries, was marketed for medicinal use.

Hahn and Meitner moved to the new Kaiser Wilhelm Institute for Chemistry in Dahlem (1912), in whose facilities, uncontaminated by radiation, they could study weakly ra-

Otto Hahn. Courtesy of German Information Center, New York.

dioactive substances. During a leave from Hahn's chemical warfare service (1915–18), he and Meitner discovered the radioactive isotope protactinium (1917). But by the time Hahn became institute director (1928), radiochemistry seemed exhausted.

James Chadwick's discovery of the neutron (1932) opened a new field, nuclear chemistry, which used neutrons to bombard heavy elements. The Hahn-Meitner partnership revived until the *Anschluss* forced her, an Austrian Jew, to emigrate (1938). Hahn and his assistant Fritz Strassmann then unexpectedly found barium in uranium that they had bombarded with neutrons. In Sweden, Meitner and her nephew Otto Frisch explained this as "nuclear fission": neutrons had split uranium nuclei, producing barium and releasing potentially vast amounts of energy.

Although Hahn's institute contributed significant basic research to Germany's wartime nuclear project, the project lacked the resources to produce a successful reactor, much less a weapon. After confinement in England with other German nuclear scientists (1945–46), Hahn returned to preside over the Kaiser Wilhelm Society and its reorganization into the Max Planck Society (1948). He guided the society's revival until his retirement (1960). He continued promoting the recovery of science in the Federal Republic and also spoke out against nuclear weapons.

Jeffrey A. Johnson

See also Atom Bomb (German Development of); Chemistry, Scientific and Industrial; Fischer, Emil; Heisenberg, Werner; Kaiser Wilhelm/Max Planck Societies and Their Institutes; Meitner, Lise; Physics

References

Hahn, Otto. *My Life: The Autobiography of a Scientist.* New York, NY: Herder and Herder, 1970. (Trans. of *Mein Leben* by Ernst Kaiser and Eithne Wilkins.)

————. *Otto Hahn: A Scientific Autobiography.* New York, NY: C. Scribner's Sons, 1966. (Trans. of *Vom Radiothor zur Uranspaltung* by Willy Ley.)

Shea, William R., ed. *Otto Hahn and the Rise of Nuclear Physics.* The University of Western Ontario Series in Philosophy of Science, 22. Dordrecht: D. Reidel Pub. Co., 1983.

Sime, Ruth L. *Lise Meitner: A Life in Physics.* Berkeley, CA: University of California Press, 1996.

Walker, Mark. *German National Socialism and the Quest for Nuclear Power, 1939–1949.* Cambridge: Cambridge University Press, 1989.

Halder, Franz (1884–1972)

Colonel General Franz Halder was the army chief of staff in the initial, victorious phase of World War II. He had loose connections with the resistance against Hitler, but never made a serious attempt to overthrow the dictator.

Halder was born on June 30, 1884, in Würzburg, Bavaria. He joined the Bavarian army in 1902 and was commissioned into an artillery regiment in 1904. He attended the Bavarian war academy and served in various General Staff assignments during World War I, emerging as a captain. During the Weimar Republic he was accepted by the Reichswehr, and employed in staff and command assignments. In 1935, as a brigadier, he was given command of the Seventh Division in Munich. In 1937 he was put in charge of the training branch of the Army General Staff, and, as a lieutenant general, took over the even more prestigious Operations Branch in 1938. When Colonel Beck, the army chief of staff, resigned over Hitler's war plans in September 1938, Halder was the natural choice as his successor. Halder despised Hitler and his policy, and hesitated for a moment before accepting. Finally, he saw the position, which had once been Moltke's, as a means of opposing Hitler's policy more effectively, and took it.

From then on, Halder encouraged any opposition to Hitler, and it is probably due to him that the Army General Staff became a hotbed of resistance. However, he himself never undertook any active measures. Halder drew up all operations plans for the campaigns from the occupation of Austria and the Sudetenland to the attack on Poland. In the preparations for the attack on France, it took some time to persuade Halder to place the point of main effort in the center rather than in the north, which would have been a mere repetition of the Schlieffen Plan of World War I. Once Halder had agreed with the new concept, he supported it enthusiastically, stressing the thrust through the Ardennes even more than its originator,

Major General (later Field Marshal) Erich von Manstein (1887–1973) had done.

Halder also masterminded the attack on Russia and was in charge of its operational planning until September 1942. Halder objected to Hitler's conduct of the war on the eastern front, but made an effort to serve him loyally, particularly when the führer assumed the office of army commander in chief himself. However, Halder became increasingly estranged from Hitler, whom he had come to regard as dangerously deluded, and his eventual dismissal came as no surprise.

After the attempt on Hitler's life on July 20, 1944, Halder, who had had nothing to do with the plot, was arrested and dismissed from the army. He survived Flossenbürg concentration camp and was taken prisoner by the Americans. From 1948 to 1961, he was head of the Historical Liaison Group of German officers who worked for the United States Army Historical Division, and thus influenced strongly the early historiography regarding the German side of World War II. His diaries, published in 1962–63, provide an important source for historians.

Winfried Heinemann

See also Beck, Ludwig; Hitler, Adolf; Manstein, Erich von; National Socialist Germany; National Socialist Germany: Military; Resistance; World War II

References

Brett-Smith, Richard. *Hitler's Generals*. San Rafael, CA: Presidio, 1977.

Halder, Franz. *The Halder War Diary, 1939–1942*. Novato, CA: Presidio, 1988.

Hartmann, Christian. *Halder: Generalstabschef Hitlers 1938–1942*. Paderborn: Schöningh, 1991.

Leach, Barry A. "Halder." *Hitler's Generals*. Ed. Correlli Barnett. London: Weidenfeld and Nicolson, 1989.

Schall-Riaucourt, Heidemarie Gräfin von. *Aufstand und Gehorsam: Offizierstum und Generalstab im Umbruch: Leben und Wirken von Generaloberst Franz Halder, Generalstabschef 1938–1942*. Wiesbaden: Limes, 1972.

Hallstein, Walter (1901–82)

As one of the close advisors to Chancellor Konrad Adenauer, Walter Hallstein played an important role in shaping the early Federal Republic's of Germany's (FRG) foreign policy. He was a staunch advocate of Western integration and one of the spiritual authors of the so-called Hallstein Doctrine, according to which the FRG claimed to be the sole legal international representative of Germany (*Alleinvertretungsanspruch*). The doctrine provided the basic paradigm of West German foreign policy from the mid-1950s to Chancellor Willy Brandt's (1913–92) *Ostpolitik* (eastern policy) some ten years later.

A lawyer from Mainz, Hallstein entered politics after an academic career in Rostock and Frankfurt (1941–48). Already during his term as a professor in Frankfurt, the Hessian state government had considered him a highly informed expert and had sought his counsel in basic economic policy

decisions. Not affiliated with any political party, he attracted Adenauer's attention and was appointed minister in the Office of the Chancellor (1950–51) and in the Foreign Ministry (1951–57).

Owing to Adenauer's heavy workload—he had appointed himself the first foreign minister of the FRG in 1951—Hallstein virtually managed the Foreign Office by himself. Hallstein, who excelled through his legal expertise and his brilliant memory, proved his diplomatic skills in 1950 when he led the German delegation at the Schuman Plan negotiations, in which Adenauer gave him a free hand, on the creation of the European Coal and Steel Community.

As minister he was a proponent of a tough stand vis-à-vis the Soviet Union. On his initiative, the foreign policy maxim that the FRG could not establish diplomatic relations with states that gave diplomatic recognition to the German Democratic Republic (GDR) was formulated and first announced by Adenauer in a speech to the Bundestag in 1955. This policy provided the rationale for the rupture of diplomatic relations with Yugoslavia (1957) and Cuba (1963).

Adenauer recommended Hallstein for the presidency of the European Economic Commission (EEC). During his presidency in Brussels from 1958 to 1967, Hallstein, who favored a federalist model of European integration, played an important part in progress toward European union. At the same time, he continued to emphasize the necessity of an Atlantic partnership. Because of French reservations, he renounced the presidency of the European Community (EC) after the fusion of the European Commissions, i.e., the EEC, the European Coal and Steel Commission (ECSC), and Euratom, in 1967. From 1968 to 1974 he occupied the office of the president of the European Movement, and he was a member of the Bundestag for the Christian Democratic Union (CDU) from 1969 to 1972.

Walter Mühlhausen

See also Adenauer, Konrad; American-German Relations; Chancellor's Office; Diplomatic Corps and Diplomacy; Federal Republic of Germany: Foreign Policy; Franco-German Relations; German-German Relations; Israeli-German Relations; Postwar European Integration and Germany; Schuman Plan; Soviet-German Relations

References

Baring, Arnulf. *Aussenpolitik in Adenauers Kanzlerdemokratie*. 2nd ed. Munich: Oldenbourg, 1982.

Die Kabinettsprotokolle der Bundesregierung. 2 vols. (1950 *ff.*), Boppard: Boldt, 1984 *ff.*

Schwarz, Hans-Peter. *Adenauer*. 2 vols. Providence, RI and Oxford: Berghahn Books, 1995–1997.

Hamburg

Located on the Elbe River about 75 miles south of its outlet into the North Sea, Hamburg has been the largest German port, as well as a major center of commerce, banking, and industry, for over a hundred years. Hamburg has a tradition of civic independence dating to the Middle Ages, when it was a founder of the Hanseatic League (together with Lübeck) and a free imperial city, like Bremen, its smaller competitor as Germany's main seaport.

Hamburg enjoyed tremendous economic and demographic growth in the Imperial period. Its economy centered on commerce, shipbuilding, shipping, and merchant banking. Numerous German emigrants left the country via Hamburg, many on ships of the Hamburg-America Steamship Company (HAPAG) headed by Albert Ballin (1857–1918). Hamburg mushroomed from 290,000 inhabitants in 1880 to 932,000 in 1910. The face of the city changed rapidly with a building boom. For example, the new *Rathaus* (city hall), a neo-Renaissance building, was completed in 1897.

Hamburg was long dominated by a bourgeois elite, which, with the help of restrictive voting laws, maintained a firm grip on the central institutions of municipal government. These were the Senate, which exercised executive power and elected two burgomasters, and the Citizens' Assembly (*Bürgerschaft*), which elected the Senate. The ruling class was cosmopolitan in outlook and more Anglophile than pro-Prussian, although a pro-Prussian faction won out after 1871. Although the Senate solidly supported free trade, Hamburg had to surrender its status as a customs-free port in 1888 and join the Imperial Customs Union (Zollverein). It was allowed to create a free port where industries could produce for export.

Though liberal, Hamburg was certainly not a democracy. The patrician elite put its own narrow class interests first in the formulation of policy. This was notable in the cholera epidemic of 1892. At first, city officials tried to conceal the outbreak of cholera, fearing quarantine measures would be detrimental to trade. As a result, cholera spread quickly, killing many more people than it did in other parts of Germany.

Hamburg became a major center of the labor movement. The dockworkers' strike of 1896–97 was the largest of the many strikes of the prewar era. The Social Democratic Party (SPD) received most of the vote in Reichstag elections in Hamburg (83 percent in 1890). In the Revolution of 1918, Hamburg came under the rule of workers' and soldiers' councils.

In the Weimar Republic, Hamburg retained its statehood, although it lost its earlier financial and political autonomy. With the dismantling of the three-class voting system (under the 1921 constitution), the Social Democrats became the strongest party. However, they ruled in coalition with non-socialist parties. As a result, representatives of the "old Hamburg" continued to serve as mayors until 1930. Nonetheless, Hamburg made strides in public-housing construction and school reform. In 1919, a university was founded, and Hamburg participated in the rich cultural life of the Weimar Republic.

The city's liberal traditions did not make Hamburg immune to the Nazi Party, which became the largest party in the Citizens' Assembly in 1932 with 31 percent of the vote. After the Nazi takeover, Hamburg came under the rule of a Nazi *Gauleiter* (district leader). The city, a center of naval shipbuilding, aircraft production, and the importation of raw materials, was vital to the Nazi war effort. As a result, Hamburg became a major target of Allied bombing, and the port facili-

Hamburg city hall and port. Courtesy of German Embassy, Ottawa.

ties and shipyards were severely damaged. Over 100,000 inhabitants died as a result of the war and of Nazi persecution, including 50,000 in the concentration camps of Fühlsbuttel and Neuengamme near Hamburg.

After World War II, the city's 1921 constitution was resurrected and Hamburg became an "independent" *Land* (state). West Germany's federal system gave Hamburg more autonomy than it had enjoyed in the Weimar Republic. The old elite-dominated political system was not resurrected, however, and the SPD has largely dominated Hamburg politics since the war.

After the war Hamburg's importance as a port declined, largely because of the loss of the city's hinterland to East Germany. This was more than compensated by Hamburg's growing importance in book and newspaper publishing, banking, insurance, and industry—notably electronics, oil refining, and the chemical industry in the 1980s. Among the major magazines and newspapers published in Hamburg are *Der Spiegel, Die Zeit, Stern,* and *Die Welt.*

Hamburg's population rose to 1.4 million in 1946 due to the influx of German refugees from the east, who eventually made up one-fifth of the population. Since the mid-1950s, large numbers of *Gastarbeiter* ("guest workers," recently mainly Turks) immigrated to Hamburg, raising the percentage of foreigners to 10 percent by the 1980s. Hamburg's population rose to 1.8 million in 1960, only to decline to some 1.6

million in 1980, due mainly to the population shift to sub-urban areas beyond the city limits.

Paradoxically, although Hamburg has had the highest per capita income of all German states in recent years, its unemployment rate has been among the highest in Germany (13.6 percent in 1987), owing to the rapid loss of jobs in industry (including shipbuilding). The sluggish economy engendered budgetary deficits. In a departure from traditional SPD politics, Mayor Klaus von Dohnanyi embarked on an austerity program in the mid-1980s. An economic upturn was in progress by the late 1980s. The demise of the German Democratic Republic (GDR) restored its hinterland to Hamburg and inaugurated a new role for the city in east-west economic relations.

The Green Party (called GAL in Hamburg) posed a challenge to the Hamburg SPD when it garnered 13 percent of the vote in 1984. A resurgence of extreme rightist activities has made itself felt since German reunification.

Dolores L. Augustine

See also Ballin, Albert; Bourgeoisie; Disease; Federalism; Press and Newspapers; Social Democracy; Urbanization; Warburg, Max

References

Chernow, Ron. *The Warburgs.* New York, NY: Random House, 1993.

Evans, Richard J. *Death in Hamburg: Society and Politics in the Cholera Years 1830–1910.* Oxford: Clarendon Press, 1987.

Grüttner, Michael. *Arbeitswelt an der Wasserkante: Sozialgeschichte der Hamburger Hafenarbeiter 1886–1914.* Göttingen: Vandenhoeck & Ruprecht, 1984.

Jochmann, Werner and Hans-Dieter Loose, eds. *Hamburg: Geschichte der Stadt und ihrer Bewohner.* Vol. 2. Hamburg: Hoffmann & Campe, 1986.

Lamar, Cecil. *Albert Ballin: Business and Politics in Imperial Germany, 1888–1918.* Princeton, NJ: Princeton University Press, 1967.

Schramm, Percy Ernst. *Neun Generationen: Dreihundert Jahre deutscher "Kulturgeschichte" im Lichte der Schicksale einer Hamburger Bürgerfamilie (1648–1948).* Vol. 2. Göttingen: Vandenhoeck & Ruprecht, 1964.

Hamm-Brücher, Hildegard (1921–)

Hildegard Hamm-Brücher, a member of the Free Democratic Party (FDP) and perhaps the most prominent woman in postwar West German politics, has held elective office on all three levels of government: she began as Munich's youngest city councilor (1948–54), then became Bavarian state legislator (1950–66; 1970–76), then a member of the Bundestag (since 1976). In 1963, she joined the FDP's national executive committee and in 1972 became its vice-chair. Her appointive posts have ranged from deputy assistant minister of culture in SPD-ruled Hesse (1967–69) to federal deputy minister of education and science (1969–72)

to minister of state at the federal Foreign Office (1977–82) during SPD-FDP coalition governments.

Hamm-Brücher was born on May 11, 1921, in Essen to a Jewish mother and a Lutheran father but was orphaned by age 11. She studied chemistry at the University of Munich (1939–45), where she received her doctorate. She received one of the first Fulbright grants to study at Harvard University (1949). In Munich she became involved with the White Rose student resistance movement. After the war, Hamm-Brücher worked as a science and education writer for the United States military government-sponsored newspaper, the *Neue Zeitung.* As a journalist she met Theodor Heuss (1884–1963), Baden-Württemberg's culture minister, who encouraged her to enter politics, in 1948. She was elected to Munich's city council that same year, and in 1950 married one of the city's Christian Social Union (CSU) department heads, Erwin Hamm.

Hamm-Brücher's primary domestic political concerns were social and educational reform and civil rights. Her criticism of religiously segregated schools and her promotion of comprehensive, non-tracked schools in the 1960s reflect the traditional anticlericalism of German liberalism and her individual commitment to the continued democratization of West German society. She advocated tolerance and understanding for the anti-authoritarian concerns of the 1968 student movement. During the height of the Red Army Faction terrorism and the state's special anti-terrorist measures in the late 1970s, Hamm-Brücher strongly defended civil rights. Although re-

Hildegard Hamm-Brücher. Courtesy of German Information Center, New York.

fusing to be identified as a left-liberal, she was more often aligned with the younger social liberals than with the old-style national liberals or the traditional economic liberals, such as Count Otto Lambsdorff. When the FDP left the coalition with the SPD in 1982, she protested the FDP's withdrawal in a speech to the Bundestag as a betrayal of the coalition agreement and advocated holding new elections to determine popular opinion. Yet she also appealed to her liberal colleagues to become reconciled and to seek ways to resolve the conflict rather than abandoning the party.

Hamm-Brücher opposed the resurgence of Nazism in the young Federal Republic of Germany (FRG). Her years of agitation against the appointment of Theodor Maunz, a former Nazi constitutional expert, as Bavarian minister of culture eventually succeeded in forcing his resignation in 1964.

Hamm-Brücher has also asserted her independence in foreign policy. In opposition to the FDP's executive committee she supported recognition of the Oder-Neisse line as a permanent German border at the 1967 annual party congress. At the Foreign Office (1977–82) she encouraged international understanding through increased cultural awareness of other countries. This commitment to international amity and her long record of support for civil rights, as well as her loyalty to the FDP, have led most recently to her being considered for the post of federal president.

Rebecca Boehling

See also Federal Republic of Germany; Federal Republic of Germany: Foreign Policy; Federal Republic of Germany: Women; Feminism in the Federal Republic of Germany; Free Democratic Party; Liberalism; Oder-Neisse Line

References
Boehling, Rebecca. "Symbols of Continuity and Change in Postwar German Liberalism: Wolfgang Haussmann and Hildegard Hamm-Brücher." *In Search of a Liberal Germany.* Ed. Konrad H. Jarausch and Larry E. Jones. Oxford: Berg, 1990.

Hamm-Brücher, Hildegard. *Kämpfen für eine demokratische Kultur: Texte aus vier Jahrzehnten.* Munich: Piper, 1986.

Hamm-Brücher, Hildegard and Norbert Schreiber. *Die aufgeklärte Republik: Eine kritische Bilanz.* Munich: Bertelsmann, 1989.

Salentin, Ursula. *Hildegard Hamm-Brücher: Der Lebensweg einer eigenwilligen Demokratin.* Freiburg i. B.: Herder, 1987.

Hammerstein-Equord, Kurt von (1878–1943)
Colonel General Kurt Freiherr von Hammerstein-Equord was born in Hinrichshagen, Mecklenburg, on September 26, 1878 and died in Berlin on April 24, 1943. He served as a major in the General Staff during the First World War, as chief of staff in Military Area Command III (Berlin) from 1924 to 1929, and from 1929 as chief of the Troop Office (the equivalent of chief of the General Staff). In 1930 he became chief of Army Command (commander in chief of the army).

At the time of Hitler's appointment as chancellor, Hammerstein-Equord was the center of rumors of a *Putsch* to prevent the Nazis from taking power. In fact, he and Brigadier General Kurt von Schleicher (1882–1934), who had preceded Hitler as chancellor, agreed that there was no alternative to Hitler. When Hammerstein-Equord, soon an outspoken opponent of the Nazis, saw his authority and influence waning, he resigned and retired in January 1934.

Hammerstein-Equord was, nevertheless, promoted to colonel general (*Generaloberst*). He kept in contact with other opposition figures such as the chief of the General Staff (1933–38) General Ludwig Beck (1880–1944), General Franz Halder (1884–1972) (Beck's successor), and Carl Goerdeler (1884–1945), all of whom plotted against Hitler. On September 9, 1939, Hammerstein-Equord was given command of Army Detachment A on the lower Rhine with headquarters in Cologne. He collaborated in plans to entice Hitler to a visit to his headquarters in order to arrest the dictator, but was relieved of his command before Hitler visited any part of the western front. In the years until his death, Hammerstein-Equord frequently figured in coup plans.

Peter Hoffmann

See also Beck, Ludwig; Goerdeler, Carl; Halder, Franz; National Socialist Germany: Military; Resistance; Schleicher, Kurt von; Weimar Germany: Army

References
Hammerstein, Kunrat Freiherr von. *Spähtrupp.* Stuttgart: Henry Goverts Verlag, 1963.

Hoffmann, Peter. *The History of the German Resistance, 1933–1945.* London: Macdonald and Jane's; Cambridge, MA: MIT Press, 1977.

Wheeler-Bennett, John W. *The Nemesis of Power: The German Army in Politics, 1918–1945.* London: Macmillan; New York, NY: St. Martin's Press, 1953.

The Handicapped
In 1980, the World Health Organization proposed a differentiation of the terms impairment, disability, and handicap: *impairment* to mean physical or mental problems, *disability* the diminished ability to work, and *handicap* the status of outsiders.

The philosophy of the end of the eighteenth century promulgated the ideal of educating all people to become accepted and active members of society. Educational institutions for young people deprived of their senses were established: for the blind in Paris (1784), Liverpool (1790), Berlin (1806), Vienna (1808), Dresden (1809), and Zürich (1810), and for the deaf and dumb in Paris (1810) and Leipzig (1778). Persons suffering from mental illness were hospitalized in new types of medical establishments, inspired by the English "moral treatment," after the 1810s; those declared incurable were nursed in special institutions, and after the 1840s, the establishments for healing and for nursing were combined in complex buildings. Orthopedia developed after the 1840s; a "journal for orthopedical surgery" was founded in 1892, and a "yearbook for the care of the crippled" in 1899. This care was primarily provided by the churches. Many of these institutions treated the impairments and provided some form of employment for the disabled.

Around 1900, eugenics became popular in Germany. Its proponents recommended that persons considered to be of diminished social value, i.e., those suffering from one of the many forms of mental illness that were thought to be hereditary, not be allowed to reproduce. Even the political left debated the issue of forced sterilization. In 1906, all "crippled" persons were counted by a census advocated by the orthopedist Konrad Biesalski (1868–1930) and by the churches. Of the 75,000 handicapped persons registered, some 42,000 were said to need institutional care. Orthopedic doctors mostly cared for "crippled" children; World War I shifted their endeavors to the wounded.

The French constitution of 1793 promulgated a society obliged to support its unfortunate citizens by providing them with work or with a means of existence for those unable to work, but Germany had no such legislation until 1919–20. The Prussian state had obliged its communes to support the poor in 1794, and published a special law in 1842–43 to support the disabled poor. No general right to be employed, educated, or supported existed. The other German states enacted similar poor laws, and the Prussian law was extended throughout Germany in 1871. In 1884, an imperial law provided support to people who suffered from work accidents, and after 1889, pensions were given to invalids.

But the "invalids of war and of work" did not gain special rights regarding employment before the end of World War I: in 1919, the Weimar Republic took over the care of disabled ex-servicemen. In 1920, all invalids of war or of work accidents—called "cripples" by a Prussian law of the same year—gained protection from dismissal, and large employers had to engage a certain percentage of disabled workers. In 1924, the "Decree of the Reich on the Obligation of Public Care" extended care for the disabled, performed widely by communal health offices.

Nazism postponed this care; the imbeciles were persecuted, some even murdered. The term "cripple," which the Protestants had advanced since the 1880s, and which had always had discriminatory connotations, was banned from official use in favor of "handicapped." After 1945, medical, vocational, and social rehabilitation expanded from the invalids of war and of work accidents to all groups of disabled persons. In 1974, this extension culminated in a law offering the same rehabilitation measures to all kinds of disabled people; there were some 600,000 of them in West Germany in 1990. These public measures, however, did not end society's discrimination against the handicapped.

Gunnar Stollberg

See also Disease; Eugenics; Galen, Clemens August von; Health; Insanity; National Socialist Germany; Old Age; Poverty; Social Insurance; Social Reform; Veterans' Organizations; Working Conditions

References

Blasius, Dirk. *Der verwaltete Wahnsinn: Eine Sozialgeschichte des Irrenhauses.* Frankfurt am Main: Fischer, 1980.

Bundesminister für Arbeit und Sozialordnung, ed. *Übersicht über die Soziale Sicherheit.* 2nd ed. Bonn: Bundesministerium für Arbeit, 1991.

Burleigh, Michael. "'Euthanasia' in the Third Reich: Some Recent Literature." *Social History of Medicine* 4 (1991), 317–28.

Fandrey, Walter. *Krüppel, Idioten, Irre: Zur Sozialgeschichte behinderter Menschen in Deutschland.* Stuttgart: Silberburg, 1990.

Haaser, Albert. "Entwicklungslinien und gesellschaftliche Bedingungen der Behindertenpolitik in Deutschland: Zur Sozialgeschichte und Soziologie der Rehabilitation." Unpublished doctoral dissertation. University of Konstanz, 1975.

Heinze, Rolf G. and Peter Runde, eds. *Lebensbedingungen Behinderter im Sozialstaat.* Opladen: Westdeutscher Verlag, 1982.

Mroczynski, Peter. *Rehabilitations-Recht.* 2nd ed. Munich: Beck, 1986.

Sachsse, Christoph and Florian Tennstedt. *Geschichte der Armenfürsorge in Deutschland.* 3 vols. Stuttgart: Kohlhammer, 1980–92.

Thomann, Klaus-Dieter. "Der 'Krüppel': Entstehen und Verschwinden eines Kampfbegriffs." *Medizinhistorisches Journal* 27 (1992), 221–71.

———. "Orthopädie im 19. Jahrhundert: Eine medizinische Spezialdisziplin für die Wohlhabenden?" *Medizin, Gesellschaft, Geschichte* 8 (1991), 27–62.

Valentin, Bruno. *Geschichte der Orthopädie.* Stuttgart: Thieme, 1961.

Weindling, Paul. *Health, Race and German Politics between National Unification and Nazism 1870–1945.* Cambridge: Cambridge University Press, 1989.

Whalen, Robert. *Bitter Wounds: German Victims of the Great War, 1914–1939.* Ithaca, NY: Cornell University Press, 1984.

Handke, Peter (1942–)

Peter Handke's literary work has secured the author a prominent position within the postmodern writing tradition. In addition to drama and prose, his oeuvre includes poems, radio plays, essays, and feature films; he has also won recognition for his excellent literary translations from French, English, Slovenian and ancient Greek.

Handke was born on December 6, 1942 in Griffen, a small town in the Austrian province of Carinthia. The regional and social narrowness of his background and the experience of rigid authority left their mark on the author and his work. He won instant notoriety after his highly publicized outburst at the 1966 Princeton meeting of the Gruppe (group) 47, where he accused the German literary establishment of "impotence of description."

Handke's initial literary success stemmed from his experimental plays, including *Publikumsbeschimpfung* (published as

Offending the Audience), 1966; *Weissagung* 1966; *Selbstbezichtigung* (published as *Self-Accusation*), 1966, *Hilferufe* (Cries for help), 1967, which expose conventional language and theater practices. The plays *Kaspar,* 1968, *Das Mündel will Vormund sein,* 1969, *Quodlibet,* 1970, and *Der Ritt über den Bodensee* (published as *The Ride across Lake Constance*), 1971, criticize stereotyped, predictable language and perceptions. They also illustrate the role of language as mediator in an authoritarian system and its devastating power over the individual.

The destruction of normative systems is the main focus of Handke's first experimental prose texts, *Der Hausierer* (The peddlar), 1966, *Die Hornissen,* (The hornets), 1967, and *Die Begrüssung des Aufsichtsrats,* 1967. The less experimental novel *Die Angst des Tormanns beim Elfmeter* (published as *The Goalie's Anxiety at the Penalty Kick*), 1970, relates the story of the alienated, unemployed construction worker Joseph Bloch, a former goalie turned murderer. The central theme is not the crime itself but Bloch's disoriented perception of reality. Social conventions and their alienating effect are central to the novel *Wunschloses Unglück* (published as *A Sorrow Beyond Dreams*), 1972, Handke's commemoration of his mother's life.

In the novel, *Der kurze Brief zum langen Abschied* (published as *Short Letter, Long Farewell*), 1972, the critical tendency of Handke's work was replaced by the concept of literature as a counter-reality that preserves individuality. With conscious reference to the German *Bildungsroman* (educational novel), Handke tells the story of self-discovery resulting from a journey across a fictitious, utopian America. Similarly, the protagonists of the two narratives, *Die Stunde der wahren Empfindung* (published as *A Moment of True Feeling*), 1975, and *Die linkshändige Frau* (published as *The Left-Handed Woman*), 1976 achieve moments of epiphany by breaking out of expected normative behavioral patterns. The themes of mystical unity, wholeness, and peace foreshadowed by these last texts now dominate the works of the tetralogy *Langsame Heimkehr* (published as *Slow Homecoming*), 1979, *Die Lehre der Sainte-Victoire,* (The lesson of Sainte-Victoire), 1980, *Kindergeschichte* (Child story), 1981 and the dramatic poem, *Über die Dörfer,* 1981.

The tetralogy marks a shift in Handke's aesthetics reflecting the influence of classical literary traditions. Handke continues his new immanent poetic style, which had already emerged in the journals *Das Gewicht der Welt* (published as *The Weight of the World*), 1977, *Die Geschichte des Bleistifts,* 1982, and *Phantasien der Wiederholung,* 1983, and in the novel *Der Chinese des Schmerzes* (1983). Here, the protagonist, Loser, an "observer," exists in a static isolation that he violates by murdering a man who has defaced nature with a swastika. Loser's existential stasis corresponds with Filip Kobal's happiness in the "emptiness" of his "landscape of freedom" in *Die Wiederholung* (Repetition), 1986. *Die Wiederholung* is a book about memory and the rediscovery of artistic and ethnic identity. The title refers to a narration that will bring back the past through conscious effort rather than unfocused remembering. Handke's subsequent fiction, *Nachmittag eines Schriftstellers* (published as *Afternoon of a Writer*), 1987, *Versuch über die Müdigkeit,* 1989, *Versuch über die Jukebox* (1990) and *Versuch*

über den geglückten Tag (1991), centers on the artistic experience and the creative process. In these works, Handke continues his intention to restore a sense of wonder at the world by aesthetic means. Yet with every work, he questions and redefines his position while constantly aiming for renewal and innovation.

The change in Handke's writing shifted his critical reception. He was no longer a rebel against the literary establishment but stood accused of narcissistic self-stylization. Critics were alienated by his grand archaic style and his ahistorical concept of a poetic utopia. These reservations notwithstanding, Handke stands among the most significant contemporary writers.

Helga Schreckenberger

See also Bildung und Bildungsbürgertum; Drama; Federal Republic of Germany: Literature; Novel

References
Arnold, Heinz L., ed. *Peter Handke.* Munich: Edition Text + Kritik Sonderband, 1969, 1971, and 1976.

Fellinger, Raimund, ed. *Peter Handke.* Frankfurt am Main: Suhrkamp, 1985.

Firda, Richard A. *Peter Handke.* New York, NY: Twayne, 1993.

Gabriel, Norbert. *Peter Handke und Österreich.* Bonn: Bouvier, 1983.

Haslinger, Adolf. *Peter Handke: Jugend eines Schriftstellers.* Salzburg: Residenz, 1992.

Hern, Nicholas. *Peter Handke.* New York, NY: Ungar, 1972.

Mixner, Manfred. *Peter Handke.* Kronberg: Athenäum, 1977.

Nägele, Rainer und Renate Voris. *Peter Handke.* Munich: C.H. Beck, 1978.

Pütz, Peter. *Peter Handke.* Munich: Edition Text + Kritik, 1978.

Scharang, Michael, ed. *Über Peter Handke.* Frankfurt am Main: Suhrkamp, 1972.

Schlueter, June, ed. *The Plays and Novels of Peter Handke.* Pittsburgh, PA: University of Pittsburgh Press, 1981.

Wolf, Jürgen. *Visualität, Form und Mythos in Peter Handkes Prosa.* Opladen: Westdeutscher Verlag, 1991.

Hanna, Gertrud (1876–1944)

A trade unionist and socialist, Gertrud Hanna represented women's interests in the independent trade unions of Germany from the 1910s to the 1930s. From 1909 to 1933, she headed the Secretariat for Women Workers of the General Commission of German Trade Unions (Arbeiterinnensekretäriat der Generalkommission der freien Gewerkschaften). She edited the *Gewerkschaftliche Frauenzeitung* (Women's trade union paper) from 1916 until 1933. A pragmatist, Hanna moved up through the ranks, guarded union autonomy, and encouraged women's involvement in the unions.

Hanna came from a poor, working-class family. At the age of 14 she took a job as a printer's aide; three years later, she joined the first Berlin local of the Printers' Aides, a female group. Against her parents' wishes, she became involved in union life and accepted a position with a different organization, the Printers' Aides Union, in 1907. For Hanna, the unions represented opportunities for intellectual and material improvement. Under her leadership, the women's secretariat moved from an emphasis on political education to a reformist stance.

Hanna supported the German war effort from 1914 to 1918 and cooperated with bourgeois organizations to mobilize women for the cause. In 1916, when union leaders launched the biweekly women's paper *Gewerkschaftliche Frauenzeitung* to counterbalance the radical socialist, anti-war *Gleichheit* (Equality) of Clara Zetkin (1857–1933), publisher Carl Legien (1861–1920) chose Hanna as editor. By 1917, subscriptions numbered 100,000; by 1919, circulation reached 375,000.

Even before the war ended, Hanna warned that stagnation of the labor market would have devastating effects on women. At the 1919 Congress of Trade Unions she introduced a resolution that recognized women's right to jobs and pledged the unions to prevent hostility to women from playing a part in dismissals. But at the Weimar Social Democratic Party Congress (1919), Hanna conceded her helplessness against the movement to remove women, especially married women, from the German work force. She could only urge women to strive for more influence in the unions and on the job.

Hanna sat in the Prussian *Landtag* (parliament) from 1919 to 1933 and represented German working women at various international conferences. Although she eschewed the label "feminist," she consistently promoted women's causes, from extended maternity leave and protection of pregnant workers on the job to equal pay for equal performance. Critical of what she considered working women's apathy, Hanna has herself been criticized for blaming women for their weak position in the unions and in the labor force as a whole.

In 1932, together with Marie Juchacz (1879–1956) from the Women's Bureau of the Social Democratic Party, Hanna called on women to join the front against fascism. During the Nazi regime, she retreated from public view. She died in 1944, apparently by suicide.

Doris L. Bergen

See also Feminism and Anti-Feminism, 1871–1918; Juchacz, Marie; Legien, Carl; Prussia; Social Democratic Party, 1871–1918; Trade Unions, 1871–1945; (Bourgeois) Women's Movement; Women's Occupations; Working Conditions; World War I

References
Arendt, Hans-Jürgen and Siegfried Scholze, eds. *Zur Rolle der Frau in der Geschichte des Deutschen Volkes (1839 bis 1945): Eine Chronik.* Frankfurt am Main: Verlag Marxistische Blätter, 1984.
Hagemann, Karen. *Frauenalltag und Männerpolitik: Alltagsleben und gesellschaftliches Handeln von Arbeiterfrauen in der Weimarer Republik.* Bonn: J.H.W. Dietz, 1990.
Juchacz, Marie. *Sie lebten für eine bessere Welt: Lebensbilder führender Frauen des 19. und 20. Jahrhunderts.* Berlin-Hanover: J.H.W. Dietz, 1955.
Quataert, Jean H. *Reluctant Feminists in German Social Democracy, 1885–1917.* Princeton, NJ: Princeton University Press, 1979.
Thönessen, Werner. *The Emancipation of Women: The Rise and Decline of the Women's Movement in German Social Democracy, 1863–1933.* Glasgow: Pluto, 1973.

Harden, Maximilian (1861–1927)

Born as Felix Ernst Witkowski, Harden used various pseudonyms, including Kent, Apostata, and Proteus. An essayist and publicist, he became the leading critic of Kaiser Wilhelm II.

At age 14, Harden fled his middle-class Jewish home and went, without having finished school, into the theater, where he changed his name to Maximilian Harden. In 1878, he converted to Protestantism. In 1888, he left the stage, audited classes at Berlin University, published essays and contributed to various newspapers and magazines. From 1892 until 1922, Harden was the sole editor and main contributor of the weekly *Die Zukunft* (The future), which reached a circulation of 23,000 and attained significant political influence.

In 1898, Harden was detained for two weeks because of an essay he had written about King Otto of Bavaria. In 1899 and 1901, he served a total of 14 months' imprisonment because of numerous articles critical of Wilhelm II. With three court cases (1907–09) against the Berlin city commander Kuno von Moltke and two against Prince Philipp zu Eulenburg (1847–1921), both suspected of homosexuality, Harden sought to expose the political influence of the "court camarilla" as well as the dilettantish politics of Wilhelm II. During the *Daily Telegraph* Affair of 1908, he demanded the removal of the kaiser.

Harden cultivated personal relationships with leading personalities in politics (Otto von Bismarck, Walther Rathenau [1867–1922], and Friedrich von Holstein), economics (Albert Ballin [1857–1918] and Hugo Stinnes [1870–1924]), and culture (Hermann Bahr, Fritz Mauthner, Max Reinhardt [1873–1943], Frank Wedekind [1864–1918] and Emil Ludwig [1881–1948]), some of whom also published in his periodical.

Although Harden had warned for years of a European war, he showed himself to be an annexation-nationalist in the summer of 1914. Only a few months later, he advocated the dominance of politics over the military and became a consistent pacifist, who pleaded for "peace for humanity." The military censors prohibited *Die Zukunft* on three occasions, for several months each time. Harden condemned the reactionary nationalism of the Weimar Republic and produced plans for a European economic community. He survived an assassination attempt by the radical right wing. The ensuing trial, in November 1922, focused more on disparaging him than on punishing the guilty parties.

Through astute analysis, prodigious knowledge, and intellectual sensibility, Harden realized his intention to make "politics by the word." Through parodies, satires, and a host of varied styles, he produced a literary journalism that influenced the following generation, in particular Kurt Tucholsky (1890–1935). His essays, still worth reading despite being affected and prolix in places, are a chapter of contemporary history. Harden aptly described himself as "the Cassandra of the Empire"; for a quarter of a century he rendered political diagnosis and prophesied decline.

Gisela Brude-Firnau

See also Ballin, Albert; *Daily Telegraph* Affair; Imperial Germany: Literature; Journalism; Ludwig, Emil; Rathenau, Walther; Reinhardt, Max; Satire; Stinnes, Hugo; Wedekind, Frank; Wilhelm II

References

Fröhlich, Hans Jürgen. "Über Maximilian Harden." *Journalisten über Journalisten.* Ed. Hans Jürgen Schulz. Munich: Kindler, 1980.
————, ed. *Köpfe: Porträts, Briefe und Dokumente.* Hamburg: Rütten & Loening, 1963.
Harden, Maximilian. *Kaiserpanorama: Literarische und politische Publizistik.* Ed. Ruth Greuner. Berlin: Buchverlag der Moderne, 1983.
————. *Köpfe.* 2 vols. Berlin: Erich Reiss, 1911–24.
————. *Krieg und Friede.* 2 vols. Berlin: Erich Reiss, 1918.
————. *Literatur und Theater.* Berlin: Freund & Jeckel, 1896.
————. *Von Versailles nach Versailles.* Hellerau bei Dresden: Avalon, 1927.
Hellige, Hans Dieter. "Rathenau und Harden in der Gesellschaft des Deutschen Kaiserreichs." *Walther Rathenau-Gesamtausgabe.* Vol. 6. Ed. Hans Dieter Hellige and Ernst Schulin. Munich-Heidelberg: Gotthold Müller-Lambert Schneider, 1983.
Weller, Bernd Uwe. *Maximilian Harden und die "Zukunft."* Bremen: Schünemann, 1970.
Young, Harry F. *Maximilian Harden: Censor Germaniae.* The Hague: Martinus Nijhoff, 1959.

Harich, Wolfgang (1923–)

One of the German Democratic Republic's (GDR) very few overt manifestations of organized intellectual opposition centered on Wolfgang Harich and a few of his associates in the aftermath of Stalin's death and the worker uprising of June 1953. At best a feeble effort, it was soon put to rest by the Ulbricht regime, but it signaled, however briefly, that independent Marxian thought survived in the GDR.

Harich, a protégé of the great Marxist philosopher Ernst Bloch (1885–1977), was at the time a lecturer in philosophy and history at the Humboldt University in Berlin, co-editor of the *Deutsche Zeitschrift für Philosophie* (German journal for philosophy), and an associate of an important publishing house, Aufbau Verlag. With Walter Janke, head of Aufbau at the time, and other colleagues from university and journalism (all Socialist Unity Party [SED] members), Harich fashioned a platform for the introduction of a democratic and humane socialism to replace the official program that emerged from the Third SED Conference of 1956. The platform echoed

some of the demands of the rebellious workers of 1953 and represented the kinds of reform proposed from within other Eastern European ruling parties later that year and again in 1968.

After the events of fall 1956 in Poland and Hungary, the state security apparatus had the group arrested. Members were tried in two judicial processes in 1957; Harich and some of his associates were sentenced to ten years in prison for crimes against the state.

Upon his release, Harich resumed his academic career but without further inclination to oppositional activity. His one noteworthy public act was to publish his *Kommunismus ohne Wachstum* (Communism without growth) in 1975. The book was published in Hamburg, although the author, who considered himself a loyal follower of the regime, would have preferred its appearance in the GDR. This study attempted to combine an environmental argument with Marxian theory and to arouse concern in the GDR over the degradation of the environment. Such a viewpoint was less than welcome in the SED and the GDR government.

In his brief career as an active dissident and advocate of reform, Harich was a victim not only of a repressive regime but also of his own naïveté. He could not even get the reform program presented to the SED leadership, still less secure support for it.

Lyman H. Legters

See also German Democratic Republic; German Democratic Republic: Marxism-Leninism; German Democratic Republic: Opposition; Socialist Unity Party; Ulbricht, Walter

References

Fricke, Karl Wilhelm. *Opposition und Widerstand in der DDR.* Cologne: Verlag Wissenschaft und Politik, 1984.
Holmes, Leslie. "The Significance of Marxist Dissent to the Emergence of Postcommunism in the GDR." *The Road to Disillusion.* Ed. Raymond Taras. Armonk, NY: M.E. Sharpe, 1992.
Harich, Wolfgang. *Keine Schwierigkeiten mit der Wahrheit: Zur nationalkommunistischen Opposition 1956 in der DDR.* Berlin: Dietz, 1993.

Harnack, Adolf von (1851–1930)

The influential church historian Adolf von Harnack was born on May 7, 1851 at Dorpat in Livonia, where his father, Theodosius Harnack, was professor of speculative and practical theology. Harnack began his own teaching career at Leipzig in 1874, and in 1888, after periods at Giessen and Marburg, he was appointed to the University of Berlin, despite the opposition of the Lutheran Church, which objected to his liberal views. In books such as his three-volume *Dogmengeschichte* (published as *History of Dogma*), 1886–89, and the popular *Das Wesen des Christentums* (published as *What Is Christianity?*), 1900, Harnack argued that history demonstrates that dogma is the product of the effort of succeeding generations to express the inner nature of Christianity in the concepts and thought patterns of their particular age. Dogma is, as it were, the wrapping making the shape of the truth it contains visible to a certain era; dogma, he maintained, is not the truth itself. He opposed, therefore, the normative status the churches have given to the early Church's efforts to express the significance of mysteries such as the Trinity and the nature of Christ. He felt that insisting on outdated conceptualizations of the New Testament message created an unnecessary tension between dogmatic faith and modern thought and betrayed the tendency of the Reformation to strip belief to the essentials.

A capable administrator as well as a prolific author of works such as *Die Mission und Ausbreitung des Christentums in den ersten drei Jahrhunderten* (published as *The Mission and Expansion of Christianity during the First Three Centuries*), 1902, *Geschichte der altchristlichen Literatur* (History of ancient Christian literature), 1893–1904, and a three-volume history of the Prussian Academy of Science, Harnack, who was ignored by his church, turned his energies toward serving society and the state while continuing his academic labors. He was appointed director general of the Royal Library in 1906 and, in 1911, president of the Kaiser Wilhelm Society, an organization concerned with the establishment of research centers. He held the latter position until his death. Harnack, the last German scholar to be raised to the hereditary nobility, was often consulted by the Ministry of Education. He declined the offer of an ambassadorship to the United States in 1921.

Harnack lived long enough to see his emphasis on the horizontal, human, and historical dimensions of Christianity overridden by the transcendental emphasis on divine revelation in the thought of his former student, Karl Barth (1886–1968).

Kenneth C. Russell

See also Barth, Karl; History; Kaiser Wilhelm/Max Planck Societies and Their Institutes; Protestantism and the Protestant Church; Protestant Theology; Ritschl, Albrecht; Schweitzer, Albert

References

Glick, Garland Wayne. *The Reality of Christianity: A Study of Adolf von Harnack as Historian and Theologian.* New York, NY: Harper and Row, 1967.

Pauck, Wilhelm. "Adolf von Harnack." *A Handbook of Christian Theologians.* Ed. Dean G. Peerman and Martin E. Marty. Nashville, TN: Abington Press, 1984.

Rumscheidt, Martin, ed. *Adolf von Harnack: Liberal Theology at Its Height.* London: Collins, 1989.

Zahn-Harnack, Agnes von. *Adolf von Harnack.* Berlin: Walter de Gruyter, 1951.

Hasenclever, Walter (1890–1940)

A key figure in German literary expressionism, Walter Hasenclever (June 8, 1890–June 21, 1940) achieved equal success during the Weimar era in comedy. As an expressionist, his major significance rests on the dramas *Der Sohn* (The

son), 1914, and *Antigone* (1917). Of his later comedies, *Ein besserer Herr* (A better gentleman), 1926, is still performed on stage and television today.

Like many of his literary contemporaries, Hasenclever dedicated his early writing—almost all in poetry and drama—to themes of individual liberty, sexual emancipation, social justice, and, with the advent of war, pacifism. Several poems from *Städte, Nächte und Menschen* (Nights and people), 1910, *Der Jüngling* (The youth), 1913, and *Tod und Auferstehung* (Death and resurrection), 1917, appear in the famous expressionist anthology of Kurt Pinthus, *Mennschheitsdämmerung* (Dawn of humanity), 1920. But it was Hasenclever's provocative *Der Sohn*, with the yet-to-become-famous Ernst Deutsch playing the parricidal son, that became a quintessential document of expressionism for its radically charged generational conflict. World War I, in which Hasenclever served briefly as a volunteer soldier, provided the stimulus for his antiwar polemic *Antigone*, a reworking of Sophocles in expressionist terms. It brought Hasenclever the Kleist Prize (1917).

Hasenclever's plays in the immediate postwar years testify to a growing political disenchantment and flight into spiritualism and theosophical ruminations, centering chiefly on Emanuel Swedenborg. But a brief stint in Paris as correspondent for the liberal newspaper *8-Uhr Abendblatt* led to a major new direction in Hasenclever's career: satiric comedy. The rest of his oeuvre—apart from memoirs—consists of comedies lampooning social manners and conventions and, sometimes, the contemporary political scene. *Ein besserer Herr* (A better gentleman) satirizes the battle of the sexes; *Ehen werden im Himmel geschlossen* (Marriages are made in heaven), 1928, challenges the religious establishment; and *Napoleon greift ein* (Napoleon intervenes), 1929, mocks European politics, particularly those of the fascist Mussolini. Other comedies, including collaborations with Ernst Toller (1893–1939) and Kurt Tucholsky (1890–1935), had brief runs on the stage and remained, until 1990, largely unpublished. One late comedy, *Münchhausen,* 1963, may well be Hasenclever's crowning achievement in this genre, but its merits still await proper critical appreciation. The same applies to his last comedy, *Konflikt in Assyrien* (Conflict in Assyria), 1990, a devastating parody of the Biblical Esther directed against the Nazi regime. Though not Jewish, Hasenclever fled Germany early in the Nazi era and settled eventually in southern France. The imminent German occupation precipitated Hasenclever's suicide just hours before a train would have taken him to safety. Two autobiographical volumes, *Die Rechtlosen* (Those without justice), 1963, and *Irrtum und Leidenschaft* (Error and sorrow), 1969, survived.

The common denominator in Hasenclever's twofold achievement, as expressionist and writer of comedy, is his overriding concern for humane values in an equitable social order.

Alfred Hoelzel

See also Comedy; Drama; Expressionism (Literature); Imperial Germany: Literature; Poetry; Toller, Ernst; Tucholsky; Kurt; Weimar Germany: Literature; World War I

References

Hasenclever, Walter. *Gedichte, Dramen, Prosa.* Ed. Kurt Pinthus. Hamburg: Rowohlt, 1963.

———. *Sämtliche Werke.* Ed. Dieter Breuer and Bernd Witte. Mainz: Hase & Köhler, 1990.

Hoelzel, Alfred. *Walter Hasenclever's Humanitarianism.* Las Vegas, NV: Peter Lang, 1983.

Raggam, Miriam. *Walter Hasenclever: Leben und Werk.* Hildesheim: Gerstenberg, 1973.

Wilder, Ania. *Die Komödien Walter Hasenclevers.* Frankfurt am Main: Peter Lang, 1983.

Hassell, Christian August Ulrich von (1881–1944)

As ambassador to Italy (1932–38) Christian Hassell opposed the ties of the Anti-Comintern Pact (November 6, 1937) because of the damaging effect a German-Italian alliance would have on relations with Great Britain. Hitler rejected this advice and retired Hassell, who then became a conservative critic of many aspects of the Nazi regime and a participant in the plotting against Hitler, which resulted in his arrest and execution after the attempt to assassinate Hitler on July 20, 1944.

Hassell was by upbringing deeply Christian and conservative, reflecting his father's views. Very early he chose a career as a diplomat and was educated in law and languages. He entered the Foreign Office in 1909 and was appointed vice-consul in Genoa in 1911, the year he married Ilse von Tirpitz, daughter of the admiral. In 1914, as a captain in the reserve, he was severely wounded at the Battle of the Marne. After recovering he held administrative positions in Prussia. A fervent monarchist, an advocate of extensive war aims, and a proponent of giving Hindenburg and Ludendorff supreme power, he opposed reform of the three-class voting system in Prussia even in 1918. In defeat, he joined the German National People's Party (DNVP), advocated "young conservatism" in some journalistic articles, denounced the Treaty of Versailles, and was at best a *Vernunftrepublikaner* (reluctant republican) in the Weimar Republic because of his hostility to parliamentary democracy.

In 1919 he returned to the foreign service, first in Rome, then as consul general in Barcelona (1921), envoy in Copenhagen (1926) and Belgrade (1930), and ambassador in Rome (1932). Attracted to Nazism before 1933, he welcomed Hitler's assumption of power as well as the achievements of his first years. Yet Hassell objected to the formation of a bloc with Italy and Japan and deplored the Nazi attack on Christianity and conservative values, and the increasing displacement of his class by socially and culturally inferior upstarts. Explicit and incautious expressions of his views are in his diaries (the 1988 German version is much fuller than previous editions), but he also warned in lectures, essays, and books against departures in foreign policy from Bismarckian precedents and examples.

In 1940, his employment by the Mitteleuropäische Wirtschaftstage (Central European Economic Organizations) facilitated travels outside Germany, especially in Switzerland and the Balkans. In the last days of August 1939, he had tried with State Secretary Weizsäcker and Ambassador Henderson to prevent war; in 1940, he sought British contacts in order to arrange a peace acceptable to plotters of a change of regime in Germany. Conservative resisters wanted British acceptance of many of Germany's territorial acquisitions, such as Austria, the Sudetenland, and the Polish Corridor, while allowing an autonomous Czechoslovakia and Poland.

Hassell consulted with Beck, Goerdeler, and Popitz about the shape of the post-Hitler state, and these discussions widened to the Kreisau Circle and some representatives of the Social Democrats. The new regime would not have been democratic or parliamentary, and would initially have relied on military rule. Hassell would probably have been foreign minister. After the July 20, 1944 attempt on Hitler's life, Hassell awaited his arrest in Berlin. A two-day trial before the People's Court resulted in his conviction on September 8 and execution the same day.

Exemplary of a type of German conservative, Hassell was less important as a diplomat than as a determined opponent of Hitler and Nazism, and his diaries are an extraordinary witness to his thoughts, actions, and relations with a wide range of people in the Third Reich from 1938 to 1944.

Leonidas E. Hill

See also Beck, Ludwig; Conservatism, 1918–45; Diplomatic Corps and Diplomacy; German National People's Party; Goerdeler, Carl; Italian-German Relations; National Socialist Germany: Foreign Policy; Resistance; Versailles, Treaty of; Weizsäcker, Ernst von

References

Gärtringen, Friedrich Freiherr Hiller von, ed. *Die Hassell-Tagebücher 1938–1944: Ulrich von Hassell, Aufzeichnungen vom andern Deutschland.* Berlin: Siedler, 1988. English translation: *The von Hassell Diaries.* New York, NY: Doubleday, 1947.

Schöllgen, Gregor. *A Conservative against Hitler: Ulrich von Hassell: Diplomat in Imperial Germany, the Weimar Republic and the Third Reich, 1881–1944.* Trans. Louise Willmot. Oxford: Macmillan Academic and Professional Ltd., 1991.

Hauptmann, Gerhart (1862–1946)

Gerhart Hauptmann became the most famous and influential dramatist since Friedrich Schiller (1759–1805) and received the Nobel Prize for literature in 1912. He eventually saw 43 of his plays premiered and also published novels, autobiographical writings, and collections of poetry, but his historical importance stems primarily from his first plays, especially *Vor Sonnenaufgang* (published as *Before Daybreak*), 1889, *Das Friedensfest* (published as *The Coming of Peace*), 1890, *Einsame Menschen* (published as *Lonely Lives*), 1891, *Kollege Crampton* (published as *Colleague Crampton*), 1892, *Die Weber* (published as *The Weavers*), 1892, *Der Biberpelz* (published as *The Beaver Coat*), 1893, *Hanneles Himmelfahrt* (published as *Hannele,* 1894), 1894, *Florian Geyer,* 1896, *Fuhrmann Henschel* (Coachman Henschel), 1899, and *Michael Krämer,* 1900, which ushered in the naturalist theater in Germany and, together with the works of his many imitators, assured its dominance for over a decade.

By drawing their inspiration first from Émile Zola and subsequently from Bjørnstjerne Bjørnson, Henrik Ibsen, Leo Tolstoy, and Walt Whitman, the first German naturalists evoked criticism as *Ausländerei* (adulators of foreigners), which seemed substantiated by their loose association with the internationally thinking socialists. With the exception of Arno Holz, scarcely any of the early naturalists, however, could claim much literary merit. Then a German writer of unquestionable talent appeared in the person of Hauptmann, who after some haphazard studies and an unsuccessful attempt to become a sculptor had moved to Berlin and taken up with the "moderns" there.

Because of the strict censorship, the first naturalist plays could be performed only for the membership of the society supporting an alternative theater, Freie Bühne, but Hauptmann's most famous work, *Die Weber*, provoked a court trial in 1892, after which this and other naturalist works could be performed on public stages. Nonetheless, after the performance of this dramatization of the Silesian weavers' exploitation and revolt in 1844, Kaiser Wilhelm II gave up his box at the theater and later twice refused Hauptmann the coveted Schiller Prize. Even after the turn of the century and the gradual disappearance of naturalism, Hauptmann, although simultaneously writing plays in a variety of styles, continued to achieve success mainly through reliance on a strongly realistic depiction of characters and their social environment, for example in *Rose Bernd,* 1903, *Die Ratten* (published as *The Rats*), 1911, and *Vor Sonnenuntergang* (Before sunset), 1932.

Despite the kaiser's animosity, Hauptmann's fame grew steadily. In 1912, he was asked to write a work to celebrate the hundredth anniversary of Napoleon's defeat at Leipzig. The playwright responded with his only solely political work, *Festspiel in deutschen Reimen* (published as *Commemoration Masque*, 1917), 1913, which, because of its ironic treatment of patriotic values and heroes, evoked a scandal reminiscent of that surrounding *Die Weber*. Yet when World War I broke out the following year, Hauptmann, a critic of Wilhelminian officialdom and militarism, wrote enthusiastically patriotic poems. After the war, his renown reached such an extent that he was considered a possible candidate for the presidency of the Weimar Republic. But when Hitler came to power, Hauptmann, now over 70, subjected himself to much criticism by staying in Germany. His remarks and actions after 1933 often seemed ambiguous, but the Nazi regime often tried to suppress celebrations in his honor and performances of his plays. When his longtime friend Max Pinkus, a Jew, died in 1934, Hauptmann and his wife were the only gentiles to attend the funeral, which then inspired him to write *Die Finsternisse: Requiem* (Darkness: a requiem), 1947.

Hauptmann cannot be called a thinker. Although he left several diaries and personal papers, none of these, or the numerous essays he wrote, contain a systematic presentation of his aesthetic or political ideas. His poetic legacy includes many admirable (albeit not totally successful) works, for example, a long verse epic on Till Eulenspiegel, 1927, and a verse te-

tralogy on the house of Atreus, 1941–48. His early novella *Bahnwärter Thiel* (Flagman Thiel), 1887, is still read in German schools. But he will undoubtedly be remembered as the playwright who brought dramatic realism to its greatest breadth and height, for despite this century's movement away from realism, his plays have to this day not disappeared from the repertoires of German theaters.

Roy C. Cowen

See also Censorship; Drama; Imperial Germany: Literature; National Socialist Germany; Naturalism; Satire; Theater; Wilhelm II

References
Cowen, Roy C. *Hauptmann-Kommentar zum dramatischen Werk.* Munich: Winkler, 1980.
———. *Hauptmann-Kommentar zum nichtdramatischen Werk.* Munich: Winkler, 1981.
Erdmann, Gustav, ed. *Gerhart Hauptmann: Neue Akzente—neue Aspekte.* Berlin: Wolfgang Stapp, 1992.
Hauptmann, Gerhart. *Sämtliche Werke: Centenar-Ausgabe zum hundertsten Geburtstag des Dichters 15. November 1962.* Ed. Hans-Egon Hass, Martin Machatzke, and Wolfgang Bungies. 11 vols. Frankfurt am Main: Propyläen, 1962–74.
Hilscher, Klaus. *Gerhart Hauptmann: Leben und Werk.* Neuausgabe. Berlin (East): Verlag der Nation, 1987; Frankfurt am Main: Propyläen, 1988.
Hoefert, Sigfrid. *Internationale Bibliographie zum Werk Gerhart Hauptmanns.* 2 vols. Berlin: Schmidt, 1986–89.
Marshall, Alan. *The German Naturalists and Gerhart Hauptmann.* Frankfurt am Main: Lang, 1982.
Maurer, Warren R. *Gerhart Hauptmann.* Boston, MA: Twayne, 1982.
McInnes, Edward. *German Social Drama 1840–1900.* Stuttgart: Heinz, 1976.
Osborne, John. *The Naturalist Drama in Germany.* Manchester: Manchester University Press, 1971.
Reichart, Walter A. *Ein Leben für Gerhart Hauptmann: Aufsätze aus den Jahren 1929–1990.* Berlin: Schmidt, 1991.
Sprengel, Peter. *Gerhart Hauptmann: Epoche-Werk-Wirkung.* Munich: Beck, 1984.

Havemann, Robert (1910–82)

One of the few critics of the East German regime to become known by name outside the German Democratic Republic (GDR) as well as within, Robert Havemann remained until his death in 1982 a steadfast advocate of a more humane socialism. He was expelled from the Socialist Unity Party. Some observers in the West denounced him for being no friend of capitalism; but his criticism from within the ranks of committed socialists was of the kind most discomfiting to the rulers of the GDR.

As a student, Havemann became a member of the Communist Party of Germany (KPD) in 1932. During the Hitler regime, he continued his studies and graduated in chemistry advancing ecological arguments to accompany his advocacy of democratization. The final years of his life were devoted largely to the unofficial peace movement in the GDR. Since he could not publish in the GDR, Havemann had a number of works issued in West Germany, of which his autobiographical *Fragen Antworten Fragen* (Questions answer questions), 1970, is perhaps the best introduction to his mature convictions.

    Lyman H. Legters

See also Biermann, Wolf; German Democratic Republic; German Democratic Republic: Marxism-Leninism; German Democratic Republic: Opposition; German Democratic Republic: Technical Intelligentsia; Pacifism and the Peace Movement; Philosophy; Resistance; Socialist Unity Party

References

Allen, Bruce. *Germany East: Dissent and Opposition.* Montreal: Black Rose Books, 1991.

Fricke, Karl Wilhelm. *Opposition und Widerstand in der DDR.* Cologne: Verlag Wissenschaft und Politik, 1984.

Havemann, Robert. *An Alienated Man.* Trans. Derek Masters. London: Davis-Poynter, 1973.

———. *Die Stimme des Gewissens: Texte eines deutschen Antistalinisten.* Reinbek bei Hamburg: Rowohlt, 1990.

———. *Warum ich Stalinist war und Antistalinist wurde.* Berlin: Dietz, 1990.

Holmes, Leslie. "The Significance of Marxist Dissent to the Emergence of Postcommunism in the GDR." *The Road to Disillusion.* Ed. Raymond Taras. Armonk: M.E. Sharpe, 1992.

Health

Since the late nineteenth century, health issues have figured prominently in German public policy debates. Concepts of health and appropriate health care have often reflected anxieties about national strength. Policymakers and the public have been preoccupied with such matters as health insurance, birth rates, and sexually transmitted diseases. Successive political regimes have transformed health policy quite dramatically. Major turning points include the creation of the world's first national health-insurance system under Chancellor Otto von Bismarck in 1883, experiments in social hygiene during the Weimar Republic, the medically legitimated barbarism of the Third Reich, and the divergence of health-care strategies in the Federal Republic of Germany (FRG) and German Democratic Republic (GDR) after 1949.

    Measured by such standard indices as average life spans, rates of infant mortality, or death rates from infectious diseases, the general level of health has improved remarkably since 1871. For example, average life expectancy had risen from 37 years at birth in 1871–75 to over 70 years in both German states by the mid-1980s, while infant mortality declined from around 240 per 1,000 live births to under 10. Despite political discontinuity and some German peculiarities, German health indices and the provision of health care have paralleled those of other advanced industrial countries.

Robert Havemann. Courtesy of Inter Nationes, Bonn.

even as he pursued his activity in the Resistance. Late in 1943, after completing his *Habilitation* (university teaching qualification thesis) in chemistry, he was sentenced to death by the Nazi People's Court, but was freed by the advancing Soviet army before the sentence could be carried out. From 1950 to 1964, he headed the institute of physical chemistry at the Humboldt University in East Berlin and was also, until 1963, a member of the East German parliament (Volkskammer). It was in the latter role that he appeared before protesting workers in June 1953, seeking in vain to respond to their complaints against the regime.

    The 1956 disclosure of Stalin's crimes shook Havemann's confidence in the prevailing order within the Soviet Bloc, and he became increasingly critical of the government and ruling party in the GDR. His insistence that the state had usurped the control that belonged properly to the working class led directly to dismissal from his university chair and expulsion from the party. One year later he was deprived of his research post in the Academy of Sciences.

    Arguing from within the framework of Marxian categories, Havemann objected to the paternalism of the regime, displaying more faith in the political sense of the working populace than did some of his fellow critics. He was inspired by the example of Czechoslovakia in 1968 and deplored East German involvement in the Soviet-led invasion. Although he continued to insist on his loyalty to the GDR, Havemann was placed under house arrest in 1975. But he continued to write,

The contribution of the medical profession to such progress is debatable, however, since changes in health are shaped by a variety of factors. Not only the availability and quality of medical treatment affect health, but also nutrition, housing, environmental conditions, social habits, and government policies. Since many of these determinants are dependent on one's social position, the health of various social strata, such as industrial workers or farmers, has often been worse than that of the middle class. The long-term trend, however, has been toward greater equality of health standards.

The foundation for modern health policy was laid in Imperial Germany in response to industrialization, urbanization, and the rise of mass politics. Policies were advanced by the municipal sanitation movement, the Imperial government, and various middle-class social-hygiene associations. Public-health proponents justified their efforts in terms of national efficiency. A healthier population meant a more productive and militarily powerful Germany.

At the time of unification, the liberal German Association for Public Health urged municipal governments to create hygienic cities by introducing modern sewer and water systems, cleaning streets, building parks, and inspecting food. By the end of the century most major German cities had constructed state-of-the-art sanitary infrastructures, which did much to eliminate typhoid and cholera. In Hamburg, where the municipal government failed to upgrade the water and sewer systems, more than 8,600 people died from the cholera epidemic in 1892 while other German cities were spared.

The central government intervened increasingly in health affairs. In response to the major smallpox epidemic that followed the Franco-Prussian War, vaccination of children became compulsory throughout Germany in 1874 despite opposition. In 1876 the Imperial Health Office was instituted to collect medical statistics, supply vaccines, and coordinate measures against disease. But the most important legislation was the enactment of a national system of health insurance in 1883.

Bismarck proposed health insurance as part of a welfare program intended to woo laborers away from the Social Democratic Party (SPD). All industrial workers and most white-collar workers were covered. Employees and employers jointly financed and administered sickness funds. Contrary to Bismarck's hopes, Social Democratic workers were often elected to oversee these funds. Moreover, since the local insurance administrations negotiated fees, many doctors resented them and organized professional bodies to bargain for higher payment. Despite such conflicts, increasing numbers of insured Germans sought professional care for illness. Between 1884 and 1914, the number of those directly insured grew from about 4 million to 15 million, while hospitals and hospital beds more than doubled. The number of people hospitalized rose at three times the rate of the population.

As general health improved, specialized health groups proliferated. These were dedicated to strengthening the country by combating tuberculosis (TB), alcoholism, and sexually transmitted disease (STDs), or by fostering school-based and maternal hygiene. Some advocated eugenics and racial hygiene, and most deplored declining birth rates. Such middle-

class organizations, the medical counterparts to patriotic associations such as the Navy League, lobbied for government measures and engaged in mass propaganda. In the prewar period, this broad social-hygiene movement exercised a growing influence on health policy.

World War I gave a fillip to social hygiene. As casualties mounted, the army and government backed an aggressively pro-natalist policy that entailed campaigns against STDs and for maternal and child care. Sanitary precautions preserved Germany from major epidemics (apart from the flu pandemic of 1918). But because of the naval blockade and the demands of the war economy, nutrition deteriorated and the incidence of TB rose. Malnutrition of children became a central health-policy issue. Medical officials avowed that to win the war, the country should be mobilized in a battle for health.

These emphases on social hygiene, natalism, family policy, and mobilization for health were bequeathed to the Weimar Republic. German states and municipalities reorganized and expanded many of their health services. They set up clinics to treat TB, STDs, and pediatric diseases and to advise prospective married couples. Doctors, teachers, and officials joined in the Reich Council for Health Education, which promoted such major events as German Health Week and a giant hygiene exhibition in Düsseldorf in 1926. A broad consensus emerged that health policies were crucial to restoring and regenerating the population after the losses of the war, but in the polarized republic there were sharp differences over the means to achieve such goals. Whereas the left favored more equalitarian health care as part of a comprehensive welfare state, the increasingly militant right pressed for coercive eugenics policies. The left's program was undermined as health provision, including urban clinics and even health insurance, was cut drastically during the Great Depression.

In keeping with their notions of forging a militarily and industrially powerful Germany by breeding a healthy and fertile Nordic racial elite, the Nazis completely overhauled health services. They abolished the democratic administration of health insurance funds in 1934 by centralizing state and municipal health care. The more than 300,000 health workers were Nazified, and individual health became subordinated to the extremist nationalist goals of Nazism. As part of their organic vision, the Nazis initially endorsed natural healing and other alternative treatments, but retreated when confronted by professional opposition. The diversion of resources to armaments probably contributed to declining health for large sectors of the population, despite initiatives in physical fitness and preventive medicine. Infant deaths appear to have risen, as did industrial accidents. Most importantly, minorities and supposed degenerates, including Jews, Gypsies, homosexuals, the genetically handicapped, and the mentally ill, were labeled "cancers" or "parasites." Already in 1933, the regime passed legislation mandating the compulsory sterilization of the mentally ill and "social deviants." In 1939, Hitler launched the secret T4 "euthanasia" program, whereby the mentally ill and physically handicapped were legally murdered under medical supervision. Between 70,000 and 95,000 died before public pressure halted T4 in 1941. Nazi medical officials even tried to legitimate the ghettoization and destruction of Eastern European Jewry as essential measures for defending German public health against Jewish-borne infectious disease. The Holocaust was implemented with the complicity of numerous medical professionals. Perverted Nazi obsessions with national health and pseudo-scientific racial hygiene paved the way for an unprecedented descent into exterminatory policies.

After the defeat of Nazi Germany, health services were reconstructed in accordance with the policies of the occupying powers. Health policy in the Soviet zone diverged sharply from that in West Germany. Faced with a breakdown of health services and epidemics of STDs and TB in 1945, the Soviets established an entirely new system, which stressed public health as well as industrial and preventive medicine. Their state-controlled system was supposed to enhance economic productivity and demonstrate the superiority of socialism. Ambulatory health care was delivered in multispecialty polyclinics or smaller clinics in neighborhoods and industrial firms. The GDR, founded in 1949, inherited and adapted this Soviet-designed system.

The medical sector of the GDR grew rapidly. By the 1970s, the health system had over 400,000 employees, about 5 percent of the workforce. Whereas in 1950 the doctor/population ratio in the GDR was half that of the FRG, by the 1970s the GDR approached parity. The number of hospitals actually decreased because of centralization, but the number of hospital beds remained virtually constant after 1950. By 1988, over 90 percent of the population had access to health care at the workplace. About 10 percent of personal income was deducted for health insurance, although the state allocated only about 5 percent of its revenues for health care, far less than in Western industrial countries. Health professionals were poorly paid and little was spent on medical research.

Nonetheless, in some areas of health care, such as the reduction of infant mortality and elimination of infectious diseases such as TB, the GDR made remarkable strides. Workplace health and safety measures brought some benefits as well. Industrial accident rates halved between the 1950s and 1980s. But official claims of declines in work-related illness may well have been statistical illusions attributable to the periodic reclassification of diseases. A 1987 survey reported that 45 percent of all employees suffered from work-related disorders. The GDR's record in treating heart disease and cancer, the two leading causes of death, was far from impressive, with death rates far higher than in most Western industrial countries. The life expectancy of men and women in the GDR fell several years short of that of West Germans. To erase this health deficit, during the final years of the GDR the German Hygiene Museum in Dresden coordinated a campaign to convince East Germans to reduce alcohol and tobacco consumption and in general to adopt healthier lifestyles. With the sudden collapse of the regime in 1989, the health-care system entered a crisis as thousands of doctors and nurses departed for better-paid jobs in the west.

In contrast to the Soviets, the Western occupying powers lacked a coherent vision of health care. Consequently, there was greater continuity in their zones with earlier German health policies, including those of the Nazi regime (although racial legislation was rescinded). Physicians' organizations played a decisive role in restoring the health-care system. Private doctors secured a monopoly over ambulatory care, despite American reservations, and moved to restrict entry into the profession. In contrast to the GDR, health care was largely individual and curative whereas industrial medicine and public health were relegated to the margins. The nationwide system of health insurance was reconstituted, but doctors were successful in limiting the scope of bargaining by elected representatives of employees. Public-health policy was decentralized and largely left to the health ministries of the federal states.

As in other industrial nations, the medical industry in the FRG burgeoned after the war. As revealed by countless polls, individual health became a central value. Between 1950 and the early 1980s, the number of doctors increased from 63,000 for 50 million people to 143,000 for slightly more than 60 million, while the number of hospital beds grew from around 500,000 to about 700,000. The ratio of doctors and hospital beds to population soared far above the average for industrial lands. By the mid-1970s, more than 1.5 million people were employed in the health-care industry. Over 90 percent of the population was covered by health insurance, which was reformed in 1957 and 1970 to accord parity of benefits to wage and salaried workers. Some 12 percent of the average German's income was spent on insurance and other health-care expenditure. Insurance paid for a broad array of medical services, including periodic checkups, hospitalization, dentistry, medical tests, and drugs. A wide variety of medical treatments was available to the consumer, ranging from homeopathy and spa cures to CAT scans.

Some analysts have expressed concern about "overdoctoring." By the 1980s, the average West German consulted a doctor 12 times and used 11 prescriptions annually, far above European averages. More than 120,000 drugs were available on the market. Costs skyrocketed after the 1960s due to the payment system, the growth of high-tech medicine, the power of the pharmaceutical industry, and an aging population. Massive health budget deficits became standard.

After complex negotiations among the political parties and major interest groups, cost-control legislation was passed in 1977. But since underlying pressures were not addressed, costs continued to rise. Because of the unexpectedly high price of unification, new cost-control legislation was enacted in late 1992.

Whatever the deficiencies of the FRG's health-care system, it has unquestionably been effective by international standards. Life expectancy is among the highest and infant mortality among the lowest in the world. Death rates from heart disease are well below those of Britain, Austria, or the United States. As Germany reunified, recasting health services in the east, containing costs, and meeting the challenge of the AIDS epidemic loomed as key health-care issues.

Derek S. Linton

See also Bacteriology; Disease; Eugenics; Euthanasia; Food; Housing; Industrialization; Infants, Children, and Adolescents; Insanity; Medicine; Morality; Old Age; Parks, Public;

Poverty; Social Insurance; Social Reform; Suicide; Temperance Movements; Urbanization; Welfare State; Women's Occupations; Working Conditions

References

Berg, Manfred and Geoffrey Cocks, eds. *Medicine and Modernity: Public Health and Medical Care in Nineteenth- and Twentieth-Century Germany.* Cambridge: Cambridge University Press, 1997.

Evans, Richard J. *Death in Hamburg: Society and Politics in the Cholera Years 1830–1910.* London: Penguin Books, 1990.

Die Gesundheitspolitik der DDR in Wandel: Probleme und Neuansätze. Bonn: Friedrich Ebert Stiftung, 1989.

Labisch, Alfons and Florian Tennstedt. *Der Weg zum "Gesetz über die Vereinheitlichung des Gesundheitswesens" vom 3. Juli 1934: Entwicklungslinien und -momente des staatlichen und kommunalen Gesundheitswesen in Deutschland.* Düsseldorf: Schriftenreihe der Akademie für Öffentliche Gesundheitswesen in Düsseldorf, 1985.

Ladd, Brian. *Urban Planning and Civic Order in Germany, 1860–1914.* Cambridge, MA: Harvard University Press, 1990.

Light, Donald W. and Alexander Schuller, eds. *Political Values and Health Care: The German Experience.* Cambridge, MA: MIT Press, 1986.

Payer, Lynn. *Medicine and Culture: Varieties of Treatment in the United States, England, West Germany and France.* New York, NY: Penguin Books, 1988.

Proctor, Robert N. *Racial Hygiene: Medicine under the Nazis.* Cambridge, MA: Harvard University Press, 1988.

Spree, Reinhard. *Health and Social Class in Imperial Germany: A Social History of Mortality, Morbidity and Inequality.* Oxford: Berg Publishers Ltd., 1988.

Weindling, Paul. *Health, Race and German Politics between National Unification and Nazism 1870–1945.* Cambridge: Cambridge University Press, 1989.

Heartfield, John (1891–1968)

John Heartfield (born Helmut Herzfeld) is well known for his photomontage book jackets for Communist publications during the Weimar Republic and for his satirical photomontages attacking the Nazis in the *Arbeiter-Illustrierte-Zeitung* (*AIZ*; Workers' illustrated newspaper), 1930–38, a Comintern newspaper published in Berlin and Prague.

Heartfield studied at the School of Applied Arts in Munich (1913) and at the Arts and Crafts School in Berlin (1914), where he associated with artists from the Sturm and Aktion circles. Drafted into the infantry, he was sent to a military hospital after feigning mental disorder (1915). Anglicizing his name as an antiwar protest while active in Berlin dada, he provided the graphic design for the antiwar and revolutionary journals published by his brother Wieland Herzfelde (1896–1988; also born Herzfeld) and George Grosz (1893–1959) from 1917 to 1924.

After the friends joined the German Communist Party (KPD), in 1919, Heartfield designed outstanding placards and election posters for the KPD, created striking didactic book covers for Herzfelde's Malik Verlag (Malik publishing) and for Willi Münzenberg's (1889–1940) Neuer Deutscher Verlag (new German publishing), and collaborated on KPD publications, including *Der Knüppel* (The cudgel), 1923–27, *Arbeiter-Kalender* (Worker calendar), 1924–33, and *Die Rote Fahne* (The red flag), 1927–33. He produced stage designs for Max Reinhardt's (1873–1943) political cabaret, Erwin Piscator's (1893–1966) proletariat theater, and KPD party revues. A member of the Communist artist organizations Red Group (1924) and Association of Revolutionary Artists of Germany (1928–33), Heartfield had his photomontages featured in major German photographic exhibitions (1929, 1931), and an exposition of his work was held in Moscow, where he gave workshops to Soviet workers on the art of photomontage (1931–32). In Berlin (1930–33) and then in Prague (1933–38), he produced 237 political photomontages for *AIZ*, created by Münzenberg for a working-class audience. These photomontages, including brilliant series attacking Hitler as a tool of capitalism and another accusing the Nazis of burning the Reichstag, faithfully followed Moscow's ideological lines. With his citizenship revoked (1934) and the Nazi government demanding his extradition, Heartfield fled to London (1938), where he continued his anti-Nazi activities.

His return to the German Democratic Republic (GDR) was complicated by illness and by charges that his work was bourgeois formalism (1950). He designed stage settings and posters for Bertolt Brecht's (1898–1956) Berlin Ensemble and the German Theater in East Berlin (1950–60), became a member of the German Academy of Arts (1956), was an honored guest in China (1957), held exhibitions throughout Eastern Europe (1958–68), and received the highest honors from the GDR (1958–67).

Beth Irwin Lewis

See also Brecht, Bertolt; Cabaret; Dada; Expressionism (Visual Arts); German Communist Party; German Democratic Republic: Arts and Politics; Grosz, George; Herzfelde, Wieland; Münzenberg, Willi; Piscator, Erwin; Reinhardt, Max; Weimar Republic

References

Evans, David. *John Heartfield/AIZ: Arbeiter-Illustrierte Zeitung: Volks Illustrierte, 1930–38.* New York, NY: Kent Fine Art, Inc., 1992.

Farner, John, ed. *John Heartfield: Photomontagen zur Zeitgeschichte.* Zürich: Schriftenreihe der Vereinigung Volk und Kultur, 1945.

Heartfield, John and Kurt Tucholsky. *Deutschland, Deutschland über Alles.* Berlin: Neuer Deutscher Verlag, 1929. English translation by Anne Halley: Amherst, MA: University of Massachusetts Press, 1972.

Herzfelde, Wieland. *John Heartfield: Leben und Werk.* Dresden: VEB Verlag, 1962.

John Heartfield 1891–1968: Photomontages. Berlin: Deutsche Akademie der Künste; London: Arts Council of Great Britain, 1969.

John Heartfield-Krieg im Frieden: Fotomontagen zur Zeit 1930–1938. Munich: Carl Hansen Verlag, 1972. English translation by Eva Berghoffen: New York, NY: Universe, 1977.

Kahn, Douglas. *John Heartfield: Art and Mass Media*. New York, NY: Tanam, 1985.

Lewis, Beth Irwin. *Grosz/Heartfield: The Artist as Social Critic*. Minneapolis, MN: University Gallery (Holmes & Meier), 1980.

März, Roland, ed. *John Heartfield: Der Schnitt entlang der Zeit: Selbstzeugnisse, Erinnerungen, Interpretationen: Eine Dokumentation*. Dresden: VEB Verlag der Kunst, 1981.

Pachnicke, Peter and Klaus Honnef. *John Heartfield*. New York, NY: Harry N. Abrams, 1992. German edition: Cologne: DuMont Buchverlag, 1991.

Siepmann, Eckhard. *Montage: John Heartfield, vom Club Dada zur Arbeiter-Illustrierten Zeitung*. Berlin: Elefanten Press, 1977.

Töteberg, Michael. *John Heartfield in Selbstzeugnissen und Bilddokumenten*. Hamburg: Rowohlt, 1978.

Heckel, Erich (1883–1970)

A founding member of the German expressionist group *Brücke* (Bridge), Erich Heckel was born in Döbeln, Saxony, the son of a railroad construction engineer. He attended Gymnasium from 1877 to 1904 in Chemnitz, where, outside of school, the works of Nietzsche, Dostoyevsky, Strindberg, and Ibsen inspired his interest in literature. While enrolled at the *Technische Hochschule* (Technical Academy) in Dresden (1904–05), and then in Aschaffenburg, he sketched local landscapes. He was deeply moved by Grünewald's *Pieta*. His friendship with Ernst Ludwig Kirchner (1880–1938) led to the formation of the *Brücke* with Karl Schmidt-Rottluff (1884–1976) and Fritz Bleyl in 1905.

Like other expressionists, Heckel at first rejected naturalism and impressionism. His earliest painting experiments, around 1904 in Dresden, emphasized process and subjectivity through vigorous impasto and a light-filled palette. The nude female figure, such as in the color woodcut *Standing Child*, 1910, became a positive expression of the forces of nature and a challenge to bourgeois morals.

Heckel moved to Berlin in 1911. Works such as *Two Men at a Table*, 1912, inspired by his rereading of Dostoyevsky, signaled a major shift in content and style. The theme of conflict and deep psychological tension is created through spatial compression, elongated figures, and an autumnal palette. Heckel had his first one-person exhibition at Fritz Gurlitt's Berlin gallery in 1913, the same year he painted the famous *Convalescence*. A spiritual melancholy, inspired by Romantic and symbolist sources, replaced the effulgent sensuality of his earlier works. The attenuated figure and the elongated but strongly three-dimensional head indicate Heckel's internalization of the forms of African and medieval sculpture. These became sources for his own sculpture after 1910.

Images of wounded soldiers, sailors, medical orderlies, and unscarred landscapes refer to Heckel's experience as a Red Cross medical orderly (1915–18) in Belgium during World War I. Though he met the artist Max Beckmann (1884–1950), who also served in the medical corps, and the Belgian artist James Ensor in 1915, his interaction with artist-followers Max Kaus, Anton Kerschbaumer, and Otto Herbig as well as the George Circle–member Ernst Morwitz affirmed the personal nature of his work. In the extraordinary color woodcut, *Portrait of a Man*, 1919, Heckel finally recorded his contemplative reaction to the physical and psychological devastation wrought by the war in a deeply introspective self-portrait.

His roles as the poet-philosopher, business manager, and organizer of exhibitions for the *Brücke* made Heckel an important force within the group. His work between 1911 and 1919 as a figurative expressionist offers a strongly spiritualized view of human relationships.

Sara Gregg Skerker

See also Artists; Beckmann, Max; Expressionism (Visual Arts); Kirchner, Ernst; Painting; Schmidt-Rottluff, Karl

References

Dube, Annemarie and Wolf-Dieter Dube, eds. *Erich Heckel: Das graphische Werk*. New York, NY: Ernst Rathenau, 1964.

Felix, Zdenek, ed. *Erich Heckel 1883–1970*. Munich: Prestel-Verlag, 1983.

Gabler, Karlheinz. *Erich Heckel und sein Kreis: Dokumente-Fotos-Briefe-Schriften*. Stuttgart: Belser-Verlag, 1983.

———. *Erich Heckel: Zeichnungen Aquarelle*. Stuttgart: Belser-Verlag, 1983.

Heller, Reinhold. *Brücke: German Expressionist Prints from the Granvil and Marcia Specks Collection*. Evanston, IL: Northwestern University, Mary and Leigh Block Gallery, 1988.

Heidegger, Martin (1889–1976)

Martin Heidegger, author of *Sein und Zeit* (published as *Being and Time*), 1927, is arguably the most outstanding German philosopher of the twentieth century. Born in humble circumstances to Roman Catholic parents in Messkirch, southern Germany, he entered the Jesuit novitiate in 1909. After a brief period of war service, he turned to the study of philosophy, eventually assuming the chair at Marburg University (1923). He succeeded Edmund Husserl (1859–1938) at Freiburg University (1928), and held that chair for the rest of his life. As rector at Freiburg (1933–34), he encouraged the reform of the German universities on lines consistent with his own philosophy and those of Nazism. Although he became disillusioned with its leaders, he never renounced what he once called the "inner greatness and grandeur" of the National Socialist movement. Moreover, Heidegger's concern with the rootedness and the destiny of peoples is thought by some to have played into the hands of the Nazi ideology of blood, soil, and folk. According to his critics, Heidegger's relationship to Nazism raises serious questions about the essential connection between his philosophy and National Socialism.

Heidegger's most important work, *Being and Time*, ana-

Martin Heidegger. Courtesy of German Information Center, New York.

lyzes human existence, which introduces his most primary and enduring concern: the essence and meaning of being. The treatise examines a variety of themes, including dread and anxiety, fear of freedom, human finitude, and death, and is often interpreted as a work of modern existentialism. But Heidegger rejected the existentialist label and always insisted that his primary goal was to remind his readers of the primacy of being and to situate humanity in this broader context.

Heidegger's later work increasingly focused on the essence of technology, which Heidegger interpreted as the natural culmination of the underlying principle of Western metaphysics. Heidegger argued that the purpose of technology is to understand reality as purely objective, that is, to turn reality, humanity included, into an object of scientific analysis. But being, he argued, is not an object and therefore it requires a different means of expression—the goal of which was the primary task of philosophy. Here, Heidegger turned to early Greek classical thought and to the eminent German poets, such as Friedrich Hölderlin, who emphasized the notion of being and who tried to develop what Heidegger called a nonobjectifying thinking and being. In his last works, he anticipated the possibility of a post-technological era—one in which a rootless humanity would be saved from the threat of global objectification.

Heidegger's philosophy continues to have an enormous impact on developments in twentieth-century philosophy, theology, and literary theory.

Colin O'Connell

See also Arendt, Hannah; Husserl, Edmund; Jaspers, Karl; National Socialist Germany; National Socialist Germany: Art; Nietzsche, Friedrich; Philosophy; Third Reich: Propaganda and Culture; Universities

References

Farias, Victor. *Heidegger and Nazism.* Ed. Joseph Margolis and Tom Rockmore. Trans. Paul Burrell, with Dominic Di Bernardi. Philadelphia, PA: Temple University Press, 1989.

Gadamer, Hans Georg. *Heidegger Memorial Lectures.* Ed. Werner Marx. Trans. Steven W. Davis. Pittsburgh, PA: Duquesne University Press, 1982.

———. *Heidegger's Ways.* Albany, NY: State University of New York Press, 1994.

Heidegger, Martin. *Basic Questions of Philosophy: Selected Problems of Logic.* Bloomington, IN: Indiana University Press, 1994.

———. *Being and Time.* Trans. John Macquarrie and Edward Robinson. New York, NY: Harper and Row, 1962.

———. *The Question Concerning Technology and Other Essays.* Trans. William Lovitt. London: Harper and Row, 1977.

Ott, Hugo. *Martin Heidegger: A Political Life.* Trans. Allan Blunden. Hammersmith: Harper Collins Publishers; New York, NY: Basic Books, 1993.

Rockmore, Tom. *On Heidegger's Nazism.* Berkeley, CA: University of California Press, 1992.

Sluga, Hans. *Heidegger's Crisis: Philosophy and Politics in Nazi Germany.* Cambridge, MA: Harvard University Press, 1993.

Wolin, Richard, ed. *The Heidegger Controversy—A Critical Reader.* Cambridge, MA: MIT Press, 1993.

Heilmann, Ernst (1881–1940)

Ernst Heilmann, as chair of the Prussian Social Democratic (SPD) caucus, contributed significantly to the continuity of the SPD government in Prussia from 1919 to 1932. He also exemplified the resistance to Nazism by democratic socialists.

Born in Berlin in 1881, he studied law and statecraft but was not allowed to take his second state examination because of his political affiliation with the SPD. He decided to become a journalist. He began as parliamentary reporter, and then from 1909 to 1917 he edited the newspaper *Chemnitzer Volksstimme* with Gustav Noske (1868–1946). During that time, he wrote a history of the labor movement in Chemnitz and its region (*Geschichte der Arbeiterbewegung in Chemnitz und im Erzgebirge,* 1912).

During World War I, Heilmann became a chauvinistic defender of the German nation-state. He volunteered for service, was seriously wounded, and lost an eye. During the war and the Weimar Republic, Heilmann remained an influential and controversial advocate of the SPD's right wing in his roles as editor, publisher, and reporter for SPD newspapers and journals.

Heilmann's most important activity after 1919 centered on the SPD's Prussian parliamentary caucus. He proved to be a brilliant parliamentarian: a convincing speaker, capable tactician, and sharp-witted observer of political developments. He recognized the dangers emanating from the political right from the beginning of the Republic. He fought the right with strong polemics and especially with policies that aimed at the democratic stability of Prussia. Those policies depended decisively on the maintenance of the SPD-Center coalition under SPD leader Otto Braun (1875–1955). For many years, Heilmann worked successfully on behalf of this coalition.

As a leading Social Democrat and as a Jew, Heilmann was in peril after Hitler's seizure of power. His friends urged him to leave Germany but he refused. He did not want to live as an emigrant and as a private person, he explained. His martyrdom lasted seven years in various concentration camps before he was murdered in Buchenwald.

Susanne Miller

See also Braun, Otto; Noske, Gustav; Prussia; Resistance; Social Democratic Party; Weimar Republic

References

Lösche, Peter. "Ernst Heilmann—Sozialdemokratischer parlamentarischer Führer im Preussen der Weimarer Republik." *Geschichte in Wissenschaft und Unterricht* 33 (1982), 420–32.
Möller, Horst. "Ernst Heilmann: Ein Sozialdemokrat in der Weimarer Republik." *Jahrbuch des Instituts für deutsche Geschichte* 11 (1982), 261–94.

Heim, Georg (1865–1938)

Georg Heim, the "Farmers' Doctor," was a secondary-school teacher who started a new career in 1892 as advocate for Bavaria's distressed farmers. He was a skilled politician and agitator, was active in state and national legislatures, and earned the title of "uncrowned king" of Bavarian politics. His party, the Bavarian Center, had done little for farmers and was threatened by the formation of a new party, the Bavarian Farmers' League. Heim responded by founding the Bavarian Christian Farmers' Associations, which regained the rural districts for the Center and attained a membership of nearly 190,000.

In 1906, Heim led the fight in the state legislature for reapportionment and the direct vote. In order to obtain the necessary two-thirds majority, Heim and the Center's left wing allied with the Social Democrats. For this reason, after the reform passed, the party's conservative leadership branded him a radical and a demagogue and ousted him from his committee posts.

During World War I, Heim launched a protest against the Reich Nutrition Office, claiming, apparently rightly, that Bavarian farmers were being exploited in favor of Prussian consumers. Even though he opposed Kurt Eisner's (1867–1919) postwar revolution, Heim may have helped to make it possible by his role in alienating Bavarian farmers from state and national governments. At one point, he proposed Bavaria's separation from the Reich and its union with Austria in a Danubian republic. He and his colleague Sebastian Schlittenbauer founded the Bavarian People's Party (BVP) in a deliberate attempt to secede from the national Center Party because of its supposed antifederalist position. The BVP was structured to ensure the domination of the farmers' associations, but Heim sought no office for himself, preferring to operate behind the scenes from his home in Regensburg.

Heim's last and most fateful political success came in 1925 when he persuaded the BVP leadership to support Hindenburg for president; this seems to have been motivated solely by his resentment of the national Center Party. When, in 1932, Bavarian autonomy was genuinely threatened with destruction by the Papen regime, Heim's Bavarian League for Homeland and King briefly contemplated restoring the Wittelsbach dynasty. With this futile gesture, the career of this agrarian populist and intransigent states' righter terminated.

Ellen L. Evans

See also Agrarian Leagues; Agriculture; Bavaria; Bavarian People's Party; Catholicism, Political; Center Party; Food; Peasantry; Pressure and Special Interest Groups

References

Möckl, Karl. *Die Prinzregentenzeit: Gesellschaft und Politik während der Ära des Prinzregenten Luitpold in Bayern.* Munich: R. Oldenbourg, 1972.
Münch, Friedrich. "Die agitatorische Tätigkeit des Bauernführer Heim." *Bayern im Umbruch: Die Revolution von 1918, ihre Voraussetzungen, ihr Verlauf und ihre Folgen.* Ed. Karl Bösl. Munich: R. Oldenbourg, 1969.
Renner, Hermann. *George Heim: Der Bauerndoktor.* Munich: BLV Verlagsgesellschaft, 1960.
Schönhoven, Klaus. *Die Bayerische Volkspartei 1924–1932.* Düsseldorf: Droste, 1972.
Schwend, Karl. *Bayern zwischen Monarchie und Diktatur.* Munich: R. Pflaum, 1954.

Heimat (Homeland)

A key word in the historical development of German notions of collectivity and place, *Heimat* denotes at the simplest level the idea of home, and homeland in particular. Over the course of the nineteenth and twentieth centuries, the word became prominent in a number of movements—aesthetic, preservationist, environmental, and historicist—that sought to impart value and, quite often, national significance to the particular characteristics of different German regions and local places. *Heimat* has thus been at the center of a way of thinking about German identity as the amalgam of locality, region, and nation, and the foundation of a number of collective efforts to embody identity in concrete social, environmental, and aesthetic programs.

The word *Heimat* has ancient German roots, according to Jacob and Wilhelm Grimm, and has been identifiably present in various German dialects since the fifteenth century. But as late as the 1780s, the word appeared infrequently enough in public German as to be worthy of a Romantic effort to revive it and incorporate it into speech and writing. The appeal of the word then—and later—was its ability to evoke an immediate sense of "homey tranquillity and happiness" (Karl Phillip Moritz). *Heimat* gradually took its place among terms such as *Nation*, *Staat*, and *Volk* (people or race) as part of the modern imagining and construction of new forms of social cohesion at a time when older forms of social life, such as that of the genuine "German hometown," were disintegrating.

The nineteenth and early twentieth centuries saw a proliferation of efforts to organize groups and to create concepts around the notion of *Heimat*. They included literary efforts, the so-called *Heimatnovelle* (regional novel) and *Heimatgedichte* (regional poetry), which attempted to depict the authentic life of the German locality, the voice of folk custom and speech, and the presence of a familiar, if not always friendly, natural setting. They also included early environmental and preservationist groups, the myriad of organizations under the general rubric of *Heimatschutz* (protection), which were dedicated to efforts to reconcile modern civilization with the natural world. Finally, efforts included a varied collection of local and regional clubs to celebrate the history, folklife, and "natural monuments" of particular German places.

The German interest in *Heimat* has always reflected a longing for the familiar in the midst of a society that constantly presented people with the new and unfamiliar. *Heimat* activities expressed the need to "feel at home" in Germany. This quality accounts for the slightly contrived nature of much German *Heimat* activism. It also accounts for the longevity of its appeal to Germans, who have continued to participate in *Heimat* organizations, purchase *Heimat* publications, and attend *Heimat* films throughout the upheavals and discontinuities of the twentieth century.

Just as capable of reflecting a suspicion, even hatred, of outsiders as of evoking "homey tranquillity and happiness," *Heimat* served the Nazi regime through many of the organizations and publications that had existed since the late nineteenth century. They took on a more explicitly nationalistic and racialist character than they had had before and became parts of the drive to centralized administration that affected many other aspects of institutional and public life in Germany. *Heimat* activism became subsumed after 1934 under a new Reichsbund Volkstum und Heimat (Reich Federation for Race and Homeland). But "homeyness" was never a controlling metaphor for the Nazi conception of the German nation.

Heimat's representation of the nation as the large home in which everyone's unique little homes find a place has had a diffuse and differentiated impact on the development of German national identity, difficult to pin down to any single pervasive and persistent era or organization.

Celia Applegate

See also Customs; Ecology; National Identity; Nationalism; *Völkisch* Ideology

References

Applegate, Celia. *A Nation of Provincials: The German Idea of Heimat.* Berkeley, CA: University of California Press, 1990.

Bausinger, Hermann and Konrad Köstlin, eds. *Heimat und Identität: Probleme regionaler Kultur.* Neumünster: Wachholtz, 1980.

Cremer, Will and Ansgar Klein, eds. *Heimat, Analysen, Themen, Perspecktiven.* Bieleteld: Westfalen Verlag, 1990.

Greverus, Ina-Maria. *Auf der Suche nach Heimat.* Munich: C.H. Beck, 1979.

———. *Der territoriale Mensch: Ein literaturanthropologischer Versuch zum Heimatphänomen.* Frankfurt am Main: Athenäum, 1972.

Heimat: Analysen, Themen, Perspektiven. Vol. 294. Bonn: Bundeszentrale für politische Bildung, 1990.

Lipp, Wolfgang. "Heimatbewegung, Regionalismus: Pfade aus der Moderne?" *Kölner Zeitschrift für Soziologie und Sozialpsychologie.* Sonderheft 27. Opladen: Westdeutscher Verlag, 1986.

Rollins, William H. "Aesthetic Environmentalism: The *Heimatschutz* Movement in Germany, 1904–1918." Ann Arbor, MI: University Microfilms, 1994.

Hein, Christoph (1944–)

Christoph Hein is an East German writer known for his novels, plays, short stories, and essays. In these, he critically confronted the effects of Stalinism on the German Democratic Republic (GDR). Many of his works could be published only after long arguments with the authorities. In 1987, he gave a much-acclaimed speech in which he openly condemned censorship and insisted on the right to self-expression. Throughout the "peaceful revolution" in the GDR in 1989, Hein played his part in helping to overcome Stalinist structures and supported attempts to establish a truly democratic socialism in East Germany.

Born in 1944, Hein grew up near Leipzig as the son of a parson. As a consequence of the anti-Christian character of GDR socialism, Hein was subjected at an early age to discrimination; he was more or less forced to attend school in West Berlin and was not allowed to study the subjects he wanted at university in Leipzig. These experiences shaped him as a writer. The mechanisms of discrimination, and their psychological effects, are a central theme in Hein's works. In his novella *Der fremde Freund* (published as *The Distant Lover*), 1982, Hein describes anti-Christian discrimination in the early years of the GDR. The novel *Horns Ende* (Horn's end), 1985, focuses on the historian Horn, who is ejected from the GDR's Socialist Unity Party because of his nonconformist views and banished to a small Saxon town. Here, when charged with writing an antisocialist essay, he hangs himself. In the novel *Der Tangospieler* (published as *The Tango Player*), 1989, lecturer Dallow is sent to prison for playing the piano in a student cabaret that mildly satirized GDR leader Walter Ulbricht (1893–1973).

Horn and Dallow pose no threat to the state and are victims of a neurotically self-protective political system. Hein examines the conformity forced on the individual by such a system. This is the central theme in *Der fremde Freund*, where Claudia lives a life of self-repression; in *Der Tangospieler*, Dallow, on his release from prison, is unable to relish his freedom because he has always lived according to instructions.

For Hein, GDR socialism was a betrayal of original socialist ideals. In his dramas, Hein explores the theme of the failed revolution. In *Cromwell,* 1980, Cromwell starts out as a revolutionary only to turn into a tyrant. In *Lassalle,* 1980, the former revolutionary Lassalle retreats into a life of lazy self-indulgence. And in *Die Wahre Geschichte des Ah Q* (The true story of Ah Q), 1983, the longed-for revolution does not bring any change in the political situation. These dramas reflect a historical continuity in the discrepancy between humanistic ideals and their realization.

Hein's most recent drama, *Die Ritter der Tafelrunde* (The knights of the round table), 1989, was performed to great acclaim during the "peaceful revolution" of 1989 in the GDR. It depicts the quarrels of aging knights as to the hopes of ever finding the Holy Grail, and was interpreted as reflecting the senility and moral bankruptcy of the socialist leadership of the GDR.

In September 1990, Hein stressed that *Die Ritter der Tafelrunde* could equally well reflect the failure of capitalism to answer human needs. Hein has never been well-disposed toward the capitalist system, which he has always seen as an *Ellbogengesellschaft* (elbowing society) with structures as repressive as those in the GDR. Since German reunification, he has often criticized capitalism. In his novel *Das Napoleonspiel* (The Napoleon game), 1993, Hein concentrates on the destructive effects of a system encouraging material gain.

Once a critic of real-existing socialism, Hein has now become a critic of, to use his own terminology, "real-existing" capitalism. He remains committed to the hope that socialism might reemerge in the future in a more humane form.

Bill Niven

See also Censorship; Drama; German Democratic Republic; German Democratic Republic: Arts and Politics; German Democratic Republic: Literature and Literary Life; German Democratic Republic: Marxism-Leninism; Novel; Satire; Socialist Unity Party

References

Arnold, Heinz Ludwig, ed. *Christoph Hein.* Munich: Text + Kritik, 1991.

Baier, Lothar, ed. *Christoph Hein: Texte, Daten, Bilder.* Frankfurt am Main: Luchterhand, 1990.

Fischer, Bernd. *Christoph Hein: Drama und Prosa im letzten Jahrzehnt der DDR.* Heidelberg: Carl Winter, 1990.

Hammer, Klaus, ed. *Chronist ohne Botschaft: Christoph Hein, ein Arbeitsbuch.* Berlin: Aufbau, 1992.

Roberts, David. "Surface and Depth: Christoph Hein's *Drachenblut.*" *The German Quarterly* 63 (1990) 478–89.

Heinemann, Gustav (1899–1976)

Gustav Heinemann, Christian Democratic (CDU) minister of the interior in the first Adenauer cabinet, Social Democratic (SPD) minister of justice (1966–69) during the Grand Coalition, and president of the Federal Republic of Germany (FRG) from 1969 to 1974, saw himself primarily as a democrat with a Christian orientation who, during his terms of office, exemplified his commitment to civic responsibilities. Democracy and pragmatic Protestantism were his guiding principles throughout his life. Already during his preparation for the bar (1918–23) he was politically active as a member of a democratic student group. After his graduation with a doctorate in law he worked first as a lawyer and subsequently as a legal advisor in industry. His experience as a member of the Confessing Church, which opposed the Third Reich, left an imprint for life. At the same time he was, however, professionally implicated in the armaments industry, being a member of the Board of Directors of the Rheinische Stahlwerke in Essen. After 1946 he was lord mayor of Essen, and in 1949, Adenauer appointed him to his cabinet as one of the co-founders of the CDU and its most prominent representative of Protestantism.

Heinemann's rupture with Adenauer's politics, his resignation from the cabinet (1950), and his withdrawal from the CDU (1952) underlined his protest against German rearmament and the one-sided integration into the West that cemented, in his view, the division of Germany. On the other hand, his rejection of Adenauer's policies was related to his experience with the church struggle during the Third Reich. Heinemann, who in 1949 signed the Stuttgart Declaration of Guilt by the German Protestant Church and who chaired the All-German Synod from 1949 to 1955, was convinced that the church must preserve a free hand vis-à-vis the state and that it must avoid endorsing the position that pitted "the

Gustav Heinemann. Courtesy of Inter Nationes, Bonn.

Christian Occident against anti-Christian Communism." In his settlement of accounts with Adenauer's German policy, Heinemann stressed in 1958 that Christ "did not die against Karl Marx, but for all of us."

Actually, this position also explains Heinemann's defection to the SPD in 1957 after the failure of the Gesamtdeutsche Volkspartei (United German People's Party), which he had co-founded in 1953. Heinemann, who sympathized with the 1947 Ahlener Program of the CDU and its Christian-social planks, found similar positions in SPD policies during the late 1950s. Even though he was a member of the party executive after 1958, he seldom espoused prevailing trends in the SPD. In 1961, for example, he refused to be a member of an SPD government as long as the Social Democrats did not clearly reject the nuclear armament of the Bundeswehr. Similarly, as a member of the Grand Coalition in 1968, he sought dialogue with the extra-parliamentary opposition (APO). As president of the FRG he did not avoid controversial discussion of the Nazi past, and he contributed significantly to the restoration of the FRG's moral reputation in the world.

Bernd Stöver

See also Adenauer, Konrad; Brandt, Willy; Christian Democratic Union; Cold War and Germany; Confessing Church; Detente and Germany; Federal Republic of Germany; Grand Coalition; *Ostpolitik*; Presidency; Protestantism and the Protestant Church; Rearmament; Social Democratic Party, 1919–90; Soviet-German Relations

References

Heinemann, Gustav. *Reden und Schriften.* 3 vols. Frankfurt am Main: Suhrkamp, 1975–77.
Jasper, Gotthard. "Gustav Heinemann." *Persönlichkeiten und Politik in der Bundesrepublik Deutschland: Porträts.* Vol. 1. Ed. Walther L. Bernecker and Volker Dotterweich. Göttingen: Vandenhoeck & Ruprecht, 1982.
Lindemann, Helmut. *Gustav Heinemann: Ein Leben für die Demokratie.* Munich: Kösel, 1978.
Stern, Carola. *Zwei Christen in der Politik: Gustav Heinemann, Helmut Gollwitzer.* Munich: Kaiser, 1979.
Vinke, Hermann. *Gustav Heinemann.* Hamburg: Dressler, 1979.
Zitelmann, Rainer. *Adenauers Gegner: Streit für die Einheit.* Erlangen: D. Straube, 1991.

Heinkel, Ernst (1888–1958)

Ernst Heinkel was an aircraft designer who initially used rather conservative technology. After daringly establishing his own company, however, he introduced a series of spectacular innovations ranging from a catapult launch for planes to the first jet and rocket aircraft. His success as an industrialist was also based on pioneering mass production of numerous types of planes.

Born January 24, 1888 at Grunbach, a small village near Stuttgart in the valley of the Rems, Heinkel studied mechani-

cal engineering at the technical college at Stuttgart. After recovering from a severe crash with his own experimental airplane, he left university in 1911 to become an industrial aircraft designer. Following two other jobs, he became in 1914 chief designer of the Brandenburgische Flugzeugwerke (Brandenburg Aircraft Works) in Briest. A promising start at constructing racing airplanes was cut short by the outbreak of World War I. The company, which had meanwhile been taken over by the Italo-Austrian industrialist Castiglioni, became one of the major manufacturers of military aircraft for Germany and Austria. Heinkel designed planes of all varieties and sizes, for marine as well as land use. About 30 types went into mass production.

In 1922, Heinkel established his own company at Warnemünde, near Rostock. After pioneering several developments in civilian and military aircraft, such as designs for launching mail planes from ships and floating platforms for use especially on the South Atlantic routes, the company expanded into international operations. Following the new emphasis on civilian and military aeronautics introduced during the Nazi era by Hermann Göring's (1893–1946) Ministry of Aviation, the company continued to grow during the mid-1930s. At the same time, Heinkel began to specialize in the development of new technologies. A series of tests in cooperation with the Army Ordnance Office's rocket group at Kummersdorf laid the ground for Heinkel's subsequent development of the world's first experimental rocket and jet planes, successfully flown in 1939.

The prolonged war markedly slowed down development work in favor of efforts to mass-produce airworthy operational craft. In 1941 Heinkel acquired the Hirth Motoren company in Stuttgart and thus became able to produce his own aircraft engines. Subsequently, his various enterprises were merged, in 1943, into the Ernst Heinkel AG with main centers at Rostock, Berlin, Vienna, and Stuttgart. In 1944 more than 50,000 people, including foreign slave laborers, worked in as many as 34 plants dispersed throughout the Reich and the occupied territories.

Most of this industrial empire, including the main facilities at Rostock, Berlin, and Vienna, was lost in 1945. The Stuttgart plant was placed under trusteeship—the usual Allied procedure—and was restituted to Heinkel in 1950. Except for some foreign contracts, aeronautical work was not yet possible in occupied Germany. The company, now based at a traditional motor factory, switched temporarily to light motor vechicles. But by 1955, aircraft production and development was resumed. The new Bundesluftwaffe (Federal Air Force) and other NATO forces became the primary customers. From the beginning, cooperation with foreign companies was an important asset.

Ernst Heinkel died on January 30, 1958 at Stuttgart. His company was later merged into Messerschmitt-Bölkow-Blohm and eventually became part of the Daimler conglomerate.

Wolfgang Kokott

See also Aeronautics; Air Force; Daimler-Benz AG; Göring, Hermann; Junkers, Hugo; Space; World War II

References

Boyne, Walter J. and D.S. Lopez. *The Jet Age.* Washington, DC: Smithsonian, 1979.

Heinkel, Ernst. *Stormy Life.* New York, NY: Dutton, 1956.

Schlaifer, Robert. *Development of Aircraft Engines.* Boston, MA: Harvard University Press, 1950.

Heisenberg, Werner Karl (1901–76)

Werner Heisenberg, one of the most celebrated physicists of the twentieth century, was a founder of quantum mechanics (1925), author of the "uncertainty principle" in atomic physics (1927), originator of the neutron-proton theory of the atomic nucleus (1932), and a major contributor to elementary-particle theory. He received the 1932 Nobel Prize for physics in 1933. Heisenberg remained in his homeland after Hitler's rise to power and eventually headed the main wartime research effort aimed at attaining controlled nuclear fission and an atomic bomb. Although much criticized abroad for his actions during the war, Heisenberg became a leading figure in the formulation and promotion of West German science policy.

Heisenberg was born in Würzburg, Germany, to an upper-middle-class academic family. The German defeat in World War I, a bloody uprising in Bavaria, and the romantic German youth movement were formative factors in his political outlook. During the 1920s he studied theoretical physics in Munich, and he received his doctorate in 1923. In 1925 he presented a breakthrough that, as further developed over the next two years, led to quantum mechanics, the new physics of the atom. Working with Niels Bohr and others in Copenhagen, in 1927 Heisenberg propounded his most famous contribution, the uncertainty or indeterminacy principle, one pillar of the "Copenhagen interpretation" of quantum mechanics that offered new and startling insights into the strange world of the atom. In the same year he was appointed professor of theoretical physics in Leipzig, at age 25 Germany's youngest full professor.

Hitler's rise to power and the imposition of Nazi rule caused Heisenberg great concern. Although never a party member, he continued to hold prominent academic positions and refused repeated appeals to emigrate. Increasing persecution of theoretical physicists, culminating in an attack on Heisenberg as a "white Jew" in 1937 (he was not Jewish), apparently reinforced his reasons for remaining and for eventually serving the regime during the war years. He seems to have convinced himself that he could best assist Germany and German physics in this way, while believing that the Nazi regime would fall by internal means.

During the formative years of the Federal Republic of Germany, Heisenberg argued in vain against a strongly federalist science policy, successfully opposed a nuclear-equipped German army, and instigated major efforts in German nuclear technology. To his death, he participated in the ongoing search for a unified field theory of elementary particles.

David C. Cassidy

See also Atom Bomb (German Development of); Hahn, Otto; Kaiser Wilhelm/Max Planck Societies and Their Institutes; Meitner, Lise; Physics; Science and National Socialism

References

Blum, Walter et al., eds. *Werner Heisenberg: Gesammelte Werke, Collected Works.* 9 vols. Berlin and Munich: Springer and Piper, 1984–92.

Cassidy, David C. *Uncertainty: The Life and Science of Werner Heisenberg.* New York, NY: W.H. Freeman, 1991.

Jammer, Marx. *The Conceptual Development of Quantum Mechanics.* New York, NY: McGraw-Hill, 1966.

Walker, Mark. *German National Socialism and the Quest for Nuclear Power: 1939–1949.* Cambridge: Cambridge University Press, 1989.

Helfferich, Karl (1872–1924)

One of Germany's most important bankers and influential politicians, Karl Helfferich came from a textile-producing family. He was born in Neustadt on July 22, 1872. He received a doctorate in Strassburg and established himself through economic-financial studies in Berlin. As a state official he directed the monetary system of Germany's colonies after 1901. By 1908, Helfferich was selected for the board of the Deutsche Bank. In 1910, he attained membership on the executive committee of the German central bank, the Reichsbank. This conservative banker left his "apolitical" post and became secretary of state of the treasury from January 1915 to May 1916. He served as secretary of state of the interior until mid-1917.

Beginning in 1915, Helfferich defended the policy of the Reichsbank's president, Havenstein. They financed Germany's war spending through deficits and domestic loans and refused to cover costs with taxes. Helfferich also accepted industry's high wartime profits. These policies led to massive inflation, which began about 1916 and continued into the postwar era. In practice, his economic neo-liberalism tended to favor industrial and especially agrarian interests.

As one of the Imperial elite that refused to acknowledge responsibility for its wartime action and escaped into myths, Helfferich joined the German National People's Party (DNVP) in 1919. As a member of the party executive he helped to foster its opposition to the Weimar Republic and to the policy of fulfilling terms of the Treaty of Versailles. He propagandized the "stab-in-the-back" legend as well as attacking Finance Minister Erzberger in a vulgar and personalized manner. The libel suit discredited both men, in addition to lowering political norms. Erzberger had to resign and was assassinated in 1921. When another advocate of "fulfillment," Walther Rathenau (1867–1922) was murdered in 1922, Helfferich was fingered with the phrase, "the enemy stands on the right."

In 1923, Helfferich developed a plan for a new currency based on goods, instead of on gold, although industry preferred a return to the gold standard. Helfferich's ideas were influential in the creation of the new currency, the rentenmark, which helped to end the hyperinflation. However, when proposed as head of the Reichsbank, he was passed over for Hjalmar Schacht (1877–1970). He died in a train accident while on a trip to Italy on April 23, 1924.

Dieter K. Buse

See also Banking; Currency; Deutsche Bank; Erzberger, Matthias; German National People's Party; Inflation and Hyperinflation; Rathenau, Walther; Schacht, Hjalmar; Stab-in-the-Back Legend; Versailles, Treaty of

References

Epstein, Klaus. *Matthias Erzberger and the Dilemma of German Democracy.* Princeton, NJ: Princeton University Press, 1959.

Feldman, Gerald D. *The Great Disorder: Politics, Economics and Society in the German Inflation, 1914–1924.* New York, NY: Oxford University Press, 1993.

Williamson, John G. *Karl Helfferich 1872–1924: Economist, Financier, Politician.* Princeton, NJ: Princeton University Press, 1971.

Helmholtz, Hermann von (1821–94)

The most prominent German scientist of his generation, Hermann von Helmholtz held chairs of physiology at the universities of Königsberg, Bonn, and Heidelberg. In 1871 he accepted the chair of physics at Berlin and in 1887, assumed the presidency of the newly founded Physikalische-Technische Reichsanstalt (imperial institute for physics and technology). His scientific creativity ranged awesomely wide.

A biological reductionist of the so-called 1847 School,

Hermann von Helmholtz. Courtesy of Inter Nationes, Bonn.

Helmholtz during the 1840s studied the chemistry and thermodynamics of muscle contraction and measured the velocity of the nerve impulse. In 1847, these interests culminated in his formulation of the principle of the conservation of energy, the most powerful generalization of nineteenth-century physics. Later he and his students introduced Maxwell's field theory of electromagnetism to the continent.

Helmholtz made his most significant contributions in sensory physiology, beginning with his invention of the ophthalmoscope in 1851. *Die Lehre von den Tonempfindungen* (Teachings on the sensation of tone), 1863, revolutionized physiological acoustics with the transformation theory of different tones, Helmholtz's theory of timbre and consonance, and his "place-theory" of cochlea function. His *Handbuch der Physiologischen Optik* (published as *Treatise on Physiological Optics*), 1856, 1860, and 1866, reformulated the theory of vision on the basis of Thomas Young's trichromatic theory of retinal color perception. Helmholtz's empiricist epistemology taught that the mind generates spatial perceptions out of the experiential data of sensation by a process of "unconscious inference." This controversial theory led him to attack Kant's teaching that the Euclidean axioms are necessarily true and to anticipate the possibility of non-Euclidean geometries.

R. Steven Turner

See also Hertz, Heinrich; Physics; Physiology

References

Cahan, David, ed. *Hermann von Helmholtz and the Foundations of Nineteenth-Century Science.* Berkeley, CA: University of California Press, 1994.

Hatfield, Gary. *The Natural and the Normative: Theories of Spatial Perception from Kant to Helmholtz.* Cambridge, MA: MIT Press, 1990.

Koenigsberger, Leo. *Hermann von Helmholtz.* Ed. and trans. Frances A. Welby. Oxford: Clarendon Press, 1906. Reprint New York: Dover, 1965.

Turner, R. Steven. *In the Eye's Mind: Vision and the Helmholtz-Hering Controversy.* Princeton, NJ: Princeton University Press, 1994.

Henkel AG

The chemical firm of Henkel AG, best known for the production of a variety of detergents and cleansers, was founded by the Hessian merchant Fritz Henkel (1848–1930). The son of a teacher, he had apprenticed in 1865 with Gebrüder Gessert, a chemical company in Elberfeld. In 1876 Henkel established his own firm in the city of Aachen; two years later, he moved the plant to Düsseldorf, which had more favorable transport facilities. In 1899 the firm constructed new production and administration buildings in the nearby suburb of Holthausen. In 1922 the company changed into two separate units, a manufacturing business (today's Henkel KGaA) and a selling organization (today's Henkel & Cie GmbH).

In 1913, the company established its first subsidiary outside of Germany. This venture had expanded to 15 European operations by 1939 in addition to the Düsseldorf parent plant. In 1993, the Henkel Group owned 200 consolidated companies in 55 different countries. The major business activities of Henkel in Europe are transacted in the European Community countries. Its most important overseas markets are located in the United States, Brazil, Mexico, and Japan. Today, over 60 percent of the group's sales are made in foreign countries.

The company's first product, Universal Detergent, was replaced after a short while by Henkel's Bleaching Soda (a powdered mixture of soda and water glass). In 1884, Henkel began to produce its own chemical raw materials: Rheinische Wasserglassfabrik of Herzogenrath was acquired and partly rebuilt at the Düsseldorf plant. In 1917, Henkel acquired Matthes & Weber, an important manufacturer of soda, that had been founded in Duisburg in 1838. In 1907, Henkel produced the world's first self-acting detergent, named Persil, made from two important components, perborate and silicate. Persil brought Henkel rapid growth and international credit and recognition.

In 1908, Henkel constructed its own soap factory for detergent production. After 1909, fatty acids, from which soap is made, were produced in the company's own fat-splitting plant. The crude glycerol ("sweet water") obtained from splitting operations was further processed in a glycerol factory built in 1910.

For more than 40 years, the company's sole purpose had been to produce washing and cleansing agents. When adhesives—used, among other uses, for sealing detergent packages—were scarce after World War I, Henkel started its own adhesives production in 1923. On the basis of new findings on the detergency of phosphates, the company developed in the late 1920s a variety of cleansers, degreasing agents, and disinfectants designed for industrial and food applications. After 1930, it began to manufacture household care products. In the late 1940s, Henkel initiated the production of textile and leather auxiliaries as well as cosmetics and personal-care products. The company has extensive research facilities in Germany and abroad.

In 1993, the number of employees in the Henkel Group reached a total of 40,480; about 16,745 work in the Federal Republic. Employees of the parent company in Düsseldorf-Holthausen receive their pension rights after ten years of service. Henkel has also operated systematic vocational training since 1925.

Wolfgang Bügel and Juergen C. Doerr

See also BASF; Chemistry, Scientific and Industrial; Inventions

References
Since 1969 the Henkel Company Archives in Düsseldorf-Holthausen has published a series of historical booklets (*Schriften des Werkarchivs*).

Henscheid, Eckhard (1941–)

This novelist, satirist, and social critic shows a distinct predilection for a manneristic, sometimes archaic, writing style in the tradition of Jean Paul or Georg Lichtenberg. He offers bizarre, yet mostly comical, plot lines, reminiscent of those of Franz Kafka. He lives and writes in Amberg and Frankfurt.

After studying literature and journalism, Eckhard Henscheid worked as a journalist in Regensburg, and in the mid-1960s joined *Pardon*, a popular satirical monthly in Frankfurt. In 1979 he co-founded *Titanic* (to date Germany's most popular satirical magazine) with writer/cartoonists Robert Gernhardt and F.W. Bernstein, collectively known as the "New Frankfurt School." With his debut novels, a trilogy depicting German small-town life in the 1970s *Trilogie des laufenden Schwachsinns* (Trilogy of everyday madness), 1973–78, Henscheid gained considerable publicity as a sharp-tongued and merciless critic and satirist—an epithet he largely rejects. Henscheid sees himself rather as a poetic realist; his fiction works justify this notion by their clearly definable historical settings in contemporary German everyday life.

Among the main themes of his works one finds uncannily exact observations of notorious *Zeitgeist* behavior and the satirization of linguistic abuse in an overcommercialized age (*Dummdeutsch—Ein Wörterbuch*), 1985–93, and its influence on the mental state of people of such an era. In this respect, his focus resembles most closely that of Karl Kraus (1874–1936) and Ödön von Horvath. Henscheid's unique and playful style cleverly blends jargon and ideas from the most heterogeneous areas, combining aesthetic theory (Adorno) with soccer (Beckenbauer), classical music (particularly opera) with excessive drinking, and Catholicism with card-playing.

Henscheid's main works include a collection of "Kafka stories" (*Rossmann, Rossmann*, 1982). In one of these stories Kafka attends the shooting of his country-doctor story by a group of highly dubious amateur filmers. In the novel *Dolce Madonna Bionda*, 1983, a mentally destabilized writer becomes fixated on finding an old girlfriend in a far-off Italian town. Other works include the "idyll" *Maria Schnee*, 1988, and a large number of shorter prose texts in a variety of genres (short stories, anecdotes, satires, and portraits, e.g., a farcical pseudo-biography of Chancellor Kohl). In his epic passages, Henscheid draws heavily on Dostoyevsky, the German romanticists, and Kafka, whose signature "off-style" he synthesizes with great mastery. In his shorter, bitingly satirical texts, Henscheid is comparable to Lichtenberg, after whom he titled a collection of satires, *Sudelblätter*, 1987. Many of his satires are pointedly directed ad hominem and have earned him several libel suits.

Although initially known mainly among younger and liberal-oriented readers, Henscheid has today become a mainstay in numerous important newspapers and magazines across the political spectrum. Henscheid must be considered one of the most productive, original, and stylistically interesting forces on the contemporary German literary scene.

Thomas Ringmayr

See also Federal Republic of Germany: Literature; Novel; Satire

References
"Eckhard Henscheid." *Text und Kritik* 107 (1990).
Ringmayr, Thomas G. "Humor und Ironie in der

"postmodernen" Literatur: Arno Schmidt, Eckhard Henscheid, Robert Gernhardt." Unpublished doctoral dissertation. University of Washington, Seattle, 1993.

Schardt, Michael M. *Über Eckhard Henscheid: Rezensionen (1973–1989)*. Paderborn: Igel-Verlag, 1990.

Henze, Hans Werner (1926–)

Hans Henze, one of the most important German theater composers of the postwar era, was born in Gütersloh in Westphalia. After military service he studied in Heidelberg with Wolfgang Fortner and in Darmstadt and Paris with Rene Leibowitz. In 1953, he turned his back on his native Germany and moved permanently to Italy. He taught in Cuba for one year (1969–70) and founded the Cantiere Internazionale in Tuscany in 1970, a workshop for young composers, and the Munich Biennale in 1988, which presents contemporary music theater. Henze enjoys a successful international career conducting his own works.

Henze is enormously prolific and has worked within many diverse styles, ranging from serialism to late romanticism to avant-garde techniques. His early to middle works, such as the ballet *Ondine*, 1956, or the operas *König Hirsch* (King stag), 1952–55, *The Prince of Homburg*, 1958, *Elegy for Young Lovers*, 1959–61, *Der junge Lord* (The young lord), 1964, and *The Bassarids*, 1965, reflect his practical dramaturgical experience gained in Constance and Wiesbaden in the early 1950s and are characteristic of his individual synthesis of serialism and neoclassicism, but with the emphasis on Italianate lyricism.

Henze adopted Marxism in the late 1960s and turned from conventional opera to music theater employing a more eclectic style; many of the compositions of this period display his commitment to socialist ideology, notably in his use of protest songs in his Sixth Symphony, 1969, or in his choice of subjects, such as the requiem for Che Guevara, *Das Floss der Medusa* (Medusa's raft), 1968. Later works, such as the opera *The English Cat*, 1983, or the Seventh Symphony, 1984, show no radical change in Henze's compositional development.

Gareth Cox

See also Composers; Opera; Theater

References

Geitel, Klaus. *Hans Werner Henze*. Berlin: Rembrandt, 1968.

Henze, Hans Werner. *Hans Werner Henze: Music and Politics: Collected Writings 1953–1981*. Translated by Peter Labanyi. Ithaca, NY: Cornell University Press, 1982.

Rexroth, Dieter, ed. *Der Komponist Hans Werner Henze*. Mainz: Schott, 1986.

Hermlin, Stephan (1915–97)

Born April 13, 1915 in Chemnitz, Saxony, Stephan Hermlin, one of the most prolific contemporary German poets and prose writers, grew up in Berlin, where he resumed living after having spent many years in foreign countries. Hermlin, who had read the Communist Manifesto as a 13-year-old, entered the German Communist Party at the age of 16. Through his life he remained a faithful, yet critical, advocate of socialism and Communism.

Politics predominate in Hermlin's poetry and political writings, such as his pamphlets for the Second World War and the "Mansfelder Oratorium"—a didactic oratorio that he wrote in memory of a war zone—as well as essays and speeches. Hermlin's poetry critically relates to the political and historical scene of his day. It manifests the author's strongly didactic purposes, his urge to address a large audience and affect them with his own critical views. In Hermlin's critical journalistic writings the reader detects a lively fusion of personal experience and the sociopolitical scene expressed in the author's sharply expressed appeal for triggering a higher level of political awareness or for change. His autobiographical work *Abendlicht* (Evening light), 1979, most openly witnesses the development of his own involvement with, and commitment to, Communist ideology and politics. The significance of Hermlin's journalistic and essayistic writings lies in his unblemished—yet at times polemical—style of expression. He openly states his aversion to fascism, to dogmatic political structure, and to a misunderstanding or underestimation of the importance of the role that politics plays for every human being. He thus evokes a historical and political consciousness in readers and challenges their views regarding the political scene.

Living in the former German Democratic Republic, Hermlin took a stand for the reunification of Germany and spoke for world peace. He wrote numerous poems that attest to his enthusiasm and underlying hope for a possible shift in people's attitudes. Not only did he include appeals to entire cities to wake up and take a stand and such topics as the concentration camps during the Hitler era, he also composed poems of devotion, personal and intimate testimonies of his own belief and conviction. His writings indeed reveal the different stages of political development in a critical light, from the point of view of a devoted socialist.

Sabine Cramer

See also German Democratic Republic: Literature and Literary Life; Poetry

References

Hermlin, Stephan. *Abendlicht*. Berlin: Klaus Wagenbach, 1979.

———. *Gesammelte Gedichte*. Munich: Hanser, 1979.

Rost, Maritta and Rosemarie Geist, eds. *Stephan Hermlin*. Vol. 1: *Bibliographie 2: Texte Materialien Bilder*. Leipzig: Reclam, 1985.

Hertling, Georg von (1843–1919)

Georg von Hertling, university professor and Center Party parliamentary delegate, is best remembered as the second-to-last chancellor of Imperial Germany. He came from a large and prominent Catholic family, but his career as a scholar of Thomist philosophy at the University of Bonn suffered because of his early willingness to promote and teach the dogma of papal infallibility. Such a position was unacceptable not only to Prussian authorities but also to many Catholic academics. Hertling entered Center Party politics during the *Kulturkampf,* and it was his success in this capacity that led to his promotion at Bonn and then in 1882 to a professorship at the University of Munich. He continued to serve in the Reichstag and became a member of the Bavarian Upper House, but he did not participate in the radical opposition tactics of the Bavarian Center Party.

Hertling raised the standards of Catholic scholarship. In 1876, he founded the Görres Society and served as its president until his death; the society published the *Historische Jahrbücher* (Historical yearbooks) and the *Staatslexikon* (a Catholic encyclopedia), both of which are still important publications for Catholic Germans today.

In 1909, when the Bavarian Center Party had adopted more conservative policies (partly owing to Hertling's influence), he consented to serve as its parliamentary leader. Three years later, he became head of the Bavarian ministry; this did not signal a change to parliamentary government in that *Land* (state), however, as he resigned his party membership and his seats in the provincial and national legislatures. Hertling arranged for the crowning of the Prince Regent as King Ludwig III, in gratitude for which service the king named him a count.

In 1917, when Bethmann Hollweg was forced from the imperial chancellorship, the Army High Command, eager to prevent parliamentary rule, suggested that the appointment of a conservative Catholic (such as Hertling) as chancellor might split the Center Party and neutralize the effects of Erzberger's Peace Resolution. Hertling refused the offer at first, but four months later accepted the post. As chancellor, Hertling proved incapable of altering the army's policies, and in October 1918 he resigned rather than preside over the parliamentarization of the government. He died four months later, heartbroken at Germany's defeat.

Hertling had begun his political career as a defiant member of the Catholic opposition, but in later years had sought entry for himself and his party into the imperial establishment. Ironically, his apparent success in reaching this goal merely signified the end of the empire.

Ellen L. Evans

See also Bavaria; Catholicism, Political; Center Party; Chancellor's Office; Erzberger, Matthias; Heim, Georg; *Kulturkampf,* Lieber, Ernst Maria; Vatican-German Relations; World War I

References

Bauer, Clemens. "Georg von Hertling als Sozialpolitiker und Sozialethiker." *Festschrift Nikolaus Grass.* Vol. 1. Ed. L. Carlen. Innsbruck: Wagner, 1974.

Becker, Winfried. *Georg von Hertling 1843–1919: Jugend und Selbstfindung: Zwischen Romantik und Kulturkampf.* Vol. 1 (to 1882). Mainz: Matthias Grünewald Verlag, 1981.

Deuerlein, Ernst, ed. *Briefwechsel Hertling-Lerchenfeld.* 2 vols. Boppard: H. Boldt Verlag, 1973.

———. *Deutsche Kanzler von Bismarck bis Hitler.* Munich: List Verlag, 1968.

Hertling, Georg von. *Erinnerungen aus meinen Leben.* 2 vols. (to 1899). Munich: J. Kosel, 1919–20.

Hertling, Karl Graf von. *Ein Jahr in der Reichskanzlei: Erinnerungen an die Kanzlerschaft meines Vaters.* Freiburg im Breisgau: Herder, 1919.

Morsey, Rudolf. "Georg Graf von Hertling." *Zeitgeschichte in Lebensbildern.* Vol. 1. Ed. Rudolf Morsey. Mainz: Matthias Grünewald Verlag, 1973.

Hertz, Heinrich Rudolf (1857–94)

Born in Hamburg as the eldest of five children, Heinrich Hertz is best known for theoretical and especially experimental work in electromagnetics.

On graduation from Gymnasium in 1875, Hertz went to Frankfurt for one year of practical experience preparatory to a career in engineering. He enrolled at the Dresden Technische Hochschule (technical academy), but left soon afterward to serve his year of mandatory military service (1876–77). Deciding that he preferred science to engineering, he studied mathematical and experimental physics for one year in Munich (1877–78).

Transferring to the University of Berlin in physics in 1878, Hertz quickly came to the attention of Hermann von Helmholtz (1821–94), who profoundly influenced the rest of Hertz's career. Through the Prussian Academy of Science in Berlin, Helmholtz proposed a prize problem, a decisive experiment reconciling Maxwell's theory with competing theories of electromagnetism, and suggested that Hertz take it for a thesis topic. Hertz concluded that the generator of electromagnetic energy (oscillator) that he needed might be feasible, but that the means for detection was not evident. This study initiated his decisive experiments in electromagnetics seven years later.

Hertz instead wisely chose a tractable thesis topic on inductive effects in charged rotating spheres, and in 1880 received his doctorate magna cum laude—a rare distinction at Berlin. For three years (1880–83), Hertz worked as demonstrator in the physical laboratory under Helmholtz. During this time, Hertz's research career blossomed. He published 16 papers on mechanics, instrumentation, friction, magnetics, meteorology, electricity, cathode rays, and electrical discharges in gases. In the two years spent at Kiel University as *Privatdozent* (assistant professor) from 1883 to 1885, Hertz was isolated from like-minded colleagues and lacked laboratory facilities, but he independently derived the equations of electromagnetics, the crucial second step toward successful electromagnetics experiments.

In 1885 Hertz moved as a professor to the Technical Institute at Karlsruhe, which had a well-equipped laboratory, a shop, and some staff. On July 31, 1886, Hertz married Elizabeth Doll, the daughter of a faculty colleague. He discovered electric waves, as predicted by Maxwell's equations formulated 22 years earlier, and in a step-by-step learning process, alternat-

*Heinrich Hertz.
Courtesy of German
Information Center,
New York.*

ing experimental with theoretical work, demonstrated detailed properties of these waves in the radio portion of the spectrum.

His work and his outlook were that of a pure scientist, but work by his successors reaped benefits that have included wireless telegraphy, radio and television broadcasting, radar, communications and information transfer, and home-entertainment electronics. A side effect observed in his experiments was traced to the action of ultraviolet light. Hertz had discovered the surface photoelectric effect, but had no way of understanding it. His keen observation and skill as an experimentalist show through in a paper that influenced the invention of the photocell, and that started a new line of investigation in physics that ultimately produced quantum physics.

Offers of professorships came from Berlin, Bonn, and Clark University in Massachusetts. Hertz moved to Bonn in 1889. Resuming his investigation of cathode rays started in Berlin, he demonstrated the passage of these rays through thin metal foil into the air. This experiment created another fruitful area of investigation for his successors.

In his final years, Hertz was physically unable to perform laboratory research. He developed a system of mechanics that traced natural phenomena to the laws of mechanics. His book *Mechanics*, and especially his introduction to that book, excited the attention of philosophers such as Mach and Wittgenstein. Hertz succumbed to a long illness a few months before his thirty-seventh birthday.

John H. Bryant

See also Electricity; Helmholtz, Hermann von; Physics

References

Bryant, John H. *Heinrich Hertz, the Beginnings of Microwaves: Discovery of Electromagnetic Waves.* Piscataway, NJ: The Institute of Electrical and Electronics Engineers, 1988.

Hertz, Gerhard. "Heinrich Hertz: Personal and Historical Background to His Discoveries." *Friedriciana* (University of Karlsruhe) 41 (1987), 3–37.

Hertz, Heinrich R. *Memoirs, Letters, Diaries.* 2nd ed. Ed. Mathilda and C. Susskind. San Francisco, CA: San Francisco Press, 1977.

———. *Miscellaneous Papers.* London: Macmillan, 1896.

———. *On the Principles of Mechanics Presented in a New Form.* Ed. Charles C. Gillispie. New York, NY: Dover Publications, 1956.

McCormmach, R. "Hertz, Heinrich Rudolph." *Dictionary of Scientific Biography.* Ed. Charles C. Gillispie. New York, NY: Scribners, 1972.

Herzfelde, Wieland (1896–1988)

Wieland Herzfelde (born Wieland Herzfeld) was a Communist writer who published radical and revolutionary literature from 1916 to 1947. With his brother John Heartfield (1891–1968) and his friend George Grosz (1893–1959), he engaged in antiwar activity in Berlin during World War I, participated in the Berlin dada group, and founded the Malik Verlag (1917–39), a publishing house that supported left-wing causes and sponsored writers from Central Europe, the Soviet Union, and the United States.

Sons of Franz Herzfeld (pseudonym Franz Held), Herzfelde and Heartfield entered Berlin expressionist circles in 1914. Herzfelde served in the army twice during the war. In Berlin, Herzfelde produced an anti-establishment expressionist journal, *Neue Jugend* (1916–17), and formed with Heartfield, Grosz, and Franz Jung the political wing of Berlin dada. An early member of the German Communist Party (KPD), he was arrested and detained in prison during the March 1919 uprising in Berlin, an experience recounted in *Schutzhaft* (Protective custody), 1919. He published Grosz's political portfolios (1917–30) and a series of radical satirical journals designed by Heartfield with Grosz's drawings: *Jedermann sein eigner Fussball* (Everyone his own football), 1919, *Die Pleite* (Bankruptcy), 1919–24, *Der Gegner* (The opponent), 1919–24, and *dada 3,* 1920. He also wrote critical analyses of the role of the artist, including *Gesellschaft: Künstler und Kommunismus* (Society, artist and communist), 1921, and, with Grosz, *Die Kunst ist in Gefahr* (published as *Art Is in Danger*), 1925. Herzfelde maintained the Malik Verlag as an independent Communist press whose list featured major Soviet and German novelists and political analysts, including the works of Upton Sinclair, Maxim Gorky, Ilja Ehrenburg, and Leo Tolstoy. Published in inexpensive formats, Malik books featured photomontage jackets designed by Heartfield.

Herzfelde fled to Prague in 1933, where he reestablished the Malik Verlag to publish works of exiled writers, such as

Bertolt Brecht, and a new literary journal, *Neue Deutsche Blätter* (New German papers). He participated in the First United Congress of Soviet Writers in Moscow (1934) and worked on projects with Willi Münzenberg. He fled to London (1938) and New York (1939), where he established the Aurora Verlag (1944–47), a cooperative press for exiled German writers. Herzfelde returned in 1949 to the German Democratic Republic (GDR), where he became a professor of modern literature at the University of Leipzig. He collaborated with Heartfield on stage designs for Brecht, executed book designs and reworked Heartfield's photomontages. Recipient of numerous awards in the GDR, he was active in the Academy of Arts and PEN.

Beth Irwin Lewis

See also Brecht, Bertolt; Cabaret; Dada; Expressionism (Visual Arts); German Communist Party; German Democratic Republic: Arts and Politics; Grosz, George; Heartfield, John; Münzenberg, Willi; Piscator, Erwin; Publishing and the Book Trade; Reinhardt, Max; Weimar Germany

References

Fraser, James and Steven Heller. *The Malik Verlag, 1916–1947: Berlin, Prague, New York.* New York, NY: Goethe House, 1984.

Hauberg, Jo, Giuseppe de Siati, and Thies Ziemke, eds. *Der Malik Verlag, 1916–1947: Chronik eines Verlages.* Kiel: Neuer Malik Verlag, 1986.

Hermann, Frank. "Barger, Gumperz, Herzfelde und die Entwicklungsjahre des Malik-Verlages." *Marginalien: Zeitschrift für Buchkunst und Bibliophile* 109 (1988), 43–52.

———. *Der Malik Verlag 1916–1947: Eine Bibliographie.* Kiel: Neuer Malik Verlag, 1989.

———. *Malik: Zur Geschichte eines Verlages: 1916–1947.* Düsseldorf: Droste Verlag, 1989.

Herzfelde, Wieland. *Immergrün: Merkwürdige Erlebnisse eines Waisenknaben.* Berlin: Aufbau Verlag, 1949.

———. *Unterwegs: Blätter aus fünfzig Jahren.* Berlin: Aufbau Verlag, 1961.

———. *Zur Sache geschrieben und gesprochen zwischen 18 und 80.* Berlin: Aufbau-Verlag, 1976.

Maier-Metz, Harald. *Expressionismus-Dada-Agitprop: Zur Entwicklung des Malik-Kreises in Berlin 1912–1924.* Frankfurt am Main: Peter Lang, 1984.

Herzog, Roman (1934–)

Roman Herzog was elected seventh president of the Federal Republic (and first president elected by the representatives of the reunited Germany) in May 1994. Herzog was born on April 5, 1934 in Landshut, Lower Bavaria. His father was Theo Herzog, who began his career in a snuff factory but advanced to become first an archivist, then a museum director. Born into a Lutheran family, Roman married the daughter of a Lutheran minister.

Herzog proved to be an exceptionally able student at Gymnasium and went on to study law at the university in Munich.

Here he first taught law. In 1965 he was appointed professor of constitutional law and politics at the Free University of Berlin. Four years later he took a similar position at the College of Administrative Sciences (a postgraduate institution for training lawyers for public service) in Speyer. During 1971–72 he served as the college's *Rektor* (chief administrative officer).

In 1973 Herzog entered politics. He had already joined the Christian Democratic Union (CDU) in 1970 and was chosen state representative in Bonn for the Rhineland-Palatinate government of Helmut Kohl. By 1978 he was persuaded by Hans Filbinger, minister-president of Baden-Württemberg at the time, to join his cabinet, first as minister of education and subsequently (1980–83) as interior minister. In the latter position he gained his reputation as a hardnosed conservative.

He joined the Federal Republic of Germany's (FRG) Constitutional Court in 1983 and chaired the First Court, which focuses on issues relating to fundamental rights. In 1987 he became chief justice of the court.

Richard von Weizsäcker's second and last term as FRG president ended in June 1994, and Herzog became the CDU/CSU candidate for the office when the first CDU nominee, Steffen Heitmann, aroused widespread opposition. Other candidates were Johannes Rau (1939–), minister-president of North Rhine–Westphalia and vice-chair of the SPD; Hildegard Hamm-Brücher (1912–), candidate of the FDP; and Jens Reich (1939–), prominent East German civil-rights activist, professor, and biochemist supported by a variety of left-of-center groups including the Greens and East German

Roman Herzog. Courtesy of German Information Center, New York.

citizen groups. Herzog won by a plurality on the third ballot. His election was greeted both within Germany and abroad by uncertainty, if not skepticism, about his ability to lend prestige to the office.

Juergen C. Doerr

See also Christian Democratic Union; Federal Republic of Germany: Constitutional System; Kohl, Helmut; Presidency; Weizsäcker, Richard von

References

Diekmann, Kai, Ulrich Reitz, and Wolfgang Stock. *Roman Herzog: Der neue Bundespräsident im Gespräch.* Bergisch-Gladbach: Bastei-Lübbe, 1994.

Filmer, W. and H. Schwan. *Roman Herzog: Die Biographie.* Munich: C. Bertelsmann, 1994.

Herzog, Roman. *Staat und Recht im Wandel: Einreden zur Verfassung und ihre Wirklichkeit.* Goldbach: Keip Verlag, 1994.

Reker, Stefan. *Roman Herzog.* Berlin: Edition q, 1994.

Herzog, Werner (1942–)

Since 1963, the self-taught filmmaker Werner Herzog (born Werner Stipetic) has been producing short films, documentaries, and feature films that—more directly than any other New German Cinema contributions—reflect a strong continuity with cinematic expressionism and its roots in the nineteenth-century German Romantic tradition. All his films portray individualistic protagonists who confront and challenge the limits of existence. Because they are extremists, not at home in the "normal" world, they generally lose or die, thereby framing his narratives with a metaphysical or mythological dimension.

Herzog's first feature-length film, *Signs of Life*, 1967, transposes a story by Romantic author Achim von Arnim to Greece during the German occupation in World War II. It portrays the hopeless and failed revolt of a German soldier who goes insane in the isolation and monotony of the arid, austere island he guards. Similarly, in Herzog's breakthrough film, *Aguirre, Wrath of God*, 1972, nature—here the Amazon jungle—defies the hero, the sixteenth-century conquistador Lope de Aguirre, who rebels against the Spanish Crown in order to seek the mythical El Dorado. The outsider as victim characterizes as well the critically acclaimed *Everyman for Himself and God against All, or The Enigma of Kaspar Hauser,* 1974, which relates the historical account of a legendary "wild child" raised without human contact in nature. This is a quintessential narrative about how authoritarian social structures deform human identity. It is the filmmaker's sacrally tinged allegory of the role of the alienated modern artist.

Herzog's fiction films, including his adaptations of *Nosferatu*, 1978, a remake of Friedrich Wilhelm Murnau's (1888–1931) expressionist masterpiece, and *Woyzeck*, 1978, based on Georg Büchner's (1813–37) drama, as well as his more recent productions of the 1980s, examine the power of irrational obsessions and fantastic visions. Equally important are the documentaries that Herzog has continued to produce throughout his career, the results of his fascination with everyday life. *Land of Silence and Darkness,* 1971, for example, also deals with outsiders, the blind and the deaf, who are not only victims of their handicaps but also heroes in the struggle to communicate.

Herzog has gained a singular position in the "New German Cinema" as the visionary who seeks and finds powerful images in exotic places and combines them with monumental music and extraordinary acting for his ethnography of the human soul.

Marc Silberman

See also Cinema; Fassbinder, Rainer Werner; Kluge, Alexander; Schlöndorff, Volker; Syberberg, Hans-Jürgen; Trotta, Margarethe von

References

Corrigan, Timothy. *The Films of Werner Herzog.* New York, NY: Methuen, 1986.

Herzog, Werner. *Drehbücher/Filmerzählungen.* Munich: Carl Hanser Verlag, 1977 *ff* (includes *Drehbücher I* and *Drehbücher II* as well as *Heart of Glass* under the imprint of Skellig; selectively translated by Alan Greenberg and Martje Herzog, Tanam Press, New York).

Peucker, Brigitte. "Werner Herzog: In Quest of the Sublime." *New German Filmmakers from Oberhausen through the 1970s.* Ed. Klaus Phillips. New York, NY: Ungar, 1984.

Pflaum, Hans Günther et al. *Werner Herzog.* Munich: Carl Hanser Verlag, 1979.

Hess, Rudolf (1894–1987)

Rudolf Hess was deputy führer of the Nazi Party, Hitler's private secretary, and Reich minister without portfolio (all posts 1933–41).

Born in Alexandria in Egypt on April 26, 1894, Hess went to Germany to attend school. Facing a career in business, he volunteered for the army at the outbreak of war (1914). He was wounded several times before transferring from the infantry to the air force. Immediately after the war he became involved in extreme nationalist politics by joining Munich's Thule Society and von Epp's *Freikorps* (volunteer troops). Hess joined the Nazi Party after hearing one of Hitler's speeches (June 1920).

While at Munich University, Hess became particularly interested in the geopolitical ideas of Karl Haushofer and in due course introduced him to Hitler. Hess participated in the Beer Hall *Putsch* and was imprisoned with Hitler (1924). During the sentence, Hitler dictated *Mein Kampf* (published as *My Struggle*) to Hess. The sections of the book dealing with *Lebensraum* (living space) ideology and the role of the British Empire in world history were influenced by Hess's ideas.

Hess was an almost religiously devoted member of Hitler's personal retinue. In recognition of his trustworthiness, Hitler appointed him replacement for Gregor Strasser (1892–1934) at the head of the party's Central Political Commission after Strasser's defection (December 1932). Following the Nazi seizure of power, Hess was appointed Hitler's private secretary and deputy führer of the Nazi Party (April 21, 1933). In theory, the latter post gave him authority over the *Gauleiter* (regional party bosses). When appointed Reich minister without portfolio (December 1933), Hess was guaranteed the right to assist any ministry in the production of any legislation. Subsequently he received the right to veto any statutes he chose (1935).

Hess's apparently extensive power, however, proved largely illusory. His office of deputy führer lacked a recognized administrative structure and the ministries generally refused to cooperate with him. By the late 1930s, Hess's office was primarily concerned with internal reorganization and the formulation of general personnel policies. Hess began to be eclipsed even by his own deputy, Martin Bormann (1900–).

Hess's bombshell came when he flew from Augsburg to the Duke of Hamilton's residence in Scotland in order to make peace overtures to the British government (May 10, 1941). The full story behind the flight is unclear to this day, but the British put Hess in prison, where he suffered a psychological breakdown. At Nuremberg he was imprisoned for life (1946).

Claims circulated periodically that the inmate of Spandau prison was not actually Hess and/or that his death in 1987 was not suicide but murder—perhaps even committed by the British government! Such sensational allegations, however, are of substantially less significance for historians than Hess's role in the development of Nazi ideology.

Martyn Housden

See also Bormann, Martin; Geopolitics; Hitler, Adolf; National Socialism; National Socialist Germany; Nazi War Crimes Trials and Investigations; Nuremberg Trials

References

Das Deutsche Führerlexikon 1934–35. Berlin: Otto Stollberg, 1934.

Fest, J. *The Face of the Third Reich.* London: Harmondsworth, 1972.

Hess, W.R. *Mord an Rudolf Hess?* Leoni am Strarnberger See: Druffel, 1990.

Padfield, P. *Hess: Flight for the Führer.* London: Weidenfeld and Nicolson, 1991.

Smelser, R. and R. Zitelmann, eds. *The Nazi Elite.* London: Macmillan, 1993.

Thomas, H. *A Tale of Two Murders.* Long Preston: Magna Print, 1990.

Wistrich, R. *Who's Who in Nazi Germany.* London: Weidenfeld and Nicolson, 1982.

Hesse

The state (*Land*) of Hesse was created through an ordinance of the United States Office of Military Government for Germany on September 19, 1945. It comprises the former Prussian province of Hesse-Nassau and the right bank of the Rhine territory of the former *Volksstaat* (citizens' state) Hesse; its capital is Wiesbaden.

In 1866, the Duchy of Nassau, the electorate of Hesse, and the Free Imperial City of Frankfurt were absorbed by Prussia and together formed the province of Hesse-Nassau, which after 1932 also included the principality of Waldeck. At the same time, the Grand Duchy of Hesse (or Hesse-Darmstadt) maintained its independence. After the Revolution of 1918, the Grand Duchy became a *Volksstaat,* which had a Social Democratic (SPD) president until 1933, even though the Nazis had become the strongest party in the *Landtag* (state legislature) in 1931.

After World War II, the SPD was the strongest party in Hesse from 1946 to 1974; at times, it had an absolute majority in the legislature. All Hessian premiers from the first state elections in 1946 to 1987 were members of the SPD; Hesse became a Social Democratic model state (the epithet "red Hesse" underlines this) at a time when the Federal Republic of Germany (FRG) was governed by the Christian Democratic Union (CDU). Several cultural and educational reforms triggered vehement discussions. The Great Hesse Plan (*Grosse Hessenplan*) of 1965 and later programs set the parameters for comprehensive measures and reforms to secure the future of the state. Hesse was the first state to see the formation of a "red/green coalition," i.e., a government consisting of the SPD and the Green Party; after its demise in 1987, a CDU–Free Democratic (FDP) government took office temporarily. Since 1991, the SPD and the Greens again have been governing together.

The territory of what is now Hesse had 1.87 million inhabitants in 1871, and has experienced a steady population growth, as the following figures show: 1911: 2.95 million; 1950: 4.32 million (including 720,000 expellees and refugees); and 1991: 5.7 million (10 percent foreigners). Owing to the rapid industrialization in the nineteenth century, the population of Hesse's cities increased exponentially from 1834 to 1910: Frankfurt am Main grew from 77,000 inhabitants to 480,000 (1987: 590,000); Wiesbaden from 26,000 to 173,000 (1987: 266,000); Kassel from 39,000 to 166,000 (1987: 185,000).

Heavy machinery and rolling-stock manufacturing, leather and textile production, and the electronic and the chemical industries led the industrial expansion after the middle of the nineteenth century. The Farbwerke Hoechst, founded in 1863, is known worldwide for its medicinal products as well as plastic and synthetic fibers. The largest industries in terms of the number of employees are the chemical industry, car manufacturing (with Opel in Rüsselsheim and a branch of Volkswagen in Baunatal), the electronics industry, and heavy machinery. The service sector, including commerce and traffic, has experienced far-above-average growth, employing 34 percent of the workforce in 1950 versus 60 percent in 1990. At the same time, the proportion of agricultural workers declined from 25 percent to 5 percent. Hesse, which consists of 40 percent wooded land and has more forests than any other state of the FRG, is also significant in terms of its tourism and viniculture.

The Rhine-Main area is the industrial heartland, and Frankfurt am Main, with its stock market, banks, and commerce, ranks among the world's leading financial centers. Hesse is one of the financially most vibrant states of the FRG. Its location in the geographical center of West Germany and of Europe has made it into an important trade hub and traffic junction. The prospects for the economic expansion of the northern region around Kassel, which had suffered economically because of its proximity to the border with the former German Democratic Republic, have been greatly enhanced by reunification. Culturally, Kassel enjoys world renown thanks to the *documenta*, a series of expositions of modern art that have been on display since 1955.

Walter Mühlhausen

See also Federalism

References

Franz, Eckhart. *Hessen: Eine politische Landeskunde.* Stuttgart: Kohlhammer, 1993.

Heidenreich, Bernd and Konrad Schacht, eds. *Hessen: Eine politische Landeskunde.* Stuttgart: Kohlhammer, 1993.

Heinemeyer, Walter, ed. *Das Werden Hessens.* Marburg: N.G. Elwert, 1986.

Mühlhausen, Walter. *". . . die Länder zu Pfeilern machen . . .": Hessens Weg in die Bundesrepublik Deutschland 1945– 1949.* Wiesbaden: Hessische Landeszentrale für politische Bildung, 1989.

———. *Hessen 1945–1950. Zur politischen Geschichte eines Landes in der Besatzungszeit.* Frankfurt am Main: Insel, 1985.

Hesse, Hermann (1877–1962)

The novelist and poet Hermann Hesse was strongly influenced by German Romanticism and Eastern philosophy. Since the heroes of his novels are often nonconformists who search for their identity outside of bourgeois society, his works became popular among North American youths during the free-spirited 1960s. Many considered the novel *Steppenwolf,* 1927, with its malcontent protagonist, Harry Haller, to be the finest literary depiction of the twentieth-century social misfit.

Hesse, the son of a missionary, grew up in a pietistic household. In 1892, he announced his refusal to follow in his father's footsteps by fleeing from the theological seminary in Maulbronn. From 1894 to 1904, Hesse tried a number of occupations; he worked in a machine shop, in book sales, and as a freelance writer for a number of magazines. Early in his career, Hesse wrote and published lyrical poetry, but it was his novels that established him as an internationally renowned author. His early prose works, *Peter Camenzind,* 1904, *Unterm Rad* (published as *The Prodigy*), 1906, and *Gertrud,* 1910, explore individual socialization and analyze the married life of the middle classes.

An individualist and pacifist, Hesse lived in Switzerland during World War I and campaigned against militaristic and nationalistic ideology. He moved to Montagnola in 1919 and acquired Swiss citizenship in 1923. Personal problems prompted his interest in psychoanalysis, preoccupation that is evident in the novel *Demian.* Hesse's involvement with East-

Hermann Hesse. Courtesy of German Embassy, Ottawa.

ern philosophy resulted in the novels *Klingsors letzter Sommer* (published as *Klingsor's Last Summer*), 1920, *Siddhartha,* 1922, and *Narziss und Goldmund* (Narcissus and Goldmund), 1930. In his later works, such as *Morgenlandfahrt* (published as *The Journey to the East*), 1932, and *Das Glasperlenspiel* (published as *Magister Ludi,* 1943), Hesse developed models of a utopian life of cosmic harmony, which combined Western mysticism and Jungian psychology with Far Eastern thought.

Hesse received many literary awards, including the prestigious Gottfried Keller Prize (1936), the Nobel Prize for literature (1946), and the highest honor awarded by the German book trade, the Friedenspreis des Deutschen Buchhandels (Peace Prize of the German Book Trade, 1955). In 1947, he accepted an honorary doctorate from the University of Bern. Hesse's works remain immensely popular and truly belong to the realm of premier world literature.

Diane Pitts

See also Imperial Germany: Literature; Novel; Pacifism and the Peace Movement; Weimar Germany: Literature

References

Field, George Wallis. *Hermann Hesse.* New York, NY: Twayne, 1970.

Hesse, Hermann. *Gesammelte Werke in zwölf Bänden.* Frankfurt am Main: Suhrkamp, 1970.

Hsia, Adrian, ed. *Hermann Hesse heute.* Bonn: Bouvier, 1980.

Koester, Rudolf. *Hermann Hesse.* Stuttgart: Metzler, 1975.

Michels, Volker, ed. *Hermann Hesse: Sein Leben in Bildern und Texten.* Frankfurt am Main: Suhrkamp, 1979.

Mileck, Joseph. *Hermann Hesse: Biography and Bibliography.* 2 vols. Berkeley, CA: University of California Press, 1977.

———. *Hermann Hesse: Life and Art.* Berkeley, CA: University of California Press, 1978.

Norton, Roger Cecil. *Hermann Hesse's Futuristic Idealism.* Bern: Lang, 1973.

Schneider, Christian Immo. *Hermann Hesse.* Munich: Beck, 1991.

Stelizig, Eugene L. *Hesse's Fictions of the Self: Autobiography and the Confessional Imagination.* Princeton, NJ: Princeton University Press, 1988.

Ziolkowski, Theodore. *Hermann Hesse.* New York, NY: Columbia University Press, 1966.

Heusinger, Adolf (1897–1982)

The first chief of staff (*Generalinspekteur*) of the Federal German Armed Forces (1957–61) and chairman of the NATO Military Committee (1961–64), Adolf Heusinger symbolized the troubled ethos of the Prussian-German general staff as it survived the union of soldiers and Nazis in the Third Reich and reemerged transformed in the Cold War. Heusinger was a leading maker of West German strategy from the late 1940s until the mid-1960s. His military life extended from the shell craters of Verdun to the explosion at Hitler's briefing hut at Rastenburg to the NATO Military Committee in Washington, DC.

Heusinger was born on August 4, 1897, into the family of a *Gymnasialdirektor* (high school principal) in Holzminden, Weser. After completing his wartime *Abitur* (senior matriculation), he joined a Thuringian regiment in 1915. Promoted the next year to lieutenant, he was seriously wounded at Verdun and again in Flanders in 1917. After a failed attempt to become a forestry official and to undertake university studies, Heusinger joined the newly formed Reichswehr in 1920. He fulfilled field-grade assignments for the next seven years until he successfully completed the sub rosa general staff training (1927–30).

As the Weimar Republic declined, Heusinger entered and remained in the Truppenamt (the clandestine General Staff) (1930–34) at the same time that secret rearmament began and Hitler ascended to the chancellorship. Heusinger was promoted to captain (1932) and received his first practical experience of strategic and operational planning under Colonel (later Field Marshal) Erich von Manstein, head of the operations section of the Truppenamt in the Reichswehr Ministry.

After three years of field service (1934–37), Heusinger returned as a major to the operations section of the General Staff in the Oberkommando des Heeres (OKH; Supreme Command of the Army) in 1937. He remained in this department without interruption until 1944. In August 1940, he became a colonel in control of the operations section of the General Staff in the OKH.

Heusinger helped to prepare Operation Barbarossa (1941), the war of annihilation against the Soviet Union. The course of the campaign against the Soviet Union brought Heusinger's repeated promotion (brigadier general, December 1942; major general, January 1943), but also Adolf Hitler's assumption of direct strategic and operational control of the eastern front. Although Heusinger knew of the plot against Hitler planned by officers, socialists, and other opponents of the Nazis in 1944, he had no direct role in the July 20 assassination attempt at Rastenburg. The Gestapo arrested him three days after the explosion and forbade his further military service for the remainder of the war.

Heusinger passed from Nazi house arrest to a United States prisoner-of-war camp (1945–48), where his captors compelled him to record his experiences. This activity brought him in contact with the United States Army Historical Section, where German and American officers initiated a kind of cautious strategic cooperation on a small scale. He remained in touch with this staff after his release in 1948. He wrote his memoirs, *Befehl im Widerstreit* (Command in dispute), an account of how the politically naïve or the mendacious among the General Staff became ensnared in the excesses and crimes of Nazism as well as losing control of strategy and operations to Adolf Hitler. At the end of the 1940s, General Reinhard Gehlen, the OKH expert on the Soviet Union, returned Heusinger to strategic planning as an advisor to the anti-Communist intelligence organization created under American sponsorship.

The Cold War brought Heusinger directly back to soldiering as a founder of the new German military establishment. As the Federal Republic of Germany (FRG) emerged in 1948–50, Heusinger, together with General Hans Speidel, provided Konrad Adenauer with strategic assessments of the diplomatic-military situation in Central Europe. The most famous of these was the "Himmerod Memorandum" of October 1950, which proposed a modern 12 division army (250, 000 men) supported by a tactical air force and coastal marine. In coordination with Western allies it would defend German territory. In October 1951, Heusinger entered the Dienststelle Blank (Department Blank) in the Adenauer chancellery. Speidel and he were the former highest-ranking officers among the handful of Wehrmacht veterans who provided military advice to the FRG government. In November 1955, he was commissioned as a lieutenant general of the new armed forces and assumed leadership of the Military Command Council in the Ministry of Defense (1955–57).

Heusinger's quiet, reserved, but efficient style impressed Minister of Defense Franz Josef Strauss (1915–88), who expedited Heusinger's further career. In April 1957 Heusinger received his fourth star, and he became *Generalinspekteur* of the Bundeswehr in June of that year. Until 1961, Heusinger supervised the troubled first years in the new army. The creation of a military force in a democracy integrated within NATO posed endless challenges at home and abroad. Heusinger became the first German Chairman of the NATO Military Committee in Washington, DC (1961–64). His stewardship of the highest military council in the Atlantic alliance consolidated the place of the FRG in NATO and won the confidence of former adversaries. Together with the political and military leadership of the FRG, they honored him on his death on November 30, 1982.

Donald Abenheim

See also Adenauer, Konrad; Blank, Theodor; Baudissin, Wolf von; Federal Republic of Germany: Armed Forces; NATO and Germany; Rearmament

References

Heusinger, Adolf. *Befehl im Widerstreit: Schicksalsstunden der deutschen Armee: 1923–1945.* Tübingen: R. Wunderlich, 1950.

———. *Reden 1956 bis 1961.* Boppard am Rhein: Boldt, 1961.

Markus Verlag, eds. *Sicherheit und Entspannung: Zum Siebzigsten Geburtstag von General a.D. Adolf Heusinger.* Cologne: Markus-Verlagsgesellschaft, 1967.

Militärgeschichtliches Forschungsamt. *Anfänge westdeutscher Sicherheitspolitik.* 3 vols. Munich: Oldenbourg, 1982–94.

Ose, Dieter, ed. *Adolf Heusinger: Ein deutscher Soldat im 20. Jahrhundert.* Bonn: 1987.

Range, Clemens. *Die Generale und Admirale der Bundeswehr.* Herford: E.S. Mittler, 1990.

Raven, Wolfram von, ed. *Armee gegen den Krieg.* Stuttgart: Seewald, 1967.

Security and Reduced Tension: On the Occasion of the 70th Birthday of General Adolf Heusinger. Cologne: Markus, 1967.

Heuss, Theodor (1884–1963)

As first president of the Federal Republic of Germany, Theodor Heuss did much to generate legitimacy and respect for the fledgling postwar democracy. More of an *homme de lettres* than a conventional party politician, Heuss brought to public life a humanistic and reflective orientation. Although he had gained some political experience and recognition in the Weimar Republic, he first reached national prominence after World War II. He was a leading liberal and a founding leader of the Free Democratic Party (FDP) before becoming head of the new West German state (1949–59).

Heuss was born in Brackenheim near Heilbronn. The Swabian homeland gave his speech an unmistakable and charming imprint. He studied economics and art history in Munich and Berlin, and completed a doctoral degree under Lujo Brentano (1844–1931), the economist, in 1905. Three years later, he married Elly (Eleonore) Knapp (1881–1953).

During his studies, Heuss was an editor of Friedrich Naumann's (1860–1919) journal, *Die Hilfe* (Help), in Berlin. Naumann became his political mentor in the reformist ideas of "social liberalism." After some years as newspaper editor in Heilbronn, Heuss returned to Berlin after World War I to become a leading executive for Naumann's Deutscher Werkbund. He continued to work as a publicist, was elected to a Berlin town council, and taught political science at the Hochschule für Politik (Academy for Politics) between 1920 and 1933.

Heuss served several terms in the Reichstag as a deputy of the German Democratic Party (1924–28) and its tiny successor, the Staatspartei (1930–32 and 1933). He had written a book, published in 1932, that was critical of Adolf Hitler. The following spring he wanted to withhold support from Hitler's Enabling Act. Having failed to persuade his small parliamentary group, however, he bowed to party unity and voted in support of the measure, as he would later recall with chagrin.

In the Third Reich, Heuss practiced political abstinence. He worked as an independent author of essays and wrote a series of biographies, including a major work on Naumann (1937). After World War II Heuss launched a new public career when the United States occupation forces appointed him minister for education in Baden-Württemberg. In 1946 he was elected to the state's constituent assembly and its parliament.

Heuss became leader of the newly formed Democratic People's Party (DVP), which soon incorporated other liberal formations within the American zone. He promoted organizational unity among liberals throughout the rest of occupied Germany, but the Cold War soon restricted his efforts to the Western zones. Heuss formed the FDP in December 1948 and was elected its first leader. By this time he was the leading liberal in the Parliamentary Council, which was drafting the Basic Law.

Heuss was elected to the first Bundestag in August 1949. One month later, he relinquished his parliamentary seat as well as the party leadership when he won election as federal president. The choice of Heuss to be West Germany's first head of

Theodor Heuss. Courtesy of German Information Center, New York.

state can be seen as a political prelude to the building of a non-socialist coalition government under Chancellor Konrad Adenauer (CDU), in which the Free Democrats served as the kingmakers of the majority. Adenauer was politically astute to support the leader of his main coalition partner for the presidency. The choice also turned out to be fortunate for the new republic.

With his cultural appreciation, historical sensitivity, and mild humor, Heuss bestowed on the new political system a sense of dignity and warmth. Such qualities were rare in a political arena marked by intense disagreement over the divided country's future course. Even as Heuss remained above partisanship, however, he managed to personify liberal democratic values to a citizenry that had little experience in such matters. His carefully crafted public speeches were widely admired and discussed. The widespread approval of his management of the office led to reelection by an overwhelming majority for a second five-year term in 1954. In 1959, he retired to his Swabian home in Stuttgart. There he continued to work on his memoirs, essays, and other writings until his death.

Christian Søe

See also Adenauer, Konrad; Basic Law; Federal Republic of Germany; Free Democratic Party; German Democratic Party; Liberalism; National Socialist Germany; Naumann, Friedrich; Presidency; Werkbund

References

Bark, Dennis L. and David R. Gress. *A History of West Germany.* Vol 1: *From Shadow to Substance.* 2nd ed. Cambridge, MA: Basil Blackwell, 1993.

Eckstein, Modris. *Theodor Heuss und die Weimarer Republik: Ein Beitrag zur Geschichte des deutschen Liberalismus.* Stuttgart: E. Klett, 1969.

Merkl, Peter H. *The Origin of the West German State.* New York, NY: Oxford University Press, 1963.

Vogt, Martin, ed. *Theodor Heuss, Politiker und Publizist: Aufsätze und Reden.* Tübingen: Wunderlich, 1984.

Winter, Ingelore M. *Unsere Bundespräsidenten von Theodor Heuss bis Richard von Weizsäcker.* Bergisch Gladbach: Bastei Lübbe, 1989.

Heydebrand und der Lasa, Ernst von (1851–1924)

Owner of a landed estate in the Prussian province of Silesia and a former district councilor (*Landrat*) (1883–95), Ernst von Heydebrand und der Lasa served as de facto leader of the German Conservative Party from 1908 to 1918. As a member of the Prussian Landtag (state legislature) from 1888 to 1918, he led the Conservative caucus there after 1906. He was also elected to represent a rural Silesian constituency in the Reichstag (1903–18). He was a member of the Conservatives' executive "Committee of Five" (1902–18), and shortly before World War I he was designated formal chairman of the party (1913–18).

In the Landtag and the Reichstag Heydebrand orchestrated his party's opposition to such government bills as the Local Government Act (1891), the Finance Reform Bill (1909), and the Prussian Franchise Reform (1910). His resistance to domestic reform and democratization continued unabated during the war, even though a younger generation of Pan-German nationalists within the party challenged his authority after 1916. A fanatical defender of Prussian—as opposed to national—interests, Heydebrand was known to contemporaries as "the uncrowned king of Prussia." Significantly, he never established a personal relationship with his monarch, Wilhelm II, and it was no empty boast when Heydebrand once confided to a colleague that "Prussian ministers dance to my tune."

In person, Heydebrand was blunt and haughty. Always conscious of the historic power of his *Junker* class and Prussian conservatism, he could be condescending and offensive, but he demanded and usually won unquestioning loyalty from his caucus followers. Remarkably small of stature and (like Bismarck) possessing a weak speaking voice, he was nicknamed "the little one." In order to be seen, he had to deliver his speeches from beside, not behind, the Reichstag podium. Yet Heydebrand was a brilliant speaker and tactician—one of perhaps half a dozen political superstars in Wilhelmine Germany. Because of his "steel-like, unbending will," one of his followers referred allusively to Heydebrand's "führer personality"; Chancellor Bethmann Hollweg spoke of his "dictatorial" and "demagogic" strains. His diminutive physical build stood in strange contrast to his Olympian political stature. As the liberal parliamentarian Eugen Schiffer (1860–1954) once observed, when Heydebrand hurled his "lightning bolts" at the left, his words were accompanied by thunderous applause from his myrmidons.

When the Prussian monarchy and the Conservative Party collapsed in November 1918, Heydebrand could not come to terms with new political realities. His final years were dissipated in futile attempts to preserve a Prussian-oriented conservative organization, and he never warmed to the new German National People's Party (DNVP). At the end of his career, Heydebrand still defended an elitist form of politics that was more appropriate to the nineteenth century than to the twentieth.

James Retallack

See also Conservatism, 1871–1918; German Conservative Party; Imperial Germany; Prussia

References

Heydebrand [und der Lasa], Dr. [Ernst von]. "Beiträge zu einer Geschichte der konservativen Partei in den letzten 30 Jahren (1888 bis 1919)." *Konservative Monatsschrift* 77 (1920), 497–504, 539–45, 569–75, 605–11, and 638–44.

———— et al. *Für Preussen!* Konservative Flugschriften, no. 6. Berlin: Konservative Schriftenvertriebsstelle, [1918].

Peck, Abraham J. *Radicals and Reactionaries: The Crisis of Conservatism in Wilhelmine Germany.* Washington, DC: University Press of America, 1978.

Retallack, James. *Notables of the Right: The Conservative*

Party and Political Mobilization in Germany, 1876–1918. London: Unwin Hyman, 1988.

———. "The Road to Philippi: The Conservative Party and Bethmann Hollweg's 'Politics of the Diagonal,' 1909–1914." *Between Reform, Reaction, and Resistance: Studies in the History of German Conservatism from 1789 to 1945.* Ed. Larry Eugene Jones and James Retallack. Oxford and Providence, RI: Berg Publishers, Inc., 1993.

Westarp, Graf Kuno von. "Heydebrand." *Deutscher Aufstieg: Bilder aus der Vergangenheit und Gegenwart der rechtsstehenden Parteien.* Ed. Hans von Arnim and Georg von Below. Berlin: Franz Schneider Verlag, 1925.

Heydrich, Reinhard Tristan Eugen (1904–42)

Reinhard Heydrich was born March 7, 1904 in Halle, Saxony. His father was Bruno Richard Heydrich, the famous composer and founder of the Halle Conservatory for Music, Theater, and Teaching. Reinhard Heydrich became an accomplished violinist and cellist himself, playing in recitals with chamber groups until a few days before his assassination. Too young for service in the German army in World War I, Heydrich enlisted in the navy in 1923 and qualified for service as a signals officer until he was dishonorably dismissed in 1931 for compromising and then refusing to marry the daughter of a senior officer. He married Lina von Osten in 1931. She was an ardent Nazi and a party member, and she and Heydrich's boyhood friend, the early Nazi and SS member Karl von Eberstein, urged Heydrich to join the Nazi Party and the SS after the disastrous end of his naval career.

Heydrich was one of the most important figures in the Third Reich. He joined the Schutzstaffel (SS) in 1931 and founded the SS Security Service (SD). After the Nazi seizure of power in 1933, Heydrich rose rapidly, accumulating enormous power as deputy chief of the Bavarian Political Police (1933), as chief of the Prussian Gestapo (1934), and as the closest associate of SS head Heinrich Himmler (1900–45).

In June, 1936, upon Himmler's appointment as Reich leader of the SS and chief of the German Police, Heydrich became chief of the Security Police and the SD, combining all of the agencies and offices of the German Criminal Police, the Gestapo, and the SD under his direct command. In 1939, he assumed control of the Reich Security Main Office (RSHA), a vastly enlarged and centralized SS and police terror apparatus that served as the executive instrument of Hitler's will within Germany and throughout the annexed and German-occupied territories in Europe during World War II.

Hitler considered Heydrich indispensable, and in September 1941 made him acting Reich protector of Bohemia-Moravia, with the charge to smash all Czech resistance to Nazi rule. By then, Heydrich had also received another assignment from Hitler, delegated through Himmler and Hermann Göring (1893–1946). On July 31, 1941, Göring authorized Heydrich to proceed with the steps necessary for the "final solution of the Jewish question"—Nazi and SS bureaucratese for the systematic extermination of all Jews living in all the areas of Europe under German control. Heydrich had begun this planning in late 1939, and had accelerated the preparations in January 1941 in anticipation of the German attack on the Soviet Union. Toward this end, he organized the special SS and police mobile killing units (SS *Einsatzgruppen*) that murdered over 500,000 Russian Jews by the spring of 1942. In addition, Heydrich supervised all the planning and preparation for construction of the extermination camps, where millions were to be killed by poison gas.

Heydrich died in Prague on June 4, 1942, from wounds inflicted in an assassination attempt on May 27 carried out by Czech parachutists flown in from England with the specific mission to kill him. At the time of his death, he was the fourth most powerful Nazi leader after Hitler, Göring, and Himmler, serving as the effective chief operating officer responsible for running the huge SS and police machinery of espionage and terror and for exploitation and mass murder throughout Nazi-occupied Europe.

Reinhard Heydrich became the twentieth century's consummate bureaucratic killer and the architect of the Holocaust.

Charles Sydnor

See also Anti-Semitism; *Einsatzgruppen*; Gestapo; Göring, Hermann; Himmler, Heinrich; Hitler, Adolf; Holocaust; National Socialist Germany; Reich Security Main Office; Security Office of SS; Schutzstaffel; Wannsee Conference; World War II

References
Aronson, Shlomo. *Reinhard Heydrich und die Frühgeschichte von Gestapo und SD.* Stuttgart: Deutsche Verlags Anstalt, 1971.

Calic, Edouard. *Reinhard Heydrich.* Trans. Lowell Bair. New York, NY: Military Heritage Press, 1982.

Deschner, Günther. *Heydrich, The Pursuit of Total Power.* London: Orbis, 1981.

Graber, G.S. *The Life and Times of Reinhard Heydrich.* London: Robert Hale, 1980.

MacDonald, Callum. *The Killing of SS Obergruppenfuehrer Reinhard Heydrich, 27 May 1942.* London: Macmillan, 1989.

Heym, Stefan (1913–)

Stefan Heym was born Helmut Flieg on April 10, 1913, in Chemnitz and now lives in Grunau near Berlin. Heym became widely known as the unofficial spokesman of the opposition movement in East Germany, where his writings were banned.

After being expelled from school for writing a pacifist poem in 1931, Heym completed his schooling in Berlin and fled to Prague in 1933, where he made his living by writing for German exile publications such as *Neue Deutsche Blätter* (new German papers) and *Die Weltbühne* (world stage). Heym also wrote a play, *Tom Sawyers grosses Abenteuer* (Tom Sawyers great adventure), which was performed in Vienna in 1937. In 1937 Heym won a scholarship from the University of Chicago, where he completed a master's degree in 1938. From 1937 to 1939 he served as editor of the Marxist anti-fascist weekly, the New York

Deutsches Volksecho (German people's echo). In 1942 Heym published his first novel, *Hostages* (in English), concerning the Nazi occupation of Prague, which became a bestseller.

In 1943 Heym, by then an American citizen, was drafted into the psychological warfare unit of the U.S. Army and took part in the European campaign. He wrote war propaganda for the U.S. station Radio Luxemburg and worked for the *Neue Zeitung*, the main American newspaper in Germany. The novel *The Crusaders* (1948) tells his military story.

Heym's postwar novels defended the Communist takeover of Czechoslovakia (*The Eyes of Reason*, 1951) and condemned American capitalism (*Goldsborough*, 1953). As a result he became a target of Senator Joseph McCarthy's anti-Communist campaigns and moved to East Berlin in 1952, renouncing his American citizenship.

After the West German weekly *Die Zeit* printed Heym's article on Stalin's declining importance in 1965, he was officially criticized by East Germany's Socialist Unity Party and his books were banned in East Germany. Subsequently, as his literature became more candid in its criticism of East German socialism, Heym continued to publish his novels in West Germany: *Der König David Bericht* (published as *The King David Report*), 1972; *Uncertain Friend* (about Germany's first socialist Ferdinand Lassalle), 1969, *Fünf Tage in Juni* (published as *Five Days in June*, about the 1953 East German workers' uprising) 1977, *Collin* (a story about a writer in conflict with the authorities), 1979, *Ahasver* (published as *The Wandering Jew*), 1981, *Schwarzenberg*, 1984, and his autobiography *Nachruf* (Obituary), 1988.

Since the collapse of East Germany's Marxist system in 1989 Heym has maintained his faith in socialism and struggles to regain the position he had enjoyed as a writer of socially relevant topics.

Reinhard K. Zachau

See also German Democratic Republic: Arts and Politics; German Democratic Republic: Literature and Literary Life; German Democratic Republic: Opposition; Novel; Poetry; Socialist Unity Party

References

Ecker, Hans-Peter. *Poetisierung als Kritik: Stefan Heyms Neugestaltung der Erzählung vom Ewigen Juden.* Tübingen: Narr, 1987.

Hutchinson, Peter. *Stefan Heym: The Perpetual Dissident.* Cambridge Studies in German. Cambridge: Cambridge University Press, 1992.

Wolfschütz, Hans. "Stefan Heym." *Kritisches Lexikon zur deutschsprachigen Gegenwartsliteratur.* Munich: Edition Text + Kritik, 1986.

Zachau, Reinhard. *Stefan Heym.* Autorenbücher vol. 28. Munich: Beck, 1982.

Heymann, Lida Gustava (1868–1943)

The feminist and pacifist Lida Gustava Heymann was prominent in the radical wing of the middle-class women's movement in Germany from the 1890s until 1933. Often associ-

ated with Minna Cauer (1841–1922), Helene Stöcker (1869–1943), and especially Anita Augspurg, Heymann championed the civil rights and sexual autonomy of women. She promoted sex education and the decriminalization of abortion, agitated for women's suffrage, opposed World War I, and helped to found the German branch of the Women's International League for Peace and Freedom (Internationale Frauenliga für Frieden und Freiheit; IFFF) in 1919.

Heymann came from a wealthy merchant family in Hamburg. In 1896, using her own funds, she started a women's center in that city that served free lunches to working women, operated a day-nursery, and provided social, sexual, and financial counseling to women. Not afraid to discuss sexuality in public, Heymann urged schools to provide girls with information about sex and spearheaded the campaign in Hamburg to abolish government-regulated prostitution. In her view, prostitution resulted from male domination rather than female immorality.

In 1902, together with Augspurg, Heymann founded the German Association for Women's Suffrage (Deutscher Verein für Frauenstimmrecht; after 1904, Deutscher Verband für Frauenstimmrecht). Proponents of a fully democratic vote for women and advocates of militant methods to attain that end, by 1912 Heymann and Augspurg had split with most supporters of women's suffrage in Germany. Heymann's call to abolish Paragraph 218 of the Criminal Code, which punished abortion, brought her further opposition from within the bourgeois women's movement.

But it was Heymann's pacifism, especially during World War I, that alienated her completely from mainstream middle-class women such as Gertrud Bäumer (1873–1954). Partici-

Lida Heymann. Courtesy of Inter Nationes, Bonn.

pation in the International Women's Peace Conference at The Hague in 1915 led to Heymann's exclusion from the Federation of German Women's Associations (Bund deutscher Frauenvereine; BDF). Bavarian police prohibited her peace activism in Munich and expelled her from the state in 1917, although she continued to live secretly with Augspurg. For Heymann, pacifism and feminism were linked; the world would find peace, she believed, only when women were free to help direct their countries.

In 1918, Heymann supported Kurt Eisner (1867–1919) and the revolutionary cause, and she criticized what she considered the harsh terms of the Treaty of Versailles. An outspoken opponent of Nazism, Heymann was vacationing in Italy when Hitler became chancellor in 1933; she remained in exile. Together with her longtime companion and collaborator Augspurg, Heymann died in Switzerland, possibly by suicide, in 1943.

Doris L. Bergen

See also Abortion; Bäumer, Gertrud; Cauer, Minna; Feminism and Anti-Feminism; Marriage and Divorce; Pacifism and the Peace Movement; Stöcker, Helene; Suffrage; (Bourgeois) Women's Movement

References

Beavan, Doris and Brigitte Faber. *"Wir wollen unser Teil fördern . . .": Interessenvertretung und Organisationsformen der bürgerlichen und proletarischen Frauenbewegung im deutschen Kaiserreich.* Cologne: Pahl-Rugenstein, 1987.

Evans, Richard J. *The Feminist Movement in Germany, 1894–1933.* London: Sage, 1976.

Gerhard, Ute. *Unerhört: Die Geschichte der deutschen Frauenbewegung.* Reinbek bei Hamburg: Rowohlt, 1990.

Greven-Aschoff, Barbara. *Die bürgerliche Frauenbewegung in Deutschland, 1894–1933.* Göttingen: Vandenhoeck & Ruprecht, 1981.

Hervé, Florence, ed. *Geschichte der deutschen Frauenbewegung.* Cologne: Papy Rossa, 1990.

Heymann, Lida Gustava and Anita Augspurg. *Erlebtes—Erschautes: Deutsche Frauen kämpfen für Freiheit, Recht und Frieden, 1850–1940.* Meisenheim am Glan: Anton Hain, 1972.

Schenk, Herrad. *Die feministische Herausforderung: 150 Jahre Frauenbewegung in Deutschland.* Munich: C.H. Beck, 1980.

Wickert, Christl. *Helene Stöcker, 1869–1943: Frauenrechtlerin, Sexualreformerin und Pazifistin.* Bonn: J.H.W. Dietz Nachf, 1991.

Hilbert, David (1862–1943)

The most influential mathematician of his era, Hilbert was born and raised in Königsberg, where he attended the local Gymnasium and university, taking his doctorate in 1885. From 1886 to 1895, he taught at Königsberg University, where he ascended from *Privatdozent* (unsalaried private lec-

David Hilbert. Courtesy of German Information Center, New York.

turer) to *Extraordinarius* (associate professor) and, finally, *Ordinarius* (full professor) in 1893. Two years later, Felix Klein (1949–1925) engineered his appointment at Göttingen, where he remained on the faculty until his retirement in 1930.

Hilbert made seminal contributions to numerous mathematical fields from invariant theory, algebraic number fields, and the foundations of geometry to integral equations, the calculus of variations, general relativity theory, and the axiomatic foundations of mathematics. After having worked in relative isolation in Königsberg, he quickly took over Klein's former role at Göttingen as the leading mathematics teacher in Germany. Between 1898 and the outbreak of World War I, Hilbert supervised the research of nearly sixty doctoral students, including such famous ones as Erhard Schmidt (1876–1959), Hermann Weyl (1885–1955), Richard Courant (1888–1972), and Erich Hecke (1887–1947). Hilbert's single most influential work stemmed from the speech he delivered at the Second International Congress of Mathematicians, held in Paris in 1900. In the extended published version, Hilbert set forth 23 unsolved problems for future consideration. These "Hilbert problems" proved to be a major source of inspiration for leading mathematicians throughout the twentieth century.

Hilbert's internationalist outlook and relatively progressive social views clashed sharply with those held by many of his colleagues in Göttingen's Philosophical Faculty. Many of the humanists regarded him as the ringleader of a liberal faction (consisting mostly of natural scientists and mathematicians) that sought to open the university's doors to various "undesirable" elements (e.g. foreigners, women, and graduates from schools other than classical *Gymnasien*). After a series of dramatic battles, the Philosophical Faculty was dissolved into two separate faculties in 1922.

In that same year, Hilbert delivered a lecture in Hamburg in which he attacked the intuitionistic views of L.E.J. Brouwer while setting forth the key principles underlying his own formalist program. The issues that sparked this conflict were embedded in the general atmosphere of cultural pessimism that marked the early years of the Weimar Republic. Hilbert, an inveterate optimist and the foremost spokesman for mathematical modernism, later engaged in a one-sided power struggle that effectively isolated Brouwer from the mathematical community. When Brouwer tried to use his connections with the Berlin mathematicians, particularly Ludwig Bieberbach (1886–1982), to stage a German boycott of the 1928 International Congress of Mathematicians in Bologna, Hilbert successfully rebuffed the effort. He personally led a large delegation of German mathematicians to the Congress, where he gave a speech in which he pleaded for international cooperation. Shortly afterward, and against strong opposition, he forced Brouwer's removal from the editorial board of the prestigious journal *Mathematische Annalen* (Mathematical yearbook).

Suffering from pernicious anemia, Hilbert spent his last years filled with sadness. The mathematical atmosphere that he, Klein, and others had cultivated in Göttingen quickly disintegrated shortly after the Nazi takeover. When he died in February 1943, only a dozen people were present at the funeral. His gravestone was marked with the famous motto from his Paris speech: "Wir müssen wissen; wir werden wissen" (we have to know; we will know).

David E. Rowe

See also Bieberbach, Ludwig; Klein, Felix; Mathematics; Weyl, Hermann

References
Browder, Felix, ed. *Mathematical Developments Arising from Hilbert Problems.* Proceedings of Symposia in Pure Mathematics, vol. 28. Providence, RI: American Mathematical Society, 1976.
Dalen, Dirk van. "The War of the Frogs and Mice, or the Crisis of the *Mathematische Annalen.*" *The Mathematical Intelligencer* 12 (1990), 17–31.
Mehrtens, Herbert. *Moderne—Sprache—Mathematik.* Frankfurt am Main: Suhrkamp, 1990.
Reid, Constance. *Hilbert.* New York, NY: Springer-Verlag, 1970.
Rowe, David E. "'Jewish Mathematics' at Göttingen in the Era of Felix Klein." *Isis* 77 (1986), 422–49.
———. "Klein, Hilbert, and the Göttingen Mathematical Tradition." *Science in Germany: The Intersection of Institutional and Intellectual Issues.* Ed. Kathryn M. Olesko. *Osiris* 5 (1989), 189–213.
Weyl, Hermann. "David Hilbert and his Mathematical Work." *Bulletin of the American Mathematical Society* 50 (1944), 612–54.

Hilferding, Rudolf (1877–1941)

As the author of *Das Finanzkapital* (published as *Finance Capital*), 1910, a prolific essayist and the editor of such leading publications as *Vorwärts* (Forward), *Die Freiheit* (Freedom), and *Die Gesellschaft* (The society), Hilferding was one of the most important European socialist economic and political theorists during the first half of the twentieth century. From 1924 to 1933, he served the Social Democratic Party (SPD) as a member of its executive committee, as a delegate in the Reichstag and as finance minister in 1923 and 1928–29. In exile after 1933, Hilferding (using the pseudonym Richard Kern) published frequently in the socialist press, edited the *Zeitschrift für Sozialismus* (Journal for socialism) and remained politically active.

Born in Vienna into a liberal Jewish middle-class family, Hilferding trained to become a physician. His real interests, however, lay in the study of political economy and the cause of Social Democracy. *Finance Capital*, Hilferding's most important economic work, described the process whereby credit institutions— specifically the banks—merged with and gained control over large-scale industry. As control over the economy became concentrated in fewer and fewer hands, he argued, the political power of the capitalist magnates also increased. They used the state to achieve three central objectives: the establishment of the largest possible economic territory, the closing of this territory to foreign competition by a wall of protective tariffs, and the reservation of this area of exploitation for the national monopolistic combines. Hilferding was convinced that the attempt by individual states to achieve these aims would lead to intensified international rivalry, the spread of radical nationalism, the acceleration of the arms race and probably—though not inevitably—to war.

Hilferding opposed the SPD's support of the German government in World War I. In 1918, he joined the antiwar Independent Social Democratic Party (USPD), in which he supported the socialization of key industrial sectors and the democratization of German politics. Although he was an internationalist, in 1920 he opposed the USPD's proposed entrance into the Communist International, which he considered too authoritarian. In 1922, he returned to the SPD and advocated the parliamentary road to socialism.

In Hilferding's view, monopoly capitalism was becoming less competitive, increasingly organized (*organisierter Kapitalismus*), and less prone to crisis, thereby creating the foundation for a Socialist economy. In addition, he thought that the major capitalist states were still reeling from the effects of World War I. They would now prefer to resolve disputes peaceably through cooperation (*realistischer Pazifismus*). In this situation, the SPD's task was to carry out the transition to socialism by peacefully gaining control of state power.

Hilferding was aware of the dangers posed by the nationalist Right, especially by the Nazis, but he remained convinced that these forces could be defeated within a parliamentary framework. The shock of the economic depression and the rapid rise of Nazism took him by surprise and, like most of his colleagues who hesitated to oppose Nazism with force, he was unable to respond decisively to the Nazi onslaught. In 1933 he fled to Denmark and later to Switzerland and France. On February 11, 1941, one day after the Vichy police handed him over to the Gestapo, he committed suicide in the prison of Le Santé in Paris.

Hilferding had worked to place the SPD's practical political strategy within a Marxist theoretical framework. The complete fiasco of that strategy in 1933 also marked his own failure. He had dedicated his life to the Social Democrats and his tragic fate mirrored that of his party.

William Smaldone

See also Independent Social Democratic Party; National Socialist Germany; Social Democratic Party; Weimar Germany

References

Breitman, Richard. *German Socialism and Weimar Democracy*. Chapel Hill, NC: University of North Carolina Press, 1981.

Edinger, Lewis J. *German Exile Politics: The Social Democratic Executive Committee in the Nazi Era*. Berkeley, CA: University of California Press, 1956.

Gottschalch, Wilfried. *Strukturveränderungen der Gesellschaft und politisches Handeln in der Lehre von Rudolf Hilferding*. Berlin: Duncker und Humblot, 1962.

Hilferding, Rudolf. *Finance Capital: A Study in the Latest Phase of Capitalist Development*. Ed. Tom Bottomore. London: Routledge and Kegan Paul, 1982.

Morgan, David W. *The Socialist Left and the German Revolution: A History of the German Independent Social Democratic Party*. Ithaca, NY: Cornell University Press, 1975.

Schorske, Carl E. *The German Social Democratic Party: 1905–1917*. Cambridge, MA: Harvard University Press, 1955.

Smaldone, William T. "Rudolf Hilferding: The Tragedy of a German Social Democrat." Unpublished doctoral dissertation. SUNY-Binghamton. Forthcoming from Berg Publishers.

Stephan, Cora, ed. *Zwischen den Stühlen oder über die Unvereinbarkeit von Theorie und Praxis: Schriften Rudolf Hilferdings*. Bonn: J.H.W. Dietz, 1982.

Wagner, F. Peter. *Rudolf Hilferding: Theory and Politics of Democratic Socialism*. Atlantic Highlands, NJ: Humanities Press, 1996.

Himmler, Heinrich (1900–45)

Heinrich Himmler was the head of the Schutzstaffel (SS) organization within the Nazi movement (1929–45) as well as chief of the German police (1936–45). He built and wielded an apparatus of party and state agencies that persecuted and terrorized designated racial and political enemies, conducted torturous medical experiments on human subjects, and perpetrated calculated mass murder on a scale which has few, if any, parallels. He was also responsible for the extermination of Slavic populations in order to clear their lands for Germans.

Born on October 7, 1900, the second of three sons of a Bavarian secondary-school teacher and a pious Catholic homemaker, the young Himmler was intelligent but awkward. With elements of the crank and the organization man, Himmler devoured books, including works by Pan-German writers, that presented Jews and Freemasons as arch-conspirators against Germany. Well before he came into direct contact with Hitler in 1926, his basic ideology was established: fear and hatred of Jews, belief in the superiority of the German race, the need for military expansion to the east, and action by a strong leader to bring these changes about.

In 1926, Himmler became assistant propaganda leader of the Nazi Party, and in 1929, Hitler appointed Himmler *Reichsführer* (Reich leader) of the SS, head of the still small paramilitary organization that Himmler would build into a huge conglomerate. In 1933–34, Himmler gained control of the state police forces and of a network of SS-run concentration camps. This enabled him to arrest, detain, and punish perceived enemies of the Third Reich.

After the outbreak of World War II, Himmler acquired new functions in conquered territories. Himmler used special militarized and mobile police formations, known as *Einsatzgruppen*, under the command of Reinhard Heydrich (1904–42) and a special office in the Reich Security Main Office, to liquidate huge numbers of perceived enemy groups—Jews, Polish nationalists, Gypsies, and Communists. Eventually, Himmler also became Reich minister of the interior (1943), commander of the Replacement Army (1944), and commander of Army Group Vistula (1944).

Himmler's SS and police empire carried out the mass murder of European Jewry. It attempted to exterminate what the Nazis considered the Jewish "race." Nazi officials employed a euphemism, the "final solution of the Jewish question," as a designation, but also as a partial disguise, for this program, which involved the deportation of Jews from most parts of Europe under Nazi control or influence to ghettos and/or new, specially constructed "extermination camps," where they were gassed to death and their bodies burned in large crematoria. Himmler frequently visited these camps and carefully supervised their operations.

On October 4, 1943, during a long speech to the top officers of the SS, Himmler boasted that the SS had carried out the "evacuation of the Jews, the extermination of the Jews" and nonetheless retained its respectability. A recording of the speech fell into Allied hands at the end of the war. It is among the best pieces of evidence of the Nazi genocide.

In late April 1945, expecting Hitler's death within days, Himmler made a desperate unilateral effort to arrange a surrender to the West and a joint German-Western alliance against the Soviet Union. The plan fell through. Just before committing suicide, Hitler angrily dismissed Himmler as *Reichsführer* of the SS (and from other offices) and appointed Silesian *Gauleiter* (district leader) Karl Hanke as his successor. On May 23, 1945, after falling into British hands, Himmler committed suicide by swallowing a cyanide pill concealed in his mouth.

Hitler's goals and Himmler's methods led directly to the

network of concentration and extermination camps that have given the twentieth century an indelible stamp.

Richard Breitman

See also Anti-Semtism; Auschwitz; Concentration Camps; *Einsatzgruppen*; Gestapo; Heydrich, Reinhard; Hitler, Adolf; Holocaust; Kripo; National Socialism; National Socialist Germany; Racism; Reich Security Main Office; Security Police; Security Service of the SS; Schutzstaffel; *Völkisch* Ideology; World War II

References

Ackermann, Josef. *Heinrich Himmler als Ideologe.* Göttingen: Musterschmidt Verlag, 1970.

Breitman, Richard. *The Architect of Genocide: Himmler and the Final Solution.* Hanover, NH: University Press of New England, 1992.

Browder, George C. *Foundations of the Nazi Police State: The Formation of the SIPO and SD.* Lexington, KY: University of Kentucky Press, 1990.

Koehl, Robert Lewis. *The Black Corps: The Structure and Power Struggles of the Nazi SS.* Madison, WI: University of Wisconsin Press, 1983.

Krausnick, Helmut et al. *Anatomy of the SS State.* New York, NY: Walker, 1968.

Padfield, Peter. *Himmler: Reichsführer SS.* New York, NY: Henry Holt, 1990.

Smith, Bradley F. *Heinrich Himmler: A Nazi in the Making.* Stanford, CA: Hoover Institution, 1971.

Smith, Bradley F. and Agnes F. Peterson. *Heinrich Himmler: Geheimreden 1933–1945 und andere Ansprachen.* Frankfurt am Main: Propyläen Verlag, 1974.

Hindemith, Paul (1895–1963)

Paul Hindemith, born on November 16, 1895, was a composer, performer, teacher, and writer, who is considered to be the most important representative of the Neoclassical style in Germany in the first half of the twentieth century. His use of traditional forms (including songs, symphonies, concertos, operas, and chamber music) attests to his knowledge of his position in the historical line of German creativity, in which he was influenced by such diverse forebears as Matthias Grünewald, Carl Maria von Weber, Rainer Maria Rilke (1875–1926), and Oskar Kokoschka (1886–1980). His philosophy as a composer and teacher is best expressed in his own remark: "Even in the wildest mixture of tones, sense and order must rule."

Hindemith's harmonic style, although dissonant, was essentially governed by tonal structure that suited the musical forms he used. Ironically, the Nazis considered him a political radical during the Third Reich. His religiosity (expressed in such works as the opera *Mathis der Maler* (Mathis the painter) and the symphony extracted from the opera), political independence (notably in the opera *Neues vom Tage*), and public association with artists who had been blacklisted by the Nazi Party were among the factors that influenced a major controversy involving factions of the Nazi establishment; ultimately Hindemith's music was banned from performance in the Third Reich.

Hindemith left his position in Berlin in 1938 and emigrated to Switzerland; two years later he went to the United States, where he eventually became an American citizen. He became influential as a teacher on the faculty of Yale University and as a theoretical writer of such works as *Unterweisung im Tonsatz* (1937), *Traditional Harmony* (1943), and *Elementary Training for Musicians* (1946). His compositional principle of controlled dissonance within a tonal framework employed in well-established forms dating to the baroque and classical periods was transmitted to many students; it is exemplified in such works as the aforementioned *Mathis der Maler*, the song cycle *Das Marienleben*, the ballet *Nobilissima Visione*, and the *Symphonic Metamorphoses on Themes of Carl Maria von Weber.*

After World War II, Hindemith made his home in Switzerland, where he continued his teaching and composition as well as performing on both violin and viola. His refusal to return to Germany (even after the Nazi period, except on an intermittent basis while on tour) resulted in a backlash against his works which has been only gradually alleviated since his death on December 28, 1963.

Susan M. Filler

See also Composers; National Socialist Germany: Music

References

Hindemith, Paul. *Catalogue of Published Works and Recordings.* London: Schott and Co., 1954. German edition: *Die Werke von Paul Hindemith.* Mainz: B. Schotts Söhne,1954.

———. *A Composer's World: Horizons and Limitations.* Cambridge, MA: Harvard University Press, 1952.

———. *A Concentrated Course in Traditional Harmony with Emphasis on Exercises and a Minimum of Rules.* 2 vols. New York, NY: Associated Music Publishers, 1943; Rev. ed. New York, NY: Associated Music Publishers; London: Schott and Co., 1944.

———. *Elementary Training for Musicians.* New York, NY: Associated Music Publishers, 1949.

———. *Selected Letters of Paul Hindemith.* Ed. and trans. Geoffrey Skelton. New Haven, CT: Yale University Press, 1995.

Noss, Luther. *Paul Hindemith in the United States.* Urbana, IL: University of Illinois Press, 1989.

Paulding, James E. "Paul Hindemith (1895–1963): A Study of His Life and Works." Unpublished doctoral dissertation. University of Iowa, 1974.

Skelton, Geoffrey. *Paul Hindemith: The Man Behind the Music.* London: Victor Gollancz, 1975.

Hindenburg, Paul von (1847–1934)

Hindenburg's name has been linked to the demise of Imperial Germany as well as of the Weimar Republic. This general became a legend for his military endeavors, but his impact was mainly political.

Paul von Beneckendorff und von Hindenburg was born on October 2, 1847 in Posen. His father came from an ancient *Junker* family; his mother was a commoner. He served as a second lieutenant at the battle of Königgrätz and was adjutant to his regiment in the Franco-Prussian War. From 1873 to 1876 he attended the War Academy, passing with distinction. He retired in 1911 when he was an army corps commander in Magdeburg.

On August 21, 1914, Hindenburg was appointed to command the Eighth Army in East Prussia. With his second-in-command, General Erich Ludendorff (1865–1937), with whom he remained closely associated until the end of the war, he won the battle of Tannenberg against the Russians. This great victory, hailed as the "second Cannae," made Hindenburg an immensely popular figure. In November 1914 he was promoted to the rank of field marshal and appointed "supreme commander east." As a result of a complex political intrigue, he was appointed to the supreme command (Third OHL) on August 29, 1916, and became to all intents and purposes the supreme commander of all the armed forces, eclipsing the Kaiser's position as supreme warlord. Although Hindenburg was essentially unpolitical, his subordinates, particularly Ludendorff and Max Bauer (1869–1929), made the OHL the center of political power during the last two years of the war. They dominated a weak political leadership but were unable to realize their schemes for the complete militarization of society, and the failure of the spring offensive in 1918 meant that their bizarre annexation plans could not be realized.

Hindenburg remained in office when Ludendorff resigned in September 1918. He supported the idea that the Kaiser should go into exile in Holland (he hoped as a temporary move), and he allowed Ludendorff's replacement, General Groener, to negotiate with Friedrich Ebert's (1871–1925) Social Democrats. He retired once again when the Treaty of Versailles was signed.

On Ebert's death in February 1925, Hindenburg allowed his name to be put forward as presidential candidate of the right-wing parties and was duly elected in April. Although neither a republican nor a democrat, and seeing himself as a kind of regent pending the return of the monarchy, Hindenburg felt himself bound by the constitution. Thus, much to the disgust of his nationalist supporters, he did nothing to hinder Gustav Stresemann's (1878–1929) "fulfillment" policies. In an unsuccessful attempt to deal with the problems of the Great Depression, he appointed the presidential "Hindenburg Cabinet" under Heinrich Brüning (1885–1970), which ruled through decree under Paragraph 48 of the constitution. In the 1932 presidential elections Hindenburg was regarded as the best guarantee against Hitler and his Nazis and against Ernst Thälmann's (1886–1944) Communists. Supported by the center and moderate left, Hindenburg won. Although he was the candidate of the democratic forces, he continued to appoint presidential cabinets, first under Franz von Papen (1879–1969) and then under Kurt von Schleicher (1882–1934). On January 30, 1933, he appointed the "Bohemian corporal," Adolf Hitler, as chancellor. He did so with considerable misgivings.

By now an old man in poor health, Hindenburg was misused by the Nazis, particularly in the cynical "Potsdam Day," which was designed to stress the links between the past and the present, between the field marshal and the corporal, between the Empire and the Third Reich. Hindenburg did almost nothing as Hitler established his dictatorship and remained silent in the face of the regime's many crimes.

A distinguished and loyal soldier, Hindenburg was hopelessly out of his depth in the world of politics, with disastrous results from 1916 to 1918 and from 1925 to 1934. He died in his home in Neudeck, on August 2, 1934, after which Hitler immediately combined the presidency and chancellorship in his own hands.

Martin Kitchen

See also Aristocracy; Bauer, Max; Brüning, Heinrich; Ebert, Friedrich; Groener, Wilhelm; Hitler, Adolf; Imperial Germany: Army; Ludendorff, Erich; Hugenberg, Alfred; National Socialism; Presidency; Prussia; Schleicher, Kurt; Seecht, Hans von; Weimar Germany; World War I

References

Asprey, Robert B. *The German High Command at War: Hindenburg and Ludendorff Conduct World War I.* New York, NY: W. Morrow, 1991.

Dorpalen, Andreas. *Hindenburg and the Weimar Republic.* Princeton, NJ: Princeton University Press, 1964.

Feldman, G.D. *Army, Industry and Labor in Germany, 1914–1918.* Princeton, NJ: Princeton University Press, 1966.

Görlitz, Walter. *Hindenburg: Ein Lebensbild.* Bonn: Athenäum, 1953.

Hindenburg, eine Auswahl aus Selbstzeugnissen des Generalfeldmarschalls und Reichspräsidenten. Bielefeld: Velhagen & Klasing, 1935.

Kitchen, Martin. *The Silent Dictatorship: The Politics of the High Command under Hindenburg and Ludendorff, 1916–1918.* London: Croom Helm, 1976.

Maser, Werner. *Hindenburg: Eine politische Biographie.* Rastatt: Moewig, 1990.

Hintze, Otto (1861–1940)

Otto Hintze's work was overshadowed by that of his more prominent colleagues, Friedrich Meinecke (1862–1954), Max Weber (1864–1920), and Ernst Troeltsch (1868–1923). He did not write many books, but in a number of articles and reviews he established a reputation as a conscientious critic of social theory and German idealism. Not until after 1945 did Hintze's writings in historical methodology and on the relationship among power politics, ethics, and internal social development begin to attract the attention of scholars in the German and English-speaking worlds.

Hintze was professor of constitutional, administrative, and economic history and politics at the University of Berlin from 1902 until 1920. His development as a historian was shaped by two important figures. As a student of Johann Gustav von Droysen (1808–84) in Berlin in the 1880s, Hintze was introduced to Prussian history. He was also influenced by Gustav Schmoller (1838–1917), with whom he worked for many years on the *Acta Borussica* (Prussian documents and materials). Although Hintze later distanced himself somewhat from

Schmoller, this collaboration was crucial in developing his interest in the social and economic aspects of the historical process.

Prior to World War I, Hintze's main interest was in the internal and external workings of the system of absolute monarchy in Prussia during the seventeenth and eighteenth-centuries. He especially saw the political, economic, and administrative achievements of Frederick the Great as a model for the Wilhelmine Empire. He was rewarded for his work with a position at the Prussian Academy of Sciences and by being named editor of the *Festschrift* in honor of the 500th anniversary of the Hohenzollern monarchy, *Die Hohenzollern und ihr Werk* (The Hohenzollerns and their work) 1916.

Hintze combined the traditional German historiographical practice of emphasizing the primacy of foreign policy with a unique understanding of social and economic forces. Although he was aware of the role that the state and international affairs played in economic development, his view of the state was not as idealistic as that of his contemporaries, and he refused to elevate it to an ethical entity as had become the custom among German scholars since Hegel.

These views were only slightly modified by Germany's defeat in World War I. He had supported without reservation the monarchy, and he never became fully reconciled to the Weimar Republic although he also did not openly oppose it. Hintze remained skeptical and increasingly turned to methodological problems, questioning the social and historical theories of such scholars as Werner Sombart (1863–1941) and Troeltsch. His studies also led him closer to Weber's understanding of the development of the modern state as the result of rationalization, rather than the traditional German emphasis on the acquisition of political power as the determining factor in international relations and the development of the modern nation-state. His work consequently can be regarded as a crucial factor in bridging the gap between traditional historical scholarship and the newer inquiries and theories of social and economic development.

John R. Hinde

See also Droysen, Johann Gustav; History; Meinecke, Friedrich; Prussia; Schmoller, Gustav von; Troeltsch, Ernst; Weber, Max

References

Gerhard, D. "Otto Hintze: His Work and His Significance in Historiography." *Central European History*. Vol. 3 (1970), 17–48.
Gilbert, Felix, ed. *The Historical Essays of Otto Hintze*. New York, NY: Oxford University Press, 1975.
Hintze, Otto. *Gesammelte Abhandlungen*. Ed. Fritz Hartung. Leipzig: Koehler und Amelang, 1943.
Koehler, E. *Bildungsbürgertum und nationale Politik: Eine Studie zum politischem Denken O. Hintzes*. Bad Homburg: Gehlen, 1970.
Simon, W.M. "Power and Responsibility: Otto Hintze's Place in German Historiography." *The Responsibility of Power*. Ed. Leonard Krieger and Fritz Stern. New York, NY: Doubleday, 1968.

Hintze, Paul von (1864–1941)

The naval leader Paul von Hintze was born at Schwedt on the Oder on February 13, 1864. The son of a tobacco merchant, Hintze entered the Imperial Navy in 1882 and attended the Naval Academy between 1894 and 1896. In 1898 Hintze served as the intermediary between his commander, Vice Admiral Otto von Diederichs, and the American commodore George Dewey when German and American cruiser squadrons threatened each other at Manila Bay. Hintze remained with the Far Eastern squadron until 1901, when he served as first officer on the battleship *Kaiser Wilhelm*. The following year he was assigned to the Admiralty Staff.

In 1903, Hintze assumed the position of naval attaché in St. Petersburg. For the next eight years he was a fixture at the Russian court. His engaging, if slightly toadying, personality won the trust of Tsar Nicholas II; his reports to Berlin drew favorable attention from Kaiser Wilhelm II, who used Hintze as an alternative to the Foreign Office in dealing with Russian affairs. Ennobled in 1908, Hintze left the navy with the rank of rear admiral in 1911, the same year that an "indiscretion" (probably an unguarded remark about the Tsarina Alexandra) necessitated his recall from St. Petersburg. His burgeoning career as a diplomat continued, however, with diplomatic missions to Mexico (1911–14), China (1914–17), and Norway (1917–18).

In June 1918, with the support of General Erich Ludendorff (1865–1937), Hintze replaced Richard von Kühlmann as State Secretary for Foreign Affairs in the cabinet of Georg von Hertling (1843–1919). Hintze soon differed with Ludendorff, however, over the proper course of action in the aftermath of the Treaty of Brest-Litovsk, which Germany had concluded with Russia three months earlier. Whereas the general sought to follow up Germany's extensive territorial and strategic gains with even more sweeping demands in the East, Hintze contended that a policy of cautious cooperation with the Bolsheviks was more likely to keep Russia in a position of dependency. Hintze's coldly pragmatic arguments found support with the Kaiser, and the series of supplementary treaties signed between Germany and Russia over the summer of 1918 reflected the admiral's relative moderation.

Hintze responded to Germany's rapidly deteriorating military and domestic conditions in the late summer and fall of 1918 with a number of proposals. He urged Wilhelm II to go to the front in order to bolster troop morale; he likewise advocated a revolution from above to forestall one from below. When Wilhelm acceded to pressure from the parliamentarians and replaced Hertling with the liberal Prince Max von Baden (1867–1929) on October 3, Hintze resigned. He remained with the Kaiser's headquarters at Spa as the Foreign Office's representative throughout the fall crisis, and, when public confidence in Wilhelm evaporated, he helped to persuade the Kaiser to seek asylum in the Netherlands.

Hintze enjoyed an active postwar career, for a time heading the German People's Party in Silesia and later serving as head of the German Overseas Institute in Stuttgart and the League of Overseas Germans. He died in Merano, less than two months after his Kaiser, on August 19, 1941.

Charles S. Thomas

See also Brest-Litovsk; German People's Party; Hertling, Georg von; Ludendorff, Erich; Naval Mutinies of 1918; Navy and Naval Policy; Tirpitz, Alfred von; Wilhelm II; World War I

References

Baden, Prince Max von. *The Memoirs of Prince Max von Baden.* 2 vols. London: Constable, 1928.

Fischer, Fritz. *Germany's Aims in the First World War.* New York, NY: Norton, 1967.

Herwig, Holger H. and Neil M. Heyman, eds. *Biographical Dictionary of World War I.* Westport, CT: Greenwood Press, 1982.

Neue Deutsche Biographie. 9th vol. Berlin: Duncker & Humblot, 1969.

Wheeler-Bennett, John W. *Brest-Litovsk: The Forgotten Peace, 1918.* New York, NY: Morrow, 1956.

Hirschfeld, Magnus (1868–1935)

Sexologist, psychiatrist, and sex reformer, Magnus Hirschfeld was the most important leader of the German homosexual emancipation movement in the pre-Hitler years. He founded the Scientific-Humanitarian Committee (Wissenschaftlich-humanitäres Komitee), the world's first homosexual-rights organization, in 1897 and the Institute for Sexology (Institut für Sexualwissenschaft, 1919), a Berlin center for research, education, sexual counseling and therapy, and advocacy on behalf of sexual privacy and reproductive rights.

Born to the family of a noted Jewish physician in Kolberg, Hirschfeld completed his medical studies in Berlin (1892). Influenced by Darwinism, he argued that homosexuals constituted a "third sex" (*drittes Geschlecht*), a natural intermediate stage between male and female, and were unjustly subjected to public and private discrimination. He later extended the notion of sexual intermediacy to include hermaphrodites and transvestites (*Transvestiten*)—a term he coined in 1910. His petition (1897) to reform Paragraph 175, the sodomy statute, was endorsed by thousands of prominent Germans. The Social Democratic Party (SPD) gave considerable, though by no means unanimous, backing to his reform efforts. Support for Hirschfeld diminished greatly because of his role as a sexological expert in the Eulenburg Affair (1907), which turned on allegations of homosexuality within the entourage of Wilhelm II leveled by the journalist Maximilian Harden (1861–1927). Harden's vindication in court, due in part to Hirschfeld's testimony, elicited an anti-Semitic and antihomosexual backlash from monarchist conservatives, and the homosexual emancipation movement was forced into quiescence until the Kaiser's abdication.

Initiatives to reform Paragraph 175 revived during the Weimar Republic, when the German Communist Party and the SPD jointly supported Hirschfeld's cause. He founded the World League for Sexual Reform (1928), which lauded the sexual politics of the pre-Stalin Soviet Union as exemplary. Brutally assaulted by Fascists (1922), excoriated in the Nazi press, and challenged by rivals within the homosexual emancipation movement for his medicalizing approach to sexuality, his political leanings, and his Jewishness, Hirschfeld de-parted (1930) for a lecture tour to the United States and Asia, residing upon his return in Switzerland and France rather than Germany. The Institute for Sexology was closed and its library burned (1933). He died in exile in Nice.

Tirelessly active as an educator, researcher, and organizer, Hirschfeld achieved international recognition as Germany's leading authority on sexuality. Within Germany he was both admired and abjured for his advocacy of homosexual rights. He was shaped by the Wilhelmine era's unquestioning faith in scientific enlightenment. His reform work advanced during the democracy of the Weimar Republic only to be destroyed by the Nazi regime.

James D. Steakley

See also Eulenburg-Hertefeld, Philipp zu; Harden, Maximilian; Homosexuality and Lesbianism; Jews, 1869–1933; Morality; Sex Reform and Birth Control

References

Herzer, Manfred. *Magnus Hirschfeld: Leben und Werk eines jüdischen, schwulen und sozialistischen Sexologen.* Frankfurt am Main: Campus, 1992.

Hirschfeld, Magnus. *Von einst bis jetzt: Geschichte einer homosexuellen Bewegung 1907–1922.* Berlin: Rosa Winkel, 1986.

Mitteilungen der Magnus-Hirschfeld-Gesellschaft 1983–1991. Hamburg: von Bockel, 1993.

Steakley, James D. *The Homosexual Emancipation Movement in Germany.* New York, NY: Arno, 1975.

———. "Iconography of a Scandal: Political Cartoons and the Eulenburg Affair." *Hidden from History: Reclaiming the Gay and Lesbian Past.* Ed. Martin Duberman et al. New York, NY: New American Library, 1989.

———, ed. *The Writings of Dr. Magnus Hirschfeld: A Bibliography.* Toronto: Canadian Gay Archives, 1985.

Wolff, Charlotte. *Magnus Hirschfeld: Portrait of a Pioneer in Sexology.* London: Quartet, 1986.

Historical Novel

As a narrative genre of the nineteenth and twentieth centuries, the historical novel depicts either authentic characters and events of history or fictional characters against a historical background. The philosophy of history that manifests itself in the interpretation of the past arises from the present-day political context of the author and introduces a second level of time. The linguistic and formal shaping of this interaction of present and past epochs, as well as of historical reality and fiction, determines the artistic value of a historical novel. The treatment of the prevailing political system occurs partly critically, partly affirmatively. This subjectivity repeatedly brings the genre into discredit.

The radical social and political changes at the beginning of the nineteenth century led to an awareness of the process by which historical events unfold and an awareness of the influence of these changes on the individual. This new interest became a fundamental prerequisite of the historical novel. The founder of the genre was Sir Walter Scott, whose historical novels for the first time depicted history for its own sake and characters whose outward and inward existences were determined by the respective epoch. The limited perspective of a "median hero" thereby provokes in the reader a search for meaning.

In Germany, the Romanticists—independently of Scott—had already turned to history, which they, to contrast to the decline of contemporary order, transfigured at the cost of historical accuracy. The first historical novels that dealt with the history of their respective countries were produced by Heinrich Zschokke (*Addrich im Moos*, 1824 and *Freihof in Aarau*, 1825) and Wilhelm Hauff (*Lichtenstein*, 1826).

Willibald Alexis provided a thoroughly researched, epically comprehensive representation of the history of Brandenburg-Prussia, and Hermann Kurz of Swabian history. In addition, both authors intended to provide democratic instruction to their contemporaries. Adalbert Stifter's *Witiko* (1865–67) glorified a social model of restoration. However, the failure of the Revolution of 1848 made the depiction of fallen social orders fundamentally impossible. The historical novel of the mid-century was influenced by the philosopher Ludwig Feuerbach, as well as the theologian David Friedrich Strauss, who emphasized the difference between legend and history.

More lasting was the influence of the historian Leopold von Ranke, who stressed the importance of precise research. Under his influence, Joseph Victor von Scheffel (*Ekkehard*, 1855) and Wilhelm Heinrich Riehl strove to synthesize historical truth and fiction. From this arose "*Professorenromane*" (professorial novels), in which academics (Felix Dahn, Gustav Ebers) often used their specialized knowledge to gloss over improbable action, causing a temporary literary debasement of the entire genre.

After the founding of the empire, the historical novel, which achieved its peak popularity, manifested a decidedly nationalistic consciousness, the desire for a perspective on Pan-German history, as well as the bourgeois fear of modern times. Representative was Gustav Freytag's (1816–95) eight-volume novel *Die Ahnen* (The Ancestor), 1872–81, which, in a transfigured way, depicted the supposed development of German national consciousness from the peoples' migration until 1848. In contrast, Conrad Ferdinand Meyer's *Jürg Jenatsch* (1876) dealt with the problems of his own day in historical guise, whereas Theodor Fontane (1819–98) presented Prussian history through various points of view in a critically differentiated way in *Vor dem Sturm* (published as *Before the Storm*), 1878 and *Schach von Wuthenow* (published as *A Man of Honor*), 1882.

Around 1900, regional art and the romantic interest in unspoiled landscapes of the past and tribal customs in each of the German-speaking countries led to a type of historical novel that though successful, was of limited literary value. A typical example, with its crass nationalistic self-glorification, was Hermann Löns's *Der Wehrwolf* (The werewolf), 1910. In contrast, Ricarda Huch combined exact source research with artistic creation and developed the historical novel into a kind of individual psychological study, which Emil Ludwig (1881–1948) and Stefan Zweig transformed into the biographical novel. The radical sociopolitical changes caused by World War I awakened different historical interest. The historical novel

served, in part, to avoid taking a position on the present or to criticize the new democratic system. Lion Feuchtwanger sought through his novels to shape the "antagonism between power and knowledge." In *Wallenstein* (1920), Alfred Döblin (1878–1957) referred to the underlying causes of the Thirty Years' War and, at the same time, to those of World War I. Joseph Roth (1894–1939) depicted the decline of the Habsburg monarchy.

The Third Reich occasioned renewed attention in the historical novel, on the one hand by authors who remained in Germany and supported the National Socialist ideology (Hans Friedrich Blunck, Erwin Guido Kolbenheyer) or covertly criticized it (Werner Bergengruen, Gertrud von Le Fort, Reinhold Schneider), and on the other hand by the exiles (Franz Werfel, Heinrich Mann [1871–1950]). These authors depicted the historical epoch as a reflection of or contrast to the present.

In the postwar period, authors turned, with the exception of the pleasure novel, more toward contemporary themes. Not until the 1970s was there a renewed return to historical novels in which problematic figures or parallels to the present day evoked interest (Peter Härtling, Christa Wolf [1929], and Christoph Ransmayer).

Gisela Brude-Firnau

See also Bergengruen, Werner; Döblin, Alfred; Feuchtwanger, Lion; Fontane, Theodor; Freytag, Gustav; Huch, Ricarda; Ludwig, Emil; Lukács, Georg; Mann, Heinrich; Novel; Ranke, Leopold von; Roth, Joseph; Wolf, Christa; Zweig, Stefan

References

Eggert, Hartmut. *Studien zur Wirkungsgeschichte des deutschen historischen Romans 1850–1875*. Frankfurt am Main: Klostermann, 1971.

Eykman, Christoph. *Geschichtspessimismus in der deutschen Literatur des zwanzigsten Jahrhunderts*. Bern: Francke, 1970.

Fleishman, Avrom. *The English Historical Novel: From Walter Scott to Virginia Woolf*. Baltimore, MD: Johns Hopkins University Press, 1971.

Geppert, Hans Vilmar. *Der "andere" historische Roman: Theorie und Strukturen einer diskontinuierlichen Gattung*. Tübingen: Niemeyer, 1976.

Hey'l, Bettina. *Geschichtsdenken und literarische Moderne: Zum historischen Roman in der Zeit der Weimarer Republik*. Tübingen: Niemeyer, 1994.

Humphrey, Robert. *The Historical Novel as Philosophy of History: Three German Contributions: Alexis, Fontane, Döblin*. London: Institute of Germanic Studies, University of London, 1986.

Limlei, Michael. *Geschichte als Ort der Bewährung: Menschenbild und Geschichtsverständnis in den deutschen historischen Romanen 1820–1890*. Frankfurt am Main: Peter Lang, 1988.

Müller, Harro. *Geschichte zwischen Kairos und Katastrophe: Historische Romane im 20. Jahrhundert*. Frankfurt am Main: Athenäum, 1988.

Schröter, Klaus. "Der historische Roman." *Exil und innere Emigration.* Ed. Reinhold Grimm and Jost Hermand. Frankfurt am Main: Athenäum, 1972.

Historikerstreit

During the late 1980s, a flood of polemical literature swamped the German book market, especially in German historical writing. This historians' debate, or *Historikerstreit,* has been largely attributed to the awakening of a new German nationalism, to the search for German identity allegedly lost, and in particular to the rise of neoconservative and revisionist trends in German political and intellectual life.

In an article on June 6, 1986, Ernst Nolte raised the rhetorical question whether the Soviet "Gulag Archipelago" did not precede Auschwitz and whether Hitler did not follow in the footsteps of Stalin. He also suggested that Nazism acted out of fear of what Bolshevism could do to Germany and Europe. He attempted to minimize Nazi crimes, to deny the "singularity" of the Holocaust, and to shift ultimate responsibility for it to others, especially to Bolshevism. This unleashed a storm of criticism among scholars and the German public. Subsequently, Nolte emphasized the need for an all-European and even a global perspective about the twentieth century and for the concept of a "global civil war" raging since 1914. He propagated the view that placing the Holocaust and twentieth century German history into the larger framework of world history, for instance Pol Pot's atrocities and those of Idi Amin, relativized Nazi excesses and made them less "singular."

Nolte's critics, in particular the philosopher Jürgen Habermas (1929–), countered that if comparisons were made with the record of other nations, they should be made with European ones, especially with developed countries, not with African or Indochinese tyrants and their largely illiterate peoples. Nor was it proper to compare Bolshevism, however brutal it was, with Nazi mass murder based on racism. There was no evidence of a causal link in the Nazi mind between the Soviet discrimination against and maltreatment of individuals of the Russian upper classes with the unprecedented mass annihilation of Jews.

The diplomatic historian Andreas Hillgruber was one of Nolte's allies in the *Historikerstreit.* According to Hillgruber, two "national catastrophies" occurred during World War II: the murder of the Jews and, immediately following, the expulsion of Germans from Eastern and Central Europe and the destruction of the Prussian-German Reich. Hillgruber saw no difference between the latter phenomenon and the outright annihilation of the Jews. He also condemned the perpetrators of the abortive anti-Hitler *Putsch* of July 1944. A successful coup would have caused a "frightful chaos" (*Durcheinander*) in German leadership, a debacle that would have accelerated the Soviets' military success. Hillgruber spurned the expression "liberation" of the German people, since this concept implied "identification with the victors." Instead, he identified with the desperate endeavors of the German army and navy in 1944–45, which aimed at protecting the German East against the "orgies of the vengeance by the Red Army."

In response to Nolte and Hillgruber, Hans-Ulrich Wehler argued against the apologetic effect of interpreting Hitler as the sole or "main culprit" of the Holocaust in order to exculpate the old German elites, the army, the bureaucracy, the judiciary, the railroad personnel and the silent mass of all of those Germans who were knowledgeable about public affairs. Wehler focused his criticism on the main participants among the neo-conservative historians—Ernst Nolte, Andreas Hillgruber, Michael Stürmer, and Klaus Hildebrand. He ridiculed the comparative attempts propounded by some German historians and he ridiculed the idea of a "Hitler era" in every great nation. Hitler, Wehler pointed out, had developed his anti-Marxist ideology long before the Russian Revolution. The same holds true of rabid anti-Semitism, which had emerged earlier, in the nineteenth century, in Germany and Austria.

Alfred D. Low

See also The Fischer Controversy; Habermas, Jürgen; History; Holocaust; Holocaust: Historiography; Memory, Collective; National Socialist Germany; *Sonderweg;* Third Reich: Historiography

References

Baldwin, Peter. *Hitler, the Holocaust and the Historians' Debate.* Boston, MA: Beacon Press, 1990.

Evans, Richard. *In Hitler's Shadow: West German Historians and the Attempt to Escape from the Nazi Past.* New York, NY: Pantheon, 1989.

Hillgruber, Andreas. *Zweierlei Untergang: Die Zerschlagung des Deutschen Reichs und das Ende des europäischen Judentums.* Berlin: Siedler, 1987.

Kershaw, Ian. *The Nazi Dictatorship: Problems and Perspectives of Interpretations.* 3rd ed. London: Edward Arnold, 1989.

Kühnl, Reinhard, ed. *Vergangenheit, die nicht vergeht: Die "Historikerdebatte": Darstellung, Dokumentation, Kritik.* Cologne: Pahl-Rugenstein, 1987.

Maier, Charles S. *The Unmasterable Past: History, Holocaust and German National Identity.* Cambridge, MA: Harvard University Press, 1988.

Nolte, Ernst. *Das Vergehen der Vergangenheit: Antwort an meine Kritiker im sogenannten Historikerstreit.* Berlin: Ullstein, 1987.

Wehler, Hans-Ulrich. *Entsorgung der deutschen Vergangenheit? Ein polemischer Essay zum "Historikerstreit."* Munich: C.H. Beck, 1988.

History

At the time of the unification of Germany under Otto von Bismarck in 1871, historical studies conducted in Germany were highly regarded throughout the world as a model for a scholarly, "scientific" approach to history. This admiration for German historical scholarship tended to overlook the limitations of the political and social context in which history emerged as a professional discipline in the Restoration period (after Napoleon) at the Prussian universities of Berlin and Bonn imposed on the vision of the German historians. Civil society, which had played a major role in the thinking of Enlightenment historians not only in Great Britain and France but also in Germany, became subordinated by Leopold von Ranke and others to the primacy of the state.

Ranke still thought in terms of the balance of power among the great European monarchies, whereas a younger generation of professional historians (J.G. Droysen [1808–84], Heinrich von Sybel [1817–95] and Heinrich von Treitschke [1834–96]) pursued their studies consciously in the service of national unification under Prussian leadership. Their liberalism became much more authoritarian than that of liberal historians elsewhere in Europe, particularly after the failure of the Revolution of 1848, when they came to rely on the power of the Prussian monarcho-military establishment to achieve national unification. Added to this was their fear of social revolution in an age of industrialization. Out of the merger of social conservatism with professional ethos a new orthodoxy emerged, that maintained itself at the German universities because of a system of recruitment that effectively prevented dissidents from obtaining university positions until well into the second half of the twentieth century.

The turn of the century witnessed a greater emphasis by Western historians generally on social, economic, and cultural factors, which they had largely neglected until then. Historians increasingly viewed history as a social science and used analytical tools analogous to those of other sciences. German historians and philosophers (Wilhelm Dilthey [1833–1911], Wilhelm Windelband [1848–1915], and Heinrich Rickert), on the other hand, stressed the distinctness of the cultural sciences (*Geisteswissenschaften*), with their concern for unique values as manifested in personalities or historical tendencies and their abhorrence of the generalizations employed in other sciences.

The Historical School of Economists (Gustav von Schmoller [1838–1917]) shared this dislike of theory and viewed the economy from the perspective of the monarchical state. Attempts by Karl Lamprecht in his *Deutsche Geschichte* (German history), 1891–1909, to introduce social analysis and cultural comparisons into historical studies were vigorously resisted by the German historical profession, which saw in Lamprecht a challenge not only to the German idealistic notion of history but also to the principles on which the established German political and social order rested. Efforts by sociologists, such as Max Weber (1864–1920), and Georg Simmel (1858–1918), and by the historian Otto Hintze (1861–1940), to bridge the gulf between history and the analytical social sciences were largely ignored by most historians.

The preoccupation of historians during the Weimar Republic with the refutation of Germany's war guilt, and the purge of the few nonorthodox historians by the subsequent Nazi regime, prevented any reorientation of historical studies until well after World War II. During the Nazi period, a number of sociologists and historians (Gunther Ipsen and Hans Freyer [1887–1969]) called for a racially oriented *Volksgeschichte* (people's history), that would pay greater attention to culture and society than the traditional history of politics had done. The majority of the orthodox historians, however, shared in a national anti-democratic and expansionist consensus that permitted them to survive unscathed in the

Third Reich and to dominate the historical profession in West Germany well into the 1960s. For them (e.g., Gerhard Ritter) Nazism represented a break with German conservative traditions and in fact had its roots in modern democracy and mass culture. However, by the 1960s, an increasing number of young German historians took up the question to what extent Germany's *Sonderweg*, i.e., its failure to follow Western patterns of liberalism and democracy in its process of modernization, had contributed to the victory of Nazism and to the Holocaust.

Taking up ideas of dissident historians of the Weimar period (Eckart Kehr and Hans Rosenberg), Hans-Ulrich Wehler, Jürgen Kocka and others rejected not only the political but also the methodological assumptions of the older school. For them, the rise of Nazism had to be understood in the context of German social structures and processes that could be comprehended only by means of analytical concepts and methods derived from the social sciences. The narrow orthodoxy that had marked the German historical discipline from Ranke to Ritter yielded to a much broader pluralism in the 1970s, which coincided with the creation of new universities and new chairs of history.

Meanwhile, in the German Democratic Republic (GDR), official historiography at first stressed the so-called progressive traditions (Münzer, the Revolution of 1848, the revolutionary working class), but then moved increasingly to a positive reconsideration of Luther and of the Prussian state

Writer and historian Ricarda Huch. Courtesy of Inter Nationes, Bonn.

(Frederick the Great and Bismarck) in order to place the socialist state in the context of the national past. In many ways, by the late 1980s the official interpretation of German history in the GDR showed closer affinities to the conservative mainstream of German historiography than to the historians in the Federal Republic of Germany (FRG) who were critical of the national past. By the mid-1970s, the latter came under attack in the FRG by historians such as Thomas Nipperdey, who resisted the emphasis on 1933 as a vantage point from which the history of modern Germany was to be analyzed. In the 1980s, conservative historians (including E. Nolte) denied the specifically German roots of Nazism and of the Holocaust, which they sought to place in the context of twentieth-century totalitarianism. Reunification gave a new impetus to efforts to rehabilitate the German past but by no means ended the controversy. Apart from these debates, many historians since the 1970s had begun to offer more attention to culture and everyday life than to the history of politics or the analysis of social structures.

Georg Iggers

See also Burckhardt, Jacob; Delbrück, Hans; Dilthey, Wilhelm; Droysen, Johann Gustav; The Fischer Controversy; Frank, Walter; *Germanistik;* Hintze, Otto; *Historikerstreit;* Holocaust: Historiography; Huch, Ricarda; Human Sciences; Kehr, Eckart; Lamprecht, Karl; Ludwig, Emil; Meinecke, Friedrich; Mommsen, Theodor; Oncken, Hermann; Rickert, Heinrich; Schmoller, Gustav von; Simmel, Georg; *Sonderweg;* Sybel, Heinrich von; Third Reich: Historiography; Treitschke, Heinrich von; Troeltsch, Ernst; Universities; Weber, Alfred; Weber, Max; Windelband, Wilhelm

References

Aly, Götz. *Macht, Geist, Wahn: Kontinuitäten deutschen Denkens.* Berlin: Argon Verlag, 1997.

Dorpalen, Andreas. *German History in Marxist Perspective: The East German Approach.* Detroit, MI: Wayne State University Press, 1985.

Faulenbach, Bernd. *Geschichtswissenschaft in Deutschland.* Munich: C. H. Beck Verlag, 1974.

Iggers, Georg G. *The German Conception of History: The German Tradition of Historical Thought from Herder to the Present.* 2nd ed. Middletown, CT: Wesleyan University Press, 1984 [1968].

McClelland, Charles E. *The German Historians and England: A Study in Nineteenth-Century Views.* Cambridge, MA: Harvard University Press, 1971.

Ringer, Fritz. *The Decline of the German Mandarins: The German Academic Community, 1890–1933.* Cambridge, MA: Harvard University Press, 1969.

Srbik, Heinrich von. *Geist und Geschichte vom deutschen Humanismus bis zur Gegenwart.* 2 vols. Munich: F. Bruckmann, 1950–51.

Streisand, Joachim, ed. *Studien über die deutsche Geschichtswissenschaft.* 2 vols. Berlin: Akademie Verlag, 1963–65.

Weber, Wolfgang. *Priester der Klio: Historisch-sozialwissenschaftliche Studien zur Herkunft und Karriere deutscher Historiker und zur Geschichte der Geschichtswissenschaft 1800–1970.* Frankfurt am Main: Peter Lang, 1984.

Wehler, Hans-Ulrich, ed. *Deutsche Historiker.* 9 vols. Göttingen: Vandenhoeck & Ruprecht, 1971–80.

Hitler, Adolf (1889–1945)

Adolf Hitler was leader of the Nazi Party (National Socialist German Worker's Party) beginning in 1921 and served as chancellor between 1933 and 1945. Following the death of President Hindenburg (August 1934), he became sole leader of Germany.

Born in provincial Austria, at Braunau am Inn (April 20, 1889), Hitler grew up dreaming of an artistic career. He left home for Vienna (October 1907), only to be rejected by the Viennese Academy of Fine Arts. Living as a virtual "down-and-outer" in the capital, Hitler encountered the anti-Semitic politics of Vienna's mayor, Karl Lueger, and read Lanz von Liebenfels's racially comic journal *Ostara* (German "goddess of spring"). From such sources, Hitler developed his own political dogma, in which Jews were responsible for everything from Marxism to capitalism, democracy to pacifism, prostitution to syphilis.

Having moved to Munich (May 1913) and swept along by the considerable tide of nationalist fervor, Hitler (still a citizen of Austria) joined the German army at the outbreak of World War I. He became a lance corporal and received the Iron Cross First Class for bravery. Blinded by gas and convalescing in Pasewalk Hospital, Hitler responded hysterically to Germany's surrender and the Revolution of 1918. The experience intensified his hatred of all of those whom he regarded as Germany's enemies.

Hitler found an outlet for his frustrations in postwar Munich. As a military spy watching political movements, he encountered and joined the German Worker's Party (September 16, 1919). After leaving the army, he had the movement renamed the National Socialist German Workers' Party (NSDAP; Nazi Party) and, during the summer of 1921, effectively became its leader. His skill as an orator, talent for political organization, and establishment of paramilitary squads facilitated the party's growth from a handful of members to over 3,000 by November 1921. The party's political ideals were expressed in a twenty-five-point program Hitler helped to produce (February 24, 1920). The document combined pseudo-socialist principles that aimed at harnessing the economy for the good of the country with the racial goal of excluding Jews from national life.

In response to a national crisis, and following a meeting in a Munich beer hall, Hitler led an unsuccessful Putsch against Bavaria's government on November 9, 1923. He was captured and sentenced to five years' imprisonment for high treason in February 1924. While in Landsberg prison, he was visited by the geopolitical analyst Karl Haushofer and developed his ideology to include the concept of *Lebensraum*—the idea that Germany required more "living space." In his cell, Hitler dictated *Mein Kampf* to fellow-prisoner Rudolf Hess (1894–1987). First published in 1925, the book sold 200,000 copies before the Nazis seized power. Frequently pornographic in tone, it stands as a chaotic epitome of antidemocratic and racialist values.

Set free after only nine months in December 1924, Hitler reestablished the Nazi Party. At the Bamberg meeting (February 1926), he made full use of his personal charisma to overcome political divisions. The coordinating reforms begun at this time enabled the party to exploit more effectively the popular dissatisfaction that sprang up during the Great Depression. Nevertheless, the Nazi Party always lacked an absolute majority in the Reichstag and so Hitler was drawn into complicated negotiations with Germany's traditional political power brokers (1932–33). Showing all the instincts of a successful gambler, he refused to accept any political appointment but the top one. Having received German citizenship the previous year, Hitler was appointed chancellor by President Hindenburg on January 30, 1933.

Just about every aspect of Hitler's chancellorship is the subject of vigorous debate. Most notably, although some (such as E. Jäckel and K. Hildebrand) believe that Hitler had a "blueprint" for action based on his early political writings, others, for example, H. Mommsen, think that he was driven much more by a nihilistic opportunism.

Within Germany, Hitler aligned the country behind himself and his party. He used the Reichstag Fire Decree (February 28, 1933) especially to persecute leftist opponents of Nazism, whereas the Enabling Law (March 23, 1933) suspended the democratic Weimar constitution in favor of a dictatorial emergency rule. When unrest surfaced in the party itself, Hitler and Heinrich Himmler (1900–45) purged the radical Sturmabteilung (SA) leadership without mercy (June 1934). Hitler and Himmler used violence once again in the form of the Crystal Night pogroms (*Kristallnacht*) on November 9, 1938. This terrorism against Jews whipped up support among the party's rank and file and confirmed the exclusion of the Jews from German life.

In international affairs, Hitler played to domestic opinion and reaffirmed his skill as a gambler. His decision, taken against the advice of military advisors, to remilitarize the Rhineland (March 1936) was a popular success. The *Anschluss* (1938) and the annexation of the Sudetenland (1938) had similar effects. The consequences of the invasion of Poland (September 1, 1939), however, were more dire.

During the ensuing war, Hitler's character showed its strengths and weaknesses most clearly. He reserved the most significant decisions for himself—for example, those to open the western front and to launch Operation Barbarossa against the Soviet Union in 1941. The modern war effort, however, proved far too complicated for one man to coordinate. Hitler often failed to appreciate strategic situations fully (for example, his refusal to withdraw from Stalingrad in 1942) and did not support adequately the most pertinent technological advances (for example, the Me 262 jet fighter and He 177 heavy bomber). These misjudgements contributed directly to Germany's defeat.

The Barbarossa campaign provided the context for the so-called "final solution to the Jewish question." Hitler's spe-

Adolf Hitler. Courtesy of German Embassy, Ottawa.

cific role here is the subject of controversy. Although there is a lack of empirical evidence to prove that he ever gave a specific order for the extermination of the Jewish people, given his interest in racial policy it is virtually inconceivable that the "cleansing" of Germany's living space (east and west) by Himmler and the Schutzstaffel (SS) could have been implemented without considerable consultation with Hitler.

Hitler pursued many of his goals opportunistically, but the contours of policy carried out in the Third Reich did resemble the basic ideological framework that he had laid down by 1925. Within Germany, democracy was replaced and socialism crushed; internationally, Germany was driven toward a resurgency, albeit a temporary one; and Europe's Jews suffered a fate in keeping with the virulence and consistency of Hitler's race hatred. This leaves the issue of whether Hitler himself really led the movement consistently toward these preformulated ends or whether his policies owed more to a spontaneous process of competition between the various and chaotically organized power blocs in the Reich, each of which competed for Hitler's patronage through the pursuit of policies broadly in line with his stated beliefs.

Both of these views have some claim to validity. As supreme ruler of a modern state, Hitler could not have involved himself actively in every aspect of each policy initiative. The depth of his involvement probably reflected the strength of his personal interest in a given topic. For example, he had considerable input regarding key foreign policy and military decisions, but was relatively happy to leave competing power groups to sort out, for instance, administrative matters.

Whether Hitler was a strong or weak dictator, the result was a system of government implementing his terrible political vision. Hence, there is no way of separating Nazism from the main strands of Hitler's personal ideology. Indeed, Hitler admitted to the futility of his vision only when the Red Army was overrunning Berlin. He committed suicide on April 30, 1945.

Martyn Housden

See also Anschluss; Anti-Semitism; Atom Bomb (German Development of); Auschwitz; Austro-German Relations; Bormann, Martin; Chamberlain, Houston Stewart; Crystal Night; Darré, Walther; Eichmann, Adolf; Euthanasia; Freisler, Roland; Fritsch, Werner von; German Christians; Gestapo; Goebbels, Joseph; Göring, Hermann; Heydrich, Reinhard; Himmler, Heinrich; Hindenburg, Paul von; Hitler Youth; Holocaust; Jews; Jodl, Alfred; Keitel, Wilhelm; League of German Girls; Ley, Robert; Ludendorff, Erich; National Socialism; National Socialist Germany; National Socialist Germany: Art; National Socialist Germany: Foreign Policy; National Socialist Germany: Military; National Socialist Germany: Music; Nuremburg Trials; Papen, Franz von; Racism; Reich Security Main Office; Resistance; Ribbentrop, Joachim von; Riefenstahl, Leni; Röhm, Ernst; Rommel, Erwin; Rosenberg, Alfred; Rust, Bernhard; Sauckel, Fritz; Schacht, Hjalmar; Schirach, Baldur von; Schleicher, Kurt von; Scholtz-Klink, Gertrud; Schutzstaffel; Science and National Socialism; Security Service of the SS; Speer, Albert; Stauffenberg, Claus von; Strasser, Gregor; Streicher, Julius; Sturmabteilung; Third Reich: Film; Third Reich: Historiography; Third Reich: Industry; Third Reich: Propaganda and Culture; *Völkisch* Ideology; Volkswagen; World War II

References

Bullock, A. *Hitler: A Study in Tyranny.* London: Odhams, 1952.

———. *Hitler and Stalin: Parallel Lives.* New York, NY: Vintage, 1991.

Carr, W. *Hitler: A Study in Personality and Politics.* London: Arnold, 1978.

Fest, J. *Hitler.* London: Penguin, 1974.

Fest, Joachim. *Plotting Hitler's Death: The German Resistance to Hitler, 1933–1945.* London: Penguin, 1974.

Graml, H. *Antisemitism in the Third Reich.* Oxford: Blackwell, 1992.

Haffner, Sebastian. *The Meaning of Hitler.* London: Weidenfeld and Nicolson, 1979.

Hiden, J. and J. Farquharson. *Explaining Hitler's Germany.* London: Batsford, 1989.

Hildebrand, K. *The Third Reich.* London: Unwin, 1984.

Jäckel, E. *Hitler's World View.* Cambridge, MA: Harvard University Press, 1981.

Kershaw, I. *Hitler.* London: Longman, 1991.

———. *The "Hitler Myth." Image and Reality in the Third Reich.* Oxford: Oxford University Press, 1987.

———. *The Nazi Dictatorship.* 3rd ed. London: Edward Arnold, 1993.

Mommsen, H. "National Socialism: Continuity and Change." *Fascism: A Reader's Guide.* Ed. W. Laqueur. London: Penguin, 1982.

Steinert, Marlis. *Hitler: A Biography.* New York, NY.: W.W. Norton, 1997.

Waite, R. *The Psychopathic God: Adolf Hitler.* New York, NY: Basic Books, 1977.

Hitler Youth

The Hitler Youth emerged from inauspicious beginnings as the youth branch of the Nazi Party to play an active and important role in the struggle for power before 1933. In the Third Reich, it swiftly destroyed almost all other groups to become the state youth organization, encompassing millions of younger Germans of both sexes and propagating to considerable effect the Nazi Weltanschauung (world view).

The Hitler-Jugend: Bund deutscher Arbeiterjugend (Hitler Youth: League of German Working-Class Youth) was established under the leadership of Kurt Gruber at the Nazi Party annual rally in Weimar in July 1926. It was only one of a number of ancillary organizations established in the mid-1920s as Hitler strove to broaden the appeal of his movement throughout German society as an essential part of a new political strategy within the democratic, parliamentary framework of the Weimar Republic. Until the early 1930s, the fulcrum of the Hitler Youth's activity lay in Gruber's home state of Saxony, which allowed the group a certain degree of independence from the Munich-based party.

With a membership before 1933 drawn mainly from working-class youngsters, the Hitler Youth developed a social-revolutionary ideological orientation that ultimately clashed with the increasingly bourgeois course of the Nazi Party. When Baldur von Schirach (1907–74) was made responsible for all Nazi Party youth groups in 1931, Gruber was dismissed and the Hitler Youth was forced to conform with the party's credo of chauvinism, anti-Marxism, and anti-Semitism. The 55,000-strong Hitler Youth helped Hitler to power by conducting noisy propaganda and acting as a recruiting agency for the party and Stormtroopers (Sturmabteilung [SA]). It also allowed the Nazi Party to sustain its image as a movement of the younger generation against the decrepit Weimar "system," ensuring that German youth would enjoy an enhanced status after 1933. It was then no longer simply the youth auxiliary of a political party, but rather the official and only youth organization of the Third Reich, charged with the mobilization of young Germans for *Führer, Volk und Vaterland* (leader, race, and fatherland).

The Hitler Youth was a new type of youth group, totalitarian in outlook and fanatical in persuasion. It wielded a ubiquitous influence over every conceivable facet of youth life in the name of National Socialism, and it set up special educational centers to train future leaders. The Law for the Hitler Youth of December 1936 formally extended legal recognition to it as a *Staatsjugend* (state-sanctioned youth movement), which all Germans under the age of 18 years were required to join. By

1939, the Hitler Youth numbered some eight million boys and girls, making it the largest organization of its kind in the world. During World War II, it was progressively militarized, and continued to display a tragic loyalty to the regime until the end.

In 1945, the Hitler Youth represented a bewildered and betrayed generation of German youth. Twenty years' dedication to Hitler and National Socialism had brought calamity instead of the glorious future so often promised.

Peter D. Stachura

See also Education; League of German Girls; National Socialism; National Socialist Germany: Education; Schirach, Baldur von; Schools; Youth; Youth Movements

References

Brandenburg, Hans-Christian. *Die Geschichte der HJ: Wege und Irrwege einer Generation.* Cologne: Verlag Wissenschaft und Politik, 1968.

Breyvogel, Wilfried. *Piraten, Swings und Junge Garde: Jugendwiderstand im Nationalsozialismus.* Berlin: Dietz, 1991.

Hellfeld, Manfred von. *Bündische Jugend und Hitlerjugend: Zur Geschichte von Anpassung und Widerstand 1930–1939.* Cologne: Verlag Wissenschaft und Politik, 1987.

Klönne, Arno. *Hitlerjugend: Die Jugend und Ihre Organisation im Dritten Reich.* Hannover: Norddeutsche Verlagsanstalt, 1956.

———. *Jugend im Dritten Reich: Die Hitler-Jugend und ihre Gegner. Dokumente und Analyse.* Düsseldorf: Diederichs, 1982.

Klose, Werner. *Generation im Gleichschritt: Eine Dokumentation.* 2nd ed. Oldenburg: Stalling, 1982.

Peukert, Detlev. *Die Edelweisspiraten—Protestbewegungen jugendlicher Arbeiter im Dritten Reich: Eine Dokumentation.* Cologne: Bund, 1980.

Scholtz, Harald. *Erziehung und Unterricht unterm Hakenkreuz.* Göttingen: Vandenhoeck & Ruprecht, 1985.

———. *NS-Ausleseschulen: Internatsschulen als Herrschaftsmittel des Führerstaates.* Göttingen: Vandenhoeck & Ruprecht, 1973.

Stachura, Peter D. *Nazi Youth in the Weimar Republic.* Oxford: ABC-Clio, 1975.

Höch, Hannah Johanne (1889–1978)

Hannah Höch's life and work were emblematic of the evolution and fate of the twentieth-century German avant-garde. As a woman and as an artist, Höch transcended the prevailing limits to break fresh ground.

Supported by enlightened bourgeois parents in Gotha, Höch had the courage to establish residence in metropolitan Berlin, where she studied applied arts at the Städtische Kunstgewerbe- und Handwerks-Schule Charlottenburg (Municipal School for Applied Arts and Crafts) until 1914. After a brief interruption of her studies caused by World War I, she became a student of Emil Orlik (1870–1932) at the teaching institute associated with the Applied Arts and Crafts Museum (1915–20). In 1915, Höch met Raoul Hausmann (1886–1971), with whom she had a seven-year relationship. Together with Hausmann, who in 1918 became one of the founders of the Club Dada in Berlin, Höch developed photo collage as a specific vehicle of the artistic expression of Berlin dadaism.

Höchst had been familiar with the collage technique since her childhood, when modern pedagogy included the manipulation of colored paper. The roots of her painting were established at this time; her first paintings were rendered in 1904. Both art forms, painting and photo montage, influenced each other in continuous creative interaction, but also found expression independent of each other. One of Höch's most famous photo collages, *Cutting with the Dada Kitchen Knife through the Last Epoch of Weimar Beer-Belly Culture,* 1919–20, was exhibited in 1920 at the First International Dada Exhibition. It offers a complex and dynamic portrait of an epoch at the beginning of the Weimar Republic. She simultaneously created pictures and collages of symbolical fantasy characters, which expound especially the realities of women's lives. Abstract-constructive compositions form another trend in the layered stylistic pluralism of her work, which developed into a network of aesthetic fragmentations and connections.

In 1926, Höch met the Dutch writer Til Brugman (1888–1956), with whom she lived until 1935, first in The Hague and from 1929 in Berlin. However, the political climate became threatening for Höch, whom the Nazis branded a "cultural Bolshevik." She therefore retreated in 1939 with her husband, Dr. Kurt Matthies (divorced after 1944), into the sheltering anonymity of Heiligensee, a Berlin suburb.

As a painter, Höch responded to political events in metaphorical, coded, cryptographic pictures. The 1933 *Wild Departure* commemorated mothers who observed with distrust and malaise the young generation's allegiance to brutality. The 1943 *Figurines with Egg,* evokes the sense of apocalyptic doom of the war years: two spectral figures, with the world-egg between them, try to avert the danger. Simultaneously, Höch developed in her collages of the 1940s a dream-like, antipodal world whose ambivalent symbols testify to the inevitability of doom.

After World War II, the congruency of motif and artistic production became increasingly important and culminated in several poetic compositions (*Konkretionen*). The former symbolic figuration of the paintings and their stylistic pluralism became internalized and absorbed by the abstract structures. They aimed at discovering and exhibiting a world composed of a multiplicity of secret shapes. These collages continued to reflect Höch's ironic-critical view of her time and its politics.

Ellen Maurer

See also Artists; Arts and Crafts; Dada; Painting

References

Adriani, G., ed. *Hannah Höch: Fotomontagen-Gemälde-Aquarelle.* Cologne: DuMont, 1980.

Berlinische Galerie, ed. *Hannah Höch: Eine Lebens-Collage: Archiv-Edition.* Berlin: Argon-Verlag, 1989.

Dech, J. *Hannah Höch: Schnitt mit dem Küchenmesser*

Dada-Spiegel einer Bierbauchkultur. Reihe Kunststück. Frankfurt am Main: Fischer Verlag, 1989.

Dech, J. and E. Maurer, eds. *Da-dazwischen Reden zu Hannah Höch: Dokumentation des Internationalen Hannah-Höch-Symposion.* Reihe "Der andere Blick." Berlin: Orlanda Verlag, 1991.

Hannah Höch. 1889–1978. Ihr Werk, ihr Leben, ihre Freunde. Exhibition catalog. Berlinische Galerie. Berlin: Argon-Verlag, 1989.

Lavin, Maud. *Hannah Höch: Photomontage and the Representation of the New Woman in Weimar Germany 1918–1933.* New Haven, CT: Yale University Press, 1993.

Maurer, Ellen. *Hannah Höch: Jenseits fester Grenzen: Das malerische Werk bis 1945.* Berlin: Gebr. Mann Verlag, 1995.

Hochhuth, Rolf (1931–)

Rolf Hochhuth is one of the best-known playwrights of West Germany. Growing up during the Third Reich had a tremendous impact on his thinking and writing.

Hochhuth gained immediate recognition and stirred up a tremendous controversy with his first play, *Der Stellvertreter* (published as *The Deputy*), 1962, which was staged in 1963 by Erwin Piscator (1893–1966). In this play Hochhuth examines to what extent Pope Pius XII was responsible for the deportation of the Roman Jews by the Nazis. His work ignited heated dispute and had political significance because of its topicality and critical approach to the Federal Republic of Germany (FRG). His 1971 comedy *Die Hebamme* (The midwife), brought the sad fate of homeless people to public attention. His latest play, *Wessis in Weimar—Szenen aus einem besetzten Land* (Westerners in Weimar—scenes from an occupied country), in which he harshly attacks the privatization trust (Treuhand-Anstalt), created a public uproar because one character proposes the assassination of the head of this organization, a fate suffered by Detlev Rohwedder, the first president of the trust.

Hochhuth's work has not only been controversial in its political stance but also with respect to its aesthetic realization. All of his dramatic work is based on detailed historical research and contains extensive authentic data and commentary. At times, it combines fictional and historical characters on stage and uses conventional theatrical codes, showing a strong debt to naturalism. Hochhuth himself has rejected the label of documentary theater and views himself in the tradition of Lessing and particularly Schiller's understanding of theater as an edifying institution.

Sabine von Dirke

See also Drama; Federal Republic of Germany: Literature; Theater

References

Bentley, Eric. *The Storm over The Deputy.* New York, NY: Grove Press, 1964.

Hochhuth, Rolf. *Alle Dramen.* 2 vols. Reinbek: Rowohlt, 1991.

———. *Eine Liebe in Deutschland.* Reinbek: Rowohlt, 1978.

———. *War hier Europa? Reden, Gedichte, Essays.* Munich: Deutscher Taschenbuch Verlag, 1987.

Rainer, Taeni. *Rolf Hochhuth.* Trans. R.W. Last. London: Oswald Wolff, 1977.

Ward, Margaret E. *Rolf Hochhuth.* Boston, MA: Twayne Publishers, 1977.

Wolff, Rudolf, ed. *Rolf Hochhuth: Werk und Wirkung.* Bonn: Bouvier, 1987.

Hödicke, Karl Horst (1938–)

Working in a variety of media—painting, object-art, film, photography and sculpture—K.H. Hödicke has come to be regarded as one of the leading renderers of contemporary *Grosstadtbilder* (urban images). From the mid-1960s on, his works have straddled the boundaries between abstraction and figuration and created potent metaphors for the contemporary experience of Berlin, the metropolis.

Hödicke began to study painting with Fred Thieler (1916–) at the Hochschule der bildenden Künste (academy of fine arts) in Berlin in 1959, where he was exposed to the abstract idioms of Informel and Tachism. By the early 1960s, he rejected pure abstraction for a more figurative, expressive painting built on experience and the visual world. He founded the group VISION with Bernd Köberling (1938–) in 1961 and the artists' cooperative *Grossgoerschen 35* with Markus Lüpertz (1941–) in 1964, both of which provided forums for young painters to develop their individual approaches to the seeming bankruptcy of abstraction.

Painting cycles such as *Reflections* (1964) and *Passages* (1965), exhibited at the Rene Block gallery in Berlin in 1965, juxtaposed the transient visions and experiences of the city, gleaned through shop windows, glass, and artificial lights, with the all-over color and gestural applications of Tachism. This dialogue between the formal, flat surface of the painting and the experience of the city continued in Hödicke's work into the 1970s, with paintings of Berlin monuments and buildings seen at night or at vertiginous angles, such as in *Schöneberg Heaven* (1974–75). Later paintings, from the 1980s, used the metaphor of the urban jungle to express the current experience of a city under siege.

From the mid-1960s on, Hödicke experimented with different media, such as photography, film, object-art, and installations, in an attempt to deemphasize style and continuity in his oeuvre. Short, experimental films, such as *Made in New York*, created during a stay in New York in 1966, and neo-dadaist objects, such as the Duchampian *European Travel Case* (1967–76), continued the theme of urban experience in media inspired by Fluxus and Happenings. By the mid-1980s, large-scale sculpture entered the artist's formal repertoire.

Since 1974, Hödicke has taught at the Hochschule der bildenden Künste in Berlin, where he is revered as a teacher and mentor to a new generation of Berlin artists. He became a member of the Akademie der Künste (academy of arts) in 1980.

Kristin Makholm

See also Artists; Cinema; Lüpertz, Markus; Painting; Photography; Sculpture

References

K.H. Hödicke. Exhibition catalog. Karlsruhe: Badischer Kunstverein, 1977.

K.H. Hödicke: Gemälde, Skulpturen, Objekte, Filme. Exhibition catalog. Düsseldorf: Kunstsammlung Nordrhein-Westfalen, 1986.

Merkert, Jorn. *K.H. Hödicke: Zu den Arbeiten von K.H. Hödicke in der Berlinischen Galerie.* Berlin: Berlinische Galerie and Argon Verlag, 1988.

Pincus-Witten, Robert. "Entries: Rebuilding the Bridge (Hödicke, Joachimides, and Berlin in the early '80s)." *Arts Magazine* 64 (March 1990), 72–7.

Hoegner, Wilhelm (1887–1980)

Hoegner's name is associated with the resistance against Nazism and the democratic reconstruction of Bavaria within a federalist Germany after World War II.

Hoegner grew up in a family of nine; his father was a railway worker. Thanks to his academic abilities, tuition fees were waived and he was able to study at the Königliches Gymnasium in Burghausen and at the Ludwigsgymnasium in Munich from 1898 to 1907. Subsequently he studied law in Berlin, Munich, and Erlangen. In 1911 he obtained his doctorate. Owing to heart problems he could not serve in World War I—much to his regret. Instead he worked as a stenography teacher and later as a volunteer in a mutual insurance company (Versicherungsbank). In 1917, he passed his assistant judge's exam; after 1920, he worked as a prosecutor and judge in Munich. In 1928 he won promotion to the rank of principal prosecutor, and in 1931 he became associate provincial court judge (*Landgerichtsrat*).

Hoegner sympathized with the moderate reformists in the Social Democratic Party (SPD) in his early years. He became a member of the party only in 1919, but he experienced quick success: in 1924, he became a member of the Bavarian Lower House, and in 1930 a member of the Reichstag. In 1933 he was, not surprisingly, ousted from these positions by the Nazis.

Hoegner had demonstrated his unflinching opposition to the Nazis by his work on the commission of inquiry into the Hitler *Putsch* of 1923, as well as by his speeches in the Reichstag. Party discipline could not prevent him from severely criticizing the SPD party leaders whom he reproached—quite perspicaciously—for being too lenient toward Hitler at the beginning of the 1930s. To escape arrest as an enemy of the Hitler regime in 1933, he embarked on an adventurous flight to Austria and Switzerland. Constantly threatened with deportation from his Swiss exile, he nevertheless continued his illegal activities. Under a variety of pseudonyms he wrote numerous articles, translated books, and gave lectures, eking out a meager living. His exile experience in Switzerland persuaded him to abandon his centralist perspective and to become a federalist.

Hoegner elaborated plans for the reconstruction of a democratic Germany in which Bavaria would play a central role; he clearly opposed all Bavarian aspirations to be a separate, Catholic state. In 1945, he returned to the Bavarian capital. After a brief prelude as president of the Senate of the Superior Provincial Court he became Bavarian minister-president and minister of justice until 1947. During his term in office he laid the foundations of the new Bavarian state. He has subsequently been considered the "father" of the Bavarian constitution and its federalist orientation. As a member of the Bavarian Lower House (1946–70), minister of justice (1946–47), minister of the interior, deputy premier (1950–54), and minister-president again (1954–57), he significantly influenced the democratic reconstruction and development of Bavaria after World War II.

Karl Heinrich Pohl

See also The Basic Law; Bavaria; Federalism; Federal Republic of Germany; Resistance; Social Democratic Party, 1919–90

References

Hoegner, Wilhelm. *Der schwierige Aussenseiter: Erinnerungen.* Munich: Isar Verlag, 1959.

———. *Die verratene Republik.* Munich: Isar Verlag, 1958.

———. *Flucht vor Hitler: Erinnerungen an die Kapitulation der ersten deutschen Republik, 1933.* Munich: Nymphenburger Verlagshandlung, 1977.

Kritzer, Peter. *Wilhelm Hoegner: Politische Biographie eines bayerischen Sozialdemokraten.* Munich: Süddeutscher Verlag, 1979.

Röder, Werner and Herbert Strauss, eds. *Biographisches Handbuch der deutschsprachigen Emigration nach 1933.* Vol. 1. Munich: K. Sauer, 1980.

Hofer, Karl (1878–1955)

Born on October 11, 1878, in Karlsruhe, Karl Hofer, a painter/graphic artist died on April 3, 1955, in Berlin.

After the death of his father in 1879, Hofer was placed in an orphanage and attended grammar school until 1892, after which he began an apprenticeship in a bookstore. From 1896 to 1901 he attended the Karlsruhe Academy on scholarship and in 1902–03 the Academy in Stuttgart. He spent 1903–08 in Rome and 1908–13 in Paris, interrupted by two trips to India, financially assisted by the Swiss collector Theodor Reinhard. In 1913, he settled in Berlin. From 1914 to 1917 he interned in France and then returned to Berlin in 1919. He was appointed professor at the Vereinigte Staatsschulen für freie und angewandte Kunst (United State Schools for Free and Applied Arts) in Berlin in 1920, elected a member of the Prussian Academy of Art in 1923, and made a senator of this institution in 1929.

Hofer's work, at first influenced by Hans von Maree, Böcklin, and Cézanne, never truly changed the forms it had already gained in the 1920s. Although he belonged to the generation of the expressionists, his expressive form has a more classical accentuation, with dominance of the contour line. His colors are subdued and devoid of light reflections. Human figures, single and in groups (many of them young female nudes), and landscapes form the bulk of his subjects. He also painted modern, frequently haunting allegories, some of which seem to point toward the catastrophe of the Nazis and World War II. He had frequently criticized the Nazis' concept of art, and in 1934 he was dismissed from his teaching position and forbidden to work or exhibit. In 1938, he was dismissed from the Academy at the same time that he won the Carnegie Institute's first prize in Pittsburgh.

Hofer remained in Berlin; 313 of his works were confiscated from German museums and eight appeared in the *Degenerate Art* exhibition of 1937. In 1943 he lost his studio and many of his works in a bombing raid on Berlin. At the end of the war, he was appointed professor and director of the Hochschule für bildende Künste (Academy of Fine Arts), which was being rebuilt. He repainted a number of his lost or destroyed works. Besides being honored by numerous exhibits of his works, he was granted an honorary doctorate by Humboldt University. He also received many prizes, such as the order of Pour le Mérite and the Cross of Merit of the Federal Republic.

Peter Guenther

See also Artists; Expressionism; National Socialist Germany: Art; Painting

References

Hartleb, Renate. *Karl Hofer.* Leipzig: P. Reclam, 1982.
Hofer, Karl. *Malerei hat eine Zukunft: Briefe, Aufsätze, Reden.* Leipzig: Kiepenheuer, 1991.
Hofer, Karl, and Theodor Reinhart. *Maler und Mäzen: Ein Briefwechsel in Auswahl.* Berlin: Henschelverlag, 1989.

Hoffmann, Heinz (1910–85)

As Minister of Defense of the German Democratic Republic (GDR) from 1960 to 1985, Heinz Hoffmann embodied the Communist German military ethos and soldierly ideals of the GDR. His service as head of the Ministry of National Defense and as ranking general of the National People's Army (NVA) reflected the Social Unity Party (SED) ideology of society and arms come to life in the person of the GDR's first soldier.

Born on November 28, 1910, into the working class of the Empire, Hoffmann moved from being a Communist apprentice machinist, to a post-1933 member of the German Communist Party underground, to political exile in France and the USSR, to combat service in the Spanish Civil War, and to Soviet political and military training that enabled his return to Germany with the Soviet military government in mid-1945. By the start of the 1960s, as the SED regime consolidated itself behind the fortifications along the inner-German border built by the new NVA, Hoffmann ascended to the leadership of defense and security organizations of the GDR. Here he remained until his death, an event that coincided with the start of the general institutional decline of the East German military establishment in the mid-1980s.

Apart from his battalion command with the Eleventh International Brigade (1936–37) in the Spanish Civil War, Hoffmann began his military career with the *Hauptabteilung*

Polit-Kultur (political directorate) of the headquarters of the *Volkspolizei* (VP; People's Police) (1950 *ff*.), later the KVP, the predecessor of the NVA. He carried out high-ranking staff functions in this paramilitary police force within the Ministry of the Interior until 1955–56. With the unveiling of the NVA in January 1956, Hoffmann attended Soviet higher general staff education at the Frunze Academy in Moscow. In the spring of 1956, he attained the rank of *Generalleutnant* (major general) of the NVA and served with the Combined Armed Forces staff of the Warsaw Pact—the strategic/operational headquarters where the Soviets directed alliance strategic planning. In March 1958, Hoffmann became chief of staff of the land forces of the NVA and in the same year chief of staff of the NVA General Staff (*Hauptstab der NVA*).

In July 1960, having been promoted to the rank of *Generaloberst* (lieutenant general), Hoffmann succeeded Willi Stoph (1914–) as Minister of National Defense. This move freed the NVA from the tutelage of the Ministry of Interior. In March 1961, Hoffmann was promoted again to the rank of *Armeegeneral* (general) and became a member of the Committee of Defense Ministers of the Warsaw Pact.

The succeeding decades of his leadership oversaw the build-up in depth of highly trained ground units, tactical air forces, and coastal naval units fitted within the offensive strategic/operational doctrine of the Warsaw Pact. From 1952, Hoffmann had been a member of the Central Committee of the SED. In October 1973, he entered the *Politbüro* of the SED. In the final decade of his tenure, the NVA came to play an ever more prominent role in the GDR state and society beyond the garrison walls. The degree of military preparation and training under Hoffmann's last years assumed an ever higher state of perfection and readiness.

This phenomenon, derived from the needs of alliance cohesion with the Soviets and political control at home, aroused the silent resistance of the man and woman on the street. Such antimilitary sentiment threatened to break into the open shortly before the end of Hoffmann's tenure. He remained Minister of National Defense and a member of the SED *Politbüro* until his death on December 2, 1985. The advent of Mikhail Gorbachev's reforms, especially in their geopolitical and social dimensions, overturned the strategic foundations on which Hoffmann and his subordinates had built their military lives. His 1981 autobiography is an example of GDR hagiography prepared by the official military historians of the Militärgeschichtliches Institut (Military Historical Institute) in Potsdam.

Donald Abenheim

See also German Democratic Republic; German Democratic Republic: National People's Army; Honecker, Erich; Mielke, Erich; Militarism

References

Fischer, Alexander, ed. *Wiederbewaffnung in Deutschland nach 1945.* Berlin: Duncker and Humblot, 1986.
Forster, Thomas. *Die NVA: Kernstück der Landesverteidigung der DDR.* 6th ed. Cologne: Markus-Verlag, 1983.

Fricke, Karl-Wilhelm. "Die Militärs in der DDR Führung." *Deutschland Archiv* 3 (1975).

Hoffmann, Heinz. *Mannheim/Madrid/Moscow: Erlebtes aus drei Jahrzehnten.* Berlin (East): Militärverlag der Deutschen Demokratischen Republik, 1981.

———. *Sozialistische Landesverteidigung: Aus Reden und Aufsätzen, 1963–1985.* 5 vols. Berlin (East): Militärverlag der Deutschen Demokratischen Republik, 1971–86.

Militärgeschichtliches Institut, ed. *Armee für Frieden Sozialismus: Geschichte der Nationalen Volksarmee.* 2nd ed. Berlin (East): Militärverlag der Deutschen Demokratischen Republik, 1987.

Thoss, Bruno, ed. *Volksarmee schaffen—ohne Geschrei!: Studien zu den Anfängen einer verdeckten Aufrüstung in der SBZ/DDR, 1947–1952.* Munich: Oldenbourg, 1994.

Hofmann, August Wilhelm von (1818–92)

August Hofmann, among the nineteenth century's leading organic chemists and chemistry teachers in Germany and England, promoted the growth of science and industry, especially in the field of aniline dyes. His leadership also shaped German chemical institutions during the 1860s and 1870s.

Hofmann was born in Giessen, where he obtained his doctorate (1841) under Justus von Liebig, whose teaching laboratory Hofmann's architect father had enlarged. After an assistantship in Giessen (1843–45), Hofmann was briefly *Privatdozent* (private scholar) in Bonn, then professor of chemistry at the Royal College of Chemistry (later the School of Mines) in London (1845–65). He became a popular teacher and an authority in the field of coal-tar chemicals, such as aniline and its derivatives. Beginning with William Perkin in 1856, Hofmann's students founded some of the first aniline dye factories, and his collaboration with some of them made him wealthy. Hofmann was primarily an extremely productive experimentalist, but his text of 1865 also promoted "modern" chemical nomenclature.

At the height of his fame, Hofmann accepted a professorship in Bonn, but before assuming it took a professorship in Berlin (1865). There Hofmann helped to lay the institutional foundations of German dominance in organic chemistry. Laboratories built to his specifications in Bonn and Berlin inaugurated a new, much larger generation of German teaching institutes supplying research-trained chemists for the rapidly growing German chemical industry. Proclaiming an alliance between science and industry, Hofmann became the first president and dominant influence in the Deutsche Chemische Gesellschaft (German Chemical Society), in 1867, whose *Berichte* (reports) presented the latest research reports in structural organic chemistry to a large international academic and industrial membership. His recommendations shaped the new German patent law (1877) to promote industrial research. At Hofmann's insistence, the Gesellschaft did not promote manufacturers' special interests, for which purpose a separate organization was established in 1877.

As university rector, Hofmann opposed the emerging anti-Semitic student movement as well as proposals to deemphasize classical secondary education and to establish a separate science faculty. A multilingual cosmopolitan, he made innumerable friends among Europe's industrial and scientific elites as well as the British and German royal families. His many honors included a title from Kaiser Friedrich III (1888). Enjoying robust health despite working long hours, Hofmann outlived three of his four wives (he had 11 children) and worked productively throughout his life.

Besides his contributions to chemistry, Hofmann was important for promoting the integration of science and industry in modern Germany.

Jeffrey A. Johnson

See also Chemistry: Scientific and Industrial; Kolbe, Hermann

References

Meinel, Christoph. "August Wilhelm Hofmann—Reigning Chemist-in-Chief." *Angewandte Chemie* (International Edition in English) 31 (1992), 1265–82.

Meinel, Christoph, and Hartmut Scholz, eds. *Die Allianz von Wissenschaft und Industrie: August Wilhelm Hofmann (1818–1892): Zeit, Werk, Wirkung.* Weinheim: VCH Verlagsgesellschaft, 1992.

Rocke, Alan J. *The Quiet Revolution: Hermann Kolbe and the Science of Organic Chemistry.* Berkeley, CA: University of California Press, 1993.

Travis, Anthony S. *The Rainbow Makers: The Origins of the Synthetic Dyestuffs Industry in Western Europe.* Bethlehem, PA: Lehigh University Press, Associated University Presses, 1993.

Hofmannsthal, Hugo von (1874–1929)

Hugo von Hofmannsthal was a poet, playwright, and novelist. His creativity is most evident in his intense and not always easy collaboration with the composer Richard Strauss (1864–1949), which resulted in the important operas *Elektra,* 1909, *Der Rosenkavalier* (The rose cavalier), 1911, and *Ariadne auf Naxos,* 1912.

Born in Vienna to a well-to-do, mixed Austrian-Jewish and Italian family of bankers, Hofmannsthal first studied law and eventually earned a doctorate in Romance literature at the University of Vienna in 1898. In 1901, he married Gertrud Schlesinger and moved to Rodaun in the vicinity of Vienna, where he lived as an independent writer until his death in 1929. His literary success started with the publication of poems and essays at the age of 17. His early verse plays, such as *Der Tor und der Tod* (Death and the fool), 1893, and *Das kleine Welttheater* (The little world theater), 1897, are characterized by a fin-de-siècle aestheticism and impressionism that Hofmannsthal later rejected in his reconsideration of the artist's endeavor in the "Brief des Lord Chandos" (Letter of Lord Chandos), 1902. That fictive letter to the philosopher Francis Bacon (1561–1626) is the best-known document of what Hofmannsthal described as a "crisis of language," his sense of the inability of words to really convey meaning, also evident in his unfinished and posthumously published novel, *Andreas oder die Vereinigten,* 1932. The "Brief des Lord

Chandos" marks as well the beginning of a new phase of literary production leading up to *Elektra,* 1904, *Ödipus und die Sphinx,* 1906, and *König Ödipus,* 1907. In these tragedies, Hofmannsthal reaches back to Greek myths but transforms them under the influence of Nietzsche and Freud. Plays such as *Jedermann* (Everyman), 1912, a reworking of a Germanic medieval theme, and essays such as "Der Dichter und diese Zeit", (The poet and these times), 1906, and "Das Schrifttum als geistiger Raum der Nation" (Literature as the spiritual realm of the nation), 1927, attest to Hofmannsthal's interest in preserving and renewing the literary heritage of the German-speaking world. Hofmannsthal's collaborations with Max Reinhardt in the 1920 production of *Jedermann* and the 1922 *Das grosse Welttheater* (The great world theater) were the beginning of the "Salzburger Festspiele" (Salzburg festival) which have continued through the twentieth century.

Hofmannsthal is best remembered for the delicacy and refinement of his language, his abundant correspondence—a unique document of the "spirit of the times"—and his collaborative genius that transformed librettos into poetic masterpieces.

Andres Nader

See also Drama; Novel; Poetry; Reinhardt, Max; Strauss, Richard

References
Bangerter, Lowell A. *Hugo von Hofmannsthal.* New York, NY: Ungar, 1977

Koch, Hans-Albrecht. *Hugo von Hofmannsthal.* Darmstadt: Wissenschaftliche Buchgesellschaft, 1989.

Renner, Ursula and Bärbel G. Schmid, eds. *Hugo von Hofmannsthal: Freundschaften und Begegnungen mit deutschen Zeitgenossen.* Würzburg: Königshausen & Neumann, 1991.

Hohenlohe-Schillingsfürst, Prince Chlodwig zu (1819–1901)

Scion of one of the great princely families of Germany and kinsman of other aristocratic magnates and European royalty, Hohenlohe was a preeminent statesman of the kingdom of Bavaria, where he was born, and the German Empire, in the service of which he held high office. A consummate cosmopolite, Hohenlohe was a Catholic with a brother who became a cardinal but had a Protestant mother. Hohenlohe was a Bavarian who had worked in his youth in the Prussian bureaucracy, a German married to a Russian princess, a large landholder who embraced liberal ideas. As a result of his hybrid background, he was uncommonly tolerant and undogmatic about religion, politics, and diplomacy.

The defeat of Bavaria in the disastrous war against Prussia in 1866 led to the fall of the government in Munich. King Ludwig II, acting on the advice of his musical protégé, Richard Wagner (1813–83), appointed Hohenlohe as his chief minister. Hohenlohe remodeled the army along Prussian lines and worked successfully to defuse the resentment felt in Munich against Berlin. He had no patience with the ultramontane leanings of many Bavarian notables and favored the

unification of Germany under the Protestant Prussians. When this was effected in 1871, Hohenlohe became a member of the new Reichstag.

Chancellor Bismarck recognized in the grand seigneur Hohenlohe a prospective diplomat and in 1873 had him appointed ambassador in Paris. Taking up his position scarcely two years after France's shattering defeat at Prussia's hands in the Franco-Prussian War, Hohenlohe made himself popular in Paris with his deft behavior, his fulsome hospitality, and his calm demeanor. In 1885, Bismarck promoted Hohenlohe to the even more sensitive post of regent of Alsace-Lorraine, where he successfully ruled with great restraint until 1894, when the young Kaiser, Wilhelm II, called him to Berlin to be chancellor.

As chancellor, Hohenlohe pursued a policy designed to avoid confrontation with the ruler and the Reichstag. His critics complained that he was without either energy or principles, but Hohenlohe argued that more was to be gained by negotiating endlessly than by taking an intractable position. During the eight years of his chancellorship, he managed to win imperial assent and Reichstag majorities for a number of reforms in the army, in the codification of the law, and in tariff policy. It was also under Hohenlohe, and with his support, that Imperial Germany acquired more colonies and built a vast navy. He could look back on many major accomplishments when late in 1900, aged and infirm, he resigned his post.

Lamar Cecil

See also Anglo-German Relations; Bülow, Bernhard von; Center Party; Chancellor's Office; Colonies and Colonial Society; Diplomatic Corps and Diplomacy; Imperial Germany: Foreign Policy; Imperialism; Ludwig II; Navy and Naval Policy; Russian-German Relations; Wilhelm II

References
Cecil, Lamar. *Wilhelm II.* Vol. I *Prince and Emperor, 1859–1900.* Vol. II *Emperor and Exile, 1900–1941.* Chapel Hill, NC: University of North Carolina Press, 1989–96.

Hohenlohe-Schillingsfürst, Prince Chlodwig zu. *Denkwürdigkeiten.* 3 vols. Leipzig: Deutsche Verlags-Anstalt, 1907–31.

Röhl, John C. G. *Germany without Bismarck: The Crisis of Government in the Second Reich.* Berkeley, CA: University of California Press, 1967.

Holocaust

Holocaust is the term customarily used in North America to refer to the murder of two-thirds of European Jewry, about six million people, by the Nazi regime during World War II. For obvious reasons, historians are uncertain about the precise number of victims, but a few statistics may be cited. The destruction amounted to about one-third of world Jewry and included over a million Jewish children. Nearly four million Jews died in internment camps. The main killing centers were in Poland, including Auschwitz-Birkenau, Chelmno, Treblinka, Sobibór, Belzec and Majdanek. Some two million perished elsewhere—mainly by shooting in the Soviet Union or through starvation and disease in the ghettos of Eastern Europe. Jews from every country occupied by the Germans were directly threatened, although the incidence of destruction varied from place to place depending on local conditions and Nazi priorities. The overwhelming majority of the victims came from Eastern Europe, where the Jewish population concentration was greatest. Poland lost the most, with close to three million Jewish victims.

Unlike many of history's massacres, the destruction of European Jewry was extensively documented. Part of the reason is the vast scale and extent of the murderous enterprise, carried out across an entire continent and administered directly and indirectly by bureaucracies and branches of the German civil service. As with conventional warfare, those who actually did the killing were a relatively small group; behind them was a great army of "desk murderers" and other workers taking charge of transportation, scheduling, construction, disposing of the Jews' former property, and so on. Another reason for the great volume of evidence is the thoroughness with which the Nazis went about their task, guided by their determination to rid the world of each and every one of their hated Jewish enemies. Historians have followed the elaborate paper trails describing the killing process itself—deportation records, reports from death camps and killing units of various sorts, and abundant evidence from bystanders, neutrals, and other witnesses, as well as the diaries, memoirs, and other testimony of victims and survivors. Scholars have also drawn upon records of the trials of some of the perpetrators—the Nuremberg and other war-crimes tribunals established immediately after the war and proceedings against perpetrators carried out in Germany and elsewhere in subsequent decades.

With this vast documentation, historians attempt to interpret the origins and course of the Holocaust. On some issues there is widespread agreement. There is no dispute about the great importance of anti-Semitism in Hitler's own ideology, to the point that one may see it as central to his worldview. Students of the Holocaust also look for origins in the intense, brutal campaign against the Jews of Germany from the moment Hitler became chancellor in 1933. Over the next six years a series of laws and decrees gradually isolated the 525,000 Jews in German society, stripping them of their rights, removing them from their employment, robbing them of their property, and subjecting them to random acts of terror. Increasingly Jews turned to emigration as their last resort, with the flow of Jews abroad intensifying particularly after the *Kristallnacht* (Crystal Night) riots against them by the Sturmabteilung (SA) and Nazi Party activists in November 1938. Just as this flow of refugees increased, new barriers to immigration were being raised everywhere. Penniless, and sometimes stateless as well, many Jews from the Greater German Reich (expanding to include Austria and western Czechoslovakia) sought in vain for a place of refuge.

Up to the outbreak of war and beyond, the German government officially called for Jewish emigration, and expelled Jews across frontiers whenever possible. The official goal of the regime was to rid the Reich of its Jews. During the first year and a half of the war the Nazis extended this goal to all the territories under their control. For a short time, in 1939, the Nazis considered placing Jews into a reservation in the Nisko region of Poland; at the same time, Heinrich Himmler's (1900–45) Schutzstaffel (SS) bureaucracy planned to move masses of Jews from Polish territory incorporated into the Reich to the General Government, the "protectorate" in the central part of the country. Haphazardly begun, these plans proved beyond the capacity of the German authorities to carry out during this period.

With the defeat of France in 1940, another solution captured the imaginations of some SS specialists as well as others in the Foreign Office—a proposal to ship the Jews to the island of Madagascar in the Indian Ocean. This project, apparently taken seriously in the Nazi hierarchy, could not be realized as long as the war continued. Then, in the following year, Nazi plans shifted once again, beginning what the German authorities themselves referred to as the "Final Solution."

It is not certain at what point and at whose direction the Nazis moved to commit Europe-wide mass murder. There is widespread agreement that Hitler had a key role in Jewish matters, although scholars differ on how closely he followed events and on what level he directed Nazi Jewish policy. Some historians, usually referred to as intentionalists, regard the Nazis' ideas about the Jews and their anti-Jewish program of the mid-1930s as pointing directly to the genocidal outcome during World War II. War, they believe, gave Hitler the opportunity to carry out a predetermined, murderous objective on a grand scale.

Other scholars, known as functionalists, stress the evolution of Nazi policy toward the Jews, contending that mass murder only emerged as a realistic option during the course of the war itself—specifically the Barbarossa campaign against the Soviet Union. They believe that the Nazis groped toward a solution of the "Jewish problem," opting for a comprehensive strategy of mass murder only when other options were blocked and when, through trial and error, they developed techniques by which an entire people could be destroyed. Some functionalists think that Hitler decided on the Final Solution during the summer of 1941, in the euphoria of victory during the first stages of the Russian campaign. Others maintain that Nazi policy crossed the line somewhat later, in the autumn of that year, when Hitler and his military leadership realized that they would not achieve an early victory over the Soviets.

Once decided, and once plans for implementation were discussed at the Wannsee Conference in January 1942, a Europe-wide bureaucracy was set into motion. Beginning with the General Government, the Nazis proceeded in an organized fashion murdering Jews in as thorough and as economic a manner as possible. Hitler put Himmler's SS in charge, although others assisted. The Wehrmacht and various police units particularly assisted in shootings and gassing in special vans in newly conquered Eastern territories. Not least were the Eastern European auxiliaries, notably in camps, ghettos, and other places of Jewish settlement; allies and satellites of the Reich in a military capacity as well as in civil and diplomatic actions; and finally officials and police in conquered countries, harnessed by the Germans to the task of mass murder in their particular localities.

As the Nazis gained experience, their techniques for mass murder slowly refined. Occupation authorities continued to stuff the ghettos of Poland and the Soviet Union with Jews from surrounding territories and even from the Reich and the West; ghettoization took a huge toll on the Jews through starvation and disease (as it was intended to do) and also proved a useful mechanism for draining the last remaining resources and personal wealth from the Jewish masses. Meanwhile, shootings in territory taken from the Soviets eliminated hundreds of thousands of those deemed undesirable in a matter of months. This proved to be "inefficient," however, and took a heavy psychological toll on the killers, for whose sensibilities the Nazi leadership expressed periodic concern.

SS officers experimented with gas vans and also gas chambers located in several camps in Poland. Moving methodically, SS troops and auxiliaries cleared the ghettos in 1942 and 1943 by dispatching most of the Jews to killing grounds. Adolf Eichmann's (1906–62) office within the Reichsicherheitshauptamt (Reich Security Main Office) of the SS organized deportation trains, mainly to Auschwitz-Birkenau, from various European countries beginning in mid-1942. During that year, the death toll soared to 2.7 million, with the massive assault on Polish Jews and the coordination of the Final Solution across Europe. The next year, with Polish Jewry practically eliminated, the toll dropped to 500,000 as the Germans' task became increasingly complex. Deportations and systematic gassing in camps continued even as the Reich began to crumble—despite obvious other needs for the men and equipment that the Nazis poured into their murderous task. Hungarian Jewry was among the very last to be destroyed—nearly half a million people were deported to the killing facilities in Auschwitz-Birkenau during the spring and summer of 1944. To the very end, the Nazis continued to murder Jews—their determination underscored by the Führer himself, when in his final testament he rehearsed his anti-Semitic fantasy and admonished Germans to scrupulously follow his racial laws.

Michael R. Marrus

See also Anti-Semitism; Auschwitz; Concentration Camps; Crystal Night; Eichmann; Adolf; *Einsatzgruppen*; Eugenics; Euthanasia; Gestapo; Göring, Hermann; Gypsies; Heydrich, Reinhard; Himmler, Heinrich; Hitler, Adolf; Höss, Rudolf; Israeli-German Relations; Jews, 1933–90; National Socialism; Nazi War Crimes Trials and Investigations; Nuremberg Trials; Polish-German Relations, 1918–45; Racism; Schutzstaffel; Wannsee Conference

References
Adam, Uwe Dietrich. *Judenpolitik im Dritten Reich.* Düsseldorf: Droste Verlag, 1972.

Bauer, Yehuda. *The Holocaust in Historical Perspective.* Seattle, WA: University of Washington Press, 1978.

———. *The Jewish Emergence from Powerlessness.* Toronto: University of Toronto Press, 1979.

Bauman, Zygmunt. *Modernity and the Holocaust.* Ithaca, NY: Cornell University Press, 1989.

Browning, Christopher. *Ordinary Men: Reserve Police Battalion 101 and the Final Solution in Poland.* New York, NY: Cambridge University Press, 1992.

———. *The Path to Genocide: Essays on Launching the Final Solution.* Cambridge: Cambridge University Press, 1992.

Fleming, Gerald. *Hitler and the Final Solution.* Berkley, CA: University of California Press, 1984.

Gilbert, Martin. *Auschwitz and the Allies.* New York, NY: Holt, Rinehart and Winston. 1981.

Goldhagen, Daniel. *Hitler's Willing Executioners: Ordinary Germans and the Holocaust.* New York, NY: Knopf, 1996.

Gutman, Israel, ed. *Encyclopedia of the Holocaust.* 4 vols. New York, NY: Macmillan, 1990.

Hilberg, Raul. *The Destruction of the European Jews.* 3 vols. Rev. ed. New York, NY: Holmes and Meier, 1985.

———. *Perpetrators, Victims, Bystanders: The Jewish Catastrophe 1933–1945.* New York, NY: HarperCollins, 1992.

Laqueur, Walter. *The Terrible Secret: An Investigation into the Suppression of Information about Hitler's Final Solution.* London: Weidenfeld and Nicholson, 1980.

Marrus, Michael R. *The Holocaust in History.* New York, NY: New American Library, 1987.

Steinert, Marlis. *Hitler: A Biography.* New York, NY: W.W. Norton, 1997.

Wyman, Davis. *The Abandonment of the Jews: America and the Holocaust 1941–1945.* New York, NY: Pantheon Books, 1984.

Yahil, Leni. *The Holocaust: The Fate of European Jewry, 1932–1945.* New York, NY: Oxford University Press, 1990.

Holocaust: Historiography

The historiography of the Holocaust may be roughly divided between works concerned with the construction and operation of the machinery of genocide (the perpetrators) and histories of the persecution and murder of the Jews (the victims). Both genres have produced an immense literature, especially in the last two decades. In many cases, there is an overlap between histories of perpetrators and of victims, and most recently, attention has also been given to the bystanders and their role in either facilitating the Final Solution or helping the victims. Nevertheless, the distinction between these two types of historical writings remains an important criterion in evaluating the historiography of the Holocaust.

This distinction may be seen in three ways. First is the manner in which the Holocaust is taught in schools or represented in the media, and the scholars and books that are used as sources. When the Holocaust is discussed as part of Jewish history, works concerned with the victims are used; when it is taught or represented as an outcome of German history or the Nazi regime, histories of the perpetrators are preferred. Second, the controversies over historical interpretations of the Nazi genocide reflect the tension between these two genres and the publics that appropriate them. Hence, Raul Hilberg's work was condemned for not paying due heed to the victims, whereas Lucy Dawidowicz's history of the Holocaust was blamed for a biased representation of Germany. Third, the preferred focus of historians on victims or perpetrators has a direct bearing on the analysis of the Nazi regime as such and of the emergence and mechanics of the machinery of genocide.

Interpretations of the Nazi regime and the Holocaust have seen the appearance of two major historiographical schools. The "intentionalist" interpretation (for instance by Dawidowicz), which is often also more concerned with the victims, sees the Final Solution as the outcome of long-range policies and intentions of the Nazi regime, and especially Hitler, possibly dating back even before their seizure of power in 1933. The "functionalist" or "structuralist" school (especially by Hans Mommsen and Martin Broszat), which focuses mainly on the perpetrators, argues that the genocide of the Jews emerged as a solution to otherwise seemingly insurmountable logistical and administrative problems that the Nazis brought upon themselves by occupying vast areas populated by large numbers of Jews and concentrating these Jews in crowded ghettos.

Heated debates between these two schools over the past two decades have now led to a certain modification of both positions and a growing consensus over some major features of the Holocaust (as seen in the work of Christopher Browning). Yet the distinction between the Holocaust written from the perpetrators' or the victims' perspective has remained, and it has most recently been given a new twist through a series of works arguing that the genocide of Jews was the outcome of an urge for modernization among middle-ranking Nazi bureaucrats in German-occupied Poland.

This interpretation, which is part of a more general historiographical trend regarding the Third Reich as a whole and its alleged modernization of German society, highlights another aspect of Holocaust writing, namely the relationship between rational policies (from the perpetrators' perspective) and ideology. The question posed here is whether the Final Solution was regarded as an economically beneficial policy for Nazi Germany, or, conversely, whether the Holocaust was the outcome of an ideological urge that functioned even when it became clear that it was wholly detrimental to Germany's war effort (see, for instance, Götz Aly and Susanne Heim and the response by Christopher Browning). This, in turn, also raises anew the question regarding the structure of the Third Reich and the relative power of Hitler, since it remains to be determined to what extent the genocide of the Jews began as the initiative of officials "on the ground" or was organized from the very beginning from the top (see, for instance, Gerald Fleming).

Another type of historical writing on the Holocaust has gained much prominence in recent years. Concerned mainly with the victims, and in some cases also with the bystanders, this genre focuses on memory and its reconstruction of the event following the end of the Holocaust. Here, interpretations of the emergence and implementation of the Final Solution are far less important, whereas the effects of genocide on the psyche of the survivors are of major concern. This genre is also accompanied by a large number of memoirs and videotaped interviews with survivors, which have gained much prominence since the 1980s (see Lawrence Langer).

Related to a general interest in the role of memory in history, this type of writing is also characterized by an emphasis on the perpetuation of the Holocaust beyond its conventional political periodization. Triggered to some extent by the realization that the witnesses to the genocide are dying out, it also stands in stark opposition to attempts made especially in the last 15 years to relativize or even wholly deny the Holocaust by political extremists and by more established scholars, ranging from Robert Faurisson in France to Ernst Nolte in the so-called *Historikerstreit* (dispute among historians) in Germany.

Omer Bartov

See also Historikerstreit; History; Memory, Collective; *Sonderweg*; Third Reich: Historiography

References

Aly, Götz and Susanne Heim. *Vordenker der Vernichtung: Auschwitz und die deutschen Pläne für eine neue europäische Ordnung*. Hamburg: Hoffmann & Campe Verlag, 1991.

Broszat, Martin. "Hitler and the Genesis of the 'Final Solution.'" *Yad Vashem Studies* 13 (1979).

Browning, Christopher R. *The Path to Genocide: Essays on Launching the Final Solution*. Cambridge: Cambridge University Press, 1992.

Dawidowicz, Lucy S. *The War against the Jews, 1933–1945*. New York, NY: Holt, Rinehart and Winston, 1975.

Fleming, Gerald. *Hitler and the Final Solution*. Berkeley, CA: University of California Press, 1984.

Friedländer, Saul. *Memory, History, and the Extermination of the Jews of Europe*. Bloomington, IN: Indiana University Press, 1993.

Hilberg, Raul. *The Destruction of the European Jews*. 3 vols. Rev. ed. New York, NY: Holmes & Meier, 1985.

Horwitz, Gordon J. *In the Shadow of Death: Living Outside the Gates of Mauthausen*. New York, NY: The Free Press, 1990.

Langer, Lawrence L. *Holocaust Testimonies: The Ruins of Memory*. New Haven, CT: Yale University Press, 1991.

Marrus, Michael R. *The Holocaust in History*. New York, NY and London: Meridian and Penguin Books, 1987.

Mommsen, Hans. "The Realization of the Unthinkable: The 'Final Solution of the Jewish Question' in the Third Reich." *The Policies of Genocide: Jews and Soviet Prisoners of War in Nazi Germany*. Ed. Gerhard Hirschfeld. London: Allen and Unwin, 1986.

Holz, Arno (1863–1929)

Arno Holz is generally regarded as the founder of German "consistent naturalism," a literature devoted to the accurate, unidealized representation of life within the lowest levels of Imperial German society. He is best known for the novella "Papa Hamlet" (1889) and the drama *Die Familie Selicke* (The

Selicke family), 1890, both co-authored with Johannes Schlaf, as well as for the poetry collection *Phantasus* (1898–1961), although he has several other plays and poetry volumes and a number of theoretical works to his credit.

Born in Rastenburg, Holz spent the bulk of his years in Berlin, where his existence was marked by constant bitterness, poverty, and strife. After quitting school, he attempted a career in journalism and, for lack of success, turned to freelance writing. While this decision had negative monetary consequences—Holz barely earned enough to maintain a tenement apartment—it proved extremely fruitful from a literary perspective because it engendered an oeuvre that contributed to German literature a measure of social relevance seldom encountered before.

Drawing on personal observations, Holz wrote unflinchingly realistic and brutal works that squarely confronted his middle-class audience with the inhumane living and working conditions of the poor, sick, and starving masses in overcrowded German cities. In "Papa Hamlet," for example, readers experience, in painfully minute detail, the tragic plight of a deranged Shakespearean actor and his starving family; in *Die Familie Selicke*, by contrast, the devastating effects of poverty and chronic alcoholism are vividly brought to the stage. Through such relentless realism, the backbone of his "consistent naturalism," Holz clearly intended to tear his audience away from the comforting caress of traditional, idealistic literature and, simultaneously, to jolt it into action toward the creation of a viable social welfare policy.

Holz's break with the artificiality of idealistic literature also extended to the matter of form, especially with reference to poetry. In his theoretical work *Revolution der Lyrik* (1899), he argued for the abandonment of such traditional poetic devices as rhyme, meter, and strophic organization in favor of a new, more realistic prose-like style in which all lines of poetry revolve around a common midpoint on the printed page. This "central axis" technique is showcased in the famous *Phantasus* collection.

Echoes of Holz's literary achievements, in terms of themes and style, may be heard far beyond the bounds of German naturalism. Its most popular representative was Gerhart Hauptmann (1862–1946). Holz's influence appears in such contexts as working-class and concrete poetry, impressionism, expressionism, and post-modernism.

Dwight Klett

See also Hauptmann, Gerhart; Imperial Germany: Literature; Naturalism; Realism; Weimar Germany: Literature; Working Conditions

References

Hechler, Manfred. *Die soziologische Dimension der Kunsttheorie von Arno Holz*. Frankfurt am Main: Peter Lang, 1981.
Mobius, Hanno. *Der Positivismus in der Literatur des Naturalismus: Wissenschaft, Kunst und soziale Frage bei Arno Holz*. Munich: Wilhelm Fink, 1980.
Oeste, Robert. *Arno Holz: The Long Poem and the Tradition of Poetic Experiment*. Bonn: Bouvier, 1982.
Schar, Oskar. *Arno Holz: Seine dramatische Technik*. Bern: Paul Haupt, 1926.
Scheuer, Helmut. *Arno Holz im literarischen Leben des ausgehenden 19. Jahrhunderts (1883–1896): Eine biographische Studie*. Munich: Winkler, 1971.
Schulz, Gerhard. *Arno Holz: Dilemma eines bürgerlichen Dichterlebens*. Munich: C.H. Beck, 1974.
Turley, Karl. *Arno Holz: Der Weg eines Künstlers*. Leipzig: Rudolf Koch, 1935.

Home Guard (Deutscher Volkssturm; 1944–45)

In the autumn of 1944, the desperate military situation forced the German High Command to raise additional formations for the defense of the Reich. An order dated September 25, 1944 created the Deutscher Volkssturm (Home Guard), which was given the task of supporting the Wehrmacht in combat within the Reich, and with protecting military installations close to the borders. SS *Reichsführer* Heinrich Himmler (1900–45) was charged with training, arming, and equipping the new formation. Only in combat was it to be subordinated to the Wehrmacht.

The Volkssturm was recruited from among the 16- to 60-year-olds who had not been drafted previously. It would include people who had been exempted in order to fulfil essential functions in the war economy or the administration. To comply with the exigencies of these employments, training was normally conducted on Sundays. Like the Wehrmacht, the Volkssturm was organized in battalions and companies. The exact number of Volkssturm battalions raised is not known but estimates range from 700 to 900.

Due to the critical economic and military situation of late 1944, the battalions could only be armed with a few weapons, mostly older captured enemy rifles. It could not be equipped or clothed properly. To make sure the Volkssturm members would be treated as combatants, they wore badges on their arms with an inscription, "Deutscher Volkssturm."

Although the first units had only been organized in the autumn of 1944, the Volkssturm was sent against the Red Army in January 1945. In the East, fear of the Russians led to high morale, while in the West, few were willing to fight.

Cooperating with the Wehrmacht and the Waffen-SS, the Volkssturm was supposed to defend the territory of the Reich until the danger of occupation by an enemy force had subsided. This concept completely disregarded the general military situation and therefore could not succeed. The Allies had superior resources in every respect, and the personnel and material reserves of the Volkssturm were by no means sufficient. The Volkssturm was unable to fulfill expectations; it had no chance of being a decisive factor in the operations of 1945. The deployment of these badly trained and insufficiently equipped formations was a senseless sacrifice in the face of an unavoidable defeat.

Klaus Schönherr

See also Himmler, Heinrich; National Socialist Germany: Military; Waffen-SS; World War II

References
Mammach, Klaus. *Der Volkssturm: Das letzte Aufgebot 1944/45.* Cologne: Pahl-Rugenstein, 1981.
Seidler, Franz W. *Deutscher Volkssturm: Das letzte Aufgebot 1944/45.* Munich/Berlin: Helbig, 1989.
Wright, Burton. "Army of Despair: The German Volkssturm 1944–1945." Unpublished doctoral dissertation. Florida State University, 1982.

Homosexuality and Lesbianism

A specifically homosexual identity and subculture have been fostered by urbanization and secularization in modern Germany, but public opinion—yielding gradually to a paradigm shift from sin to sickness—has generally remained discriminatory, with a concomitant tendency to pity, to seek to cure, or to eradicate what is perceived as a pathology. Most homosexuals have continued to conceal their orientation. An activist minority has campaigned for social equality, and this century has witnessed unprecedented tolerance of homosexuality as well as drastic persecution. Statutory law has consistently stigmatized male homosexuality while ignoring lesbianism, manifesting the patriarchal bias at the core of Germany's value system.

Unification (1871) brought the extension of the harsh Prussian sodomy statute, Paragraph 175 of the Penal Code, to the entire country, including German states that had been guided by the French Enlightenment to legalize homosexuality during the nineteenth century. Prussian hegemony was contested by Karl Heinrich Ulrichs (1825–95), who pioneered the concept of homosexuals as an oppressed minority. Ulrichs advanced a psychological explanation for homosexuality, and his hypotheses influenced a generation of forensic psychiatrists, notably Richard von Krafft-Ebing (1840–1902), whose *Psychopathia sexualis* (1886) called for the repeal of Paragraph 175. Published case histories documented growing self-awareness on the part of homosexuals, and lesbian and homosexual literature proliferated around the turn of the century.

An urban subculture emerged when the Berlin police discontinued closing homosexual bars (1895). The world's first homosexual rights organization (1897) was founded by Magnus Hirschfeld (1868–1935), and a rival group (1902) was initiated by Adolf Brand (1874–1945). This movement was impeded when two members of the Kaiser's entourage were smeared as homosexuals (1907), resulting in a moral backlash and Reichstag deliberations on criminalizing lesbianism (1909). The subculture burgeoned during the Weimar Republic, when liberalized press laws allowed the appearance of some 20 lesbian and homosexual periodicals. Most were published by new organizations that aimed more at creating support through social activities than at legal reform. The largest, the League for Human Rights (Bund für Menschenrechte), claimed a membership of 25,000. Social Democratic and Communist Reichstag delegates voted to reform Paragraph 175 (1929), but this measure was scathingly denounced by the rising Nazi party, which promised to wipe out homosexuality.

On coming to power, the Nazis moved quickly to ban all public manifestations of homosexuality (1933) and to toughen the law by promulgating Paragraph 175a (1935); the criminalization of lesbianism was once again debated. The Nazis arrested 90,000 homosexuals, consigning some 10,000 to concentration camps, where their uniforms were marked with pink triangles (*rosa Winkel*); others avoided internment by submitting to castration.

Paragraph 175a was struck down in the German Democratic Republic (GDR) (1949), and Paragraph 175 was reformed in 1968 and entirely repealed in 1988. Homosexual organizations and periodicals were nonetheless banned in the GDR; not until the 1980s could gay discussion groups meet under the protection of the Evangelical Church.

In the Federal Republic of Germany (FRG), homosexual organizations and periodicals emerged cautiously during the Adenauer years, but Paragraph 175a remained until the Social Democrats came to power (1969). Gay liberationists have challenged the continued existence of Paragraph 175 and during the 1980s responded to the AIDS epidemic. At the initiative of the Greens, the FRG granted belated restitution to pink-triangle survivors in 1988. Unification opened the issue of extending Paragraph 175 to the former GDR, and a two-year moratorium was imposed.

James D. Steakley

See also Eugenics; Eulenburg-Hertefeld, Philipp zu; Harden, Maximilian; Hirschfeld, Magnus; Jews, 1869–1933; Morality; Sex Reform and Birth Control

References
Bollé, Michael, ed. *Eldorado: Homosexuelle Frauen und Männer in Berlin 1850–1950: Geschichte, Alltag und Kultur.* Berlin: Frölich & Kaufmann, 1984.
Freunde eines schwulen Museums in Berlin e.V. *Die Geschichte des §175: Strafrecht gegen Homosexuelle.* Berlin: Rosa Winkel, 1990.
Herzer, Manfred. *Bibliographie zur Homosexualität.* Berlin: Rosa Winkel, 1982.
Hoffschildt, Rainer. *Olivia: Die bisher geheime Geschichte des Tabus Homosexualität und der Verfolgung der Homosexuellen in Hannover.* Hannover: Privately published, 1992.
Jellonek, Burkhard. *Homosexuelle unter dem Hakenkreuz.* Paderborn: Ferdinand Schöningh, 1990.
Johansson, Warren, and William A. Percy. "Homosexuals in Nazi Germany." *Simon Wiesenthal Center Annual* 7 (1990), 225–63.
Kennedy, Hubert. *Ulrichs: The Life and Works of Karl Heinrich Ulrichs, Pioneer of the Modern Gay Movement.* Boston, MA: Alyson, 1988.
Kokula, Ilse. *Weibliche Homosexualität um 1900 in zeitgenössischen Dokumenten.* Munich: Frauenoffensive, 1981.
Kowalski, Gudrun von. *Homosexualität in der DDR: Ein historischer Abriss.* Marburg: Arbeiterbewegung und Gesellschaftswissenschaften, 1987.
Oosterhuis, Harry, and Hubert Kennedy, eds. *Homosexuality and Male Bonding in Pre-Nazi Germany.* New York, NY: Haworth, 1992.

Steakley, James D. *The Homosexual Emancipation Movement in Germany*. New York, NY: Arno, 1975.

Stümke, Hans-Georg. *Homosexuelle in Deutschland: Eine politische Geschichte*. Munich: C.H. Beck, 1989.

Honecker, Erich (1912–94)

Erich Honecker was the leader of the German Democratic Republic's (GDR) ruling party, the Socialist Unity Party (SED), from May 1971 until his fall in October 1989. In 1976, he also assumed the position of chairman of the GDR's State Council, making him the de facto head of state.

Honecker was born in 1912 in Neunkirchen in the Saar; he was the son of a miner who, after World War I, became an activist in the newly-founded German Communist Party (KPD). Honecker, who was trained as a roofer, joined the Communist youth organization in 1926 and, after undergoing schooling in Moscow in 1930, became one of its leaders. After the Nazi seizure of power, Honecker continued his then illegal activities until his arrest in 1935. Convicted in 1937, he was incarcerated in Brandenburg prison and remained there until 1945. After his release, Honecker was put in charge of building a new Communist youth organization, the Free German Youth (FDJ); he remained its leader until 1955. Many of the functionaries who worked with him in the FDJ in those years assumed prominent positions in the ruling party after he became its leader. In 1956–57 he returned to the Soviet Union for schooling, and after his return to Germany was put in charge of security affairs. In this capacity he coordinated the construction of the Berlin Wall in 1961.

Although earlier a loyal supporter, and the designated successor, of the GDR's longtime leader Walter Ulbricht (1893–1973), Honecker joined other members of the *Politbüro* in conspiring with the Soviet leadership to have Ulbricht removed from power in 1971. As the SED's first secretary (his title was changed to general secretary in 1976 in accordance with Brezhnev-era usage), Honecker was identified with the international recognition of the GDR that followed the signing of a series of East-West treaties and with what regime propaganda called the "unity of economic and social policy." In practice, this emphasized the technological modernization of the GDR and the gradual expansion of social programs and benefits for East German citizens, most notably an ambitious program of housing construction.

The weakness of this policy was that it made the GDR increasingly dependent on foreign loans and various subsidies from the Federal Republic of Germany (FRG). Nevertheless, for some time it allowed Honecker to enjoy a modest degree of popularity, which reached its height with his brief defiance of the Soviet leadership in 1984 over the issue of maintaining close relations with the FRG. By 1987, however, when Honecker made his triumphant state visit to West Germany, the signs of crisis in the GDR were mounting. When he was removed in October 1989 in the wake of the exodus of many GDR citizens and the rising tide of popular demonstrations, many of his colleagues blamed his blind pursuit of the reckless policies developed by his economic chieftain, Günter Mittag, as well as his growing remoteness from or-

Erich Honecker and Helmut Kohl, 1984. Courtesy of Inter Nationes, Bonn.

dinary GDR citizens, for the regime's impending demise.

Early in 1993, judicial proceedings against Honecker were halted on the grounds of his ill health, and he was permitted to join his wife Margot, the GDR's former education minister, in exile in Chile. He died in May 1994.

Thomas A. Baylis

See also Ackermann, Anton; Axen, Hermann; Basic Treaty; Berlin; Berlin Wall; Fischer, Oskar; Free German Trade Union Federation; Free German Youth; German Communist Party; German Democratic Republic: Arts and Politics; German Democratic Republic : Churches; German Democratic Republic: Collapse; German Democratic Republic: Constitutions; German Democratic Republic: Economy; German Democratic Republic: Education; German Democratic Republic: Foreign Relations; German Democratic Republic: Government System; German Democratic Republic: Marxism-Leninism; German Democratic Republic: Media; German Democratic Republic: National People's Army; German Democratic Republic: Nationalism; German Democratic Republic: Opposition; German Democratic Republic: Political Culture; German Democratic Republic: Political Party System; German Democratic Republic: Sports; German Democratic Republic: State Security; German Democratic Republic: Technical Intelligentsia; German-German Relations; Gorbachev and the German Question; Honecker, Margot; Mielke, Erich; Mittag, Günter; Modrow, Hans; *Ostpolitik*; Reunification; Science in the Postwar Germanys; Sindermann, Horst; Socialist Unity Party; Soviet-German Relations; Stoph, Willi; Tisch, Harry; Ulbricht, Walter; Verner, Paul; Wolf, Markus

References

Fulbrook, Mary. *Anatomy of a Dictatorship: Inside the GDR, 1949–1989*. New York, NY: Oxford University Press, 1995.

Honecker, Erich. *From My Life*. London: Pergamon Press, 1980.

Lippmann, Heinz. *Honecker and the New Politics of Europe*. London: Macmillan, 1972.

Pryzybylski, Peter. *Tatort Politbüro.* 2 vols. Berlin: Rowohlt, 1991 and 1992.

Der Sturz: Erich Honecker im Kreuzverhör. Berlin: Aufbau-Verlag, 1990.

Honecker, Margot Feist (1927–)

From 1963 to 1989, Margot Honecker served as East German minister of education.

Margot Feist was born on April 17, 1927, in the industrial town of Halle. Her father, Gotthard Feist, a shoemaker and active member of the German Communist Party (KPD) was briefly sent to a Nazi concentration camp.

Margot Feist became a telephone operator. In 1945 she joined the KPD and one year later the Socialist Unity Party (SED). After the war, Feist was one of the founders of anti-Fascist youth committees in Halle. She became an active member in the newly founded Free German Youth (FDJ). After some party education she worked from 1949 to 1953 as the chair of the Young Pioneers' Organization. In 1950, at the age of 22, she became the youngest member of the Volkskammer (People's Chamber). In the same year, she became a candidate of the SED Central Committee and one year later, a full member.

In 1953, she married Erich Honecker (1912–94), who was at that time chairman of the FDJ. Their daughter, Sonja, who was born in 1951, is married to a Chilean Communist and lives in Chile. From 1953 to 1954, Feist attended the Moscow Komsomol College. For the next four years, she headed a department in the Education Ministry. In 1958, she became the minister's deputy; in 1963, she took over the office.

As minister of education for nearly a quarter of a century until 1989, she followed an orthodox Communist line in order to form "socialist personalities." In 1964, she introduced the "polytechnical principle," a combination of intellectual and practical endeavors. In 1978 she introduced—against the resistance of the church—military training for 15- and 16-year-old students. In October 1988 she expelled four students from school because they complained about military parades. At any given time she decisively influenced the situation of 300,000 teachers and 2.6 million children. Honecker had a reputation as an arrogant and power-conscious minister.

Two days after her husband was forced to step down as SED chairman and head of state on October 18, 1989, Margot Honecker also left office. After closing down the *Politbüro* settlement in Wandlitz, the Honecker couple lived from January 1990 in a pastor's home near Berlin. In April 1990, they found refuge in the Soviet military hospital in Beelitz, near Potsdam, and in March 1991 fled to Moscow. On November 16, 1991, the Russian government expelled the Honeckers, but they found political asylum in the Chilean embassy in Moscow. Erich Honecker had to return to Germany on July 29, 1992, to stand trial before a court on charges of manslaughter. His wife went to Chile. Erich Honecker followed her after being set free on January 13, 1993 because of his illness. They lived with their daughter Sonja in Chile.

Heinrich Bortfeld

See also German Democratic Republic: Education; Honecker, Erich

References
Childs, David. *The GDR: Moscow's German Ally.* 2nd ed. London: Unwin Hyman, 1988.

Dennis, Mike. *German Democratic Republic: Politics, Economics and Society.* London: Pinter Publishers, 1988.

Honecker, Erich. *From My Life.* London: Pergamon Press, 1980.

Horkheimer, Max (1895–1973)

As director of the Institut für Sozialforschung (Institute of Social Research) from 1930 until after World War II, Max Horkheimer was the doyen of a group of scholars (including Theodor Adorno [1903–69], Erich Fromm, Leo Lowenthal [1900–93], Herbert Marcuse [1898–1979], and Friedrich Pollock, [1900–80], who sought to understand and criticize the history of bourgeois society by combining economic analysis with psychology. Between 1932 and 1940, he edited the journal *Zeitschrift für Sozialforschung* (Journal for social research). In the late 1960s, Horkheimer's early writings had a significant influence on the leaders of the student movement.

A pivotal social thinker of the twentieth century, Horkheimer was born into an affluent Jewish family in Stuttgart. After completing dissertations on Immanuel Kant, he joined the Institute of Social Research at the University of Frankfurt and soon became its head. Anticipating the Nazi seizure of power, Horkheimer relocated the Institute to New York City,

Max Horkheimer. Courtesy of German Information Center, New York.

where most of the members continued their close collaboration around what came to be called "critical theory." In 1945, Horkheimer became director of research for an important survey on prejudice funded by the American Jewish Congress. In 1948, he returned to Frankfurt, where he helped to rebuild and later to lead the new Institute of Social Research.

Horkheimer's contribution to social theory is fragmentary and is best understood as a sequence of stages. Upon becoming director, he refocused the activities of the Frankfurt Institute toward an interdisciplinary approach that stressed research and didactics by combining Kantian epistemology with Marxism and an openness to psychoanalysis. Some of his major essays from these years—including "Materialism and Metaphysics" (Materialismus und Metaphysik), 1933, as well as "Traditional and Critical Theory" (Traditionelle und kritische Theorie), 1937—are collected in *Critical Theory* (1972). By the late 1930s, Horkheimer and his colleagues had completely lost their earlier confidence in the proletariat as a revolutionary force; they focused now on totalitarianism as the excrescence of the enlightenment and of liberalism. Their most despairing and nihilistic observations are reflected in the book *Dialektik der Aufklärung* (published as *Dialectic of Enlightenment*), 1972, perhaps the seminal work of the Institute, composed by Horkheimer in collaboration with Adorno in the early 1940s.

Upon his return to Frankfurt in 1948, Horkheimer became increasingly reactionary and tried to gloss over his earlier Marxian convictions. He allowed his own essays from the 1930s to be republished only after pirated editions began to circulate openly. In conversations, Horkheimer supported the American presence in Vietnam by endorsing a German version of the "domino theory." In the later years, his interviews were characterized by the sorts of ideology and mysticism he had ridiculed when he was younger.

Horkheimer's collected works are available in German in 18 volumes.

Gerd Schroeter

See also Adorno, Theodor; Benjamin, Walter; Frankfurt School; Fromm, Erich; Habermas, Jürgen; Lowenthal, Leo; Marcuse, Herbert; Marx, Karl; Neumann, Franz; Weber, Max

References

Dubiel, Helmut. *Theory and Politics: Studies in the Development of Critical Theory.* Trans. Benjamin Grigg. Cambridge, MA: M.I.T. Press, 1985.

Gumnior, Helmut, and Rudolf Ringguth. *Max Horkheimer.* Reinbek: Rowohlt, 1973.

Held, David. *Introduction to Critical Theory: Horkheimer to Habermas.* Berkeley, CA: University of California Press, 1980.

Jay, Martin. *The Dialectical Imagination: A History of the Frankfurt School and the Institute of Social Research 1923–1950.* Boston, MA: Little, Brown and Co., 1973.

Schmidt, Alfred, and Norbert Altwicker, eds. *Max Horkheimer heute: Werk und Wirkung.* Frankfurt am Main: Fischer, 1986.

Stirk, Peter M.R. *Max Horkheimer: A New Interpretation.*
Hemel Hempstead: Harvester Wheatsheaf, 1992.

Höss, Rudolf (1900–47)

Rudolf Höss was an early member of the Schutzstaffel (SS) and served at the Dachau concentration camp from 1934 to 1938. He gained international notoriety as the commandant of the Auschwitz-Birkenau concentration camp complex in German-occupied Poland from 1940 to 1945.

Born in southern Germany, Höss was raised in German East Africa, where his father served in the German colonial army. Höss served briefly in the colonial army during World War I and later returned to Germany, where he joined the Rossbach faction of the postwar volunteer corps (*Freikorps*), which was active in East Prussia and in the Baltic states. A young rabble-rouser, Höss was also involved in the *Freikorps'* anti-French and anti-Polish activities in the Ruhr and Silesia, respectively, in the early 1920s. Höss joined the Nazi Party in late 1922.

Throughout the 1920s, Höss continued to participate in *Freikorps* activities and was arrested in 1923 for his role in a political murder. He was sentenced to ten years in prison but was pardoned and released in 1928. At this time, he came under the direct influence of Heinrich Himmler (1900–45); he and his wife joined Himmler's nationalist Artamanen Society and became deeply involved in its activities.

Höss joined the SS in 1934 and was assigned to the Dachau concentration camp, where he served in an administrative capacity under Theodore Eicke until 1938. He was transferred to occupied Poland in 1940 with the order to establish a concentration camp at Auschwitz. Within two years, Höss expanded the Auschwitz-Birkenau complex into Nazi Germany's largest extermination center. He remained commandant of the camp until late 1943, when he returned to Berlin to assume responsibility for the Central Office for Camp Operation within the SS Economic and Administrative Main Office. He returned to Auschwitz in June 1944 following the deportation of the Hungarian Jews and once again supervised the killing operations.

Höss assumed an alias after the war and avoided detection and arrest until early 1946. He was extradited to Poland to stand trial for war crimes. Following his conviction, Höss was returned to the site of the Auschwitz camp, where he was hanged on April 16, 1947.

Steven B. Rogers

See also Anti-Semitism; Auschwitz; Concentration Camps; Himmler, Heinrich; Holocaust; Nazi War Crimes Trials and Investigations; Nuremberg Trials; Schutzstaffel

References

Arendt, Hannah. *Eichmann in Jerusalem.* New York, NY: Penguin, 1984.

Breitman, Richard. *Architect of Genocide: Himmler and the Final Solution.* New York, NY: Knopf, 1991.

Höss, Rudolf. *Death Dealer: Memoirs of the SS Kommandant at Auschwitz.* Buffalo, NY: Prometheus Books, 1992.

Segev, Tom. *The Commanders of Nazi Concentration Camps.* Ann Arbor, MI: Xerox University Microfilms, 1977.

Housing and Slums

Housing conditions often left much to be desired in Germany's rural areas, but it was urban conditions that alarmed many observers. The housing of the urban poor became a measure of German society's response to social problems.

Attention to urban housing was stimulated by periodic dwelling shortages that accompanied booms in industrial and urban growth between 1871 and 1914. World War I virtually stopped residential construction, creating a severe housing shortage that lingered in the weak postwar economy. During World War II, the massive destruction of the cities redoubled the problem, which was solved only slowly in the postwar years—more rapidly in the West than in the East.

The "housing question," a prominent topic of debate in the late nineteenth century, reflected a concern with the quality as well as the availability of housing. The periodic shortages drew attention to both issues because of overcrowding in existing units, which made housing conditions appear worse to observers. These observers—mainly prosperous middle-class reformers—defined the "housing question" in terms of perils to health and morals. Their reports identified the dirty, damp, and overcrowded living conditions of the urban working class as a cause of disease—notably tuberculosis, cholera, and typhoid. Fear of contamination was accompanied by an uneasiness with the lack of clearly separated family and gender spaces common in working-class housing. Many poor families, who could not afford the entire rent of an apartment, sublet rooms or beds to lodgers, or they shared common corridors and toilets with neighbors. These conditions made it impossible to create the spatial ideals of home that middle-class reformers typically held.

In the growing cities of the late nineteenth century, land prices grew rapidly and large apartment buildings became the dominant housing stock for middle-class as well as poor families. Typical buildings in the eastern cities—above all Berlin—were particularly massive; they became known as *Mietskasernen* (rental barracks). Many reformers saw them as inherently inferior housing and sought to promote model projects of smaller, more spread-out buildings, usually located in outer districts of the cities where land was cheaper.

The efforts of middle-class housing reformers often met with opposition by real-estate promoters, who saw little to be gained by tampering with the private housing market. Some members of the Social Democratic Party (SPD) supported housing reforms, but they encountered resistance within their own ranks. Following the position outlined by Friedrich Engels (1820–95) in an essay, "Die Wohnungsfrage" (The housing question), 1872, many socialists saw miserable housing conditions as a symptom of capitalism itself and denied the utility of attempts to improve them without addressing their underlying causes.

Before 1914, municipal governments strengthened housing codes and inspection but were reluctant to intervene in real-estate markets. Model housing projects were few in number and were erected by employers or by nonprofit organizations. During the 1920s, Social Democratic influence and the virtual collapse of the private housing market led to a much more active role for government. Many cities had thousands of small apartments built in dispersed housing estates. As alternatives to the *Mietskasernen*, they betrayed the influence of the prewar reformers; however, in some cities, avant-garde architects gave them a strikingly modern appearance. To the extent that it built residential housing, the Third Reich promoted designs considered less international and more German, but it, too, followed the decentralization trend. This approach added an increased emphasis on single-family houses. Similarly, after 1949, cities in East and West Germany built many satellite housing estates in their efforts to overcome the shortage of apartments.

Turn-of-the-century British and French visitors to Germany's relatively new cities saw few slums that were as bad as the worst they knew. In many German cities, the worst areas were neglected pockets of the ancient city center, filled with centuries-old houses that had been expanded and subdivided many times. They provided homes to many families, but municipal leaders saw them as impenetrable warrens of disease, criminality, prostitution, and potential social unrest. Perhaps the most notorious were the *Gängeviertel* (alley quarter) of Hamburg and the *Scheunenviertel* (shed quarter) of Berlin. They were the target of some of the few slum-clearance efforts undertaken in the early twentieth century. In the decades after World War II, many nineteenth century *Mietskasernen*—deteriorated and out of favor in West Germany and West Berlin—were razed. By the 1980s, however, it had become fashionable to renovate them. In East Germany, such districts were almost completely neglected to the point of becoming uninhabitable. After 1990, the eastern cities of the unified German state were faced with the question of what to do with these slums.

Brian Ladd

See also Architecture and Urban Design; Depression, 1873–96; Disease; Engels, Friedrich; Holz, Arno; Industrialization; Morality; Postwar Reconstruction; Social Democratic Party; Social Reform; Urbanization; Welfare State

References

Bullock, Nicholas, and James Read. *The Movement for Housing Reform in Germany and France, 1840–1914.* Cambridge: Cambridge University Press, 1985.

Engels, Friedrich. *The Housing Question.* New York, NY: International Publishers, 1935.

Evans, Richard J. *Death in Hamburg: Society and Politics in the Cholera Years, 1830–1910.* Oxford: Oxford University Press, 1987.

Honhart, Michael. "Company Housing as Urban Planning in Germany, 1870–1940." *Central European History* 23 (1990), 3–21.

Ladd, Brian. *Urban Planning and Civic Order in Germany, 1860–1914.* Cambridge, MA: Harvard University Press, 1990.

Lane, Barbara Miller. *Architecture and Politics in Germany, 1918–1945.* Cambridge, MA: Harvard University Press, 1968.

Silverman, Dan P. "A Pledge Unredeemed: The Housing Crisis in Weimar Germany." *Central European History* 3 (1970), 112–39.

Teuteberg, Hans Jürgen, and Clemens Wischermann, eds. *Wohnalltag in Deutschland 1850–1914*. Münster: Coppenrath, 1985.

Wiedenhoeft, Ronald. *Berlin's Housing Revolution: German Reform in the 1920's*. Ann Arbor, MI: UMI Research Press, 1985.

Zimmermann, Clemens. *Von der Wohnungsfrage zur Wohnungspolitik: Die Reformbewegung in Deutschland 1845–1914*. Göttingen: Vandenhoeck & Ruprecht, 1991.

Huch, Ricarda (1864–1947)

Ricarda Huch was one of Germany's, if not Europe's, most respected writers during her lifetime, although her literary work is largely forgotten today. She was an author of tremendous diversity—her work included poetry and novels as well as historical works and literary criticism. Huch's career spanned two world wars and much of that turmoil is reflected in her novels. She was also politically active, playing an influential role in the early German women's movement, and in later years was an outspoken critic of the Nazis.

Huch came to maturity in the turbulent years of the fin-de-siècle. A critic of the Empire, she was confronted by discrimination early in her life and was forced to study in Zürich (1887) because German universities were still closed to women. In Zürich she developed a lifelong admiration for the Swiss model of democracy. She completed a doctorate in history in 1892 and shortly thereafter published her first novel, *Erinnerungen von Ludolf Ursleu dem Jüngeren* (Remembrance of Ludolf Ursleu the younger), 1893, which describes the fall of a bourgeois family in a north German Hansa city, a theme taken up a few years later by Thomas Mann (1875–1955) in *Buddenbrooks*. She continued to write historical novels and works of scholarship. She disapproved somewhat of the German historian Leopold von Ranke (1795–1886) for writing history from the perspective of the elites, and she sought instead to portray sympathetic accounts of the people. Some of her most important historical works dealt with the Revolutions of 1848 and Italy during the *Risorgimento*. In these works, and particularly in her historical treatment of the Thirty Years' War, *Der Dreissigjährige Krieg* (1912–14), she tried to combine subtle literary character portraits with historical accuracy. Despite the popularity of her historical works, they remained largely literary in nature and are not generally accepted as scholarship.

In 1896, Huch returned briefly to Germany before going to Vienna in 1897. As one of the first women to break down the barriers of discrimination, she became involved in the German women's movement. Her support for the movement, however, was at times contradictory, and she did not exert much influence. Although Huch shared some of the ideals of conservative feminism, she could not support the nationalistic, militaristic policies of the Bund deutscher Frauenvereine (Federation of German Women's Associations).

Shortly after the Nazis came to power in 1933, Huch resigned from the Prussian Academy of Arts. In her letter of resignation, she openly expressed her opposition to the Nazis' brutality, their anti-Semitism, and their destruction of civil rights. Although she remained in Germany during the war, her opposition to the Nazi regime did not lead to open persecution. Nonetheless, she was often the target of vilification in the Nazi press. This was particularly true following the publication of the first volume of her *Geschichte Deutschlands* (History of Germany), 1934, in which she condemned the historical treatment of the Jews. Nonetheless, Huch's support for democratic institutions and personal liberty never wavered, a fact witnessed in her life and her work.

John R. Hinde

See also Feminist Writing; Historical Novel; History; Imperial Germany: Literature; Prussian Art Academy; Resistance; Weimar Germany: Literature

References
Frank, M.H. "Ricarda Huch and the German Women's Movement." Unpublished doctoral dissertation. New York University, 1977.

Hoppe, Else. *Richarda Huch: Weg, Persönlichkeit, Werk*. Stuttgart: Riederer, 1951.

Huch, Ricarda. *Gesammelte Werke*. Ed. W. Emrich. Berlin: Kiepenheuer und Witsch, 1966–71.

Peter, Hans-Werner, ed. *Ricarda Huch: Studien zu ihrem Leben und Werk*. 4 vols. Braunschweig: P-P Verlag GmbH, 1988–93.

Skidmore, James M. "History with a Mission: Ricarda Huch's Historiography during the Weimar Republic." Unpublished doctoral dissertation. Princeton University, 1993.

Hugenberg, Alfred (1865–1961)

As a founder of the Pan-German League and a member of Adolf Hitler's first cabinet, Alfred Hugenberg championed the rabid nationalism of the Wilhelmine era and the birth of the Third Reich. From 1909 to 1918, he played a key role in the Ruhr as the director of the Krupp directorium at Essen; after the war, he organized the powerful right-wing press syndicate, the Scherl concern. His economic power led to his election as chairman of the right-wing German National People's Party (DNVP) in 1928.

Though Hugenberg helped to organize the Pan-German League, he concentrated his efforts before World War I on his business career, which won him the respect of many important leaders in the Ruhr. His advocacy of expansionist war aims after 1914 led to his creation of a newspaper syndicate to influence public opinion. His Scherl concern in Berlin printed three daily newspapers. He also directly controlled 14 provincial papers, and his syndication services supplied material for hundreds of others. In 1927, his consortium bought control of Germany's largest film corporation, the Universum Film Aktiengesellschaft (Ufa). Hugenberg used the profits to support right-wing movements.

In 1919, Hugenberg became a member of the DNVP and entered the Reichstag. He advocated radical nationalist opposition ideas and in 1928, after DNVP moderates had participated in the government, he rallied the dissidents who took over the party. His decision to champion a plebiscite against the Young Plan for reparations facilitated some of the most radical changes at the end of the Weimar era. By sponsoring a cooperative right-wing bloc that included the Nazis, Hugenberg helped to endow Hitler with respectability and at the same time drive the moderates out of the DNVP. In the elections of September 1930, the combination of radical rhetoric, which his papers headlined, and unemployment, which the depression caused, made not the DNVP but the Nazis the most important right-wing movement.

Hugenberg had hoped to include Nazi radicals in a broad-based coalition, a *Sammlung*, under the control of traditional nationalists, but disaffected voters from 1930 through 1933 preferred Hitler to Hugenberg. The old Pan-German repeatedly tried to grasp the initiative, as at the Bad Harzburg rally in October 1931, but he continually failed. His conflicts with Hitler focused not merely on generational differences in style and tactics, but on opposition to the socialism of the Nazis. Nevertheless, the DNVP leader preferred Hitler to any democratic alternative.

In January 1933, Hugenberg accepted the position of "economic dictator" in the Hitler cabinet; he controlled four major economic departments in Prussia and the federal government. The Nazis manipulated opposition to his policies and he resigned on June 26, 1933. Shortly thereafter the DNVP dissolved itself.

After the war, a series of de-Nazification proceedings ultimately classified Hugenberg as a *Mitläufer*, or fellow traveler, of the Nazis. His large but incomplete *Nachlass* (papers) is available at the Federal Archives in Koblenz.

John A. Leopold

See also Conservatism, 1918–45; German National People's Party; Hitler, Adolf; Nationalism; National Socialist Germany; Press and Newspapers; Publishing and the Book Trade; Ufa; Young Plan

References

Guratzsch, Denkwart. *Macht durch Organisation: Grundlegung des Hugenbergschen Presseimperiums.* Hamburg: Bertelsmann Universitätsverlag, 1974.

Leopold, John A. *Alfred Hugenberg: The Radical Nationalist Campaign Against the Weimar Republic.* New Haven, CT: Yale University Press, 1977.

Human Sciences (*Geisteswissenschaften*)

Covering roughly the disciplines of humanities and social sciences, the term *Geisteswissenschaften* has become the generic name for the various investigations concerned with human beings, society, culture, and human mind or "spirit"—most often in contradistinction to the natural or physical sciences. The term became standard German usage in the latter decades of the nineteenth century, following its gradual disengagement from transcendental idealist and speculative Hegelian thought, while drawing concurrently on long-established textual and philological practices.

With special connotations of inner spirituality and outward affinity for other kindred minds, "spirits," cultures, or mentalities, the German usage was the outcome of a long and manifold process combining theoretical and sociocultural aspects. Renaissance humanism, Reformation theology, the Enlightenment, the French Revolution, industrial technology, and modern individualism all stressed the emancipation of humanity from bondage or alienation in "otherness" (i.e., nature, myth, "being," servile labor, social hierarchy, the unconscious, or the masks of ideology).

In the strictly academic context, the demand for critical-methodical study of human manifestations, actions, and institutions arose concurrently. This incipient body of disciplines became the core of Wilhelm von Humboldt's idea of the "philosophical faculty" of the German university at the time of the liberation from Napoleonic rule, when German national identity was being defined—above all in terms of spirit, culture, and language. Moreover, the "sciences of spirit" emerged as offshoots of Hegel's dialectic—turned against its own metaphysical premises but still under the sway of historical idealism. The link between these disciplines and German "identity" or self-understanding has remained strong.

This body of disciplines combined many strands of modern thought, by no means mainly German in origin or character. The Cartesian division of all reality into nature and consciousness, postulating the primacy of the latter; Vico's anti-Cartesian "new science" combining history, philology, and philosophy; Kant's transcendental turn to the universal forms of consciousness; Fichte's "science of freedom"; Hegel's phenomenology of mind in concrete historical circumstance; the "moral sciences" of British utilitarian tradition; and the general European "historical sense" of the nineteenth century were combined in this cluster of sciences. Developed in opposition to the positivistic or "scientistic" premises that privileged the natural sciences, the human sciences were thought to provide practical norms or orienting values for individuals and collectivities. They were expected to yield activating knowledge to shape the personality and the human world at large.

A pioneering attempt to found these disciplines was the unfinished *Einleitung in die Geisteswissenschaften* (published as *Introduction to the Human Sciences*), 1883, by Wilhelm Dilthey (1833–1911) and his subsequent studies on interpretative understanding and the historical sense. Rejecting both positivist and metaphysical positions, Dilthey founded the human sciences on an expanded theory of knowledge, deriving from *Verstehen* (everyday empathetic understanding), which apprehends the meaning immanent to all human awareness of life, lived experience, and signification. From decidedly more transcendental premises, the Baden school of neo-Kantianism (Wilhelm Windelband [1848–1915] and Heinrich Rickert [1863–1936]) insisted on the term "cultural sciences" and argued that these sciences presupposed universal cultural values. Whether these sciences are distinct from the natural sciences primarily with respect to their object or to their method has remained a matter of dispute.

In the twentieth century, efforts to find the unity and/or fundamentals of the human sciences have raised more perplexities. Such fundamentals remain difficult to clarify and today the human sciences coexist as heterogeneous specialties, with some vague sense of connectedness. Recent German theorists (Jürgen Habermas [1929–] and Manfred Riedel) have tended to differentiate the human sciences into three groupings: the empirical/analytical, the historical/ hermeneutical (i.e., interpretative), and the systematic/behavioral.

In the past, the *Geisteswissenschaften* were sometimes invoked to defend the embattled essence of the German spirit against the "levelling" and dehumanizing encroachments of modernity. The definition and role of the human sciences in modern society are bound to remain deeply contested, as they bring values, technology, and self- and other-regarding attitudes into play. Whether they are "provable" or not, these disciplines are believed to harbor the self-understanding of humankind.

Michael H. Ermarth

See also Bildung und Bildungsbürgertum; Dilthey, Wilhelm; Habermas, Jürgen; History; Kultur; Mythology, Classical and Germanic; Philosophy; Rickert, Heinrich; Understanding; Universities; Windelband, Wilhelm

References

Apel, Karl-Otto. *Analytic Philosophy of Language and the Geisteswissenschaften*. Dordrecht: D. Reidel, 1967.

Bodammer, Theodor. *Philosophie der Geisteswissenschaften*. Freiburg: K. Alber, 1987.

Dilthey, Wilhelm. *Introduction to the Human Sciences*. Princeton, NJ: Princeton University Press, 1988.

French, Peter, ed. *The Philosophy of the Human Sciences*. Notre Dame, IN: University of Notre Dame Press, 1990.

Kimmerle, Heinz. *Philosophie der Geisteswissenschaften als Kritik ihrer Methoden*. The Hague: M. Nijhoff, 1978.

Olafson, Frederick. *The Dialectic of Action: A Philosophical Interpretation of the Humanities*. Chicago, IL: University of Chicago Press, 1979.

Rickman, H. P. *Understanding and the Human Studies*. London: Heinemann, 1967.

Rothacker, Erich. *Einleitung in die Geisteswissenschaften*. 2nd ed. Tübingen: Mohr, 1930.

Taylor, Charles. *Philosophy and the Human Sciences*. Cambridge: Cambridge University Press, 1985.

Winch, Peter. *The Idea of a Social Science and Its Relation to Philosophy*. London: Routledge and Kegan Paul, 1990.

Husserl, Edmund (1859–1938)

Edmund Husserl, born in Prossnitz, Moravia, was the founder of phenomenology as a philosophical movement. The central goal of this movement was to establish philosophy as a rigorous science.

Husserl received a Ph.D. in mathematics from the University of Berlin in 1881. After studying with Franz Brentano (1838–1917) in Vienna, he turned his attention from mathematics to philosophy. Husserl was made a *Dozent* (assistant professor) at the University of Halle from 1887 to 1901, and from 1901 to 1916 he was a professor at the University of Göttingen. From 1916 until his retirement in 1928, Husserl was at the University of Freiburg. Husserl published six books during his lifetime, although he left various manuscripts that have been published posthumously (*Husserliana*, 1950–). Only a small portion of his writings has been translated into English.

Husserl's first systematic discussion of phenomenology appeared in his *Logische Untersuchungen* (1900–01; Logical Investigations), in which he suggested that consciousness is the only source of objective data on which a universal philosophical system could be based. The phenomena of consciousness included memories, feelings, moods, thoughts, and fantasies. Consciousness had to be studied, according to Husserl, using the phenomenological method. Husserl's writings on phenomenology had an important impact on a number of twentieth-century philosophers and psychologists, especially Mar-

tin Heidegger (1889–1976), Maurice Merleau-Ponty (1908–61), and Jean-Paul Sartre (1905–80).

James D. A. Parker

See also Heidegger, Martin; Philosophy

References

Edie, J.M. *Edmund Husserl's Phenomenology: A Critical Commentary.* Bloomington, IN: Indiana University Press, 1987.

Farber, M. *The Foundation of Phenomenology: Edmund Husserl and the Quest for a Rigorous Science of Philosophy.* 3rd ed. Albany, NY: State University of New York Press, 1967.

Harvey, C.W. *Husserl's Phenomenology and the Foundations of Natural Science.* Athens, OH: Ohio University Press, 1989.

Kockelmans, J.J. *A First Introduction to Husserl's Phenomenology.* Pittsburgh, PA: Duquesne University Press, 1967.

Ricoeur, P. *Husserl: An Analysis of His Phenomenology.* Evanston, IL: Northwestern University Press, 1967.

I

I.G. Farbenindustrie AG (1925–45)

By most measures (e.g., book or market value of stock, total sales, size of the workforce), this giant chemicals-based firm was the largest private enterprise in Germany during the Weimar and Nazi periods. Formed in 1925 by the merger of eight companies, I.G. Farben manufactured products ranging from pharmaceuticals to light metals but concentrated on monopolizing a succession of coal-based substitutes for key raw materials: dyes, nitrogen, fuel, and rubber. Though for many years it was Germany's leading industrial exporter, the firm also became indispensable to the country's attempts at expansion through conquest.

Contrary to legend, the concern neither backed Hitler prior to his takeover of power nor dominated economic policymaking and investments under the Nazi Four Year Plan (1936–42). Increasingly, however, it adapted to the Third Reich's economic priorities in order to retain its prosperity and commercial position. Its investments and output became militarized, and it was drawn into active participation in the most heinous of Nazi activities, from spoliation of foreign-owned property to the employment of slave labor, most notoriously at a factory built just three miles east of the Auschwitz concentration camp. A subsidiary in which I.G. Farben held 42.5 percent of the stock marketed the infamous Zyklon B used to gas hundreds of thousands to death. By the final years of World War II the concern had 334 plants, a workforce of 333,000 people (just under half of them voluntary, conscripted, or enslaved foreign laborers), and total sales of over three billion reichsmarks; it provided 25 percent of German output of synthetic fibers, 33 percent of fuel, 100 percent of synthetic rubber and stabilizers for explosives, and between one-third and one-half of all German chemical production. In 1947–48, 23 of the firm's principal officers were tried for war crimes by an American military tribunal and 13 were convicted.

Long treated in oversimplified fashion as the epitome of a Nazified corporation, I.G. Farben has been the subject of numerous unreliable publications. These include not only the many propagandistic accounts produced in the former Ger-

man Democratic Republic (GDR) but also several American works that appeared in the immediate aftermath of World War II and the sensationalist and tendentious book by Joseph Borkin, *The Crime and Punishment of I.G. Farben.*

Peter Hayes

See also Auschwitz; BASF; Bayer AG; Bosch, Carl; Cartels; Chemistry, Scientific and Industrial; Coal Industry; Duisberg, Carl; Four Year Plan; Holocaust; National Socialist Germany; Nazi War Crimes Trials and Investigations; Nuremberg Trials; Schmitz, Hermann; State and Economy; Third Reich: Industry

References

Hayes, Peter. *Industry and Ideology: IG Farben in the Nazi Era.* New York, NY: Cambridge University Press, 1987.

Plumpe, Gottfried. *Die I.G. Farbenindustrie AG: Wirtschaft, Technik und Politik 1904–1945.* Berlin: Duncker & Humblot, 1990.

Trials of the War Criminals Before the Nürnberg Military Tribunals under Control Council Law. Vols. 7–8. No. 10. Washington, DC: U.S. Government Printing Office, 1953.

Imbusch, Heinrich (1878–1945)

As head of the Christian Miners' Union and later also of the Christian-National German Trade Union Federation, Heinrich Imbusch was one of the most influential labor leaders in the Weimar Republic. Despite his anti-Marxist beliefs, Imbusch shared the fate of many other trade unionists when the Nazis came to power. Although he escaped imprisonment, he died from starvation, a hunted man in his home town of Essen, four months before the war ended.

Imbusch wrote extensively on labor matters, social legislation and national policies. From 1905 he was editor of, as well as the major contributor to, the Catholic miners' journal, *Der Bergknappe* (The miner). His study *Arbeitsverhältnis und Arbeits-Organisationen im deutschen Bergbau* (working conditions and work organization in the German coal industry), 1908, was among the first historical treatments of mining from a worker's perspective.

Born on September 1, 1873 as the son of a coal miner, Imbusch belonged to the long-settled, skilled labor force in the Ruhr Valley, which still lived in a semi-rural area. His upbringing in a Catholic milieu helped to define his anti-Marxism and his moralistic approach to economics and politics. Yet he strongly believed in workers' rights to full social and political equality, which he defended against encroachments from the Catholic clergy as well as from politicians. After World War I, his monarchist beliefs faded quickly. He was elected to the first parliament of the Weimar Republic and cooperated with the socialist trade unions to fight Communist radicalism among miners. At the same time, he strongly supported business and trade union cooperation, shop stewards, and co-determination.

In the later Weimar years, he increasingly became an outspoken critic of right-wing tendencies in his own Catholic Center Party and scathingly denounced the reactionary policies of heavy industry. Feared by his adversaries for his sharp pen and tongue as well as his business acumen, Imbusch was first and foremost a champion of the coal miners, although he had a loyal following among other Catholic and nationalist workers. Despite his past prominence he is all but forgotten today. In part, this can be related to the merger among the socialist, Christian, and liberal trade union movements after 1945, which seems to have made Imbusch's arguments about the incompatibility of Christian principles and socialist beliefs not only obsolete but irrelevant. Nevertheless, the ideal of moral rectitude and a good fighting spirit that Heinrich Imbusch personified as a trade union leader and politician lives on in the German trade union movement.

Irmgard Steinisch

See also Catholicism, Political; Center Party; Christian Trade Unions; Coal Industry; Trade Unions, 1871–1945; Weimar Germany; Working Conditions

References
Patch, William. *The Christian Trade Unions in the Weimar Republic, 1918–1933: The Failure of "Corporate Pluralism."* New Haven, CT: Yale University Press, 1985.
Schäfer, Michael. *Heinrich Imbusch: Christlicher Gewerkschaftsführer und Widerstandskämpfer.* Munich: Verlag C.H. Beck, 1990.
Steinisch, Irmgard. "Der Gewerkverein Christlicher Bergarbeiter." *Glückauf Kameraden. Die Bergarbeiter und ihre Organisationen in Deutschland.* Ed. Hans Mommsen and Ulrich Borsdorf. Cologne: Bund Verlag, 1979.

Immendorff, Jörg (1945–)
More than any other present-day artist, Jörg Immendorff embodies the ideas of a "neo-expressionism," a utopian, figurative response to contemporary social ills. His allegorical sculptures and paintings, such as the *Café Deutschland* series (1978–1984), reinsert the artist into a tradition of sociopolitical engagement and comment on his position in a fractured Germany.

Early in his career, Immendorff came under the influence of the dean of sociocritical art, Joseph Beuys (1921–86), with whom he studied at the Düsseldorf Academy of Art from 1964 to 1970. Immendorff became involved with Beuys in a variety of agitprop activities and student protests, and produced a body of work that challenged the role of art and the artist to effect social change. Works such as *Teine Tunst mehr mache* (baby talk for "Make no more art") and his *Lidl* actions (1968–70), influenced by Happenings and Fluxus, play with notions of kitsch and the infantile to question the relevancy of art in an increasingly radicalized, skeptical world. In the early 1970s Immendorff became a Maoist and produced paintings such as *How's your painting going, colleague?* (1973), which contrasts the dreamy concerns of an artist with the workers' revolution unfolding in the street. Later involvement with the Greens and the Düsseldorf Rainbow Coalition Initiative continued to activate Immendorff's concerns regarding the aesthetic versus the political nature of art.

In 1978, Immendorff began the *Café Deutschland* series, a group of paintings that treats the political, social, and moral divisions of modern Germany. Inspired by the situation of the East German painter A.R. Penck (1939–), whom he met in East Berlin in 1977, and his viewing of Renato Guttoso's painting *Café Greco* at the Venice *Biennale*, Immendorff decided to allegorize the divisions between East and West in a modern, conceptual space that juxtaposes recognizable politicians and artists in a chaotic, painterly setting. Using concepts of didactic theater developed by Bertolt Brecht (1898–1956), a political artist with whom he closely identified, Immendorff injected Nazi and Cold War imagery, such as swastikas, barbed wire, eagles, and gun turrets, into a hermetic world buffeted by fire and ice, with figures who fight lethargy and panic in a messianic struggle for existence.

In the mid to late 1980s, after teaching at the art academies in Stockholm, Hamburg, Zurich, Trondheim, Cologne, and Munich, and after gaining a considerable international reputation, Immendorff expanded his conceptual spaces to include artists' studios, the academy, the art gallery, and the theater. In these highly allegorical works, such as *Nachtmantel* (Night coat), 1987, Immendorff presents himself surrounded by the whole of the contemporary art world, creating modern-day group portraits that comment on the precarious role of the artist as a fashionable luminary enmeshed in art-world intrigue.

Since 1989, Immendorff has been a professor at the Stadelschule in Frankfurt and currently lives in Düsseldorf, Frankfurt, and Hamburg.

Kristin Makholm

See also Artists; Beuys, Joseph; Brecht, Bertolt; The Cold War and Germany; Expressionism; The Greens: Movement, Party, Ideology; Painting; Penck, A. R.; Sculpture

References

Adams, Brooks. "Anarchy and Innocence." *Art in America* 80, no. 2 (February 1992), 93–7.

Immendorff. Exhibition catalog. Rotterdam: Museum Boymans-van Beuningen; The Hague: Haags Gemeentemuseum, 1992.

Immendorff: Café Deutschland/Adlerhälfte. Exhibition catalog. Düsseldorf: Kunsthalle, 1982.

Jörg Immendorff. Exhibition catalog. Zürich: Kunsthaus, 1983.

Jörg Immendorff: Cafe Deutschland and Related Works. Exhibition catalog. Oxford: Museum of Modern Art, 1984.

Imperial and Free Conservative Party (1867–1918)

Leaders of the Reichs- und freikonservative Partei (RFKP) always imagined theirs to be the quintessential "national" party of Imperial Germany. It was founded in 1867 by conservatives who embraced Otto von Bismarck's solution to the national question. These men claimed that they represented an "up-to-date" brand of conservatism until the party collapsed in December 1918. Yet from beginning to end, the RFKP was dominated by political notables (*Honoratioren*) who can best be described as "generals without troops." They were well-connected and influential, including representatives of heavy industry, owners of large estates, career diplomats, state ministers, and Prussian administrators. Aristocrats, other "independents," and Catholics were also well-represented in the party's parliamentary caucuses. But because its leaders neglected grass-roots organizational work, the Imperial Party (as it was known nationally) and the Free Conservative Party (in Prussia) began to lose strength as soon as the age of mass politics dawned. Although the RFKP retained a strong contingent of deputies (50–65) in the Prussian *Landtag* (state legislature), its fortunes in Reichstag elections plummeted from 1878, when it won almost 14 percent of the popular vote and 57 seats, to just three percent and 12 seats in 1912.

Between 1867 and 1890 the RFKP was the "Bismarckian party *sans phrase*." It supported the *Kulturkampf*, protective tariffs, anti-socialist repression, and the preservation of monarchical rule. Yet despite its persistent effort to bridge the gap between the National Liberal Party on its left and the German Conservative Party (DKP) on its right, the RFKP's heterogeneity spawned sharp intra-party disputes. That the party's leaders never agreed on an official program was one sign that they recognized how difficult it was to stress only what united their followers. Wilhelm von Kardorff, the pro-agrarian party leader from 1880 to 1907, disagreed with the Saarland industrialist Carl Ferdinand von Stumm-Halberg (1836–1901) in the early 1890s over whether to support a reduction of agrarian tariffs. Around the same time, the National Party, though stillborn, threatened to detach party members with Pan-German sympathies. Still, Free Conservative leaders always influenced government policy out of all proportion to the number of their followers or voters. Some, such as Stumm and Friedrich Alfred Krupp, had the ear of the Kaiser. Some, such as the later party chairman, Oktavio von Zedlitz-Neukirch, were considered chancellor material. And some, such as Hans Delbrück (1848–1929), edited influential newspapers or journals.

Although the common struggle against the Social Democrats animated all three right-wing parties after 1903, the RFKP never convinced the electorate that its policies were more "progressive" or "moderate" than those of the larger German Conservative Party. Its dismal showing in the Reichstag campaigns of 1881, 1903, and 1912 showed that a protest vote on any number of "fairness issues" tarred both parties with the same brush.

Like the other two parties on the right, the RFKP was eventually compelled to consider how high-level influence-peddling could be supplemented with a more systematic or "popular" approach to politics. Nonetheless, one cannot accurately establish even the rough contours of a formal party membership. Free Conservatives were never organized into a network of associations with clear lines of authority or communication that bound together the national leadership, regional groupings, and local clubs. The wish to avoid "partisanship" consistently undermined the efforts of the RFKP to sharpen its own profile and broaden its following.

A number of party insiders observed retrospectively that the RFKP remained locked in an insulated, artificial world of high politics. Political talent was not lacking in the RFKP. But in the final years before the war, when the party verged on extinction, other politicians proved more adept at mobilizing a mass following by displaying the political insight, the determination, and—in some instances—the ruthlessness that the Free Conservatives found so alien.

James Retallack

See also Conservatism, 1871–1918; Delbrück, Hans; German Conservative Party; Imperial Germany; Krupp: Family and Firm; Political Parties and Politics; Prussia; Stumm-Halberg, Carl Ferdinand von

References

Aandahl, Friedrich. "The Rise of German Free Conservatism." Unpublished doctoral dissertation. Princeton University, 1955.

Arnim, Hans von, and Georg von Below, eds. *Deutscher Aufstieg, Bilder aus der Vergangenheit und Gegenwart der rechtsstehenden Parteien*. Berlin: Schneider Verlag, 1925.

Fricke, Dieter. "Reichs und freikonservative Partei (RFKP) 1867–1918." *Lexikon zur Parteiengeschichte 1789–1945*. 4 vols. Ed. D. Fricke et al. Leipzig: VEB Bibliographisches Institut, 1983-86. Vol. 3, 745–72.

Hellwig, Fritz. *Carl Ferdinand Freiherr von Stumm-Halberg 1836–1901*. Heidelberg and Saarbrücken: Westmark, 1936.

Kardorff, Siegfried von. *Wilhelm von Kardorff: Ein nationaler Parlamentarier im Zeitalter Bismarcks und Wilhelms II: 1828–1907*. Berlin: E.S. Mittler & Sohn, 1936.

Imperial Germany

The history of Imperial Germany has been a highly contentious issue since at least 1961, when the Hamburg historian Fritz Fischer labeled Germany as having been more responsible than the other great powers for precipitating World War I. Since Fischer described the built-up tensions in German society and what German statesmen perceived to be a stalemate in peaceful diplomacy, sharp differences of interpretation have arisen among historians about the basic nature of social change and political decisionmaking in the Empire. These differing views have caused important advances in empirical research, for instance on the everyday lives of working-class families, the Kaiser's court, local politics, and the role of women in society. Perhaps just as important, new research has also contributed to a more sophisticated understanding of how social, economic, political, and cultural developments were interrelated.

In older accounts, the birth of the Empire in 1871 was little more than a sequence of political, military, and international developments. As the grandmaster of European diplomacy, Chancellor Otto von Bismarck used three quick and decisive wars (1864–71) as a means to impose his own—Prussian—model on the process of German unification. Older views also emphasized how German liberals succumbed to the lure of national unity: humbled by the failed Revolution of 1848 and the constitutional crisis of the 1860s, they had abandoned their bid for hegemony in state and society by 1890 at the latest. By this reading, conservative elites in the Prussian civil service, court, and army, together with the *Junker* class in eastern Prussia and the barons of industry in the west, preserved an unhealthy dominance in public affairs because German liberals failed to dislodge them. This "failure," moreover, allegedly explains an incongruence in German history that had important short- and long-run implications. Because Germany's rapidly expanding capitalist economy remained under the control of social and political elites from a "premodern" era, Germans embraced first authoritarian and then Fascist solutions to the problem of containing the advance of liberal democracy.

More recently, however, historians have begun to stress the diverse ways in which liberals imposed their own stamp on the process of unification and its consolidation, for instance with the Civil Code of 1900. Thus, it is not the conservative but the liberal character of the Empire that was encoded in the rule of law, the freedoms of speech, association, and the press, the nationalization of political culture under the impact of universal manhood suffrage, the *Kulturkampf* against the Catholic Church in the 1870s, and the inauguration of Bismarck's anti-socialist laws, in effect from 1878 to 1890. Similarly, the rise of the educated and propertied bourgeoisie appears to have been facilitated by Bismarck's willingness to embrace liberal economic doctrine in the late 1860s and 1870s; it also spelled the end of conservative notions of a cohesive, corporative, and conflict-free society.

Bismarck's legacy and the role of Wilhelm II in decisionmaking after 1890 is another contentious area of debate. The 1890s are now regarded as a watershed in German political development, for three principal reasons. First, the struggle against the labor movement and its political wing, the Social Democrats, underwent a number of decisive phases, from attempted rapprochement to attempted repression to reform. After 1900, the government remained ambivalent as to how the "forces of revolution" could be contained with measures that would not alienate most German citizens.

Second, the final years of economic depression up to 1895 witnessed the rapid rise of protest movements, especially in the countryside and among the lower middle classes, that have been described as "demagogic" and "populist." The challenge posed by these protest movements wrenched the traditional political parties, kicking and screaming, into the age of mass politics.

Third, the so-called "personal rule" of Wilhelm II was established by 1900, and during Chancellor Bülow's term of office (1900–09) it destabilized German policy in numerous unfortunate ways, especially in foreign affairs. The Kaiser's beloved program of battleship-building virtually bankrupted the Reich government, which caused severe political conflict over proposed new taxes in 1909. It did not, however, achieve its objective of driving the British to adopt a policy of neutrality. By 1914, the unwieldy—some would say unworkable—parliamentary constellation at home and the determined enmity of Great Britain, Russia, and France abroad had driven

Emperor Wilhelm II. Courtesy of Inter Nationes, Bonn.

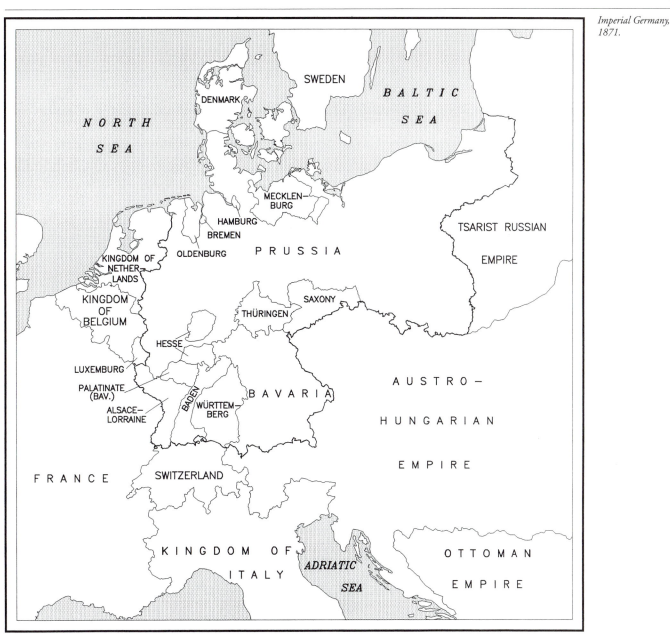

*Imperial Germany,
1871.*

German statesmen into a perceived deadlock. Whether either the domestic or the diplomatic outlook was quite as bleak in reality is less clear.

Social and political ferment also focused attention on the role of minorities in the Empire and contributed to the assault on traditional values. In Bismarck's time, the repression of Catholics, Poles, and socialists set the tone. After 1890, women, youth, national and religious minorities, and those who valued local allegiances more than national ones all staked a claim to independence and autonomy. Yet simultaneously, German nationalism became more broadly based and chauvinistic.

Just as these developments contributed to a stridency in political life that had been unknown in Bismarck's day, they also began to detach members of the bourgeoisie from their complacent beliefs regarding the virtues of individualism, rea-

son, and progress. Especially in the last 20 years of the Empire, cultural modernism fueled such doubts, even though it often juxtaposed contradictory themes—for instance, nostalgia for the past and abandonment of orthodox belief. Although conceived as a critique of staid bourgeois values, modernism accurately reflected the conflicting yearnings—backward- and forward-looking—that characterized Wilhelmine Germany as a whole.

During World War I, Germans appeared to meet many new challenges: on the field of battle, in the building of a war economy, in overcoming the gulf between socialist and nonsocialist parties, and (more briefly) in galvanizing all classes and political parties to defend the country. By September 1918, a good possibility existed that constitutional reform might introduce genuine democracy and responsible government. By then, however, the bankruptcy of the old regime was patently clear. In the second week of November, Kaiser Wilhelm II abdicated and fled to Holland. The Empire vanished and the Weimar Republic was erected in its place.

Not surprisingly, historians continue to disagree about the trajectory of German history over the Imperial period. Some emphasize all that remained in place from Bismarck's constitutional "construct" of 1871. Some choose to highlight the many ways in which life remained brutal, precarious, and unfair. Others, by contrast, stress everything that changed during the Empire, and still others note that Germany had good reason to trumpet its pioneering role in such spheres as higher education, local self-government, or industrial productivity. Yet as Germans abandoned social, economic, and cultural forms dating from the nineteenth century, they seemed always to embrace modernity with a mixture of fervor and fear. Whatever interpretation is favored, Imperial Germany is currently regarded as an immeasurably more complex historical phenomenon than had seemed conceivable just 30 years ago. Now it challenges the Weimar Republic and the Third Reich for the attention of every historian of modern Germany.

James Retallack

See also Agriculture; Agrarian Leagues; Anti-Semitism; Aristocracy; Bismarck, Otto von; Bethmann Hollweg, Theobald von; Bourgeoisie; Bülow, Bernhard von; Caprivi, Leo von; Catholicism, Political; Center Party; Conservatism; Constitutions; Ebert, Friedrich; Elections; The Fischer Controversy; Founding Years; Friedrich III; Hohenlohe-Schillingsfürst, Chlodwig zu; Imperial Germany: Army; Imperial Germany; Foreign Policy; Imperial Germany: Literature; Industrialization; Judicial System of Imperial and Weimar Germany; *Kulturkampf*; Liberalism; Militarism; Nationalism; Navy and Naval Policy; Parliamentary System; Parties and Politics; Peasantry; Protestantism and the Protestant Church; Prussia; Radical Nationalism; Revolution of 1918–19; Roman Catholic Church; Social Democratic Party, 1871–1918; Social Imperialism; Social Reform; *Sonderweg*; State and Economy; Trade Unions, 1871–1945; *Weltpolitik*; Wilhelm I; Wilhelm II; World War I

References

Abrams, Lynn. *Bismarck and the German Empire, 1871–1918.* London and New York, NY: Routledge, 1995.

Berghahn, Volker R. *Imperial Germany 1871–1914: Economy, Society, Culture and Politics.* Providence, RI and Oxford: Berghahn Books, 1994.

Blackbourn, David. *The Fontana History of Germany, 1780–1918.* London: Fontana, 1997.

———. *Populists and Patricians: Essays in Modern German History.* London: Allen and Unwin, 1987.

Eley, Geoff, ed. *Society, Culture, and the State of Germany, 1970–1930.* Ann Arbor: University of Michigan Press, 1996.

Iggers, Georg, ed. *The Social History of Politics: Critical Perspectives in West German Historical Writing since 1945.* Leamington Spa: Berg, 1985.

Mommsen, Wolfgang J. *Imperial Germany 1867–1918: Politics, Culture, and Society in an Authoritarian State.* London: Edward Arnold, 1995.

Nipperdey, Thomas. *Deutsche Geschichte, 1866–1918.* 2 vols. Munich: C.H. Beck, 1990–92.

Pflanze, Otto. *Bismarck and the Development of Germany.* Vols. 2 and 3. Princeton, NJ: Princeton University Press, 1990.

Porter, Ian, and Ian D. Armour. *Imperial Germany, 1890–1918.* London: Longman, 1991.

Retallack, James. *Germany in the Age of Kaiser Wilhelm II.* Basingstoke, London and New York, NY: Macmillan and St. Martin's Press, 1996.

Wehler, Hans-Ulrich. *The German Empire, 1871–1918.* Leamington Spa: Berg, 1985.

———. *Deutsche Gesellschaftsgeschichte, 1849–1914.* Vol. 3. Munich: C.H. Beck, 1995.

Imperial Germany: Army

The army of Imperial Germany was rooted in Prussian traditions. Nevertheless, the system of territorial recruitment insured the persistence of local traditions and attitudes, particularly in Bavaria. Paradoxically, the army's strong local identities fostered national integration after 1871 by facilitating the absorption of successive generations of conscripts into the principal symbolic institution of the Empire. Military service became a generalized male rite of passage, while the Empire's middle classes sought officers' commissions as a means of integration into the new order.

The Imperial Army was authoritarian, disdaining even the rudimentary principles of a free society and a parliamentary government. The army was arrogant, imbued with the hubris of quick and decisive victories. Neither Social Democrats nor Liberals successfully challenged the army's privileged position. Even Chancellor Otto von Bismarck controlled the army by playing its principal agencies—the War Ministry, the General Staff, and the Military Cabinet—against each other rather than risk a direct confrontation. Yet the army was also anxiety-ridden. Germany's precarious geographic position left the country vulnerable. Her increasingly entropic domestic situation indicated that a long war might split the "restless Reich" into fragments. As a result, the army concentrated on preparing for the next war rather than resting on the laurels of the last ones.

Even before the Franco-Russian alliance of 1894, the General Staff was convinced that the next war must be fought on enemy territory. The army grew obsessed with shaving every possible hour from its increasingly elaborate mobilization plan and with developing an offensive strategy with every detail planned in advance. The result was the Schlieffen Plan of 1905. A massive sweep through Belgium and northern France, it strained logistical systems to their utmost while leaving little or no room for the "fog and friction" that Carl von Clausewitz had described as characterizing modern war.

The army never demanded total mobilization of either human or material resources prior to World War I. The War Ministry was reluctant to risk diluting a politically reliable officer corps by expansion. The Reichstag was reluctant to increase budgets already strained by the demands of the new navy. By 1914 the army's peacetime establishment stood at 800,000. The war footing was 3,822,000. These impressive figures, however, concealed the fact that fully half of the men eligible for conscription in a given year saw no active service. Nor had any systematic preparations been made to integrate the economy into war planning.

As a result, Imperial Germany fought World War I by improvisation. The German people withstood the stresses of total war far better than anticipated; not until 1918 did army and home front alike collapse from exhaustion. Economic mobilization was forced and haphazard, resulting in the waste of resources that Germany could not spare. An already ramshackle political system offered no significant resistance to military interference that by 1917 established Chief of Staff Paul von Hindenburg (1847–1934) and Quartermaster-General Erich Ludendorff (1865–1937) as de facto rulers of the Empire. Out of its depth in total war, the team proved unable either to achieve a negotiated peace or to win a decisive victory.

The army's chief failure, however, was its refusal to develop more than a tactical approach to questions of grand strategy and national policy. As late as 1918, Ludendorff could emerge with no plan to end the war other than punching a hole in the Allied line and hoping for the best. The ultimate result was catastrophe: the destruction of the Empire that the army ostensibly existed to protect.

Dennis E. Showalter

See also Aristocracy; Armaments Policy; Bismarck, Otto von; Einem, Karl von; Falkenhayn, Erich; Hindenburg, Paul von; Imperial Germany; Imperial Germany: Foreign Policy; Ludendorff, Erich; Militarism; Moltke, Helmuth von (the Elder); Moltke, Helmuth von (the Younger); Navy and Naval Policy; Officer Corps; Prussia; Schlieffen, Alfred von; Waldersee, Alfred von; Weimar Germany: Army; Wilhelm I; Wilhelm II; World War I

References
Bucholz, Arden. *Moltke, Schlieffen, and War Planning.* New York, NY: Berg, 1991.

Düffler, Jost, and Karl Modd, eds. *Bereit zum Krieg: Kriegsmentalität im Wilhelminischen Deutschland 1890–1914.* Göttingen: Vandenhoeck & Ruprecht, 1986.

Förster, Stig. *Der doppelte Militarismus: Die deutsche Heeresrüstung zwischen Status-Quo Sicherung und Aggression 1890–1913.* Stuttgart: F. Steiner Verlag, 1985.

Kessel, Eberhard. *Moltke.* Stuttgart: Koehler, 1957.

Rothenberg, Günther. "Moltke, Schlieffen, and the Doctrine of Strategic Envelopment." *Makers of Modern Strategy.* Ed. Peter Paret et al. Princeton, NJ: Princeton University Press, 1986.

Schulte, Bernd. *Die Deutsche Armee 1900–1914: Zwischen Beharren und Veränderung.* Düsseldorf: Droste, 1977.

Imperial Germany: Foreign Policy

After the wars of unification and the remarkably moderate peace treaties concluded with Austria (1866) and the onerous one with France (1871), Chancellor Otto von Bismarck predicated German diplomacy on the dual device of isolating France and arranging alliances with all the other major powers in such a way that it became impossible for anyone to exert political pressure on Germany. In October 1873, Bismarck induced Kaiser Wilhelm I (1871–88) to expand the Habsburg Austria–Tsarist Russia accord into the Three Emperors' League. But when the German chancellor attempted to cajole the French Third Republic into submission in the "War in Sight" Crisis (May 1875), London and St. Petersburg intervened and demonstrated that they desired France to remain an independent actor in the European balance of power. Rather than isolating the Reich, Bismarck settled the conflicting interests of Russia and the Habsburg monarchy, which were triggered by the impending dissolution of the Ottoman Empire and the ambitions of the small Balkan states, and he drew Great Britain into his diplomatic balancing acts. At the 1878 Congress of Berlin, Bismarck earned his reputation as the "honest broker"; Russia, however, felt betrayed because it had to surrender its battlefield gains and renounce its Peace Treaty of San Stefano (March 1878) imposed on the Sultan.

The turn toward economic protectionism and competitive rearmament (1876–79), exacerbated by nationalist-imperialist propaganda campaigns, increased political tensions, especially between Germany and Russian Pan-Slavism. Bismarck attempted to reconcile the contradictory demands of his Russian and Austrian allies, and at the same time to exploit the conflicting interests between Great Britain and France in Africa and Indochina as well as between Russia and Great Britain in Asia. Bismarck wanted to ensure that each of these powers appreciated the need for Germany's support. Against the background of a highly complicated interplay between domestic pressures and foreign-policy ambitions within the European states as well as the struggle for colonies, Bismarck wove a network of seemingly irreconcilable alignments and alliances: The Dual Alliance between the Reich and the Habsburg Monarchy (1879), extended into the Triple Alliance by including Italy (May 1882); the Reinsurance Treaty between the Reich and Russia (June 1887), and—fearing a rapprochement between Russia and France—an arrangement that would tie Great Britain to Germany's Mediterranean allies (Italy and Austria-Hungary) and thus permit Germany and Great Britain to retain control over the "Oriental troubles," i.e., the Balkans and the Middle East.

The rationale behind Bismarck's juggling was to reaffirm Germany's standing as a saturated power. This explains Bismarck's reluctance to join the race for overseas colonies, which, in turn, ensured the German "newcomer" the position that no European affair involving the powers would and could be resolved without the willing cooperation of Berlin.

The new Emperor, Wilhelm II (1888–1918), and Bismarck's enemies (Fritz von Holstein) abandoned this juggling act after the forced resignation of Bismarck in 1890. Instead, the "New Course" aimed at German-British cooperation in Europe (Helgoland-Zanzibar accord, July 1890) and above all at a firmly entrenched power base in *Mitteleuropa* (central Europe), centered around a series of commercial treaties that would guarantee that Eastern European countries patronized Berlin rather than Paris. By the conclusion of the Franco-Russian Military Convention (August 1892) and through the promotion of capital exports, France established a hold on Russia. But their formal alliance offered no guarantee that Russia and France would necessarily back each other in conflicts with third parties, although Russia did come to the aid of France in the 1898 Fashoda Crisis with Great Britain. Frustrated that Great Britain did not assume its share in defending the position of its traditional partners, the Habsburg and Ottoman Empires, but also exhilarated by the prospect of matching Great Britain's economic production, Wilhelmine Germany from the mid-1890s onward began to challenge Great Britain's position as arbiter of Europe.

Based on the military might of the German army and the hub position of Germany within continental Europe's commercial relationships, the Kaiser's new men, later Chancellor Bernhard von Bülow (1849–1929) and Secretary of State of the Navy Alfred von Tirpitz (1849–1930), initiated in 1896–97 the policy of the "free hand." The international situation, i.e., the perennial conflicts between Great Britain and Russia and between France and Great Britain on one hand and the "truce" between Russia and Austria-Hungary (1897–1907) on the other, provided German diplomacy a range of opportunities. Berlin, however, misused these chances. First, Berlin overestimated Great Britain's interest, under Secretary of State for Colonies Joseph Chamberlain, in closer cooperation with Germany and, by deciding to build a battle fleet as a means to exert political pressure on London, induced Great Britain to prepare to meet the German threat.

Second, Germany attempted to exploit the political weaknesses of the French Third Republic and to demonstrate to France—in the Moroccan crises of spring 1905 and summer 1911—that neither Great Britain nor Russia was a reliable ally; Berlin provoked the opposite reaction. Germany became isolated as a warmonger or—in German terminology—it became encircled by a host of enemies. The German response, massive naval and military armament (1911–13), was also prompted by the fact that Berlin could not depend on external support; Italy virtually shifted its allegiance toward France (November 1902) and Russia (Racconigi Agreement, October 1909), and Austria-Hungary was perplexed by its own internal crises and the conflicts with Serbia (after December 1904).

Third, Russia, after its defeat in the war with Japan (1904–05), reemerged as a "European" power, resolved to buttress its claims for a hold over Istanbul and the Turkish Straits. Having failed to force Russia into friendly relations with the Reich (Björkö Accord, July 1905), Berlin used blackmailing strategies on Russia (in the Bosnian Crisis, March 1909, and the two Balkan wars, 1912–13).

Although German diplomacy under Chancellor Theobald von Bethmann Hollweg (1856–1921) tried to reverse course and temporarily succeeded in restoring accords with France (1909–10), Russia (1912) and Great Britain (1912–13), the attempts at reconciliation did not prevail. On the one hand, neither the Kaiser, nor Tirpitz, nor the Chiefs of Staff were prepared to place any of Germany's instruments of strength on the negotiating table, nor were they seriously considering to dispense with the security guarantee tendered to the Habsburg Monarchy. On the other hand, the partners of the Triple Entente (France, Russia, and Great Britain) interfered whenever they suspected that another of them was about to court Berlin.

The outbreak of World War I in the July crisis of 1914 resulted from the German resolve to bolster Austria-Hungary's claim to a strong position in the European state system and from Tsarist Russia's resolve to back Serbia, and for that matter, to put the alliance with France to the test. Inasmuch as diplomacy was deemed inadequate to attain "national security," the various governments of the two alliance systems, facing ultranationalistic agitations at home, were willing to consider war as a solution to their perception of the security dilemma.

Gustav Schmidt

See also Anglo-German Relations; Austro-German Relations; Bismarck, Otto von; Bethmann Hollweg, Theobald von; Bülow, Bernhard von; Caprivi, Leo von; Central Powers; Diplomatic Corps and Diplomacy; Franco-German Relations; Hohenlohe-Schillingsfürst, Chlodwig zu; Imperialism; Kiderlen-Wächter, Alfred von; Marschall von Bieberstein, Adolf; Navy and Naval Policy; Russian-German Relations; Schweinitz, Lothar von; *Weltpolitik*; Wilhelm II; World War I

References

Berghahn, Volker R. *Germany and the Approach of War in 1914*. 2nd ed. London: Macmillan, 1993.

Fischer, Fritz. *Germany's Aims in the First World War*. New York, NY: W. W. Norton, 1967.

———. *War of Illusions: German Policies from 1911 to 1914*. New York, NY: Norton, 1975.

Hildebrand, Klaus. *Deutsche Aussenpolitik 1871–1918*. Munich: Oldenbourg, 1989.

———. *German Foreign Policy from Bismarck to Adenauer: The Limits of Statecraft*. London: Unwin Hyman, 1989.

Hillgruber, Andreas. *Germany and the Two World Wars*. Cambridge, MA: Harvard University Press, 1981.

Kennan, George. *The Decline of Bismarck's European Order: Franco-Russian Relations, 1875–1890*. Princeton, NJ: Princeton University Press, 1979.

Mommsen, Wolfgang J. *Grossmachtstellung und Weltpolitik: Die Aussenpolitik des Deutschen Reiches 1870–1914*. Frankfurt am Main: Ullstein Verlag, 1993.

Rich, Norman. *Great Power Diplomacy, 1814–1914*. New York, NY: McGraw-Hill, 1992.

Schmidt, Gustav. *Der europäische Imperialismus*. Munich: R. Oldenbourg, 1985.

Schöllgen, Gregor. *Angst vor der Macht: Die Deutschen und ihre Aussenpolitik*. Berlin: Ullstein: 1993.

———. *Escape into War? The Foreign Policy of Imperial Germany.* Oxford: Berg, 1990.

Stürmer, Michael. *Das ruhelose Reich: Deutschland 1866–1918.* Berlin: Severin & Siedler, 1983.

Imperial Germany: Literature

Hardly any time in the history of German literature shows a greater diversity of style and artistic purpose than the nearly fifty years of the Imperial era. The major literary currents of those years often overlap and thus defy systematic periodization.

The years 1871 to 1888, roughly corresponding to the so-called *Gründerzeit* (founding years), were marked by the nationalistic euphoria immediately following Chancellor Otto von Bismarck's unification of Germany, by the growing pains of the new national economy, by Bismarck's *Kulturkampf,* and by the anti-socialist Laws. Among the writers who dominated the literary scene were the older realists: Theodor Storm with his novellas, Conrad Ferdinand Meyer with *Huttens letzte Tage* (Hutten's last days), 1871, *Jürg Jenatsch,* 1883, and Wilhelm Raabe with *Das Odfeld,* 1888, and *Stopfkuchen,* 1891; for the most part, these writers take a distant, often skeptical attitude toward the new Germany, with the possible exception of Meyer who discovered his German identity during the Franco-Prussian War of 1870–71. The monumental, historicizing style of Felix Dahn's *Ein Kampf um Rom* (A fight for Rome), 1875, and Gustav Freytag's cycle of novels *Die Ahnen* (The ancestors), 1873–81, perhaps better represents popular sentiment, with its annual celebrations of the battle of Sedan of 1870 and mythologizing reverence for the House of Hohenzollern and its Iron Chancellor. Remarkably, however, nearly all of the major authors refrained from flaunting the "hurrah-patriotism" that characterized the German middle class at that time.

Theodor Fontane (1819–98) emerged as the major portraitist of the 1880s and 1890s. His lovingly ironic exposure of his contemporaries' insecurities and anxieties also shows that their nationalism lacked the strength of inner conviction. Simultaneously, the concerns of the young naturalists, such as Gerhart Hauptmann (1862–1946), *Die Weber* (published as *The Weavers*), 1892, Hermann Sudermann, *Heimat* (Homeland), 1893, and Max Halbe, *Jugend* (Youth), 1893, were social concerns that did not permit an identification with the dominant political culture in Germany.

Naturalism was not only a movement of European dimensions and thus more or less immune to nationalistic ideologies—it had as one of its stated goals the revelation of the inherent conflicts within society, i.e., those involving the classes, the sexes, and the family, thus clearly calling into question the notion of a national body of which everybody was an integral part. This does not mean, however, that ideological Germanization did not exist; on the contrary, Paul de Lagarde (1827–91) *Deutsche Schriften* (German writings), 1878, Julius Langbehn's (1851–1907) *Rembrandt als Erzieher* (Rembrandt as educator), 1891, and especially Houston Stewart Chamberlain's (1855–1927) *Die Grundlagen des 19. Jahrhunderts* (published as *The Foundations of the 19th Century*), 1899, became the models for subsequent conservative and nationalist thought. The romantic ideas of *Volk* and

Reich were just beginning to gather political strength.

The "pluralism of styles" (Jost Hermand) around 1900, in which naturalism, impressionism, *Jugendstil* (art nouveau), and symbolism occur nearly simultaneously, obscured the fact that Germany's intelligentsia had turned against what it regarded as the crude materialism of Wilhelmine imperialism after 1895. It was ready to fill the vacuum with visions of race and *Kultur,* or a cosmic mysticism that paralleled the lust for colonial expansion in a good section of the German bourgeoisie. Thomas Mann's (1875–1955) short story, *Beim Propheten* (At the prophets), 1904, is a sardonic sketch of the cosmic milieu. Stefan George (1868–1933) made a serious attempt in his poetry to combine the critique of imperialism with the search for a new national substance. His poetic cycles *Der siebente Ring* (The seventh ring), 1907, and *Der Stern des Bundes* (The star of the covenant), 1914, were meant as a continuation of Friedrich Nietzche's earlier critique of the Bismarck Reich. George and his circle grew in influence considerably even after the end of the Wilhelmine Empire, but the elitism of George's language and that of his disciples prevented the message from being widely received.

The educated middle class of the *Bildungsbürger* (cultivated bourgeoisie) reacted more favorably to the apotheosis of such past German figures as Jakob Böhme and Paracelsus in the works of Erwin Guido Kolbenheyer, whose *Meister Joachim Pausewang* appeared in 1910 and whose Paracelsus trilogy first reached the public in 1917. Kolbenheyer became one of the leading writers during the Third Reich. Perhaps the theme of *Heimat* (homeland) presents the one unifying idea that links Pan-German imperialist nationalism with introspective, xenophobic regionalism that is a permanent characteristic of all German nationalism. The success of Hermann Burte's novel *Wiltfeber der ewige Deutsche: Die Geschichte eines Heimatsuchers* (Wiltfeber the eternal German: the story of a searcher for home)1912 and the popularity of the novels of Hermann Stehr, *Der begrabene Gott* (The buried God), 1905, and *Der Heiligenhof,* 1918, as well as the ballads of Börries von

Some of the many translations of Thomas Mann's Buddenbrooks. *Courtesy of German Embassy, Ottawa.*

Münchhausen, *Balladen,* 1900, Lulu von Strauss und Torney, *Balladen und Lieder,* (Ballads and lieder), 1902, and Agnes Miegel, *Balladen und Lieder,* 1907, are cases in point. All of these authors understood and exploited the longings and fears of large segments of the German public, its anti-urbanism and its constant sense of being threatened by enemies of the Reich. Thus, much of the subsequent Nazi ideology was well represented prior to World War I.

These tendencies evoked powerful counter-currents, as the emergence of expressionism around 1910 demonstrated. The war did not fundamentally change this constellation of forces, even though the initial national euphoria moved a poet such as Rilke to write his *Fünf Gesänge* (Five songs), 1915, and someone as normally non-nationalistic as Thomas Mann to contribute such essays as "Gedanken im Kriege" (My thoughts in wartime), 1914, and *Friedrich und die grosse Koalition* (published as *Frederick the Great and the Great Coalition*), 1915.

The nationalism of German writing during the war was primarily expressed in the language of solidarity, comradeship, and self-sacrifice that grew on the battlefields of Flanders. Walter Flex's best-selling memoir, *Der Wanderer zwischen beiden Welten* (The wanderer between both worlds), 1916, is a most poignant example of the mystification of death that rooted a national experience shaped by the war. Thomas Mann's *Betrachtungen eines Unpolitischen* (published as *Reflections of a Nonpolitical Man*), 1918, dealt at length with the entire range of experiences that characterize this peculiarly German brand of nationalism, which followed the disillusionment of 1848 and never left the sphere of German inwardness protected by the power of the state (*machtgeschützte Innerlichkeit*).

Thomas Mann's self-analysis as a German conservative resulted in the recognition of the nonpolitical nature of that conservatism, its romanticism, and its potential for imperialistic expansionism at any time. It was Thomas Mann's brother Heinrich (1871–1950) who had portrayed the seamy side of that conservatism in his novel *Der Untertan* (published as *The Patrioteer*), 1918. Heinrich Mann's political engagement was closely tied to that of the expressionists, whose role as critics of Germany's war aims has been widely discussed. The expressionists' search for a new man and new forms of society in all its complexity appeared most clearly in the plays of Georg Kaiser, *Von morgens bis mitternachts* (From morn to midnight), 1916, Fritz von Unruh, *Ein Geschlecht* (A dynasty), 1917, and Ernst Toller (1893–1939), *Die Wandlung* (Transfiguration), 1919. Together with Kurt Pinthus's anthology of expressionist poetry, *Menschheitsdämmerung* (End of the world), 1919, and Oswald Spengler's *Der Untergang des Abendlandes* (published as *The Decline of the West*), 1918, these plays symbolize the extent to which the collapse of the monarchy resulted in the most profound identity crisis of modern Germany.

Thomas Hollweck

See also Bernstein, Elsa; Busch, Wilhelm; Chamberlain, Houston Stewart; Children's Literature; Comedy; Drama; Expressionism; Fairy Tales; Feminist Writing; Fontane, Theodor; Founding Years; Freytag, Gustav; George, Stefan; *Germanistik;* Hasenclever, Walter; Hauptmann; Gerhart; *Heimat;* Holz, Arno; Huch, Ricarda; Kaiser, Georg; Lagarde, Paul de; Langbehn, Julius; Mann, Heinrich; Mann, Thomas; Nationalism; Naturalism; Nietzsche, Friedrich; Patriotic Literature; Raabe, Wilhelm; Realism; Rilke, Rainer Maria; Satire; Spengler, Oswald; Storm, Theodor; Theater; *Völkisch* Ideology

References

Berman, Russell A. *Cultural Studies of Modern Germany: History, Representation and Nationhood.* Madison, WI: University of Wisconsin Press, 1993.

———. *The Rise of the Modern German Novel: Crisis and Charisma.* Cambridge, MA: Harvard University Press, 1986.

Hamann, Richard and Jost Hermand. *Epochen deutscher Kultur von 1870 bis zur Gegenwart,* Vol. 1: *Gründerzeit.* Vol. 4: *Stilkunst um 1900.* Munich: Nymphenburger Verlagsbuchhandlung, 1971 and 1973.

Hermand, Jost. *Von Mainz nach Weimar (1793–1919): Studien zur deutschen Literatur.* Stuttgart: Metzler, 1969.

Hüppauf, Bernd, ed. *Expressionismus und Kulturkrise.* Heidelberg: Carl Winter Universitätsverlag, 1983.

Marshall, Alan. "Naturalism and Nationalism." *German Life and Literature* 37 (1983–84), 91–104.

Pascal, Roy. *From Naturalism to Expressionism: German Literature and Society 1880–1918.* New York, NY: Basic Books, 1973.

Trommler, Frank, ed. *Jahrhundertwende: Vom Naturalismus zum Expressionismus (1880–1918).* Reinbek: Rowohlt, 1983.

Imperial League against Social Democracy (1904–14)

The Reichsverband gegen die Sozialdemoraktie (Imperial League against Social Democracy) formed in the aftermath of the Social Democratic Party's (SPD) success in the 1903 elections, brought together several related initiatives and was officially launched on May 9, 1904. Steered by a circle of Conservative, Free Conservative, and right-wing National Liberal politicians in cooperation with leading heavy industrialists, it was essentially an outgrowth of *Sammlungspolitik* (coalition politics), intended to provide the latter with a national clearing house for anti-socialist propaganda. More ambitiously, it aimed to expedite local coalitions of the Right while conducting anti-socialist agitation in the *Mittelstand* (middle class) and the working class. As Eduard von Liebert (1850–1934), the chairman (also a Free Conservative parliamentarian and leading Pan-German), put it, the aim was to fight the SPD on two fronts: by working for anti-socialist unity in elections and by providing social supports for "all those who are oppressed by Social Democracy," whether small businessmen, artisans, or workers.

In the scale of its activity, the Reichsverband was a success. It enrolled 211,000 members in 702 local branches by 1909, distributed 47 million copies of 170 different leaflets and over one million pamphlets between 1904 and 1914, trained speakers, organized National Labor Secretariats, and coordinated local anti-socialist unity agreements for elections. But it also ran up against the existing political identities of the right-wing parties, whose leaders were nervous of too active a drive for cross-party unity. The Reichsverband also contained a cadre of radical-nationalist activists committed to precisely such a logic of right-wing unification, for which independent organization and popular mobilization would prepare the way.

It was these ambitions that the party establishments behind the organization's creation would not allow. This conflict of perspective remained basically unresolved. The apogee of the Reichsverband's influence was the successful brokering of anti-socialist unity for the 1907 elections, but afterwards its ability to take new organizational and agitational initiatives (such as the launching of a patriotic labor movement, or the institutionalization of local unity agreements) remained stymied by existing party divisions and the indecision of its leaders. The league was dissolved early in World War I.

Geoff Eley

See also Central Association of German Industrialists; German Conservative Party; Imperial and Free Conservative Party; Imperial Germany; Nationalism; National Liberal Party; Pan-German League; Radical Right; *Sammlungspolitik*; Social Democratic Party, 1871–1918; *Weltpolitik*

References

Eley, Geoff. *Reshaping the German Right: Radical Nationalism and Political Change after Bismarck.* Ann Arbor, MI: University of Michigan Press, 1991.

Fricke, Dieter. "Der Reichsverband gegen die Sozialdemokratie von seiner Gründung bis zu den Reichstagswahlen von 1907." *Zeitschrift für Geschichtswissenschaft* 7 (1959), 237–80.

Saul, Klaus. *Staat, Industrie, Arbeiterbewegung im Kaiserreich: Zur Innen- und Sozialpolitik des Wilhelminischen Deutschland 1903–1914.* Düsseldorf: Droste, 1974.

Imperialism

"Imperialism" in the German Empire encompassed attempts (actual and proposed) to extend control over areas beyond Germany's borders, the political forces that led to such attempts, and the ways of thinking that framed and legitimated them. Imperialism was simultaneously a phenomenon of policy, politics, and ideology, all of which interacted to help bring Germany into World War I.

German imperialist ideology had two main tendencies. The first was to regard German expansion, whether through overseas colonies, informal overseas economic hegemony, or a German-dominated trading area in Central Europe, as an extension of Germany's economic modernization. Imperialists who developed the notion of *Weltpolitik* (world power) and advocated a *Mitteleuropa* (central Europe) centering on German industry focused on the goal of securing and extending the capitalist economy. This economic imperialism became strongly rooted after 1890 in finance, business, and the bureaucracy. The other tendency emphasized the need to protect the basis on which the German *Volk* existed as a cultural and racial entity. Ideologists of this tendency, strongly represented in radical nationalist organizations such as the Pan-

German League, described colonies as places where Germans might settle as farmers or as a master race and saw German domination of Central Europe as a means of expanding the scope of German peasant agriculture. They often, although not universally, displayed an anti-industrial bias. The idea of *Lebensraum* (living space) was a sophisticated manifestation of this view.

The politics of imperialism within Germany were closely connected to differing ideologies, to the interplay of social and economic interests, and to party politics. The groups that formed the radical nationalist opposition to late Wilhelmine governments regarded imperialism as a vehicle for criticizing government policies and creating a consensus among themselves. Industrial and financial lobbies used the idea of *Weltpolitik* to advance particular economic interests and to legitimate their political roles in general. Certain parties, especially the National Liberals and the Free Conservatives, consistently identified themselves with imperialism, and even the Social Democrats acquired an imperialist wing. Political disputes over imperial matters tended to be linked to controversies in domestic German politics.

Imperialism was relatively weak as an influence on German foreign policy under Chancellor Otto von Bismarck (except for Bismarck's colonial foray in the 1880s). Succeeding governments, however, together with Wilhelm II, identified imperialist aims (usually defined in terms of *Weltpolitik* and the need for parity with Great Britain) as major policy goals. The desire to use imperialism as a national unifying force partly underlay Alfred von Tirpitz's naval building program. Economic imperialist elements of *Weltpolitik,* and the need of the Bülow and Bethmann Hollweg governments to defend themselves against radical nationalist attack, informed German actions in the Moroccan crises (1905–06, 1911). By 1914, large segments of the German political elite had come to believe that the country's future (and their own political survival) depended on successfully pursuing imperialist policies—a conviction that strongly influenced German decision making leading up to World War I and the conduct of politics and governance during the war.

Woodruff D. Smith

See also Anglo-German Relations; Bismarck, Otto von; Bülow, Bernhard von; Colonies and Colonial Society; Imperial and Free Conservative Party; Imperial Germany: Foreign Policy; National Liberal Party; Navy and Naval Policy; Navy League; Pan-German League; Radical Right; Social Imperialism; Tirpitz, Alfred von; *Völkisch* Ideology; *Weltpolitik*; Wilhelm II

References

Berghahn, Volker R. *Germany and the Approach of War in 1914.* 2nd ed. London: Macmillan, 1993.

Chickering, Roger. *We Men Who Feel Most German: A Cultural Study of the Pan-German League 1886–1914.* London: Allen & Unwin, 1984.

Eley, Geoff. *Reshaping the German Right: Radical Nationalism and Political Change after Bismarck.* Ann Arbor, MI: University of Michigan Press, 1991.

Fischer, Fritz. *Germany's Aims in the First World War.* New York, NY: Norton, 1967.

————. *War of Illusions: German Policies from 1911 to 1914.* New York, NY: Norton, 1972.

Kennedy, Paul M. *The Rise of the Anglo-German Antagonism 1860–1914.* London: Allen & Unwin, 1980.

Moses, J.A. *The Politics of Illusion: The Fischer Controversy in German Historiography.* New York, NY: Barnes and Noble, 1975.

Smith, Woodruff D. *The Ideological Origins of Nazi Imperialism.* New York, NY: Oxford University Press, 1986.

Wehler, Hans-Ulrich. *Bismarck und der Imperialismus.* Cologne: Kiepenheuer & Witsch, 1969.

Impressionism (1890–1914)

Toward the close of the nineteenth century, a group of painters—led by Max Liebermann (1848–1935), Max Slevogt (1868–1932) and Lovis Corinth (1858–1925)—abandoned their early naturalism to develop an unconventional, looser and more broadly painted representative style, strongly influenced by, though not identical to, French impressionism. Institutionalized in the Berlin Secession (founded 1898), these painters represented modernism and internationalism in the arts and for a time became the focus of a nationwide German cultural controversy.

The term "impressionist"—first applied as a derogatory label by nationalist critics who opposed alien influences and who accused the artists of importing French impressionism into Germany—is only a partially accurate label for their work, which was as much influenced by such earlier masters as Vélasquez, Goya, Rembrandt, and Hals as by more recent French artists. During the 1890s, German modernists became increasingly interested in French impressionist painters and adopted some of the French artists' innovations in articulating space. Yet, in contrast to the French, who dissolved material into color and light, German impressionists more thoroughly emphasized line and movement.

In 1898, the Berlin Secession was formed as an independent exhibition society by artists seeking to free themselves from the constraints of the Academy and its annual salon. The Secession was not limited to impressionism, but it became a magnet for impressionists working in different parts of Germany. Slevogt and Corinth, for example, moved to Berlin chiefly because the Secession drew them. Within two years, the Secession had become a powerful voice for modernism and a major cultural force in Germany.

The critics of impressionism not only objected to a changing visual "language" that they could not understand, but perceived in it alien influences that threatened traditional German values. Among the strongest critics was Wilhelm II, who, directly and through such intermediaries as Anton von Werner (1843–1915), energetically opposed modernism as being foreign and unconcerned with traditional standards of beauty. A controversy over whether or not German impressionism should be represented in the German art exhibition at the 1904 St. Louis World's Fair led to an important debate in the Reichstag in which the efforts by the Kaiser to impose his personal tastes in art as government policy were rejected by a wide range of political parties.

Impressionism and modernism in Germany weathered, and even gained from, the attacks of cultural conservatives, but already in the last years before World War I, German impressionism as an avant-garde movement was being overtaken by the bold innovations of the early expressionists. Liebermann, Slevogt, and Corinth all lived and worked well into the Weimar era, but only Corinth in his late paintings evolved a style of visual distortion that carried him into expressionism, and it was Corinth who among the impressionists received the most international attention. Despite the international character of the impressionists' aesthetic development, and notwithstanding their institutional revolt in the Berlin Secession, their artistic innovations have never been regarded as sufficiently original to earn widespread recognition outside of Germany. The importance of German impressionism, which ultimately remained a national or regional style, lies in its confrontation with Germany's conservative art establishments, which paved the way for expressionism and exemplifies the conflicts between the traditional and the modern in Wilhelmine Germany.

Paul Paret

See also Artists; Berlin Secession; Corinth, Lovis; (Visual) Expressionism; *Jugendstil*; Liebermann, Max; Munich Secession; Naturalism; Slevogt, Max; Stuck, Franz von; Uhde, Fritz von; Werner, Anton von; Wilhelm II

References
Brauner, Lothar. *Malerei der deutschen Impressionisten.* Berlin: Staatliche Museen zu Berlin, Nationalgalerie, 1979.

Kern, Josef. *Impressionismus im Wilhelminischen Deutschland: Studien zur Kunst- und Kulturgeschichte des Kaiserreichs.* Würzburg: Königshausen & Neumann, 1989.

Paret, Peter. *The Berlin Secession: Modernism and Its Enemies in Imperial Germany.* Cambridge, MA: The Belknap Press of Harvard University Press, 1980.

Römpler, Karl. *Der Deutsche Impressionismus.* Dresden: Verlag der Kunst, 1958.

Independent Social Democratic Party

On April 6, 1917, dissident former members of the German Social Democratic Party (SPD) met in the city of Gotha to discuss their future. Formally expelled from the SPD earlier that year and from the SPD parliamentary caucus in 1916, the dissidents voted to abandon the sacrosanct principle of socialist unity and found a separate political party, the German Independent Social Democratic Party (Unabhängige Sozialdemokratische Partei Deutschlands; USPD). Until its demise in September 1922, the USPD played a crucial role in German politics, especially during the Revolution of 1918 and the formation of the Weimar Republic.

The membership of the new party represented a curious mixture of ideologies. Doctrinal purists such as Karl Kautsky

(1854–1938) and disillusioned SPD functionaries such as Hugo Haase (1863–1919) collaborated with the radical labor leader Emil Barth and the revisionist Eduard Bernstein (1850–1932). On the extreme left stood the Spartacus League of Karl Liebknecht (1871–1919) and Rosa Luxemburg (1870–1919), which hoped that the war would produce a true socialist revolution. The only common thread binding these diverse elements was their antiwar sentiment. A lack of ideological coherence plagued the party throughout its existence.

The founding manifesto reflected the tensions within the new party. Calls for a general amnesty, freedom of the press, and universal elections were followed by demands for reasserting the international solidarity of the working classes. Radicals were disturbed that the manifesto issued no call for a revolution.

Once constituted at Gotha, the USPD set out to accomplish its immediate goal, to end the war. USPD branches established in most German cities challenged the local SPD organizations and achieved spectacular successes in several cities. Leipzig and Halle in particular became USPD strongholds. Despite its formation as a national party, the USPD always enjoyed as its main source of strength its local party units.

Food shortages caused by the war contributed to the growing strength of the USPD through 1917 and into 1918, but the party's prominent role in the strikes of January 1918 revealed inner tensions. Most Independents were more concerned with ending the war than with generating a Bolshevik-style revolution, which brought them into conflict with their own radical elements. Consequently, the USPD leadership was unable to provide the strikers with decisive direction.

The lack of direction became even more evident when the Imperial government collapsed in the chaos of November 1918. The speed with which the SPD under Friedrich Ebert (1871–1925) and Philipp Scheidemann (1865–1939) consolidated the revolution caught the USPD leaders by surprise. An SPD offer to form a coalition government was hotly debated and finally accepted, but only after further alienating leftist radicals. The Spartacus League seceded from the USPD in January 1919 to form the German Communist Party (KPD).

The end of the war forced the USPD to justify its existence. Formed around antiwar groups, the party either had to dissolve or redefine itself. In particular, it had to decide whether it favored a council system or a parliamentary one. The USPD's continued indecisiveness, and the bitterness engendered during the months after the November Armistice when the SPD-led provisional government crushed leftist opposition across Germany, made reconciliation between the SPD and the USPD impossible. In the eighteen months following the end of the war, growing disillusionment with the SPD among workers caused the USPD vote to rise dramatically, from less than two and a half million in January 1919 to over five million in June 1920 against the six million won by the SPD in the latter Reichstag elections. USPD vote totals declined thereafter, as political stability returned to Germany.

The final years of the USPD were filled with conflicts between its radical and moderate factions concerning the party's relationship to the Weimar government. The USPD found itself caught between the SPD and the KPD without offering workers a viable alternative to either faction's views. These debates culminated in another split within the USPD in October 1920 over the question of whether to join the Third Communist International. The divided party limped along for another two years, still searching for an identity. After the September 1922 Gera USPD Party Congress, moderate Independents formally reentered the SPD, whereas radicals joined the KPD.

David McKibbin

See also Bernstein, Eduard; Ebert, Friedrich; German Communist Party; Haase, Hugo; Kaustky, Karl; Liebknecht, Karl; Luxemburg, Rosa; Mehring, Franz; Revolution of 1918–19; Spartacus League; Social Democratic Party; Trade Unions; Weimar Germany; World War I; Zetkin, Clara; Zietz, Luise

References

Krause, Hartfrid. *USPD: Zur Geschichte der Unabhängigen Sozialdemokratischen Partei Deutschlands.* Frankfurt am Main: Europäische Verlagsanstalt, 1975.

Miller, Susanne. *Burgfrieden und Klassenkampf: Die deutsche Sozialdemokratie im Ersten Weltkrieg.* Düsseldorf: Droste, 1974.

Morgan, David W. *The Socialist Left and the German Revolution.* Ithaca, NY: Cornell University Press, 1975.

Schorske, Carl E. *German Social Democracy, 1905–1917: The Development of the Great Schism.* Cambridge, MA: Harvard University Press, 1955.

Wheeler, Robert F. *USPD und Internationaler Sozialistischer Internationalismus in der Zeit der Revolution.* Frankfurt am Main: Ullstein, 1975.

Industrialization and Its Social and Political Consequences

According to most historians, Germany experienced the economic transformation known as the "industrial revolution" more quickly and thoroughly than did other European countries. The social consequences may not have been quite as horrendous as in Great Britain in terms of child labor, pauperization, and destruction of the rural-artisan way of life. However, the political consequences of the social and cultural changes effected by industrialization have been related to the aggressive foreign policy of Imperial Germany, to the internal tensions of the Weimar Republic, and to the rise of Nazism.

In 1800, under 20 percent of the population of the German-speaking lands engaged in industrial production; the census of 1907 recorded over 40 percent. Views among historians vary on whether the decisive increase came before or after unification in 1871. All concur that only in some regions did a majority of the populace became involved in industrial production before World War I. Those were the Ruhr–north Rhine area, part of Silesia, Saxony, and Berlin, plus pockets in the large northern port cities of Hamburg and Bremen.

As elsewhere, industrialization involved a high incidence of child and female labor in the new form of concentrated production by machinery in factories. Coal mining, metal working, and textile milling became the predominant industrial occupations. This type of cheap, unskilled labor possessing no capital contrasted with the male-dominated artisan trades. The latter, though, were not displaced except in some urban areas, because craftsmen often provided the minimal training that factory hands received. As the economic spurt of the 1890s brought Germany onto the world stage competing with Great Britain in manufactures, steel, coal, and trade, the social results of urban growth and suburban development accompanying industrialization became notable: poverty, inadequate housing, and dangerous work conditions. The spatial redistribution of the social classes and the public health dangers have been well illustrated in the case of Hamburg by Richard Evans.

Two traits reminiscent of other industrializing economies marked Germany during the late nineteenth century: 1) economic cycles of boom and bust, with a depression in 1873 and downturns in 1891–92 and 1913; and 2) the high mobility of migrant and largely unskilled labor prepared to participate in strikes and protest. Whether spatial mobility brought social mobility remains open to debate.

Special about German industrialization by the end of the nineteenth century was the degree of cartelization, the size of firms and factories, the success of family enterprises—such as the Krupps, Mannesmanns, Thyssens, and Stumms—and the alliance of agricultural and industrial interests in fostering protectionism for the producer at the expense of consumers. The commensurate growth and unity of the labor movement in its economic and political wings too made Germany a special case of large industry facing large labor organizations. The Social Democratic Party, with its million members by 1914, and the trade union federation, with two and a half million, demonstrated the bifurcated society engendered, according to some scholars, by industrialization. Industrialization not only extended the stratification of Germany vertically but enhanced regional differences. While some areas remained rural and backward, a few urban centers and firms led the world in technological advances, primarily in two new areas in which the Germans dominated, especially in Europe: chemistry and electricity. In examining the special features (magnitude of units, the state's benevolent role, and types of banking) of Germany's intense industrialization phase, Ralf Dahrendorf described the result as a "faulted nation."

Some authors (for instance, Hans-Ulrich Wehler) regard Germany's path through the process of industrialization as special, in that they think a feudal ethos continued to dominate among a technological, modern elite. Further, the Imperial state had sheltered the middle class during the transitional upheaval by providing stability, status, and secure salaries. After World War I, only the feudal ethos and resentment about lack of state protection against inflation and loss of status vis-à-vis labor remained. Hence many of the old elite and the middle classes were prepared to accept the temptations and promises of Nazism. This viewpoint has been challenged by authors (in particular by Geoff Eley and David Blackbourn) who think that Fascism had European roots and that the social upheavals and divisions in the industrial process in Germany were little different than elsewhere.

Dieter K. Buse

See also Cartels; Coal Industry; Exports and Foreign Trade; Factory Laws and Reform; Food; Housing; Migration; Protectionism; Social Democratic Party, 1871–1918; Social Imperialism; Social Insurance; Social Reform; State and Economy; Steel Industry; Trade Unions, 1871–1945; Urbanization; Working Conditions

References

Barkin, Kenneth D. "Germany's Path to Industrial Maturity." *Laurentian University Review* 5 (1973), 11–33.

Blackbourn, David, and Geoff Eley. *The Peculiarities of German History*. Oxford: Oxford University Press, 1984.

Blackbourn, David, and Richard J. Evans, eds. *The German Bourgeoisie*. London: Routledge, 1993.

Dahrendorf, Ralf. *Society and Democracy in Germany*. Garden City, NY: Doubleday Anchor, 1969.

Evans, Richard. *Death in Hamburg: The Cholera Years, 1830–1910*. Oxford: Oxford University Press, 1987.

Henderson, William O. *The Rise of German Industrial Power, 1834–1914*. London: Temple Smith, 1975.

Kitchen, Martin. *The Political Economy of Germany, 1834–1914*. London: Croom Helm, 1978.

Landes, David. *The Unbound Prometheus: Technological Change and the Industrial Development in Western Europe from 1750 to the Present*. Cambridge: Cambridge University Press, 1970.

Lees, W. R., ed. *Industrialization and Industrial Growth in Germany*. London: Croom Helm, 1986.

Köllmann, Wolfgang. *Bevölkerung in der industriellen Revolution*. Göttingen: Vandenhoeck & Ruprecht, 1974.

Wehler, Hans-Ulrich. *Imperial Germany*. Leamington Spa: Berg, 1985.

Infants, Children, and Adolescents

The lives of infants, children, and adolescents have been affected by political and economic upheaval and by demographic trends. At the same time, the importance of German youth has extended beyond their own experience. Even as their representation in the population has declined (people under 20 comprised 45 percent of the population in 1890 and 25 percent in 1983), youth have often generated social and political conflict.

Perhaps the most significant change in the lives of infants has been the improved likelihood of their survival. At the time of the 1871 unification, nearly 25 percent of infants died in their first year; by the 1970s, the figure had declined to about 1.5 percent. Families with babies have also undergone considerable change. A child born early in this century was likely to have three or four siblings; most children born in the last few decades have either had one sibling or none. Until World War II, most youngsters had mothers who were not employed or who worked in the home. After the war, small children increasingly had mothers who worked outside the home; this situation was nearly universal in the German Democratic Republic (GDR). A large majority of infants and small children in the East attended nurseries, while small children in the West were cared for by nurseries, "day mothers," or relatives.

In the decades following unification, educational opportunities gradually opened to girls, and state-sponsored education replaced confessional schools in some provinces. Nevertheless, the school system remained highly stratified by class. On the eve of World War II, 90 percent of youth of both sexes still left school at the age of 14. Some four percent remained in the educational system until age 16; the remainder completed an additional three years in preparation for university.

This educational system remained static until well into the post–World War II period. In the GDR beginning in 1965, all children attended ten years of school; approximately ten percent took an additional two years of university preparation. In the Federal Republic of Germany (FRG), grouping according to ability and need still begins early in a child's school career and still largely follows class lines, but interclass movement has been considerably eased. In 1983, 20 percent of West German youth completed university preparation, 40 percent the "middle level," and 40 percent only the basic schooling to age 14. Since the Weimar era, however, three years of vocational training have been mandatory for youth leaving school at age 14. The rapid growth of the university population—without corresponding reform in the institutions themselves—contributed to the student protests in the 1960s and 1970s.

By 1893, legislation prohibited child labor and limited the work day for 12- to 14-year-olds to six hours, but most youth began full-time work at the age of 14, when they completed school. Middle-class observers grew concerned that working-class male youth might be attracted to rowdy behavior and socialism, and that their female peers might fall into prostitution; guidance for young people's free time seemed a good preventive measure. At the same time, many working-class youth desired meaningful recreational activities, and some middle-class youth found the strict style of education stifling. An expansion of traditional youth institutions, such as religious and athletic clubs, as well as the creation of new organizations, including the socialist Workers' Youth and the middle-class *Wandervogel*, resulted. By the Weimar period, 50 percent of young people belonged to some sort of organization.

Membership in the Hitler Youth became nearly universal for racially approved boys during the Nazi years; it was technically obligatory for girls, but female membership was ill-enforced. Most young people of both sexes in the GDR belonged to the Free German Youth. The attempts to coax or coerce young people into organizations, as well as battles over religious versus public schooling, indicate the extent to which political, social, and religious groups have felt it necessary to win over Germany's youth. Young people, for their part, often enjoyed the activities and contact with their peers, regardless of political or religious overtones. The formative events of the lives of many infants, children, and adolescents, however, have not been the battles over their minds and souls, but rather the same events that shaped the lives of German adults: economic crises that plunged their families into poverty, wars, and

waves of persecution that cost them relatives, and eras of well-being that provided comfort and security.

Elizabeth Heineman

See also Abortion; Childbirth and Motherhood; Education; Factory Laws and Reform; Family; Federal Republic of Germany: Women; Fertility; German Democratic Republic: Education; German Democratic Republic: Women; Hitler Youth; League of German Girls; Marriage and Divorce; Technical Training, Technical Institutes, and Universities; Women; Women's Occupations; Working Conditions; Youth; Youth Movements

References

Albisetti, James. *Schooling German Girls and Women: Secondary and Higher Education in the Nineteenth Century.* Princeton, NJ: Princeton University Press, 1988.
———. *Secondary School Reform in Imperial Germany.* Princeton, NJ: Princeton University Press, 1983.
Jaide, Walter. *Generationen eines Jahrhunderts: Wechsel der Jugendgenerationen im Jahrhunderttrend: Zur Sozialgeschichte der Jugend in Deutschland 1871–1985.* Opladen: Leske & Budrich, 1988.
Lamberti, Marjorie. *State, Society, and the Elementary School in Imperial Germany.* New York, NY: Oxford University Press, 1989.
Laqueur, Walter. *Young Germany: A History of the German Youth Movement.* London: Routledge & Kegan Paul, 1962.
Linton, Derek S. *"Who Has the Youth, Has the Future": The Campaign to Save Young Workers in Imperial Germany.* New York, NY: Cambridge University Press, 1991.

Inflation and Hyperinflation (1914–24)

The German inflation was a protracted episode of monetary depreciation that began in World War I and culminated in the hyperinflation of July 1922 to November 1923. The progress of the inflation was uneven rather than linear, and the causative factors varied in character and intensity at different times. Germany was not unusual in having a wartime inflation, although its full measure was veiled by the severe reduction of its international trade. The exchange rate went from 4.20 marks per dollar in July 1914 to 7.43 in November 1918. The dangerous future potential of the wartime inflation lay in Germany's decision to finance the war by domestic loans (rather than through taxation), the inability to borrow abroad, the development of monetary mechanisms that increased the liquidity of the economy while pretending to maintain coverage requirements, and the failure to control excessive profits and high wages after the launching of the exorbitant Hindenburg weapons and munitions program in 1916.

Four major periods in the history of the inflation may be identified. The first (November 1918–March 1920) encompassed the Revolution of 1918, the signing of the Treaty of Versailles, and the Kapp Putsch. The exchange rate was 15.08 marks per dollar in July 1919 and 99.11 in February 1920. Domestic factors largely induced the significant depreciation of the mark during this period, particularly the government's efforts to maintain social peace through work creation, high unemployment supports, and benevolence toward price and wage increases. The signing of the peace treaty damaged confidence in the currency, and reparations payments in kind played a secondary role in promoting inflation.

A second period of relative stabilization, begun in the spring of 1920, lasted through the spring of 1921, when the dollar averaged 60 marks. The depreciated mark enabled Germany to enjoy strong export advantages, maintain relatively high employment, and avert the severe deflationary and depression cycle experienced contemporaneously by Great Britain and the United States. Although Germany's deficit increased substantially during this period, international confidence in the capacity of Germany to set its house in order generated massive speculative investments, especially by Americans, in the mark and in mark-denominated assets. During this period, the most important steps were taken to reconstruct Germany's industrial infrastructure and global market position.

A third period characterized by galloping inflation began following Germany's acceptance of the London Ultimatum on reparations in May 1921 and the first payment under its schedule in August 1921. The murder of Matthias Erzberger (1875–1921) in August, the failures of the Wirth governments to find a satisfactory domestic basis for its policy of treaty fulfillment and taxation programs, refusal by industrialists to support the reparations effort, and the breakdown of labor's wage restraint contributed to the depreciation of the mark from 84.31 to the dollar in August 1921 to 493 to the dollar in July 1922.

A similar combination of circumstances—failures in Germany's reparations negotiations, growing internal unrest, and the murder of Foreign Minister Walther Rathenau (1867–1922) in June 1922—precipitated the final period of hyperinflation. Wirth and Rathenau had utilized the policy of fulfillment to persuade the Allies that Germany could not pay under the London Schedule and that it needed breathing space and a large foreign loan to stabilize its currency and set its house in order.

The Allies rejected the balance-of-payments theory of inflation on which the German policy was based, namely, that the Germans had to print money as long as they had a negative balance of payments. Arguing from the quantity theory perspective, the Allies insisted that Germany stabilize its currency first and thereby qualify itself for a foreign loan. The resulting deadlock increased tensions within Germany regarding how the costs of the lost war and reparations were to be paid. Germans now joined foreigners in fleeing from the mark. Prior to the Ruhr occupation in January 1923, the chief motor of the hyperinflation was the decision of the Reichsbank under Rudolf von Havenstein to discount commercial bills as a solution to the growing credit crisis. As these credits were regularly rediscounted and ultimately repaid in depreciated currency, a private inflation was thereby added to the public one arising from the Reichsbank's discounting of treasury bills to fund the deficit. Between August 1922 and the end of the year, the mark depreciated from 1,134 to 7,589 to the dollar.

The financing of passive resistance against the French occupation of the Ruhr completed the process of destroying the currency, once the Reichsbank's attempt to support the mark at a level of approximately 21,000 to the dollar collapsed in mid-April 1923. By the summer of 1923, the farmers were refusing to accept paper marks. Most of the population was calculating in foreign currencies, and the Reichsbank could not print enough marks to meet the demand.

Faced with the danger of starvation and unrest, a new government, formed under Gustav Stresemann (1878–1929) in August, terminated passive resistance, began an austerity program, imposed taxation, and undertook a major currency reform. The latter measure, inspired by Karl Helfferich (1872–1924) and carried out by Hjalmar Schacht (1877–1970), involved the creation of a new temporary currency, the rentenmark, which was to be issued by a Rentenbank in strictly limited quantities, and to which the government was to have only limited recourse in the coverage of its expenses. Formally secured by all the landed and industrial wealth in Germany, the rentenmark and the new reichsmark, which replaced it in 1924, became ultimately stabilized in a "shock therapy." This involved the issuing of a limited currency, high taxes, austerity, longer working hours, lower wages, and the prospect of international loans—secured through the Dawes Plan as a reward for these measures. The old paper mark was formally pegged to the dollar at a rate of 4.2 trillion to one in November 1923, and to the gold-denominated rentenmark and reichsmark at the rate of one billion to one.

There is general agreement that the inflation and hyperinflation precipitated a massive transfer of wealth from those who held liquid assets to those in control of real goods and that they benefited debtors at the expense of creditors. There is much disagreement with respect to the evaluation of the inflation. Some economic historians, most notably Carl-Ludwig Holtfrerich, have argued that the inflation and hyperinflation benefited Germany by creating full employment, promoting economic reconstruction, and wiping out Germany's domestic debts as well as the speculative investments of foreigners in Germany's currency. Others—the author of this article among them—do not contest that the inflation contributed to reconstruction. They argue, however, that the total destruction of the currency produced a legacy of bitterness and sense of unfairness that severely burdened the Weimar Republic's social and political future and promoted right and left radicalism. The expropriation of international creditors made it impossible for Germany to borrow at reasonable interest rates and the inflationary reconstruction itself produced destabilizing distortions in the economy. It may be impossible to measure the economic benefits of the inflation against its sociopolitical and economic costs scientifically; but the trauma of hyperinflation clearly injured the Republic politically, weighed heavily on policymaking during the Great Depression, and has remained a powerful element in German political culture to this day.

Gerald D. Feldman

See also Currency; Dawes Plan; (Great) Depression; Erzberger, Matthias; Helfferich, Karl; Luther, Hans; Rathenau, Walther; Reparations; Ruhr Crisis; Schacht, Hjalmar; State and Economy; Stinnes, Hugo; Stresemann, Gustav; Versailles, Treaty of; Weimar Germany; Wirth, Joseph; World War I

References

Bresciani-Turroni, Costantino. *The Economics of Inflation: A Study of Currency Depreciation in Post-War Germany, 1914–1923*. London: Allen and Unwin, 1937. Reprinted 1968; original Italian edition 1931.

Feldman, Gerald D. *The Great Disorder: Politics, Economics, and Society in the German Inflation, 1914–1924*. Oxford: Oxford University Press, 1993.

Graham, Frank D. *Exchange, Prices, and Production in Hyperinflation: Germany, 1920–1923*. Princeton, NJ: Princeton University Press, 1930.

Holtfrerich, Carl-Ludwig. *The German Inflation 1914–1923*. Berlin: de Gruyter, 1986; German edition 1980.

Laursen, Karsten, and Jørgen Pedersen. *The German Inflation 1918–1923*. Amsterdam: North Holland, 1964.

Webb, Steven B. *Hyperinflation and Stabilization in Weimar Germany*. New York, NY: Oxford University Press, 1989.

Information Processing (Electronic)

The worldwide proliferation and present universal importance of electronic computers has created a new field of technology generally known as information processing. The term means generation of new information with machines from given information subdivided into elementary signs.

In its early stages, information processing was characterized by manipulating numbers with calculators or with punched-card machines. Germany was one of the leading countries with regard to the manufacture and the application of mechanical calculators as well as the punch-card systems. Germany had been manufacturing calculators since the 1890s.

The war economy during World War I and the rationalization of business during the 1920s extended applications. The new possibilities were utilized in scientific and practical industrial management, modernization of insurance business and administration, and the increasing use of mathematics in all scientific, technological, and social-science research.

After the late 1950s, foreign and German-made electronic computers became publicly available, primarily in scientific institutions. They spread rapidly in highly industrialized countries, including the Federal Republic of Germany (FRG). In the German Democratic Republic (GDR) this process was delayed and less intensive because of the isolation from Western technology. In spite of the important preliminary theoretical and practical computer design work of Konrad Zuse during the 1930s and 1940s, American enterprises controlled the technological development of computers in Germany.

In both German states, large-scale research and development information processing was supported by the governments. Beginning in the 1960s, facilities for education and instruction in computer technology were established at all levels from universities to skilled trades. Because of the Allied prohibition at the end of World War II, the German computer industry developed independently of armament projects, in contrast to those in the United States and Japan, although some firms, such as Nixdorf, developed their own hardware systems.

The general transition in telecommunication technologies to digital processing during the 1960s and 1970s marked a turning point not only in technological development but also in cultural and political history. Computers became part of telecommunication networks, with important consequences. In the FRG, the introduction of a machine-readable identity card and the installation of large-scale police computer networks for seizing and transmitting personal data produced critical discussions and a fear of "big brother" by the citizen. Despite state laws on the use of personal data according to European Community agreements—supervised by data-protection officals in state administrations and private firms—a popular anti–data-collecting movement emerged during the 1980s. At least one census was delayed.

After 1974 microprocessors were designed and manufactured in the United States. Within a few years, corporations in the FRG and GDR manufactured them under licenses. Since the end of the 1970s, these mass-produced, cheap "computers on one chip" determined the projects and products of German industries for the home and export market. An innovation boom shaped the concepts of automation of all types of manufacturing equipment. A main marketing point became the "intelligence" of automobiles and household appliances. The ability to manufacture microprocessors and highly integrated memory chips became an ideologically crucial point in both German states. In the GDR, it was styled as a milestone in the development of socialism; in the FRG, it was a measure of technological advancement compared to the United States and particularly Japan. In both German states the importance of computers and of the need for high-level technology in the manufacture and use of computers was fully recognized. Foreign competence in computer technology seemed to threaten national independence.

In the mid-1970s, pocket computers and "personal computers" began spreading into private homes in the FRG, as was the case in other Western countries. Computers became favored toys for children. Officials and scientists in the GDR desperately, though unsuccessfully, sought to keep pace.

Harmut Petzold

See also Electrical Information Transmission; Inventions; Technology

References

Aly, Götz, and Karl Heinz Roth. *Die restlose Erfassung: Volkszählen, Identifiziern, Aussondern im Nationalsozialismus*. Berlin: Rotbuch, 1984.

Beauclair, Wilfried de. *Rechnen mit Maschinen*. Braunschweig: F. Vieweg, 1968.

Bölsche, Jochen. *Der Weg in den Überwachungsstaat.* Reinbeck bei Hamburg: Rowohlt, 1979.

Braun, Ernest and Stuart Macdonald. *Revolution in Miniature: The History and Impact of Semiconductor Electronics.* Cambridge: Cambridge University Press, 1978.

Petzold, Hartmut. *Moderne Rechenkünstler.* Munich: C.H. Beck, 1992.

Taeger, Jürgen, ed. *Die Volkszählung.* Reinbek bei Hamburg: Rowohlt, 1983.

Zuse, Konrad. *Der Computer, Mein Lebenswerk.* 2nd ed. Berlin: Springer-Verlag, 1984.

Insanity

In Germany, as in other European countries, mental illness became a special subject of medical studies in the nineteenth century. By 1901, it was a compulsory subject of examination in the German medical approbation regulations. From about 1850, psychiatry had developed on two different levels. One was "university psychiatry," i.e., theoretical research carried out in universities; the other was "institutional psychiatry," whose primary concern was the confinement and treatment of mentally ill patients. Starting in the 1970s, institutional psychiatry became gradually replaced by community psychiatry aimed at resocializing these patients.

Psychiatric Concepts and "University Psychiatry"

Wilhelm Griesinger (1817–68), director of the Clinic for Psychiatry and Diseases of the Nervous System in Berlin, with his concept of *Einheitspsychose* ("unitary psychosis"), had the greatest influence on psychiatry in Germany. Griesinger interpreted the various forms of mental illness as different stages in a homogeneous pathological process localized in the brain. This view became the basis of the scientific approach toward mental illness, culminating in "brain psychiatry" during the 1870s and 1880s, which tried to prove the derivation of all forms of mental disorders from anatomical changes in the brain and the nervous system. Working with scientific methods, this concept gained academic recognition which was denied, at least at that time, to the predominantly philosophico-anthropologically oriented psychiatry. The price paid for its integration into modern, natural-science-oriented medicine was its separation from institutional care.

As psychiatric neuropathology failed to prove that pathological changes in the brain and nervous system were the general cause of mental illness, around the turn of the century the emphasis shifted to the psychopathologically oriented "clinical psychiatry," whose leading and internationally influential representative was Emil Kraepelin (1856–1926), professor at the University of Munich. He complemented neuroanatomical research by including clinical findings on the course of the disease, clinical descriptions of a patient's psychopathology, and experimental psychology studies. With the help of this extension in methodological parameters, he succeeded in differentiating certain clinical pictures (dementia praecox and manic-depressive psychosis) and in establishing a classification of mental illnesses that still pertains. The Swiss clinician Eugen Bleuler (1857–1939) supplemented this classification with the term "schizophrenia."

As of World War I, the increasingly important field of genetics gained considerable influence on the predominantly somatics- and science-oriented line of thought in German psychiatry. In his concept of constitutional biology, which displays affinity with eugenics, Ernst Kretschmer (1888–1964) associated certain forms of psychic disorders with certain types of physique. Around the turn of the century, supporters of "racial hygiene," such as Ernst Ruedin (1874–1952), started to consider hereditary predisposition to be the decisive factor in the occurrence of mental illness.

As of 1933, the one-sided, strictly science-committed psychiatry, which reduced patients with psychological problems to mere experimental subjects and totally neglected their individuality, represented the most extreme form of "racial hygiene" under the influence of eugenics and the racial doctrines of Nazism. This approach allowed scientists who felt uncompromisingly committed to the revival of "brain psychiatry" (e.g., Carl Schneider, 1891–1946) to conduct studies in psychiatric patients murdered by the state whom they had already examined while they were still living.

After World War II, the experiences of the psychiatry of the Third Reich led to a return to the intellectual and philosophical elements in psychiatry. Although Bleuler had introduced elements of depth psychology into psychiatry, it was not until the 1950s that Sigmund Freud's (1856–1939) psychoanalysis gained influence in German psychiatry which, up to the recent past, was also strongly phenomenology-oriented and sought to achieve a more profound understanding by reference to philosophical thinking (Max Scheler [1874–1928], Henri Bergson, and Martin Heidegger [1889–1976]).

Already before World War I, Karl Jaspers (1883–1969) had claimed that a psychiatrist could get truly close to his patient only by empathizing and imaginatively recreating his patient's experience, not by means of examination of the patient's brain. With regard to psychopathology, Jaspers put the humanistic "understanding" on the same level as the etiological "explaining" in natural sciences. Social psychiatry called attention to the social dimension of being ill by interpreting psychic illness as a social process and by viewing patients' problems as a product of their environment.

During the politically turbulent and reformist 1960s and early 1970s, social psychiatry met with the "antipsychiatry" movement, which held the general attitude then prevailing in West German psychiatry accountable for inhumane conditions in mental institutions. The criticism of psychiatric care jointly expressed by these two groups resulted in the "Enquete on the Situation of Psychiatry in the Federal Republic of Germany" that was prepared for the Bundestag in 1975, and in the "Recommendations of the Experts' Commission of the Federal German Government for the Reform of Patient Care in the Fields of Psychiatry and Psychotherapy/Psychosomatics" in 1988. With similar conditions in the German Democratic Republic, the East German government drew up the Rodewischen Theses on Psychiatric Rehabilitation in 1963 and the Brandenburg Theses on the Therapeutic Community in 1974.

"Institutional Psychiatry"

The unification of Germany in 1871 spurred a marked increase in the architectural expansion of already existing mental institutions and in the establishment of new psychiatric clinics (in 1877 there were 93 public institutions with 33,023 patients; in 1904, 180 institutions with 111,951 patients). This development was due to an increase in population, microsocial changes that precluded the toleration of psychically ill patients, and the intention of state and society to marginalize maladjusted persons. Although the external appearance of mental institutions changed from that of "prisons" to that of "palaces," the internal structures basically remained the same for decades. The main objective of these institutions was the confinement of patients for the sake of "public safety" and to "protect" these patients from themselves.

Unsatisfactory therapeutic outcomes, resulting from a lack of specific remedies, led to a persistent therapeutic helplessness in which the conceptual analysis of various mental illnesses had no effect on the actual therapeutic practice. Although mental institutions increasingly refrained from the use of physical restraint, only a few of them actually abandoned the employment of traditional therapeutic methods, because, as a rule, calming patients down was still the primary objective in psychiatric treatment. This approach included baths, drugs (narcotics and hypnotics), bed rest, and occupational therapy. Removing patients from their environments, i.e., institutionalizing them, was justified by the argument that this eliminated the harmful influence of the environment and thus eliminated the actual cause of a patient's disease.

After World War I, a process of reform started that was hastened by economic pressures. Various forms of open psychiatric care (rural "loony colonies," patient care in the family) that had originated in the 1880s were extended because they were expected to save expenses. In addition, the mentally numbing "bed therapy" was superseded by occupational therapy (Hermann Simon, 1867–1947) designed for all mental patients without distinction.

The Nazis destroyed these efforts of restructuring by charging psychiatry with the task of selecting and eliminating "inferior" and "incurable" patients. As a consequence, 350,000 people were forcibly sterilized between 1933 and 1939, and up to 200,000 institutionalized patients were murdered by means of different measures of "euthanasia" (the T4 action, for example) which were carried out under medical supervision (e.g., by Paul Nitsche, 1876–1948) in special killing institutions between 1939 and 1945. At the same time, patients classified as curable became subject to drug and active therapy, mainly the newly discovered shock treatment.

After 1945, West German psychiatry condemned the medical killings but was disinclined to classify forcible sterilization as a crime. The institutional psychiatry of the postwar period at first continued along the lines of old traditions and then increasingly tried to apply methods of psychotherapy. It was fundamentally changed, however, by the introduction of psychotropic agents such as antidepressants, neuroleptic drugs, and tranquilizers in the 1950s, as these drugs made the use of the rather stressful shock treatment and physical restraints superfluous while frequently allowing outpatient treatment and enhancing social reintegration.

The initial euphoria, however, overlooked the considerable side effects and risk of substance dependency of many of these new drugs. In the late 1960s, the wide use of these drugs in psychiatric therapy was questioned (social psychiatry and the antipsychiatric movement), and not only in the FRG. This dispute led to harsh criticism of mental institutions in general. According to this criticism, drug-induced immobilization and hospitalization devalued the patient's personality and kept the patient from leading a regular social life.

Under the impact of the "Psychiatry Enquete," efforts were made to reduce the size of large mental institutions and to establish psychiatric departments in general hospitals, plus therapeutic centers working in close association with local authorities. Outpatient living under the supervision of a specialist social worker, sheltered work, and ambulant services were expected to help patients lead their lives as independently as possible. In 1990, 115 departments of psychiatry in general hospitals cared for as many patients as did the 70 mental institutions in the FRG, with individual forms of outpatient care differing from region to region and from state to state.

Psychiatry in the GDR basically developed along the same lines as in the Federal Republic, yet those involved in efforts to reform psychiatric care had to struggle with conservative forces among their own ranks and with the ideology of a socialist society and the bureaucratic, centralistic style of their political leadership. Starting in the early 1980s, the acute lack of physicians (on account of migration from East to West Germany) as well as the gradual dilapidation of the buildings made themselves felt. Contrary to conditions in West Germany, large-scale mental institutions were the dominating organs in charge of psychiatric care in the GDR up to 1990. Questions regarding the political abuse of psychiatry in the GDR, such as forcible commitment of political dissidents, for example, were posed after unification but have yet to be answered.

Georg Lilienthal

See also Disease; Eugenics; Health; Medical Profession; Medicine; Poverty; Psychiatry; Psychoanalysis; Psychology

References

Bauer, M., R. Engfer, and J. Rappl, eds. *Psychiatrie-Reform in Europa*. Bonn: Psychiatrie-Verlag, 1991.

Benzenhofer, Udo. *Bibliographie der zwischen 1975 und 1989 erschienenen Schriften zur Geschichte der Psychiatrie im deutschsprachigen Raum*. Tecklenburg: Burgverlag, 1992.

Blasius, Dirk. *Umgang mit Unheilbarem: Studien zur Sozialgeschichte der Psychiatrie*. Bonn: Psychiatrie-Verlag, 1986.

Eulner, Hans-Heinz. "Psychiatrie und Neurologie." *Die Entwicklung der medizinischen Spezialfächer an den Universitäten des deutschen Sprachgebietes*. Ed. Hans-Heinz Eulner. Stuttgart: Ferdinand Enke Verlag, 1970.

Pauleihkoff, Bernhard. *Das Menschenbild im Wandel der Zeit: Ideengeschichte der Psychiatrie und der Klinischen Psychologie.* Vols. 1–7. Hurtgenwald: Guido Pressler Verlag, 1983–92.

Siemen, Hans Ludwig. *Menschen blieben auf der Strecke: Psychiatrie zwischen Reform und Nationalsozialismus.* Gütersloh: Verlag Jakob van Hoddis, 1987.

Thom, Achim, ed. *Zur Geschichte der Psychiatrie im 19. Jahrhundert.* Berlin (East): VEB Verlag Volk and Gesundheit, 1984.

———. *Psychiatrie im Wandel: Erfahrungen und Perspektiven in Ost und West.* Bonn: Psychiatrie-Verlag, 1990.

Trenckmann, Ulrich. *Mit Leib and Seele: Ein Wegweiser durch die Konzepte der Psychiatrie.* Bonn: Psychiatrie-Verlag, 1988.

Inventions

Most inventions partially solve well-defined technological problems. It is not uncommon for identical inventions to be made at approximately the same time by different inventors in different countries. This explains why many people in technologically advanced societies have an exaggerated idea of their own country's inventive genius. Adolf Hitler suffered from this delusion. Hitler's speeches abound with examples of a perverted romanticism that depicts the German *Volk* as the preeminent inventive race and the German inventor as a modern hero, the incarnation of the ancient Germanic warrior imbued with unmatched technological powers. Such notions were an integral part of Hitler's worldview and account for the underestimation of his enemies and his faith in wonder weapons during World War II.

Hitler carried these ideas to pathological extremes, but he was not alone in his illusions about the power of German inventiveness. Many of his compatriots to a greater or lesser extent shared them, because Germany had in fact accumulated a truly remarkable record of inventions and technological innovations since the middle of the nineteenth century. Starting with the Siemens brothers' creativity in electricity and metallurgy, Germans could boast of inventive achievements that include among countless others the Otto internal combustion engine, the diesel engine, aspirin, salvarsan, margarine, synthetic dyes and detergents, perlon (the German counterpart to nylon), the Bosch-Haber process for synthesizing nitrates and explosives, synthetic rubber and fuels, the swept aircraft wing, magnetic tape, color photography, the jet engine, and modern rocketry.

All these inventions—and inventions in general—belong to one of two types: radical or conservative. Radical inventions, historically the province of independent inventors, are fundamental breakthroughs associated with the rise of new technological systems, replacing or superimposing themselves on older systems (e.g., the automobile vs. the railroad, electric vs. gas lighting). Conservative inventions are improvements and refinements of existing technologies (e.g., fuel injection vs. spark plugs). They are usually associated with organized research and development (R&D) by corporations employing salaried inventors and industrial scientists. Although Germany has had its share of radical inventions, relative to the United States its technological culture has been weighted toward conservative inventions and started moving in that direction as early as the decade before World War I. The reasons have to do with the school-based professionalization of most German technologists, the country's bureaucratic tradition, sharp divisions between technological specialties, the institutional and financial advantages of corporations over independent and salaried inventors, general economic conditions, and a patent system inimical to the individual inventor.

In the Weimar Republic, a perception of inventive slowdown and anticapitalist critiques stimulated plans to create a more inventor-friendly climate. The aim was to rekindle economic and technological dynamism and improve the financial rewards of salaried inventors. Such plans were in fact implemented by the Nazi government, which in 1936 introduced a new patent law disposing of anonymous corporate inventions and placing the actual inventor center stage. During World War II, the regime went a step further and introduced statutory royalties for patented inventions by employed inventors. While expediency—the expectation of speeding up innovation and forcing technological breakthroughs for military purposes—played a large role in these reforms, ideological considerations were an important factor. The Nazi reforms remained on the books in both East and West Germany after 1945, and with minor modifications are the basis of current law in the Federal Republic.

The effect of Germany's pro-inventor laws is difficult to measure, but they do not seem to have done much to stimulate radical inventions. If anything, the royalty system for salaried inventors may have strengthened impulses toward conservative inventions. Although Germany has retained a technologically dominant position in older industries where it has long excelled, it has not become a leader in new fields such as biotechnology or computers.

Kees Gispen

See also Abbe, Ernst; Aeronautics; Benz, Karl; Bosch, Robert; Braun, Wernher von; Chemistry, Scientific and Industrial; Daimler, Gottlieb; Diesel, Rudolf; Dornberger, Walter; Electricity; Haber, Fritz; Heinkel, Ernst; Junkers, Hugo; Lilienthal, Otto; Linde, Carl von; Mannesmann: Firm and Family; Optics; Porsche, Ferdinand; Röntgen, Wilhelm; Siemens, Werner von; Space; Technical Training, Technical Institutes, and Universities; Technology; Zeppelin, Count Ferdinand

References

Bijker, Wiebe E., Thomas P. Hughes, and Trevor J. Pinch, eds. *The Social Construction of Technological Systems: New Directions in the Sociology and History of Technology.* Cambridge, MA: The MIT Press, 1984.

Gispen, Kees. "National Socialism and the Technological Culture of the Weimar Republic." *Central European History* 25 (1992), 387–406.

———. *New Profession, Old Order: Engineers and German Society, 1815–1914.* Cambridge: Cambridge University Press, 1989.

Hughes, Thomas P. *American Genesis: A Century of Invention and Technological Enthusiasm 1870–1970*. New York, NY: Viking and Penguin, 1989.

———. *Networks of Power: Electrification in Western Society (1880–1930)*. Baltimore, MD: The Johns Hopkins University Press, 1983.

Jewkes, John, David Sawers, and Richard Stillerman. *The Sources of Invention*. 2nd ed. New York, NY: W.W. Norton & Co., 1969.

Radkau, Joachim. *Technik in Deutschland: Vom 18. Jahrhundert bis zur Gegenwart*. Frankfurt am Main: Suhrkamp Verlag, 1989.

Zitelmann, Rainer. *Hitler: Selbstverständnis eines Revolutionärs*. Hamburg: Berg Publishers, 1987.

Israeli-German Relations

Since the proclamation of the state of Israel in 1948 and the founding of the Federal Republic of Germany (FRG) and the German Democratic Republic (GDR) in 1949, German-Israeli relations have been complicated by a fundamental tension between the burdens of the past and the imperatives of the present. Whereas the FRG and Israel gradually built up wide-ranging and intensive relations, the GDR not only refused to deal with the Jewish state (or other Jewish representatives) over the issues of restitution and reparations but also flanked its anti-Zionist propaganda with massive verbal and material support for radical Arab and Palestinian positions and groups. Erich Honecker's (1912–94) feeble attempt to reverse course (beginning in 1985) proved too little too late.

The initial phase of postwar German-Israeli relations was dominated by the issue of compensation for the burdens assumed by the 600,000 citizens of the newly independent and financially strapped state of Israel in integrating over 300,000 Central and Eastern European Jewish refugees. These survivors of the Holocaust, almost all of whom were too old or too frail to contribute to the economy, were arriving while Israel was attempting to absorb an additional 600,000 immigrants fleeing Islamic countries.

In November 1949, West German Chancellor Konrad Adenauer signaled the readiness of his government to offer material compensation. In January 1951, the Israeli government decided on an indirect approach and on March 12 addressed a diplomatic note to the four Allied powers requesting their assistance in obtaining reparations from both German states. The Soviet Union did not reply at all, but the United States urged Israel to engage in direct negotiations with the Bonn government. Adenauer further smoothed the way with a declaration before the Bundestag on September 27. In Israel, however, the government of Prime Minister David Ben-Gurion was forced to overcome vehement resistance both inside and outside the Knesset. Opposition leader Menachem Begin objected strenuously and on principle to negotiations over "blood money."

Following negotiations between representatives of Israel, diaspora Jewish organizations (forming the "Claims Conference"), and the FRG beginning in March 1952, the Luxembourg Agreement (signed in the capital of the Grand Duchy on September 9) provided for $1 billion to be provided to Israel (primarily in the form of material goods from German industrial production) and $500 million to the Claims Conference over a period of ten years.

Included in the Claims Conference structure were representatives of the tiny German Jewish community, organized since 1950 under the umbrella of the "Central Council of Jews in Germany," a name indicative of the ambivalent identity of the community (not "German Jews" but "Jews in Germany"), about three-quarters of whom were displaced persons from Eastern Europe. From some 15,000 persons in 1950, the membership of the Jewish community in West Germany reached a plateau of 25,000–28,000 in the 1960s, where it stayed until the late 1980s. When the Berlin Wall fell in late 1989, only a few hundred Jews remained in the GDR. Because of history, identity and sheer numbers—and because the GDR chose to isolate itself—German-Israeli history since 1948–49 is largely the story of the relations between the FRG and the state of Israel.

Although the Adenauer government repeatedly showed interest in establishing formal diplomatic relations with Israel in the early 1950s, Jerusalem hesitated. Extensive ties nevertheless developed, especially after the Suez Crisis of 1956, when the FRG refrained from pressuring Israel to withdraw (as did the United States and the USSR) and continued its reparations deliveries and aid without interruption. Relations soon came to include a military component, which both sides strove to keep secret and which led to several coalition crises in Israel, including Ben-Gurion's resignation in 1957.

The high point of this phase of German-Israeli relations was the meeting between Adenauer and Ben-Gurion in New York in 1960, which led to more intensive relations on many levels, again including the military. Ben-Gurion agreed to this meeting despite intense domestic and international concern over a wave of apparent neo-Nazi desecration incidents in West Germany in 1959 and 1960, which, it is now known, were coordinated by Eastern Bloc agents.

By the late 1950s, a role reversal had taken place: Israel desired official ties but Bonn hesitated out of fear that Arab countries might retaliate by recognizing the GDR, thus undermining both the Hallstein Doctrine and Germany's increasing trade with the Arab world. The publication of details of secret German arms deliveries to Israel, the debate over the West German statute of limitations for Nazi crimes, and tensions over the presence of German rocket technicians in Egypt contributed to a crisis in relations in late 1964, but by early 1965 the chief issues were resolved and, following a visit to Egypt by East German leader Walter Ulbricht (1893–1973), the FRG and Israel established full diplomatic relations in May. In 1966 the two countries concluded an economic agreement initiating the continuing tradition of annual West German low-interest credits for Israel.

The Six Day War of 1967 brought an outpouring of public sympathy for Israel among the West German public and ever more shrill anti-Israel propaganda from East Berlin. The decade of the 1970s was marked by an increasing routinization of relations between Bonn and Jerusalem, including mutual visits by the foreign ministers and heads of government, but it was also a period in which sympathies cooled, as West Germany, especially after the oil shock in the wake of the 1973 Yom-Kippur War, repeatedly joined its partners in the European Community (EC) in declarations perceived in Israel as one-sidedly pro-Arab and pro-Palestinian. In a UN General Assembly debate in 1974, the FRG became the first EC country to publicly support the right of the Palestinians to self-determination.

In 1977, the Likud assumed power for the first time in Israel. Prime Minister Menachem Begin became increasingly embittered by the lack of EC support for the Camp David peace process and by Chancellor Helmut Schmidt's (1913–) efforts to improve German-Arab and German-Saudi relations in particular (including the proposed sale of Leopard-2 tanks). Under intense pressure in the election campaign of 1981, and incensed by Schmidt's failure in televised remarks to even mention the Jews while listing nations and peoples victimized by the Nazis, Begin a few days later lashed out not only at Schmidt but at what he defined as the collective guilt of the German people in general. The shadow of the past effectively thwarted Bonn's attempt to demonstrate "normalcy" in its relations with Israel and the Arab countries. In the face of massive opposition in his own ranks, the Social Democratic chancellor was forced to drop the Saudi arms deal.

The continuing presence of the past—and a certain continuity in German Middle East policy—became apparent in Israeli reactions to Christian Democratic Chancellor Helmut Kohl's effort to emphasize "normalcy" during his visit to Israel in early 1984. Even more dramatic was the controversy over Kohl's arrangements in 1985 for American President Ronald Reagan's visit to the Bitburg military cemetery, which also contains the graves of Waffen-SS soldiers.

Sympathy for Israel among the West German public declined precipitously in the wake of the Lebanon intervention beginning in 1982 and again after the outbreak of the Palestinian uprising (*Intifada*) in late 1987. By the end of 1990, in reunited Germany, Israel proved the least popular country on the list submitted to the German public in an Infratest poll.

The Israeli public reacted with equanimity and even sympathy toward German reunification. The involvement of German firms in Saddam Hussein's weapons program and Bonn's reluctance to make an open military commitment to the Allied effort in the war against Iraq, however, led to a crisis in relations. While Israeli sympathy for Germany plummeted (but with a great majority still desiring "better relations"), the German public exhibited great concern over the threat to the Jewish state, but a majority remained firmly opposed to military involvement in the Persian Gulf region. The predictable result was Foreign Minister Genscher's "checkbook diplomacy"—and a further loss of prestige both at home and abroad.

Despite dramatic short-term swings in public sympathies, Germany and Israel have continually expanded governmental, economic, academic, and cultural relations over a period of four and a half decades. One indicator of the status of these relations is the fact that Germany was the second country (after the United States) visited by Prime Minister Rabin following his election victory in 1992. Other official gestures of Israeli goodwill followed despite the wave of xenophobic and anti-Semitic terrorist acts that continued to rock Germany in 1992 and 1993.

Neither Germany's past nor anti-Semitic incidents in the present served to deter thousands of Eastern European Jews from flocking to Germany, especially to Berlin, after the fall of the Communist regimes. The number of Jewish immigrants might have been far greater had not the German government, at Israel's strong urging, maintained restrictions and cooperated in directing immigration toward the Jewish state. Nevertheless, the size of the registered Jewish community in Germany increased by nearly half to some 40,000 persons. The internal debate over the ambivalent identity of that community continues, and many Germans who are above suspicion as anti-Semites have difficulty accepting that an individual can be both Jewish and German. The renewed growth and vitality of contacts is a further significant indicator of the state of German-Israeli relations in the 1990s.

Douglas Bokovoy

See also Abs, Hermann; Adenauer, Konrad; Anti-Semitism; Bitburg; Federal Republic of Germany: Foreign Policy; German Democratic Republic: Foreign Relations; German-Jewish Organizations; Hallstein, Walter; Holocaust; Jews; Kohl, Helmut; Schmidt, Helmut; Springer, Axel

References

Balabkins, Nicholas. *West German Reparations to Israel.* New Brunswick, NJ: Rutgers University Press, 1971.

Brumlik, Micha et al., eds. *Jüdisches Leben in Deutschland seit 1945.* Frankfurt am Main: Athenäum, 1986.

Feldman, Lily Gardener. *The Special Relationship between West Germany and Israel.* Boston, MA: George Allen and Unwin, 1984.

Gilman, Sander L., and Karen Remmler, eds. *Reemerging Jewish Culture in Germany: Life and Literature since 1989.* New York, NY: New York University Press, 1994.

Sagi, Nana. *German Reparations: A History of the Negotiations.* Trans. Dafna Alon. New York, NY: St. Martin's Press; Jerusalem: Magnes Press, Hebrew University, 1986.

Wolffsohn, Michael. *Eternal Guilt? Forty Years of German-Jewish-Israeli Relations.* Trans. Douglas Bokovoy. 2nd ed. New York, NY: Columbia University Press, 1994.

Zweig, Ronald W. *German Reparations and the Jewish World: A History of the Claims Conference.* Boulder, CO: Westview Press, 1987.

Italian-German Relations

Italy and Germany function in two different spheres; Italy is a Mediterranean power and Germany a continental one. They have tended to unite against France and to divide over south-central Europe, notably Austria-Hungary in the nineteenth century and Austria in the twentieth. Whenever German power has encouraged Italian adventurism, it has traditionally spelled doom for Italy.

In the nineteenth century, Italy profited from an alliance with Chancellor Otto von Bismarck's Prussia in the Austro-Prussian War (1866) to incorporate the Veneto into Italy. Frustration with the French occupation of Tunis (1881) led to Italian adhesion to the Triple Alliance with Germany and Austria-Hungary (1882). This alliance served to pressure France not to attempt to reverse the 1871 German unification as well as to reassure Austria-Hungary that Italy would not seek to reclaim Italian-speaking subjects of the Dual Monarchy. Membership in the Triple Alliance led to Italy's "tariff war" with France (1888–92) and fueled Italy's imperial ambitions in Africa. The result was disastrous in terms of both the economic crisis exacerbated by the tariff war and the defeat of Italy by Abyssinia at the battle of Adowa (1896). Rapprochement with France in 1902 weakened the links of the Triple Alliance, resulting in Italy's declaration of neutrality in 1914 on the grounds that the Triple Alliance did not oblige her to fight against England, her traditional friend.

Promises of extensive territorial gains for Italy at Austrian expense brought Italy into World War I against the Central Powers through the secret Treaty of London (1915) with France and Britain. The disintegration of the Austro-Hungarian Empire in 1918 into successor states based on the principle of national self-determination, however, frustrated many Italian territorial claims at the Versailles Peace Conference (1919). Subsequently, Italy, one of the victors, echoed the vanquished Germany in demanding revision of the peace. At the same time, the demise of Austria-Hungary allowed Italy considerable freedom in the Balkans and on the Danube because a great power was no longer situated on her northeastern frontier. An independent Austria, acting as a buffer between Germany and Italy, protected this freedom, while the threat of *Anschluss*, which would unite Germany and Austria, menaced it.

French domination of continental Europe in the 1920s was challenged by Italy's Fascist government. Benito Mussolini sought to organize the revisionist states and to create Balkan and central European clients in order to contest French hegemony in the region. The reassertion of German strength under Adolf Hitler in the 1930s threatened Italian power in central Europe. When Hitler attempted an *Anschluss* in 1934, Mussolini marched Italian troops to the Austrian frontier as a warning. This threat to the independence of Austria drove Italy temporarily into the arms of the French. In January 1935, by the Franco-Italian Agreement, Italy agreed to join France in opposing German revision of the Treaty of Versailles and, in return, France agreed to the extension of Italian influence in Abyssinia.

In *Mein Kampf* (1924), Adolf Hitler had defined Italy's role as a future ally of Germany to deter and neutralize the French. When the Abyssinian War (1935–36) alienated Italy from France and Britain, Hitler offered support and sympathy to the Italians. Fearful of the spread of Nazi and Fascist power in the early 1930s, the Communist International adopted the anti–Fascist program of left-wing unity known as the Popular Front (1935). Election victories by Popular Front coalitions in Spain (February 1936) and France (May 1936), followed by the outbreak of the Spanish Civil War (1936–39), drove the German and Italian regimes into the anti-Bolshevik entente of the Rome-Berlin Axis (November 1936) and, later, Italian adhesion to the Anti-Comintern Pact (1937). The Axis, ending German and Italian isolation, was consolidated by Italian acceptance of the *Anschluss* (March 1938), which gave Germany the dominant role in the partnership.

In spite of assertions of friendship and common purpose, Hitler would not share his plans with Mussolini, and as a result Italy declared nonbelligerence when the German invasion of Poland (September 1939) led to a European war. German victory over France (May-June 1940) prompted Italian entry (June 10, 1940) to fight a "parallel war" for control of the Mediterranean Sea. Italian military failures in Greece and North Africa (1940–1941), however, meant that German armies had to assist Italy, ending her independent military aspirations. With the fall of Mussolini (July 1943), Italy surrendered to the Allies and joined the anti-German camp, only to be occupied by German troops (September 1943) for the duration of the war.

Since the 1950s, the relationship between Italy and Germany has flourished within supranational institutions and has been challenged by ethnic nationalism. Italy and West Germany have cooperated within the European Economic Community (EEC) and the North Atlantic Treaty Organization (NATO). Both countries prospered through the EEC in the 1960s and 1970s, with Germany receiving the largest share of Italian exports and sending the most tourists to Italy. German factories were the preferred destination for many Italian migrants during the period of the Economic Miracle (1958–63), although, with the beginning of recession in the early 1970s, these foreign workers were the first to be released. Italy and Germany cooperated within NATO to negate the anti-American stance of France's Charles de Gaulle. With a German-speaking population in the South Tyrol, Italy has remained sensitive, however, to any resurgence of German nationalism. A dispute with Austria over the South Tyrol was resolved by compromise in the early 1960's to avoid a new wave of pan-Germanism.

Peter Kent

See also Anschluss; Austro-German Relations; Central Powers; Federal Republic of Germany: Foreign Policy; Hassell, Christian August Ulrich von; Hitler, Adolf; Imperial Germany: Foreign Policy; National Socialist Germany: Foreign Policy; Postwar European Integration and Germany; Versailles, Treaty of; Weimar Germany: Foreign Policy; World War I; World War II

References

Bosworth, R.J.B. *Italy, the Least of the Great Powers: Italian Foreign Policy Before the First World War.* London: Cambridge University Press, 1979.

Cassels, Alan. *Mussolini's Early Diplomacy*. Princeton, NJ: Princeton University Press, 1970.

Deakin, F.W. *The Brutal Friendship: Mussolini, Hitler, and the Fall of Italian Fascism*. 2 vols. London: Weidenfeld and Nicolson, 1962.

Hiden, John. *Germany and Europe, 1919–1939*. London: Longman, 1977.

Knox, Macgregor. *Mussolini Unleashed*. Cambridge: Cambridge University Press, 1982.

Kogan, Norman. *A Political History of Italy: The Postwar Years*. New York, NY: Praeger, 1983.

Lowe, C.J., and F. Marzari. *Italian Foreign Policy, 1870–1940*. London: Routledge and Kegan Paul, 1975.

Robertson, Esmonde M. *Hitler's Prewar Policy and Military Plans*. London: Longman, 1963.

Rusinow, D. *Italy's Austrian Heritage, 1919–1946*. Oxford: Clarendon, 1969.

Toscano, Mario. *The Origins of the Pact of Steel*. Baltimore, MD: Johns Hopkins University Press, 1968.

Wiskemann, Elizabeth. *The Rome-Berlin Axis: A Study of the Relations between Hitler and Mussolini*. London: Collins, 1966.

J

Japanese-German Relations

The first Germans to arrive in Japan were in the service of the Dutch during the seventeenth century. In 1860, after the forced opening of Japan in the mid-1850s, a small Prussian fleet arrived to conclude a treaty with the Japanese government. After four months of difficult negotiations, a treaty of friendship, trade, and shipping was signed in January 1861. However, the treaty was valid only for Prussia and excluded all the other member states of the North German Confederation, unlike as intended by the German side. This restriction relaxed the following year.

After the defeat of France and the foundation of the German Empire in 1871, Germany was widely admired in Japan. The government employed many German scientists in a variety of capacities, above all in law (including the constitution and establishment of a bureaucracy), medicine, education and the military. The army, which had been originally modernized by French officers, was now remodeled along Prussian lines. This included the position of the military in the state structure: the general staff—and later the navy general staff—gained independence from the government and became responsible to the Emperor only. The modern Japanese state, which had been founded by the samurai warrior class, became even more militaristic. The constitution adopted many Prussian elements by creating a system with a weak parliament and a three-class election system.

Education and compulsory military service in both countries became an indoctrination instrument in a nationalistic sense. Japan's military victories over China (1894–95) and Russia (1904–05) were—at least insofar as land battles were concerned—widely regarded as having resulted from German military education. At the same time, however, relations between the two countries became strained because of both countries' imperialism. In 1895, Germany, together with France and Russia, forced Japan by a joint intervention to restore a part of the privileges extorted from defeated China. Furthermore, Germany founded a colony in China (Tsingtao) and obtained territories in Micronesia, virtually in Japan's immediate vicinity. When World War I broke out, Japan, Great Britain's ally since 1902, declared war against Germany, occupied Tsingtao, and seized the Micronesian islands north of the equator.

After World War I, relations between Germany and Japan became rapidly normalized but did not become close. In both countries democracy attained deeper roots but then became weakened in response to the Great Depression. In the 1930s revisionism brought Japan and Germany together. Enmity against Communism and the USSR engendered the conclusion of the Anti-Comintern Pact in 1936, joined by Italy in the following year. After the outbreak of the Sino-Japanese war in 1937, Germany reluctantly sacrificed its strong economic and political relations with China in favor of Japan. In 1938 negotiations for a military alliance linking Japan, Germany, and Italy commenced, but they were protracted because Tokyo refused to get involved in a treaty that would apply not only against the USSR but against the Western countries as well. Japan's hesitation caused Hitler to follow a policy of conciliation with Stalin. In 1939, Germany and the Soviet Union concluded a non-aggression treaty, which prepared the ground for the outbreak of World War II.

Japan was on the brink of defeat in an undeclared border war with Soviet troops at that time. The Japanese government was shocked by Germany's behavior and kept at a cool distance in the following months. Only after the German victory over the Netherlands, Belgium, and France in the spring of 1940 did it show renewed interest in closer relations with Berlin. Expecting a British defeat, Japan hoped to seize the colonies of the European powers in Southeast Asia. In September 1940, the Tripartite Pact linked Japan, Germany, and Italy in a defensive alliance against American intervention in Europe as well as in Asia. It recognized Asia as Japan's sphere of influence and Europe as that of Germany and Italy. The idea of a Japanese understanding with the USSR, perhaps with German support, also became part of this global vision. At the same time, the political parties were dissolved in Japan and became united in a single organization, which broadly followed in the footsteps of the totalitarian states in Europe without ever reaching an equal degree of efficiency or becoming an instrument of terror against its own citizens.

Japanese occupation of French South Indochina in July 1941 provoked an embargo, including oil deliveries, by the Western countries. Rather than retreat, Japan started a war against the United States in December 1941. Three days later, Germany and Italy declared war against the United States, whereas Japan stayed neutral in Hitler's war against the Soviet Union. Cooperation, including trade, between Japan and the other Tripartite powers, whose battlefields were thousands of miles away, was almost nil.

After the war, Japan and Germany were temporarlily suspended from engaging in diplomatic activities. In 1952, the Federal Republic of Germany established limited diplomatic relations with Japan under a chargé d'affaires. Only in 1955 did the two countries exchange ambassadors. Relations became friendly again, documented in cultural-educational activities and trade. Both countries became key allies of the United States. In 1973, the German Democratic Republic established diplomatic relations. German reunification found a warm welcome in Japan.

Gerhard Krebs

See also Exports and Foreign Trade; Federal Republic of Germany: Foreign Policy; Hitler, Adolf; Imperial Germany: Foreign Policy; National Socialist Germany: Foreign Policy; Weimar Germany: Foreign Policy; World War II

References

Boyd, Carl. *Hitler's Japanese Confidant: General Oshima Hiroshi and Magic Intelligence, 1941–1945.* Lawrence, KS: University Press of Kansas, 1993.

Fox, John P. *Germany and the Far Eastern Crisis 1931–1938: A Study in Diplomacy and Ideology.* Oxford: Oxford University Press, 1982.

Krebs, Gerhard. *Japans Deutschlandpolitik 1935–1941: Eine Studie zur Vorgeschichte des Pazifischen Krieges.* 2 vols. Hamburg: OAG, 1984.

Kreiner, Josef, ed. *Japan und die Mittelmächte im Ersten Weltkrieg und in den zwanziger Jahren.* Bonn: Bouvier, 1986.

Kreiner, Josef, and Regine Mathias, eds. *Deutschland-Japan in der Zwischenkriegszeit.* Bonn: Bouvier, 1990.

Martin, Bernd. *Deutschland und Japan im Zweiten Weltkrieg: Vom Angriff auf Pearl Harbor bis zur deutschen Kapitulation.* Göttingen: Musterschmidt, 1969.

Morley, James, ed. *Deterrent Diplomacy: Japan, Germany, and the USSR, 1935–1940.* New York, NY: Columbia University Press, 1976.

Pauer, Erich, ed. *Technologietransfer Deutschland—Japan von 1850 bis zur Gegenwart.* Munich: Iudicium, 1992.

Presseisen, Ernst L. *Before Aggression: Europeans Prepare the Japanese Army.* Tucson, AZ: University of Arizona Press, 1965.

Schwalbe, Hans, and Heinrich Seemann, eds. *Deutsche Botschafter in Japan 1860–1973.* Tokyo: OAG, 1974.

Siemes, Johannes. *Hermann Roessler and the Making of the Meiji State.* Tokyo: Sophia University Press, 1968.

Wippich, Rolf-Harald. *Japan und die deutsche Fernostpolitik 1894–1898.* Stuttgart: Steiner, 1987.

Jaspers, Karl (1883–1969)

Karl Jaspers is often called the founder of modern existentialism, although he was much closer to Immanuel Kant than those who followed his lead and built a philosophical system that had many traditional features. He was a cultural nationalist who believed German thought to be essential to the future of philosophy, and a democrat and liberal who protested against the postwar banning of the German Communist Party. Politically, he argued for a world order that would transcend the limitations of Western thought. His philosophy centered on the notion of *Das Umgreifende*—the "encompassing" reality that transcends all systems and limitations.

Jaspers began his career as a doctor and moved to psychology through psychiatry. He published his first book, *Allgemeine Psychopathologie* (General Psychopathology), in 1913. The three-volume *Philosophie* (published as *Philosophy*), 1932, was his first major work (and some believe his magnum opus) in the specialty he ultimately chose, although *Existenzphilosophie* (published as *The Philosophy of Existence*), 1938, is the work most commonly associated with his name. In all, he published 34 books, culminating in *Philosophie und Welt* (published as *Philosophy and the World*) in 1958.

Karl Jaspers. Courtesy of German Information Center, New York.

Jaspers' entire academic career until 1948, when he moved to Basel, Switzerland, was spent at Heidelberg. He wanted to develop the possibilities of a universal moral and legal system and to reconcile science, religion, and traditional metaphysics. Like Kant, he also wanted to develop history as an intelligible basis for human action. Hannah Arendt (1906–75) called him Kant's sole genuine disciple. But his system was distinct and built around a central paradox. He found the bases of religion, of human dignity, and of a political order that would respect the individual in the fact that human existence transcends the limits of all systems: there are always more possibilities than those of which we are aware. He was an "existentialist" in the precise sense that he believed in human existence as being central for the understanding of value and knowledge. He doubted that such an existence could ever be fully captured or compressed. He remained devoted to his Jewish wife and struggled against the Nazi regime, although he was banned from teaching and publishing from 1936 until the end of World War II, when he became rector of the University of Heidelberg. After moving to Basel, he wrote *Wohin treibt die Bundesrepublik*, translated as *The Future of Germany* (1967). In it, he argued that the Federal Republic had still failed to grasp the essence of democracy.

Leslie Armour

See also Arendt, Hannah; Federal Republic of Germany; Heidegger, Martin; Philosophy

References

Allen, E.L. *The Self and Its Hazards: A Guide to the Thought of Karl Jaspers*. London: Hodder and Stoughton, 1950.

Jaspers, Karl. *Allgemeine Psychopathologie*. Berlin: Springer, 1963. Published as *General Psychopathology*. Trans. J. Hoenig and M. Hamilton. Chicago, IL: University of Chicago Press, 1963.

———. *Die Atombombe und die Zukunft des Menschen.* Munich: Piper, 1958. English translation: *The Future of Mankind*. Trans. E.B. Ashton. Chicago, IL: University of Chicago Press, 1961.

———. *Philosophie.* 3 vols. Berlin: Springer, 1932. English translation: *Philosophy*. Trans. E.B. Ashton. Chicago, IL: University of Chicago Press, 1969.

———. *Philosophie und Welt.* Munich: Piper, 1958. English translation: *Philosophy and the World.* Trans. E.B. Ashton. Chicago, IL: Henry Regnery, 1963.

———. *Wohin treibt die Bundesrepublik.* Munich: Piper, 1967. English translation: *The Future of Germany.* Trans. E.B. Ashton. Chicago, IL: University of Chicago Press, 1967.

Lichtigfeld, Adolph. *Jaspers' Metaphysics*. London: Colibri, 1954.

Schilpp, P.A., ed. *The Philosophy of Karl Jaspers*. New York, NY: Tudor, 1949.

Schrag, Oswald. *Existence, Existenz, and Transcendence: An Introduction to the Philosophy of Karl Jaspers.* Pittsburgh, PA: Duquesne University Press, 1971.

Young-Bruehl, Elisabeth. *Freedom and Karl Jaspers's Philosophy*. New Haven, CT: Yale University Press, 1981.

Jewish Women, League of (1904–38)

In 1904, progressive members of the traditional Jewish women's religious societies as well as Jewish women who were involved in the German feminist movement formed the nucleus of the Jüdischer Frauenbund (JFB; League of Jewish Women). Its founder and president, Bertha Pappenheim, was a dedicated feminist and a devout Jew. Her organization, which attracted a large following—50,000 women, or about 20 percent of all Jewish women over the age of 30—played a vital role within the Jewish community until 1938. It maintained a cooperative and supportive role within the bourgeois women's movement, the Bund deutscher Frauenvereine (BDF; Federation of German Women's Associations), from 1907 until 1933. In contrast, the Catholic women's organization never joined the BDF and the Protestant women's association joined, but withdrew, in 1918.

The JFB combined feminist goals with a strong sense of Jewish identity. It sought to strengthen community consciousness among Jews; further the ideals of the women's movement; expand the participation of women in the Jewish community on the basis of equality with men; provide Jewish women with career training; and combat all forms of immorality, specifically the traffic in women. Its demands were essentially reformist, shaped by the omnipresence of anti-Semitism and the intransigence (within the Jewish community and in German society) of anti-feminism.

League members reflected the overwhelmingly middle-class socioeconomic position of German Jews. Although several prominent leaders remained single, most JFB members were middle-class housewives who did not work for pay. They belonged to a generation of volunteers whose daughters would later enter professions such as social work or teaching.

Despite the considerable tensions involved in being both feminists and observant Jews, JFB members insisted on remaining in both camps, desiring to be accepted by their German sisters, while also guarding their own ethnic and religious distinctiveness. Its major campaigns reflected the JFB's feminist aspirations as well as the insecurity of Jews in Germany. In attempting to provide career training for women, the JFB established employment offices, vocational guidance centers, night courses, and several home-economics schools to improve job skills. As feminists they hoped to professionalize housework and increase respect for it. At the same time, they insisted that woman's place was not only in the home. As Jews, concerned with a job profile heavily skewed toward commerce—and aware of anti-Semitic criticisms of this fact—they hoped to shift Jewish youth toward occupations that were more typical of those of the general population.

Through prevention and rescue efforts, the JFB fought prostitution, particularly among Jewish women from Eastern Europe who were lured abroad and sold or forced into prostitution by traffickers. To thwart procurers, the JFB established railroad and harbor outposts for women traveling alone and offered food, hostels, financial aid, and information to needy young women. It also supported vocational and educational institutions for Jewish girls in Eastern Europe, sent teachers and nurses there, and published leaflets and warnings on the dangers of white slavery. The JFB cooperated with national and international volunteer organizations to suppress the traffic and founded the first Jewish home for delinquent girls, unwed mothers, and children of unwed mothers in Germany.

The fight for political power within the Jewish community entailed the League's longest and most arduous battle. The JFB lobbied and petitioned rabbis and community leaders for gaining a voice in community governance. Meeting with orthodox opposition and liberal indifference, the JFB nonetheless helped women to wrest the vote in six of seven Jewish communities in major German cities by the end of the 1920s. After the Nazi seizure of power, the JFB focused on social work within the Jewish community. It was forcibly disbanded by the Nazis following the November Crystal Night pogrom of 1938.

Marion Kaplan

See also Anti-Semitism; Catholic Women's Association; Crystal Night; Feminism and Anti-Feminism; Jews; Nationalist Women's Associations; (German) Protestant Women's League; Women; (Bourgeois) Women's Movement

References

Kaplan, Marion. *The Jewish Feminist Movement in Germany: The Campaigns of the Jüdischer Frauenbund, 1904–1938.* Westport, CT: Greenwood Press, 1979.

Jews, 1869–1933

From their full emancipation in 1869 to their disemancipation by the Nazis in 1933, German Jews experienced opportunities for advancement and assimilation as well as continuing social and political anti-Semitism. Their notable contributions to Germany's economic and cultural life demonstrated deepening integration into the life of the host country. However, as a small minority of approximately one percent of the German population, they had to place their fate heavily on the fortunes of German liberalism.

The North German Confederation 1869 Law on the Equality of All Confessions, adopted by the German Empire as a whole upon its creation two years later, completed the emancipation of German Jewry and opened the door to its modernization. The Jews rapidly became largely urbanized and middle class. Although the majority of them moved upward in various commercial trades, increasing numbers of Jews took university degrees and entered careers in law, medicine, and journalism. Middle-class Jews, like their gentile counterparts, married later and tended to have fewer children, which slowed the Jewish birthrate. Only the continued immigration of Eastern European Jews kept the Jewish population of Germany growing, from 512,000 at the beginning of the period to 615,000 in 1910. Thereafter, it declined markedly, reaching 503,000 in 1933. Declining birthrates and increasing

numbers of conversions and mixed marriages raised questions about the long-term viability of German Jewry. Jews also moved further away from religious orthodoxy. By 1900, most of them had come to adhere to Reform Judaism with varying degrees of commitment. A few members of the Jewish elite became fully secularized.

That this integration of the Jews into German society did not lead to full assimilation resulted from the interaction of persistent Jewish ethnicity and widespread social anti-Semitism. Ethnic identity and fears of being snubbed influenced most Jews to live, associate, and work mainly with their coreligionists. Although German Jews could pursue many occupations after 1869, most of them preferred to remain in commercial trades traditionally associated with Jews, especially textiles, printing, metals, and banking. Jewish otherness annoyed some Germans, who felt that the Jews had violated an unwritten social contract exchanging emancipation for complete assimilation. Faulting the Jews for insufficient German-mindedness, anti-Semites generated widespread social discrimination and, in moments of economic stress, political movements dedicated to repealing Jewish emancipation. Prejudice, in turn, impelled most Jews to cast their political fortunes with left liberalism: the Progressive Party in Imperial Germany and the Democratic Party in the Weimar Republic, principled foes of Judeophobia. A number of Jewish intellectuals became Marxists to express a broader view of emancipation.

These social and political asymmetries patterned Jewish contributions to German life and culture. Jews in business and politics sought to build bridges. Bankers such as Gerson von Bleichröder (1822–93), Max Warburg (1867–1946) and Jakob Goldschmidt (1882–1955) assisted in financing Germany's industrialization before World War I and its recovery afterward. The shipping magnate Albert Ballin (1857–1918) and the founder of the German General Electric Company, Emil Rathenau (1838–1915), contributed to Germany's status as an economic powerhouse. Fewer Jews held prominent political posts. Rathenau's son Walther (1867–1922) organized Germany's critical raw materials during World War I and served as foreign minister of the Weimar Republic until his assassination in 1922. The initial draft of the Weimar constitution was the work of Hugo Preuss (1860–1925). On the other hand, Jewish intellectuals often took advantage of their status as outsiders to act as cultural critics and innovators. Especially during the Weimar years, Jews were overrepresented in avant-garde movements. The expressionist dramas of Ernst Toller (1893–1939), the atonal music of Arnold Schönberg (1874–1951), and the naturalistic psychological novels of Alfred Döblin (1878–1957) are but three of the most important examples.

Although German Jews were initially reluctant to risk irritating German sensibilities by creating a nationwide Jewish organization, in 1893 they established the Central Union of German Citizens of the Jewish Faith to combat anti-Semitism and promote German patriotism and Jewish consciousness among its members. Four years later, the Zionist minority founded the Zionist Federation of Germany to support the resettlement of persecuted Eastern European Jews in Palestine and press German Jews to adopt a more exclusively Jewish point of view. Growing anti-Semitism during and after World War I estranged the two Jewish organizations. Whereas the Central Association affirmed the patriotism of German Jewry at every opportunity, the Zionists advised Jews to distance themselves from German politics and look to a future in Palestine. The need to forge a common front against Nazism in the last years of the Weimar Republic only partially healed the rift. Behind-the-scenes efforts by the Central Association to support anti-Nazi and pro-republican political parties helped to deny Adolf Hitler an electoral majority, even though they could not prevent him from slipping into power. Leaders of the liberal Jewish majority, like most other Germans, had underestimated Hitler, but they had not been passive during the rise of his Nazi movement.

Donald L. Niewyk

See also Anti-Semitism; Bleichröder, Gerson von; Citizenship and Foreigners; Döblin, Alfred; German Democratic Party; Jews, 1933–1990; Jewish Women, League of; Liberalism; Minorities, Ethnocultural and Foreign; Racism; Rathenau, Walther; Schönberg, Arnold; Toller, Ernst; *Völkisch* Ideology; Warburg, Aby; Warburg, Max; Warburg, Otto

References

Brenner, Michael. *The Renaissance of Jewish Culture in Weimar Germany*. New Haven, CT: Yale University Press, 1996.

Gay, Ruth. *The Jews of Germany: A Historical Portrait*. New Haven, CT: Yale University Press, 1992.

Kaplan, Marion A. *The Making of the Jewish Middle Class: Women, Family, and Identity in Imperial Germany*. New York, NY: Oxford University Press, 1991.

Kauders, Anthony. *German Politics and the Jews: Düsseldorf and Nuremberg, 1910–1933*. New York, NY: Oxford University Press, 1996.

Lamberti, Marjorie. *Jewish Activism in Imperial Germany: The Struggle for Civil Equality*. New Haven, CT: Yale University Press, 1978.

Mosse, Werner E. *Jews in the German Economy: The German-Jewish Economic Elite, 1820–1935*. Oxford: Clarendon Press, 1986.

Niewyk, Donald L. *The Jews in Weimar Germany*. Baton Rouge, LA: Louisiana State University Press, 1980.

Poppel, Stephen M. *Zionism in Germany, 1897–1933*. Philadelphia, PA: Jewish Publication Society of America, 1976.

Pulzer, Peter. *Jews and the German State: The Political History of a Minority, 1848–1933*. Oxford and Cambridge: Blackwell, 1992.

Richarz, Monika, ed. *Jewish Life in Germany: Memoirs from Three Centuries*. Bloomington, IN: Indiana University Press, 1991.

Schorsch, Ismar. *Jewish Rections to German Anti-Semitism, 1870–1914*. New York, NY: Columbia University Press, 1972.

Jews (1933–90)

Between 1933 and 1945, the German Jews were first marginalized and then totally excluded from Nazi society. The majority emigrated, and most of the rest were exterminated in the Holocaust. Although a small Jewish community revived in postwar Germany, it had almost no roots in traditional German Jewry.

During the first four years of Hitler's rule, German Jews had difficulty understanding Nazi anti-Semitic policies that fluctuated between severity and restraint. Jews were fired from government jobs and subjected to hateful propaganda attacks and a one-day national boycott on April 1, 1933, causing thousands to flee the country. Otherwise, apart from occasional physical attacks by Nazi stormtroopers, most German Jews were left pretty much alone at first. Psychologically unprepared to abandon their German identity, they hoped for a restoration of sanity and the rule of law. Their initial response to Nazi persecution was to table religious and political differences and establish the Reich Representation of German Jews (renamed "of the Jews in Germany" at Nazi insistence in 1935). It helped to coordinate aid to Jews left unemployed by boycotts and firings and those who had fled persecution in small towns and villages for the shelter of large urban communities. The organization also provided schools for Jewish children victimized by anti-Semitism in public institutions. Especially after the promulgation of the Nuremberg Laws in 1935, it helped to prepare younger Jews for emigration to various countries. This included support for Zionist projects that sent around 30,000 Jews to Palestine, accomplished with the full cooperation of German authorities.

By 1937, the Nazis were more securely in power than ever, and their intensifying policies of isolating the Jews, confiscating ("Aryanizing") their businesses, and banning them from the professions were destroying their means of existence. Jews who had hoped to hold out in Germany reluctantly sought out scarce opportunities to settle abroad. Their desperation was intensified by the Crystal Night pogroms of November 9–10, 1938, when thousands of Jews were arrested, beaten, and killed. More than ever before, the welfare and cultural activities of the Reich Representation were crucial to their material and emotional survival. In February 1939, the Nazis replaced it with the Reich Association of the Jews in Germany, which was made directly responsible to the Gestapo. By that time the Jews' economic basis had been demolished, their ties to German society had been severed, and their advanced cultural integration had been extinguished. Difficulties of obtaining visas notwithstanding, a total of approximately 280,000 Jews managed to emigrate from Nazi Germany. Nearly half of them entered the United States, and about 20 percent fled to Palestine. Most of the remainder went to other European countries or Latin America.

Following the outbreak of war in September 1939, the emigration of German Jews slowed to a trickle. Those remaining were concentrated in special apartment houses and conscripted as forced laborers in defense factories. In October 1940, the first group of seven thousand Jews was deported from southwestern Germany to concentration camps in France, to be shipped to Madagascar. When that plan fell through, the German Jews were transported to ghettos, labor camps, and extermination centers in Eastern Europe between October 1941 and February 1943. Around 10,000 Jews in mixed marriages were exempted from the deportations, and an additional 3,000–4,000 Jews successfully hid themselves in Germany with the aid of gentile friends. They were among the very few who survived the Holocaust.

Of the nearly 200,000 Jews in Germany at the end of World War II, most were Eastern European slave laborers who had been brought to Germany by the Nazis in the last year of the war. The great majority of them left as soon as possible. A small postwar German Jewish community was rebuilt by two groups that had little in common: German Jews who had survived in Germany or else returned from Nazi camps and foreign havens and the remaining Eastern European displaced persons. The latter increasingly predominated because the German Jews tended to be older and more assimilated.

By the 1950s, the community numbered about 26,000, largely foreign-born and virtually all in West Germany. It enjoyed material comfort arising from the postwar economic boom and generous West German restitution and reparation policies, but it coexisted uncomfortably with a German society wrestling with a sense of guilt and seeking a new national identity. With the destabilization of the U.S.S.R. in the late 1980s, Soviet Jews fleeing anti-Semitism and economic distress settled in the reunited Germany in numbers that doubled the size of the Jewish community. This influx held out possibilities of reinvigorating Jewish culture and life in Germany.

Donald L. Niewyk

See also Anti-Semitism; Civil Service; Crystal Night; Expulsion and Exile of Scientists and Scholars; Holocaust; Israeli-German Relations; Jewish Women, League of; Jews, 1869–1933; Minorities, Ethnocultural and Foreign; Polish-German Relations, 1918–45; Racism; Schindler, Oskar; *Völkisch* Ideology

References
Angress, Werner T. *Between Fear and Hope: Jewish Youth in the Third Reich.* New York, NY: Columbia University Press, 1988.

Baker, Leonard. *Days of Sorrow and Pain: Leo Baeck and the Berlin Jews.* New York, NY: Macmillan, 1978.

Barkai, Avraham. *From Boycott to Annihilation: The Economic Struggle of German Jews, 1933–1945.* Hanover, NH: University Press of New England, 1989.

Boehm, Eric H., ed. *We Survived: Fourteen Histories of the Hidden and Hunted of Nazi Germany.* Santa Barbara, CA: ABC Clio, 1966.

Paucker, Arnold, ed. *The Jews in Nazi Germany, 1933–1943.* Tübingen: J.C.B. Mohr, 1986.

Rabinbach, A., and J. Zipes, eds. *Germans and Jews since the Holocaust.* New York, NY: Holmes and Meier, 1986.

Jodl, Alfred (1890–1946)

Colonel-General Alfred Jodl was chief of operations in the German High Command (Oberkommando der Wehrmacht).

As one of Chancellor Adolf Hitler's closest military advisers, he became Hitler's personal chief of staff. He had known Adolf Hitler personally since 1923. Jodl proved to be a conservative general who tried to remain apolitical.

Jodl was born in Würzburg on May 10, 1890. He joined the Bavarian Cadet Corps at the age of 13 and was commissioned as a second lieutenant in 1910. During World War I he fought in the artillery as a first lieutenant. He joined the Reichswehr in 1919 as a captain; after completing the General Staff course, he was transferred to the Seventh Division's staff in Munich. In the autumn of 1932, he was moved to a department of the Truppenamt, which later became the General Staff.

In July 1935, as part of Germany's general military build-up, Jodl took over the National Defense section of the Department of War. This posting allowed him to exert a decisive influence on operational planning throughout the 1930s. After promoting him to major general in April 1939, Hitler entrusted Jodl with the task of chief of operations in the German High Command. Jodl was to advise Hitler on strategic and tactical aspects of warfare. As chief of operations, Jodl organized the conduct of war on all fronts from the North Cape to the Sahara, with the exception of the eastern front. Hitler appreciated Jodl's efficiency and promoted him to general of artillery in July 1940 and colonel-general in February 1944.

Jodl did not always agree with Hitler, and he voiced his criticism openly. But these disagreements with Hitler were operative-strategic differences, not ideological ones, and Jodl generally submitted to the orders of Hitler as the supreme commander. Jodl remained convinced of Hitler's military and political genius until the end of the Third Reich. This prevented him from forcing his own views on the Führer and from resigning his position over the major differences of opinion between him and his master.

As the war drew to a close, Jodl wanted to surrender only to the Americans and British. This approach proved as illusory as his idea that the Operation Staff of the German High Command (Wehrmachtführungsstab) might be preserved as a kind of liaison office serving the individual Allied Military governments. On May 8, 1945, Jodl had to sign an instrument of unconditional surrender. Soon after, he was arrested by the British and charged with planning a war of aggression. The International Military Tribunal at Nuremberg found him guilty and sentenced him to death. He was hanged on October 1, 1946.

Klaus Schönherr

See also Hitler, Adolf; National Socialist Germany: Military; Nuremberg Trials; World War II

References
Brett-Smith, Richard. *Hitler's Generals.* San Rafael, CA: Presido Press, 1976.

Jodl, Luise. *Jenseits des Endes: Leben und Sterben des General-Oberst Alfred Jodl.* Munich: Molden, 1976.

Scheurig, Bodo. *Alfred Jodl: Gehorsam und Verhängnis.* Berlin: Propyläen, 1991.

Johnson, Uwe (1934–84)

One of the most respected postwar novelists writing in German, Uwe Johnson left the German Democratic Republic in 1959 after his first published novel, *Mutmassungen über Jakob* (published as *Speculations about Jakob*), was perceived as being too critical of the state. His novels received numerous awards, as did his shorter prose pieces from the 1960s, collected in *Berliner Sachen,* 1974, which have been read as commentaries on the division of the city and as Johnson's theory of writing. Receiving particular praise were the four volumes of *Jahrestage. Aus dem Leben von Gesine Cresspahl* (published as *Anniversaries: From the Life of Gesine Cresspahl*), 1970–83.

After emigrating to the West, Johnson probed the consequences of German nationalism in the postwar world, exploring the division of Germany against the background of a "German" heritage. Often compared stylistically to William Faulkner, Johnson in his early works, such as *Das dritte Buch über Achim* (published as *The Third Book about Achim*), 1961, and *Zwei Ansichten* (published as *Two Views*), 1965, represented life under socialism by reexamining the problem of the possibility of actually "knowing" personal or national histories. The heroization of individuals and the reification of historical narratives, integral to the ideologies of National Socialism, Stalinism, and bourgeois capitalism, find no footing in either the form or content of Johnson's work on German history. The family histories and personal relationships remembered within specific historical contexts synthesize all his novels without ever creating the illusion that the complete picture has been received.

Johnson was among the first of his generation to recognize the importance of the United States in structuring German history and in generating a contemporary sense of German identity. *Jahrestage* sensitively follows the interwoven threads of the nature of German history, the late 1960s, the United States presence and a German woman's attempt to negotiate those forces within her own life as a single mother. This interweaving of the personal and political parallels tendencies by younger artists, the "new subjectivity" of Peter Handke (1942–) and Wim Wenders, for example. Rather than trusting or privileging a single position for narrating history, however, Johnson maintains a multiplicity of viewpoints and voices and thus avoids the romantic self-centeredness that marks much of the younger generation's work.

John Davidson

See also Federal Republic of Germany: Literature; German Democratic Republic: Literature and Literary Life; German Democratic Republic: Nationalism; Handke, Peter; Memory, Collective; National Identity; Novel

References

Gerlach, Rainer, and Matthias Richter, eds. *Uwe Johnson.* Frankfurt am Main: Suhrkamp, 1984.
Neumann, Bernd. *Utopie und Mimesis: Zum Verhältnis von Ästhetik, Gesellschaftsphilosophie und Politik in den Romanen Uwe Johnsons.* Kronberg: Athenäum Verlag, 1977.
Riedel, Nicolai. *Untersuchungen zur Geschichte der internationalen Rezeption Uwe Johnsons.* Hildesheim: Georg Olms, 1985.
Riordan, Colin. *The Ethics of Narration: Uwe Johnson's Novels from Ingrid Babendererde to Jahrestage.* London: Institute of Germanic Studies, 1989.

Johst, Hanns (1890–1978)

Following a brief encounter with pacifist-oriented expressionism, the writer Hanns Johst became a German nationalist. He openly supported Hitler during the final phase of the Weimar Republic and remained a loyal stalwart of the Third Reich until its collapse in 1945. Johst was active in all the traditional genres of literature, including poetry, drama, prose fiction, and essay writing; however, his reputation in Nazi Germany was primarily as a dramatist. This is remarkable because Johst stopped publishing dramatic works after Hitler's advent in 1933. Because of his involvement in Nazi cultural politics, most notably his presidency of the Reichsschrifttumskammer (Reich Chamber for Literature) from 1935 to 1945, his works, with the exception of a late novel and a few samples from his expressionist period, have not been published since 1945.

The son of a small-town schoolteacher and a farmer's daughter, Johst attended high school in Leipzig and planned to become a missionary. He interrupted his training in order to study medicine, philosophy, and history in Leipzig, Vienna, Munich, and Berlin. For some time he was also an actor. At the outbreak of the war in 1914 he volunteered to the front, and at war's end he became a mercenary soldier.

Johst made his literary debut with a one-act play, *Die Stunde der Sterbenden* (The hour of the dying), 1914, which made him one of the first German writers to express negative reactions to World War I. Among Johst's full-length expressionist plays, the one which has become best known (especially since it also served as a kind of inspiration for Brecht's play *Baal*, written from an opposing and ideological perspective), is *Der Einsame: Ein Menschenuntergang* (The lonely one: the ruin of a human being), 1917. The play focuses upon the life and ill-fated literary career of Christian Grabbe, an early-nineteenth-century German dramatist known for his personal excesses. From this and Johst's following dramas it soon became apparent that, apart from a few themes, the expressionism in Johst's works was primarily a stylistic ploy rather than a genuine belief in the modern intellectual's obligation to serve as the conscience of society.

After the war, Johst, one of the first expressionists to adopt a more realistic style of writing, turned to nationalist themes and goals. His play *Propheten* (Prophets), 1922, which takes place during the sixteenth century, depicts as one of its heroes Martin Luther, who comes across as less of a religious reformer than a spokesman and fighter for Germany's national liberation and unification. Another play, the comedy *Wechsler und Händler* (Money exchangers and traders), 1923, satirizes the inadequacy of German politicians to cope with the country's high inflation rate caused by the huge national debt and political corruption. While Johst's contemptuous treatment of the Weimar Republic may have indirectly aided the nationalist forces whose goal it was to undermine and overthrow it, his last two published plays were entirely unconcealed calls for nationalist action and the demise of democracy in Germany. *Thomas Paine,* 1927, became one of Johst's most successful plays in Germany, although the work aroused almost no interest in the United States. In contrast to the historical Paine, who died in his bed in New York, Johst's hero drowns himself in Boston harbor after being released from a French prison and learning that he had been forgotten in his homeland, which had in the meantime gained independence. In Johst's last play, *Schlageter,* 1933, the nationalist action is set in Germany's Ruhr region during the French occupation (1923). The hero is one of those Nazi fighters later emulated by countless members of the SA and SS and glorified in Nazi songs and literature. The play, which the author dedicated to Hitler, was first performed simultaneously in several German cities on the Führer's first birthday celebration after his ascent to power in 1933 and became part of the Third Reich's standard literary canon for schools.

In the course of postwar German de-Nazification, Johst was prohibited from further publication for ten years. He died in Oberallmannshausen, the Bavarian village in which he had lived since the days of his early successes.

Helmut F. Pfanner

See also Expressionism (Literature); Hitler, Adolf; Nationalism; National Socialist Germany; National Socialist Germany: Literature; Patriotic Literature; Weimar Germany; Weimar Germany: Literature

References

Cuomo, Glenn R. "Hanns Johst und die Reichsschrifttumskammer: Ihr Einfluss auf die Situation des Schriftstellers im Dritten Reich." *Leid der Worte: Panorama des literarischen Nationalsozialismus.* Ed. Jörg Thuneke. Bonn: Bouvier Verlag Herbert Grundmann, 1987.

Denkler, Horst. "Hanns Johst." *Expressionismus als Literatur: Gesammelte Studien.* Ed. Wolfgang Rothe. Bern: Francke, 1969.

Pfanner, Helmut F. *Hanns Johst: Vom Expressionismus zum Nationalsozialismus.* The Hague: Mouton, 1970.

Ritchie, J.M. "Johst's 'Schlageter' and the End of the Weimar Republic." *Weimar Germany: Writers and Politics.* Ed. A.F. Bance. Edinburgh: Scottish Academic Press, 1982.

Willoughby, L.A. "Hanns Johst." *German Life and Letters* 1 (1936–37), 73–6.

Joos, Joseph (1878–1965)

Joseph Joos was the editor of the *Westdeutsche Arbeiterzeitung* (West German Workers' Newspaper, the principal organ of the Catholic Workers' Associations) and a prominent member of the left wing of the Center Party. An Alsatian worker's son, Joos was trained as a pattern-maker but became involved in Catholic social work and politics at an early age. Under the guidance of Johannes Giesberts, he attended courses given by the Volksverein für das katholische Deutschland (People's Association for Catholic Germany) in Mönchengladbach and began writing for the *Westdeutsche Arbeiterzeitung,* becoming its editor in 1905. For Joos, the primary mission of the workers' associations was to raise the social status of workers through spiritual and educational work, rather than to fulfill an economic role like the interconfessional Christian labor unions.

During World War I, Joos as editor avoided strident nationalism and annexationism and supported the Peace Resolution of 1917 and Prussian electoral reform. He welcomed the Weimar Republic and served in the Reichstag from 1920 until 1933 as a follower of Matthias Erzberger (1875–1921) and Joseph Wirth (1879–1956) in the Center Party's left wing. He was a natural mediator and compromiser and because of these qualities was urged to become party chairman in 1928, but he refused to campaign actively for the position and failed to win election.

By 1932, Joos had become much more conservative and enthusiastically supported Heinrich Brüning's (1885–1970) authoritarian government. He even used his talents as a mediator to try to bring the Nazis into a coalition government with the Center, but he quickly became disillusioned about that possibility. During the Nazi period, Joos tried to carry on his activities with the Catholic Workers' Associations, which had been guaranteed continued existence in the 1933 Concordat, but this proved to be impossible. He was eventually arrested for Resistance sympathies and spent five years in Dachau concentration camp. After 1945, Joos worked for a time in social counseling but did not reenter politics; he died a few years after moving to Switzerland.

It was Joos's fate to outlive by more than 30 years the workers' associations to which he had devoted most of his life. It was largely through his efforts, however, that the associations' goal of integrating Catholic workers into the mainstream of German life was fully achieved.

Ellen L. Evans

See also Brüning, Heinrich; Catholicism, Political; Center Party; Christian Trade Unions; Erzberger, Matthias; Wirth, Joseph

References

Evans, Ellen L. *The German Center Party 1870–1933.* Carbondale, IL: Southern Illinois University Press, 1981.

Grebing, Helga. *The History of the German Labour Movement: A Survey.* Abridged by Mary Saran. Trans. Edith Körner. Leamington Spa: Berg, 1985.

Joos, Joseph. *Am Räderwerk der Zeit: Erinnerungen aus der katholischen und sozialen Bewegung und Politik.* Augsburg: Verlag Winfried-Werk, 1950.

Patch, William L., Jr. *Christian Trade Unions in the Weimar Republic, 1918–1933.* New Haven, CT: Yale University Press, 1985.

Wachtling, Oswald. "Joseph Joos." *Zeitgeschichte in Lebensbildern.* Vol. 1. Ed. Rudolf Morsey. Mainz: Matthias-Grünewald-Verlag, 1973.

———. *Joseph Joos: Journalist—Arbeiterführer—Parlamentarier: Politische Biographie 1878–1933.* Mainz: Matthias-Grünewald-Verlag, 1974.

Journalism

Anyone who is engaged in the dissemination of information or opinion distributed via mass media such as the press, radio, and television is considered to be a journalist. In 1993 this broad definition described the activities of about 31,000 professional journalists in Germany. Of those, about 10,000 are affiliated as editors, reporters, or correspondents with daily newspapers. Another 5,000 each are employed by magazines and press and information offices, and about 4,000 pursue their careers in radio and television stations. About 1,000 represent news agencies and press bureaus. Furthermore, about 5,000 freelance journalists contribute to several mass media.

About 70 percent of all journalists in Germany are represented by a professional organization. The largest single organization, with a membership of 24,000, is the Deutscher Journalisten-Verband-e.V. (DJV; German Journalists' Association, Inc.), headquartered in Bonn. Mainly print journalists comprise the membership of this organization, which traces its lineage to the Reichsverband der Deutschen Presse (Reich Association of the German Press), which was founded in 1910. A strictly trade-union organization is the powerful Industriegewerkschaft Medien (Media Union) with a membership of 245,000. It represents the combined interests of print, bookbinding and paperwork, broadcasting, and pictorial and theater-arts unions.

One reason for the desire to join a professional organization and/or trade union may be found in the rather unconventional career path that journalism seems to represent. Journalism is essentially a free profession. There is no fixed, prescribed educational path, nor is there a fixed job description. Collective wage agreements and conditions of employment (*Manteltarifverträge*), arrived at between the trade union and the employer, have become the defining parameters for the professional journalist. However, in today's changing multimedia world, education and the acquisition of specialized knowledge have become an essential requisite for anyone aspiring to become a journalist. Therefore, there are several discernible pathways to the journalism profession in Germany.

The oldest and most frequent path to journalism is a two-year on-the-job training commitment in an editorial office of a newspaper or television/radio station, known as *Volontariat* (journalist trainee). In addition to extensive on-the-job vocational training, the aspiring journalist also has to master a four-to six-week curriculum based on diverse theoretical journalistic subjects. These courses and seminars are cosponsored by publishers and professional/trade-union organizations. They are conducted at such institutions as the Deutsches Institut für Publizistik (Hamburg) and the Akademie der Bayrischen Presse (Munich).

Of the 2,200 *Volontäre* (journalist trainees) who embarked on this two-year training path in 1992, for example, some 1,400 were placed with daily newspapers, 500 with magazines, about 40 with news agencies, and 220 at radio/TV stations. About 60 percent of these *Volontäre* were university graduates.

An alternative path to the profession is to enroll in one of eight schools, cosponsored by the private sector, that engage in a holistic journalism education. All of these schools share in a common belief: to combine theory and practice as the foundation of all journalism education. This is true for the Deutsche Journalistenschule in Munich as well as the Kölner Schule-Institut für Publizistik e.V. in Cologne. The curriculum in Munich lasts only fifteen months (with an option to pursue futher course work at the University of Munich); the curriculum at Cologne takes from four to six years, because it is officially linked to an academic major (mainly in the social sciences or business) at the University of Cologne.

Grooming their future editors is the mission of several in-house schools, underwritten by major publishers. For example, the Journalisten-Schule Axel Springer (publisher Axel Springer A.G.) and the Henri-Nannen-Schule (financed jointly by the publisher Verlag Gruner+Jahr and the weekly newspaper *Die Zeit* [publisher Gerd Bucerius]), located in Hamburg, accept about 20 applicants each per calendar year. The Georg von Holtzbrinck-Schule für Wirtschaftsjournalismus (business journalism) in Düsseldorf and the Burda-Journalistenschule in Munich are likewise financed by press groups, who have some degree of influence as to their curriculum.

Universities throughout Germany also offer special courses in journalism. In general, they are of an introductory nature. Their relation to the real world is quite limited, however. Realizing this shortcoming, several universities are trying to combine theory and practice in integrated courses. Internships in publishing houses, radio/TV stations, and public-relations facilities are a compulsory component of the universities' programs. Universities at Bamberg, Dortmund, Eichstatt, Hamburg, and Munich have begun to expand their journalism/communication curriculum in this fashion.

Practicing journalists have recognized that lifelong, on-going vocational training is a necessity. It is achieved through specialized in-service training programs. ARD (Arbeitsgemeinschaft der öffentlich-rechtlichen Rundfunkanstalten der Bundesrepublik Deutschland) and ZDF (Zweites Deutsches Fernsehen) are cosponsoring two such schools for their employees. The Schule für Rundfunktechnik (School for Broadcast Engineering) in Nuremberg is attended annually by some 1,000 technical staff members affiliated with various radio/television stations representing public broadcasting organizations from throughout Germany. The Zentralstelle Fortbildung Programm (In-Service Training Center) in Frankfurt am Main offers 80 to 90 seminars yearly, attended by some 1,500 trainees and editors of ARD and ZDF. The press also supports a similar institution, the Deutsche Institut für publizischtische Bildungsarbeit in Hagen.

In contemporary Germany, the professional journalist has to continually adapt to new and challenging working conditions. As new media technologies evolve, so does the journalist. The opening of radio and television to the private sector, as well as the creation of extensive cable networks and the distribution of radio and television signals via satellite throughout Germany, has created new opportunities for many. In a modern, democratic society such as Germany's, journalism has a strong presence and a large sphere of influence affecting every segment of public and private life.

Manfred K. Wolfram

See also Dietrich, Otto; Dirks, Walter; Dönhoff, Marion; Freyer, Hans; Freytag, Gustav; Goebbels, Joseph; Harden, Maximilian; Joos, Joseph; Jung, Edgar Julius; Jünger Ernst; Kogon, Eugen; Magazines; Moeller van den Bruck, Arthur; Mosse, Rudolf; Mühsam, Erich; Münzenberg, Willi; Niekisch, Ernst; Ossietzky, Carl von; Press and Newspapers; Professions; Publishing and the Book Trade; Radio; Rohrbach, Paul; Satire; Schwarzer, Alice; Television; Tucholsky, Kurt; Wallraff, Günter; Wolff, Theodor; Zehrer, Hans

References

Hellack, Georg. "Press, Radio and Television in the Federal Republic of Germany." Special Topic: SO-11. Code No. 720 Q 0716. Bonn: Inter Nationes, 1992.

Noelle-Neumann, Elisabeth, Winfried Schulz, and Jürgen Wilke, eds. *Publizistik Massen-Kommunikation*. Frankfurt am Main: Fischer Taschenbuch Verlag, 1993.

Juchacz, Marie (1879–1956)

Juchacz was one of the most important Social Democrats to work in social welfare and protective legislation. She chaired the Workers' Welfare Organization (*Arbeiterwohlfahrt*), which she founded in 1919, and also defended workers' welfare interests in the Reichstag from 1919 to 1933.

Born in Landsberg in the Warthe area, Juchacz typified the Social Democrats who rose to leading positions in the Weimar Republic. As a servant girl, factory worker, and nurse she had contributed to the support of her family. She educated

Marie Juchacz. Courtesy of Inter Nationes, Bonn.

herself and became a good agitator. After her divorce in 1903, she lived as a single parent with her two children and her sister, the Social Democratic Party (SPD) representative to the National Assembly, Elisabeth Röhl-Kirschmann (1888–1930), while finding time for her volunteer work in Social Democracy. From 1913, she served as women's secretary for the SPD in the Cologne and Aachen region.

After the SPD split in 1917, she was elected to replace Luise Zietz (1865–1922) as the main woman representative in the SPD executive, to which she belonged until 1933. Simultaneously, she became the successor of Clara Zetkin (1857–1933) as the editor of *Die Gleichheit*, the SPD women's journal.

As a member in the National Assembly of 1919, Juchacz was the first woman to speak in a national parliament. In that address of February 19, 1919, she emphasized social policy as the special task of women. She expressed her own focus on social welfare through the Workers' Welfare system, which she organized via the SPD at the end of 1919. From 1919 to 1933, she chaired the directing committee, which operated on the principle of aid to anticipate need. She helped to establish welfare homes, kindergartens, and old-age homes in order to fill voids left by the state.

In 1933, Juchacz emigrated via the Saar, France, and Martinique to the United States and organized support for those persecuted under the Nazis. Later, she championed postwar aid to Germany. After her return to Germany in March 1949, she became honorary chair of the Workers' Welfare bureau. As a former emigrant she was unable to reestablish ties to party friends who had remained in Germany during the Nazi years, and she never returned to political life.

Walter Mühlhausen

See also Braun, Lily; Factory Laws and Reform; Hanna, Gertrud; Social Democratic Party; Weimar Germany; Women; (Bourgeois) Women's Movement

References

Dertinger, Antje. *Die bessere Hälfte kämpft um ihr Recht: Der Anspruch der Frauen auf Erwerb und andere Selbstverständlichkeiten.* Cologne: Bund Verlag, 1980.

Marie Juchacz: Gründerin der Arbeiterwohlfahrt—Leben und Werk. Bonn: Arbeiterwohlfahrt Bundesverband, 1979.

Roehl, Fritzmichael. *Marie Juchacz und die Arbeiterwohlfahrt.* Hannover: Neue Gesellschaft, 1961.

Judicial System of Imperial and Weimar Germany

When the German Empire came into existence in 1871, each of its constituent states possessed its own system of substantive law and its own judicial system. Larger states included recently acquired territories (such as the Prussian Rhineland), with their own systems of laws, procedures, and courts. Since the 1830s, liberals and nationalists had viewed this fragmented condition as one of the signal ills of the German condition and had pressed in 1848 and afterward for unification of the multifarious systems. The close association of judges and lawyers with the German liberal movement made the connection between reform of the judicial system and solution of the national question even more urgent. Despite steps taken toward common legal legislation in the final years of the German Confederation and the North German Confederation, the task of creating a uniform national system of courts remained to be addressed.

The National Liberal Party, together with Bismarck's government, enacted a legislation package known as the Imperial Justice Laws, effective October 1, 1879, which created a uniform and national judicial system for the first time in German history. This Constitution of the Courts (*Gerichtsverfassungsgesetz*) established a four-tiered structure of courts of ordinary jurisdiction. Although judges remained state appointees, national legislation prescribed their training and qualifications as well as the system of courts in which they served.

Local district courts (*Amtsgerichte*), consisting of single judges, had exclusive initial jurisdiction over most criminal misdemeanors and civil cases in which less than 300 marks (later increased to 600 marks and stabilized in the 1920s at 500 reichsmarks) were in dispute. Superior courts (*Landgerichte*) had exclusive initial jurisdiction over criminal felonies, in which the cases were heard by both judges and juries (*Schwurgerichte*) or by a mixed panel of judges and lay people (*Schöffengerichte*), exclusive initial jurisdiction in civil cases in which amounts of more than 300 marks were contested, and appellate jurisdiction over criminal and civil cases from the district courts.

Courts of appeal (*Oberlandesgerichte*), whose districts coincided roughly with state or provincial boundaries, heard appeals from decisions of the superior courts. Finally, crowning the pyramid, the Imperial Supreme Court (*Reichsgericht*) in Leipzig provided the final appellate review of cases from the courts of appeal. In 1901, the German Empire had 1,932 district courts, 173 superior courts, and 28 courts of appeal, with a total of 8,397 judges. All higher courts were collegial courts, in which panels of several judges heard and decided cases. This system remained substantially unchanged down to 1933.

The system of courts of ordinary jurisdiction described above did not include all matters of judicial review. Disputes between citizens and governmental agencies, whether local, state, or federal, remained outside the jurisdiction of ordinary courts and within that of administrative courts (*Verwaltungsgerichte*), which were creatures of state rather than national legislation. As the social welfare net began to grow after the social insurance laws of the 1880s, other extraordinary courts were added, such as the social courts (*Sozialgerichte*) for claims involving social benefits and the finance courts (*Finanzgerichte*) for claims involving taxes. Finally, special legislation carved out exceptions from the jurisdiction of ordinary courts, beginning with the industrial courts (*Gewerbegerichte*) of 1890 and the merchants' courts (*Kaufmannsgerichte*) in 1904, culminating in the labor courts (*Arbeitsgerichte*) of 1926. All of these courts provided summary procedures to settle employment contract disputes. Parties were forbidden to be represented by lawyers, and the aim was to increase the speed and decrease the cost of litigation.

The liberal reformers of the 1860s and 1870s had anticipated that their efforts would ensure the independence of the judiciary from government policy and protect the civil and political liberties of the German people. Since 1848, judges had acted as bulwarks of resistance to arbitrary acts of the bureaucracy, provoking frustration from government ministers, especially in Prussia, and attracting persecution and disciplinary rebukes for their involvement. The Constitution of the Courts thus secured for judges in courts of ordinary jurisdiction protection from arbitrary dismissal or transfer. Although the selection process for legal education ensured that most judges during the Imperial period favored the monarchical status quo, and although persecuted minorities such as the Social Democratic Party (SPD) complained of "class injustice," the courts served in some cases as protection against the abuse of civil and political power. Administrative courts also served in notable cases, such as attempts to censor performances of Gerhart Hauptmann's (1862–1946) play *Die Weber*, to limit intrusions into political liberties.

During the Weimar Republic, however, the continuity in office of judges loyal to the monarchy, coupled with hostility toward the judicial system by the SPD and the economic and political turmoil of the early 1920s, led to an even sharper conflict of values under the rubric of "political justice." Highly contentious civil trials, such as the "treason trial" of President Friedrich Ebert (1871–1925) in 1924, and highly controversial criminal sentences, such as those of the assassins of former Finance Minister Matthias Erzberger (1875–1921) in 1921 and Foreign Minister Walther Rathenau (1867–1922) in 1922, poisoned the political atmosphere of the Weimar Republic and heightened tensions between the judicial system and forces supporting the republic. Explanations for opposition to the Republic have been sought in the dominance of legal positivism, reduction of judicial salaries as cost-cutting measures, and status anxieties of judges with the increased power of the Reichstag; regardless, much of the judicial system greeted the Nazi seizure of power with enthusiasm and eagerly applied Nazi "new values" to the administration of justice.

Kenneth F. Ledford

See also The Basic Law; Constitutions; Federal Republic of Germany: Judicial System; Freisler, Roland; German Democratic Republic: Judicial System; Law (German Conception of); National Liberal Party; People's Court; Third Reich: Legal Profession

References

Angermund, Ralph. *Deutsche Richterschaft 1919–1945: Krisenerfahrung, Illusion, politische Rechtsprechung.* Frankfurt am Main: Fischer, 1990.

Döhring, Erich. *Geschichte der deutschen Rechtspflege seit 1500.* Berlin: Duncker & Humblot, 1953.

Engelmann, Bernt. *Die unsichtbare Tradition.* 2 vols. Vol. 1: *Richter zwischen Recht und Macht: Ein Beitrag zur Geschichte der deutschen Strafjustiz von 1779 bis 1918.* Vol. 2: *Rechtsverfall, Justizterror und das Schwere Erbe: Ein Beitrag zur Geschichte der deutschen Strafjustiz von 1919 bis heute.* Cologne: Pahl-Rugenstein, 1988–89.

Ensor, Robert C.K. *Courts and Judges in France, Germany, and England.* Oxford: Oxford University Press, 1933.

Hannover, Heinrich, and Elisabeth Hannover-Druck. *Politische Justiz 1918–1933*. Frankfurt am Main: Fischer, 1966.

Kern, Eduard. *Geschichte des Gerichtsverfassungsrechts*. Munich: Beck, 1954.

Ledford, Kenneth F. *From General Estate to Special Interest: German Lawyers 1878–1933*. Cambridge (U.K.) and New York, NY: Cambridge University Press, 1996.

Müller, Ingo. *Furchtbare Juristen: Die unbewältigte Vergangenheit unserer Justiz*. Munich: Knaur, 1989. English translation: *Hitler's Justice: The Courts of the Third Reich*. Trans. by Deborah Lucas. Cambridge, MA: Harvard University Press, 1991.

Jugendstil

Jugendstil, the German version of the French Art Nouveau and the Viennese Secession style, peaked around 1900 and disappeared before World War I.

The name, "style of youth," derives from an art journal, *Die Jugend*, founded in 1896 in Munich by the publisher and writer Georg Hirth (1841–1915). This German version of the British art journal *The Studio* addressed all aspects of artistic life. In 1899 the name *Jugendstil* was first used by its critics. The main centers of *Jugendstil* were Munich, Darmstadt, and Dresden. The style combined the contributions of a variety of quite different artists, such as Peter Behrens (1868–1940), August Endell (1871–1925), Otto Eckmann (1865–1902), Hermann Obrist (1863–1927), Bernhard Pankok (1872–1943), Bruno Paul (1874–1968), and Richard Riemerschmid (1868–1957). Many of them were painters before they turned to design and architecture.

Jugendstil artists were aiming to reform the arts and crafts. The movement started in Great Britain and through *The Studio* soon became popular throughout Europe. The first general evaluations of *Jugendstil* were published as early as 1925, 1935, and 1941, but only in the late 1950s and 1960s did the style return to fashion. Big exhibitions in Zürich (1952), Munich (1958), and New York (1959) made the neglected and despised style known and appreciated by a broader public. The earliest and most important show was organized by Hans Curijel and Johannes Itten in Zürich in 1952.

Generally, *Jugendstil* was perceived (as in the view of Nikolaus Pevsner) as paving the way for modern style and less as a value unto itself. Most surveys treat *Jugendstil* as a decorative art rather than as an architectural style. In 1988, the UNESCO included *Jugendstil* architecture in its study program in order to help to catalogue and protect designated buildings. The most recent literature deals with the individual artists.

Jugendstil had its specific national components but was influenced by British and, via Henry van de Velde (1863–1957), by Belgian ideas. It hardly ever had socialist connotations, as had, for example, the British Arts and Crafts movement. *Jugendstil* combines two different stylistic tendencies, a floral and a more abstract ornamental version, as is also found in the Viennese Secession style. Occasionally, it incorporates a poetical and irrational component, as with the art of August Endell and Hermann Obrist. These two artists created the first icons of *Jugendstil*, the Fassade and interior de-

sign of the Atelier Elvira in Munich (1897–98; now destroyed) and the so-called *Alpenveilchen* or *Peitschenhieb*, an embroidered wallhanging (1895). Martin Dülfer (1859–1942) built the first *Jugendstil* villa in Munich in 1896–98.

Numerous art journals and exhibitions promoted the new style around 1900. Two major 1897 exhibitons, in Munich and Dresden, displayed modern decorative art next to examples of fine art. Munich exhibited only German artists' works. Dresden displayed the designs of the Belgian artist Henry van de Velde. The movement culminated with the major exhibition in 1902 by the artist colony Mathildenhöhe in Darmstadt, where several artists designed furnished houses and thus created a *Gesamtkunstwerk* (total art work). The first of these artists had arrived in 1899 in Darmstadt by the invitation of the Duke of Hesse. Among others, Peter Behrens and Joseph Maria Olbrich (1867–1908), the architect of the Viennese Secession building, participated.

The *Jugendstil* artists' products never sold well. The 1906 Dresden exhibition marked the end of the style and inaugurated the subsequent foundation of the German Werkbund in 1907. Most *Jugendstil* artists left Munich at the beginning of the century in search of better economic opportunities. They assumed teaching positions in Berlin, Stuttgart, and elsewhere.

Christina Melk-Haen

See also Architecture and Urban Design; Artists; Arts and Crafts; Behrens, Peter; Decorative Arts; Painting; Werkbund

References

Ahlers-Hestermann, Friedrich. *Stilwende—Aufbruch der Jugend um 1900*. Berlin: Gebrüder Mann, 1941.

Curijel, Hans, and Johannes Itten, eds. *Um 1900—Art Nouveau und Jugendstil*. Zürich: Kunstgewerbemuseum, 1952.

German Commission for the UNESCO, ed. *Art Nouveau/Jugendstil Architecture in Europe*. Vol. 26. Bonn: 1988.

Hamann, Richard, and Jost Hermand. *Stilkunst um 1900: Deutsche Kunst und Kultur von der Gründerzeit bis zum Expressionismus*. Vol. 4. Berlin: Akademie Verlag, 1967.

Heskett, John. *German Design 1870–1918*. New York, NY: Taplinger, 1986.

Hiesinger, Kathy. *Art Nouveau in Munich*. Katalog Philadelphia Art Museum. Munich: Prestel Verlag, 1988.

Pevsner, Nikolaus. *Pioneers of the Modern Movement from William Morris to Walter Gropius*. London: Faber and Faber, 1936.

Schmutzler, Robert. *Art Nouveau. Jugendstil*. Stuttgart: Hatje, 1977, [1962].

Selz, Peter and Mildred Constantine. *Art Nouveau; Art and Design at the Turn of the Century*. Exhibition catalogue. New York, NY: Museum of Modern Art, 1959.

Jung, Carl Gustav (1875–1961)

Carl Jung, a Swiss psychiatrist, founded the school of analytical psychology. Born in Kesswil, near Lake Constance, Switzerland, the son of a Protestant pastor, Jung received a medical degree from the University of Basel in 1900. That same year he went to work at the Burghölzli Psychiatric Clinic of the

University of Zürich, then under the directorship of Eugen Bleuler (1857–1939). In 1902, Jung spent several months studying psychopathology in Paris, where he attended lectures by Pierre Janet (1859–1947). Jung published his first papers on psychiatric topics, including his pioneering work on the use of the word-association test in psychiatric research, while working at the Burghölzli. *Psychologie der Dementia praecox* (1907), which outlined a psychogenic model for this mental disorder, was one of Jung's first major works.

Jung was one of the first medical specialists outside of Vienna to take an active interest in the psychoanalytic theories of Sigmund Freud (1856–1939). For several years, between 1907 and 1914, Freud and Jung developed a close working relationship. Jung left the Burghölzli in 1910 to concentrate on his clinical practice and various professional activities involved in promoting psychoanalysis. In 1911, Jung became the first president of the International Psychoanalytic Society, although he had begun to have problems reconciling a number of psychoanalytic theories, especially the importance of sexuality in Freudian psychoanalysis, with his own ideas. Jung outlined many of his conflicting theories in one of his most important books, *Wandlungen und Symbole der Libido* (published as *Psychology of the Unconscious: A Study of the Transformation and Symbolism of the Libido*), 1912. By 1914, Jung had distanced himself from Freud to such an extent that the two men severed personal and professional relations. Jung resigned from the International Psychoanalytic Society in 1914 and spent the remainder of a long and productive career developing his ideas about analytic psychology, many outlined in another influential book, *Psychologische Typen* (published as *Psychological Types*), 1921.

One of the most important differences between analytic psychology and Freudian psychoanalysis is Jung's treatment of the concept of libido. Unlike Freud, who emphasized sexual instinct, Jung regarded libido as a generalized life force. Jung also modified the role played by the unconscious in the development of personality and psychopathology by distinguishing between the personal and the collective unconscious. Analytic psychology has had a limited impact on scientific psychology. Jung's ideas, however, have been influential in a variety of other disciplines, such as anthropology, art, literature, literary criticism, and psychotherapy.

James D.A. Parker

See also Freud, Sigmund; Psychoanalysis; Psychology; Psychiatry; Symbolism

References
Homans, P. *Jung in Context: Modernity and the Making of a Psychologist.* Chicago, IL: University of Chicago Press, 1979.
Jung, C.G. *The Collected Works of C.G. Jung.* 19 vols. Princeton, NJ: Princeton University Press, 1953–79.
Samuels, A. *Jung and the Post-Jungians.* London: Routledge, 1985.
Steele, R.S. *Freud and Jung: Conflicts of Interpretation.* London: Routledge, 1982.
Storr, A. *C.G. Jung.* New York, NY: Viking Press, 1973.

Jung, Edgar Julius (1894–1934)

Edgar Jung, one of the Weimar Republic's leading neoconservative political writers, was a major catalyst in the events that precipitated the Röhm purge on June 30, 1934.

After World War I, Jung established himself as a spokesman for the "front generation" and its efforts to rebaptize German political life in the spirit of the "front experience." At the outset, Jung was a passionate nationalist who earned for himself a measure of notoriety by his role in the assassination of the Palatinate separatist Franz Josef Heinz-Orbis (1884–1924) in January 1924. His efforts to win a seat in the Reichstag, however, ended in failure, with the result that in the second half of the 1920s Jung began to cultivate increasingly close ties with the antirepublican right. The publication of his magnum opus, *Die Herrschaft der Minderwertigen* (published as *The Rule of the Inferior*), 1927, established Jung as one of the most uncompromising critics of the Weimar system. This book represented a sustained assault against the revolutionary tradition of 1789 and called for a conservative revolution that would overcome the fragmentation of modern political life through the spiritual and moral regeneration of state and society.

Shortly thereafter Jung cast his lot with the young conservative elements within the German National People's Party (DNVP) and joined them in founding the People's Conservative Reich Association (Volkskonservative Vereinigung) in January 1930 and the Conservative People's Party (Konservative Volkspartei) the following July. These ventures, however, only strengthened Jung in his belief that the existing political system was hopelessly moribund and that its complete overthrow constituted an essential precondition for Germany's national revival.

Jung's revolutionary conservatism attracted the attention of Franz von Papen (1879–1969), who engaged Jung to write his speeches in the campaign for the March 1933 Reichstag elections. Without Papen's knowledge or approval, Jung worked closely with Herbert von Bose (1893–1934) and other members of the Papen Vice-Chancellery to organize conservatives disillusioned with the Nazi regime in hopes that they might be able to regain the reins of power. In this context, Jung wrote the ringing indictment of the Nazi regime that Papen delivered at the University of Marburg on June 17, 1934, thereby activating the series of events that culminated in Hitler's strike against the Sturmabteilung (SA) on the morning of June 30, 1934, as well as in Jung's own murder in a small forest on the outskirts of Berlin that night.

Larry Eugene Jones

See also Conservatism, 1918–45; German National People's Party; Journalism; Papen, Franz von

References
Forschbach, Edmund. *Edgar Julius Jung: Ein konservativer Revolutionär 30. Juni 1934.* Pfullingen: G. Neske, 1984.
Grass, Karl-Martin. "Edgar Jung, Papenkreis und Röhm-

krise 1933–34." Unpublished doctoral dissertation. Universität Heidelberg, 1966.

Jenschke, Bernhard. *Zur Kritik der konservativ-revolutionären Ideologie in der Weimarer Republik: Weltanschauung und Politik bei Edgar Julius Jung.* Munich: Beck, 1971.

Jones, Larry Eugene. "The Limits of Collaboration: Edgar Jung, Herbert von Bose, and the Origins of the Conservative Resistance to Hitler, 1933–34." *Between Reform, Reaction, and Resistance: Studies in the History of German Conservatism from 1789 to 1945.* Ed. Larry Eugene Jones and James Retallack. Providence, RI: Berg, 1993.

Jung, Edgar Julius. *Die Herrschaft der Minderwertigen, ihr Zerfall und ihre Ablösung durch ein Neues Reich.* 2nd ed. Berlin: Beutsche Rundschau, 1930.

———. *Sinndeutung der deutschen Revolution.* Oldenburg: G. Stalling, 1933.

Jünger, Ernst (1895–)

Ernst Jünger is an author whose productivity spans an exceptionally long and eventful period, from the early Weimar Republic to reunited Germany. His main work consists of literary diaries, essays, and allegorical novels influenced initially by Friedrich Nietzsche (1844–1900) and later by Martin Heidegger (1889–1976).

Born the son of a pharmacist on March 29, 1895, Jünger grew up in Heidelberg and Hannover. In 1914, he volunteered for service in the German army and fought on the western front for four years. He was wounded many times and highly decorated for his courage. The war experience formed the theme of his first publications, most prominently, *In Stahlgewittern* (published as *The Storm of Steel*), 1920, and influenced most of his later works.

Jünger was both fascinated and repelled by technological mass warfare. Although enemy artillery often made soldiers in the trenches feel utterly powerless, Jünger insists that courage and determined leadership still mattered. Without embellishing trench life, he interprets it as the means to an ecstatic self-realization of individuals and, ultimately, of a fighting nation. It symbolizes both the serializing aspects of modern existence and ways to transcend them by infusing them with heroic and esthetic meaning. Jünger probed the social implications of the war experience in *Die totale Mobilmachung* (Total mobilization), 1931, and *Der Arbeiter: Herrschaft und Gestalt* (The worker: rule and form), 1932.

As a spiritual leader of revolutionary nationalism, Jünger helped to undermine the Weimar Republic but rejected association with the Nazi regime after 1933. His novel, *Auf den Marmorklippen* (published as *On the Marble Cliffs*), 1939, describes the rise of a barbaric but well-organized dictatorship that threatens the highly cultured and contemplative life of two brothers. It was read as a critique of the Third Reich.

Jünger's later diaries cover his experiences as a captain in the German occupation army in Paris from 1940 to 1944 and his frequent extended journeys. His novels written after 1945, continue earlier themes. In *Gläserne Bienen* (published as *The Glass Bees*), 1957, insect populations serve as an allegory of serialized mass life. *Annäherungen: Drogen und Rausch* (Approach: drugs and intoxication), 1970, reports Jünger's drug experiences. *Eine gefährliche Begegnung* (A dangerous meeting), 1985, concerns the clash of aristocratic characters with the machine age.

Jünger explores ecstasy and intoxication—whether through drugs, struggle, or the proximity of death—as a means to preserve individuality in modern existence and to overcome a ghastly spiritual void. His lifelong aestheticism, antidemocratic elitism, and celebration of sacrificial death have met with widespread criticism. His work and his style, nevertheless, are highly original and forceful.

Raffael Scheck

See also Federal Republic of Germany: Literature; Heidegger, Martin; National Socialist Germany: Literature; Nationalism; Nietzsche, Friedrich; Radical Right; Weimar Germany: Literature; World War I

References
Arnold, Heinz Ludwig, ed. *Ernst Jünger.* Text + Kritik 105/106. Munich: Edition Text + Kritik, 1990.

Bullock, Marcus Paul. *The Violet Eye: Ernst Jünger's Visions and Revisions on the European Right.* Detroit, MI: Wayne State University Press, 1992.

Herf, Jeffrey. *Reactionary Modernism: Technology, Culture, and Politics in Weimar and the Third Reich.* Cambridge: Cambridge University Press, 1984.

Hermand, Jost. *Old Dreams of a New Reich: Völkisch Utopias and National Socialism.* Trans. Paul Levesque and Stefan Soldovieri. Bloomington, IN: Indiana University Press, 1992.

Kaempfer, Wolfgang. *Ernst Jünger.* Stuttgart: Metzler, 1981.

Loose, Gerhard. *Ernst Jünger.* Twayne's World Authors Series. New York, NY: Twayne Publishers, 1974.

Prümm, Karl. *Die Literatur des soldatischen Nationalismus der 20er Jahre (1918–1933): Gruppenideologie und Epochenproblematik.* 2 vols. Kronberg (Taunus): Scriptor Verlag, 1974.

Schwilk, Heimo, ed. *Ernst Jünger: Leben und Werk in Bildern und Texten.* Stuttgart: Klett-Cotta, 1988.

Sontheimer, Kurt. *Antidemokratisches Denken in der Weimarer Republik.* 3rd ed. Munich: Deutscher Taschenbuch Verlag, 1978.

Theweleit, Klaus. *Male Fantasies.* Trans. S. Conway, E. Carter, and C. Turner. 2 vols. Minneapolis, MN: University of Minnesota Press, 1987–89.

Woods, Roger. *Ernst Jünger and the Nature of Political Commitment.* Stuttgarter Arbeiten zur Germanistik 116. Stuttgart: Akademischer Verlag, 1982.

Junkers, Hugo (1859–1935)

A gifted mechanical engineer and prolific inventor, Hugo Junkers pioneered the full-metal passenger aircraft as well as applied thermodynamics for aviation and other purposes, from household appliances to heavy-duty ship motors. The

Hugo Junkers. Courtesy of German Information Center, New York.

international scope of his economic ventures and his close cooperation with the government of the Weimar Republic resulted in his nearly immediate ousting by Third Reich authorities.

Born on February 3, 1859, at Rheydt, the third of seven sons of a textile factory owner, Junkers studied at Berlin, Karlsruhe, and Aachen. After graduation (1883), he worked as a design engineer for several employers and, in 1888, joined the Continental Gas Company at Dessau to design and develop gas engines. His successful work led, in 1890, to a cooperative partnership with his erstwhile employer. By 1892 Junkers registered himself as a civil engineer, and in 1893 his calorimeter won a prize at the Chicago World's Fair. From 1897 through 1912, Junkers held a professorship at the Aachen Institute of Technology, paralleling his Dessau en-

terprise. Prior to 1914 Junkers motors were produced under license agreements by as many as seven manufacturers in Germany and abroad; his heavy ship motors became especially important in Great Britain and the United States. A joint venture with British partners, the Junkers Motor Works at Magdeburg, founded in 1913, closed down during World War I.

Junkers designed his first experimental aircraft in 1909. These new industrial activities led to the construction of the first experimental wind tunnels in prewar Germany and, during World War I, to military airplane production. Junker's aircraft were based on full-metal technology, and by 1916, he introduced aluminum alloy as a basic material. Postwar civilian aviation first got off to a promising start, with Junkers supplying mail and passenger aircraft for Germany and the United States. In 1921, these activities were temporarily suspended by restrictions imposed on Germany by the Allies according to terms of the Treaty of Versailles. Meanwhile, mail aviation to South America as well as throughout Europe flourished, thanks to the use of Junkers planes. His line of closed-cabin aircraft later proved capable of flying at altitudes of up to 10,000 feet (1929).

Numerous activities abroad followed, from branch factories in the Soviet Union to freight lines in numerous countries. The Moscow connection provided a convenient excuse for the Nazi government to bring charges of alleged treason against Junkers. Although no trial resulted from these fabrications, Junkers was forced to sell his enterprises to the Reich. He died on February 3, 1935 at Gauting, near Munich.

Wolfgang Kokott

See also Air Forces; Aeronautics; Inventions; Technology

References

Fritzsche, Peter. *A Nation of Fliers: German Aviation and the Popular Imagination.* Cambridge, MA: Harvard University Press, 1992.

Groehler, Olaf. *Hugo Junkers: Ein politisches Essay.* Berlin: Militärverlag der DDR, 1989.

Meyer, Henry Cord. *Airshipmen, Businessmen and Politics, 1890–1940.* Washington, DC: Smithsonian Institution Press, 1991.

Schmitt, Günther. *Hugo Junkers: Ein Leben für die Technik.* Planegg (Munich): Aviatic, 1991.

K

Kaas, Ludwig (1881–1952)

Ludwig Kaas, the Catholic theologian and politician, was born in Trier on May 23, 1881 and died in Rome on April 15, 1952. He was ordained priest in 1906. His political career began in 1919 as a delegate to the National Assembly, and from 1920 to 1933 he served as a member of the Reichstag, specializing in foreign-policy questions. During the crucial years 1928 to 1933, he was chairman of the Center Party. After 1934, he went to Rome, where he occupied himself with ecclesiastical work.

From 1918 to 1924, Kaas was a professor of canon law in Trier. After entering the Reichstag, he became the Center Party's Reichstag delegation chairman in 1920 and succeeded Wilhelm Marx as party chairman in 1928. After 1917, he was a close associate of and advisor to Eugenio Pacelli, papal nuncio to Bavaria and after 1925 to the Reich. Kaas represented the conservative wing of the Center Party and opposed cooperation with all forms of organized Marxism. As a priest, he especially emphasized the aims of the Roman Catholic Church in such matters as school laws and the rights and privileges of the Church. He opposed, for example, the introduction of interconfessional schools. As a result, he sought allies among the rightist parties.

Although in the early 1920s he at first favored separation of the Rhineland from Germany, he became a strong nationalist and reluctantly supported Stresemann's efforts at reconciliation with France. He supported the Heinrich Brüning government, but opposed Franz von Papen and contributed to his downfall. After Brüning's ouster in 1932, Kaas advocated a government of national consolidation, including the Nazis. In 1932–33, he continued to seek some accommodation with the Nazis. He hoped to obtain a concordat for Germany along the lines of the Italian Lateran Accords. Kaas urged the Center to vote for Hitler's Enabling Act on the basis of Hitler's verbal assurances of safeguards for the Church. The promised written assurances from Hitler never arrived. Shortly after the passage of the Enabling Act, Kaas left for Rome, where at the request of Pacelli and Papen he played a leading role in the negotiations for the Concordat of July 1933, which was signed speedily. Kaas's role in the passage of the Enabling Act, the dissolution of the Center Party in 1933, and the connection of these events with the signing of the Concordat are still debated.

Stewart Stehlin

See also Brüning, Heinrich; Catholicism, Political; Center Party; National Socialist Germany; Papen, Franz von; Vatican-German Relations; Weimar Germany

References

Hömig, Herbert. *Das preussisches Zentrum in der Weimarer Republik.* Mainz: Matthias Grünewald Verlag, 1979.
May, Georg. *Ludwig Kaas, der Priester, der Politiker, und der Gelehrte aus der Schule von Ulrich Stutz.* 4 vols. Amsterdam: Grüner, 1981–82.
Stehlin, Stewart. *Weimar and the Vatican, 1919–1933.* Princeton, NJ: Princeton Universtiy Press, 1983.
Wynen, A. *Ludwig Kaas: Aus seinem Leben und Wirken.* Trier: Paulinus Verlag, 1953.

Kafka, Franz (1883–1924)

Franz Kafka was one of the most influential German-language authors of the twentieth century. Although his writings (primarily three novel fragments, several novellas, and a larger number of short narrative prose works) are limited to a few volumes, the vast scholarship on Kafka reflects all trends in literary interpretation since the author's death.

Kafka was the oldest of six children of a Jewish merchant in Prague who had little or no understanding of his son's literary inclinations. Following his university studies in law and German literature, the young Kafka worked for 14 years as an insurance clerk. He died of tuberculosis at a time when he had not yet achieved much recognition as a writer. In his time, Prague was torn among various nationalistic factions, foremost among them Austro-Germans (transplants and officials from Austria), Bohemian Germans, Czechs, and Jews (divided into four groups: Germanophones, Czechophones, advocates of the Hebrew language, and Yiddish speakers). The Jewish community to which Kafka's family belonged was culturally entrenched in the German tradition. However, Kafka realized that full assimilation into German culture was an unfulfillable dream for a Jewish individual. He found himself isolated from all ethnic groups, including those Jews who sought assimilation with either the Germans or the Czechs. Other factors, e.g., a strong father-son conflict, unfulfilled female relationships despite three engagements, and a boring office job, added to his feeling of alienation, which forms the central theme of his works.

The suspension between two distant and unattainable poles received many expressions in Kafka's works, sometimes tragic and at other times more humorous or sarcastic. A typical example is the story "Vor dem Gesetz" (published as *In Front of the Law*), which is a key passage in the novel *Der Prozess* (published as *The Trial*), 1946. This work, like his two other novels, *Amerika* (America) and *Das Schloss* (published as *The Castle*), was published posthumously. The story's plot involves a "man from the country" who tries to gain access to the "Law" but never gets past the first door, which is guarded by a heavily armed doorkeeper. When old and prepared to die, the man inquires why no one else had tried to enter during his long wait. The guard replies that this door was meant only for the man from the country and, since he was now dying, it would be shut. The numerous obscure expressions in the story, which also characterize Kafka's longer works, raise the possibility of different interpretations, including the author's view of the Jews' frustrated aspirations to assimilate into German culture.

Aware of the impossibility of being accepted into the German cultural community, Kafka sought other ways of ethnic fulfillment. Having for some time shared the self-critical, downright anti-Semitic views of some contemporary Jewish intellectuals (e.g., Theodor Herzl, Karl Kraus [1874–1936]), he came to experience a strong feeling of "national" identity with the Jews of Eastern Europe, some of whom he met in person as they arrived in Prague as members of a Yiddish theater troupe. He also heard Martin Buber (1878–1965) speak and thus developed an understanding of the Hasidic beliefs and practices of eastern Judaism. Although Kafka did not identify with the Zionist movement in the political sense, he came to terms with it on the cultural level. His critical attitude toward his and his Jewish contemporaries' uprootedness and his admiration for the happier situation before the "fall" are reflected in his parables, e.g., the title story *In der Strafkolonie* (published as *In the Penal Colony*), 1950, written in 1914, and "Ein Bericht für eine Akademie" (a report for an academy), published in *Ein Landarzt* (A country doctor), 1919.

In his quest for a firm cultural identity in a modernizing, polyethnic society, Kafka experienced the frustrations often felt by alienated intellectuals who are intent on reaching the unattainable goal of social and ethnic integration. His failure to be attracted by any specific cultural norm caused Kafka considerable psychic pain and bred disillusionment with all facets of contemporary Central European society. Instead (or by way of compensation), he found an outlet through which to express his understanding—timeless and universally applicable symbols, and the bizarre and the absurd in his literary allusions.

Helmut F. Pfanner

See also Imperial Germany: Literature; Jews, 1869–1933; Novel; Weimar Germany: Literature

References

Anderson, Mark, ed. *Reading Kafka: Prague, Politics, and the Fin de Siècle*. New York, NY: Schocken Books, 1989.

Gross, Ruth V., ed. *Critical Essays on Franz Kafka*. Boston, MA: G.K. Hall, 1990.

Hayman, Ronald. *Kafka: A Biography*. New York, NY: Oxford University Press, 1982.

Karl, Frederick R. *Franz Kafka: Representative Man*. New York, NY: Ticknor and Fields, 1991.

Robertson, Ritchie. *Kafka: Judaism, Politics, and Literature*. Oxford: Clarendon Press, 1985.

Spann, Meno. *Franz Kafka*. Twayne World Author Series, vol. 381. Boston, MA: Twayne Publishers, 1976.

Kaiser, Georg (1878–1945)

Georg Kaiser was the most prolific playwright of German expressionism. A school dropout at seventeen in Magdeburg, his birthplace, he became a member and co-founder of Sappho, a reading association where he began his literary career with *Schellenkönig* (King of diamonds), 1895, an eccentric play that contains germinal ideas of his later period, mainly the renewal of humanity.

Kaiser's first publication was the dramatic treatment of the biblical Judith in *Die jüdische Witwe* (The Jewish widow), 1911; the year 1915 saw the first performance of a play at the Neue Bühne in Vienna, *Der Fall des Schülers Vehgesack* (The case of the pupil). The decisive breakthrough came with the staging of *Die Bürger von Calais* (The burghers of Calais), 1917, one of his few idealistic plays that are still widely read in German schools. Among Kaiser's best-known plays are *Von morgens bis mitternachts* (published as *From Morn to Midnight*), 1912, a "Stationendrama" (station drama), and the so-called Gas Trilogy: *Die Koralle* (published as *The Coral*), 1916–17, *Gas I*, and *Gas II* (1917–19). The structured and experimental nature of his dramas initially earned Kaiser the label *Denkspieler* (mental player); more recent critics, however, have recognized Kaiser's predominant concerns with ideology over mere theatrical effects. His plays reflect the turmoil before and after World War I and point to the necessity of improving society through a renewal of the individual. Seldom does Kaiser show the renewal achieved—for which he has been criticized—but offers only a glimmer of hope against a background of demise and destruction.

Lifelong financial difficulties prompted Kaiser to pawn some contents of a luxurious villa that he had rented at the Starnberger See. During the resulting sensational trial for embezzlement in 1921, Kaiser took exception to being treated as a common criminal. While serving a one-year jail term in 1921, he wrote the play *Noli me tangere*. The following years

(1921–33) brought an astounding success of over 40 pre-
mieres on the German stage with plays that clearly showed the
influence of Georg Büchner and Frank Wedekind (1864–
1918). His dramatic aims and techniques remained controversial, yet found wide recognition among other writers, especially Bertolt Brecht (1896–1958). A number of composers,
notably Kurt Weill (1900–50) and Mischa Spolianky, collaborated with Kaiser by providing musical scores to a number of
his plays.

Although Kaiser had outperformed all other contemporary dramatists, his membership in the Preussische Akademie
der Künste (Prussian Academy of Art) was withdrawn in 1933,
and his works were outlawed and publicly burned. Warned of
impending arrest, Kaiser escaped to Switzerland, where he
created scripts for movies, narratives, and lyrical and dramatic
works with classical and anti-Fascist themes. His legacy includes 70 dramas, three novels, several hundred poems, and
numerous theoretical essays.

Manfred Kuxdorf

See also Brecht, Bertolt; Drama; Expressionism; Imperial
Germany: Literature; Wedekind, Frank; Weill, Kurt; Weimar
Germany: Literature; World War I

References

Arnold, Armin, ed. *Interpretationen zu Georg Kaiser.* Munich:
    Klett, 1980.
Kaiser, Georg. *Five Plays.* Trans. B.J. Kenworthy, Rex Last,
    and J.M. Ritchie. London: Calder and Boyars, 1971.
———. *The Raft of the Medusa.* Trans. Ulrich Weisstein.
    First Stage 1 (Spring 1962), 35–48.
———. *Werke.* 6 vols. Ed. Walther Huder. Berlin:
    Propyläen, 1971–72.
Kenworthy, Brian J. *Georg Kaiser.* Oxford: Blackwell, 1957.
Kuxdorf, Manfred. *Die Suche nach dem Menschen im
    Drama Georg Kaisers.* Bern: Lang, 1971.
Petersen, Klaus. *Georg Kaiser: Künstlerbild und Künstlerfigur.*
    Bern: Lang, 1976.
Reichert, Herbert W. "Nietzsche and Georg Kaiser." *Studies
    in Philology* 61 (1964), 85–108.
Schrer, Ernst. *Georg Kaiser.* New York, NY: Twayne, 1971.
Tyson, Peter K. *The Reception of Georg Kaiser 1915–1945.*
    New York: Lang, 1984.

Kaiser, Jakob (1888–1961)

Jakob Kaiser, an official of the Christian Trade Unions during the Weimar era and later an active member of the German
resistance to Hitler, was one of the founders of the Christian
Democratic Union (CDU). Late in 1945, Kaiser succeeded
Andreas Hermes as chair of the CDU in the Soviet-occupied
zone of Germany. In December 1947, the Soviets purged and
"coordinated" the eastern CDU, and Kaiser, like Hermes before him, was forced to relinquish his post. As head of the
Christian Democratic Social Committees, Kaiser continued
to bring labor interests to bear within the western CDU. A
living symbol of national democratic resistance to Soviet oppression in eastern Germany, Kaiser served in the first two
cabinets of West German Chancellor Konrad Adenauer
(1876–1967) as minister for all-German affairs.

Kaiser combined avid nationalism with a streak of social
radicalism. A protégé of the Christian trade union leader and
fellow Catholic Franconian Adam Stegerwald (1874–1945),
he returned from combat in World War I to serve as regional
secretary of the Christian unions in the Rhineland and
Westphalia. Kaiser was a member of the Center Party and a
Reichstag deputy in the last parliament (1933) of the Weimar
Republic. Peripherally implicated in the plot to assassinate
Hitler in July 1944, Kaiser had to hide in a cellar in Berlin for
the remainder of World War II.

Believing that labor disunity had given Nazism its opening, Kaiser and his colleague in the Resistance, the socialist
trade-union leader Wilhelm Leuschner (1890–1944), hoped
to form a unified, nonideological labor party after the war. But
when the Social Democratic Party (SPD) reconstituted itself,
Kaiser fell back on a second option: an interdenominational,
socially diverse populist party, somewhat along the lines advocated by Stegerwald in his Essen program of 1920. Asserting that "the bourgeois age is over," Kaiser nonetheless rejected
Marxism, whose antireligious prejudice and materialistic concept of class struggle he deemed intolerant and undemocratic.
Instead, like Karl Arnold in the British zone, Kaiser wanted
the CDU to stand for "Christian socialism." Under this rubric, the socialist emphasis on the common good was to be
tempered by Christian respect for the freedom and dignity of
the individual. To the CDU's chairman in the British zone
(Adenauer), "Christian socialism" was a contradiction in
terms. In the Soviet zone, however, it provided Kaiser with a
rationale for carrying on an adversarial relationship with the
Communist-dominated Socialist Unity Party (SED) even
within the "socialist" constraints of the Soviet-mandated all-
party Anti-Fascist Unity Bloc.

During the first years of the postwar occupation, Kaiser
staked the claim of the Berlin CDU to lead the party nationwide. This aspiration was vehemently countered by Adenauer,
who feared that the party might be hindered everywhere by
the constraints it faced in the Soviet zone. Calling for Germany to be a "bridge" between East and West, Kaiser feuded
bitterly with Adenauer, whom he accused of building a wall
between the zones. But Kaiser's own fate at the hands of the
Soviets soon compelled him to accept Adenauer's thesis that
only through the Western integration of the "free" part of
Germany could the rest of Germany be saved.

Nevertheless, Kaiser continued to balk at the consequences of this position. As Adenauer's "Germany" minister,
he often clashed with the chancellor when a short-term choice
had to be made between steps that promoted Western integration and those that promoted German national unification.
The most notable clashes occurred over the Saar, a continual
problem in Franco-German relations until its return to Germany in 1956. Whereas Kaiser consistently asserted that
Germany ought to pursue a more resolute national line,
Adenauer moved cautiously on this matter, fearing consequences disruptive to Western integration. In the end, Kaiser
believed himself to have been vindicated in regard to the

recovery of this German territory. But he was no more successful than Adenauer in keeping Western integration from calcifying the division of Germany in the east.

Noel D. Cary

See also Adenauer, Konrad; Anti-Fascism; Berlin; Center Party; Christian Democratic Union; Christian Trade Unions; Federal Republic of Germany: Foreign Policy; German Democratic Republic; Leuschner, Wilhelm; Nationalism; Resistance; Saar; Socialist Unity Party; Soviet Occupation of Germany; Stegerwald, Adam

References

Cary, Noel D. *The Path to Christian Democracy: German Catholics and the Party System from Windthorst to Adenauer.* Cambridge, MA: Harvard University Press, 1996.

Conze, Werner, Erich Kosthorst, and Elfriede Nebgen. *Jakob Kaiser.* 4 vols. Stuttgart: W. Kohlhammer GmbH, 1967–72.

Heidenheimer, Arnold. *Adenauer and the CDU.* The Hague: Martinus Nijhoff, 1960.

Patch, William Jr. *Christian Trade Unions in the Weimar Republic, 1918–1933: The Failure of "Corporate Pluralism."* New Haven, CT: Yale University Press, 1985.

Kaiser Wilhelm/Max Planck Societies and Their Institutes

The Max Planck-Gesellschaft zur Förderung der Wissenschaften (MPG; Max Planck Society for the Advancement of the Sciences), with its component Max Planck Institutes, is the premier research institution of the Federal Republic of Germany (FRG). It was established in Göttingen in 1948 to replace the Kaiser Wilhelm-Gesellschaft (KWG), constituted in 1911. These two institutions have employed a large proportion of the German scientific elite; about half of the German Nobel laureates in science have been members. The KWG began as a quasi-private endowment supporting research institutes with minimal teaching functions and loose ties to the existing system of state universities and academies. The KWG and MPG have maintained a separate institutional identity and nominal autonomy, but since the destruction of the original endowment of nearly fifteen million marks through hyperinflation (1920–23), their support has come mostly from the federal government and the *Länder* (states).

The KWG's original base was the Berlin suburb of Dahlem, where the Prussian educational bureaucrat Friedrich Althoff had dreamed of creating a "scientific colony." There the KWG opened its first two research institutes, for chemistry and for physical chemistry (1912), born of efforts by academic and industrial chemists to establish a national research center. The organic chemist Emil Fischer (1852–1919) joined the KWG's administrative committee and became a significant influence on its first president, the church historian Adolf von Harnack (1851–1930).

Fischer helped to set the KWG's early emphasis on chemistry, biology, and their applications. His efforts to rally ad-

ditional industrial support for research enabled the KWG to expand beyond Dahlem with the Kaiser Wilhelm Institute for Coal Research in Mühlheim (1914). Its work with strategic raw materials during World War I made it a model for a series of institutes in industrial regions performing basic research on critical materials such as iron and steel, nonferrous metals, leather, and textiles. At the same time, Fritz Haber's (1868–1934) physical chemistry institute developed most of Germany's chemical weapons.

Apart from autonomous groups of corporate investors that supported the chemical institute and the materials institutes, the bulk of the KWG's initial endowment came from an elite of fewer than two hundred Prussian businessmen and bankers who joined the society in response to a membership campaign by Prussian and Imperial bureaucrats, that stressed the Kaiser's personal interest and involvement. Respondents included a disproportionate number of status-seeking assimilated or converted Jews (such as Leopold Koppel, sole endower of the institute for physical chemistry). At the same time, a significant number of the institutes' initial scientific members or directors were of Jewish origin, such as Haber and Richard Willstätter (1872–1942) in chemistry, Otto Warburg (1883–1970) in biology, later cell physiology, and Albert Einstein (1879–1955) in physics.

Aided by government support and the Rockefeller Foundation during the 1920s, the KWG expanded from some 20 institutes in 1921 to about 30 by the time of Harnack's death (1930). Under the presidency of Max Planck (1858–1947) from 1930 to 1937, the society suffered economic and political setbacks, losing more than 70 scientists and staff during the National Socialist "coordination" (*Gleichschaltung*). Although the KWG continued to support much basic research that was not overtly political or military, especially in biology, Planck's successors, corporate directors Carl Bosch (1874–1940; 1937–1940) and Albert Vögler (1877–1945; president 1941–45), secured increased funding as KWG institutes were integrated into German autarky policy, military research (including the nuclear work of scientists such as Werner Heisenberg [1901–76] and Otto Hahn [1879–1968]), and elements of the Holocaust.

The war destroyed or caused the removal of many of the institutes, and the occupation and division of Germany forced the division and dissolution of the KWG. In the Western zones it was reconstituted under Hahn's leadership as the MPG (1948) and gained support from the new federal government in 1949. Most older institute buildings in Dahlem eventually became part of the Free University of Berlin. Surviving institutes in the Soviet zone were mostly incorporated into the Academy of Sciences of the German Democratic Republic (GDR).

Under Hahn (1946–60) the MPG increased its budget from some 12.5 million to 62 million deutsche marks (DM) and its number of institutes to 40 (with 3,000 full-time staff members). Under Adolf Butenandt (1903–95; president 1960–72) the most dramatic growth occurred, as the MPG shifted its headquarters to Munich and increased its budget to about 580 million DM, with 47 institutes or research centers employing 8,000 full-time staff. The society simultaneously grew increasingly dependent on government subsidies, which accounted for about 90 percent of its income (shared, by a 1975–76 agreement, equally between Bonn and the states). Under Butenandt's successors, the budget no longer grew substantially in real terms, prompting fears that the society would lose its innovative edge.

The most significant postwar research area of the society was physics and related fields, whose large, costly experimental facilities consumed about half of the total budget. Another third was allocated to biomedical research. By 1990, the MPG was operating 60 research centers with a budget of 1.3 billion DM and 8,700 full-time staff. The collapse of the GDR and reunification opened a new era of potential expansion in the east, with the closure of competing East German academic research institutes and their partial absorption into the MPG.

Throughout its history, the KWG/MPG has been an elite institution, employing a disproportionate number of the most innovative German scientists. Its development exemplifies a host of issues in the relationship between science and social change in the twentieth century.

Jeffrey A. Johnson

See also Althoff, Friedrich; Bosch, Carl; Butenandt, Adolf; Biochemistry; Chemistry, Scientific and Industrial; Fischer, Emil; Foundations and Research Institutes; Franck, James; Haber, Fritz; Hahn, Otto; Harnack, Adolf von; Heisenberg, Werner; Inflation and Hyperinflation; Physics; Planck, Max; Science and National Socialism; Science in the Postwar Germanys; Universities

References

Gerwin, Robert, and Barbara Holzt. *The Max-Planck-Gesellschaft and Its Institutes: Portrait of a Research Organization: Objectives, Activities, Structure, Development.* 3rd ed. Munich: Max-Planck-Gesellschaft zur Förderung der Wissenschaften, 1984. (Trans. of *Die Max-Planck-Gesellschaft und ihre Institute*, 3d ed.; the 4th ed., 1991, has not been translated.)

Johnson, Jeffrey Allan. *The Kaiser's Chemists: Science and Modernization in Imperial Germany.* Chapel Hill, NC: University of North Carolina Press, 1990.

Macrakis, Kristie. *Surviving the Swastika: Scientific Research in Nazi Germany.* Oxford: Oxford University Press, 1993.

Renneberg, Monika, and Mark Walker. *Science, Technology, and National Socialism.* Cambridge, UK: Cambridge University Press, 1994.

Kaltenbrunner, Ernst (1903–46)

Ernst Kaltenbrunner was one of the leading personalities of the Third Reich. A prominent Austrian Nazi, he assumed a high-ranking position in the police following the 1938 *Anschluss.* He succeeded Reinhard Heydrich (1904–42) as the head of the Reich Security Main Office (RSHA) in Berlin and later served as chief of the Security Police and the SD (Security Service).

Born in Reid, Upper Austria, in 1903, Kaltenbrunner was raised in a household dominated by a father who instilled in his son a strong German chauvinism and a fanatical aversion to Catholicism and Judaism. Kaltenbrunner followed in his father's footsteps and studied law at Graz. After completing his studies, Kaltenbrunner joined a local *Heimatschutz* (defense of home [nation]) organization, but he grew disappointed with its lack of clear focus and soon allied himself with the Austrian Nazis. He joined the Nazi Party (NSDAP) in 1930 and the Schutzstaffel (SS) in 1931. Heinrich Himmler (1900–45) appointed him leader of the entire Austrian SS in January 1937 and he held this position until the *Anschluss* with Germany.

From 1938 to 1942, Kaltenbrunner served as the secretary for public security in the new Ostmark (formerly Austria) and as the higher SS and police leader in Vienna. Following the assassination of Heydrich in June 1942, Himmler, who was impressed with Kaltenbrunner's ability to coordinate the political functions of the SS and the police with the goals of the Nazi Party, the Wehrmacht, and the state, summoned him to Berlin to succeed Heydrich as the head of the RSHA. Kaltenbrunner also took his predecessor's title of chief of the Security Police and the SD, and he used his new position to further advance his radical racial and political policies against those who refused to give full and total allegiance to the Nazis. He focused a great deal of time and attention on the "final solution of the Jewish question" in Europe, including Aktion Reinhard and the deportation of elderly Jews from Theresienstadt to Auschwitz.

Kaltenbrunner was one of the most powerful and bloodthirsty men in Nazi Germany. He survived the war only to be captured and tried as a major Nazi war criminal at Nuremberg. He feigned ignorance of his leading role in the Final Solution, blaming his actions and decisions on his subordinates. Kaltenbrunner was convicted of participation in crimes against humanity and was hanged in October 1946. His name remains synonymous with the barbarism practiced by the Hitler regime.

Steven B. Rogers

See also Anschluss; Anti-Semitism; Auschwitz; Austro-German Relations; Heydrich, Reinhard; Himmler, Heinrich; Hitler, Adolf; Holocaust; National Socialist Germany; Nuremberg Trials; Reich Security Main Office; Schutzstaffel; Security Service of the SS

References

Black, Peter. *Ernst Kaltenbrunner: Ideological Soldier of the Third Reich.* Princeton, NJ: Princeton University Press, 1984.

Houston, Wendell Robert. "Ernst Kaltenbrunner: A Study of an Austrian SS and Police Leader." Unpublished doctoral dissertation. Rice University, 1972.

Pauley, Bruce F. *Hitler and the Forgotten Nazis: A History of Austrian National Socialism.* Chapel Hill, NC: University of North Carolina, 1981.

Reitlinger, Gerald. *The Final Solution.* 2nd ed. London: Vallentine, Mitchell, 1968.

*1911 Painting,
Komposition IV—
Schlacht (Battle)
by Wassily Kandinsky.
Courtesy of Inter
Nationes, Bonn.*

Kandinsky, Wassily (1866–1944)

Wassily Kandinsky's concept of abstraction as an international language that could transcend the boundaries of class, race, and nation attracted the attention of artists and critics all over Europe before the onset of World War I. His manifesto *Über das Geistige in der Kunst* (On the Spiritual in Art), a description of abstract painting as a stimulus to a new world order, was published in 1912 by the Munich publisher R. Piper and Co. His establishment, with the painter Franz Marc (1880–1916), of the exhibition group and yearbook the *Blaue Reiter*, helped to insure the fame of his large-scaled and vividly colored oils, some bearing titles such as *Composition* and *Improvisation* to reinforce the association of painting with music, then thought to be the highest of the arts.

Born in Moscow, Kandinsky moved to Munich in 1896 to study painting. He never lost contact with his Russian heritage and returned there when World War I began. He became a supporter of the cultural aims of the new Soviet Union, serving on committees for the reform of art education and briefly chairing the Moscow Institute of Artistic Culture. As painting came under criticism as nonproductive by the constructivists, Kandinsky returned to Germany, and in 1922 Walter Gropius (1883–1969) appointed him to the faculty of Weimar's most famous art school, the Bauhaus. Along with Paul Klee (1879–1940), he taught aspects of the preliminary course, and he remained with the Bauhaus as it moved from Weimar to Dessau and finally to Berlin. Shortly after the Nazis closed the school in 1933, Kandinsky emigrated to Paris. He continued to be productive until his death 11 years later.

In his early years, symbolist, theosophical, and anarchist ideas guided Kandinsky's slow evolution toward abstraction; he used hidden images based on apocalyptic notions of good and evil, subtitling major paintings *Last Judgement* and *Garden of Love*, to deal with the problem of evoking meaning in abstract art. Even when he no longer offered these imagistic or verbal clues to the thematic content of his work and turned to structured architectural forms (1920s), and to biomorphic shapes (in the 1930s), Kandinsky continued to have faith in the utopian notion of a universal language of form and color communicating transnational and transcendental truths.

Rose-Carol W. Long

See also Aesthetics; Artists; Bauhaus; *Blaue Reiter*; Expressionism; Gropius, Walter; Klee, Paul; Marc, Franz; Painting

References

Barnett, Vivian, and Armin Zweite, eds. *Kandinsky: Watercolors and Drawings.* Munich: Prestel Verlag, 1992.

Kandinsky, Wassily, and Franz Marc, eds. *The Blaue Reiter Almanac.* Ed. Klaus Lankheit. New York, NY: Viking, 1974.

Lindsay, Kenneth C., and Peter Vergo, eds. *Kandinsky: Complete Writings on Art.* 2 vols. Boston, MA: G. K. Hall and Co., 1982.

Long, Rose-Carol Washton. *Kandinsky: The Development of an Abstract Style.* Oxford: Clarendon Press, 1980.

———. "Occultism, Anarchism, and Abstraction: Kandinsky's Art of the Future." *Art Journal* 46 (Spring 1987), 38–45.

Roethel, Kans K., and Jean K. Benjamin. *Kandinsky: Catalogue Raisonné of the Oil-Paintings.* 2 vols. Ithaca, NY: Cornell University Press, 1982.

The Solomon R. Guggenheim Museum. *Kandinsky: Russian and Bauhaus Years, 1915–1933.* New York, NY: Guggenheim Museum, 1983.

Kant, Hermann (1926–)

The writer and essayist Hermann Kant, president of the Writers' Association of the German Democratic Republic (GDR) from 1978 until 1989, was twice awarded the National Prize of the GDR. He is best known for his novel, *Die Aula* (The aula), 1965.

Kant was born in Hamburg and apprenticed as an electrician before serving in the Wehrmacht. He was a prisoner of war in Poland from 1945 to 1949, then a student and teacher at the Workers' and Peasants' Faculty (ABF) of the University of Greifswald, which was established to open up higher education to wider sectors of the population. Kant went on to study German in East Berlin and worked as a journalist on the Socialist Unity Party (SED) newspaper, *Neues Deutschland.* He has been a professional author and essayist since 1962.

Kant's novel *Die Aula,* based on his own experiences in Greifswald, presented the ABF as a model of the new society being developed in the GDR and the new educated class being formed to govern that society. Its modernist narrative structure was innovative for the GDR, and it used humor and satire to criticize the resistance of the middle classes, the overenthusiasm of the students, and, in particular, dogmatism and lack of humanity where it occurred among those in positions of power. In this work, Kant's narrative style of anecdotes, wordplay and jokes does not overwhelm the content. In *Der Aufenthalt* (The stay), 1977, Kant adopted a more serious and reflective style, suited to his material: Germany's war crimes and its relationship with its eastern neighbors. The narrator, a young German soldier, is taken prisoner in Poland and through his experiences with Poles and fellow-prisoners is brought to reflect on past attitudes.

As president of the Writers' Association of the GDR, Kant was involved in the expulsion of a number of critical authors, including Stefan Heym (1913–) in 1979. Kant has insisted that he did everything in his power to protect writers from political repercussions, but his critics within the Writers' Association forced his resignation during the events of 1989. Since then, Kant has published his autobiography, *Abspann* (Unyoking), 1991.

Kant's anecdotal, humorous style was effective in *Die Aula* but later developed into a mannerism: relentless facetiousness as sugar-coating for a missionary didacticism, for instance in his novel *Das Impressum* (The imprint), 1972, dealing with a newspaper editor who is called on to serve as a minister in the government. Only in some of his short stories that satirize the more farcical aspects of GDR everyday life, such as *Bronzezeit* (Bronze age), 1986, do form and content remain in balance. Kant's reputation as an author suffered in the wake of the controversy surrounding his activity in the Writers' Association, but *Die Aula* and *Der Aufenthalt* nevertheless remain important literary treatments of aspects of Germany's history in the twentieth century.

James A. Mellis

See also German Democratic Republic; German Democratic Republic: Literature and Literary Life; Novel

References

Durzak, Manfred. *Der deutsche Roman der Gegenwart, Entwicklungsvoraussetzungen und Tendenzen.* 3rd ed. Stuttgart: Kohlhammer, 1979.

Kant, Hermann. *Selections, 1981.* Berlin: Aufbau-Verlag, 1981.

———. *Abspann: Erinnerung an meine Gegenwart.* Berlin: Aufbau-Verlag, 1991.

Krenzlin, Leonore. *Hermann Kant, Leben und Werk.* Berlin: Volk & Wissen, 1979.

Langenbruch, Theodor. *Dialectical Humor in Hermann Kant's Novel "Die Aula": A Study in Contemporary East German Literature.* Bonn: Bouvier, 1975.

Karajan, Herbert von (1908–89)

The most celebrated Austrian/German conductor of the postwar era, Herbert von Karajan united technical mastery, interpretive vitality, and personal charisma in his innumerable performances and recordings. His legacy numbers over 800 audio and video recordings. With the Berlin Philharmonic as his chief conducting engagement between 1955 and 1989, Karajan molded the orchestra to attain his musical goals. His repertory ranged from Bach to Henze, encompassing orchestral, operatic, and choral music, with an emphasis on German romantic and late-romantic symphonic music and opera.

At an early age, Karajan studied piano at the Salzburg Mozarteum, but he then decided on a career in conducting, which he pursued in Vienna at the Academy of Music. His student conducting debut was on December 17, 1928, his professional debut (with the Salzburg Orchestra) one month later. He conducted at the Stadttheater (city theater) Ulm for five years (1929–34), then served as *Generalmusikdirektor* (general music director) in Aachen between 1935 and 1942. In 1938, Karajan amazed Berlin audiences in debuts with the Berlin Philharmonic and at the *Staatsoper* (state opera). From that point onward, his star was in rapid ascendancy, with guest engagements throughout Western Europe. The conductor eventually settled in Berlin in 1941.

The 1930s and 1940s were also characterized by Karajan's fascination with the Nazi Party, which led him to join in 1933 and ensured Karajan's continued activity throughout the war years. Although initially forbidden to conduct after World War II, Karajan was de-Nazified in 1947 and entered into a ten-year relationship with the Vienna Philharmonic beginning in 1948. He also served as conductor of the Philharmonia Orchestra of London between 1948 and 1954. In 1955, Karajan succeeded Wilhelm Furtwängler as conductor of the Berlin Philharmonic, where he remained until his retirement in April 1989. He also was artistic director of the Salzburg Festival (1956–60) and of the Vienna Staatsoper (1957–64), which solidified his domination of the European art-music scene.

Karajan maintained ties with Salzburg, establishing the renowned Easter Festival there in 1967. He became conductor for life of the Berlin Philharmonic in 1967. During his tenure with that orchestra, the Philharmonie (the orchestra's concert hall) was constructed; the Philharmonic toured Europe, Japan, China, and the Soviet Union; and the orchestra accepted its first woman member. Karajan remained active as conductor until shortly before his death.

By virtue of his organizational skills, strength of will, and talents as a conductor, Karajan could immerse himself in the music (he conducted from memory) and make it come alive for the audience. Karajan had the solid basis for an "empire"

Herbert von Karajan. Courtesy of Inter Nationes, Bonn.

that would last almost 30 years. His plastic sense of line, dramatic flair, and timbal effect created a characteristic "sensual" sound that some critics have labeled as overindulgent. But no critic can dispute the significance of the phenomenon that Karajan was in the second half of the twentieth century. He is likely to remain a measure for others for decades to come.

James Deaville

See also Composers; Conductors; Furtwängler, Wilhelm; National Socialist Germany; National Socialist Germany: Music; Opera; Operetta; Orchestras; Walter, Bruno

References

Bachmann, Robert C. *Karajan: Notes on a Career*. Trans. Shaun Whiteside. London: Quartet Books, 1990.

Csobadi, Peter, ed. *Karajan: Oder die kontrollierte Ekstase: Eine kritische Hommage von Zeitzeugen*. Vienna: P. Neff, 1988.

Häussermann, Ernst. *Herbert von Karajan: Biographie*. Vienna: Verlag Fritz Molden, 1978.

Karajan, Herbert von. *My Autobiography: Herbert von Karajan as Told to Franz Endler*. Trans. S. Spencer. London: Sidgwick & Jackson, 1989.

Vaughan, Roger. *Herbert von Karajan: A Biographical Portrait*. New York, NY: W.W. Norton, 1986.

Kaschnitz, Marie Luise (1901–74)

Marie Luise Kaschnitz, a writer, constantly traversed uncomfortable borderlands in search of places of relative security. She would then position herself in order to gain a vantage point from which she could carefully observe and critique the everyday horrors of modern life. Although often skeptical of the ability of a writer to address the complex moral dilemmas faced by people in an age of technology gone amok, she never failed to address such issues in her poetry and prose. She believed that humankind would be worse off without the efforts of writers like herself. In short stories, novels, essays, radio plays, and poetry, and finally in the laconic language of her later autobiographical sketches, Kaschnitz probed her own psyche (*Das Haus der Kindheit* [The house of childhood], 1956) and the world around her (*Orte: Aufzeichnungen* [Places: notes], 1973). Like the photographer behind the hedge in her famous poem "Hiroshima," Kaschnitz wanted to be "das Auge der Welt" (the eye of the world), "nirgends mehr und überall zu Hause sein" (at home nowhere and everywhere). An increasing sense of resignation marked her old age, but even in her last essay ("Rettung durch Phantasie," [Rescue through imagination], 1974), she still considered the possibility that the power of the imagination could help to rescue humanity.

The daughter of an officer, Kaschnitz was raised in Berlin and Potsdam. The family moved to the village of Bollschweil in Baden during World War I. It was one of the three places she would always call home (*Beschreibung eines Dorfes* [Description of a village], 1966). Kaschnitz met her husband, archeologist Guido von Kaschnitz-Weinberg, while working as a bookseller in Rome in the 1920s. Their daughter, Iris, was born there, but the couple spent the 1930s and 1940s in Königsberg, Marburg, and Frankfurt am Main. Rome remained the eternal city for Kaschnitz, a place of renewal, of memory and longing expressed in poetry and prose (*Ewige Stadt* [Eternal city], 1951; *Engelsbrücke: Römisches Tagebuch* [Bridge of angels: Roman diary], 1955). Frankfurt was always associated in her mind with the ugliness of the war and the postwar Economic Miracle.

The security provided by her marriage granted Kaschnitz 30 years of productivity. Major collections of poetry and prose appeared regularly during the 1940s: *Griechische Mythen* (Greek myths), 1944; *Gedichte 1928–44* (Poetry), 1947. Kaschnitz gained wider recognition in the 1950s, including the prestigious Georg Büchner Prize (1955). She was invited to offer the lectures on poetics at the University of Frankfurt in 1960. But she remained modest, citing her lack of ambition, her reluctance to engage in public debates, and—as a woman—the primacy of her family life.

Her husband's painful illness and death in 1958 unleashed a personal crisis even more devastating than the experience of World War II. Kaschnitz remained silent at first, while she repositioned herself. Then she renewed her engagement with the world through her writing, repeatedly posing the difficult queries "Wohin sind wir gekommen?" (Whence have we come?), and "Wohin gehe ich?" (Where am I going?), 1963. She claimed that old age was not a prison, but rather a balcony providing a vantage point from which she could see farther and more accurately. At the time of her death, she had just completed a cycle of poems, *Gedicht vom Menschenleben* (Song of a human life), 1974, on which she had labored for years.

Margaret E. Ward

See also Autobiography; Federal Republic of Germany: Literature; Novel; Poetry

References

Gersdorff, Dagmar von. *Marie Luise Kaschnitz: Eine Biographie*. Frankfurt am Main: Insel, 1993.

Kaschnitz, Marie Luise. *Circe's Mountain: Stories*. Trans. Lisel Mueller. Minneapolis, MN: Milkweed Editions, 1990.

———. *Gesammelte Werke*. 7 vols. Ed. Christian Buttrich and Norbert Miller. Frankfurt am Main: Insel, 1981–85.

Pulver, Elsbeth. *Marie Luise Kaschnitz: Autorenbücher*. Munich: C.H. Beck; *Text + Kritik*, 1984.

Reichardt, Johanna Christiane. *Zeitgenössin: Marie Luise Kaschnitz: Eine Monographie*. Frankfurt am Main: Peter Lang, 1984.

Schweikert, Uwe. *Marie Luise Kaschnitz: Materialien*. Frankfurt am Main: Suhrkamp, 1984.

Stephan, Inge. "Männliche Ordnung und weibliche Erfahrung: Überlegungen zum autobiographischen Schreiben bei Marie Luise Kaschnitz." *Frauenliteratur ohne Tradition? Neun Autorinnenporträts*. Ed. Inge Stephan, Regula Venske, and Sigrid Weigel. Frankfurt am Main: Fischer Taschenbuch, 1987.

Kästner, Erich (1899–1974)

The theater critic and journalist Erich Kästner became famous as a writer during the 1920s and early 1930s with his lyrical poetry, as well as his humorous and often satirical novels. He belonged to the *Neue Sachlichkeit* (New objectivity) movement of the mid-1920s, was involved with the cabaret scene in Berlin, and worked for the weekly political magazine *Die Weltbühne*. His greatest successes, however, were his children's books. The most celebrated of his children's novels written in rapid succession during the last years of the Weimar Republic included *Emil und die Detektive* (published as *Emil and the Detectives*), 1928, *Pünktchen und Anton* (published as *Annaluise and Anton*), which appeared in 1931, and *Das fliegende Klassenzimmer* (published as *The Flying Class Room*), which came out in 1933.

Kästner was born in Dresden on February 23, 1899. He studied German literature, philosophy, and the history of the theater in Dresden, Rostock, Berlin, and Leipzig. After receiving his doctorate with a dissertation on Frederick the Great's *De la littérature allemande*, he moved to Berlin. While working as a journalist and freelance writer, he penned four volumes of poetry. In 1931 he published *Fabian*, a humorous but tragic novel that contains all the major components of his writing: melancholy, satire, humor, and a strong belief in humanitarian principles.

Because of the moralistic and satirical elements in his works, Kästner was not permitted to write or publish after 1933. He was twice arrested by the Gestapo, and the novels he wrote during the Nazi years had to be printed in Switzerland. After World War II, Kästner worked as an editor for the newspaper, *Neue Zeitung*, in Munich and continued to write children's books and poems. During the last decade of his life, two autobiographical volumes appeared: *Als ich ein kleiner Junge war* (published as *When I Was a Little Boy*), 1957, and *Notabene '45* (1961). He died in Munich on July 29, 1974.

Because of his witty and humorous style, Kästner is still well-known to a large readership today. Among the literary prizes he received, the Literaturpreis der Stadt München (1956) and the Georg Büchner Prize (1957) are the most distinguished.

Ulrich Scheck

See also Cabaret; Children's Literature; *Die Weltbühne*; Federal Republic of Germany: Literature; Journalism; National Socialist Germany: Literature; Novel; Poetry; Satire; Theater; Weimar Germany: Literature

References

Bäumler, Marianne. *Die aufgeräumte Wirklichkeit des Erich Kästner*. Cologne: Prometh, 1984.

Bemmann, Helga. *Humor auf Taille: Erich Kästner, Leben und Werk*. Frankfurt am Main: Fischer, 1985.

Benson, Renate. *Erich Kästner: Studien zu seinem Werk*. Bonn: Bouvier, 1973.

Enderle, Luiselotte. *Erich Kästner in Selbstzeugnissen und Bilddokumenten*. Reinbek bei Hamburg: Rowohlt, 1966.

Kästner, Erich. *Gesammelte Schriften*. Frankfurt am Main: Büchergilde Gutenberg, 1958.

———. *Gesammelte Schriften für Erwachsene*. Munich: Droemer-Knaur, 1969.

Kiesel, Helmuth. *Erich Kästner*. Munich: Beck, 1981.

Lämmerzahl-Bensel, Uta, ed. *Erich Kästner: Eine Personalbibliographie*. Giessen: Dux, 1988.

Last, R.W. *Erich Kästner*. London: Wolf, 1974.

Mank, Dieter. *Erich Kästner im nationalsozialistischen Deutschland 1933–1945: Zeit ohne Werk?* Frankfurt am Main: Lang, 1981.

Walter, Dirk. *Zeitkritik und Idyllensehnsucht: Erich Kästners Frühwerk, 1928–1933, als Beispiel linksbürgerlicher Literatur in der Weimarer Republik*. Heidelberg: Winter, 1977.

Winkelman, John. *The Poetic Style of Erich Kästner*. Lincoln, NE: University of Nebraska Press, 1957.

Kautsky, Karl (1854–1938)

Among the most important theoreticans of the Social Democratic Party (SPD), Karl Kautsky tried to validate Marxism within the labor movement. Together with Friedrich Engels (1820–95) he popularized, and some think vulgarized, Karl Marx's (1818–83) ideology.

Born in Prague to a middle-class family, Kautsky came to Social Democracy in Vienna during his university studies. In the 1870s he was influenced by the positivist, natural-science outlook of Ernst Haeckel (1834–1919) and other proponents of Charles Darwin's ideas. He worked for the socialist press in Austria and then in Switzerland. In 1883 Kautsky founded the journal *Neue Zeit* (New times), which became his and the SPD's main theoretical voice for 30 years. Together with Eduard Bernstein (1850–1932), he studied the major Marxist writings and moved to London from 1885 to 1888 to work with Engels. Publication in 1887 of *Karl Marx' oekonomische Lehren* (The economic doctrines of Karl Marx) established him as a major socialist thinker and intellectual heir to Marx and Engels.

Kautsky led in drafting the Erfurt Program of the SPD in 1891. For the rest of his life he propagated and defended this program. He coined phrases, such as "revolutionary party but not a revolution-making party" to explain the SPD focus on change combined with avoidance of action (what Dieter Groh termed attentism). Together with August Bebel (1840–1913), Kautsky warded off every effort to alter the militant stance of the Erfurt Program even while the party undertook primarily organizing and agitation. In every major debate—whether on the role of the peasantry, Bernstein's proposal to revise the party ideology, the mass-strike disputes with the trade unions, or support for state budgets—Kautsky maintained the centrist position between the reformists on the right and the radicals on the left. His short study of 1909, *Der Weg zur Macht* (The road to power), seemed a shift leftward, but the more strident stance of the leading radicals such as Rosa Luxemburg (1870–1919) realigned Kautsky with the party's centrist leadership.

During World War I Kautsky sided with the co-leader of the party minority, Hugo Haase (1863–1919), in opposition to war credits. In 1917 the majority under Friedrich Ebert (1871–1919) dismissed him from *Neue Zeit*, though by that time Kautsky's influence had waned. Despite being one of their spokespersons, Kautsky disagreed with the Independent Social Democrats' (USPD) positive outlook toward the Bolsheviks and the Russian Revolution; he crossed swords with Leon Trotsky, among others, in defense of parliamentary democracy.

During the Revolution of 1918–19 Kautsky served as undersecretary in the Foreign Office, being responsible for the publication of German documents on the origins of the war. The state officials had little difficulty in misdirecting his investigations. Within the USPD, he fostered a parliamentary approach and nearly resigned when the party shifted leftward during 1919. By 1920 he knew he was isolated in the USPD and later encouraged reunification with the SPD. He moved to Vienna in 1925, recognizing that he had little influence and no official position in the reunited party.

Dieter K. Buse

See also Bebel, August; Bernstein, Eduard; Ebert, Friedrich; Engels, Friedrich; Haase, Hugo; Independent Social Democratic Party; Luxemburg, Rosa; Marx, Karl; Revolution of 1918–19; Social Democratic Party, 1871–1918; World War I

References

August Bebels Briefwechsel mit Karl Kautsky. Ed. Karl Kautsky Jr. Assen: Van Gorcum, 1971.

Groh, Dieter. *Negative Integration und revolutionärer Attentismus: Die deutsche Sozialdemokratie am Vorabend des Ersten Weltkrieges*. Frankfurt am Main: Propyläen Verlag, 1973. English summary: "Waiting For and Avoiding Revolution: Social Democracy and the Reich." *Laurentian University Review* 5 (1973), 83–109.

Kautsky, Karl. *The Dictatorship of the Proletariat*. Ann Arbor, MI: University of Michigan Press, 1964.

Pierson, Stanley. *Marxist Intellectuals and the Working Class Mentality in Germany 1887–1912*. Cambridge, MA: Harvard University Press, 1993.

Rogers, Homer K. *Before the Revisionist Controversy: Kautsky, Bernstein and the Meaning of Marxism, 1895–1898*. New York, NY: Garland Publishing, 1992.

Salvadori, Massimo L. *Karl Kautsky and the Socialist Revolution, 1880–1938*. London: NLB, 1979.

Schorske, Carl E. *German Social Democracy 1905–1917: The Development of the Great Schism*. Cambridge, MA: Harvard University Press, 1955.

Steenson, Gary P. *Karl Kautsky, 1854–1938: Marxism in the Classical Years*. Pittsburgh, PA: Pittsburgh University Press, 1978.

Trotsky, Leon. *Terrorism and Communism: A Reply to Karl Kautsky*. 2nd ed. Ann Arbor, MI: University of Michigan Press, 1961.

Kehr, Eckart (1902–33)

With the publication of his dissertation, "Schlachtflottenbau und Parteipolitik 1894–1901" (published as *Battleship Building and Party Politics in Germany 1894–1901*), 1930, and a series of articles, later published as *Der Primat der Innenpolitik* (published as *Economic Interest, Militarism, and Foreign Policy: Essays on German History*), 1965, Eckart Kehr became established as one of the twentieth century's most important and innovative historians, one who critically challenged orthodox assumptions in German history and methodology. The high quality of his work was soon recognized in the United States, and in 1932 he was awarded a Rockefeller scholarship. He died on May 29, 1933 in Washington. Despite his early death and his lack of acceptance during the years of Nazi rule, Kehr was never totally forgotten and his posthumous influence on the development of German historiography has been extraordinary, particularly since the 1960s when his work was rediscovered and republished under the auspices of Hans-Ulrich Wehler.

Kehr's path as a historian was largely influenced by the conclusions he drew from Germany's defeat in World War I. He believed that answers to the causes of Germany's catastrophe could not be found in the idealist tradition of historical writing associated with his teacher, Friedrich Meinecke (1862–1954), or the staunch nationalistic political history characterized by the German School. Influenced by Karl Marx (1818–83) and Max Weber (1864–1920), Kehr instead attempted to provide a new critical orientation in German historiography by analyzing social and economic structures. In "Schlachtflottenbau und Parteipolitik," Kehr emphasized the primacy of domestic politics over foreign affairs and stressed the significance of material interests and socioeconomic factors in the formation of the modern capitalist state by studying economic interest groups and considering their relationship to the German naval buildup and imperialism in the 1890s. One of his conclusions was that German military expansion and imperialist ventures at the turn of the century were the result of domestic political considerations—namely, the need to support and sustain industry and agriculture against the growing working class.

In the political climate of the Weimar Republic, Kehr's work was severely criticized, and some prominent scholars took steps to hinder his career. Nevertheless, his attempt to transform traditional historicism into a historical social science has influenced an entire generation of contemporary historians. Rather than discussing history in traditional categories of politics, the state, and foreign affairs, he used new concepts, such as class, party, and ideology, to understand the structural development of society. Sometimes called the "Kehrites," the group of scholars centered around Hans-Ulrich Wehler at the University of Bielefeld elaborated notions first developed by Kehr. To a large degree, his work became a model for studying the role of interest groups in Wilhelmine Germany and was a forerunner of the highly influential *Sonderweg* thesis, which argued that Germany's failed revolutionary experience and the continued political and economic power of the feudal elites prevented the emergence of a modern democratic state.

John R. Hinde

See also History; Imperial Germany: Foreign Policy; Meinecke, Friedrich; Navy and Naval Policy; *Sonderweg*

References

Iggers, Georg G. *New Directions in European Historiography.* Middletown, CT: Wesleyan University Press, 1975.

Kehr, Eckart. *Battleship Building and Party Politics in Germany 1894–1901.* Ed. Pauline R. Anderson and Eugene N. Anderson. New York, NY: Kraus Reprint, 1975.

———. *Economic Interest, Militarism, and Foreign Policy: Essays on German History.* Berkeley, CA: University of California Press, 1977.

Rüsen, Jörn. *Geschichte des Historismus.* Munich: Beck, 1992.

Wehler, Hans-Ulrich. "Eckart Kehr." *Deutsche Historiker.* Vol. 1. Ed. Hans-Ulrich Wehler. Göttingen: Vandenhoeck & Ruprecht, 1971.

Keim, August (1845–1926)

August Keim is best remembered not for his service as a career officer in the German army but rather for his role as one of the leaders of the German popular nationalist movement of the late nineteenth and early twentieth centuries. Great ambition as well as a commitment to infusing German military policy with new ideas (such as modern technology and a broader-based officer corps) and to instilling the German public with a keener sense of national pride led Keim to found the German Army League (Deutscher Wehrverein) in 1912. A diligent student of the military, Keim prepared himself for the challenge of the Army League, the last of the patriotic societies (*Nationale Verbände*), by first serving as an executive officer in two of its predecessors, the German Navy League and the Pan-German League.

Born into an established Hessian military family in 1845, Keim fought in the Wars of Unification and afterward found consolation in military journalism. Keim's pen proved mightier than the sword (and certainly sharper). Through the publication of numerous articles and pamphlets and in his position as Chancellor Leo von Caprivi's (1831–99) military spokesman for the Army Bill of 1893, Keim was able to espouse a kind of ultra-nationalism that in theory, at least, elicited the participation of the German public and in practice offended the sensibilities of the traditional German military elite.

As president of the German Army League, Keim led the charge by pressing for quantitative increase and qualitative improvement as embodied in the Army Bills of 1912 and 1913. He served as military governor of the Belgian province of Limburg during World War I, and after 1918 resumed his journalistic ventures until his death from cancer in 1926. Keim's vitriolic brand of militaristic nationalism foreshadowed the mood of 1914. But the initial optimism that war would revitalize the German nation faded with its reality—death and destruction.

Marilyn Shevin-Coetzee

See also Caprivi, Leo von; German Army League; Imperial Germany; Militarism; Nationalism; Navy League; Radical Nationalism; Pan-German League; World War I

References

Chickering, Roger. *We Men Who Feel Most German: A Cultural Study of the Pan-German League, 1886–1914.* London: Allen and Unwin, 1984.

Eley, Geoff. *Reshaping the German Right: Radical Nationalism and Political Change after Bismarck.* New Haven, CT: Yale University Press, 1980.

Keim, August. *Erlebtes und Erstrebtes: Lebenserinnerungen.* Hannover: Ernst Letsch, 1925.

Shevin-Coetzee, Marilyn. *The German Army League: Popular Nationalism in Wilhelmine Germany.* New York, NY: Oxford University Press, 1990.

Keitel, Wilhelm (1882–1946)

Field Marshal Wilhelm Keitel was one of Adolf Hitler's most loyal and devoted generals. From 1938 through 1945, he was chief of the German High Command (Oberkommando der Wehrmacht; OKW). During this period, he was Hitler's military adviser as well as the executor of his orders, which he did without remonstrating. He owed his rise partly to nepotism (he was the son-in-law of General Blomberg) and partly to his industriousness. He had little imagination or intellectual power and seldom took a decision on his own. By his fervent Nazi attitude and admiration for Hitler, Keitel led the army astray—he neglected to exploit his titular power as chief of the OKW and allowed the strategic direction of the war to pass unquestioned into Hitler's hand.

Keitel was born near Brunswick on August 22, 1882. After his final examination at secondary school in 1901, he decided to become an army officer. During World War I, he served as a captain, mainly in General Staff positions. At the same rank, he entered the Reichswehr in 1919, and he served in various command and staff assignments until 1929. From 1929 through 1933, he commanded the Department of Army Organization, which determined the structures of what was

Field Marshal Keitel signing unconditional surrender documents. Berlin, May 9, 1945. Courtesy of Inter Nationes, Bonn.

later to be the Wehrmacht. In 1935, he was appointed head of the Wehrmacht Bureau (Wehrmachtsamt) within the Department of War, which later became the OKW.

During the Blomberg-Fritsch Incident of 1938, Hitler made himself commander-in-chief of the Wehrmacht. No new secretary of war was appointed. Instead, Hitler created the OKW and made Keitel its chief. Keitel was now charged with the leadership of the Wehrmacht as well as with administrative duties formerly performed by the secretary of war. But in this position Keitel had no authority of command, so he was completely dependent on Hitler.

Keitel assisted Hitler in a fashion that far exceeded traditional military loyalty. Any dispute between Hitler and his generals would see Keitel on the Führer's side. His servile obedience involved him in major war crimes. As a close adviser, he was involved in all major decisions. Due to his unwillingness to contradict Hitler, Keitel was disliked by most generals. However, his servility earned him swift promotion (colonel-general, 1938; field marshal, 1940).

On May 9, 1945, Keitel signed Germany's unconditional surrender in Berlin. Five days later, he was arrested by the Allies and charged with war crimes before the Nuremberg Military Tribunal. He was hanged on October 16, 1946.

Klaus Schönherr

See also Blomberg, Werner von; Hitler, Adolf; Jodl, Alfred; National Socialist Germany: Military; Nazi War Crimes Trials and Investigations; Nuremberg Trials; Weimar Germany: Army; World War I; World War II

References

Brett-Smith, Richard. *Hitler's Generals.* San Rafael, CA: Presidio Press, 1976.

Görlitz, Walter, ed. *Generalfeldmarschall Keitel: Verbrecher oder Offizier? Erinnerungen, Briefe, Dokumente des Chefs des Oberkommandos der Wehrmacht.* Göttingen: Musterschmidt, 1961.

Moll, Otto E. *Die deutschen Generalfeldmarschälle 1935–1945.* Ed. E. Marck. Rastatt: Pabel, 1961.

Mueller, Gene Albert. *Wilhelm Keitel: Chief of the Oberkommando der Wehrmacht 1938–1945.* Ann Arbor, MI: University Microfilms International, 1978.

Kekulé, August (1829–96)

Friedrich August Kekulé (ennobled as Kekule [sic] von Stradonitz in 1895), the most influential German theoretical organic chemist of the mid-nineteenth century, was best known for formulating the six-membered ring structure of the key aromatic compound benzene (1865).

Born in Darmstadt, Kekulé obtained his doctorate (1852) in Giessen and went on to assistantships in Zürich and London before beginning his academic career as *Privatdozent* (private lecturer) in Heidelberg (1856). Earlier work with Charles Gerhardt in Paris and contact with A.W. Williamson in London had brought him into the most advanced French-English theoretical debates over chemical structure, to which he became a leading contributor in Heidelberg and as full professor in Ghent, Belgium (1860–67). In dynamic lectures and the early parts of his massive *Lehrbuch der organischen Chemie* (Textbook of organic chemistry), 1859–67, as well as at the first international congress of chemists in Karlsruhe, organized by Kekulé and his allies (1861), he set forth the newest ideas on the classification and structure of carbon compounds. His vision that carbon atoms could form chains and ultimately the benzene ring, and that the valence linkages between all the atoms in a compound could be represented by structural formulae, provided crucial tools to organic chemists.

After August Wilhelm von Hofmann (1818–92) exchanged his professorship in Bonn for Berlin, Kekulé took the post and occupied the large new institute that had been built for Hofmann (1867). At the same time, a consensus in favor of the new structural chemistry was emerging, especially among younger German organic chemists who saw Kekulé as their chief authority. Supported by an able research group, Kekulé refined his benzene theory and synthesized triphenylmethane and anthraquinone (1869–72), thereby stimulating innovation in the growing German aniline dye industry for which these were key structural components.

After 1874, Kekulé lost his leadership to others, his energy drained by health problems and a troubled second marriage (his first wife had died after giving birth to his son Stephan in 1863). Kekulé never completed his text and published only ten more papers. His colleagues remembered the twenty-fifth anniversary of his benzene theory with a gala celebration in Berlin (1890). There, in a speech still debated by historians, he recalled the visions that had led him to the benzene ring.

More than anyone else, Kekulé presented structural organic chemistry in a form accessible to his German colleagues, thus laying the intellectual foundations for their emergence as world leaders in this discipline.

Jeffrey A. Johnson

See also Chemistry, Scientific and Industrial; Hofmann, Wilhelm von

References

Benfey, Otto Theodor, ed. *Kekulé Centennial.* Washington, DC: American Chemical Society, 1966.

Rocke, Alan J. *The Quiet Revolution: Hermann Kolbe and the Science of Organic Chemistry.* Berkeley, CA: University of California Press, 1993.

Wotiz, John H., ed. *The Kekulé Riddle: A Challenge for Chemists and Psychologists.* Clearwater, FL: Cache River Press, 1993.

Kelly, Petra (1947–92)

Petra Kelly was the most internationally prominent politician and activist of the West German Green Party from its founding in 1979 until its unsuccessful bid for election to the united German national parliament in December 1990. She was one of three spokespersons for the party's executive committee (1980–82) and a member of the Green parliamentary group's executive committee (1983–84). Kelly was the sole parliamentary deputy to represent the Green Party from their first national parliamentary success in 1983 through 1990. This long tenure was facilitated by her exemption from the rotation principle of the party, whereby all Green deputies were to rotate their posts halfway through the legislative period.

In the early 1980s, Kelly promoted the idealistic positions of the 1970s' antinuclear, pacifist, feminist, and environmentalist nonviolent protest movements that had formed the core of the early party. She also stressed the anti-party, grassroots social-movement nature of the party's origins in her acts of civil disobedience, particularly in response to the planned stationing of American cruise missiles in West Germany. Later she came to stress the global issues of human rights, social justice, fair treatment for the peoples of the Third World, international relations based on the encouragement of grassroots democratic movements, and nuclear and conventional disarmament. She was awarded the Alternative Nobel Peace Prize in 1982 and the Woman of the Year Prize in 1983 by Women Strike for Peace, a United States women's peace organization.

Kelly was born on November 29, 1947, in Günzburg, where she attended a Catholic girls' boarding school until the age of 13. Because of her mother's marriage to an American military officer, Kelly spent the next ten years in the United States. She became active in the civil rights, women's, and anti-Vietnam War movements while studying political science at the American University in Washington, DC. Returning to Europe in 1970, Kelly received her M.A. from the University of Amsterdam (1971). She worked as the only woman political administrator with the Economic and Social Committee of the European Economic Community from 1972 until 1983. After her ten-year-old sister died of cancer in 1970, Kelly founded a children's cancer research society and became so involved in antinuclear and alternative-health issues that she helped to found the Green Party.

Within the Green Party, Kelly steadfastly rejected any political coalition with the Social Democratic Party (SPD) because of her fear of the cooptation of Green principles. When the party factionalized in the mid-1980s, Kelly refused to align herself with either the so-called fundamentalist faction, which she saw as too dogmatic, or the so-called realistic faction, which she regarded as too willing to compromise Green ideals and join in coalitions for the sake of the traditional power politics she firmly rejected.

From the mid-1980s, Kelly came to have less influence within the party and in German politics in general, but she continued to be deemed the foremost representative of the Greens internationally. She continued to dedicate her life, often to the point of sheer exhaustion, to her own view of the Greens' principles of nonviolent, grassroots democratic change. After her Bavarian district voted to restrict Green candidates from serving for more than two legislative periods in 1989, Kelly could not run in 1990 for re-election. But she had been designated as one of the Green candidates for the 1994 European Parliament elections shortly before her mysterious death, together with her longtime companion, Gerd Bastian, in October 1992.

Rebecca Boehling

See also American-German Relations; Disarmament; Ecology; Federal Republic of Germany; Feminism in the Federal Republic; The Greens: Movement, Party, Ideology; Pacifism and the Peace Movement; Parties and Politics

References

Kelly, Petra Karin. *Fighting for Hope*. Trans. Marianne Howarth. London: Hogarth Press, 1984. Translation of *Um Hoffnung kämpfen: Gewaltfrei in eine grüne Zukunft* (1983).

———. *Mit dem Herzen denken: Texte für eine glaubwürdige Politik*. Munich: C.H. Beck, 1990.

———. *Nonviolence Speaks to Power*. Honolulu, HI: Spark M. Matsunaga Institute for Peace, 1992.

Kelly, Petra Karin, and Gerd Bastian. *Plädoyer für Tibet: Mahnung an Politiker und Intellektuelle*. Stuttgart: A. Tykve, 1992.

Parkin, Sara. *The Life and Death of Petra Kelly*. London: Harper, 1994.

Sperr, Monika. *Petra Karin Kelly: Politikerin aus Betroffenheit*. Munich: C. Bertelsmann, 1983.

Kempowski, Walter (1929–)

Walter Kempowski is the author of dozens of children's books, radio plays, television films and novels. His work has a strong central focus: it documents the lives of ordinary individuals engaged with the tribulations of the twentieth century. His "meganovel," *Die deutsche Chronik* (The German chronicle), traces the history of the Kempowski family, paralleling the history of Germany, Europe, and the world, from the beginning of the century to 1984 (with one more novel projected to round out the century).

Kempowski's works consist of seven novels and three "factual books" (*Sachbücher*), containing hundreds of answers by contemporaries to Kempowski's pointed questions, e.g., "Did you ever see Hitler?" "Did you know about the concentration camps?" and "What are your memories of your schooldays (did school prepare you to live in a democratic society)?"

These works are buttressed by items from his enormous private archive of diaries, photo albums, autobiographies, common objects of the period, and letters, which is stored in his house, especially constructed for the purpose. They range from the perspective of a farm wife on the rise of Fascism and the Holocaust to that of a German officer captured by Soviet troops on the eastern front to that of a young American bomber crewman shot down in an air raid over Germany and imprisoned in Stalag 17.

The inverse complement of the grand structural scale of Kempowski's macroscopic "meganovel" is the unusual microscopic style in which it is written. He writes in small blocks of prose, like verbal snapshots on the pages of photo albums, all seemingly unconnected slices of streams of consciousness. The author himself refrains almost entirely from commentary and symbolism in the conventional sense. Only in the juxtaposition of the snapshots, in recurring motifs and language patterns such as idioms and the titles of popular songs and films, in an extremely complex tapestry of microsymbolic "red threads" that emerge on occasion in proximity to each other after the fashion of a kaleidoscope, does he invest the works with symbolic meaning.

Das Echolot (Echo or sonar sounding), a "collective diary" of January and February 1943, covers a mere two months in four volumes, including 3,000 pages of original letters, diary entries, communiqués, and obituaries, ranging from those of Hitler, Stalin, Churchill, and Roosevelt to housewives, Holocaust victims and wounded infantrymen. Kempowski is working on a second "Echolot" of equal or greater size.

Walter Kempowski grew up as the third child in a relatively well-to-do family of shipowners in the port city of Rostock. After the death of his father on the eastern front in World War II and the Russian occupation of Rostock, 16-year-old Walter acquired some bills of lading from his older brother, who had continued to work in the shipping business, and took them to Wiesbaden, in the American zone, where he contacted the American Counter Intelligence Corps (CIC), the precursor of the CIA. He hoped to get their help in finding a job and a place to live. In return, his documents demonstrated the extent to which the Soviet occupation forces were systematically dismantling and shipping to Russia German industrial plants and machine tools.

When he returned home to Rostock for a visit, he was arrested by the Soviets, along with his brother and his mother, charged with espionage, and sentenced to 25 years in prison. He was released during an "amnesty" after eight years. He went to West Germany, attended university, and became an elementary-school teacher.

The account of his imprisonment became the tip of the literary monolith yet to come, *The German Chronicle*, and it was the beginning of a great, mnemonic life's work.

Alan Keele

See also Federal Republic of Germany: Literature; Memory, Collective

References
Drews, Jörg, and Charlotte Heinritz. *Walter Kempowski zum 60. Geburtstag.* Munich: Albrecht Knaus Verlag, 1989.
Fischer, André. *Inszenierte Naivität: zur ästhetischen Simulation von Geschichte by Günter Grass, Albert Drach und Walter Kempowski.* Munich: W. Fink, 1992.

Ketteler, Wilhelm Emmanuel von (1811–77)
Born into a Westphalian noble family, Wilhelm Ketteler studied law at the universities of Göttingen (where he lost the tip of his nose in a student duel), Berlin, Heidelberg, and Munich. In 1833, he entered the legal department of the Prussian civil service. Whatever prospects he might have had in a bureaucratic career were abruptly terminated when in 1838 he resigned his position in protest against Prussia's arrest and incarceration of the Archbishop of Cologne during the *Kölner Wirren*, a church-state dispute over the religious education of children from mixed marriages. Estranged from his old profession, Ketteler turned instead to an ecclesiastical career. Following the completion of his theo-

logical training in Munich and his ordination at age 33, he served as chaplain in Beckum (1844–46), pastor in Hopsten (1847–49), and dean of St. Hedwig's church in Berlin (1849–50). In 1850 he was named Bishop of Mainz, a post he held until his death in 1877.

As one of the leading Catholic churchmen in nineteenth-century Germany, Ketteler wielded enormous influence among his coreligionists. That power owed something to his command of the political process and the strength of his character. He was a delegate to the Frankfurt Assembly in 1848, a Reichstag deputy from 1871 to 1872, and a pleader for the church's interests with Chancellor Otto von Bismarck himself. Ketteler also appreciated that persuasion and public opinion were the ingredients of success in ecclesiastical politics and church diplomacy. Nowhere was this understanding more evident than in his political writing. Ketteler was a prodigious author and publicist, unrivaled among his German episcopal colleagues in the volume of his literary output and in the breadth of his interests. His writings ranged from a defense of the Jesuits to an appeal to his coreligionists to accommodate themselves to the seismic political shifts caused by Prussia's victory over Austria in the Seven Weeks' War, and from protests against the *Kulturkampf* and calls for passive resistance to criticism of Adalbert Falk (1827–1900), Prussia's minister of ecclesiastical affairs and the official most responsible for the enforcement of Bismarck's church policies. Even when these writings sometimes suffered from weaknesses of argument, lack of tact, or carelessness, their force remained undiminished because of Ketteler's courage, grit, and determination together with his reputation for personal integrity.

Ketteler's influence and prominence, however, owed most to his ability to shape the social conscience of his church and its adherents. In *Die Arbeiterfrage und das Christentum* (The labor question and Christianity), 1864, together with other pronouncements, he criticized the extremes of poverty and wealth associated with capitalism. To close that gap and to ameliorate Germany's social problems, Ketteler advocated worker cooperatives, Christian trade unions, and various forms of self-help. His calls for social justice earned Ketteler numerous encomiums, even the appellation of "worker bishop."

Ronald J. Ross

See also Bismarck, Otto von; Catholicism, Political; Center Party; Christian Trade Unions; Falk, Adalbert; *Kulturkampf*; Roman Catholic Church; Working Conditions

References
Birke, Adolf M. *Bischof Ketteler und der deutsche Liberalismus: Eine Untersuchung über das Verhältnis des liberalen Katholizismus zum bürgerlichen Liberalismus in der Reichsgründungszeit.* Mainz: Matthias Grünewald Verlag, 1971.
Ketteler, Wilhelm Emmanuel von. *Hirtenbriefe.* Ed. Joh. Michael Raich. Mainz: Druckerei Lehrlingshaus, 1904.
Lenhart, Ludwig. *Bischof Ketteler.* 3 vols. Mainz: Hase u. Koehler, 1966–68.

Mumbauer, Johannes, ed. *Wilhelm Emmanuel von Kettelers Schriften*. 3 vols. Kempten: Verlag der Jos. Kösel'schen Buchhandlung, 1911.

Pfülf, Otto. *Bischof von Ketteler (1811–1877): Eine geschichtliche Darstellung*. 3 vols. Mainz: Verlag von Franz Kirchheim, 1899.

Raich, J.M., ed. *Briefe von und an Wilhelm Emmanuel Freiherr von Ketteler, Bischof von Mainz*. Mainz: Verlag von Franz Kirchheim, 1879.

———. *Predigten des Hochwürdigsten Herrn Wilhelm Emmanuel Freiherrn v. Ketteler, Bischof von Mainz*. 2 vols. Mainz: Verlag von Franz Kirchheim, 1878.

Vigener, Fritz. *Ketteler: Ein deutsches Bischofsleben des 19. Jahrhunderts*. Munich: R. Oldenbourg, 1924.

Keyboard Music

From late nineteenth century, the keyboard largely used in solo works has been the piano, although the organ and other keyboard instruments have occasionally been used as well. The piano was also often used in orchestral and chamber music. The style of the romantic, postromantic, and modern periods was governed by two major factors. The composer was generally a pianist who performed before audiences who were insatiable for new works. This was a corollary of the profession of touring pianist made popular by Franz Liszt (1811–86). Works involving more than one pianist (whether at a single keyboard or separate ones) were by no means as common, because they involved cooperation between equals that was ill-suited to the cult of the soloist. An increasing popularity of keyboard transcriptions of operas, symphonies and other works originally written for voice or orchestra may be considered a form of popularization and education in which the participants usually did not work alone. The most common form of such transcriptions was the piano duet.

There was much diversity in the forms of works purposely written for the piano; while the sonata promulgated by Mozart, Haydn, and Beethoven remained in frequent use by composers such as Hans Bronsart von Schellendorf and his wife Ingeborg (both of whom had been students of Liszt and, in her case, Adolf von Henselt as well), the scope of such works was greatly expanded almost to symphonic proportions, and the number of compositions in this form diminished proportionately.

Individual character pieces, first exploited by Felix Mendelssohn and Robert Schumann, were increasingly favored over sonatas because they could be adapted in form depending on possible extramusical influences. However, not all such works were based on tone painting of literary or artistic works. Established forms dating back as far as the baroque period (including toccatas, fugues, and variations) remained the backbone of keyboard works written by composers who favored absolute music during the Romantic period and continued into the twentieth century, when neoclassicism affected composers such as Paul Hindemith (1895–1963); they were embraced by the Second Viennese School in the revolt against giganticism. However, works based on literary models became increasingly inventive in their solutions of problems of form, because the composers were ready to modify form in order to accommodate dramatic consideration of the programmatic basis for such works. Sometimes a work was given an extramusical title to conceal the use of an established form.

There were some instances of multimovement cycles that were not classifiable as sonatas, suites for example. Even in such works, however unclassifiable outwardly, the composers were influenced by extramusical factors (including visual art and literature) more than they publicly acknowledged.

Transcriptions of works originally written for other performing media fell into two general categories. The first was concerned with popularization in public performances. Virtuoso pianists chose a recognizeable melody (from an opera or other such work) and reworked the material into showcases for use in concert. Most such compositions were recognizably in the theme-and-variations form even when they were given titles like "Concert Fantasy," and they proved popular with audiences. They were, however, a phenomenon of the nineteenth century, and lost favor in the twentieth—except in a few cases.

The transcription of serious concert works for orchestra into piano duets and other forms (occasionally solos) was most often for educational purposes at universities and conservatories, or occasionally for entertainment at home. These works were rarely performed in public, a curious phenomenon because many had no deletions and were therefore quite demanding for the performers. Easier piano solo material was introduced in anthologies such as *Musik für Alle* that were meant for entertainment at home; such collections included transcriptions of songs and arias and occasional sections of movements from symphonic works.

Many transcriptions were made at the publishing houses by staff employees, whose names are not recognizable today. However, in a surprising number of cases the names of the transcriptionists are quite familiar. The most striking example was Johannes Brahms' (1833–97) own transcription of his four symphonies. In the case of the symphonies of Gustav Mahler (1860–1911), transcriptionists were usually answerable directly to him in the course of the publication process; among those working on such projects were Alexander von Zemlinsky (1871–1942), Bruno Walter (1876–1962), Alfredo Casella (1883–1947), and, after Mahler's death, Alban Berg (1885–1935).

The popularity of this form of keyboard music continued for several decades into the twentieth century, until it was supplanted in terms of educational technique by the increasing availability of recordings, in which the composer's original work could be heard as he had written it. By that time, the piano transcription had lost its use even as a source of revenue for publishers.

Susan M. Filler

See also Chamber Music; Choral Music; Composers; Conductors; National Socialist Germany: Music; Orchestral Music

References

Dale, Kathleen. *Nineteenth Century Piano Music*. New York, NY: Da Capo Press, 1972.

Gillespie, John. *Five Centuries of Keyboard Music: An Historical Survey of Music for Harpsichord and Piano.* New York, NY: Dover Publications, 1972.

Kirby, Frank E. *A Short History of Keyboard Music.* New York, NY: Free Press, 1966.

Wolf, Henry S. "The Twentieth Century Piano Sonata." Unpublished doctoral dissertation. Boston University, 1957.

Kiderlen-Wächter, Alfred von (1852–1912)

Alfred von Kiderlen-Wächter played a major role in Imperial Germany's prewar diplomacy. The son of a Stuttgart banker, he received a hereditary title of nobility from the King of Württemberg in 1868 and participated in the Franco-Prussian War two years later. After completing the study of law, Kiderlen-Wächter joined the German diplomatic service in 1879. He subsequently represented his government in St. Petersburg, Paris, and Constantinople and acted as a Middle East specialist in the Foreign Office. Energetic and outspoken, he frequently accompanied Kaiser Wilhelm II on his cruises during the 1890s but eventually incurred the monarch's wrath by his barbed comments at the expense of the Imperial court. In 1899, the irreverent Swabian was therefore "banished" to the Bucharest legation, where he remained (with some important interruptions) until 1910.

Toward the end of Bülow's chancellorship, in the fall of 1908, Kiderlen-Wächter was brought to Berlin to manage the Foreign Office during the illness of Wilhelm von Schoen. Although the latter was able to resume his duties as state secretary in December 1908, Kiderlen-Wächter stayed on in Berlin until the following April and, in fact, played a key role in the settlement of the Bosnian Crisis. Despite the Kaiser's continued misgivings about Kiderlen-Wächter's personality and manners, Chancellor Theobald von Bethmann Hollweg (1856–1921) persuaded the monarch in June 1910 that the abrasive Swabian should be appointed state secretary. Kiderlen-Wächter presided over the Foreign Office until December 30, 1912, when he was felled without warning by a stroke.

Kiderlen-Wächter's accomplishments are a matter of scholarly controversy. Some have regarded him as the premier German diplomatist after Bismarck, but many others have taken a dim view of his performance, calling him unnecessarily ruthless and inclined to bluster and swagger. It seems clear that in the last phases of his career he favored a rapprochement with Great Britain and France but also believed that Germany must act "firmly" in order to improve her standing as a great power. This prompted him to advocate a hard line toward Russia during the Bosnian Crisis of 1908–09 and to use a muscular gesture, the dispatch of the gunboat *Panther* to Agadir, two years later. Whether he would have performed more effectively in 1914 than Gottlieb von Jagow, his successor in the Foreign Office, is anyone's guess, but his record between 1908 and 1912 suggests that under his management the July Crisis might have led to hostilities even sooner.

Ulrich Trumpener

See also Anglo-German Relations; Austro-German Relations; Bülow, Bernhard von; Diplomatic Corps and Diplomacy; Franco-German Relations; Imperial Germany: Foreign Policy; Russian-German Relations; *Weltpolitik*

References
Cecil, Lamar. *The German Diplomatic Service, 1871–1914.* Princeton, NJ: Princeton University Press, 1976.

Fischer, Fritz. *Krieg der Illusionen: Die deutsche Politik von 1911 bis 1914.* Düsseldorf: Droste, 1969.

Hull, Isabel V. *The Entourage of Kaiser Wilhelm II, 1888–1918.* Cambridge, MA: Cambridge University Press, 1982.

Jäckh, Ernst, ed. *Kiderlen-Wächter, der Staatsmann und Mensch: Briefwechsel und Nachlass.* 2 vols. Berlin: Deutsche Verlagsanstalt, 1925.

Jarausch, Konrad. *The Enigmatic Chancellor: Bethmann Hollweg and the Hubris of Imperial Germany.* New Haven, CT: Yale University Press, 1973.

Nichols, J. Alden. *Germany after Bismarck: The Caprivi Era 1890–1894.* Cambridge, MA: Harvard University Press, 1958.

Rich, Norman. *Friedrich von Holstein: Politics and Diplomacy in the Era of Bismarck and Wilhelm II.* 2 vols. Cambridge, UK: Cambridge University Press, 1965.

Vietsch, Eberhard von. *Bethmann Hollweg: Staatsmann zwischen Macht und Ethos.* Boppard: Harald Boldt, 1969.

Kiefer, Anselm (1945–)

Anselm Kiefer has succeeded more than any other contemporary artist in challenging the myths and taboos surrounding Germany's recent past. Since the early 1970s, his monumental paintings, sculptures, and unique, hand-made books have confronted the ways in which memory and history are constructed in the post-Nazi era.

Kiefer studied painting in Freiburg (1966–68) and Karlsruhe (1969) before coming under the influence of the conceptual artist Joseph Beuys (1921–86) in Düsseldorf in 1970. By this time, Kiefer had already shocked the German public with a series of photographs entitled *Occupations* (1969), which depict the artist himself with his arm raised in the Fascist salute in different locales in France, Italy and Switzerland, a series that prompted many to accuse Kiefer of being a neo-Nazi.

After his move to Hornbach in the Odenwald in 1971, Kiefer continued to be interested in the volatility of German legends, writers and symbols. The mythical spirit of the German landscape, including the oak forest and the March Sands of Brandenburg, he treats in unique artists' books and paintings, such as *March Heath* (1974), in which fire threatens to destroy an already charred and mutilated earth. The legends of the *Niebelungen* and the *Edda*, Richard Wagner's *Meistersinger*, and Goethe's *Faust*, aspects of German culture adopted by the Nazis to celebrate German nationalism, are recalled in large-scale paintings of oil, lead, straw, and woodcut, exposing the vulnerability of their foundations as cultural constructs. In the 1980s, Kiefer turned to sources outside the German pantheon, such as Jewish mysticism, the poems of the German-Romanian Jew Paul Celan (1920–70), and the writings of Dionysius the Areopagite, a first-century Greek convert to Christianity, in order to broaden his view of human beings' interpretation of history and creation. Many of these paintings, including *Shulamith* (1983) and *The Order of Angels* (1983–84), gain additional potency with their references to gas chambers and nuclear holocaust.

Since 1969, Kiefer has created unique artists' books that use photographs of Kiefer's studio or woodcuts of the Rhine River to show the diachronic nature of myth and experience. By 1980, the image of a book as sign was elevated to a central position in the artist's oeuvre in works such as *The Book* (1979–85) and *The Breaking of the Vessels* (1990), a monumental bookshelf made of lead, copper wire, and broken glass based on the myths of creation from the Jewish cabala. Along with the ubiquitous image of the winged artist's palette, books in Kiefer's oeuvre point to the importance of the artist, culture, and language in shedding light on ways we reconfigure the world and give it meaning.

In 1980, Kiefer exhibited in the West German Pavilion at the Venice *Biennale*, provoking hostility from many who believed that his images dealt too closely with volatile issues of German nationalism. The United States and the international community embraced Kiefer in the 1980s, but he was virtually shunned by the German establishment from 1984 to 1990, when a retrospective of his books was mounted in Stuttgart. Kiefer has lived in southwestern France since 1991.

Kristin Makholm

See also Artists; Beuys, Joseph; Celan, Paul; Holocaust; Memory, Collective; Mythology; National Identity; National Socialist Germany; Painting; Symbolism

References

Adriani, Götz, ed. *The Books of Anselm Kiefer, 1969–1990*. Trans. Bruni Mayor. New York, NY: George Braziller, 1991.

Haxthausen, Charles W. "Kiefer in America: Reflections on a Retrospective." *Kunstchronik* 42 (January 1989), 1–16.
——————. "The World, the Book, and Anselm Kiefer." *Burlington Magazine* 133 (December 1991), 846–51.

Huyssen, Andreas. "Anselm Kiefer: The Terror of History, and the Temptation of Myth." *October* 48 (Spring 1989), 25–45.

Rosenthal, Mark. *Anselm Kiefer*. Exhibition catalog. The Art Institute of Chicago and Philadelphia Museum of Art. Munich: Prestel-Verlag, 1987.

Schjeldahl, Peter. "Our Kiefer." *Art in America* 76 (March 1988), 116–27.

Kiesinger, Kurt Georg (1904–88)

Kurt Georg Kiesinger's political career began in the Swabian Christian Democratic Union (CDU) in 1947. From 1949 until 1958, he served as a member of the Bundestag. When he was not appointed foreign minister in the Adenauer cabi-

Portrait of Kurt Georg Kiesinger by Günther Rittner. Courtesy of German Information Center, New York.

net formed after the 1957 elections, Kiesinger returned to *Land* (state) politics as minister-president of Baden-Württemberg. His return to national prominence in 1966 was made possible by the crisis within the governing coalition that led to the fall of Ludwig Erhard (1897–1977). In the CDU leadership contest against Gerhard Schröder (1910–89) and Rainer Barzel (1924–), Kiesinger won by advocating a Grand Coalition. He then assumed the chancellorship of the first federal CDU-SPD (Social Democratic Party) coalition, which lasted from 1966 to 1969.

As chancellor during this exceptional era, Kiesinger had his political control limited by the balance of power within the coalition, where the CDU/CSU (Christian Social Union) held ten cabinet positions, while the SPD claimed nine. Kiesinger had to govern through a delicate process of elite bargaining and compromise that was institutionalized in the weekly meeting of top ministers from the CDU/CSU and SPD known as the Kressbronn Circle.

Kiesinger contributed significantly to the establishment of *Ostpolitik*, a new direction in foreign policy based on a reduction of tensions with East Germany and a reconciliation with the Soviet Union and Eastern Europe. These initiatives amounted to an implicit abandonment of the Hallstein Doctrine of nonrecognition, although Kiesinger continued to oppose full recognition for East Germany.

Kiesinger was subject to harsh criticism for having joined the Nazi Party in 1933, but this nominal membership did not damage his popularity as chancellor. He stood as CDU/CSU chancellor candidate in 1969 against Willy Brandt (1913–92) and left office following the formation of an SPD–FDP (Free Democratic Party) coalition.

In part because he was overshadowed in public opinion by the popular SPD leaders Brandt and Karl Schiller (1911–95), Kiesinger remains the least known of West Germany's postwar chancellors, despite the fact that he presided over a unique transition period and played a crucial role during a time of substantial policy innovation.

William M. Chandler

See also Baden-Württemberg; Brandt, Willy; Chancellor's Office; Christian Democratic Union; Erhard, Ludwig; Grand Coalition; *Ostpolitik*

References

Bark, Dennis L., and David R. Gress. *Democracy and Its Discontents: A History of West Germany.* 2nd ed. Vol. 2. Oxford: Blackwell, 1993.

Hancock, Donald. *West Germany, the Politics of Democratic Corporatism.* Chatham: Chatham House, 1989.

Mintzel, Alf, and Heinrich Oberreuter. *Parteien in der Bundesrepublik Deutschland.* 2nd ed. Opladen: Leske & Budrich, 1992.

Rudzio, Wolfgang. *Das politische System der Bundesrepublik Deutschland.* 3rd ed. Opladen: Leske & Budrich, 1991.

Kirchner, Ernst Ludwig (1880–1938)

The painter, graphic artist, and sculptor Ernst Kirchner, was born on May 6, 1880 in Aschaffenburg and died on June 15, 1938 in Frauenkirch bei Davos by suicide. Kirchner was the most important artist and leader of early expressionism's first artistic group, the Bridge.

After completing high school in Chemnitz in 1901, Kirchner enrolled at the *Technische Hochschule* (Technical Academy) in Dresden to study architecture. He transfered to Munich (1903–04) and studied with Wilhelm von Debschitz and Hermann Obrist, but returned to Dresden in 1904. He decided to become a painter, and on June 7, 1905 he formed, with his friends Erich Heckel (1883–1970), Fritz Bleyl, and Karl Schmidt-Rottluff (1884–1976) (all architecture students), the *Künstlergruppe Brücke* ("artist group bridge"). Working in various storefront studios, the group gained (for some time) Emil Nolde (1867–1956), Curt Amiet, Max Pechstein (1881–1955), Akseli Gallen-Kallela, and Otto Mueller as members. For a fee, they offered a yearly graphics portfolio to "passive members." The friends painted their models as nudes in motion at the Moritzburg Lakes near Dresden and at the shores of the Baltic Sea.

Bridge members had their first exhibitions during 1907 in Leipzig and Dresden. After some visits to Berlin (where he saw a Matisse and a Cézanne exhibit), Kirchner moved to Berlin and founded with Max Pechstein a short-lived art school (MUIM-Institut). In 1912, he created with Erich Heckel wall paintings for the chapel at the Sonderbund-Ausstellung in Cologne; the group exhibited graphic works in the second exhibition of *Der Blaue Reiter* (The Blue Rider) in Munich. Kirchner's first one-man exhibitions were held in

1913 at the Folkwang Museum, Hagen, and the Gurlitt Gallery in Berlin and in 1914 at the Kunstverein (Art Association) in Jena. His chronicle of the *Brücke* caused the dissolution of the group in 1913.

Kirchner's dependence on narcotics during military service led to a nervous breakdown and periods at sanatoriums in Königstein (1916) and Berlin. After his release from military service in 1917, Kirchner moved to Davos, Switzerland. After a further stay at a sanatorium in Kreuzlingen, he moved to the Stafelalb near Frauenkirch, where he—as he had done in Dresden and Berlin—sculpted his own furniture. In 1921, 50 of his works were exhibited at the Kronzprinzen Palais in Berlin (Department of Modern Art of the National Gallery). A retrospective exhibition of his work was held in 1923 at the Kunsthalle (Art Gallery) in Basel. Dr. Gustav Schiefler prepared the graphic oeuvre catalogue. At this time Kirchner moved into a large farmhouse at Wildboden near Frauenkirch. In 1924, a large-scale exhibition was held at Winterthur and in 1925 at the Schames Gallery in Frankfurt. The museum in Bern showed a large exhibition of his works in 1933. After 1935, Kirchner suffered from recurring intestinal cancer and nervous conditions (partly because of the news from Nazi Germany) and began to depend on medications again. Wilhelm R. Valentiner organized the first large Kirchner exhibition at the Art Institute of Detroit (January 1937), and in the same year the Nazis confiscated 639 of his works and exhibited 32 of them in the *Degenerate Art* exhibition in Munich. Kirchner began to destroy a number of his works, and on June 15, 1938, he committed suicide.

Peter Guenther

See also Artist; *Blaue Reiter*; Exhibitions; Expressionism (Visual Arts); Heckel, Erich; Museums; National Socialist Germany: Art; Nolde, Emil; Painting; Pechstein, Max; Schmidt-Rottluff, Karl; Sculpture

References

Dube, Annemarie, and Wolf-Dieter Dube. *Ernst Ludwig Kirchner, das graphische Werk.* 2 vols. Munich: Prestel Verlag, 1967.

Gordon, D.E. *Ernst Ludwig Kirchner, with a Critical Catalogue of All Paintings.* Munich: Prestel Verlag, 1968.

Kornfeld, Eberhard. *Ernst Ludwig Kirchner, Nachzeichnung seines Lebens.* Bern: Verlag Kornfeld & Co., 1979.

Löfler, Fritz. *Ernst Ludwig Kirchner: Oeuvre der Gemälde.* Recklinghausen: Verlag Aurel Bongers, 1981.

Kirsch, Sarah (Ingrid Bernstein) (1935–)

Born to working-class parents in 1935, Ingrid Bernstein changed her name to Sarah as a young woman in order to demonstrate solidarity with Jews who perished in the Holocaust. Trained as a biologist at the East German University of Halle, she married the poet Rainer Kirsch and joined a circle of young writers around the critic Gerhard Wolf. Her first publications, children's literature and a volume of poetry (*Gespräch mit dem Saurier* [Discussion with the saurier], 1965), were written in collaboration with her husband. Like many contemporary writers, Kirsch attempted to pursue the officially promulgated ideal of solidarity between writers and workers ("Bitterfelder Weg" [Bitterfeld path]) through experiences in industry and agriculture, but her writing has always reflected much more attention to details of nature, her personal landscape, and interpersonal relationships. Recognition of her talent led to admission to the Johannes R. Becher Institute for Literature in Leipzig and association of her name with the so-called Sächsische Dichterschule (Saxon School of Poets) of controversial poets emerging from Saxony. Her first independent volume of poetry, *Landaufenthalt* (Country visit), appeared in 1967.

Newly divorced, she moved to East Berlin in 1968, where in addition to poetry (*Zaubersprüche* [published as *Conjurations*, 1985], 1973, and *Rückenwind* [Tailwind], 1976), she began to publish prose that focused on the lives of women in East Germany. *Die Pantherfrau: Fünf unfrisierte Erzählungen aus dem Kassetten-Recorder* (published as *The Panther Woman: Five Unadorned Tales from the Cassette Recorder*, 1989], 1973, commissioned as a documentary for the "Year of the Woman," employed the very words of her subjects to confront the contradictions and problems of women who, like the *dompteuse* (trainer) of the title, were typical only in being untypical. *Die ungeheuren bergehohen Wellen auf See* (The monstrous mountainous waves on the sea) of the same year consists of short stories in a similarly unconventional vein. The best known of these, "*Blitz aus heiterem Himmel*" (Lightening out of the clear blue sky), a witty exploration of the improvements effected in a woman's life by a sudden sex change, became the title story of a controversial 1975 anthology of sex-change stories edited by Edith Anderson, an American resident in East Germany.

Sarah Kirsch. Courtesy of Inter Nationes, Bonn.

Political events in East Germany, particularly reprisals against writers who attempted to support Wolf Biermann in 1976, led to Kirsch's separation from the Socialist Unity Party (SED) and the Writers' Association and her decision to move to West Germany in 1977. Her next volume of poems (*Drachensteigen* [Kite-flying], 1979) reflected this break in her life as well as subsequent travels in Italy and French Provence. Later volumes of poetry drew on her experiences in the United States and West Berlin (*Erdreich* [Earthly kingdom], 1982) and her new life in rural Schleswig-Holstein (*Katzenleben* [published as *Catlives*, 1991], 1984; *Schneewärme* [Warmth of snow], 1989; and a prose volume, *Eine reizende Menagerie* [A wonderful zoo], 1994). Kirsch also published prose poems (*La Pagerie* [Pages], 1980; *Irrstern* [False star], 1986), as well as a longer narrative, *Allerlei-Rauh* (Varying coarseness), 1988. Her most recent collection, *Das simple Leben* (The simple life), 1994, reveals similar autobiographical traces. Always laconic, often ironic, increasingly bleak, her poetry is characterized by distinctive rhythms (the so-called "Sarah sound"), that derive from freely structured verses, enjambment, and a suggestive lack of punctuation. This, together with the startlingly evocative power of her sensuous, often intensely personal images, has led critics to call her the most important woman writing German poetry in the late twentieth century.

Patricia Herminghouse

See also Biermann, Wolf; Children's Literature; Feminist Writing; German Democratic Republic: Literature and Literary Life; German Democratic Republic: Women; Poetry

References

Cosentino, Christine. *"Ein Spiegel mit mir darin:" Sarah Kirschs Lyrik.* Tübingen: Francke, 1990.

Graves, Peter J., ed. *Three Contemporary German Poets: Wolf Biermann, Sarah Kirsch, Reiner Kunze.* Leicester: Leicester University Press, 1985.

Mabee, Barbara. *Die Poetik von Sarah Kirsch: Erinnerungsarbeit und Geschichtsbewusstsein.* Amsterdam: Rodopi, 1989.

Klee, Paul (1879–1940)

Although born in Switzerland, Paul Klee is primarily associated with the various manifestations of modernism that developed in Germany. Acclaimed for his oils, watercolors, and graphic works as well as his theoretical writings on art, Klee became an associate of *Der Blaue Reiter* (The Blue Rider) in 1911 and in 1921 an instructor at the Bauhaus, where he remained for ten years. He taught at the Düsseldorf Academy in 1931, but soon after the Nazi ascension to power in 1933 he left Germany permanently and settled in Bern, his birthplace.

Klee began to study art in Munich in 1898. His involvement with the tenets and practices of international modernism in the years before World War I led to his embrace of expressionism and cubism. He was concerned with uncovering elemental forms that could evoke the cosmological, and he turned to children's art and the art of the mentally ill for creative sources. At the Bauhaus, witty and ironic images, apparent in such works as *Twittering Machine* (1922) and *Fish Magic* (1925), alternated with geometrically abstract forms, evident in such works as *Architecture* (1923) and *Highroad and Byroads* (1929). He drew on both tendencies in his teaching and theoretical formulations, publishing his *Pedagogical Sketchbook* in the Bauhaus book series in 1924. The French surrealists admired his work, and during the 1930s an awareness of surrealist biomorphism emerged in his paintings. During the last years of his life, when he was ill with scleroderma, his output increased dramatically and he produced some of his major works, such as *The Key* (1938) and *Death and Fire* (1940).

Rose-Carol W. Long

See also Artists; Bauhaus; *Blaue Reiter*; Exhibitions; Expressionism (Visual Arts); Museums; National Socialist Germany: Art; Painting

References

Franciscono, Marcel. *Paul Klee: His Work and Thought*. Chicago, IL: The University of Chicago Press, 1991.

Haxthausen, C.W. *Paul Klee: The Formative Years*. New York, NY: Garland Publishing, Inc., 1981.

Klee, Felix, ed. *The Diaries of Paul Klee, 1898–1918*. Berkeley, CA: The University of California Press, 1968.

Lanchner, Carolyn, ed. *Paul Klee*. New York, NY: The Museum of Modern Art, 1987.

Werckmeister, O.K. *The Making of Paul Klee's Career, 1914–1920*. Chicago, IL: The University of Chicago Press, 1989.

Zweite, Armin, ed. *Paul Klee: Das Frühwerk, 1883–1922*. Munich: Städtische Galerie im Lenbachhaus, 1979.

Klein, Felix (1849–1925)

Mathematician Felix Klein was born and raised in Düsseldorf, the son of a Prussian civil servant. He attended Bonn University, where he studied with the geometer and physicist Julius Plucker (1801–68). Following the latter's death, Klein took his doctorate under Rudolf Lipschitz (1832–1903) at Bonn before proceeding to Göttingen. There he became closely associated with the geometrical school surrounding Alfred Clebsch (1833–72). After a brief study tour in Berlin and Paris, he returned home and volunteered for an ambulance crew during the Franco-Prussian War. He witnessed the battles at Metz and Sedan, celebrating the events that brought down Napoleon III and set the stage for the founding of the Second Reich. Like nearly all Germans of his generation, Klein remained loyal to the Kaiser throughout his life, although his nationalism was tempered by an internationalist outlook regarding scientific affairs.

Klein taught as a *Privatdozent* (private lecturer) in Göttingen until 1872, when he was appointed to a full professorship (*Ordinariat*) at Erlangen. Only 23 years of age, he presented the faculty an expository essay, the so-called Erlangen Program, that would later come to be regarded as a milestone in the history of geometry. During his early career at Erlangen, the *Technische Hochschule* (Technical University)

in Munich, and Leipzig University, Klein emerged as the most dynamic figure in German mathematics. His mathematical style, a mixture of geometry and analysis informed by *anschauliche* (graphically clear) elements, stood in sharp contrast to the methodological trends promoted by the Berlin school of mathematicians. This unusually creative period ended abruptly, however, in 1883, after Klein could no longer keep pace with the even more brilliant work of the young French mathematician Henri Poincaré (1854–1912).

Klein's career entered a new phase when he accepted a chair at Göttingen in 1886. Supported by the Prussian ministerial official Friedrich Althoff (1839–1908), Klein orchestrated a series of judicious appointments, beginning in 1895 with the brilliant Königsberg mathematician David Hilbert (1862–1943). After the turn of the century, the Göttingen faculty added Hermann Minkowski (1864–1909), Carl Runge (1856–1927), Ludwig Prandtl (1875–1953), and Edmund Landau (1877–1938) to its ranks. Göttingen emerged as the dominant mathematical center in Germany, far surpassing its traditional rival, Berlin University.

In an effort to promote technological research, Klein enlisted the support of Henry Böttinger (1848–1920) and other leading German industrialists in the founding of the Göttingen Association for the Advancement of Applied Physics. This organization, established in 1898, provided funding for a number of new institutes at Göttingen for research in applied physics and mathematics. These developments, however, drew Klein into a headlong conflict with leading representatives of the *Technische Hochschulen*. Tensions largely subsided, however, after 1899, when Wilhelm II decreed that the latter institutions would henceforth have the right to confer doctoral degrees.

Health problems forced Klein to retire in 1913, although he continued to hold private lectures afterward in his home. During World War I, he lectured on the history of modern mathematics; the lectures were published posthumously in *Vorlesungen über die Entwicklung der Mathematik im 19. Jahrhundert* (1926–27). Afterward he prepared the publication of his own scientific work, *Gesammelte Mathematische Abhandlungen* (1921–23), to which he added many personal and historical remarks. His plans to build a mathematics institute at Göttingen fell by the wayside after the war, along with the German Empire. Shortly after Klein's death, his successor, Richard Courant, obtained funding for this project from the Rockefeller Foundation. The new Göttingen Mathematical Institute, the building Klein had dreamed about for years, was dedicated in December 1929. The glory years of Göttingen mathematics, however, would soon be snuffed out with the dawning of a new Reich.

David E. Rowe

See also Althoff, Friedrich; Hilbert, David; Landau, Edmund; Mathematics; Universities; Wilhelm II

References

Klein, Felix. *Gesammelte Mathematische Abhandlungen*. 3 vols. Berlin: Springer, 1921–23.

———. *Vorlesungen über die Entwicklung der Mathematik im 19. Jahrhundert.* 2 vols. Berlin: Springer, 1926–27.

Manegold, Karl-Heinz. *Universität, Technische Hochschule und Industrie: Ein Beitrag zur Emanzipation der Technik im 19. Jahrhundert unter besonderer Berücksichtigung der Bestrebungen Felix Kleins.* Berlin: Duncker & Humblot, 1970.

Mehrtens, Herbert. *Moderne—Sprache—Mathematik.* Frankfurt am Main: Suhrkamp, 1990.

Parshall, Karen H., and David E. Rowe. *The Emergence of the American Mathematical Research Community, 1876–1900: J.J. Sylvester, Felix Klein, E.H. Moore.* Providence, RI: American Mathematical Society, 1994.

Pyenson, Lewis. *Neohumanism and the Persistence of Pure Mathematics in Wilhelmian Germany.* Memoirs of the American Philosophical Society, vol. 150. Philadelphia, PA: American Philosophical Society, 1983.

Rowe, David E. "'Jewish Mathematics' at Göttingen in the Era of Felix Klein." *Isis* 77 (1986), 422–49.

———. "Klein, Hilbert, and the Göttingen Mathematical Tradition." *Science in Germany: The Intersection of Institutional and Intellectual Issues.* Ed. Kathryn M. Olesko. *Osiris* 5 (1989), 189–213.

Tobies, Renate. *Felix Klein. Biographien hervorragender Naturwissenschaftler, Techniker und Mediziner.* Vol. 50. Leipzig: Teubner, 1981.

Kluge, Alexander (1932–)

Trained in law, professor of sociology at the University of Frankfurt, author of historical and theoretical studies as well as fiction, Alexander Kluge is also an important mentor and tireless advocate of postwar German cinema. Kluge, the media politician, initiated the 1962 Oberhausen Manifesto announcing the expectations of the German New Wave directors. Since then he has lobbied incessantly for the revision of film subsidy laws, focusing attention on the cinema beyond mass culture commodity and aesthetic avant-gardism. Kluge's continuing interest in the relationship between theory and practice became most evident in his administrative and teaching functions at the Film Institute of the Hochschule für Gestaltung in Ulm (1963–70), the first film production school in Germany.

Kluge's filmmaking is characterized by its interruptive editing and historical resonances. *Abschied von Gestern* (Yesterday girl), 1966, his first feature-length narrative film, is a loosely structured portrait of a young woman drifting through cities, jobs, petty criminality, and love affairs. Jump cuts, fast and slow motion, printed titles, and handheld tracking shots resist illusionism and invite spectators to construct the film's meaning (Kluge: "The final editing takes place in the viewer's head"). Intermingled with the fragmented narrative are historical "documents" that suggest the significance of memory but also its nonlinear quality: interviews, old photographs, a 1920s children's story, and music from the 1940s and 1950s.

Die Artisten in der Zirkuskuppel: ratlos (Artists under the big top: perplexed), 1967, radicalizes such digressions and serves as a manifesto of sorts for Kluge's convictions about the necessarily utopian nature of art. The allegorical heroine's extravagant plans to create a "reform circus" that allows animals their authenticity is a self-ironical representation of the filmmaker's dilemma, caught among the contradictions of tradition, entertainment, and state subsidies. Kluge's ongoing concern with historical representation and Germany's "work of mourning" culminated in *Die Patriotin* (The patriot), 1979. The story of Gabi Teichert, intermingled with the reflections of a "knee joint" of a dead World War II soldier, questions official versions of history while constructing almost archeologically the popular memory of the German past.

Kluge continues to explore the formal, thematic, and organizational possibilities of the visual medium in omnibus projects (e.g., the highly acclaimed film about terrorism, *Deutschland im Herbst* [Germany in autumn], 1978), documentaries, shorts, and, increasingly since 1985, television broadcasting. His subtle, witty films are full of dry humor and yet appeal to the imagination and the senses.

Marc Silberman

See also Cinema; Fassbinder, Rainer Werner; Herzog, Werner; Schlöndorff, Volker; Television; Trotta, Margarethe von

References
Arnold, Heinz Ludwig, ed. "Alexander Kluge." *Text + Kritik* 85–86 (January 1985).

Böhm-Christl, Thomas, ed. *Alexander Kluge.* Frankfurt am Main: Suhrkamp, 1983.

Fiedler, Theodore. "Alexander Kluge: Mediating History and Consciousness." *New German Filmmakers from Oberhausen Through the 1970s.* Ed. Klaus Phillips. New York: Ungar, 1984.

Hansen, Miriam. "Alexander Kluge." Special issue. *New German Critique* 49 (Winter 1990).

Lewandowski, Rainer. *Alexander Kluge.* Munich: Verlag C. H. Beck and Edition *Text + Kritik*, 1980.

———. *Die Filme von Alexander Kluge.* Hildesheim: Olms Presse, 1980.

Liebman, Stuart. "Alexander Kluge: Theoretical Writings, Stories, and an Interview." Special issue. *October* 46 (Fall 1988).

Kluge, Günther Hans von (1882–1944)

Field Marshal Günther Hans von Kluge was one of the most successful commanders on the eastern front. He was marginally involved with the plot against Adolf Hitler, but after his transfer to the western theater did not make himself available to the Resistance. He committed suicide when he had reason to fear that his involvement had been discovered.

Kluge was born into a Prussian military family and was commissioned into a field artillery regiment in 1901. He attended the War Academy and was transferred to the Prussian General Staff. During World War I, he saw service as a general staff officer on the western front. In the postwar Reichswehr, Kluge rose through the ranks and was promoted to brigadier general in 1933. From being a divisional commander in 1934, he was elevated to the command of an army by 1938. His Fourth Army was successful in the Polish campaign, and Kluge was promoted to full general in October 1939. During the offensive against France in May and June 1940, the Fourth Army was the right half of the spearhead that split open the French front. The Seventh Panzer Division, commanded by Brigadier General Erwin Rommel and operating within the Fourth Army, was the first unit to force a crossing over the Meuse River.

Kluge was made a field marshal after the conclusion of the campaign in France and was appointed commander in chief of Army Group Center in December 1941. During the previous campaigns he had learned the merits of highly mobile warfare. Now Hitler was forcing him into a rigid defense without opportunity to maneuver. Kluge was becoming estranged from the Führer, and under the influence of his operations officer, Colonel (later Brigadier) Henning von Tresckow (1901–44), Kluge began to show sympathies for the German resistance against Hitler.

On October 12, 1943, Kluge was severely injured in a car accident. After a lengthy recovery, he was appointed commander in chief west, replacing Field Marshal Gerd von Rundstedt (1875–1953), whom Hitler had found too pessimistic. Rundstedt's natural successor would have been Field Marshal Rommel, who commanded Army Group B under him and who was understandably annoyed at Kluge's appointment. Kluge and Rommel initially fell out with each other, Kluge reproaching Rommel for a lack of vigor. However, Kluge soon came to see that Rommel's pessimistic views were all too justified. On July 15, 1944, he forwarded Rommel's memorandum to Hitler, which declared the war could not be won and called for "consequences," i.e., requesting negotiations with the Allies.

When Rommel was severely wounded on July 17, Kluge took over as commander in chief, Army Group B. On July 20, during the attempted coup against Hitler, Kluge was faced with the choice of siding with the conspirators and opening the western front, or quenching the revolt in the west. Kluge had always vacillated in critical situations, earning himself the nickname "der Kluge Hans" ("clever Hans"). Now, he proved himself too timid and let the occasion pass.

On August 15, Hitler tried several times unsuccessfully to contact Kluge, who had gone to visit front-line units. Hitler suspected (wrongly) that Kluge was trying to contact the Western Allies. He sent Field Marshal Model to replace him immediately, and recalled Kluge to Berlin. Kluge feared (wrongly, as well) that his contacts with the conspirators had been revealed, and took poison on August 19.

Winfried Heinemann

See also Imperial Germany: Army; National Socialist Germany: Military; Resistance; Rommel, Erwin; Runstedt, Gerd von; Tresckow, Henning von; Weimar Germany: Army; World War I; World War II

References
Hoffmann, Peter. *The History of the German Resistance, 1933–1945.* Cambridge, MA: MIT Press, 1977.

Lamb, Richard. "Kluge." *Hitler's Generals.* Ed. Correlli Barnett. London: Weidenfeld and Nicolson, 1989.
Ose, Dieter. "Generalfeldmarschall von Kluge im Western: Das Ende eines Heerführers." *Europäische Wehrkunde* 29 (1980), 30–34.
Reinhardt, Klaus. *Moscow—The Turning Point: The Failure of Hitler's Strategy in the Winter of 1941–42.* Studies in Military History, vol. 3. Oxford: Berg, 1992.
Scheurig, Bodo. *Henning von Tresckow: Eine Biographie.* Oldenburg: Stalling, 1973.

Koch, Robert (1843–1910)

Heinrich Hermann Robert Koch was a physician best known for his pioneering work resulting in the isolation and identification of the tubercle bacillus, anthrax, and cholera. He and Louis Pasteur are regarded as the founders of modern medical bacteriology.

Koch received his medical degree from the University of Göttingen in 1866. He practiced medicine as a country doctor. When the Franco-Prussian War broke out, he enlisted in the medical corps and saw service in many field hospitals.

Koch was employed at the Berlin Health Department from 1880 to 1885. He was professor and administrator of Berlin University between the years 1885 and 1890 and director of the Institut für Infektionskrankheiten (Institute for Communicable Diseases) in Berlin from 1891 to 1904. Throughout his career in the medical corps, and later as director of the Institut für Infektionskrankheiten, Koch led efforts to control diseases in various countries. Koch played a major role in writing the government regulations for public health in Germany. In 1883, he led a group of German investigators in Egypt to help with the cholera epidemic and was later decorated by the Prussian Crown for this work. In 1896, Koch went to the Cape Colony in South Africa to help overcome rinderpest, and while there he devised procedures for active immunization.

In 1877, Koch proved that a specific organism could cause a specific disease. Koch was recognized as the first bacteriologist to isolate bacteria in pure culture. In 1881, he described the use of a semi-solid medium containing gelatin as the solidifying agent. This discovery enabled many other workers to preserve and isolate bacteria in pure culture, one of the most significant practical developments in establishing bacteriology as a separate scientific discipline. In 1882 he discovered the cause of tuberculosis (TB).

Bacteriologists throughout the world have benefited from Koch's meticulous work in defining the conditions for recognizing a specific bacterium as the cause of a particular disease. His legacy continues to the present because of his formulation, in 1884, of the fundamental laws of infectious disease causation, which have become known as Koch's Postulates.

According to Koch's Postulates, before an organism can be attributed as the cause of a particular disease, the organism (1) must be found to be constantly associated with that disease, (2) must be isolated from a lesion of that disease

Robert Koch. Courtesy of German Information Center, New York.

apart from other organisms, (3) must reproduce the disease in a suitable animal upon inoculation in pure culture, and (4) must be found again in the lesions of this artificially produced disease.

Koch also contributed significantly to the discipline of cellular immunology with his work with the tubercle bacillus. In 1891 he described the delayed-type skin test, whereby tuberculin (a sterile filtrate of tubercle bacilli suspension) elicited a severe local inflammatory reaction in TB patients upon intradermal application. This is still used for the identification of patients infected with *Mycobacterium tuberculosis* (TB).

The significance of Robert Koch's achievements may be realized by the awards he received. The first monument dedicated to Koch was erected on the Italian island of Brioni for his help in eradicating malaria there in 1900. Five years later Koch was awarded the Nobel Prize for Medicine for his achievements. He received the Harben Medal in 1901 and the Prussian order Pour le Mérite in 1906 and was given the rank of *Exzellenz* in 1907. That year also saw the founding of the Robert Koch Grant Fund for the control of tuberculosis. The first Robert Koch Medal was given to Koch posthumously in 1908. The medal is still used as an honor of excellence in research. His importance brought recognition to Germany as a leading force in the new discipline of bacteriology after the period of the Franco-Prussian War.

Lori Walsh

See also Bacteriology; Disease; Hamburg; Health; Medicine

References

Barlow, C. *Robert Koch.* Portland, OR: Heron Books, 1971.

Brock, Thomas. *Milestones in Microbiology.* Washington, DC: American Society for Microbiology, 1961.

———. *Robert Koch.* New York, NY: Springer-Verlag Publishers, 1988.

Bullock, William. *History of Bacteriology.* New York, NY: Dover Publications, 1938.

Green, Gareth M., Daniel M. Thomas, and Wilmot C. Ball, Jr. *Koch Centennial Memorial.* New York, NY: American Lung Association, 1982.

Koch, Robert. "Zur Untersuchung von pathogenen Organismen." *Mittheilungen aus dem Kaiserlichen Gesundheitsamte* 1 (1881), 1–48.

Lechevalier, Hubert A., and Morris Solotorovsky. *Three Centuries of Microbiology.* New York, NY: McGraw-Hill Book Company, 1965.

"Methods for Studying, Preserving and Photographing Bacteria." *Microbiology Contributions from 1776–1908.* New Brunswick, NJ: Rutgers University Press, 1960.

Schlessinger, Bernard S., and H. June. *The Who's Who of Nobel Prize Winners 1901–1990.* 2nd ed. Phoenix, AZ: Oryx Press, 1991.

Koch-Weser, Erich (1875–1944)

Erich Koch-Weser was a lawyer, a liberal politician, the leader of the German Democratic Party (DDP) in the Weimar Republic (1924–30), a minister in several national governments (1919–21, 1928–29), and the author of many articles, pamphlets, and books. His collected papers in the German Federal Archives are an important source for the history of the Weimar Republic. He changed his name from Koch to Koch-Weser in 1925.

After some 18 years in municipal politics as mayor (first of Delmenhorst then Kassel), Koch-Weser began a career in national politics after World War I by joining the newly founded DDP and was elected to the National Assembly in January 1919. He was a member of the Reichstag throughout the 1920s. Because of his Jewish ancestry on the maternal side, and also for political reasons, he left Germany after the Nazi takeover in 1933 and lived in Brazil thereafter.

During World War I, Koch-Weser attracted considerable attention with his writings about urban problems and by his espousal of parliamentary reform in Prussia. But it was his significant contribution to the drafting of the Weimar constitution in 1919 that established his reputation as a rising star in the DDP. His work on federal-state (*Reich-Länder*) relations helped to support centralism against separatist tendencies. Subsequently he became a committed and controversial champion of constitutional reform and relentlessly pursued his elusive goal of the "decentralized unitary state." As minister of the interior (1919–21) and vice-chancellor (1920–21) he earned a great deal of respect for his commitment, competence, and imaginative reform plans, though few were implemented.

As national leader of the DDP after 1924, he was preoccupied with the problems of German liberalism, such as the existence of two liberal parties and the DDP's relations with the Social Democrats. He regarded the ultimate merger of the two liberal parties as desirable, but his conviction that liberals had to cooperate with the Social Democrats to ensure governmental stability made the realization of liberal unity more difficult. He unsuccessfully fostered the creation of a Grand Coalition in 1925 and served as Minister of Justice under Hermann Müller's (1876–1931) short-lived one (1928–29). During the late 1920s, the steady erosion of popular support for the Democrats, shrinking membership, and the frightening polarization in German political life prompted him in 1930 to undertake a desperate attempt to unite all liberals and other moderate, pro-republican forces in a new State Party. The dismal failure of that party in the elections of 1930 led directly to his retirement from active politics.

Koch-Weser was a man of boundless energy and ambition, with a sharp intellect and impressive negotiating skills. He was a tireless defender of the Weimar Republic, although he became highly critical of its party-political system as it was practiced. By unconditionally supporting Chancellor Gustav Stresemann's (1878–1929) foreign policy in 1923 and by propagating ideas of international reconciliation and cooperation, he sought to help the Republic's unsuccessful struggle against the intransigent and aggressive forces of nationalism.

Attila Chanady

See also Federalism; German Democratic Party; Liberalism; Prussia; Weimar Germany

References

Frye, Bruce B. *Liberal Democrats in the Weimar Republic: The History of the German Democratic Party and the German State Party.* Carbondale, IL: Southern Illinois University Press, 1985.

Hess, Jürgen C. "Das ganz Deutschland soll es sein.": *Demokratischer Nationalismus in der Weimar Republik am Beispiel der Deutschen Demokratischen Partei.* Stuttgart: Klett-Cotta, 1978.

Jones, Larry E. *German Liberalism and the Dissolution of the Weimar Party System 1918–1933.* Chapel Hill, NC: University of North Carolina Press, 1988.

Koch-Weser, Erich. *Germany in the Post-war World.* Philadelphia: Dorrance and Co., 1930. (English translation of *Deutschlands Aussenpolitik in der Nachkriegszeit.* Berlin: K. Vowinkel, 1929.)

———. *Hitler and Beyond: A German Testament.* Trans. Olga Marx. New York, NY: A.A. Knopf, 1945.

Papke, Gerhard. *Der Liberale Politiker Erich Koch-Weser in der Weimarer Republik.* Baden-Baden: Nomos, 1989.

Portner, Ernst. *Die Verfassungspolitik der Liberalen—1919: Ein Beitrag zur Deutung der Weimarer Reichsverfassung.* Bonn: Röhrscheid, 1973.

Schneider, Werner. *Die Deutsche Demokratische Partei in der Weimarer Republik 1924–1930.* Munich: Fink, 1978.

Stephan, Werner. *Aufstieg und Verfall des Linksliberalismus 1918–1933: Geschichte der Deutschen Demokratischen Partei.* Göttingen: Vandenhoeck & Ruprecht, 1973.

Koeppen, Wolfgang (1906–1996)

Wolfgang Koeppen's reputation as one of the most important contemporary German writers rests largely on his postwar trilogy of novels, which critically portray developments in West Germany. His novels and their characters reflect his concept of the modern writer as an observer and outsider. Koeppen is also known for his travelogues, which demonstrate his abilities as a careful observer. After being awarded the Georg Büchner Prize (1962), he published no major works.

Born in Greifswald in 1906, Koeppen went to sea after leaving school, followed by a variety of laboring jobs and a period of university study before he became a newspaper editor with the *Berliner Börsen-Courier* in 1931. His early novels, *Eine unglückliche Liebe* (An unhappy love), 1934, and *Die Mauer schwankt* (The wall is shaking), 1935, deal with the outsider and the isolation of the individual. The latter, written in exile in Holland, contains hidden criticism of the Nazi regime. Koeppen nevertheless spent the war years in Germany as a film scriptwriter.

Koeppen's three postwar novels appeared in rapid succession. *Tauben im Gras* (published as *Pigeons on the Grass*), 1951, *Das Treibhaus* (The hothouse), 1953, and *Der Tod in Rom* (published as *Death in Rome*), 1954, harshly criticize the political and social situation in West Germany. Koeppen's themes encompass the political restoration under Chancellor Konrad Adenauer and the reemergence of elements of National Socialist ideology in German society. His main characters are outsiders who question society but are unable or unwilling to influence political developments and consequently become resigned to the situation.

Koeppen's postwar novels enraged many critics because of their condemnation of the new Federal Republic. In the meantime, the importance of the trilogy has been recognized, both as to Koeppen's assessment of postwar Germany and as to his experimental narrative technique. The influence of Alfred Döblin (1878–1957), John Dos Passos (1896–1970), and James Joyce (1882–1941) is apparent in Koeppen's novels. He used the literary montage technique, which abandons the traditional linear plot development in favor of a shifting narrative perspective and the contrast and juxtaposition of scenes and characters. Extracts from newspaper headlines, advertising slogans, and songs are integrated into the text to provide a link with current events. Mythological and literary references add a further dimension.

Critics and public alike responded enthusiastically to Koeppen's travelogues. In *Nach Russland und anderswohin* (To Russia and elsewhere), 1958, *Amerikafahrt* (Voyage to America), 1959, and *Reisen nach Frankreich* (Trips to France), 1961, Koeppen assumes the role of a distanced observer and avoids direct political comment. His prose is frequently exquisite and rich in classical allusions.

After receiving the Georg Büchner Prize (1962), Koeppen published numerous essays and reviews. *Romänisches Cafe* (Rumanian cafe), 1972, contains a selection of prose pieces, and the semi-autobiographical short story *Jugend* (Youth), 1976, became a bestseller. Koeppen's trilogy is part of the literature that opposed political restoration in West Germany, but his novels appeared before the large-scale politicization of literature and consequently received a particularly hostile response. The experimental techniques in his trilogy are typical of the modern novel. His publications, although successful, illustrate Koeppen's rejection of political and social comment.

Steven W. Lawrie

See also Federal Republic of Germany; Federal Republic of Germany: Literature; Journalism; Novel

References

Brink-Friederici, Christl. *Wolfgang Koeppen: Die Stadt als Pandämonium.* Frankfurt am Main: Lang, 1990.

Craven, Stanley. *Wolfgang Koeppen: A Study in Modernist Alienation.* Stuttgart: Akademischer Verlag Hans-Dieter Heinz, 1982.

Erlach, Dietrich. *Wolfgang Koeppen als zeitkritischer Erzähler.* Uppsala: Studia Germanistica, 1973.

Hanbidge, Carole. *The Transformation of Failure: A Critical Analysis of Character Presentation in the Novels of Wolfgang Koeppen.* New York, NY: Lang, 1983.

Koeppen, Wolfgang. *Gesammelte Werke.* 6 vols. Ed. Marcel Reich-Ranicki. Frankfurt am Main: Suhrkamp, 1986.

Siblewski, Klaus. "Wolfgang Koeppen." *Kritisches Lexikon zur deutschsprächigen Gegenwartsliteratur.* Ed. Heinz Ludwig Arnold. Munich: *Text + Kritik*, 1978–80.

Kogon, Eugen (1903–87)

Eugen Kogon was a German journalist and political scientist and an active opponent of Nazism. Interned in Buchenwald in 1939, Kogon survived the ordeal and published a highly influential book, *Der SS Staat* (published as *The Theory and Practice of Hell*, 1950), 1946, which described the conditions in, and the organization of, the SS concentration-camp empire and analyzed the role of the SS as a powerful "state within a state" in Nazi Germany.

Kogon was born in Munich on February 2, 1903 and was educated in sociology and economics at the universities of Munich, Florence, and Vienna. From 1927 to 1934 Kogon worked with the conservative Catholic newspaper *Schöne Zukunft*. Because of his active anti-Nazi stance and connections with circles considered politically unreliable by the Nazis, Kogon was arrested following the *Anschluss* of Austria in 1938. In 1939 he was sent to Buchenwald, where he remained until April 1945. His experiences in Buchenwald are vividly described in *Der SS Staat*, which had originated as his official report for the Psychological Warfare Division of the Supreme Headquarters, Allied Expeditionary Forces (SHAEF). *Der SS Staat* was published in numerous editions and languages, and represented one of the first scholarly investigations into the Nazi SS. Kogon's argument that the SS constituted an all-powerful elite "superstate" or "state within a state" was generally accepted and further developed by other scholars.

In 1946, Kogon helped to found the *Frankfurter Hefte*, a journal concerning political and cultural affairs; he remained actively involved with this endeavor until his death. From 1949 to 1953, Kogon served as the first chairman of the Europa-Union, an organization promoting Western European

Eugen Kogon. Courtesy of German Information Center, New York.

unity. In 1951, Kogon took a post as professor of political science at the College of Engineering in Darmstadt, serving until his retirement in 1968.

Throughout his retirement, Kogon remained an active scholar, continuing to write and edit a number of works addressing issues relating to Germany's Nazi past in addition to other political and historical topics. Kogon died on December 24, 1987, in Falkenstein (zu Königstein im Taunus).

Mark P. Gingerich

See also Concentration Camps; Catholicism, Political; Dirks, Walter; Journalism; National Socialist Germany; Political Science; Schutzstaffel

References

Habicht, Hubert, ed. *Eugen Kogon—ein politischer Publizist in Hessen: Essays, Aufsätze, Reden zwischen 1946 und 1982.* Frankfurt am Main: Insel, 1982.

Kogon, Eugen. *Die Stunde der Ingenieure: Technologische Intelligenz und Politik.* Düsseldorf: VDI-Verlag, 1976.

———. *The Theory and Practice of Hell: The German Concentration Camps and the System behind Them.* New York, NY: Octagon Books, 1973.

Kogon, Eugen, ed. *Terror und Gewaltkriminalität: Herausforderung für den Rechtsstaat: Diskussionsprotokoll Reihe Hessenforum.* Frankfurt am Main: Aspekte, 1975.

Kogon, Eugen, Hermann Langbein, and Adalbert Ruckerl, eds. *Nazi Mass Murder: A Documentary History of the Use of*

Poison Gas. Trans. Mary Scott and Caroline Lloyd-
   Morris. New Haven, CT: Yale University Press, 1994.
Prumm, Karl. *Walter Dirks und Eugen Kogon als katholische
   Publizisten der Weimarer Republik.* Heidelberg:
   C. Winter, 1984.
Rein, Gerhard. *Dienstagsgespräche mit Zeitgenossen.*
   Stuttgart and Berlin: Kreuz-Verlag, 1976.

Kohl, Helmut (1930–)

Born in Ludwigshafen in 1930, Helmut Kohl joined the
Christian Democratic Union (CDU) youth wing (Junge
Union) at the age of 17. He was first elected to the *Land* (state)
legislature of Rhineland-Palatinate in 1959 and within ten
years became minister-president of the state.

After the defeat of the Christian Democratic Union/
Christian Social Union (CDU/CSU) in the 1972 Bundestag
elections, Kohl was elected chairman of the federal CDU and
catapulted into national politics. As chancellor candidate for
the CDU/CSU in 1976, Kohl revived his party to its highest
vote share (48.8 percent) since 1957, but he still fell short of
winning a majority.

In the aftermath of this defeat, Kohl wanted to lead the
parliamentary party in opposition against the popular in-
cumbent chancellor, Helmut Schmidt (1913–). Although
CSU leader Franz Josef Strauss (1915–88) was chosen over
Kohl to be chancellor candidate for the CDU/CSU in 1980,
Kohl retained the chairmanships of the party and the parliamentary caucus (*Fraktion*), thereby leaving himself posi-
tioned to exploit the eventual breakup of the social-liberal

*Helmut Kohl.
Courtesy of German
Information Center,
New York.*

coalition. On the basis of the constitutional procedure of the
"constructive vote of no confidence" in October 1982, Kohl
was elected chancellor. At age 52 he was the youngest chancellor in the history of the FRG. The 1983 Bundestag election confirmed the new Christian-liberal majority and Kohl's
chancellorship.

After Kohl's reelection in 1987, the CDU suffered a series of defeats in regional elections, and the chancellor's popularity began to fade. However, when the "Gorbachev revolution" signaled the end of the Cold War and prompted the
collapse of the East German regime in 1989, a new political
opportunity presented itself to Kohl, who sensed the inevitability of unification earlier than most other political leaders.
Starting with his Ten Point Plan, which foresaw only an eventual confederation of the two Germanys, he initiated the revolutionary transformation rather than reacting to it.

By early 1990, the mounting exodus of easterners to the
West intensified pressures for unification. This crisis transformed the chancellor into a figure around whom Germans
from East and West could rally. The first crucial test of public sentiment came with the Volkskammer (People's Chamber)
election in East Germany on March 18, 1990. Led by the
chancellor, the CDU-backed coalition (Alliance for Germany)
promised fast-track unity with currency parity. This strategy
produced a resounding victory. The Kohl agenda for unity was
ratified, and the chancellor's prestige soared.

Kohl's historic meetings with Gorbachev in July 1990
resolved the possibility of an international deadlock over unification. The ensuing Caucasus Agreements provided a comprehensive accord in which Moscow agreed to permit a unified Germany to remain within NATO. In return, Bonn
promised the Soviet Union economic aid and military concessions, including the acceptance of existing Eastern European
borders, a renunciation of nuclear, biological, and chemical
weapons, and reimbursement for Soviet troop withdrawals.
With this last serious obstacle removed, unification was formalized within three months. Kohl became the first chancellor of a reunited postwar Germany. This accomplishment,
comparable to Bismarck's creation of the German Empire in
1871 and Adenauer's postwar rebuilding of democracy in the
FRG, has ensured Kohl his place in history.

With the five new eastern *Länder* (states) constitutionally joined to the FRG, the burdens and challenges of unification, compounded by the onset of a severe recession, bred
disillusionment and brought Kohl's popularity to a low point.
However, by early 1994, economic recovery was again under
way, and the pendulum of public opinion began to swing back
toward optimism. The June 1994 European elections demonstrated a surprising revival of support for the CDU/CSU and
a corresponding stagnation for the Social Democratic Party
(SPD). The way was cleared for Kohl's narrow reelection in
October 1994. One month later, the Bundestag reinstalled the
chancellor, but only by a one-vote margin—exactly as with
Adenauer in 1949.

Kohl's capacity for political adaptation and comeback
has been consistently underestimated by critics and supporters alike. His extraordinary durability may best be under-

stood as a function of his patient yet tenacious leadership style and his skills as a professional party and coalition manager. In contending with political opponents, coalition partners, and intraparty rivals, Kohl has balanced interests and marginalized potential threats. Based on years of experience in regional and federal government, he has always relied on internal control within his own party and within his coalition, even during periods of unpopularity and electoral setbacks. His effective management of the CDU has never been seriously questioned.

As a policy maker, Chancellor Kohl is a generalist rather than an expert. His strategy on major issues has been either to seek the middle ground or to await the resolution of controversial issues. Unlike his conservative contemporaries, Margaret Thatcher and Ronald Reagan, Kohl has remained primarily a pragmatist and a consensus-seeker. Although no "ism" has ever been attached to his name, Kohl does not lack firm beliefs. His is an embedded conservatism based on the traditional values of family and fatherland. Helmut Kohl is a unity chancellor who cannot be described as a narrow nationalist. The building of a united Europe stands in the primary place in his system of priorities. He has repeatedly argued that German unification must go hand in hand with European integration.

William M. Chandler

See also Adenauer, Konrad; American-German Relations; Anglo-German Relations; Chancellor's Office; Christian Democratic Union; Christian Social Union; Constitutions; Federal Republic of Germany; Federal Republic of Germany: Foreign Policy; Franco-German Relations; Free Democratic Party; Genscher, Hans-Dietrich; German Democratic Republic; German-German Relations; Gorbachev and the German Question; Honecker, Erich; *Ostpolitik*; Parties and Politics; Polish-German Relations (after 1945); Postwar European Integration and Germany; Reunification; Rhineland-Palatinate; Schmidt, Helmut; Social Democratic Party, 1919–90; Soviet-German Relations; Strauss, Franz Josef; Weizsäcker, Richard von

References

Dönhoff, Marion Gräfin. *Deutschland deine Kanzler.* Munich: Goldmann, 1992.

Jarausch, Konrad, H. *The Rush to German Unity.* New York, NY: Oxford, 1994.

Kohl, Helmut. *Ich wollte Deutschlands Einheit.* Berlin: Propyläen, 1996.

Merkl, Peter H. *German Unification in the European Context.* University Park, PA: Pennsylvania State University Press, 1992.

Potthoff, Heinrich. *Die "Koalition der Vernunft": Deutschlandpolitik in den 80er Jahren.* Munich: Deutscher Taschenbuck Verlag, 1995.

Pruys, Karl Hugo. *Kohl, Genuis of the Present: A Biography of Helmut Kohl.* Chicago, IL, 1996.

Smith, Gordon. "The Resources of a German Chancellor." *West European Politics.* 14 (April 1991), 48–61.

Köhler, Wolfgang (1887–1967)

The scientist, philosopher, and co-founder of Gestalt psychology Wolfgang Köhler was born in Reval (now Tallinn, Estonia) to a Baltic German family; his father was a Gymnasium director. He attended the Gymnasium (high school) in Wolfenbüttel and studied physics, chemistry, psychology, and philosophy at the universities of Bonn and Berlin, obtaining his doctoral degree in Berlin in 1909 for experimental studies on the psychology of hearing.

While working as an assistant in the Frankfurt psychological laboratory in 1910, he met Max Wertheimer (1880–1943) and became, with Wertheimer and Kurt Koffka (1886–1941), one of the three chief exponents of Gestalt theory. The central claim of the new approach was that wholes and meaningful relationships are the primary constituents of experience and behavior, which should not be reduced to arbitrary sums of allegedly more basic units. In 1913, Köhler became director of the Anthropoid Research Station of the Prussian Academy of Sciences on Tenerife, in the Canary Islands. Interned there during World War I, he produced now-classical studies of "insight" into animal problem solving and perception (*Intelligenzprüfungen an Menschenaffen* [published as *The Mentality of Apes*, 1925], 1917). On Tenerife he also wrote a major philosophical work, *Die physischen Gestalten in Ruhe und im stationären Zustand* (Physical structures at rest and in a stationary state), 1920, in which he argued that self-organizing, nonreducible structures analogous to those in human perception are also present in the physical world.

In 1922, Köhler became professor of philosophy and director of the Psychological Institute of the University of Berlin. Together with Wertheimer, he made the institute one of the leading psychological laboratories in the world. Visiting professorships in the United States and publication of the book *Gestalt Psychology* (1929) in English helped to introduce the Gestalt viewpoint in that country. His association with Hans Reichenbach's Society for Scientific Philosophy clearly expressed his commitment to combining holism and natural science.

Köhler was one of the few German professors to protest publicly against Nazi firings of Jews in 1933. He tried for a time to retain his position in Berlin but resigned and went to Swarthmore College in 1935. His William James Lectures, given at Harvard University that year, appeared in 1938 as *The Place of Value in a World of Facts*. A monograph, *Dynamics in Psychology* (1940), began a series of studies in the 1940s and 1950s in which he attempted to record directly the brain events correlated with perceived forms. His discovery and measurement of direct cortical currents was widely acknowledged, but the theory he advanced to explain them was not accepted. He was elected to the National Academy of Sciences and the American Academy of Arts and Sciences, and was chosen president of the American Psychological Association in 1959. He was also named an Honored Citizen (*Ehrenbürger*) of the Free University of Berlin.

Köhler remained committed throughout his career to the union of rigorous science and humanistic values. His Gestalt viewpoint is coming to be appreciated again as scientists pay increasing attention to self-organizing systems and the spontaneous emergence of order in nature.

Mitchell G. Ash

See also Expulsion and Exile of Scientists and Scholars; Philosophy; Psychology; Wertheimer, Max

References

Asch, Solomon E. "Wolfgang Köhler." *American Journal of Psychology* 81 (1968), 110–19.

Ash, Mitchell G. *Gestalt Psychology in German Culture: Holism and the Quest for Objectivity*. Cambridge: Cambridge University Press, 1995.

Henle, Mary. "One Man Against the Nazis: Wolfgang Köhler." *American Psychologist* 33 (1978), 939–44.

Jaeger, Siegfried, ed. *Briefe Wolfgang Köhlers an Prof. Dr. Geitel*. Passau: Passavia Universitätsverlag, 1989.

Köhler, Wolfgang. *Selected Papers of Wolfgang Köhler*. Ed. Mary Henle. New York, NY: Liveright, 1971.

Kokoschka, Oskar (1886–1980)

The painter, portraitist, graphic artist, and playwright Oskar Kokoschka was born on March 1, 1886 in Pöchlarn, Austria and died on February 22, 1980 in Villeneuve, Montreux, Switzerland.

This most eminent portraitist of the first half of the twentieth century studied from 1905 to 1909 at the Kunstgewerbeschule (Art Trade School) in Vienna, while also working for the *Wiener Werkstätten* (Viennese Workshops). His first important portraits were painted in 1908 and his portrait drawings were published in 1910 in the important expressionist journal *Der Sturm* (The storm). His first plays, *Sphinx und Strohmann* (Sphinx and strawman) and *Mörder, Hoffnung der Frauen* (published as *Murder, Hope of Women*), were performed in 1909. During one year, he served as assistant at the Kunstgewerbeschule, exhibited at the Sturm Gallery, and illustrated his poem "Allos Makar" and Karl Kraus's (1874–1936) "Die Chinesische Mauer" (The Chinese wall).

Kokoschka's friendship with Alma Mahler lasted from 1911 until 1914 ("Die Windsbraut" [The wind's bride] is a document of their love); he volunteered for the army and was severely wounded in 1915. While in Berlin and Dresden, he saw to the publication of his portfolios, "Der Gefesselte Columbus" (The bound Columbus) and "O Ewigkeit, Du Donnerwort" (Oh eternity, you thundrous word [Bach Kantate]); large numbers of his portraits and other works were exhibited during 1916 in Berlin at the Sturm Gallery. In 1919 he was appointed professor at the Dresden Art Academy. Paul Hindemith (1895–1963) wrote the music to the play, *Murder, Hope of Women*, which was performed in Frankfurt in 1921. His works were exhibited in several galleries in Germany and at the *Biennale* in Venice. In 1924 he left his professorship and for nearly ten years traveled throughout Europe and North Africa while his works were shown also in London and Paris.

When the Nazis began their rule in Germany, Kokoschka moved to Prague, married, painted a portrait of Czechoslo-

vak President Thomas Masaryk, and worked on his drama, "Comenius." The Nazis confiscated a volume of his drawings edited by Ernst Rathenau and no fewer than 417 of his works in German museums. They exhibited nine paintings, a portfolio of drawings, and other of his productions at the *Degenerate Art* exhibition in 1937. After the Nazi occupation of Czechoslovakia in March 1939, Kokoschka fled with his wife to England, where they arrived penniless. He immediately became active in a number of emigrant organizations and dedicated the price for a portrait of the Soviet Ambassador Ivan Maisky to a Stalingrad hospital fund.

In 1947 Kokoschka became a British citizen and visited his large retrospective exhibit in Basel. He was honored with the exhibition of 16 works at the *Biennale* and lectured at Boston and Minneapolis during exhibitions of his works. He received a large number of prizes and medals, and in 1953 opened his art school, Schule des Sehens (School of Vision), in Salzburg. He continued to paint cityscapes as portraits of various cities, designed theater and opera sets and costumes (among others, for Mozart's *Magic Flute*), and in 1953 moved to Villeneuve in Switzerland, where he died in 1980. His largest retrospective, in Vienna with 682 works (1958), made his works well known; he received the order of Pour le Mérite as well as many honors (honorary doctorate from Oxford University, the Erasmus Medal, and the honorary citizenship of Vienna, among many others). His play, *Comenius*, was shown on television in 1975.

Peter Guenther

See also Artists; Expressionism (Visual Arts); National Socialist Germany: Art; Poetry; Theater

References

Calvocoressi, Richard. *Oskar Kokoschka*. New York, NY: Rizzoli, 1992.

Kokoschka, Olda, and Alfred Marnau. *Oskar Kokoschka: Letters 1905–1976*. Trans. Mary Whittal. London: Thames and Hudson, 1992.

Kokoschka, Oskar. *My Life*. Trans. David Britt. New York, NY: Macmillan, 1974.

Wingler, Hans Maria. *Oskar Kokoschka, das druckgraphische Werk*. Salzburg: Gallerie Welz, 1975.

———. *Oskar Kokoschka, The Work of the Painter*. 2 vols. Salzburg: Gallerie Welz, 1958–81.

Kolbe, Georg (1877–1947)

The prolific sculptor Georg Kolbe was born on April 15, 1877 in Waldheim, Saxony, and died on November 2, 1947 in Berlin.

Kolbe began his career as a painter (Dresden, Munich, and Academie Julian, Paris). A longer stay in Rome and the example and advice of Louis Tuaillon made him turn to sculpture. In 1905, he received the Villa Romana Prize and spent one year in Florence. He settled in Berlin, where friendships with Richard Scheibe and Karl Schmidt-Rottluff (1884–1976) strongly influenced his development.

Kolbe became famous with his nude dancer figures (especially the one of 1912) and obtained the commission of the city of Frankfurt for a Heinrich Heine monument (destroyed by the Nazis). He also worked in wood. His clothed figures *Mourning* and *Anger*, as well as his nudes (*Call of the Earth*), showed a close relationship to expressionism. After his wife died in 1927, nude figures (*Lonely One* and *Pieta*) again dominated his oeuvre. From 1926 until his death, he worked on a Beethoven monument that originally had been rejected in a competition.

By 1928, his figures gained monumentality and their quiet movements were frequently considered as being close to the Nazi-preferred forms, especially since he began to add attributes (swords and bows). He never gained full Nazi backing (his earlier portrait of Max Liebermann [1848–1935] and the Rathenau Fountain were not forgotten). In the first post–World War II exhibition in Dresden he showed *The Liberated One*, after completing *Fallen* and *Zarathustra*. In his later years, his health deteriorated and he became nearly blind. He was one of Germany's important sculptors of the first half of the twentieth century, honored in many catalogues and in displays of early versions of his works at the Georg Kolbe Museum in Berlin.

Peter Guenther

See also Artists; National Socialist Germany: Art; Schmidt-Rottluff, Karl; Sculpture

References
Andrew Dickson White Museum, Cornell University, Ithaca. *Georg Kolbe—Sculpture from the Collection of B. Gerald Cantor*. Exhibition Catalog. Ithaca, NY: Cornell University Press, 1972.
Hartog, Arie. "Georg Kolbe, receptie in Duitslandtussen 1920 en 1950." Unpublished doctoral dissertation. Catholic University, Nijmegen, 1989.
Heller, Reinhold. "Georg Kolbe Revaluated." *Apollo* 99 (1972), 50–55.
Kolbe, Georg. *Auf Wegen der Kunst: Schriften, Skizzen, Plastiken*. Berlin: K. Lemmer, 1949.

Kolbe, Hermann (1818–84)

Hermann Kolbe was one of the most prominent German organic chemists during the period in which German chemistry rose to a preeminent position in European academia and industry. He was perhaps the most important of the founders of the concepts and methodology of chemical synthesis.

Born in Elliehausen, just outside of Göttingen in the Kingdom of Hannover, Kolbe studied chemistry at the nearby university under Friedrich Wöhler; his doctorate, however, was supervised by Robert Bunsen at Marburg in Hesse-Kassel (1843). After a period as Bunsen's assistant, an 18-month postdoctoral sojourn in London, and finally a four-year period as writer and editor in Braunschweig, Kolbe succeeded Bunsen in Marburg in 1851. In 1865, he was called to the University of Leipzig, where he remained until his death.

Kolbe's reputation was founded on some of the earliest work on organic synthetic methods (1842–47), including the first "total synthesis" of an organic compound—acetic acid—

in 1844. A second period, between 1859 and 1865, produced ingenious and fruitful methods for synthesizing novel substances and for investigating their detailed chemical structures. All of these studies represented basic rather than applied science, but Kolbe was always sensitive to technological and entrepreneurial possibilities—especially after 1858, when synthetic organic dyes emerged as an important industry.

In 1873, Kolbe discovered an inexpensive way to synthesize salicylic acid, a constituent of a natural product that had long been known to have analgesic and febrifugal properties. He and a partner founded a factory for the production of this substance; the concern grew rapidly and eventually became the largest chemical factory in Saxony. The product was used in pharmaceuticals and as a food preservative. A minor modification of the compound (1899) resulted in the invention of aspirin.

Kolbe had a cantankerous and self-righteous personality. At the time of the Franco-Prussian War, his attitudes hardened into virulent xenophobia, chauvinism, and anti-Semitism. Privately and publicly he contested priority for the theories of valence and structure with such offensive invective that he gradually alienated even those inclined to see the matter from his point of view. He was an excellent and much-loved teacher, but as a result of his incessant attacks he was ineffective in placing even highly talented students in good positions. Nonetheless, Kolbe was one of the best chemists of the nineteenth century and a principal founder of pure and applied organic synthesis.

Alan J. Rocke

See also Chemistry, Scientific and Industrial; Nationalism

References
Rocke, A.J. *The Quiet Revolution: Hermann Kolbe and the Science of Organic Chemistry*. Berkeley, CA: University of California Press, 1993.

Kollwitz, Käthe (1867–1945)

Käthe Kollwitz, an influential, stylistically traditional graphic artist and sculptor, was a fiercely independent, politically progressive social critic during the Wilhelmine and Weimar eras.

Born Käthe Schmidt in Königsberg, Kollwitz was raised in an atmosphere of left-leaning liberalism; her maternal grandfather, Julius Rupp, founded and led the first Protestant Free Religious Congregation in Germany, and her father and brother were socialists. After attending the School for Women Artists in Berlin (1885–86) and studying further in Königsberg and Munich, she moved to Berlin in 1891 with her new husband, Karl Kollwitz, a physician, and settled in the working-class district of Prenzlauer Berg, where she lived throughout her life.

After gaining recognition at the Great Berlin Art Exhibition of 1898 for her print cycle *A Weavers' Rebellion* (1893–98), based on Gerhart Hauptmann's play *The Weavers*, Kollwitz joined the Berlin Secession, of which she became the most important female member. Kollwitz continued to work on impressive graphic cycles, including *Peasants' War* (1902–08), *War* (1923), and *Proletariat* (1925), and in 1909 made

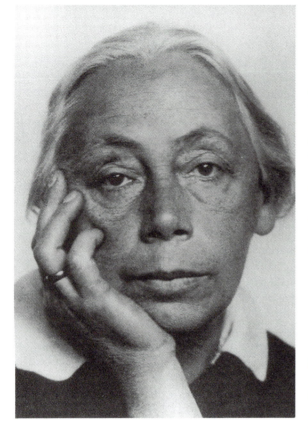

Käthe Kollwitz.
Courtesy of German
Embassy, Ottawa.

her first sculptures. Her 50th birthday was celebrated with exhibitions at the Paul Cassirer gallery in Berlin and the Kunsthalle Bremen. Two years later, in 1919, Kollwitz was elected to the Prussian Academy of Arts and appointed professor at the teaching institution associated with it. Despite these successes, Kollwitz, throughout her 50-year working life, was plagued by self-doubts about her artistic competence and the efficacy of her social engagement.

A nonideological socialist, Kollwitz was deeply skeptical, and her independent will kept her from joining any political party. After the death of her second son, Peter, on the western front in 1914, Kollwitz became an unyielding pacifist. The ambiguity of her position is demonstrated in several versions of *Memorial Sheet to Karl Liebknecht* (1919–20), in which Kollwitz emphasizes the mourners rather than the murdered Spartacist leader—for whom she had strong sympathies, but whose advocacy of violence she could not support. Under the Third Reich, Kollwitz was removed from the Prussian Academy of Arts, and by 1936 she was unofficially prohibited from exhibiting.

In her work and life, Kollwitz consistently expressed compassion for human suffering. Today she is recognized as an important feminist voice. Her best work evokes powerful emotions and is strongly critical of social injustice, but it tends to adhere to a fairly conservative academic social realism. Recently, some scholars have stressed her experimentation with innovative printing techniques. As a sculptor, Kollwitz did not develop a strong personal style, but in her graphic cycles and in her best drawings of working-class women and children she

achieved a unique combination of combative idealism, sharp observation, and technical mastery.

Paul Paret

See also Artists; Berlin Secession; Hauptmann, Gerhart; Pacifism and the Peace Movement; Prussian Art Academy; Sculpture

References

Guratzsch, Herwig, ed. *Käthe Kollwitz: Druckgraphik, Handzeichnungen. Plastik.* Stuttgart: Gerd Hatje, 1990.
Kilpstein, August. *Käthe Kollwitz: Verzeichnis der graphischen Werke.* Bern: Klipstein & Co., 1955.
Klein, Mina C., and H. Arthur Klein. *Käthe Kollwitz, Life in Art.* New York, NY: Schocken Books, 1975.
Kollwitz, Käthe. *Die Tagebücher.* Ed. Jutta Bohnke-Kollwitz. Berlin: Seidler, 1989.
Prelinger, Elizabeth, with Alessandra Comini and Hildegard Bachert. *Käthe Kollwitz.* New Haven, CT: National Gallery of Art, Washington, DC and Yale University Press, 1992.

Kopf, Hinrich Wilhelm (1893–1961)

Hinrich Wilhelm Kopf was born on May 6, 1893 in Neuenkirchen, in the Prussian province of Hannover. His father was a farmer. He attended grammar school and passed the *Abitur* examination in 1913. At the age of 16, before finishing school, he left his parents' house and spent nine months in the United States.

Kopf studied law and economics at the universities of Marburg and Göttingen in 1913 and 1914. At the beginning of World War I he joined the army, but because of an injury he soon left the services and resumed his education at Göttingen. After his examination in 1917, he started a traineeship in the civil service (*Referendariat*). During his traineeship he spent some time with the Imperial Navy, became involved in the revolutionary uprisings of the sailors in 1918, and joined the Council of Workers and Soldiers (Arbeiter- und Soldatenrat) in Hamburg.

Kopf appreciated the achievements of the early revolutionary period, such as the eight-hour day, freedom of assembly and coalition, and especially universal suffrage. Unlike the left wing of the revolutionary sailors and soldiers, he did not support a "dictatorship of the proletariat."

During the turmoil of the postwar period Kopf engaged himself in the support of the democratic Weimar Republic. He became a member of the Social Democratic Party (SPD) and associated with the more conservative or right-wing Social Democrats, such as Carl Severing and Gustav Noske.

Kopf found employment in different occupations in the civil service as well as in the private economy. In 1928, he was nominated and appointed head of the administration of his native district (Landkreis), Hadeln. He held this office until 1932, when he was appointed to a new post in Oppeln, Upper Silesia. In 1934, when the civil service was "cleansed" of Social Democrats and other opponents of Nazism, Kopf lost his position. From 1934 until 1945, Kopf lived in Berlin and

Upper Silesia. At the end of the war, he and his family fled to North Germany. Their flight ended south of Hannover, in the British Occupation Zone.

Already before the surrender of the German army, Kopf had reestablished contacts with Social Democratic acquaintances. He was appointed Regierungspräsident (head of the administration) of the province of Hannover by the British military government. When the *Land* (state) Hannover was restored in the fall of 1945, he became its first (and only) postwar prime minister.

Kopf engaged himself in the administrative reform of North Germany. He advocated an amalgamation of the states, in particular Hannover with Brunswick and Oldenburg. Finally, by order of the British military government, the *Land* Lower Saxony was established in November 1946. Kopf became its first prime minister. The first elections of the diet (*Landtag*) of Lower Saxony on April 20, 1947 confirmed Kopf in his office.

Kopf held office until 1955, when a coalition of "non-socialist" parties formed a government without the SPD. This government lasted for two years. It was succeeded by a coalition of the Christian Democrats and the SPD. Within this government, Kopf held office as minister of domestic affairs. After the 1959 diet election, Kopf resumed the office of prime minister, which he held until his death on December 21, 1961.

Wolfgang Renzsch

See also Federalism; Federal Republic of Germany; Lower Saxony; Social Democratic Party, 1919–90; Weimar Germany

References
Vogelsang, Thilo. *Hinrich Wilhelm Kopf und Niedersachsen.* Hannover: Verlag für Literatur & Zeitgeschehen, 1963.

Kracauer, Siegfried (1889–1966)

Siegfried Kracauer is known primarily as a historian of Weimar cinema and a film theoretician in the realist tradition. As one of the foremost critics during the Weimar Republic, he also played an essential role in promoting the study of modern mass culture and synthesizing the perspectives of sociology, phenomenology, and critical theory.

Born on February 8, 1889 in Frankfurt am Main, Kracauer studied architecture, philosophy, and sociology and worked briefly as an architect. In 1921 he joined the newpaper *Frankfurter Zeitung,* and became head of its Berlin feuilleton office in 1930. The big city inspired many articles about urban culture and a sociological study on white-collar workers (*Die Angestellten*) in 1930. Kracauer left Germany for Paris in 1933, where he wrote *Jacques Offenbach und das Paris seiner Zeit* (Offenbach and the Paris of his time), 1937, and emigrated to the United States in 1941. Scholarships from the Guggenheim, Rockefeller, and Bollingen foundations, as well as his association with the Voice of America, the Museum of Modern Art, and Columbia University, allowed him to complete a history of Weimar cinema, *From Caligari to Hitler,* 1947, and his magnum opus, *Theory of Film: The Redemption of Physical Reality,* 1960. While working on *History: The Last Things Before the Last,* 1969, Kracauer died on November 26, 1966.

Kracauer's work resists easy classification. His writings range from semi-autobiographical novels and scholarly books on sociology and the philosophy of history to critical articles and essays on film, literature, architecture, fashion, and other aspects of modern consumer culture. The study of surface phenomena in the tradition of Georg Simmel characterizes his early work. Discussions with Ernst Bloch (1885–1977), Walter Benjamin (1892–1940), and Theodor W. Adorno (1903–69) brought a stronger commitment to left-liberal causes and sociological methods that continued in his American studies on mass propaganda. Despite the diversity, Kracauer's work remains integrated by a continuous exploration of the ephemeral and marginal and an awareness of the function of critical discourse that makes his writings on culture and society an important precursor of contemporary cultural studies.

Sabine Hake

See also Adorno, Theodor; Benjamin, Walter; Bloch, Ernst; Cinema; Journalism; Simmel, Georg; Sociology

References
Kessler, Michael, and Thomas Y. Levin, eds. *Siegfried Kracauer: Neue Interpretationen.* Tübingen: Stauffenburg, 1990.

Kracauer, Siegfried. *From Caligari to Hitler: A Psychological History of the German Film.* Princeton, NJ: Princeton University Press, 1974.

———. *History: The Last Things Before the Last.* New York, NY: Oxford University Press, 1969.

———. *Theory of Film: The Redemption of Physical Reality.* New York, NY: Oxford University Press, 1960.

———. *Werke.* Ed. Karsten Witte and (after 1990) Inka Mülder-Bach. Frankfurt am Main: Suhrkamp, 1971 *ff.*

Mülder, Inka. *Siegfried Kracauer—Grenzgänger zwischen Theorie und Literatur: Seine frühen Schriften 1913–1933.* Stuttgart: Metzler, 1985.

Kraus, Karl (1874–1936)

Karl Kraus was the most influential satirical writer and cultural critic in Vienna during the first three decades of the twentieth century. In 1899 he founded the literary and political review *Die Fackel,* which he edited until 1936. From 1911 onward he was also the magazine's sole author. Countless Austrian writers have been inspired by Kraus's analytical wit, critical dissection of bourgeois morality, and satirical attacks against the Viennese newspapers and the literary scene.

Kraus was born on April 28, 1874, in Jičin in Bohemia. Soon thereafter, his family moved to Vienna. There he attended the Franz-Josephs-Gymnasium, studied law for a few years, and wrote his first literary reviews for the newspaper *Wiener Literatur-Zeitung.* On April 1, 1899 the inaugural issue of *Die Fackel* appeared. From the beginning, Kraus did not shy away from personal attacks against all those who—in his view—abused language. On the one hand he charged Franz Werfel, Maximilian Harden (1861–1927), and Alfred Kerr with being responsible for the superficiality of cultural life; on the other hand he supported Else Lasker-Schüler (1869–1945), Frank Wedekind (1864–1918), and Peter Altenberg and was instrumental in the revival of Jacques Offenbach's and Johann Nepomuk Nestroy's works. His main target was the Viennese press, which he regarded as the great manipulator of public opinion.

The most famous of Kraus's dramas is the monumental *Die letzten Tage der Menschheit* (The last days of mankind), 1922, an apocalyptic picture of his time and a condemnation of war in over two hundred scenes. Kraus was a pacifist who vehemently opposed the emerging radical right-wing forces. However, after the Nazis seized power in Germany he fell silent, because he no longer believed in the effectiveness of satire. *Die dritte Walpurgisnacht* (The third walpurgis night), published posthumously in 1952, opens with Kraus's much-quoted statement: "Mir fällt zu Hitler nichts ein" (I can't think of anything to say about Hitler).

Ulrich Scheck

See also Pacifism and the Peace Movement; Press and Newspapers; Satire

References

Arntzen, Helmut. *Karl Kraus und die Presse.* Munich: Fink, 1975.

Fischer, Jens Malte. *Karl Kraus.* Stuttgart: Metzler, 1974.

Grimstad, Kari. *Masks of the Prophet: The Theatrical World of Karl Kraus.* Toronto: University of Toronto Press, 1982.

Kerry, Otto. *Karl-Kraus-Bibliographie.* Munich: Kösel, 1970.

Kraus, Karl. *Die Fackel.* 12 vols. Frankfurt am Main: Zweitausendeins, 1977.

———. *Werke.* 14 vols. Ed. Heinrich Fischer. Munich: Kösel, 1954–67.

Scheichl, Sigurd Paul, and Edward Timms, eds. *Karl Kraus in a New Perspective: London Kraus Symposium.* Munich: *Text + Kritik*, 1986.

Schick, Paul. *Karl Kraus in Selbstzeugnissen und Bilddokumenten.* Reinbek bei Hamburg: Rowohlt, 1965.

Schneider, Manfred. *Die Angst und das Paradies des Nörglers: Versuch über Karl Kraus.* Frankfurt am Main: Syndikat, 1977.

Timms, Edward. *Karl Kraus, Apocalyptic Satirist: Culture and Catastrophe in Habsburg Vienna.* New Haven, CT: Yale University Press, 1986.

Wagner, Nike. *Geist und Geschlecht: Karl Kraus und die Erotik der Wiener Moderne.* Frankfurt am Main: Suhrkamp, 1982.

Zohn, Harry. *Karl Kraus.* New York, NY: Twayne, 1971.

Kreuzzeitung (1848–1939)

First published in Berlin on June 16, 1848, the newspaper, *Neue Preussische (Kreuz-) Zeitung,* was known as the *Kreuzzeitung* because of the prominent Iron Cross on its masthead. Through decades of social and political upheaval that first favored Prussian conservatives and then pushed them to the wall, the *Kreuzzeitung* remained the favorite newspaper of Germans who enjoyed the privileges of wealth, rank, and power. As hundreds of other newspapers came and went, and as conservatives strove (without success) to establish a party press rivaling those of liberals and socialists, the *Kreuzzeitung* survived and thrived. It did so because it offered what Prussian officers, courtiers, estate owners, civil servants, and other conservatives wanted most: a chronicle of Berlin high society, a window on political intrigue in the capital, and an unabashedly partisan defense of aristocratic privilege, agrarianism, the monarchy, and the Protestant church. The *Kreuzzeitung's* motto was "Forward with God for King and Fatherland." Yet it repeatedly suffered scandal when its most famous chief editors—Hermann Wagener (1848–53), Philipp von Nathusius-Ludom (1872–81), and Baron Wilhelm von Hammerstein-Schwartow (1881–95)—associated themselves with campaigns against Chancellor Otto von Bismarck or the Jews. Ironically, this staunchly monarchist newspaper was banned more than once from the royal palace.

The *Kreuzzeitung's* founding in mid-1848 provided a crucial rallying point for Prussian conservatives, who had floundered since March in the grip of revolutionary events. Among the most important backers of the new undertaking were Leopold and Ludwig von Gerlach, Friedrich Julius Stahl, and Otto von Bismarck—soon known collectively as the "*Kreuzzeitung* party." Immediately profitable and popular despite its relatively high price, the *Kreuzzeitung* provided conservatives with the program and the self-confidence they needed to regain their feet in mid-1848 and to consolidate the counter-revolution in 1849.

When party life in Germany again became moribund in the reactionary 1850s, the *Kreuzzeitung* continued to offer a crucial organizational focus for Prussian conservatives, although its opinions were not unchallenged on the right. In the 1860s and 1870s, conservative unity was further fractured by questions of national unity, constitutional reform, economic modernization, and the *Kulturkampf.* In this era, the *Kreuzzeitung* lost some of its influence and readership; yet throughout its history, the newspaper retained its circulation in the respectable range of 5,000 to 11,000 copies, not least because it attracted such talented writers as Theodor Fontane (1819–98) and George Ludwig Hesekiel. When Hammerstein in the 1880s injected his characteristic "salty style" into its lead editorials, the *Kreuzzeitung* once again rose to unequaled prominence. In 1888, it became one of few political organs that could afford the luxury of supplementing its evening edition with a morning offering.

For Bismarck and Kaiser Wilhelm II, the *Kreuzzeitung's* unparalleled stature was unwelcome, because it allowed its editors to challenge the leaders of the governmental wing of the Conservative Party. This challenge began in the mid-1870s, when the *Kreuzzeitung's* "Era Articles" (June-July 1875) charged that Bismarck, the liberals, and the Jews were jointly responsible for the financial scandals that hit Germany after 1873. By the late 1880s, Hammerstein and the anti-Semitic leader Adolf Stoecker (1835–1909) headed a powerful faction of conservatives attempting to steer Wilhelm II onto a radical right-wing course. This so-called "*Kreuzzeitung* group" staged a palace revolt within the Conservative Party in 1892, overthrowing the chairman and introducing sharply populist, anti-establishment rhetoric into the party's program, including calls to combat the "dominance" of Jews in public life.

In 1896, however, the *Kreuzzeitung* group episode ended when Stoecker left the party and Hammerstein was convicted of fraud for having purchased newsprint at vastly inflated prices. Thereafter, the *Kreuzzeitung* influenced conservative policy less directly. Nonetheless, throughout the Wilhelmine and Weimar periods, other party leaders contributed to it regularly, and it remained essential reading for those wishing to gauge conservative opinion. Like many other conservative organs, it placed itself at the service of those who opposed the Weimar Republic, including the Stahlhelm (Steel Helmets) and, later, the Nazis. After contributing to the radicalization of the German Right that helped to set the stage for National Socialism, the *Kreuzzeitung* ceased publication on January 31, 1939.

James Retallack

See also Anti-Semitism; Bismarck, Otto von; Conservatism, 1871–1918; German Conservative Party; Press and Newspapers; Prussia; Stoecker, Adolf; Wilhelm II

References

Leuss, Hans. *Wilhelm Freiherr von Hammerstein 1881–1895: Chefredakteur der Kreuzzeitung.* Berlin: H. Walther, 1905.

Merbach, Paul Alfred. "Die Kreuzzeitung 1848–1923. Ein geschichtlicher Rückblick." *Neue Preussische Zeitung (Kreuz-Zeitung)* 75, no. 274 (June 16, 1923), 1–17. Special anniversary issue.

Orr, William James, Jr. "The Foundation of the Kreuzzeitung Party in Prussia, 1848–50." Unpublished doctoral dissertation. University of Wisconsin, 1971.

Rohleder, Meinolf and Burkhard Treude. "*Neue Preussische (Kreuz-) Zeitung (1848–1939).*" *Deutsche Zeitungen des 17. bis 20. Jahrhunderts.* Ed. Heinz-Dietrich Fischer. Munich-Pullach: Dokumentation, 1972, 208–224.

Treude, Burkhard. *Konservative Presse und National-sozialismus: Inhaltsanalyse der "Neuen Preussischen (Kreuz-) Zeitung" am Ende der Weimarer Republik.* Bochum: Brockmeyer, 1975.

Kripo (Reich Kriminalpolizei, 1936–45)

Kripo had long been an acronym for detective police, but when Heinrich Himmler (1900–45) became chief of all German police in 1936, he created Germany's first national detective force and the term acquired new significance. The new national Kripo became coordinated with the Gestapo in the newly-created Sipo (Sicherheitspolizei) to serve as the executives for prosecution of all perceived enemies of the *Volksgemeinschaft* (racial community). As such, they enforced the Nazi ideal of national homogeneity.

When Hitler became chancellor, Germany had about 12,000 plain-clothes detectives scattered among the state and municipal police forces. Like detectives anywhere, they investigated conventional and political crimes. Internationally, they had a high reputation for professionalism and efficiency, but they prided themselves especially on an aloofness from politics.

When the Nazis purged the police, whom they believed to be infected by Social Democratic politics, the detectives suffered numerical losses of perhaps four percent. Nevertheless, the ranks of the regular detectives declined further as many were detached to form independent political police in the *Länder* (states), such as the Gestapo of Prussia. After 1934, when Himmler became commander of the political police of each *Land*, Wilhelm Frick (1877–1946), Reich and Prussian minister of the interior, formed a centralized Prussian Kripo under the leadership of Arthur Nebe, one of the earliest Nazi detectives in Prussia. Although they had hoped that the Kripo could provide the basis for displacing Himmler's extraordinary political police, their plans came to naught in 1936 when Himmler became chief of all police. Himmler completed the nationalization of the detectives as a force to round out his emerging Schutzstaffel (SS) police state.

Under Himmler, the numerical strength of the new Reich Kripo rose rapidly to over 15,000 in 1942. The effects of this and of SS penetration on their professionalism has never been studied. The Nazi claim to have reduced crime represents another complex and problematic issue. In any case, Nazi commitments declined as Kripo ranks plummeted to 12,000 by 1944 and undoubtedly well below that thereafter.

By 1936, most detectives had joined Nazi organizations, but SS penetration of their ranks had not been marked. From 1937, pressure on all police to join the Party increased, until most did so. With the creation of the Reich Kripo as part of Sipo, they came under the command of Reinhard Heydrich (1904–42), also chief of the Sicherheitsdienst (SD). From 1938, he increasingly sought to bring them into the SS as members of his SD. The needs of the war years disrupted the process, and the extent of actual interpenetration remains unknown. Nebe remained the actual leader of the Reich Kripo, a useful concession to the detectives' sense of their separateness, but he, like all commanding officers in the Sipo, was drawn into the SS/SD.

Despite any limits to SS penetration, the detectives lost much of their alleged aloofness from Nazi and SS ideology and contamination. Joint training, indoctrination, and coordinated efforts with the Gestapo colored their professional lives. Nebe surrendered all future generations of detective recruits to a complete fusion with the SS. Most of all, Himmlerian racial-biological theories permeated the new orthodox criminology, which included proactive crime prevention. The procedure involved permanently incarcerating known offenders and misfits. Kripo personnel could be assigned not only to Gestapo work, but to Sipo posts in occupied territories and to the *Einsatzgruppen*, where they became directly involved in the execution of racial programs. Himmlerian theories led to their special responsibility for enforcing the "euthanasia" program as an aspect of the elimination of all sources of deviant genes.

George C. Browder

See also Euthanasia; Frick, Wilhelm; Gestapo; Heydrich, Reinhard; Himmler, Heinrich; Racism; Schutzstaffel; Security Service of the SS; Security Police

References

Browder, George C. *The Foundations of the Nazi Police State: The Formation of Sipo and SD.* Lexington, KY: University Press of Kentucky, 1990.

———. *Hitler's Enforcers: the Gestapo and the SS Security Service in the Nazi Revolution.* New York, NY: Oxford University Press, 1996.

Terhorst, Karl-Leo. *Polizeiliche planmässige Überwachung und polizeiliche Vorbeugungschaft im Dritten Reich.* Heidelberg: C.F. Müller Juristischer Verlag, 1985.

Krupp: Family and Firm

In 1811, Friedrich Krupp (1787–1826) founded the cast iron, steel, and foundry works in Essen which, under his son Alfred (1812–1887) expanded into a huge industrial empire. As one of the world's leading steel and armaments producers, the Krupp firm played a key role in the industrial development of Germany and in its wars.

The House of Krupp, as it was called, became a symbol of Germany's economic success and of German militarism. Numerous popular biographies offered adulation of, or heaped criticism on, a firm whose history has been inadequately surveyed by historians.

The public image of the firm and family was lastingly shaped by Alfred Krupp. Under his direction, the Krupp firm expanded rapidly and became world-famous for its pioneering role in the production of specialty steels and alloys and the manufacture of seamless steel locomotive wheels and axles as well as guns. Alfred also pioneered labor management and welfare policies. The draconian discipline that he enforced in his plants was frequently compared to military drill.

This severity, however, went hand in hand with a system of paternalistic welfare. As early as 1836, the Krupp firm established a health-insurance plan for its workers, followed later by extensive company housing and a company pension plan. In addition, sons and relatives of loyal workers enjoyed preferred employment. As Alfred Krupp shrewdly recognized well ahead of his time, benevolent paternalism profited business. Entirely wedded to his business pursuits and the sense of his own grandeur, "King Alfred," as family and contemporaries called him, also built the colossal family residence, Villa Hügel, in Essen.

In 1887, Alfred's sole heir, Friedrich Alfred Krupp (1854–1902) took over the family firm. Expansion into armaments production became even more pronounced with the acquisition of the Grusonwerk AG in 1893 and the addition of the Germaniawerft in 1902. This navy yard was added to the firm in order to profit from the building of the Imperial Navy. Friedrich Alfred's friendship with Kaiser Wilhelm II most likely facilitated business, as did the traditional practice of recruiting highly placed civil servants into the Krupp upper management.

When Friedrich Alfred Krupp died in 1902, only 48 years old and possibly by his own hand, he left a business that had more than doubled its sales under his tutelage (91 million marks annually) and also doubled its number of employees to 40,000. Under the direction of the board of directors—a management structure dating to Alfred Krupp—the Krupp firm continued to grow even more rapidly in the next decade, despite the lack of entrepreneurial leadership.

Without a male heir, Friedrich Alfred Krupp left the largest heavy industrial enterprise in Germany to his oldest daughter, Bertha Krupp (1886–1957), who, although nominally in charge, left business decisions to her husband, Gustav von Bohlen und Halbach, a diplomat and lawyer by training who was descended from a German-American family. Both were deeply committed to orderly family life and proper social etiquette. They had six sons and two daughters. Probably for reasons of her highly publicized role as a privately and publicly caring mother after World War II, Bertha Krupp remains to this day somewhat of an icon among the older people in Essen.

Bertha's husband who headed the Krupp firm from 1909 until 1943, was granted the royal privilege to incorporate Krupp into his name and that of his heir. Like his father-in-law, Gustav Krupp von Bohlen und Halbach was on friendly terms with Kaiser Wilhelm II, who attended his wedding. In business, Gustav followed the expansionist policies of his predecessors and was probably even more successful in identifying the business interests of Krupp as being those of Imperial Germany at large. As the most important German armaments manufacturer, the Krupp firm experienced an unprecedented boom during World War I, and when the war was lost, Gustav

Alfred Krupp and son Arndt. Courtesy of Inter Nationes, Bonn.

was, to some extent, rather proud to be named a war criminal along with Kaiser Wilhelm II by the Allied powers.

Despite his nostalgia for Imperial Germany, Gustav did not hesitate to seek and accept financial support from the governments of the Weimar Republic in order to keep the firm afloat during the difficult times of restructuring and downsizing after 1918. The production of Krupp coal mines and steel mills was geared to the manufacture of rails and locomotives, farm implements, heavy machinery and a range of other diverse products such as cash registers and medical instruments.

There is little doubt that, in violation of the Treaty of Versailles of 1919, Krupp subsidiaries were also engaged in the secret development of new weaponry and armaments. Significantly, the Krupp firm did not join the United Steel Trust, formed in 1926. Instead, it remained an independent shareholding company exclusively owned by the Krupp family. Not politically inclined, Gustav Krupp played a minor role in the various political intrigues of his colleagues in heavy industry. But he certainly shared their general hostility toward trade unions and collective bargaining, as well as their increasing contempt for the democratic political system of the Weimar Republic. He also participated in the inner circle of heavy industry and was a member of its secret high council, the "Ruhrlade." But his election as chair of the influential Federation of German Industry in 1931 marked his first major public position.

Although Krupp had actively opposed the political machinations of his former general director, Alfred Hugenberg (1865–1961), who as head of the right-wing German National People's Party looked to Hitler and the Nazis for his political fortune, he quickly forgot his earlier antipathy towards the Nazis in the early 1930s. From 1933 onward, Krupp's financial contributions to the various causes of the Nazi Party and also the Schutzstaffel (SS) were substantial. In the course of rearmament, the Krupp firm once again experienced extraordinary economic growth, and it resumed its role as Germany's armory. It adjusted to the anti-Semitic policies of the Third Reich, and during the war it extensively utilized the forced labor of foreign workers and inmates of concentration camps and prisoner-of-war camps. Many thousands of these workers, mainly Jews but also Gypsies, Poles, and Russians, were worked to death or died because of the horrid conditions in the camps.

Unlike his oldest son and designated heir, Alfried Krupp von Bohlen und Halbach (1907–1967), who assumed a leading role in organizing the war production and expansion of the Krupp firm and its many subsidiaries, Gustav Krupp was too ill to play a major role after the outbreak of war. He spent the last years of the war at castle Blöhnbach, the family estate in Austria. In 1943, Alfried Krupp took charge officially and became the sole owner of the vast Krupp empire. His connections to the highest Nazi authorities were excellent.

After the war, Alfried was charged as a war criminal along with his father, who was too ill to be tried; Alfried was sentenced to twelve years' imprisonment by the Nuremberg Military Tribunal. His immense personal and corporate property was confiscated. He served his sentence until 1951, when a general amnesty issued by the American High Commissioner, John J. McCloy (1895–1989), freed him. His property was restored to him on the understanding that he would divest himself of his coal and steel holdings. This did not happen. Alfried Krupp systematically expanded his firm, aided by his young and talented general director, Berthold Beitz (1913–).

By 1960, Alfried Krupp emerged as the leading steel producer in Europe as well as the sole owner of a diversified industrial empire that employed over 100,000 people and netted annual sales of more than one billion dollars. He was again one of the most influential industrialists in Europe and one of the richest. But by the end of the decade, he had overextended himself and his firm was in severe financial difficulties. Like his father, Gustav, and his great-grandfather, "King Alfred," Alfried Krupp was rescued by the government in 1967. Forced to relinquish sole control, he saw his enterprise restructured as a joint-stock company. He died the same year and left all his corporate property to the Krupp Foundation, which, under the direction of Beitz, was founded in 1968. Alfried's only heir, Arndt von Bohlen und Halbach (1938–1986), Alfried's son from his first, short marriage, was never regarded as a "true" Krupp by his father or the family. His death ended the Krupp dynasty.

Irmgard Steinisch

See also Beitz, Berthold; Coal Industry; Concentration Camps; Foundations and Research Institutes; Hitler, Adolf; Hugenberg, Alfred; National Socialist Germany; Navy and Naval Policy; Nazi War Crimes Trials and Investigations; Nuremberg Trials; Ruhr Region; Ruhrlade; Schutzstaffel; Steel Industry; Third Reich: Industry; Wilhelm II; Working Conditions; World War I; World War II

References

Boelcke, Willi A., ed. *Krupp und die Hohenzollern in Dokumenten: Krupp-Korrespondenz mit Kaisern, Kabinettschefs und Ministern 1850–1918*. Frankfurt am Main: Akademische Verlagsanstalt Athenäion, 1970.

Engelmann, Bernt. *Krupp: Legenden und Wirklichkeit*. Munich: Franz Schneekluth Verlag KG, 1969.

Feldman, Gerald D. *Iron and Steel in the German Inflation 1916–1923*. Princeton, NJ: Princeton University Press, 1977.

Friz, Diana Maria. *Alfried Krupp und Berthold Beitz: Der Erbe und sein Statthalter*. Zürich: Orell Füssli, 1988.

Klass, Gert von. *Krupps: The Story of an Industrial Empire*. Trans. James Cleugh. London: Sidgwick and Jackson, 1963.

Manchester, William. *The Arms of Krupp 1587–1968*. New York, NY: Bantam Books, 1970.

Neebe, Reinhard. *Grossindustrie, Staat und NSDAP 1930–1933*. Göttingen: Vandenhoeck & Ruprecht, 1981.

Turner, Henry Ashby, Jr. *German Big Business and the Rise of Hitler*. New York, NY: Oxford University Press, 1985.

Kubel, Alfred (1909–)

Alfred Kubel was born on May 25, 1909, in Brunswick, Germany. After finishing secondary school, he started professional training as a commercial clerk and later became a druggist. In 1926, Kubel joined the Internationaler Sozialistischer Kampfbund (International Socialist Combat Group), which advocated a non-Marxist socialism, primarily based on neo-Kantian philosophy, for ethical reasons.

After Adolf Hitler's seizure of power in 1933 Kubel moved to Berlin and became an active member of the anti-Nazi resistance. During the 1936 Olympic Games in Berlin, he distributed anti-Nazi leaflets. Kubel was imprisoned in 1937 and sentenced to one year's imprisonment for high treason. Having served his sentence, he worked in the chemical industry.

After the end of the war, Kubel resumed political activity. He was a leading person in reorganizing the Social Democratic Party in Brunswick. In 1946, he was appointed Prime Minister of the *Land* (state) Brunswick. When Brunswick became part of the newly created Lower Saxony in November 1946, he joined its government. From 1946 until 1970—with an interruption from 1955 through 1957—Kubel served in various ministries of Lower Saxony; he was minister of economics, labor and reconstruction, finance, and agriculture and was finally elected prime minister in 1970. He resigned in 1976.

In various endeavors, such as agriculture or public finance, Kubel initiated reforms guided by the principle of "liberal socialism": individual freedom and market economy combined with equal opportunities and support for underprivileged people. In addition to being a member of the government of Lower Saxony for 28 years, Kubel was one of the founders of the Hannover Fair. Until 1978, he was a member and chairman of the board of the Deutsche Messe AG.

After his resignation from public office, Kubel engaged himself in the support of the Georg-Eckert-Institut for international school book research and comparison in Brunswick.

Wolfgang Renzsch

See also Lower Saxony; Social Democratic Party, 1919–90; Trade Fairs and Exhibitions

References
Renzsch, Wolfgang. *Alfred Kubel—30 Jahre Politik für Niedersachsen: Eine politische Biographie.* Bonn: Neue Gesellschaft, 1985.

Kultur

In order to understand *Kultur* (culture), as used in Germany, one needs to consider cultural achievements and appreciate how the concept of *Kultur* has been revised. As mass production and consumption undermined cultural exclusivity, the struggle to control cultural forms, ranging from art to lifestyle, intensified. *Kultur* faced a myriad of demands: to cement a German nation whose history was fragmented and diverse and to provide the distinctions for a changing social order.

Friedrich Nietzsche (1844–1900) voiced a stringent cul-ture in *Unzeitgemässige Betrachtungen* (published as *Untimely Meditations*),1873, which attacked the "educated philistine" who "doesn't know what culture is, namely unity of style." Cultural unity preoccupied the new Prussian state, which sought to enforce its authenticity by the *Kulturkampf* against Roman Catholicism, by silencing undesirable artists, and by inculcating a national culture from the classroom and museum.

Government control over culture did not go uncontested. New "cultural scientists" and social thinkers joined with veterans of voluntary associations, the *Vereine*, to stake out a cultural realm beyond state purview. Drawing on Kant's juxtaposition of the intrinsically "cultivated" person to "civilized" improvements in social interrelations, they made *Kultur* their bulwark against a "civilization" of laws and mere good manners—a privatized sphere also more open to women's participation.

The strain of cultural pessimism within this debate concerned contemporaries and historians alike. Together with illiberalism, *Kultur* was used to explain the withdrawal of a discouraged *Bildungsbürgertum* (cultivated bourgeoisie) from politics. Nonetheless, other members of these educated classes, along with business and trade leaders, saw industrialization in a positive light. In a spate of newly founded cultural journals, modernist hostility to mass culture confronted the enthusiastic social and aesthetic interventions of a variegated avant-garde.

The constitution of cultural activity was regarded as separate from everyday life and politics. Negotiating the boundaries of culture proper and proper culture had very much to do with public power, because the state had designated culture as a state-making activity. An autonomous *Kultur* also served as a staging ground for resistance and renewal. The state edited vibrant local cultural life into *kleindeutsch* or other rigid "German"-ness. Articulating a different *Kultur* could thwart the imposition of state cultural hegemony.

The acknowledgment of many cultures as distinctly "German" corrects the nationalizing drive of German historiography and the apolitical characterization of culture. Recent work details cultural production and consumption as state representation at exhibitions abroad and invention of tradition at home, demographics of the *Bildungsbürgertum* and other reading publics, artistic and cultural movements, and the politics of design.

The discursive dichotomy between culture and civilization maintained itself in social theory. Ferdinand Tönnies' (1855–1936) *Gemeinschaft und Gesellschaft* (published as *Community and Society*), 1887, framed the discussion of social transformation, positing a unified culture of values and customs (*Gemeinschaft*), which preceded rationalized but fragmented civilization (*Gesellschaft*). In his 1912 address, "The Sociological Concept of *Kultur*," Alfred Weber (1868–1958) elaborated a unique, coherent culture of intellectual and moral capacities against rational, accumulative civilization. Weber's *Kultur* studies also prompted involvement with the German Werkbund. In practical terms, the Werkbund wanted to bring a competitive German style onto the international market. Moreover, *Stil* (style) was to restore the cultural unity destroyed by urbanization, commodity production, and division of labor.

The upheaval following World War I highlighted how mass production could overcome a culturally and socially conflicted modernity. City planners promoting *Das Neue Frankfurt* (the new Frankfurt), for example, combined mass-produced housing with a municipally sponsored culture movement to unite Frankfurt citizens. Together with Bertolt Brecht (1898–1956), Walter Benjamin (1892–1940) explored the implications of modern technology for collective-political art forms in order to combat the Fascist deployment of tradition against modernity.

Benjamin's vision of transformative potential in new modes of cultural production and response found little support among his associates at the Institute for Social Research. A critical approach to mass culture characterized the Frankfurt School analyses of cultural institutions in capitalist society. In place of popular culture rising from the concerns of the people, Theodor Adorno (1903–69) saw an administered world of bureaucracy and "culture industry," where Fascism followed the surrender of individual autonomy. The Nazi takeover closed the Frankfurt School in Germany, one episode in their eradication of "un-German" culture and culture-makers.

Adorno's remark, "To write poetry after Auschwitz is barbaric" (1955), reflected the strife over reconciling the *Kultur* tradition with genocidal politics. Another controversy surrounded the cultural engagement of Thomas Mann (1875–1955), whose years in exile, so the argument ran, had compromised his ability to judge German cultural needs.

The Frankfurt School continued to shape thinking about culture in the postwar period. The pervasiveness of administered culture, warned Hans Magnus Enzensberger (1929–), would culminate in a "consciousness industry." Herbert Marcuse's (1898–1979) *One-Dimensional Man* (1964) stands as the classic Frankfurt School analysis of how advanced industrial society absorbs oppositional forces, although in other writings Marcuse found a critical, emancipatory capacity in culture. The 1960s protests sparked interest in alternative cultures and subcultures; subversive and ironic twists could destabilize even a totalized system from within. The backdrop for postwar *Kultur* discussions remained the division of the German *Kultur* nation into two states. Each state claimed the *Kultur* tradition for its own, yet fostered a cultural identity predicated in many respects in the construction of its postwar counterpart.

Carol Scherer

See also Adorno, Theodor; Benjamin, Walter; *Bildung und Bildungsbürgertum*; Brecht, Bertolt; Censorship; Education; Enzensberger, Hans Magnus; Frankfurt School; *Germanistik; Kulturkampf;* Marcuse, Herbert; Nietzsche, Friedrich; Schools; Tönnies, Ferdinand; Weber, Alfred; Werkbund

References

Berman, Russell A. *Modern Culture and Critical Theory: Art, Politics, and the Legacy of the Frankfurt School.* Madison, WI: University of Wisconsin Press, 1989.

Bürger, Peter. *Theory of the Avant-Garde.* Minneapolis, MN: University of Minnesota Press, 1984.

Glaser, Hermann. *The Rubble Years: The Cultural Roots of Postwar Germany.* New York, NY: Paragon, 1986.

Huyssen, Andreas. *After the Great Divide: Modernism, Mass Culture, Postmodernism.* Bloomington, IN: Indiana University Press, 1986.

Jackman, Jarrell C., and Carla M. Borden, eds. *The Muses Flee Hitler: Cultural Transfer and Adaptation 1930–1945.* Washington, DC: Smithsonian, 1983.

Paret, Peter. *The Berlin Secession: Modernism and Its Enemies in Imperial Germany.* Cambridge, MA: Harvard University Press, 1980.

Selle, Gert. *Design-Geschichte als in Deutschland: Produktkultur Entwurf und Erfahrung.* Cologne: DuMont, 1987.

Stark, Gary D., and Bede Karl Lackner, eds. *Essays on Culture and Society in Modern Germany.* College Station, TX: Texas A&M University Press, 1982.

Kulturkampf (1871–87)

Few conflicts in Imperial Germany were more important than the *Kulturkampf,* a bitter and protracted dispute between the Roman Catholic Church and the Prussian and Imperial German state. The *Kulturkampf* began in 1871, gathered in intensity and bitterness until 1878, and then continued with diminishing severity down to 1887.

This dispute owed much to Protestant Germany's distrust of Rome, dismay among non-Catholics at Pope Pius IX's 1864 Syllabus of Errors and the far-reaching claim of papal infallibility promulgated by the Vatican Council in 1870, resentment in governmental circles regarding the reappearance of the Catholic-dominated Center Party in the Reichstag and in the Prussian *Landtag* (diet), and Chancellor Otto von Bismarck's conviction that the Catholic clergy used its influence in Prussia's eastern districts to retard the assimilation of the local Polish populace into the German nation.

What transformed this distrust, fear, and animosity into political action was Bismarck's decision to launch an "internal preventive war" against the alleged revolutionary potential of Catholics, Poles, and socialists that he believed threatened the consolidation of the newly unified German Reich.

Following a series of preliminary skirmishes, the *Kulturkampf* quickly escalated into a broad campaign against the Roman Catholic Church chiefly in Prussia, and to a lesser degree in the German Empire as a whole. The Pope denounced the *Kulturkampf* as a "massive persecution" reminiscent of anti-Christian outrages perpetrated in ancient Rome. Bismarck's church regulations, however, avoided a frontal assault on religious belief itself in favor of specific limitations and controls on the practice of religion.

In 1871, Bismarck and his collaborators abolished the "Catholic Section" in the Prussian Ministry of Ecclesiastical Affairs and amended the Empire's criminal code to prevent the use of the pulpit for political propaganda. In 1872, they eliminated ecclesiastical influence in curricular matters and in the supervision of Prussia's schools, and expelled the Jesuit Order from Germany. With the *Landtag*'s adoption of the so-called May Laws in 1873, the training and appointment of clergy in Prussia came under state jurisdiction. The Prussian government also introduced compulsory civil marriage in 1874, a step extended to the entire Empire a year later. Additional Prussian legislation in 1875 abolished religious orders and congregations, choked off state subsidies to the Church, and deleted religious guarantees from the Prussian constitution. With Bismarck's sanction, furthermore, Prussian authorities in 1874 and 1875 enacted statutes permitting state agents to take charge of vacated bishoprics and authorized laymen to assume administrative responsibilities at the parish level.

The *Kulturkampf* produced an increasingly pervasive, almost palpable atmosphere of anti-Catholicism, shared by high and low alike. Within this climate of hostility, and as a consequence of the *Kulturkampf*'s regulations, Catholics suffered grievously. The bishops and lower clergy were the most conspicuous victims of governmental persecution, but laymen too were harassed, victimized, and sometimes imprisoned. All Catholics experienced a decade and more of constant strain. By the end of the 1870s, when the *Kulturkampf* began to wane, more than half of Prussia's Catholic episcopate was either in exile or in prison, and nearly a quarter of all parishes were without pastors. Less severe but painful nonetheless were the hardships that needlessly complicated and saddened the lives of ordinary Catholics. The last rites could not be administered to the dying, burials sometimes became the focus of unseemly quarrels, and regularity of sacramental observance became increasingly difficult to maintain.

Despite these setbacks, Catholics continued to oppose Bismarck's church regulations. Confronted by massive Catholic disaffection and disobedience, and faced with domestic political challenges that dictated compromise, Bismarck after 1878 relaxed the ecclesiastical laws, came to terms with the Center Party and the Church, and slowly dismantled the *Kulturkampf*. Although the *Kulturkampf* failed to break the Church, Bismarck and his allies wrested certain concessions from Rome in the diplomatic accord that brought the conflict to an end in 1887. The state retained curricular influence over church-run schools and seminaries, the appointment of clergy, the Pulpit Decree of 1871, even compulsory civil marriage. But when assessed in terms of Bismarck's larger purpose—as a means to eliminate Catholicism as a major force in German politics—the *Kulturkampf* was a failure and a disappointment to those responsible for its enforcement.

Ronald J. Ross

See also Bismarck, Otto von; Catholicism, Political; Center Party; Education; Falk, Adalbert; Ketteler, Wilhelm; Liberalism; National Liberal Party; Polish-German Relations, 1871–1918; Prussia; Puttkamer, Robert Viktor von; Roman Catholic Church; Schools; Vatican-German Relations; Windthorst, Ludwig

References

Anderson, Margaret Lavinia. *Windthorst: A Political Biography*. Oxford: Clarendon Press, 1981.

Blackbourn, David. *Marpingen: Apparitions of the Virgin Mary in Nineteenth-Century Germany*. Oxford: Clarendon Press, 1993.

Bornkamm, Heinrich. "Die Staatsidee im Kulturkampf." *Historische Zeitschrift* 170 (1950), 41–72; 273–306.

Constabel, Adelheid, ed. *Die Vorgeschichte des Kulturkampfes: Quellenveröffentlichung aus dem Deutschen Zentralarchiv*. Berlin: Rütten & Loening, 1956.

Kissling, Johannes B. *Geschichte des Kulturkampfes im Deutschen Reiche*. 3 vols. Freiburg: Herder, 1911–16.

Lill, Rudolf, ed. *Vatikanische Akten zur Geschichte des deutschen Kulturkampfes: Leo XIII*. Tübingen: M. Niemeyer, 1970.

Pflanze, Otto. *Bismarck and the Development of Germany*. 3 vols. Princeton, NJ: Princeton University Press, 1990.

Ross, Ronald J. "Enforcing the Kulturkampf: The Bismarckian State and the Limits of Coercion in Imperial Germany." *The Journal of Modern History* 56 (1984), 456–82.

Schmidt-Volkmar, Erich. *Der Kulturkampf in Deutschland 1871–1890*. Göttingen: Musterschmidt, 1963.

Smith, Helmut Walser. *German Nationalism and Religious Conflict*. Princeton, NJ: Princeton University Press, 1995.

Sperber, Jonathan. *Popular Catholicism in Nineteenth-Century Germany*. Princeton, NJ: Princeton University Press, 1984.

Kunert, Günter (1929–)

A contemporary writer, presently residing in Itzehoe, Schleswig-Holstein, Günter Kunert belongs to the group of intellectuals who were widely discussed in both the former East and West Germany.

Growing up in Nazi Germany as the son of a Jewish mother, Kunert experienced persecution and discrimination. Only after the end of World War II was he able to study graphic art at the Institute for Applied Arts in Berlin. His interest, however, soon shifted to literature. In 1947 his first satirical poems and short stories appeared in the magazine *Ulenspiegel*. After the establishment of the German Democratic Republic (GDR) he joined the Socialist Unity Party (SED), believing in the humanitarian goals proclaimed by its members. Under the influence of Bertolt Brecht (1898–1956), Kunert devoted his literary work to didactic poems and epigrams that warned of the evils of a Fascist past.

Through the 1960s and 1970s, Kunert's poems criticized socialist society. In addition, he alerted his readers to the threat associated with the advancements of technology. Although he had criticized the East German government, an act resulting in prosecution, he was able to spend a year as a visiting professor at the University of Texas in Austin, and in 1975 at the University of Warwick in England. His poetic writings reflect detailed descriptions and critical observations of the countries he visited. In 1976, when the GDR government revoked Wolf Biermann's (1936–) citizenship while he was on a concert tour in the West, Kunert signed a letter of protest with other leading GDR artists such as Christa Wolf (1929–), Sarah Kirsch (1935–), and Fritz Cremer (1906–93). As a result, Kunert was expelled from the SED in 1977 and moved to West Germany.

Kunert's literary productivity did not cease in the west. In addition to numerous prestigious awards, he received the Heinrich Heine Prize of the city of Düsseldorf in 1985. Despite persecution and political repression by National Socialism and by a divided Germany, Kunert has treated his concerns with utmost sensibility and integrity while repudiating any ideological stagnation. He is perceived as a nihilist and pessimist, but his literary work confronts the reader with the undeniable dilemmas of our time.

Silvia A. Rode

See also Brecht, Bertolt; Cremer, Fritz; Federal Republic of Germany: Literature; German Democratic Republic; German Democratic Republic: Literature and Literary Life; German Democratic Republic: Opposition; Poetry; Satire; Socialist Unity Party; Wolf, Christa

References
Jonsson, Dieter. *Kunert: Literatur im Widerspruch, Mit Materialien.* Stuttgart: Klett-Cotta, 1980.
Kunert, Günter. *Unterwegs nach Utopie: Gedichte.* Munich: Hanser, 1977.
Reese, James R. "Cultural Politics and the Literary Avant Garde in East Germany: The Case of Günter Kunert." *Journal of the Pacific Northwest Council on Foreign Languages* 2 (1981), 142–46.

Küng, Hans (1928–)

Ordained a Roman Catholic priest in 1954, Hans Küng has been on the faculty at the University of Tübingen since 1963, where he has directed the Institute for Ecumenical Research. He served as an official theological consultant at Vatican II and subsequently became a leading scholar on the *magisterium* (authority) of the Church.

A proponent of church reform, Küng, in his work *Die Kirche* (The church), 1968, asserted that today's Christian message is the result of a two-thousand-year historical transmission. As a mediating process, history can help the individual and the ecclesiastical community to guard against subjectivity so that both can perceive the truth more comprehensively. Küng has insisted that Scripture be read within the environment of the present faith experience as well as within church tradition. Sensitive to past developments, he has warned against turning the magisterium into a "super-criterion" or the gospel into an uncritical, subjectivistic criterion. The theologian is to strive for a balanced comprehension by using the historical-critical method.

This theoretical methodology illuminates the lively tension between faith and historical experience, which Küng sees as fruitful for those engaged in the theological enterprise. History conditions but does not determine faith. From this foundation, Küng has offered what some have suggested are controversial views on reconciling Catholic and Protestant theology. In 1973, the Vatican's Sacred Congregation for the Doctrine of the Faith ordered Catholics to reject Küng's theories. His books have appeared in about a hundred foreign-language editions outside of Germany and have been considered by progressives as being on the cutting edge of theology.

A persistent emphasis in Küng's post–Vatican II books and essays on the Church has been the need for continuous institutional reform. Küng characterized the Church as an ever-reforming institution, and as a community marked not only by faith, hope and love but also by truthfulness and freedom (*Christ sein* [published as *On Being a Christian*], 1976). All the authority in the Church, he has insisted, must ultimately be invested in the service of the Kingdom and only immediately in the service of the Church itself. The institutional *magisterium*, therefore, cannot be the sole criterion of orthodoxy, since the gospel urges a continuing response as Christians assimilate their culture.

Donald J. Dietrich

See also Catholicism, Political; Roman Catholic Church

References
Kirvan, John, ed. *The Infallibility Debate.* New York, NY: Paulist Press, 1971.
Kiwiet, John. *Hans Küng.* Waco, TX: Word Book, 1985.
LaCugna, Catherine Mowry. *The Theological Methodology of Hans Küng.* New York, NY: The Scholars Press, 1982.
Norwell, Robert. *A Passion for Truth: Hans Küng.* London: Collins, 1981.
Swidler, Leonard, ed. *Küng in Conflict.* Garden City, NY: Doubleday, 1982.

Kunze, Reiner (1933–)

Slim volumes of lyric poetry and short prose comprise the bulk of Reiner Kunze's literary production. In addition, Kunze has published children's books and translations from Czech (Jan Skácel et al.). In the 1960s and 1970s, Kunze's was one important dissenting voice in the German Demo-

Reiner Kunze. Courtesy of Inter Nationes, Bonn.

cratic Republic (GDR). To escape state censorship, Kunze left East Germany in 1977 and settled in Bavaria. During that year, he received the Georg-Trakl-Preis für Lyrik, the Andreas Gryphius Prize and the Georg Büchner Prize. His works have been translated into more than 20 languages and honored with literature prizes in several European countries.

Kunze studied and then taught journalism at the Karl-Marx-Universität in Leipzig until 1959. In the 1960s, he worked as an independent writer and became involved in the debate concerning content and function of lyric poetry in socialist culture. The publication in the Federal Republic of Germany (FRG) of *Sensible Wege,* 1969, a poetry collection about communication under state surveillance and the Soviet invasion of Czechoslovakia in 1968, led to a publication ban in the GDR. The poems of *Zimmerlautstärke* (published as *With the Volume Turned Down*), 1973, and the short prose of *Die wunderbaren Jahre* (published as *The Wonderful Years*), 1976, established Kunze's reputation in the FRG as a sensitive critic of GDR socialism. In response, the GDR Writers' Union expelled Kunze. *Auf eigene Hoffnung* (Upon one's own hope), 1981, and *Eines jeden einziges Leben* (Every individual's own life), 1986, analyze the author's impressions of life in the FRG and other Western countries, including the United States. In *Deckname "Lyrik"* (Cover name), 1990, Kunze compiled excerpts from his GDR State Security files.

With their youthful protagonists, Kunze's texts have become parts of German high school curricula. The reception of Kunze's works must be seen in the context of the East-West conflict. Independently of political developments, the author continues to probe into questions of individual existence in the face of inhumanity, which, Kunze insists, is by no means limited to the former East German state.

Katherina Gerstenberger

See also Federal Republic of Germany: Literature; German Democratic Republic: Literature and Literary Life; German Democratic Republic: Opposition; Poetry

References

Feldkamp, Heiner, ed. *Reiner Kunze: Materialien zu Leben und Werk.* Frankfurt am Main: Fischer, 1987.

Graves, Peter, ed. *Three Contemporary German Poets: Wolf Biermann, Sarah Kirsh, Reiner Kunze.* Leicester: Leicester University Press, 1985.

Mytze, Andreas W., ed. *Über Reiner Kunze.* Berlin: europäische ideen, 1976.

Wallmann, Jürgen P., ed. *Reiner Kunze: Materialien und Dokumente.* Frankfurt am Main: Fischer, 1977.

Wolff, Rudolf, ed. *Reiner Kunze: Werk und Wirkung.* Bonn: Bouvier, 1983.

GERMANY, 1990

NORTH SEA

DENMARK

SWEDEN

BALTIC SEA

SOVIET UNION

Schleswig–Holstein

Bremen

Mecklenburg

Hamburg

Lower Saxony

Berlin

West   East

POLAND

KINGDOM OF NETHER-LANDS

North Rhine–Westphalia

Brandenburg

Saxony–Anhalt

KINGDOM OF BELGIUM

Hessen

Thüringia

Saxony

Rhineland Palatinate

LUXEMBURG

Saan

Baden–Württemberg

Bavaria

CZECHOSLOVAKIA

FRANCE

SWITZERLAND

AUSTRIA

HUNGARY

ROMANIA

ITALY

YUGOSLAVIA

ADRIATIC SEA